CIVIL PROCEDURE

CIVIL PROCEDURE

Sixth Edition

STEPHEN C. YEAZELL

David G. Price & Dallas P. Price Professor of Law
University of California, Los Angeles

PUBLISHERS

76 Ninth Avenue, New York, NY 10011
http://lawschool.aspenpublishers.com

Aspen Publishers
Attn: Permissions Department
76 Ninth Avenue, 7th Floor
New York, NY 10011-5201

Printed in the United States of America.

2 3 4 5 6 7 8 9 0

ISBN 0-7355-4511-1

Library of Congress Cataloging-in-Publication Data

Yeazell, Stephen C.
    Civil procedure / Stephen C. Yeazell. — 6th ed.
      p. cm.
    Includes bibliographical references and index.
    ISBN 0-7355-4511-1 (alk. paper)
    1. Civil procedure—United States—Cases. I. Title.

KF8839.Y43 2004
347.73'5—dc22

                          2004045138

About Aspen Publishers

Aspen Publishers, headquartered in New York City, is a leading information provider for attorneys, business professionals, and law students. Written by preeminent authorities, our products consist of analytical and practical information covering both U.S. and international topics. We publish in the full range of formats, including updated manuals, books, periodicals, CDs, and online products.

Our proprietary content is complemented by 2,500 legal databases, containing over 11 million documents, available through our Loislaw division. Aspen Publishers also offers a wide range of topical legal and business databases linked to Loislaw's primary material. Our mission is to provide accurate, timely, and authoritative content in easily accessible formats, supported by unmatched customer care.

To order any Aspen Publishers title, go to *www.aspenpublishers.com* or call: 1-800-638-8437.

To reinstate your manual update service, call 1-800-638-8437.

For more information on Loislaw products, go to *www.loislaw.com* or call: 1-800-364-2512.

For Customer Care issues, e-mail *CustomerCare@aspenpublishers.com*; call: 1-800-234-1660; or fax 1-800-901-9075.

Aspen Publishers
A Wolters Kluwer Company

For Ruth, Owen, and Emmet

SUMMARY OF CONTENTS

CONTENTS

PART A

THE CONSTITUTIONAL FRAMEWORK
FOR U.S. LITIGATION

XII. RESPECT FOR JUDGMENTS

PART C

TESTING THE BOUNDARIES: ADDITIONAL
CLAIMS AND PARTIES

XIII. JOINDER

PREFACE

Process lies at the core of our legal system: It expresses many of our culture's basic ideas about the meaning of fairness; it determines the victor in close cases; and it further determines which cases will be close ones. Procedure is also the area of law least understood and most maligned by lay observers. We root for underdogs and insist that rules not be stacked against them. But we are equally quick to condemn a case for having been decided on a "legal technicality," a phrase commonly signifying that a procedural rule has come into operation.

A similar ambivalence pervades debate about the behavior of courts and lawyers. As a society we demonstrate a strong belief in the efficacy of lawsuits to solve social, business, and personal problems, and we extol the rule of law as a distinguishing virtue of our culture. But at the same time we worry about what many believe is an excessive willingness to seek legal solutions. The ensuing debate ranges from the role of courts in restructuring social institutions to the question of whether lawyers exacerbate disputes and waste social resources by reflexively behaving in competitive, adversarial ways.

All these issues are procedural. Lawyers thus need to understand process as a tool of their trade, as a constitutive element of the legal system, and as a focus of debate about social values. Yet civil procedure is, by most accounts, a difficult and frustrating first-year course. Students come to law school with little experience in thinking explicitly about procedure and with an impression that cases simply arrive at the point of decision. Moreover, students sense that procedure may be the area in which lawyers' skill counts most; the notion that meritorious cases can be lost because of bad lawyering outrages their sense of justice even as it creates anxiety.

This book seeks to show procedure as an essential mechanism for presenting substantive questions and as a system that itself often raises fundamental issues regarding social values. I hope that students will begin to appreciate that lawyers move the system and that, to a large extent, clients' fates depend on the wisdom, skill, and judgment of their lawyers. Moreover, although all would agree that cases should not be decided on the basis of "mere" technicalities, fierce debate quickly arises when one tries to distinguish rules that merely direct traffic from those that guard the boundaries of fairness.

In addition to considering such theoretical issues, the book has some practical goals. It seeks to give students a working knowledge of the procedural system and its sometimes arcane terminology. The course also introduces the techniques of statutory analysis. It should give students a better understanding of the procedural context of the decisions they read in other courses. To these ends I have tried to select cases that are factually interesting and do not involve substantive matters beyond the experience of first-year students. The problems following the cases are intended to be answerable by first-year students and to present real-life issues. Finally, the book incorporates a number of dissenting opinions to dispel the notion that most procedural disputes present clear-cut issues.

The organization of the book adapts it to the most common sequences in contemporary procedure courses. After a brief overview of the procedural system in Chapter I, some courses will initially consider the materials in Part A, which covers jurisdiction and choice of law. Other courses will begin with discussion of remedies, pleading, discovery, resolution without trial, identifying the trier, trial, appeal, and former adjudication which are addressed in Part B. Part C, on joinder and complex litigation, recapitulates much of the material in Parts A and B and can be used either as a culmination of the course or as an insertion that follows pleading.

Cases have been severely edited to eliminate citations (without indicating their omission), and they read somewhat differently from real case reports; I hope they err in the direction of smoothness. Citations are retained only when they seem significant. Footnotes have been eliminated without indication. Those that survive retain their original numbers, while the editor's footnotes employ symbols. We have used several special citation forms: F. James, G. Hazard, and J. Leubsdorf, Civil Procedure (5th ed. 2001), is cited as James, Hazard, and Leubsdorf; C. Wright, Federal Courts (5th ed. 1994), is cited as Wright, Federal Courts; J. Moore, Federal Practice and Procedure (1969), is cited as Moore; C. Wright, A. Miller, and E. Cooper, Federal Practice and Procedure (1969), is cited as Wright and Miller.

We gratefully acknowledge the permissions granted to reproduce the following materials. The excerpts from Kamp, The History Behind Hansberry v. Lee, 20 U.C. Davis L. Rev. (1987), are reprinted by permission of the author and the Regents of the University of California (copyright © 1987 by the Regents of the University of California).

Those whose assistance was acknowledged in the preface of earlier editions built the foundations on which this book rests. This revision has incurred additional debts of its own, including the suggestions received from teachers and students using the book. This edition has continued to benefit greatly from the perceptive comments of Allen M. Katz, Esq. A distinguished litigator, Mr. Katz has shared his insights about the way in which doctrine matters in the shaping of a lawsuit and has offered many valuable suggestions about the way in which pretrial rulings affect litigation strategy. Without giving him any responsibility for the errors that doubtless still remain, I also want to thank him for having read and commented on the draft of each chapter. I want also to thank Professors Richard Epstein, and Richard D. Friedman, for detailed, thoughtful, and constructive comments. As with past editions, this one has been greatly improved by the library staff at UCLA's Hugh & Hazel Darling Law Library, whose ingenuity is exceeded only by their helpfulness. This edition has also benefited from the help of Stephanie Thomas-Hodge, UCLAW Class of '03 and Joseph Socher who tracked down citations, indexed, and improved the book's comprehensibility.

This edition bears the name of only one author. In many respects, however, it continues to be the work of Jonathan Landers and the late James Martin, on whose intellectual framework and approach I have continued to build; though neither bears any responsibility for errors of judgment or detail, both should get credit for much that is right and helpful about the book.

Stephen C. Yeazell

April 2004

CIVIL PROCEDURE

AN OVERVIEW OF PROCEDURE

I

A. The Idea and the Practice of Procedure

1. Locating Procedure

Civil procedure is about truth and justice — about how we define those words, how we seek the goals they express, and how we sometimes lose them. Civil procedure is also about lawyers — about their relation to their clients, to their profession, and to the courts. It is also, inevitably, a course about greed, venality, and oppression, and the running battle waged against these eternal human characteristics.

Mixed with these lofty themes are the minutiae of lawyers' work. Most of the first year of law school concerns what lawyers call substantive law, the rules governing behavior in ordinary life: property, criminal law, torts, and contract. Everyone needs to know at least a little about these topics simply to function in the everyday world. But procedure is insiders' law, of special importance to those administering the legal system.

Those insiders turn to procedure to describe steps in the elaborate game called litigation. At one level, procedure is the etiquette of ritualized battle, defining the initiation, development, and conclusion of a lawsuit. What does one have to say to get a court to pay attention? Supposing my adversary wants to invoke a court's help — can I instead take the dispute to a different forum? From whom may a person with a grievance seek relief? What kind of relief? If I believe my adversary has information that would help me to develop my case, may I demand it of her? All these questions — involving what lawyers would call pleading, forum selection, joinder, remedies, and discovery — are dealt with in a course in civil procedure. The answers to such questions are important to any lawyer who needs to help a client in a lawsuit. Because these answers sometimes enable prediction of the probable results of suits, they are equally important to clients who want to stay out of litigation. Lawyers need to know this body of esoteric knowledge; it is part of what makes them lawyers.

But if procedure were no more than a set of rules about the etiquette of lawsuits, it would be hard to justify its place in the first-year curriculum. Another facet of procedure justifies that place: Procedure mirrors our most basic notions of fairness and about the meaning of justice. Procedure tries to capture our ideas about the acceptable forms of settling disputes — about whether we most desire peace or truth, efficiency or justice. Procedure in this aspect embodies not just the rules governing "the way we do things here" but the reasons we do them that way.

If coming to a quick decision were all that mattered, we could flip coins to decide lawsuits. We don't flip coins because solving an important dispute without reference to its merits strikes us as unfair: The decision, we believe, ought to reflect more than chance. This belief that procedure ought to promote decisions on the merits informs the resolution of procedural questions ranging from the global — why does the system generally require a hearing before reaching a decision? — to the minute — how much time should a defendant have to reply to a complaint?

Many of the values embodied in current procedural law are now under renewed scrutiny. Some argue that our system's obsession with permitting the adversarial airing of grievances has created a monster. Proposed solutions range from the streamlining of adjudication to nonadjudicative dispute resolution. The system's defenders have not been silent, arguing both that the critics overstate the problem and that adjudication has proved to be a major force for social justice and political stability over the past two centuries. Such issues lurk in the background at every turning of our path.

This chapter seeks to give you some feel for procedural issues while offering you a first view of the life cycle of a civil lawsuit. It will raise more questions than it answers, but it will offer you a sense of the course of civil litigation and a taste of the kind of problems lawyers describe as procedural.

We start with a simple and plausible fact situation: Peters, a student at the University of Michigan, spent his winter vacation at his parents' home in Champaign, Illinois. While there, he was seriously injured in an automobile accident with Dodge, a lifelong resident of Champaign. The remainder of this chapter deals with issues that might flow from this everyday occurrence.

2.   Procedure, Lawyers, and Clients

Consider first whether and how this accident might enter the formal legal system. Most such episodes will never get near lawyers or courts. If Peters had adequate medical insurance and no lost wages, he might have little reason to sue Dodge. Alternatively, Dodge (or his insurer) might well offer Peters a satisfactory settlement before suit was filed. Or, Peters might be interested in a lawsuit but be unable to find a lawyer who would take the case. These three alternatives account for most disputes that arise in our society, with the consequence that they will never enter the official judicial system. For the rest of this book — and for the rest of law school — you will be dealing with the exceptional instances, the disputes that do find their way into the official mechanism.

How would that happen? The first step would probably involve Peters's finding a lawyer. (In the United States individuals can prosecute their cases themselves — *in pro. per.* or *pro se*, in the jargon of the law* — but most find lawyers worthwhile

---

* *In pro. per.* is an abbreviation for the Latin in propria persona, meaning "in his or her own person" (rather than by an agent or attorney). *Pro se* means "for him- or herself." Like most Latin terms in law, they don't convey very important concepts but instead serve as shorthand.

for litigation, in part because lawyers know their way around the procedural system.) Having a lawyer to represent Peters has substantial consequences. Peters wants the lawyer to navigate the procedural system to bring him to his goal — in this case a recovery of damages to compensate Peters for his injuries. The lawyer presumably shares that goal, but she will also have other goals: her other cases, her professional success, and her nonprofessional interests — family, friends, religious obligations, and the like. Most of the time lawyers are able to represent clients without serious interference from these potentially divided loyalties. But when tension between lawyer and client surfaces, it frequently does so in ways that affect the procedural system.

In order for legal representation to work, the legal system has to treat the lawyer's choices as if they were Peters's choices. For example, if Lawyer files a suit seeking recovery for Peters's personal injuries but not for damage to his car, the legal system will treat that choice as if Peters himself had made it. But what if Lawyer's behavior results not from Peters's choice but from Lawyer's carelessness — her failure to ask Peters whether his car was damaged? In that situation, the procedural system faces a dilemma. If the system allows Lawyer to correct her mistake by later adding the claim for property damage, it will thereby harm Dodge, who may have been relying on the original claim to be a complete statement of Peters's grievance. But if the procedural system insists that Peters stand by the original version of the claim — without the property damages — it will thereby harm Peters, by forcing him to forgo compensation for his damaged car.

The system has hit on three solutions to this essentially insoluble problem — all of which you will see repeatedly in procedural cases. The first is make the party who did the wrong suffer. Peters can sue his lawyer if her negligence has caused him to forgo part of his recovery. The second is to tell the party suffering the harm — here Dodge — that harm really isn't so bad, and that he should suffer the expense and inconvenience of allowing Peters to fix the mistake. If the procedural system allows Peters's lawyer to fix her mistake, then Peters will again be adequately represented, but Dodge will suffer. Finally, the system can try to buy its way out of the problem by allowing Peters to amend his claim but granting Dodge extra time to prepare a defense. In that case neither of the two parties to the lawsuit suffers greatly — but only because other parties with other claims bear the cost of having to wait longer for a hearing. Each solution to the dilemma has a corresponding drawback. If the system insists that Peters is bound by his lawyer's slip — and that his only remedy is a malpractice action — it will force him to start a second lawsuit (against his lawyer), with all the attendant uncertainty, expense, and delay. If the system allows Peters's lawyer to cure her slip by amending the complaint, it will undermine the efficiency that flows from treating lawyers' actions as those of their clients and will inflict the costs of Peters's lawyer's sloppiness on Dodge. And if it tries a solution that hurts neither Peters nor Dodge, it will inflict costs on other litigants.

Because no solution is very attractive and because procedural choices have consequences for clients, you will repeatedly encounter the procedural system resolving this trilemma. As you do, consider whether the choices it has made are reasonable.

B. Where Can the Suit Be Brought?

Once Peters has selected a lawyer, that lawyer will have to begin making procedural choices, each of which may have consequences — sometimes unforeseeable ones — for the outcome of the suit. One of the first such choices is where to bring the action. The 50 states and the federal government all operate systems of courts, and Peters's lawyer must find out whether she can bring his suit in one or more state courts or in a federal court. If she has a choice, she will have to decide which would be most advantageous.

Why should Peters's lawyer care which court hears his suit? A complete answer to that question could take one deep into the tactics of lawyering, but a sketch of the possibilities should suffice as background to the next case. Convenience provides one possible answer: If Peters (and his lawyer) are both in Ann Arbor, Michigan, they may find it cheaper and more convenient to have a court (state or federal) hear the case there rather than in Champaign, Illinois — if the court has the power to do so. All things being equal, most lawyers would rather try a case where they know the small folkways of the court and perhaps some of the judges, and are generally comfortable with the system. Moreover, convenience for Peters is likely to mean inconvenience for Dodge (or his insurer), a factor that may not make Peters's lawyer unhappy. Beyond convenience lies tactics. Will an Ann Arbor jury be more sympathetic to Peters or to Dodge? Do courts in one state or the other have large case backlogs that would delay Peters's claim?

The choice between state and federal courts turns in part on these factors and brings some new elements into the calculation. First, the fact that all federal judges are appointed for life (Article III of the U.S. Constitution permits their removal only by impeachment) can be important in a case in which judicial insulation from political pressure may play a role (not likely in the Dodge-Peters case). Second, in some districts federal courts have smaller caseloads than their state court counterparts and are therefore likely to bring a case to trial faster. For Peters, anxious to collect a judgment or settlement, that will be a plus; for Dodge, it may be a minus. Third, tactical factors may influence the lawyer: Sometimes the belief that the opponent will be unfamiliar with the greater formality or faster pace of federal court litigation will lead a lawyer to seek that forum. Finally, a number of idiosyncratic factors — ranging from the greater freedom to question prospective jurors in state courts to the desire to obtain or avoid a particular judge in the case — may influence the lawyer. While reading Hawkins v. Masters Farms, infra, you might speculate about why the plaintiff's lawyer sought a federal court when state courts would have been available for the claim.

With a sense of where she might prefer to bring suit in mind, the lawyer now needs to know what the possibilities are. The rules governing where a suit can be brought come under the headings of subject matter jurisdiction, personal jurisdiction, and venue.

1. Subject Matter Jurisdiction

Subject matter jurisdiction is the term used to denote whether a court can hear a particular type of dispute. For example, a small claims court has subject matter jurisdiction over claims below a set amount (for example, $25,000). If a suit for $50,000 were brought in such a court, the court would lack subject matter jurisdiction. Similarly, a family court may have jurisdiction over matters relating to marital status, child custody, name change, and other matters affecting families or family status. Such a court would lack subject matter jurisdiction over Peters's claim against Dodge.

To describe the subject matter jurisdiction of a court, two different terms are used. Some courts are said to be courts of *general jurisdiction*. This means that they can hear any kind of claim between any persons unless there is legal authority saying that they cannot hear a particular kind of case. For example, it is common for probate matters (wills, trusts, and so on) to be excluded from the purview of courts of general jurisdiction. Other courts are said to be courts of *limited jurisdiction*. These courts can hear only those cases that are specifically authorized by the statutes that set up the particular court. All states have at least one court of general jurisdiction that would be competent to hear Peters's claim. In Illinois and Michigan, that court is the circuit court, but in other states it may be called a district court, superior court, court of common pleas, or, in New York, the supreme court. Thus, one alternative open to Peters is the Circuit Court of Illinois; another alternative open for consideration might be the Circuit Court of Michigan.

Can Peters also bring his case in a federal court? Unlike state courts, all federal courts are courts of limited jurisdiction. The outer bounds of that jurisdiction are set by Article III, Section 2 of the Constitution. There is, however, no requirement that the federal courts be granted the broadest jurisdiction allowable under the Constitution. Instead, it is up to Congress to decide the precise subject matter jurisdiction of the federal courts. The only limitation is that Congress cannot grant more subject matter jurisdiction than is permitted by the Constitution. Congress has enacted a number of statutes authorizing subject matter jurisdiction. The most important at this point are 28 U.S.C. §§1331 and 1332.*

You will note from these sections that the subject matter jurisdiction of the federal courts is based on two kinds of considerations. Certain claims may be brought in the federal courts because of the nature of the claim — "arising under" the Constitution, laws, or treaties of the United States. Other claims may be

---

* This citation form means that the text of this statute is found in title 28 of the United States Code, a compilation of the statutes that make up part of federal law. The "titles" are divisions of the code according to topic; title 28 is also known as the Judiciary Code, and governs matters of procedure in federal courts.

brought in the federal courts because of the citizenship of the parties to the suit; the case below applies this statute to circumstances like Peters's, in which someone has two places he might plausibly call "home." Does it tell Peters's lawyer whether he can file his claim in federal court?

Hawkins v. Masters Farms, Inc.

2003 WL 21555767 (D. Kan. 2003)

VAN BEBBER, Senior J.

Plaintiffs, Mary Ann Hawkins [and Rachel Baldwin, representing] the Estate of James Patrick Creal . . . bring this action . . . aris[ing] from a December 8, 2000 traffic accident in which a tractor driven by Defendant Masters collided with Mr. Creal's automobile, resulting in the death of Mr. Creal. Plaintiffs filed this action in federal court alleging the existence of diversity jurisdiction under 28 U.S.C. §1332. Defendants dispute that there is complete diversity among the parties, and the matter is before the court on Defendants' motion to dismiss for lack of subject matter jurisdiction. For the reasons set forth below, Defendants' motion is granted.

I.   Rule 12(b)(1) Motion to Dismiss Standard

Fed. R. Civ. P. 12(b)(1) motions for lack of subject matter jurisdiction generally take one of two forms: (1) a facial attack on the sufficiency of the complaint's allegations as to subject matter jurisdiction; or (2) a challenge to the actual facts upon which subject matter jurisdiction is based. A court reviewing a facial challenge must accept the plaintiff's factual allegations regarding jurisdiction as true. In contrast, a court reviewing a factual attack may not presume that the plaintiff's allegations are true. Rather, "[a] court has wide discretion to allow affidavits, other documents, and a limited evidentiary hearing to resolve disputed jurisdictional facts under Rule 12(b)(1) ."

Here, Defendants mount a factual attack on Plaintiffs' allegations of diversity subject matter jurisdiction. In addition to Plaintiffs' complaint itself, deposition testimony and other documents have been submitted for the court's review. As the party seeking to invoke federal jurisdiction, Plaintiffs bear the burden of proving that jurisdiction is proper. Because federal courts are courts of limited jurisdiction, the presumption is against federal jurisdiction.

II.   Factual Background

On December 8, 2000, Mr. Creal was killed in an automobile accident on Mineral Point Road, just south of Troy, Kansas, when his 1988 Chevrolet van collided with a New Holland tractor driven by Defendant Masters [a citizen of Kansas]. At the time of his death, Mr. Creal was living in Troy with his wife, Elizabeth Creal, and her children. He was approximately forty-four years old when he died.

James and Elizabeth Creal first met in St. Joseph, Missouri in November 1999. Mr. Creal had lived in St. Joseph for most of his life, while Mrs. Creal resided in Troy for the majority of her life. When the couple first met, Mr. Creal was living at his mother's home in St. Joseph, where he had been residing since obtaining a divorce from his previous wife.

Beginning in January 2000, Mr. Creal began spending the night at the apartment Mrs. Creal shared with her children on South Park Street in Troy. Initially, Mr. Creal would return to his mother's house every evening after work, shower, gather some clothes, and proceed to the apartment to retire for the evening. Mrs. Creal paid the rent for the apartment on South Park Street, while Mr. Creal contributed by buying the groceries for himself, Mrs. Creal, and her two children. Mr. and Mrs. Creal split the cost of utilities for the apartment.

When Mrs. Creal and her children moved into an apartment on 1st Street in Troy in March 2000, Mr. Creal brought his clothes, some furniture, pictures, photo albums, and other memorabilia to the new apartment. Mr. and Mrs. Creal also purchased a bedroom set for the apartment. When they moved into the apartment, Mr. Creal stopped going to his mother's house in St. Joseph to shower and change after work, and instead came directly back to Troy to spend the night. Also at that time, Mr. and Mrs. Creal opened a joint checking account into which Mr. Creal began depositing his paychecks to help pay the household bills. Mr. and Mrs. Creal were married in July 2000.

In November 2000, Mr. and Mrs. Creal moved into a house on Streeter Creek Road in Troy. Mr. Creal died approximately two weeks later. His death certificate lists Kansas as his residence.

From the time Mr. and Mrs. Creal first met until Mr. Creal's death in December 2000, Mr. Creal retained certain connections with the State of Missouri. In November 1999, he applied for a Missouri title and license for his Chevrolet van using his mother's St. Joseph address. In December 1999, he applied for automobile insurance on the van using the same address. In March 2000, he listed the address when he took out a loan and applied for a new Missouri title on the van to name a new lien holder. In April 2000, he renewed his Missouri driver's license for three more years under the address. In May 2000, he filled out a form for life insurance listing the address. Mr. Creal also received mail and his paycheck stubs at his mother's house, where he stopped by every week to visit. After his death, an estate was opened for Mr. Creal in Buchanan County, Missouri alleging that he resided at his mother's address at the time of his death.

Finally, although Mr. and Mrs. Creal left open the possibility of leaving Troy to move to a location closer to Kansas City, Missouri, such as Platte City or Faucett, Missouri, they never looked for houses elsewhere and never made any specific plans to leave. Mrs. Creal testified in deposition that she was, for the most part, satisfied living in Troy.

III.   Discussion

. . . The parties do not dispute that all Defendants are citizens of the State of Kansas and that Plaintiff Baldwin is a citizen of the State of Missouri. Although

Plaintiff Hawkins, as an individual, is also a citizen of the State of Missouri, her role in this case as Personal Representative of the Estate of Mr. Creal mandates that the court focus on the citizenship of Mr. Creal at the time of his death, not the citizenship of Plaintiff Hawkins herself. 28 U.S.C. §1332(c)(2) ("[T]he legal representative of the estate of a decedent shall be deemed to be a citizen only of the same State as the decedent . . ."). Whether Mr. Creal was a citizen of the State of Kansas or the State of Missouri at the time of his death is the central dispute currently before the court.

defining citizenship

For purposes of determining whether diversity jurisdiction exists, a person is a "citizen" of the state in which he or she is "domiciled." "For adults, domicile is established by physical presence in a place in connection with a certain state of mind concerning one's intent to remain there." Miss. Band of Choctaw Indians v. Holyfield, 490 U.S. 30, 48 (1989).

Here, the court concludes that at the time of his death, Mr. Creal had not only established a physical presence in the State of Kansas, but also displayed an intent to remain there. Although Mr. Creal lived the majority of his life in St. Joseph, Missouri, he had been living in Troy, Kansas with his wife of five months for nearly one year at the time he died. Among other things, he had moved his clothes, some furniture, pictures, photo albums, and other memorabilia into the home he shared with Mrs. Creal and her children; he contributed to household costs; and he purchased a new bedroom set with his wife. Although Mr. Creal retained some connections with the State of Missouri, the court does not find these connections sufficient to overcome the evidence that his actions from January 2000 until the time of his death demonstrated an intent to remain with his wife in the State of Kansas. In fact, the only evidence presented by Plaintiffs that directly calls Mr. Creal's intent into question is the deposition testimony of Mrs. Creal that the couple left open the possibility of leaving Troy to move to a location like Platte City or Faucett, Missouri, but that they never looked for houses there or made any specific plans to leave. At most, Mrs. Creal's testimony evidences a "floating intention" of Mr. Creal to return to his former domicile, which is insufficient to overcome the evidence that he was domiciled in the State of Kansas at the time of his death.

In conclusion, the court has considered all of the evidence and arguments presented by the parties and holds that Mr. Creal was a citizen of the State of Kansas at the time of his death. Because Plaintiffs have failed to carry their burden of showing that complete diversity exists among the parties, the court grants Defendants' motion to dismiss for lack of subject matter jurisdiction.

IT IS, THEREFORE, BY THE COURT ORDERED that Defendants' motion to dismiss is granted.

The case is closed.

NOTES AND PROBLEMS

1. In an auto accident case, one expects that the parties will argue about whose careless driving caused the accident. Why aren't these parties asking the judge to decide that question?

2. Why do plaintiffs lose?

a. Troy, Kansas, where the Creals lived during their short marriage, is about sixteen miles from St. Joseph, Missouri, which lies on the eastern bank of the Missouri River. Mr. Creal still conducted most of his business affairs — car registration and insurance, life insurance and paycheck address — in Missouri. Why wasn't this enough to make him a "citizen" of Missouri.

b. What's the smallest factual change that would, you think, lead to a different outcome? If the Creals had signed a lease in St. Joseph, but not yet moved there? If Mr. Creal had not moved his "memorabilia" into their Kansas apartment? If the Creals had not married?

3. What does it mean that plaintiffs have lost this motion?

a. Can plaintiffs file the claim again in federal court?

b. Can plaintiffs file the claim again in a state court?

c. The answer to the latter question is "probably." One might think that during the federal litigation, the statute of limitations would expire but Kansas, like many states, has a "savings" statute, which provides:

> If any action be commenced within due time, and the plaintiff fail in such action otherwise than upon the merits, and the time limited for the same shall have expired, the plaintiff, or, if the plaintiff die, and the cause of action survive, his or her representatives may commence a new action within six (6) months after such failure.

K.S.A. §60-518.

The action in federal court apparently "was commenced within due time," that is, within the statute of limitations, and it failed for a reason "otherwise than upon the merits," namely a jurisdictional dismissal.

4. Why did the parties have this fight in the first place?

a. If plaintiff can refile her claim in a Kansas court, why did defendants (or more likely the lawyer hired by their insurance carrier) spend time and money getting the case dismissed from federal court? Does it help to know that interest on claims like this one will not start to accrue until judgment is entered?

b. Conversely, if there was any doubt about the existence of federal diversity jurisdiction, why did plaintiffs (or, more likely, their lawyer who is probably working on a contingent fee arrangement) waste time and effort on a losing gamble when they could have been proceeding with state court litigation? Mrs. Creal's lawyer's goal was to achieve a satisfactory outcome for his client. Filing in federal court was one possible route. What advantages might such a filing have?

i. Speed might be one: Some federal courts have shorter waiting times to trial than do state courts. At the time the case was filed, the Kansas state courts were experiencing a fiscal crisis that had led to staff hiring freezes, and might be expected to lead to longer case processing times.

ii. Tactical advantage might be another: There are only two state judges in Doniphan county, where Troy is located, so Ms. Creal's lawyer could make a pretty good guess who would be hearing the case. Was he trying to avoid a judge who he feared might not be sympathetic to his client's claim?

5. How did the court come to know all of the facts about the Creals which the court relied upon in making its ruling?

a. For the most part, issues that arise before trial are decided based on written presentations of evidence, usually affidavits (sworn statements) from witnesses. The affidavits may incorporate documentary evidence: bills, correspondence, photographs, and the like. If you were representing plaintiff, whom would you have contacted to obtain an affidavit?

b. In this case, because there was a dispute over the facts relating to the question of jurisdiction, the court says that it considered deposition testimony as well. At a deposition, a witness is questioned under oath before a court reporter by lawyers for all parties, usually at one attorney's offices. The witness can also be requested to bring documents in her possession to the deposition, which then can be reviewed and possibly marked as exhibits. The transcript and exhibits from the deposition are then submitted to the court as evidence. If you were representing defendant, whom would you have liked to depose to obtain evidence to support your argument that the court lacked jurisdiction? What documents would you have asked the witness to bring to the deposition? What questions would you have asked?

c. As you read cases in this book, and in your other law school courses, consider in each instance how the court came to know the facts that the court relies upon in its opinion. Much of lawyering consists of marshalling the facts and trying to persuade the court that your client's version of the facts is more credible than your opponent's version.

6. On the basis of cases like *Hawkins*, you decide to bring Peters's case in a federal court. Peters will return to school next week. Do you think that it is a better idea to file the case now or to wait? If you think waiting is a good idea, do you have any advice concerning things Peters might do when he returns to school?

2.   Personal Jurisdiction

After deciding whether to file Peters's suit in a federal or state court, we still have to decide in which state to bring the case. Whether the suit is commenced in a state court or in a federal court located in a particular state, it may be brought only in a state where the defendant is subject to personal jurisdiction. That is, the state court or federal court in that state must have the power to render a judgment against this particular defendant — Dodge, in our hypothetical case. For present purposes, you may assume that the personal jurisdiction of a federal court within a given state is the same as that of a state court in the same state. Federal Rule of Civil Procedure 4(k)(1)(A).* That is, if Peters can obtain personal jurisdiction over Dodge in the state court in a given state, he can also obtain personal jurisdiction in a federal court in the same state.

Traditionally, obtaining personal jurisdiction over a defendant required service of process on such defendant (that is, someone's handing to the defendant papers containing the complaint and an order to come to court to explain his conduct)

---

* Hereafter, we will simply cite these as Rule _____. The Federal Rules of Civil Procedure, which govern procedure in the district courts, are promulgated by the U.S. Supreme Court pursuant to 28 U.S.C. §2072.

within the particular state. Today, courts assert jurisdiction over persons who were not personally served within the state. For example, a person permanently residing in Illinois is subject to jurisdiction in that state even if served outside of its borders. Courts have also held that persons who engaged in certain types of activities in a state are subject to jurisdiction for claims arising from those activities. For example, in the early part of the last century, many states enacted so-called nonresident motorist statutes, which provided that any nonresident who drove within a state was subject to personal jurisdiction in the state for claims arising from accidents. The notion of personal jurisdiction has since expanded far beyond that, as you will see in Chapter II.

NOTES AND PROBLEMS

1. So far as federal subject matter jurisdiction is concerned, if one federal district court has jurisdiction, all have it.

2. How does the doctrine of personal jurisdiction narrow Peters's choice of courts?
   a. Is Dodge subject to personal jurisdiction in Illinois?
   b. Is Dodge subject to personal jurisdiction in Michigan?

3. Venue

There is a third set of rules regulating the place where Peters can bring his action, and these are rules of *venue*. The term "venue" means, quite simply, "place of trial," and venue rules are an attempt to allocate business among those courts that have subject matter and personal jurisdiction. A suit lies open to a defendant's challenge unless the court has subject matter jurisdiction, personal jurisdiction, *and* venue.

Where would venue be proper if Peters brought his suit in a federal court? To apply the federal venue rules, a brief word must be said about the structure of the federal court system. There are three levels of federal courts. Actions are commenced and tried in the *district courts*. A district sometimes comprises part of a state and sometimes the entire state. Thus, Illinois has three districts; Michigan, two districts; California, four districts; and Kansas, a single district.

Assume we have decided to file our case in a federal court in Illinois, which is divided into three districts—the Northern District (the northern part of the state, including Chicago); the Central District (the southeastern part of the state, including Champaign); and the Southern District (the southwestern part of the state).

NOTES AND PROBLEMS

1. Examine 28 U.S.C. §1391(a). On the facts of Peters v. Dodge, where will venue be proper ("lie" in lawyer's jargon)?

2. Why won't venue lie in the Eastern District of Michigan (which includes Ann Arbor, Michigan, where Peters attends school)?

If Peters's case had been brought in a state court, we would encounter similar venue rules. Most often, the states have set up a number of judicial districts with one court of general jurisdiction for each district. Usually the judicial districts are set up along county lines, although for less populous counties, one judicial district may cover several counties. The state venue rules would tell us in which judicial district to bring the case. Although state venue rules vary widely, most permit the case to be brought where either party resides, where the claim arose, or where a defendant is doing business. Thus, if our case had been brought in the Circuit Court of Illinois, proper venue would lie in the Circuit Court for Champaign County.

4.   Service of Process

Once we (as advisers to Peters's lawyer) have decided where to bring the suit, we must begin the action and notify the defendant that it has begun. The first thing to do is to draft a *complaint.* See Forms 9-12 for examples of common sorts of claims.* A copy of the complaint must be filed with the court. Rule 3.

Then the plaintiff's lawyer must decide how to notify the defendant. Rule 4 sets forth two basic means of notice, one inexpensive and informal, the other more expensive and formal. The inexpensive method, called waiver of service, involves mailing the defendant the complaint and Forms 1A and 1B; if the defendant mails back a signed copy of Form 1B, the suit can proceed. The expensive method, used if the defendant refuses to cooperate, requires the lawyer to draft a *summons* (see Form 1), and take it to the clerk of the court, who will sign and seal it. See Rule 4(a) and (b). The summons and complaint must then be "served" — that is, delivered to the defendant in one of the ways authorized by Rule 4 — by private process servers or, in exceptional cases, a federal marshal. See Rule 4(c).

C.   Stating the Case

1.   The Lawyer's Responsibility

The preceding paragraphs referred in passing to the lawyer's drafting of a complaint. Do not be misled by that casual reference: A complaint asks the

----

* The drafters of the Federal Rules have compiled an Appendix of Forms for use with the Rules. See Rule 84. These will be cited as Form _____.

formal legal system to use governmental power to grant plaintiff relief. Those invoking that system also bear the responsibility not to invoke it for improper purposes. Lawyers bear special burdens in this respect. Read Rule 11 and consider it in connection with the next case.

Bridges v. Diesel Service, Inc.

1994 U.S. Dist. LEXIS 9429 (E.D. Pa. 1994)

HUYETT, J.

Rule 11

I. Background

James Bridges ("Plaintiff") commenced this action against Diesel Service, Inc. ("Defendant") under the Americans with Disabilities Act ("ADA"), 42 U.S.C. §12101 et seq. [Bridges alleged that Diesel Service dismissed him from his job as a result of a disability and thus violated the ADA.] By Order dated June 29, 1994, the Court dismissed Plaintiff's Complaint without prejudice for failure to exhaust administrative remedies. In particular, Plaintiff did not file a charge with the Equal Employment Opportunity Commission ("EEOC") until after commencement of this action. Defendant now moves for sanctions pursuant to Fed. R. Civ. P. 11. . . .

II. Discussion

. . . [A]s explained in this Court's June 29 Order, the filing of a charge with the EEOC is . . . a condition precedent to maintenance of a discrimination suit under the ADA. The parties do not dispute that administrative remedies must be exhausted before commencement of an action under the ADA. . . .

Rule 11 "imposes an obligation on counsel and client analogous to the railroad crossing sign, 'Stop, Look and Listen.' It may be rephrased, 'Stop, Think, Investigate and Research' before filing papers either to initiate the suit or to conduct the litigation." Gaiardo v. Ethyl Corp., 835 F.2d 479, 482 (3d Cir. 1987). Rule 11 is violated only if, at the time of signing, the signing of the document filed was objectively unreasonable under the circumstances. "The Rule does not permit the use of the 'pure heart and an empty head' defense." *Gaiardo*. Rather, counsel's signature certifies the pleading is supported by a reasonable factual investigation and "a normally competent level of legal research." Lieb v. Topstone Industries, Inc., 788 F.2d 151, 157 (3d Cir. 1986).

The Court is not convinced that Plaintiff's counsel displayed a competent level of legal research. A brief review of case law would have revealed the EEOC filing requirement. Further, an award of sanctions for failure to exhaust administrative remedies is not unprecedented.

Notwithstanding, the Court will not grant sanctions. Rule 11 is not intended as a general fee-shifting device. The prime goal of Rule 11 sanctions is deterrence of improper conduct. In this case, monetary sanctions are not necessary to deter future misconduct. Plaintiff's counsel immediately acknowledged its error and attempted to rectify the situation by filing a charge with the EEOC and moving to place this action in civil suspense. In fact, the Complaint has been dismissed without prejudice. The Court expects that Plaintiff's counsel has learned its lesson and will demonstrate greater diligence in future.

Further, Rule 11 sanctions should be reserved for those exceptional circumstances where the claim asserted is patently unmeritorious or frivolous. The mistake in the present case was procedural rather than substantive. It is also possible that Plaintiff's counsel was confused by the different interpretations of the Supreme Court's holding in [a case interpreting the EEOC filing requirement]. Finally, the Court is aware of the need to avoid "chilling" Title VII litigation.

III.   Conclusion

For the above stated reasons, Defendant's motion pursuant to Fed. P. Civ. P. 11 is DENIED. However, this Opinion should not be read as condoning the conduct of Plaintiff's counsel. As stated above, the standard of pre-filing research was below that required of competent counsel. Plaintiff's case has been dismissed without prejudice. If the action is refiled, the Court fully expects to see a high standard of legal product from Plaintiff's counsel—in particular attorney London, who signed the Complaint.

NOTES AND PROBLEMS

1. What did the plaintiff's lawyer do wrong according to the court? What should she have done? What provision of Rule 11(b) was violated?

2. The court concludes that the plaintiff's lawyer violated Rule 11 by signing and filing a complaint that was "objectively unreasonable under the circumstances." But the court nevertheless declines to impose a sanction. What word in Rule 11(c) gives the court this discretion?

3. The judge, the defendant, and the plaintiff agree that the complaint was defective and that it will be easy to cure the defect by filing the right piece of paper with the Commission. If the defect is so minor and so easy to cure, why did the defendant bother to file a motion for sanctions?

a. One possibility is that the defendant hoped to collect fees for the relatively small amount of time necessary to bring the preceding motion to dismiss. Possible, but not likely: Most judges would view such a motion as a waste of time —and think ill of the defendant's lawyer for imposing on the court.

So why wouldn't the defendant's lawyer just write plaintiff's lawyer a letter pointing out the error and ask the plaintiff's counsel to dismiss the action without prejudice, hopefully avoiding a formal motion? If the defendant's lawyer had done so and plaintiff's counsel had persisted in refusing to dismiss the action, do you think the court's decision on sanctions might have been different?

b. Consider another possibility. Many employment discrimination lawyers would say that the EEOC filing requirement as a precondition of suit was quite elementary, and that a lawyer unfamiliar with it was likely not familiar with this area of the law. Supposing such an assessment to be correct, consider what signals the defendant's lawyer would be sending to the judge with such a motion. Are there signs in the opinion that the judge has heard those between-the-lines signals?

2. The Complaint *(17)*

Bridges illustrates one facet of a lawyer's responsibility in drafting a complaint. But even if Peters's lawyer is entirely comfortable that the claim is well grounded in fact and in law, she must still confront the task of setting forth that claim in a formal document. What should be in a complaint? Should it contain a simple statement that Peters is suing Dodge for injuries suffered in an accident, a detailed recitation of what each party did on the day of the accident, and a blow-by-blow account of plaintiff's injuries and recovery, or something else? The model forms furnish some guidance. See, for example, Form 9.

Bell v. Novick Transfer Co.

17 F.R.D. 279 (D. Md. 1955)   *Rule 8*

THOMPSEN, J.

In this tort action, originally filed in the Court of Common Pleas of Baltimore City, and removed to this court pursuant to 28 U.S.C. §§1441 and 1446, defendants have moved to "dismiss the Declaration" because (1) it "fails to state a claim against the defendants and each of them upon which relief can be granted"; (2) it "alleges only that an accident occurred due to the negligence of the defendants as a result of which the plaintiffs were injured"; and (3) it "fails to allege the specific acts of negligence by the defendants of which the plaintiffs complain."

The [complaint, known in Maryland as a] declaration[,] alleges that [1] "on or about August 14, 1954, while the Infant Plaintiff, Ronald Bell, was riding in an automobile headed in a northerly direction on Race Road at its intersection with Pulaski Highway, both said road and highway being public highways of Baltimore County, State of Maryland, the automobile in which the infant plaintiff was riding was run into and struck by an automobile tractor-trailer outfit owned by the Defendants, Novick Transfer Company, Inc., and Katie Marie Parsons, and operated at the time by their agent, servant or employee, the Defendant, Morris Jarrett Coburn, III, in a careless, reckless and negligent manner, in a westerly direction on Pulaski Highway at the intersection aforesaid, [2] so that" the infant plaintiff was injured. The declaration also alleges the injuries and damage, and that they were "the direct result of the negligence on the part of the defendants" without any negligence on the part of the plaintiffs contributing thereto.

Although this declaration may not be sufficient under Maryland practice, Jeter v. Schwind Quarry Co., it meets the requirements of Rule 8, Fed. Rules Civ. Proc., which requires only "a short and plain statement of the claim showing that the pleader is entitled to relief." See Official Form 9 in Appendix to Rules.

Nor is defendant entitled in this case to "a more definite statement" by motion under Rule 12(e). Although some courts have held that such a motion is the correct procedure to follow if a party needs further information to prepare his defense, the better rule of law is that such information should be obtained by interrogatories under Rule 33, or other discovery procedure, unless it is really necessary to enable the party to frame his responsive pleading.

Defendant may obtain by interrogatories or other discovery procedure the facts upon which plaintiff based its allegations that the truck was being operated in a careless, reckless and negligent manner, and that such negligence was the direct cause of the injury to the infant plaintiff.

The motion is hereby overruled.

NOTES AND PROBLEMS

1. To understand what this fight is about, reread the second paragraph of the opinion, which quotes the significant parts of the complaint, which are preceded by numbers in square brackets (e.g., [1]). Imagine yourself in the position of the defendant. What other information would defendant want the complaint to contain?

a. If the plaintiff knew this information, why not require him to state it in the complaint?

b. If the plaintiff did not know this information, would filing the complaint violate Rule 11? (The case arose before the current version of Rule 11.)

2. Notice that the plaintiff alleged that his own negligence did not contribute to the accident.

a. Was this necessary? Rule 8(c).

b. Supposing it was not necessary, why might the plaintiff nevertheless want to include it in a complaint?

3. The court in passing notes that the complaint was not sufficiently detailed to pass muster under the then-prevailing Maryland state court pleading rules.

a. Where was the suit originally filed?

b. How did it get to federal court? The case tells us it was "removed." As you will see, under some circumstances it is possible for a defendant to second-guess plaintiff's original choice of a court. Defendant here did so, by "removing" the case to federal district court. Does the outcome of this case suggest that doing so was a mistake?

On the basis of *Novick Transfer Co.*, Peters's attorney has drafted the following complaint:

United States District Court for the Central District of Illinois

Paul Peters, Plaintiff	COMPLAINT FOR NEGLIGENCE
v.	File No._____
Dan Dodge, Defendant	

Plaintiff, Paul Peters, for his complaint, alleges as follows:

1. Plaintiff, Paul Peters, is a citizen of the state of Michigan, and defendant, Dan Dodge, is a citizen of the state of Illinois. The matter in controversy exceeds $75,000, exclusive of interest and costs.

2. On January 1, 2004, Paul Peters was operating his car on Main Street in Champaign, Illinois.

3. At 4:00 P.M. on that date, a car owned and operated by defendant Dan Dodge negligently collided with plaintiff's car, causing damage to plaintiff's car and injury to plaintiff's person.

4. Plaintiff suffered a sprained neck, broken arm, and numerous bruises and lacerations, and incurred medical expenses in the amount of $25,000.

WHEREFORE, plaintiff demands judgment for $100,000, together with the costs of this action.

> *Ursula Sands*
> Attorney for Plaintiff
> 123 Church Street
> Champaign, Illinois 61820
> 217/353-5775

3.   The Response — Motions and Answer

Once the defendant has been properly notified of the claim, attention shifts to his response — the defense of the action. Although it would be possible to have a system in which defendant was not required to do anything until trial, both the Federal Rules and state codes of procedure require some response by the defendant. Generally, that response takes one of two forms: a *motion* attacking the summons and complaint in some way or a responsive pleading (usually called an *answer*).

Theoretically, six types of responses are available to a defendant:

Preanswer Motions

Motions are simply requests to the court that it do something; lawyers speak of "moving" or of "making a motion" to have the court take some step — dismiss the case, enter judgment on a verdict, and so on. At the early stages of the complaint, there are various motions that a defendant may make to end the case or to alter its shape.

1. There may be reasons, having nothing to do with the claim itself, why the action should not proceed. These reasons typically relate to the court in which the action is brought or the method by which the defendant was brought into that court. For example, the defendant may contend that the case should be dismissed because it does not belong in federal court (subject matter jurisdiction); such a motion brought forth the decision in Hawkins v. Masters Farms, the first case in this chapter. See Rule 12(b)(1).

2. The defendant may say that, even if everything in the complaint is true, under the substantive law plaintiff has no right to relief. The typical elementary example is a complaint that alleges that the defendant made a face at the plaintiff or that the defendant drove a car of an offensive color. At common law, the defendant would *demur* to such claims; now we say that the complaint fails to state a claim upon which relief can be granted. See Rule 12(b)(6). Bell v. Novick Transfer was written in response to the defendant's Rule 12(b)(6) motion.

3. The defendant may be unsure of what is being asserted, finding the complaint either vague or confused and complicated. In this case, defendant might want a "more definite statement" of the complaint. See Rule 12(e). (Defendant in Bell v. Novick Transfer made a Rule 12(e) motion.)

The Answer

Notice an important characteristic of the motions described above: *they take no position on the truth or falsity of plaintiff's allegations.* By contrast, an *answer*, as the name suggests, does respond to the allegations of the complaint. There are only two essential variations on the answer:

1. In the most common response to a complaint the defendant denies the truth of one or more of the allegations of the complaint, or, if the defendant does not know whether an allegation is true, he may deny the allegation until he finds out. See Rule 8(b).

2. The defendant may want to assert additional matters that will wholly or partially defeat plaintiff's claim. For example, the defendant may claim that the applicable statute of limitations has run or that the plaintiff has released her claim. We call such assertions *affirmative defenses.* See Rule 8(c).

These five categories of motions and answers exhaust most possible responses to the complaint. It is common, however, for the defendant to want to assert his own claims against the plaintiff, another defendant, or a new party. Such claims are called, respectively, *counterclaims, cross-claims,* and *third-party* claims. See Rules 13(a), (b), (g), and 14. We will discuss this sixth category of responses in a subsequent section.

In modern procedure a defendant may respond to the complaint using several of the categories sketched above. For example, the defendant in Bell v. Novick Transfer made both Rule 12(b)(6) and Rule 12(e) motions. With a little effort one can hypothesize situations in which a defendant would want to assert all six possible responses to the complaint.

Once you have digested this catalogue of responses to the complaint, it is important to know that there is still one procedural distinction among them. The Rules (and analogous state procedural systems) permit the defendant to make some responses in a *pre-answer motion*. Rule 12(a). Others may be made only in an answer. This distinction matters because a pre-answer motion, unlike an answer, offers the defendant the possibility of getting an immediate dismissal of plaintiff's claim (or, at a minimum, a significant delay before he refiles it). An answer, by contrast, establishes the battle lines for what may prove a long course of litigation. Moreover, to answer the defendant must take a position as to the truth of the plaintiff's allegations. So if a pre-answer motion is available, defendants often find it attractive.

NOTES AND PROBLEMS

1. If the defendant makes a pre-answer motion, what does she want the court to do? (Consider Hawkins v. Masters Farms and Bell v. Novick Transfer as examples.) If the court grants the motion, why is the defendant not required to answer the complaint?

2. Can the defendant make a pre-answer motion on the ground

a. that everything the plaintiff alleges is false?

b. that she was not properly served with a copy of the complaint?

c. that venue is improper?

3. If Dodge wants to make a pre-answer motion, he will prepare and file a series of papers with the court and serve them on Peters:

a. A notice of the motion — which simply tells the other side that the defendant plans to make a motion, what that motion is (here, a motion to dismiss for want of subject matter jurisdiction), and the time and place at which the motion will be heard by the judge;

b. A memorandum of points and authorities (a short brief discussing his case and the reasons the court should grant his motion);

c. Any evidence pertinent to the motion — perhaps an affidavit (a sworn declaration) and copies of documents concerning Dodge's and Peters's residence and local affiliations.

4. The judge will typically have read the "motion papers" before the hearing and will usually hear oral argument from the lawyers. She may decide the motion on the spot or she may "reserve" her ruling, making it after additional thought or research. Sometimes a judge will issue a tentative ruling based on the papers, which is given to the lawyers when they arrive for the hearing. The judge then allows the "losing" party to argue against the tentative ruling.

If the defendant does not make a pre-answer motion or if the court denies a pre-answer motion, the defendant must then answer. See Rules 7(a), 12(a). Generally, the defendant can include any or all of the possible responses in his answer.* Thus a defendant may claim that the complaint does not state a claim

---

* There are exceptions if the defendant has made a pre-answer motion and has not included certain defenses. See Rule 12(g), (h). We shall save these more intricate rules for later.

upon which relief can be granted, deny various allegations of the complaint, and allege various affirmative defenses. See Form 20.

Turning to Peters's case, one can surmise that Dodge's attorney will conclude that there is no question relating to personal jurisdiction or venue and that there are no problems with the process itself or service of process. On the other hand, Dodge may very well question the subject matter jurisdiction of the court; it may be that Peters's case is distinguishable from *Hawkins*. And Dodge probably will want to deny certain allegations of the complaint, such as the allegation that defendant was negligent, and also may want to allege various affirmative defenses. For example, in such a case it is quite common for a defendant to claim that the plaintiff's contributory negligence was, at least in part, the cause of the accident. Such contributory negligence will act as a complete or partial defense to recovery.

Before drafting our answer, we also must ask whether defendant wants to make any claim of his own, which would have to be included in the answer. There are three such possibilities: counterclaims, cross-claims, and third-party claims.

NOTES AND PROBLEMS

1. Within what category does Dodge's claim for personal injuries in the collision fall? See Rule 13.

2. What if Dodge had earlier lent Peters money, and Peters had not repaid it. Can Dodge bring a claim for the debt as a counterclaim? What kind of counterclaim?

Cross-claims. Often, a plaintiff will sue several defendants; one of those defendants might then want to sue another for claims arising out of the same transaction. For example, if a pedestrian had been injured in the Peters-Dodge auto accident, he might sue both Peters and Dodge. In such a case, Peters might deny the pedestrian's claim of negligence and also may claim that Dodge was at fault and is liable to Peters for his injuries in the same accident. If Peters asserted such a claim against Dodge, it would be called a cross-claim. See Rule 13(g). Counterclaims involve parties on opposite sides of the "v." that divides plaintiff from defendant in the name of the lawsuit; cross-claims involve parties on the same side of the "v."

NOTES AND PROBLEMS

1. On the facts just noted, can Peters cross-claim against Dodge for breach of a contract for the sale of goods?

2. In the original Peters-Dodge action, there will not be any cross-claims because there is only one party on each side of the lawsuit, and cross-claims

are possible only when there are at least two parties on the same side of the suit.

Third-party claims.   In some cases, a defendant may want to assert a claim against a party not in the action. Rule 14 would permit Dodge to file a third-party complaint against (*implead*) any party that is liable to Dodge for Peters's claim against Dodge. Suppose Dodge was engaged on an assignment for Tucker at the time of the accident and Tucker had agreed to indemnify Dodge for any liabilities Dodge incurred in performing this mission. Dodge could implead Tucker as a third-party defendant. In such a suit, Peters would be the plaintiff, Dodge would be the defendant and third-party plaintiff, and Tucker would be the third-party defendant.*

After considering the possible responses and possible counterclaims, cross-claims, and third-party claims, Dodge's attorney has drafted the following answer to Peters's complaint.

Answer

**United States District Court for the Central
District of Illinois**

Paul Peters,
      Plaintiff   ANSWER AND COUNTERCLAIM

  v.

                            File No. _____

Dan Dodge,
      Defendant

Defendant, Dan Dodge, answers the complaint of plaintiff herein as follows:

1. Admits that defendant is a citizen of the state of Illinois, and, except as admitted, denies the allegations of paragraph 1 of the complaint.

2. Admits that, at approximately 4:00 PM on January 1, 2004, plaintiff was operating a car on Main Street in Champaign, Illinois, and, except as admitted, states that defendant is without information or belief sufficient to form a belief as to the truth of the allegations in paragraph 2 of the complaint and, on that basis, denies the allegations of paragraph 2 of the complaint.

3. Admits that, at approximately 4:00 PM on January 1, 2004, there was a collision between a car owned and operated by defendant and a car owned and operated by plaintiff and that plaintiff's vehicle was damaged and plaintiff suffered some injury as a result of said collision and, except as admitted, defendant denies the allegations of paragraph 3 of the complaint.

---

* If a third party is brought in, it may be possible for each of the parties to make claims against the others. We will save discussion of issues related to such multiple claims until later.

4. Defendant states that he is without information sufficient to form a belief as to the truth of the allegations in paragraph 4 of the complaint and, on that basis, denies the allegations of paragraph 4 of the complaint.

FIRST DEFENSE

5. The court lacks jurisdiction over the subject matter of this action because plaintiff and defendant are not citizens of different states.

SECOND DEFENSE

6. Defendant alleges that plaintiff drove his car carelessly and recklessly, and that such careless and reckless operation was a cause of the accident.

COUNTERCLAIM

7. On January 1, 2004, at approximately 4:00 PM at Main Street in Champaign, Illinois, Paul Peters drove a car in a careless, reckless, and negligent manner and thereby caused said car to collide with a car owned and operated by Dan Dodge.

8. As a result of said collision, Dodge's car was damaged, and Dodge also suffered a whiplash injury, as well as numerous cuts and bruises, and incurred expenses for medical treatment of $1,800.

WHEREFORE, defendant demands judgment dismissing Peters's action and judgment against Peters on the counterclaim in the amount of $12,000, together with the costs thereof.

_____

Yvonne O. Upton
Attorney for Defendant
125 Church Street
Champaign, Illinois 61820
217/353-7531

NOTES AND PROBLEMS

1. Contrast this answer with the hypothetical preanswer motion discussed in the previous section.

a. Note first the difference in scope. Unlike the motion, the answer responds to all the allegations of the complaint, rather than selecting one or two vulnerable aspects.

b. Unlike the motion, the answer seeks no immediate relief from the court; instead it sets the stage for various future battles. For example, if Dodge had not made a pre-answer motion on this basis, he could, on the basis of his first defense, seek to have the case dismissed for want of subject matter jurisdiction, but the answer itself does not seek this immediate termination of the lawsuit.

2. What would happen if the answer failed to respond to some of the allegations of the complaint? See Rule 8(d).

3. What is the purpose and effect of stating that the defendant lacked information or belief sufficient to admit or deny some of the allegations of the complaint? See Rule 8(b).

4. Reread paragraph 3 of the complaint. Could Dodge have made a blanket denial of this paragraph on the grounds that he thought he wasn't negligent? What potential confusion might this lead to? See Rule 8(b).

5. Are the allegations in paragraph 7 of the answer ambiguous? What exactly is Dodge alleging? Having filed such a counterclaim, could Dodge seek to introduce evidence that Peters's brakes failed because he had not properly maintained them?

6. Now that Yvonne Upton has drafted the answer, what should she do with it? See Rule 5(a), (d).

4. Amendment of Pleadings

The Federal Rules reject the view that the case is "set in stone" once the pleadings are completed. Instead, the Rules reflect a liberal policy toward changes (called *amendments*) to the pleadings. The discovery rules, which enable parties to gather information about the case, would mean little if new information could not be reflected in amended pleadings. For example, the Peters v. Dodge complaint assumes that Dodge was both the owner and driver of the vehicle. Discovery might reveal that Dodge's parents are co-owners on the vehicle title (perhaps they cosigned a loan to purchase the car). Under the substantive law, all owners of the vehicle are liable for accidents negligently caused by a permissive driver. Dodge's parents could then be added as defendants (which might make a difference if the amount of liability exceeded the insurance coverage).

Rule 15(a) sets forth the basic amendment rules and states that "leave to amend shall be freely given when justice so requires." Rule 15(c) deals with amendments that are interposed after the statute of limitations on the "new" claim has run. Rule 15(b) deals with amendments interposed during the course of trial to reflect the introduction of evidence that is not within the scope of the pleadings.

D. Parties to the Lawsuit

Our Peters-Dodge lawsuit is an action by a single plaintiff against a single defendant, but litigation often is not so simple; the events giving rise to a lawsuit may affect more than two persons, sometimes many more. The procedural issues raised by the involvement of multiple parties are discussed under a variety of headings. First, who *may* be joined as a plaintiff or a defendant in the lawsuit? See Rule 20. Second, who *must* be joined as a plaintiff or a defendant in the lawsuit? See Rule 19. Third, are there persons who are not in the lawsuit who can join as parties if they so choose? See Rule 24. Fourth, may some of the parties in the lawsuit represent others who are not in the lawsuit, so that the final decision will determine the rights of all? See Rule 23. There are other party issues as well, but these will give you their flavor.

1.   Permissive and Compulsory Joinder

Rule 20 governs permissive joinder. Note that the plaintiff has a choice of whom to join as a coplaintiff as well as whom to join as a codefendant. Imagine that Peters was riding in the car with Passenger, and that the car had been struck by two other vehicles, one driven by Dodge and the other by Dusty. Could Peters and Passenger sue Dodge and Dusty in one lawsuit? Could they also sue Mechanic, whom Dusty believes badly repaired his brakes and may thus have contributed to the accident? Does the next case, which reflects a collision between Hollywood and Nashville, answer your question?

Bridgeport Music, Inc. v. 11C Music

202 F.R.D. 229 (M.D. Tenn., Nashville Division 2001)

CAMPBELL, District Judge.

I.   Introduction . . .

Plaintiffs, entities engaged in publishing, recording, and distributing music, bring this action against over 770 [music and entertainment companies]. Plaintiffs assert a variety of claims arising out of numerous instances of what they describe as the "sampling" of music in which they claim an ownership interest.[1] They allege copyright infringement. . . . Due primarily to the number of Defendants, Plaintiffs' complaint is an exceptionally large document. It includes 486 counts, most of which contain multiple claims. It is 901 pages long not including exhibits.

Defendants argue that Plaintiffs have violated Rules 8 and 20 of the Federal Rules of Civil Procedure because Plaintiffs' complaint does not give a "short and plain statement" of its claims, see Fed. R. Civ. P. 8, and because Defendants are not properly joined, see Fed. R. Civ. P. 20. . . .

II.   Analysis

Defendants argue that they are not properly joined. Federal Rule of Civil Procedure 20(a) provides that:

> [a]ll persons . . . may be joined in one action as defendants if there is asserted against
> them jointly, severally, or in the alternative, any right to relief in respect of or arising
> out of the same transaction, occurrence, or series of transactions or occurrences and
> if any question of law or fact common to all defendants will arise in the action.

Rule 20(a) is designed to promote judicial economy and trial convenience. This accords with the general principle under the Federal Rules of Civil

---

1. "Sampling," according to the complaint, is the copying of portions of prior master sound recordings of earlier musical compositions directly onto new sound recordings.

Procedure to allow "the broadest possible scope of action consistent with fairness to the parties." United Mine Workers of Am. v. Gibbs, 383 U.S. 715, 724 (1966) ("[J]oinder of claims, parties and remedies is strongly encouraged.").

Permissive joinder is circumscribed, however, by the dual requirements of a common question and transactional relatedness. The first of these, the common question test, is usually easy to satisfy. The transactional test, however, is more forbidding. It requires that, to be joined, parties must assert rights, or have rights asserted against them, that arise from related activities — a transaction or an occurrence or a series thereof. See, e.g., Michaels Bldg. Co. v. Ameritrust Co., 848 F.2d 674, 682 (6th Cir. 1988) (finding that a loan made to the plaintiff by one defendant was unrelated to loans made to the plaintiff by other defendants and that joinder was therefore improper); Demboski v. CSX Transp., Inc., 157 F.R.D. 28, 29-30 (S.D. Miss. 1994) (holding that four separate railway accidents involving the same defendant did not constitute a series of occurrences); Rappoport v. Steven Spielberg, Inc., 16 F. Supp. 2d 481, 496 (D.N.J. 1998) (severing a plaintiffs' claims against defendants where plaintiff alleged copyright infringement in separate works in different media). This test is easy to articulate, but it is often difficult to apply. Because it does not lend itself to bright line rules, it generally requires a case by case analysis. . . .

Defendants argue that . . . Plaintiffs' 477 counts of alleged copyright infringement "are really 477 separate lawsuits rolled into one enormous pleading;" each allegedly infringing song represents a separate transaction or occurrence. They suggest that each infringement count brought by Plaintiffs will require a unique set of proof. . . .

Plaintiff responds that . . . 1) that Defendants and the claims against them are intricately interrelated; 2) that Defendants have inflicted the same harm against Plaintiffs; 3) that certain Defendants repeatedly infringed Plaintiffs' copyrights, often in different capacities (e.g., as publisher, administrator, label, or entertainment company); and 4) that a small number of clearance companies, manufacturers, and distributors were involved in most of the allegedly infringing songs giving rise to Plaintiffs' claims. . . .

The Court finds that . . . [e]ach song and the alleged sampling contained therein represents a discrete occurrence. The fact that certain Defendants were involved in the production, publishing, and distribution of more than one allegedly offending song does not, in itself, cause these songs to be related occurrences in the manner contemplated by Rule 20(a). In this respect, this case is similar to *Demboski*, where the fact that a single railway Defendant was involved in separate train crashes did not create a series of occurrences sufficient to allow joinder of plaintiffs. . . .

Even if the counts in Plaintiffs' complaint arose from the same series of occurrences, the Court would exercise the discretion afforded it to order a severance to avoid causing unreasonable prejudice and expense to Defendants and to avoid a great inconvenience in the administration of justice. . . . As a practical matter, this case is unmanageable in its current form. Because this Court's courtroom would seat only a small fraction of Defendants and their attorneys, it cannot even hold a hearing on the motions currently pending; it cannot host a management conference; it certainly cannot try all — or even most — of the Plaintiffs' counts together. If joined in one action, hundreds of Defendants will be subjected to an overwhelming onslaught of materials and information unrelated to the specific claims against them — all of which they must pay their attorneys to review. . . .

Based on the above, it appears that the severed copyright infringement counts should proceed separately as 477 individual cases. . . . However, in order to give all parties, including non-moving parties, a full opportunity to comment on how severance shall be accomplished, the parties shall have until July 31, 2001, to submit supplemental briefs on the most appropriate method for severance. Finally, as a result of the Court's determination, Defendants' Rule 8 motions are now moot. . . .

NOTES AND PROBLEMS

1. The case presents both basic procedural doctrine and strategy. Start with doctrine:
   a. What exactly, were defendants asking the court to do?
   b. What Rules were they invoking in so arguing?
   c. Who won and why?
   d. What will happen now?

2. As with most procedural decisions, this one does not purport to say who will ultimately prevail in the case. But, as with most procedural decisions, this one makes the road to victory easier for one party and harder for the other. Whom does this decision favor and why?

Returning to our hypothetical case, what happens if the reason for Dodge's dissatisfaction with the defendant lineup is that he believes Daniels, who serviced Dodge's car, should also be in the lawsuit? Under some conditions Dodge may bring in Daniels as a third-party defendant pursuant to Rule 14(a). The Rule's text permits such joinder when Daniels "is or may be liable to [Dodge] for all or part of the plaintiff's claim against him." Such a situation might occur if Dodge alleged that his failure to stop resulted from Daniels's faulty adjustment of the car's brakes. Under those circumstances, Dodge, as the driver of the car, would be liable to Peters, but he could seek to pass that liability on to Daniels.

All the joinder rules surveyed thus far involve the question of when parties to a lawsuit may bring another party into the action. The third party might not be happy about the prospect of being brought in, but from the standpoint of those parties already in the suit, joinder is permissive — that is, they voluntarily sought to bring an additional party into the action. *Compulsory joinder*, on the other hand, involves bringing a party into a lawsuit by order of the court, even though the opposing party might not want him there. The subject has a convoluted history. Born of an important realization — that lawsuits may affect persons who are not formally parties — the principles of compulsory joinder aim at bringing into suits those who may be affected by their results. Rule 19 represents the present codification of this idea, an idea that has proved both difficult and controversial. The difficulty with compulsory joinder is that its impulse to do entire justice, and to do it in one lawsuit, runs afoul of two other principles: the principle of party autonomy (the idea that it is the parties in the lawsuit who should control their own claims and their own litigative strategy); and the principle that courts should seek to decide the claims of the parties now before them.

In general, courts call for joinder when the underlying substantive law in a suit involves rights or liabilities that are *joint*, when two or more parties are claiming the same property, or when granting relief to one party would necessarily affect the rights of another party. Common examples arise in cases involving property that is jointly owned or whose ownership is disputed. If Husband and Wife own property together, then they should both be joined as plaintiffs in a lawsuit for injury to the property, or as defendants in a lawsuit against them for misuse of the property. Similarly, if Trustee is unsure whether to give an antique vase to Son or Daughter, both should be joined in any litigation involving ownership of the vase.

2. Intervention

The rules on intervention mirror those on permissive and compulsory joinder. As noted, it is for the plaintiff to decide whom to join in the first instance, and the defendant can "force" parties into the lawsuit who should be present to avoid possible prejudice to both existing and excluded parties. But if the plaintiff does not wish to join a party, and the defendant either does not wish to join a party or is unable to convince a court that the party should be joined, the absent party can still seek to come into the suit. We call this *intervention*. Rule 24 divides intervention into two categories: *intervention as of right* and *permissive intervention*. Crudely put, a party has a right to intervene when a lawsuit conducted without him has the potential to inflict real hardship on him.

NOTES AND PROBLEMS

1. There is a collision between cars driven by Peters and Dodge. Peters sues Dodge. Passenger, who was riding in Dodge's car, seeks to intervene to assert a claim against Dodge. Although such a mode of proceeding might seem efficient, it interferes with Peters's autonomy. Consequently courts will typically refuse to allow intervention under such circumstances, reasoning that Passenger is free to bring his own lawsuit.

2. Intervention is common in land-use litigation. Suppose the city of Dogpatch at M's request rezones certain land from residential/single-family to residential/multi-family, so that M can use the land to build garden apartments. P, owner of adjacent property, sues City and M, claiming the zoning change is unlawful. Use your intuition to decide who among the following should be permitted to intervene:

a. N, who lives next door to the proposed apartment complex;

b. T, who lives two blocks away and claims that the apartment complex will lower the value of his property (estimated at $250,000);

c. the Sierra Club of Dogpatch; and
d. the Board of Realtors of Dogpatch.

3.   Class Actions

The idea of a *class action* is simple enough. Assume that a given claim or claims involve a large number of plaintiffs or defendants. It would theoretically be possible to join all the plaintiffs or defendants in accordance with Rule 20. But if the number is large enough — for example, over 30 — the multiplicity of parties (and lawyers) would make the action cumbersome indeed. To the extent that the claims of the plaintiffs or defendants are similar, it would seem to make little sense to require joinder of such an excessive number of parties. Thus the solution: Allow some parties to stand in for the entire group.

The subject of class actions attracted comparatively little attention prior to 1966; in that year, however, Rule 23 of the Federal Rules was extensively revised, and that revision served as a catalyst for the development of a vast amount of legal learning and case development of issues surrounding class actions. Indeed, shortly after Professor Wright noted that it would be possible to write a book on class actions of the length of his treatise on federal courts (more than 550 pages), another author proved his estimate decidedly low by writing no fewer than six full volumes.*

The development of the class action has received mixed reviews, some arguing that in the class action lies the solution to the role of law in a mass society, others contending that it represents at best a nuisance, at worst an abuse of the judicial process. The debate over the merit of class actions reflects the uncertainty surrounding the question of what it means to represent another person — an important and troubling question that is fundamental to the idea of procedure in an adversarial system. These issues are too large to be addressed in this introductory survey. Students should scan Rule 23 to know that it exists, but should recognize however, that scanning will provide little of the flavor of the disputes that have raged around its text.

E.   Factual Development — Discovery

Questions of jurisdiction, pleading, and parties typically arise at what may be called the pleading stage of a lawsuit. In order to draft a complaint or answer, the parties must have some understanding of the facts underlying the suit. They can gather those facts in any of the ways in which ordinary citizens, unaided by official sanction, find out about things — through observation, personal knowledge, or conversations with anyone who will talk to them. Before the Federal Rules,

---

* Herbert B. Newberg, Newberg on Class Actions (1977).

factual development largely came about through such efforts of the parties. Much of it still does. Such private inquiry is difficult to "study" in law school, and is consequently often overlooked in civil procedure courses. The limits of such self-help inquiries are not well defined; use your common sense and intuition on the following problems.

NOTES AND PROBLEMS

1. In the Peters-Dodge case, assume that one of the issues in the suit is the seriousness of Peters's injuries and that Peters has been active in college athletics. Upton (Dodge's counsel) wishes to speak to coaches and the athletic department about Peters's pre-accident and post-accident performance. Can Upton question these people on the issue and, if so, how should she go about it?

2. Same facts except that Upton knows that Fred McGolf, an assistant coach, will be a major witness for plaintiff on the issue of Peters's injuries. Can Upton question McGolf?

3. Upton wants to know whether it is proper for her to employ a photographer for either of the following purposes:

a. to stand on the edge of the field where Peters's team practices (on university property, which is open to the public) to photograph Peters while he practices;

b. to sit in a car on the street outside Peters's dormitory to do "surveillance" videotaping.

———————————

In many cases, private inquiry by the parties simply won't work. For example, neither Peters nor Dodge is likely to voluntarily provide information to opposing counsel, and the prospects for obtaining information from witnesses such as Peters's parents, friends, or coach are low. People are sometimes reluctant to become involved in litigation or to produce pertinent information in the absence of legal compulsion. Accordingly, the Rules provide mechanisms for a party to obtain information about the case both from other parties in the case and from third parties not in the case. These rules are grouped under the heading of *discovery*.

The discovery rules, which compel the parties and others involved in a lawsuit to cooperate in the unearthing of factual background, are a major innovation of modern procedure (though they have antecedents in earlier practices). They are also a source of much dispute, both among the parties seeking and resisting discovery and among the commentators debating whether the effort and expense involved in discovery yields real returns either to the judicial system or to the parties.

There are five primary means of discovery. First, unless the court otherwise orders, a party must, without being asked, reveal to each other certain basic information supporting that party's claims or defenses — names of witnesses, the existence of documents, bases for damage calculations, and the like. See Rule 26(a)(1). Beyond these *disclosures*, the parties may seek additional information through several means.

Probably most important is the request for the *production of documents*. See Rules 34 and 45(a)(1)(C). The term "documents" includes everything from printed and written papers to photographs, videotapes, sound recordings, and email. In many cases such records — often in the hands of third parties — will provide the backbone of evidence; in virtually every case such documents will be significant. In Peters v. Dodge, items records might include medical records and receipts for car maintenance. If the records are in the hands of the opposing party, the requesting party uses Rule 34 to demand the production of "specified" documents, and the opposing party must produce the documents at the appointed time and place. Frequently, significant records will be in the hands of nonparties — financial institutions, physicians and hospitals, law enforcement authorities, and the like. If so, Rule 34 will not help because it applies only to parties. To bring non-parties within the power of the court, and thus to obtain documents from them, parties can use a subpoena pursuant to Rule 45 or, in the case of public agencies, by a simple request for public records. In Peters v. Dodge, such a document might be the police report of the accident.

Armed with such documents, the parties may want to conduct *oral depositions*. See Rules 30, 45. An oral deposition may be loosely described as a procedure for questioning a witness under oath before trial. Anyone with information about the lawsuit may be deposed. To begin the process, the attorney taking the deposition serves a notice (and perhaps a subpoena), the person to be questioned shows up (often with an attorney) at the appointed time and place (usually the office of the questioning party), and takes an oath; questions are then asked of and answered by the witness, and the responses are recorded either by audio- or videotape or by a stenographer. There are procedures for handling objectionable questions and for terminating the deposition if it becomes abusive or exceeds the bounds of propriety. In Peters v. Dodge, it's likely that lawyers will want to depose at least the two parties, Peters and Dodge.

Next in importance are *written interrogatories*. See Rule 33. These are written questions to be answered, also in writing, by the opposing party. Written interrogatories can be used only against a party, not against nonparty witnesses. As might be expected, the party's lawyer plays a substantial role in formulating the answers. The most frequently productive use of such interrogatories is to locate relevant documents. In Peters v. Dodge, the parties might ask each other for the location of any records regarding maintenance of their cars and about the existence of medical records and treating physicians.

Finally, there are *physical and mental examinations*. See Rule 35. This discovery device differs from the others in that a motion first must be made to obtain the desired examination. Also, the party seeking the examination must demonstrate that the condition to be examined is in controversy and that there is good cause for the examination. Often, the existence of good cause is not seriously disputed. For example, physical examinations are allowed almost as a matter of course when the plaintiff seeks damages for personal injuries, thereby putting his physical condition at issue. It is much more difficult to obtain an examination for purposes other than showing physical injury. Note, too, that physical and mental examinations are permitted only against parties or those persons in their control (such as children). If there were a significant dispute about the extent of injuries in Peters v. Dodge, the parties might seek such a physical examination.

Rule 26 applies generally to all discovery methods. Read Rule 26(b)(2) and (c) and the following case. As with all discovery cases, frame the issues by asking yourself what is sought to be discovered and why you think the party is seeking that information.

Butler v. Rigby

1998 U.S. Dist. LEXIS 4618 (E.D. La. 1998)

SARAH VANCE, J.

American Medical Group ("AMG") and Midtown Health Care ("MHC") object to Magistrate Judge Chasez's ruling of February 20, 1998. For the reasons that follow, Magistrate Judge Chasez's order is affirmed in part, and reversed in part.

I.   Background

This lawsuit arises out of an automobile accident. . . . AMG and MHC are not parties to this lawsuit, but doctors from both groups provided medical treatment to all of the plaintiffs. Defendants filed identical notices of depositions on AMG and MHC, in which defendants requested certain documents and information. Pertinent to this motion, defendants asked for the following:

> 2) Any and all documents, computer printouts, records, charts, accounting records, tax records, canceled checks, written contracts, letters of guarantee, correspondence and any and all other tangible evidence which reflects:
>> a) A listing of the total number of patients treated at your facility which are involved in litigation since January 1992.
>> b) A listing of the total number of patients treated at your facility that have been referred to you by attorneys since January 1992.
>> c) A listing of the total number of patients/patient accounts for individuals referred you by Evan Tolchinsky, . . . Jose Castro, and/or the Personal Injury Law Center. . . .
>> e) Any and all letters of guarantee or contracts with attorneys or law firms relating to individuals seen, treated, or examined at your facility since 1992.

AMG and MHC moved the Court for a protective order prohibiting defendants from discovering the information requested in 2(a)-(e) on the grounds that it is not relevant to the lawsuit, some of it is protected by the health care provider-patient privilege, and the request is overly burdensome. Magistrate Judge Chasez concluded that most of the information was discoverable. . . .

AMG and MHC object to the Magistrate Judge's ruling. They insist that the information is not relevant to the lawsuit, it is unduly burdensome to non-parties, and some of the information is privileged. . . .

II.   Discussion . . .

B.   Scope of Discovery in General

The Federal Rules contemplate liberal discovery and provide for a flexible treatment of relevance. Under Rule 26(b)(1) of the Federal Rules of Civil Procedure, the scope of discovery includes any matter, not privileged, that is relevant to "the claim or defense [of any party,] including the existence, description, nature, custody, condition, and location of any books, documents, or other tangible things and the identity and location of persons having knowledge of any discoverable matter." Fed. R. Civ. P. 26(b)(1). The rules make clear that the discovery need not be admissible at trial "if the information sought appears reasonably calculated to lead to the discovery of admissible evidence." Id.

Discovery may be limited by the court if it determines that "the discovery sought is unreasonably cumulative or duplicative." Fed. R. Civ. P. 26(b)(2). The court may also restrict discovery if it concludes that "the burden or expense of the proposed discovery outweighs its likely benefit, taking into account the needs of the case, the amount in controversy, the parties['] resources, the importance of the issues at stake in the litigation, and the importance of the proposed discovery in resolving the issues." Id. Further, the federal rules provide that the court "may make any order which justice requires to protect a party or person from annoyance, embarrassment, oppression, or undue burden or expense." Fed. R. Civ. P. 26(c).

C.   The Discovery in Dispute

*1. A listing of the total number of patients referred to AMG and/or
   MHC by Castro, Tolchinsky, and/or the PILC*

AMG and MHC argue that this information has no relevance to plaintiffs' lawsuit, and the request is unduly burdensome. Defendants contend that they seek this information in order to show that the medical groups receive substantial income from the attorneys who initially represented the plaintiffs in this matter, and they argue that such evidence is relevant to show potential bias.

Magistrate Judge Chasez's conclusion that the sought-after information was discoverable was not contrary to law. Evidence of a special relationship between an expert witness and legal counsel is relevant to demonstrate the possible bias of the expert witness, and discovery that is reasonably calculated to lead to such evidence should be permitted. . . .

Further, it was not clearly erroneous for Magistrate Judge Chasez to conclude that the expense or burden of producing this information did not outweigh its likely benefits. . . . However, in light of the medical groups' concerns of time and expense and the sworn affidavit that states that compiling the requested information would require that each individual chart be manually pulled and reviewed, the Court orders that defendants shall pay one-half the costs associated with composing the list of the total number of patients. . . .

3.   *A computer printout of AMG's and MHC's current patients*

Magistrate Judge Chasez ordered that the medical groups are to provide defendants with a computer printout listing their current patients as well as any patient lists that were previously generated. AMG and MHC insist that lists of their current or past patients are privileged from discovery pursuant to La. R.S. 13:3734. The Court agrees and concludes that the magistrate judge's ruling was contrary to law. Rule 501 of the Federal Rules of Evidence provides that [the state law of privilege — here, that of Louisiana — shall govern in diversity cases.] . . .

. . . Louisiana courts have broadly interpreted the scope of the health care provider-patient privilege. [Louisiana's] First Circuit Court of Appeal has concluded that "when an individual walks into a doctor's office and opens his mouth, that everything spilling out of it, whether it be his identity or his false teeth . . . , is presumptively privileged and beyond the reach of discovery." Sarphie v. Rowe, 618 So. 2d 905, 908 (La. App. 1st Cir.), writ. denied, 620 So. 2d 1324 (La. 1993). . . .

In light of this precedent, the Court concludes that the AMG/MHC lists of current and/or past patients is privileged, and the information is therefore not discoverable. Moreover, this Court does not see how the identity of these patients could be relevant to this litigation in any event. Magistrate Judge Chasez's order compelling AMG and MHC to disclose their patient lists was contrary to law, and it is reversed.

For all of the foregoing reasons,

IT IS ORDERED that Magistrate Judge Chasez's ruling of February 20, 1998 is affirmed in part, and reversed in part, in accordance with the Court's conclusions as set forth above.

NOTES AND PROBLEMS

1. From whom are defendants seeking discovery? By what procedural means did defendants seek the documents in question? See Rules 34(a), (c); 45(a)(1)(C), (c)(2)(B).

2. Why are defendants seeking this information?

a. Try to hypothesize information that would help defendant's case.

b. Perhaps defendants seek this information less because they believe it will help their case than because they think it will impede the plaintiffs' efforts. How did the clinics try, unsuccessfully, to object that the discovery sought more to harass than to produce useful information?

3. The court denies defendants access to the names of current and past patients: Why?

a. At the end of the opinion the court says it "does not see how the identity of these patients could be relevant to this litigation. . . ." That statement is probably too hasty. Suppose defendants, armed with these names, interview some of the former patients, who describe how the physicians exaggerated their injuries in order to increase recoverable damages. That would surely be relevant information; would it therefore be discoverable?

b. The answer to the preceding question is no: relevance does not render something discoverable if it is privileged, as the court says that these names are under Louisiana law (though not in some other states). Another way to put it is to say that privilege usually protects disclosure of even highly relevant information.

c. Consider why. The legal system has devised such privileges as the doctor-patient and lawyer-client privileges and the privilege against self-incrimination, to list only a few well-known ones. What is the justification for barring the introduction of highly relevant evidence?

F.   Pretrial Disposition — Summary Judgment

Under the Federal Rules, it is uncommon for cases to be dismissed at the pleading stage. A combination of relaxed pleading rules and a policy that readily permits amendment of defective pleadings tends to minimize the role of pleadings in disposing of cases before trial. Indeed, the provisions for broad discovery implicitly suggest that dismissals should not be granted before each party has had a full opportunity to obtain factual information about the case.

Despite such a policy, orderly and efficient procedure requires some mechanism for deciding cases without trials, if possible. A trial involves substantial financial and social costs, and little purpose is served by having one unnecessarily. In consequence, the Federal Rules have adopted the device of *summary judgment* to provide a mechanism for deciding cases for which a trial is not necessary and would serve no purpose. Of course, deciding when a trial is not necessary and would serve no purpose is no mean task.

Rule 56 regulates summary judgment. Although a party may make a motion for summary judgment at any stage of the proceedings, within the scheme of the Federal Rules such motions are not ordinarily granted until after the factual development of the case is complete — that is, after discovery. In fact, Rule 56(f) specifically contemplates that the decision on a motion for summary judgment will be delayed if an opposing party has not been able to complete discovery.

When may it be said, as required by Rule 56(c), that there is "no genuine issue as to any material fact"? For example, suppose in the Peters v. Dodge case that Dodge moves for summary judgment and asserts that the collision occurred at the intersection of Massachusetts Avenue and Boylston Street, that Peters was driving down Massachusetts and Dodge down Boylston, and that the light was red for Massachusetts traffic and green for Boylston traffic. To support the motion, Dodge submits his own affidavit stating that the Boylston light was green and submits the affidavit of a truck driver who was immediately behind Peters on Massachusetts saying that the light on Massachusetts was red. On this showing, with nothing contrary in the record, most courts would grant summary judgment for Dodge.

By contrast, if in response to these affidavits from Dodge, Peters submitted his own affidavit in opposition stating that he had the green light, this would show the presence of a factual issue for trial: Who was accurately perceiving and telling the truth about the traffic lights? In such a situation, a court would deny Dodge's motion for summary judgment. The court would reason that summary judgment is not for weighing evidence but for determining whether there is any evidence to weigh; the conflicting affidavits would establish that there was an issue for trial.

Often, however, it is not as easy to tell whether there is a factual issue for trial. Consider the following case.

Houchens v. American Home Assurance Co.
927 F.2d 163 (4th Cir. 1991)

Ervin, C.J.

Alice Houchens brought suit against American Home Assurance Company ("American") for breach of contract involving two insurance policies in the United States District Court for the Eastern District of Virginia. American made a motion for summary judgment, and a hearing was held on the motion. The district court granted American's motion for summary judgment,[1] and Houchens appealed. Finding no error in the granting of summary judgment in favor of American, we affirm.

I

Coulter Houchens disappeared in August 1980 and has not been heard from since. His wife, Alice Houchens, is trying to collect upon either of two life insurance policies issued by American, which covered Mr. Houchens. One policy was an occupational accidental injury and death insurance policy. The other policy was a non-occupational accident insurance policy. . . . Both policies required that the insured's death be caused by accident in order to be covered.

Evidence shows that Mr. Houchens was . . . [employed by the] International Civil Aviation Organization in Montreal, Canada (ICAO) . . . [and] stationed in Dharan, Saudi Arabia.

Sometime around August 14, 1980, Mr. Houchens received a week of vacation leave. He traveled to Bangkok, Thailand on or before August 14 via Thai Airlines. Immigration records show that he arrived in Bangkok on August 15, 1980. His entry permit was valid through August 29, 1980.

---

1. The court stated its reasoning as follows:

Under the *Celotex Case*, of course, when met with a motion for summary judgment such as this it is incumbent upon the plaintiff to come forward with evidence that would allow a fact finder to infer that the death resulted from an injury which was caused by accident. I don't think that the plaintiff has met that burden. The disappearance, and that is really all we have here, of the decedent is not, in my opinion, disappearance and not being found, is all that the plaintiff really can show here. I don't think they are such from which a jury or other fact finder could infer a death caused or accidental injury caused by an accident which resulted in death.

No one has heard from Mr. Houchens since that time. The State Department, the FBI, ICAO, Mrs. Houchens, and the Red Cross have searched for him to no avail. In 1988, Mrs. Houchens brought an action to declare Mr. Houchens legally dead under Virginia law. On April 29, 1988, an order was issued by the Circuit Court of Loudoun County, Virginia, declaring that Mr. Houchens is presumed to have died between August 15 and August 29, 1980.

Houchens sued American for breach of contract because American refused to pay under either of two accidental death policies covering Mr. Houchens, which were issued by American. Both policies provided coverage in the event of death by accident. American maintained that there was no evidence of Mr. Houchens' death, nor was there evidence of *accidental death*. American moved for summary judgment, and the district court granted the motion. This appeal followed. . . .

III

Section 64.1-105 of the Virginia Code provides that a person who has been missing for 7 years is presumed to be dead. Va. Code Ann. §64.1-105 (1987). Therefore, Mr. Houchens is presumed to be dead, and Mrs. Houchens is entitled to that presumption. However, in order for Mrs. Houchens to recover under the American policies, she must prove that Mr. Houchens died as a result of an accident. The term "accident" is not defined in the policies. In such cases, the courts of Virginia have said that an accident is an "event that takes place without one's foresight or expectation; an undesigned, sudden, and unexpected event." Harris v. Bankers Life & Cas. Co., 222 Va. 45, 46, 278 S.E.2d 809, 810 (1981) (quoting Ocean Accident & Guaranty Corp. v. Glover, 165 Va. 283, 285, 182 S.E. 221, 222 (1935)).

"Under the general rule . . . a beneficiary who makes a death claim under an accident policy or the double indemnity clause of a life policy, has the burden of proving that the insured's death was caused by violent, external and accidental means within the terms of the policy." Life & Cas. Ins. Co. of Tennessee v. Daniel, 209 Va. 332, 335, 163 S.E.2d 577, 580 (1968). Therefore, the burden is on Mrs. Houchens to prove that her husband died by accidental means.

The district court granted summary judgment to American in this case under the rationale of Celotex Corp. v. Catrett, 477 U.S. 317 (1986). The Supreme Court set out the standard for granting summary judgment as follows:

> In our view, the plain language of Rule 56(c) mandates the entry of summary judgment, after adequate time for discovery and upon motion, against a party who fails to make a showing sufficient to establish the existence of an element essential to that party's case, and on which that party will bear the burden of proof at trial.

Celotex, 477 U.S. at 322. We elaborated on that standard in Helm v. Western Maryland Ry. Co.:

> The appellate court, therefore, must reverse the grant of summary judgment if it appears from the record that there is an unresolved issue of material fact; the inferences to be drawn from the underlying facts contained in the materials before the trial court must be viewed in the light most favorable to the party opposing the motion.

838 F.2d 729, 734 (4th Cir. 1988). On this appeal, then, we must view the evidence in the light most favorable to Houchens to ascertain whether she made a sufficient showing that Mr. Houchens died accidentally.

Mrs. Houchens asserts that the presumption that Mr. Houchens is dead somehow translates into the presumption that he died accidentally; therefore, she made a sufficient showing. She relies upon three cases from the western part of the country as support for the fact that she met her burden. The first case is Martin v. Insurance Co. of America, 1 Wash. App. 218, 460 P.2d 682 (1969). There, the "deceased" had been seen hunting elk in the American River Ridge. He was last seen alive at 9 A.M. at 3,000 foot level, without the aid of a compass, asking for directions. Conditions were inclement: snow on the ground, fog obscuring vision, and steep and wooded mountainside. The court explained the issue as follows:

Plaintiff arg [handwritten margin note]

> Defendant contends that because of the two-fold nature of the ultimate fact — both of which are dependent upon circumstantial evidence — the jury was first asked to infer death from the proven facts and thereafter to infer the manner of death — and that this process constitutes "the piling of inferences upon inferences." If this process constituted plaintiff's logical development of the ultimate fact, we would be obliged to affirm the judgment. . . . A jury will not be permitted to extrapolate conjecturally beyond a legal conclusion which is itself arrived at circumstantially by inference from a proven fact. But a given set of facts may radially project two (or more) separate inferences. In such event, one inferential conclusion is not pyramided upon another; each is drawn independently from the same evidence.

Martin, 460 P.2d at 684-85. The *Martin* court was persuaded that the surrounding circumstances of the missing person's disappearance gave rise to two separate inferences: (1) that he was dead; and (2) that the death was caused by accident. The plaintiff there was not piling inferences on inferences. Rather, the evidence gave rise to two separate inferences.

The other two cases Houchens relies upon have equally bizarre and telling circumstances surrounding the disappearances. In Englehart v. General Electric Co., 11 Wash. App. 922, 527 P.2d 685 (1974), the missing person told some people that he was going fishing. His car was discovered at the yacht club. His boat was found adrift with the ignition on, throttle at one-quarter speed in a forward running position. His children testified that he was not a good swimmer, and that the boat had recently had some problems requiring their father to lean over the back of the boat or to get into the water behind the boat in order to repair the problems. The court held that an inference of accidental death could be drawn from the circumstances surrounding his disappearance. . . .

In Valley Natl. Bank of Arizona v. J. C. Penney Ins. Co., 628 P.2d 991, 129 Ariz. 108 (Ct. App. 1981), the missing person disappeared while camping in California with his wife and step-daughter. They all three disappeared. The deceased's skeletal remains were discovered at a campsite, with bullet casings nearby. The court relied upon the bizarre circumstances of his death to infer that the death was accidental.

These three cases are readily distinguishable from the case at bar. Here, there is only evidence of a disappearance. Mr. Houchens went to Bangkok and was never heard from again. There are no bizarre circumstances surrounding his disappearance. He was not last seen in a position of peril as in *Martin*. He simply vanished. The circumstances surrounding his disappearance do not give us a clue that he actually died, as did the circumstances in *Martin, Englehart,* and *Valley National*. Viewed in the light most favorable to Mrs. Houchens, we can only conclude that Mr. Houchens disappeared, and then presume that he died under Virginia law. We cannot conclude that he died accidentally. To do so would be to pile inferences on inferences. . . .

[handwritten margin notes: Differs from precedent / No clues as to how he died — can't pile on inferences]

To summarize, Houchens relies on the presumption given her by §64-1.105 of the Virginia Code to establish that Mr. Houchens is dead. She then relies upon the facts surrounding his disappearance as a basis for a jury finding that his death was accidental. However, the meager circumstances would not allow a jury to reasonably conclude that it is more likely that Mr. Houchens died from an accident than in some other manner. Because of the sparse evidence concerning his disappearance, we cannot say that the district court erred in granting summary judgment in favor of American under the *Celotex* standard. Therefore, the order of the district court is affirmed. . . .

NOTES AND PROBLEMS

1. Be sure that you understand what it means to move for summary judgment. What pieces of paper did defendant's lawyer use? What did he do with them? What pieces of paper did Mrs. Houchens's lawyer use? What did he do with them?

2. The court says that it can distinguish the cases cited by plaintiff because in those cases the circumstances of the deaths suggested accidents. Is that a fair reading of those cases or should the court simply concede that it is not following them? (Since all of them are from states other than Virginia, whose law governs, the court is not bound to follow them as precedent.)

3. Would it be irrational to conclude that Mr. Houchens died accidentally? If such a conclusion would not be irrational, why did the court not permit the case to go to trial? What does its ruling tell us about the function of a trial and the burdens placed on the parties?

4. To understand summary judgment, one needs to understand what additional evidence would have enabled Mrs. Houchens to avoid summary judgment. Consider several possibilities; in each the question is whether there is a genuine issue of material fact, making summary judgment improper.

a. Suppose Mrs. Houchens produced a witness, a former college friend of Mr. Houchens who had not seen him for more than 10 years. The friend is prepared to testify that, while vacationing in Thailand during the time in question, he saw Mr. Houchens (or someone who looked like him) hit by a bus in a busy intersection. He caught only a brief glimpse; moreover, his vision is not good. The Thai police have no record of a bus accident on the day in question. Can Mrs. Houchens avoid summary judgment with this showing?

b. What if, in response to Mrs. Houchens's production of the witness above, the insurance company comes forward with two affidavits of its own. From two Thai government officials, the affidavits state that Mr. Houchens was shot and killed by Thai police when they intercepted a drug smuggling effort. (Assume that such a death would not be accidental, as the Virginia courts define that term.) In support of these affidavits, the Thai officials state that they are prepared to produce Mr. Houchens's passport. The judge, then, is faced with conflicting affidavits — one from the near-sighted former roommate, the other from Thai government officials. Summary judgment for the insurer?

c. Finally, what if, as in *Houchens* itself, neither side had been able to find information about the circumstances of Mr. Houchens's death. But assume that Virginia law specified that seven years' unexplained absence would give rise to a presumption of death, and, in the absence of contrary evidence, such presumed death would be further presumed to be accidental. Summary judgment for the insurer? For Mrs. Houchens?

There are other methods of pretrial disposition that should be briefly mentioned here. In some cases, defendant will fail to answer the complaint entirely, or will otherwise fail to defend, and a *default judgment* will be granted. See Rule 55. Similarly, if plaintiff does not obey an order of the court during the proceedings, a *dismissal* may be granted. The most common reasons for dismissal are persistent failure to comply with discovery orders, failure to prosecute the case, and failure to appear for calendar calls, motions, or pretrial conferences. See Rule 41(b). In addition, plaintiff may seek a so-called *voluntary dismissal* of the case if, for some reason, he thinks that he would be better off starting over. See Rule 41(a). We will discuss these matters in more detail later; for now, the student simply should be aware of their existence.

G.   Trial

All pretrial activities, from pleading through summary judgment, anticipate the ultimate trial, yet few cases actually reach that point. Fewer than 5 percent of all cases commenced in the federal courts go to trial, and a sizable number of the remainder are settled during trial or even at the appellate stage. Nevertheless, the trial process acts as a dominant influence on pretrial because pretrial is, by definition, an attempt to prepare for trial and also because a party's estimate of what is likely to happen at the trial has an important bearing on its pretrial preparation and its approach to settlement.

To summarize a typical trial process, we shall assume that the Peters-Dodge case is now ready for trial. The first step, which has an important effect on mechanics, is simply for the court to notify the lawyers of the trial date. In some courts, there is no fixed trial date; instead, the lawyers are told that the case will be called within a given one- or two-week period. Or, a court may set multiple cases for trial on the same day. The reason for both of these trial management practices is that most cases end up settling, and if the court set only one case for trial on a given day, there would be a significant likelihood the court would end up having nothing to do that day. Obviously, both practices strain the lawyer's ability to "peak" preparation at the correct moment and may create serious scheduling problems for active trial lawyers and for cases involving out-of-town and expert witnesses.

Once the case is called, the first step is to select the *jury*. Methods of choosing the jury pool and the jurors for a particular case differ widely. From those called to hear the particular case, twelve (or six) will be seated in the jury box (the *panel*). Generally, someone (usually the judge, but sometimes a jury clerk or the attorneys) will tell the jurors something about the case, the names of parties and witnesses, and any other information that may help to identify persons who might not be suitable jurors. For example, Peters, Dodge, and their attorneys and witnesses will be identified so that jurors who know any of them might be excluded. Then the jurors are questioned as a group and individually; the questioning is by the judge, the lawyers, or both. Both parties may challenge jurors for cause (that is, for a stated legally sufficient reason), and each has a number of so-called *peremptory challenges*, for which reasons need not be stated. The method of using challenges and the timing of challenges differ widely among courts.

Once the jury is selected, the actual trial starts. In trial the parties' lawyers typically take turns at each stage of the proceeding. Peters's attorney begins the trial with an *opening statement*, which provides the jury with an overview of the case. Then Dodge's attorney may either deliver her opening statement or delay making it until later in the case.

Then Peters puts on his case-in-chief. As each witness is called, that witness is *examined* by Peters's attorney and *cross-examined* by Dodge's attorney. (Occasionally this symmetrical questioning will extend into other stages: *redirect testimony*, then *recross*, and so on.) During the testimony various documents are introduced, and these are either accepted into evidence or excluded. When Peters is finished, he rests his case.

At this point, Dodge may make a motion for a *judgment as a matter of law* (also called a *directed verdict*). See Rule 50(a). This motion says, in effect, that even if all the evidence that plaintiff has offered is true and all legitimate inferences from such evidence are made, there is no right to relief. In deciding this motion, the judge must assume that what the witnesses have said is true and then decide whether a reasonable person could find for Peters. If the answer is negative, the motion is granted; otherwise, Dodge proceeds with his case.

If Dodge's attorney did not present her opening statement after Peters's attorney, she does so at this point. The defense then presents its case, with the same sequence of direct examination, cross-examination. At the conclusion of Dodge's case, she rests. It is now open to plaintiff to move for a directed verdict, although in the typical case in which plaintiff has the burden of proof, this is rarely granted.

It is now the plaintiff's turn to rebut the defendant's case, then for the defendant to rebut the plaintiff's rebuttal, and so on. Technically, each rebuttal phase is limited to refuting new matters raised during the prior phase, but the judge may exercise some discretion to permit introduction of matters into evidence that were inadvertently overlooked during earlier phases. Finally, both parties rest their cases.

At this point, either party may move for *judgment as a matter of law*. See Rule 50(a). Most often, the defendant makes the motion, claiming that plaintiff has not satisfied her burden of proof. The judge may grant the motion, although typically he reserves judgment.

The case concludes with the arguments to the jury and the judge's instructions to the jury. Closing arguments provide the attorneys with an important opportunity to bring together all the evidence, marshal it in logical order, and present it in a light most favorable to their particular points of view. These arguments also provide an opportunity to persuade, cajole, humor, and win the sympathy of the jurors. Generally, attorneys are given considerable leeway in summing up, although they are bound to adhere to the evidence in the case and not go beyond the bounds of propriety.

After the arguments, the judge instructs or *charges* the jury. The charge tells the jury what law applies to the evidence received. Beforehand, the parties usually have the opportunity to propose jury instructions, and the judge rules on such proposed charges before making the actual charge. The attorneys must listen carefully to the charge as delivered because failure to object promptly to anything that they think is erroneous usually means waiver of the right to raise the error as a ground for appeal. See Rule 51.

Then the jury retires to deliberate and informs the judge when it has reached a *verdict*. The verdict is read in open court, and the jurors are ordinarily polled (asked) to make sure that they agree with the verdict as read. At this point, the jury is dismissed (usually with the court's thanks), and the trial ends.

The losing party is not without hope. Within ten days of an adverse verdict, the loser may again move for a *judgment as a matter of law* (at this stage sometimes called a *judgment notwithstanding the verdict* or a j.n.o.v.*), or a new trial, or both. See Rules 50(b), 59. The motion for judgment as a matter of law asserts that even if all the winner's evidence is true and the winner is given all reasonable inferences from that evidence, the loser is entitled to a verdict as a matter of law. The motion for a new trial may be based either on an error of law, such as the erroneous admission or rejection of evidence, on an erroneous charge, or on so-called discretionary grounds, such as misconduct of counsel, newly discovered evidence, or the verdict being against the weight of the evidence.

The losing party may also *appeal* the decision. It is not necessary to make a postverdict motion in order to appeal, but it is usually necessary for the loser to have perfected at least one ground for appeal by raising the point at a proper time in the proceedings in the trial court.

There is one other option open to the loser, although even a statement of it tends to overstate its availability. In limited cases it may be possible for a party against whom a judgment has been rendered to make a motion under Rule 60(b)

---

* The "n.o.v." comes from the Latin phrase for "notwithstanding the verdict," *non obstante veredicto*.

to *set aside* the judgment. The grounds for setting aside a judgment are limited, and even those grounds are construed narrowly. For example, while it might be possible to have a judgment set aside on the ground that a witness had been bribed, it will not be set aside on the ground that a witness now realizes he made a mistake in his testimony.

The Seventh Amendment of the U.S. Constitution and comparable provisions in state constitutions demonstrate a strong commitment to the idea of jury trial. This commitment makes it difficult to define the circumstances under which the jury ought not to be permitted to decide the case. That is, when should the court enter judgment as a matter of law before a jury verdict, and when should the court set aside a verdict in favor of one side and enter a judgment as a matter of law in favor of the other? There is general agreement that if a party who has the burden of proof on an issue offers no evidence at all on that issue, judgment must be directed against him. There is similar agreement in cases in which the party with the burden of proof offers evidence that is simply too weak to be worthy of belief. But what about a case involving evidence that, although weak, conceivably could be credited? Courts are scrupulous in asserting that it is the jury's job to evaluate the credibility of witnesses and that, in passing on motions for judgments as a matter of law and judgments n.o.v., they will not consider whether witnesses are telling the truth. Courts are equally firm, however, in their belief that the function of judgment as a matter of law is to avoid jury trials in cases in which a jury could reasonably come to only one verdict. The next case involves a collision of these two principles.

Norton v. Snapper Power Equipment

806 F.2d 1545 (11th Cir. 1987)

CLARK, J.

Plaintiff James L. Norton was injured while using a riding lawn mower manufactured by defendant Snapper Power Equipment. The issue on appeal is whether the district court erred in granting a judgment notwithstanding the verdict to Snapper on Norton's strict liability claim. We reverse.

I. Facts

Norton was, and still is, in the commercial lawn mowing business. He bought a Snapper riding mower in July 1981. On January 24, 1983, Norton was using this mower to clear leaves from a yard . . . adjacent to a creek. At the end of his third circular route through the yard, he drove up an incline, traveling in the direction away from the creek. Norton testified that as he reached the top of the incline, approximately six feet from the creek, the mower began to slide backwards toward the creek. Norton says he applied the brakes, but he continued to slide backwards. The lawn mower, with Norton still aboard, crashed into the creek. Norton testified that he kept both hands on the handle bars until the impact of the mower hitting the water knocked him off the seat. . . . [A]t some point during this crash, Norton's hand was caught in the lawn mower's blades, thereby amputating four of his fingers. It is not known . . . precisely how the injury occurred. . . .

At the close of the plaintiff's case, and again at the close of all evidence, Snapper moved for a directed verdict. The court dismissed Norton's negligence and warranty claims, but left the strict liability "defect" claim for the jury. The jury returned a verdict for Norton, holding Snapper liable for 80% of the injuries.

Immediately after dismissing the jury, the district court indicated it would enter a judgment notwithstanding the verdict:

The Court:

All right. Gentlemen, I allowed this case to go to the jury reserving a ruling on the motions prior to submission to the jury. The court at this time must give a judgment notwithstanding the verdict of the jury for the defense. The court cannot allow this case to proceed under any of the present law in this case. The court finds that the jury could not have considered in 1981 that the equipment used in the normal course of the equipment as it was designed could have had a defect which was the legal cause of this injury, and that the injury was caused of course by a turnover of the equipment and there is not sufficient evidence presented which a jury could find that there was an inherent defect in the product at that time. So the court must over-turn the jury's verdict. . . .

II.   *Substantive Objections to Judgment Notwithstanding the Verdict*

The test for granting a judgment notwithstanding the verdict is the same as the test for granting a directed verdict. The court considers the evidence in the light most favorable to the non-moving party and should grant the judgment notwith-standing the verdict only where the evidence so strongly and so favorably points in the favor of the moving party that reasonable people could not arrive at a contrary verdict. . . .

The issues in this case were: (1) whether the failure to install "dead man" devices rendered the 1981 Snapper mower defective; and (2) if the lawn mower was defective, whether the lack of a "dead man" control caused Norton's injury. Snapper claims that there was little or no evidence to support the jury's verdict. . . .

Norton claims the Snapper mower was unreasonably dangerous because it did not have a "dead man" device. Although there are several types of such devices, the basic principle is the same in each type. In order to keep the lawn mower blades spinning, the operator has to remain in a certain position or has to contin-uously apply pressure to a pedal or handle. When the operator disengages the blades, they are quickly brought to a stop. The 1981 Snapper mowers were designed so that the blades would spin for three to five seconds after the power was turned off. Norton offered evidence that more sophisticated "dead man" devices are able to stop the blades in less than one second after the operator applies the brakes or releases the handle.

[After reviewing the law on product defects, the appellate court concluded that the jury could reasonably have found the mower defective.]

B.   Causation

. . . Since Norton did not know exactly when or how his hand got caught in the blades, and since a reconstruction of the accident was impossible, Snapper contends that the jury could not determine whether a blade stopping device would have eliminated or lessened Norton's injury.

Snapper correctly points out that "plaintiffs are not entitled to a verdict based on speculation and conjecture." Fenner v. General Motors Corp., 657 F.2d 647, 651 (5th Cir. 1981), cert. denied, 455 U.S. 942 (1982). . . . The jury is, however, permitted to "reconstruct the series of events by drawing an inference upon an inference." Id. at 650.

In *Fenner*, plaintiff contended his automobile veered off the highway because of a defective steering mechanism. The steering problem would only manifest itself if a stone got caught in the steering mechanism. Because plaintiff's vehicle was not examined by any experts and since plaintiff's experts were only able to say that theoretically the accident could have been caused by a stone in the steering mechanism, the district court entered a judgment notwithstanding the verdict for defendant. . . .

The causation evidence in this case, although circumstantial, was far more impressive than the evidence presented in *Fenner*. Norton testified that the lawn mower slid six feet from the top of the hill into the creek. . . . Expert testimony revealed that when Norton applied the brakes, an effective dead man device could have stopped the blades in as little as .7 seconds. The blades on the 1981 Snapper would continue to spin for three to five seconds. . . . Each of Snapper's experts testified that, given the amount of time the mower would have taken to slide six feet and given Norton's testimony that both of his hands were on the handle bars until the mower hit the creek, a two or three second difference in blade stopping time would have avoided the injury. . . . Snapper was given every opportunity to point out the weaknesses in Norton's proof, but apparently was unpersuasive. . . .

Reversed and Remanded.

NOTES AND PROBLEMS

1. Keep in mind that in a case involving a motion for judgment as a matter of law or a judgment notwithstanding the verdict, the court is deciding whether a reasonable jury could reach a verdict in favor of the party opposing the motion. In this case the jury's verdict for plaintiff depended on its finding that the absence of a device on the lawn mower capable of quickly stopping the mower blades caused Norton's injury. The trial court concluded that there was insufficient evidence for the jury to reach this decision; the court of appeals ruled that the jury could reasonably have reached its verdict. Who is right?

2. Is the case really distinguishable from *Fenner*? In *Fenner* the plaintiff's experts testified that a stone in the steering device could have caused the car to crash; in *Norton* the plaintiff and his experts testified that Norton's injuries could have been caused by the blades' failure to stop spinning quickly enough. But isn't

it equally possible that the injury could have occurred even if the blades stopped sooner? Norton, after all, did not remember just how the accident happened.

3. Is *Norton* distinguishable from *Houchens*? That question can be addressed on two levels — of procedural theory and of factual inference.

a. Start with procedural theory. *Houchens* was decided on a motion for summary judgment, under Rule 56; *Norton* was decided after trial on a motion for judgment notwithstanding the verdict (now called a motion for judgment as a matter of law), under Rule 50. Both result in a judge's decision that one party is entitled to victory because there just isn't any evidence to support the other side. But the two motions come at different stages: The summary judgment motion asserts that there just isn't any conflicting evidence that a trial could resolve; a motion for judgment as a matter of law comes during trial when the evidence for one or both sides has already been presented.

If the two motions cover similar ground, why is there ever any need for the judgment as a matter of law? Shouldn't summary judgment have been granted if there really was no evidence to support one side? Logically, that question makes sense. Practically, however, it often happens that what looks at the pretrial stage like an evidentiary conflict evaporates at trial: A witness fails to appear or tells a different story at trial than in the lawyer's office. In that situation the motion for judgment as a matter of law serves as a back-up to summary judgment.

b. Now turn to the facts of the two cases. In *Houchens* the court affirmed a grant of summary judgment while conceding it was possible that Houchens had died accidentally. Does the jury verdict in *Norton* rest on more than a finding that the absence of a dead-man mechanism *might* have caused the accident?

4. What will happen to this case now that the court of appeals has reversed and remanded?

H.   Former Adjudication

Most of us are vaguely familiar with the criminal law notion of double jeopardy, which prevents a person from being tried twice for the same crime. Not surprisingly, there is a similar notion in civil procedure: A plaintiff who brings a case, or a defendant who defends one, should not be able to try again if he is not satisfied with the result. This principle is easy enough to state, but it is often difficult to determine which claims and issues should be permitted to be litigated in a second action. Lawyers speak of such questions under the general heading of former adjudication or, in its Latin equivalent, *res judicata* (literally, (some)thing adjudicated); they subdivide former adjudication into *claim preclusion* and *issue preclusion.*

To take the easiest case of claim preclusion, if plaintiff sues for personal injuries suffered in a car accident with defendant and loses or is dissatisfied with the amount of damages awarded by the jury, she may not sue again. Similarly, if plaintiff wins, the defendant cannot bring a second action to set aside the first judgment. In such a case, we say that the first claim precludes the second (or is res judicata to the second).

For claim preclusion to apply, the claim must be the same in both the first and second action. As might be expected, deciding what is and is not the same claim is sometimes difficult. For example, there is general agreement that an injured party cannot sue for damage to his arm in one action and to his leg in another. But, as the next case demonstrates, not all courts agree that plaintiff's claims for personal injuries and property damage arising out of the same accident are part of the same claim.

The doctrine of former adjudication also encompasses issue preclusion. Suppose *A* sues *B* on a promissory note, and *B* defends on the ground of fraud. *A* wins, the court ruling that there was no fraud. *A* then sues *B* on another promissory note executed at the same time, and *B* again claims fraud based on the same events as those in the first suit. *A*'s claim would not be precluded (because the law sees the second note as involving a distinct claim), but under the doctrine of issue preclusion *B* would be precluded from claiming fraud a second time because that issue was determined in the first litigation between the parties.

The next case involves a court wrestling with a problem involving both claim and issue preclusion. The court uses older but still common terminology in its discussion, calling claim preclusion (and also the whole topic of former adjudication) *res judicata* and issue preclusion *collateral estoppel*. The latter term derives from the idea that the litigant is being precluded (estopped) from relitigating an issue in a second (that is, collateral) proceeding. The opinion — like many you will encounter in law school and practice — is written in a somewhat opaque style; see if you can discern the real issue being debated.

Rush v. City of Maple Heights

167 Ohio St. 221, 147 N.E.2d 599, cert. denied, 358 U.S. 814 (1958)

, [Plaintiff owned a motorcycle. While her husband was driving, she was injured after being thrown to the ground when the motorcycle ran into a hole in the road. Plaintiff first sued the City for damage to the motorcycle. The Municipal Court found that the City was negligent in not repairing the road and that such negligence was the proximate cause of the accident; it awarded plaintiff damages of $100. That judgment was affirmed by the Court of Appeals and the Supreme Court.

Subsequently, plaintiff commenced the present action to recover damages for personal injuries suffered in the same accident. The trial court held that the issues of negligence and proximate cause had been determined in the prior action against the defendant and were binding. At a trial solely on the question of damages, the jury awarded plaintiff $12,000. The Court of Appeals affirmed this judgment.]

HERBERT, J.

The eighth error assigned by the defendant is that "the trial and appellate courts committed error in permitting plaintiff to split her cause of action and to file a separate action in the Cleveland Municipal Court for her property damage and reduce same to judgment, and, thereafter, to proceed, in the Cuyahoga County Common Pleas Court, with a separate action for personal injuries, both claims arising out of a single accident." . . .

In the case of Vasu v. Kohlers, Inc., 145 Ohio St. 321, 61 N.E.2d 707, 709, 166 A.L.R. 855, plaintiff operating an automobile came into collision with defendant's truck, in which collision he suffered personal injuries and also damage to his automobile. At the time of collision, plaintiff had coverage of a $50 deductible collision policy on his automobile. The insurance company paid the plaintiff a sum covering the damage to his automobile, whereupon, in accordance with a provision of the policy, the plaintiff assigned to the insurer his claim for such damage.

In February 1942, the insurance company commenced an action . . . against Kohlers, Inc., the defendant in the reported case to recoup the money paid by it to cover the damage to Vasu's automobile.

In August 1942, Vasu commenced an action in the same court against Kohlers, Inc., to recover for personal injuries which he suffered in the same collision.

In March 1943, in the insurance company's action, a verdict was rendered in favor of the defendant, followed by judgment.

Two months later [the defendant in the second suit sought to have it dismissed on grounds of former adjudication. The Ohio Supreme Court said that Vasu's suit could proceed, and in the "syllabus," prepared by the court reporter, summarized its reasoning:]

1. If the owner of a single cause of action arising out of a single tortious act brings an action against his tort-feasor, he may have but one recovery; and, in case he fails to recover, he may not maintain a subsequent action on the same cause of action, even though he has failed to include his entire cause of action or elements of damage in his original action.

2. If an owner of a single cause of action has a recovery thereon, the cause of action is merged in the judgment; but if he fails to recover on his claimed cause of action and judgment goes against him, such judgment is res judicata and a bar to a second action on the same cause of action. . . .

4. Injuries to both person and property suffered by the same person as a result of the same wrongful act are infringements of different rights and give rise to distinct causes of action, with the result that the recovery or denial of recovery of compensation for damages to the property is no bar to an action subsequently prosecuted for the personal injury, unless by an adverse judgment in the first action issues are determined against the plaintiff which operate as an estoppel against him in the second action.

5. A right, question or fact in issue which was necessarily determined by a court of competent jurisdiction in a judgment which has become final, cannot be disputed or litigated in a subsequent suit between the same parties, although the subsequent suit is based upon a different cause of action. . . .

[C]ases distinguishing and explaining the Vasu case have not changed the rule established in paragraph four of the syllabus of the latter case, holding that injuries to both person and property suffered by the same person as a result of the same wrongful act are infringements of different rights and give rise to distinct causes of action.

However, it is contended here that that rule is in conflict with the great weight of authority in this country and has caused vexatious litigation. The following quotation from 1 American Jurisprudence, 494, Section 114, states this question well:

> It sometimes happens that a single wrongful or negligent act causes damage in respect of both the person and the property of the same individual, as, for instance, where the owner of a vehicle is injured in a collision which also damages the vehicle. In such a case, the question arises as to whether there are two causes of action or only one, and the authorities are in conflict concerning it. The majority rule is that only one cause of action arises, the reason of the rule being that as the defendant's wrongful act is single, the cause of action must be single, and that the different injuries occasioned by it are merely items of damage proceeding from the same wrong. . . .
>
> In other jurisdictions, the rule is that two causes of action result from a negligent act which inflicts injury on a person and his property at the same time. This conclusion has been reached in different jurisdictions by different lines of reasoning.
>
> Upon examination of decisions of courts of last resort, we find that the majority rule is followed in the following cases in each of which the action was between the person suffering injury and the person committing the tort, and where insurers were not involved, as in the case here. . . .

[The court cited 20 cases supporting the majority rule and five cases supporting the minority rule.]

The reasoning behind the majority rule seems to be well stated in the case of Mobile & Ohio Rd. Co. v. Matthews, as follows:

> The negligent action of the plaintiff in error constituted but one tort. The injuries to the person and property of the defendant in error were the several results and effects of one wrongful act. A single tort can be the basis of but one action. It is not improper to declare in different counts for damages to the person and property when both result from the same tort, and it is the better practice to do so where there is any difference in the measure of damages, and all the damages sustained must be sued for in one suit. This is necessary to prevent multiplicity of suits, burdensome expense, and delays to plaintiffs, and vexatious litigation against defendants. . . .

Indeed, if the plaintiff fails to sue for the entire damage done him by the tort, a second action for the damages omitted will be precluded by the judgment in the first suit brought and tried.

The minority rule would seem to stem from the English case of Brunsden v. Humphrey (1884), 14 Q.B. 141. The facts in that case are set forth in the opinion in the *Vasu* case concluding with the statement:

> The Master of the Rolls, in his opinion, stated that the test is "whether the same sort of evidence would prove the plaintiff's case in the two actions," and that, in the action relating to the cab, "it would be necessary to give evidence of the damage done to the plaintiff's vehicle. In the present action it would be necessary to give evidence of the bodily injury occasioned to the plaintiff, and of the sufferings which he has undergone, and for this purpose to call medical witnesses. This one test shows that the causes of action as to the damage done to the plaintiff's cab, and as to the injury occasioned to the plaintiff's person, are distinct."

The fallacy of the reasoning in the English court is best portrayed in the dissenting opinion of Lord Coleridge, as follows: ". . . [I]t seems to me a subtlety not warranted by law to hold that a man cannot bring two actions, if he is injured in his arm and in his leg, but can bring two, if besides his arm and leg being injured, his trousers which contain his leg, and his coat sleeve which contains his arm, have been torn."

There appears to be no valid reason in these days of code pleading to adhere to the old English rule as to distinctions between injuries to the person and damages to the person's property resulting from a single tort. It would seem that the minority rule is bottomed on the proposition that the right of bodily security is fundamentally different from the right of security of property and, also, that, in actions predicated upon a negligent act, damages are a necessary element of each independent cause of action and no recovery may be had unless and until actual consequential damages are shown.

Whether or not injuries to both person and property resulting from the same wrongful act are to be treated as injuries to separate rights or as separate items of damage . . . a plaintiff may maintain only one action to enforce his rights existing at the time such action is commenced. . . .

[The court carved out an exception to the rule it was announcing in cases where the first suit was brought by an insurer who had paid for property damage and the second suit by the injured driver—as was the case in *Vasu*.]

Apparently, much of the vexatious litigation, with its attendant confusion, which has resulted in recent years from the filing of separate petitions by the same plaintiff, one for personal injuries and one for property damage although sustained simultaneously, has grown from that one decision, this case presenting a good example.

In the light of the foregoing, it is the view of this court that the so-called majority rule conforms much more properly to modern practice, and that the rule declared in the fourth paragraph of the syllabus in the *Vasu* case, on a point not actually at issue therein, should not be followed.

We, therefore, conclude and hold that, where a person suffers both personal injuries and property damage as a result of the same wrongful act, only a single cause of action arises, the different injuries occasioned thereby being separate items of damage from such act. It follows that paragraph four of the syllabus in the *Vasu* case must be overruled. . . .

Judgment reversed and final judgment for defendant.

WEYGANDT, C.J., and STEWART, TAFT, MATTHIAS and BELL, J.J., concur.

STEWART, J. (concurring).

In the case of Vasu v. Kohlers, Inc., Judge Hart stated in part: "The rule at common law and in a majority of the states of the union is that damages resulting from a single wrongful act, even though they include both property and personal injury damages, are, when suffered by the same person, the subject of only one action against the wrongdoer."

However, he referred to the fact that there were a number of state jurisdictions which followed the English rule, laid down in Brunsden v. Humphrey, L.R.,

14, Q.B. Div., 141, and known as the two-causes-of-action rule, and then proceeded to announce that rule as the Ohio rule, and it was written into the fourth paragraph of the syllabus of the *Vasu* case. If it had been necessary to decide the question whether a single tort gives rise to two causes of action as to the one injured by such tort, I would be reluctant to disturb that holding. However, neither the discussion in the *Vasu* case as to whether a single or double cause of action arises from one tort nor the language of the fourth paragraph of the syllabus was necessary to decide the issue presented in the case, and obviously both such language and such paragraph are obiter dicta and, therefore, are not as persuasive an authority as if they had been appropriate to the question presented. . . .

ZIMMERMAN, J. (dissenting).

I am not unalterably opposed to upsetting prior decisions of this court where changing conditions and the lessons of experience clearly indicate the desirability of such course, but, where those considerations do not obtain, established law should remain undisturbed in order to insure a stability on which the lower courts and the legal profession generally may rely with some degree of confidence. . . .

NOTES AND PROBLEMS

1. Both plaintiff and defendant were asserting that the first action affected the second in some way.
   a. How did plaintiff think the first case should affect the second?
   b. How did defendant think the first case should affect the second?
   c. Which of the parties was arguing for issue preclusion? Which for claim preclusion?

2. Do you think that a court would reach the same result in this case if plaintiff's husband had sued to recover for his own injuries?

3. If plaintiff had lost the first action because the court found that the city was not negligent in maintaining the street and plaintiff's husband then sued for his own injuries, do you think that the decision in the first action would be binding on him?

4. Normally a court will follow earlier decisions on principles of law, even though the parties currently before the court were not parties to the earlier case. For example, assume that, in plaintiff's action, the court established a rule that the city is not liable for holes in the pavement unless it has actual notice of the holes (as opposed to mere reason to know). That rule ordinarily would be followed not only in an action by plaintiff's husband but also in one by an unrelated plaintiff whose cycle fell into a different hole, on a different street, on a different day. This principle is called *stare decisis*. The majority and the concurring and dissenting opinions in *Rush* are arguing in part about whether the court is departing from stare decisis in their treatment of *Vasu*.
   a. Is it?
   b. If so, is the departure justified?

5. Imagine that Ms. Rush, before she filed the property damage claim, consulted her lawyer, who told her that it was well established law in Ohio that one could bring separate claims for property damage and personal injury. She (and her lawyer) now know that advice was wrong. Can she recover from her lawyer for malpractice? Very unlikely: To prevail on such a claim, Rush must show two things: (a) that a lawyer of ordinary competence would have known that Ohio was likely to change its rule of former adjudication; and (b) that, but for the lawyer's error, she would have prevailed in the original lawsuit. Under the circumstances of *Rush*, the second showing will be easy—after all, she prevailed in the property damage action before it was reversed. But it isn't likely that a court will let a jury find that Rush's lawyer was negligent for failing to predict the Ohio Supreme Court's reversal of *Vasu*—ordinary competence doesn't include prescience. Where does that leave Ms. Rush?

I. Appeals

Our judicial system permits a losing party to appeal an adverse judgment of the trial court to a higher court. Appeals address the correctness of trial court rulings that are likely to have affected the outcome. Appeals cannot be used to correct strategic decisions made by counsel during trial, or during pretrial proceedings, even if those strategic decisions could be shown to have affected the outcome. For example, a party cannot appeal on the ground that his lawyer has now thought of a more effective closing argument, or has now decided he should have had different witnesses testify at trial. Moreover, while erroneous trial court rulings can be challenged on appeal, the right of appeal does not ensure the "correctness" of *all* trial court rulings. To understand this apparent contradiction, one must understand the interaction of procedural rules that determine: (1) when in the course of a given lawsuit an adverse ruling can be appealed; and (2) how closely an appellate court will scrutinize any alleged error. To comprehend their interaction, imagine that a trial judge has made an important discovery ruling, one that both parties believe will affect the outcome of the case. Further, suppose that the ruling is at least questionable and that the party on the losing end of the ruling appeals. The next case shows what will happen.

Apex Hosiery Co. v. Leader

102 F.2d 702 (3d Cir. 1939)

PER CURIAM.

The defendants in an action for treble damages under the Sherman Anti-Trust Act, have appealed from an order of the court below made under Federal Rule of Civil Procedure 34 for the discovery and production by them of documents for inspection, copying and photographing by the plaintiff for use at the trial of the action. An order of this nature is interlocutory and, therefore, not appealable. This has been expressly decided by the Supreme Court in Cogen v. United States, 278 U.S. 221 (1929). In the former case Mr. Justice Brandeis said ([278 U.S.] 223, 224): "The disposition made of the motion will necessarily determine the conduct of the trial and may vitally affect the result. In essence, the motion resembles others made before or during a trial to secure or to suppress evidence, such as applications to suppress a deposition; to compel the production of books or documents; for leave to make physical examination of a plaintiff; or for a subpoena duces tecum. The orders made upon such applications, so far as they affect the rights only of parties to the litigation, are interlocutory. It is only when disobedience happens to result in an order punishing criminally for contempt, that a party may have review by appellate proceedings before entry of the final judgment in the cause." Union Tool Co. v. Wilson, 259 U.S. 107, 110, 111 [1922].

While the appeal must be dismissed for want of jurisdiction, we think it may fairly be said that the order entered by the learned District Judge was most carefully drawn to prevent the plaintiff from unduly prying into the defendants' affairs.

Appeal dismissed.

NOTES AND PROBLEMS

1. Be sure you understand what has happened in this case.

a. Did the court rule on defendants' contention that discovery was improper? What did it do? Why?

b. Notice the court's discomfort with this disposition, discomfort evident in the second-to-last sentence ("While the appeal must be dismissed. . . ."). Having said it has no jurisdiction over the appeal, the court nevertheless tries to reassure the losing side that the lower court has not been careless. This sentence is dictum of the purest sort — since the court has just said it has no jurisdiction over the case. Why does the court write this sentence?

2. The *final judgment* rule (as the doctrine expressed in *Apex Hosiery* is called) finds its current statutory expression in 28 U.S.C. §1291, which gives the federal courts of appeals jurisdiction "of appeals from all final decisions" of the federal district courts. The negative corollary is just as important: that the courts of appeal have no jurisdiction over appeals from judgments or rulings that are not "final." Such nonfinal rulings are called *interlocutory* orders.

One can justify the final judgment rule in several ways. Probably the most telling argument is that many trial court decisions that seem wrong at the time turn out not to matter because the party on the losing end of that decision goes on to prevail. Another justification is that a rule permitting interlocutory appeals from every trial decision would enormously protract litigation and that it is more important to bring litigation to an end than to assure that every trial court ruling was perfectly correct.

The argument against the final judgment rule relies on a different kind of pragmatic reasoning. Most cases will not end in a judgment of any sort: The parties will settle. Judicial rulings that precede settlements are not appealable, but those rulings may have dictated the terms of the settlement — by greatly advantaging one party. In those cases — the majority of all cases — it seems unjust to allow what may be practically dispositive judicial rulings to escape appellate review. Some states, New York most notable among them, have adopted this reasoning by providing for liberal interlocutory appeal of significant trial court rulings. Others (the federal courts included) weasel a bit with judge-made doctrines that slightly soften the final judgment rule. It is nevertheless still fair to say that the rule poses an insuperable barrier to immediate appeal of most trial court rulings.

3. Apply the final judgment rule to some of the cases we have already considered in this chapter. From which of the following decisions would an immediate appeal lie, according to 28 U.S.C. §1291:

a. A trial court order granting dismissal for want of subject matter jurisdiction (as in Hawkins v. Masters Farms)?

b. A trial court order refusing to dismiss for want of subject matter jurisdiction?

c. A trial court order denying a 12(b)(6) motion (as in Bell v. Novick Transfer)?

d. A trial court order granting a 12(b)(6) motion?

e. A trial court order granting or denying requested discovery (as in Butler v. Rigby)?

4. With these exercises in mind, consider how the final judgment rule affects the dynamics of litigation. Plaintiff files a lawsuit and defendant, before answering, makes a modest settlement offer. Plaintiff's lawyer advises plaintiff to reject the offer, which he does. Plaintiff then seeks discovery of some information vital to the lawsuit, but the defendant resists and the judge refuses to grant discovery. Plaintiff cannot appeal unless the case goes to final judgment, but it will cost plaintiff considerable time and money to get to that stage. Will the defendant's original settlement offer look better? Will defendant still be willing to make even that modest offer, having won the battle over discovery?

5. The final judgment rule affects the timing of appeals. Other doctrines affect how the courts of appeals will decide those cases that do reach final judgment. Put in very simplified form, existing doctrine tells the appellate courts that they should scrutinize trial court rulings in two different ways: (a) findings of fact should be affirmed unless "clearly erroneous"; (b) by contrast, rulings of law should be subject to reversal if wrong in any respect, if there is a genuine reason to believe the error affected the outcome of the lawsuit.

a. Consider what it means to say that a trial judge may be reversed by an appellate court only when factual findings are "clearly erroneous." Doesn't that standard imply that it's permissible for a trial judge to be "a little wrong," so long as her error is factual? How would one defend such a standard?

b. Conversely, why should the appellate courts be so concerned that the trial judge get the law exactly right? What is at stake?

c. Finally, in many areas, the law itself gives the trial judge discretion to balance competing concerns in making a ruling — for example, whether the potential information to be gained from a particular discovery request is outweighed by the financial burden of complying with that discovery request. In those areas, the issue on appeal is not whether the appellate court judges would themselves have balanced the competing interests the same way, but whether the trial court can be said to have abused its discretion.

NOTE ON APPELLATE STRUCTURE AND JURISDICTION

In this and other law school courses you will read a good many appellate opinions from state and federal courts. What determines which court will hear such an appeal?

In the federal system, parties who lose in the district court can appeal to the court of appeals. The courts of appeals hear cases from district courts in regions covering several states, each region being called a "circuit." There are 11 circuits covering the 50 states, a twelfth for the District of Columbia, and a thirteenth, the Court of Appeals for the Federal Circuit, which hears appeals in certain specialized cases — patent actions, for example. Thus the Court of Appeals for the Second Circuit hears cases from the district courts in Connecticut, Vermont, and New York; the Court of Appeals for the Seventh Circuit hears cases from the district courts in Indiana, Illinois, and Wisconsin. Atop the courts of appeals is the Supreme Court of the United States.

Parties who lose in the court of appeals do not, in most cases, have an automatic right to appeal to the U.S. Supreme Court. Instead, they must apply to the U.S. Supreme Court to have the case heard, which they do by asking the Court to grant a *writ of certiorari*.

Most states have a similar appellate structure — a trial court of general jurisdiction, an intermediate appellate court to which all cases may be appealed, and a state supreme court* that has discretion over which cases it will hear. In some states, however, there is no intermediate appellate court, so appeals go directly to the state supreme court. If the case is not brought in a court of general jurisdiction but in an inferior court (for example, a court whose jurisdiction is limited to claims under $10,000), there may be a different and more limited appellate structure. Finally, some decisions of the highest state court can be reviewed by the U.S. Supreme Court.

As the preceding discussion indicates, the U.S. Supreme Court can hear cases that have originated in either the federal or the state system. But an important caveat is necessary: The U.S. Supreme Court can hear cases that arise in the state system only if they present an issue of federal law. It cannot hear cases from the state supreme court that involve solely questions of state law. For example, assume that a case is brought in the state courts of Florida and that on appeal the Florida Supreme Court adopts a rule to the effect that a retailer is liable for criminal acts suffered by customers on adjacent premises, if reasonably foreseeable. The Supreme Court of the United States cannot review this ruling because the issue is one of state tort law (unless the retailer were contending that Florida tort law was unconstitutional). On the other hand, if the Florida Supreme Court were to rule that a person attempting to sell magazines on a private college campus is not protected by the First Amendment, that ruling would present an issue of federal constitutional law, which could be reviewed by the U.S. Supreme Court.

---

* New York has particularly challenging terminology: The state calls its trial court of general jurisdiction the "Supreme Court," its intermediate appellate court the "Appellate Division," and its highest court the "Court of Appeals."

Supreme Court review is governed by 28 U.S.C. §§1253-1258; in exercising its power of review, the Court enjoys broad discretion in selecting which cases it will hear. An important, though widely misunderstood, point is that a decision by the Supreme Court not to review a case does not signify approval of the decision rendered by the court below. The Court's members may roundly disapprove of both the law applied and the results reached by the lower court but nevertheless determine not to grant review because, for example, they think the issue is not sufficiently important to warrant review.

NOTE: CIVIL PROCEDURE IN YOUR SUBSTANTIVE COURSES

In the course of the year you will encounter repeated discussion of procedural issues in various substantive courses. Discussing a case in contracts, your instructor may ask about the procedure by which the case reached the appellate court; a torts class may focus on the question of what additional evidence would have enabled plaintiff to avoid defendant's motion for a directed verdict. A property class may explore the defects in plaintiff's complaint for trespass that led the court to sustain a demurrer. These scenarios do not represent efforts by your other instructors to seize pedagogical territory by conquest. Instead they reflect the role that substantive law plays in procedural decisions and that procedure plays in substantive law.

Lawsuits grow from disputes. Parties may dispute what happened and what consequences the law attaches to those happenings. At several stages of litigation procedure establishes hurdles that a party must jump. Demurrers or Rule 12(b)(6) motions are one such hurdle; motions for summary judgment, a directed verdict, or a judgment n.o.v. are others. All these procedural devices require the judge to reflect on the substantive law that applies to the case and to describe the way in which that law applies to the facts as they then appear.

Focusing on the procedural stance of the case clarifies two points. First, seeing that the case arises on an appeal from a demurrer, an objection to jury instructions, or the like explains why the judge is engaging in a recitation of the substantive law. Second, understanding the procedural stance of the case enables you to see how much of what the court says depends purely on a legal assessment of the case and how much depends on a factual assessment. For example, on a demurrer or Rule 12(b)(6) motion, the court considers whether the plaintiff's allegations, if proved, would entitle him to the court's help; it does not consider whether it is likely that the plaintiff could prove the truth of the statements. On a motion for summary judgment or a directed verdict, by contrast, the court must consider both the law that applies to the case and the evidence that the parties have presented. These propositions might take concrete form in a case in which plaintiff claimed that defendant had injured him by shooting him with a ray gun. However unlikely such a claim sounds, it would survive a demurrer — even if the judge firmly believed that plaintiff's injuries were figments of an overworked imagination — because a demurrer asks whether the alleged facts, if they were true, would form the basis for relief. That same claim might well succumb to a motion for summary judgment or a motion for a directed verdict, not because the law of ray-gun-inflicted injuries had changed but because, for instance, doctors' examinations had revealed that, although plaintiff might be slightly deranged, he had suffered no physical injury.

Procedure will thus play two roles in your substantive courses. First, various procedural hurdles will provide the occasion for judicial expositions of the law of torts, property, contract, and crimes. Second, by understanding the procedural stage at which the issue under discussion arose, you will also understand the extent to which the court is considering the facts of the particular case. Comprehending this dual role will enable you to see both the way in which procedure shapes substantive law and the reason procedural discussions will often play a central role in learning that substantive law.

THE CONSTITUTIONAL FRAMEWORK FOR U.S. LITIGATION

A. Approaching Civil Procedure

One can study the procedural system from the top down or from the bottom up. The top-down approach starts with the constitutional environment in which the individual lawsuit exists. That approach takes the student into both the history and the current interpretation of the Constitution of the United States. Studying the Constitution reveals several limits on the ways in which state and federal court systems conduct their business — limits that have major consequences for individual litigants. The bottom-up approach begins with the life cycle of an individual lawsuit: how the parties initially state their grievances, develop information about them, and bring them to resolution. This approach emphasizes features and problems of the contemporary procedural system, which is in many respects a bold experiment. Studying the process of litigation reveals how these features shape and constrain the litigants' responsibilities and choices.

As you have probably already guessed, anyone wanting to become a lawyer has to understand both approaches, to comprehend the constitutional environment as well as the modes for processing disputes. This book accordingly contains materials about both approaches, and most courses will examine both. But one can with equal validity start at the top and look down or begin at the bottom and work up. The three parts of this book are labeled to emphasize these different starting points. Some courses may begin with Part A: The Constitutional Framework for U.S. Litigation, comprising Chapters II-IV. This starting point represents the "top-down" approach. Other classes may move first to Part B: The Process of Litigation, comprising Chapters V-XII and representing the "bottom-up" approach. The last part of this book, Part C: Testing the Limits of the Litigation System: Additional Claims and Parties, combines significant elements of both the other parts and may be studied either at the end of the course, as a reprise, or in conjunction with either of the other two parts. The next three chapters represent an approach to litigation starting at the top — with the constitutional framework.

B. Constitutional Limits in Litigation

The U.S. Constitution dictates many fundamental aspects of a lawsuit — not only in landmark cases but in ordinary civil litigation. For example, someone looking at the U.S. system from outside might conclude that it would be more efficient to have a single, unitary court system for all disputes rather than 51 separate systems (one for each state and one for the federal government). Efficient it might be, but it would also be unconstitutional, for reasons you will come to understand. The next three chapters develop several of the most important ways the Constitution shapes litigation in the United States. Two of those ways involve "jurisdiction," a protean and important word in U.S. litigation; the third involves "choice of law."

1.   The Idea of Jurisdiction

No legal system in the world claims the power to decide all disputes arising anywhere. Which cases, then, will a legal system resolve? Consider this question concretely. Imagine that you live in Illinois and come to California to attend law school. A particularly contentious sort, you become involved in two disputes during your first year there: You think your landlord is failing to maintain your apartment, and you think one of your instructors unfairly rejects you for a position as a part-time research assistant. In the first case, you might start by complaining to the landlord; in the second, to the instructor or the dean. You would *not* seek relief from the landlord of the building next door or from the dean of another law school. You would not do so because the landlord of the other building and the dean of the other school have no power over the conditions in your apartment or school. Putting the matter very loosely, one could say the condition of your apartment and employment decision fall outside of their *jurisdictions*: Say what they might about the poor state of garbage collection or the unfairness of the failure to hire you, they are powerless to remedy either.

You will repeatedly encounter the concept of jurisdiction while studying law and will soon discover that the term is used in several different ways. More or less literally, "jurisdiction" means the power to declare the law. By extension, it has acquired several other meanings. Lawyers may speak of "the law of a jurisdiction" or of a suspected felon's having "fled the jurisdiction," using the term in both instances to signify a state or territory. In civil procedure it has a narrower meaning. Lawyers sometimes refer to jurisdiction in this narrower sense as "judicial jurisdiction": the power of a court to render a judgment that other courts and government agencies will recognize and enforce.

You might encounter jurisdiction in this narrower legal sense if your two imaginary disputes escalated and you sued either the landlord or the instructor. If during the dispute with your landlord you returned to Illinois for the summer and there filed an action against your California landlord, you might well be met with the defense that courts in Illinois had no jurisdiction over the landlord. If you filed suit in federal court in California against either the instructor, a different kind of jurisdiction question might arise. While conceding that both the instructor could be sued in California, the defendants might challenge the jurisdiction of *federal* courts over the lawsuit: Whether the challenge was successful would depend on whether you could either frame your challenge to the hiring decision as a claim "arising under federal law" or convince the court that you were still a "citizen" of Illinois and that you and the defendant(s) were of diverse citizenship.

2.   Jurisdiction and the Constitution

The next two chapters explore the ways in which courts in the United States conceive of and resolve questions like those raised in the preceding hypothetical case. Exploring the topic will be easier if you have some sense of both the terminology and the context in which jurisdictional issues arise. The basic terminology requires the student to distinguish between "personal" jurisdiction, the focus of Chapter II, and "subject matter" jurisdiction, the focus of Chapter III. Lawyers would describe the challenge to the Illinois suit against your California landlord as involving a question of *personal jurisdiction* — the power of an Illinois court to render a judgment binding someone who may have never set foot in Illinois. They would describe the challenge to the federal courts' power to decide the question whether you were wrongly refused a part-time job as raising the issue of federal courts' *subject matter jurisdiction* — the power of federal (as opposed to state) courts to decide certain kinds of cases. At the outset you need only bear in mind that personal and subject matter jurisdiction are *both* necessary ingredients of any court's power to render a binding decision in a case; that is, a court must have both subject matter and personal jurisdiction to render a valid judgment.

The deep concern with jurisdiction ranks high among the distinguishing characteristics of the Anglo-American legal system. The concept has special significance in the United States, where government power is divided among states and between the states as a whole and the federal government: No single government entity has plenary power. This system of limited and overlapping authority means that government agencies — including courts — must repeatedly decide which agency has the power to exercise authority in a given situation. Because the federal Constitution defines the lines of authority among the competing centers of power, courts look to the Constitution for their basic framework in deciding issues of judicial jurisdiction. This aspect of civil procedure will be for many students their first law school encounter with the Constitution, the text of which appears in the Rules supplement that accompanies the casebook.

Three parts of the Constitution bear on jurisdiction. Article III authorizes the establishment of the system of federal courts and in Section 2 sets the limits of federal judicial authority. Federal courts cannot exceed those jurisdictional boundaries, and Congress has the power in many instances to restrict the scope of federal judicial authority more narrowly than does the Constitution. The constraints imposed by Article III and the legislation implementing it are the focus of Chapter III, on subject matter jurisdiction.

Article IV, Section 1 requires that "Full Faith and Credit . . . be given in each State to judicial proceedings of every other State." The Supreme Court has interpreted this clause to require that one state recognize and enforce judgments of another state. For example, suppose a court in State A enters a money judgment against D, but plaintiff cannot find any assets of D within State A to satisfy the judgment. *D*'s only assets turn out to be a large bank account at a bank located in State *B*. Under the Full Faith and Credit Clause, plaintiff commences a summary proceeding in a court in State *B*, records State *A*'s judgment and obtains a writ of execution from the State *B* court enforcing State *A*'s judgment against any assets of *D* located in State *B*.

As you are about to see, however, the Full Faith and Credit Clause has an important unstated condition — such judgments are entitled to full faith and credit only if the court rendering them had jurisdiction to do so. Finally, Section 1 of the Fourteenth Amendment provides that no "State [shall] deprive any person of life, liberty or property without due process of law." This clause, known as the Due Process Clause, has proved one of the cornerstones of modern constitutional and procedural theory. It derives its relation to jurisdiction from Pennoyer v. Neff, a case that might be termed the great-grandparent of personal jurisdiction, the topic of Chapter II. As you will see, *Pennoyer* made the question of what we now call personal jurisdiction part of the Constitution.

3.   The Constitution and Choice of Law

Beyond personal and subject matter jurisdiction, the Constitution shapes U.S. litigation in a third way: It sometimes dictates which set of laws a court must apply to a dispute. There are two key ways in which the Constitution dictates choice of law. First, Article VI provides that the Constitution and federal laws "shall be the supreme Law of the Land; and the Judges in every State shall be bound thereby, any Thing in the Constitution or Laws of any State to the Contrary notwithstanding." This provision is commonly referred to as the Supremacy Clause. Although the import of the Supremacy Clause is typically covered in a Constitutional Law class rather than in Civil Procedure, for present purposes it is enough to understand that the clause means that if Congress has validly enacted a statute dealing with a particular subject, both federal and state courts are required to enforce the federal statute, regardless of whether there is a contrary state statute or state common law rule.

The second way in which the Constitution dictates choice of law is that, in the absence of a controlling federal statute, the federal court system is required to respect both the statutory and common law rules of the several states. For an example of how such an issue might arise, imagine that your hypothetical dispute with your California landlord found its way to a federal court. What law would the court apply to the dispute? Would it be bound by the California law of landlord and tenant? Or would it be free to apply what it thought was a more sensible or just system of regulation to the dispute before it? That question is the focus of Chapter IV, on the *Erie* problem, so-called from the name of its leading case, Erie Railroad v. Tompkins. *Erie* is a case of constitutional dimensions — or so it insists — but, unlike personal or subject matter jurisdiction, one cannot readily locate the constitutional provisions from which it flows; that enigma itself is part of the problem. Together with personal and subject matter jurisdiction, the Supremacy Clause and the *Erie* doctrine shape the environment in which U.S. litigation operates.

PERSONAL JURISDICTION

II

A.   The Origins

Personal jurisdiction is a part of U.S. constitutional law because of Pennoyer v. Neff, a case whose deceptively simple facts spawned a truly splendid doctrinal elaboration. To understand those facts you need to have some background. One of the more difficult parts of a lawsuit often comes at its end, when a victorious plaintiff tries to collect the judgment from the defendant, who declines to pay. When this happens, the plaintiff may obtain a writ of execution from the court, which will authorize the sheriff to seize any property belonging to the defendant, sell it, and give the resulting money to the plaintiff (up to the amount of the judgment). When that sale occurs, the sheriff gives to whoever buys the defendant's property a "sheriff's deed" as evidence of title. The second piece of background you need for Pennoyer concerns the idea of "constructive" notice. In law "constructive" generally means "fictional" or "pretend." As you have already seen, defendants generally receive service of process, but what happens if no one can find the defendant? Under those conditions some states provide for a notice in a newspaper — in those fine-print columns no one reads. Under such conditions service is "constructive" because it is highly unlikely that the defendant will actually see it. Finally, you need to know that "attachment" is the legal term for an officially sanctioned seizure of property: Real estate, cars, and other property may be "attached." Sometimes "attachment" means literal seizure; other times it means posting notices on property or on records of title so that prospective buyers know it cannot be sold.

Pennoyer v. Neff

95 U.S. 714 (1877)

Mr. Justice FIELD delivered the opinion of the Court.

[The case concerned two lawsuits. The first suit grew from an unpaid legal fee. Marcus Neff hired Mitchell, a lawyer living and practicing in Oregon, to do some legal work. When Neff failed to pay Mitchell's fee, Mitchell sued him in state court. At the time of this first suit Neff was, in the court's words, "a non-resident of the State [who] was not personally served with process, and did not appear [i.e., did not come to court or otherwise resist the lawsuit]. . . . [J]udgment was entered upon his default in not answering the complaint, upon a constructive service of

61

Mitchell sues Neff who defaults
Sheriff seizes + sells Neff's land and Pennoyer buys

summons by publication." *After* this default judgment, Neff acquired 300 acres of land in Oregon from the federal government. To satisfy his judgment Mitchell had the sheriff seize and sell the land. Pennoyer bought it and received a sheriff's deed as evidence of title. The sheriff then turned the sale proceeds over to Mitchell. Sometime after these events Neff reappeared, and when he discovered what had become of his land, brought the second lawsuit with which *Pennoyer* is concerned. Neff sued Pennoyer in federal court "to recover the possession of [the] tract of land." As evidence of their respective titles, Neff pointed to the original government deed, and Pennoyer pointed to the sheriff's deed. In this second suit the court thus had to decide whether the first lawsuit and the sheriff's sale had extinguished Neff's title. The opinion begins with an analysis of the form of notice in the first suit.]

The Code of Oregon provides for such [constructive] service when an action is brought against a non-resident and absent defendant, who has property within the State. It also provides, where the action is for the recovery of money or damages, for the attachment of the property of the non-resident. And it also declares that no natural person is subject to the jurisdiction of a court of the State, "unless he appear in the court, or be found within the State, or be a resident thereof, or have property therein; and, in the last case, only to the extent of such property at the time the jurisdiction attached." Construing this latter provision to mean that, in an action for money or damages where a defendant does not appear in the court, and is not found within the State, and is not a resident thereof, but has property therein, the jurisdiction of the court extends only over such property, the declaration expresses a principle of general, if not universal, law. The authority of every tribunal is necessarily restricted by the territorial limits of the State in which it is established. Any attempt to exercise authority beyond those limits would be deemed in every other forum, as has been said by this court, an illegitimate assumption of power, and be resisted as mere abuse. D'Arcy v. Ketchum et al., 11 How. 165. In the case against the plaintiff, the property here in controversy sold under the judgment rendered was not attached, nor in any way brought under the jurisdiction of the court. Its first connection with the case was caused by a levy of the execution. It was not, therefore, disposed of pursuant to any adjudication, but only in enforcement of a personal judgment, having no relation to the property, rendered against a non-resident without service of process upon him in the action, or his appearance therein. The court below did not consider that an attachment of the property was essential to its jurisdiction or to the validity of the sale, but held that the judgment was invalid from defects in the affidavit upon which the order of publication was obtained, and in the affidavit by which the publication was proved.

There is some difference of opinion among the members of this court as to the rulings upon these alleged defects. [The disagreement centered on whether the statute required an affidavit from the "printer," as the statute specified, or whether one from the editor would suffice.]

If, therefore, we were confined to the rulings of the court below upon the defects in the affidavits mentioned, we should be unable to uphold its decision. But it was also contended in that court, and is insisted upon here, that the judgment in the

Jurisdiction extends only over property if non-resident

State court against the plaintiff was void for want of personal service of process on him, or of his appearance in the action in which it was rendered, and that the premises in controversy could not be subjected to the payment of the demand of a resident creditor except by a proceeding in rem; that is, by a direct proceeding against the property for that purpose. If these positions are sound, the ruling of the Circuit Court as to the invalidity of that judgment must be sustained, notwithstanding our dissent from the reasons upon which it was made. And that they are sound would seem to follow from two well-established principles of public law respecting the jurisdiction of an independent State over persons and property. The several States of the Union are not, it is true, in every respect independent, many of the rights and powers which originally belonged to them being now vested in the government created by the Constitution. But, except as restrained and limited by that instrument, they possess and exercise the authority of independent States, and the principles of public law to which we have referred are applicable to them. One of these principles is, that every State possesses exclusive jurisdiction and sovereignty over persons and property within its territory. As a consequence, every State has the power to determine for itself the civil status and capacities of its inhabitants; to prescribe the subjects upon which they may contract, the forms and solemnities with which their contracts shall be executed, the rights and obligations arising from them, and the mode in which their validity shall be determined and their obligations enforced; and also to regulate the manner and conditions upon which property situated within such territory, both personal and real, may be acquired, enjoyed, and transferred. The other principle of public law referred to follows from the one mentioned; that is, that no State can exercise direct jurisdiction and authority over persons or property without its territory. Story, Confl. Laws, c. 2; Wheat. Int. Law, pt. 2, c. 2. The several States are of equal dignity and authority, and the independence of one implies the exclusion of power from all others. And so it is laid down by jurists, as an elementary principle, that the laws of one State have no operation outside of its territory, except so far as is allowed by comity; and that no tribunal established by it can extend its process beyond that territory so as to subject either persons or property to its decisions. "Any exertion of authority of this sort beyond this limit," says Story, "is a mere nullity, and incapable of binding such persons or property in any other tribunals." Story, Confl. Laws, sect. 539.

But as contracts made in one State may be enforceable only in another State, and property may be held by non-residents, the exercise of the jurisdiction which every State is admitted to possess over persons and property within its own territory will often affect persons and property without it. To any influence exerted in this way by a State affecting persons resident or property situated elsewhere, no objection can be justly taken; whilst any direct exertion of authority upon them, in an attempt to give ex-territorial operation to its laws, or to enforce an ex-territorial jurisdiction by its tribunals, would be deemed an encroachment upon the independence of the State in which the persons are domiciled or the property is situated, and be resisted as usurpation.

Thus the State, through its tribunals, may compel persons domiciled within its limits to execute, in pursuance of their contracts respecting property elsewhere situated, instruments in such form and with such solemnities as to transfer the title, so far as such formalities can be complied with; and the exercise of this jurisdiction in no manner interferes with the supreme control over the property by the State within which it is situated.

So the State, through its tribunals, may subject property situated within its limits owned by non-residents to the payment of the demand of its own citizens against them; and the exercise of this jurisdiction in no respect infringes upon the sovereignty of the State where the owners are domiciled. Every State owes protection to its own citizens; and, when non-residents deal with them, it is a legitimate and just exercise of authority to hold and appropriate any property owned by such non-residents to satisfy the claims of its citizens. It is in virtue of the State's jurisdiction over the property of the non-resident situated within its limits that its tribunals can inquire into that non-resident's obligations to its own citizens, and the inquiry can then be carried only to the extent necessary to control the disposition of the property. If the non-residents have no property in the State, there is nothing upon which the tribunals can adjudicate. . . .

If, without personal service, judgments *in personam*, obtained ex parte against non-residents and absent parties, upon mere publication of process, which, in the great majority of cases, would never be seen by the parties interested, could be upheld and enforced, they would be the constant instruments of fraud and oppression. Judgments for all sorts of claims upon contracts and for torts, real or pretended, would be thus obtained, under which property would be seized, when the evidence of the transactions upon which they were founded, if they ever had any existence, had perished.

Substituted service by publication, or in any other authorized form, may be sufficient to inform parties of the object of proceedings taken where property is once brought under the control of the court by seizure or some equivalent act. The law assumes that property is always in the possession of its owner, in person or by agent; and it proceeds upon the theory that its seizure will inform him, not only that it is taken into the custody of the court, but that he must look to any proceedings authorized by law upon such seizure for its condemnation and sale. Such service may also be sufficient in cases where the object of the action is to reach and dispose of property in the State, or of some interest therein, by enforcing a contract or a lien respecting the same, or to partition it among different owners, or, when the public is a party, to condemn and appropriate it for a public purpose. In other words, such service may answer in all actions which are substantially proceedings in rem. But where the entire object of the action is to determine the personal rights and obligations of the defendants, that is, where the suit is merely in personam, constructive service in this form upon a non-resident is ineffectual for any purpose. Process from the tribunals of one State cannot run into another State, and summon parties there domiciled to leave its territory and respond to proceedings against them. Publication of process or notice within the State where the tribunal sits cannot create any greater obligation upon the non-resident to appear: Process sent to him out of the State, and process published within it, are equally unavailing in proceedings to establish his personal liability. . . .

[The court explained that to acquire jurisdiction by attachment Oregon would have had to attach the property before the lawsuit; doing so afterward did not suffice to establish jurisdiction.]

The force and effect of judgments rendered against non-residents without personal service of process upon them, or their voluntary appearance, have been the subject of frequent consideration in the courts of the United States and of the several States, as attempts have been made to enforce such judgments in States other than those in which they were rendered, under the provision of the Constitution requiring that "full faith and credit shall be given in each State to the public acts, records, and judicial proceedings of every other State"; and the act of Congress [current version at 28 U.S.C. §1738] providing for the mode of authenticating such acts, records, and proceedings, and declaring that, when thus authenticated, "they shall have such faith and credit given to them in every court within the United States as they have by law or usage in the courts of the State from which they are or shall be taken." In the earlier cases, it was supposed that the act gave to all judgments the same effect in other States which they had by law in the State where rendered. But this view was afterwards qualified so as to make the act applicable only when the court rendering the judgment had jurisdiction of the parties and of the subject-matter, and not to preclude an inquiry into the jurisdiction of the court in which the judgment was rendered, or the right of the State itself to exercise authority over the person or the subject-matter. M'Elmoyle v. Cohen, 13 Pet. 312. . . .

Since the adoption of the Fourteenth Amendment to the Federal Constitution, the validity of such judgments may be directly questioned, and their enforcement in the State resisted, on the ground that proceedings in a court of justice to determine the personal rights and obligations of parties over whom that court has no jurisdiction do not constitute due process of law. Whatever difficulty may be experienced in giving to those terms a definition which will embrace every permissible exertion of power affecting private rights, and exclude such as is forbidden, there can be no doubt of their meaning when applied to judicial proceedings. They then mean a course of legal proceedings according to those rules and principles which have been established in our systems of jurisprudence for the protection and enforcement of private rights. To give such proceedings any validity, there must be a tribunal competent by its constitution — that is, by the law of its creation — to pass upon the subject-matter of the suit; and, if that involves merely a determination of the personal liability of the defendant, he must be brought within its jurisdiction by service of process within the State, or his voluntary appearance.

Except in cases affecting the personal status of the plaintiff, and cases in which that mode of service may be considered to have been assented to in advance, as hereinafter mentioned, the substituted service of process by publication, allowed by the law of Oregon and by similar laws in other States, where actions are brought against non-residents, is effectual only where, in connection with process against the person for commencing the action, property in the State is brought under the control of the court, and subjected to its disposition by process adapted to that purpose, or where the judgment is sought as a means of reaching such property or affecting some interest therein; in other words, where the action is in the nature of a proceeding in rem. As stated by Cooley in his Treatise on Constitutional Limitations, 405, for any other purpose than to subject the property of a non-resident to valid claims against him in the State, "due process of law would require appearance or personal service before the defendant could be personally bound by any judgment rendered." . . .

It follows from the views expressed that the personal judgment recovered in the State court of Oregon against the plaintiff herein, then a non-resident of the State, was without any validity, and did not authorize a sale of the property in controversy.

To prevent any misapplication of the views expressed in this opinion, it is proper to observe that we do not mean to assert, by anything we have said, that a State may not authorize proceedings to determine the status of one of its citizens towards a non-resident, which would be binding within the State, though made without service of process or personal notice to the non-resident. The jurisdiction which every State possesses to determine the civil status and capacities of all its inhabitants involves authority to prescribe the conditions on which proceedings affecting them may be commenced and carried on within its territory. The State, for example, has absolute right to prescribe the conditions upon which the marriage relation between its own citizens shall be created, and the causes for which it may be dissolved. . . .

Neither do we mean to assert that a State may not require a non-resident entering into a partnership or association within its limits, or making contracts enforceable there, to appoint an agent or representative in the State to receive service of process and notice in legal proceedings instituted with respect to such partnership, association, or contracts, or to designate a place where such service may be made and notice given, and provide, upon their failure, to make such appointment or to designate such place that service may be made upon a public officer designated for that purpose, or in some other prescribed way, and that judgments rendered upon such service may not be binding upon the non-residents both within and without the State. . . . Nor do we doubt that a State, on creating corporations or other institutions for pecuniary or charitable purposes, may provide a mode in which their conduct may be investigated, their obligations enforced, or their charters revoked, which shall require other than personal service upon their officers or members. Parties becoming members of such corporations or institutions would hold their interest subject to the conditions prescribed by law.

In the present case, there is no feature of this kind, and, consequently, no consideration of what would be the effect of such legislation in enforcing the contract of a non-resident can arise. The question here respects only the validity of a money judgment rendered in one State, in an action upon a simple contract against the resident of another, without service of process upon him, or his appearance therein.

Judgment affirmed.

[Mr. Justice HUNT dissented.]

NOTES AND PROBLEMS

1. Before considering anything else, look back at the facts.

a. Do we know whether Neff ever learned about the existence of Mitchell's original lawsuit?

b. If not, isn't the absence of notice a strong objection to the way in which the first lawsuit was conducted?

c. Did the court discuss this objection?

2. The case operates on two levels — simple facts and lofty doctrine. According to the opinion, what facts would have to be different for the Oregon courts to have had jurisdiction to enter a valid judgment in Mitchell's original suit against Neff?

3. The Supreme Court confronted not just a case but a significant political and economic problem. The transcontinental railroad, completed eight years before the Court's decision, made relatively fast travel a reality. Someone could buy a piece of property in Oregon, and be in New York a week later. If title proved defective, could Buyer sue Seller of the property in New York? If Buyer's check bounced, could Oregon Seller sue Buyer in Oregon?

4. The Court's resolution of these questions is framed in lofty Latinate phrases that divided the world into two jurisdictional categories: *in personam* and *in rem*. The case assumes that jurisdiction is about power and that one can divide power into two apparently distinct categories — power over persons and power over property. Making that distinction implied that one could sensibly think about Oregon's having power over Neff's property (had it gone about acquiring it in the proper way) as a question separate from its having power over Neff himself. Power over Neff himself came to be known as jurisdiction *in personam* (over the person); power over his property came to be known as jurisdiction *in rem* (over the thing). Modern legal scholars have tended to believe that the distinction doesn't hold up. The best critique appears in Geoffrey C. Hazard, Jr., A General Theory of State Court Jurisdiction, 1965 S. Ct. Rev. 241. As you will see, in recent years the Supreme Court has also reconsidered this distinction.

a. *In personam* jurisdiction looks, at first, refreshingly simple. To obtain jurisdiction over a non-resident person one must personally serve that person with process within the borders of the state in question. So, to recur to the hypothetical in Note 3, Buyer could sue Seller in New York only if he could serve him with process in New York; otherwise he would be beyond the range of the New York court's power. In *Pennoyer's* view, serving him by other means (e.g., by mail or by personal service in a different state) in other places does not work. Working with the facts of *Pennoyer*, explain why the Oregon court did not obtain *in personam* jurisdiction over Neff.

b. *In rem* jurisdiction, the more obscure category, seems to flow from a problem created by the rules for *in personam* jurisdiction: People sometimes own property distant from their usual personal residence. Returning to the hypothetical case in Note 3, suppose that, after Buyer of the Oregon land returned to New York, the check tendered as the purchase price bounces, and Seller argues that he still owns the property. Can Buyer, by remaining out of state — perhaps for years at a time — prevent Oregon from giving clean title back to Seller (and thus enabling him to sell to a solvent purchaser)? If *in personam* jurisdiction is the only possibility, nothing can be done until the owner returns and can be served with process. Unwilling to see that result, the court created a procedure by which a court located in the same state as the property could enter a judgment disposing of that property—by seizing it at the outset of the lawsuit. *Pennoyer* calls that procedure *in rem* jurisdiction. Working with the facts of *Pennoyer*, explain why the Oregon court did not obtain *in rem* jurisdiction over Neff.

c. So far, so good. The waters begin to cloud in the paragraph that begins "To prevent any misapplication . . . ," in which the opinion qualifies and retracts some of the broad statements it makes in the preceding section. Can you explain how this section changes some of the jurisdictional principles (or at least the way in which they will be applied in practice) of the second section?

5. *Pennoyer* established fundamental jurisdictional doctrine whose main outlines prevailed for a century and which is still good law in many fundamental respects. *Pennoyer* proclaims that its holding rests on the Constitution, and the opinion mentions both the Due Process and the Full Faith and Credit Clauses. That assertion has two implications. First, because the Due Process Clause restricts the power of state governments, the boundaries of personal jurisdiction proclaimed by the Supreme Court bind state courts.

Pennoyer's mention of the Full Faith and Credit Clause (U.S. Const. Art. IV, §1) pointed to a second constitutional issue. The opinion links full faith and credit to jurisdiction: the courts of State Y need not heed a judgment entered by the courts of State X if X lacked personal jurisdiction over the defendant. That proposition is sometimes described as the doctrine of collateral attack: A defendant may under some circumstances attack in a second—collateral—proceeding a judgment rendered without jurisdiction. What circumstances? It is difficult in a brief space to sketch all the variations, but, at a minimum, it is possible to attack collaterally a judgment entered without personal jurisdiction if the challenging party did not appear at all in the proceedings that led to the assertedly invalid judgment. Explain how this proposition applied to Neff in *Pennoyer*.

6. To understand *Pennoyer*'s general principles and its specific holding, consider the following variations. To which does *Pennoyer* give a clear answer? In each assume that A, a resident of Minnesota, is suing B, a resident of North Dakota, in Minnesota (where B owns some land).

a. A serves B in North Dakota; B moves to dismiss the Minnesota action for lack of personal jurisdiction.

b. Same as (a) except that instead of appearing to object to the Minnesota court's jurisdiction, B defaults and the court enters judgment against her. A then takes that judgment to North Dakota to enforce; B appears in the enforcement proceeding and argues that the judgment is invalid and should not be enforced.

c. A serves B while B is traveling on business in Minnesota; B moves to dismiss for lack of personal jurisdiction.

d. Same as (c) except that instead of moving to dismiss, B defaults; A recovers a default judgment, which he then takes to North Dakota to enforce; B appears in the enforcement proceeding and argues that the judgment is invalid and should not be enforced.

e. A attaches B's land in Minnesota and obtains a judgment against B. A then seeks to have the land sold to satisfy the judgment. B sues to enjoin the sale, arguing that the court lacked jurisdiction over her or her land because she was not personally served.

f. Without attaching B's land, A serves B by publication, obtains a default judgment, and sues to enforce that judgment in North Dakota. B appears in North Dakota and objects.

g. A and B are married, and the suit is for divorce. A notifies B in North Dakota. B's lawyer moves to dismiss on the ground that the Minnesota court lacks personal jurisdiction.

h. Same facts as in (g), except that, in addition to a divorce, A seeks child support and alimony.

i. Finally, consider a question that Pennoyer does not answer: A attempts to serve B while B is on a fishing trip on the Minnesota-Wisconsin border. B moves to dismiss the Minnesota suit, claiming she was served in Wisconsin. B loses the motion to dismiss. A then gets a judgment and sues on the judgment in North Dakota. B appears in the North Dakota enforcement proceeding and argues that the judgment should not be enforced because the Minnesota court lacked jurisdiction — because she, B, was not in Minnesota when served with process. In principle, how should the court in this second enforcement action respond to B's argument?

7. *Pennoyer* is rooted both in constitutional history and in the colorful personal biographies of its participants.

a. Mitchell's original suit against Neff occurred in 1866. The Fourteenth Amendment — part of a revolution in state-federal relations following the Civil War — was not ratified until 1868. Is it surprising to find that amendment applied retroactively?

b. Prof. Linda Silberman has told the personal stories well:

> Mitchell was a well-known Portland lawyer specializing in land litigation and railroad right-of-way cases. In 1872 Mitchell was elected a United States Senator. Allegations of vote fraud were made against Mitchell, and indictments were sought but later dismissed. Interestingly, Judge Deady — who rendered the lower court decision in *Pennoyer* — actively supported the attempts to seek indictments for vote fraud. It is somewhat surprising that Mitchell was ever elected to public office given his somewhat sordid past. At the age of 22, Mitchell was forced to marry a fifteen-year-old girl "he had seduced and made pregnant." He soon abandoned his first wife and took up with a "schoolmarm." Mitchell next entered a bigamous marriage, and eventually fell "in love with his wife's sister and carr[ied] on an open affair for many years." [Citing and quoting from E. MacColl, The Shaping of a City 201-203 (1976).]
>
> Pennoyer was also active in public life. Educated at Harvard, he was both governor of Oregon and mayor of Portland. Something of a political maverick, Pennoyer proclaimed Oregon's Thanksgiving Day holiday one week later than the rest of the Nation.

Linda Silberman, Shaffer v. Heitner: The End of an Era, 53 N.Y.U.L. Rev. 33, 44 n.53 (1978).

c. Pictures of some of the participants (but sadly not of Marcus Neff, who started it all, survive); they suggest that the possession of a beard was a key feature of the early law of personal jurisdiction:

Sylvester Pennoyer   John Mitchell   Justice Stephen Field

8. Focus on *Pennoyer's* conceptual scheme. That scheme involves three elements: power, consent, and notice. Each element persists, though in altered form, as a theme in today's jurisdictional cases.

a. *Power.*   We have already considered the main outlines of *Pennoyer's* division of power into two categories, *in personam* and *in rem* jurisdiction (see Note 4, supra). *In personam* jurisdiction, suggested *Pennoyer,* was necessary when one wanted to obtain either a money judgment or injunctive relief against a defendant; it would also suffice to decide the ownership of property. *In rem* jurisdiction was available if one wanted to decide the ownership of property when one could not acquire *in personam* jurisdiction over a defendant claiming title. By extension, *in rem* jurisdiction could also be used to adjudicate claims unrelated to the property itself. For example, in *Pennoyer,* Mitchell's claim was for legal fees; he was interested in Neff's property only as a way of satisfying his contract claim. Some courts refer to this extended use of in rem jurisdiction as *quasi in rem.*

Pennoyer, as if anticipating the problems its absolute scheme would create, immediately softened it by establishing a number of exceptions that appear in the latter part of the opinion. One such exception is the mysterious jurisdiction over the "status of one of its citizens toward a nonresident." The reference, as the remainder of the discussion makes clear, is to marriage and family relations. Even under the strictest interpretation of *Pennoyer,* a deserted spouse could sue for divorce — though not alimony or child support — even if the absent wife or husband could not be served within the state. See notes 6(g) and 6(h) above.

More obscure was the question of whether *Pennoyer's* language about service of process as a requirement of *in personam* jurisdiction applied to *residents* of the state in question. Would Oregon have jurisdiction over a lifelong resident who could not be located and served with process? Was domicile — actual residence combined with the intent to remain indefinitely—enough to establish jurisdiction? With its attention focused on nonresidents, the opinion did not directly answer this question, although parts hint that the answer might be yes. We shall consider these questions in more detail later.

b. *Consent.*   *Pennoyer* allowed one other escape from the rigors of its jurisdictional scheme. In several parts of the opinion the Court indicated that nonresidents who had no property in the state were nevertheless subject to its jurisdiction if they had consented to its exercise—for example, by designating an agent in the state who would accept service of process on their behalf. So, if Neff in his agreement with Mitchell had appointed a friend living in Oregon to receive service of process in any suit arising from the agreement, Oregon would, according to this part of *Pennoyer*, have jurisdiction to enter a valid judgment in Mitchell's suit for his fees. (Put aside for a moment any concern whether it would be ethical for a lawyer to present his client with such an agreement.) The penultimate paragraph of the opinion goes further, saying that the state might *require* persons and organizations to appoint such agents (and thereby to "consent" to jurisdiction). If that rather loose idea of consent were taken far enough, a state could obtain jurisdiction over a wide variety of nonresidents by requiring them to agree to jurisdiction as a condition of engaging in various sorts of transactions in the state. For corporations, such required consent became a widespread way of obtaining jurisdiction; for persons, it was much more problematic because other portions of the Constitution give persons the right to travel between states and to do business: Could a state require someone to "consent" to jurisdiction as the price of doing something he had a constitutional right to do in any case? For example, could Oregon require that any person—such as Neff—contracting for legal services to be rendered in that state had "consented" to jurisdiction for claims arising from that contract? Again, we shall return to that theme later.

c. *Notice.*   The final, almost concealed strand of *Pennoyer* dealt with notice, a topic about which the court appears to have contradictory ideas. On the one hand, the opinion contains a paragraph ("If without personal service. . . .") suggesting the importance of notice in *in personam* actions. On the other hand, it is perfectly willing to permit notice by publication in *in rem* actions. This judicial schizophrenia led to two lines of apparently contradictory decisions.

For *in personam* actions, the terms of *Pennoyer*'s scheme almost guaranteed that defendants would receive notice: So long as personal service of process was the primary way of obtaining *in personam* jurisdiction, the questions of notice and power would collapse into one inquiry. By personally serving a person with process within its borders, a state would simultaneously give notice and assert power. Only after states attempted service by means other than personal service did the questions of notice and power separate themselves. We shall consider the question of the constitutional sufficiency of notice in Mullane v. Central Hanover Bank & Trust, infra page 146.

For *in rem* actions the court lapsed into wishful thinking and fictions. Justifying notice by publication, *Pennoyer* says, "Substituted service by publication, or in any other authorized form, may be sufficient to inform parties of the object of proceedings taken where property is once brought under the control of the court by seizure or some equivalent act. The law assumes that property is always in the possession of its owner, in person or by agent; and it proceeds upon the theory that its seizure will inform him. . . ." Using this rationale, courts for almost a century upheld very scanty notice, so long as the action in question could be called *in rem*. One can be more forgiving of the apparently cavalier assumption by reminding oneself of the situation confronting the Court. Large tracts of land in the Western U.S. were held by absentee owners — like Neff himself. Unless the state courts could adjudicate title to those lands, endless disputes and uncertainty about title could delay the social and economic development of perhaps half of the nation. *In rem* jurisdiction and constructive notice may have been a clumsy solution, but the problem was real. As we shall see, Mullane v. Central Hanover Bank & Trust ended this scheme.

9. *Pennoyer* in a modern economy.   *Pennoyer* has its feet planted in a pre-industrial world with uncertain communications. The Court seemed to assume that the instance of the nonresident defendant would be an occasional problem that could be averted in most cases by the availability of property as an alternative basis of jurisdiction. The Court proved a poor prophet; the decade following *Pennoyer* saw enormous railroad construction. The last quarter of the nineteenth century also witnessed both a great expansion of industrial production and the proliferation of often interlocking corporations organizing that production. Within 50 years of the decision other developments — the automobile, telegraph, and telephone — had nationalized economic life and even leisure activities in a way unforeseen by *Pennoyer*'s authors. In consequence, many of the most difficult problems facing the courts after *Pennoyer* dealt with entities and situations to which *Pennoyer* only passingly alluded.

To solve them later courts repeatedly resorted to two concepts that appeared in *Pennoyer*: consent and presence. Under *Pennoyer* a state could acquire jurisdiction over a defendant who consented to its assertion of power; likewise over a defendant present in the state when served with process. For 70 years after *Pennoyer*, the courts stretched these ideas of consent and presence considerably.

a. "*Consent.*"   Consent had its easiest application to corporations. Initially, courts held that corporations could be subject to service only where they were incorporated, and this view found support in a Supreme Court dictum that "a corporation can have no legal existence out of the boundaries of the sovereignty by which it is created." Bank of Augusta v. Earle, 38 U.S. (13 Pet.) 519 (1839). Later it was held that corporations could operate outside the state that created them, but that the "host" state could place conditions on foreign corporations (meaning U.S. corporations operating outside their home state). The condition most important for present purposes was that of requiring consent to jurisdiction. Such consent might be express or implied, but if implied it was limited to suits arising from the transaction of business in the state.

With persons, the notion of consent was less clear. Thus, in Flexner v. Farson, 248 U.S. 289 (1919), the Supreme Court held that Kentucky did not have jurisdiction over a partnership doing business in Kentucky through an agent. But eight years later, in Hess v. Pawloski, 274 U.S. 352 (1927), the Court sustained jurisdiction over a nonresident defendant who had been involved in an accident on the Massachusetts highways. The statute involved provided that

> the acceptance by a nonresident of the rights and privileges [of driving on the Massachusetts highways] shall be deemed equivalent to the appointment [of a local official] upon whom may be served all lawful processes . . . growing out of any accident or collision in which said nonresident may be involved while operating a motor vehicle on such a way, and said acceptance or operation shall be a signification of his agreement that any such process against him . . . . shall be of the same legal force and validity as if served on him personally.

The Court sustained the statute based on the implied consent of the nonresident, the rather dubious power to exclude nonresidents absent consent, and the "state's power to regulate the use of its highways."

b. *"Presence."* A corporation does not have a physical existence that permits personal service where it is located. Initially the problem was solved by *Bank of Augusta*, supra, which held that a state could exact "consent" to jurisdiction as a price of permitting a corporation to operate. Then courts began to reject the *Bank of Augusta* dictum and held that a corporation was "present" (that is, subject to jurisdiction) if it conducted a certain level of activity in the state. Once present, the corporation was subject to jurisdiction for all claims (just as under *Pennoyer* an individual was subject to jurisdiction for all claims if personally served in the forum).

The courts used both consent and presence alternatively; the confusion was compounded because they used the same test — doing business — to determine both issues. That is, a corporation doing business might be held either to have "consented" to jurisdiction or to be "present" in the state. Such manipulation of consent and presence achieved bearable results — states could regulate activities conducted within their borders — but getting to those results required some rather creaky doctrinal machinery. The modern reworking of that machinery is the focus of the next section.

NOTE ON THE MECHANICS OF JURISDICTION: CHALLENGE AND WAIVER

Before further exploring the development of personal jurisdiction, the student will find it useful to understand how lawyers bring jurisdictional challenges to bear on actual cases. The workings of such procedures grow from *Pennoyer* and expose some otherwise hidden assumptions about the meaning of jurisdiction.

Assume Abe, a resident of Illinois, sues Barbara, a resident of California, in Illinois, and Barbara thinks that she is not subject to personal jurisdiction. How does she proceed?

The simplest but riskiest course is for Barbara to do nothing. If she is very sure indeed that the court lacks jurisdiction, she may simply decline to appear, suffer a default judgment, and attack the judgment only when Abe seeks to enforce it in a subsequent proceeding — for example, when Abe records the Illinois judgment in a California court and obtains a writ of execution from the California court enforcing the Illinois judgment against Barbara's assets in California. Even before *Pennoyer*, that route — known as collateral attack — lay open. D'Arcy v. Ketchum, 52 U.S. 165 (1850). It carries, however, a serious risk, for if the second court rejects the jurisdictional challenge, Barbara can raise no other defenses on the merits. Jurisdiction, but only jurisdiction, is open to collateral attack.

What happens if Barbara wishes to pursue a less risky course of action; how does she raise jurisdictional objections in the first proceeding?

a. Under the Federal Rules (and state statutes patterned on them), Barbara may raise her jurisdictional defense either in the answer or, if she makes a pre-answer motion, at that time. Read Rule 12(b), (h), and (g). They make sequence critical. Making any preanswer motion that omits a defense of personal jurisdiction is treated as a waiver of jurisdiction. By the same token, making an appearance or litigating other issues but failing to challenge personal jurisdiction in one of these two ways results in waiver of the jurisdictional defense. If Barbara raises the objection at the proper time, she does not waive it by joining it with other defenses or objections, but she must raise it the first time she raises any issue, either by way of motion, appearance, or answer. Moreover, she must litigate the claim promptly. This happens as a matter of course if she makes a pre-answer motion. If she makes no such motion but challenges jurisdiction in her answer, she must promptly move for dismissal on this ground. Although the Rules do not say so, courts will not look kindly on a defendant who waits until the end of discovery to see how the "wind is blowing" on the merits of the case before moving to dismiss for want of personal jurisdiction.

b. In a few state systems (and in many older cases), Barbara would raise the jurisdictional claim by making a "special appearance." See, for example, 735 Ill. Comp. Stat. 5/2-301(b) (Bender 2004); Tex. R. Civ. P. 120a (Bender 2003). The procedure is so-called for reasons you can now understand: In *Pennoyer*'s scheme, a defendant who "appeared" might be held to have consented to the state's exercise of power. What was needed was a form of "appearance" that would not be equated with "presence" or consent. A "special" appearance permitted the defendant to object to jurisdiction without the action of objecting being itself the basis for jurisdiction.

c. Finally, what happens if the defendant has availed herself of the system's opportunity to challenge jurisdiction but loses? May she immediately appeal that decision? Some states do permit such an immediate appeal. Other states and the federal system treat a jurisdictional defense like other pretrial rulings and require that an appeal await final judgment. If you were a defendant with a jurisdictional defense, which pattern would you prefer? If you were a plaintiff, which would you prefer?

NOTES AND PROBLEMS

1. Jurisdictional challenges raise technical, strategic, and theoretical issues. Start with the technical. Reread Rules 12(b), (h), and (g) and apply them to the

following scenarios. Each assumes that the plaintiff has filed a complaint and the defendant then makes one of the following responses. The question is whether the defendant has waived her jurisdictional objection.

a. Defendant makes a pre-answer 12(b)(6) motion; upon its denial she files a second pre-answer motion based on Rule 12(b)(2), seeking a dismissal for want of personal jurisdiction.

b. Defendant makes a pre-answer 12(b)(6) motion; upon its denial she files an answer containing both a defense on the merits and a 12(b)(2) motion to dismiss for want of personal jurisdiction.

c. Defendant makes no pre-answer motion but answers the complaint, including in her answer a defense based on personal jurisdiction.

d. Defendant makes a pre-answer 12(b)(1) motion, which is denied; she then makes a 12(b)(2) motion.

e. Defendant makes a 12(f) motion to strike a scandalous allegation from the complaint; she then makes a 12(b)(2) motion.

f. Defendant moves to transfer venue under 28 U.S.C. §1404; after transfer is denied she moves to dismiss under 12(b)(2).

2. Other actions by the defendant, apart from motions under Rule 12(b) and answers to the complaint, may result in waiver of the jurisdictional issue, and a defendant who wishes to object to personal jurisdiction must carefully consider any litigation activity preceding such an objection. For example, litigating the propriety of a preliminary injunction or filing a permissive counterclaim before an answer or 12(b) motion have sometimes been held to constitute waiver. See Wright, Federal Courts 463.

3. Now that you have avoided future malpractice claims with this technical knowledge, consider what the technical pattern means. Why is such a premium placed upon arguing the jurisdictional issue at the same time as or before other issues? What does that say about the nature of this defense that defendants can so easily — even by inattention — waive objections to personal jurisdiction?

4. As you have seen, Rule 12(b) allows a defense of lack of personal jurisdiction to be raised either by pre-answer motion or as part of the answer (if but only if there has been no pre-answer motion). Why would a defendant choose a pre-answer motion rather than simply bundling everything into her answer to the complaint?

a. To get an idea of one possible reason, read Rules 8(b) and 11, which puts the lawyer's professional standing — and also her pocketbook — behind the allegations of an answer.

b. Rule 13 supplies another reason: It requires that an answer contain any counterclaim arising out of the same transaction as the claim.

c. Not only money and professional requirements but also time is at stake. Rule 12(b) gives the defendant just 20 days to answer (unless time is extended or the defendant waives service of process). That may be a short time if the lawyer has to do substantial factual investigation to decide on the strategy of the answer. Rule 12(a)(4) extends the time to answer until ten days after the court has ruled on a pre-answer motion.

B.   The Modern Constitutional Formulation of Power

Each of the elements found in *Pennoyer* — power, consent, and notice — continues to play a role in modern jurisdictional thought. But each has taken on a different shape, one that sometimes makes the original assumptions difficult to recognize. This section traces the evolution of these three themes in the modern law of personal jurisdiction.

1.   Redefining Constitutional Power

Operating under the framework established by *Pennoyer*, state and federal courts encountered several situations for which its schema seemed ill-adapted. As noted above, one of the most frequent involved *in personam* jurisdiction over a defendant corporation. Ironically, the way out of the tangled path was suggested in a case involving not a corporation but a person. In Milliken v. Meyer, 311 U.S. 457 (1940), two partners in an oil well sued each other. Meyer, the defendant, had been a resident of Wyoming but was at the time of the suit served personally in Colorado; Meyer did not appear in Wyoming, where the court rendered a judgment against him. Meyer attacked the Wyoming judgment collaterally (does this sound a lot like *Pennoyer* so far?). The U.S. Supreme Court held that the Wyoming judgment was valid, and in a paragraph that laid the groundwork for much future law said:

> Domicile in the state is alone sufficient to bring an absent defendant within the reach of the state's jurisdiction for purposes of a personal judgment by means of appropriate substituted service. Substituted service [i.e., service other than personal service in the forum state] in such cases has been quite uniformly upheld where the absent defendant was served at his usual place of abode in the state as well as where he was personally served without the state. That such substituted service may be wholly adequate to meet the requirements of due process was recognized by this Court in McDonald v. Mabee despite earlier intimations to the contrary. See Pennoyer v. Neff, 95 U.S. 714. Its adequacy so far as due process is concerned is dependent on whether or not the form of substituted service provided for such cases and employed is reasonably calculated to give him actual notice of the proceedings and an opportunity to be heard. If it is, the traditional notions of fair play and substantial justice (McDonald v. Mabee, supra) implicit in due process are satisfied. Here there can be no question on that score. Meyer did not merely receive actual notice of the Wyoming proceedings. While outside the state, he was personally served in accordance with a statutory scheme which Wyoming had provided for such occasions. And in our view the machinery employed met all the requirements of due process. Certainly then Meyer's domicile in Wyoming was a sufficient basis for that extraterritorial service. As in case of the authority of the United States over its absent citizens, the authority of a state over one of its citizens is not terminated by the mere fact of his absence from the state. The state which accords him privileges and affords protection to him and his property by virtue of his domicile may also exact reciprocal duties. "Enjoyment of the privileges of residence within the state, and the attendant right to invoke the protection of its laws, are inseparable" from the various incidences of state citizenship. See

Lawrence v. State Tax Commission. The responsibilities of that citizenship arise out of the relationship to the state which domicile creates. That relationship is not dissolved by mere absence from the state. The attendant duties, like the rights and privileges incident to domicile, are not dependent on continuous presence in the state. One such incidence of domicile is amenability to suit within the state even during sojourns without the state, where the state has provided and employed a reasonable method for apprising such an absent party of the proceedings against him.

Id. at 462-463. The next case took these suggestions and ran with them, rearranging the landscape of personal jurisdiction; most contemporary debate concerns its application and interpretation. It thus bears careful study.

International Shoe Co. v. Washington

326 U.S. 310 (1945)

Mr. Chief Justice STONE delivered the opinion of the Court.

Questions

The questions for decision are (1) whether, within the limitations of the due process clause of the Fourteenth Amendment, the appellant, a Delaware corporation, has by its activities in the State of Washington rendered itself amenable to proceedings in the courts of that state to recover unpaid contributions to the state unemployment compensation fund enacted by state statutes, Washington Unemployment Compensation Act, and (2) whether the state can exact those contributions consistently with the due process clause of the Fourteenth Amendment.

The statutes in question set up a comprehensive scheme of unemployment compensation, the costs of which are defrayed by contributions required to be made by employers to a state unemployment compensation fund. The contributions are a specified percentage of the wages payable annually by each employer for his employees' services in the state. The assessment and collection of the contributions and the fund are administered by appellees. Section 14(c) of the Act authorizes appellee Commissioner to issue an order and notice of assessment of delinquent contributions upon prescribed personal service of the notice upon the employer if found within the state, or, if not so found, by mailing the notice to the employer by registered mail at his last known address. . . .

Method for notice

In this case notice of assessment for the years in question was personally served upon a sales solicitor employed by appellant in the State of Washington, and a copy of the notice was mailed by registered mail to appellant at its address in St. Louis, Missouri. Appellant appeared specially before the office of unemployment and moved to set aside the order and notice of assessment on the ground that the service upon appellant's salesman was not proper service upon appellant; that appellant was not a corporation of the State of Washington and was not doing business within the state; that it had no agent within the state upon whom service could be made; and that appellant is not an employer and does not furnish employment within the meaning of the statute. . . .

Π arg

The facts as found by the appeal tribunal and accepted by the state Superior Court and Supreme Court, are not in dispute. Appellant is a Delaware corporation, having its principal place of business in St. Louis, Missouri, and is engaged in the manufacture and sale of shoes and other footwear. It maintains places of business in several states, other than Washington, at which its manufacturing is carried on and from which its merchandise is distributed interstate through several sales units or branches located outside the State of Washington.

Appellant has no office in Washington and makes no contracts either for sale or purchase of merchandise there. It maintains no stock of merchandise in that state and makes there no deliveries of goods in intrastate commerce. During the years from 1937 to 1940, now in question, appellant employed eleven to thirteen salesmen under direct supervision and control of sales managers located in St. Louis. These salesmen resided in Washington; their principal activities were confined to that state; and they were compensated by commissions based upon the amount of their sales. The commissions for each year totaled more than $31,000. Appellant supplies its salesmen with a line of samples, each consisting of one shoe of a pair, which they display to prospective purchasers. On occasion they rent permanent sample rooms, for exhibiting samples, in business buildings, or rent rooms in hotels or business buildings temporarily for that purpose. The cost of such rentals is reimbursed by appellant.

The authority of the salesmen is limited to exhibiting their samples and soliciting orders from prospective buyers, at prices and on terms fixed by appellant. The salesmen transmit the orders to appellant's office in St. Louis for acceptance or rejection, and when accepted the merchandise for filling the orders is shipped f.o.b. from points outside Washington to the purchasers within the state. All the merchandise shipped into Washington is invoiced at the place of shipment from which collections are made. No salesman has authority to enter into contracts or to make collections. . . .

Appellant . . . insists that its activities within the state were not sufficient to . . . [confer] jurisdiction. . . . And appellant further argues that since it was not present within the state, it is a denial of due process to subject it to taxation or other money exaction. It thus denies the power of the state to lay the tax or to subject appellant to a suit for its collection.

Historically the jurisdiction of courts to render judgment in personam is grounded on their de facto power over the defendant's person. Hence his presence within the territorial jurisdiction of a court was prerequisite to its rendition of a judgment personally binding him. Pennoyer v. Neff. But now that the capias ad respondendum has given way to personal service of summons or other form of notice, due process requires only that in order to subject a defendant to a judgment in personam, if he be not present within the territory of the forum, he have certain minimum contacts with it such that the maintenance of the suit does not offend "traditional notions of fair play and substantial justice."

Since the corporate personality is a fiction, although a fiction intended to be acted upon as though it were a fact, it is clear that unlike an individual its "presence" without, as well as within, the state of its origin can be manifested only by activities carried on in its behalf by those who are authorized to act for it. To say that the corporation is so far "present" there as to satisfy due process requirements, for purposes of taxation or the maintenance of suits against it in the courts of the state, is to beg the question to be decided. For the terms "present" or "presence" are used merely to symbolize those activities of the corporation's agent within the state which courts will deem to be sufficient to satisfy the demands of due process. Those demands may be met by such contacts of the corporation with the state of the forum as to make it reasonable, in the context of our federal system of government, to require the corporation to defend the particular suit which is brought there. An "estimate of the inconveniences" which would result to the corporation from a trial away from its "home" or principal place of business is relevant in this connection.

"Presence" in the state in this sense has never been doubted when the activities of the corporation there have not only been continuous and systematic, but also give rise to the liabilities sued on, even though no consent to be sued or authorization to an agent to accept service of process has been given. Conversely it has been generally recognized that the casual presence of the corporate agent or even his conduct of single or isolated items of activities in a state in the corporation's behalf are not enough to subject it to suit on causes of action unconnected with the activities there. To require the corporation in such circumstances to defend the suit away from its home or other jurisdiction where it carries on more substantial activities has been thought to lay too great and unreasonable a burden on the corporation to comport with due process.

While it has been held, in cases on which appellant relies, that continuous activity of some sorts within a state is not enough to support the demand that the corporation be amenable to suits unrelated to that activity, there have been instances in which the continuous corporate operations within a state were thought so substantial and of such a nature as to justify suit against it on causes of action arising from dealings entirely distinct from those activities.

Finally, although the commission of some single or occasional acts of the corporate agent in a state sufficient to impose an obligation or liability on the corporation has not been thought to confer upon the state authority to enforce it, other such acts, because of their nature and quality and the circumstances of their commission, may be deemed sufficient to render the corporation liable to suit. True, some of the decisions holding the corporation amenable to suit have been supported by resort to the legal fiction that it has given its consent to service and suit, consent being implied [sic] from its presence in the state through the acts of its authorized agents. But more realistically it may be said that those authorized acts were of such a nature as to justify the fiction.

It is evident that the criteria by which we mark the boundary line between those activities which justify the subjection of a corporation to suit, and those which do not, cannot be simply mechanical or quantitative. The test is not merely, as has sometimes been suggested, whether the activity, which the corporation has seen fit to procure through its agents in another state, is a little more or a little less. Whether due process is satisfied must depend rather upon the quality and nature of the activity in relation to the fair and orderly administration of the laws which it was the purpose of the due process clause to insure. That clause does not contemplate that a state may make binding a judgment in personam against an individual or corporate defendant with which the state has no contacts, ties, or relations.

But to the extent that a corporation exercises the privilege of conducting activities within a state, it enjoys the benefits and protection of the laws of that state. The exercise of that privilege may give rise to obligations, and, so far as those obligations arise out of or are connected with the activities within the state, a procedure which requires the corporation to respond to a suit brought to enforce them can, in most instances, hardly be said to be undue.

Applying these standards, the activities carried on in behalf of appellant in the State of Washington were neither irregular nor casual. They were systematic and continuous throughout the years in question. They resulted in a large volume of interstate business, in the course of which appellant received the benefits and protection of the laws of the state, including the right to resort to the courts for the enforcement of its rights. The obligation which is here sued upon arose out of those very activities. It is evident that these operations establish sufficient contacts or ties with the state of the forum to make it reasonable and just, according to our traditional conception of fair play and substantial justice, to permit the state to enforce the obligations which appellant has incurred there. Hence we cannot say that the maintenance of the present suit in the State of Washington involves an unreasonable or undue procedure.

We are likewise unable to conclude that the service of the process within the state upon an agent whose activities establish appellant's "presence" there was not sufficient notice of the suit, or that the suit was so unrelated to those activities as to make the agent an inappropriate vehicle for communicating the notice. It is enough that appellant has established such contacts with the state that the particular form of substituted service adopted there gives reasonable assurance that the notice will be actual. Nor can we say that the mailing of the notice of suit to appellant by registered mail at its home office was not reasonably calculated to apprise appellant of the suit. . . .

Appellant having rendered itself amenable to suit upon obligations arising out of the activities of its salesmen in Washington, the state may maintain the present suit in personam to collect the tax laid upon the exercise of the privilege of employing appellant's salesmen within the state. For Washington has made one of those activities, which taken together establish appellant's "presence" there for purposes of suit, the taxable event by which the state brings appellant within the reach of its taxing power. The state thus has constitutional power to lay the tax and to subject appellant to a suit to recover it. The activities which establish its "presence" subject it alike to taxation by the state and to suit to recover the tax.

Affirmed.

Mr. Justice BLACK delivered the following opinion. . . .

I believe that the Federal Constitution leaves to each State, without any "ifs" or "buts," a power to tax and to open the doors of its courts for its citizens to sue corporations whose agents do business in those States. Believing that the Constitution gave the States that power, I think it a judicial deprivation to condition its exercise upon this Court's notion of "fair play," however appealing that term may be. Nor can I stretch the meaning of due process so far as to authorize this Court to deprive a State of the right to afford judicial protection to its citizens on the ground that it would be more "convenient" for the corporation to be sued somewhere else.

There is a strong emotional appeal in the words "fair play," "justice," and "reasonableness." But they were not chosen by those who wrote the original Constitution or the Fourteenth Amendment as a measuring rod for this Court to use in invalidating State or Federal laws passed by elected legislative representatives. No one, not even those who most feared a democratic government, ever formally proposed that courts should be given power to invalidate legislation under any such elastic standards. . . .

True, the State's power is here upheld. But the rule announced means that tomorrow's judgment may strike down a State or Federal enactment on the ground that it does not conform to the Court's idea of natural justice. . . .

NOTES AND PROBLEMS

1. *International Shoe* is an unusual case in several respects.

a. In most cases the briefs, argument, and ensuing opinion occupy the same conceptual universe — that is, the parties and the court agree, for example, that this is a contract case and that the central issue is whether the "offer" was definite enough to be accepted. *International Shoe* is different. The parties briefed and argued the case in the then-traditional categories of "presence" and "consent." The Court responded in quite different terms, with a conceptual scheme focusing on "minimum contacts" and "substantial justice and fair play." Should a court tell the parties in advance that it is contemplating such a doctrinal shift?

b. Moreover, the Court redrew the conceptual boundaries although it did not have to do so in order to reach the result in question: It could, as the Washington Supreme Court had done, simply have held that International Shoe was "present" in that state for the jurisdictional purposes of this suit. What was so important about the new conceptual framework?

c. Perhaps because it was redrawing the doctrinal map as well as deciding the case before it, the opinion is remarkably vague about the application of the principles it announces to the facts before it. What facts would have to change for the Court to have reached a different result?

2. When the Court writes that, to be subject to a state's jurisdiction, a defendant must "have certain minimum contacts with it such that the maintenance of suit does not offend 'traditional notions of fair play and substantial justice,'" does it provide a workable standard for the lower courts to follow in deciding future cases? In later cases, if the salespeople in question are freelancers who work for several companies, will each of the companies be subject to the jurisdiction of the State of Washington under the *International Shoe* rationale? What if their activities are not confined to Washington but also take them to Oregon and California? One commentator has suggested that the basic test of *International Shoe* is a good one but that because of its generality it must be subjected to a process of "arbitrary particularization" in order to come up with workable rules.

Geoffrey C. Hazard, Jr., A General Theory of State-Court Jurisdiction, 1965 Sup. Ct. Rev. 241, 283.

3. *General and specific jurisdiction.* Consider the following paragraph of *International Shoe*:

> While it has been held, in cases on which appellant relies, that continuous activity of some sorts within a state is not enough to support the demand that the corporation be amenable to suits *unrelated to that activity*, there have been instances in which the continuous corporate operations within a state were thought so substantial and of such a nature as to justify suit against it on causes of action arising from dealings *entirely distinct from those activities.* (Emphasis added.)

Many have implied from this sentence an entire vision of jurisdiction.

a. *General jurisdiction*   In some cases the defendant will have such substantial contacts with the forum state to make it fair to assert jurisdiction even over claims unrelated to those contacts. For example, General Motors has its chief place of business in Michigan. Under the theory of general jurisdiction, General Motors could be sued in Michigan even over contracts or torts concluded or committed in Idaho or Germany. *International Shoe* did nothing to disturb the rule that when a corporation is doing business in a state such that its contacts are "substantial," even cases unrelated to the corporation's activities within the state may be brought against the corporation there. Such cases fall within the category described above as instances "in which the continuous corporate operations within a state were thought so substantial and of such a nature as to justify a suit against it on causes of action arising from dealings entirely distinct from those activities." As the Court put it in Helicopteros Nacionales de Colombia v. Hall, 466 U.S. 408, 414 (1984), "Even when the cause of action does not arise out of or relate to the foreign corporation's activities in the forum State, due process is not offended by a State's subjecting the corporation to its in personam jurisdiction when there are sufficient contacts between the State and the foreign corporation."

b. *Specific jurisdiction.*   By contrast, where the defendant's activities fall short of general jurisdiction, the minimum contacts analysis of *International Shoe* becomes important. In those cases courts worry both about the extent of those contacts and about the relation between those contacts and the claim on which plaintiff is suing. Suppose, for example, Driver has never been in Missouri but, in the course of a vacation trip, enters the state. Specific jurisdiction would allow an injured pedestrian to sue Driver on a claim arising from that accident. Commentators describe such cases as instances of specific jurisdiction, in which jurisdiction exists for the specific claim in question but not necessarily for other claims. All other things being equal, the more closely related the contacts and the facts giving rise to the claim, the more likely the court is to uphold jurisdiction.

The classic and influential discussion of this jurisdictional scheme is that of Arthur von Mehren and Donald Trautman, Jurisdiction to Adjudicate: A Suggested Analysis, 79 Harv. L. Rev. 1121 (1966).

4. For practice in using the concepts of specific and general jurisdiction, consider the following variations on the facts in *International Shoe*. As stated in

the case, assume that International Shoe is incorporated in Delaware and has its headquarters and principal manufacturing operations in Missouri. Further assume that International Shoe has no salespeople in Wyoming, sells no shoes there, buys no cowhide there, and does no business there of any sort — except use the roads for transporting its wares to other states.

a. A truck loaded with shoes, owned by International Shoe Co. and driven by one of its employees, traveled through Wyoming on its way to the State of Washington. While in Wyoming, the truck collided with a pickup driven by a rancher, who was injured in the accident. The rancher filed suit against International Shoe in Wyoming, alleging negligence by the International Shoe driver. Jurisdiction in Wyoming?

b. In Wyoming there also lives a former employee of International Shoe, who used to work for the company at its Missouri headquarters. Alleging that she was wrongfully discharged from her job in Missouri, she files suit against International Shoe in Wyoming. Jurisdiction?

What is the rationale on which one could explain a different jurisdictional outcome in 4a and 4b?

c. Same facts except the plaintiff sues in Missouri. In this instance would it make any difference whether the plaintiff was the rancher in 4a or the former employee in 4b?

d. Same facts except the plaintiff sues in Delaware. Would it make any difference whether the plaintiff was the rancher or the former employee?

e. Same facts as 4a, except that plaintiff rancher owns some shares of International Shoe bonds on which the corporation has failed to pay interest when due. He brings suit on two claims — personal injury and for the unpaid interest. Suppose there is jurisdiction as to the claim for personal injury; does it follow that the rancher can also sue for the bond interest?

5. *Domicile, incorporation, and jurisdiction.* If one accepts the notion of general jurisdiction, a question arises: Are there easily identifiable circumstances in which a defendant invariably may be sued for all claims?

a. The circumstances most closely approaching such a rule are the state of incorporation (for corporations) and domicile (for individuals). It is generally accepted that a corporation may be sued in its state of incorporation for all claims, even though that state serves primarily as an address of convenience — as Delaware does for many corporations. The result is sometimes justified by pointing out that the incorporating state has "created" the corporation (by granting its charter) and therefore can put whatever conditions it wishes on that grant. Can you see the shadow of *Pennoyer*'s notion of induced consent lurking here?

b. An analogous rule applies to the domicile (place of permanent residence) for individuals. Milliken v. Meyer, 311 U.S. 457, 462-464 (1940).

2.   Absorbing *In Rem* Jurisdiction

International Shoe provided a new framework for thinking about *in personam* jurisdiction over corporations. But the case left open other jurisdictional questions.

International Shoe involved a corporate defendant (as did many of the most difficult jurisdictional questions), and it therefore did not discuss the applicability of its
approach to jurisdiction over individuals. The second issue left untouched by
International Shoe was *in rem* and *quasi in rem* jurisdiction. Under the line of cases
descended from *Pennoyer*, the presence of property could be the basis for jurisdiction over claims of any sort.

While it lasted, such *quasi in rem* jurisdiction created some striking doctrinal
possibilities. The most unexpected elaboration of this branch of *Pennoyer* came
in a series of cases holding that plaintiffs could obtain jurisdiction by seizing not
only tangible property — land and chattels — but also debts owed to the defendant. Harris v. Balk, 198 U.S. 215 (1905), is probably the most bizarre of this line
of cases. Harris owed Balk money, and Balk owed Epstein money; Balk lived in
North Carolina, Epstein in Maryland. Harris journeyed from North Carolina to
Maryland. While Harris was in Maryland, Epstein had him served with process,
and a Maryland court entered a judgment saying that Harris should pay the
money he owed Balk to Epstein instead. Balk challenged the Maryland court's
power to enter this judgment (arguing that only personal service on him in
Maryland would have justified such a judgment), but the Supreme Court upheld
it. The consequence of Harris was that a state could acquire jurisdiction over
persons whenever their debtors were present in that state by "attaching" the debts.
The result was to make creditors liable (to the extent of amounts owed them) in
any state in which their debtors set foot.

Under *Harris*'s extension of *Pennoyer*, for example, if Alfred Manhattanhite
had lent money to his friend Jane Gotham and she took a trip to Florida, that
state had the power to enter a judgment directing Jane to pay someone besides
Alfred the money she owed him — if Jane's debt to Alfred were "attached" during
her visit.

Lurking behind these somewhat extravagant results was an undiscussed
circumstance: *in rem* jurisdiction provided an escape from the results yielded by
Pennoyer's somewhat restrictive doctrines. To the extent, then, that *International
Shoe* provided a more sensible way of thinking about *in personam* jurisdiction,
one might not need *in rem* jurisdiction. Two cases decided by the Supreme Court
about a decade after *International Shoe* suggested the Court thought that it had
found such a framework. The two cases, still frequently cited, present paradig-
matic instances of the issues that arise in applying *International Shoe*.

McGee v. International Life Insurance Co.

355 U.S. 220 (1957)

Opinion of the Court by Mr. Justice BLACK, announced by Mr. Justice DOUGLAS.
The material facts are relatively simple. In 1944, Lowell Franklin a resident of
California, purchased a life insurance policy from [an insurer subsequently
bought by respondent, who] then mailed a reinsurance certificate to Franklin in
California offering to insure him. . . . He accepted this offer and from that time
until his death in 1950 paid premiums by mail from his California home to

respondent's Texas office. [When the beneficiary notified International Life of Franklin's death,] it refused to pay, claiming that he had committed suicide. It appears that neither [the original insurer] nor respondent has ever had any office or agent in California. . . .

Looking back over this long history of [jurisdiction cases] a trend is clearly discernible toward expanding the permissible scope of state jurisdiction over foreign corporations and other nonresidents. In part this is attributable to the fundamental transformation of our national economy. . . . With this increasing nationalization of commerce has come a great increase in the amount of business conducted by mail across state lines. At the same time modern transportation and communication have made it much less burdensome for a party sued to defend himself in a State where he engages in economic activity. Turning to this case we think it apparent that the Due Process Clause did not preclude the California court from entering a judgment binding on respondent. It is sufficient for purposes of due process that the suit was based on a contract which had substantial connection with that State. The contract was delivered in California, the premiums were mailed from there and the insured was a resident of that State when he died. It cannot be denied that California has a manifest interest in providing effective means of redress for its residents when their insurers refuse to pay claims. These residents would be at a severe disadvantage if they were forced to follow the insurance company to a distant State in order to hold it legally accountable. . . . There is no contention that respondent did not have adequate notice of the suit or sufficient time to prepare its defenses and appear.

Hanson v. Denckla

357 U.S. 235 (1958)

Mr. Chief Justice WARREN delivered the opinion of the Court.

[The case arose from a family fight over the assets of Mrs. Donner, a deceased mother who had established a trust in Delaware and some years later moved to Florida, where she died. The contest was whether Florida or Delaware courts had jurisdiction over the trust assets; that issue turned on whether Florida could acquire jurisdiction over the Delaware trustee. If Florida had jurisdiction, two daughters got entire estate, at the expense of the third daughter; if it didn't, the three daughters shared equally. The Supreme Court said Florida had no jurisdiction.]

. . . [P]rogress in communications and transportation has made the defense of a suit in a foreign tribunal less burdensome. In response to these changes, the requirements for personal jurisdiction over nonresidents have evolved from the rigid rule of Pennoyer v. Neff to the flexible standard of International Shoe Co. v. Washington. But it is a mistake to assume that this trend heralds the eventual demise of all restrictions on the personal jurisdiction of state courts. Those restrictions are more than a guarantee of immunity from inconvenient or distant litigation. They are a consequence of territorial limitations on the power of the respective States. However minimal the burden of defending in a foreign tribunal, a defendant may not be called upon to do so unless he has had the "minimal contacts" with that State that are a prerequisite to its exercise of power over him. See International Shoe Co. v. Washington.

We fail to find such contacts in the circumstances of this case. The defendant trust company has no office in Florida, and transacts no business there. . . . [T]he record discloses no solicitation of business in that State either in person or by mail. . . .

The first relationship Florida had to the agreement was years later when [Mrs. Donner] became domiciled there, and the trustee remitted the trust income to her in the State. From Florida Mrs. Donner carried on several bits of trust administration. . . . But the record discloses no instance in which the trustee performed any acts in Florida. . . .

The unilateral activity of those who claim some relationship with a nonresident defendant [Mrs. Donner] cannot satisfy the requirement of contact with the forum State. The application of that rule will vary with the quality and nature of the defendant's activity, but it is essential in each case that there be some act by which the defendant purposefully avails itself of the privilege of conducting activities within the forum State, thus invoking the benefits and protections of its laws. International Shoe Co. v. Washington. . . .

[Justices BLACK, BURTON, BRENNAN, and DOUGLAS dissented, the latter separately.]

NOTES AND PROBLEMS

1. *McGee* and *Hanson*, decided a year apart, come to different conclusions about jurisdiction on remarkably similar facts: business conducted by mail with an out-of-state financial institution, which was then sued in plaintiff's state. Notice as well the emphasis both cases place on modern transport and communication.

a. *McGee* is often thought to represent a high-water mark of jurisdictional aggressiveness. Was its result justified?

b. Can you identify a factual difference that justifies the difference in outcomes in the two cases?

2. If cases like *McGee* and *Hanson* provided a working framework, two problems still remained.

a. Did *International Shoe* apply to individuals as well as corporations? Cases like *Hanson* and *McGee*, because they involved corporate defendants, did not address this question.

b. Were *in rem* and *quasi in rem* jurisdiction available where *in personam* jurisdiction was not? Throughout this period plaintiffs continued to attach real property, bank accounts, debts, and the like, and courts, respecting the teaching of cases like Harris v. Balk, would uphold jurisdiction under those circumstances.

c. These two themes — the applicability of *International Shoe* to individuals and the role of *in rem* jurisdiction — came together in Shaffer v. Heitner, the most important jurisdictional case since *International Shoe*. A bit of substantive law background will help the jurisdictional point emerge more clearly. Directors of corporations are trustees, charged with guiding the corporation's affairs in a prudent manner. Like other trustees, they can be sued by their beneficiaries. But because the corporation is the beneficiary and is controlled by the directors, the prospect of such a suit to enforce the directors' fiduciary duties is nil — unless a representative of the corporation who is independent of the directors may sue. American law has developed such a procedure, called the shareholder's derivative suit. In a derivative action, a shareholder steps forward and sues the directors or officers in the name of the corporation, alleging some breach of fiduciary duty. If the suit is successful, the proceeds go to the corporation. Such suits have spawned numerous complex issues of procedural and corporate law as well as a good deal of controversy.

Shaffer v. Heitner

433 U.S. 186 (1977)

Mr. Justice MARSHALL delivered the opinion of the Court.

The controversy in this case concerns the constitutionality of a Delaware statute that allows a court of that State to take jurisdiction of a lawsuit by sequestering any property of the defendant that happens to be located in Delaware. Appellants contend that the sequestration statute as applied in this case violates the Due Process Clause of the Fourteenth Amendment both because it permits the state courts to exercise jurisdiction despite the absence of sufficient contacts among the defendants, the litigation, and the State of Delaware and because it authorizes the deprivation of defendants' property without providing adequate procedural safeguards. We find it necessary to consider only the first of these contentions.

I

Appellee Heitner, a nonresident of Delaware, is the owner of one share of stock in the Greyhound Corporation, a business incorporated under the laws of Delaware with its principal place of business in Phoenix, Ariz. On May 22, 1974, he filed a shareholder's derivative suit in the Court of Chancery for New Castle County, Del., in which he named as defendants . . . 28 present or former officers or directors of one or both of the corporations. In essence, Heitner alleged that the individual defendants had violated their duties to Greyhound by causing it and its subsidiary to engage in actions that resulted in the corporation's being held liable for substantial damages in a private antitrust suit and a large fine in a criminal contempt action. The activities which led to these penalties took place in Oregon.

Simultaneously with his complaint, Heitner filed a motion for an order of sequestration of the Delaware property of the individual defendants pursuant to 10 Del. C. §366. This motion was accompanied by a supporting affidavit of counsel which stated that the individual defendants were nonresidents of Delaware. The affidavit identified the property to be sequestered as common stock, 3% Second Cumulative Preferred Stock and stock unit credits of the Defendant Greyhound Corporation, a Delaware corporation, as well as all options and all warrants to purchase said stock issued to said individual Defendants and all contractral [sic] obligations, all rights, debts or credits due or accrued to or for the benefit of any of the said Defendants under any type of written agreement, contract, or other legal instrument of any kind whatever between any of the individual Defendants and said corporation.

The requested sequestration order was signed the day the motion was filed. Pursuant to that order, the sequestrator "seized" approximately 82,000 shares of Greyhound common stock belonging to 19 of the defendants, and options belonging to another two defendants. These seizures were accomplished by placing "stop transfer" orders or their equivalents on the books of the Greyhound Corporation. So far as the record shows, none of the certificates representing the seized property was physically present in Delaware. The stock was considered to be in Delaware, and so subject to seizure, by virtue of 8 Del. C. §169, which makes Delaware the situs of ownership of all stock in Delaware corporations.

All 28 defendants were notified of the initiation of the suit by certified mail directed to their last known addresses and by publication in a New Castle County newspaper. The 21 defendants whose property was seized (hereafter referred to as appellants) responded by entering a special appearance for the purpose of moving to quash service of process and to vacate the sequestration order. They contended that the ex parte sequestration procedure did not accord them due process of law and that the property seized was not capable of attachment in Delaware. In addition, appellants asserted that under the rule of International Shoe Co. v. Washington, they did not have sufficient contacts with Delaware to sustain the jurisdiction of that State's courts.

[The Delaware courts rejected all of defendants' arguments. They distinguished seizure for jurisdictional purposes from other forms of ex parte seizure. And they contended that the assertion of jurisdiction need not meet *International Shoe* standards because Delaware was asserting in rem, rather than in personam, jurisdiction.]

II

The Delaware courts rejected appellants' jurisdictional challenge by noting that this suit was brought as a quasi in rem proceeding. Since quasi in rem jurisdiction is traditionally based on attachment or seizure of property present in the jurisdiction, not on contacts between the defendant and the State, the courts considered appellants' claimed lack of contacts with Delaware to be unimportant. This categorical analysis assumes the continued soundness of the conceptual structure founded on the century-old case of Pennoyer v. Neff.

[The Court discussed the development of jurisdictional ideas from the time of Pennoyer v. Neff. In reviewing *International Shoe* itself the opinion explained in footnote 19, that "the *International Shoe* court believed that the standard it was setting forth governed actions against natural persons as well as corporations, and we see no reason to disagree. The differences between individuals and corporations may, of course, lead to the conclusion that a given set of circumstances establishes State jurisdiction over one type of defendant but not over the other." The note cited McGee v. International Life as a "see also" citation for this proposition.]

[The relationship among the defendant, the forum, and the litigation, rather than the mutually exclusive sovereignty of the States on which the rules of *Pennoyer* rest, became the central concern of the inquiry into personal jurisdiction.[20] The immediate effect of this departure from *Pennoyer's* conceptual apparatus was to increase the ability of the state courts to obtain personal jurisdiction over nonresident defendants.

No equally dramatic change has occurred in the law governing jurisdiction in rem. There have, however, been intimations that the collapse of the in personam wing of *Pennoyer* has not left that decision unweakened as a foundation for in rem jurisdiction. [The court cited lower court opinions, commentators, and oblique hints in Supreme Court cases.] . . .

It is clear, therefore, that the law of state-court jurisdiction no longer stands securely on the foundation established in *Pennoyer*. We think that the time is ripe to consider whether the standard of fairness and substantial justice set forth in *International Shoe* should be held to govern actions in rem as well as in personam.

State court jurisdiction no longer stands as established in Pennoyer

III

The case for applying to jurisdiction in rem the same test of "fair play and substantial justice" as governs assertions of jurisdiction in personam is simple and straightforward. It is premised on recognition that "[t]he phrase, 'judicial jurisdiction over a thing,' is a customary elliptical way of referring to jurisdiction over the interests of persons in a thing." Restatement (Second) of Conflict of Laws §56, introductory note. This recognition leads to the conclusion that in order to justify an exercise of jurisdiction in rem, the basis for jurisdiction must be sufficient to justify exercising "jurisdiction over the interests of persons in a thing."[23] The standard for determining whether an exercise of jurisdiction over the interests of persons is consistent with the Due Process Clause is the minimum contacts standard elucidated in *International Shoe*.

This argument, of course, does not ignore the fact that the presence of property in a State may bear on the existence of jurisdiction by providing contacts among the forum State, the defendant, and the litigation. For example, when claims to

---

20. Nothing in Hanson v. Denckla [infra page 85] is to the contrary. The Hanson Court's statement that restrictions on state jurisdiction "are a consequence of territorial limitations on the power of the respective states," simply makes the point that the States are defined by their geographical territory. After making this point, the Court in Hanson determined that the defendant over which personal jurisdiction was claimed had not committed any acts sufficiently connected to the State to justify jurisdiction under the International Shoe standard.

23. It is true that the potential liability of a defendant in an in rem action is limited by the value of the property but that limitation does not affect the argument. The fairness of subjecting a defendant to state-court jurisdiction does not depend on the size of the claim being litigated.

the property itself are the source of the underlying controversy between the plaintiff and the defendant, it would be unusual for the State where the property is located not to have jurisdiction. In such cases, the defendant's claim to property located in the State would normally indicate that he expected to benefit from the State's protection of his interest. The State's strong interests in assuring the marketability of property within its borders and in providing a procedure for peaceful resolution of disputes about the possession of that property would also support jurisdiction, as would the likelihood that important records and witnesses will be found in the State.[28] The presence of property may also favor jurisdiction in cases, such as suits for injury suffered on the land of an absentee owner, where the defendant's ownership of the property is conceded but the cause of action is otherwise related to rights and duties growing out of that ownership.

It appears, therefore, that jurisdiction over many types of actions which now are or might be brought in rem would not be affected by a holding that any assertion of state-court jurisdiction must satisfy the *International Shoe* standard. For the type of quasi in rem action typified by Harris v. Balk and the present case, however, accepting the proposed analysis would result in significant change. These are cases where the property which now serves as the basis for state-court jurisdiction is completely unrelated to the plaintiff's cause of action. Thus, although the presence of the defendant's property in a State might suggest the existence of other ties among the defendant, the State, and the litigation, the presence of the property alone would not support the State's jurisdiction. . . .

Since acceptance of the *International Shoe* test would most affect this class of cases, we examine the arguments against adopting that standard as they relate to this category of litigation. Before doing so, however, we note that this type of case also presents the clearest illustration of the argument in favor of assessing assertions of jurisdiction by a single standard. For in cases such as *Harris* and this one, the only role played by the property is to provide the basis for bringing the defendant into court. Indeed, the express purpose of the Delaware sequestration procedure is to compel the defendant to enter a personal appearance. In such cases, if a direct assertion of personal jurisdiction over the defendant would violate the Constitution, it would seem that an indirect assertion of the jurisdiction should be equally impermissible.

The primary rationale for treating the presence of property as a sufficient basis for jurisdiction to adjudicate claims over which the State would not have jurisdiction if *International Shoe* applied is that a wrongdoer "should not be able to avoid payment of his obligations by the expedient of removing his assets to a place where he is not subject to an in personam suit." Restatement §66, Comment a. This justification, however, does not explain why jurisdiction should be recognized without regard to whether the property is present in the State because of an effort to avoid the owner's obligations. Nor does it support jurisdiction to adjudicate the underlying claim. . . .

---

28. We do not suggest that these illustrations include all the factors that may affect the decision, nor that the factors we have mentioned are necessarily decisive.

It might also be suggested that allowing in rem jurisdiction avoids the uncertainty inherent in the *International Shoe* standard and assures a plaintiff of a forum.[37] . . . [W]hen the existence of jurisdiction in a particular forum under *International Shoe* is unclear, the cost of simplifying the litigation by avoiding the jurisdictional question may be the sacrifice of "fair play and substantial justice." That cost is too high.

We are left, then, to consider the significance of the long history of jurisdiction based solely on the presence of property in a State. . . . "[T]raditional notions of fair play and substantial justice" can be as readily offended by the perpetuation of ancient forms that are no longer justified as by the adoption of new procedures that are inconsistent with the basic values of our constitutional heritage. Cf. *Sniadach v. Family Finance Corp.* The fiction that an assertion of jurisdiction over property is anything but an assertion of jurisdiction over the owner of the property supports an ancient form without substantial modern justification. Its continued acceptance would serve only to allow state court jurisdiction that is fundamentally unfair to the defendant.

We therefore conclude that all assertions of state court jurisdiction must be evaluated according to the standards set forth in *International Shoe* and its progeny.[39]

IV

The Delaware courts based their assertion of jurisdiction in this case solely on the statutory presence of appellants' property in Delaware. Yet that property is not the subject matter of this litigation, nor is the underlying cause of action related to the property. Appellants' holdings in Greyhound do not, therefore, provide contacts with Delaware sufficient to support the jurisdiction of that State's courts over appellants. If it exists, that jurisdiction must have some other foundation.

Appellee Heitner did not allege and does not now claim that appellants have ever set foot in Delaware. Nor does he identify any act related to his cause of action as having taken place in Delaware. Nevertheless, he contends that appellants' positions as directors and officers of a corporation chartered in Delaware provide sufficient "contacts, ties, or relations," International Shoe Co. v. Washington, with that State to give its courts jurisdiction over appellants in this stockholder's derivative action. This argument is based primarily on what Heitner asserts to be the strong interest of Delaware in supervising the management of a Delaware corporation. That interest is said to derive from the role of Delaware law in establishing the corporation and defining the obligations owed

---

37. This case does not raise, and we therefore do not consider, the question whether the presence of a defendant's property in a State is a sufficient basis for jurisdiction when no other forum is available to the plaintiff.

39. It would not be fruitful for us to re-examine the facts of cases decided on the rationales of *Pennoyer* and *Harris* to determine whether jurisdiction might have been sustained under the standard we adopt today. To the extent that prior decisions are inconsistent with this standard, they are overruled.

to it by its officers and directors. In order to protect this interest, appellee concludes, Delaware's courts must have jurisdiction over corporate fiduciaries such as appellants.

This argument is undercut by the failure of the Delaware Legislature to assert the state interest appellee finds so compelling. Delaware law bases jurisdiction not on appellants' status as corporate fiduciaries, but rather on the presence of their property in the State. Although the sequestration procedure used here may be most frequently used in derivative suits against officers and directors, the authorizing statute evinces no specific concern with such actions. Sequestration can be used in any suit against a nonresident, and reaches corporate fiduciaries only if they happen to own interests in a Delaware corporation, or other property in the State. But as Heitner's failure to secure jurisdiction over seven of the defendants named in his complaint demonstrates, there is no necessary relationship between holding a position as a corporate fiduciary and owning stock or other interests in the corporation. If Delaware perceived its interest in securing jurisdiction over corporate fiduciaries to be as great as Heitner suggests, we would expect it to have enacted a statute more clearly designed to protect that interest. . . .

Appellee suggests that by accepting positions as officers or directors of a Delaware corporation, appellants performed the acts required by Hanson v. Denckla. He notes that Delaware law provides substantial benefits to corporate officers and directors, and that these benefits were at least in part the incentive for appellants to assume their positions. It is, he says, "only fair and just" to require appellants, in return for these benefits, to respond in the State of Delaware when they are accused of misusing their powers.

But like Heitner's first argument, this line of reasoning establishes only that it is appropriate for Delaware law to govern the obligations of appellants to Greyhound and its stockholders. It does not demonstrate that appellants have "purposefully avail[ed themselves] of the privilege of conducting activities within the forum State," Hanson v. Denckla, in a way that would justify bringing them before a Delaware tribunal. Appellants have simply had nothing to do with the State of Delaware. Moreover, appellants had no reason to expect to be haled before a Delaware court. Delaware, unlike some States, has not enacted a statute that treats acceptance of a directorship as consent to jurisdiction in the State. And "[i]t strains reason . . . to suggest that anyone buying securities in a corporation formed in Delaware 'impliedly consents' to subject himself to Delaware's . . . jurisdiction on any cause of action." Appellants, who were not required to acquire interests in Greyhound in order to hold their positions, did not by acquiring those interests surrender their right to be brought to judgment only in States with which they had "minimum contacts."

The Due Process Clause "does not contemplate that a state may make binding a judgment . . . against an individual or corporate defendant with which the state has no contacts, ties, or relations." International Shoe Co. v. Washington. Delaware's assertion of jurisdiction over appellants in this case is inconsistent with that constitutional limitation on state power. The judgment of the Delaware Supreme Court must, therefore, be reversed.

It is so ordered.

Mr. Justice REHNQUIST took no part in the consideration or decision of this case.

Mr. Justice POWELL, concurring.

I agree that the principles of International Shoe Co. v. Washington should be extended to govern assertions of in rem as well as in personam jurisdiction in state court. I also agree that neither the statutory presence of appellants' stock in Delaware nor their positions as directors and officers of a Delaware corporation can provide sufficient contacts to support the Delaware courts' assertion of jurisdiction in this case.

I would explicitly reserve judgment, however, on whether the ownership of some forms of property whose situs is indisputably and permanently located within a State may, without more, provide the contacts necessary to subject a defendant to jurisdiction within the State to the extent of the value of the property. In the case of real property, in particular, preservation of the common law concept of quasi in rem jurisdiction arguably would avoid the uncertainty of the general International Shoe standard without significant cost to "traditional notions of fair play and substantial justice."

Subject to that reservation, I join the opinion of the Court.

Mr. Justice STEVENS, concurring in the judgment.

The Due Process Clause affords protection against "judgments without notice." International Shoe Co. v. Washington (opinion of Black, J.). . . .

One who purchases shares of stock on the open market can hardly be expected to know that he has thereby become subject to suit in a forum remote from his residence and unrelated to the transaction. As a practical matter, the Delaware sequestration statute created an unacceptable risk of judgment without notice. . . . I therefore agree with the Court that on the record before us no adequate basis for jurisdiction exists and that the Delaware statute is unconstitutional on its face.

How the Court's opinion may be applied in other contexts is not entirely clear to me. . . . My uncertainty as to the reach of the opinion, and my fear that it purports to decide a great deal more than is necessary to dispose of this case, persuade me merely to concur in the judgment.

Mr. Justice BRENNAN, concurring and dissenting.

I join Parts I-III of the Court's opinion. I fully agree that the minimum contacts analysis developed in International Shoe Co. v. Washington represents a far more sensible construct for the exercise of state court jurisdiction than the patchwork of legal and factual fictions that has been generated from the decision in Pennoyer v. Neff. It is precisely because the inquiry into minimum contacts is now of such overriding importance, however, that I must respectfully dissent from Part IV of the Court's opinion. . . .

I am convinced that as a general rule a state forum has jurisdiction to adjudicate a shareholder derivative action centering on the conduct and policies of the directors and officers of a corporation chartered by that State. Unlike the Court, I therefore would not foreclose Delaware from asserting jurisdiction over appellants were it persuaded to do so on the basis of minimum contacts.

It is well settled that a derivative lawsuit as presented here does not inure primarily to the benefit of the named plaintiff. . . . "The cause of action which such a plaintiff brings before the court is not his own but the corporation's. . . . Such a plaintiff often may represent an important public and stockholder interest in bringing faithless managers to book."

Viewed in this light, the chartering State has an unusually powerful interest in insuring the availability of a convenient forum for litigating claims involving a possible multiplicity of defendant fiduciaries and for vindicating the State's substantive policies regarding the management of its domestic corporations. I believe that our cases fairly establish that the State's valid substantive interests are important considerations in assessing whether it constitutionally may claim jurisdiction over a given cause of action.

In this instance, Delaware can point to at least three interrelated public policies that are furthered by its assertion of jurisdiction. First, the State has a substantial interest in providing restitution for its local corporations that allegedly have been victimized by fiduciary misconduct, even if the managerial decisions occurred outside the State. . . . Second, state courts have legitimately read their jurisdiction expansively when a cause of action centers in an area in which the forum state possesses a manifest regulatory interest. . . . Finally, a State like Delaware has a recognized interest in affording a convenient forum for supervising and overseeing the affairs of an entity that is purely the creation of that State's law. . . .

I, therefore, would approach the minimum contacts analysis differently than does the Court. Crucial to me is the fact that appellants voluntarily associated themselves with the State of Delaware, "invoking the benefits and protections of its laws," Hanson v. Denckla; International Shoe Co. v. Washington, by entering into a long term and fragile relationship with one of its domestic corporations. They thereby elected to assume powers and to undertake responsibilities wholly derived from that State's rules and regulations, and to become eligible for those benefits that Delaware law makes available to its corporations' officials. E.g., 8 Del. C. §§143 (interest-free loans); 145 (indemnification). While it is possible that countervailing issues of judicial efficiency and the like might clearly favor a different forum, they do not appear on the meager record before us; and, of course, we are concerned solely with "minimum" contacts, not the "best" contacts. I thus do not believe that it is unfair to insist that appellants make themselves available to suit in a competent forum that Delaware might create for vindication of its important public policies directly pertaining to appellants' fiduciary associations with the State.

NOTES AND PROBLEMS

1. Do not let the corporate context or the caption of this suit mislead you into assuming that jurisdiction over the corporation was at issue. The defendants challenging jurisdiction were the 21 individual members of Greyhound's board of directors, none of whom were residents of Delaware but who held stock in

Greyhound. No one suggested that Delaware lacked jurisdiction over Greyhound itself, which was a Delaware corporation.

2. Explain why *Shaffer* did not decide:

a. That property is irrelevant to the existence of jurisdiction;

b. That stock is not property;

c. That directors of a corporation cannot be sued in the state of incorporation;

d. That Greyhound's board of directors had not "consented" to be sued in Delaware;

e. That attachment of property is an unconstitutional way for a state to assert its jurisdiction.

3. If all these statements are misreadings of the case, what did *Shaffer* decide? Approach that question by imagining two variations on *Pennoyer*. How would these cases be decided under *Pennoyer*? Does *Shaffer* alter that result?

a. Neff, who has never been to Oregon, inherits property there. Mitchell, from whom Neff has borrowed money, sues Neff in Oregon for the unpaid debt, asserting jurisdiction by attaching the property.

b. Neff, who has never been to Oregon, hires Mitchell to help him buy some property in Oregon. Mitchell does so, but Neff fails to pay Mitchell's fees. Mitchell sues Neff in Oregon, attaching the property.

4. Why does the majority, in the second-to-last paragraph of its opinion, suggest that Delaware could have required the corporate officers to submit to Delaware jurisdiction as a condition of becoming corporate officers? Wasn't that whole line of reasoning rejected in *International Shoe*, which said at one point, "True, some of the decisions holding the corporation amenable to suit have been supported by resort to the legal fiction that it has given its consent to service and suit, consent being implied [sic] from its presence in the state through the acts of its authorized agents. But more realistically it may be said that those authorized acts were of such a nature as to justify the fiction."

After the decision in *Shaffer*, the Delaware legislature enacted a statute purporting to give its courts jurisdiction over officers and directors of Delaware corporations in cases related to their corporate activities. See 10 Del. Code §3114. The Delaware Supreme Court upheld the statute against constitutional attack in Armstrong v. Pomerance, 423 A.2d 174 (Del. 1980). Does *Shaffer* permit Delaware to assert such jurisdiction regardless of the extent of directors' and officers' other contacts with the state?

5. Notice Justice Brennan's contention that one ought to take into account not only the defendant's circumstances but the interests of the forum state. As you will see in subsequent cases, the Court has not entirely agreed about how to take this factor into account. Notice that it will usually favor the assertion of jurisdiction and the plaintiff, who is likely to be at least a temporary resident of the forum state.

6. Footnote 37 of the Court's opinion suggests that attachment jurisdiction might still be available when "no other forum is open to the plaintiff." When would that be the case? When the defendant is domiciled outside the country? Would that discriminate against foreign defendants?

7. *In rem* jurisdiction, an old idea, and the Internet, a newer one, have come together in an interesting way. Like other trademarks, Internet domain names are

valuable pieces of intellectual property, and legislation protects them from various sorts of abuse and poaching. Because of the ease of establishing a Web site and the ubiquity of the Internet, plaintiffs seeking to protect domain names sometimes have difficulty in locating the defendant. Even if the defendant's whereabouts are known, the defendant may not be subject to personal jurisdiction in the United States. Congress has responded with the Anti-Cybersquatting Consumer Protection Act (15 U.S.C. §1125(d)(2) (2000)), whose procedural portions exploit the architecture of the Internet and the concept of *in rem* jurisdiction. Understanding the statutory scheme requires understanding how the network routes traffic in cyberspace. Individual computers in the Internet have numerical "addresses." But long strings of numbers are more difficult to remember than, for example, ibm.com, so the Internet uses a domain name system, which is a table of names associated with computer addresses. Whenever an Internet user requests a domain name site, its numerical address has to be matched with a number by searching a list acquired from "directory computers" that maintain lists matching site names with numerical addresses. The domain name registrar keeps the most current tables matching names and numbers. The registrar thus functions both as a keeper of title records and as a continually updated directory that facilitates the matching process that allows the Internet to function.

In addition to establishing liability for various forms of "cybersquatting," the statute exploits this system. It allows a plaintiff to bring an *in rem* action in the location of the registrar of domain names:

> The owner of a mark may file an in rem civil action against a domain name in the judicial district in which the domain name registrar, domain name registry, or other domain name authority that registered or assigned the domain name is located if: . . .
> (A) (ii) the court finds that the owner —
> (I) is not able to obtain in personam jurisdiction over a person who would have been a defendant in a civil action under paragraph (1); or
> (II) through due diligence was not able to find a person who would have been a defendant in a civil action under paragraph (1) by —
> (aa) sending a notice of the alleged violation and intent to proceed under this paragraph to the registrant of the domain name at the postal and e-mail address provided by the registrant to the registrar; and
> (bb) publishing notice of the action as the court may direct promptly after filing the action.
> (B) The actions under subparagraph (A)(ii) shall constitute service of process.

Upon receiving such a notice, the domain name registrar is to "deposit" the disputed domain name with the court during the suit's pendency. Consider some issues raised by these provisions:

a. Are they fair to defendants, many of whom believe they have either legitimate property rights or free speech rights to their domain names? Consider López, an Arizona defendant who establishes a "SmithBad.com" site, criticizing the actions of Smith, Inc. The domain registry of SmithBad is in Virginia, the location of Network Solutions, Inc., the world's largest domain name registrar (with more than a million registrations). Smith Inc. brings an action in Virginia, invoking the statute just quoted. What objections might López have to the invocation of the *in rem* procedure? What additional facts would you want to know?

b. Are these provisions consistent with your understanding of *Shaffer*? Suppose a defendant located in California allegedly infringes a domain name of a New York plaintiff, who brings suit in the Eastern District of Virginia, What will the domain name registrar do when it receives notice of the action? Is the *in rem* solution as applied to these facts constitutional?

8. In Carolina Power & Light Co. v. Uranex, 451 F. Supp. 1044 (N.D. Cal. 1977), the plaintiff sought to garnish a debt owed by a California corporation to Uranex, a French company. (Garnishment is a form of attachment in which the property attached is in the hands of a third party.) Plaintiff was already arbitrating a contract dispute against Uranex in New York. Plaintiff feared, however, that even if it won the arbitration, it would be unable to collect the award against Uranex, which had few assets in the United States. Plaintiff therefore filed a suit in California to attach a debt owed Uranex by another corporation. Uranex argued that *Shaffer* forbade the seizure of the debt in question. The court disagreed, noting that while *Shaffer* forbade adjudication of the merits of a case simply on the basis of the presence of property, in the present case plaintiff was seeking seizure of the property not to determine the merits but rather to have security for the New York determination on the merits. We will see in Chapter V that such cases of prejudgment seizure of property, even when there are minimum contacts, may require prior notice and hearing to the owner of the property.

9. Because the defendants in *Shaffer* were individuals (even though the case arose in a corporate context), a necessary implication of the holding (as well as of footnote 19, quoted supra page 88) is that *International Shoe* applies to individuals as well as to corporations. But what exactly does that statement mean? One part of the picture is clear enough: In order for a state to exercise jurisdiction over a person not present in the state, contacts are necessary. Those contacts may include the ownership of property, but mere ownership of property does not conclusively establish jurisdiction, as it did under the regime of *Pennoyer* and Harris v. Balk.

The picture gets murkier if the question is whether the mere physical presence of the defendant — without any other contacts — is sufficient to establish jurisdiction for all claims. For a long time before *Shaffer* the answer was yes. The Restatement (Second) of Conflict of Laws §28 (1971) said so: "A state has power to exercise judicial jurisdiction over an individual who is present within its territory, whether permanently or temporarily." A series of colorful cases took this view; the most striking of them, Grace v. MacArthur, 170 F. Supp. 442 (E.D. Ark. 1959), upheld Arkansas jurisdiction over a defendant who was served with process in an airplane flying over that state. Do those cases upholding this rule of so-called transient jurisdiction survive *Shaffer*? Consider this question again after reading Burnham v. Superior Court, infra page 152.

3.   Specific Jurisdiction: The Modern Cases

Having understood how Shaffer v. Heitner eliminated *in rem* jurisdiction and consolidated the regime of *International Shoe*, the student needs to think about two issues. First, one needs practice in applying the concepts of *International Shoe* and its two strands — specific and general jurisdiction. Specific jurisdiction has produced more recent Supreme Court cases, and in those cases the Court has shown some restlessness with the doctrinal categories of *International Shoe*. The Court's restlessness raises the second question, one you should consider as you work through the intricacies of modern jurisdictional doctrine: Does the current doctrinal framework make sense?

The cases represent a sampling of the Supreme Court's cases in the years since *International Shoe*. As you read them, work on two levels of analysis. Initially, consider the analytical framework the Court is applying: To what extent is it working within, and to what extent modifying or departing from, the framework of *International Shoe*? Second, try to understand how the particular facts of each case led to its holding; what is the smallest alteration in facts that would lead the Court to a different result?

World-Wide Volkswagen Corp. v. Woodson

444 U.S. 286 (1980)

Mr. Justice WHITE delivered the opinion of the Court.

The issue before us is whether, consistently with the Due Process Clause of the Fourteenth Amendment, an Oklahoma court may exercise in personam jurisdiction over a nonresident automobile retailer and its wholesale distributor in a products-liability action, when the defendants' only connection with Oklahoma is the fact that an automobile sold in New York to New York residents became involved in an accident in Oklahoma.

I

Respondents Harry and Kay Robinson purchased a new Audi automobile from petitioner Seaway Volkswagen, Inc. (Seaway) in Massena, N.Y., in 1976. The following year the Robinson family, who resided in New York, left that State for a new home in Arizona. As they passed through the State of Oklahoma, another car struck their Audi in the rear, causing a fire which severely burned Kay Robinson and her two children.[1]

The Robinsons subsequently brought a products-liability action in the District Court for Creek County, Okla. claiming that their injuries resulted from defective design and placement of the Audi's gas tank and fuel system. They joined as defendants the automobile's manufacturer, Audi NSU Auto

---

1. The driver of the other automobile does not figure in the present litigation.

Union Aktiengesellschaft (Audi); its importer, Volkswagen of America, Inc. (Volkswagen); its regional distributor, petitioner World-Wide Volkswagen Corporation (World-Wide); and its retail dealer, petitioner Seaway. Seaway and World-Wide entered special appearances,[3] claiming that Oklahoma's exercise of jurisdiction over them would offend the limitations on the State's jurisdiction imposed by the Due Process Clause of the Fourteenth Amendment.

The facts presented to the District Court showed that World-Wide is incorporated and has its business office in New York. It distributes vehicles, parts and accessories, under contract with Volkswagen, to retail dealers in New York, New Jersey, and Connecticut. Seaway, one of these retail dealers, is incorporated and has its place of business in New York. Insofar as the record reveals, Seaway and World-Wide are fully independent corporations whose relations with each other and with Volkswagen and Audi are contractual only. Respondents adduced no evidence that either World-Wide or Seaway does any business in Oklahoma, ships or sells any products to or in that State, has an agent to receive process there, or purchases advertisements in any media calculated to reach Oklahoma. In fact, as respondents' counsel conceded at oral argument, there was no showing that any automobile sold by World-Wide or Seaway has ever entered Oklahoma with the single exception of the vehicle involved in the present case. . . .

. . . Petitioners then sought a writ of prohibition in the Supreme Court of Oklahoma to restrain the District Judge, respondent Charles S. Woodson, from exercising in personam jurisdiction over them.

The Supreme Court of Oklahoma denied the writ. . . . The Court's rationale was contained in the following paragraph:

> In the case before us, the product being sold and distributed by the petitioners is by its very design and purpose so mobile that petitioners can foresee its possible use in Oklahoma. This is especially true of the distributor, who has the exclusive right to distribute such automobile in New York, New Jersey and Connecticut. The evidence presented below demonstrated that goods sold and distributed by the petitioners were used in the State of Oklahoma, and under the facts we believe it reasonable to infer, given the retail value of the automobile, that the petitioners derive substantial income from automobiles which from time to time are used in the State of Oklahoma. This being the case, we hold that under the facts presented, the trial court was justified in concluding that the petitioners derive substantial revenue from goods used or consumed in this State.

We granted certiorari to consider an important constitutional question with respect to state-court jurisdiction and to resolve a conflict between the Supreme Court of Oklahoma and the highest courts of at least four other States. We reverse.

---

3. Volkswagen also entered a special appearance in the District Court, but unlike World-Wide and Seaway did not seek review in the Supreme Court of Oklahoma and is not a petitioner here. Both Volkswagen and Audi remain as defendants in the litigation pending before the District Court in Oklahoma.

II

. . . As has long been settled, and as we reaffirm today, a state court may exercise personal jurisdiction over a nonresident defendant only so long as there exist "minimum contacts" between the defendant and the forum State. International Shoe Co. v. Washington. The concept of minimum contacts, in turn, can be seen to perform two related, but distinguishable functions. It protects the defendant against the burdens of litigating in a distant or inconvenient forum. And it acts to ensure that the States, through their courts, do not reach out beyond the limits imposed on them by their status as coequal sovereigns in a federal system.

The protection against inconvenient litigation is typically described in terms of "reasonableness" or "fairness." We have said that the defendant's contacts with the forum State must be such that maintenance of the suit "does not offend 'traditional notions of fair play and substantial justice.'" International Shoe Co. v. Washington, quoting Milliken v. Meyer. The relationship between the defendant and the forum must be such that it is "reasonable . . . to require the corporation to defend the particular suit which is brought there." Implicit in this emphasis on reasonableness is the understanding that the burden on the defendant, while always a primary concern, will in an appropriate case be considered in light of other relevant factors, including the forum State's interest in adjudicating the dispute; the plaintiff's interest in obtaining convenient and effective relief, at least when that interest is not adequately protected by the plaintiff's power to choose the forum, cf. Shaffer v. Heitner; the interstate judicial system's interest in obtaining the most efficient resolution of controversies; and the shared interest of the several States in furthering fundamental substantive social policies.

The limits imposed on state jurisdiction by the Due Process Clause, in its role as a guarantor against inconvenient litigation, have been substantially relaxed over the years. As we noted in McGee v. International Life Ins. Co., this trend is largely attributable to a fundamental transformation in the American economy. . . .

The historical developments noted in *McGee*, of course, have only accelerated in the generation since that case was decided. Nevertheless, we have never accepted the proposition that state lines are irrelevant for jurisdictional purposes, nor could we and remain faithful to the principles of interstate federalism embodied in the Constitution. The economic interdependence of the States was foreseen and desired by the Framers. In the Commerce Clause, they provided that the Nation was to be a common market, a "free trade unit" in which the States are debarred from acting as separable economic entities. But the Framers also intended that the States retain many essential attributes of sovereignty, including, in particular, the sovereign power to try causes in their courts.

The sovereignty of each State, in turn, implied a limitation on the sovereignty of all of its sister States — a limitation express or implicit in both the original scheme of the Constitution and the Fourteenth Amendment. . . .

Thus, the Due Process Clause "does not contemplate that a state may make binding a judgment in personam against an individual or corporate defendant with which the state has no contacts, ties, or relations." International Shoe Co. v. Washington. Even if the defendant would suffer minimal or no inconvenience from being forced to litigate before the tribunals of another State; even if the forum State has a strong interest in applying its law to the controversy; even if the forum State is the most convenient location for litigation, the Due Process Clause, acting as an instrument of interstate federalism, may sometimes act to divest the State of its power to render a valid judgment. Hanson v. Denckla.

III

Applying these principles to the case at hand, we find in the record before us a total absence of those affiliating circumstances that are a necessary predicate to any exercise of state-court jurisdiction. Petitioners carry on no activity whatsoever in Oklahoma. They close no sales and perform no services there. They avail themselves of none of the privileges and benefits of Oklahoma law. They solicit no business there either through salespersons or through advertising reasonably calculated to reach the State. Nor does the record show that they regularly sell cars at wholesale or retail to Oklahoma customers or residents or that they indirectly, through others, serve or seek to serve the Oklahoma market. In short, respondents seek to base jurisdiction on one, isolated occurrence and whatever inferences can be drawn therefrom: the fortuitous circumstance that a single Audi automobile, sold in New York to New York residents, happened to suffer an accident while passing through Oklahoma.

It is argued, however, that because an automobile is mobile by its very design and purpose it was "foreseeable" that the Robinsons' Audi would cause injury in Oklahoma. Yet "foreseeability" alone has never been a sufficient benchmark for personal jurisdiction under the Due Process Clause. In Hanson v. Denckla, supra, it was no doubt foreseeable that the settlor of a Delaware trust would subsequently move to Florida and seek to exercise a power of appointment there; yet we held that Florida courts could not constitutionally exercise jurisdiction over a Delaware trustee that had no other contacts with the forum State. . . .

If foreseeability were the criterion, a local California tire retailer could be forced to defend in Pennsylvania when a blowout occurs there; a Wisconsin seller of a defective automobile jack could be haled before a distant court for damage caused in New Jersey; or a Florida soft drink concessionaire could be summoned to Alaska to account for injuries happening there. Every seller of chattels would in effect appoint the chattel his agent for service of process. His amenability to suit would travel with the chattel. We recently abandoned the outworn rule of Harris v. Balk, that the interest of a creditor in a debt could be extinguished or otherwise affected by any State having transitory jurisdiction over the debtor. Shaffer v. Heitner. Having interred the mechanical rule that a creditor's amenability to a quasi in rem action travels with his debtor, we are unwilling to endorse an analogous principle in the present case.

This is not to say, of course, that foreseeability is wholly irrelevant. But the foreseeability that is critical to due process analysis is not the mere likelihood that a product will find its way into the forum State. Rather, it is that the defendant's conduct and connection with the forum State are such that he should reasonably anticipate being haled into court there. The Due Process Clause, by ensuring the "orderly administration of the laws," gives a degree of predictability to the legal system that allows potential defendants to structure their primary conduct with some minimum assurance as to where that conduct will and will not render them liable to suit.

When a corporation "purposefully avails itself of the privilege of conducting activities within the forum State," it has clear notice that it is subject to suit there, and can act to alleviate the risk of burdensome litigation by procuring insurance, passing the expected costs on to customers, or, if the risks are too great, severing its connection with the State. Hence if the sale of a product of a manufacturer or distributor such as Audi or Volkswagen is not simply an isolated occurrence, but arises from the efforts of the manufacturer or distributor to serve, directly or indirectly, the market for its product in other States, it is not unreasonable to subject it to suit in one of those States if its allegedly defective merchandise has there been the source of injury to its owner or to others. The forum State does not exceed its powers under the Due Process Clause if it asserts personal jurisdiction over a corporation that delivers its products into the stream of commerce with the expectation that they will be purchased by consumers in the forum State. Cf. Gray v. American Radiator.

But there is no such or similar basis for Oklahoma jurisdiction over World-Wide or Seaway in this case. Seaway's sales are made in Massena, N.Y. World-Wide's market, although substantially larger, is limited to dealers in New York, New Jersey, and Connecticut. There is no evidence of record that any automobiles distributed by World-Wide are sold to retail customers outside this tri-State area. It is foreseeable that the purchasers of automobiles sold by World-Wide and Seaway may take them to Oklahoma. But the mere "unilateral activity of those who claim some relationship with a nonresident defendant cannot satisfy the requirement of contact with the forum State." Hanson v. Denckla.

In a variant on the previous argument it is contended that jurisdiction can be supported by the fact that petitioners earn substantial revenue from goods used in Oklahoma. The Oklahoma Supreme Court so found, drawing the inference that because one automobile sold by petitioners had been used in Oklahoma, others might have been used there also. While this inference seems less than compelling on the facts of the instant case, we need not question the Court's factual findings in order to reject its reasoning.

This argument seems to make the point that the purchase of automobiles in New York, from which the petitioners earn substantial revenue, would not occur but for the fact that the automobiles are capable of use in distant States like Oklahoma. Respondents observe that the very purpose of an automobile is to travel, and that travel of automobiles sold by petitioners is facilitated by an extensive chain of Volkswagen service centers throughout the Country, including some in Oklahoma.[12] However, financial benefits accruing to the defendant from a collateral relation to the forum State will not support jurisdiction if they do not stem from a constitutionally cognizable contact with that State. In our view, whatever marginal revenues petitioners may receive by virtue of the fact that their

12. As we have noted, petitioners earn no direct revenues from these service centers.

products are capable of use in Oklahoma is far too attenuated a contact to justify that State's exercise of in personam jurisdiction over them.

Because we find that petitioners have no "contacts, ties, or relations" with the State of Oklahoma, the judgment of the Supreme Court of Oklahoma is reversed.

Mr. Justice BRENNAN, dissenting.

. . . Because I believe that the Court reads *International Shoe* and its progeny too narrowly, and because I believe that the standards enunciated by those cases may already be obsolete as constitutional boundaries, I dissent.

I

The Court's opinions focus tightly on the existence of contacts between the forum and the defendant. In so doing, they accord too little weight to the strength of the forum State's interest in the case and fail to explore whether there would be any actual inconvenience to the defendant. . . .

II . . .

B

[T]he interest of the forum State and its connection to the litigation is strong. The automobile accident underlying the litigation occurred in Oklahoma. The plaintiffs were hospitalized in Oklahoma when they brought suit. Essential witnesses and evidence were in Oklahoma. See Shaffer v. Heitner. The State has a legitimate interest in enforcing its laws designed to keep its highway system safe, and the trial can proceed at least as efficiently in Oklahoma as anywhere else.

The petitioners are not unconnected with the forum. Although both sell automobiles within limited sales territories, each sold the automobile which in fact was driven to Oklahoma where it was involved in an accident. It may be true, as the Court suggests, that each sincerely intended to limit its commercial impact to the limited territory, and that each intended to accept the benefits and protection of the laws only of those States within the territory. But obviously these were unrealistic hopes that cannot be treated as an automatic constitutional shield.[9]

An automobile simply is not a stationary item or one designed to be used in one place. An automobile is intended to be moved around. Someone in the business of selling large numbers of automobiles can hardly plead ignorance of their mobility or pretend that the automobiles stay put after they are sold. It is not merely that a dealer in automobiles foresees that they will move. The dealer actually intends that the purchasers will use the automobiles to travel to distant States

---

9. Moreover, imposing liability in this case would not so undermine certainty as to destroy an automobile dealer's ability to do business. According jurisdiction does not expand liability except in the marginal case where a plaintiff cannot afford to bring an action except in the plaintiff's own State. In addition, these petitioners are represented by insurance companies. They not only could, but did, purchase insurance to protect them should they stand trial and lose the case. The costs of the insurance no doubt are passed on to customers.

where the dealer does not directly "do business." The sale of an automobile does *purposefully* inject the vehicle into the stream of interstate commerce so that it can travel to distant States. . . .

The Court accepts that a State may exercise jurisdiction over a distributor which "serves" that State "indirectly" by "deliver[ing] its products into the stream of commerce with the expectation that they will [be] purchased by consumers in other States." It is difficult to see why the Constitution should distinguish between a case involving goods which reach a distant State through a chain of distribution and a case involving goods which reach the same State because a consumer, using them as the dealer knew the customer would, took them there. In each case the seller purposefully injects the goods into the stream of commerce and those goods predictably are used in the forum State. . . .

III

It may be that affirmance of the judgments in these cases would approach the outer limits of *International Shoe*'s jurisdictional principle. But that principle, with its almost exclusive focus on the rights of defendants, may be outdated. . . .

The Court's opinion suggests that the defendant ought to be subject to a State's jurisdiction only if he has contacts with the State "such that he should reasonably anticipate being haled into court there."[18] . . .

I would also, however, strip the defendant of an unjustified veto power over certain very appropriate fora — a power the defendant justifiably enjoyed long ago when communication and travel over long distances were slow and unpredictable and when notions of state sovereignty were impractical and exaggerated. But I repeat that that is not today's world. If a plaintiff can show that his chosen forum State has a sufficient interest in the litigation (or sufficient contacts with the defendant), then the defendant who cannot show some real injury to a constitutionally protected interest should have no constitutional excuse not to appear.[21] . . .

[Two dissenting opinions, one by Justice MARSHALL, joined by Justice BLACKMUN, and another by Justice BLACKMUN writing separately, are omitted.]

NOTES AND PROBLEMS

1. Consider the case as doctrine, as strategy, and as a guide to future litigation. Begin by clarifying what the case did and didn't decide:

a. Which defendants were before the Supreme Court?

b. Audi, the manufacturer, did not challenge personal jurisdiction; Volkswagen of America, the national distributor, originally objected to the Oklahoma court's

---

18. The Court suggests that this is the critical forseeability rather than the likelihood that the product will go to the forum State. But the reasoning begs the question. A defendant cannot know if his actions will subject him to jurisdiction in another State until we have declared what the law of jurisdiction is. . . .

21. Frequently, of course, the defendant will be able to influence the choice of forum through traditional doctrines, such as venue or forum non conveniens, permitting the transfer of litigation.

jurisdiction, but did not appeal the trial court's rejection of that defense. Because their case was not before the Court, the case does not hold that these parties are subject to jurisdiction, but suggests that they would be:

> Hence if the sale of a product of a manufacturer or distributor such as Audi or Volkswagen is not simply an isolated occurrence, but arises from the efforts of the manufacturer or distributor to serve, directly or indirectly, the market for its product in other States, it is not unreasonable to subject it to suit in one of those States if its allegedly defective merchandise there has been the source of injury to others. . . .

c. Apply the case to the following hypothetical: Assume that, as purchased, the Robinsons' car lacked a radio. Before leaving on the trip to Arizona, they went to a Massena, N.Y., retailer who specialized in sound equipment for cars and purchased a sound system for the Audi. The system was manufactured in Japan and sold all over the United States. The national distributor was located in California. Further assume that the cause of the car fire was traced to defective wiring in the sound system. If the Robinsons sue in Oklahoma, naming the Massena retailer, the Japanese manufacturer, and the California distributor, who will be subject to personal jurisdiction?

2. If the manufacturer and importer are subject to jurisdiction in Oklahoma, but the regional distributor and dealer are not, *World-Wide Volkswagen* can result in unnecessary multiplicity of lawsuits. Suppose Audi discovered a gas tank problem and sent a service bulletin to Seaway and World-Wide requiring them to correct the problem — but they had failed to do so. Their failure to correct the defect would not be a defense in the Robinsons' actions against Audi, but it might be the basis for requiring Seaway and World-Wide to indemnify Audi. Under these circumstances, Audi would have to sue Seaway and World-Wide separately, probably in New York. But because World-Wide and Seaway would not have been parties to the Oklahoma litigation, they would not be bound by the finding of a product defect. The result might be inconsistent judgments — Oklahoma holding Audi responsible for a design defect, but New York courts finding that there was no defect and that Audi was therefore not entitled to indemnity. Is this result of a no-jurisdiction holding a problem?

3. Personal jurisdiction motions are strategic tools in defendant's arsenal, and therefore something plaintiffs must anticipate.

a. In theory, a successful motion to dismiss for want of personal jurisdiction only delays the suit: At least as to a U.S. defendant, there will be some jurisdiction (permanent domicile, state of incorporation) where suit can be brought. So why do defendants bother?

b. In a marginal case, the suit might go away entirely. The statute of limitations in the news forum state may have run. Or, unlike the Robinsons case, which involved very serious permanent injuries, suppose a much lower damage bill. Plaintiff's lawyer has to locate a competent practitioner in another case and arrange for her to take the case over, a process involving some expense. If witnesses have to travel, the added expense might make the suit irrational to bring.

c. Even if the case persists, the defendant has done two things. He's delayed the date at which he may have to pay damages (in many tort suits interest does not run until judgment is entered). And he's moved the case to a different forum, which, for reasons having nothing to do with jurisdiction, may be friendlier.

d. But plaintiffs too can behave strategically. Modern jurisdictional doctrine often permits plaintiff a choice of several fora in which to sue. In *World-Wide* the plaintiffs could have sued Audi in New York, in Oklahoma, and perhaps in Arizona, where the Robinsons were moving on their ill-fated trip.

4. *World-Wide* is not only an important part of jurisdictional doctrine, but an example of both parties maneuvering for strategic advantage by deploying jurisdictional doctrine. Reading the case, you may have wondered, first, why the driver of the car that collided with the plaintiffs did not seem to be in the case, and, second, why the plaintiffs bothered to name the local dealer as a defendant. Professor Charles Adams, who has looked into the story behind the case in World-Wide Volkswagen v. Woodson — The Rest of the Story, 72 Neb. L. Rev. 1122 (1993), provides an account:

> Lloyd Hull knew he had a serious drinking problem. Ever since his retirement from the Navy two years before, it seemed as though he needed to get a little high, or better, every day. After getting off work on September 21, 1977, in Berryville, Arkansas, Lloyd was on his way to visit his older sister in Okarche, Oklahoma. Next to the bottle of Jim Beam on the front seat was a loaded .22 Magnum pistol for shooting jack rabbits on his sister's farm. . . .
>
> As he drove along, Lloyd took shots from the bottle of bourbon. . . . Later he assumed he must have been driving too fast on account of the liquor. Lloyd did not notice the small car ahead of him until he was nearly on top of it. . . .
>
> Lloyd Hull was an obvious defendant, but he had no liability insurance. . . .

Id. at 1122-1123, 1127.

But, according to plaintiffs' theory of the case, the seriousness of the injuries, if not the accident itself, had been caused by a product defect. Where would such a claim be tried?

a. Start with the plaintiff, who has the initial choice. Why did the Robinsons' lawyer choose Oklahoma? According to Professor Adams, Creek County, Oklahoma, was "a blue collar community that . . . [had] become known to personal injury lawyers throughout the state as being particularly sympathetic to personal injury plaintiffs." Id. at 1128.

b. But a successful strategy to try the case in Creek County would not only have to bring it there but keep it there. As you will see in the next chapter, noncitizen defendants may "remove" to federal court an action if the requisites of diversity have been met. Any good plaintiffs' lawyer would know that if he sued a German manufacturer and its national distributor (located in Michigan), the defendants could, at a minimum, remove the case to a federal district court by invoking diversity jurisdiction. Since the federal district court nearest to Creek County is in Tulsa, and since that court would draw its jurors from a number of counties in the Eastern District of Oklahoma, the defendants could, by making such a move, dilute what plaintiff thought would be a favorable jury pool.

c. Could the plaintiff prevent such removal? For diversity jurisdiction to exist, none of the defendants can be of the same state as the plaintiffs (a principle explored more fully in the next chapter). The Robinsons' lawyer argued that the

Robinsons, although they were on their way to Arizona, remained New York citizens. Hence the importance of naming World-Wide and Seaway, both New York corporations, as defendants: So long as they remained in the lawsuit, the case could not be removed to federal court and would therefore be tried before a Creek County jury.

d. The defendants' counter was the motion to dismiss the two New York defendants for want of personal jurisdiction. Do you now understand why there was such a fierce battle about personal jurisdiction over two apparently irrelevant defendants?

e. Given this background, what would you expect to be the remaining defendants' next procedural move after the case has been sent back to Oklahoma courts with the holding that there is no jurisdiction over Seaway and World-Wide?

5. *World-Wide Volkswagen* is emblematic of the modern economy. A car is a complicated product, assembled from components made by many "upstream" manufacturers and then sold through a national network of "downstream" distributors and dealers. Many goods — from simple ones like toasters and bicycles to complex ones like autos, electronic equipment — have similar profiles. When something goes wrong with such a product and a lawsuit results, the legal system has to answer the question of who will be subject to suit.

Part of the answer lies in substantive law, which has evolved dramatically over the last hundred years. Another part is jurisdictional. Everyone seems to agree that the manufacturer of the product — the entity that designed and assembled it (like Audi in *World-Wide Volkswagen*) — will be subject to suit where that product causes injury. The hard question comes when one thinks about those who precede and follow the manufacturer — the potential upstream and downstream defendants. The *World-Wide Volkswagen* case itself dealt with those downstream parts of the network. Suppose that, as the suit against World-Wide proceeded, attention had focused on the manufacturer of the gas tank — a Polish company, let us imagine. Could Audi have joined this "upstream" component manufacturer in the Oklahoma litigation? The next case responds to that question.

Asahi Metal Industry Co. v. Superior Court

480 U.S. 102 (1987)

Justice O'CONNOR announced the judgment of the Court and delivered the unanimous opinion of the Court with respect to Part I; the opinion of the Court with respect to Part II-B, in which THE CHIEF JUSTICE, J[ustices] BRENNAN, WHITE, MARSHALL, BLACKMUN, POWELL, and STEVENS join; and an opinion with respect to Parts II-A and III, in which THE CHIEF JUSTICE, Justice[s] POWELL and SCALIA join.

This case presents the question whether the mere awareness on the part of a foreign defendant that the components it manufactured, sold, and delivered outside the United States would reach the forum State in the stream of commerce constitutes "minimum contacts" between the defendant and the forum State such that the exercise of jurisdiction "does not offend 'traditional notions of fair play and substantial justice.'" International Shoe Co. v. Washington, quoting Milliken v. Meyer.

On September 23, 1978, on Interstate Highway 80 in Solano County, California, Gary Zurcher lost control of his Honda motorcycle and collided with a tractor. Zurcher was severely injured, and his passenger and wife, Ruth Ann Moreno, was killed. In September 1979, Zurcher filed a product liability action in the Superior Court of the State of California in and for the County of Solano. Zurcher alleged that the 1978 accident was caused by a sudden loss of air and an explosion in the rear tire of the motorcycle, and alleged that the motorcycle tire, tube, and sealant were defective. Zurcher's complaint named, inter alia, Cheng Shin Rubber Industrial Co., Ltd. (Cheng Shin), the Taiwanese manufacturer of the tube. Cheng Shin in turn filed a cross-complaint [that is, what the Federal Rules would call a third-party complaint] seeking indemnification from its codefendants and from petitioner, Asahi Metal Industry Co., Ltd. (Asahi), the manufacturer of the tube's valve assembly. Zurcher's claims against Cheng Shin and the other defendants were eventually settled and dismissed, leaving only Cheng Shin's indemnity action against Asahi.

California's long-arm statute authorizes the exercise of jurisdiction "on any basis not inconsistent with the Constitution of this state or of the United States." Cal. Code Civ. Proc. Ann. §410.10 (West 1973). Asahi moved to quash Cheng Shin's service of summons arguing the State could not exert jurisdiction over it consistent with the Due Process Clause of the Fourteenth Amendment.

. . . Asahi is a Japanese corporation. It manufactures tire valve assemblies in Japan and sells the assemblies to Cheng Shin, and to several other tire manufacturers, for use as components in finished tire tubes. . . . Cheng Shin bought and incorporated into its tire tubes [between 100,000 and 500,000 assemblies annually in the years from 1978 to 1982; those sales] accounted for 1.24 percent of Asahi's income in 1981 and 0.44 percent in 1982. Cheng Shin alleged that approximately 20 percent of its sales in the United States are in California. Cheng Shin purchases valve assemblies from other suppliers as well, and sells finished tubes throughout the world.

. . . . An affidavit of a manager of Cheng Shin whose duties included the purchasing of component parts stated: "'In discussions with Asahi regarding the purchase of valve stem assemblies the fact that my Company sells tubes throughout the world and specifically the United States has been discussed. I am informed and believe that Asahi was fully aware that valve stem assemblies sold to my Company and to others would end up throughout the United States and in California.'" An affidavit of the president of Asahi, on the other hand, declared that Asahi "'has never contemplated that its limited sales of tire valves to Cheng Shin in Taiwan would subject it to lawsuits in California.'" The record does not include any contract between Cheng Shin and Asahi.

Primarily on the basis of the above information, the Superior Court denied the motion to quash summons, stating that "Asahi obviously does business on an international scale. It is not unreasonable that they defend claims of defect in their product on an international scale."

We granted certiorari and now reverse.

II

A

. . . Applying the principle that minimum contacts must be based on an act of the defendant, the Court in World-Wide Volkswagen Corp. v. Woodson rejected the assertion that a *consumer's* unilateral act of bringing the defendant's product into the forum State was a sufficient constitutional basis for personal jurisdiction over the defendant. Since *World-Wide Volkswagen*, lower courts have been confronted with cases in which the defendant acted by placing a product in the stream of commerce, and the stream eventually swept defendant's product into the forum State, but the defendant did nothing else to purposefully avail itself of the market in the forum State. Some courts have understood the Due Process Clause, as interpreted in *World-Wide Volkswagen*, to allow an exercise of personal jurisdiction to be based on no more than the defendant's act of placing the product in the stream of commerce. Other courts have understood the Due Process Clause and the above-quoted language in *World-Wide Volkswagen* to require the action of the defendant to be more purposefully directed at the forum State than the mere act of placing a product in the stream of commerce.

The reasoning of the Supreme Court of California in the present case illustrates the former interpretation of *World-Wide Volkswagen*. The Supreme Court of California held that, because the stream of commerce eventually brought some valves Asahi sold Cheng Shin into California, Asahi's awareness that its valves would be sold in California was sufficient to permit California to exercise jurisdiction over Asahi consistent with the requirements of the Due Process Clause. The Supreme Court of California's position was consistent with those courts that have held that mere foreseeability or awareness was a constitutionally sufficient basis for personal jurisdiction if the defendant's product made its way into the forum State while still in the stream of commerce.

Other courts, however, have understood the Due Process Clause to require something more than that the defendant was aware of its product's entry into the forum State through the stream of commerce in order for the state to exert jurisdiction over the defendant. . . .

We now find this latter position to be consonant with the requirements of due process. The "substantial connection," between the defendant and the forum State necessary for a finding of minimum contacts must come about by *an action of the defendant purposefully directed toward the forum State*. The placement of a product into the stream of commerce, without more, is not an act of the defendant purposefully directed toward the forum State. Additional conduct of the defendant may indicate an intent or purpose to serve the market in the forum State, for example, designing the product for the market in the forum State, advertising in the forum State, establishing channels for providing regular advice to customers in the forum State, or marketing the product through a distributor who has agreed to serve as the sales agent in the forum State. But a defendant's awareness that the stream of commerce may or will sweep the product into the forum State does not convert the mere act of placing the product into the stream into an act purposefully directed toward the forum State.

[R]espondents have not demonstrated any action by Asahi to purposefully avail itself of the California market. . . . On the basis of these facts, the exertion of personal jurisdiction over Asahi by the Superior Court of California* exceeds the limits of due process.

B

The strictures of the Due Process Clause forbid a state court from exercising personal jurisdiction over Asahi under circumstances that would offend "traditional notions of fair play and substantial justice." International Shoe v. Washington, quoting Milliken v. Meyer.

We have previously explained that the determination of the reasonableness of the exercise of jurisdiction in each case will depend on an evaluation of several factors. A court must consider the burden on the defendant, the interests of the forum state, and the plaintiff's interest in obtaining relief. It must also weigh in its determination "the interstate judicial system's interest in obtaining the most efficient resolution of controversies; and the shared interest of the several States in furthering fundamental substantive social policies." World-Wide Volkswagen.

A consideration of these factors in the present case clearly reveals the unreasonableness of the assertion of jurisdiction over Asahi, even apart from the question of the placement of goods in the stream of commerce.

Certainly the burden on the defendant in this case is severe. Asahi has been commanded by the Supreme Court of California not only to traverse the distance between Asahi's headquarters in Japan and the Superior Court of California in and for the County of Solano, but also to submit its dispute with Cheng Shin to a foreign nation's judicial system. The unique burdens placed upon one who must defend oneself in a foreign legal system should have significant weight in assessing the reasonableness of stretching the long arm of personal jurisdiction over national borders.

When minimum contacts have been established, often the interests of the plaintiff and the forum in the exercise of jurisdiction will justify even the serious burdens placed on the alien defendant. In the present case, however, the interests of the plaintiff and the forum in California's assertion of jurisdiction over Asahi are slight. All that remains is a claim for indemnification asserted by Cheng Shin, a Taiwanese corporation, against Asahi. The transaction on which the indemnification claim is based took place in Taiwan; Asahi's components were shipped from Japan to Taiwan. Cheng Shin has not demonstrated that it is

---

* We have no occasion here to determine whether Congress could, consistent with the Due Process Clause of the Fifth Amendment, authorize federal court personal jurisdiction over alien defendants based on the aggregate of national contacts, rather than on the contacts between the defendant and the State in which the federal court sits.

more convenient for it to litigate its indemnification claim against Asahi in California rather than in Taiwan or Japan.

Because the plaintiff is not a California resident, California's legitimate interests in the dispute have considerably diminished. . . . The possibility of being haled into a California court as a result of an accident involving Asahi's components undoubtedly creates an additional deterrent to the manufacture of unsafe components; however, similar pressures will be placed on Asahi by the purchasers of its components as long as those who use Asahi components in their final products, and sell those products in California, are subject to the application of California tort law.

World-Wide Volkswagen also admonished courts to take into consideration the interests of the "several States," in addition to the forum State, in the efficient judicial resolution of the dispute and the advancement of substantive policies. In the present case, this advice calls for a court to consider the procedural and substantive policies of other nations whose interests are affected by the assertion of jurisdiction by the California court . . . "Great care and reserve should be exercised when extending our notions of personal jurisdiction into the international field." United States v. First National City Bank.

Considering the international context, the heavy burden on the alien defendant, and the slight interests of the plaintiff and the forum State, the exercise of personal jurisdiction by a California court over Asahi in this instance would be unreasonable and unfair.

III

Because the facts of this case do not establish minimum contacts such that the exercise of personal jurisdiction is consistent with fair play and substantial justice, the judgment of the Supreme Court of California is reversed, and the case is remanded for further proceedings not inconsistent with this opinion. It is so ordered.

[Justice BRENNAN, with whom Justices WHITE, MARSHALL, and BLACKMUN joined, concurred in part and concurred in the judgment.]

I do not agree with the interpretation in Part II-A of the stream-of-commerce theory, nor with its conclusion that Asahi did not "purposely avail itself of the California market." I do agree, however, with the Court's conclusion in Part II-B that the exercise of personal jurisdiction over Asahi in this case would not comport with "fair play and substantial justice." *International Shoe.* This is one of those rare cases in which "minimum requirements inherent in the concept of 'fair play and substantial justice' . . . defeat the reasonableness of jurisdiction even [though] the defendant has purposefully engaged in forum activities." Burger King Corp. v. Rudzewicz. I therefore join Parts I and II-B of the Court's opinion, and write separately to explain my disagreement with Part II-A.

[Justice Brennan argued that injecting goods into a stream of commerce should suffice to support jurisdiction.] The endorsement in Part II-A of what appears to be the minority view among Federal Courts of Appeals represents a marked retreat from its analysis in World-Wide Volkswagen v. Woodson. . . .

. . . Accordingly, I cannot join the plurality's determination that Asahi's regular and extensive sales of component parts to a manufacturer it knew was making regular sales of the final product in California is insufficient to establish minimum contacts with California.

[Justice STEVENS, joined by Justices WHITE and BLACKMUN, concurred in part and concurred in the judgment.]

The judgment of the Supreme Court of California should be reversed for the reasons stated in Part II-B of the Court's opinion. While I join Parts I and II-B, I do not join Part II-A for two reasons. First, it is not necessary to the Court's decision. An examination of minimum contacts is not always necessary to determine whether a state court's assertion of personal jurisdiction is constitutional. See Burger King Corp. v. Rudzewicz. Part II-B establishes, after considering the factors set forth in World-Wide Volkswagen Corp. v. Woodson, that California's exercise of jurisdiction over Asahi in this case would be "unreasonable and unfair." This finding alone requires reversal; this case fits within the rule that "minimum requirements inherent in the concept of 'fair play and substantial justice' may defeat the reasonableness of jurisdiction even if the defendant has purposefully engaged in forum activities." *Burger King* (quoting International Shoe Co. v. Washington). Accordingly, I see no reason in this case for the Court to articulate "purposeful direction" or any other test as the nexus between an act of a defendant and the forum State that is necessary to establish minimum contacts.

Second, even assuming that the test ought to be formulated here, Part II-A misapplies it to the facts of this case. The Court seems to assume that an unwavering line can be drawn between "mere awareness" that a component will find its way into the forum State and "purposeful availment" of the forum's market. Over the course of its dealings with Cheng Shin, Asahi has arguably engaged in a higher quantum of conduct than "[t]he placement of a product into the stream of commerce, without more. . . ." Whether or not this conduct rises to the level of purposeful availment requires a constitutional determination that is affected by the volume, the value, and the hazardous character of the components. In most circumstances I would be inclined to conclude that a regular course of dealing that results in deliveries of over 100,000 units annually over a period of several years would constitute "purposeful availment" even though the item delivered to the forum state was a standard product marketed throughout the world.

NOTES AND PROBLEMS

1. The caption of the case is potentially confusing. As in *World-Wide Volkswagen,* the defendants challenged the trial court's ruling by seeking an interlocutory writ of mandate. In that writ the nominal defendant is the trial court — hence the caption of the case. Ordinarily, as here, the party who stands to gain from the trial court's ruling (the "real party in interest"), here Cheng Shin, assumes responsibility for defending the ruling in question.

2. Having figured out the parties, sort out holding and dicta, majority and concurrences.

a. Somewhat unusually, the Court agreed unanimously on a result but split sharply on the reasoning leading to its conclusion. What parts of Justice O'Connor's opinion commanded a majority? (Note that only these parts are precedent.)

b. Can you infer the views of the majority that endorsed the result but declined to join Parts II-A and III?

c. Can you infer the position of Justice Scalia, who endorsed Parts II-A and III but *not* Part II-B, which the other eight Justices signed?

d. What do lower courts do when the U.S. Supreme Court produces such a split opinion on a frequently litigated topic like personal jurisdiction? U.S. Law Week reported the following reaction:

> *Asahi Metal* . . . failed to produce a majority opinion. Subsequently, the circuits have divided over the appropriate test to draw from Asahi Metal: the Fifth and Eighth circuits have adopted the test advocated by Justice Brennan; the First Circuit has adopted the test advocated by Justice O'Connor; the other circuits have not adopted a specific test; and the Eleventh Circuit has issued conflicting decisions. For its part, the Third Circuit [has] recognized this division of authority but found it unnecessary to choose a specific test.

Circuit Split Roundup, 67 U.S. L. Wk. 2158 (1998). One imagines similar confusion among state courts. Should such results persuade the justices to do everything they can to arrive at a majority opinion?

3. Would the outcome have been different:

a. If Asahi had been a U.S. manufacturer of tire valves that had sold them to a U.S. tire manufacturer for incorporation in motorcycles manufactured in the United States?

b. If Asahi had been one of the primary defendants rather than a third-party defendant?

c. If the suit against the primary defendants had not been settled?

d. If Asahi also sold some of its tire valves to tire stores in California, for sale as replacements?

e. If Cheng Shin had presented evidence that, because of a chill in foreign relations, Japan's courts were closed to Taiwanese plaintiffs?

4. Put *World-Wide Volkswagen* and *Asahi* together. Both grew from tort actions involving a complicated product assembled from many components and sold nationally. Both assume without so holding that the manufacturer — Audi and Honda — can be sued wherever the product is sold. Both limit jurisdiction over those who precede and follow the manufacturer in the "stream of commerce."

Assume that Volvo, a Swedish car maker partly owned by General Motors, buys brake components from BrakeCo, a U.S. manufacturer located in Illinois. Volvo has a national distributor, located in New Jersey, and a network of dealers throughout the United States. Consumer buys a Volvo in Florida; the brakes fail and it crashes. Consumer brings suit in Florida against Volvo, BrakeCo, National Distributor, and Dealer. Who will be subject to personal jurisdiction? What more facts do you want to know — and why?

5. Doctrinally, *Asahi* is interesting because of its suggestion that "substantial justice and fair play" is not a synonym for minimum contacts but an independent

requirement. In *Asahi* the substantial justice requirement defeated jurisdiction, even though a majority of the justices seemed prepared to say that Asahi did have minimum contacts with California, the forum state. The next case suggests that substantial justice may also play a positive role — pushing the court toward assumption of jurisdiction, even when contacts are quite thin.

Burger King Corp. v. Rudzewicz

471 U.S. 462 (1985)

Justice BRENNAN delivered the opinion of the Court.

[Burger King operates an extensive fast food franchise system in which it trains franchisees and regulates their operations in great detail. Headquarters are in Florida, but regional offices supervise franchisees in their areas.]

The instant litigation grows out of Burger King's termination of one of its franchisees, and is aptly described by the franchisee as "a divorce proceeding among commercial partners." The appellee John Rudzewicz, a Michigan citizen and resident, is the senior partner in a Detroit accounting firm. In 1978, he was approached by Brian MacShara, the son of a business acquaintance, who suggested that they jointly apply to Burger King for a franchise in the Detroit area. MacShara proposed to serve as the manager of the restaurant if Rudzewicz would put up the investment capital; in exchange, the two would evenly share the profits. Believing that MacShara's idea offered attractive investment and tax-deferral opportunities, Rudzewicz agreed to the venture.

Rudzewicz and MacShara jointly applied for a franchise to Burger King's Birmingham, Michigan, district office in the autumn of 1978. Their application was forwarded to Burger King's Miami headquarters, which entered into a preliminary agreement with them in February 1979. During the ensuing four months it was agreed that Rudzewicz and MacShara would assume operation of an existing facility in Drayton Plains, Michigan. MacShara attended the prescribed management courses in Miami during this period, and the franchisees purchased $165,000 worth of restaurant equipment from Burger King's Davmor Industries division in Miami. Even before the final agreements were signed, however, the parties began to disagree over site-development fees, building design, computation of monthly rent, and whether the franchisees would be able to assign their liabilities to a corporation they had formed. During these disputes Rudzewicz and MacShara negotiated both with the Birmingham district office and with the Miami headquarters. With some misgivings, Rudzewicz and MacShara finally obtained limited concessions from the Miami headquarters, signed the final agreements, and commenced operations in June 1979. By signing the final agreements, Rudzewicz obligated himself personally to payments exceeding $1 million over the 20-year franchise relationship.

[Shortly after the agreement was signed, business at the franchise began to deteriorate. When rent payments fell behind, Burger King first negotiated, then sued in federal district court in Florida, invoking both diversity and trademark jurisdiction. Rudzewicz and MacShara challenged personal jurisdiction. The district court rejected their challenge. The case went to trial, at which the judge awarded Burger King both damages and injunctive relief. A divided] panel of [the Eleventh] Circuit reversed the judgment, concluding that the District Court could not properly exercise personal jurisdiction over Rudzewicz pursuant to Fla. Stat. §48.193(1)(g) (Supp. 1984) because "the circumstances of the Drayton Plains franchise and the negotiations which led to it left Rudzewicz bereft of reasonable notice and financially unprepared for the prospect of franchise litigation in Florida." [W]e . . . reverse.

II

A

The Due Process Clause protects an individual's liberty interest in not being subject to the binding judgments of a forum with which he has established no meaningful "contacts, ties, or relations." International Shoe Co. v. Washington.[13] By requiring that individuals have "fair warning that a particular activity may subject [them] to the jurisdiction of a foreign sovereign," Shaffer v. Heitner (Stevens, J., concurring in judgment), the Due Process Clause "gives a degree of predictability to the legal system that allows potential defendants to structure their primary conduct with some minimum assurance as to where that conduct will and will not render them liable to suit," World-Wide Volkswagen Corp. v. Woodson.

Where a forum seeks to assert specific jurisdiction over an out-of-state defendant who has not consented to suit there, this "fair warning" requirement is satisfied if the defendant has "purposefully directed" his activities at residents of the forum and the litigation results from alleged injuries that "arise out of or relate to" those activities. . . .

. . . Although it has been argued that foreseeability of causing injury in another State should be sufficient to establish such contacts there when policy considerations so require, the Court has consistently held that this kind of foreseeability is not a "sufficient benchmark" for exercising personal jurisdiction. World-Wide Volkswagen Corp. v. Woodson. Instead, "the foreseeability that is critical to due process analysis . . . is that the defendant's conduct and connection with the forum State are such that he should reasonably anticipate being haled into court there." Id. In defining when it is that a potential defendant should "reasonably anticipate" out-of-state litigation, the Court frequently has drawn from the reasoning of Hanson v. Denckla:

> The unilateral activity of those who claim some relationship with a nonresident defendant cannot satisfy the requirement of contact with the forum State. The application of that rule will vary with the quality and nature of the defendant's activity, but it is essential in each case that there be some act by which the defendant

13. Although this protection operates to restrict state power, it "must be seen as ultimately a function of the individual liberty interest preserved by the Due Process Clause" rather than as a function "of federalism concerns." Insurance Corp. of Ireland, Ltd. v. Compagnie des Bauxites de Guinee, 456 U.S. 694, 702-703, n.10 (1982).

purposefully avails itself of the privilege of conducting activities within the forum State, thus invoking the benefits and protections of its laws. . . .

Once it has been decided that a defendant purposefully established minimum contacts within the forum State, these contacts may be considered in light of other factors to determine whether they comport with "fair play and substantial justice." International Shoe Co. v. Washington. Thus courts in "appropriate case[s]" may evaluate "the burden on the defendant," "the forum State's interest in adjudicating the dispute," "the interstate judicial system's interest in obtaining the most efficient resolution of controversies," and the "shared interest of the several States in furthering fundamental substantive social policies" World-Wide Volkswagen v. Woodson. These considerations sometimes serve to establish the reasonableness of jurisdiction upon a lesser showing of minimum contacts than would otherwise be required. On the other hand, where a defendant who purposefully has directed his activities at forum residents seeks to defeat jurisdiction, he must present a compelling case that the presence of some other considerations would render jurisdiction unreasonable. Most such considerations usually may be accommodated through means short of finding jurisdiction unconstitutional. For example, the potential clash of the forum's law with the "fundamental substantive social policies" of another State may be accommodated through application of the forum's choice-of-law rules. Similarly, a defendant claiming substantial inconvenience may seek a change of venue. Nevertheless, minimum requirements inherent in the concept of "fair play and substantial justice" may defeat the reasonableness of jurisdiction even if the defendant has purposefully engaged in forum activities. World-Wide Volkswagen Corp. v. Woodson. As we previously have noted, jurisdictional rules may not be employed in such a way as to make litigation "so gravely difficult and inconvenient" that a party unfairly is at a "severe disadvantage" in comparison to his opponent.

B

(1)

Applying these principles to the case at hand, we believe there is substantial record evidence supporting the District Court's conclusion that the assertion of personal jurisdiction over Rudzewicz in Florida for the alleged breach of his franchise agreement did not offend due process. . . .

In this case, no physical ties to Florida can be attributed to Rudzewicz other than MacShara's brief training course in Miami. Rudzewicz did not maintain offices in Florida and, for all that appears from the record, has never even visited there. Yet this franchise dispute grew directly out of "a contract which had a substantial connection with that State." McGee v. International Life Insurance Co. Eschewing the option of operating an independent local enterprise, Rudzewicz deliberately "reach[ed] out beyond" Michigan and negotiated with a Florida corporation for the purchase of a long-term franchise and the manifold benefits that would derive from affiliation with a nationwide organization. . . . [H]e entered into a carefully structured 20-year relationship that envisioned continuing and wide-reaching contact with Burger King in Florida. In light of Rudzewicz's voluntary acceptance of the long-term and exacting regulation of his business from Burger King's Miami headquarters, the "quality and nature" of his relationship to the company in Florida can in no sense be viewed as "random," "fortuitous," or "attenuated." Hanson v. Denckla. . . . Rudzewicz most certainly knew that he was affiliating himself with an enterprise based primarily in Florida. . . . When problems arose over building design, site-development fees, rent computation, and the defaulted payments, Rudzewicz and MacShara learned that the Michigan office was powerless to resolve their disputes and could only channel their communications to Miami. . . .

Moreover, we believe the Court of Appeals gave insufficient weight to provisions in the various franchise documents providing that all disputes would be governed by Florida law. The franchise agreement, for example, stated:

> This Agreement shall become valid when executed and accepted by BKC at Miami, Florida; it shall be deemed made and entered into in the State of Florida and shall be governed and construed under and in accordance with the laws of the State of Florida. The choice of law designation does not require that all suits concerning this Agreement be filed in Florida.

. . . As Judge Johnson argued in his dissent below, Rudzewicz "purposefully availed himself of the benefits and protections of Florida laws" by entering into contracts expressly providing that those laws would govern franchise disputes.[24] . . .

III

Notwithstanding these considerations, the Court of Appeals apparently believed that it was necessary to reject jurisdiction in this case as a prophylactic measure, reasoning that an affirmance of the District Court's judgment would result in the exercise of jurisdiction over "out-of-state consumers to collect payments due on modest personal purchases" and would "sow the seeds of default judgments against franchisees owing smaller debts." We share the Court of Appeals' broader concerns and therefore reject any talismanic jurisdictional formulas. . . . We . . . have emphasized that jurisdiction may not be grounded on a contract whose terms have been obtained through "fraud, undue influence, or overweening bargaining power" and whose application would render litigation "so gravely difficult and inconvenient that [a party] will for all practical purposes be deprived of his day in court." . . .

For the reasons set forth above, however, these dangers are not present in the instant case. . . . The judgment of the Court of Appeals is accordingly reversed, and the case is remanded for further proceedings consistent with this opinion.

Justice POWELL took no part in the consideration or decision of this case.

---

24. In addition, the franchise agreement's disclaimer that the "choice of law designation does not *require* that all suits concerning this Agreement be filed in Florida" (emphasis added) reasonably should have suggested to Rudzewicz that by negative implication such suits *could* be filed there. . . .

Justice STEVENS, with whom Justice WHITE joins, dissenting.

In my opinion there is a significant element of unfairness in requiring a franchisee to defend a case of this kind in the forum chosen by the franchisor. It is undisputed that respondent maintained no place of business in Florida, that he had no employees in that State, and that he was not licensed to do business there. Respondent did not prepare his French fries, shakes, and hamburgers in Michigan, and then deliver them into the stream of commerce "with the expectation that they [would] be purchased by consumers in" Florida. To the contrary, respondent did business only in Michigan, his business, property, and payroll taxes were payable in that state, and he sold all of his products there.

Throughout the business relationship, respondent's principal contacts with petitioner were with its Michigan office. Notwithstanding its disclaimer, the Court seems ultimately to rely on nothing more than standard boilerplate language contained in various documents, to establish that respondent "'purposefully availed himself of the benefits and protections of Florida's laws.'" Such superficial analysis creates a potential for unfairness not only in negotiations between franchisors and their franchisees but, more significantly, in the resolution of the disputes that inevitably arise from time to time in such relationships.

Judge Vance's opinion for the Court of Appeals for the Eleventh Circuit adequately explains why I would affirm the judgment of that court. I particularly find the following more persuasive than what this Court has written today:

> Nothing in the course of negotiations gave Rudzewicz reason to anticipate a Burger King suit outside of Michigan. The only face-to-face or even oral contact Rudzewicz had with Burger King throughout months of protracted negotiations was with representatives of the Michigan office. . . .
>
> We discern a characteristic disparity of bargaining power in the facts of this case. There is no indication that Rudzewicz had any latitude to negotiate a reduced rent or franchise fee in exchange for the added risk of suit in Florida. He signed a standard form contract whose terms were non-negotiable and which appeared in some respects to vary from the more favorable terms agreed to in earlier discussions. In fact, the final contract required a minimum monthly rent computed on a base far in excess of that discussed in oral negotiations. Burger King resisted price concessions, only to sue Rudzewicz far from home. In doing so, it severely impaired his ability to call Michigan witnesses who might be essential to his defense and counterclaim.
>
> In sum, we hold that the circumstances of the Drayton Plains franchise and the negotiations which led to it left Rudzewicz bereft of reasonable notice and financially unprepared for the prospect of franchise litigation in Florida. Jurisdiction under these circumstances would offend the fundamental fairness which is the touchstone of due process.

Accordingly, I respectfully dissent.

NOTES AND PROBLEMS

1. What does *Burger King* mean to a lawyer?

a. Short of not entering into the franchise agreement, is there any way that Rudzewicz could have avoided Florida jurisdiction?

b. If you were advising Burger King, would you tell them that the opinion means that they can henceforth sue any franchisee in Florida courts? Or would you have qualifications?

c. You are a lawyer who has read *Burger King*. You are consulted by another Burger King franchisee who is in a dispute with the franchisor and foresees litigation. You want to avoid the Florida forum, thinking another venue may be more sympathetic. What can you do?

2. How does *Burger King* fit into the doctrinal landscape?

a. Can you distinguish *Burger King* from *World-Wide Volkswagen*? Why is the local automobile dealer not subject to jurisdiction in Oklahoma, while the local hamburger dealer is subject to jurisdiction in Florida?

b. Compare *Burger King* with *Asahi*. In the elaborate doctrinal discussion in Part IIA of the opinion, Justice Brennan articulates a relationship between minimum contacts and substantial justice. For him, the first inquiry is whether "a defendant purposefully established minimum contacts within the forum State." If the answer is yes, then

> courts in "appropriate case[s]" may evaluate "the burden on the defendant," "the forum State's interest in adjudicating the dispute," "the interstate judicial system's interest in obtaining the most efficient resolution of controversies," and the "shared interest of the several States in furthering fundamental substantive social policies" *World-Wide Volkswagen v. Woodson*. These considerations sometimes serve to establish the reasonableness of jurisdiction upon a lesser showing of minimum contacts than would otherwise be required.

Is this the same role that substantial justice plays in *Asahi*?

3. Compare *Burger King* with Diamond HealthCare of Ohio, Inc. v. Humility of Mary Health Partners, 229 F.3d 448 (4th Cir. 2000). Diamond, based in Virginia, contracted with HMH, in Ohio, to provide various health services, including hospitalization for the elderly. Diamond had approached HMH in Ohio, where the contract was negotiated, where most of the services were to be performed and whose law governed the contract. But all the paperwork passed through Virginia, and some parts of the agreement were also performed there. Diamond sued HMH for breach of contract in federal district court in Virginia. The two-judge majority rejected Virginia's jurisdiction; the dissent, citing *Burger King*, said that case was indistinguishable and governed. Who's right?

4. Unlike *World-Wide Volkswagen* and *Asahi*, *Burger King* was initiated in a federal court. The *Burger King* opinion silently assumes that the analysis is identical — that the jurisdictional reach of a federal court matches that of a state court sitting in the same state. The reason for that assumption at one level is straightforward: Federal Rule of Civil Procedure 4(k)(1)(A) gives a federal court the same jurisdictional reach as a court of the state in which it sits, except when either a specific federal statute extends that reach.

a. Exceptions to this provision occur when a specific federal statute or Rule authorizes more extensive personal jurisdiction. Rule 4(k)(1)(B)-(D). In several notable instances Congress has purported to give the federal courts expansive powers of personal jurisdiction. For example, the Federal Interpleader Act,

28 U.S.C. §2361, gives federal courts the power to serve process anywhere in the nation, a power that has been interpreted to include personal jurisdiction. Various laws regulating federal securities do the same. Is such jurisdictional reach constitutional? Under a jurisdictional model deriving from *Pennoyer*, the question was fairly simple. If jurisdictional power flowed from sovereignty, and if the federal government was in some sense sovereign within the borders of the nation, then jurisdiction existed: The only restraint lay in Congress's self-denial, the limitations of venue, and the doctrine of forum non conveniens.

b. *International Shoe* (and its reaffirmation in *Shaffer* and subsequent cases) made the question much harder. If personal jurisdiction was a matter of inconvenience to the defendant, then was it not equally possible for that inconvenience to exist in a federal as in a state forum? Suppose a state court could not constitutionally exercise jurisdiction because to do so would violate due process. May a federal court, sitting in the same state, disregard that limitation? (A small technical note: The Constitution contains two Due Process Clauses, one in the Fourteenth Amendment, applying to state governments, and one in the Fifth Amendment, applying to the federal government; courts have generally interpreted them in identical ways.)

5. It is both a strength and a weakness of contemporary jurisdictional doctrine that the broad categories of *International Shoe* require contextualization in differing circumstances. A recent challenge to the doctrine has arisen from its application to the Internet.

Pavlovich v. Superior Court

29 Cal. 4th 262, 58 P.3d 2 (2002)

BROWN, J.

. . . Not surprisingly, the so-called Internet revolution has spawned a host of new legal issues as courts have struggled to apply traditional legal frameworks to this new communication medium. Today, we join this struggle and consider the impact of the Internet on the determination of personal jurisdiction. In this case, a California court exercised personal jurisdiction over a defendant based on a posting on an Internet Web site. Under the particular facts of this case, we conclude the court's exercise of jurisdiction was improper.

I

Digital versatile discs (DVDs) "provide high quality images, such as motion pictures, digitally formatted on a convenient 5-inch disc. . . ." Before the commercial release of DVDs containing motion pictures, the Content Scrambling System (CSS), a system used to encrypt and protect copyrighted motion pictures on DVDs, was developed. The CSS technology prevents the playing or copying of copyrighted motion pictures on DVDs without the algorithms and keys necessary to decrypt the data stored on the disc.

Real party in interest DVD Copy Control Association, Inc. (DVD CCA) . . . [,] a nonprofit trade association organized under the laws of the State of Delaware with its principal place of business in California . . . acquired the licensing rights to the CSS technology and became the sole licensing entity for this technology in the DVD video format.

Petitioner Matthew Pavlovich is currently a resident of Texas and the president of Media Driver, LLC, a technology consulting company in Texas. During the four years before he moved to Texas, he studied computer engineering at Purdue University in Indiana, where he worked as a systems and network administrator. Pavlovich does not reside or work in California. He has never had a place of business, telephone listing, or bank account in California and has never owned property in California. Neither Pavlovich nor his company has solicited any business in California or has any business contacts in California.

At Purdue, Pavlovich was the founder and project leader of the LiVid video project (LiVid), which operated a Web site located at "livid.on.openprojects.net." The site consisted of a single page with text and links to other Web sites. The site only provided information; it did not solicit or transact any business and permitted no interactive exchange of information between its operators and visitors.

According to Pavlovich, the goal of LiVid was "to improve video and DVD support for Linux and to . . . combine the resources and the efforts of the various individuals that were working on related things. . . ." To reach this goal, the project sought to defeat the CSS technology and enable the decryption and copying of DVDs containing motion pictures. Consistent with these efforts, LiVid posted the source code of a program named DeCSS on its Web site. . . . DeCSS allows users to circumvent the CSS technology by decrypting data contained on DVDs and enabling the placement of this decrypted data onto computer hard drives or other storage media.

At the time LiVid posted DeCSS, Pavlovich knew that DeCSS "was derived from CSS algorithms" and that reverse engineering these algorithms was probably illegal. He had also "heard" that "there was an organization which you had to file for or apply for a license" to the CSS technology. He did not, however, learn that the organization was DVD CCA or that DVD CCA had its principal place of business in California until after DVD CCA filed this action.

In its complaint, DVD CCA alleged that Pavlovich misappropriated its trade secrets by posting the DeCSS program on the LiVid Web site. . . . The complaint sought injunctive relief but did not seek monetary damages. In response, Pavlovich filed a motion to quash service of process, contending that California lacked jurisdiction over his person. . . .

II

California courts may exercise personal jurisdiction on any basis consistent with the Constitutions of California and the United States. (Code Civ. Proc., § 410.10.) . . .

. . . A court may exercise specific jurisdiction over a nonresident defendant only if: (1) "the defendant has purposefully availed himself or herself of forum benefits" (2) "the 'controversy is related to or "arises out of" [the] defendant's contacts with the forum'" and (3) "the assertion of personal jurisdiction would comport with "fair play and substantial justice[.]""

[The opinion reviewed cases applying the purposeful availment test, focusing on the analogy of this case with defamation.]

In the defamation context, the United States Supreme Court has described an "effects test" for determining purposeful availment. In [Jones v.] Calder, a reporter in Florida wrote an article for the National Enquirer about Shirley Jones, a well-known actress who lived and worked in California. The president and editor of the National Enquirer reviewed and approved the article, and the National Enquirer published the article. Jones sued, among others, the reporter and editor (individual defendants) for libel in California. The individual defendants moved to quash service of process, contending they lacked minimum contacts with California.

The United States Supreme Court disagreed and held that California could exercise jurisdiction over the individual defendants "based on the 'effects' of their Florida conduct in California." . . . The court . . . noted that the individual defendants wrote or edited "an article that they knew would have a potentially devastating impact upon [Jones]. And they knew that the brunt of that injury would be felt by [Jones] in the State in which she lives and works and in which the National Enquirer has its largest circulation." . . .

[C]ourts have "struggled somewhat with *Calder*'s import, recognizing that the case cannot stand for the broad proposition that a foreign act with foreseeable effects in the forum state always gives rise to specific jurisdiction." . . .

. . . In this case, Pavlovich's sole contact with California is LiVid's posting of the DeCSS source code containing DVD CCA's proprietary information on an Internet Web site accessible to any person with Internet access. . . .

Although we have never considered the scope of personal jurisdiction based solely on Internet use, other courts have considered this issue, and most have adopted a sliding scale analysis. "At one end of the spectrum are situations where a defendant clearly does business over the Internet. If the defendant enters into contracts with residents of a foreign jurisdiction that involve the knowing and repeated transmission of computer files over the Internet, personal jurisdiction is proper. At the opposite end are situations where a defendant has simply posted information on an Internet Web site which is accessible to users in foreign jurisdictions. A passive Web site that does little more than make information available to those who are interested in it is not grounds for the exercise of personal jurisdiction. The middle ground is occupied by interactive Web sites where a user can exchange information with the host computer. In these cases, the exercise of jurisdiction is determined by examining the level of interactivity and commercial nature of the exchange of information that occurs on the Web site." Zippo Manufacturing Co. v. Zippo Dot Com, Inc. (W.D. Pa. 1997) 952 F. Supp. 1119, 1124.

Here, LiVid's Web site merely posts information and has no interactive features. There is no evidence in the record suggesting that the site targeted California. Indeed, there is no evidence that any California resident ever visited, much less downloaded the DeCSS source code from, the LiVid Web site. Thus, Pavlovich's alleged "conduct in . . . posting [a] passive Web site[] on the Internet is not," by itself, "sufficient to subject" him "to jurisdiction in California." "'Creating a site, like placing a product into the stream of commerce, may be felt nationwide — or even worldwide — but, without more, it is not an act purposefully directed toward the forum state.'" (*Cybersell*, quoting Bensusan Restaurant Corp. v. King (S.D.N.Y. 1996) 937 F. Supp. 295, 301, affd. (2d Cir. 1997.) Otherwise, "personal jurisdiction in Internet-related cases would almost always be found in any forum in the country." (GTE New Media Services Inc. v. BellSouth Corp. 199 F.3d 1343, 1350 (D.C. Cir. 2000)) Such a result would "vitiate long-held and inviolate principles of" personal jurisdiction.

Nonetheless, DVD CCA contends posting the misappropriated source code on an Internet Web site is sufficient to establish purposeful availment in this case because Pavlovich knew the posting would harm not only a licensing entity but also the motion picture, computer and consumer electronics industries centered in California. According to DVD CCA, this knowledge establishes that Pavlovich intentionally targeted California and is sufficient to confer jurisdiction under the *Calder* effects test. Although the question is close, we disagree.

As an initial matter, DVD CCA's reliance on Pavlovich's awareness that an entity owned the licensing rights to the CSS technology is misplaced. Although Pavlovich knew about this entity, he did not know that DVD CCA was that entity or that DVD CCA's primary place of business was California until *after* the filing of this lawsuit. . . .

Thus, the only question in this case is whether Pavlovich's knowledge that his tortious conduct may harm certain industries centered in California — i.e., the motion picture, computer, and consumer electronics industries — is sufficient to establish express aiming at California. As explained below, we conclude that this knowledge, by itself, cannot establish purposeful availment under the effects test. . . .

[C]onsider the ramifications of a contrary holding. According to DVD CCA, California should exercise jurisdiction over Pavlovich because he *should have known* that third parties *may* use the misappropriated code to illegally copy movies on DVDs and that licensees of the misappropriated technology resided in California. In other words, DVD CCA is asking this court to exercise jurisdiction over a defendant because he *should have known* that his conduct *may* harm — not a California plaintiff — but industries associated with that plaintiff. . . .

Indeed, such a broad interpretation of the effects test would effectively eliminate the purposeful availment requirement in the intentional tort context for select plaintiffs. . . . For example, any creator or purveyor of technology that enables copying of movies or computer software — including a student in Australia who develops a program for creating backup copies of software and distributes it to some of his classmates or a store owner in Africa who sells a device that makes digital copies of movies on videotape — would be subject to suit in California because they should have known their conduct may harm the motion picture or computer industries in California. . . . Under this logic, plaintiffs connected to the auto industry could sue any defendant in Michigan, plaintiffs connected to the financial industry could sue any defendant in New York, and plaintiffs connected to the potato industry could sue any defendant in Idaho.

Because finding jurisdiction under the facts in this case would effectively subject all intentional tortfeasors whose conduct may harm industries in California to jurisdiction in California, we decline to do so.

We, however, emphasize the narrowness of our decision. A defendant's knowledge that his tortious conduct may harm industries centered in California is undoubtedly relevant to any determination of personal jurisdiction and may support a finding of jurisdiction. We merely hold that this knowledge *alone* is insufficient to establish express aiming at the forum state as required by the effects test. Because the only evidence in the record even suggesting express aiming is Pavlovich's knowledge that his conduct may harm industries centered in California, due process requires us to decline jurisdiction over his person.

In addition, we are not confronted with a situation where the plaintiff has no other forum to pursue its claims and therefore do not address that situation. DVD CCA has the ability and resources to pursue Pavlovich in another forum such as Indiana or Texas. Our decision today does not foreclose it from doing so. Pavlovich may still face the music — just not in California.

III

Accordingly, we reverse the judgment of the Court of Appeal and remand for further proceedings consistent with this opinion.

KENNARD, WERDEGAR and MORENO, JJ concur.

BAXTER, J., joined by GEORGE, C.J. and CHIN J., dissenting

I respectfully dissent. That this case involves a powerful new medium of electronic communication, usable for good or ill, should not blind us to the essential facts and principles. The record indicates that, by intentionally posting an unlicensed decryption code for the Content Scrambling System (CSS) on their Internet Web sites, defendant and his network of "open source" associates sought to undermine and defeat the very purposes of the licensed CSS encryption technology, i.e., *copyright protection* for movies recorded on digital versatile discs (DVDs) and *limitation of playback* to operating systems licensed to unscramble the encryption code. The intended targets of this effort were not individual persons or businesses, but entire industries. Defendant knew at least two of the intended targets — the movie industry and the computer industry involved in producing the licensed playback systems — either were centered in California or maintained a particularly substantial presence here. Thus, the record amply supports the trial court's conclusion, for purposes of specific personal jurisdiction, that defendant's intentional act, even if committed outside California, was "expressly aimed" at California. (See Calder v. Jones).

In the particular circumstances, it cannot matter that defendant may not have known or cared about the *exact identities* or *precise locations* of each individual target, or that he happened to employ a so-called passive Internet Web site, or whether any California resident visited the site. By acting with the broad intent to harm *industries he knew were centered or substantially present in this state,* defendant forged sufficient "minimum contacts" with *California* "that he should reasonably anticipate being haled into court [*here*]" (*World-Wide Volkswagen Corp*) for litigation "'arising out of'" his forum-related conduct. . . .

NOTES AND PROBLEMS

1. The Court split 4 to 3 in this case. Did it reach the right result?

2. The majority opinion focuses on Pavlovich's knowledge that his action would cause damage in California.

a. The premise is that a state has jurisdiction over a defendant who acts in a way that he knows will cause harm in another state. Firing a bullet over a state line supplies a classic example. A less violent example occurred in *Calder* (discussed in the case), in which the defendant newspaper knew that plaintiff lived in California and that, if its defamatory article caused her harm, it would occur there.

b. Suppose that the lawyers for DVD Copy Control located a former classmate of Pavlovich, who will under oath swear that he heard defendant say of his decryption program, "This ought to show those creeps in Silicon Valley that they aren't as smart as they think they are." Would such a statement, if properly in evidence, be enough to lead to a different outcome in this case? Or is there something else that leads the court to deny jurisdiction?

c. In *Calder* the defendant newspaper profited from the scandalous (and allegedly defamatory statements) about the plaintiff. In *Pavlovich* the defendant, although reducing the value of others' intellectual property, did not himself profit. Suppose he had; should the case have come out differently if Pavlovich had sold copies of his decrypting programs?

3. The plaintiff's lawyers were hired by the holders of the intellectual property at stake in this case. Pavlovich was represented pro bono by a lawyer located in Silicon Valley. Pavlovich is not the average pro bono client; why do you suppose his lawyer took on this uncompensated representation?

4. General Jurisdiction

The cases in the previous section all concerned the relationship to the forum state necessary to support specific jurisdiction. For example, *Burger King* holds that Florida had jurisdiction to hear a lawsuit against Mr. Rudzewicz arising out of his dealings with Burger King; the case does not stand for the proposition that Florida could hear a lawsuit brought by Mr. Rudzewicz's Michigan neighbor claiming that his tree roots had clogged the neighbor's drains, or a suit by an Iowa motorist claiming that Rudzewicz had collided with her on a Colorado road.

Under what circumstances will defendant be subject to jurisdiction for all claims — even those without any connection to the forum state? In passing,

International Shoe suggests that at least for U.S. defendants, there will always be a state in which suit may be brought on all claims. For corporations, the state of incorporation will be such a forum; so will the state that is the principal place of business (if different from the state of incorporation). To return to an example used in a previous section, General Motors, incorporated in Delaware and with its principal place of business in Michigan, may be sued in either of those states even for claims unrelated to its activities there. Thus an Oregon automobile owner claiming injuries due to a defectively designed GM vehicle could sue in either Michigan or Delaware. That would be true even if the vehicle had been manufactured at a GM plant in Texas, Mexico, or Germany.

A similar situation holds true for individuals. As already noted, Milliken v. Meyer (supra page 76) stands for the proposition that individuals can be sued in the state of their domicile for all claims. Thus Mr. Rudzewicz could be sued in Michigan for claims arising out of an auto accident that occurred while he was vacationing in Colorado.

The states of domicile (for individuals) and incorporation and principal place of business (for corporations) comprise the easy instances of general jurisdiction, instances where defendants are being sued in what is self-evidently their "base of operations." The language of *International Shoe* and the cases elaborating on it suggest that the principle of general jurisdiction extends further than this, and that, given some absolute level of activity, a defendant may be subject to suit beyond this base of operations.

As a way of framing the next case consider a variation on the facts of Pavlovich v. Superior Court. Suppose that the entity making the "no-copy" codes for DVDs had sent Pavlovich a letter threatening him with legal action if he did not remove his site from the worldwide web. Suppose that Pavlovich had then filed a declaratory judgment suit in a state court in Texas against DVD CCA seeking a declaration that his Web site was lawful. (A declaratory judgment action is a lawsuit in which the plaintiff seeks a declaration of the parties' rights without requesting coercive relief such as damages or an injunction. See infra pp. 285.) Would a Texas court have personal jurisdiction over DVD CCA? Is there a difference between requiring a party to go to another state if it wants to pursue an action as plaintiff, and requiring a party to appear in another state as a defendant? Consider these questions when you read the following case, which is an action for declaratory relief in which the plaintiff loses its bid for specific jurisdiction but is offered a slight hope of holding on to its chosen forum by demonstrating general jurisdiction.

Coastal Video Communications Corp. v. The Staywell Corp.

59 F. Supp. 2d 562 (E.D. Va. 1999)

Rebbeca Beach Smith, District Judge.

This matter comes before the court on the motion of . . . Krames Communications ("Krames"), to dismiss for lack of personal jurisdiction pursuant to Rule 12(b)(2) of the Federal Rules of Civil Procedure and plaintiff's motion seeking discovery on the issue of personal jurisdiction. For the reasons stated below, the plaintiff's motion for discovery is granted, pursuant to the guidelines contained in this opinion, and defendant's motion to dismiss is taken under advisement pending the outcome of the limited discovery granted herein.

I.   *Factual Background*

Plaintiff, Coastal Video Communications . . . ("Coastal"), is a Virginia corporation engaged in the business of producing employee handbooks, video training programs, posters, and interactive CD-ROM courses. Coastal sells these products to companies throughout the United States. One of Coastal's products is an employee handbook titled "Defending Your Safety Zone: Back Protection."

. . . Krames Communications ("Krames"), . . . a Delaware corporation with its principal place of business in California . . . , is in the business of publishing patient education, health promotion, safety, and injury prevention training materials. As part of this effort, Krames publishes "Safety Zone: Using Natural Limits to Protect Your Back," for which it holds U.S. Copyright Registration. . . .

. . . On February 6, 1999, Coastal filed the instant action [in Virginia], seeking a declaration that the handbook, "Defending Your Safety Zone: Back Protection," does not infringe on copyrighted material contained in Krames's "Safety Zone" handbook. On April 8, 1999, the instant motion to dismiss for lack of personal jurisdiction was filed.

. . . Coastal, through . . . affidavits . . . offers the following facts in support of its argument that the court has personal jurisdiction over Krames. None of plaintiff's assertions summarized here are disputed by the defendant.

Krames sells its products to managed care organizations, more than seventy percent of hospitals in the United States, and to more than 100,000 physicians, nurses, and health educators in private practice and hospitals. Krames also sells its products to customers in fifty countries on six continents. Krames has also sold and distributed products in Virginia in the past and currently. Krames mailed product catalogs to individuals in Virginia, as recently as Winter, 1998. Krames has also sent mailings to Virginia residents at their homes and business addresses containing order forms for Krames products and free product samples. According to the Rice Affidavit, Krames also has apparently distributed and sold products to at least three hospitals located in Virginia: Chesapeake General Hospital, Virginia Beach General Hospital, and Sentara Norfolk General Hospital. However, there is no indication in plaintiff's affidavits that Krames's "Safety Zone" publication was ever purchased by any of these hospitals. Furthermore, apart from allegations that the "Defense of the Safety Zone" publication is available for sale through the website and catalog and generic "products" have been sold in Virginia, there is no indication in the affidavits provided by plaintiff that any copies of Krames's "Safety Zone" publication were actually sold in Virginia. Krames is qualified to do business in Virginia and maintains a registered agent in Virginia.

. . . Krames's World Wide Web site advertises over 850 Krames products and allows customers to order products directly over the Web by completing order forms online. The Krames website also provides an "Ask Krames" service by which potential customers may e-mail questions about Krames products and services to the company. Krames offers the "Safety Zone" product over its website. In addition to the Krames site, there is also a separate site for Staywell[, an affiliated company]. Staywell's website states that it is the "premier provider of integrated health improvement and behavior change programs." According to the site, Staywell is the exclusive creator and publisher of American Red Cross health and safety training programs and manuals. These materials are distributed by more than 1,300 local American Red Cross chapters around the country, including, presumably, those located in Virginia. Staywell publishes student course books, instructor training materials, videos, and slides for American Red Cross courses in First Aid, CPR, Aquatics, and mission-related care giving, such as child care, babysitting, and HIV/AIDS.

The website also describes Staywell products in the areas of health risk assessment, focused intervention, disease management, workplace wellness, and newsletter publishing, among others. The site lists a toll-free number to call with inquiries about Staywell products. Visitors to the site may download a free demonstration of a Staywell/Krames on-line "On Demand Patient Education Program." The Staywell site also lists job opportunities available with the company, and permits interested individuals to send a resume to the company over the Internet, as well as provides an e-mail address and fax number to contact the company concerning employment opportunities.

II. Discussion

Federal Rule of Civil Procedure 12(b)(2) permits dismissal of an action lacking the requisite personal jurisdiction. . . . The plaintiff bears the burden of demonstrating personal jurisdiction by a preponderance of the evidence once its existence is questioned by the defendant. Resolution of the jurisdictional issue is a matter for the court. . . .

A. Specific Jurisdiction

In arguing that the court has specific, personal jurisdiction over Krames, Coastal claims the case is controlled by Virginia's long-arm statute, which states "[a] court may exercise personal jurisdiction over a person, who acts directly or by an agent, as to a cause of action arising from the person's . . . [t]ransacting any business in this Commonwealth[.]" Va. Code Ann. §8.01-328.1 (Michie 1992). . . .

Plaintiff argues the sale of defendant's "Safety Zone" publication in Virginia constitutes "transacting business" and that the declaratory judgment action arises from these transactions. . . .

Even if plaintiff was able to demonstrate that defendant sold the "Safety Zone" publication in Virginia, the court would still not have specific, personal jurisdiction over defendant because the declaratory judgment action currently before the court does not "arise from" the sale of defendant's publication. . . .

B. General Jurisdiction

The lack of specific jurisdiction, however, does not end the inquiry. Even though the present action does not "arise from" defendant's in-state sales of "Safety Zone," the court may still exercise personal jurisdiction over a defendant if it has "general jurisdiction," in which the requisite "minimum contacts" between the defendant and the forum state are "fairly extensive." . . . Only when the "continuous corporate operation within a state [is] thought so substantial and of such a nature as to justify suit against it on causes of action arising from dealings entirely distinct from those activities" may a court assert general jurisdiction over a corporate defendant. [*International Shoe*]

The facts of this case, however, present the court with difficulties in applying traditional general jurisdiction principles. . . . [I]n the instant case, it is undisputed that the Krames/Staywell websites went well beyond mere advertising and solicitation of products. The sites allow the on-line visitor to purchase all of Krames's products through the website, without ever speaking to a Krames representative. In addition, if a customer did have questions, the site also provides a mechanism for those questions to be posed and answered through an exchange of e-mail. In essence, Krames/Staywell has established an on-line storefront that is readily accessible to every person in Virginia with a computer, a modem, and access to the World Wide Web. Thus, instead of using physical assets such as sample-bearing salesmen, or traditional business offices to reach their Virginia-based hospital, Red Cross, and health care provider customers, Krames is able to provide the same level of service via the Internet's instant connections. . . .

One of the few cases to exercise general personal jurisdiction over a defendant grounded, in substantial part, on the Internet-based contacts with the forum state was *Mieczkowski*[,] a products liability action brought against the North Carolina manufacturer of a bunk bed owned by the Texas plaintiffs. . . . The plaintiffs presented evidence that over the previous six years defendant sold and shipped $5.7 million in products to Texas residents; consummated 250 business transactions totaling $717,000 in the year prior to the filing of the lawsuit; and, received 3.2 percent of its gross sales income from Texas residents in the previous four years. The district court also found it significant that defendant maintained a World Wide Web site accessible to over two million Texas residents. In *Mieczkowski*, the defendant's website provided categories of furniture and allowed a visitor to the site to view individual furniture pieces. A visitor to the site could print an order form to complete their purchase after reviewing their selections on-line. In addition, customers could check the status of their order through the Internet site as well. Finally, visitors to the site could communicate directly with defendant's on-line sales representatives via e-mail. . . .

Superficially, the facts in *Mieczkowski* are very analogous to those of the present case. As in *Mieczkowski*, defendant in this case maintains a World Wide Web site with a high degree of interactivity. In addition, it also appears from the record that defendant maintains traditional business contacts with Virginia through its product sales to at least three Virginia hospitals. However, it appears that the record before the district court in Texas was much more developed, especially with regard to the traditional business contacts. . . .

. . . As with traditional business contacts, the most reliable indicator of the nature and extent of defendant's Internet contact with the forum state will be the amount of sales generated in the state by or through the interactive website. In addition, it may also be possible to determine how many times a website has been accessed by residents or businesses located in a specific state. Such information, if available, would also be relevant to the determination of general personal jurisdiction. . . .

Given the significant gaps in the record as to the nature and extent of both defendant's traditional business contacts with Virginia and also defendant's Internet-based contacts with Virginia, information that is uniquely in the control of the defendant, the court grants plaintiff's motion for discovery on the issue of general personal jurisdiction over the defendant. In accordance with the principles contained in this opinion, plaintiff is directed to seek discovery of information relevant to the issue of the court's general personal jurisdiction over defendant within fifteen (15) days of the date of this order. Within seventy-five (75) days of the date of this order, the parties are directed to set a hearing with the calendar clerk on defendant's motion to dismiss. . . .

It is so ordered.

NOTES AND PROBLEMS

1. Consider the suit as a bit of jurisdictional strategy:

a. In what states would there have been unquestioned jurisdiction over Krames?

b. Why do you suppose Coastal chose Virginia instead?

c. Why do you think Coastal chose to file a declaratory relief action against Krames/Staywell rather than just wait for Krames/Staywell to sue? Should the fact that Coastal has brought a declaratory relief action when it is arguably a "defendant" in the underlying dispute have an impact on the analysis of personal jurisdiction?

d. Did Coastal win or lose its gamble?

2. What facts will Coastal's lawyer hope to uncover in the sixty days of discovery allowed by the judge?

a. Suppose Coastal can show that Krames/Staywell do about $500,000 worth of business annually in Virginia, from a combination of catalog and Internet sales; this business amounts to about 3 percent of the defendants' annual sales. Jurisdiction?

b. Does the following excerpt from an appellate opinion in a case where a plaintiff succeeded in convincing the court that general jurisdiction existed help or harm Coastal?

Given the high standard the Ninth Circuit has set, the presence of general jurisdiction in the instant case is a close question. Admittedly, L.L. Bean has few of the factors traditionally associated with physical presence, such as an official agent or incorporation. Nevertheless, we find that there is general jurisdiction in light of L.L. Bean's extensive marketing and sales in California [amounting to about 6 percent of its total sales], its extensive contacts with California vendors, and the fact that, as alleged by Gator, its website is clearly and deliberately structured to operate as a sophisticated virtual store in California.

First, L.L. Bean's overall commercial contacts with California meet the continuous and systematic contacts test applied in *Davies, Bancroft* and *Helicopteros* . . . : it makes sales, solicits business in the state, and serves the state's markets. In addition, unlike the defendant in *Bancroft*, Gator alleges that L.L. Bean "targets" its electronic advertising at California and maintains a highly interactive, as opposed to "passive," website from which very large numbers of California consumers regularly make purchases and interact with L.L. Bean sales representatives. Unlike the defendant in *Helicopteros*, L.L. Bean has not merely made a single "package" purchase from a forum vendor or cashed a check on a forum bank; instead, it ships very large numbers of products to California and maintains ongoing contacts with numerous California vendors. Nor are any of L.L. Bean's contacts occasional or infrequent. L.L. Bean's contacts are part of a consistent, ongoing, and sophisticated sales effort that has included California for a number of years.

In short, even under the heightened standard applied to general jurisdiction, the "consistent and substantial pattern of business relations" represented by these facts is sufficient to confer general jurisdiction. There is nothing "random, fortuitous, or attenuated" about subjecting L.L. Bean to the authority of the court as L.L. Bean has deliberately and purposefully availed itself, on a very large scale, of the benefits of doing business within the state. Second, even if the only contacts L.L. Bean had with California were through its virtual store, a finding of general jurisdiction in the instant case would be consistent with the "sliding scale" test that both our own and other circuits have applied to internet-based companies. This test requires both that the party in question "clearly [do] business over the Internet," *Zippo Mfg. Co. v. Zippo Dot Com, Inc.*, 952 F. Supp. 1119, 1124 (W.D. Pa. 1997), and that the internet business contacts with the forum state be substantial or continuous and systematic. Recognizing that an online store can operate as the functional equivalent of a physical store, the test does not require an actual presence in the state. Rather, the nature of the commercial activity must be of a substantial enough nature that it "approximate[s] physical presence."

Applying this test, the District of Columbia Circuit recently found general jurisdiction after finding that a defendant online brokerage firm was "through its website . . . doing business in the District of Columbia" where customers could use the website to open accounts, transmit funds to those accounts electronically, use the accounts to buy and sell securities, and enter into binding contracts with the defendant. . . . The Fourth Circuit has also adopted the "sliding scale" test without explicitly applying it in the general jurisdiction context, noting that "something more" than systematic transmission of electronic signals would be required in order to assert general jurisdiction.

Under the sliding-scale analysis, L.L. Bean's contacts with California are sufficient to confer general jurisdiction. L.L. Bean's website is highly interactive and very extensive: L.L. Bean "clearly does business over the Internet." Moreover, millions of dollars in sales, driven by an extensive, ongoing, and sophisticated sales effort involving very large numbers of direct email solicitations and millions of catalog sales, qualifies as "substantial" or "continuous and systematic" commercial activity. . . .

Even if there are sufficient contacts to support general jurisdiction in a particular case, it is still limited by a reasonableness analysis. The reasonableness test set out by *Amoco* is the same as the test for reasonableness in the specific jurisdiction context, requiring an analysis of seven factors:

[T]he extent of purposeful interjection, the burden on the defendant to defend the suit in the chosen forum, the extent of conflict with the sovereignty of the defendant's state, the forum state's interest in the dispute; the most efficient forum for judicial resolution of the dispute; the importance of the chosen forum to the plaintiff's interest in convenient and effective relief; and the existence of an alternative forum.

[The court found the assertion of jurisdiction by California reasonable.]

Gator.com Corp. v. L.L. Bean, Inc. 341 F.3d 1072, 1078-1080 (9th Cir. 2003).

3. As a quick review, explain briefly why Coastal Video was not subject to jurisdiction on a specific jurisdiction theory: after all, it unquestionably did some business in Virginia.

4. What will it mean if after additional discovery the court rules that Krames is subject to general jurisdiction?

a. Obviously it will mean that Coastal can pursue in Virginia its contention that it is not infringing Krames's copyright.

b. In theory, it also means that any plaintiff with any claim could sue Krames in Virginia. For example, if there is general jurisdiction in Virginia, a former employee of Krames, which, you'll recall, has its principal place of business in California, could sue in Virginia for wrongful discharge. Or an end user of Krames's educational materials in North Dakota could sue in Virginia on allegations that the instructions for heavy lifting were medically inappropriate and caused him to injure his back. Does that sound intuitively like the right result? Or is it the right result only if Krames does a very high volume of business in Virginia?

5. *Coastal Video* wrestles with applying general jurisdiction to a corporation. For persons general jurisdiction also exists in the place of their permanent residence. Does it also exist wherever they happen to be momentarily present? That appeared to be the rule in *Pennoyer* and in Milliken v. Meyer, supra; does it still hold true?

Burnham v. Superior Court

495 U.S. 604 (1990)

Justice SCALIA announced the judgment of the Court and delivered an opinion in which the CHIEF JUSTICE and Justice KENNEDY joined, and in which Justice WHITE joined as to Parts I, II-A, II-B, and II-C.

The question presented is whether the Due Process Clause of the Fourteenth Amendment denies California courts jurisdiction over a nonresident, who was personally served with process while temporarily in that State, in a suit unrelated to his activities in the State.

[handwritten: 1. Served while in state 2. Temporarily in state 3. Unrelated to activities]

I

Petitioner Dennis Burnham married Francie Burnham in 1976, in West Virginia. In 1977 the couple moved to New Jersey, where their two children were born. In July 1987 the Burnhams decided to separate. They agreed that Mrs. Burnham, who intended to move to California, would take custody of the children. Shortly before Mrs. Burnham departed for California that same month, she and petitioner agreed that she would file for divorce on grounds of "irreconcilable differences."

In October 1987, petitioner filed for divorce in New Jersey state court on grounds of "desertion." Petitioner did not, however, obtain an issuance of summons against his wife, and did not attempt to serve her with process. Mrs. Burnham, after unsuccessfully demanding that petitioner adhere to their prior agreement to submit to an "irreconcilable differences" divorce, brought suit for divorce in California state court in early January 1988.

In late January, petitioner visited southern California on business, after which *[handwritten: Visits CA on business & to visit Children]* he went north to visit his children in the San Francisco Bay area, where his wife resided. He took the older child to San Francisco for the weekend. Upon returning the child to Mrs. Burnham's home on January 24, 1988, petitioner was served with a California court summons and a copy of Mrs. Burnham's divorce petition. He then returned to New Jersey.

Later that year, petitioner made a special appearance in the California Superior Court, moving to quash the service of process on the ground that the court lacked personal jurisdiction over him because his only contacts with California were a few short visits to the State for the purpose of conducting business and visiting his children. The Superior Court denied the motion, and the *[handwritten: CA cts say there is PJ]* California Court of Appeal denied mandamus relief, rejecting petitioner's contention that the Due Process Clause prohibited California courts from asserting jurisdiction over him because he lacked "minimum contacts" with the State. The court held it to be "a valid jurisdictional predicate for in personam jurisdiction" that the "defendant [was] present in the forum state and personally served with process." We granted certiorari.

II

A

. . . To determine whether the assertion of personal jurisdiction is consistent with due process, we have long relied on the principles traditionally followed by American courts in making out the territorial limits of each State's authority. That criterion was first announced in Pennoyer v. Neff, in which we stated that due process "mean[s] a course of legal proceedings according to those rules and principles which have been established in our systems of jurisprudence for the protection and enforcement of private rights," including the "well-established principles of public law respecting the jurisdiction of an independent State over persons and property." In what has become the classic expression of the criterion, we said in International Shoe Co. v. Washington, 326 U.S. 310 (1945), that a State Court's assertion of personal jurisdiction satisfies the Due Process Clause if it does not violate "'traditional notions of fair play and substantial justice'" [quoting Milliken v. Meyer]. Since *International Shoe*, we have only been called upon to decide whether these "traditional notions" permit States to exercise jurisdiction over absent defendants in a manner that deviates from the rules of jurisdiction applied in the 19th century. We have held such deviations permissible, but only with respect to suits arising out of the absent defendant's contacts with the State.[1] The question we must decide today is whether due process requires a similar connection between the litigation and the defendant's contacts with the State in cases where the defendant is physically present in the State at the time process is served upon him.

B

Among the most firmly established principles of personal jurisdiction in American tradition is that the courts of a State have jurisdiction over nonresidents who are physically present in the State. The view developed early that each State had the power to hale before its courts any individual who could be found within its borders, and that once having acquired jurisdiction over such a person by properly serving him with process, the State could retain jurisdiction to enter judgment against him, no matter how fleeting his visit. See, e.g., Potter v. Allin, 2 Root 63, 67 (Conn. 1793); Barrell v. Benjamin, 15 Mass. 354 (1819). That view had antecedents in English common-law practice, which sometimes allowed "transitory" actions, arising out of events outside the country, to be maintained against seemingly nonresident defendants who were present in England. . . .

Recent scholarship has suggested that English tradition was not as clear [as Supreme Court Justice and treatise writer Joseph Story thought it was.] . . . Accurate or not, however, judging by the evidence of contemporaneous . . . decisions, one must conclude that Story's understanding was shared by American courts at the crucial time for present purposes: 1868, when the Fourteenth Amendment was adopted.

---

1. We have said that "[e]ven when the cause of action does not arise out of or relate to the foreign corporation's activities in the forum state, due process is not offended by a State's subjecting the corporation to its *in personam* jurisdiction when there are sufficient contacts between the state and the foreign corporation." Helicopteros Nacionales de Colombia v. Hall, 466 U.S. at 414. Our only holding supporting that statement, however, involved "regular service of summons upon [the corporation's] president while he was in [the forum state] acting in that capacity." See Perkins v. Benguet Consolidated Mining Co., 342 U.S. 437 (1952). It may be that whatever special rule exists permitting "continuous and systematic" contacts . . . to support jurisdiction with respect to matters unrelated to activity in the forum, applies *only* to corporations, which have never fitted comfortably within a jurisdictional regime based primarily upon "de facto power over the defendant's person." *International Shoe*. . . . We express no views on these matters — and, for simplicity's sake, omit reference to this aspect of "contacts"-based jurisdiction in our discussion.

C

Despite this formidable body of precedent, petitioner contends, in reliance on our decisions applying the *International Shoe* standard, that in the absence of "continuous and systematic" contacts with the forum, see note 1, supra, a nonresident defendant can be subjected to judgment only as to matters that arise out of or relate to his contacts with the forum. This argument rests on a thorough misunderstanding of our cases. . . .

[Cases following *International Shoe* upheld jurisdiction over defendants who were *not* present in the forum state.]

Nothing in *International Shoe* or the cases that have followed it, however, offers support for the very different proposition petitioner seeks to establish today: that a defendant's presence in the forum is not only unnecessary to validate novel, nontraditional assertions of jurisdiction, but is itself no longer sufficient to establish jurisdiction. . . .

The short of the matter is that jurisdiction based on physical presence alone constitutes due process because it is one of the continuing traditions of our legal system that define the due process standard of "traditional notions of fair play and substantial justice." That standard was developed by analogy to "physical presence," and it would be perverse to say it could now be turned against that touchstone of jurisdiction.

D

Petitioner's strongest argument, though we ultimately reject it, relies upon our decision in Shaffer v. Heitner.

It goes too far to say, as petitioner contends, that *Shaffer* compels the conclusion that a State lacks jurisdiction over an individual unless the litigation arises out of his activities in the State. *Shaffer*, like *International Shoe*, involved jurisdiction over an absent defendant, and it stands for nothing more than the proposition that when the "minimum contact" that is a substitute for physical presence consists of property ownership it must, like other minimum contacts, be related to the litigation. Petitioner wrenches out of its context our statement in *Shaffer* that "all assertions of state-court jurisdiction must be evaluated according to the standards set forth in *International Shoe* and its progeny." 433 U.S., at 212. When read together with the two sentences that preceded it, the meaning of this statement becomes clear:

> The fiction that an assertion of jurisdiction over property is anything but an assertion of jurisdiction over the owner of the property supports an ancient form without substantial modern justification. Its continued acceptance would serve only to allow state-court jurisdiction that is fundamentally unfair to the defendant.
>
> "We *therefore conclude* that all assertions of state-court jurisdiction must be evaluated according to the standards set forth in *International Shoe* and its progeny." Ibid. (emphasis added).

Shaffer was saying, in other words, not that all bases for the assertion of in personam jurisdiction (including, presumably, in-state service) must be treated alike and subjected to the "minimum contacts" analysis of *International Shoe*;

but rather that quasi in rem jurisdiction, that fictional "ancient form," and in personam jurisdiction, are really one and the same and must be treated alike — leading to the conclusion that quasi in rem jurisdiction, i.e., that form of in personam jurisdiction based upon a "property ownership" contact and by definition unaccompanied by personal, in-state service, must satisfy the litigation-relatedness requirement of *International Shoe*. . . . *International Shoe* confined its "minimum contacts" requirement to situations in which the defendant "be not present within the territory of the forum," and nothing in *Shaffer* expands that requirement beyond that.

It is fair to say, however, that while our holding today does not contradict *Shaffer*, our basic approach to the due process question is different. . . . While in no way receding from or casting doubt upon the holding of *Shaffer* or any other case, we reaffirm today our time-honored approach. For new procedures, hitherto unknown, the Due Process Clause requires analysis to determine whether "traditional notions of fair play and substantial justice" have been offended. *International Shoe*. But a doctrine of personal jurisdiction that dates back to the adoption of the Fourteenth Amendment and is still generally observed unquestionably meets that standard. . . .

III

A few words in response to Justice Brennan's opinion concurring in the judgment. . . .

The subjectivity, and hence inadequacy, of [Justice Brennan's] approach becomes apparent when the concurrence tries to explain why the assertion of jurisdiction in the present case meets its standard. . . . Justice Brennan lists the "benefits" Mr. Burnham derived from the State of California — the fact that, during the few days he was there, "[h]is health and safety [were] guaranteed by the State's police, fire, and emergency medical services; he [was] free to travel on the State's roads and waterways; he likely enjoy[ed] the fruits of the State's economy." Three days' worth of these benefits strike us as powerfully inadequate to establish, as an abstract matter, that it is "fair" for California to decree the ownership of all Mr. Burnham's worldly goods acquired during the 10 years of his marriage, and the custody over his children. We daresay a contractual exchange swapping those benefits for that power would not survive the "unconscionability" provision of the Uniform Commercial Code. . . .

Suppose . . . that a defendant in Mr. Burnham's situation enjoys not three days' worth of California's "benefits," but 15 minutes' worth. Or suppose we remove one of those "benefits" — "enjoy[ment of] the fruits of the State's economy" — by positing that Mr. Burnham had not come to California on business, but only to visit his children. . . .

. . . What if Mr. Burnham were visiting a sick child? Or a dying child? Cf. *Kulko v. Superior Court of California, City and County of San Francisco*, 436 U.S. 84, 93 (1978) (finding the exercise of long-arm jurisdiction over an absent parent unreasonable because it would "discourage parents from entering into reasonable visitation agreements"). . . .

The difference between us and Justice Brennan has nothing to do with whether "further progress [is] to be made" in the "evolution of our legal system." It has to do with whether changes are to be adopted as progressive by the American people or decreed as progressive by the Justices of this Court. . . .

[Justice WHITE'S concurrence is omitted.]

Justice BRENNAN, with whom Justice MARSHALL, Justice BLACKMUN, and Justice O'CONNOR join, concurring in the judgment.

I agree with Justice Scalia that the Due Process Clause of the Fourteenth Amendment generally permits a state court to exercise jurisdiction over a defendant if he is served with process while voluntarily present in the forum State.[1] I do not perceive the need, however, to decide that a jurisdictional rule that "'has been immemorially the actual law of the land,'" quoting Hurtado v. California, 110 U.S. 516, 528 (1884), automatically comports with due process simply by virtue of its "pedigree." Although I agree that history is an important factor in establishing whether a jurisdictional rule satisfies due process requirements, I cannot agree that it is the only factor such that all traditional rules of jurisdiction are, ipso facto, forever constitutional. Unlike Justice Scalia, I would undertake an "independent inquiry into the . . . fairness of the prevailing in-state service rule." I therefore concur in the judgment.

I

I believe that the approach adopted by Justice Scalia's opinion today — reliance solely on historical pedigree — is foreclosed by our decisions in International Shoe Co. v. Washington, 326 U.S. 310 (1945), and Shaffer v. Heitner, 433 U.S. 186 (1977). . . . In *Shaffer*, we stated that "all assertions of state-court jurisdiction must be evaluated according to the standards set forth in *International Shoe* and its progeny." 433 U.S. at 212 (emphasis added). The critical insight of *Shaffer* is that all rules of jurisdiction, even ancient ones, must satisfy contemporary notions of due process. . . .

II

. . . Tradition, though alone not dispositive, is of course relevant to the question. . . .

. . . [T]he historical background [is] relevant because, however murky the jurisprudential origins of transient jurisdiction, the fact that American courts have announced the rule for perhaps a century (first in dicta, more recently in holdings) provides a defendant voluntarily present in a particular State *today* "clear notice that [he] is subject to suit" in the forum. Regardless of whether Justice Story's account of the rule's genesis is mythical, our common understanding now, fortified by a century of judicial practice, is that jurisdiction is often a function of

---

1. I use the term "transient jurisdiction" to refer to jurisdiction premised solely on the fact that a person is served with process while physically present in the forum State.

geography. The transient rule is consistent with reasonable expectations and is entitled to a strong presumption that it comports with due process. . . . "If I visit another State, . . . I knowingly assume some risk that the State will exercise its power over my property or my person while there. My contact with the State, though minimal, gives rise to predictable risks." *Shaffer*, 433 U.S., at 218 (Stevens, J., concurring in judgment). . . . [11]

By visiting the forum State, a transient defendant actually "avail[s]" himself of significant benefits provided by the State. His health and safety are guaranteed by the State's police, fire, and emergency medical services; he is free to travel on the State's roads and waterways; he likely enjoys the fruits of the State's economy as well. Moreover, the Privileges and Immunities Clause of Article IV prevents a state government from discriminating against a transient defendant by denying him the protections of its law or the right of access to its courts. . . . Without transient jurisdiction, an asymmetry would arise: a transient would have the full benefit of the power of the forum State's courts as a plaintiff while retaining immunity from their authority as a defendant.

The potential burdens on a transient defendant are slight. "'[M]odern transportation and communications have made it much less burdensome for a party sued to defend himself'" in a State outside his place of residence. *Burger King*, 471 U.S. at 474, quoting McGee v. International Life Insurance Co. That the defendant has already journeyed at least once before to the forum—as evidenced by the fact that he was served with process there—is an indication that suit in the forum likely would not be prohibitively inconvenient. . . .

In this case, it is undisputed that petitioner was served with process while voluntarily and knowingly in the State of California. I therefore concur in the judgment.

Justice STEVENS, concurring in the judgment.

As I explained in my separate writing, I did not join the Court's opinion in Shaffer v. Heitner because I was concerned by its unnecessarily broad reach. The same concern prevents me from joining either Justice Scalia's or Justice Brennan's opinion in this case. For me, it is sufficient to note that the historical evidence and consensus identified by Justice Scalia, the considerations of fairness identified by Justice Brennan, and the common sense displayed by Justice White, all combine to demonstrate that this is, indeed, a very easy case.[*]

NOTES AND PROBLEMS

1. As in *Asahi*, the Court in *Burnham* is unanimous as to the result but cannot agree as to why its members reach that result.

---

11. As the Restatement suggests, there may be cases in which a defendant's involuntary or unknowing presence in a State does not support the exercise of personal jurisdiction over him. The facts of the instant case do not require us to determine the outer limits of the transient jurisdiction rule.

[*] Perhaps the adage about hard cases making bad law should be revised to cover easy cases.

a. Should they have agreed about the result? Justice Stevens characterizes *Burnham* as an easy case; was it? Which Justice's views could you most easily turn into a dissent?

b. Perhaps the answer to the preceding question turns on how broadly one reads *Burnham*: as a marital property case or a case applicable to all settings. If one limits *Burnham* to its domestic relations context, it begins to look easy. After all, there are only two possible states that could take jurisdiction (New Jersey, where the husband lives, and California, where the wife lives); isn't one as reasonable as the other? Moreover, Mr. Burnham, having allegedly reneged on his pre-separation agreement to divide marital property equally with Mrs. Burnham, was not a particularly sympathetic litigant.

c. But nothing in the opinion suggests such a limitation. Read broadly, it revives "tag" jurisdiction, in which mere presence and service with process conclusively establishes jurisdiction. Is that a good rule?

2. Could Mr. Burnham (or his lawyer) have avoided this outcome?

a. Recall that Mr. Burnham had filed a divorce action in New Jersey, but he had not served Mrs. Burnham. If he had done so — and divorce and marital property litigation was under way in another state — California courts would not have proceeded with the action. Could New Jersey have acquired jurisdiction over the absent Mrs. Burnham based on the substantial duration of the marriage and location of at least some of the marital property in that state?

b. The Uniform Interstate Family Support Act, now mandatory in all states by virtue of federal law, seeks to establish guidelines for jurisidiction over child and marital property litigation. The Act, of course, cannot establish jurisdiction on an unconstitutional basis, but one could argue that a court facing a due process claim under this Act should be cognizant of the kinds of mess, represented by *Burnham* into which matters fall if unregulated by statutory guidelines.

3. *Burnham* concerns an individual defendant.

a. What if a registered agent of a corporation were served with process, the corporation having no other contacts with the state? Siemer v. Learjet Acquisition Corp., 966 F.2d 179 (5th Cir. 1992), cert. denied, 506 U.S. 1080 (1993) (*Burnham* not applicable to corporate defendants).

b. Is it fair to subject the casual visitor to general jurisdiction but not the corporation that does unrelated business in the state?

4. *Burnham* suggests that the courts applying its principles will need to confront an issue that arose regularly under the regime of *Pennoyer*: When does service of process obtained by force or fraud confer jurisdiction? Consider the following examples.

a. If the defendant were kidnapped, brought across state borders, served with process, and then released, would that establish jurisdiction? A number of cases assert that under such conditions service of process did not establish jurisdiction, although the situation seems to have arisen so infrequently in civil suits that it is difficult to locate a holding on point.

b. What would have happened if Mrs. Burnham had called Mr. Burnham and falsely told him one of the children was seriously ill, and, when he arrived to visit the "sick" child, had served him with process? On analogous facts the court in

Wyman v. Newhouse, 93 F.2d 313 (2d Cir.), cert. denied, 303 U.S. 664 (1937), held that the court lacked personal jurisdiction. See also Voice Systems Marketing Co. v. Appropriate Technology Corp., 153 F.R.D. 117 (E.D. Mich. 1994) (called to state to resolve customer problems, defendant was asked to extend stay for a day for a "meeting," at which he was served with process; service quashed).

c. What would be the result if the defendant were present in the state to participate in court proceedings, whether as a lawyer, a party, a witness, or a criminal defendant? By and large U.S. courts have given witnesses immunity from service of process. They have wavered on parties to civil actions (some courts granting immunity to nonresident defendants but not to nonresident plaintiffs) and on criminal defendants (some courts distinguishing between the defendants who voluntarily surrender and those who are extradited). See James, Hazard, and Leubsdorf §2.15.

d. Is the necessity to work out rules in such cases an argument against reverting to the rule of *Pennoyer*? Or is the clarity of the rule sufficient to outweigh the occasional attempted abuse?

C.   Consent as a Substitute for Power

Recall *Pennoyer*'s indication that either power or consent could establish jurisdiction. That proposition remains true today: A defendant may, either at the outset of the lawsuit itself or before it, consent to jurisdiction in a forum. But the significance of consent as a basis for jurisdiction long remained buried. Before *International Shoe* the cases that spoke of consent often referred to consent implied from presence, or from what modern jurisdictional analysis would refer to as contacts. Such contacts can provide a perfectly adequate basis for jurisdiction, but they are not consent in any strong sense of the word. Since *International Shoe* recharacterized implied consent cases in terms of contacts, it has once again become possible to focus on what one might call "real" consent, a specific agreement to submit to jurisdiction.

The starting point is National Equipment Rental v. Szukhent, 375 U.S. 311 (1964). The Szukhents, Michigan farmers, leased farm equipment from a New York concern. On the back of the lease form was a clause saying that the Szukhents "designate[ ] Florence Weinberg [at a New York City address] as agent for the purpose of accepting service of process." When the Szukhents defaulted on the lease, plaintiff sued in New York, serving process on Ms. Weinberg (who notified defendants of the suit), and basing jurisdiction on such service. The Supreme Court upheld this procedure, treating the quoted clause as consent to personal jurisdiction and holding that under the circumstances the clause did not violate due process.

In *National Equipment Rental* the parties manipulated jurisdictional rules contractually, the Szukhents consenting to a New York jurisdiction that would not likely have existed without that clause. Notice, however, that the clause in

National Equipment Rental permitted, but did not require, suit to be brought in New York; so far as the contract was concerned, the Szukhents could have sued National Equipment Rental in Michigan. The next case takes matters further. (A word about substantive background may ease understanding: Federal courts have jurisdiction over admiralty matters, which include the interpretation of contracts calling for carriage of passengers by sea.)

Carnival Cruise Lines, Inc. v. Shute

499 U.S. 585 (1991)

Justice BLACKMUN delivered the opinion of the Court.

In this admiralty case we primarily consider whether the United States Court of Appeals for the Ninth Circuit correctly refused to enforce a forum-selection clause contained in tickets issued by petitioner Carnival Cruise Lines, Inc., to respondents Eulala and Russel Shute.

I

The Shutes, through an Arlington, Wash., travel agent, purchased passage for a 7-day cruise on petitioner's ship, the Tropicale. Respondents paid the fare to the agent who forwarded the payment to petitioner's headquarters in Miami, Fla. Petitioner then prepared the tickets and sent them to respondents in the State of Washington. The face of each ticket, at its left-hand lower corner, contained this admonition: "SUBJECT TO CONDITIONS OF CONTRACT ON LAST PAGES IMPORTANT! PLEASE READ CONTRACT — ON LAST PAGES 1, 2, 3."

The following appeared on "contract page 1" of each ticket:

Terms and Conditions of Passage Contract Ticket. . . .

3. (a) The acceptance of this ticket by the person or persons named hereon as passengers shall be deemed to be an acceptance and agreement by each of them of all of the terms and conditions of this Passage Contract Ticket. . . .

8. It is agreed by and between the passenger and the Carrier that all disputes and matters whatsoever arising under, in connection with or incident to this Contract shall be litigated, if at all, in and before a Court located in the State of Florida, U.S.A., to the exclusion of the Courts of any other state or country.

The last quoted paragraph is the forum-selection clause at issue.

II

Respondents boarded the Tropicale in Los Angeles, Cal. The ship sailed to Puerto Vallarta, Mexico, and then returned to Los Angeles. While the ship was in international waters off the Mexican coast, respondent Eulala Shute was injured when she slipped on a deck mat during a guided tour of the ship's galley. Respondents filed suit against petitioner in the United States District Court for the Western District of Washington, claiming that Mrs. Shute's injuries had been caused by the negligence of Carnival Cruise Lines and its employees.

Petitioner moved for summary judgment, contending that the forum clause in respondents' tickets required the Shutes to bring their suit against petitioner in a court in the State of Florida. . . .

III

We begin by noting the boundaries of our inquiry. First, this is a case in admiralty, and federal law governs the enforceability of the forum-selection clause we scrutinize. Second, we do not address the question whether respondents had sufficient notice of the forum clause before entering the contract for passage. Respondents essentially have conceded that they had notice of the forum-selection provision. Brief for Respondents 26 ("The respondents do not contest the incorporation of the provisions nor [sic] that the forum selection clause was reasonably communicated to the respondents, as much as three pages of fine print can be communicated."). . . .

Within this context, respondents urge that the forum clause should not be enforced because, contrary to this Court's teachings in *The Bremen* [v. Zapata Off-Shore Co., 407 U.S. 1 (1972)], the clause was not the product of negotiation, and enforcement effectively would deprive respondents of their day in court. . . .

IV

A

. . . [R]espondents' passage contract was purely routine and doubtless nearly identical to every commercial passage contract issued by petitioner and most other cruise lines. In this context, it would be entirely unreasonable for us to assume that respondents — or any other cruise passenger — would negotiate with petitioner the terms of a forum-selection clause in an ordinary commercial cruise ticket. Common sense dictates that a ticket of this kind will be a form contract the terms of which are not subject to negotiation, and that an individual purchasing the ticket will not have bargaining parity with the cruise line. . . .

Including a reasonable forum clause in a form contract of this kind well may be permissible for several reasons: First, a cruise line has a special interest in limiting the fora in which it potentially could be subject to suit. Because a cruise ship typically carries passengers from many locales, it is not unlikely that a mishap on a cruise could subject the cruise line to litigation in several different fora. Additionally, a clause establishing ex ante the forum for dispute resolution has the salutary effect of dispelling any confusion about where suits arising from the contract must be brought and defended, sparing litigants the time and expense of pretrial motions to determine the correct forum and conserving judicial resources that otherwise would be devoted to deciding those motions. Finally, it stands to reason that passengers who purchase tickets containing a forum clause like that at issue in this case benefit in the form of reduced fares reflecting the savings that the cruise line enjoys by limiting the fora in which it may be sued. . . .

It bears emphasis that forum-selection clauses contained in form passage contracts are subject to judicial scrutiny for fundamental fairness. In this case, there is no indication that petitioner set Florida as the forum in which disputes were to be resolved as a means of discouraging cruise passengers from pursuing legitimate claims. Any suggestion of such a bad-faith motive is belied by two facts: Petitioner has its principal place of business in Florida, and many of its cruises depart from and return to Florida ports. Similarly, there is no evidence that petitioner obtained respondents' accession to the forum clause by fraud or overreaching. Finally, respondents have conceded that they were given notice of the forum provision and, therefore, presumably retained the option of rejecting the contract with impunity. In the case before us, therefore, we conclude that the Court of Appeals erred in refusing to enforce the forum-selection clause. . . .

[handwritten margin note: No evidence of unfairness]

Justice STEVENS, with whom Justice MARSHALL joins, dissenting. . . .

Forum-selection clauses in passenger tickets involve the intersection of two strands of traditional contract law that qualify the general rule that courts will enforce the terms of a contract as written. Pursuant to the first strand, courts traditionally have reviewed with heightened scrutiny the terms of contracts of adhesion, form contracts offered on a take-or-leave basis by a party with stronger bargaining power to a party with weaker power. Some commentators have questioned whether contracts of adhesion can justifiably be enforced at all under traditional contract theory because the adhering party generally enters into them without manifesting knowing and voluntary consent to all their terms. . . .

The second doctrinal principle implicated by forum-selection clauses is the traditional rule that "contractual provisions, which seek to limit the place or court in which an action may . . . be brought, are invalid as contrary to public policy." Although adherence to this general rule has declined in recent years, particularly following our decision in The Bremen v. Zapata Off-Shore Co., 407 U.S. 1 (1972), the prevailing rule is still that forum-selection clauses are not enforceable if they were not freely bargained for, create additional expense for one party, or deny one party a remedy. . . .

NOTES AND PROBLEMS

1. To see the effect of the forum selection clause in this case, begin by imagining that the ticket had contained no such clause. Under such circumstances the questions that arise are a recapitulation of the material in the preceding sections of this chapter:

  a. Where might the lawsuit plausibly have been brought?

  b. What jurisdictional issues would arise in each of those locations?

2. Now consider the forum selection clause. One of the hallmarks of U.S. law is the extent to which the rules of procedure are "default" rules, rules that govern if the parties have not agreed to something else. Forum selection clauses provide

an example of the parties' ability to make agreements that displace ordinary procedural rules. The clause is a contractual provision. As Justice Stevens's dissent
suggests, courts approaching such clauses will always have at least two questions
to consider:

a. As a matter of contract law, is the clause enforceable?

b. Apart from the law of contract, is there some overriding reason that such
clauses should not be enforceable?

c. On the facts of *Carnival Cruise Lines*, which of these two issues provided the
better argument against enforcement of the clause? Can you summarize the
reasons the majority rejected this argument?

d. Does the majority suggest any circumstances under which it would have
been unwilling to enforce a forum selection clause?

3. *Carnival Cruise Lines* stands as evidence of the Court's willingness to
enforce forum selection clauses. Until the middle of this century, courts often
looked on forum selection and similar clauses skeptically; *Carnival Cruise Lines*
is one of a number of cases that accept such clauses, thereby opening the door to
substantial party choice about forum and procedure.

a. Consider the personal jurisdiction cases you have already read; in which of
them could the jurisdictional dispute have been eliminated by a forum selection
clause?

b. After *Carnival Cruise Lines*, does a lawyer commit malpractice if she does
not consider such a clause in any important agreement?

4. A forum selection clause lies in the middle of a spectrum of contractual
provisions that affect procedure:

a. Choice of law clauses do not purport to say where suit shall be brought but
do provide that the substantive law of a particular jurisdiction will govern disputes
arising under the contract. The contract in *Burger King* (supra page 114)
contained such a clause, which specified that Florida law would govern the
agreement.

b. Consent-to-jurisdiction clauses say that the parties (or one of the parties)
consents to suit in a particular place, thus waiving challenges to personal jurisdiction. Such clauses permit, but do not require, that the suit be brought in the
consented-to place. The Supreme Court upheld such a clause in National
Equipment Rental v. Szukhent, described supra page 140.

c. Forum selection clauses, exemplified in *Carnival Cruise Lines*, take things
one step further, limiting the forum to a single location.

d. Arbitration clauses (discussed in Chapter VIII infra) take disputes out of the
hands of the judicial system altogether and place them in an arbitration procedure.

e. *Cognovit* clauses represent the outer limits of the parties' ability to contract
out of procedural law. The cognovit is a contract that

> authorizes an attorney to confess judgment against the person or persons signing it. It
> is written authority of a debtor and a direction by him for the entry of a judgment
> against him if the obligation set forth in the note is not paid when due. Such a judg-
> ment may be taken by any person . . . holding the note, and it cuts off every defense
> which the maker of the note may otherwise have. It likewise cuts off all rights of
> appeal from any judgment taken on it.

Jones v. John Hancock Mutual Life Ins. Co., 289 F. Supp. 930, 935 (W.D. Mich. 1968). The cognovit thus involves not only consent to jurisdiction but also a waiver of the right to assert a defense and the right to trial and appeal. Notice that the cognovit need not deprive the signer of a hearing, but it does mean that any hearing will come only if that signer brings an action to set aside the judgment authorized by the cognovit. The person who would ordinarily be the defendant becomes the plaintiff in such an action, and assumes the burden of instituting litigation and of producing evidence to show that entry of judgment was not warranted. In D. H. Overmyer Co. v. Frick Co., 405 U.S. 174 (1972), the Court upheld the constitutionality of a cognovit, but did so in a way suggesting the device will be limited to circumstances in which the party signing the note understands its effect and receives something in exchange for consent.

D. The Constitutional Requirement of Notice

Pennoyer established an analytic scheme with three branches — power, consent, and notice. This exploration of personal jurisdiction has so far focused on the first two of these branches. Before taking up notice, it may help to refine the relationship of power and consent. Reflecting on the case law examined so far, one could conclude that in order to exercise jurisdiction over a defendant a forum state must have *either* power (flowing from the kind of relationships discussed in the contacts cases) *or* the defendant's consent. Consent may come either in the form of a prelitigation agreement (as in Carnival Cruise Lines v. Shute) or by waiver (when defendant appears but fails to challenge jurisdiction).

The facts of *Pennoyer*, however, suggested another basic objection to the exercise of a state's power. In Mitchell v. Neff, the lawsuit preceding Pennoyer v. Neff, the only notice given to the defendant was a small-print advertisement appearing in the pages of a legal newspaper. In the lower courts Neff argued that the statute authorizing notice in this form had not been complied with, and the lower court had reversed on this ground. The U.S. Supreme Court split on the question of statutory interpretation and went on to rest its decision on the absence of power. Because the Court equated power with personal service of process, the question of notice was for some decades buried: Personal service of process on the defendant within the state simultaneously asserted power and gave notice.

The issues of power and notice began to diverge as states expanded the concept of consent. For example, in Wuchter v. Pizzutti, 276 U.S. 13 (1928), a precursor of Mullane v. Central Hanover Bank & Trust, infra, the Supreme Court considered a New Jersey nonresident motorist statute. It treated the use of the state's roads by nonresidents as consent to both jurisdiction and to the appointment of the Secretary of State as the agent of the defendant for service of process. But the statute did not explicitly direct the Secretary to give notice to the nonresident driver. Even though the defendant had in fact received notice, the Court struck down the statute.

Cases like *Wuchter* made it clear that individuals being sued *in personam* must receive some form of notice. But again recall the distinction, established by *Pennoyer*, between *in personam* and in *rem jurisdiction*. As the *Pennoyer* Court saw things, because it was perfectly permissible for a state to assume that people kept an eye on their property, a state could presume that the seizure of property (a necessary prerequisite to *in rem jurisdiction*, you will recall) would also accomplish notice. Lying behind this rather cavalier assumption may have been an understandable concern. If states were to exercise control over land titles, they had to have some method of rendering binding judgments; a rule that permitted landowners to avoid jurisdiction simply by wandering off without leaving an address would be intolerable. The willingness to presume notice from seizure was a rough but effective way of insuring that this situation did not arise. But it also posed a potentially troubling question — could a state also dispense with notice if the whereabouts of the property owner *were* known? The next case, a constitutional landmark, addresses that question.

Mullane v. Central Hanover Bank & Trust Co.

339 U.S. 306 (1950)

Mr. Justice JACKSON delivered the opinion of the Court.

This controversy questions the constitutional sufficiency of notice to beneficiaries on judicial settlement of accounts by the trustee of a common trust fund established under the New York Banking Law. . . .

Common trust fund legislation is addressed to a problem appropriate for state action. Mounting overheads have made administration of small trusts undesirable to corporate trustees. In order that donors and testators of moderately sized trusts may not be denied the service of corporate fiduciaries, the District of Columbia and some thirty states other than New York have permitted pooling small trust estates into one fund for investment administration. The income, capital gains, losses and expenses of the collective trust are shared by the constituent trusts in proportion to their contribution. By this plan, diversification of risk and economy of management can be extended to those whose capital standing alone would not obtain such advantage.

Statutory authorization for the establishment of such common trust funds is provided in the New York Banking Law . . . [which provides] for accountings twelve to fifteen months after the establishment of a fund and triennially thereafter. The decree in each such judicial settlement of accounts is made binding and conclusive as to any matter set forth in the account upon everyone having any interest in the common fund or in any participating estate, trust or fund.

In January, 1946, Central Hanover Bank and Trust Company established a common trust fund in accordance with these provisions, and in March, 1947, it petitioned the Surrogate's Court for settlement of its first account as common trustee. During the accounting period a total of 113 trusts, approximately half inter vivos and half testamentary, participated in the common trust fund, the gross capital of which was nearly three million dollars. The record does not show the number or residence of the beneficiaries, but they were many and it is clear that some of them were not residents of the State of New York.

The only notice given beneficiaries of this specific application was by publication in a local newspaper in strict compliance with the minimum requirements of N.Y. Banking Law §100-c(12): "After filing such petition [for judicial settlement of its account] the petitioner shall cause to be issued by the court in which the petition is filed and shall publish not less than once in each week for four successive weeks in a newspaper to be designated by the court a notice or citation addressed generally without naming them to all parties interested in such common trust fund and in such estates, trusts or funds mentioned in the petition, all of which may be described in the notice or citation only in the manner set forth in said petition and without setting forth the residence of any such decedent or donor of any such estate, trust or fund." Thus the only notice required, and the only one given, was by newspaper publication setting forth merely the name and address of the trust company, the name and the date of establishment of the common trust fund, and a list of all participating estates, trusts or funds.

At the time the first investment in the common fund was made on behalf of each participating estate, however, the trust company, pursuant to the requirements of §100-c(9), had notified by mail each person of full age and sound mind whose name and address were then known to it and who was "entitled to share in the income therefrom . . . [or] . . . who would be entitled to share in the principal if the event upon which such estate, trust or fund will become distributable should have occurred at the time of sending such notice." Included in the notice was a copy of those provisions of the Act relating to the sending of the notice itself and to the judicial settlement of common trust fund accounts.

Upon the filing of the petition for the settlement of accounts, appellant was, by order of the court pursuant to §100-c(12), appointed special guardian and attorney for all persons known or unknown not otherwise appearing who had or might thereafter have any interest in the income of the common trust fund; and appellee Vaughan was appointed to represent those similarly interested in the principal. There were no other appearances on behalf of any one interested in either interest or principal.

Appellant appeared specially, objecting that notice and the statutory provisions for notice to beneficiaries were inadequate to afford due process under the Fourteenth Amendment, and therefore that the court was without jurisdiction to render a final and binding decree. Appellant's objections were entertained and overruled, the Surrogate [*] holding that the notice required and given was sufficient. A final decree accepting the accounts has been entered, affirmed by the Appellate Division of the Supreme Court and by the Court of Appeals of the State of New York.

The effect of this decree, as held below, is to settle "all questions respecting the management of the common fund." We understand that every right which beneficiaries would otherwise have against the trust company, either as trustee of the

* [In New York the court with jurisdiction over trusts and estates is the Surrogate's Court; its judges are known as Surrogates. — Ed.]

common fund or as trustee of any individual trust, for improper management of the common trust fund during the period covered by the accounting is sealed and wholly terminated by the decree.

We are met at the outset with a challenge to the power of the State — the right of its courts to adjudicate at all as against those beneficiaries who reside without the State of New York. It is contended that the proceeding is one in personam in that the decree affects neither title to nor possession of any res, but adjudges only personal rights of the beneficiaries to surcharge their trustee for negligence or breach of trust. Accordingly, it is said, under the strict doctrine of Pennoyer v. Neff, the Surrogate is without jurisdiction as to nonresidents upon whom personal service of process was not made.

Distinctions between actions in rem and those in personam are ancient and originally expressed in procedural terms what seems really to have been a distinction in the substantive law of property under a system quite unlike our own. The legal recognition and rise in economic importance of incorporeal or intangible forms of property have upset the ancient simplicity of property law and the clarity of its distinctions, while new forms of proceedings have confused the old procedural classification. American courts have sometimes classed certain actions as in rem because personal service of process was not required, and at other times have held personal service of process not required because the action was in rem.

Judicial proceedings to settle fiduciary accounts have been sometimes termed in rem, or more indefinitely quasi in rem, or more vaguely still, "in the nature of a proceeding in rem." It is not readily apparent how the courts of New York did or would classify the present proceeding, which has some characteristics and is wanting in some features of proceedings both in rem and in personam. But in any event we think that the requirements of the Fourteenth Amendment to the Federal Constitution do not depend upon a classification for which the standards are so elusive and confused generally and which, being primarily for state courts to define, may and do vary from state to state. Without disparaging the usefulness of distinctions between actions in rem and those in personam in many branches of law, or on other issues, or the reasoning which underlies them, we do not rest the power of the State to resort to constructive service in this proceeding upon how its courts or this Court may regard this historic antithesis. It is sufficient to observe that whatever the technical definition of its chosen procedure the interest of each state in providing means to close trusts that exist by the grace of its laws and are administered under the supervision of its courts is so insistent and rooted in custom as to establish beyond doubt the right of its courts to determine the interests of all claimants, resident or nonresident, provided its procedure accords full opportunity to appear and be heard.

Quite different from the question of a state's power to discharge trustees is that of the opportunity it must give beneficiaries to contest. Many controversies have raged about the cryptic and abstract words of the Due Process Clause but there can be no doubt that at a minimum they require that deprivation of life, liberty or property by adjudication be preceded by notice and opportunity for hearing appropriate to the nature of the case.

In two ways this proceeding does or may deprive beneficiaries of property. It may cut off their rights to have the trustee answer for negligent or illegal impairments of their interests. Also, their interests are presumably subject to diminution in the proceeding by allowance of fees and expenses to one who, in their names but without their knowledge, may conduct a fruitless or uncompensatory contest. Certainly the proceeding is one in which they may be deprived of property rights and hence notice and hearing must measure up to the standards of due process.

Personal service of written notice within the jurisdiction is the classic form of notice always adequate in any type of proceeding. But the vital interest of the State in bringing any issues as to its fiduciaries to a final settlement can be served only if interests or claims of individuals who are outside of the State can somehow be determined. A construction of the Due Process Clause which would place impossible or impractical obstacles in the way could not be justified.

Against this interest of the State we must balance the individual interest sought to be protected by the Fourteenth Amendment. This is defined by our holding that "The fundamental requisite of due process of law is the opportunity to be heard." This right to be heard has little reality or worth unless one is informed that the matter is pending and can choose for himself whether to appear or default, acquiesce or contest.

The Court has not committed itself to any formula achieving a balance between these interests in a particular proceeding or determining when constructive notice may be utilized or what test it must meet. Personal service has not in all circumstances been regarded as indispensable to the process due to residents, and it has more often been held unnecessary as to nonresidents. We disturb none of the established rules on these subjects. No decision constitutes a controlling or even a very illuminating precedent for the case before us, but a few general principles stand out in the books.

An elementary and fundamental requirement of due process in any proceeding which is to be accorded finality is notice reasonably calculated, under all the circumstances, to apprise interested parties of the pendency of the action and afford them an opportunity to present their objections. The notice must be of such nature as reasonably to convey the required information, and it must afford a reasonable time for those interested to make their appearance. But if with due regard for the practicalities and peculiarities of the case these conditions are reasonably met, the constitutional requirements are satisfied. . . .

But when notice is a person's due, process which is a mere gesture is not due process. The means employed must be such as one desirous of actually informing the absentee might reasonably adopt to accomplish it. The reasonableness and hence the constitutional validity of any chosen method may be defended on the ground that it is in itself reasonably certain to inform those affected, or, where conditions do not reasonably permit such notice, that the form chosen is not substantially less likely to bring home notice than other of the feasible and customary substitutes.

It would be idle to pretend that publication alone, as prescribed here, is a reliable means of acquainting interested parties of the fact that their rights are before the courts. It is not an accident that the greater number of cases reaching this

Court on the question of adequacy of notice have been concerned with actions founded on process constructively served through local newspapers. Chance alone brings to the attention of even a local resident an advertisement in small type inserted in the back pages of a newspaper, and if he makes his home outside the area of the newspaper's normal circulation the odds that the information will never reach him are large indeed. The chance of actual notice is further reduced when, as here, the notice required does not even name those whose attention it is supposed to attract, and does not inform acquaintances who might call it to attention. In weighing its sufficiency on the basis of equivalence with actual notice, we are unable to regard this as more than a feint.

Nor is publication here reinforced by steps likely to attract the parties' attention to the proceeding. It is true that publication traditionally has been acceptable as notification supplemental to other action which in itself may reasonably be expected to convey a warning. The ways of an owner with tangible property are such that he usually arranges means to learn of any direct attack upon his possessory or proprietary rights. Hence, libel of a ship, attachment of a chattel or entry upon real estate in the name of law may reasonably be expected to come promptly to the owner's attention. When the state within which the owner has located such property seizes it for some reason, publication or posting affords an additional measure of notification. A state may indulge the assumption that one who has left tangible property in the state either has abandoned it, in which case proceedings against it deprive him of nothing, or that he has left some caretaker under a duty to let him know that it is being jeopardized. . . .

In the case before us there is, of course, no abandonment. On the other hand these beneficiaries do have a resident fiduciary as caretaker of their interest in this property. But it is their caretaker who in the accounting becomes their adversary. Their trustee is released from giving notice of jeopardy, and no one else is expected to do so. Not even the special guardian is required or apparently expected to communicate with his ward and client, and, of course, if such a duty were merely transferred from the trustee to the guardian, economy would not be served and more likely the cost would be increased.

This Court has not hesitated to approve of resort to publication as a customary substitute in another class of cases where it is not reasonably possible or practicable to give more adequate warning. Thus it has been recognized that, in the case of persons missing or unknown, employment of an indirect and even a probably futile means of notification is all that the situation permits and creates no constitutional bar to a final decree foreclosing their rights.

Those beneficiaries represented by appellant whose interests or whereabouts could not with due diligence be ascertained come clearly within this category. As to them the statutory notice is sufficient. However great the odds that publication will never reach the eyes of such unknown parties, it is not in the typical case much more likely to fail than any of the choices open to legislators endeavoring to prescribe the best notice practicable.

Nor do we consider it unreasonable for the State to dispense with more certain notice to those beneficiaries whose interests are either conjectural or future or, although they could be discovered upon investigation, do not in due course of business come to knowledge of the common trustee. Whatever searches might be required in another situation under ordinary standards of diligence, in view of the character of the proceedings and the nature of the interests here involved we think them unnecessary. We recognize the practical difficulties and costs that would be attendant on frequent investigations into the status of great numbers of beneficiaries, many of whose interests in the common fund are so remote as to be ephemeral; and we have no doubt that such impracticable and extended searches are not required in the name of due process. The expense of keeping informed from day to day of substitutions among even current income beneficiaries and presumptive remaindermen, to say nothing of the far greater number of contingent beneficiaries, would impose a severe burden on the plan, and would likely dissipate its advantages. These are practical matters in which we should be reluctant to disturb the judgment of the state authorities.

Accordingly we overrule appellant's constitutional objections to published notice insofar as they are urged on behalf of any beneficiaries whose interests or addresses are unknown to the trustee.

As to known present beneficiaries of known place of residence, however, notice by publication stands on a different footing. Exceptions in the name of necessity do not sweep away the rule that within the limits of practicability notice must be such as is reasonably calculated to reach interested parties. Where the names and post-office addresses of those affected by a proceeding are at hand, the reasons disappear for resort to means less likely than the mails to apprise them of its pendency.

The trustee has on its books the names and addresses of the income beneficiaries represented by appellant, and we find no tenable ground for dispensing with a serious effort to inform them personally of the accounting, at least by ordinary mail to the record addresses. Certainly sending them a copy of the statute months and perhaps years in advance does not answer this purpose. The trustee periodically remits their income to them, and we think that they might reasonably expect that with or apart from their remittances word might come to them personally that steps were being taken affecting their interests.

We need not weigh contentions that a requirement of personal service of citation on even the large number of known resident or nonresident beneficiaries would, by reasons of delay if not of expense, seriously interfere with the proper administration of the fund. Of course personal service even without the jurisdiction of the issuing authority serves the end of actual and personal notice, whatever power of compulsion it might lack. However, no such service is required under the circumstances. This type of trust presupposes a large number of small interests. The individual interest does not stand alone but is identical with that of a class. The rights of each in the integrity of the fund and the fidelity of the trustee are shared by many other beneficiaries. Therefore notice reasonably certain to reach most of those interested in objecting is likely to safeguard the interests of all, since any objection sustained would inure to the benefit of all. We think that under such circumstances reasonable risks that notice might not actually reach every beneficiary are justifiable. "Now and then an extraordinary case may turn up, but constitutional law like other mortal contrivances has to take some chances, and in the great majority of instances no doubt justice will be done."

The statutory notice to known beneficiaries is inadequate, not because in fact it fails to reach everyone, but because under the circumstances it is not reasonably calculated to reach those who could easily be informed by other means at hand. However it may have been in former times, the mails today are recognized as an efficient and inexpensive means of communication. Moreover, the fact that the trust company has been able to give mailed notice to known beneficiaries at the time the common trust fund was established is persuasive that postal notification at the time of accounting would not seriously burden the plan.

In some situations the law requires greater precautions in its proceedings than the business world accepts for its own purposes. In few, if any, will it be satisfied with less. Certainly it is instructive, in determining the reasonableness of the impersonal broadcast notification here used, to ask whether it would satisfy a prudent man of business, counting his pennies but finding it in his interest to convey information to many persons whose names and addresses are in his files. We are not satisfied that it would. Publication may theoretically be available for all the world to see, but it is too much in our day to suppose that each or any individual beneficiary does or could examine all that is published to see if something may be tucked away in it that affects his property interests. We have before indicated in reference to notice by publication that, "Great caution should be used not to let fiction deny the fair play that can be secured only by a pretty close adhesion to fact." McDonald v. Mabee.

We hold that the notice of judicial settlement of accounts required by the New York Banking Law §100-c(12) is incompatible with the requirements of the Fourteenth Amendment as a basis for adjudication depriving known persons whose whereabouts are also known of substantial property rights. Accordingly the judgment is reversed and the cause remanded for further proceedings not inconsistent with this opinion.

NOTES AND PROBLEMS

1. To see the force of *Mullane*, consider following:

a. Imagine the thought processes of the drafters of the New York Banking Law: What led them to think that the published form of notice would be constitutionally adequate?

b. What was wrong with their thinking, according to the Court?

2. What does the decision mean in practical terms? After the decision, what steps would have to occur to assure that the proceeding would bind the beneficiaries? How, in light of this decision, should New York have amended its statute to create a constitutionally valid procedure for examining and approving trustees' accounts? See N.Y. Banking Law §100-c(6) (Consol. 2003).

3. Written in broad terms, *Mullane* is a central case for the meaning of due process in civil litigation. But it is less explicit about its implications than about its holding:

a. In *Mullane* mass mailings were deemed satisfactory. The Court acknowledged that some letters would not get through to their intended recipients but reasoned that under the particular circumstances, in which all intended recipients had the same interests, contacting a certain number of people in the group would serve approximately the same function as contacting them all. How would this principle apply to ordinary litigation, in which only a few parties are involved: Is mail adequate then? The answer matters because mail notice reduces the cost of serving process while also increasing the risk that the mail will not arrive. One court has suggested *Mullane* prohibits service of process by ordinary mail. Miserandino v. Resort Properties, Inc., 691 A.2d 208 (Md.), cert. denied, 522 U.S. 963 (1997). Is that an accurate reading of *Mullane*?

b. Does *Mullane* require individual notice whenever one can identify and locate a person whom litigation may affect — even if the cost of such notice will be high? The issue matters greatly in class actions — where both sides in the debate cite *Mullane*, one stressing its requirement of individual notice, the other stressing its emphasis on practicality. Who's right?

4. Although the *Mullane* court dropped some hints, some courts and lawyers thought it did not answer the question whether notice was required in traditional in rem actions. In Walker v. Hutchinson, 352 U.S. 112 (1956), the Court applied *Mullane* to require that personal notice be given a landowner whose property was being taken by condemnation and whose name and address were listed in the city's land records. Similar reasoning was applied in Schroeder v. City of New York, 371 U.S. 208 (1962) (planned diversion of water; published notice not sufficient when property owner's address known) and in Tulsa Professional Collection Services, Inc. v. Pope, 485 U.S. 478 (1985) (settlement of decedent's estate; published notice to creditors in general insufficient when estate knew of claim of particular creditor). Given this line of cases, should a lawyer assume that published notice will never suffice for a defendant whose identity and whereabouts are known and who is not seeking to evade service?

5. The student should be alert to a potential confusion that arises when courts or statutes speak of service of process and personal jurisdiction.

a. In speaking of "service of process," courts sometimes refer to the way in which the defendant is given notice of the action — the question with which *Mullane* deals. At other times they refer instead to the issues involving the extent of a court's adjudicatory power — minimum contacts and the like. This blending occurs because, unless transient jurisdiction is no longer valid, service of process within a state's borders may confer jurisdiction (as in Burnham v. Superior Court, supra page 132). There is thus a tendency in some contexts to speak of "service of process" although what is meant is jurisdiction or a combination of jurisdiction and service. (The Federal Interpleader Act, 28 U.S.C. §2361, for example, speaks in terms of nationwide process rather than nationwide jurisdiction.)

b. Conversely, courts that conclude that a defendant did not receive constitutionally adequate notice (as in *Mullane*) will sometimes express that conclusion by saying that the court lacked "jurisdiction"; that is, it lacked one of the constitutional requisites for exercising adjudicatory power: proper notice.

NOTES AND PROBLEMS ON SERVICE OF PROCESS

1. Assuming that some constitutionally adequate notice is required, one must then decide what form notice must take. That form is widely regulated by statute. Rule 4 provides that regulation in federal courts.

The current Rule 4 consolidates a gradual informalizing of the practice of service of process that has taken place over the last few decades, an evolution enabled in part by *Mullane*'s suggestion that forms of notice other than personal service would satisfy due process. In pursuit of informality, Rule 4 makes service by an officer of the court (a U.S. marshal) exceptional rather than ordinary. In its place the Rule provides for service by any individual who is not a party and is at least eighteen years old.

More fundamentally, Rule 4 proposes to replace even this personal but "unofficial" service with a still less formal procedure called "waiver of service" (see Rule 4(d)). Waiver of service uses first-class mail to send a copy of the complaint to the defendant, together with a request that the defendant return by mail a form (Form 1B) waiving formal service of a summons. If the defendant does return that form, the case proceeds as if process had been served. If the defendant does not return the form within the time specified in the Rule, the plaintiff must then proceed to have a summons served more formally, using the procedures set forth in Rule 4(e)-(j). The defendant who waives service does not thereby waive objections to venue or jurisdiction, or any defenses to the merits of the lawsuit. By waiving service the defendant does, however, give up any objections to the sufficiency of the summons or the method by which it was served (Rule 12(b)(4) and (5)).

Why should the defendant want to make things easy for the plaintiff by waiving formal service of process? Rule 4 provides two answers to that question—a stick for failing to waive and a carrot for doing so. The Rule imposes on defendants the "duty to save costs of service." Enforcing that duty is a provision of Rule 4(d)(2) requiring a "defendant located within the United States" to pay the costs of subsequent service if he has without good cause refused to waive service of process. On the other hand, the Rule gives defendants additional time to answer the complaint if they do waive service—extending the time from twenty to sixty days for domestic defendants and from twenty to ninety days for foreign defendants. The accompanying notes reflect a hope that this combination of procedural sticks and carrots will make waiver the predominant form of "service" in federal litigation.

If the defendant fails to waive service, Rule 4 goes on to specify various means by which a plaintiff may serve defendants. Plaintiff must also use these means to serve defendants from whom a waiver of service cannot be demanded. Such defendants include the U.S. government, infants and incompetents, and others whose service is thought to require special formality so as to reduce the possibility of inadvertent default.

Where such formal service is required, its form depends on the nature of the defendant—individuals and corporations, domestic and foreign defendants, and federal and state government entities all have sections. The amended Rule specifies the means of serving foreign defendants, a source of special problems and growing concern as the volume of international business increases. Rules 4(f) and (h) set forth a list of ways in which such foreign defendants may be served, incorporating the provisions of the Hague Service Convention of 1969, an important international treaty.

2. Read Rule 4 and answer the following questions:

a. Plaintiff wishes to sue an individual located in the United States and wants to commence the suit at minimum cost. What steps should she take?

b. Defendant, located in the United States, receives a complaint together with copies of Forms 1A and 1B, requesting waiver of summons. Defendant seeks advice from Lawyer about the effect of ignoring this request. What should Lawyer tell defendant?

c. Defendant, located in the United States, receives a complaint together with copies of Forms 1A and 1B, requesting waiver of summons. The request is dated September 1. If defendant wishes to waive summons, by when must she respond? See Rule 4(d)(2)(F).

d. Defendant, located in the United States, receives a complaint together with copies of Forms 1A and 1B, requesting waiver of summons. The request is dated September 1; defendant signs and returns Form 1B by September 20 but does not file an answer to the complaint. On October 20 plaintiff moves to enter a default, citing Rule 12(a), which requires defendant to answer the complaint within 20 days. How should the court rule on plaintiff's motion?

e. Defendant, located in the United States, receives a complaint together with copies of Forms 1A and 1B, requesting waiver of summons. The request is dated September 1. Three months elapse, and plaintiff has received no response. What should plaintiff do?

f. Plaintiff wishes to sue defendant, located in the United States, on a claim in diversity jurisdiction on which the statute of limitations will run in 45 days. Should plaintiff request a waiver of service from defendant? Why?

g. Plaintiff requests a waiver of summons from a defendant located in the United States, receives no waiver, and incurs the costs of personal service. After service has been completed, plaintiff moves pursuant to Rule 4(d)(2) to recover the increased costs from defendant. Defendant resists the motion, arguing that the underlying lawsuit is without merit and that it denies him due process of law to require him to help his adversary bring a meritless action. How should plaintiff respond to this argument?

h. Plaintiff wishes to sue the United States. May plaintiff request a waiver of summons from this defendant?

i. Plaintiff wishes to sue a defendant located in the United States who has failed to return the request for a waiver of summons within a reasonable time. What information must plaintiff have in order to know what form of service to employ?

3. Service of process gives defendant notice and thus overcomes what would otherwise be a constitutional obstacle to a valid judgment. Service may also avoid a defense based on the statute of limitations; in many states the statute is satisfied not by filing the suit but by serving defendant with process. For claims based on federal law, Rule 3 provides that the statute of limitations stops running

when the complaint is filed with the court. But defendant must still be notified; how long does plaintiff have to do so? Read Rule 4(m) and respond to the following questions.

a. Suppose a claim is based on federal law. Plaintiff has filed his complaint with the court but has been unable to serve process because defendant has gone into hiding. Time is running out on the 120-day period for service of process; what should plaintiff do?

b. Can a court extend the time for service *without* a showing of good cause? The second half of Rule 4(m) contains a good cause requirement; the first half, which allows a court to "direct that service be effected within a specified time," contains no such requirement.

4. The current Rule 4 also makes explicit one proposition that has been implicit since Pennoyer v. Neff and another that the Rules have long skirted: the nature of the relation between personal jurisdiction and service of process and the relation between the reach of personal jurisdiction of the state and federal courts.

a. On the first issue, Rule 4(k)(1) states that service (or waiver) establishes jurisdiction over defendants subject to personal jurisdiction. That formula is as important for what it does not say as for what it does. It does not say that service establishes jurisdiction. That had been the assumption of *Pennoyer*, at least for defendants served in the forum state. Instead, the Rule states that if the requisites of personal jurisdiction exist, proper service establishes jurisdiction. Thus a defendant who waives process, or who has been properly served, remains free to challenge the existence of personal jurisdiction.

b. How does waiver of service interact with tag jurisdiction under *Burnham*? Plaintiff wishes to sue defendant who has no constitutionally adequate contacts with the forum state but has recently visited the state. Had plaintiff served defendant with process while he was in the state, *Burnham* suggests that jurisdiction would be established. Can plaintiff request a waiver and argue that the forum state has jurisdiction because he could have served defendant while in the forum state? Or is this a bit too cute?

c. On the second issue — the personal jurisdiction of federal courts — Rule 4 establishes a four-tier scheme. First, it says that federal courts, at a minimum, have personal jurisdiction over any defendant over whom the state court of the forum state would have such jurisdiction (Rule 4(k)(1)(A)). To that extent — and this provision covers the vast majority of all cases — the personal jurisdiction of state and federal courts "match." Thus a federal court sitting in California or Georgia has the same jurisdictional reach as a state court in that state — no less, but also no more.

The three remaining provisions deal with situations in which the Rule defines a longer jurisdictional reach for the federal courts than the state courts would have. One occurs when a party is joined to litigation under Rule 14 or 19; in these instances the Rules provide for a "100-mile bulge" in the personal jurisdiction of a federal district court, even if a state court would not have had such jurisdiction (Rule 4(k)(1)(B)). This provision is particularly useful where federal district courts lie close to state lines: the Southern and Eastern Districts of New York

(Manhattan and Brooklyn) and the district courts in New Jersey, Washington, D.C., Philadelphia, and Delaware provide examples.

The second special situation arises when federal legislation specifically provides for broad, national power of a federal court. One example is a federal statute providing for nationwide service of process (for example, see 28 U.S.C. §1335); another is the enforcement of a civil contempt order arising from litigation involving a federal question (Rule 4.1(b)).

Finally, the Rule purports to define a new form of personal jurisdiction, limited to federal claims against defendants no subject to personal jurisdiction in any state. Such defendants will inevitably be foreign persons or entities that have insufficient contacts with any single state to create personal jurisdiction. In that situation, Rule 4(k)(2) provides:

> If the exercise of jurisdiction is consistent with the Constitution and laws of the United States, serving a summons or filing a waiver of service is also effective, with respect to claims arising under federal law, to establish personal jurisdiction over the person of any defendant who is not subject to the courts of general jurisdiction of any state. . . .

This provision seems to rest on the proposition that the Due Process Clause permits aggregation of the defendant's contacts with the United States as a whole for jurisdictional purposes.

5. As international litigation grows with international business, more lawyers find themselves faced with the necessity to serve process on foreign defendants. When they do, they discover that matters can quickly become complicated. This note cannot be comprehensive, but it can sketch the issues.

a. The Hague Service Convention, an important international treaty covering service of process, aims at clarifying the means of serving judicial process abroad. The Hague Convention would, for example, guide a Japanese firm seeking to serve an American defendant in a suit brought in Japanese courts; it would also guide a U.S. plaintiff seeking to sue a Spanish defendant. The Convention provides that each signatory nation must designate a "Central Authority" responsible for serving process on its nationals. So long as a plaintiff submits its request to this Central Authority in proper form, the Authority assumes responsibility for serving process in whatever way plaintiff directs.

b. Unfortunately, the Convention's flexibility sometimes creates complications, and other complications arise from the interaction of the Convention and Rule 4. For example, the Convention permits the Central Authority to serve process in any of three ways: (1) in any manner specified by the receiving nation for its own civil litigation (thus the United States might employ Rule 4); (2) in a manner specified by the plaintiff, so long as that manner does not violate the receiving nation's laws; or (3) by the defendant's voluntarily accepting service. If one asks the Central Authority to use the first of these procedures, it is clear that one must submit translations of all the relevant documents; under the remaining two that requirement is less clear. The difference matters because translations involve

---

* In the United States the Central Authority is a division of the U.S. Department of Justice.

expense and delay. The question matters because if one does not effect proper service, the nation in question may refuse to enforce any subsequent judgment.

c. Lawyer represents plaintiff, a former wife domiciled in the United States, who seeks to collect delinquent child support from her former husband, who now resides in Italy but has assets in the United States. The courts of plaintiff's state permit mail service on defendants located out of state. Italy does not allow mail service in its courts. How should plaintiff proceed? See Rule 4(f). What risks does plaintiff run if she uses mail service? Are those risks worth running? How would your answer change if defendant had assets only in Italy?

d. Nations' rules for voluntary acceptance of service differ; for example, in some countries the defendant must retrieve process from the local police station. Rule 4(d) allows foreign defendants to waive service of process by mail. Suppose a product liability suit against a foreign manufacturer, who waives service under Rule 4(d). The suit goes to judgment with defendant suffering a money judgment against it. Plaintiff now seeks to enforce the judgment abroad. Do you see what defense the defendant might raise?

6. Assuming one knows the proper mode of service, questions still arise over whether the attempt has complied with a suitable mode. For example, has the process server left process with a "person of suitable age and discretion" as required by Rule 4(e)(2)? Or what if the process server submits an affidavit that the defendant was served, but defendant denies it? Such questions will often require a hearing and judicial resolution. They may arise, for example, in a motion made under Rule 60(b) to set aside a judgment. They may also arise in those states in which the statute of limitations does not stop running until process is served. And, ironically, service may be quashed on defendant's motion at the preliminary stages of the case for improprieties of form even though the service has performed its chief function — that of notifying the defendant of the commencement of the case.

a. Failure to deliver service may be to the benefit of the process server if his failures are not caught, because he can collect the fees and not do the work. Such intentional failure to serve process, accompanied by a false affidavit of service, is called "sewer service" by reference to the place where process eventually finds itself. Such abuses may also benefit the plaintiff, who may be able to collect a default judgment based on the sewer service because the defendant was intimidated by the judgment collection process, was ignorant of his rights, or could not afford a lawyer.

b. On the other side of the coin, defendants may sometimes take unfair advantage of service-of-process rules. Wily prospective defendants have sometimes dodged process for long periods, thereby requiring process servers to display ingenuity and sometimes even physical bravery. What should be done with such defendants, who refuse to waive service and then evade the process server? Rule 4(d), which imposes the duty to minimize costs of service on defendants and shifts those costs to a defendant who makes expensive personal service necessary, is one response; Rule 4(m), extending the time for service "for good cause," is another. But such a defendant must be served as a prerequisite even for collecting those costs of service, not to speak of the relief sought on the merits of the lawsuit. The provision of Rule 4(e) allowing process to be left at the defendant's home is a partial answer. Some states permit notice by publication in such circumstances. Another solution is found in Michigan Gen. Ct. R. 105.8, which empowers the judge in any case to "allow service of process to be made upon a defendant in any other manner which is reasonably calculated to give him actual notice of the proceedings and an opportunity to be heard, if an order permitting such service is entered before service of process is made upon a showing to the court that service of process cannot reasonably be made in the manner provided for under other rules."

c. Finally, one case involving service of process should not go unnoticed. In United States ex rel. Mayo v. Satan and His Staff, 54 F.R.D. 282 (W.D. Pa. 1971), plaintiff complained that the defendant had "on numerous occasions caused plaintiff misery" and that the defendant had caused his downfall. The court refused to allow the plaintiff to proceed in forma pauperis in part because he had failed to include in his complaint instructions for service of process on the defendant.

E.   Self-Imposed Restraints on Jurisdictional Power: Long-Arm Statutes, Venue, and Discretionary Refusal of Jurisdiction

Our discussion of jurisdiction has thus far proceeded as if the only relevant questions are constitutional power and notice. Each case has silently assumed that the state or federal court in question was authorized to assert jurisdiction if doing so was constitutionally permissible. The issue has been whether the Constitution permitted such an assertion of jurisdiction. We now go behind that assumption in three settings: long-arm statutes, venue laws, and the doctrine of forum non conveniens. Each represents a situation in which the legislature or courts have framed rules that restrict where a lawsuit may take place—even when the Constitution would pose no obstacles.

1.   Long-Arm Statutes as a Restraint on Jurisdiction

A court may exercise jurisdiction over a defendant only when the state or federal government authorizes it to do so (and the authorization must be constitutional as applied to the case in question). In the world of *Pennoyer* such authorization was usually a simple matter: Had the state provided for service of process on a defendant in this situation? As the doctrines of personal jurisdiction expanded (especially in the years after *International Shoe*), many states began to authorize service (often by mail) on defendants beyond their borders. Because *Pennoyer* had conceived of such extensions of state court jurisdiction as near-physical exertions of state power, statutes authorizing courts to reach beyond their own borders came to be known as "long-arm" statutes: states were extending their jurisdictional "arms." The name has stuck.

Some states have enacted long-arm statutes that reach for as much jurisdiction as the Constitution allows. California provides a well-known example:

California Code of Civil Procedure §410.10 (West 2003)

A Court of this state may exercise jurisdiction on any basis not inconsistent with the Constitution of this state or of the United States.

Under such a statute there is no separate problem of analyzing the coverage of the long-arm statute: If jurisdiction is constitutional, it is also authorized by the statute. (A common variation on this pattern occurs when the words of the statute appear to limit jurisdiction to specified instances but the state's courts have construed the statute to permit jurisdiction whenever constitutionally permissible.) Other states have long-arm statutes limiting jurisdiction to specified occurrences. The next case displays a court wrestling with such a statute.

Gibbons v. Brown

716 So. 2d 868 (Fl. Dist. Ct. App. 1998)

PER CURIAM.

[In 1994 Martine Gibbons and Mr. and Mrs. Brown were driving together in Montreal, Canada. Ms. Gibbons gave allegedly faulty directions to Mr. Brown, who was driving, causing him to turn the wrong way onto a one-way street, resulting in a head-on collision that injured both passengers. In 1995 Ms. Gibbons, a Texas resident, sued Mr. Brown in Florida; Mrs. Brown was not a party. Two years later Mrs. Brown, seeking to recover for her own injuries, brought this Florida action against Ms. Gibbons.]

In her complaint . . . Mrs. Brown alleged 1) that she is a resident of Florida; 2) that Ms. Gibbons has subjected herself to the personal jurisdiction of the Florida court by bringing [the prior] lawsuit. . . . In her motion to quash service of process and, alternatively, motion to dismiss, Ms. Gibbons . . . challenged the allegations in the 1997 complaint as . . . inadequate to satisfy the strict requirements of the Florida long-arm statute. . . .

Obtaining in personam jurisdiction over a non-resident defendant requires a two-pronged showing. First, the plaintiff must allege sufficient jurisdictional facts to bring the defendant within the coverage of the long-arm statute, section 48.193, Florida Statutes. If that prong is satisfied, then the second inquiry is whether sufficient "minimum contacts" are shown to comply with the requirements of due process. International Shoe Co. v. Washington. Generally speaking, Florida's long-arm statutes are of a class that requires more activities or contacts to allow service of process than are currently required by the decisions of the United States Supreme Court.

As to the first part of the inquiry, Mrs. Brown contends that the allegations in her complaint satisfy section 48.193(2), Florida Statutes (1995), which states:

A defendant who is engaged in substantial and not isolated activity within this state, whether such activity is wholly intrastate, interstate, or otherwise, is subject to the jurisdiction of the courts of this state, whether or not the claim arises from that activity.

The parties agree that as a general rule in Florida, a plaintiff, by bringing an action, subjects herself to the jurisdiction of the court and to subsequent lawful orders entered regarding the same subject matter of that action. Mrs. Brown broadly construes this general rule to mean that by initiating the 1995 action, Ms. Gibbons subjected herself to Florida jurisdiction with respect to any "lawful orders" that were entered subsequently regarding "the subject matter of the action." On the other hand, Ms. Gibbons notes that her prior suit was brought in 1995, whereas Mrs. Brown did not file her complaint until October 20, 1997. Although Ms. Gibbons acknowledges that her prior action arose from the same vehicular accident as Mrs. Brown's instant suit, Ms. Gibbons notes that Mrs. Brown was not a party in the earlier action. Furthermore, several years separate the filing of the two proceedings. For purposes of the resolution of the question on appeal, we assume that the 1995 proceedings were over by the time Mrs. Brown brought her 1997 suit.

In Milberg Factors, Inc. v. Greenbaum, 585 So. 2d 1089 (Fla. 3d DCA 1991) . . . [o]bserving that an entity cannot control where its account debtors choose to relocate, the court stated that "the filing of lawsuits unrelated to this action against account debtors in Florida does not subject Milberg to the jurisdiction of our courts."

Even if we assume (without deciding) that bringing an action in a Florida court can constitute a "substantial and not isolated activity" in some instances, we nevertheless note that Mrs. Brown has not shown that Ms. Gibbons "is engaged" in any activity in this state whatsoever other than defending the present suit. A current defendant's prior decision to bring a suit in Florida should not act indefinitely as a sword of Damocles hanging perilously over the head of that defendant if she later challenges jurisdiction in a separate suit (albeit a suit arising from the same subject matter). . . . Given the length of time between the two actions and the fact that the prior suit named as the defendant a non-party in the instant proceedings, we conclude that Mrs. Brown has not alleged a satisfactory ground for personal jurisdiction pursuant to statutory subsection (2). The appellee does not suggest, nor do we find, that the appellant's filing the 1995 action in the Florida court would, by itself, satisfy any of the alternative grounds for jurisdiction set forth in section 48.193(1)(a)-(1)(h). . . .

Absent sufficient jurisdictional allegations to show that Ms. Gibbons' acts satisfy the prerequisites in the Florida long-arm statute . . . the trial court is directed to DISMISS Mrs. Brown's complaint.

NOTES AND PROBLEMS

1. Be sure you understand why the opinion above does not say that it would be unconstitutional for Florida to assert personal jurisdiction over Ms. Gibbons.

a. Why does Ms. Gibbons's activity not satisfy the Florida statute?

b. Suppose Florida had a long-arm statute like that of California (quoted supra), extending state court jurisdiction to the boundaries permitted by the Due

Process Clause. On the facts of this case, would it have been constitutional for Florida to exercise jurisdiction over Ms. Gibbons?

c. In answering the preceding question, it may help to compare the facts of Gibbons to those of Adam v. Saenger, 303 U.S. 59 (1938). Saenger, a Texas citizen, brought suit in California against Adam, a California resident. Adam counterclaimed against Saenger, whereupon Saenger abandoned his action. Adam then recovered a default judgment on the counterclaim against Saenger. When Adam sued in Texas to enforce his judgment, Saenger defended on the ground that the California court lacked personal jurisdiction. So far as the record showed, Saenger's one and only contact with California was the filing of the lawsuit in question. That was enough, held the U.S. Supreme Court: "The plaintiff having, by his voluntary act in demanding justice from the defendant, submitted himself to the jurisdiction of the court, there is nothing arbitrary or unreasonable in treating him as being there for all purposes for which justice to the defendant demands his presence." Id. at 67-68. Is Gibbons distinguishable?

2. Gibbons points out that "Florida's long-arm statutes are of a class that requires more activities or contacts to allow service of process than are currently required by the decisions of the United States Supreme Court."

a. New York is another populous state that has decided not to extend its jurisdictional reach to the full extent permitted by the constitution:

> [NY]CPLR 302 (a) (3), the provision of New York's long-arm statute at issue here, permits a court to exercise personal jurisdiction over a nondomiciliary who:
>> "3. commits a tortious act without the state causing injury to person or property *within the state* . . . if he
>>> "(i) *regularly* does or solicits business, or engages in any other persistent course of conduct, or derives substantial revenue from goods used or consumed or services rendered, *in the state*, or
>>> "(ii) expects or should reasonably expect *the act to have consequences in the state* and derives substantial revenue from *interstate* or international *commerce*"
>> (CPLR 302[a][3] [emphasis supplied]).
>
> Under this provision, the appellant must show both that an injury occurred "within the state," and that the elements of either clause (i) or (ii) have been satisfied. It is appropriate to point out that establishment of long-arm jurisdiction in connection with a New York injury under either clause does not implicate constitutional due process concerns. "[T]he subdivision [302 (a) (3)] was not designed to go to the full limits of permissible jurisdiction. The limitations contained in subparagraphs (i) and (ii) were deliberately inserted to keep the provision 'well within constitutional bounds'" (1 Weinstein-Korn-Miller, NY Civ Prac P 302.14, quoting 12th Ann Report of NY Jud Conf, at 341).

Ingraham v. Carroll, 90 N.Y.2d 592, 596 (1997). Which portions of the quoted statute would you amend to make its limits as broad as the Due Process Clause?

b. Apply the New York statute to the following facts. Mrs. Ingraham "was a patient of Community Health Plan (CHP), a New York HMO with clinic located in Hoosick Falls, New York," near the Vermont border. On several occasions her HMO physicians referred her to Dr. Carroll, who practices in Bennington,

Vermont. Dr. Carroll is not under contract with CHP for consultation services. However, he frequently sees CHP patients on an ad hoc/fee-for-service basis, on referral. Dr. Carroll allegedly misdiagnosed Mrs. Ingraham, whose survivors sued in New York. Assuming that defendant's contacts satisfied the Due Process Clause, did they fall within the New York Statute? Held, no. Ingraham v. Carroll, 90 N.Y.2d 592 (1997).

3. What is the relation between long-arm statutes and the Due Process Clause?

a. Analytically, the two involve distinct inquiries. The Constitution sets the outer boundaries of personal jurisdiction, but nothing requires that a state assert the entire jurisdiction permitted by the Constitution. A legislature might decide that it did not want to be as jurisdictionally aggressive as the Constitution would permit. As in *Gibbons*, a court convinced that the long-arm statute does not cover the facts would simply stop there, without needlessly deciding the constitutionality of asserting personal jurisdiction. Only if one decides that the long-arm statute does reach the facts of the lawsuit need one make the second, constitutional inquiry.

b. Why would a state want to restrict its jurisdictional reach more than the Constitution already requires? Imagine advising a state legislative committee revising a long-arm statute. Having read the cases in this chapter, can you develop an argument that a state ought to adopt a rule more restrictive than the Constitution requires?

c. Encountering a long-arm statute that appears to be more restrictive than the Constitution, the lawyer must be careful not to assume that it is as limited as the text suggests. State courts have often interpreted such statutes to reach beyond what the text implies. For example, see Sifers v. Horen, 385 Mich. 195 (1971) (interpreting "transaction of any business within the state" as expressing legislative intent to go to limits of Due Process Clause).

4. *Gibbons* is a state case and applies a state long-arm statute. How do long-arm statutes apply in the federal courts? Mrs. Brown was apparently a Florida citizen, and Ms. Gibbons a citizen of Texas. As you will see in the following chapter, if more than $75,000 was in controversy, Ms. Gibbons could have sued in federal district court, invoking diversity jurisdiction. Suppose she had; would the Florida long-arm statute still apply? Reread Rule 4(k)(1)(A).

5. In several notable instances Congress has enacted federal long-arm statutes, which purport to give the federal courts expansive powers of personal jurisdiction. Provisions of the federal securities laws provide one example. Another is the Federal Interpleader Act, 28 U.S.C. §2361, which gives federal courts the power to serve process anywhere in the nation, a power that has been interpreted to include personal jurisdiction.

a. Is such an extended federal jurisdictional reach constitutional? One court has limited this power by interpreting "service of process" to be distinct from personal jurisdiction. In Peay v. Bellsouth Medical Assistance Plan, 205 F.3d 1206 (10th Cir. 2000), the court held that the nationwide service of process in federal pension legislation did not confer personal jurisdiction, whose requirements had to be separately satisfied.

b. Suppose a defendant is properly served under such a "nationwide service" statute attached to a federal claim. Plaintiff also brings related state-law claims against the same defendant. The federal long-arm statute is constitutional as applied to defendant and reaches far enough to bring defendant into the federal court, but the state's statute doesn't reach as far as the federal long-arm statute. May plaintiff bring the state-law claims, invoking what some have called "pendent personal jurisdiction"? One court has so held:

> [W]e recognize pendent personal jurisdiction of a district court which has obtained personal jurisdiction over a defendant by reason of a federal claim to adjudicate state claims properly within the court's subject matter jurisdiction, even though that state's long-arm statute could not authorize service over the defendants with respect to the state claims. . . . Once a court has a constitutional case, in the Article III sense, properly before it, service by a court sufficient to assert personal jurisdiction over a defendant by any authorized mechanism consistent with due process may be held to apply to the entire constitutional case.

ESAB Group, Inc. v. Centricut Inc., 126 F.3d 617, 628-629 (4th Cir. 1997). Can you frame an argument that this result runs counter to the last fifty years of jurisdictional doctrine? Is it nonetheless the right result?

2.   Venue as a Further Localizing Principle

Venue, like personal jurisdiction, determines where litigation will take place. Unlike personal jurisdiction, venue flows solely from statutory rather than constitutional sources. The general federal venue statute is 28 U.S.C. §1391. Surveying this statute will show that it typically tries to place suits in areas connected either to the parties or to the events giving rise to the action. See, for example, the portions of 28 U.S.C. §1391(a) and (b), which put venue "where any defendant resides" or where "a substantial part of the events or omissions giving rise to the claim occurred." In many respects, then, the inquiries necessary under present venue statutes duplicate those involved in personal jurisdiction questions.

Why, then, have both a law of personal jurisdiction and one of venue? At a technical level the answer to that question is easy: Unlike personal jurisdiction, venue locates litigation not just in a state but in a particular federal judicial district within that state. For example, suppose a defendant is clearly subject to personal jurisdiction in Florida, which has three federal judicial districts. See 28 U.S.C. §133(a). Principles of jurisdiction tell plaintiff that she can sue in Florida, but the venue statutes and cases interpreting them will tell her in which of the three districts venue will lie.

The federal venue statute took its present form in 1990, following a century-long evolution during which it was sometimes impossible to find a judicial district in which venue lay even when there was both personal and subject matter jurisdiction over the case and parties. Of the present statute one commentator has remarked: "It is still possible to conceive of cases in which there will be no federal district in which suit can be brought, but those cases are more likely to arise in classroom hypotheticals than in real life." Wright, Federal Courts 262. The following problems survey a range of common federal venue problems under the current statute; we shall concentrate on what Professor Wright called the "real life" problems, saving a few of the other sort for the end.

NOTES AND PROBLEMS

After reviewing 28 U.S.C. §§1391-1392, answer the following questions by deciding the states (or districts) in which venue lies. (You may assume that all requirements of federal subject matter jurisdiction have been met.) Notice that §1391(a) and (b) differ slightly and that their application depends on whether the case contains any claim based on federal law.

1. Plaintiff sues defendant, a resident of the Southern District of New York, on a claim of breach of contract. The contract called for the manufacture and delivery of a machine. The machine was designed in New Mexico and assembled in the Northern District of Illinois from parts made in Ohio, California, and Pennsylvania.

a. Where will venue certainly lie?

b. What additional information would one need to decide whether there were other available venues?

2. Plaintiff sues A, a resident of the Southern District of New York, and B, who resides in New Jersey but conducts his business from an office in the Southern District of New York, on a claim of breach of contract. The contract called for the manufacture and delivery of a machine in Japan, from parts made in Mexico.

3. The problems thus far have assumed that the defendants are individuals. For corporations, §1391(c) provides a more expansive definition of "jurisdiction": Quite simply, a corporate defendant is deemed, for venue purposes, to reside wherever it is subject to personal jurisdiction.

4. Special venue provisions apply to aliens:

a. C, a Canadian citizen, wishes to sue D, a resident of the Eastern District of California, alleging personal injury damages arising from an automobile accident in Nevada. Where will venue lie?

b. D, a resident of the Eastern District of California, wishes to sue C, a Canadian citizen, alleging personal injury damages arising from an automobile accident in Nevada. Where will venue lie?

c. Section 1391(d) also applies to alien corporations, subjecting them to suit not just where they do business, but in any judicial district.

d. Before deciding that §1391(d) is extremely harsh on aliens, consider how doctrines of personal jurisdiction will limit its application. In Problem 4b, venue will lie in any judicial district in the United States; assuming that C is a tourist who has since returned to Canada, where will personal jurisdiction lie?

5. What is the difference between §1391(a)(3) and §1391(b)(3)? Section 1391(a)(3) requires that a defendant be subject to personal jurisdiction in a district; §1391(b)(3) allows for venue whenever a defendant "may be found" in that district. Is "be[ing] found" a less rigorous test than being subject to personal jurisdiction? May a defendant ever be "found" in a district in which personal jurisdiction is unavailable? After Burnham v. Superior Court, supra, the answer

may be "never" in the case of an individual. If service of process on an individual satisfies the requirements of jurisdiction, being "found" will be the same as being subject to personal jurisdiction, at least if one is "found" by a process server. The next case wrestles with the problem.

Dee-K Enterprises, Inc., v. Heveafil Sdn. Bhd.

982 F. Supp. 1138 (E.D. Va. 1997)

ELLIS, J.

In this antitrust action, two American purchasers of extruded rubber thread sue various foreign manufacturers and distributors of the thread alleging an international conspiracy to restrain trade in, and fix prices of, the thread in the United States. Defendants' several motions to dismiss raise the following threshold issues:

(1) whether there is personal jurisdiction over an Indonesian manufacturer-defendant that consummates its sales of thread in Indonesia;

(2) whether venue is proper in the Eastern District of Virginia; . . .

[Plaintiffs Dee-K and Asheboro, Virginia and North Carolina corporations respectively, bought rubber thread from defendants to make, among other things, bungee cords. Plaintiffs sued a number of corporations producing the rubber thread, corporations in Malaysia (including defendants Heveafil, Rubfil, and Rubberflex), in Indonesia (defendants Bakrie and Perkebunan), and in Thailand. Plaintiffs alleged a broad conspiracy among defendants to fix prices and restrain competition in rubber thread. Defendants challenged jurisdiction and venue.]

The prerequisites for obtaining personal jurisdiction are well established. . . . First, the plaintiff must point to a statute (usually a state's long-arm statute) or rule that authorizes service of process over the defendant. Second, the service of process pursuant to the specified statute or rule must comport with due process. . . .

In the instant circumstances, the first prerequisite is met both by §12 of the Clayton Act, 15 U.S.C. §22, and by Rule 4(k)(2), Fed. R. Civ. P. Section 12 of the Clayton Act provides for nationwide-indeed worldwide-service of process when the antitrust defendant is a corporation. See 15 U.S.C. §22 (providing for service "wherever [defendant] may be found").[9] Further, under Rule 4(k)(2), a defendant not subject to the jurisdiction of any state court that is served with process is subject to personal jurisdiction in the federal courts as long as the assertion of jurisdiction (i) is consistent with federal law, and (ii) does not offend the Constitution.

In this case, Bakrie was properly served in Indonesia pursuant to Rule 4(f)(2)(C)(ii), Fed. R. Civ. P. Because the Clayton Act provides for worldwide service, service in Indonesia was consistent with federal law. Thus, plaintiffs need only show under Rule 4 that the service effected did not offend the

---

9. Of course, §12 provides only that service may be effected worldwide; it does not prescribe the proper means for accomplishing the service. In that regard, a plaintiff must comply with Rule 4, Fed. R. Civ. P.

Constitution. . . . Thus, under either the Clayton Act or Rule 4, any challenge to personal jurisdiction is governed by the familiar constitutional test of "fair play and substantial justice." *International Shoe*. In essence, the statutory analysis regarding service of process collapses into the constitutional inquiry. . . .

[Applying *International Shoe* to the facts, the court found that due process was satisfied by defendants' appointment of exclusive U.S. sales agents and its customizing of its products for the U.S. market.]

Next, there is the matter of venue. Defendants contend that even if in personam jurisdiction is established on the basis of aggregated, national contacts, venue in the Eastern District of Virginia is improper.

Section 12 of the Clayton Act lays venue in any district where the defendant is "found" or where it "transacts business." At first blush this would seem to be an insurmountable obstacle to suit in this district, as the foreign defendants here apparently cannot be found in any judicial district in the United States because they conduct their business abroad. Yet, this is not fatal to venue, for the Supreme Court has held that 28 U.S.C. §1391(d), which provides that aliens may be sued in any district, overrides any special venue statute (such as the one contained in 12 of the Clayton Act). Thus, §1391(d) eliminates any venue impediment to suit in this district with respect to the foreign defendants because they, as aliens, may be sued in any federal judicial district.

As to the American defendants, [under 28 U.S.C. §1391(b)] venue is proper in (1) a judicial district where any defendant resides, if all defendants reside in the same State, (2) a judicial district in which a substantial part of the events or omissions giving rise to the claim occurred . . . or (3) a judicial district in which any defendant may be found, if there is no district in which the action may otherwise be brought. In the case at bar, neither (1) nor (2) applies; thus, venue is proper as to all the American defendants in any district where one of them may be found.[24]

Plaintiffs have alleged some Virginia-related contacts of defendants, but the allegations are quite sparse. In addition to the boilerplate statement that defendants "are found or do business in the district or the state," Second Amended Complaint P 2, plaintiffs assert that Heveafil sold its rubber thread in Virginia; that Rubfil had customers in Virginia and sold to them with the aid of its subsidiary, Rubfil-USA; that Rubberflex sold its thread in Virginia with the aid of its subsidiaries Flexfil (RI) and Flexfil (NC); and that Consortium sold Perkebunan's product in this state. Several defendants contend—and plaintiffs have yet to dispute—that these Virginia contacts were located in the Western District of Virginia, not the Eastern District, and thus that venue here is improper. Not all defendants, however, have objected to venue being laid in this

---

24. The fact that the foreign defendants can be sued in this district pursuant to 28 U.S.C. §1391(d) does not mean that they can also be found in this district, thereby creating a basis for proper venue as to the domestic defendants pursuant to 1391(b)(3). Were this not so, in a case involving foreign and domestic defendants, 1391(d) could be used as to the foreign defendants to circumvent the requirements of 1391(b) as to the domestic defendants. Neither the statute as a whole, nor sensible policy, permits such a result. When, as here, there are both foreign and domestic defendants, 1391(b) must be satisfied as to the domestic defendants.

No allegation in complaint that venue should be in E.D. va

district. That fact might suggest that there are indeed sufficient contacts with this district such that at least one of the American distributors can be "found" here, thus satisfying 1391(b)(3). Yet no specific allegation to that effect is found in the second amended complaint. At this time, therefore, it is unclear whether venue is proper in the Eastern District of Virginia. Accordingly, plaintiffs must show that venue in this district is proper, or the action may be transferred to the Western District of Virginia. . . .

NOTES AND PROBLEMS

1. *Dee-K Enterprises* reviews many of the topics considered in this chapter as it illustrates how they relate to each other.

a. Explain why "the statutory analysis regarding service of process collapses into the constitutional inquiry" in this case.

b. The opinion says that process was served under Rule 4(f)(2)(C)(ii) — certified mail with return receipt. Why not under the Hague Service Convention, described supra at page 157? Indonesia had not signed the Convention.

2. Wrap yourself around footnote 24, which explores the relationship of §§1391(b)(3) and (d).

a. If this suit were solely against Bakrie, the Indonesian defendant, where would venue lie?

b. Why, in the court's view, does this change when Bakrie is joined with the other defendants?

c. The opinion ends by sending the parties out to develop additional information about domestic defendants' contacts with the Eastern District of Virginia. Why?

3. Having surveyed the basic issues of the contemporary federal venue statute, we can reconsider the overlap between personal jurisdiction and venue: Why have both? At a basic level, the question of whether venue is redundant has no easy answer. Historically, venue statutes preceded concepts of personal jurisdiction and were, until Pennoyer v. Neff, the only law regulating the place where suit might be brought. Moreover, until a few decades ago venue was in some respects more restrictive than the law of personal jurisdiction. But as the requirements for venue have come ever more closely to approximate those of personal jurisdiction, it is fair to ask whether we need both doctrines, or would jurisdiction alone suffice? Note that because venue is statutory, one could contemplate its abolition: It is safe to say that the abolition of venue requirements might cause some housekeeping problems but would not violate the Due Process Clause.

When an action is brought in state court, federal venue statutes are irrelevant; they apply only to actions originally brought in the federal courts. (Cases removed to the federal courts from state courts are similarly not subject to federal venue requirements; venue lies in the district encompassing the state court from which the case is removed.) States, however, have their own venue statutes that indicate in which county an action must be brought. Professors James, Hazard, and Leubsdorf have summarized the state venue rules as follows:

> In transitory actions, state venue rules follow variegated patterns that employ one or more of the following tests: (a) where the cause of action, or part thereof, arose or accrued; (b) where some fact is present or happened; (c) where the defendant resides; (d) where the defendant is doing business; (e) where the defendant has an office or place of business, or an agent, or representative, or where an agent or officer of defendant resides; (f) where the plaintiff resides; (g) where the plaintiff is doing business; (h) where the defendant may be found; (i) where the defendant may be summoned or served; (j) in the county designated in the plaintiffs complaint; (k) in any county; (l) where the seat of government is located. The tests that give plaintiff the widest choice are often applicable only where defendant is a nonresident of the state. The defendant's residence is the most common provision for venue.[*]

Another principle that is sometimes given the label "venue" is the local-action rule for certain causes of action, chiefly those involving real property. The rule states that only the courts of the state where land is located will hear cases that raise any question concerning title to the land. In the early case of Livingston v. Jefferson, 15 F. Cas. 660 (C.C.D. Va. 1811) (No. 8,411), Livingston sought to sue Thomas Jefferson for trespass to land located in Louisiana. As Jefferson was a resident of Virginia and not subject to jurisdiction elsewhere, and as the court ruled that under English common law the action was local and had to be brought where the land was located, the plaintiff was effectively left without a remedy. The rule has since been changed by statute in many states and was rejected by court decision in Reasor-Hill Corp. v. Harrison, 220 Ark. 521, 249 S.W.2d 994 (1952). Another traditional local action is an action by a state to collect taxes, although increasingly that restriction has been abandoned. E.g., Oklahoma ex rel. Oklahoma Tax Committee v. Neely, 225 Ark. 230, 282 S.W.2d 150 (1955).

3.   Declining Jurisdiction: Transfer and Forum Non Conveniens

Both state and federal courts possess the power to decline to exercise jurisdiction even though they possess it. You have already encountered one example of this power: long-arm statutes that do not extend as far as the Constitution would permit. As personal jurisdiction has expanded under modern analyses and as state and federal courts perceive themselves to be working with greater caseloads, the power of declining to hear cases has been exercised more frequently. This section examines two of the rationales for declining to exercise jurisdiction. One — transfer among federal judicial districts under 28 U.S.C. §1404 — has special significance for federal courts because they are located throughout the United States and its possessions. The other — forum non conveniens — affects both state and federal courts.

---

[*] James, Hazard, and Leubsdorf 97, citing Stevens, Venue Statutes: Diagnosis and Proposed Cure, 49 Mich. L. Rev. 307, 310-315 (1951).

Both §1404(a) transfer and forum non conveniens dismissals flow from the same perception: that there will be circumstances in which a court has the power to hear a case but, for reasons of justice or efficiency, should not do so. One might think that for a court applying the jurisdictional principles enunciated in *International Shoe*, such situations would be rare. They can, however, occur. For example, the judge may conclude that although jurisdiction is clear, a strong local prejudice against one of the parties will make a fair trial difficult to achieve. Or the preponderance of witnesses, perhaps some of them severely disabled, will have to travel long distances to testify. Under these or similar circumstances, a federal court may decide to either transfer the case to another federal court under §1404(a) or dismiss it under the forum non conveniens doctrine for trial in another country. A state court might take a similar action, transferring (under a state statute analogous to §1404(a)) to another court in the same state or dismissing under the forum non conveniens doctrine for refiling in another state or country. We start with the more basic doctrine, forum non conveniens.

a. Forum Non Conveniens

Piper Aircraft v. Reyno

454 U.S. 235 (1981)

Justice MARSHALL delivered the opinion of the Court. . . .

I

A

In July 1976, a small commercial aircraft crashed in the Scottish highlands during the course of a charter flight from Blackpool to Perth. The pilot and five passengers were killed instantly. The decedents were all Scottish subjects and residents, as are their heirs and next of kin. There were no eyewitnesses to the accident. At the time of the crash the plane was subject to Scottish air traffic control.

The aircraft, a twin-engine Piper Aztec, was manufactured in Pennsylvania by petitioner Piper Aircraft Co. (Piper). The propellers were manufactured in Ohio by petitioner Hartzell Propeller, Inc. (Hartzell). . . . [The aircraft was owned and maintained by Air Navigation and] was operated by McDonald Aviation, Ltd. (McDonald), a Scottish air taxi service. Both Air Navigation and McDonald were organized in the United Kingdom. The wreckage of the plane is now in a hanger in Farnsborough, England.

[A] British Department of Trade [report] . . . found no evidence of defective equipment and indicated that pilot error may have contributed to the accident. The pilot, who had obtained his commercial pilot's license only three months earlier, was flying over high ground at an altitude considerably lower than the minimum height required by his company's operations manual.

In July 1977, a California probate court appointed respondent Gaynell Reyno administratrix of the estates of the five passengers. Reyno is not related to and does not know any of the decedents or their survivors; she was a legal secretary to the attorney who filed this lawsuit. Several days after her appointment, Reyno commenced separate wrongful-death actions against Piper and Hartzell in the Superior Court of California, claiming negligence and strict liability. . . . Reyno candidly admits that the action against Piper and Hartzell was filed in the United States because its laws regarding liability, capacity to sue, and damages are more favorable to her position than are those of Scotland. Scottish law does not recognize strict liability in tort. Moreover, it permits wrongful-death actions only when brought by a decedent's relatives. The relatives may sue only for "loss of support and society."

[The defendants first removed to federal district court in California. Piper then sought transfer to transfer under §1404(a) to the Middle District of Pennsylvania, where Piper does business, on grounds of convenience. Hartzell moved to dismiss for want of personal jurisdiction, or in the alternative to transfer the case to the Middle District of Pennsylvania under 28 U.S.C. §1631, where Hartzell's business with Piper supported jurisdiction; the district court transferred. With both cases now moved to federal district court in Pennsylvania, both defendants then sought to dismiss the case on grounds of forum non conveniens.]

B

. . . The District Court granted these motions in October 1979. It relied on the balancing test set forth by this Court in Gulf Oil Corp. v. Gilbert, 330 U.S. 501 (1947), and its companion case, Koster v. Lumbermens Mut. Cas. Co., 330 U.S. 518 (1947). In those decisions, the Court stated that a plaintiff's choice of forum should rarely be disturbed. However, when an alternative forum has jurisdiction to hear the case, and when trial in the chosen forum would "establish . . . oppressiveness and vexation to a defendant . . . out of all proportion to plaintiff's conve-nience," or when the "chosen forum [is] inappropriate because of considerations affecting the court's own administrative and legal problems," the court may, in the exercise of its sound discretion, dismiss the case. To guide trial court discretion, the Court provided a list of "private interest factors" affecting the convenience of the litigants, and a list of "public interest factors" affecting the convenience of the forum.[6]

---

6. The factors pertaining to the private interests of the litigants included the "relative ease of access to sources of proof; availability of compulsory process for attendance of unwilling, and the cost of obtaining attendance of willing, witnesses; possibility of view of premises, if view would be appropriate to the action; and all other practical problems that make trial of a case easy, expeditious and inexpensive." Gilbert, 330 U.S., at 508. The public factors bearing on the question included the administrative difficulties flowing from court congestion; the "local interest in having localized controversies decided at home"; the interest in having the trial of a diversity case in a forum that is at home with the law that must govern the action; the avoidance of unnecessary problems in conflict of laws, or in the application of foreign law; and the unfairness of burdening citizens in an unrelated forum with jury duty.

3d Circuit reverses dismissal

[The Third Circuit reversed, on the ground that dismissal for forum non conveniens is never appropriate where the law of the alternative forum is less favorable to the plaintiff.]

II

It can't defeat motion to DC other forum is less favorable

The Court of Appeals erred in holding that plaintiffs may defeat a motion to dismiss on the ground of forum non conveniens merely by showing that the substantive law that would be applied in the alternative forum is less favorable to the plaintiffs than that of the present forum. The possibility of a change in substantive law should ordinarily not be given conclusive or even substantial weight in the forum non conveniens inquiry.

We expressly rejected the position adopted by the Court of Appeals in our decision in Canada Malting Co. v. Paterson Steamships, Ltd., 285 U.S. 413 (1932)....

The Court of Appeals' decision is inconsistent with this Court's earlier forum non conveniens decisions in another respect. Those decisions have repeatedly emphasized the need to retain flexibility....

[I]f conclusive or substantial weight were given to the possibility of a change in law, the forum non conveniens doctrine would become virtually useless. Jurisdiction and venue requirements are often easily satisfied. As a result, many plaintiffs are able to choose from among several forums. Ordinarily, these plaintiffs will select that forum whose choice-of-law rules are most advantageous. Thus, if the possibility of an unfavorable change in substantive law is given substantial weight in the forum non conveniens inquiry, dismissal would rarely be proper. . . .

Litigation in US would increase even more

Upholding the decision of the Court of Appeals would result in other practical problems. At least where the foreign plaintiff named an American manufacturer as defendant, a court could not dismiss the case on grounds of forum non conveniens where dismissal might lead to an unfavorable change in law. The American courts, which are already extremely attractive to foreign plaintiffs, would become even more attractive. The flow of litigation into the United States would increase and further congest already crowded courts.[19] . . .

We do not hold that the possibility of an unfavorable change in law should never be a relevant consideration in a forum non conveniens inquiry. Of course, if the remedy provided by the alternative forum is so clearly inadequate or unsatisfactory that it is no remedy at all, the unfavorable change in law may be given

19. In holding that the possibility of a change in law unfavorable to the plaintiff should not be given substantial weight, we also necessarily hold that the possibility of a change in law favorable to defendant should not be considered. Respondent suggests that Piper and Hartzell filed the motion to dismiss, not simply because trial in the United States would be inconvenient, but also because they believe the laws of Scotland are more favorable. She argues that this should be taken into account in the analysis of the private interests. We recognize, of course, that Piper and Hartzell may be engaged in reverse forum-shopping. However, this possibility ordinarily should not enter into a trial court's analysis of the private interests. If the defendant is able to overcome the presumption in favor of plaintiff by showing that trial in the chosen forum would be unnecessarily burdensome, dismissal is appropriate — regardless of the fact that defendant may also be motivated by a desire to obtain a more favorable forum.

substantial weight; the district court may conclude that dismissal would not be in the interests of justice. In these cases, however, the remedies that would be provided by the Scottish courts do not fall within this category. Although the relatives of the decedents may not be able to rely on a strict liability theory, and although their potential damages award may be smaller, there is no danger that they will be deprived of any remedy or treated unfairly. . . .

III

The Court of Appeals also erred in rejecting the District Court's *Gilbert* analysis. . . .

A

The District Court acknowledged that there is ordinarily a strong presumption in favor of the plaintiff's choice of forum, which may be overcome only when the private and public interest factors clearly point towards trial in the alternative forum. It held, however, that the presumption applies with less force when the plaintiff or real parties in interest are foreign.

The District Court's distinction between resident or citizen plaintiffs and foreign plaintiffs is fully justified. In *Koster*, the Court indicated that a plaintiff's choice of forum is entitled to greater deference when the plaintiff has chosen the home forum. When the home forum has been chosen, it is reasonable to assume that this choice is convenient. When the plaintiff is foreign, however, this assumption is much less reasonable. Because the central purpose of any forum non conveniens inquiry is to ensure that the trial is convenient, a foreign plaintiff's choice deserves less deference.

B

The forum non conveniens determination is committed to the sound discretion of the trial court. It may be reversed only when there has been a clear abuse of discretion. . . .

(1)

In analyzing the private interest factors, the District Court stated that the connections with Scotland are "overwhelming." This characterization may be somewhat exaggerated. Particularly with respect to the question of relative ease of access to sources of proof, the private interests point in both directions. As respondent emphasizes, records concerning the design, manufacture, and testing of the propeller and plane are located in the United States. She would have greater access to sources of proof relevant to her strict liability and negligence theories if trial were held here.[25] However, the District Court did not act unreasonably in

---

25. In the future, where similar problems are presented, district courts might dismiss subject to the condition that defendant corporations agree to provide the records relevant to the plaintiff's claims.

concluding that fewer evidentiary problems would be posed if the trial were held in Scotland. A large proportion of the relevant evidence is located in Great Britain . . .

The District Court correctly concluded that the problems posed by the inability to implead potential third-party defendants clearly supported holding the trial in Scotland. Joinder of the pilot's estate, Air Navigation, and McDonald is crucial to the presentation of petitioners' defense. If Piper and Hartzell can show that the accident was caused not by a design defect, but rather by the negligence of the pilot, the plane's owners, or the charter company, they will be relieved of all liability. . . .

(2)

The District Court's review of the factors relating to the public interest was also reasonable. On the basis of its choice-of-law analysis, it concluded that if the case were tried in the Middle District of Pennsylvania, Pennsylvania law would apply to Piper and Scottish law to Hartzell. It stated that a trial involving two sets of laws would be confusing to the jury. It also noted its own lack of familiarity with Scottish law. Consideration of these problems was clearly appropriate under *Gilbert*. . . .

Scotland has a very strong interest in this litigation. The accident occurred in its airspace. All of the decedents were Scottish. Apart from Piper and Hartzell, all potential plaintiffs and defendants are either Scottish or English. As we stated in *Gilbert*, there is "a local interest in having localized controversies decided at home." Respondent argues that American citizens have an interest in ensuring that American manufacturers are deterred from producing defective products, and that additional deterrence might be obtained if Piper and Hartzell were tried in the United States, where they could be sued on the basis of both negligence and strict liability. However, the incremental deterrence that would be gained if this trial were held in American court is likely to be insignificant. The American interest in this accident is simply not sufficient to justify the enormous commitment of judicial time and resources that would inevitably be required if the case were to be tried here.

IV

The Court of Appeals erred in holding that the possibility of an unfavorable change in law bars dismissal on the ground of forum non conveniens. It also erred in rejecting the District Court's *Gilbert* analysis. The District Court properly decided that the presumption in favor of the respondent's forum choice applied with less than maximum force because the real parties in interest are foreign. It did not act unreasonably in deciding that the private interests pointed towards trial in Scotland. Nor did it act unreasonably in deciding that the public interests favored trial in Scotland. Thus, the judgment of the Court of Appeals is

Reversed.

[Justices POWELL and O'CONNOR took no part in the decision of these cases. The concurring opinion of Justice WHITE and the dissent of Justices STEVENS and BRENNAN are omitted.]

NOTES AND PROBLEMS

1. Be sure you understand the issue at stake. By the time the case came to rest in Pennsylvania, defendants were not challenging the court's personal jurisdiction; what were they arguing?

2. What change in facts should lead to a different outcome — that is, the denial of the motion to dismiss for forum non conveniens?

a. If the decedents had been U.S. citizens?

b. If the plane had crashed into the sea, making it unavailable for examination?

c. If Scotland permitted no recovery for wrongful death?

3. What will happen now that the case has been dismissed? One possibility is that the plaintiffs, deprived of the advantageous U.S. product liability law, will drop the lawsuit. Another possibility is that they will refile in Scotland. But what if, in the meantime, the statute of limitations has run? It seems unfair to permit a defendant to move for dismissal on the grounds that forum A is less convenient than forum B, only to raise a defense that makes forum B entirely unavailable.

a. To obviate this unfairness, courts regularly require that a defendant moving to dismiss on grounds of an inconvenient forum agree in advance to waive the statute of limitations defense in the alternative forum.

b. The same requirement sometimes applies to personal jurisdiction and venue: Occasionally defendants will argue that a forum lacking either jurisdiction or venue is more convenient. When courts accept such arguments, they often condition dismissal on an agreement to waive jurisdictional or venue defenses in the new forum.

4. *Piper* exemplifies two adversaries determined to wring every ounce of advantage from the procedural system.

a. Who was the plaintiff? Why do you suppose she filed suit in California, where none of the obviously relevant events occurred?

b. How did defendants respond to plaintiff's initial strategy? Enumerate the steps defendants used as they maneuvered toward the eventual outcome.

5. The opinion hints at the possibility that dramatic differences in procedure in the alternative forum would make dismissal inappropriate. How different would a foreign legal system have to be for a U.S. court to refuse to dismiss on grounds that there was no adequate alternative forum?

a. One can think of this question in two ways — in terms of formal procedural differences, such as the inability of a litigant to cross-examine a witness — or in terms of the practical obstacles to a lawsuit, such as the speed of the legal system.

b. Most legal systems differ substantially from those of the United States. None, for example, affords the widespread right to a civil jury; few permit discovery on the scope allowed by the United States. Not surprisingly, courts do not hold that differences in procedural systems are a sufficient reason to bar forum non conveniens dismissals.

c. In In re Union Carbide Gas Plant Disaster, 809 F.2d 195 (2d Cir. 1987), the Indian plaintiffs injured in a gigantic industrial explosion, opposed a forum non conveniens motion that would have sent the case from New York to India, where the explosion had occurred. They did so on grounds, initially supported by the

Indian government that the court system was entirely unable to handle the number of claims involved. The court nevertheless dismissed the case, citing the extreme difficulties of bringing hundreds of Indian witnesses to the United States.

6. Contrast two applications of *Piper*'s doctrine. Are the cases distinguishable?

a. Guidi v. Inter-Continental Hotels Corp., 224 F.3d 142 (2d Cir. 2000). Plaintiffs were U.S. citizens, survivors and heirs of the victims of shootings in an Egyptian hotel operated by defendant, where a gunman had shot six. Plaintiffs brought a federal diversity action in New York against the New York-based corporate hotel operator. The district court dismissed on forum non conveniens grounds, finding that an Egyptian court would be more familiar with Egyptian law, which governed the action, that Egypt's commitment to tourism assured that the suit would be handled properly, and that there was already related litigation pending in Egypt — suits brought by the families of French and Italian victims. The Second Circuit reversed, holding that the district court had abused its discretion in dismissing. The inconvenience and "emotional burden" on plaintiffs outweighed the "slight[ly]" greater convenience of litigation in Egypt, said the court. Can you distinguish *Piper*?

b. Gonzales v. Chrysler Corp., 301 F.3d 377 (5th Cir. 2002). Plaintiff, a Mexican national, sued for the wrongful death of his child as a result of an air bag accident. The court explained:

> Mexican law caps the maximum award for the loss of a child's life at approximately $2,500 (730 days' worth of wages at the Mexican minimum wage rate). Thus, according to Gonzalez, Mexico provides an inadequate alternative forum for this dispute. . . .
>
> Gonzalez argues that because of the damage cap, the cost of litigating this case in Mexico will exceed the potential recovery. As a consequence, the lawsuit will never be brought in Mexico. Stated differently, the lawsuit is not economically viable in Mexico. . . .
>
> The practical and economic realities lying at the base of this dispute are clear. At oral argument, the parties agreed that this case would never be filed in Mexico. In short, a dismissal on the ground of forum non conveniens will determine the outcome of this litigation in Chrysler's favor.[9] We nevertheless are unwilling to hold as a legal principle that Mexico offers an inadequate forum simply because it does not make economic sense for Gonzalez to file this lawsuit in Mexico. . . .
>
> [I]f we allow the economic viability of a lawsuit to decide the adequacy of an alternative forum, we are further forced to engage in a rudderless exercise of line drawing with respect to a cap on damages: At what point does a cap on damages transform a forum from adequate to inadequate? Is it, as here, $2,500? Is it $50,000? Or is it $100,000? Any recovery cap may, in a given case, make the lawsuit economically unviable. We therefore hold that the adequacy inquiry under *Piper Aircraft* does not include an evaluation of whether it makes economic sense for Gonzalez to file this lawsuit in Mexico.

Is *Piper* distinguishable? Is *Guidi*, described in the preceding note?

---

9. This fact is not unique to this lawsuit. A survey found that between 1945 and 1985, of 85 transnational cases dismissed on the ground of forum non conveniens, only 4 percent ever reached trial in a foreign court. See David Robertson, Forum Non Conveniens in America and England: "A Rather Fantastic Fiction," 103 L.Q. Rev. 398, 418-419 (1987).

b.   Transfer under 28 U.S.C. §§1404, 1406, and 1631

Reading *Piper* carefully, one notices that before seeking dismissal under forum non conveniens, the defendants first removed to federal court and then sought transfer to a different judicial district under 28 U.S.C. §1404. That statute permits transfer "[f]or the convenience of parties and witnesses, in the interest of justice." It thus gives to federal courts the ability to move cases within the system without the necessity for dismissal and refiling, which would be necessary under the doctrine of forum non conveniens.

NOTES AND PROBLEMS

1. *Piper* was filed in a California state court, then removed to federal court in California, where the defendants made the §1404 motion. Using the facts in the opinion, reconstruct the arguments defendants would have made in support of their motion to transfer the case to the Middle District of Pennsylvania.

2. Why could defendants not invoke §1404(a) when they sought to move the litigation to Scotland?

3. Although the statutory scheme of §1404(a) closely resembles the common law doctrine of forum non conveniens, there are differences worth noting:

a. Section 1404(a) governs only in the federal courts. State courts may make use of the forum non conveniens doctrine to dismiss a case or of state statutes analogous to §1404(a) to transfer between districts within the state, but they lack power to transfer a case to another state.

b. Forum non conveniens dismissal is available only to the defendant, because the plaintiff may voluntarily dismiss the first action, which he brought. But plaintiffs may seek transfer under §1404. Ferens v. John Deere Co., 494 U.S. 516 (1990).

c. The district judge has a bit more discretion under §1404 than under the forum non conveniens doctrine. In Norwood v. Kirkpatrick, 349 U.S. 29 (1955), the Supreme Court upheld a transfer even though the plaintiff was a resident of the district in which he had brought suit. The traditional deference to the plaintiff's choice of forum (if jurisdiction and venue were proper) meant that forum non conveniens was unavailable in such circumstances.

4. Section 1404 does not exhaust the possibilities of transfer within the federal system.

a. Section 1406 allows transfer from a district in which venue is improper. (Dismissal is also allowed.)

b. When venue is proper but jurisdiction is lacking, 28 U.S.C. §1631 permits transfer to a court with jurisdiction. In such a case, the statute specifies that "the action . . . shall proceed as if it had been filed in . . . the court to which it is transferred." It further stipulates that the transferred action relates back to date of the original filing.

5. Section 1407 of 28 U.S.C. sets up a judicial panel on multidistrict litigation and authorizes it to transfer cases pending in different districts to a single district

for coordinated or consolidated pretrial proceedings. The transferee district need not be one in which venue was originally proper. The theory underlying such consolidation is efficiency: It is needless to have multiple courts deciding identical pretrial motions and numerous parties conducting duplicative discovery. This quest for efficiency halts, however, at the threshold of trial, as §1407 proceedings are limited to the pretrial stage. Trial takes place in the original district in which the action is brought (unless it is transferred under §1404 or §1406). Lexecon v. Milberg Weiss, 523 U.S. 26 (1998) (assigned multidistrict court cannot "transfer" case to itself for trial). Typical cases for the application of §1407 are airplane crash cases.

This chapter has explored the elaborate law developed to answer a single question: Where can this lawsuit against this defendant be brought? The complexity of the doctrine answering that question testifies both to its practical importance and to a constitutional structure that recognizes a degree of independent autonomy and sovereignty in the several states. Simply put: It matters whether Alabama or California courts will hear a case because the constitutional structure gives to the governments of Alabama and California, including their respective courts, the last word on many important questions. Under our federal structure, however, there is an overarching — but limited — federal sovereignty with its own court system. So, in each case, the question is not simply whether the case belongs in State *A* or State *B*, but whether can the case be heard in a federal court instead of a state court. The next chapter explores the answer to that question.

SUBJECT MATTER JURISDICTION OF THE FEDERAL COURTS

III

A. The Idea and the Structure of Subject Matter Jurisdiction

The law of personal jurisdiction limits both state and federal courts in relation to particular defendants. If the defendant lacks the requisite connection with the forum state, due process prevents courts sitting in that state from rendering a judgment that will bind that defendant. The Constitution thereby guards the boundary between fair and unfair assertions of judicial power over a particular defendant by courts in a given geographic location.

Courts in the United States must also cope with a second and quite different jurisdictional boundary. The Constitution created a federal government but made the federal government supreme only in certain areas. In other areas the states are sovereign, and in still others federal and state governments share power. The centuries since the ratification of the Constitution have seen numerous political struggles and a bloody civil war fought over the location of the line between state and federal power. That continuing struggle is reflected in the realm of civil procedure. Because both state and federal governments have court systems, litigants, their lawyers, and judges need to know which kinds of cases belong in which courts. Lawyers describe this sorting of cases between court systems as "subject matter jurisdiction."

A sketch of constitutional history reveals several political compromises that shape the structure of federal judicial jurisdiction. Read Article III, the portion of the Constitution devoted to the judiciary. You won't be surprised to see that §1 of this Article establishes a Supreme Court. But you may be surprised to learn that the Constitution views the other federal courts as optional. Section 1 authorizes, but does not require, Congress to establish lower federal courts — what we know today as the courts of appeals and the district courts. Putting the question of lower federal courts into Congress's hands represented a compromise between those who feared an overly powerful federal government and those who viewed the establishment of federal courts as one of the most important goals of the new government. The compromise left the issue subject to changeable legislative wishes. In fact, the first Congress created lower federal courts, and their existence has never been in serious question since, though the exact scope of their powers has often been questioned.

Section 2 of Article III contains a second compromise, one whose terms have been fiercely contested for more than 200 years. Article III limits federal courts' jurisdiction to the list set forth in §2: By implication a case not there enumerated may not be heard in a federal court. Such a case could be heard only in a state court. Within the boundaries of Article III, however, Congress remains free to bestow all or some of the constitutionally permissible jurisdiction on the lower federal courts.

This history has implications even in ordinary lawsuits. Because the federal courts are courts of *limited jurisdiction*, two questions lurk at the threshold of every case brought in a federal court: Does the case fall within one of the enumerated categories of Article III, §2; and has Congress further authorized the lower federal courts to assume that jurisdiction? Rule 8(a) reflects these concerns by requiring every federal complaint to begin with a "short and plain statement of the grounds upon which the court's jurisdiction depends." In judging those jurisdictional statements, the courts look to three bodies of law—the Constitution, the statutes conferring jurisdiction, and the case law interpreting both.

Skimming the jurisdictional statutes, one might not suspect another important feature: Federal courts share most of their jurisdiction with state courts. Look, for example, at the so-called general federal question statute, 28 U.S.C. §1331. It grants federal courts jurisdiction over cases that arise under federal law. That federal courts have such jurisdiction does not seem surprising, but it may be surprising to learn that they do not have exclusive jurisdiction over such cases. So far as Congress and the Constitution are concerned, cases arising under this statute can be brought in state as well as federal courts. Lawyers speak of such shared jurisdiction as *concurrent*. Like general federal question cases, diversity jurisdiction (28 U.S.C. §1332) is also concurrent. In some instances Congress has made federal jurisdiction exclusive. See, for example, 28 U.S.C. §§1333 (admiralty), 1334 (bankruptcy), and 1337 (antitrust). For an example of a statute carefully discriminating between grants of concurrent and exclusive federal jurisdiction, read 28 U.S.C. §1338. In still other instances Congress has specifically forbidden federal courts from hearing cases that might otherwise fall within their jurisdiction; for example, 28 U.S.C. §1341 forbids federal courts from enjoining state tax collection in most circumstances.

Why would a lawyer or a litigant care whether a state or federal court heard her case? Assuming some court is available, why should it matter which one? The answer has both practical and political dimensions. As a tactical matter, the reasons for seeking a federal rather than a state court range from the mundane (some federal courts presently have shorter waiting times until trial than their state counterparts) to the strategic (is the defendant likely to get a more sympathetic hearing from the local state judge than from the federal judge in the nearest large city; will a six-person federal jury, drawn from a broader geographic area and required to reach a unanimous verdict, be likely to award higher—or lower—damages than the state jury, which may have 12 members and may be allowed to reach a non-unanimous majority verdict; are federal judges more inclined to enforce arbitration agreements than state judges; is the federal bench generally more liberal or conservative than the state court bench in the particular jurisdiction?) to the crafty (is the opposing lawyer uncomfortable with the generally more formal conduct and faster pace of federal litigation?).

On a somewhat different plane, one might note that Article III, §1 gives federal judges lifetime tenure, a protection that is supposed to shield them from political pressure. So a litigant with a legally strong but unpopular claim or defense might prefer federal courts. The limited jurisdiction of the federal courts also shields them, however, from certain kinds of cases: Family law disputes, for example, are not part of the federal docket. These dual insulations — from political pressure and from a broad caseload — may work in opposite directions. Arguing that federal courts possess a range of virtues ranging from greater competence to "class-based predilections favorable to constitutional enforcement," one civil rights litigator has argued that in virtually every conceivable situation the federal courts would be more hospitable to his clients' claims. Bert Neuborne, The Myth of Parity, 90 Harv. L. Rev. 1105 (1977). Another experienced litigator has argued that for his gay and lesbian clients, the state courts' closer ties both to the local community and their broad mix of cases make them the superior forum. William Rubenstein, The Myth of Superiority, 16 Const. Commentary 599 (2000). For us the significance of the debate lies in the fact that experienced lawyers could believe it matters whether a state or a federal court hears the case — even in instances when the two courts would be applying the same law. This proposition sets the stage for an exploration of federal subject matter jurisdiction.

B.   Federal Question Jurisdiction

Although many Americans today assume that federal trial courts have jurisdiction to hear all cases involving federal law, that assumption has not been true for most of the nation's history and is true today only in a limited and sometimes counter-intuitive form. The first Congress passed a Judiciary Act that exercised the option given it by Article III to expand the federal judiciary beyond the Supreme Court. In choosing to create what the Constitution calls "inferior" federal courts, Congress bestowed on those courts some but not all of the jurisdiction allowed under Article III. Among the most important grants of jurisdiction were diversity and admiralty. Most striking from a modern perspective, however, is the absence of any general federal question jurisdiction. Individual statutes contained juris-dictional grants — patents and federal pension laws are two early examples — but no general power was given to federal courts to entertain claims based on federal law. Consider what that meant: Unless covered by one of the specific and gener-ally narrowly drawn statutes, a claim based directly on the Constitution or a federal statute could not be brought in federal court; the federal question would come to a federal forum (the Supreme Court) only on appeal from a state court judgment. Not until after the Civil War had reshaped understanding of federal-ism and, in particular, the federal courts' role in the enforcement of civil rights, did Congress in 1875 enact a general federal question statute. Its contemporary successor is found in 28 U.S.C. §1331.

The key provision of that statute gives district courts jurisdiction over cases "arising under" the Constitution, statutes, or treaties of the federal government.

The difficulty comes in deciding what it means for a case to "arise under" federal law. About the interpretation of that phrase, one scholar has said, "Though the meaning of this phrase has attracted the interest of such giants of the bench as Marshall, Waite, Bradley, the first Harlan, Holmes, Cardozo, Frankfurter, and Brennan, and has been the subject of voluminous scholarly commentary, it cannot be said that any clear test has yet been developed to determine which cases 'arise under' the Constitution, laws or treaties of the United States." Wright, Federal Courts 101. Before you despair, bear in mind that the basics are quite straightforward and that the difficult problems arise in a narrow band of cases. As a preface to our exploration, consider the following two cases.

1. Worker contends that Employer has violated the federal Fair Labor Standards Act, which, among other things, establishes a minimum wage for certain employees. Employer does not contest the applicability of the statute or the amount of the minimum wage but instead asserts that Worker has overstated the number of hours he has worked and is for that reason not entitled to the pay he seeks. Consider what issues will be contested.

2. Plaintiff claims that Newspaper has libeled her. Newspaper's defense rests on a body of law that the courts have extrapolated from the First Amendment. Specifically, it relies on a body of U.S. Supreme Court cases holding that media defendants in libel cases may prevail — even if they have published false and injurious information — so long as they have not been negligent in, for example, checking their sources. Newspaper concedes the inaccuracy of its article but nevertheless believes that it has such a First Amendment defense. Consider what the contested issues in the second case will be.

As an intuitive matter, which, if either, of these cases should be in federal court? Why? Now consider how the following case affects the answers to those questions.

Louisville & Nashville Railroad v. Mottley

211 U.S. 149 (1908)

[Erasmus and Annie Mottley were injured in a railway accident. To settle their claims, the railroad in 1871 gave them a lifetime pass good for free transportation on the line. Several decades later, Congress, believing that railroads were using free transportation to bribe public officials, made free passes unlawful. The railroad thereupon refused to honor the Mottleys' passes, citing the new federal legislation. The Mottleys sued in federal court seeking specific performance of their contract. "The bill [, that is the complaint,] further alleges: First, that the act of Congress referred to does not prohibit the giving of passes under the circumstances of this case; and, second, that if the law is to be construed as prohibiting such passes, it is in conflict with the Fifth Amendment of the constitution, because it deprives the plaintiffs of their property without due process of law. The defendant demurred to the bill." [The federal trial court overruled the demurrer and granted the Mottleys the relief they had requested. Defendant railroad appealed to the Supreme Court.]

Mr. Justice MOODY . . . delivered the opinion of the court.

Two questions of law were raised by the demurrer to the bill, were brought here by appeal, and have been argued before us. They are, first, whether that part of the act of Congress of June 29, 1906 (34 Stat. 584), which forbids the giving of free passes or the collection of any different compensation for transportation of passengers than that specified in the tariff filed, makes it unlawful to perform a contract for transportation of persons, who in good faith, before the passage of the act, had accepted such contract in satisfaction of a valid cause of action against the railroad; and, second, whether the statute, if it should be construed to render such a contract unlawful, is in violation of the Fifth Amendment of the Constitution of the United States. We do not deem it necessary, however, to consider either of these questions, because, in our opinion, the court below was without jurisdiction of the cause. Neither party has questioned that jurisdiction, but it is the duty of this court to see to it that the jurisdiction of the Circuit Court, which is defined and limited by statute, is not exceeded. This duty we have frequently performed of our own motion.

There was no diversity of citizenship and it is not and cannot be suggested that there was any ground of jurisdiction, except that the case was a "suit . . . arising under the Constitution and laws of the United States." [The Court cited the then-current version of the "arising under" jurisdiction statute.] It is the settled interpretation of these words, as used in this statute, conferring jurisdiction, that a suit arises under the Constitution and laws of the United States only when the plaintiff's statement of his own cause of action shows that it is based upon those laws or that Constitution. It is not enough that the plaintiff alleges some anticipated defense to his cause of action and asserts that the defense is invalidated by some provision of the Constitution of the United States. Although such allegations show that very likely, in the course of the litigation, a question under the Constitution would arise, they do not show that the suit, that is, the plaintiff's original cause of action, arises under the Constitution. In Tennessee v. Union & Planters' Bank, 152 U.S. 454, the plaintiff, the State of Tennessee, brought suit in the Circuit Court of the United States to recover from the defendant certain taxes alleged to be due under the laws of the State. The plaintiff alleged that the defendant claimed an immunity from the taxation by virtue of its charter, and that therefore the tax was void, because in violation of the provision of the Constitution of the United States, which forbids any State from passing a law impairing the obligation of contracts. The cause was held to be beyond the jurisdiction of the Circuit Court, the court saying, by Mr. Justice Gray, "a suggestion of one party, that the other will or may set up a claim under the Constitution or laws of the United States, does not make the suit one arising under that Constitution or those laws." Again, in Boston & Montana Consolidated Copper & Silver Mining Company v. Montana Ore Purchasing Company, 188 U.S. 632, the . . . cause was held to be beyond the jurisdiction of the Circuit Court, the court saying, by Mr. Justice Peckham:

> It would be wholly unnecessary and improper in order to prove complainant's cause of action to go into any matters of defence which the defendants might possibly set up and then attempt to reply to such defence, and thus, if possible, to show that a

Federal question might or probably would arise in the course of the trial of the case. To allege such defence and then make an answer to it before the defendant has the opportunity to itself plead or prove its own defence is inconsistent with any known rule of pleading so far as we are aware, and is improper.

The rule is a reasonable and just one that the complainant in the first instance shall be confined to a statement of its cause of action, leaving to the defendant to set up in his answer what his defence is and, if anything more than a denial of complainant's cause of action, imposing upon the defendant the burden of proving such defence.

Conforming itself to that rule the complainant would not, in the assertion or proof of its cause of action, bring up a single Federal question. The presentation of its cause of action would not show that it was one arising under the Constitution or laws of the United States.

The only way in which it might be claimed that a Federal question was presented would be in the complainant's statement of what the defence of defendants would be and complainant's answer to such defence. Under these circumstances the case is brought within the rule laid down in Tennessee v. Union & Planters' Bank, 152 U.S. 454. That case has been cited and approved many times since. . . .

. . . The application of this rule to the case at bar is decisive against the jurisdiction of the circuit court.

It is ordered that the judgment be reversed and the case remitted to the circuit court with instructions to dismiss for want of jurisdiction.

NOTES AND PROBLEMS

1. Explain why the federal trial court lacked jurisdiction.

a. How did the federal issue arise in *Mottley*?

b. Look back at the two hypothetical cases in the text preceding *Mottley*. Under the principle applied in *Mottley*, which case will "arise under" federal law?

2. Who raised the question of federal jurisdiction in *Mottley*?

a. If both parties were prepared to argue the merits of the case, how could a court justify dismissal on a ground unrelated to those merits? See Federal Rule 12(h)(3) for another example of the importance federal courts attach to their subject matter jurisdiction.

b. After suffering dismissal in the Supreme Court, the Mottleys refiled their suit in state court; it again made its way to the U.S. Supreme Court. The Mottleys lost again, this time on the merits. 219 U.S. 467 (1911). Is this any way to run either a railroad or a judicial system? Before answering, consider the next two notes.

3. *Mottley* exemplifies the "well-pleaded complaint" rule, one rather rigid — but widely used — approach to a difficult problem. Can one justify this approach? An enormous number of claims have some federal ingredient in their background. For example, as Charles Wright points out, land title in most western states can be traced back to U.S. land grants. Wright, Federal Courts 102. Large numbers of checks clear through federal reserve banks. Does every question of land title or every suit on a bad check arise under federal law and thus belong in

federal court? If one answers that question "no," then one has to find a principled way of sorting claims in which federal questions have some central importance from those in which they are merely background assumptions.

Mottley chooses to sort roughly, based on the pleadings: The federal claim must appear as part of a well-pleaded complaint. That approach has at least one important advantage: It permits the sorting to occur at the opening of the lawsuit before the parties and court have invested much time. To see the force of this point, consider the opposite extreme: One could, theoretically, postpone a decision on jurisdiction until after trial, to see whether an important question of federal law had emerged, and dismiss if it had not, allowing the case to start all over in state court. Not too surprisingly, not even the fiercest critic of *Mottley* has suggested taking things this far.

There are also some disadvantages to the *Mottley* approach. First, it eliminates cases, like *Mottley* itself, in which the central issue of federal law was a defense rather than a part of the plaintiff's claim. Second, the rule may make less sense now than it did when framed. In 1908, pleadings (under either common law or code pleading regimes, discussed in Chapter VI) required considerably more detail than do the Federal Rules. Under the current notice pleading regime, in some cases it may be difficult to apply the approach used in *Mottley* because the notice pleading regime of the Rules often give rather little information.

4. It is clear that the restrictive reading *Mottley* (and numerous other cases) gives to "arising under" is not constitutionally required. Why? After all, both Article III and §1331 speak of cases "arising under" federal law; could that phrase mean different things in the Constitution and in the statute? Yes; the Supreme Court in several cases has said that the meaning of "arising under" in Article III is broader than the same phrase in §1331. The different constitutional and statutory constructions of "arising under" have several implications.

a. Because the constitutional meaning of "arising under" is broader than its statutory meaning, the Supreme Court (operating under the broader constitutional definition) had jurisdiction to hear and decide *Mottley* the second time around, even though it previously decided that the district court (operating under the narrower statutory definition) did not have jurisdiction.

b. As a further corollary, Congress could change the result in *Mottley* by amending §1331. It might, for example, provide that the district courts have original jurisdiction over cases "in which an essential element either of a claim or defense rests on federal law." Should Congress do so?

5. When a defendant challenges federal question jurisdiction, one of three questions commonly arises:

a. Is there a federal issue at all? If the plaintiff's claim is based on some federal statute or regulation, the problem consists in interpreting legislation. If the plaintiff claims the right to relief under federal common law, the question is whether such federal common law exists.

b. Assuming there is a federal issue, does it "give rise to" plaintiff's claim? That is the question in *Mottley*.

c. If there is a federal issue that is not, strictly speaking, part of the basis for plaintiff's claim, is it sufficiently important to "federalize" the case?

6. *Mottley*'s bright-line test suggests that the answer to 5c is simple: No. But alongside this broad and tightly channeled mainstream flows a narrow and meandering rivulet. In this second line of cases the federal courts have assumed "arising under" jurisdiction on the basis of something less — or different — than a claim depending on federal law.

a. Smith v. Kansas City Title & Trust Co., 255 U.S. 180 (1921), is the poster child of this more expansive view. In *Smith* the plaintiff alleged that the defendant bank as trustee had violated a state law allowing it to invest only in legal securities. Thus stated, the suit would seem to arise entirely under state law regulating trustees. But the allegedly "illegal" securities were bonds issued by a federal agency under a federal law that plaintiff claimed was unconstitutional. Held: "arising under" jurisdiction. Is *Mottley*, not cited in *Smith*, distinguishable?

b. With *Smith* contrast T. B. Harms Co. v. Eliscu, 339 F.2d 823 (2d Cir. 1964), another well-known case in the *Mottley* tradition, which nicely summarizes the problem:

> A layman would doubtless be surprised to learn that an action wherein the purported sole owner of a [federal] copyright alleged that persons claiming partial ownership had recorded their claim in the Copyright Office and had warned his licensees against disregarding their interests was not one "arising under any Act of Congress relating to copyrights" over which 28 U.S.C. §1338 gives the federal courts exclusive jurisdiction. Yet precedents going back for more than a century teach that lesson and lead us to affirm Judge Weinfeld's dismissal of the complaint.
>
> The litigation concerns four copyrighted songs[, but the issue raised by the complaint was not whether the copyright had been infringed — a federal question — but whether the owner of the copyright had assigned it to another — a question of property and contract arising under state law]. Defendants moved to dismiss the complaint for failure to state a claim on which relief can be granted and for lack of federal jurisdiction; voluminous affidavits were submitted. The district court dismissed the complaint for want of federal jurisdiction. . . .
>
> Just as with western land titles, the federal grant of a patent or copyright has not been thought to infuse with any national interest a dispute as to ownership or contractual enforcement turning on the facts or on ordinary principles of contract law. Indeed, the case for an unexpansive reading of the provision conferring exclusive jurisdiction with respect to patents and copyrights has been especially strong since expansion would entail depriving the state courts of any jurisdiction over matters having so little federal significance.
>
> In an endeavor to explain precisely what suits arose under the patent and copyright laws, Mr. Justice Holmes stated that "(a) suit arises under the law that creates the cause of action"; in the case sub judice, injury to a business involving slander of a patent, he said, "whether it is a wrong or not depends upon the law of the State where the act is done" so that the suit did not arise under the patent laws. American Well Works Co. v. Layne & Bowler Co., 241 U.S. 257, 260 (1916). . . .
>
> [But] we cannot halt at questions hinging only on the language of the Copyright Act. For a new and dynamic doctrine, taking its name from Clearfield Trust Co. v. United States, 318 U.S. 363 (1943), instructs us that even in the absence of express statute, federal law may govern what might seem an issue of local law because the federal interest is dominant. Sola Elec. Co. v. Jefferson Elec. Co., 317 U.S. 173 (1942), is relevant here, not only for its holding that the radiations of the antitrust

laws governed an estoppel question in a patent license case but also for the Court's unwillingness to say whether the estoppel rule would have been "local" or "federal" even if the antitrust laws had not been invoked. If this "federal common law" governed some disputed aspect of a claim to ownership of a copyright or for the enforcement of a license, federal jurisdiction might follow. . . . But there is not the slightest reason to think that any legal question presented by Harms' complaint falls in the shadow of a federal interest suggested by the Copyright Act or any other source. . . .

c. What's going on in the "broader" *Smith* line of cases? One way of explaining is to say that the courts thought the federal law interests were very important. Important in what way? A monumentally important case with a federal ingredient will likely make its way to the Supreme Court, which, you'll recall, has a broader "arising under" jurisdiction than do the district courts. But the Supreme Court hears only about a hundred cases a year, so as a practical matter most federal interests litigated in state courts have little chance of federal review. The battle in the statutory "arising under" cases is fought over which federal interest cases should be heard in federal trial and intermediate appellate courts. One thoughtful analysis puts the question like this:

> Federal issues might be raised in a large number of cases, but the claimants of federal rights often are wrong in their view that federal law protects them. They would there-fore lose on the federal issue, and they could win only on state law grounds. If "arising under" were interpreted expansively, many cases in federal court on the basis of "arising under" jurisdiction would be disposed of on state law grounds. . . . What is needed is a test that will screen out cases in which federal interests are unlikely to be strongly implicated. Can the following considerations be combined to produce a "test"? (i) What is the national interest in disposing of the case as a whole—with federal fact-finding—in the federal courts, as compared to the interest of disposing of it in the state courts? (ii) How likely is it that the national interest will in fact be implicated? (iii) How likely is it that the Supreme Court will use its limited resources to decide the federal issue where the record is made in the state court?

Howard Fink & Mark Tushnet, Federal Jurisdiction: Policy and Practice 396 2d ed. (1987). Recall that these questions—if these are the right questions—must be decided at a very early stage, with nothing more than the pleadings before the court, and you will understand why courts and scholars have struggled over the question for a century.

7. As you will see in Chapter V, under the federal Declaratory Judgment Act, 28 U.S.C. §§2201-2202, the federal courts are empowered to hear certain cases in which a potential defendant seeks not a coercive remedy but a declaration of rights. Thus, for example, an insurance company might seek a declaration of nonliability under an insurance contract. How does one apply the well-pleaded complaint rule to such cases? The question is made more difficult by a well-established understanding that the Declaratory Judgment Act did not expand the jurisdiction of the federal courts.

a. Some cases are simple. Suppose a patent-holder believes that a competing business is infringing his patent. He could sue for damages or file an injunction, and such a suit would "arise under" federal law. Believing that proof of damages or of the requisites for injunctive relief would be expensive to prove, he simply sues for a declaration that the competitor is infringing his patent. The claim for relief arises under federal law.

b. Reverse the situation. This time Competitor sues, seeking a declaration that she is not infringing the patent, perhaps so she can convince a bank or investor to give her funds to expand her factory. It's well established that a federal district court has jurisdiction to hear Competitor's claim for relief. Wright, Federal Courts 111. Why? Before the Declaratory Judgment Act, the suit couldn't have been brought in federal district court; if we now say there is federal jurisdiction, haven't we allowed the Act to expand federal question jurisdiction? The standard answer is that the exact issue — patent validity and scope — could have been tried, although in a suit brought by the patent-holder, so the Act isn't really "expanding" jurisdiction. This approach reverses the normal "plaintiff" and "defendant" labels, asking whether the federal court would have had jurisdiction if the defendant had brought a coercive suit in the declaratory action.

c. Now a harder case. Suppose "a party seeks a declaration that it is immune, by virtue of federal law, from a nonfederal claim that the other party may have." Wright, Federal Courts 112. For example, imagine that the Louisville & Nashville Railroad had brought a declaratory action against the Mottleys (seeking a declaration that their refusal of passage was lawful). Would that action have been within the jurisdiction of the federal courts? As Professor Wright puts it,

> On the narrow view [the railroad] could not, for absent the declaratory procedure, the federal claim would arise only as a defense to the passholders' [state law] action for breach of contract, and the only possible coercive action, that by the Mottleys for specific performance, would raise no federal question. The broader view would permit the declaratory action since in that suit the railroad's federal claim of an immunity to the [state law] action would appear on the face of the railroad's complaint.

Wright, Federal Courts 111. After some struggle, the Supreme Court appears to have taken the narrower view, though conceding that it reached its view "for reasons involving perhaps more history than logic. . . ." Franchise Tax Board v. Construction Laborers Vacation Trust for Southern California, 463 U.S. 1, 4 (1983).

8. A case can start out as a federal case, but then lose its federal status after a judgment or settlement.

a. Plaintiffs sue defendants on a claim arising under federal law. The parties then settle the case by signing an agreement. The case is dismissed by agreement of the parties in an order that makes no reference to the settlement agreement. Plaintiff then sues defendant for violation of the agreement. Is there federal question jurisdiction? The Fourth Circuit ruled "no" in Fairfax Countywide Citizens Association v. County of Fairfax, 571 F.2d 1299 (4th Cir.), cert. denied, 439 U.S. 1047 (1978). The settlement agreement is an ordinary contract, whose breach does not arise under federal law. But if the agreement were embodied in the court's judgment of dismissal, its breach would arise under federal law, because federal courts have jurisdiction to enforce their own judgments. What should plaintiff have done to ensure continuing federal jurisdiction over the settlement?

b. Sally borrowed money from Frank, giving him a mortgage as security. She then declared bankruptcy, and, in a federal bankruptcy proceeding, Frank's interest was transferred to Joe. (Recall that there is exclusive federal jurisdiction over bankruptcy.) Through an error, however, the transfer to Joe was never properly recorded. Frank now sues Joe, alleging that he still holds a mortgage on the property. Joe seeks to remove the case to federal district court, arguing that Frank's lawsuit calls into question the validity of the federal bankruptcy judgment and thus "arises under" federal law. Held: No, in Rivet v. Regions Bank, 522 U.S. 470 (1998) (claim preclusion based on a prior federal judgment is a defense, so the claim does not arise under federal law, citing Mottley).

NOTE: CHALLENGING FEDERAL SUBJECT MATTER JURISDICTION

Suppose you represent a defendant in a case filed in federal court and you think that there isn't a basis for federal subject matter jurisdiction. How do you get the court to dismiss the case? The obvious answer seems to be to move for dismissal under Rule 12(b)(1), asserting the absence of federal subject matter jurisdiction. In diversity cases the obvious method is also the only method. In federal question cases there is a special twist, however. Because "arising under" jurisdiction depends on the substance of the plaintiff's claim, one can think of the challenge as attacking either the claim (there's no federal claim, therefore no federal jurisdiction) or jurisdiction (there's no jurisdiction because there's no claim arising under federal law). So a party arguing that a complaint does not state a claim arising under federal law could move for dismissal invoking either Rule 12(b)(1) or Rule 12(b)(6). Addressing this situation, the Court has said that if there's any arguable basis for a federal claim, the district court should examine the federal question not as a matter of jurisdiction but on a Rule 12(b)(6) motion to dismiss the substantive claim.

NOTES AND PROBLEMS

1. Why does it matter how that question is decided?

a. Suppose defendant moves for dismissal under Rule 12(b)(1) and the federal court, ruling that the case does not arise under federal law, dismisses it. Plaintiff now refiles the same claim in state court; can defendant argue that the federal dismissal requires dismissal of the state claim?

b. Suppose defendant moves for dismissal under Rule 12(b)(6) and the federal court, ruling that the federal law invoked does not apply to the facts stated, dismisses the claim. Plaintiff now refiles the same claim in state court; can defendant argue that the federal dismissal requires dismissal of the state claim?

c. The choice of grounds has another consequence if the plaintiff combines state law claims with her federal claim:

Bell v. Hood, 327 U.S. 67, 939 (1946), is often taken as indicating that if a complaint comes close enough to presenting a federal claim that the court has trouble in deciding that it doesn't, dismissal of that claim should be for "failure to state a claim upon which relief can be granted" rather than for lack of jurisdiction. . . . The only apparent consequence of Bell v. Hood as applied to this case is that if the complaint is close enough to the line to give "jurisdiction," the court may have power to adjudicate a "pendent" or "ancillary" state claim. But a federal court need not try such a state claim when the non-existence of the federal claim has been determined on motion prior to trial on the merits — and the case against its doing so is particularly strong when, as here, a prior suit for the same relief is pending in a state court.

T. B. Harms v. Eliscu, 339 F.2d 823, 828-829 (2d Cir. 1964). Pendent and ancillary jurisdiction are now subsumed under the concept of supplemental jurisdiction, discussed later in this chapter.

2. But suppose that the defendant does not move to dismiss under either Rule 12(b)(1) or 12(b)(6) and the case proceeds.

a. Is the objection to jurisdiction waived? No: As _Mottley_ demonstrates, the requirement of subject matter jurisdiction is held to be so fundamental that a court is required to raise the issue _sua sponte_ (on the court's own motion) and dismiss if it finds a lack of jurisdiction. Moreover, the case must be dismissed even if the lack of jurisdiction is discovered for the first time at the appellate stage. Thus, in Capron v. Van Noorden, 6 U.S. 126 (1804), plaintiff sued defendant in federal court and lost. On appeal in the Supreme Court (there was no court of appeals at the time), plaintiff suggested a lack of jurisdiction because of lack of diversity. The Supreme Court dismissed the case, leaving the plaintiff free to bring suit in state court (assuming that the statute of limitations had not yet run).

b. With _Capron_ and _Mottley_ contrast Caterpillar, Inc. v. Lewis, infra page 214. Lewis sued Caterpillar for personal injuries, in state court. At the start of the suit there were nondiverse parties. Caterpillar nevertheless removed, over Lewis's objection, but the district court erroneously ruled that there was diversity jurisdiction. During pretrial proceedings the nondiverse parties settled and thus vanished from the party configuration. After losing at trial, Lewis renewed his objections to jurisdiction. The Supreme Court affirmed Caterpillar's trial court victory. True, Lewis should have prevailed in seeking to have the case remanded to state court, but by the time the trial occurred there was diversity; the values of efficiency and finality overcame the validity of Lewis's timely objections. Explain how one can distinguish _Capron_ and _Caterpillar_.

c. In one respect _Capron_ and _Caterpillar_ agree: Both treat challenges to subject matter jurisdiction in a way that differs sharply from personal jurisdiction. Personal jurisdiction may be waived by failing to raise it at the threshold of litigation: Imagine the outcome if in _Mottley_ or _Capron_ the problem had been personal jurisdiction and was raised for the first time on appeal.

3. Given draconian rules about the nonwaivability of federal subject matter jurisdiction, one might ask if it would be easy to mount a collateral attack on a judgment alleged to be without federal jurisdiction. In fact, the answer is "probably not," though the few cases that have dealt with this question have not been resolved consistently. Moreover, the legal principles have been slowly evolving. In 1940, the First Restatement of Judgments took the position that collateral attack was presumptively available. In 1982 the Restatement (Second) of Judgments took the position collateral attack was presumptively unavailable — justified only by

special circumstances. To get a feel for the problem, consider three situations: (1) defendant appears, challenges subject matter jurisdiction and loses; (2) defendant appears, fails to challenge subject matter jurisdiction, but loses on the merits; (3) defendant defaults. In each case the question is whether in a second lawsuit the former defendant may seek to avoid the effect of the first judgment by arguing that the court lacked subject matter jurisdiction.

a. Parties who appear, challenge the subject matter jurisdiction of a federal court, and lose are bound by that determination; just as with personal jurisdiction, they may not thereafter challenge the judgment in a second action. Stoll v. Gottlieb, 305 U.S. 165 (1938); Durfee v. Duke (infra, page 716).

b. Similarly, and again as with personal jurisdiction, parties who have appeared but failed to challenge the subject matter jurisdiction of a district court may generally not thereafter attack its judgment in another court, state or federal, for lack of diversity or federal question jurisdiction. Chicot County Drainage District v. Baxter State Bank, 308 U.S. 371 (1939).

To this general principle the Supreme Court has, however, added an exception of indeterminate size. In the same term in which the Supreme Court decided *Chicot County Drainage District* came Kalb v. Feuerstein, 308 U.S. 433 (1940). *Kalb* held that a state court foreclosure proceeding against a farmer during the pendency of federal bankruptcy proceedings was not binding on the federal court because the automatic stay provision of the federal bankruptcy laws had divested the state courts of jurisdiction. The result would follow, the Court indicated, even if the jurisdictional issue had been litigated in the state court in favor of that court's jurisdiction. This allowance of collateral attack, the Court said, was simply an application of legislative intent: Congress had meant to permit such collateral challenges to foreclosure proceedings. The difficulty arises because Congress had not in so many words decreed that result; it was rather implied from the general circumstances of the legislation.

c. What about defendants who entirely default? Were they objecting to personal jurisdiction, they would be entitled to attack collaterally under the doctrine of *Pennoyer*. May they collaterally attack subject matter jurisdiction in the same way? Here one cannot be certain. If one extends *Chicot County Drainage District*, one concludes that collateral attack is not available — that a party wishing to challenge subject matter jurisdiction must appear in the first suit. *Kalb*, however, points in the opposite direction: A party who had appeared (in the foreclosure proceeding) was nevertheless able to raise a collateral challenge. To be sure, *Kalb* involved a statute that, as the Court saw things, permitted collateral challenge. The only entirely safe statement is that the Court has not clearly resolved that question. As one commentator put it:

> The proverbial case involves a justice of the peace who has undertaken to grant a divorce [thus clearly overstepping his jurisdictional power]. [W]ould [one] require the respondent in such a case to appear before the justice under penalty that otherwise the divorce would be legally valid [?] I cannot believe that any court would hold that.

Geoffrey C. Hazard, Jr., Revisiting the Second Restatement of Judgments: Issue Preclusion and Related Problems, 66 Cornell L. Rev. 564, 591 (1981).

4. Finally, what about defendants who combine challenges to subject matter and personal jurisdiction?

a. Suppose, defendant files a pre-answer motion seeking dismissal based on Rule 12(b)(1) *and* 12(b)(2). If either challenge is well-founded, the case will be dismissed. But a dismissal will have different consequences for a refiled suit, depending on which ground is used for dismissal.

b. If a case is dismissed for want of federal subject matter jurisdiction, a plaintiff is free to refile the suit in state court because the judgment establishes only the lack of federal jurisdiction, presumably leaving the state court open.

c. If the case is dismissed for want of personal jurisdiction, a plaintiff is precluded from refiling in state court in the same state because the federal court's decision that personal jurisdiction is lacking will bind the state court under the principles of issue preclusion.

d. Under those circumstances, should a federal court faced with motions to dismiss on both grounds always take subject matter jurisdiction first, because that will have the narrowest subsequent effect? No, the Supreme Court has said; the discretion of a trial court to handle its docket allows it to dismiss for want of personal jurisdiction if that is the most obvious ground. Ruhrgas AG v. Marathon Oil Co., 526 U.S. 574 (1999).

C.   Diversity Jurisdiction

Diversity jurisdiction was among the earliest congressional grants to the lower federal courts. The underlying justification, however, has remained obscure, and the grant has come under considerable attack. The following excerpt from a congressional committee report sums up the standard learning.

> Federal diversity of citizenship jurisdiction is made possible by Article III of the Constitution which was drafted to permit, but not mandate, Federal court jurisdiction based on "controversies between citizens of different States" and "between a State, or the citizens thereof, and foreign States, citizens or subjects." . . .
>
> The debates of the Constitutional Convention are unclear as to why the Constitution made provision for such jurisdiction; nor is pertinent legislative history much aid as to why the First Congress exercised its prerogative to vest diversity jurisdiction in the Federal courts.
>
> Many legal scholars who have researched this issue have concluded that it was based on a fear that State courts would be biased or prejudiced against those from out of State. A minority view is that the Nation's early lawmakers shared misgivings as to whether at least some of the State courts would be fair to the interests of creditors, out-of-staters or in-staters. Another position is that, the Federal courts being better than the State, it was preferable to route as many cases into the former as possible.

Abolition of Diversity of Citizenship Jurisdiction, H.R. Rep. No. 893, 95th Cong., 2d Sess. 2 (1978). In the midst of this uncertainty about the basis for diversity jurisdiction, courts must nevertheless decide whether it exists. The cases that follow illustrate some of the strategic maneuvers and interpretive problems that grow from diversity jurisdiction.

Redner v. Sanders

2000 WL 1161080 (S.D.N.Y. 2000)

GRIESA, J.

Plaintiff in this action asserts that federal jurisdiction is based on diversity of citizenship. Defendants move under Fed. R. Civ. P. 12(b)(1) to dismiss for lack of jurisdiction. The motion is granted.

The complaint alleges that plaintiff "is, and at all times herein mentioned was, a citizen of the United States residing in France," and that two individual defendants are residents of the State of New York and the corporate defendant has its principal place of business in New York. The complaint avers that diversity jurisdiction exists because plaintiff "is a resident of a foreign state, while defendants are residents of the State of New York."

The applicable statute is 28 U.S.C. §1332, which provides in pertinent part:

> (a) The district courts shall have original jurisdiction of all civil actions where the matter in controversy exceeds the sum or value of $75,000, exclusive of interest and costs, and is between —
>> (1) citizens of different States;
>> (2) citizens of a State and citizens or subjects of a foreign state; . . .

Plaintiff apparently seeks to invoke subsection (a)(2) as a basis for jurisdiction. However, plaintiff's complaint speaks of *residence* whereas the statute speaks of *citizenship*. The two are not synonymous.

It appears in fact that defendants are citizens of the State of New York. But for jurisdiction to exist under (a)(2) plaintiff would need to be a citizen of a foreign state, not merely a resident, and the complaint itself alleges that plaintiff is a citizen of the United States. Thus the case does not involve an action between citizens of the United States and a citizen of a foreign state. There is no jurisdiction under §1332(a)(2).

In responding to the motion, plaintiff does not really defend the idea of jurisdiction based upon his location in France, but shifts the ground to a discussion of his connection with California. Plaintiff has filed an affidavit stating that he was raised and educated in California commencing in 1948, and that while he has resided in France for the last several years (his attorney's brief says since 1990), he has maintained certain contacts with California, including a license to practice law, and a law office there which he states he has visited at least four times a year since living abroad. He has a California drivers' license. He recently solicited two San Francisco law offices for possible employment, although there is no indication of any affirmative response. Plaintiff's affidavit states that he has "not given up the idea of returning to California" and that he considers California as his domicile.

To the extent that plaintiff now argues for a California domicile, it would appear that he might be attempting to lay a basis for jurisdiction under §1332(a)(1). This subsection would, of course, allow a citizen of California to invoke diversity juris-diction in a suit against citizens of New York. A person is a citizen of a state of the United States within the meaning of 28 U.S.C. §1332 if he is a citizen of the United States and is domiciled within the state in question. Newman-Green Inc. v. Alfonzo-Larrain, 490 U.S. 826, 828 (1989).

However, plaintiff's factual submission is not sufficient to demonstrate a California domicile. Plaintiff's affidavit is entirely lacking in details about what his living in France has involved. Plaintiff provides no information about exactly where he lives, what kind of a residence he has, whether he has any family in France, or what professional activities he carries out in France.

Moreover, despite the discussion of domicile to some extent, neither plaintiff's affidavit nor his attorney's brief actually asserts the claim that there is jurisdiction on the basis of a California domicile or makes a request to amend the complaint to assert such a claim.

The action is dismissed for lack of subject matter jurisdiction. This dismissal is without prejudice.

SO ORDERED.

NOTES AND PROBLEMS

1. Does this mean that Redner cannot sue Sanders in the United States?

2. How did Redner's lawyer make such an elementary mistake? Putting aside the possibility of carelessness or ignorance, consider the possibility that the error was induced by the way in which the underlying statute has been interpreted.

a. On one hand the courts read the statute's sections quite literally; if a given case does not fit into one of §1332's several categories, it does not fall within diversity jurisdiction — regardless of whether one might, in a very loose and intuitive way, perceive the parties as "diverse."

b. On the other hand, because the statute does not define the meaning of state "citizenship," and because, unlike the national government, states do not issue any formal documents to show that one is a "citizen" of California or Florida or Illinois, courts have developed a test of state citizenship. The standard doctrinal formulation says that state citizenship depends on present domicile and intent to remain indefinitely. That test is easy to apply for most people, who have a single clear affiliation.

c. But, like Mr. Redner, many people may reside "temporarily" in a different place for considerable periods. Thus a student who was attending law school in New York might for diversity purposes still be a citizen of Florida. In such cases much may turn on intent, as demonstrated by external indicia. Consider, for example, Hawkins v. Masters Farms, supra page 6.

Notice that the factual issues involved in such determinations can require significant inquiry at the outset of the lawsuit, inquiry unrelated to the merits of the case. Does this make the relatively mindless simplicity of the well-pleaded complaint rule look better by comparison?

d. Moreover, the time for measuring citizenship for diversity purposes is as of the date on which the complaint is filed in federal court. That is true even if the plaintiff has moved to another state for the sole purpose of establishing diversity:

> On May 5, 1997, plaintiff filed an identical action in Kansas state court. At the time, plaintiff was domiciled in Kansas. Shortly after filing suit, plaintiff moved to Oklahoma and became domiciled there. Plaintiff voluntarily dismissed his state action on January 10, 2000, then filed this case on February 1, 2000.
>
> Plaintiff alleges that this Court has diversity jurisdiction under 28 U.S.C. §1332. Defendant contends that the parties are not truly diverse. The complaint shows otherwise. Diversity of citizenship is determined at the commencement of the action. Commencement of the action occurs at the time the complaint is filed. When plaintiff filed his complaint here, he was a citizen of Oklahoma. Defendant does not contend otherwise. Rather, defendant argues that the Court must refer back to May 5, 1997, when plaintiff filed his state action. . . .
>
> Defendant notes that plaintiff could not have removed his original state action to federal court and argues that plaintiff should not be allowed the "tactical advantage" of doing essentially the same thing now. While defendant is correct that plaintiff could not have removed his state action, this does not mean that the Court can look back to plaintiff's prior action to determine its jurisdiction. Regardless of plaintiff's intent, the fact remains that federal subject matter jurisdiction now exists. Despite defendant's implied argument, federal subject matter jurisdiction, by removal or otherwise, does not focus on whether a party is attempting to gain a tactical advantage. Litigants constantly attempt to gain so-called tactical advantages in various ways, including both removing cases and avoiding removal. Defendant cites no authority for the proposition that subject matter jurisdiction is defeated if it somehow affords one party a tactical advantage. Indeed, defendant's argument that plaintiff is attempting to gain a "tactical advantage" rings entirely hollow because defendant's argument for lack of jurisdiction appears to be nothing more than an attempt to gain his own tactical advantage—a return to state court. . . .

Smith v. Kennedy, 2000 WL 575024 (D. Kan. 2000).

3. Suppose Redner's lawyer, after explaining with some embarrassment to his client (also a lawyer!) why his case has been dismissed, still believes that federal court is by far the best forum for the case and would like to refile it in federal court. Describe how one might go about establishing diversity jurisdiction.

4. Consider two variations on the facts of the case:

a. Suppose Redner had been a French citizen. Diversity?

b. Suppose Redner had been a French citizen who had moved to the United States and, while not becoming a U.S. citizen, had become a permanent resident alien domiciled in New York. Read the last sentence of §1332(a).

5. Suppose Redner convinces a judge that he is a citizen of California. At that point a citizen of California is suing two citizens of New York. Assuming the amount in controversy requirement is met, diversity jurisdiction exists. But what if Redner (whom we are now assuming is a California citizen) wants to join with Jones, a New York citizen, in suing the two New York defendants. Diversity?

a. No. Although 28 U.S.C. §1332 does not by its terms require that each plaintiff be diverse from each defendant, that interpretation was attached to the predecessor statute by Chief Justice Marshall in Strawbridge v. Curtiss, 7 U.S. 267 (1806), and has been unquestioned law every since. Thus even in a case with multiple diverse parties the existence of a single party with the same state citizenship as that of an opposing party will destroy diversity.

b. Some question remained after *Strawbridge* as to whether the constitutional language of Article III, from which the statutory language was taken, required the same interpretation. It is now settled that the Constitution, as opposed to §1332, requires only minimal diversity, that is, at least one claimant diverse in citizenship from another. State Farm v. Tashire, 386 U.S. 523 (1967). The principle matters in applying statutes not requiring complete diversity — for example, the Federal Interpleader Act, 28 U.S.C. §1335.

[handwritten margin note: Some statutes don't require Complete diversity]

c. Suppose a court faces a case where there is diversity, but also a nondiverse party. Must the entire case have had to be dismissed? Newman-Green, Inc. v. Alfonzo-Larrain, 490 U.S. 826 (1989), permitted a court to retain jurisdiction by dismissing a party not held to be indispensable. See Rule 19 and infra page 762.

6. Apply the following cases to the statutory language, assuming that in each case, the amount in controversy requirement is met:

a. A citizen of Mexico sues a citizen of Japan. §1332(a)(1)(4).

b. A citizen of California sues citizens of Mexico and Japan. §1332(a)(2).

c. A citizen of California and a citizen of Mexico sue a citizen of New York and a citizen of Japan. See §1332(a)(3).

d. Finally, suppose things are as in the preceding problem, and the citizen of New York drops out. At that point a citizen of California and a citizen of Mexico are suing a citizen of Japan. The case no longer falls within §1332(a); do you see why? Should diversity jurisdiction extend to this situation? In what might be called a strong dictum, the Supreme Court has suggested not. Ruhrgas AG v. Marathon Oil, 526 U.S. 574 (1999) ("Marathon joined an alien plaintiff (Norge) as well as an alien defendant (Ruhrgas). If the joinder of Norge is legitimate, the complete diversity required by 28 U.S.C. §1332 (1994 ed. and Supp. III), but not by Article III, . . . is absent.").

7. For diversity purposes, partnerships are not considered as entities but as collections of individuals; thus the citizenship of each of the members of a partnership must be considered. In a state court the State of Wisconsin sues a New York law firm for malpractice. The defendant firm would like to remove to federal court, where it believes that a jury pool drawn from a wider area will be more sympathetic to its defense. The firm, with more than 250 partners, has no offices and no partners in Wisconsin but has several U.S. offices and several located overseas. Each of these overseas offices has at least one U.S. citizen partner assigned to it. What will you want to know about each of these partners to decide whether defendant can invoke diversity jurisdiction to remove to federal court?

8. Beyond the requirement of complete diversity, the other principal difficulty presented by diversity jurisdiction has to do with determining the citizenship of a corporation. The rules for determining such citizenship for diversity purposes are set out in 28 U.S.C. §1332(c).

a. The corporation has dual citizenship: where it is incorporated and where it has its chief place of business. The purpose of the dual citizenship is to prevent what Congress thought were essentially local state claims between a citizen and a local corporation, incorporated elsewhere for convenience, from burdening the federal courts. Many corporations incorporate under the law of a state deemed to have more permissive corporation laws than those of the state of their chief place of business. Delaware, for example, is more often the legal "home" of corporations than it is their chief place of business.

b. The chief place of business of a corporation is said to be a question of fact. Though there can be only one such chief place of business, there are various tests for locating it. One is to emphasize the corporate "nerve" center where the executive and administrative functions are controlled. Another is to concentrate on the everyday business activities of the company — sometimes called the "muscle" in an extension of the anatomical metaphor. Many courts look to both; for example, see Northeast Nuclear Energy Co. v. General Electric Co., 435 F. Supp. 344 (D. Conn. 1977). Northeast Nuclear referred to the purpose of diversity jurisdiction — to avoid prejudice against outsiders — in order to emphasize the place where the company has its greatest contact with the public. How would one apply that test to a company such as an airline that might be incorporated in Delaware, have chief executive offices in New York, have its greatest number of flights out of O'Hare Airport in Chicago, have training facilities in Kansas City, and have its greatest number of employees living in Kansas City and Chicago?

9. *Strawbridge's* rule of complete diversity limits the scope of §1332 beyond what one would expect from reading its text. Another doctrine has a similar effect. In Ankenbrandt v. Richards, 504 U.S. 689 (1992) the Court reaffirmed a nineteenth-century decision holding that suits for divorce, alimony, or child custody fell outside the scope of diversity jurisdiction, even if the spouses were citizens of different states when suit was brought. *Ankenbrandt* went on to hold that some "domestic" cases could invoke diversity; for example, one former spouse could sue the other in tort for child abuse. It is fair to say that neither *Ankenbrandt* nor its nineteenth-century predecessor, Barber v. Barber, 62 U.S. 582 (1858), are masterpieces of judicial persuasion. *Ankenbrandt* essentially says that *Barber* was wrong when decided but that its holding has become settled practice without congressional response, so that the passage of time has made bad law into good law.

a. Does the federal judiciary's reluctance to hear "domestic" cases, even in the face of a statute that suggests such actions fall within its jurisdiction, flow from gender bias — the idea that such cases are "beneath" the federal judiciary? See Judith Resnik, "Naturally" Without Gender: Women, Jurisdiction, and the Federal Courts, 66 N.Y.U.L. Rev. 1682 (1991).

b. Against the backdrop of agonizing child custody disputes, Congress has enacted 28 U.S.C. §1738A (the Parental Kidnapping Prevention Act), which sets forth criteria for the interstate recognition and modification of child custody decrees. The statute does not confer federal jurisdiction but instead purports to tell state courts when they must heed and when they can modify a sister state's decree.

c. Notice that §1738A will only come into effect when there is diversity between the parties — when the custodial and noncustodial parents are in different states. Should Congress have solved this problem by creating diversity jurisdiction for these cases instead of telling the state courts what to do?

10. Section 1359 of 28 U.S.C. deprives district courts of jurisdiction in those cases in which a party has been "improperly or collusively . . . joined" to invoke diversity jurisdiction. The courts are not unanimous in what is "improper." The statute resolves one situation: For diversity purposes the representative of a child, an incompetent, or a deceased person (appointed to administer the estate) has the same citizenship as the individual represented. 28 U.S.C. §1332(a)(2).

11. Is a citizen of the District of Columbia (or of Puerto Rico, Guam, or another American territory not a state) a citizen of a "state" for diversity purposes? 28 U.S.C. §1332(d) says so, and its constitutionality was upheld in National Mutual Ins. Co. v. Tidewater Transfer Co., 337 U.S. 582 (1949).

12. Congress, while unwilling to repeal diversity jurisdiction, has restricted it in a number of small ways. It has regularly increased the amount in controversy requirement. And in 1988 it amended the statute to add the last sentence in §1332(a). Reread that section.

a. In so amending the statute Congress presumably had in mind something like the following. Suppose an ordinary auto accident, giving rise to a tort claim for personal injuries, the most common form of lawsuit in the U.S. If, as is usually the case, the parties involved are both citizens of the same state, the suit will — and must — be heard by the state courts. But suppose that one of those involved in the accident is a permanent resident alien — perhaps a resident of the state in question for decades. Before the enactment of the amendment in question, there would be federal diversity jurisdiction; afterwards not.

b. But the amendment, apparently drafted to restrict the availability of diversity jurisdiction, can be read to expand it in some situations. In the next case the court had to decide whether to follow the language of the statute or what it thought was the intent of Congress.

Saadeh v. Farouki

107 F.3d 52 (D.C. Cir. 1997)

ROGERS, J.

[Mr. Farouki, a businessman with wide international investments, borrowed funds from Mr. Saadeh and defaulted on the loan. By the time suit was filed, Farouki, a Jordanian citizen residing in Maryland, had achieved "permanent resident" immigration status in the United States. Saadeh, a Greek citizen, brought suit on the several written contracts allegedly breached, invoking diversity jurisdiction. While the litigation was under way, Farouki became a citizen of the United States. The district court rendered a judgment for Saadeh, and Farouki appealed on the merits. The Court of Appeals asked that the parties brief jurisdiction and, without reaching the merits, ordered the case dismissed for lack of subject matter jurisdiction.]

. . . Article III of the Constitution . . . requires only minimal diversity, that is, diversity of citizenship between any two parties on opposite sides of an action, regardless of whether other parties may be co-citizens. Congress has never granted the district courts the full measure of diversity jurisdiction permitted by the Constitution, however. . . . The Supreme Court has never addressed the scope of the complete diversity rule in cases involving alien parties. Prior to 1988, however, this court held, as have others, that the diversity statute did not confer jurisdiction over a lawsuit involving an alien on one side, and an alien and a citizen on the other side.

. . . Congress amended the diversity statute in 1988 to add what now appears as the last sentence of 28 U.S.C. §1332(a). This sentence provides in pertinent part that for the purposes of §1332(a) "an alien admitted to the United States for permanent residence shall be deemed a citizen of the State in which such alien is domiciled." Under this amendment, diversity of citizenship no longer exists in an action between a citizen of State A and an alien admitted to the United States for permanent residence who resides in State A. Read literally, however, the amended statute would create diversity between Saadeh and . . . Farouki[ ]. As permanent residents of Maryland at the time Saadeh filed his complaint, Mr. . . . and Mrs. Farouki would be "deemed" citizens of Maryland. Thus the amended statute would also appear to abrogate partially the rule of complete diversity by permitting a non-resident alien and a resident alien to be present on opposite sides of this lawsuit. Courts and commentators have differed as to whether this latter result is permissible under the amended statute.

[The opinion first affirmed the principle that citizenship at the time suit is filed is the relevant test, so that Farouki's subsequent acquisition of U.S. citizenship did not create diversity.]

Thus, the remaining question is whether, at the time Saadeh filed his complaint, Farouki qualified as a "citizen of a State" under the 1988 amendment to §1332. In resolving a question of statutory interpretation, a court's starting point is always the language of the statute. . . .

A literal reading of the 1988 amendment to §1332(a) would produce an odd and potentially unconstitutional result. It would both partially abrogate the longstanding rule of complete diversity, and create federal diversity jurisdiction over a lawsuit brought by one alien against another alien, without a citizen of a state on either side of the litigation. The judicial power of the United States does not extend to such an action under the Diversity Clause of Article III. Hodgson v. Bowerbank, 9 U.S. 303 (1809). Under the circumstances, it behooves the court to examine the legislative history of the 1988 amendment in order to determine congressional intent.

The 1988 alienage amendment was added to the Judicial Improvements Act during the Senate debate, and the legislative history consists of what is in the Congressional Record. So far as appears, the idea for the addition of an alienage provision originated in a recommendation of the Judicial Conference of the United States. The Judicial Conference supported the addition of the alienage provision in order to restrict diversity jurisdiction:

> There is no reason why actions involving persons who are permanent residents of the United States should be heard by federal courts merely because one of them remains a citizen or subject of a foreign state or has not yet become a citizen of the United States. Accordingly, the Conference agreed to recommend that Congress amend 28 U.S.C. §1332(a) to treat a permanent resident alien as a citizen of the state of his or her domicile.

The intentions of the Judicial Conference are mirrored by the comments of Senator Heflin, the sponsor of the Senate bill, during the debate on the Judicial Improvements Act. Referring to Title II, on diversity jurisdiction, he stated:

Intent is to reduce basis for SMJ

> The provisions of this title make modest amendments to reduce the basis for Federal court jurisdiction based solely on diversity of citizenship. . . .

A section-by-section analysis introduced into the Congressional Record similarly reveals the intent to reduce diversity jurisdiction through the alienage provision. Describing Title II as "making modest adjustments to the scope of diversity jurisdiction to relieve the caseload pressures on the Federal Courts," the analysis paralleled the language of the Judicial Conference report. . . .

Given the reasoning underlying the recommendation for the alienage provision and the general expressions of legislative intent for the Judicial Improvements Act, in the absence of contrary evidence, we conclude that Congress intended to contract diversity jurisdiction through the 1988 amendment to §1332(a), not to expand it by abrogating the longstanding rule that complete diversity is destroyed in lawsuits between aliens. . . . [W]e do not view these concerns about the workload of the federal judiciary and the burdens imposed by diversity jurisdiction as consistent with the conclusion that Congress intended what a literal reading of the statute suggests. It would be illogical to conclude that Congress intended to eliminate diversity jurisdiction in cases between a citizen and an alien permanently residing in the same state, but simultaneously intended to expand diversity jurisdiction in cases between an alien permanently residing in one state and an alien permanently residing in another state. Despite the plain language of §1332(a), the alienage amendment "clearly appears to have been intended only to eliminate subject matter jurisdiction of cases between a citizen and an alien living in the same state." Lloyds Bank v. Norkin, 817 F. Supp. at 419. There is no reason to conclude, however, that the amendment was intended to create diversity jurisdiction where it did not previously exist. . . .

[T]his appears to be one of those rare cases where the most literal interpretation of a statute is at odds with the evidence of Congressional intent and a contrary construction is necessary to avoid "formidable constitutional difficulties."

NOTES AND PROBLEMS

1. *Saadeh* is another case, like *Mottley*, in which an appellate court, rather than the parties, raised the jurisdictional question. Why would Farouki, who had objected to jurisdiction at the outset of the case, abandon this argument and brief only the merits of the case on appeal?

a. By the time of the appeal, three circumstances had changed: (a) the other parties who were nondiverse had been dropped from the case; (b) Farouki had become a U.S. citizen; (c) Farouki had lost on the merits at trial. Explain how these events might lead Farouki's lawyer to ignore the jurisdictional question.

b. What do you suppose Saadeh's lawyer will do after reading this case?

2. The opinion proceeds on several levels. Most obviously it is a case about the interpretation of §1332(a) and of Article III of the Constitution.

a. The court says that if it construes the statute to mean what it appears to mean — and upholds jurisdiction in this case — that interpretation presents "formidable constitutional difficulties." Explain what those difficulties are.

b. Can you construct an argument — apparently one not made in Congress — that the sentence in question should be construed evenhandedly to deprive resident aliens of diversity jurisdiction in suits against the fellow residents of their home state but to grant them diversity in suits against foreign nationals?

3. Other courts have reached different conclusions about the statutory language in question.

a. As *Saadeh* noted:

> The Third Circuit reached a contrary conclusion in Singh [v. Daimler Benz]. It reasoned that although "Congress may not have intended to enlarge diversity jurisdiction, . . . the possible unintended effect of permitting a permanent resident alien to invoke diversity jurisdiction when that party could not have done so before the amendment is not sufficient reason for us to torture or limit the statutory language." The Third Circuit concluded that the legislative history of the Judicial Improvements Act did not provide an "overriding reason" to depart from the plain language of §1332(a). In particular, the court rejected the claim that the overall purpose of the Act was "to reduce diversity jurisdiction to relieve caseload pressures."

107 F.3d 52, 60 (D.C. Cir. 1997).

b. At a second level *Saadeh* deals with conflicting approaches to statutory interpretation. In courts and academic circles a debate rages about the circumstances — if there are any — in which a court should look beyond the test of a statute to consider its legislative history. Is the opinion in *Saadeh* convincing in its conclusion that one should look to the legislative history in this case? Might someone think that a court should be most wary of invoking legislative history when: (a) Part of that history was drafted by judges (who comprise the entire membership of the Judicial Conference); and (b) the statute in question involves the court's own jurisdiction?

4. The opinion also gives us a glimpse of the concern of some members of the federal judiciary about caseloads, which in recent decades have risen faster than the number of judges. One result has been recommendations by such bodies as the Judicial Conference, the administrative voice of the federal judiciary, to restrict federal judicial jurisdiction.

Very roughly speaking, one could keep caseloads at manageable levels in three ways: by increasing the number of judges to keep pace with caseloads; by restricting jurisdiction and thus reducing the number of cases; and by ending cases at an early stage of litigation. One can find all three themes in recent law. Which approch one thinks is preferable may depend in part on one's notion of the functions of the federal judiciary and on the nature of civil litigation.

5. Finally, the opinion gives us a glimpse of the continuing debate about the existence of diversity jurisdiction.

a. Although diversity was among the first of the jurisdictional grants to be passed by Congress, since the 1960s regular proposals to abolish or limit it have been introduced in Congress. The argument against diversity generally has two prongs. The first is that diversity cases constitute a substantial portion of the federal courts' civil caseload — ranging between 20 and 25 percent in recent years. So, if those courts are feeling pressed by caseloads, as they increasingly have been since the mid-1960s, diversity is an obvious candidate for elimination — unless, of course, it serves a vital function.

The second prong of the argument is that diversity serves no such function. The argument is that prejudice based on state citizenship is simply no longer an important factor in contemporary U.S. society. As a congressional report put the matter, "although there is still far too much prejudice in the United States (especially on grounds of race, religion, economic class, sex, nationality and age), it is . . . doubtful that prejudice against an individual because he is from another State is any longer a significant factor in this country's State courts." H.R. Rep. No. 893, 95th Cong., 2d Sess. 3-5 (1978).

Supporters of diversity argue that prejudice in state courts continues to exist, that a system of concurrent jurisdiction results in a beneficial interplay between state and federal procedures, that federal judges benefit from the regular exposure to run-of-the-mill state law, and that federal courts are superior to state courts.

b. While unwilling to eliminate diversity jurisdiction, Congress has been willing to limit its availability by increasing the required amount in controversy and by restricting the availability of supplemental jurisdiction in diversity cases. One can read *Saadeh* as another case in this tradition.

NOTE: AMOUNT IN CONTROVERSY

Besides diversity, §1332 requires an amount greater than $75,000 in controversy. Congress has from time to time increased this amount, most recently in 1997, from $50,000 to the present figure. The courts have treated this requirement in much the same way as they have the issue of federal question jurisdiction — that is, they have by and large viewed the allegations of the pleading as all but controlling, rather than engaging in judicial guessing about the likelihood that the plaintiff would succeed in collecting as much as he had prayed for. The leading Supreme Court case, St. Paul Mercury Indemnity Co. v. Red Cab Co., 303 U.S. 283, 289 (1938), stated as follows:

> It must appear to a legal certainty that the claim is really for less than the jurisdictional amount to justify dismissal. The inability of plaintiff to recover an amount adequate to give the court jurisdiction does not show his bad faith or oust the jurisdiction. Nor does the fact that the complaint discloses the existence of a valid defense of the claim. But if, from the face of the pleadings, it is apparent, to a legal certainty, that the plaintiff cannot recover the amount claimed, or if, from the proofs, the court is satisfied to a like certainty that the plaintiff never was entitled to recover that amount, and that his claim was therefore colorable for the purpose of conferring jurisdiction, the suit will be dismissed.

But their trust in the pleadings is not boundless. Consider, for example, a plaintiff who brought a diversity action against a hotel, alleging its security personnel had assaulted him; the likely compensatory damages were small, but the plaintiff relied on a punitive damage count to lift him over the amount in controversy:

> Although the Plaintiff has alleged in each count of the Complaint that the controversy is "in excess of $75,000," Defendant argues that Plaintiff cannot satisfy this amount because he did not sustain any calculable compensatory damages in the alleged altercation. D.T. Management attaches to its Motion and relies upon the Ft. Lauderdale police report of the incident. Officer Coffin, who issued the report, noted that he arrived at the Doubletree Oceanfront on October 10 while the EMS was treating Salmi. Officer Coffin noted that Plaintiff "Salmi had a small cut to his forehead area. EMS advised later that it was a minor cut and only need a bandaid [sic]." The report further noted that "after talking to both parties involved and witnesses and EMS it was determined that Salmi [had a] small injury" and "did not have any other red marks on his face." The reporting officer concluded that it "should be noted that Salmi was extremely intoxicated and needed assistance to walk." . . .
>
> Plaintiff has not provided "competent proof" to meet his burden of demonstrating the requisite amount in controversy. Instead, he argues that he satisfies the jurisdictional requirement because he is entitled to recovery of punitive damages that could result in a verdict in excess of $75,000.
>
> . . . Salmi has pled that the Defendants acted "intentionally," thus punitive damages are potentially recoverable under Illinois law if Salmi can prove what he has alleged.
>
> Even assuming Salmi can recover punitive damages, [however,] . . . he would have to recover multiple times his actual damages to satisfy the $75,000 amount. Such a recovery certainly would "stretch[] the normal ratio, and would face certain remittitur." Plaintiff's mere hope for an extreme punitive award cannot be the sole basis for jurisdiction. See 75 F.3d at 318 (no subject matter jurisdiction where average class action plaintiff would have to recover more than 17 times the compensatory damages amount through punitive damages to reach requisite amount). With no competent evidence offered to support his claim for compensatory and punitive damages in excess of the requisite $75,000, Plaintiff has failed to establish proof to a reasonable probability that subject matter jurisdiction exists. Accordingly, Salmi's Complaint is dismissed.

Salmi v. D.T. Management, Inc., 2002 U.S. Dist. LEXIS 17970 (N.D. Ill. 2002).

Other significant issues in determining the amount in controversy for jurisdictional purposes are:

1. What should be done if the plaintiff asks for an injunction rather than money damages? At least four approaches have been used: Determine the value of the injunction to the plaintiff; determine the cost to the defendant of complying; determine the cost or value to the party invoking federal jurisdiction (the plaintiff, if the action is brought in federal court, and the defendant, if the action was brought in state court and defendant is attempting to remove); and allow jurisdiction if any of the tests above yields a figure of the statutory amount. For a discussion of these approaches (and an application of the fourth), see McCarty v. Amoco Pipeline Co., 595 F.2d 389 (7th Cir. 1979).

2. May a plaintiff aggregate claims? In some circumstances, different claims may be aggregated to meet the statutory amount; saying when that can happen is harder:

> The law on aggregation . . . is in a very unsatisfactory state. The traditional rules in this area evolved haphazardly and with little reasoning. They serve no apparent policy and "turn on a mystifying conceptual test." . . . Thus it is not altogether easy to say what the law is in this area and it is quite hard to say why it is as it seems to be.

Wright, Federal Courts 209. Some guidelines from the case law:

a. A single plaintiff with two or more unrelated claims against a single defendant may aggregate claims to satisfy the statutory amount.

b. If two plaintiffs each have claims against a single defendant, they may not aggregate if their claims are regarded as "separate and distinct."

c. If one plaintiff has a claim in excess of the statutory amount and a second plaintiff has a claim for less than the statutory amount, both against the same defendant, the first plaintiff can sue in federal court. What about the second? In Stromberg Metal Works, Inc. v. Press Mechanical, 77 F.3d 928 (7th Cir. 1996), the court allowed the second plaintiff to invoke supplemental jurisdiction under 28 U.S.C. §1367, where the claims were related.

d. In situations involving multiple plaintiffs or multiple defendants with a common undivided interest and single title or right, the value of the total interest will be used to determine the amount in controversy. This is not the case if the various claims are considered several and distinct, and they may be so considered even though the claims arose from a single instrument or the parties have a community of interest.

e. The preceding rules have been extended to cover class actions. Simply aggregating the claims of all the class members cannot satisfy the amount in controversy; at least some members must have claims that individually satisfy the jurisdictional amount. Snyder v. Harris, 394 U.S. 332 (1969). One case held that *each* class member had to have a claim that satisfied the jurisdictional amount. Zahn v. International Paper Co., 414 U.S. 291 (1973). But several lower courts have now held that the 1990 enactment of §1367, discussed in the next section, changed this result — permitting a class action as long as the class representative satisfies the jurisdictional limit. Free v. Abbott Labs., 51 F.3d 524 (5th Cir. 1995); Garza v. National American Ins. Co., 807 F. Supp. 1256 (M.D. La. 1992). The issue remains unresolved by the Supreme Court, which affirmed the *Free* decision by an evenly divided vote when Justice O'Connor recused herself from participation in the case.

3. Counterclaims are treated differently, depending on their classification under Rule 13 as either compulsory or permissive. Basically, when a plaintiff's claim exceeds $75,000 (the statutory amount), a compulsory counterclaim may be heard regardless of amount, while a permissive counterclaim requires an independent jurisdictional basis. The law is unsettled, however, when plaintiff's claim falls short of $75,000 but defendant's counterclaim increases the amount in controversy to more than $75,000. See generally Wright, Federal Courts 216-221.

4. Apply these principles to a hypothetical variation on Louisville & Nashville Railroad v. Mottley. Suppose the plaintiffs, Erasmus and Annie Mottley, having

learned they cannot state an arising under claim, still want a federal forum for the trial of their case. So, taking advantage of the fact that diversity is measured at the time of filing, they move out of state and file their action as a diversity case. In each variation, assume that the requisite diversity exists and only the amount in controversy is an issue.

a. Erasmus sues Railroad for $75,000 for breach of contract.

b. Erasmus sues Railroad for $100,000 for breach of contract; Railroad counterclaims for $5,000, alleging that on some occasions Erasmus, in violation of the settlement terms, allowed a friend to use his pass.

c. Erasmus sues Railroad on two unrelated claims: breach of the settlement agreement ($72,000) and a due but unpaid Railroad bond ($5,000).

d. Annie and Friend sue Railroad. Annie, alleging breach of the settlement agreement, seeks $60,000, Friend, alleging she was riding the train with Annie when a luggage rack fell off and injured her, seeks $40,000.

e. Erasmus and Annie both sue Railroad for breach of the settlement agreement, each seeking $50,000.

D.   Supplemental Jurisdiction

Thus far we have examined aspects of federal subject matter jurisdiction that narrow the doors to federal courts in ways that neither intuition nor the texts of the Constitution and the statutes might suggest. We turn now to a doctrine that broadens federal jurisdiction, in equally unexpected ways. This doctrine, now known as supplemental jurisdiction, originated in case law and has recently taken statutory form.

Supplemental jurisdiction originated in decisions that stretched federal jurisdiction to cover parts of cases that, if brought independently, would not have fit within the district courts' subject matter jurisdiction. Examine the statute, 28 U.S.C. §1367, and consider structure and its application to some basic problems.

NOTES AND PROBLEMS

1. What is the distinction between the cases covered in §1367(a) and those in §1367(b)?

2. In these problems, assume the litigation occurs in federal district court and that amount-in-controversy requirements, if they apply, are satisfied. Also assume the joined party or claim would fall within the applicable joinder Rule (see Chapter XIII). In working out your analysis, first identify the portion of §1367 that applies, and then apply that section to the facts.

a. A, a citizen of Illinois, sues B, also a citizen of Illinois, alleging that B violated federal civil rights statutes in firing her. A seeks to add a state law claim alleging that her firing also violated a state wrongful discharge law. Is there supplemental jurisdiction?

b. A, a citizen of Illinois, sues B, also a citizen of Illinois, alleging that B violated federal civil rights statutes in firing her. A seeks to add a state law claim alleging that *B* caused her injuries when his car backed into hers in the company parking lot. Is there supplemental jurisdiction?

c. *A*, a citizen of Illinois, sues *B*, also a citizen of Illinois, alleging that *B* violated federal civil rights statutes by permitting co-workers to engage in sexual harassment. *A* invokes Rule 20 to join *C*, a co-worker, who actually engaged in the harassment. State tort law is the basis of *A*'s claim against *C*. Because *C* is not *A*'s employer, the claim against him does not arise under federal law. Is there supplemental jurisdiction over the claim against *C*?

d. *A*, a citizen of Illinois, sues *B*, a citizen of Wisconsin, alleging breach of an employment contract and seeking a recovery in excess of $75,000. *A* invokes Rule 20 to join *C*, a citizen of Illinois; *A* alleges that *C* conspired with *B* to breach the employment contract. Is there supplemental jurisdiction over the claim against *C*?

e. Arthur, a citizen of New York, sues Barbara, a citizen of Pennsylvania, in federal district court. He alleges several claims: federal antitrust violations, federal securities law violations, and state law breach of contract. He pays more than $100,000 in damages for each claim. Will the district court have to analyze how closely related the federal and state law claims are for purposes of deciding whether supplemental jurisdiction exists or whether any of the reasons in §1367(c) for declining to exercise jurisdiction apply? Why not?

3. Having applied the statute to some cases, step back and consider its constitutional underpinnings.

a. A statute that gave federal district courts jurisdiction to decide a case based entirely on state law between two Florida citizens would be unconstitutional because beyond the power granted by Article III.

b. How then can it be constitutional for a district court to hear such a claim when the same parties also are embroiled in litigation over a federal claim?

The statute contains a clue in the language of subsection (a), which speaks of "claims that are so related to claims in the action within such original jurisdiction that they form part of the same case or controversy under Article III of the Constitution." Article III says that federal "judicial Power . . . extend[s] to all Cases" of the sorts enumerated and to "Controversies" of sorts that are further enumerated. From this phrase the courts have drawn the idea that:

> [Supplemental] jurisdiction, in the sense of judicial power, exists whenever there is a claim [within the Constitutional jurisdiction], and the relationship between that claim and the [claim outside the constitutionally enumerated jurisdiction of the federal courts] permits the conclusion that the entire action before the court comprises but one constitutional "case." The federal claim must have substance sufficient to confer subject matter jurisdiction on the court. The state and federal claims must derive from a common nucleus of operative fact. But if, considered without regard to their federal or state character, a plaintiff's claims are such that he would ordinarily be expected to try them all in one judicial proceeding, then, assuming substantiality of the federal issues, there is power in federal courts to hear the whole.[13]

United Mine Workers v. Gibbs, 383 U.S. 715, 725 (1966).

13. While it is commonplace that the Federal Rules of Civil Procedure do not expand the jurisdiction of federal courts, they do embody "the whole tendency of our decisions . . . to require a plaintiff to try his . . . whole case at one time," Baltimore S. S. Co. v. Phillips, [274 U.S. 316], and to that extent emphasize the basis of pendent jurisdiction.

c. United Mine Workers v. Gibbs and §1367 espouse a principle that may look surprising at first glance. Its rationale emerges more clearly if one recalls that a central feature of the Federal Rules is the ease with which they permit joinder of claims. See, e.g., Rule 18(a). It would be logically possible, but awkward, to permit parties to join closely connected claims but then deny the federal courts power over claims that did not bring their own jurisdictional basis with them. In such situations, whichever court (state or federal) tried the related claim second would have to engage in elaborate analyses of which issues were precluded in the first lawsuit. Section 1367 allows some — but not all — of these related claims to come to federal court under the wing of supplemental jurisdiction.

4. Consider the constitutional and statutory application to the next case.

Jin v. Ministry of State Security

254 F. Supp. 2d 61 (2003)

URBINA, District Judge.

This multi-count civil rights and RICO[1] action comes before the court on defendant China Television Corporation's ("CTC") motion to dismiss. The plaintiffs, 51 Falun Gong practitioners who are visiting Chinese nationals, U.S. residents, or U.S. citizens, allege violations of their rights under the Constitution and federal and state law by persons and entities associated with the People's Republic of China ("PRC"). CTC now moves to dismiss the defamation claim against it pursuant to Federal Rule of Civil Procedure 12(b)(1) and (6). . . .

A. Factual Background

The plaintiffs all practice Falun Gong, a self-improvement practice or discipline similar to Tai Chi that is rooted in ancient Chinese culture. According to the plaintiffs, Falun Gong has become a very popular form of exercise and meditation in China since the government loosened controls after the Cultural Revolution. The plaintiffs report that since its introduction into China in 1992, the number of Falun Gong practitioners has grown rapidly, reaching more than 70 million in number by 1999.

The plaintiffs alleged that at first, Falun Gong was well received in China for its health benefits. . . . The plaintiffs claim, however, that the Chinese government began to perceive the spectacular growth of Falun Gong as a threat to state security, stability, and economic development. The plaintiffs assert that in 1996, after the government's early efforts to control the practice met with only limited success, the government began a campaign to marginalize and eventually eradicate Falun Gong by publishing a series of negative articles about the practice in state-run newspapers. . . .

In the United States, the Chinese government allegedly engaged in many of the same tactics of threats and coercion that it used in China. The plaintiffs assert

---

1. Racketeer Influenced and Corrupt Organizations Act ("RICO"), 18 U.S.C. §1961 *et seq.*

that in a propaganda campaign aimed at overseas Chinese residents, the government sought to use mass media outlets to disparage Falun Gong leadership and vilify the Falun Gong practice. . . . In particular, the plaintiffs allege that on January 30, 2001, the government staged a limited-access news event ("the staged news event") at which several individuals identified as Falun Gong practitioners set themselves on fire in Tiananmen Square. In February 2001, CTC promoted and distributed the television footage of the staged news event throughout the United States. According to the plaintiffs, the CTC footage was accompanied by a narrative that defamed certain Falun Gong practitioners living in the United States as advocates of suicide, intra-family violence, anti-family values, and cult worship. . . .

Based on these and other actions, nine of the plaintiffs [joined to their RICO claim that invoked arising under jurisdiction] one count of defamation against CTC, CCTV, the defendant ministries, and the embassy and consulate officials. . . .

[handwritten margin note: Joined defamation to federal Claim]

B.   Procedural History

. . . On August 19, 2002, CTC filed a motion to dismiss the defamation claim pursuant to Rule 12(b)(1) and (6).

III.   *Analysis*

A.   The Court Denies Defendant CTC's Motion to Dismiss for Lack of Subject-Matter Jurisdiction

1. Legal Standard for a Motion to Dismiss Pursuant to Rule 12(b)(1)

On a motion to dismiss for lack of subject matter jurisdiction pursuant to Federal Rule of Civil Procedure 12(b)(1), the plaintiff bears the burden of establishing that the court has subject-matter jurisdiction. In considering a motion to dismiss for lack of subject-matter jurisdiction, the court should accept as true all of the factual allegations contained in the complaint.

Because subject-matter jurisdiction focuses on the court's power to hear the plaintiff's claim, however, a court resolving a motion to dismiss under Rule 12(b)(1) must give the complaint's factual allegations closer scrutiny than required for a motion to dismiss pursuant to Rule 12(b)(6) for failure to state a claim. . . .

2. The Court Has Subject-Matter Jurisdiction Over the Plaintiffs' Defamation Claim

In this case, the plaintiffs assert subject matter jurisdiction pursuant to several statutory grants of jurisdiction. Because the defamation claim arises under state law, CTC's jurisdictional challenge focuses on the plaintiffs' assertion of supplemental jurisdiction pursuant to 28 U.S.C. §1367. Asserting that the defamation claim is "completely different from and unrelated to the other causes of action asserted in the complaint" because it pertains to Falun Gong practitioners as a group while the other claims pertain to individual plaintiffs, and that there are "complex questions of state law" raised by the defamation claim, CTC urges the court to dismiss the defamation count. In response, the plaintiffs argue that the court has the discretion to assert supplemental jurisdiction for claims that a plaintiff ordinarily would expect to try in one proceeding. . . .

In this case, because the plaintiffs' claims include claims under federal civil rights and conspiracy statutes, they have an independent basis for federal jurisdiction. Accordingly, applying the two-part test for supplemental jurisdiction, the court first looks to see whether the plaintiffs' defamation claim shares a common nucleus of operative facts with the other claims, and concludes that it does.

Here, the facts on which the plaintiffs base their defamation claim allege a series of steps — including the production and distribution of video, print, and other communications targeted at the Chinese-American community and public officials — taken by various defendants to vilify and defame the defendants. Whether or not the claim identifies the plaintiffs individually or collectively, the facts supporting the defamation claims are linked to the facts supporting the remaining claims because they form a key part of an alleged overarching campaign to abridge and nullify the plaintiffs' rights and liberties. Because the defamation claim and the federal claims are related to the point that the plaintiffs "would ordinarily be expected to try them all in one judicial proceeding," the court concludes that the claims do derive from a common nucleus of operative fact. *Women Prisoners*, 93 F.3d at 920-21 (finding a common nucleus because the state and federal claims revolved around the city's decision to re-assume custody of its female prisoners and its alleged failure to provide for their needs); LaShawn v. Barry, 87 F.3d 1389, 1391 (D.C. Cir. 1996) (concluding that a common nucleus existed because the state and federal claims related to the city's allegedly inept administration of its foster care system); Prakash v. Am. Univ., 727 F.2d 1174, 1183 (D.C. Cir. 1984) (determining that a common nucleus existed because the local and federal labor claims were related to the plaintiff's employment contract dispute with the defendant). The court therefore has the power to hear the state claim. . . .

As for the second part of the test, the court concludes that the interests of judicial economy, convenience, and fairness support the exercise of supplemental jurisdiction. CTC contends that because the plaintiffs are domiciled in different states, the defamation claim implicates the defamation laws of multiple jurisdictions. According to CTC, the resulting choice-of-law issues and the diverse applications of defamation elements by state courts create complexities that weigh against supplemental jurisdiction. The court is reluctant, however, to equate difficulty with complexity. Here, CTC asserts only that the states differ in their application of the elements of defamation. While determining the correct application of the elements may be time-consuming, it does not mean the local law is "so important and so unsettled" that the court must decline jurisdiction. Rather, complexity exists when there is significant uncertainty as to the law itself. Accordingly, the court concludes that the defamation claim does not raise complex issues of state law that outweigh the court's interest in promoting judicial economy.

In sum, because the state and federal claims share a common nucleus of operative facts, and the court has decided to exercise its discretion to hear the state claim, the court may assert supplemental jurisdiction in this case.

B.   The Court Grants Defendant CTC's Motion to Dismiss for Failure to State a Claim

1. Legal Standard for a Motion to Dismiss Pursuant to Rule 12(b)(6)

For a complaint to survive a Rule 12(b)(6) motion to dismiss, it need only provide a short and plain statement of the claim and the grounds on which it rests. . . . Thus, the court may dismiss a complaint for failure to state a claim only if it is clear that no relief could be granted under any set of facts that could be proved consistent with the allegations.

A defendant may raise the affirmative defense of statute of limitations via a Rule 12(b)(6) motion when the facts that give rise to the defense are clear from the face of the complaint. . . . If "no reasonable person could disagree on the date" on which the cause of action accrued, the court may dismiss a claim on statute of limitations grounds.

2. The Plaintiffs' Defamation Claim Is Time-Barred

The plaintiffs' sole claim against CTC is that of defamation. CTC argues, however, that the defamation claim is barred by the District of Columbia's one-year statute of limitations. CTC points out that the basis for the plaintiffs' defamation claim against CTC is its alleged February 2001 promotion and distribution of the staged news event in target markets in the United States. Because the plaintiffs did not file their complaint until April 2002, CTC concludes that the plaintiffs' defamation claim falls outside the one-year statute of limitations and therefore is time-barred. In response, the plaintiffs argue that since February 2001, CCTV and various embassy officials have continued to re-broadcast the staged news event footage that CTC originally published and distributed, thereby effectively tolling the statute of limitations. . . .

In the District of Columbia, the statute of limitations for defamation claims is one year from the date of first publication. . . . Moreover, the District of Columbia follows the "single publication" rule, whereby publication of defamatory matter "gives rise to but one cause of action for libel, which accrues at the time of the original publication." Because the statute of limitations runs from the date of the original publication, any subsequent sale or delivery of a copy of the publication does not create a new cause of action. . . .

Accordingly, the court grants CTC's motion to dismiss the plaintiffs' defamation claim as outside the one-year period prescribed by the statute of limitations. . . .

NOTES AND PROBLEMS

1. As a review of the chapter so far — and to be clear why this case turned entirely on supplemental jurisdiction — explain why plaintiffs could not rely on either arising under or diversity jurisdiction for their defamation claims.

a. If the defamation claims proceeded, the defendant broadcaster would almost certainly raise a First Amendment argument — that the allegations in the broadcast were substantially true, or, if false, were not recklessly so — and thus constitutionally protected. Why doesn't this federal ingredient in the case provide a basis for arising under jurisdiction?

b. Why couldn't the plaintiffs rely on diversity jurisdiction? (Assume that the amount in controversy requirement was satisfied.)

2. The court decides it has supplemental jurisdiction.

a. What portion of §1367 covered this case?

b. Why was a defamation claim against CTC part of the same case or controversy as a claim arising under the federal antiracketeering statute invoked as the basis of original jurisdiction? Among other distinctions, defamation claims are subject to complicated First Amendment defenses that in many instances dominate the case. Recall that such defenses do *not* under the well-pleaded complaint rule provide a basis for federal arising under jurisdiction.

c. The opinion, quoting case law, says that the claims are related because the parties "would ordinarily be expected to try them all in one judicial proceeding." Is this test circular? The parties would "be expected" to do so if courts regularly allow them to and otherwise not. Looking to parties' expectations when those expectations are a function of what courts usually do doesn't help the courts decide what to do.

d. Is there another, unarticulated reason for keeping this case in a federal district court? The claim is against a sovereign nation (a very large one at that) and its agencies. That makes it a matter of significant foreign policy concern. Is it desirable to have such a case in a federal court, which may be more attentive to briefs and submissions on behalf of the Department of State, than in a state court perhaps more inclined to disregard such "outsiders"? Is this a reason for the court to exercise its discretion in favor of supplemental jurisdiction? If so, should the opinion have made this explicit?

3. Plaintiffs' procedural strategy delivered a small victory — supplemental jurisdiction — and a large defeat — dismissal on the merits.

a. Suppose plaintiffs had lost on their bid for supplemental jurisdiction and had then refiled in state court. Could a state court hear their defamation claim?

b. Suppose after this decision they refile their defamation claim in a state court; what will happen?

4. Section 1367(c) tells us that courts need not exercise supplemental jurisdiction even when they have the constitutional power to do so. Consider how it might apply to the following situations.

a. Robert files a federal employment discrimination claim and a state law wrongful discharge claim, which the district court finds to be within the scope of §1367. His federal civil rights claim is dismissed on a Rule 12(b)(6) motion after he fails to plead his membership in any of the racial, religious, or other categories protected by the civil rights statutes as a factor in his dismissal. Should the court continue to exercise supplemental jurisdiction over the state claim?

b. Same claim, but Robert pleads racial discrimination and the case proceeds to discovery. After substantial discovery Employer moves for summary judgment on the discrimination claim and the court grants the motion, ruling that Robert has failed to produce evidence that race was a factor in his dismissal. Trial is set to begin two weeks later. Should the court decide the state claim?

c. Same as in 4(b) but the state law in question is a newly enacted statute in which it is unclear whether plaintiff must prove that his discharge is wrongful or defendant must show that it was for good cause.

5. Supplemental jurisdiction can create difficult problems for plaintiffs who guess wrong in invoking federal question jurisdiction. Suppose plaintiff has an employment discrimination claim. Believing the claims involve both state and federal law and preferring a federal forum, plaintiff files in federal court, invoking supplemental jurisdiction for the state claims. It turns out that plaintiff was wrong about the federal claims: After the state statute of limitations has run, the federal court dismisses the federal claims and declines to exercise jurisdiction over the remaining state law claims. What can plaintiff do?

a. Some states have "savings" statutes that toll the state statute of limitations under such circumstances, so plaintiff could refile in state court.

b. But not all states have such statutes. In such cases §1367(d) seeks to address the problem by opening a 30-day "window." Suppose our hypothetical plaintiff is in a state which has no "savings" statute; how does §1367(d) help her? What should she do?

c. Courts have wrestled with interpreting §1367(d). The U.S. Supreme Court has held the 30-day extension unconstitutional as applied to a claim against a state agency that has not consented to such a provision. Raygor v. Regents, 534 U.S. 533 (2002).

E. Removal

Jurisdictional statutes give plaintiffs an initial choice of state or federal courts for cases in which federal and state court jurisdiction overlap. Congress has also given defendants the power to second-guess plaintiffs who choose a state court through a process known as removal. The basic text is 28 U.S.C. §1441; consider its operation in the following problems.

NOTES AND PROBLEMS

1. Which of the following cases would be removable?

a. *P* sues *D* for defamation in state court; *D* believes the statement she published is protected under the First Amendment.

b. *P* sues *D* in state court, alleging violation of *P*'s rights under the equal protection clause of the U.S. Constitution.

c. *P*, a citizen of Florida, sues *D*, a citizen of New Jersey, on a personal injury claim, in a Florida state court, seeking $100,000 in damages.

d. *P*, a citizen of Florida, sues *D*, a citizen of New Jersey, on a personal injury claim in New Jersey state court, seeking $100,000 in damages.

e. The facts are as in Problem 1(d), except that P adds a claim that D has violated her federal civil rights.

f. P, a citizen of Florida, sues D, a citizen of New Jersey, and E, a citizen of New York, on a personal injury claim in New York state court, seeking $100,000 in damages.

g. P, a citizen of California, sues D, a citizen of California, for infringement of copyright. P brings the suit in California state courts. D seeks to remove. Until 1988 there was an unexpected result: Although the federal courts have exclusive jurisdiction over copyright claims, D could not remove—because the California courts never had jurisdiction. There was no validly pending "case" that could be removed to federal court. In 1988 Congress amended §1441, adding what is now section (f). What result in the case just posed?

2. The procedure for removal is set forth in 28 U.S.C. §1446; that for challenging removal in §1447. Read these statutes and apply them to the following questions.

a. Plaintiff, a citizen of Pennsylvania, files a complaint in Pennsylvania state court naming Danielle as defendant and seeking $100,000 in damages. Danielle is a citizen of Georgia. If Danielle wishes to remove, what must her notice of removal say?

b. If in her notice of removal Danielle falsely states that she is a citizen of Georgia, what risks does she run?

c. Danielle files her notice of removal two months after being served with the state court complaint. Assuming that the conditions for diversity exist, can she remove?

d. Same problem as in (a), except that plaintiff's initial complaint seeks only $10,000 in damages. Six months later, after some discovery, plaintiff amends his state complaint to add an additional cause of action, so he now seeks $85,000 in damages. May Danielle now remove?

e. Same problem as in (d), except the damage prayer is well below the jurisdictional amount. Danielle seeks to remove, claiming that if she is liable, which she denies, the damages are far more than the jurisdictional amount. May she remove?

f. Same problem as in (d), except that plaintiff amends his complaint a year after the original complaint. No removal is possible, even though the requisites of diversity jurisdiction are met. Why?

g. Finally, §1447 (c) contains a pair of provisions concerning remand to the state courts. The first, a motion to remand "on the basis of any defect other than lack of subject matter jurisdiction," has a 30-day time limit. The second requires remand if the "district court lacks subject matter jurisdiction." What's the difference? Courts have interpreted the first to apply to problems that would prevent removal but would not have destroyed federal jurisdiction—for example, if one or more of the defendants seeking removal was a citizen of the state where suit was brought. See §1441(b). The second refers to facts that negate federal subject matter jurisdiction—for example, the absence of diversity or a federal question.

The problems discussed above deal with the basic situations in which removal is available. There are, however, more difficult situations, illustrated by the next case.

Caterpillar, Inc. v. Lewis

519 U.S. 61 (1996)

Justice GINSBURG delivered the opinion of the Court. . . .

The question presented is whether the absence of complete diversity at the time of removal is fatal to federal-court adjudication. We hold that a district court's error in failing to remand a case improperly removed is not fatal to the ensuing adjudication if federal jurisdictional requirements are met at the time judgment is entered.

Respondent James David Lewis, a resident of Kentucky, filed this lawsuit in Kentucky state court on June 22, 1989, after sustaining injuries while operating a bulldozer. Asserting state-law claims based on defective manufacture, negligent maintenance, failure to warn, and breach of warranty, Lewis named as defendants both the manufacturer of the bulldozer — petitioner Caterpillar Inc., a Delaware corporation with its principal place of business in Illinois — and the company that serviced the bulldozer — Whayne Supply Company, a Kentucky corporation with its principal place of business in Kentucky.

Several months later, Liberty Mutual Insurance Group, the insurance carrier for Lewis' employer, intervened in the lawsuit as a plaintiff. A Massachusetts corporation with its principal place of business in that State, Liberty Mutual asserted subrogation claims against both Caterpillar and Whayne Supply for workers' compensation benefits Liberty Mutual had paid to Lewis on behalf of his employer.

Lewis entered into a settlement agreement with defendant Whayne Supply less than a year after filing his complaint. Shortly after learning of this agreement, Caterpillar filed a notice of removal, on June 21, 1990, in the United States District Court for the Eastern District of Kentucky. Grounding federal jurisdiction on diversity of citizenship, Caterpillar satisfied with only a day to spare the statutory requirement that a diversity-based removal take place within one year of a lawsuit's commencement, see 28 U.S.C. §1446(b). Caterpillar's notice of removal explained that the case was nonremovable at the lawsuit's start: Complete diversity was absent then because plaintiff Lewis and defendant Whayne Supply shared Kentucky citizenship. Proceeding on the understanding that the settlement agreement between these two Kentucky parties would result in the dismissal of Whayne Supply from the lawsuit, Caterpillar stated that the settlement rendered the case removable.

Lewis objected to the removal and moved to remand the case to state court. Lewis acknowledged that he had settled his own claims against Whayne Supply. But Liberty Mutual had not yet settled its subrogation claim against Whayne Supply, Lewis asserted. Whayne Supply's presence as a defendant in the lawsuit, Lewis urged, defeated diversity of citizenship. Without addressing this argument, the District Court denied Lewis' motion to remand on September 24, 1990, treating as dispositive Lewis' admission that he had settled his own claims against Whayne Supply.

In June 1993, [Liberty Mutual and Whayne settled]. . . . With Caterpillar as the sole defendant adverse to Lewis, the case proceeded to a 6-day jury trial in November 1993, ending in a unanimous verdict for Caterpillar. . . .

We note, initially, two "givens" in this case as we have accepted it for review. First, the District Court, in its decision denying Lewis' timely motion to remand, incorrectly treated Whayne Supply, the nondiverse defendant, as effectively dropped from the case prior to removal. Second, the Sixth Circuit correctly determined that the complete diversity requirement was not satisfied at the time of removal. We accordingly home in on this question: Does the District Court's initial misjudgment still burden and run with the case, or is it overcome by the eventual dismissal of the nondiverse defendant? . . .

Having preserved his objection to an improper removal, Lewis urges that an "all's well that ends well" approach is inappropriate here. He maintains that ultimate satisfaction of the subject-matter jurisdiction requirement ought not swallow up antecedent statutory violations. The course Caterpillar advocates, Lewis observes, would disfavor diligent plaintiffs who timely, but unsuccessfully, move to check improper removals in district court. Further, that course would allow improperly removing defendants to profit from their disregard of Congress' instructions, and their ability to lead district judges into error.

Concretely, in this very case, Lewis emphasizes, adherence to the rules Congress prescribed for removal would have kept the case in state court. Only by removing prematurely was Caterpillar able to get to federal court inside the 1-year limitation set in §1446(b). Had Caterpillar waited until the case was ripe for removal, i.e., until Whayne Supply was dismissed as a defendant, the 1-year limitation would have barred the way, and plaintiff's choice of forum would have been preserved.[14]

These arguments are hardly meritless, but they run up against an overriding consideration. Once a diversity case has been tried in federal court, with rules of decision supplied by state law under the regime of Erie R. Co. v. Tompkins, 304 U.S. 64 (1938), considerations of finality, efficiency, and economy become overwhelming . . .

Our view is in harmony with a main theme of the removal scheme Congress devised. Congress ordered a procedure calling for expeditious superintendence by district courts. The lawmakers specified a short time, 30 days, for motions to remand for defects in removal procedure, 28 U.S.C. §1447(c), and district court orders remanding cases to state courts generally are "not reviewable on appeal or otherwise," §1447(d). Congress did not similarly exclude appellate review of refusals to remand. But an evident concern that may explain the lack of symmetry relates to the federal courts' subject-matter jurisdiction. Despite a federal trial court's threshold denial of a motion to remand, if, at the end of the day and case, a jurisdictional defect remains uncured, the judgment must be vacated. See Fed. Rule Civ. Proc. 12(h)(3) ("Whenever it appears by suggestion of the parties or otherwise that the court lacks jurisdiction of the subject matter, the court shall dismiss the action.") In this case, however, no jurisdictional defect lingered through judgment in the District Court. To wipe out the adjudication postjudgment, and return to state court a case now satisfying all federal jurisdictional

14. Lewis preferred state court to federal court based on differences he perceived in, inter alia, the state and federal jury systems and rules of evidence.

[handwritten margin note: would impose exorbitant cost to return to state court]

requirements, would impose an exorbitant cost on our dual court system, a cost incompatible with the fair and unprotracted administration of justice. Lewis ultimately argues that, if the final judgment against him is allowed to stand, "all of the various procedural requirements for removal will become unenforceable"; therefore, "defendants will have an enormous incentive to attempt wrongful removals." In particular, Lewis suggests that defendants will remove prematurely "in the hope that some subsequent developments, such as the eventual dismissal of nondiverse defendants, will permit the case to be kept in federal court." We do not anticipate the dire consequences Lewis forecasts.

The procedural requirements for removal remain enforceable by the federal trial court judges to whom those requirements are directly addressed. Lewis' prediction . . . rests on an assumption we do not indulge — that district courts generally will not comprehend, or will balk at applying, the rules on removal Congress has prescribed. The prediction furthermore assumes defendants' readiness to gamble that any jurisdictional defect, for example, the absence of complete diversity, will first escape detection, then disappear prior to judgment. The well-advised defendant, we are satisfied, will foresee the likely outcome of an unwarranted removal — a swift and nonreviewable remand order, see 28 U.S.C. §1447(c), (d), attended by the displeasure of a district court whose authority has been improperly invoked. The odds against any gain from a wrongful removal, in sum, render improbable Lewis' projection of increased resort to the maneuver.

For the reasons stated, the judgment of the Court of Appeals is reversed, and the case is remanded for proceedings consistent with this opinion. . . .

NOTES AND PROBLEMS

1. *Caterpillar*, written by a former civil procedure teacher,[*] splendidly illustrates the pitfalls of removal.

a. Explain why removal was improper at the time Caterpillar attempted it.

b. Explain why removal would still have been improper had Caterpillar waited until the point in the lawsuit when complete diversity existed.

2. Removal is not an entirely popular idea, either with states or with plaintiffs who find their initial choice of a forum thwarted.

a. Why did Congress place a one-year "statute of limitations" on removal petitions in diversity cases — even in cases like *Caterpillar* where the basis for removal did not present itself until after that date? See §1446(b). Notice that in some cases this time limit allows plaintiffs an opportunity to manipulate jurisdiction, joining nondiverse parties and then dropping them after a year.

b. Can plaintiff prevent the removal of a diversity case by filing her claim in state court but asking for less than $75,000 in damages, waiting a year, and then amending her pleading to seek a greater amount? What's the risk that plaintiff runs?

---

[*] Justice Ginsburg taught civil procedure for more than a decade before being appointed to the bench.

c. Apparently post-removal manipulation of the amount in controversy will not work. In Rogers v. Wal-Mart Stores Inc., 230 F.3d 868 (6th Cir. 2000), plaintiff filed a state law negligence action seeking $950,000 in damages. Defendant removed, invoking diversity. After the case was removed, plaintiff sought remand to state court, offering to stipulate that she would seek less than $75,000 in damages and the case therefore fell below the amount in controversy requirement. The Sixth Circuit affirmed a denial of the remand petition, saying that the removal petition should be judged by the apparent amount in controversy at the time removal is sought.

d. Nor can the state legislature help much. Ohio sought to discourage removal by enacting a statute providing that any out-of-state insurer that removed a case to federal court was barred from doing business in the state for three years. Held: unconstitutional. International Insurance Co. v. Duryee, 96 F.3d 837 (6th Cir. 1996).

3. In Capron v. Van Noorden, supra page 190, the Supreme Court dismissed a case in which plaintiff had improperly invoked diversity jurisdiction, then lost at trial. On appeal, plaintiff pointed to the lack of jurisdiction — and won. Contrast *Caterpillar*, in which the plaintiff properly and accurately objected to removal. But the Court in *Caterpillar*, acknowledging that diversity did not exist at the time of filing, nevertheless affirmed the federal judgment. Why?

4. Subsection (c) of §1441 poses unexpected difficulties. Until 1990 this subsection contained a snarl of statutory construction (involving its application to diversity cases) so tangled that we shall not try to describe it. Congress cut this knot by specifying that subsection (c) applies only to federal question cases. But when can §1441(c) apply to a federal question case? Consider two possible constructions:

a. In a suit in which the parties are not of diverse citizenship, plaintiff brings a pair of claims, one based on federal law, the other on state law. Defendant seeks to remove. If the two claims are closely related, defendant can remove without regard to subsection (c); the two claims are part of the same constitutionally related "case or controversy." Recall 28 U.S.C. §1367, which says that a federal court has jurisdiction over state law claims that are closely related to federal claims. In that situation the entire case would be removable under §1441(b) because it would be "a civil action of which the district courts have original jurisdiction." If, however, the two claims are entirely unrelated, they will not be part of the same case or controversy and therefore will be beyond the constitutional reach of the federal courts' jurisdiction. If jurisdiction under those circumstances is unconstitutional, a mere statute cannot alter the situation. Under this analysis §1441(c) is either unnecessary or unconstitutional.

b. Now imagine the same situation, with the two claims unrelated to each other. But imagine that one of the claims contains a federal element; for example, a fired employee sues, invoking a state law barring religious discrimination and, in addition, a federal law claim for alleged violations of the federal pension laws. The pension claim, let us imagine, arises directly under federal law and would thus be removable if brought alone; the state law discrimination claim is not removable, however. Nor are the two claims sufficiently related to be removable under 28 U.S.C. §1367. Does §1441(c) give the courts jurisdiction over a "separate and independent" claim with a federal ingredient, even if that ingredient would not suffice for federal jurisdiction if brought separately? See Wisconsin Dept. of Corrections v. Schacht, 524 U.S. 381 (1998) (federal court retains jurisdiction over remaining claim).

c. One can cut this Gordian knot by supposing that the federal court will promptly determine that the unrelated state claim should be remanded to the state courts. At a pragmatic level this solves the problem; at a conceptual level the statute still appears to give federal courts temporary jurisdiction over cases they cannot constitutionally hear.

5. In addition to 28 U.S.C. §1441, which is the general removal statute, there are statutes permitting removal in specific cases. For example, §1442 permits removal of suits by federal officers or agencies sued for the performance of their duties. By contrast, some actions that otherwise would be removable under §1441 are made specifically nonremovable by §1445. Examine that statute and consider why Congress might have made such actions nonremovable and thus allowed plaintiffs to dictate the choice between state and federal court.

6. Finally, consider an interesting use of removal that takes us full circle back to the premises of *Mottley*, with which this chapter began. The Securities Litigation Uniform Standards Act of 1998 does three things. First, it preempts state securities class actions alleging fraud in the sales of securities; it provides, in other words, that in such cases federal law displaces otherwise applicable state law. 15 U.S.C. §77p(b). Second, it provides that securities fraud class actions based entirely on state law "shall be removable to the federal district court for the district in which the action is pending." 15 U.S.C. §77p(c). Finally, it orders dismissal of the removed class actions. This three-step process provides a review of much of this chapter.

a. The first step is substantive and takes us beyond the boundaries of procedure. Without going into great detail, one can conclude that Congress could constitutionally displace—preempt—all state securities law. If Congress can do that, can it take the half-way step of allowing state law to continue to exist in suits brought by individual plaintiffs but preempting state law in securities class actions?

b. If one assumes that Congress has the power suggested in (a), one reaches the procedural curiosity. The Securities Litigation Uniform Standards Act has created a federal defense to a state law claim—the defense of preemption. Ordinarily the system relies on state courts to recognize federal defenses. If state courts err, the remedy—the only remedy—is review by the U.S. Supreme Court. One can think of *Mottley* in these terms: The Supreme Court dismissed the case, requiring the Mottleys to refile in state court and to await review by the Supreme Court as the only way to get a federal court to pass on the federal question involved. Notice that this scheme creates some slippage; if the U.S. Supreme Court had not reviewed the case the second time around, the Mottleys would have hung onto their free pass even though federal law outlawed it.

c. The Securities Litigation Uniform Standards Act eliminates this slippage. The statute does two things: It creates a federal defense to certain state law claims, and then it creates removal based on that defense. Recall from the start of the chapter that the well-pleaded complaint rule as interpreted in *Mottley* is a statutory rather than a constitutional matter and that Congress can statutorily create a broader jurisdiction for the federal courts under removal than under original jurisdiction. It has done so here. As a consequence, one can expect that all such claims will be removed — and dismissed — by federal district courts.

d. Should Congress use this technique more widely? For all federal defenses? Should Congress use it at all?

THE *ERIE* PROBLEM

IV

Recall the theme of this section — the constitutional framework for U.S. litigation. The two preceding chapters have illustrated the two principal means by which the Constitution creates that framework: It limits the powers of states, and it enumerates (thereby limiting) the powers of the federal government. The first limitation appears in the doctrines of personal jurisdiction, the second in those of federal subject matter jurisdiction. The Constitution thus requires state courts to share power with one another and with a federal judiciary. This chapter explores an entailment of that shared power: How does the Constitution ensure that these two court systems respect each other's spheres of power?

The question arises because state and federal courts not only share power, but they exercise overlapping jurisdiction. For example, under modern understandings of personal jurisdiction, several different states may have jurisdiction to hear a case against a particular defendant. Similarly, state courts can hear cases arising under federal law, and federal courts, sitting in diversity, can hear cases that could also be tried in state courts. Under these circumstances both state and federal courts frequently face a question that arises from this overlapping jurisdiction: What law applies to the case before us?

Seen abstractly, this question has many applications. Must a state court in a criminal trial apply federal constitutional law? Should a state court, hearing a question arising under federal law, follow the Federal Rules of Civil Procedure instead of its usual procedural code? The *Erie* problem, from which this chapter takes its title, involves a very specific subset of these questions: When a federal court sits in diversity jurisdiction, what law does it apply?

This question, though phrased narrowly, opens the door onto a much larger set of questions about the relations of state and federal courts and of constitutional interpretation. Speaking about part of this problem, one distinguished commentator has written, "No issue in the whole field of federal jurisprudence has been more difficult. . . ."* This chapter will seek to explain why someone might take that view — but also to make the problems less difficult than this quotation implies.

---

* Wright, Federal Courts 369.

A.   State Courts as Lawmakers in a Federal System

1.   The Issue in Historical Context

To understand how the issue arises, one needs a very brief historical introduction. The first judiciary provided for federal diversity jurisdiction and also contained a section now codified at 28 U.S.C. §1652 and known as the Rules of Decision Act:

> The laws of the several states, except where the Constitution or Acts of Congress otherwise require or provide, shall be regarded as rules of decisions in civil actions in the courts of the United States, in cases where they apply.

On its face, one might think that that statute, in effect since the earliest days of the Republic, would resolve the question. Since diversity cases are in federal court only because of the parties' citizenship, there isn't any federal law to apply, so one might think that such cases would be "cases where they [i.e., state laws] apply." The story is not that simple, however, because people have disagreed sharply about what "the laws of the several states" means.

The leading pre-*Erie* case, the case *Erie* overrules, was Swift v. Tyson, 41 U.S. 1 (1841). *Swift* involved a "bill of exchange," a halfway step between a promissory note and a modern check. With promissory notes, there are numerous defenses assertable by anyone sued for breach; with checks those defenses are much more limited. The substantive issue in *Swift* was how many defenses could be asserted and thus how much like a contract and how much like a check the "bill" was. Procedurally and jurisprudentially (the aspect with which we shall be concerned), the issue was how one decided which law applied to the substantive question. *Swift* was a diversity case filed in a federal court sitting in New York. New York courts had spoken on the substantive issue, ruling that bills were subject to a number of defenses. Were these New York cases part of "the laws" of that state and thus binding on the federal district court? No, held the U.S. Supreme Court; the New York precedents were not "laws"; instead, the federal courts sitting in diversity were free to ignore them:

> But, admitting the doctrine to be fully settled in New York, it remains to be considered whether it is obligatory upon this court if it differs from the principles established in the general commercial law. It is observable that the Courts of New York do not found their decisions upon this point upon any local statute, or positive, fixed, or ancient usage; but they deduce the doctrine from the general principles of commercial law. It is, however, contended that [the Rules of Decision Act] furnishes a rule obligatory on this Court to follow the decisions of state tribunals in all cases to which they apply. . . . In order to maintain the argument, it is essential . . . that the word "laws" [in the Rules of Decision Act] includes within the scope of its meaning the decisions of local tribunals. In the ordinary use of language it will hardly be contended that the decisions of Courts constitute laws. They are at most evidence of what the laws are; and are not themselves laws. . . . The laws of a state are more usually understood to mean the rules and enactments promulgated by the legislative authority thereof. . . . [The court said it would be bound by state legislation and by state judge-made law on matters of peculiarly "local usages," generally understood to involve land title, but not on more general topics.] Undoubtedly, the

decisions of the local tribunals upon such subjects are entitled to, and will receive, the most deliberate attention and respect of this Court; but they cannot furnish positive rules on conclusive authority. . . .

Swift went on to reach a conclusion different from that reached by the New York courts.

In the next century *Swift* came to be seen by many not only as momentous but also as pernicious, not because of its holding on the negotiability of bills of exchange, but because of its treatment of state law. For many federal courts *Swift* became a charter of judicial independence, a declaration that they could ignore state law even when sitting in cases that were not explicitly governed by federal law. Often decisions in the *Swift* line of cases seemed to favor business interests. One commentary argues:

> The furor can only be understood against the background of 19th-century mercantile expansion westward, although it is rarely presented so. In the latter part of the 19th century, and the early part of the 20th, the federal courts came to be seen as protectors of mercantile and corporate interests against agrarian and workingmen's interests. . . .*

Notice that *Swift* reached its conclusion as an interpretation of the Rules of Decision Act, which Congress could have amended during. Congress did not amend the Act. The next step in the story took matters out of Congress's hands.

2. Constitutionalizing the Issue

This step grew out of homely circumstances. On Thursday, July 26, 1934, Harry Tompkins visited his mother-in-law's house in Hughestown, a village of 2,800 people in northwestern Pennsylvania's coal-mining country. He received a ride part of the way home and walked the remaining distance along the railroad tracks of the Erie Railroad, keeping several feet between himself and the tracks. A train passed, and an open door on a refrigerator car struck him and knocked him partially under the train. His right arm was severed. After recovering from his injuries, he sought a lawyer and found 27-year-old Bernard Nemeroff. Hoping to benefit from Swift v. Tyson, Nemeroff and his partner, 21-year-old Aaron Danzig, chose to bring suit against the railroad in the federal District Court for the Southern District of New York.

Under Pennsylvania law, for whose application the railroad's lawyer argued, Tompkins was a trespasser, and the railroad was therefore liable only for "wanton" negligence, a finding unlikely given the facts. The judge, relying on the freedom given by Swift v. Tyson, instructed the jury according to the "general law," that the railroad was liable even if it was guilty of only "ordinary" negligence. The jury returned a verdict for Tompkins in the amount of $30,000 (about $390,000 in 2000 dollars). The railroad appealed, but the Second Circuit upheld Tompkins's verdict. The railroad then sought a writ of certiorari from the Supreme Court. In

---

* Howard Fink and Mark V. Tushnet, Federal Jurisdiction: Policy and Practice 179 (2d ed. 1987).

the meantime the railroad asked Justice Cardozo to stay the judgment until the Supreme Court could consider the certiorari petition, and Justice Cardozo obliged. The railroad then made Tompkins a settlement offer — $7,500 plus the withdrawal of its certiorari petition — but Danzig and Nemeroff talked him out of accepting and then hid him from the railroad's lawyers.

The Supreme Court granted certiorari, even though it rarely did so in negligence cases. On April 25, 1938, the Supreme Court decided the case in one of the last opinions written by Justice Brandeis. The decision went unnoticed until Justice Stone wrote privately to Arthur Krock of the New York Times calling to his attention "the most important opinion since I have been on the court."[*]

Erie Railroad v. Tompkins

304 U.S. 64 (1938)

Mr. Justice BRANDEIS delivered the opinion of the Court.

The question for decision is whether the oft-challenged doctrine of Swift v. Tyson shall now be disapproved. . . .

First. Swift v. Tyson held that federal courts exercising jurisdiction on the ground of diversity of citizenship need not, in matters of general jurisprudence, apply the unwritten law of the State as declared by its highest court; that they are free to exercise an independent judgment as to what the common law of the State is — or should be; and that, as there stated by Mr. Justice Story:

> [T]he true interpretation of the [Rules of Decision Act] limited its application to state laws strictly local, that is to say, to the positive statutes of the state, and the construction thereof adopted by the local tribunals, and to rights and titles to things having a permanent locality, such as the rights and titles to real estate, and other matters immovable and extraterritorial in their nature and character. It never has been supposed by us, that the section did apply, or was intended to apply, to questions of a more general nature, not at all dependent upon local statutes or local usages of a fixed and permanent operation, as, for example, to the construction of ordinary contracts or other written instruments, and especially to questions of general commercial law, where the state tribunals are called upon to perform the like functions as ourselves, that is, to ascertain upon general reasoning and legal analogies, what is the true exposition of the contract of instrument, or what is the just rule furnished by the principles of commercial law to govern the case.

. . . The federal courts assumed, in the broad field of "general law," the power to declare rules of decision which Congress was confessedly without power to enact as statutes. Doubt was repeatedly expressed as to the correctness of the construction given [the Act], and as to the soundness of the rule which it introduced. But it was the more recent research of a competent scholar, who examined the original document, which established that the construction given to it

---

[*] This summary comes from Younger, Observation: What Happened in Erie, 56 Tex. L. Rev. 1011 (1978), and Rizzi, Erie Memoirs Reveal Drama, Tragedy, 63 Harv. L. Record 2 (Sept. 24, 1976).

by the Court was erroneous; and that the purpose of the section was merely to make certain that, in all matters except those in which some federal law is controlling, the federal courts exercising jurisdiction in diversity of citizenship cases would apply as their rules of decision the law of the State, unwritten as well as written.[5]

Criticism of the doctrine became widespread after the decision of Black & White Taxicab Co. v. Brown & Yellow Taxicab Co. There, Brown and Yellow, a Kentucky corporation owned by Kentuckians, and the Louisville and Nashville Railroad, also a Kentucky corporation, wished that the former should have the exclusive privilege of soliciting passenger and baggage transportation at the Bowling Green, Kentucky, railroad station; and that the Black and White, a competing Kentucky corporation, should be prevented from interfering with that privilege. Knowing that such a contract would be void under the common law of Kentucky, it was arranged that the Brown and Yellow reincorporate under the law of Tennessee, and that the contract with the railroad should be executed there. The suit was then brought by the Tennessee corporation in the federal court for Western Kentucky to enjoin competition by the Black and White; and injunction issued by the District Court was sustained by the Court of Appeals; and this Court, citing many decisions in which the doctrine of Swift v. Tyson had been applied, affirmed the decree.

Second. Experience in applying the doctrine of Swift v. Tyson had revealed its defects, political and social; and the benefits expected to flow from the rule did not accrue. Persistence of state courts in their own opinions on questions of common law prevented uniformity; and the impossibility of discovering a satisfactory line of demarcation between the province of general law and that of local law developed a new well of uncertainties.

On the other hand, the mischievous results of the doctrine had become apparent. Diversity of citizenship jurisdiction was conferred in order to prevent apprehended discrimination in State courts against those not citizens of the State. Swift v. Tyson introduced grave discrimination by non-citizens against citizens. It made rights enjoyed under the unwritten "general law" vary according to whether enforcement was sought in the state or in the federal court; and the privilege of selecting the court in which the right should be determined was conferred upon the non-citizen. Thus, the doctrine rendered impossible equal protection of the law. In attempting to promote uniformity of law throughout the United States, the doctrine had prevented uniformity in the administration of the law of the State.

The discrimination resulting became in practice far-reaching. This resulted in part from the broad province accorded to the so-called "general law" as to which federal courts exercised an independent judgment. [The opinion cited many fields of law.]

In part the discrimination resulted from the wide range of persons held entitled to avail themselves of the federal rule by resort to the diversity of citizenship jurisdiction. . . .

---

5. Charles Warren, New Light on the History of the Federal Judiciary Act of 1789, 37 Harv. L. Rev. 49, 51-52, 81-88, 108 (1923).

The injustice and confusion incident to the doctrine of Swift v. Tyson have been repeatedly urged as reasons for abolishing or limiting diversity of citizenship jurisdiction. Other legislative relief has been proposed. If only a question of statutory construction were involved, we should not be prepared to abandon a doctrine so widely applied throughout nearly a century. But the unconstitutionality of the course pursued has now been made clear and compels us to do so.

Third. Except in matters governed by the Federal Constitution or by Acts of Congress, the law to be applied in any case is the law of the State. And whether the law of the State shall be declared by its Legislature in a statute or by its highest court in a decision is not a matter of federal concern. There is no federal general common law. Congress has no power to declare substantive rules of common law applicable in a State whether they be local in their nature or "general," be they commercial law or a part of the law of torts. And no clause in the Constitution purports to confer such a power upon the federal courts. . . .

The fallacy underlying the rule declared in Swift v. Tyson is made clear by Mr. Justice Holmes. The doctrine rests upon the assumption that there is "a transcendental body of law outside of any particular State but obligatory within it unless and until changed by statute," that federal courts have the power to use their judgment as to what the rules of common law are; and that in the federal courts "the parties are entitled to an independent judgment on matters of general law":

> [B]ut law in the sense in which courts speak of it today does not exist without some definite authority behind it. The common law so far as it is enforced in a State, whether called common law or not, is not the common law generally but the law of that State existing by the authority of that State without regard to what it may have been in England or anywhere else. . . . The authority and only authority is the State, and if that be so, the voice adopted by the State as its own [whether it be of its Legislature or of its Supreme Court] should utter the last word.

Thus the doctrine of Swift v. Tyson is, as Mr. Justice Holmes said, "an unconstitutional assumption of powers by courts of the United States which no lapse of time or respectable array of opinion should make us hesitate to correct." In disapproving that doctrine we do not hold unconstitutional §34 of the Federal Judiciary Act of 1789 or any other Act of Congress. We merely declare that in applying the doctrine this Court and the lower courts have invaded rights which in our opinion are reserved by the Constitution to the several States.

Fourth. The defendant contended that by the common law of Pennsylvania as declared by its highest court in Falchetti v. Pennsylvania R. Co., 160 A. 859, the only duty owed to the plaintiff was to refrain from willful or wanton injury. The plaintiff denied that such is the Pennsylvania law. In support of their respective contentions the parties discussed and cited many decisions of the Supreme Court of the State. The Circuit Court of Appeals ruled that the question of liability is one of general law; and on that ground declined to decide the issue of state law. As we hold this was error, the judgment is reversed and the case remanded to it for further proceedings in conformity with our opinion.

Reversed.

Mr. Justice REED.

I concur in the conclusion reached in this case, in the disapproval of the doctrine of Swift v. Tyson, and in the reasoning of the majority opinion except insofar as it relies upon the unconstitutionality of the "course pursued" by the federal courts. . . .

To decide the case now before us and to "disapprove" the doctrine of Swift v. Tyson requires only that we say that the words "the laws" [in the Rules of Decision Act] include in their meaning the decisions of the local tribunals. . . . [T]his Court is now of the view that "laws" includes "decisions," [and] it is unnecessary to go further and declare that the "course pursued" was "unconstitutional," instead of merely erroneous.

[handwritten margin note: Not necessary to say uncont.]

The "unconstitutional" course referred to in the majority opinion is apparently the ruling in Swift v. Tyson that the supposed omission of Congress to legislate as to the effect of decisions leaves federal courts free to interpret general law for themselves. I am not at all sure whether, in the absence of federal statutory direction, federal courts would be compelled to follow state decisions. There was sufficient doubt about the matter in 1789 to induce the first Congress to legislate. . . . If the opinion commits this Court to the position that the Congress is without power to declare what rules of substantive law shall govern the federal courts, that conclusion also seems questionable. The line between procedural and substantive law is hazy but no one doubts federal power over procedure. The Judiciary Article and the "necessary and proper" clause of Article One may fully authorize legislation, such as this section of the Judiciary Act.

In this Court, stare decisis, in statutory construction, is a useful rule, not an inexorable command. It seems preferable to overturn an established construction of an Act of Congress, rather than, in the circumstances of this case, to interpret the Constitution. . . .

[Dissenting opinion of Justices BUTLER and MCREYNOLDS is omitted.]

NOTES AND PROBLEMS

1. What is the connection between the doctrine announced in the decision and the outcome?

a. Under the circumstances of this case, why did it matter to Harry Tompkins (or to the Erie Railroad) whether *Swift* was overruled?

b. Tompkins won in the trial court. The U.S. Supreme Court seems to assume that if the tort law of Pennsylvania applied to the facts of the case, the railroad would owe Tompkins only the duty of refraining from wanton or willful negligence. Tompkins had a better chance of preserving his verdict if the railroad owed him a higher degree of care. Tompkins's lawyers pointed to a different source of law, one requiring such a higher standard of care. What was that source?

2. With the practical consequences framed, turn to the doctrine.

a. According to the opinion, what is the source of the federal courts' duty to follow Pennsylvania judge-made law in this case?

b. The most obvious answer is to point to the Rule of Decision Act, requiring federal courts to apply state law in appropriate cases. Why won't that work as a fair reading of *Erie*?

c. The *Erie* Court says that it is handing down a constitutional decision. Does the opinion ever identify a part of the Constitution that leads to its holding?

d. If *Erie* isn't a constitutional decision, Congress could change its result. How?

3. Since *Erie* was decided, lawyers and political scientists have argued about whether it was a constitutional decision, and, if so, how it ought to be understood. One plausible candidate is the opinion's statement that "Congress has no power to declare substantive rules of common law applicable in a State whether they be local in their nature or 'general,' be they commercial law or a part of the law of torts."

a. Assume for the moment that this statement is accurate as a matter of constitutional law. Congress has no power to make general tort law, and nothing in Article III gives the federal courts that power either. It would therefore follow that a federal court, like the district court in *Erie*, that purported to be declaring substantive law in such a setting would be acting unconstitutionally — because it would be exercising a power not given it by any part of the Constitution.

b. Now alter the assumption about Congressional power. Understandings of constitutional law have changed considerably since the *Erie* decision was handed down. Today's Supreme Court would likely uphold a federal statute establishing rules for liability for injury incurred along the right-of-way of a railroad engaged in interstate commerce. Indeed, Congress has gone much further than that: To choose just one example, a federal statute regulating debt collectors purports to specify venue for a state law lawsuit seeking to enforce a simple debt governed by state contract law. 15 U.S.C. §1692i(a). If such statutes are constitutional, should *Erie*, though not overruled, be considered obsolete because its underlying assumptions have been eroded?

c. One answer to the preceding question is to distinguish between Congress's power to make such a law and the federal courts' power to do so. Because of its structure (giving each state a voice), Congress gives considerable deference to state interests; the courts have no such structural characteristics. One might therefore think that it continues to be unconstitutional for the federal courts to displace state law, even if the federal government as a whole could do so. Does the mere grant of diversity jurisdiction to the district courts include the power to legislate — judicially — whenever Congress itself could do so?

d. Historians of American law have vigorously debated this question, with some urging a more charitable view of Swift v. Tyson, and others that arguing that it represented an evil more pervasive than suggested in *Erie*. The most comprehensive recent study of *Erie* has urged a broader view of the case as part of a social system of litigation and as an often-misunderstood constitutional milestone:

> In 1938 *Erie* stood — indeed still stands — as a potential cornerstone for a fundamental proposition that goes far beyond the narrow and historically specific issue of federal-state forum shopping under Swift v. Tyson. The proposition is as follows: legal analysis should systematically examine the dynamics of litigation practice, consider more thoroughly the role of social inequalities in determining the results of procedural and jurisdictional rules applied in the various de facto litigation processes that mark different fields of practice, and seek continually to recreate those rules in

order to maximize the ability of litigants — particularly the weak, unsophisticated, and practically disadvantaged — to secure practical justice.*

To this one might add only that Harry Tompkins might be somewhat perplexed about why it was necessary to overturn his jury verdict in order to vindicate the "practically disadvantaged."

4. If one moves from broad constitutional significance back to a more technical plane, one notes that Tompkins' lawyers filed *Erie* in the Southern District of New York, yet the Court assumed that Pennsylvania law had to be applied. Why?

a. Each state has a body of law called its conflict of laws rules, which specify the circumstances in which courts of that state should follow laws of other jurisdictions, such as those of other states, federal law, or foreign law. Two inferences are possible from the *Erie* Court's silence on this point. The Court might have thought it absolutely clear that New York courts would have applied Pennsylvania law, or the Court might have thought that the New York conflict of laws rules were irrelevant.

b. In the latter case, conflict of laws rules would themselves be an exception to *Erie* — that is, the federal courts on their own would be free to choose which state's law would apply to a case connected to more than one state. Some have suggested that the federal courts, as a neutral forum, would be well-suited to decide which state's law should apply.

Such speculation was laid to rest, however, in Klaxon Co. v. Stentor Elec. Mfg. Co., 313 U.S. 487 (1941), in which the Supreme Court applied Erie principles to conflicts rules: Under *Erie* a federal court sitting in diversity must apply the conflicts principles of the forum state. Failure to refer to New York conflicts rules in *Erie* presumably came about because in the simple case presented by *Erie,* all states' conflicts rules (at the time) pointed to the law of Pennsylvania.

5. Much of the Court's discussion in *Erie* is devoted to the evils of forum-shopping. By "forum-shopping" the Court seems to mean the practice of a litigant's selecting one rather than another court in which to sue, in the hope that the court will in some way treat the litigant more favorably than another court that might have heard the case. For example, under Swift v. Tyson there were several circumstances in which federal courts would enforce contracts that state courts would have refused to enforce. In such an instance, a plaintiff hoping to enforce such an agreement would "shop" for a forum (in this case the federal courts) that would enforce it.

a. What's wrong with different outcomes? If a federal judge believes that she has come up with the just and proper solution to a particular legal problem, doesn't it deny justice to the parties to rule to the contrary simply to imitate the state court's predicted result? Isn't that behaving as if two wrongs will somehow make a right?

b. What's wrong with forum-shopping? *Erie* seems to assume that forum-shopping between state and federal courts is the major problem; what about

---

* Edward A. Purcell, Jr., Brandeis and the Progressive Constitution: *Erie,* the Judicial Power, and the Politics of the Federal Courts in Twentieth-Century America 297 (New Haven: 2000).

forum-shopping among states? Seven years after *Erie*, the Court decided *International Shoe*, thus giving its constitutional blessing to an extended jurisdictional reach for state courts. With this extension, plaintiffs will often have a choice of several different states in which to sue a defendant, states that may have different substantive laws. Indeed, even at the time of *Erie*, Tompkins could have sued the railroad in Pennsylvania, in New York, and perhaps in several other states where it did business; each of those states would likely have taken a slightly different approach to his case. So, if forum-shopping is both inevitable and constitutionally permissible, why does it become unconstitutional in *Erie*?

6. *Erie* was the first civil case heard by Judge Mandelbaum, the trial judge. Judge Mandelbaum was a product of Tammany politics and, over strong protest from the bar, was appointed to the bench by President Roosevelt. Before his appointment Mandelbaum had visited the federal courthouse only once, to see what it looked like. His notes, penned in the margin of his copy of the Supreme Court's Erie opinion and reported in Younger, Observation: What Happened in Erie, 56 Tex. L. Rev. 1011, 1030 (1978), suggest a different perspective on the case: "Because the Swift Tyson case although before this case I never knew of its existence to be truthful and for the confusion this decision brought about, it might have been better to leave it alone and stand by good old Swifty."

NOTE: *ERIE* AND THE PERSISTENCE OF FEDERAL COMMON LAW

Erie says that "there is no federal general common law." One can easily understand this sentence to mean more than it does. In fact, federal common law continues to flourish. *Erie* holds only that "general" federal common law may not displace that of the states in areas in which the Constitution grants lawmaking power to the states. The Constitution grants substantive lawmaking power to the federal government; because the courts are part of that government, and because courts in the United States have traditionally exercised lawmaking powers, the Constitution thus grants potential lawmaking power to the federal courts in many areas.

The grant of judicial power in admiralty and maritime cases under Article III invites federal courts to create common law for such cases. Federal statutes may also provide an opportunity for federal common law to fill gaps in the statutory scheme. Much of antitrust law, for example, is judge-made law that fills the gaps left by vague and general statutes. Perhaps the most famous case in which the Court has found the existence of a jurisdictional statute authority for the federal courts to elaborate a body of federal common law is Textile Workers Union of America v. Lincoln Mills, 353 U.S. 448 (1957).

In *Lincoln Mills*, the Supreme Court was faced with an attack on the constitutionality of §301 of the Taft-Hartley Act, 29 U.S.C. §185 (1947). The statute was challenged on the ground that it purported to confer jurisdiction on the federal courts for disputes arising between employers and labor unions, without suggesting substantive rules to govern such disputes. The problem arose in this case because there was neither obvious federal question jurisdiction nor diversity of citizenship among the parties. The Court said Congress must have intended by the grant of jurisdiction in §301 to give the federal courts substantive rulemaking power in the area — in other words, the courts were to develop a federal common law under the Taft-Hartley Act (often by borrowing from state contract law and the like).

In light of *Lincoln Mills*, could Congress amend the Rules of Decision Act to provide that the federal courts can form their own common law? Or is a narrower grant, limited to a single field like labor law, a necessary condition for such a delegation?

B. The Limits of State Power in Federal Courts

Having struggled with the constitutional ambiguities, the student will be distressed to learn that, constitutional basis aside, *Erie* was an easy case for the application of the principle it announced. The remainder of this chapter will consider decisions in which the issue is whether and how to apply the *Erie* doctrine — decisions that require a much more subtle look at what that case held.

Erie established that federal courts sitting in a diversity action were bound to replicate state practice in some circumstances: What were those circumstances? Though *Erie* did not say so, its setting suggested that at the very least federal courts sitting in diversity should observe state substantive law, whether made by legislatures or by judges. But what about other "laws"? For example, were federal courts sitting in diversity bound to apply state statutes of limitations? If the courts of the state in question did not generally enforce arbitration agreements, could federal courts nevertheless do so if authorized by a federal statute? If a suit in state court could be decided only by a judge, was a federal court precluded from using a jury? If a state statute required personal service of process, did that requirement also apply to process served in a federal diversity action? If a state court were bound to refuse to honor a contractual forum selection clause, were federal courts sitting in that state required to do likewise? If a state legislature orders its appellate courts to reduce excessive damages awarded by juries, does a federal appellate court have the same power?

In the years since *Erie* the Supreme Court has addressed each of these questions (as well as others) in an effort to mediate between two opposing principles: that *Erie* requires deference to state courts as lawmaking bodies, and that federal courts are an independent judicial system with the autonomy that statement implies. Justice Reed's *Erie* concurrence in *Erie* raised but did not resolve the question: "The line between procedural and substantive law is hazy, but no one doubts federal power over procedure." Notice that many of these questions involve issues that could be described as "procedural." As you read the next cases, consider whether it is true that "no one doubts" federal power over procedure.

1.   Interpreting the Constitutional Command of Erie

Guaranty Trust Co. v. York

326 U.S. 99 (1945)

Mr. Justice FRANKFURTER delivered the opinion of the Court. . . .

[Plaintiffs sued a bond trustee in a federal diversity action alleging misrepresentation and breach of trust. New York substantive law governed. Among other defenses, defendant invoked the New York statute of limitations. Plaintiffs argued that the statute of limitations did not bar the suit because it was on the "equity side" of federal court. The courts of equity had traditionally considered the length of time elapsing between the maturing of a claim and the bringing of suit but had not thought themselves strictly bound by statutes of limitations. Referring to that equitable tradition, the Second Circuit ruled that plaintiffs' suit was not barred. The Supreme Court disagreed.]

Our starting point must be the policy of federal jurisdiction which Erie R. Co. v. Tompkins embodies. In overruling Swift v. Tyson, Erie R. Co. v. Tompkins did not merely overrule a venerable case. It overruled a particular way of looking at law which dominated the judicial process long after its inadequacies had been laid bare. Law was conceived as a "brooding omnipresence" of Reason, of which decisions were merely evidence and not themselves the controlling formulations. Accordingly, federal courts deemed themselves free to ascertain what Reason, and therefore Law, required wholly independent of authoritatively declared State law, even in cases where a legal right as the basis for relief was created by State authority and could not be created by federal authority and the case got into a federal court merely because it was "between Citizens of different States" under Art. III, §2 of the Constitution of the United States. . . .

And so this case reduces itself to the narrow question whether, when no recovery could be had in a State court because the action is barred by the statute of limitations, a federal court in equity can take cognizance of the suit because there is diversity of citizenship between the parties. . . .

And so the question is not whether a statute of limitations is deemed a matter of "procedure" in some sense. The question is whether such a statute concerns merely the manner and the means by which a right to recover, as recognized by the State, is enforced, or whether such statutory limitation is a matter of substance in the aspect that alone is relevant to our problem, namely, does it significantly affect the result of a litigation for a federal court to disregard a law of a State that would be controlling in an action upon the same claim by the same parties in a State court?

It is therefore immaterial whether statutes of limitation are characterized either as "substantive" or "procedural" in State court opinions in any use of those terms unrelated to the specific issue before us. Erie R. Co. v. Tompkins was not an endeavor to formulate scientific legal terminology. It expressed a policy that touches vitally the proper distribution of judicial power between State and federal courts. In essence, the intent of that decision was to insure that, in all cases where a federal court is exercising jurisdiction solely because of the diversity of citizen-ship of the parties, the outcome of the litigation in the federal court should be substantially the same, so far as legal rules determine the outcome of a litigation, as it would be if tried in a State court. . . .

[handwritten: Intent to generate same outcome]

The judgment is reversed and the case is remanded for proceedings not inconsistent with this opinion.

So ordered.

[The dissenting opinion of Justice RUTLEDGE is omitted.]

NOTES AND PROBLEMS

1. *Guaranty Trust* displays a ferocity that impedes analysis.

a. The opinion sharply attacks the proposition that if something is "procedural" it is not governed by the rule in *Erie*. Why? The main opinion in *Erie* had asserted no such proposition; is Justice Frankfurter disputing Justice Reed's concurrence about federal power over procedure?

b. Even in the midst of this attack, however, Justice Frankfurter conceded that federal courts need not follow state law that "concern[ed] merely the manner and means by which a right to recover is . . . enforced." Isn't this saying that Justice Reed was right?

c. As you read the rest of the cases in the *Erie* line, consider whether they don't come down to the question of defining "the manner and means by which a right to recover is . . . enforced." (A procedure casebook can be excused for omitting "merely" from the phrase.)

2. To solve the problem of distinguishing between such "manner and mode" issues and the other (dare one say "substantive"?) kind, *Guaranty Trust* proposed what came to be known as the "outcome-determinative test." A state rule that was outcome-determinative was to be followed, no matter how it might be labeled. *[handwritten: Outcome determinative test]*

What does that mean? At one time, the federal government used paper measuring 8 x 10 1/2 inches. The standard sizes are 8 1/2 x 11 and 8 1/2 x 14. If a litigant offered the clerk of a federal district a complaint typed on 8 1/2 x 14 inch paper, but the clerk refused to accept it on the grounds that the rules required shorter paper and the filing cabinets couldn't hold paper 14 inches long, would you call the rule invoked by the clerk substantive because it was outcome-determinative? After all, the plaintiff might very well win in state court but can hardly win in federal court if the complaint can't be filed. If you conclude that the "paper size" rule is not substantive for *Erie* purposes, how would you modify the outcome-determinative rule to exclude cases of this sort?

3. *Guaranty Trust* not only decided a lawsuit; it also asserted that *Erie* marked a revolution in legal thought, a rejection of "Law . . . as a 'brooding omnipresence' of Reason," a view presumably attributed to those judges (perhaps especially to Justice Story) who had adhered to Swift v. Tyson. *Erie* and *Guaranty Trust* asserted that such a view was not only jurisprudentially bankrupt but historically false — that the understanding of the Rules of Decision Act held by its

framers was in accordance with that enunciated by *Guaranty Trust* and *Erie*. Though that understanding has been challenged by some historians, it exercised a powerful influence over the *Erie* line of cases. After *Guaranty Trust* the Supreme Court for more than a decade regularly upheld state practices (whether called substantive or procedural) whenever they conflicted with the practice the federal court would have used in the absence of *Erie*. All these cases involved conflicts between a federal statute or Rule of Civil Procedure and a state practice:

a. Ragan v. Merchants Transfer & Warehouse Co., 337 U.S. 530 (1949), held that state law, rather than federal, would determine when an action was "commenced" for purposes of satisfying the state statute of limitations. Federal Rule 3 provides that an action is commenced by filing a complaint; the state rule provided that a case was commenced by service on the defendant. *Guaranty Trust* was invoked as controlling.

b. Cohen v. Beneficial Indus. Loan Corp., 337 U.S. 541 (1949), held that a federal diversity court must apply a state statute allowing a corporation to require plaintiff to post a bond for the expenses of defense of a shareholder's derivative suit; the corporation could recover its expenses if the plaintiff lost. Federal Rule 23 (now 23.1) did not require such a bond. The purpose of the bond and requirement that the plaintiff pay expenses was to discourage so-called strike suits brought to coerce settlements rather than win on the merits.

c. Bernhardt v. Polygraphic Co. of America, 350 U.S. 198 (1956), narrowly construed the federal arbitration statute (which requires federal courts to enforce arbitration agreements in contracts affecting interstate commerce) and held, under the influence of *Erie*, that state law concerning the enforceability of arbitration agreements should control in a diversity action.

d. Woods v. Interstate Realty Co., 337 U.S. 535 (1949), held that a state statute closing the doors of the state courts to out-of-state corporations that had not qualified to do business (by paying taxes) in Mississippi would close the Mississippi federal courts to those same corporations. *Woods* did not consider the effect of Rule 17(b), which says that the state of incorporation, and by inference not the forum state, should determine the capacity of a corporation to sue.

4. The cases in Note 3 are remarkable for several reasons:

a. Each involved a conflict between a state practice and an arguably applicable federal statute or rule of procedure. Such conflicts have characterized the *Erie* cases for the past 40 years.

b. They represent a high-water mark of *Erie*-compelled deference to state courts. Starting only two years after *Bernhardt Polygraphic*, the last of the series, the Court began to retreat from its almost reflexive bowing to state law.

c. Finally, one can ask whether all — or any — of these cases described in Note 3 are correctly decided. As you will see, later cases have questioned several of these results. As you will also see, the *Erie* cases from the late 1950s onward broke with the pattern of invariably favoring state practice and suggested a different framework for analyzing the *Erie* problem, in the process to retreating from *Guaranty Trust*.

Byrd v. Blue Ridge Rural Electric Cooperative

356 U.S. 525 (1958)

Mr. Justice BRENNAN delivered the opinion of the Court.

[Plaintiff was injured while on a construction job for defendant; he sued in tort. Although plaintiff was employed by an independent contractor, defendant contended plaintiff was doing the same work as defendant's regular employees and, therefore, was a "statutory" employee whose exclusive remedy was under the South Carolina Workmen's Compensation Act.]

[Presenting evidence on the statutory employee defense,] respondent's manager testified on direct examination that three of its substations were built by the respondent's own construction and maintenance crews. When pressed on cross-examination, however, his answers left his testimony in such doubt as to lead the trial judge to say, "I understood he changed his testimony, that they had not built three." But the credibility of the manager's testimony, and the general question whether the evidence in support of the affirmative defense presented a jury issue, became irrelevant because of the interpretation given [the state statute] by the trial judge.

[The Court first decided that the lower courts had incorrectly interpreted the state statute.]

II

A question is also presented as to whether on remand the factual issue is to be decided by the judge or by the jury. The respondent argues on the basis of the decision of the Supreme Court of South Carolina in Adams v. Davison-Paxon Co., that the issue of immunity[*] should be decided by the judge and not by the jury. . . .

The respondent argues that this state-court decision governs the present diversity case and "divests the jury of its normal function" to decide the disputed fact question of the respondent's immunity under §72-111. This is to contend that the federal court is bound under Erie R. Co. v. Tompkins to follow the state court's holding to secure uniform enforcement of the immunity created by the State.

First. It was decided in *Erie* R. Co. v. Tompkins that the federal courts in diversity cases must respect the definition of state-created rights and obligations by the state courts. We must, therefore, first examine the rule in Adams v. Davison-Paxon Co. to determine whether it is bound up with these rights and obligations in such a way that its application in the federal court is required.

The Workmen's Compensation Act is administered in South Carolina by its Industrial Commission. The South Carolina courts hold that, on judicial review of actions of the Commission under §72-111, the question whether the claim of an injured workman is within the Commission's jurisdiction is a matter of law for

[* The employer would be immune from a tort suit if the worker were covered by Workers' Compensation, which bars tort actions against employers. — Ed.]

decision by the court, which makes its own findings of fact relating to that jurisdiction. The South Carolina Supreme Court states no reasons in Adams v.
Davison-Paxon Co. why, although the jury decides all other factual issues raised
by the cause of action and defenses, the jury is displaced as to the factual issue
raised by the affirmative defense under §72-111. . . . We find nothing to suggest
that this rule was announced as an integral part of the special relationship created
by the statute. Thus the requirement appears to be merely a form and mode of
enforcing the immunity, Guaranty Trust Co. v. York, and not a rule intended to
be bound up with the definition of the rights and obligations of the parties. . . .

Second. But cases following *Erie* have evinced a broader policy to the effect
that the federal courts should conform as near as may be — in the absence of other
considerations — to state rules even of form and mode where the state rules may
bear substantially on the question whether the litigation would come out one way
in the federal court and another way in the state court if the federal court failed to
apply a particular local rule. E.g., Guaranty Trust Co. v. York; Bernhardt v.
Polygraphic Co. Concededly the nature of the tribunal which tries issues may be
important in the enforcement of the parcel of rights making up a cause of action
or defense, and bear significantly upon achievement of uniform enforcement of
the right. It may well be that in the instant personal-injury case the outcome
would be substantially affected by whether the issue of immunity is decided by a
judge or a jury. Therefore, were "outcome" the only consideration, a strong case
might appear for saying that the federal court should follow the state practice.

But there are affirmative countervailing considerations at work here. The
federal system is an independent system for administering justice to litigants who
properly invoke its jurisdiction. An essential characteristic of that system is the
manner in which, in civil common-law actions, it distributes trial functions
between judge and jury and, under the influence — if not the command[10] — of
the Seventh Amendment, assigns the decisions of disputed questions of fact to the
jury. The policy of uniform enforcement of state-created rights and obligations,
see, e.g., Guaranty Trust Co. v. York, supra, cannot in every case exact compliance with a state rule[12] — not bound up with rights and obligations — which
disrupts the federal system of allocating functions between judge and jury. Thus
the inquiry here is whether the federal policy favoring jury decisions of disputed
fact questions should yield to the state rule in the interest of furthering the objective that the litigation should not come out one way in the federal court and
another way in the state court.

We think that in the circumstances of this case the federal court should not
follow the state rule. It cannot be gainsaid that there is a strong federal policy
against allowing state rules to disrupt the judge-jury relationship in the federal
courts. . . . Perhaps even more clearly in light of the influence of the Seventh

10. Our conclusion makes unnecessary the consideration of — and we intimate no view upon —
the constitutional question whether the right of jury trial protected in federal courts by the Seventh
Amendment embraces the factual issue of statutory immunity when asserted, as here, as an affirmative defense in a common-law negligence action.

12. This Court held in Sibbach v. Wilson & Co. that Federal Rule of Civil Procedure 35 should
prevail over a contrary state rule.

Jury is essential factor [handwritten annotation]

Amendment, the function assigned to the jury "is an essential factor in the process for which the Federal Constitution provides." . . .

Third. We have discussed the problem upon the assumption that the outcome of the litigation may be substantially affected by whether the issue of immunity is decided by a judge or a jury. But clearly there is not present here the certainty that a different result would follow, cf. *Guaranty Trust Co. v. York, supra,* or even the strong possibility that this would be the case. There are factors present here which might reduce that possibility. The trial judge in the federal system has powers denied the judges of many States to comment on the weight of evidence and credibility of witnesses, and discretion to grant a new trial if the verdict appears to him to be against the weight of the evidence. We do not think the likelihood of a different result is so strong as to require the federal practice of jury determination of disputed factual issues to yield to the state rule in the interest of uniformity of outcome. . . .

Not certain that different result would follow [handwritten annotation]

Reversed and remanded.

[The opinions of Justices WHITTAKER, FRANKFURTER, and HARLAN are omitted.]

NOTES AND PROBLEMS

1. State the holding of *Byrd.*

2. *Byrd* could have been decided under the criterion of *Guaranty Trust:* Unlike previous cases in which the outcome-determinative test had been applied, using a jury rather than a judge in these circumstances might, but would not necessarily, determine the outcome of the case. The Court thus seemed to be going out of its way to find another analysis by which to approach *Erie* problems. That process continued in the next case in this line, to which we now turn.

2.   De-Constitutionalizing Erie

Under both *Guaranty Trust* and *Byrd, Erie* questions are constitutional matters; whether federal courts should follow the state practice is a constitutional question. That framing of the issue is consistent with *Erie* itself, which rejected the invitation to reach its decision as an interpretation of the Rules of Decision rather than the Constitution. The next case, while purporting to overrule none of the cases in the *Erie* line, reframes the issue as one of statutory rather than constitutional interpretation.

Hanna v. Plumer

380 U.S. 460 (1965)

Mr. Chief Justice WARREN delivered the opinion of the Court.

The question to be decided is whether, in a civil action where the jurisdiction of the United States district court is based upon diversity of citizenship between

the parties, service of process shall be made in the manner prescribed by state law
or that set forth in Rule 4(d)(1) of the Federal Rules of Civil Procedure.

[The case arose out of a diversity suit for personal injuries. The defendant was
the estate of one of the drivers involved. The issue arose because Massachusetts
law provided that suits required personal service of process on the executor of
the estate. Process was instead served under Rule 4(d)(1), which allowed for the
summons and complaint to be left with a competent adult at the residence of
the defendant. The district court and First Circuit, citing *Ragan* (see Note 3a,
supra page 234), ruled that the claim should be dismissed because plaintiff had
failed to comply with the state method of serving process within the applicable
statute of limitations.]

We conclude that the adoption of Rule 4(d)(1), designed to control service of
process in diversity actions, neither exceeded the congressional mandate embodied in the Rules Enabling Act nor transgressed constitutional bounds, and that
the Rule is therefore the standard against which the District Court should have
measured the adequacy of the service. Accordingly, we reverse the decision of the
Court of Appeals.

The [version of the] Rules Enabling Act, 28 U.S.C. §2072 [then in effect]
provide[d] in pertinent part:

> The Supreme Court shall have the power to prescribe, by general rules, the forms of
> process, writs, pleadings, and motions, and the practice and procedure of the district
> courts of the United States in civil actions.
>
>   Such rules shall not abridge, enlarge or modify any substantive right and shall
> preserve the right of trial by jury. . . .[*]

Under the cases construing the scope of the Enabling Act, Rule 4(d)(1) clearly
passes muster. Prescribing the manner in which a defendant is to be notified that
a suit has been instituted against him, it relates to the "practice and procedure of
the district courts." "The test must be whether a rule really regulates procedure —
the judicial process for enforcing rights and duties recognized by substantive law
and for justly administering remedy and redress for disregard or infraction of
them." Sibbach v. Wilson & Co. . . .

Thus were there no conflicting state procedure, Rule 4(d)(1) would clearly
control. However, respondent, focusing on the contrary Massachusetts rule, calls
to the Court's attention another line of cases, a line which — like the Federal
Rules — had its birth in 1938. Erie R. Co. v. Tompkins, overruling Swift v. Tyson,
held that federal courts sitting in diversity cases, when deciding questions of
"substantive" law, are bound by state court decisions as well as state statutes. The
broad command of *Erie* was therefore identical to that of the Enabling Act:
federal courts are to apply state substantive law and federal procedural law.
However, as subsequent cases sharpened the distinction between substance and
procedure, the line of cases following *Erie* diverged markedly from the line
construing the Enabling Act. . . .

[* The current version of §2072 is substantially identical in all respects relevant to this case —
Ed.]

Respondent, by placing primary reliance on *York* and *Ragan*, suggests that the *Erie* doctrine acts as a check on the Federal Rules of Civil Procedure, that despite the clear command of Rule 4(d)(1), *Erie* and its progeny demand the application of the Massachusetts rule. . . .

In the first place, it is doubtful that, even if there were no Federal Rule making it clear that in-hand service is not required in diversity actions, the *Erie* rule would have obligated the District Court to follow the Massachusetts procedure. "Outcome-determination" analysis was never intended to serve as a talisman. Byrd v. Blue Ridge Cooperative. Indeed, the message of *York* itself is that choices between state and federal law are to be made not by application of any automatic, "litmus paper" criterion, but rather by reference to the policies underlying the *Erie* rule.

The *Erie* rule is rooted in part in a realization that it would be unfair for the character or result of a litigation materially to differ because the suit had been brought in a federal court. . . . The decision was also in part a reaction to the practice of "forum-shopping" which had grown up in response to the rule of Swift v. Tyson. That the *York* test was an attempt to effectuate these policies is demonstrated by the fact that the opinion framed the inquiry in terms of "substantial" variations between state and federal litigation. Not only are nonsubstantial, or trivial, variations not likely to raise the sort of equal protection problems which troubled the Court in *Erie*; they are also unlikely to influence the choice of a forum. The "outcome-determination" test therefore cannot be read without reference to the twin aims of the *Erie* rule: discouragement of forum-shopping and avoidance of inequitable administration of the laws.

The difference between the conclusion that the Massachusetts rule is applicable, and the conclusion that it is not, is of course at this point "outcome-determinative" in the sense that if we hold the state rule to apply, respondent prevails, whereas if we hold that Rule 4(d)(1) governs, the litigation will continue. But in this sense *every* procedural variation is "outcome-determinative." . . . [I]t is difficult to argue that permitting service of defendant's wife to take the place of in-hand service of defendant himself alters the mode of enforcement of state-created rights in a fashion sufficiently "substantial" to raise the sort of equal protection problems to which the *Erie* opinion alluded.

There is, however, a more fundamental flaw in respondent's syllogism: the incorrect assumption that the rule of Erie R. Co. v. Tompkins constitutes the appropriate test of the validity and therefore the applicability of a Federal Rule of Civil Procedure. The *Erie* rule has never been invoked to void a Federal Rule. It is true that there have been cases where this Court has held applicable a state rule in the face of an argument that the situation was governed by one of the Federal Rules. But the holding of each such case was not that *Erie* commanded displacement of a Federal Rule by an inconsistent state rule, but rather that the scope of the Federal Rule was not as broad as the losing party urged, and therefore, there being no Federal Rule which covered the point in dispute, *Erie* commanded the enforcement of state law. . . . (Here, of course, the clash is unavoidable; Rule 4(d)(1) says — implicitly, but with unmistakable clarity — that in-hand service is not required in federal courts.) At the same time, in cases adjudicating the validity of Federal Rules, we have not applied the *York* rule or other refinements of *Erie*, but have to this day continued to decide questions concerning the scope of the Enabling Act and the constitutionality of specific Federal Rules in light of the distinction set forth in *Sibbach*.

Nor has the development of two separate lines of cases been inadvertent. The line between "substance" and "procedure" shifts as the legal context changes. . . . It is true that both the Enabling Act and the *Erie* rule say, roughly, that federal courts are to apply state "substantive" law and federal "procedural" law, but from that it need not follow that the tests are identical. For they were designed to control very different sorts of decisions. When a situation is covered by one of the Federal Rules, the question facing the court is a far cry from the typical, relatively unguided *Erie* choice: the court has been instructed to apply the Federal Rule, and can refuse to do so only if the Advisory Committee, this Court, and Congress erred in their prima facie judgment that the Rule in question transgresses neither the terms of the Enabling Act nor constitutional restrictions. . . .

Erie and its offspring cast no doubt on the long-recognized power of Congress to prescribe housekeeping rules for federal courts even though some of those rules will inevitably differ from comparable state rules. . . . Thus, though a court, in measuring a Federal Rule against the standards contained in the Enabling Act and the Constitution, need not wholly blind itself to the degree to which the Rule makes the character and result of the federal litigation stray from the course it would follow in state courts, it cannot be forgotten that the *Erie* rule, and the guidelines suggested in York, were created to serve another purpose altogether. To hold that a Federal Rule of Civil Procedure must cease to function whenever it alters the mode of enforcing state-created rights would be to disembowel either the Constitution's grant of power over federal procedure or Congress' attempt to exercise that power in the Enabling Act. Rule 4(d)(1) is valid and controls the instant case.

Reversed.

Mr. Justice BLACK concurs in the result.

Mr. Justice HARLAN, concurring. . . .

Erie was something more than an opinion which worried about "forum-shopping and avoidance of inequitable administration of the laws," although to be sure these were important elements of the decision. I have always regarded that decision as one of the modern cornerstones of our federalism, expressing policies that profoundly touch the allocation of judicial power between the state and federal systems. *Erie* recognized that there should not be two conflicting systems of law controlling the primary activity of citizens, for such alternative governing authority must necessarily give rise to a debilitating uncertainty in the planning of everyday affairs.[1] And it recognized that the scheme of our Constitution envisions an allocation of law-making functions between state and federal legislative

---

1. Since the rules involved in the present case are parallel rather than conflicting, this first rationale does not come into play here.

processes which is undercut if the federal judiciary can make substantive law affecting state affairs beyond the bounds of congressional legislative powers in this regard. Thus, in diversity cases *Erie* commands that it be the state law governing primary private activity which prevails.

The shorthand formulations which have appeared in some past decisions are prone to carry untoward results that frequently arise from oversimplification. . . . To my mind the proper line of approach in determining whether to apply a state or a federal rule, whether "substantive" or "procedural," is to stay close to basic principles by inquiring if the choice of rule would substantially affect those primary decisions respecting human conduct which our constitutional system leaves to state regulation. If so, *Erie* and the Constitution require that the state rule prevail, even in the face of a conflicting federal rule.

The Court weakens, if indeed it does not submerge, this basic principle by finding, in effect, a grant of substantive legislative power in the constitutional provision for a federal court system, and through it, setting up the Federal Rules as a body of law inviolate. . . . So long as a reasonable man could characterize any duly adopted federal rule as "procedural," the Court, unless I misapprehend what is said, would have it apply no matter how seriously it frustrated a State's substantive regulation of the primary conduct and affairs of its citizens. Since the members of the Advisory Committee, the Judicial Conference, and this Court who formulated the Federal Rules are presumably reasonable men, it follows that the integrity of the Federal Rules is absolute. Whereas the unadulterated outcome and forum-shopping tests may err too far toward honoring state rules, I submit that the Court's "arguably procedural, ergo constitutional" test moves too fast and far in the other direction.

The courts below relied upon this Court's decisions in Ragan v. Merchants Transfer Co. . . .

Ragan . . . was wrong. At most, application of the Federal Rule [3] would have meant that potential Kansas tort defendants would have to defer for a few days the satisfaction of knowing that they had not been sued within the limitations period. The choice of the Federal Rule would have had no effect on the primary stages of private activity from which torts arise, and only the most minimal effect on behavior following the commission of the tort. In such circumstances the interest of the federal system in proceeding under its own rules should have prevailed. . . .

[Justice Harlan, applying his test to the facts of the case, found the federal rule controlling because it would have at most a negligible effect on the parties' out-of-court behavior.]

NOTES AND PROBLEMS

1. Briefly explain why the federal court could disregard the state practice in this case.

2. *Byrd* and *Hanna* reach similar results: Both hold that the federal court need not behave as a state court would if it were hearing the case. Moreover, both enunciate multi-tiered "tests" for determining whether federal or state practice

should prevail. And they complement each other in one respect: *Hanna*, narrowly construed, tells a federal court what to do when a Rule or federal statute dictates the federal practice; *Byrd* deals with a federal practice not dictated by a specific federal statute or Rule. However similar in result, the two cases diverge sharply in their texture. *Byrd* is nuanced, "soft," and, in many cases, indeterminate — and grounds its analysis directly in the Constitution. *Hanna* is hard-edged and more determinate — and insists that a statute — the Rules Enabling Act — is as important as the Constitution in many *Erie* cases.

3. Analytically it is easier to begin with *Hanna's* framework. Start with the proposition that one faces an *Erie* problem only when a federal court, left to its own devices, would ordinarily behave differently from a state court: At that point a federal court sitting in diversity must decide whether it should follow its usual practice. According to *Hanna*, one's analysis of the problem differs, depending on the source of the federal practice.

a. *Hanna* says that the answer to that question is relatively easy if the federal practice in question is dictated by a Federal Rule of Civil Procedure (or, by extension, a federal statute). If so, one has to ask whether the statute itself is constitutional. One can hear in this question an echo of *Erie*, with its assertion that Congress could not constitutionally dictate tort law to the states. The converse proposition is that Congress can dictate rules of procedure to the federal courts it creates. If the statute is constitutional and tells a federal court to do something, the court must follow the dictates of that statute. At that point, the "*Erie*" issue ceases to be directly constitutional, becoming instead a matter of statutory construction: What does the governing statute tell the federal court to do? In the case of a Federal Rule of Civil Procedure, the analysis requires two steps, because the Rules are not themselves statutes but a delegation to the Supreme Court to make statute-like rules. Theoretically, one must consider whether the initial delegation (in the Rules Enabling Act, 28 U.S.C. §2072) was constitutional; the few cases to consider the question have said it is. E.g., Sibbach v. Wilson, 312 U.S. 1 (1941). As a practical matter, the open questions thus become: (a) whether the Rule promulgated under the authority of the Rules Enabling Act in fact fits its description, "rules of practice and procedure" and (b) whether the Rule itself is constitutional. If the Rule passes both these tests, then it must be applied, even if it differs from the state practice in a significant way.

If the Rule fails either test (that is, if it is not "procedural" as the Rules Enabling Act uses that term) or if it is unconstitutional, then the state practice applies. No case has ever held a Rule to be beyond the scope of the Rules Enabling Act, though some have suggested that particular Rules come close to the line. Jonathan M. Landers, Of Legalized Blackmail and Legalized Theft: Consumer Class Actions and the Substance Procedure Dilemma, 47 S. Cal. L. Rev. 842 (1974). Nor has any Rule ever been held unconstitutional, though several have been revised in light of constitutional developments that might have made them subject to attack. See., e.g., Rule 65(b).

b. To test your understanding of this scheme, apply it to the facts of *Hanna* itself, explaining the source of the conflict between state and federal practice and the reason for following the federal practice.

c. *Hanna's* principle will yield a result different from *Guaranty Trust* whenever the federal practice is dictated by a federal statute or Rule (so long as the statute or Rule is constitutional and within the scope of the Rules Enabling Act). Explain why this first part of *Hanna's* doctrine would not have yielded a different result in *Guaranty Trust* itself.

4. Consider now the second part of *Hanna's* doctrine, the problem with which *Byrd* deals: What if the usual federal practice is not dictated by a specific statute or Rule, but has its roots either in the common law of federal procedure or in mere custom? How then should a court think about whether to follow the federal or the state practice? One example would be the issue in *Byrd* itself—whether a question would be decided by a judge or submitted to a jury. Another might be differences in the manner in which prospective jurors were questioned: Many states, either by law or custom, permit extensive colloquies between jurors and lawyers during jury selection; no statute or Rule governs the matter, but in many federal courts judges do all the questioning and do so very quickly. In a clash, should state or federal practice prevail? *Byrd* and *Hanna* approach that question in different ways.

a. For *Byrd* there are three questions: (1) is the state practice "bound up with the definition of the rights and obligations of the parties?"; if so, state law governs; (2) even if it isn't part of the substantive rights and obligations, would its application determine the outcome of the case?; (3) if so, are there "affirmative countervailing" considerations of federal judicial administration present? The *Byrd* Court assumes that if the first question is answered affirmatively, state practice should prevail. The idea seems to be that some procedural practices are so much a part of the substantive law that they should be followed; burden of proof would supply an example. *Byrd's* distinctive doctrinal contribution lies in its third question, which requires courts to balance state against federal interests. As with all balancing tests, the results will be fact-bound.

b. Under the same circumstances (in the absence of a federal Rule or statute dictating federal practice), *Hanna* asks a different question: Would following the federal practice lead to forum-shopping or inequitable administration of the laws? The implication is that if one finds either of these likely, the state rather than the federal practice should prevail. One difficulty in applying this standard lies in knowing what those two phrases mean. In some respect these terms seem to be *Hanna's* rephrasing of what *Guaranty Trust* and *Byrd* called "outcome-determination." It remains to be seen if the rephrasing is helpful. Forum-shopping refers to the practice, widely followed by lawyers, of seeking a court that will be most hospitable to the client's claims or defenses. As suggested earlier, almost any imaginable procedural difference in systems could lead to such a choice; perhaps one should therefore limit the inquiry to differences that, before the lawsuit began, seem significant enough to cause forum-shopping. Does even that version give state practice too much power? "Inequitable administration of the laws" is more difficult. It seems to refer to patterns of federal practice that regularly result in different applications of what is nominally the same substantive law, such as federal courts' pre-*Erie* willingness to enter injunctions in situations where state courts would not.

The problem with both of *Hanna*'s criteria is that for federal diversity jurisdiction to have any usefulness, it should sometimes lead to different results, and if lawyers can predict that, their obligation to their clients requires them to shop for the most advantageous forum.

c. *Hanna* did not overrule *Byrd*, which it cited with approval. Both cases suggest an approach to a federal practice not dictated by a federal statute or Rule. Which is preferable? One finds courts citing both.

3. Determining the Scope of Federal Law: Avoiding and Accommodating Erie

Under *Hanna*'s reading of *Erie*, many "*Erie*" questions will not require resort to the Constitution because Congress by statute will have told federal courts what to do in the situation. So long as the statute is constitutional and one knows what the statute requires, the choice of law problem is solved. Because the constitutionality of the major procedural statutes seems clear, this route to the solution of *Erie* problems has proved tempting. So long as a judge can find a federal statute governing the situation, it prevails over the state practice, and a difficult, perhaps indeterminate, *Erie* analysis is unnecessary.

Two examples will illustrate the technique. In Burlington Northern Railroad v. Woods, 480 U.S. 1 (1987), the Court confronted an Alabama statute providing that if a defendant appealed a money judgment and lost on appeal, the successful plaintiff-appellate should be awarded an additional 10 percent on the judgment. Should that rule apply in a diversity action? The Supreme Court said no, because the state law conflicted with Federal Rule of Appellate Procedure 38 which in its entirety states: "If a court of appeals shall determine that an appeal is frivolous, it may award just damages and single or double costs to the appellee." That Rule, said the Court, conflicted with the Alabama statute and, because it was constitutional and conformed with the Rules Enabling Act, prevailed.

In Stewart Organization v. Ricoh, 487 U.S. 22 (1988), the Court confronted another diversity case from Alabama. This time the issue was whether to enforce a contractual forum selection clause, which called for a Manhattan forum for all suits arising from the contract. The Alabama courts, however, in a series of decisions had refused to enforce such clauses. The Alabama plaintiff argued that a federal court sitting in diversity was bound to honor that state judge-made law and thus to refuse enforcement to the forum selection clause. One might have thought this judge-made rule was just the sort of "substantive" state law that *Erie* required to be observed in diversity actions. But the Supreme Court again rejected application of state law because it found that state law conflicted with a valid federal procedure. In this instance the federal procedure was found not in a Rule but in 28 U.S.C. §1404 (discussed in Chapter II), which provides:

> For the convenience of the parties, in the interest of justice, a district court may transfer any civil action to any other district or division where it might have been brought.

Guiding the lower courts on remand, the Supreme Court suggested that in deciding how to apply §1404 they were free to take the state's policy on forum selection clauses into account as one factor, but not necessarily to view it as a dispositive one.

These two cases suggested that the Supreme Court would stretch rather far to find an applicable federal law covering the situation. But recent developments demonstrate that there are limits to this practice and that federal procedure will sometimes itself have to do the stretching. Gasperini v. Center for Humanities, Inc., 518 U.S. 415 (1996) involved a collision between a New York statute; as Justice Ginsburg stated the issue:

> Under the law of New York, appellate courts are empowered to review the size of jury verdicts and to order new trials when the jury's award "deviates materially from what would be reasonable compensation." Under the Seventh Amendment, which governs proceedings in federal court, but not in state court . . . "no fact, tried by a jury, shall be otherwise reexamined in any Court of the United States, than according to the rules of the common law." The compatibility of these provisions [in a diversity case] is the issue we confront. . . .

The difficulty arose because the majority found that both state and federal interests were significant—the state had clearly evinced a policy to rein in excessive verdicts, and the federal courts allocated power between trial and appellate courts under a constitutional command. The majority found that the two interests could be accommodated by requiring that the federal district courts, not the appellate panels envisioned by state law, do the examination and reduction of jury verdicts.

The next case goes further; is it rightly decided?

Semtek Intl. Inc. v. Lockheed Martin Corp.

531 U.S. 497 (2001)

Justice SCALIA delivered the opinion of the Court.

This case presents the question whether the claim-preclusive effect of a federal judgment dismissing a diversity action on statute-of-limitations grounds is determined by the law of the State in which the federal court sits.

I

Petitioner filed a complaint against respondent in California state court, alleging breach of contract and various business torts. Respondent removed the case to the United States District Court for the Central District of California on the basis of diversity of citizenship, and successfully moved to dismiss petitioner's claims as barred by California's 2-year statute of limitations. In its order of dismissal, the District Court, adopting language suggested by respondent, dismissed petitioner's claims "in [their] entirety on the merits and with prejudice." . . . Petitioner . . . brought suit against respondent in the State Circuit Court for Baltimore City, Maryland, alleging the same causes of action, which were not time barred under

Maryland's 3-year statute of limitations. . . . Following a hearing, the Maryland state court granted respondent's motion to dismiss on the ground of res judicata. . . . The [Maryland] Court of Special Appeals affirmed, holding that, regardless of whether California would have accorded claim-preclusive effect to a statute-of-limitations dismissal by one of its own courts, the dismissal by the California federal court barred the complaint filed in Maryland, since the res judicata effect of federal diversity judgments is prescribed by federal law, under which the earlier dismissal was on the merits and claim preclusive. . . .

II

Petitioner contends that the outcome of this case is controlled by Dupasseur v. Rochereau, 21 Wall. 130, 135 (1875), which held that the res judicata effect of a federal diversity judgment "is such as would belong to judgments of the State courts rendered under similar circumstances," and may not be accorded any "higher sanctity or effect." Since, petitioner argues, the dismissal of an action on statute-of-limitations grounds by a California state court would not be claim preclusive, it follows that the similar dismissal of this diversity action by the California federal court cannot be claim preclusive. While we agree that this would be the result demanded by *Dupasseur*, the case is not dispositive because it was decided under the Conformity Act of 1872 [the pre-Rules legislation] which required federal courts to apply the procedural law of the forum State in nonequity cases. . . .

Respondent, for its part, contends that the outcome of this case is controlled by Federal Rule of Civil Procedure 41(b), which provides as follows:

Involuntary Dismissal: Effect Thereof

For failure of the plaintiff to prosecute or to comply with these rules or any order of court, a defendant may move for dismissal of an action or of any claim against the defendant. Unless the court in its order for dismissal otherwise specifies, a dismissal under this subdivision and any dismissal not provided for in this rule, other than a dismissal for lack of jurisdiction, for improper venue, or for failure to join a party under Rule 19, operates as an adjudication upon the merits.

Since the dismissal here did not "otherwise specify" (indeed, it specifically stated that it *was* "on the merits"), and did not pertain to the excepted subjects of jurisdiction, venue, or joinder, it follows, respondent contends, that the dismissal "is entitled to claim preclusive effect."

Implicit in this reasoning is the unstated minor premise that all judgments denominated "on the merits" are entitled to claim-preclusive effect. That premise is not necessarily valid. The original connotation of an "on the merits" adjudication is one that actually "passes directly on the substance of [a particular] claim" before the court. Restatement §19, Comment *a*, at 161. That connotation remains common to every jurisdiction of which we are aware. . . . And it is, we think, the meaning intended in those many statements to the effect that a judgment "on the merits" triggers the doctrine of res judicata or claim preclusion. See, e.g., Parklane Hosiery Co. v. Shore, 439 U.S. 322, 326, n.5 (1979).

But over the years the meaning of the term "judgment on the merits" "has gradually undergone change," R. Marcus, M. Redish, & E. Sherman, Civil Procedure: A Modern Approach 1140-1141 (3d ed. 2000), and it has come to be applied to some judgments (such as the one involved here) that do *not* pass upon the substantive merits of a claim and hence do *not* (in many jurisdictions) entail claim-preclusive effect.

In short, it is no longer true that a judgment "on the merits" is necessarily a judgment entitled to claim-preclusive effect; and there are a number of reasons for believing that the phrase "adjudication upon the merits" does not bear that meaning in Rule 41(b). . . .

And even apart from the purely default character of Rule 41(b), it would be peculiar to find a rule governing the effect that must be accorded federal judgments by other courts ensconced in rules governing the internal procedures of the rendering court itself. Indeed, such a rule would arguably violate the jurisdictional limitation of the Rules Enabling Act: that the Rules "shall not abridge, enlarge or modify any substantive right," 28 U.S.C. §2072(b). . . . In the present case, for example, if California law left petitioner free to sue on this claim in Maryland even after the California statute of limitations had expired, the federal court's extinguishment of that right (through Rule 41(b)'s mandated claim-preclusive effect of its judgment) would seem to violate this limitation.

Moreover, as so interpreted, the Rule would in many cases violate the federalism principle of Erie R. Co. v. Tompkins, 304 U.S. 64, 78-80 (1938), by engendering "'substantial' variations [in outcomes] between state and federal litigation" which would "likely . . . influence the choice of a forum," Hanna v. Plumer. See also Guaranty Trust Co. v. York. With regard to the claim-preclusion issue involved in the present case, for example, the traditional rule is that expiration of the applicable statute of limitations merely bars the remedy and does not extinguish the substantive right, so that dismissal on that ground does not have claim-preclusive effect in other jurisdictions with longer, unexpired limitation periods. Out-of-state defendants sued on stale claims in California and in other States adhering to this traditional rule would systematically remove state-law suits brought against them to federal court — where, unless otherwise specified, a statute-of-limitations dismissal would bar suit everywhere.[1]

We think the key to a more reasonable interpretation of the meaning of "operates as an adjudication upon the merits" in Rule 41(b) is to be found in Rule 41(a), which, in discussing the effect of voluntary dismissal by the plaintiff, makes

---

1. Rule 41(b), interpreted as a preclusion-establishing rule, would not have the two effects described in the preceding paragraphs — arguable violation of the Rules Enabling Act and incompatibility with Erie R. Co. v. Tompkins — if the court's failure to specify an other-than-on-the-merits dismissal were subject to reversal on appeal whenever it would alter the rule of claim preclusion applied by the State in which the federal court sits. No one suggests that this is the rule, and we are aware of no case that applies it.

clear that an "adjudication upon the merits" is the opposite of a "dismissal without prejudice":

> Unless otherwise stated in the notice of dismissal or stipulation, the dismissal is without prejudice, except that a notice of dismissal operates as an adjudication upon the merits when filed by a plaintiff who has once dismissed in any court of the United States or of any state an action based on or including the same claim.

The primary meaning of "dismissal without prejudice," we think, is dismissal without barring the defendant from returning later, to the same court, with the same underlying claim. That will also ordinarily (though not always) have the consequence of not barring the claim from *other* courts, but its primary meaning relates to the dismissing court itself. . . .

We think, then, that the effect of the "adjudication upon the merits" default provision of Rule 41(b) — and, presumably, of the explicit order in the present case that used the language of that default provision — is simply that, unlike a dismissal "without prejudice," the dismissal in the present case barred refiling of the same claim in the United States District Court for the Central District of California. That is undoubtedly a necessary condition, but it is not a sufficient one, for claim-preclusive effect in other courts.[2]

III

Having concluded that the claim-preclusive effect, in Maryland, of this California federal diversity judgment is dictated neither by Dupasseur v. Rochereau, as petitioner contends, nor by Rule 41(b), as respondent contends, we turn to consideration of what determines the issue. Neither the Full Faith and Credit Clause, U.S. Const., Art. IV, §1,[3] nor the full faith and credit statute, 28 U.S.C. §1738,[4] addresses the question. By their terms they govern the effects to be given only to state-court judgments (and, in the case of the statute, to judgments by courts of territories and possessions). And no other federal textual

2. We do not decide whether, in a diversity case, a federal court's "dismissal upon the merits" (in the sense we have described), under circumstances where a state court would decree only a "dismissal without prejudice," abridges a "substantive right" and thus exceeds the authorization of the Rules Enabling Act. We think the situation will present itself more rarely than would the arguable violation of the Act that would ensue from interpreting Rule 41(b) as a rule of claim preclusion; and if it is a violation, can be more easily dealt with on direct appeal.

3. Article IV, §1 provides as follows:

> Full Faith and Credit shall be given in each State to the public Acts, Records, and judicial Proceedings of every other State. And the Congress may by general Laws prescribe the Manner in which such Acts, Records and Proceedings shall be proved, and the Effect thereof.

4. Title 28 U.S.C. §1738 provides in relevant part as follows:

> The records and judicial proceedings of any court of any . . . State, Territory or Possession . . . shall have the same full faith and credit in every court within the United States and its Territories and Possessions as they have by law or usage in the courts of such State, Territory or Possession from which they are taken.

provision, neither of the Constitution nor of any statute, addresses the claim-preclusive effect of a judgment in a federal diversity action.

It is also true, however, that no federal textual provision addresses the claim-preclusive effect of a federal-court judgment in a federal-question case, yet we have long held that States cannot give those judgments merely whatever effect they would give their own judgments, but must accord them the effect that this Court prescribes. The reasoning of [the cases so holding] suggests, moreover, that even when States are allowed to give federal judgments (notably, judgments in diversity cases) no more than the effect accorded to state judgments, that disposition is by direction of *this* Court, which has the last word on the claim-preclusive effect of *all* federal judgments. . . .

It is left to us, then, to determine the appropriate federal rule. And despite the sea change that has occurred in the background law since *Dupasseur* was decided — not only repeal of the Conformity Act but also the watershed decision of this Court in *Erie* — we think the result decreed by *Dupasseur* continues to be correct for diversity cases. Since state, rather than federal, substantive law is at issue there is no need for a uniform federal rule. And indeed, nationwide uniformity in the substance of the matter is better served by having the same claim-preclusive rule (the state rule) apply whether the dismissal has been ordered by a state or a federal court. This is, it seems to us, a classic case for adopting, as the federally prescribed rule of decision, the law that would be applied by state courts in the State in which the federal diversity court sits. See Gasperini v. Ctr. for Humanities, Inc. As we have alluded to above, any other rule would produce the sort of "forum-shopping . . . and . . . inequitable administration of the laws" that *Erie* seeks to avoid, *Hanna*, since filing in, or removing to, federal court would be encouraged by the divergent effects that the litigants would anticipate from likely grounds of dismissal. See Guaranty Trust Co. v. York.

This federal reference to state law will not obtain, of course, in situations in which the state law is incompatible with federal interests. If, for example, state law did not accord claim-preclusive effect to dismissals for willful violation of discovery orders, federal courts' interest in the integrity of their own processes might justify a contrary federal rule. No such conflict with potential federal interests exists in the present case. Dismissal of this state cause of action was decreed by the California federal court only because the California statute of limitations so required; and there is no conceivable federal interest in giving that time bar more effect in other courts than the California courts themselves would impose.

Because the claim-preclusive effect of the California federal court's dismissal "upon the merits" of petitioner's action on statute-of-limitations grounds is governed by a federal rule that in turn incorporates California's law of claim preclusion (the content of which we do not pass upon today), the Maryland Court of Special Appeals erred in holding that the dismissal necessarily precluded the bringing of this action in the Maryland courts. The judgment is reversed, and the case remanded for further proceedings not inconsistent with this opinion.

It is so ordered.

NOTES AND PROBLEMS

1. Frame the issue before the court.

a. Unlike any of the *Erie* cases we have so far encountered, this was not a question of the law to be applied by a *federal* court in a diversity action. It was instead a question of how a state court, in a subsequent case, should understand a federal judgment in a diversity action. Specifically, the question was whether the state court should give the federal diversity judgment a broader scope than it would have given a state judgment, had the diversity case remained in state court. Held: no.

b. Further, bear in mind that in claims which might plausibly be brought in several states, states often apply their own statute of limitations. So, if the *Semtek* claim had remained in a California state court, which had concluded that the statute of limitations had run, one can imagine the plaintiff's refiling in Maryland and having Maryland decide to apply its longer statute of limitations.

c. Thus put, *Semtek* might sound like an application of *Guaranty Trust*. Suppose California courts wouldn't insist that Maryland treat their judgment of dismissal as binding on Maryland; should the outcome be different just because defendant took advantage of diversity and removed the case to a federal court in California? Didn't *Hanna* say that rules should not create incentives to shop for a federal forum in diversity cases?

2. The preceding note leaves something out of the discussion, doesn't it?

a. The Maryland court thought it was applying Rule 41, which required it to give broad application to a federal judgment. Moreover, the Maryland court was correct in one respect. As you will see in Chapter XII, federal courts have regularly said that involuntary dismissals under Rule 41(b) bar not only the claim pleaded but all claims arising from the transaction or occurrence behind the pleaded claim. To see the breadth of this doctrine, suppose the claim in question had arisen under federal law, and the federal court had dismissed with prejudice, and that the plaintiff then sought to bring a related claim under state law, in state courts. The state courts would be required to bar the claim. Federated Dept. Stores v. Moitie, 452 U.S. 394 (1981).

b. Moreover, *Hanna* says that a Federal Rule, if constitutional and within the Rules Enabling Act, overcomes a contrary state rule, even in a diversity case. How did the Court deal with this objection?

c. The first step is to say that the Rule doesn't quite cover this situation or, that, if it does, it may go beyond the authority granted by the Rules Enabling Act. Can you locate the part of the opinion where the Court makes this move?

On at least two prior occasions the Supreme Court had made a similar move, and it is instructive to compare these situations with *Semtek*. Rule 3 deals with commencing a lawsuit and says, in entirety, "A civil action is commenced by filing a complaint with the court." One might think that "commencement" involved stopping the statute of limitations from running, and in fact in cases arising under federal law that is exactly what Rule 3 means: filing the complaint with the court satisfies the statute of limitations, and the plaintiff can proceed to serve the complaint in accord with Rule 4. But some states treat their statutes of limitations as not satisfied until defendant is served with process. The Supreme Court has twice said that in diversity cases a plaintiff must comply with the state practice to satisfy the statute of limitations. Ragan v. Merchants Transfer & Warehouse Corp. (described in Note 5a, following *Guaranty Trust* and criticized by Justice Harlan in his *Hanna* concurrence) and again in Walker v. Armco Steel Corp., 446 U.S. 740 1980), largely on the grounds of stare decisis. The Court accommodated Rule 3 by holding that it did not explicitly command the result in question. Is that what it is doing in *Semtek*?

3. It would have been relatively easy to write an opinion saying that Rule 41 means the same in diversity as in federal question cases and that it should therefore apply in the same way. What was it about the case that led the court, in a rarely unanimous *Erie* case, to go in the other direction, reinterpreting the Rule so it did not occupy the entire territory?

4. Finally, notice that some of *Byrd's* concerns surface in the opinion. Suppose a federal court sitting in diversity dismisses a case under Rule 41(b) for plaintiff's repeated failure to comply with scheduling guidelines. The state courts operate under a much more relaxed scheduling regime. Plaintiff refiles his complaint in state court and, when defendant moves to dismiss on res judicata grounds, cites *Semtek*. What result?

4. Determining the Scope of State Law: An Entailment of *Erie*

Erie requires federal courts sitting in a diversity action to use state law under various circumstances. That holding requires the federal court to declare state law. State courts face such questions all the time; a state trial judge must often decide what law applies to the case before her. Sometimes determining the answer will be a simple matter: A recent state supreme court case has carefully defined it, or the matter is covered in an authoritative statute.

But the question can be far more difficult. What happens if there is no precedent on point, or the only available precedent is some years old, and the area of law has recently shown signs of change? Or what if the question is complicated by a horizontal choice of law problem like the one that brought forth Judge Henry Friendly's quip: "Our principal task, in this diversity of citizenship case, is to determine what the New York courts would think the California courts would think on an issue about which neither has thought." Nolan v. Transocean Air Lines, 276 F.2d 280, 281 (2d Cir. 1960). For a state trial judge, such a situation presents difficulties, but she at least has the assurance that if she is wrong, the state appellate courts will straighten things out. Federal judges, compelled to follow *Erie*, generally lack that assurance.

What, then, should the federal judge do? Should she predict what the state court would probably do under such circumstances? Should she act as she thinks a state court should act in these circumstances, even if she thinks they would not behave that way? For that matter, which state court should the federal district court seek to resemble — the state trial court, which is often hesitant to depart from precedent — or the state supreme court? The district court judge must exercise his best judgment about how the state courts would resolve the issue, but appeal from that decision lies only within the federal system.

The same predicament faces the federal courts of appeals. On appeal from the district court's judgment, a federal court of appeals must do its best to decide what the state appellate courts would do when faced with the same appeal. Nor may the courts of appeals simply defer to the district court (on the ground that federal district judges, who have almost invariably practiced in the state in question, are more likely to be familiar with state practice). Salve Regina College v. Russell, 499 U.S. 225 (1991) (federal court of appeals required to review de novo district court's determination of state law).

Under such circumstances, one finds federal courts of appeals making such statements as, "Because we are persuaded by a careful review of the Ohio decisional law, as well as other relevant sources,[*] that the Supreme Court of Ohio would not construe its statute of limitations so as to preclude recovery in this case, we [do likewise]." McKenna v. Ortho Pharmaceutical Corp., 622 F.2d 657, 659 (3d Cir. 1980). Holdings based on such predictions of state court views are awkward, particularly if the predictions later turn out to be wrong.

Consider, for example, the tangle in Pierce v. Cook & Co., 518 F.2d 720 (10th Cir. 1975), cert. denied, 423 U.S. 1079 (1976). Driver and three passengers were involved in a collision with a truck driven by an independent contractor hauling wheat for Cook. Driver and Passengers each brought actions. Two of the suits were removed to federal courts; the third remained in state courts. In the federal court actions defendants won a summary judgment on the basis of thirty-year-old precedent making Cook not responsible for the negligence of an independent contractor, and the case was affirmed on appeal. Meanwhile, the state trial court had also granted summary judgment — on the basis of the same precedent — but plaintiff appealed to the state supreme court, which overruled the precedent. The state supreme court decision became final more than three years after the original federal appeal.

Six months later, the two federal plaintiffs moved to vacate the federal appellate decision under Rule 60(b), which permits the reopening of a final judgment under limited circumstances (see Chapter XII). In setting aside the federal judgment, the court of appeals emphasized that there had been "divergent results from a common vehicular accident," that plaintiffs had been forced into the federal courts, and that plaintiffs had received substantially different results in the federal courts than they would have in the state courts, in violation of the *Erie* principle. *Pierce* received considerable attention. See Note, Pierce v. Cook & Co.: Rule 60(b)(6) Relief from Judgment for Change of State Law in a Diversity Case, 62 Va. L. Rev. 414 (1976) (raising the question whether it is rational to limit the rule to common-accident cases); Note, Federal Rule of Civil Procedure 60(b): Standards for Relief from Judgments Due to Changes in Law, 43 U. Chi. L. Rev. 646 (1976).

Contrast with *Pierce* DeWeerth v. Baldinger, 38 F.3d 1266 (2d Cir. 1994), cert. denied, 513 U.S. 1001 (1994). In 1987 plaintiff sued a New York art dealer to

[* What other sources could be relevant? Presumably only ones that the Ohio appellate courts themselves would find persuasive. — Ed.]

recover a Monet painting stolen from his family during World War II. The federal court ruled that DeWeerth had failed to satisfy what they understood to be a required showing of reasonable diligence in locating stolen property. Four years later the New York courts in a similar case held that a showing of reasonable diligence was not required under the relevant statute. DeWeerth moved to reopen his federal judgment under Rule 60(b), the same Rule used in *Pierce*. The Second Circuit sharply rejected the attempt:

> *Erie* simply does not stand for the proposition that a plaintiff is entitled to reopen a federal court case that has been closed for several years in order to gain the benefit of a newly announced decision of a state court, a forum in which she specifically declined to litigate her claim.

In an effort to render cases like *Pierce* and *DeWeerth* less frequent, several states have adopted a process called certification. In certification the federal court asks the state supreme court for an answer to a question about state law. There are, however, several defects in this system. First, the state must have a certification procedure; many do not. Even when the procedure is available and is used, the results are not always satisfactory.

PART B

THE PROCESS OF LITIGATION

A. Approaching Civil Procedure

In studying the procedural system used in U.S. courts one can take at least two different paths. One path starts from the bottom, examining the way in which an individual lawsuit develops: how the parties state cases, develop information about them, and bring them to resolution. This approach emphasizes features and problems of the contemporary procedural system, which is in many respects a bold experiment. Studying the process of litigation reveals how these features shape and constrain the litigants' responsibilities and choices. The other approach starts from the top, examining the constitutional environment in which the individual lawsuit exists. That approach takes the student into both the history and the current interpretation of the Constitution of the United States. Studying that document reveals several limits on the ways in which state and federal court systems conduct their business, limits that have major consequences for individual litigants.

Anyone wanting to become a lawyer has to understand *both* approaches, comprehending the constitutional environment as well as the modes for processing disputes. This book accordingly contains materials about both, and most courses will examine both. But one can with equal validity start at the top and look down or begin at the bottom and work up. The three Parts of this book are labeled to emphasize those different starting points. Some courses may begin with this section, "Part B: The Process of Litigation," comprising Chapters V-XII and representing the "bottom-up" approach. Other classes may start with "Part A: The Constitutional Framework for U.S. Litigation," comprising Chapters II-IV, the "top-down" approach.

The third part of this book, "Part C: Expanding the Framework of Litigation — Additional Claims and Parties" combines significant elements of both the other parts and may be studied either at the end of the course, as a reprise, or in conjunction with either of the other two parts.

B. Choosing Procedure

Beginning with the process of litigation, one finds oneself exploring the development of the individual lawsuit. The themes here transcend boundaries of time and culture. Since disputing began (which, according to several religious traditions, was shortly after the first humans appeared on the face of the earth), disputants and whoever helped them resolve their disputes have been faced with procedural choices. One way of framing the choices is as between speed and quality. Everyone wants disputes to be decided quickly; everyone also wants them to be decided correctly — after full exploration of the facts and careful weighing of the law. But even in a world of unlimited resources these two goals are in conflict, and ours is hardly a world of unlimited resources. Another way to frame the conflict is as between fairness and justice. Everyone wants the judge to be fair as between the parties; everyone also wants the judge to decide in favor of the party on whose side truth lies. But in some cases these goals will conflict; the party who makes the best presentation of the evidence may not be the side that should win.

These conflicts force those who design procedure (legislators, lawyers, judges) to choose; moreover, they must choose not just once but at every stage of the process. Should all cases go to trial — on the ground that trials may best uncover the truth — or should we weed out most cases before trial, thus speeding the resolution of disputes while increasing the risk of error? Should plaintiffs have to state their cases in detail — in the hope that we can sort weak from strong cases at an early stage — or does a requirement of detailed pleading trip up plaintiffs with good cases who need access to facts possessed by the defendant? How much factual investigation should we permit, bearing in mind that free access to discovery will turn up more information but also increase cost and delay? How much should we delegate matters to the parties — which will require fewer judges and less public expense — and how much should we insist on judicial responsibility — which may increase public confidence in the outcome but will increase public cost?

Behind all these questions lies another, more generalized issue: Is a lawsuit an official quest for truth, or is it primarily a means of settling a dispute? The more we think litigation is an inquiry into truth, the more likely we are to want judges rather than the adversaries to control the inquiry. The more confident we are that litigation reveals the truth, the more likely we are to extend the results of one lawsuit into other, similar ones. Conversely, the more we see litigation as a battle between the parties, the greater our comfort with giving the parties control over the terms of that battle, but the less we shall be inclined to think that the personalized battle yields the truth.

These and similar questions lie just beneath the surface of contemporary procedural rules; each rule, and often even innocuous-looking individual words and phrases within rules, represent a choice among procedural values. In exploring the development of a lawsuit, we shall be doing at least two things: seeing how a procedural system has made particular choices; and looking beneath those choices at the values they imply. That exploration is particularly apt because the procedural system we shall explore — that set forth in the Federal Rules of Civil Procedure — represents a self-conscious choice of flexibility. The drafters of the Rules (and those who have since amended them) sought above all to break free from what they thought were rigidities of earlier procedural systems. They largely succeeded, but critics have begun to ask whether lawsuits have become unstructured, expensive monsters as a result.

C.   A Roadmap for Exploring Choices

This book explores the answers to such questions by following the development of a lawsuit in roughly chronological order. The first chapter in this section (Chapter V) looks at why people litigate. The chapter explores the demography of contemporary litigation, the arsenal of remedies courts can grant, including a look at the financing of litigation. Having decided to commence a lawsuit, one needs to know how to get things started; Chapter VI — on pleading — does that. Logically, one can proceed in two ways at this point. One approach moves from pleading (the setting forth of claims) to the exploration of facts underlying those claims — that is discovery, explored in Chapter VII. The other direction explores a second aspect of pleading, how one adds additional parties and additional claims to a lawsuit (joinder, the topic of Chapter XIII in Part C) before examining discovery.

Most modern lawsuits reach the discovery stage; the real question is whether they will go further. Chapter VIII examines a variety of official and unofficial ways in which lawsuits can end at this stage. If they do not end here, they proceed to trial. Chapter IX examines the doctrines that determine who will participate in that trial — whether it is a judge alone or a judge and jury and, further, which judge or which jury. Chapter X examines a central issue in the trial itself — the law's efforts to assure a rational result. Once the trial is over, the loser may appeal; the availability of and limits on appeals constitute Chapter XI. Whether a lawsuit ends on appeal or at some earlier stage, there may come a quite difficult question: Just what is it that the concluded lawsuit has decided? That question, which goes under several doctrinal names, is explored in Chapter XII, Respect for Judgments.

INCENTIVES TO LITIGATE

V

People don't litigate for fun. Lawsuits cost money. Worse, they are for most participants miserable experiences whether one wins or loses. In considering the litigation process, one might therefore begin asking why anyone brings a lawsuit. That
inquiry should extend to defendants: Plaintiffs almost always seek something in
defendant's power to grant; why does defendant choose to add the insult of litigation to what may be the eventual injury of an adverse judgment? And to make the
inquiry complete, one should also ask whether the expense and unpleasantness of
litigation are desirable or undesirable. Should it be easier to commence or defend
a lawsuit, or is it already too easy? Lawyers give two labels to these inquiries: remedies (comprising the question of what courts can do to and for litigants) and access
to justice (the question of whether barriers to litigation are too high or too low).

A. Litigation in the United States at the Start of the Twenty-First Century

1. How Much Litigation?

Answering any of the inquiries posed above is silly without at least a sketch of
the existing litigation system. For one's answer to the question of whether litigation should be easier — or whether it is already too easy — should turn on one's
view of the way things are now. There is, for example, presently a debate
conducted in legislatures, editorial pages, and scholarly journals about whether
litigation in the U.S. is "out of control." Some of this debate turns on factual
premises. To be a participant in this debate or a well-informed lawyer one needs
to know how much litigation there is in the contemporary United States, what it
consists of, and how long it takes and what its results are.

Because of jurisdictional limits on the federal courts, about 98 percent of civil
litigation in the United States occurs in state courts. In 2000 (the most recent
year for which complete data are available), about 91 million cases were filed in
the United States.* If the population of the United States is about 275 million,

---

* State court statistics in this discussion come from Brian J. Ostrom et al., Examining the Work of
State Courts, 1995: A National Perspective from the Court Statistics Project (National Center for
State Courts 1996). Federal statistics come from the Annual Report, Administrative Office of the
United States Courts 1998, on line at http://www.uscourts.gov/dirrpt98/index.html.

that is one case per year for about every 2.75 persons. Of the 91 million cases, three-fifths are traffic and other ordinance violations. Some of these cases can have significant effects on people's lives — lost driving licenses, towed cars, and increased insurance premiums — but they are not typically what we think of when we think of serious litigation.

The remaining 36 million cases — 1 for every 7.6 persons — could be thought of as "serious." They consist of two large groups — civil and criminal cases — and two smaller ones — juvenile and family cases. In the most recent year for which good data are available there were:

- about 14 million criminal filings: about 15% of all filings and about 39% of non-traffic filings
- about 15 million civil cases: about 16% of all filings and about 41 % of non-traffic filings
- about 5 million family (divorce, support, and custody filings): about 6% of all filings and 14% of non-traffic filings
- about 2 million juvenile filings: about 2% of all filings, 6% of non-traffic filings:

Non-Traffic Case Distribution, 2000

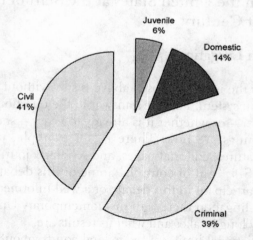

This course focuses on civil lawsuits, the most numerous of the filings. Over the past two decades, the number of civil filings has risen, then steadied, and started to decline slightly:

* Christian Wollschlager, Exploring Global Landscapes of Litigation Rates, (indicating high litigation rates in developed economies, with Germany, Sweden, Israel, and Austria having higher per capita rates of litigation than the U.S.)

Civil Litigation in U.S. Courts, 1984-2000

Comparative studies of legal systems suggest that, roughly speakings civil litigation correlates with people and with economic activity: All things being equal more people and more economic activity means more civil litigation.* One would therefore expect that the U.S., with a large population and the world's largest Gross Domestic Product, would have a relatively high, and growing, rate of litigation. It does: Over the past two decades, the "civil litigation rate" has hovered around 20 — one civil lawsuit filed per year per 20 persons. Perhaps more striking is that U.S. litigation rates have grown far more slowly than the economy, just slightly outpacing the rate of population growth:

People, $ & Lawsuits: Growth Rates, 1985-2000

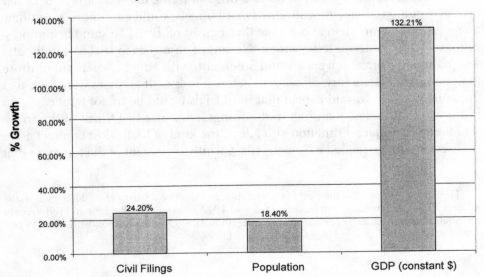

Focusing on the civil lawsuits within this group, one can ask what they are about. For filings — lawsuits begun — the answer today, as it has been for most of the past few decades is "contracts":

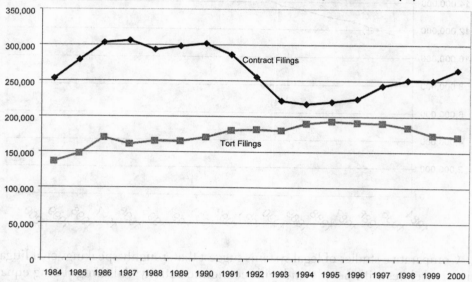

Contract & Tort Fillings — A 14-State Sample 1990-95 (...)

Source Examining the Work of State Courts, 2001, National Center for State Courts.

One gets a slightly varying picture depending on the size of the sample (for example, on a national basis tort filings briefly exceeded contract cases for a few years in the mid-1990s), but the overall trends are fairly clear. Contracts, once heavily dominant, are still the most common form of lawsuit, but tort filings, though they have dropped in very recent years, have grown by more than 20 percent. The most recent statistics suggest about a 45 percent/55 percent division between the categories.

At first glance, one might not think a litigator trying to predict the fate of her case or a public official allocating judicial budgets would care more about how many cases there are than about what they consist of. But, like some first impressions, this one turns out to be wrong. No sort of case goes to trial at a high rate: The national average hovers around 3 percent, with about 70 percent of those trials coming before a jury, 30 percent before a judge.[*] If all cases went to trial at the same rate, one would expect that most trials would be in contract cases. In fact, torts, though less than half of the filings, comprise two thirds of the trials. And the tort/contract distinction also affects the kind of trial: Most contract cases are tried to a judge (called a "bench" trial), while 85 percent of the tort cases that

---

[*] The findings reported in the next few paragraphs are based on a survey of civil litigation in the nation's 75 largest counties, conducted in the mid-1990s; it comprises the best and most recent information about national patterns of civil litigation. U.S. Dept. of Justice, Bureau of Justice Statistics, *Civil Trial Cases in Large Counties, 1996* (1999).

reach trial go before a jury. Because bench trials are a bit easier to schedule and usually a little faster than jury trials, the median time to judgment in a bench trial (the route chosen by most contract litigants) was about 18 months; for jury trials (dominated by torts) the figure was about 22 months. Bear in mind that such averages conceal large regional variations: If one drives the few hours north from Chicago to Milwaukee, one moves from the nation's longest median disposition time (861 days) for a tort case to the shortest (217).

Who wins these trials? Again, the answer differs depending on whether one is looking at tort or contract cases. In tort cases, by a very narrow margin (51 percent to 49 percent) defendants win, the plaintiff recovering nothing. Contract trials, by contrast, are dominated by plaintiffs, who win about 62 percent of the time.

When plaintiffs win, how much do they recover? News accounts suggest fabulous sums; reality is different. The median recovery in tort cases was $31,000 (recall that most tort plaintiffs do not win at trial); in contract cases the median plaintiff's judgment was a bit higher, $37,000. (These figures come from the mid-1990s, but no data suggest that there has been much change.) In about 15 percent of all plaintiff wins, there is a recovery of greater than $250,000; in about 5 percent it is greater than $1 million. Put simply these numbers mean that the stakes in almost all civil litigation are about the median family income for a year. This is hardly a trivial amount but neither is it the stuff of urban legend and professional folktales. Another way to put it is that plaintiffs will recover seven-figure sums in less than 5 percent of cases, and that defendants and their insurers will work hard to avoid being on the wrong side of such high-figure verdicts — and will mostly succeed.

NOTES AND PROBLEMS

1. Consider some implications of the statistical picture sketched above:

a. You walk into a courtroom in a big U.S. city. A civil jury trial is in progress. Without knowing more you can make a very good guess about what kind of case it is. Explain.

b. You walk into another big-city courtroom, where another trial is in progress, this one before a judge without a jury. You can be pretty sure what kind of case it is, who will win, and make a prediction about how much the judgment will be for. Explain.

c. Legislation is introduced to streamline litigation by reducing the amount of time spent in jury selection. Explain why the legislation, though it may make jurors' lives more pleasant, will have no effect on the time of disposition of an average case.

d. State court administrators and judges, staggering under heavy caseloads, sometimes oppose federal legislation that would limit federal diversity jurisdiction on the grounds that the state courts already have too many cases and the "dumped" federal cases would overwhelm them. Explain why that argument is weak.

e. A civil trial lawyer complains that her breach of contract case will never get to court because "all courts do these days is try drug cases." Explain why she's wrong.

2. Be clear about what trial rates do and do not mean. Although most civil cases will not end in trial, many will end with a judicial decision — about jurisdiction, about the sufficiency of pleadings, about discovery issues, about summary judgment — even though there is no trial. For example, in the federal system, for which we have elaborate statistics, such rulings are dispositive (that is, case-ending) in about a third of all filings. So a low trial rate does not mean a low "decision" rate. As you will see, a good part of the contemporary litigation process involves such pretrial rulings. It may not be a great exaggeration to say that contemporary litigation *is* the pretrial process. Indeed, some cases end almost as soon as they begin, with a default judgment: about 14 percent of the total cases and about a quarter of the contract cases end with default judgments, probably because a debtor has no defense to a claim for breach of contract.

3. Notice that most civil cases end in an event that is ambiguous: settlement or abandonment. These events may represent a response to the merits: As facts are uncovered, the plaintiff or defendant recognizes that what he thought was a strong case has a fatal flaw. Alternatively, settlement or abandonment may represent surrender to financial exigency: A plaintiff gives up a strong case because she cannot afford to litigate any further; a defendant offers something to make a plaintiff with a trumped up claim go away because defeating the claim on the merits will cost more than the settlement offered. When financial exigency rather than the merits of the claim dictate the result, one confronts the central topic of this chapter, the relation of the incentives and costs of litigation to the merits of the claims involved.

2. Why Litigate?

The people filing 15 million civil lawsuits each year want something; the people against whom they are filed want to know what they stand to lose. To a lawyer, those questions translate into inquiries about what remedies a court will order — what acts it will require of the defendant if plaintiff prevails on the merits. Remedies in our legal system aim to "cure" a legal harm. Remedies can be divided into two groups — those that seek to restore directly and specifically that which the defendant has taken from the plaintiff (*specific* remedies) and those that seek to provide the plaintiff with a reasonable substitute (*substitutionary* remedies). If, for example, defendant takes plaintiff's car unlawfully, a specific remedy would be an order (either to the defendant or the sheriff) commanding the return of the car; a substitutionary remedy would be a judgment that defendant pay plaintiff an amount sufficient to purchase an equivalent car. (In one instance, the two remedies merge: If a debtor owes a creditor money, a judgment for money is simultaneously a specific and a substitutionary remedy because money is fungible.) One of the issues we shall examine below is the extent to which plaintiffs have a choice between these two forms of remedies.

Aside from what courts can do for them, clients are interested in how much it will cost them to get that relief. Most of the bar in the United States is private and charges its clients fees for its services. In addition to attorneys' fees are other costs: filing fees, the fees of court reporters, the cost of expert witnesses, and the like. Such costs can form a significant barrier to litigation such that the harmed plaintiff finds the costs of litigation greater than the potential recovery. To that extent there are legal rights for which there is no practical remedy. That anomaly resolves itself if the successful plaintiff can recover attorneys' fees as part of the remedy. Since the mid-1970s, large changes have occurred in the extent to which such costs can be shifted to the other side of the lawsuit.

B. Substitutionary Remedies

Most remedies in the modern U.S. legal system are substitutionary. Most suits seek money damages, making damages also the most common substitutionary remedy. This frequency of money damages has several sources. One is that in a credit economy many claims are for debts, and a successful debt claim will always result in a damage judgment. Second, for many common claims specific remedies are impossible: Defendant cannot replace an injured limb or erase the pain of disfigurement or insult. Under such conditions money may be a poor substitute, but only a substitute is possible. Because damages are a substitute, however, the law encounters difficulty in deciding how to measure them. In settlement negotiations the parties bargain directly about how much (or how little) they would accept to dispose of the case. In trials, courts must resort to less direct methods for estimating the value of a substitute. Many of these methods depend on the existence of a market in which the substitute can be priced, but some substitutionary remedies involve damages for which there is no market.

1. Compensatory Damages

Rules of substantive law often contain rules for the measurement and proof of damages. For example, in contracts a party can typically recover only "expectation damages," and even these will be limited by doctrines of foreseeability. In intentional torts, by contrast, I am liable for all harm my acts cause, even if I did not foresee the extent of that harm.

Courts enforce these principles of substantive law through rules of procedure and evidence. If plaintiff brings a claim in contract, he will need to prove, not just that defendant breached a valid agreement, but also that plaintiff purchased substitute goods at the then-prevailing market prices; failure to do so will mean that defendant wins a motion for summary judgment or a directed verdict. Analogous rules govern tort claims. If Pedestrian shows only that Driver negligently struck him in a crosswalk, Pedestrian will lose the case unless he goes further, offering in evidence his medical bills, the amount of lost wages, and the like. This failure of proof will be enforced, again, by a summary judgment or directed verdict. Procedural rules thus serve as the gatekeepers of substantive law.

All the damages thus far mentioned are what courts and legislatures sometimes call "economic" damages: the damages at stake will compensate the plaintiff for money he has either lost (when vendor did not supply the goods or he was home from work with a broken leg for two weeks) or has had to pay (the higher price of oil in the spot market, physicians' and hospital bills). In some cases, however, damages reach beyond such economic losses. Consider, for example, "pain and suffering." If Driver's negligence breaks Pedestrian's leg, it will hurt. For some severe injuries, the pain may last for a lifetime. Or suppose the dean of students at your law school falsely accuses you of cheating on an examination. That accusation, uncorrected, might cost you a job (or even a career), for which economic compensation would lie. It would also cost you, likely, sleepless nights and great worry — emotional distress. Like pain and suffering, emotional distress may be an element of damages in some cases. So may, in appropriate cases, loss of consortium (harm to a relationship), humiliation, and harm to reputation.

Contemporary U.S. law compensates for these non-economic harms as well, using damages. As you might expect, measuring such damages provides a challenge. Experienced lawyers and insurance adjusters often use rules of thumb in settling such cases: three times the amount of economic damages for pain and suffering is one common guideline. But these guidelines are not part of law, so juries cannot be instructed to use them, and how they assess such non-economic damages. A litigation technique popular among attorneys required to offer such "proof" in physical pain and suffering cases is to ask the jury how much it would take to compensate the plaintiff for a single hour's (or day's) suffering, and then to multiply that number by the expected duration of the pain — sometimes a lifetime. In Beagle v. Vasold, 65 Cal. 2d 166, 417 P.2d 673, 53 Cal. Rptr. 129 (1966), a trial court was reversed for abuse of discretion because it had refused to permit such an argument. Such efforts are in part a result of jury instructions that do not give many guidelines:

> Reasonable compensation for any pain, discomfort, fears, anxiety and other mental and emotional distress suffered by the plaintiff and caused by the injury and for similar suffering reasonably certain to be experienced in the future from the same cause.
>
> No definite standard or method of calculation is prescribed by law by which to fix reasonable compensation for pain and suffering. Nor is the opinion of any witness required as to the amount of such reasonable compensation. Furthermore, the argument of counsel as to the amount of damages is not evidence of reasonable compensation. In making an award for pain and suffering you should exercise your authority with calm and reasonable judgment and the damages you fix must be just and reasonable in the light of the evidence.

California Jury Instructions, Civil: Book of Approved Jury Instructions, §14.3 (9th ed. West 2003).

As one might expect in such circumstances, jury awards vary widely. Their variation has, in turn, prompted legislative efforts to create predictability. One approach is to bar non-economic damages entirely for certain categories of cases. E.g., Cal. Civ. Code §3333.4 (West 2002) (no recovery for non-economic damages for vehicular negligence if plaintiff was operating his vehicle under influence of alcohol at time of accident). Another approach is simply to put a cap on non-economic damages in some or all cases:

> "In no action [for medical malpractice] shall the amount of damages for noneconomic losses exceed two hundred fifty thousand dollars."

Cal. Civ. Code §3333.2(b) (Deering 2003).

> In any action for personal injury, property damage, or wrongful death, based upon principles of comparative fault, the liability of each defendant for non-economic damages shall be several only and shall not be joint. Each defendant shall be liable only for the amount of non-economic damages allocated to that defendant in direct proportion to that defendant's percentage of fault, and a separate judgment shall be rendered against that defendant for that amount.

Cal. Civ. Code §1431.2 (Deering 2003).

NOTES AND PROBLEMS

1. Test your grasp of procedural and strategic implications of these principles.

a. Plaintiff's complaint alleges negligence and harm but does not mention damages; what should defendant do?

b. In a breach of contract case, plaintiff asks the court to instruct the jury to award as much damages as it will take to "send the defendant a message" about breaking its promise; what ruling on the request?

c. Sometimes the need for proof of damages is not a barrier but an aid to recovery. In a claim for personal injuries, the very badly injured plaintiff seeks to introduce evidence of her cries of pain during physical therapy; defendant objects that such evidence will prejudice the jury. What is plaintiff's best response?

d. Suppose a plaintiff is severely and permanently injured in a car accident. Defendant has some questions about the claimed cost of medical care, and also believes it has a very strong case that plaintiff's own carelessness, not defendant's, caused the injuries. In a pretrial conference the judge suggests that the case has two phases — liability and damages. How might defendant seek to prevent evidence on damages from affecting the verdict on liability?

2. The issues sketched above represent a sample of problems in measuring compensatory damages.

a. Sometimes the damage in question has no market. In ascertaining such damages courts do not simply ask the plaintiffs how much it would take to compensate them for the harm they have suffered. One reason for not doing so is the parties' temptation to exaggerate the amount.

b. At other times there is a market, but plaintiff has no access to it. For example, contract doctrines require that the plaintiff mitigate damages by trying to find a substitute for defendant's breach, even if plaintiff has to borrow money to buy the substitute. But what if plaintiff doesn't have good credit? See Valencia v. Shell Oil

Co., 23 Cal. 2d 840, 845, 147 P.2d 558, 560 (1944): "The duty to minimize damages does not require an injured person to do what is unreasonable or impracticable, and, consequently, when expenditures are necessary for minimization of damages, the duty does not run to a person who is financially unable to make such expenditures."

c. A third problem arises from the law's efforts to individualize damages. Such insistence reflects the goal of what might be called the "perfect remedy" — that which provides an exact compensation for the harm suffered by this plaintiff. The goal is noble, but it has its costs, chiefly in the time it takes to establish the precise level of harm. If lawyers and insurance companies regularly use multipliers as rules of thumb, and if predictability is the goal, would statutory schedules (e.g., three times economic damages as pain and suffering in personal injury cases) be a better approach?

3. Courts insisting on such individualization do not mention the cost of vindicating the legal right to compensation — court fees, attorneys' fees, and the like. The reason for this omission is simple: As you will see in Section E of this chapter, American courts do not typically compensate successful litigants for the cost of litigation. This feature of remedial law means that an award of compensatory damages, no matter how precisely calculated, will always fall short of full compensation.

4. As you have seen in the preceding section, lawsuits take time. In the world of finance, time costs money. Courts take account of it by adding interest to the damages. Rules for awarding interest vary depending on whether it is calculated from the time the claim accrues (prejudgment interest) or only during the time between the entry of judgment and the moment when the judgment amount is paid (postjudgment interest).

a. In most jurisdictions, the nature of the harm sued for will determine whether prejudgment interest accrues. The Restatement (Second) of Torts §913 provides for prejudgment interest for the taking of property and for other pecuniary harms if necessary to avoid injustice, but not for bodily injury, emotional distress, or reputational harms. What theory underlies such a distinction? The Restatement (Second) of Contracts, §354 provides for prejudgment interest on actions brought to enforce a sum certain (for example, a promissory note), and for interest on other contracts if justice requires.

b. After judgment is entered, most jurisdictions provide for interest to accrue until the judgment is paid, but the rate of interest varies considerably. Federal law (28 U.S.C. §1961) ties such postjudgment interest to the rate of one-year U.S. Treasury Bills. Some states, however, have fixed rates, which may be above or below the prevailing rate (for example, 10 percent in California. Civ. Proc. Code §685.010 (West 1991)).

2.   Liquidated, Statutory, and Punitive Damages

Given the difficulty of calculating compensatory damages, in some situations the parties try to agree beforehand about price of the harm. The most common such situations are contractual, in which the parties may agree to such *liquidated* damages for breach of contract. Their power to so agree is limited in several ways. First, they may not agree to liquidated damages unless the actual damages would be difficult to calculate. The parties could not, for example, agree to liquidated damages of $1,000 for failure to repay a $500 debt. An example of a statute simultaneously permitting and limiting liquidated damages is UCC §2-718(1):

> Damages for breach by either party may be liquidated in the agreement but only at an amount which is reasonable in light of the anticipated or actual harm caused by the breach, the difficulties of proof of harm caused by the breach, the difficulties of proof of loss, and the inconvenience or nonfeasibility of otherwise obtaining an adequate remedy. A term fixing unreasonably large liquidated damages is void as a penalty.

Using a logic somewhat resembling that of liquidated damage clauses, statutes sometimes set minimum damages not specifically tied to the amount of the loss suffered. For example, the Copyright Act gives holders whose rights have been infringed a choice between proving lost profits and accepting statutory damages in an amount between $500 and $20,000 for a negligent violation and up to $100,000 for a willful violation. 17 U.S.C. §504(c); Feltner v. Columbia Pictures Television, Inc., 523 U.S. 340 (1998) (holding that a jury must set the amount of statutory damages between the applicable minimum and maximum). Minimum damage provisions (often coupled with separate provisions for attorneys' fees) also arise in the context of small transactions (bad-check statutes provide a common example); they are designed to offset the costs of litigation over matters that are often small in dollar amount and to encourage plaintiffs to enforce public policy by bringing suit.

The theory underlying minimum damage amounts is also partly punitive. *Punitive damages*, by contrast, aim entirely at punishment. Specifically designed to punish the defendant for wrongful behavior, merge the goals of criminal and civil actions and provide an exception to the general rule that damages serve only to compensate the plaintiff. Both substantive law and rules of evidence reflect the change in emphasis. For example, as in criminal law, mere negligence will generally not support an award of punitive damages; "willfulness" or some malicious intent is generally required. Because punitive damages aim to punish defendants rather than compensate plaintiffs, in some jurisdictions plaintiffs seeking punitive damages may introduce testimony as to the defendant's net worth; the idea is that one has to know the defendant's wealth in order to decide how much a given award will hurt — a monetary instance of suiting the punishment to the criminal.

Punitive damage awards play several roles in the strategy of litigation. Mention punitives and you can start a vigorous argument among lawyers and scholars. One view is that they are wildly unpredictable and "out of control," striking hapless defendants like lightning bolts without much correlation with the harm done or the badness of behavior. Reading the newspapers for a month one can find some evidence for this view, which may also be reflected in the next case, State Farm v. Campbell. On the other side of the debate lie a set of empirical inquiries, which suggest, first, that punitive damages are relatively rare, occurring in about 6 percent of cases that go to judgment, and, second, that the median award of punitives is about $50,000, an amount about equal to the amount of compensatory damages awarded in the median case. Theodore Eisenberg et al., The Predictability of Punitive Damages, 26 J. Legal Stud. 623, 634 (1997). Some draw from these studies the conclusion that the "problem" of punitive damages is easily exaggerated. Others counter that these studies fail to take account of two factors: first, that many cases may settle in ways that reflect the fear of punitive damages, and that the median punitive award masks a very small set of extremely high awards thousands of times greater.

Over the last fifteen years the U.S. Supreme Court repeatedly struggled with the question of punitive damages as a matter of constitutional law and decided a number of cases in which it tried to find a congenial approach to the question.

The sequence started with Browning-Ferris Indus. v. Kelco Disposal, 492 U.S. 257 (1989), in which the Court rejected the argument that the Eighth Amendment (barring cruel and unusual punishments) spoke to punitive damages but said that "[t]here is some authority in our opinions for the view that the Due Process Clause places outer limits on the size of a civil damages award made pursuant to a statutory scheme." That cause, in the second sentence of §1 of Fourteenth Amendment to the U.S. Constitution forbids "any State" from "depriv[ing] any person of life, liberty, or property without due process of law." The Court has struggled to fit review of punitive damage awards into a due process framework.

After some false starts, in which the justices affirmed punitive damage awards without explaining very precisely why they were doing so, the Court established two approaches — one procedural, one substantive. Both are summarized in the next case, which also establishes presumptive arithmetic limits on such awards. The case refers to an action for "bad faith" against an insurer. As you will see in the next section, liability insurers usually have the power to settle claims against their insureds. Many states control this power by holding insurers liable if they unreasonably refuse an opportunity to settle a claim against their insured, and the result is a judgment in excess of the policy limits. Such an outcome sets the stage for the Supreme Court's decision in the next case.

State Farm Mutual Automobile Insurance Co. v. Campbell

123 S. Ct. 1513 (2003)

Justice KENNEDY delivered the opinion of the Court.

We address once again the measure of punishment, by means of punitive damages, a State may impose upon a defendant in a civil case. The question is whether, in the circumstances we shall recount, an award of $145 million in punitive damages, where full compensatory damages are $1 million, is excessive and in violation of the Due Process Clause of the Fourteenth Amendment to the Constitution of the United States.

I

In 1981, Curtis Campbell (Campbell) was driving with his wife, Inez Preece Campbell, in Cache County, Utah. He decided to pass six vans traveling ahead of them on a two-lane highway. Todd Ospital was driving a small car approaching from the opposite direction. To avoid a head-on collision with Campbell, who by then was driving on the wrong side of the highway and toward oncoming traffic, Ospital swerved onto the shoulder, lost control of his automobile, and collided with a vehicle driven by Robert G. Slusher. Ospital was killed, and Slusher was rendered permanently disabled. The Campbells escaped unscathed.

In the ensuing wrongful death and tort action, Campbell insisted he was not at fault. Early investigations did support differing conclusions as to who caused the accident, but "a consensus was reached early on by the investigators and witnesses that Mr. Campbell's unsafe pass had indeed caused the crash." Campbell's insurance company, petitioner State Farm Mutual Automobile Insurance Company (State Farm), nonetheless decided to contest liability and declined offers by Slusher and Ospital's estate (Ospital) to settle the claims for the policy limit of $50,000 ($25,000 per claimant). State Farm also ignored the advice of one of its own investigators and took the case to trial, assuring the Campbells that "their assets were safe, that they had no liability for the accident, that [State Farm] would represent their interests and that they did not need to procure separate counsel." To the contrary, a jury determined that Campbell was 100 percent at fault, and a judgment was returned for $185,849, far more than the amount offered in settlement.

At first State Farm refused to cover the $135,849 in excess liability. Its counsel made this clear to the Campbells: "'You may want to put for sale signs on your property to get things moving.'" Nor was State Farm willing to post a supersedeas bond to allow Campbell to appeal the judgment against him. Campbell obtained his own counsel to appeal the verdict. During the pendency of the appeal, in late 1984, Slusher, Ospital, and the Campbells reached an agreement whereby Slusher and Ospital agreed not to seek satisfaction of their claims against the Campbells. In exchange the Campbells agreed to pursue a bad faith action against State Farm and to be represented by Slusher's and Ospital's attorneys. The Campbells also agreed that Slusher and Ospital would have a right to play a part in all major decisions concerning the bad faith action. No settlement could be concluded without Slusher's and Ospital's approval, and Slusher and Ospital would receive 90 percent of any verdict against State Farm.

In 1989, the Utah Supreme Court denied Campbell's appeal in the wrongful death and tort actions. State Farm then paid the entire judgment, including the amounts in excess of the policy limits. The Campbells nonetheless filed a complaint against State Farm alleging bad faith, fraud, and intentional infliction of emotional distress. . . .

[The Utah Supreme Court described State Farm's stance in the bad faith case:]

> State Farm argued . . . that its decision to take the case to trial was an "honest mistake" that did not warrant punitive damages. In contrast, the Campbells introduced evidence that State Farm's decision to take the case to trial was a result of a

national scheme to meet corporate fiscal goals by capping payouts on claims company-wide. This scheme was referred to as State Farm's "Performance, Planning and Review," or PP &; R, policy. To prove the existence of this scheme, the trial court allowed the Campbells to introduce extensive expert testimony regarding fraudulent practices by State Farm in its nation-wide operations. . . .

Evidence pertaining to the PP&R policy concerned State Farm's business practices for over 20 years in numerous States. Most of these practices bore no relation to third-party automobile insurance claims, the type of claim underlying the Campbells' complaint against the company. The jury awarded the Campbells $2.6 million [later reduced to $1 million] in compensatory damages and $145 million in punitive damages. . . .

II

We recognized in Cooper Industries, Inc. v. Leatherman Tool Group, Inc., that in our judicial system compensatory and punitive damages, although usually awarded at the same time by the same decisionmaker, serve different purposes. Compensatory damages "are intended to redress the concrete loss that the plaintiff has suffered by reason of the defendant's wrongful conduct" (citing Restatement (Second) of Torts §903, pp. 453-454 (1979)). By contrast, punitive damages serve a broader function; they are aimed at deterrence and retribution. . . .

Although these awards serve the same purposes as criminal penalties, defendants subjected to punitive damages in civil cases have not been accorded the protections applicable in a criminal proceeding. This increases our concerns over the imprecise manner in which punitive damages systems are administered. . . .

In light of these concerns, in [BMW of North America v.] *Gore*, we instructed courts reviewing punitive damages to consider three guideposts: (1) the degree of reprehensibility of the defendant's misconduct; (2) the disparity between the actual or potential harm suffered by the plaintiff and the punitive damages award; and (3) the difference between the punitive damages awarded by the jury and the civil penalties authorized or imposed in comparable cases. We reiterated the importance of these three guideposts in *Cooper Industries* and mandated appellate courts to conduct de novo review of a trial court's application of them to the jury's award. Exacting appellate review ensures that an award of punitive damages is based upon an "'application of law, rather than a decisionmaker's caprice.'"

[handwritten margin note: Guidelines for imposing punitive damages]

III

[handwritten margin note: Holding]

Under the principles outlined in BMW of North America, Inc. v. Gore, this case is neither close nor difficult. It was error to reinstate the jury's $145 million punitive damages award. We address each guidepost of *Gore* in some detail.

A

"[T]he most important indicium of the reasonableness of a punitive damages award is the degree of reprehensibility of the defendant's conduct." *Gore*. We have

Points for considering reprehensibility

instructed courts to determine the reprehensibility of a defendant by considering whether: the harm caused was physical as opposed to economic; the tortious conduct evinced an indifference to or a reckless disregard of the health or safety of others; the target of the conduct had financial vulnerability; the conduct involved repeated actions or was an isolated incident; and the harm was the result of intentional malice, trickery, or deceit, or mere accident. The existence of any one of these factors weighing in favor of a plaintiff may not be sufficient to sustain a punitive damages award; and the absence of all of them renders any award suspect. It should be presumed a plaintiff has been made whole for his injuries by compensatory damages, so punitive damages should only be awarded if the defendant's culpability, after having paid compensatory damages, is so reprehensible as to warrant the imposition of further sanctions to achieve punishment or deterrence.

Applying these factors in the instant case, we must acknowledge that State Farm's handling of the claims against the Campbells merits no praise. The trial court found that State Farm's employees altered the company's records to make Campbell appear less culpable. State Farm disregarded the overwhelming likelihood of liability and the near-certain probability that, by taking the case to trial, a judgment in excess of the policy limits would be awarded. State Farm amplified the harm by at first assuring the Campbells their assets would be safe from any verdict and by later telling them, postjudgment, to put a for-sale sign on their house. While we do not suggest there was error in awarding punitive damages *Too high an award* based upon State Farm's conduct toward the Campbells, a more modest punishment for this reprehensible conduct could have satisfied the State's legitimate objectives, and the Utah courts should have gone no further.

This case, instead, was used as a platform to expose, and punish, the perceived deficiencies of State Farm's operations throughout the country. The Utah Supreme Court's opinion makes explicit that State Farm was being condemned for its nationwide policies rather than for the conduct direct[ed] toward the Campbells. . . .

A State cannot punish a defendant for conduct that may have been lawful where it occurred. *Gore.* . . . Nor, as a general rule, does a State have a legitimate concern in imposing punitive damages to punish a defendant for unlawful acts committed outside of the State's jurisdiction. Any proper adjudication of conduct that occurred outside Utah to other persons would require their inclusion, and, to those parties, the Utah courts, in the usual case, would need to apply the laws of their relevant jurisdiction. Phillips Petroleum Co. v. Shutts, [casebook page 813] (1985). . . .

For a more fundamental reason, however, the Utah courts erred in relying upon this and other evidence: The courts awarded punitive damages to punish and deter conduct that bore no relation to the Campbells' harm. A defendant's dissimilar acts, independent from the acts upon which liability was premised, may not serve as the basis for punitive damages. A defendant should be punished for the conduct that harmed the plaintiff, not for being an unsavory individual or business. Due process does not permit courts, in the calculation of punitive damages, to adjudicate the merits of other parties' hypothetical claims against a defendant under the guise of the reprehensibility analysis, but we have no doubt the Utah Supreme Court did that here. . . .

The Campbells have identified scant evidence of repeated misconduct of the sort that injured them. Nor does our review of the Utah courts' decisions convince us that State Farm was only punished for its actions toward the Campbells. Although evidence of other acts need not be identical to have relevance in the calculation of punitive damages, the Utah court erred here because evidence pertaining to claims that had nothing to do with a third-party lawsuit was introduced at length. Other evidence concerning reprehensibility was even more tangential. For example, the Utah Supreme Court criticized State Farm's investigation into the personal life of one of its employees and, in a broader approach, the manner in which State Farm's policies corrupted its employees. . . .

B

Turning to the second *Gore* guidepost, we have been reluctant to identify concrete constitutional limits on the ratio between harm, or potential harm, to the plaintiff and the punitive damages award. . . . We decline again to impose a bright-line ratio which a punitive damages award cannot exceed. Our jurisprudence and the principles it has now established demonstrate, however, that, in practice, few awards exceeding a single-digit ratio between punitive and compensatory damages, to a significant degree, will satisfy due process. [The Court reviewed its cases, summing up as follows:] They demonstrate what should be obvious: Single-digit multipliers are more likely to comport with due process, while still achieving the State's goals of deterrence and retribution, than awards with ratios in range of 500 to 1 or, in this case, of 145 to 1.

Nonetheless, because there are no rigid benchmarks that a punitive damages award may not surpass, ratios greater than those we have previously upheld may comport with due process where "a particularly egregious act has resulted in only a small amount of economic damages." The converse is also true, however. When compensatory damages are substantial, then a lesser ratio, perhaps only equal to compensatory damages, can reach the outermost limit of the due process guarantee. . . .

In the context of this case, we have no doubt that there is a presumption against an award that has a 145-to-1 ratio. The compensatory award in this case was substantial; the Campbells were awarded $1 million for a year and a half of emotional distress. This was complete compensation. The harm arose from a transaction in the economic realm, not from some physical assault or trauma; there were no physical injuries; and State Farm paid the excess verdict before the complaint was filed, so the Campbells suffered only minor economic injuries for the 18-month period in which State Farm refused to resolve the claim against them. The compensatory damages for the injury suffered here, moreover, likely were based on a component which was duplicated in the punitive award. Much of the distress was caused by the outrage and humiliation the Campbells suffered at the actions of their insurer; and it is a major role of punitive damages to condemn such conduct. . . .

The remaining premises for the Utah Supreme Court's decision bear no relation to the award's reasonableness or proportionality to the harm. . . . The wealth of a defendant cannot justify an otherwise unconstitutional punitive damages award. *Gore* ("The fact that BMW is a large corporation rather than an impecunious individual does not diminish its entitlement to fair notice of the demands that the several States impose on the conduct of its business"); ("[Wealth] provides an open-ended basis for inflating awards when the defendant is wealthy. . . . That does not make its use unlawful or inappropriate; it simply means that this factor cannot make up for the failure of other factors, such as 'reprehensibility,' to constrain significantly an award that purports to punish a defendant's conduct"). The principles set forth in *Gore* must be implemented with care, to ensure both reasonableness and proportionality.

C

The third guidepost in *Gore* is the disparity between the punitive damages award and the "civil penalties authorized or imposed in comparable cases." . . . Here, we need not dwell long on this guidepost. The most relevant civil sanction under Utah state law for the wrong done to the Campbells appears to be a $10,000 fine for an act of fraud, an amount dwarfed by the $145 million punitive damages award. . . .

IV

An application of the *Gore* guideposts to the facts of this case, especially in light of the substantial compensatory damages awarded (a portion of which contained a punitive element), likely would justify a punitive damages award at or near the amount of compensatory damages. The punitive award of $145 million, therefore, was neither reasonable nor proportionate to the wrong committed, and it was an irrational and arbitrary deprivation of the property of the defendant. The proper calculation of punitive damages under the principles we have discussed should be resolved, in the first instance, by the Utah courts.

The judgment of the Utah Supreme Court is reversed, and the case is remanded for proceedings not inconsistent with this opinion.

It is so ordered.

[Justices Scalia and Thomas dissented separately on the grounds that neither the due process clause nor the rest of the Constitution provided a basis for controlling states' awards of punitive damages.]

[Justice Ginsburg dissented on two grounds: that it was unwise for the Court to use the Constitution to lay down the kind of rules that were essentially legislative; and that in this case the behavior of State Farm (which included the apparent destruction of materials that had been requested in discovery) warranted the award in question:]

I remain of the view that this Court has no warrant to reform state law governing awards of punitive damages. Even if I were prepared to accept the flexible guides prescribed in *Gore*, I would not join the Court's swift conversion of those guides into instructions that begin to resemble marching orders. For the reasons stated, I would leave the judgment of the Utah Supreme Court undisturbed.

NOTES AND PROBLEMS

1. Start by summarizing doctrine.

a. What procedural requirement does the due process clause place on courts awarding punitive damages?

b. What does the Court say are the substantive tests for punitive damages?

2. Apply those principles to the case at hand.

a. Explain why the Utah decision affirming an award of $145 million in punitive damages was not vulnerable to attack under the *Oberg-Cooper Industries'* procedural requirements. How had the Utah courts complied with that case?

b. Why was the Utah decision vulnerable under *Gore*, according to the majority?

3. *What* should the Utah courts — and the plaintiffs — do on remand? They know that $145 million is too much, maybe a lot too much. What else?

a. Is an award of any punitives justified? Does the opinion speak clearly to this point?

b. If so, how much? The opinion suggests that "single-digit" multipliers (1-9 times the compensatory damages) will usually mark the outer bounds of due process. Does this mean that a $9 million award should be upheld? Or, as the majority suggests, is the fact that this is a case in which substantial compensatory damages were awarded justify only a lower multiplier? How much lower?

4. What does *Campbell* say about other applications of its principles?

a. The opinion stresses that the Campbells suffered no physical injuries. Suppose they had, and that State Farm had also declined to pay their medical expenses (on the grounds that they were exaggerating their condition or seeking medically unnecessary treatment). All other things being equal, the opinion suggests a higher multiplier than with solely economic damages. How much higher? Higher than the single-digit presumption?

b. Suppose the same compensatory damages (economic loss only) but evidence that defendant had used the same tactic multiple times in Utah (thus eliminating problem of applying Utah punitives to out-of-state conduct). What multiplier?

5. To what extent does the opinion require state and federal courts to alter their approach to punitive damage cases?

a. At the moment courts give juries relatively open-ended instructions; consider a fairly typical instruction:

> If you find that plaintiff suffered actual injury, harm, or damage caused by (cause of action), you should then consider whether you should award punitive damages against defendant, for the sake of example and by way of punishment. You should in your discretion award punitive damages, if, but only if, you find by clear and convincing evidence that the defendant was guilty of oppression, fraud, or malice in the conduct on which you base your finding of liability. [After defining oppression, fraud, and malice, the instruction continues:]
>
> The law provides no fixed standards as to the amount of such punitive damages, but leaves the amount to the jury's sound discretion, exercised without passion or prejudice.
>
> In arriving at any award of punitive damages, consider the following factors:
> (1) The reprehensibility of the conduct of the defendant. (2) The amount of punitive damages which will have a deterrent effect on the defendant in the light of

defendant's financial condition. (3) That the punitive damages must bear a reasonable relation to the injury, harm, or damage actually suffered by the plaintiff.

California Jury Instructions, BAJI 14.71 (9th ed. West 2003).

b. Does *Campbell* suggest that this instruction is no longer valid? If so, how would you rewrite it?

c. Specifically, does the opinion suggest that trial courts may (or should) instruct juries in multipliers, telling them to choose among single-digits, except in egregious cases? Suppose a revision that revised the sentence that now says "the law provides no fixed standards." Should this sentence now say: "The law provides no fixed standards as to the amount of punitive damages, but in most cases punitive damages will not exceed nine times the compensatory damages."

d. Or is the doctrine about multiples directed primarily to judges? If the courts should not instruct juries as to multipliers, can lawyers use them in arguments directed to juries? Suppose on remand plaintiffs' lawyer says to the jury: "I suggest to you that an award of $1 million would adequately compensate the Campbells for the ordeal to which the defendants have subjected them; and I suggest that another $9 million would send defendant the right kind of message about the evil of its conduct." Error?

e. Many states now allow plaintiffs to introduce evidence of defendants' wealth in punitive damage cases, on the grounds that such evidence allows juries to fit the punishment not just to the "crime" but to the defendant. The instruction quoted above is typical. Reread the last paragraph in section III B of the opinion. What does it mean to say that a defendant's great wealth cannot make constitutional an otherwise unconstitutional award? Suppose an award would be just outside the outer limits of constitutionality for a $100 million corporation. Could it nevertheless be inside the limits of constitutionality for a $10 billion corporation? If not, is the wealth of a defendant irrelevant? The answers matter, because the ability to introduce defendant's wealth in evidence is a powerful tool, many lawyers would say.

6. When the opinion came down, the legal press suggested it was a big victory for insurers and "repeat defendants." Matters may be more complicated than that.

a. If the empirical studies cited above are correct, punitive damages are awarded at trial only in the 5-7 percent of cases. Moreover, in these cases the median amount awarded was about $50,000, a ratio of about 1:1 with compensatory damages: whether consciously or not judges and jurors were essentially matching the amount of compensatory damages. Theodore Eisenberg et al., The Predictability of Punitive Damages, 26 J. Legal Stud. 623, 634 (1997). If this data is representative, the decision will not reduce many punitive awards. In fact, if the *Campbell* multiplier range (from 1 to 9 times compensatory damages) reaches the ears of jurors, either through instructions or lawyers' argument, it might, by encouraging juries not just to "match" compensatory damages but to multiply them, actually increase the median punitive damage award.

b. But the median awards don't tell the whole story. Empirical studies of litigation suggest that a high proportion of damage awards comes in a very small number of trials. One study reported that in the nation's largest jurisdiction, California, half of all the damages "were awarded in 3% of the 1985-86 trials and in 1% of the 1990-91 trials."[*] Statisticians would say that the mean (arithmetic average) and median (mid-point of all awards) differ significantly. That means that for "repeat defendants" (State Farm is a good example), the importance of *Campbell* lies less in its potential for increasing the ordinary punitive damage judgments and more in its reduction of the very occasional but very high awards. Put arithmetically, even if one multiplied the median punitive judgment ($50,000) by nine, it would take more than three hundred such judgments to equal one award the size of that in *Campbell*. From this perspective, *Campbell* substantially reduces the risk of taking a case involving punitive damages to trial. How will *Campbell* affect defendants' settlement calculations?

C.   Specific Remedies

1.   The Idea of Specific Relief

Though damages are the most commonly sought remedy, they are not the only available one. Courts may order parties to do things or to refrain from doing them; they also can enlist the help of officials in recapturing personal or real property from defendants wrongfully possessing or occupying it. Legal writers sometimes refer to such remedies as *specific* (as opposed to *substitutionary*) remedies. Suppose that in *Campbell*, the plaintiffs had taken their insurance company's original advice and put their house on the market to satisfy the uninsured portion of the damage award against them, that a buyer had agreed to their terms, but the Campbells had then had second thoughts and refused to sign the deed conveying the property to their buyers. The buyers might have sued for damages, the difference between the contract price and the market price of the house — a substitutionary remedy. But another remedy would also be available — an order from the court commanding the Campbells, under penalty of contempt, to convey the property. Such a "decree for specific performance" is one of the array of specific remedies available from U.S. courts.

Suppose the Campbells had conveyed their house, but then refused to vacate for the new buyers. Under those circumstances the buyers could seek to *eject* the Campbells, getting a court order that required the sheriff to remove them from the premises. Or, suppose when the Campbells left (with or without the presence of the sheriff), they mistakenly left behind some of Mrs. Campbell's jewelry. Under those circumstances the Campbells could *replevy* the jewels: a successful action of *replevin* results in a court order requiring a sheriff or marshal return an item to its owner. In addition to these specialized remedies, U.S. courts have broad power to enter *injunctions* (court orders directed to parties) commanding them to do or stop doing any of a range of acts. Some of these orders can be

---

[*] Samuel R. Gross & Kent D. Syverud, *Don't Try: Civil Jury Verdicts in a System Geared to Settlement*, 44 UCLA L. Rev. 1, 37 (1996).

narrow and specific — stop dumping waste on plaintiff's property; others can be complex and subtle: establish a system of outpatient psychiatric assistance that meets the need of psychotic patients currently institutionalized. In the twentieth century many of the most interesting and controversial remedies have been specific: racial integration of schools and places of employment; changes in the operation of prisons, hospitals, and other institutions.

Given the existence of both substitutionary and specific remedies, a lawyer who is thinking about filing a lawsuit must consider which among the array of potential remedies is actually available in this case. To answer this, some historical background is needed.

2. An Excursus on Equity and Specific Relief

The English legal system, whose structure and suppositions the colonies inherited, had in the sixteenth and seventeenth centuries (when the founders of those colonies emigrated) not one or two but a group of court systems, each with a rather specialized jurisdiction. The most significant of these systems were the courts of common law and the Court of Chancery (sometimes referred to as a court of equity). For our purposes the important point is that each court administered different remedies. Courts of common law administered legal remedies; the Court of Chancery administered equitable remedies. To call a remedy "equitable" thus simply means that it would, historically, have been granted by the Court of Chancery rather than by one of the common law courts.

Injunctions are by far the most prevalent form of equitable relief. But the fact that injunctions are common should not blind you to their potentially dramatic effects. One of the consequences of a court's issuing an injunction is that it is prepared to enforce it if the party to whom it is directed does not comply. Injunctions are enforced by contempt proceedings. A party who is held in contempt of court for refusing to obey an injunction may be fined or put in jail until she obeys the order. That makes the injunction an extremely powerful weapon; one writer has compared it to a criminal statute drafted and enforced at the behest of a party to civil litigation.*

Although injunctions are the most frequently sought form of equitable relief, there are others that remain important. Suppose Collector asks Art Dealer to sell a painting and deliver the proceeds to Buyer; Dealer sells, but instead of delivering the money, buys another painting, which appreciates greatly in value because the artist and most of his other paintings perish in a fire. Collector may seek the declaration of a *constructive trust* over the newly valuable painting, preventing Dealer from profiting from his abuse of trust. A party to a contract may seek *rescission* of the contract or its *cancellation,* or may seek to have it *reformed* to comply with the true intent of the parties. In complex financial transactions in which it is impossible for the plaintiff to calculate his actual money damages, he may ask the

---

* Owen Fiss, The Civil Rights Injunction 7-37 (1978).

court to require an *accounting* of the defendant in order to determine what is owed. And an owner in possession of land may seek to *quiet title* to it or to *remove clouds from the title.*

This list of equitable remedies can easily — but wrongly — lead you to assume that all specific remedies are equitable. In fact, several legal remedies are specific rather than substitutionary. As already noted, an action in *replevin* to recover personal property is classified as legal, as is an action in *ejectment* to recover land wrongfully in the possession of another. The writ of *mandamus*, through which a court orders a lower court or a public official to perform an act required by law, is also officially categorized as legal. So is *habeas corpus* (a civil writ, though it has its most frequent use in criminal cases). The reason for the "legal" label in these cases is, again, simply historical: Courts of law (rather than Chancery, the court of equity) had jurisdiction to grant those forms of relief.

Unfortunately, the distinction between legal and equitable remedies was not founded on any neat concept. As the list in the preceding paragraph makes clear, it is not true, for example, that equity granted only specific remedies and common law only substitutionary remedies. Just as the courts of law administered several specific remedies, so Chancery sometimes ordered the payment of damages as part of its decrees, thus administering substitutionary remedies. By and large, however, Chancery issued orders directing defendants to act or refrain from acting — to perform the contract, stop dumping waste on the plaintiff's land, hand over the deed to Blackacre, render an accounting to the beneficiary of the trust, and the like. And, by and large (with the notable exceptions just listed), the common law awarded damages — to pay the plaintiff the amount promised, compensate him for injuries inflicted, and so on.

With law and equity operating as separate courts, the system required some rules of priority. Was the choice between legal and equitable remedies (and the two court systems that delivered those remedies) entirely up to the plaintiff? Could law and equity undo each other's decrees — equity granting injunctions against the enforcement of damage awards and law awarding damages to undo the effect of injunctions? In 1616 the problem rose to a fever pitch in what came to be known as the Coke-Ellesmere dispute (named after the judges involved rather than the litigants). In that case, King James I himself rendered a judgment that worked a truce between the two systems. If courts of equity and courts of law were to continue to coexist, one had to defer to the other. Equity did the deferring. The accepted maxim was that in order to be entitled to an equitable remedy, the plaintiff had to show that her legal remedy was "inadequate" — that some injustice would result if Chancery (equity's court) did not come to the rescue.

In Great Britain and in most judicial systems in the United States the two court systems have merged. Rule 1 accomplishes such a merger for the federal system. Merger makes things much easier for the litigant and lawyer in one respect: No longer need they worry which court system can grant relief. And no longer need the sovereign referee fights between the two systems. The question remains whether there is still a need for a remedial hierarchy — and whether one exists.

3. Is There a Remedial Hierarchy?

One frequently encounters statements suggesting that a hierarchy of remedies persists, that courts prefer legal to equitable remedies. Courts sometimes refer to the requirement that a plaintiff seeking an equitable remedy (usually an injunction) demonstrate that the legal remedy (usually damages) is inadequate. Other times courts will insist that the plaintiff demonstrate that the harm is "irreparable," meaning that money damages will not provide an adequate remedy. In such standard doctrinal formulations the plaintiff who prevails on the merits will receive the equitable remedy only if she demonstrates the irreparability of the harm or the inadequacy of the legal remedy, a showing amounting to the same thing.

Despite these statements, one writer has denied that, in practice, U.S. courts still insist that legal remedies be preferred to equitable ones:

> The . . . statement [that] damages [are] the rule and specific relief "a most extraordinary exception" . . . is not the law. It is not even close to the law. It is merely a spectacular example of the confusion created by one of our archaic "rules" for choosing among remedies. It states an extreme but recognizable version of the most general and most misleading of those rules — the irreparable injury rule. But it is wildly wrong as a description of what courts do.[*]

Others would disagree with the broad form of this statement, but even they acknowledge that courts are readier than they once were to grant injunctive relief and other forms of equitable remedies:

> The courts have altered their application of the inadequacy prerequisite without changing their terminology. More and more plaintiffs seek injunctions to protect statutory, common law, and constitutional entitlements to less and less palpable interests. Commentators note that litigants raise the inadequacy prerequisite less frequently and that contemporary judges grant more injunctions than their predecessors. The inadequacy prerequisite has been eroded, operating today in a less formidable, more limited fashion.[**]

Neither statement should be understood to mean that all plaintiffs who win on the merits and want injunctions get them. Courts regularly deny injunctions for a variety of reasons. Sometimes they describe those reasons by asserting that the legal remedy is adequate or that the plaintiff's harm is not irreparable. A classic example is the proposition that a court will not enjoin a libelous publication. Is that because the legal remedy, damages, is truly adequate? Or because the injunction will be too effective, interfering with other values (free speech and press) that we think valuable as well? A similar reason for denying injunctive relief is that the injunction will work too great a hardship on the defendant. The next case considers and rejects such an argument.

---

[*] Douglas Laycock, The Death of the Irreparable Injury Rule, 103 Harv. L. Rev. 688 (1990).
[**] Doug Rendleman, The Inadequate Remedy at Law Prerequisite for an Injunction, 33 U. Fla. L. Rev. 346, 347 (1981).

Sigma Chemical Co. v. Harris

605 F. Supp. 1253 (E.D. Mo. 1985)

NANGLE, C.J.

This case was tried to this Court sitting without a jury. This Court . . . hereby makes the following findings of fact and conclusions of law as required by Rule 52 of the Federal Rules of Civil Procedure.

A.   Findings of Fact

1. Sigma Chemical Company . . . is a Missouri corporation . . . selling 16,000 esoteric or fine chemicals used in research, production and analysis in laboratories, universities and hospitals. . . . Of these 16,000 chemicals, 10,000 are purchased from supplies in the United States and all over the world. . . . Purchases are made from 2,300 suppliers, many of whom are small "mom and pop" operations. The heart of Sigma's business is matching the right supplier with the product sold by Sigma. Although Sigma's suppliers send out catalogues and advertisements to many buyers, including Sigma's competitors, and although the chemicals and their names are in the public domain, Sigma's knowledge of which supplier sells a particular chemical of a certain quality that satisfies a particular purpose at the right price is not in the public domain. . . .

[Foster Harris, the defendant, went to work for Sigma in 1979, after signing an agreement that he would not work for a competitor for two years after leaving Sigma and even after that period would not disclose any confidential information acquired from Sigma.]

19. After becoming dissatisfied with Sigma, Harris started sending out resumes to pharmaceutical companies . . . [including] ICN . . . one of Sigma's five major competitors. . . .

20. Harris accepted a job with ICN as a purchasing agent and began employment on November 29, 1983. Prior to leaving Sigma, Harris lied about the identity of his future employer. . . .

[Harris used information acquired during his employment at Sigma, suggesting to ICN new sources of various chemicals. He also violated the terms of a temporary restraining order by continuing to do work for ICN after being ordered to stop.]

B.   Conclusions of Law

This Court has subject matter jurisdiction because the parties are of diverse citizenship and the amount in controversy exceeds [the statutory minimum]. . . .

1.   Validity of Restrictive Covenant

The benchmark in determining the validity of a restrictive covenant is whether it is reasonable. . . . Reasonableness has three components: 1) the covenant must be reasonably necessary to protect the employer's legitimate interest; 2) the covenant must be reasonable in terms of temporal scope; and 3) the covenant must be reasonable in terms of geographic scope. . . . [After a detailed analysis the court concluded that the covenant Harris signed was valid and enforceable.]

2.   Propriety of Permanent Injunctive Relief

The principles which guide this court in determining whether permanent injunctive relief is appropriate in this case are well known. "[T]he determination whether to issue an injunction involves a balancing of the interests of the parties who might be affected by the Court's decision — the hardship on plaintiff if relief is denied as opposed to the hardship to defendant if it is granted. . . ." 11 C. Wright & A. Miller, Federal Practice and Procedure: Civil §2942 at 366-67 (1973). Moreover, "the main prerequisite to obtaining injunctive relief is a finding that plaintiff is being threatened by some injury for which he has no adequate legal remedy." Id. at 368-69. In the opinion of this Court, Sigma is entitled to permanent injunctive relief in this case.

First, it is clear that Harris is violating or would violate the restrictive covenant in his employment contract by working for ICN as a purchasing agent. Given Harris' responsibilities and activities at ICN. . . . Harris is contributing his knowledge to a service or product which is competitive with and similar to a service or product on which Harris worked at Sigma. In addition, Harris is in a position where it is very likely that he will, directly or indirectly, use or disclose trade secret information that Harris learned from Sigma's product files. Under these circumstances, there is a strong threat of irreparable injury to Sigma. Plaintiff stands to lose part of a competitive edge that has taken over forty years to develop. The threat that Harris poses to Sigma is particularly great in view of defendant's own testimony that he had memorized some information through daily use and that he was the "best source person" at Sigma. . . .

On the other hand, the harm that would occur to Harris if a permanent injunction were granted is not insubstantial. By the terms of the restrictive covenant Harris will be prevented from working for ICN until November 22, 1985. In addition, Harris may be barred from utilizing his knowledge of Sigma's sources in the fine chemical business, so long as Sigma's trade secret information remains secret. . . . The potential harm to Harris is . . . diminished by the fact that other Sigma former employees have not had difficulty obtaining other employment [with employers that did] not compete with Sigma. Further, the balance of the equities do not favor Harris because he was aware of the restrictions imposed on him by his contract with Sigma and he took a voluntary, knowing and calculated risk by deciding to violate that contract.

On balance, it is the opinion of this Court that the threat of harm to Sigma if an injunction were not granted greatly outweighs the threat of harm to Harris if an injunction were granted. Accordingly, Sigma is entitled to permanent injunctive relief. . . .

IT IS HEREBY ORDERED, ADJUDGED AND DECREED that defendant be and is hereby restrained and enjoined from: 1) rendering services directly or indirectly to or for ICN Pharmaceuticals, Inc., as a purchasing agent involved in the purchase of, or the selection of sources of supply for, chemicals which are also sold by Sigma, until November 22, 1985, or further Order of this Court, whichever first occurs; and 2) using or disclosing any trade secret or other confidential information that is the property of plaintiff which defendant acquired by reason of his employment with plaintiff.

NOTES AND PROBLEMS

1. One might cite *Sigma Chemical* as an example both for those who think that the irreparable injury rule has disappeared and for those who think it persists.

a. Those who think it persists could point to the fact that the court refers to the rule at one point.

b. Those who think it has disappeared could point to the sparse analysis of the reasons Sigma's legal remedy was inadequate. In *Sigma*, as in many inadequacy-of-remedy cases, the court reaches a conclusion without truly analyzing the alternative legal remedies, which here would be damages. Consider what such an analysis might have looked like:

> The damage remedy in this case would have consisted of the profits Sigma lost as a result of ICN's acquiring its trade secrets about suppliers. Two circumstances make this remedy unsuitable. First, it would be horrendously difficult to calculate just how much business ICN took away from its competitor as a result of Harris's actions. Second, even if that calculation could be made, defendant Harris would be extremely unlikely to have the money to pay such damages. In ruling that the legal remedy is inadequate, this court concludes that awarding damages would be a nuisance, and probably a futile nuisance at that. We prefer the equitable remedy because it's simpler and it will work.

Does this imaginary analysis make some sense out of the "inadequacy" requirement?

2. In discussing the propriety of issuing an injunction, the court mentions two factors: the inadequacy of the legal remedy and the balance of hardships to the two parties.

a. What is the relationship between these two factors? If the denial of an injunction works crushing hardship to the plaintiff, that presumably demonstrates the inadequacy of the legal remedy. But if the legal remedy is inadequate, why does it matter whether the defendant will be disadvantaged by the issuance of the injunction? Remedies always inflict hardship on defendants, and courts generally don't stop ordering them on that account alone. For the hardship standard to make sense, it has to mean that the court might choose the legal remedy if the equitable remedy is too adequate. Is the idea behind the phrase "equitable discretion" beginning to take shape?

b. Assuming hardship does matter, how much would there have to be to change the decision in *Sigma*?

c. Notice the terms of the injunction: How has the court arguably taken Harris's hardship into account?

3. On appeal the injunction was modified. Harris could work for ICN, but not as a purchasing agent. Moreover, the case was remanded so the district court could modify the injunction so that it forbade the disclosure of proprietary information only for so long as it would "take a 'legitimate competitor' to independently reproduce the information contained in the product and vendor files." Sigma was unsuccessful in its argument on cross-appeal, contending that Harris should not have been allowed to work for ICN in any capacity. Sigma Chemicals v. Harris, 794 F.2d 371 (8th Cir. 1986). Imagine that you are Sigma Chemical's lawyer, arguing for an en banc rehearing in the 8th Circuit — a procedure in which the case is reargued before all or most of the Circuit's judges (instead of the usual three-judge panel). Argue that the appellate panel's modification of the injunction makes it ineffective and unenforceable.

4. Notice who decided this case in the trial court: the judge. Historically, cases in equity were decided not by a jury but by the judge (the chancellor and various assistant judges). Even after merger that tradition persists; as you will see in Chapter IX, cases seeking solely equitable relief (like the injunction in *Sigma Chemical*) are tried to judges. The choice of a remedy can therefore determine not only what relief the plaintiff will get but also what trier will decide on whether he gets any relief.

D.   Declaratory Relief

Occasionally a party has a legal problem that neither damages nor a specific remedy can solve. Imagine, for example, that Alice, whose signature appears on a promissory note due in five years, denies the note's validity. How is Sam, holding the note, to determine whether he has a valuable asset or a worthless piece of paper? He cannot sue for damages until the note is due, and there is no claim for injunctive relief on the facts stated. Meanwhile, however, witnesses' recollections are fading and Sam, who wants to raise money for a small business, cannot with certainty list the note as an asset. Or suppose a theater owner wants to show a film declared obscene by the local prosecutor, who has threatened to prosecute anyone who exhibits the film. Thinking that the film is not obscene, the owner wishes to show it. He wants to abide by the law, however, and doesn't want to risk a jail sentence as the price of guessing wrong about the law of obscenity.

Under the federal Declaratory Judgment Act, 28 U.S.C. §§2201 and 2202, and similar legislation in almost every state, parties in such circumstances may seek a declaration of their rights without any coercive relief such as damages or an injunction. The procedure for *declaratory judgment* in the federal courts is governed by Rule 57.

Who actually uses declaratory judgments? "Declaratory judgments are probably sought most often in insurance and patent litigation, but they are available and used in all types of civil litigation" with two exceptions: state and federal taxes. Wright, Federal Courts 715. Declaratory judgment actions are also used for testing the constitutionality of legislation, though the Supreme Court has demonstrated some reluctance to adjudicate public issues without the factual record that often accompanies suits for coercive relief.

One controversy about declaratory judgments concerns the line between a hypothetical case and a concrete factual controversy. In the federal courts, Article III of the Constitution is viewed as limiting the availability of declaratory judgments to actual cases or controversies; hypothetical questions may not be answered by the courts. "Necessarily the difference between an abstract question and an actual controversy is one of degree, and where there is a substantial dispute touching some real and proximate interest of the party, the fact that he has taken action in order to provoke a test case does not make the case inappropriate for a declaratory judgment." Wright, Federal Courts 714.

Unlike equitable relief, which is available only in the absence of adequate legal remedies, declaratory relief may be chosen by a party even though other avenues are open to her. See Rule 57.

Declaratory relief can raise jurisdictional problems, some of which flow from the interaction of the well-pleaded complaint rule (exemplified in Louisville & Nashville RR v. Mottley, supra page 182) and the requirements of federal question jurisdiction. The basic problem is that an action for declaratory relief does not fit comfortably inside the idea of the well pleaded complaint rule. As a result, the decisions do not line up very clearly. The courts have said that a party who would assert a federal defense in an action for coercive relief cannot create federal jurisdiction by asserting that defense as a claim for declaratory relief. But the courts have also suggested that if either party could state a claim for coercive relief that would arise under federal jurisdiction, then an action for a declaratory judgment will "arise under" federal law; it is safe to say that not much more is clear, and that when you study federal jurisdiction in an advanced course you will better understand how vexed the question is.

What about nonjurisdictional issues? If P sues D for breach of contract, P bears the burden of producing evidence and the burden of persuasion. But if D sues P for a declaration that D has not violated the contract in question, who should bear these burdens? The case law is again muddled on the subject. And if D sues P for a declaration that D has not breached a contract on which P might have sued either for damages or for specific performance, is either entitled to a jury trial? See Chapter IX. And finally, what happens if P sues D for a declaration of nonliability on an insurance contract and loses, but D does not counterclaim for damages under the contract? Is D forever barred under Rule 13(a) from collecting the money to which the court's judgment implies he is entitled? As a practical matter, must the defendant in a declaratory judgment action always counterclaim in a jurisdiction with a compulsory counterclaim statute?

NOTES AND PROBLEMS

1. Arthur, a citizen of Georgia, agrees that he will build an expensive house for Barbara, a citizen of Florida, using "only top-quality materials." As construction proceeds, Barbara regularly complains that Arthur is skimping on the quality of

the materials. Arthur brings an action for declaratory relief in federal court, invoking diversity jurisdiction. Barbara challenges the claim, arguing that there is no case or controversy because she hasn't sued Arthur for breach. What decision?

2. Sam, from Texas, sues Joe, from California, in federal court, seeking a declaration that Joe's new modem design infringes Sam's similar patented device, which account for $1 million in annual sales. Joe challenges diversity jurisdiction, on the grounds that Sam's complaint does not satisfy the amount in controversy requirement because he seeks no monetary damages. What ruling?

3. Newspaper, about to publish an expose of corruption in the mayor's office, has concerns about a libel suit. It believes that its statements are true, and, beyond that, that the "public official" principles of First Amendment doctrine will protect it because none of the statements are recklessly false. Newspaper files an action for declaratory relief, invoking federal question jurisdiction and seeking a declaration that its statements are protected by the First Amendment. What outcome?

E. Financing Litigation

Lawsuits cost money. Civil lawsuits transfer money (or control over resources) between the parties. To understand litigation, one therefore has to understand who is paying for it, how that payment is made, and how the resulting financing affects both sides' strategic decisions.

Some of the expenses — the courtroom, the judge, clerical staff, and bailiffs — are borne by society generally, paid for by taxes. This public subsidy is not trivial; in the early 1990s one state estimated that each "judge-day" of civil litigation cost about $4,000. Cal. Code Civ. Proc. §1775(f) (West 2002). Other expenses are paid by the parties. Some take the form of fees paid directly either to a court or to nonlawyers who perform some service (e.g., expert witnesses, private investigators, court reporters). But attorneys' fees account for most of the cost of litigation in the United States; those fees are often substantial. Relatively high legal fees result in part from the design of the U.S. legal system, which assigns to parties (and their lawyers) responsibility for conducting the suit: Virtually every other step of the lawsuit occurs because the lawyer on one side or the other takes some initiative. In other societies a judge or similar official paid by the state assumes some of these responsibilities, resulting in lower legal fees and higher taxes.

Legal fees shape contemporary litigation. Any fee system in which the parties bear any costs of litigation will cause cases to be brought, abandoned, or settled on bases other than their legal and factual merits. Financing systems will affect not only how many suits are brought but also which ones; for example, the availability of punitive damages in a particular case category, combined with contingent fees, will, all other things being equal, move legal resources toward such cases. Conversely, limitations on damage awards, such as those enunciated in State Farm v. Campbell, supra page 270, will move resources away from such cases. Understanding civil litigation therefore requires comprehending the incentives and barriers to litigation posed by the way in which lawyers are paid. That understanding is particularly important because the fee system is changing in ways that affect those incentives. In thinking about fee systems, consider three sorts of incentives: those for the client (when will a prospective litigant be encouraged or discouraged?); those for the lawyer (how will the fee system affect the lawyer's work on the case once it is under way?); and those for the opposing party, who will know or can make educated guesses about financing mechanisms (how will those guesses about financing affect opposition strategy?).

1.   The "American" Rule

Who pays for lawyers' work? Essentially there are four candidates: the client, the opposing party, society generally (via subsidies), and the lawyer herself (because she does the work for free). Each of these accounts for a portion of U.S. civil litigation.

The system in which each party pays its own legal fees has come to be known as the *American Rule*. It is so called to distinguish it from the *English Rule*, under which (in its purest form) the losing party pays both its own fees and those of the other side. In practice, to an increasing extent someone other than the client pays U.S. legal fees, and in Great Britain less than the full amount of actual fees is generally taxed to the other side. Thus these two "rules" do not accurately describe present practice in either country; they are, however, useful as models with which to explore the subject.

The English Rule in its pure form fully compensates the winner: She gets both the damages (or other remedy) and the costs of litigation. By contrast, under the pure American Rule, a winning litigant has to subtract from any damages the amount charged by his lawyer, and is to that extent made less than whole. Defenders of the American Rule point out that it permits litigants, typically plaintiffs, with tenable but less-than-certain cases to invoke the legal system without fear of having to bear the expense both of their own and the opposition's attorney. That incentive may be particularly important in a political system in which the courts play a significant role (as they do not in Britain) in protecting the constitutional rights of unpopular groups. One might not wish to burden an unsuccessful effort to protect a constitutional right with the legal fees of the victor. Let us begin to explore the structure of fee arrangements with a common situation — the client who agrees to pay the lawyer's fee. Often, but not always, agreements take the form of a written contract between lawyer and client, sometimes called "a retainer letter" (from the still-occasional practice of requiring a deposit — a retainer — from a client). In some states such written agreements are required in some categories of cases. One common form of agreement calls for the client to pay the lawyer at a specified hourly rate for legal services, plus various costs — photocopying, telephone calls, and the like.

The hourly fee is probably the single most common financing mechanism for U.S. litigation. In the United States hourly fees range from fifty to hundreds of dollars per hour; one study done at the end of the twentieth century found that the median hourly rate for legal fees was about $100 per hour; this average masks wide variations, with senior lawyers in large urban practices charging more than $400 per hour and rural solo practitioners charging as little as $75 per hour. Most contract and commercial litigation, which, as you may recall, accounts for the majority of civil filings, is financed this way.

Flat rates mean a lawyer charges a set amount for a particular kind of work: an uncontested divorce, a will, a stock offering, and so on. Some lawyers use such a system or use it in combination with other kinds of compensation. It has the obvious advantage of a predictable, guaranteed fee. Its disadvantages are equally clear. Underestimates are possible: What begins as an uncomplicated conveyance can turn into a nightmare of legal research into the Rule against Perpetuities. Yet if the lawyer tries to allow for such contingencies, she risks charging more than the matter warrants. As a consequence, flat rates are most often used for kinds of work that the lawyer thinks will have predictable investments of time: Wills are probably the most common example. Because of its unpredictability, most lawyers will not handle contested litigation on a flat-rate basis, but some insurance defense firms who do high volumes of work have entered into per-case agreements with insurance carriers.

NOTES AND PROBLEMS

1. What incentives does the American Rule create for litigants?

a. Andy has a claim for $1,000 arising out of a dispute with a merchant. A competent lawyer estimates that handling the claim in even the most economical way will take 20 hours. What will Andy do?

b. Irma's Grocery is a small family business that does not carry liability insurance. One day Irma receives a summons and complaint from a customer who alleges injuries from a slip and fall. Irma remembers the episode and strongly doubts the customer was injured at all, much less seriously. But when she consults a lawyer she learns that it will cost perhaps $7,000 to defend the claim. The plaintiff's lawyer tells Irma his client is willing to settle for $1,500. What will Irma do?

2. How does one defend a legal system in which some meritorious claims and defenses are simply too expensive to vindicate?

3. Nor are matters simple even if one posits a claim that is economical to bring or defend. Assume that the client hires a lawyer, engaging her on an hourly fee basis. Consider the incentives that such a payment system creates for the lawyer. Some argue that such a payment scheme encourages the lawyer to invest unneeded hours in the case because each hour can be billed. Such undesirable incentives may not operate if the lawyer has other work on her desk; nevertheless, fear of such incentives can cause clients to spend time and money monitoring legal fees to try to detect unnecessary expenditure.

4. Given the American Rule, legal rules that increase the amount of damages potentially available will increase the availability of lawyers to take a claim. For example, if a fraud claim can be added to a breach of contract action, the availability of punitive damages may make it economical to bring a claim that would

otherwise be irrational to pursue. By the same token, the potential for such "super-damages" may enable a plaintiff to pursue a claim marginal on the merits.

5. The American Rule has at least one chink in its armor. Read Rule 54 and 28 U.S.C. §1920. Most states have similar provisions.

a. Explain how they temper the American Rule; what expenses do they routinely shift to the losing side of a lawsuit?

b. Imagine a fairly typical civil case arising out of an auto accident, which, atypically (because most cases settle), leads to a four-day trial. In that trial, again typically, both sides called three ordinary (non-expert) witnesses, who each incurred travel expenses of $50 each. Both parties also employed two expert witnesses — an engineer on the causation of the accident, a physician on the extent of permanent physical damages — both sides offered in evidence attested photocopies of various medical and employment records, both sides ordered "daily" transcripts of the preceding day's trial to use overnight in preparation for the next day, and both sides paid filing and docket fees to the clerk's office for various papers. And, of course, each side incurred substantial attorneys' fees. Which of these expenses will be taxable to the losing party under Rule 54?

c. Now read Rule 68. How does it change the costs payable under Rule 54? Suppose that, six months after suit is filed, the plaintiff has incurred $500 in costs that would be taxable under Rule 54 if he won the lawsuit. Defendant makes an offer, complying with the requirements of Rule 68, to settle the suit for $10,000; plaintiff rejects the offer. In the ensuing six months, which include the trial, the plaintiff incurs another $500 in taxable costs. At trial, plaintiff wins, recovering a verdict for $8,000. How much in costs will plaintiff recover under Rule 54?

d. In the preceding example, suppose that plaintiff recovered a verdict for $30,000. How much in costs would he recover?

e. In any of the preceding scenarios, will attorneys' fees be awarded as a part of costs?

2.   Insurance and the Contingent Fee

Thus far, the discussion has assumed that the client will pay legal fees directly out of current assets. Often, however, that will not be the case. Consider an everyday occurrence — an automobile accident in which Driver A sues Driver B for injuries and property damage. In that most common source of litigation in the United States it is unlikely that either side will pay its legal expenses directly. Both plaintiff and defendant will probably have their fees paid through schemes that spread the costs among other similarly situated persons.

Take first the defendant. If he has liability insurance (required in some states and by all auto-finance lenders), the insurance company will provide the defense as part of the policy benefits. Large numbers of vehicle owners have thus purchased a form of legal insurance. Homeowners' and tenants' insurance policies typically contain similar provisions for claims arising from household accidents, thereby creating a widespread form of legal insurance for potential defendants.

NOTES AND PROBLEMS

1. Consider how the existence of insurance affects litigation.

a. You are involved in a vehicle collision in which you sustain substantial uninsured personal injuries and property damage (you carry liability but no collision coverage on your car). You believe it's the other driver's fault, but she declines to pay for your damage. What determines whether you will sue?

b. Same scenario, but the other driver is insured for the minimum amount ($10,000 in your state). You consult a lawyer, who concludes that, given contested responsibility for the accident and for the extent of your injuries, it will require at least $8,000 in expert witness fees to bring the case. What likely result?

2. Most liability policies that undertake to pay eventual damage claims also promise to undertake the insured's legal defense and require that the insurer's lawyers conduct the lawsuit. Almost all such policies also give the insurer the power to settle a claim within policy limits without the insured's consent (some medical malpractice insurers require the insured's consent).

a. Why would an insurance company be reluctant to issue such a policy without a provision giving it control over employing the lawyer?

b. Why do you suppose the insurers also want to control settlement? Are policies without such settlement power — such as some medical malpractice policies — likely to be more or less expensive than policies with such a clause?

c. For some categories of liability insurance, insurers write policies to provide that both legal fees and the amount of the judgment or settlement are subject to the policy limits — this is, for example, a common term in legal malpractice insurance. Under such a policy, $1 million in coverage would support a $200,000 defense and an $800,000 settlement but would not cover all of a $100,000 defense and a $1 million judgment.

3. In addition to such legal insurance included within liability policies, one finds a small number of "pure" legal insurance policies. Such policies typically provide for a limited amount of prepaid office or telephone consultation and a few standard services at a flat rate. Almost none of them will cover the expenses of any form of litigation. Why not?

What about the plaintiff in the automobile accident scenario? Her automobile liability policy will provide a *defense* against any counterclaim the other driver may bring, but it will not finance her claim as a plaintiff. A uniquely American fee arrangement — the contingent fee — may, however, perform a similar function. In the contingent fee system, the lawyer typically agrees to provide legal representation, with the fee to be paid from the proceeds of any settlement or recovery. A standard contingent fee arrangement might provide that the lawyer will receive 20 percent of a settlement reached before filing suit, 25 percent if suit is filed but no further steps taken, 33 percent if the case goes to trial, and perhaps 50 percent if the case goes to appeal. In return for these hefty chunks taken from the plaintiff's recovery, the lawyer agrees to forgo a fee entirely if there is no recovery: The plaintiff thus eliminates the risk of paying legal fees in a losing cause. For the client with limited funds the idea is often inviting — he pays only if he recovers something. No recovery means no fee.

Most individual plaintiffs seeking damages for personal injuries enter into contingent fee arrangements, even when their finances would permit them to hire a lawyer on an hourly basis.

People sometimes praise or malign the contingent fee system without understanding it. To do so one must consider several perspectives: that of the individual client, the lawyer's other clients, and the lawyer. The client gains the assurance that he will not suffer out-of-pocket expenses for lawyer's fees, which may make the client more willing to bring a case where recovery is doubtful: He risks no loss and he may gain. Some have criticized and others have praised the system for this characteristic. This assurance (of a risk-free lawsuit) comes at a cost that becomes apparent if one considers the position of the lawyer and the lawyer's other clients. The lawyer, to be sure, does not charge the plaintiff any fees if the case is lost, but the lawyer has incurred expenses on the case — if only such overhead items as rent and secretarial services. Those expenses must be paid, and the only source of payment is the fees generated by clients who have recovered or settled. In setting fees, the lawyer must take the probability of success into account; fees from successful cases must cover the expenses incurred in unsuccessful cases. To that extent *contingent fees cause the successful clients to bear part of the costs attributable to the unsuccessful clients.* To describe it thus is not to condemn the arrangement; the winners are only going to pay legal fees if in fact they recover something, and the guarantee of no fee if they lose may be an assurance for which they would willingly pay the higher fee if they win. Indeed, the prevalence of such arrangements may suggest that all concerned find them satisfactory. An elaborate study of contingent fee lawyers found that their "effective hourly rate" (their mean hourly earnings including both winning and losing cases) was just a few dollars more than their counterparts in the insurance-retained defense bar. Herbert M. Kritzer, The Wages of Risk: The Returns of Contingency Fee Legal Practice, 47 De Paul L. Rev. 267 (1998).

NOTES AND PROBLEMS

1. One can think of the contingent fee in several ways. For medieval and early modern lawyers it was an antisocial charge that stirred up dissension and disserved society. This view, still prevalent in most of the world today, makes a contingent fee a form of criminal activity.

2. Alternatively, one can see the contingent fee as a form of insurance. The client buys insurance against losing the case; the "premium" is her agreement that if she wins she'll pay a share of her winnings to the lawyer. Just as all drivers who insure with a given insurance company share risks with their fellow-insureds, each contingent fee client pools his risk with that of the other clients of the same lawyer. So long as the lawyer is a good estimator of risks (or has a sufficiently large inventory of cases), the winners and the losers will balance out.

3. One can also think of the contingent fee as a credit system in which the client borrows from the lawyer and repays him only when (and if) there is a recovery.

a. Because repayment is contingent on success, the rate of interest is considerably higher than it would be if the money were borrowed directly.

b. Theoretically, a meritorious claim could serve as collateral for an ordinary bank loan. In practice, a banker would have apoplexy if a client walked into a bank and announced, "I have a perfectly splendid little lawsuit, and I'd like you to lend me some money to pursue it."

In fact, that does happen, only it happens indirectly. One reason for the banker's hypothesized reaction is that bankers are not very expert in assessing the merits of legal claims. Lawyers, however, are, and it therefore makes sense for the lawyer to assess the claim. But the lawyer will typically need to pay the rent and support her family while the suit is in progress; to get this working capital she is quite likely to seek a line of credit from a bank. When the bank lends in such a situation, it is indirectly lending against the expected proceeds, not from a single lawsuit, but from the lawyer's whole inventory of claims. As one banker who writes loans to lawyers put it:

> One thing we do is to look at a firm's collateral base — its receivables, its inventory, how much it makes. . . . With a plaintiffs' firm, there is no asset base. What they offer is an income stream of several types of cases that will come in over time. So you research their reputation in the marketplace, the size of the organization, the number of cases coming in. . . .
>
> If a lawyer tells you, "I'm going to invest $1 million in this case and it's the only one I have, and I'm sure I'll get paid on June 30," we know that's not how it always works. We are more inclined to lend money to someone who says, "I have seven cases and a business plan that includes a worst-case scenario of what may happen to them."

Michael Grinfeld, Justice on Loan, 19 Calif. Lawyer 39, 40 (1999).

4. A fourth way of thinking about the contingent fee is as a partnership entered into by the lawyer and the client. Each brings something to the partnership: The client has a potentially valuable asset; the lawyer has human capital in the form of her education and experience. They agree ahead of time to divide the proceeds of this mutual investment in a particular way. If there are no proceeds, the two "partners" go their separate ways, sadder but wiser. (Note that this theoretical model of the contingent fee is sometimes illegal: Some rules of professional ethics make it unlawful for a lawyer to practice law in partnership with a nonlawyer. In recent years some have proposed substantial changes to these rules, to allow lawyers to share practices with other disciplines in a collaboration called "multi-disciplinary practice.")

5. An alternative to the contingent fee would be the purchase and assignment of legal claims. In theory, a client might go to a lawyer and describe the claim, whereupon the lawyer would buy it outright, paying client immediate cash; the lawyer would then prosecute the case in his own name. Such a system would work only if it were possible for the client to sell ("assign") claims to the lawyer. With a limited set of exceptions, such purchases are illegal (and have been since the Middle Ages, when they were known as "champerty"). But some interesting recent exceptions to the champerty laws have appeared.

a. Several enterprises will "buy" part of a damage judgment on appeal. According to a press account, it works like this: After a plaintiff has won a damage judgment but while the case is on appeal, the law firm examines the record and briefs and then offers to "invest" in the judgment. For example, one such lender paid $200,000 for a $400,000 share of a $1.5 million compensatory damage award. Large Verdicts for Sale, Nat'l L.J., Jan. 11, 1999, at 1. As in a contingency fee contract, if the damage judgment is reversed on appeal, the lender gets nothing; if the judgment is affirmed and paid, at least to the tune of $400,000, the lender gets that amount. The advantage for the plaintiff is that the immediate proceeds may enable him to wait out a protracted appeals process rather than settling for a smaller amount.

b. At least a few entrepreneurs are prepared to go further, lending directly to finance the early phases of the suit. According to one report, what one might call a venture capital firm for lawsuits advances money to plaintiffs and their lawyers based on the firm's assessment of the strength of the case:

> The . . . cases are generally funded by RSC in exchange for an equity position in the case. RSC evaluates proposed expenses for a large case and undergoes weeks of intensive due diligence to determine the extent to which the plaintiff has a sufficiently strong position to warrant RSC's involvement. Following the due diligence process, RSC will either advance or deny funds.[*]

An interview with Perry Walton, the entrepreneur behind this firm, indicates that the lender wishes at all costs to avoid plaintiffs who are litigating "on principle" rather than to maximize their eventual recovery. Richard B. Schmidt, Staking Claims, Wall St. J., Sept. 15, 2000 at A1.

Consider the contingent fee from the lawyer's perspective as she evaluates a prospective client. Ideally, she would like to minimize the number of unsuccessful clients; unlike the hourly-fee lawyer, each such client costs her money. She may screen her cases differently from the hourly-fee lawyer and seek to eliminate those in which a recovery is unlikely or damages are likely to be low or uncollectible. Does the effect of this screening offset the greater incentives of contingent fee clients to sue? The question would be very hard to answer with any assurance; at this point it is important for the student to see that this fee system involves complex and offsetting incentives.

Another of those incentives may affect the lawyer's behavior once she takes the contingent fee case. All lawyers owe their clients the duties of loyalty and competence; financial self-interest sometimes creates a tension with these ethical obligations. We have already seen that the hourly-fee lawyer may have some incentive to spend too much time on the case. At first glance, one might think that the contingent fee would correct this tendency by linking the lawyer's fee to the client's recovery. Recall, however, that the lawyer's economic interest lies not in the maximum absolute fee, but in the maximum profit after subtracting the cost of time and overhead, and, if she has a desk full of work, at the maximum fee per hour of her time.

[*] Web page http://www.franchisegator.com/cgi-bin/profile.php?key=12&f_type=5 (Site visited June 24, 2003).

NOTES AND PROBLEMS

1. The contingent fee lawyer can approach cases in two rather different ways: a large inventory of cases with varying merit or a small inventory of carefully screened cases. Either approach may yield a steady income for the lawyer, but the two approaches will have different consequences for the client and different ethical challenges for the lawyer.

a. The low-volume, high-screening approach would be to accept only those cases in which the chances of recovery seem high. At its most extreme, this approach involves taking only those cases in which liability is clear and in which damages are the only issue. Such a lawyer will devote substantial time to each case, knowing he has a high probability of success. Correspondingly, he will refuse many unpromising cases.

b. The high-volume, low-screening approach would be to accept almost all cases in which there is any prospect of a money recovery. The lawyer will then devote modest amounts of time to each case, hoping that a sufficient percentage of the cases will yield a sufficient recovery to result in an acceptable hourly rate of compensation.

c. If we think of the lawyer as an "investor" in cases, both methods are defensible. The first relies on "stock-picking," with the lawyer hoping that careful research will identify winners in which he will then invest his time heavily. The second relies on "indexing," with the lawyer hoping that small amounts invested in a broad "portfolio" will yield good results on average — with diversification offering some protection against bad picks.

2. Even if both approaches are defensible from the lawyer's standpoint, they have different consequences for the client and bring with them corresponding ethical issues.

a. Consider first the ethical challenges to the lawyer who does substantial screening of his cases. Some have criticized contingent fees under such circumstances on the ground that the fee is really not contingent. If the lawyer has carefully screened his clients, there is a high probability of recovery in each case. Such lawyers, the argument continues, cannot justify the increased-percentage fee for successive stages of litigation.

One proposal to deal with this criticism is to allow defendants to make offers to settle at an early stage of the litigation. If the plaintiff accepted the offer, the lawyer would be entitled only to fees for the hours worked plus a small percentage of the settlement (10 percent or less). If the offer was refused, the lawyer would be entitled to a contingent fee *only if the amount recovered was greater than the original offer*. Lester Brickman, Michael Horowitz, and Jeffrey O'Connell, Rethinking Contingency Fees (Manhattan Institute 1994). No jurisdiction has thus far adopted this proposal: Should it be adopted?

b. Now consider the challenges confronting the lawyer who does minimal screening. A lawyer has agreed to take a case on a sliding scale: 25 percent if it settled before the complaint is filed or 33 percent for any settlement short of trial itself. After three hours of work — interviewing the client and ascertaining some basic facts — the lawyer calls the prospective defendant, who makes a settlement offer of $10,000. If the client accepted that settlement, the lawyer's share would be $2,500, or more than $800 per hour for the lawyer's time. Client asks what the lawyer expects from the case. Lawyer believes that with about 300 hours of work, the case will settle on the courthouse steps for about $100,000. The lawyer's share of that recovery will be $33,000, a per hour return of $110. Which scenario is more profitable for lawyer if she has other, equally profitable cases on her desk? Recall that the lawyer owes her client the duties of loyalty and competence.

3. Client comes to you with a story involving a serious injury for which it appears a solvent prospective defendant is responsible. You do almost all such representation on a contingent fee basis. Client asks you if you would represent him at an hourly rate instead and also asks you to explain what difference it might make. What should you tell him? Should you explain that it might be to his financial advantage to hire you on an hourly basis? Cf. N.J. Gen. Ct. R. 1-21-7(b) (West 2003) (requiring that lawyer raise possible hourly-rate alternatives to prospective contingent fee client).

4. One form of the sliding contingent fee scale — in which the fee increases as later stages of litigation are reached — is described supra. Some states have by statute enacted a different form of contingency arrangement in which the lawyer is entitled to a *decreasing* percentage of the recovery or settlement as the absolute amount increases — for example, 33-1/3 percent of damages up to $500,000, 30 percent on the next $500,000, 25 percent on the next, 20 percent on the next, and a fee set by the court on any recovery above $2,000,000. See N.J. Gen. Ct. R. 1:21-7(c) (West 2003); Cal. Bus. & Prof. Code §6146 (Deering 2003) (applying only to medical malpractice actions). What would be the justification for such statutes?

3.   Public Subsidies and Professional Charity

Insurance will help only those who have it. Contingent fee systems will help only those who seek to recover money damages (and enough money damages to justify the lawyer's investment of time). That leaves substantial numbers of people who could benefit from legal counsel but who have no means to pay for it. But how substantial? Much depends on how the question is asked. Some would ask how many people would benefit — in the sense of improving their present position — from legal advice or representation but do not think they can spare the money for such assistance. Others would ask how many people handed say, $2,000 (about 20 hours of lawyer's time at about the national median rate), would choose to spend it on legal fees. The response to the first question yields a picture of widespread unmet legal need; the response to the second suggests that the demand is much lower. Much debate occurs over which form of the question is the appropriate one.

However great the need, it's concentrated in pockets. Contingent fee arrangements "cover" people with meritorious claims for significant amounts — providing a market-based form of legal insurance for plaintiffs. In a market society, people with no insurance and no assets have a grim form of protection against lawsuits: Almost no one intentionally sues a judgment-proof defendant for damages. That leaves two good-sized groups without access to representation: persons with small claims (for whom the legal system has no good answer, regardless of wealth) and persons without liquid assets who are nevertheless sued. These defendants comprise two large subgroups: holdover tenants (their "asset" is the property they are occupying); and spouses and parents sued for divorce and child custody (one cannot legally end a marriage or transfer custody of a child without a court order).

Whatever the measure of need, various local, state, and national efforts address it with varying degrees of success. Some of this representation is done by volunteers operating outside formal organization — lawyers who donate time either as a professional obligation (some bar associations have established minimum amounts of donated time to be an obligation of membership) or as a personal act of charity. The oldest form of legal assistance to those in need, such professional volunteerism suffers from a certain randomness in the large urban settings where most Americans now live. If a poor citizen has a legal problem, where should he go? It seems unfair to burden the lawyers whose offices happen to be geographically closest to poor areas, and it leaves many lawyers who might wish to participate without a way of linking up with needy prospective clients.

At the opposite pole from these individual acts of charity lie the institutions generically referred to as "legal aid." Funded with a combination of tax dollars from all levels of government and private philanthropic support, legal aid offices typically employ full- or part-time lawyers who deliver assistance directly to clients who seek it. These institutions focus on people of small means who find themselves in the position of defendants faced with eviction or with creditors' suits. The theory is that for most suits that would yield a money recovery, it is possible to find a lawyer who would take the matter on a contingency basis. Some challenge that assumption — one that often represents a concession to segments of the local bar that opposed the establishment of Legal Aid as unnecessary. Others have argued that such a defensive posture robs Legal Aid of the ability to challenge the conditions that underlie poverty and oppression in the United States. In the past, such programs have mounted challenges to the existing legal and social order. Evans v. Jeff D., the next case in this section, was conducted by Legal Aid. The last case in this chapter, Fuentes v. Shevin, challenging a centuries-old common law procedure, was also conceived and financed by Legal Aid lawyers. Such challenges have sometimes created opposition, especially when publicly subsidized lawyers question some part of the existing political order. In some instances legislatures have responded by trying to limit the kinds of legal work publicly subsidized lawyers can perform for their clients — for example, by forbidding them to sue state and local governments.

If volunteer efforts by individual lawyers mark one end of the spectrum and institutionalized, publicly funded legal aid marks the other, intermediate forms have emerged in recent years that combine features of both systems. In one model private firms pledge support, of both money and professional time, to a small organization that functions as a point of client contact and a referral system, matching clients' needs with available professional services. This enables a relatively small organization to deliver legal services many times greater than its budget. It also enables lawyers and firms to participate in pro bono activities with some assurance that they will get a steady flow of such work and that it will match their legal expertise and capacity. Because such organizations are funded by private donations, they also avoid some of the restrictions on practice that governmentally funded aid encounters.

Still another form of subsidized legal services is that formed around a cause — an ethnic, religious, or affinity group with an agenda for social change. The hallmark of such groups is that they solicit funds and memberships with the aim of using those funds to finance litigation that furthers the group's goals. Such groups have been behind major social impact litigation on a range of issues, on both ends of the political spectrum. The most prominent example is undoubtedly Brown v. Board of Education, 347 U.S. 443 (1954) (striking down racial segregation in public education), financed largely by the Legal Defense Fund of the National Organization for the Advancement of Colored People, a pioneer civil rights group. Analogous affinity groups have funded litigation seeking to advance agenda of reproductive rights, environmental causes, and more. In recent decades groups from the right side of the political spectrum have mounted their own litigation challenges, sometimes seeking to undo or roll back earlier impact litigation. In 2003 the Supreme Court decided Gratz v. Bollinger, 123 S. Ct. 2411 (2003), striking down a racial preference in admissions for the undergraduate college at the University of Michigan; the challenge was financed by the Center for Individual Rights, an organization describing itself as "an attempt to duplicate the success of liberal public interest law firms in the conservative public interest realm."*

Finally, note that every lawsuit receives some public subsidy: the amounts necessary to maintain the judicial establishment — everything from judges' salaries to the electricity bill for the courthouse. Each federal district judgeship (including law clerks, secretarial help, and bailiffs) costs in excess of $250,000 annually just in salaries. This amount does not include real estate costs, the central clerks' office, or general overhead. State judgeships, which are less well supported, would typically have lower costs, but even those costs are substantial: in the early 1990s the California Legislature made a finding that each "judge day" entailed about $4,000 in public costs. Cal. Code Civ. Proc. §1775(f) (West 2003) (urging early mediation of civil disputes as a remedy). No litigant pays for these direct costs of adjudication. Moreover, the amount of the subsidy falls unevenly. For the great majority of litigants who file a complaint, engage in modest procedural maneuvering, and then settle, the subsidy is small. For litigants who proceed to trial, the subsidy is quite large.

NOTES AND PROBLEMS

1. A friend has just separated from her abusive husband and is facing eviction for nonpayment of rent. Unemployed and assetless, she asks you where she can find legal representation. What can you tell her?

---

* Web page http://www.cir-usa.org/index.html (visited July 1, 2003).

2. Just out of law school, you join a small firm in a rapidly expanding suburban area. Because of the spate of recent growth, population has outrun the capacities of a one-person legal aid office largely funded by the county. A number of small law firms have opened practice in this area, and at a Young Lawyers meeting several raise concerns. Two proposals are made: to lobby the county supervisors for increased Legal Aid funding; and to organize a system for referring clients to private firms who volunteer to do pro bono representation. You are asked to prepare a short paper outlining the pros and cons of the two proposals. What are your major headings?

4.   From Fee Spreading to Fee Shifting

Thus far we have examined means of spreading attorneys' fees, usually the major expense of litigation. Contingent fees and insurance spread fees among particular groups of litigants; public subsidies spread costs among all citizens. There is one more spreading device that begins to shade into fee shifting.

a.   The Common Fund

Plaintiff brings a lawsuit that benefits him, but in the process also benefits other similarly situated persons. Should those others have an obligation to contribute to the plaintiff's attorneys' fees? The origin of this theory came in a suit in which a bondholder sued the bond issuer to force payment of the bond. The plaintiff won and in the process established that the issuer had to pay other similarly situated bondholders: He had, by vindicating his interest, helped others to win a valuable legal right. In that case the court held that the original plaintiff could recover part of his attorney's fee from the *fund* that his efforts had created — the sum from which the other bondholders would be paid. Trustees v. Greenough, 105 U.S. 527 (1881). Notice that this *common fund* theory requires that the plaintiff's efforts create some fund from which the lawyer's fee can be deducted. This judicially created doctrine has proved very important in financing class actions, in which one party or a few parties may represent a class of many thousands. If in such a case the class representatives win a judgment or settlement for money damages, they regularly seek a contribution to their fees from the fund created for the benefit of the class. Observe that the common fund theory does not itself shift fees from one party to the other; instead it requires that all who benefit from the recovery share its cost. The common fund theory *shares* fees among similarly situated persons rather than shifting them to the opposing party in a lawsuit.

NOTES AND PROBLEMS

In which of the following situations will the common fund theory apply?

1. Student A sues the Regents of State University, alleging that they have without legal authority increased tuition payments; she sues on behalf of all

students and recovers $4 million in excess tuition payments, to be distributed among those paying the excess tuition.

2. Student *B* sues the Regents of State University, alleging that the tuition increase about to go into effect is unauthorized. He prevails, and the court enters an injunction forbidding the tuition increase. If Student *B* had not brought this suit, all students would have been required to pay a higher tuition, the total sum amounting to some $4 million.

Because the common fund theory depends on a fund created by a judgment or settlement against the adversary, it straddles the line between fee spreading and fee shifting. We turn now to purer forms of fee shifting, in which the losing party pays the winner's attorneys' fees. When that happens, the so-called American Rule begins to shade into something closer to the English Rule. Since the early 1970s, an increasing amount of U.S. litigation has involved the possibility for such fee shifting, a circumstance that has in turn created sublitigation about the conditions and circumstances for such shifting. Notice that such systems fall into two groups. In their purest form, such fee shifts are symmetrical; that is, the loser pays the winner's fees. An increasingly common form is asymmetrical (also called "one-way fee shifting"), in which a prevailing plaintiff collects at least partial fees from a defendant, but a prevailing defendant does not collect fees from a losing plaintiff unless the plaintiff has sued in bad faith.

b.   By Contract

In the contemporary United States, a common form of symmetrical fee shifting arises from contractual agreements. Parties to contracts may provide that if litigation over the contract arises, the loser will pay the winner's legal fees. Such agreements may in theory be asymmetrical (tenant pays landlord's lawyer if evicted; landlord doesn't have to pay tenant's lawyer if effort to evict fails), but courts and legislatures have often required that such asymmetrical clauses be interpreted as symmetrical — loser pays winner's lawyer. Loan agreements and leases often contain such clauses. When a landlord sues a tenant for rent, the tenant may be ordered to pay both the rent and the fee of the landlord's lawyer. The reverse would be true if the tenant sued the landlord for constructive eviction. If the tenant's lease had such a clause, how would it affect her incentives to sue or defend? One often finds such clauses in contracts where the amount in dispute will be relatively small. Do you see the reason for that pattern?

c.   By Common Law

Even when the parties have not agreed to shift fees, there are exceptions to the American Rule. A well-established situation in which one side may pay the other's legal fee occurs when a plaintiff has groundlessly brought a suit; in most states one element of damages in a subsequent action for *malicious prosecution* is attorneys' fees for defending the first suit. Beyond any specific statutory authority lies the inherent power of the court to control behavior designed to thwart the just operation of the legal system. Chambers v. NASCO, Inc., 501 U.S. 32 (1991) (upholding imposition of nearly $1 million in fees on party acting in bad faith). In an influential opinion, the U.S. Supreme Court refused to create a generalized common law doctrine shifting fees in "public interest" cases but said that the legislature remained free to do so. Alyeska Pipeline Service v. Wilderness Society, 421 U.S. 240, 257 (1975).

d.   By Statute

Over the past few decades legislatures have enthusiastically accepted the invitation in *Alyeska*. Several hundred federal and several thousand state statutes shift attorneys' fees in various categories of cases. Those "exceptions" to the American Rule have now grown so numerous that some have asked whether the rule still exists in the country that supplied its name. That assessment probably stretches things — in the most common forms of litigation, fees will still not shift — but it properly highlights the importance of such statutes.

In their most general form, such statutes authorize courts to award fees to parties "in any action which has resulted in the enforcement of an important right affecting the public interest." Cal. Code Civ. P. §1021.5 (West 2002). Most legislatures have been less sweeping, enacting fee shifting statutes to cover particular substantive areas. Such statutes cover many topics — mine safety, truth in lending, consumer product safety, endangered species — but among the most important such federal statutes have been those concerning the enforcement of civil rights. The basic provision is contained in 42 U.S.C. §1988(b):

> In any action or proceeding to enforce . . . [various listed civil rights statutes] . . . , the court, in its discretion, may allow the prevailing party, other than the United States, a reasonable attorney's fee as part of the costs.

The quoted statute speaks of a "prevailing party" being entitled to fees, a phrase that has brought forth at least two unsuspected readings. One might think such language created symmetrical fee shifting — that an employee who unsuccessfully sues her employer alleging job discrimination will not only lose the suit but also have to pay the defendant's legal fees. Not so, held Christianburg Garment Co. v. Equal Employment Opportunity Commission, 434 U.S. 412 (1978). In light of the legislative history suggesting that Congress wanted to make it easier, not harder, to enforce civil rights, the *Christianburg* court interpreted such statutes to permit routine attorneys' fees awards to prevailing *plaintiffs* but not to defendants. The exception, in which a two-way shift was permissible, occurred only when the plaintiff's claim was "frivolous, unreasonable, or groundless, or that the plaintiff continued to litigate after it clearly became so." *Christianburg* at 422. *Christianburg* has had an important influence: It has meant that the predominant form of fee shifting statute in the United States has been one-way shifting.

NOTES AND PROBLEMS

1. Consider the effect of fee shifting on the filing and conduct of litigation. Client has been recently discharged from her job. Your investigation suggests a breach of the employment contract. There is also a possible racial discrimination claim, which is much more difficult to prove. The potential amounts at stake are not large. Does the choice make any difference so far as the financing of the case is concerned?

2. Suppose you and your client decide to press both claims, with the client agreeing to a contingent fee for any sums recovered. In spite of your best efforts the employment discrimination claim is dismissed at an early stage. How will this affect your estimate of whether this case will pay for itself? Professional ethics limit the ability of a lawyer to withdraw from representation once it has begun but allow a lawyer to withdraw from representation if "the representation will result in an unreasonable financial burden on the lawyer." Model Rule 1.16(a)(5). Losing money on a case in which the lawyer thought he would make money probably does not qualify as an unreasonable financial burden. Could the lawyer have avoided this situation?

3. When are such awards of fees to plaintiffs called for? A plaintiff who prevails at trial will obviously receive such an award; see Rule 54(d)(2), which establishes a procedure for seeking, contesting, and awarding such fees. But most cases do not go to trial; a majority will settle. In such cases, the parties can negotiate about fees as well as the portion of the settlement going to the plaintiff. This situation provides an opportunity for the defendant to drive a wedge between lawyer and client, a wedge whose sharpness and power the next case illustrates.

Evans v. Jeff D.

475 U.S. 717 (1986)

Justice STEVENS delivered the opinion of the Court.

The Civil Rights Attorney's Fees Awards Act of 1976 (Fees Act) provides that "the court, in its discretion, may allow the prevailing party . . . a reasonable attorney's fee" in enumerated civil rights actions. 42 U.S.C. §1988(b).

. . . In this case, we consider the question whether attorney's fees must be assessed when the case has been settled by a consent decree granting prospective relief to the plaintiff class but providing that the defendants shall not pay any part of the prevailing party's fees or costs. We hold that the District Court has the power, in its sound discretion, to refuse to award fees. . . .

I

[The plaintiff class of emotionally and mentally handicapped children sued the State of Idaho seeking injunctive relief that would improve the treatment of institutionalized class members. Johnson, the class's attorney, was employed by the Idaho Legal Aid Society; his representation agreement with the class representatives contained no provision covering legal fees.]

[O]ne week before trial, petitioners presented respondents with a new settlement proposal . . . "offer[ing] virtually all of the injunctive relief . . . sought in the[ ] complaint[,]" [but] includ[ing] a provision for a waiver by respondents of any claim to fees or costs. Originally, this waiver was unacceptable to the Idaho Legal Aid Society, which had instructed Johnson to reject any settlement offer conditioned upon a waiver of fees, but Johnson ultimately determined that his ethical obligation to his clients . . . "forced," [him] by an offer giving his clients "the best result [they] could have gotten in this court or any other court," to waive his attorney's fees.[6] The District Court, however, evaluated the waiver in the context of the entire settlement and rejected the ethical underpinnings of Johnson's argument. . . .

. . . Rule 23(e) wisely requires court approval of the terms of any settlement of a class action, but the power to approve or reject a settlement negotiated by the parties before trial does not authorize the court to require the parties to accept a settlement to which they have not agreed. . . . The question we must decide, therefore, is whether the District Court had a duty to reject the proposed settlement because it included a waiver of statutorily authorized attorney's fees.

That duty, whether it takes the form of a general prophylactic rule or arises out of the special circumstances of this case, derives ultimately from the Fees Act rather than from the strictures of professional ethics. Although respondents contend that Johnson, as counsel for the class, was faced with an "ethical dilemma" when petitioners offered him relief greater than that which he could reasonably have expected to obtain for his clients at trial (if only he would stipulate to a waiver of the statutory fee award), and although we recognize Johnson's conflicting interests between pursuing relief for the class and a fee for the Idaho Legal Aid Society, we do not believe that the "dilemma" was an "ethical" one in the sense that Johnson had to choose between conflicting duties under the prevailing norms of professional conduct. Plainly, Johnson had no ethical obligation to seek a statutory fee award. His ethical duty was to serve his clients loyally and competently.[14] Since the proposal to settle the merits was more favorable

---

6. Johnson's oral presentation to the District Court reads in full as follows:

In other words, an attorney like myself can be put in the position of either negotiating for his client or negotiating for his attorney's fees, and I think that is pretty much the situation that occurred in this instance. I was forced, because of what I perceived to be a result favorable to the plaintiff class, a result that I didn't want to see jeopardized by a trial or by any other possible problems that might have occurred. And the result is the best result I could have gotten in this court or any other court and it is really a fair and just result in any instance and what should have occurred years earlier and which in fact should have been the case all along. That result I didn't want to see disturbed on the basis that my attorney's fees would cause a problem and cause that result to be jeopardized.

14. Generally speaking, a lawyer is under an ethical obligation to exercise independent professional judgment on behalf of his client; he must not allow his own interests, financial or otherwise, to influence his professional advice. ABA, Model Code of Professional Responsibility EC 5-1, 5-2 (as amended 1980); ABA, Model Rules of Professional Conduct 1.7(b), 2.1 (as amended 1984). Accordingly, it is argued that an attorney is required to evaluate a settlement offer on the basis of his client's interest, without considering his own interest in obtaining a fee; upon recommending settlement, he must abide by the client's decision whether or not to accept the offer, see Model Code of Professional Responsibility EC 7-7 to EC 7-9; Model Rules of Professional Conduct 1.2(a).

than the probable outcome of the trial, Johnson's decision to recommend acceptance was consistent with the highest standards of our profession. The District Court, therefore, correctly concluded that approval of the settlement involved no breach of ethics in this case.

The defect, if any, in the negotiated fee waiver must be traced not to the rules of ethics but to the Fees Act. Following this tack, respondents argue that the statute must be construed to forbid a fee waiver that is the product of "coercion." They submit that a "coercive waiver" results when the defendant in a civil rights action (1) offers a settlement on the merits of equal or greater value than that which plaintiffs could reasonably expect to achieve at trial but (2) conditions the offer on a waiver of plaintiffs' statutory eligibility for attorney's fees. Such an offer, they claim, exploits the ethical obligation of plaintiffs' counsel to recommend settlement in order to avoid defendant's statutory liability for its opponents' fees and costs. . . .

III

The text of the Fees Act provides no support for the proposition that Congress intended to ban all fee waivers offered in connection with substantial relief on the merits. On the contrary, the language of the Act, as well as its legislative history, indicates that Congress bestowed on the "prevailing party" (generally plaintiffs) a statutory eligibility for a discretionary award of attorney's fees in specified civil rights actions. It did not prevent the party from waiving this eligibility anymore than it legislated against assignment of this right to an attorney, such as effectively occurred here. . . . The statute and its legislative history nowhere suggest that Congress intended to forbid all waivers of attorney's fees — even those insisted upon by a civil rights plaintiff in exchange for some other relief to which he is indisputably not entitled[20] — anymore than it intended to bar a concession on damages to secure broader injunctive relief. . . . In fact, we believe that a general proscription against negotiated waiver of attorney's fees in exchange for a settlement on the merits would itself impede vindication of civil rights, at least in some cases, by reducing the attractiveness of settlement. [As we said in] Marek v. Chesney, 473 U.S. 1 (1985) . . . [:]

20. Judge Wald has described the use of attorney's fees as a "bargaining chip" useful to plaintiffs as well as defendants. In her opinion concurring in the judgment in Moore v. National Assn. of Security Dealers, Inc., she wrote:

On the other hand, the Jeff D. approach [taken by the 9th Circuit] probably means that a defendant who is willing to grant immediate prospective relief to a plaintiff case, but would rather gamble on the outcome at trial than pay attorneys' fees and costs up front, will never settle. In short, removing attorneys' fees as a "bargaining chip" cuts both ways. It prevents defendants, who in Title VII cases are likely to have greater economic power than plaintiffs, from exploiting that power in a particularly objectionable way; but it also deprives plaintiffs of the use of that chip, even when without it settlement may be impossible and the prospect of winning at trial may be very doubtful.

762 F.2d, at 1112.

. . . Some plaintiffs will receive compensation in settlement where, on trial, they might not have recovered, or would have recovered less than what was offered. And, even for those who would prevail at trial, settlement will provide them with compensation at an earlier date without the burdens, stress, and time of litigation. In short, settlements rather than litigation will serve the interests of plaintiffs as well as defendants.

. . . We conclude, therefore, that it is not necessary to construe the Fees Act as embodying a general rule prohibiting settlements conditioned on the waiver of fees in order to be faithful to the purposes of that Act.

Court's ruling on Fees Act argument

IV

The question remains whether the District Court abused its discretion in this case by approving a settlement which included a complete fee waiver. As noted earlier, Rule 23(e) wisely requires court approval of the terms of any settlement of a class action. The potential conflict among members of the class — in this case, for example, the possible conflict between children primarily interested in better educational programs and those primarily interested in improved health care — fully justifies the requirement of court approval.

The Court of Appeals, respondents, and various amici supporting their position, however, suggest that the court's authority to pass on settlements, typically invoked to ensure fair treatment of class members, must be exercised in accordance with the Fees Act to promote the availability of attorneys in civil rights cases. . . .

[The court rejected this proposition, holding that the question was instead the overall fairness of the settlement agreement; in deciding whether to approve such a settlement, the court could consider the demand for a fee waiver.]

District Court must rule on overall fairness of agreement

Remarkably, there seems little disagreement on these points. . . . The Solicitor General, for example, has suggested that a fee waiver need not be approved when the defendant had "no realistic defense on the merits," or if the waiver was part of a "vindictive effort . . . to teach counsel that they had better not bring such cases." . . .

[The court found no such evidence.]

In light of the record, respondents must — to sustain the judgment in their favor — confront the District Court's finding that the extensive structural relief they obtained constituted an adequate quid pro quo for their waiver of attorney's fees. . . .

What the outcome of this settlement illustrates is that the Fees Act has given the victims of civil rights violations a powerful weapon that improves their ability to employ counsel, to obtain access to the courts, and thereafter to vindicate their rights by means of settlement or trial. For aught that appears, it was the "coercive" effect of respondents' statutory right to seek a fee award that motivated petitioners' exceptionally generous offer. Whether this weapon might be even more powerful if fee waivers were prohibited in cases like this is another question,[34] but it is in any event a question that Congress is best equipped to answer. Thus far,

---

34. We are cognizant of the possibility that decisions by individual clients to bargain away fee awards may, in the aggregate and in the long run, diminish lawyers' expectations of statutory fees in civil rights cases. If this occurred, the pool of lawyers willing to represent plaintiffs in such cases

the Legislature has not commanded that fees be paid whenever a case is settled. Unless it issues such a command, we shall rely primarily on the sound discretion of the district courts to appraise the reasonableness of particular class-action settlements on a case-by-case basis, in the light of all the relevant circumstances. In this case, the District Court did not abuse its discretion in upholding a fee waiver which secured broad injunctive relief, relief greater than that which plaintiffs could reasonably have expected to achieve at trial. . . .

[Justice BRENNAN dissented, expressing concern that settlment offers of this sort would cause public interest litigation to dry up.]

NOTES AND PROBLEMS

1. Start by recognizing the circumstances in which Johnson, the lawyer for the plaintiff class, found himself.

a. Recall that Johnson was working for the Legal Aid Society. In most areas such organizations work on perennially tight budgets. Imagine the following quite plausible scenario. After interviewing his clients, Johnson consults his supervising attorney, who, after discussing the case for a bit, tells him that the society is very strapped for personnel and funds right now, but, with some misgivings, she'll let Johnson take the case *because* — as a result of §1988(b) — it has the potential for generating at least enough fees to pay the overhead on the case.

b. Now comes the settlement offer. The court tells us that Johnson faced no ethical dilemma because the professional ethics are quite clear that the lawyer is obliged to pursue his client's interest, not his own or that of his employer (the Legal Aid Society). What kind of dilemma did Johnson face? Should that dilemma, of whatever sort it is, have any bearing on the outcome of the case?

2. The opinion hints that Johnson had found himself in this dilemma because his clients had not instructed him to refuse any settlement requiring a waiver of fees.

a. If one pursues the implications of that suggestion, lawyers wishing to avoid such a problem will simply ask their clients to sign a standard form instructing the lawyer to refuse all settlement offers that do not provide for attorneys' fees.

b. Is it that simple? Model Rule of Professional Responsibility 1.7(b) provides that:

> A lawyer shall not represent a client if the representation of that client may be materially limited by the lawyer's responsibility to another client . . . or by the lawyer's own interests unless:

---

might shrink, constricting the "effective access to the judicial process" for persons with civil rights grievances which the Fees Act was intended to provide. H.R. Rep. No. 94-1558, p. 1 (1976). That the "tyranny of small decisions" may operate in this fashion is not to say that there is any reason or documentation to support such a concern at the present time. Comment on this issue is therefore premature at this juncture. We believe, however, that as a practical matter the likelihood of this circumstance arising is remote.

(1) the lawyer reasonably believes the representation will not be adversely affected; and

(2) the client consents after consultation. . . .

Put yourself in Johnson's shoes at two stages. First, imagine how you would explain to the clients what you were asking them to sign. Can you meet the two conditions of Model Rule 1.7(b) (quoted above)? Second, suppose your clients do sign and Idaho now makes its offer. Assume you believe that the settlement (fees aside) is as good a job as you can do for the handicapped children. On the other hand, you realize that Legal Aid might do much for your other clients with the fees received if you can bargain your way into some. Are you free, by refusing to accept the settlement offer (as the agreement with your clients provides), to trade off the interests of your present clients against other clients?

3. The opinion reports no evidence that the defendant state was trying to "teach counsel a lesson that they had better not bring such cases." Presumably the Court thought it necessary to announce that finding because the bare facts of the case might otherwise lead to such a surmise. Try, however, to put yourself in defendant's shoes for a moment. Recall that this suit was financed by the Idaho Legal Aid Society. Recalling what you know about how such organizations are funded, give a nonvindictive explanation for the state's conditioning a settlement on the waiver of fees.

4. One fee-shifting statute applies only in civil litigation against the United States. 28 U.S.C. §2412. The Equal Access to Justice Act provides that, unless a specific statute prohibits it, a court shall award fees to a party that prevails against the United States, unless the government's position was "substantially justified." 28 U.S.C. §2412(d)(1)(A). The statute is complex (it limits fee awards to individuals and businesses below a certain size, exempts tort actions, and caps fees at $125 an hour) and frequently amended. Its exception for "substantially justified" litigative positions suggests an interesting alternative to 42 U.S.C. §1988(b). The same phrase appears in Rule 37(a)(4), governing sanctions for failure to comply with discovery.

5. *Jeff D.* displays hardball tactics deployed by a defendant. The next case shows us a defendant who sought to "win" by giving up entirely.

Buckhannon Board and Care Home, Inc. v. West Virginia Department of Health and Human Resources

532 U.S. 598 (2001)

Chief Justice REHNQUIST delivered the opinion of the Court.

Numerous federal statutes allow courts to award attorney's fees and costs to the "prevailing party." The question presented here is whether this term includes a party that has failed to secure a judgment on the merits or a court-ordered consent decree, but has nonetheless achieved the desired result because the lawsuit brought about a voluntary change in the defendant's conduct. We hold that it does not.

Buckhannon Board and Care Home, Inc., which operates care homes that provide assisted living to their residents, [ran afoul of a state regulation that required residents to be sufficiently ambulatory to get out of burning buildings]. On October 28, 1997, after receiving cease and desist orders requiring the closure of its residential care facilities within 30 days, Buckhannon Board and Care Home, Inc., on behalf of itself and other similarly situated homes and residents (hereinafter petitioners), brought suit in the United States District Court for the Northern District of West Virginia against the State of West Virginia . . . seeking declaratory and injunctive relief[1] that the "self-preservation" requirement violated the Fair Housing Amendments Act of 1988 (FHAA), 102 Stat. 1619, 42 U.S.C. §3601 *et seq.*, and the Americans with Disabilities Act of 1990 (ADA), 104 Stat. 327, 42 U.S.C. §12101 *et seq.*

Respondents agreed to stay enforcement of the cease-and-desist orders pending resolution of the case and the parties began discovery. In 1998, the West Virginia Legislature enacted two bills eliminating the "self-preservation" requirement, and respondents moved to dismiss the case as moot. The District Court granted the motion, finding that the 1998 legislation had eliminated the allegedly offensive provisions and that there was no indication that the West Virginia Legislature would repeal the amendments.[2]

Petitioners requested attorney's fees as the "prevailing party" under the FHAA, 42 U.S.C. §3613(c)(2) ("[T]he court, in its discretion, may allow the prevailing party . . . a reasonable attorney's fee and costs"). . . . Petitioners argued that they were entitled to attorney's fees under the "catalyst theory," which posits that a plaintiff is a "prevailing party" if it achieves the desired result because the lawsuit brought about a voluntary change in the defendant's conduct. [Most Courts of Appeals recognized the "catalyst theory."]

In the United States, parties are ordinarily required to bear their own attorney's fees — the prevailing party is not entitled to collect from the loser. . . . Congress, however, has authorized the award of attorney's fees to the "prevailing party" in numerous statutes in addition to those at issue here. . . .

In designating those parties eligible for an award of litigation costs, Congress employed the term "prevailing party," a legal term of art. Black's Law Dictionary 1145 (7th ed. 1999) defines "prevailing party" as "[a] party in whose favor a judgment is rendered, regardless of the amount of damages awarded [in certain cases, the court will award attorney's fees to the prevailing party]. —Also termed *successful party*." This view that a "prevailing party" is one who has been awarded some relief by the court can be distilled from our prior cases. . . .

In addition to judgments on the merits, we have held that settlement agreements enforced through a consent decree may serve as the basis for an award of attorney's fees. . . . These decisions, taken together, establish that enforceable judgments on the merits and court-ordered consent decrees create the "material

---

1. The original complaint also sought money damages, but petitioners relinquished this claim on January 2, 1998. See App. to Pet. for Cert. A11.
2. The District Court sanctioned respondents under Federal Rule of Civil Procedure 11 for failing to timely provide notice of the legislative amendment. App. 147.

alteration of the legal relationship of the parties" necessary to permit an award of attorney's fees. . . .

We think, however, the "catalyst theory" falls on the other side of the line from these examples. It allows an award where there is no judicially sanctioned change in the legal relationship of the parties. . . . A defendant's voluntary change in conduct, although perhaps accomplishing what the plaintiff sought to achieve by the lawsuit, lacks the necessary judicial *imprimatur* on the change . . .

Petitioners nonetheless argue that the legislative history of the Civil Rights Attorney's Fees Awards Act supports a broad reading of "prevailing party" which includes the "catalyst theory." . . .

The House Report to §1988 states that "[t]he phrase 'prevailing party' is not intended to be limited to the victor only after entry of a final judgment following a full trial on the merits," while the Senate Report explains that "parties may be considered to have prevailed when they vindicate rights through a consent judgment or without formally obtaining relief[.]" . . . Petitioners argue that these Reports . . . indicate Congress' intent to adopt the "catalyst theory." We think the legislative history cited by petitioners is at best ambiguous as to the availability of the "catalyst theory" for awarding attorney's fees. Particularly in view of the "American Rule" that attorney's fees will not be awarded absent "explicit statutory authority," such legislative history is clearly insufficient to alter the accepted meaning of the statutory term. . . .

Petitioners finally assert that the "catalyst theory" is necessary to prevent defendants from unilaterally mooting an action before judgment in an effort to avoid an award of attorney's fees. They also claim that the rejection of the "catalyst theory" will deter plaintiffs with meritorious but expensive cases from bringing suit. We are skeptical of these assertions, which are entirely speculative and unsupported by any empirical evidence.

Petitioners discount the disincentive that the "catalyst theory" may have upon a defendant's decision to voluntarily change its conduct, conduct that may not be illegal. "The defendants' potential liability for fees in this kind of litigation can be as significant as, and sometimes even more significant than, their potential liability on the merits," Evans v. Jeff D., and the possibility of being assessed attorney's fees may well deter a defendant from altering its conduct.

And petitioners' fear of mischievous defendants only materializes in claims for equitable relief, for so long as the plaintiff has a cause of action for damages, a defendant's change in conduct will not moot the case. . . .[10]

We have also stated that "[a] request for attorney's fees should not result in a second major litigation," and have accordingly avoided an interpretation of the fee-shifting statutes that would have "spawn[ed] a second litigation of significant dimension." If among other things, a "catalyst theory" hearing would require analysis of the defendant's subjective motivations in changing its conduct, an analysis

10. Only States and state officers acting in their official capacity are immune from suits for damages in federal court. See, e.g., Edelman v. Jordan, 415 U.S. 651, 94 S. Ct. 1347, 39 L. Ed. 2d 662 (1974). Plaintiffs may bring suit for damages against all others, including municipalities and other political subdivisions of a State, see Mt. Healthy City Bd. of Ed. v. Doyle, 429 U.S. 274, 97 S. Ct. 568, 50 L. Ed. 2d 471 (1977).

that "will likely depend on a highly factbound inquiry and may turn on reasonable inferences from the nature and timing of the defendant's change in conduct." . . . .

The judgment of the Court of Appeals is *Affirmed*.

[A concurrence by Justice SCALIA, with whom Justice THOMAS joined is omitted.]

Justice GINSBURG, with whom Justices STEVENS, SOUTER, BREYER joined dissented:]

The Court today holds that a plaintiff whose suit prompts the precise relief she seeks does not "prevail," and hence cannot obtain an award of attorney's fees, unless she also secures a court entry memorializing her victory. The entry need not be a judgment on the merits. Nor need there be any finding of wrongdoing. A court-approved settlement will do.

The Court's insistence that there be a document filed in court — a litigated judgment or court-endorsed settlement — upsets long-prevailing Circuit precedent applicable to scores of federal fee-shifting statutes. The decision allows a defendant to escape a statutory obligation to pay a plaintiff's counsel fees, even though the suit's merit led the defendant to abandon the fray, to switch rather than fight on, to accord plaintiff sooner rather than later the principal redress sought in the complaint. Concomitantly, the Court's constricted definition of "prevailing party," and consequent rejection of the "catalyst theory," impede access to court for the less well heeled, and shrink the incentive Congress created for the enforcement of federal law by private attorneys general.

In my view, the "catalyst rule," as applied by the clear majority of Federal Circuits, is a key component of the fee-shifting statutes Congress adopted to advance enforcement of civil rights. Nothing in history, precedent, or plain English warrants the anemic construction of the term "prevailing party" the Court today imposes. . . .

NOTES AND PROBLEMS

1. Exactly what was the fight about?

a. Did plaintiffs avoid the threatened shutdown of their nursing homes?

b. How did they win?

c. Essentially, the State decided to throw in the towel, either deciding that the plaintiffs' interpretation of federal regulations was correct or that the fight was not worth it. When parties reach that conclusion (and the plaintiffs want the long-term behavior of the defendants to remain as agreed), they sometimes enter into a consent decree, in which the court orders the parties to do what they have already agreed to do. If that had been the end of *Buckhannon*, would the plaintiffs have been able to collect attorneys' fees under the court's decision?

d. If so, does it make sense that they cannot collect those fees if the way the State "gives up" is to repeal the offending legislation?

2. A broader way of asking the preceding question is to ask how to apply a fee rule based on adjudicated termination of a case to a world in which most cases end by settlement rather than adjudication.

a. In principle, the answer is that settlements will often reflect the law that will be applied if there is adjudication. But that answer works only if one can hold the defendant in the litigation until either adjudication or a settlement reflecting the likely outcome of adjudication occurs. Mootness — the principle that a court will dismiss a case if the grounds of dispute have vanished — provides an escape hatch for a defendant willing to give up immediately, if the only relief sought by plaintiff is prospective, an injunction or similar forward-looking relief.

b. Suppose the plaintiffs had anticipated the *Buckhannon* principle. Is there any way they could have prevented the dismissal for mootness of their claims — and thus forced the defendant to settle or litigate?

3. When *Buckhannon* was decided, many legal aid and affinity groups that regularly litigate believed that *Buckhannon* posed a significant threat to their financing. Because they often litigate against public entities, they expressed concern that the principle of *Buckhannon* would enable such defendants, whenever they appeared to be losing, to back down, thereby mooting the case and forcing the plaintiff organization to bear the whole cost of the lawsuit that had resulted in the changed policy.

a. First, describe the circumstances in which this scenario could happen: What conditions have to exist?

b. Second, suppose, after *Buckhannon,* you represent a client facing a similar situation: A state has enacted a regulation that you believe invalid. You have volunteered to assist a privately supported affinity group, specializing in helping poor people, in a lawsuit challenging a new welfare regulation that would cut off assistance to many who now receive aid. The regulation goes into effect at the start of next month. The group you are assisting is perennially short of funding and is counting on the lawsuit to be at least partially self-funding, by collecting attorneys' fees under 42 U.S.C. §1988(b). The lawyers have heard of *Buckhannon* and ask you if it poses problems for them. Explain the possible scenarios, suggest ways of avoiding those scenarios, and describe any ethical problems you see posed by your courses of action.

4. The issue *Buckhannon* poses globally is posed in a smaller way by Rule 68. Recall the preceding discussion of Rule 68, page 290 supra; typically that Rule enables a defendant to avoid part of what would otherwise be costs taxed to a losing party. Usually those "costs" will be a minor part of the total expenses of a lawsuit; specifically they do *not* in an ordinary case include attorneys' fees.

a. But the Supreme Court has said that in some cases, other statutes define attorneys' fees as part of the "costs" affected by a Rule 68 offer. Marek v. Chesney, 473 U.S. 1 (1985). Deciding whether a given fee-shifting statute includes such fees is a statute-by-statute inquiry, but the Court has decided that many of the principal fee-shifting statutes, like 42 U.S.C. §1988(b), should be so read.

b. Consider how a fee-shifting statute and Rule 68 interact to affect the strategy of settlement. Employee sues Employer for violating federal laws forbidding employment discrimination; a fee-shifting statute applies to such cases, so a successful plaintiff will collect attorneys' fees from the defendant, whether in a judgment or as a part of a settlement agreement. As the case proceeds, suppose Employee's lawyer has reasonably incurred about $10,000 in fees. (That would be about 40 lawyer-hours at $250 per hour, the rate of the median civil rights fee-shift award in California state and federal courts in 2002, or 100 hours at the national median lawyers' fee of $100 per hour.) Defendant calls plaintiff's lawyer on the telephone and offers to settle the entire case for $15,000 including fees. As a preliminary matter, has defendant made a Rule 68 offer?

c. Now assume the defendant has complied with the requirements of a Rule 68 offer — of $15,000, including fees. (The Supreme Court has held that such fee-inclusive offers are valid under Rule 68 and the relevant statutes. Marek v. Chesney.) How should the plaintiff think about accepting or declining this offer? Obviously the merits of the case and educated guesses (notoriously unreliable) about possible outcomes and recoveries are important. But what additional uncertainty has defendant introduced by making this Rule 68 offer?

d. Now suppose that plaintiff declines the offer and proceeds toward trial, incurring another $10,000 in reasonably incurred legal fees. At trial plaintiff wins a verdict for $12,000. Plaintiff will recover, in addition to this amount and ordinary costs, how much in attorneys' fees? Explain your reasoning. What if the verdict had been for $50,000; how much would plaintiff recover in attorneys' fees.

e. One imaginative pro se plaintiff challenged a public entity's alleged practice of offering only lump-sum settlements of civil rights suits, on the grounds that they so impeded her ability to find counsel that they constituted a violation of the Supremacy Clause (the constitutional provision making federal law supreme). In a very narrow opinion a court suggested she might have a point — at least a good enough one to entitle her to a preliminary injunction barring the defendant from using the alleged practice in her case. Bernhardt v. Los Angeles County, 339 F.3d 920 (9th Cir. 2003).

F. Provisional Remedies

A remedy that comes too late is useless — worse than useless if the client has incurred costs to obtain it. In state and federal courts currently the median time to trial (for those cases that do go to trial) is a bit more than eighteen months. Litigants cannot always wait for the ponderous mechanisms of the law. Interest added to money judgments is one recognition of the importance of timing. But life sometimes demands speed from the legal system. The battered spouse needs a protective order immediately, not after a year's wait for trial. The small business threatened by a competitor's unlawful action will be bankrupt if it has to wait for full-blown adjudication. Provisional remedies — relief pending final adjudication of the dispute — are the legal system's response to this need.

But provisional remedies present a problem: Because, by definition, they must be granted or denied before the case has been heard on the merits, the judge (all such cases will be decided by judges, not juries) must base her decision on incomplete information, acting without the full adversarial exchange that would accompany a trial. The stage of the proceedings at which the issue arises and the need for a quick resolution pose at least two problems: (1) How should a court decide whether to grant temporary relief when all the relevant information is not yet available? (2) When does the curtailment of ordinary procedures in granting provisional relief amount to a denial of due process?

1. Preliminary Injunctions and Temporary Restraining Orders: The Basic Problem

William Inglis & Sons Baking Co. v. ITT Continental Baking Co.

526 F.2d 86 (9th Cir. 1976)

SKOPIL, J.

In 1971 William Inglis & Sons Baking Co. (Inglis) and four other wholesale baking companies filed this antitrust action against various competitors within relevant geographic markets in Washington, Oregon, and California. The complaint charged violations of §§1 and 2 of the Sherman Act, 15 U.S.C. §§1 and 2; §2(a) of the Robinson-Patman Act, 15 U.S.C. §13(a); §§3 and 7 of the Clayton Act, 15 U.S.C. §§14 and 18; and applicable state laws.

In 1974 Inglis moved for a preliminary injunction in the Northern California market against five of the defendants: ITT Continental Baking Co., Inc., American Bakeries Company, Rainbo Baking Co. of Sacramento Valley, Kilpatrick's Bakeries, Inc., and San Joaquin Bakeries, Inc. The latter three defendants are subsidiaries of defendant Campbell Taggart, Inc. The preliminary injunction sought involved only alleged violations of §2(a) of the Robinson-Patman Act and §17000 et seq. of the California UPA [Unfair Practices Act].

The district court conducted extensive hearings on the motion, reviewed voluminous briefs submitted by the parties, and ordered preparation of cost studies by the defendants. On January 21, 1975, the court issued a memorandum opinion and order denying issuance of the preliminary injunction requested by Inglis. Plaintiff appeals from that denial pursuant to 28 U.S.C. §1292(a)(1). We vacate and remand.

Our disposition of this case makes a detailed discussion of the facts unnecessary. Basically, plaintiff contends that the defendants are guilty of discriminatory and below-cost pricing of their "private label" bread products.[1] As one of their defenses to these allegations, defendants assert that their bread prices were established in a good faith effort to meet competition. The meeting competition defense is a statutory defense to violations of both §2(a) of the Robinson-Patman Act and the UPA.

The district court stated that a plaintiff is entitled to a preliminary injunction only if the court finds that (1) the plaintiff will suffer irreparable injury if injunctive relief is not granted, (2) the plaintiff will probably prevail on the merits, (3) in balancing the equities, the defendants will not be harmed more than plaintiff is helped by the injunction, and (4) granting the injunction is in the public inter-

---

1. "Private label" bread products are produced by the wholesale baker for sale under the retail grocer's own label rather than under a nationally-advertised brand label.

est. The district court denied the injunction sought in this case because of its "serious reservations as to the probability of success on the merits. In brief, while the evolution of this market does indicate a tendency toward monopoly, the court is unconvinced that the purpose of defendants' conduct was to injure competition or monopolize." Even assuming that Inglis had shown a prima facie violation of §2(a) of the Robinson-Patman Act and the UPA, the court found that the defendants had adequately negated such violation by the meeting competition defense.

The grant or denial of a preliminary injunction is subject to reversal only if the lower court based its decision upon an erroneous legal premise or abused its discretion. As a court of appeals, our review is extremely limited: "An appeal from an order granting or refusing an interlocutory injunction does not invoke the judicial discretion of the appellate court. The question is not whether or not that court in the exercise of its discretion would make or would have made the order. It was to the discretion of the trial court, not to that of the appellate court, that the law entrusted the granting or refusing of these injunctions, and the only question here is: Does the proof clearly establish an abuse of that discretion?" The district court was faced with the difficult task of resolving conflicting evidence in an extremely complex case. We are unable to find an abuse of discretion in its conclusion that plaintiff failed to satisfy the standard for granting a preliminary injunction applied by the district court.

There is, however, an alternative test that the district court did not apply. As the Second Circuit stated in Charlie's Girls, Inc. v. Revlon, Inc.: "One moving for a preliminary injunction assumes the burden of demonstrating either a combination of probable success and the possibility of irreparable injury or that serious questions are raised and the balance of hardships tips sharply in his favor." The alternative test was also stated in one of the cases cited by the district court: "It is not necessary that the moving party be reasonably certain to succeed on the merits. If the harm that may occur to the plaintiff is sufficiently serious, it is only necessary that there be a fair chance of success on the merits." This court has adopted the alternative test.

Since the district court did not consider whether a preliminary injunction should issue under the alternative test, we remand for a consideration of that question. In the event it becomes necessary, the district court shall also consider other questions bearing upon the propriety of injunctive relief not previously reached because of its conclusion that relief was barred in any event by plaintiff's failure to establish probability of success on the merits. We wish to make it unmistakably clear that in remanding for further consideration we intimate no position whatsoever as to whether a preliminary injunction should issue.

Reversed and remanded for proceedings consistent with this opinion.

NOTES AND PROBLEMS

1. Focus first on the case itself.

a. What did Inglis want from the district court? What would the requested order have done?

b. Why did the district court refuse to grant that relief?

c. Why did Inglis want a preliminary injunction? How would its lawyer have tried to convince the district court to persuade it to issue this extraordinary relief?

d. Having been given a brief reprieve, what can Inglis's lawyer add to his previous argument to convince the district judge to issue the preliminary injunction?

2. The opinion enunciates two standard doctrinal tests for the issuance of preliminary injunctions. How are they different? What parties are more likely to succeed under the second than under the first?

3. Do not be misled by the "preliminary" label. Not only in Inglis & Sons but in many other cases, the decision about the preliminary injunction will, as a practical matter, end the case. For example, in many business transactions, market conditions will mean that even a short delay makes the transaction financially infeasible. Raider Corporation wants to buy Sluggish Co. for several million dollars. The management of Sluggish seeks a preliminary injunction, alleging that the acquisition will violate securities laws and mean the loss of scores of jobs if Raider tries to cut expenses. Raider opposes the injunction, contending that Sluggish's management is only trying to protect their ill-deserved salaries, and arguing that even a three-week delay (until a fuller hearing can occur) will mean the expiration of their financing for the acquisition. How should a trial court rule on such a motion? Consult Rule 65(a). Does it suggest a way to accommodate both parties' interests?

4. John Leubsdorf has analyzed the problem of the preliminary injunction as follows:

> A court considering a motion for interlocutory relief faces a dilemma. If it does not grant prompt relief, the plaintiff may suffer a loss of his lawful rights that no later remedy can restore. But if the court does grant immediate relief, the defendant may sustain precisely the same loss of his rights.
>
> The dilemma, of course, exists only because the court's interlocutory assessment of the parties' underlying rights is fallible in the sense that it may be different from the decision that ultimately will be reached. The danger of incorrect preliminary assessment is the key to the analysis of interlocutory relief. . . .
>
> The court need not consider every harm resulting from an erroneous preliminary decision, but only harm that final relief cannot address.

John Leubsdorf, The Standard for Preliminary Injunctions, 91 Harv. L. Rev. 525, 541 (1978).

If this analysis is valid, does it imply that the more certain a judge is about the correctness of the decision on the merits, the less she need worry about the special problems of a preliminary injunction?

5. *Inglis* is an excellent example of a private dispute in which the public interest is at stake. Put baldly, the plaintiff is asking the judge or order defendant to charge more for each loaf of bread during the time it takes for the antitrust suit to be decided, perhaps several years. That burden will fall disproportionately on poor families, who spend most of their incomes on housing and food.

a. The doctrine requires the judge to find that "granting the injunction is in the public interest." How should the judge consider this interest?

b. May — or must — the judge create an opportunity for groups adversely affected by the grant of a preliminary injunction to participate in this phase of the lawsuit. Suppose a coalition of local poverty advocacy groups seeks to intervene in the lawsuit under Rule 24 (treated infra at page 772) to argue that increasing the price of a basic foodstuff like bread will hurt their members; should the judge let them participate? If so, it will delay the decision on the preliminary injunction, thus, plaintiff will say, thwarting its need for speed and indirectly helping the plaintiff to put defendant out of business by predatory price-cutting. Could ITT Baking, the defendant, offer to foot the legal bill for such a coalition?

6. If preliminary relief is granted but the court's final decision is in defendant's favor, defendant may have suffered harm during the time the preliminary injunction was in effect. For example, if the *Inglis & Sons* court had granted a preliminary injunction that later was dissolved, ITT Continental Baking Co. might have lost customers and profits from being forced, during the pendency of the preliminary injunction, to charge higher prices. One response to this concern is to require plaintiffs seeking preliminary relief to post a bond intended to cover such losses. See Rule 65(c).

a. Notice the problems of setting an appropriate bond on the facts of a case like *Inglis & Sons.* If one of the grounds for seeking injunctive relief in the first place is the difficulty of calculating damages, how would one decide how large the bond should be?

b. What happens if plaintiff makes a showing of likely irreparable harm but lacks money to post the bond? Though Rule 65 on its face requires a bond ("No . . . preliminary injunction shall issue except upon the giving of security. . . ."), some courts have created an exception for plaintiffs who show a hardship (which can be true indigence, or in some cases, the mere need for cash in running a business). Other courts have demanded bonds in such cases but allowed the amounts to be very low (a few hundred dollars). Does the issuance of a preliminary injunction under such circumstances deny due process to a defendant? Or is it a denial of due process to the plaintiff to insist on a bond as the price of an otherwise available remedy? Think again about this question as you read Fuentes v. Shevin, the next case.

c. Exacerbating the problem posed in Note 6 is the circumstance that the federal courts adhere to rule that the defendant's *only* remedy for an erroneously issued preliminary injunction is an action against the bond; no separate action for damages lies. Russell v. Farley 105 U.S. 433 (1882). So if a court sets a very low bond, or none at all, the defendant cannot recover damages.

d. Finally, notice that only the defendant can recover against a bond, if one exists. The residents of the region covered by the preliminary injunction in *Inglis Sons* won't be able to collect the higher prices they paid for bread during the pendency of an erroneously issued preliminary injunction.

7. Though appeals in the federal courts generally lie only from final judgments of the district courts (28 U.S.C. §1291), §1292(a)(1) creates an exception allowing interlocutory appeals from orders "granting, continuing, modifying,

refusing or dissolving injunctions, or refusing to dissolve or modify injunctions." Preliminary injunctions are "injunctions" for purposes of the statute. Do the circumstances of *Inglis* explain why Congress permitted immediate appeals?

8. Preliminary injunctions are a provisional form of injunctive relief. There are also processes that are in effect provisional monetary relief—attachment and garnishment. The first involves seizure of property (in the case of real property the "seizure" may be accomplished by anything from physical occupation of the land to the symbolic posting of a notice at the recorder's office). Garnishment involves asking some third party—often the defendant's bank or employer—not to pay defendant money due him because the plaintiff has a claim on it. The justification for these provisional remedies resembles that for the preliminary injunctions: Without them the plaintiff may suffer severe hardship, in some cases extreme enough to render a final remedy meaningless. A plaintiff seeking damages may believe that the defendant will, if given enough time, either dissipate or conceal the assets from which a judgment could be satisfied. Under such circumstances, the plaintiff needs relief before a final judgment. That relief comes, however, at a price to the defendant. As with preliminary injunctive relief, these remedies can work great hardship on the defendant and give significant power to the plaintiff who obtains such an order. Not only does the attachment or garnishment guarantee the plaintiff that there will be some assets from which a judgment may be satisfied, but it may also provide significant leverage in settlement negotiations.

2.   Provisional Remedies and Due Process

Preliminary injunctions exist because final remedies can be too slow. Is it possible for provisional remedies to be too fast?

The problem arises because in some situations, the very procedural steps required to obtain a preliminary injunction will cause or exacerbate the threatened harm. For example, a defendant served with notice of an application for an order garnishing her bank account may transfer the assets abroad or flee the jurisdiction to avoid service of process. A defendant accused of battering a spouse might instigate new violence if served with a notice of hearing on a preliminary injunction. In these and similar cases the desire for an effective remedy collides with another principle, the guarantee of due process. The next case illustrates the collision; it is important in its own right and as a reminder that all procedures are subject to examination under the Due Process Clause. The procedure under scrutiny, replevin, was a common law action more than eight hundred years old when its modern use was challenged. Historically, replevin arose because feudal landlords, if they thought their tenants were not paying rents and other obligations when due, would, without judicial authorization, seize ("distrain") the tenants' goods, often livestock. The tenants, in turn, would "replevy" the cattle, by getting an order telling the sheriff to return them until a court had sorted out who owed whom what.

Fuentes v. Shevin

407 U.S. 67 (1972)

Mr. Justice STEWART delivered the opinion of the Court.

We here review the decisions of two . . . federal District Courts that upheld the constitutionality of Florida and Pennsylvania laws authorizing the summary seizure of goods or chattels in a person's possession under a writ of replevin. Both statutes provide for the issuance of writs ordering state agents to seize a person's possessions, simply upon the ex parte application of any other person who claims a right to them and posts a security bond. Neither statute provides for notice to be given to the possessor of the property, and neither statute gives the possessor an opportunity to challenge the seizure at any kind of prior hearing. The question is whether these statutory procedures violate the Fourteenth Amendment's guarantee that no State shall deprive any person of property without due process of law.

I

. . . Margarita Fuentes, . . . a resident of Florida[,] . . . purchased a gas stove and service policy from the Firestone Tire and Rubber Co. (Firestone) under a conditional sales contract calling for monthly payments over a period of time. A few months later, she purchased a stereophonic phonograph from the same company under the same sort of contract. The total cost of the stove and stereo was about $500, plus an additional financing charge of over $100. Under the contracts, Firestone retained title to the merchandise, but Mrs. Fuentes was entitled to possession unless and until she should default on her installment payments.

For more than a year, Mrs. Fuentes made her installment payments. But then, with only about $200 remaining to be paid, a dispute developed between her and Firestone over the servicing of the stove. Firestone instituted an action in a small-claims court for repossession of both the stove and the stereo, claiming that Mrs. Fuentes had refused to make her remaining payments. Simultaneously with the filing of that action and before Mrs. Fuentes had even received a summons to answer its complaint, Firestone obtained a writ of replevin ordering a sheriff to seize the disputed goods at once.

In conformance with Florida procedure, Firestone had only to fill in the blanks on the appropriate form documents and submit them to the clerk of the small-claims court. The clerk signed and stamped the documents and issued a writ of replevin. Later the same day, a local deputy sheriff and an agent of Firestone went to Mrs. Fuentes' home and seized the stove and stereo. . . .

[The second case challenged Pennsylvania's prejudgment replevin process, which, like Florida's, allowed for seizure without prior notice or hearing.]

II

Under the Florida statute challenged here, "[a]ny person whose goods or chattels are wrongfully detained by any other person . . . may have a writ of replevin to

recover them. . . ." Fla. Stat. Ann. §78.01 (Supp. 1972-1973). There is no requirement that the applicant make a convincing showing before the seizure that the
goods are, in fact, "wrongfully detained." Rather, Florida law automatically relies
on the bare assertion of the party seeking the writ that he is entitled to one and
allows a court clerk to issue the writ summarily. It requires only that the applicant
file a complaint, initiating a court action for repossession and reciting in conclusory fashion that he is "lawfully entitled to the possession" of the property, and
that he file a security bond

> in at least double the value of the property to be replevied conditioned that plaintiff
> will prosecute his action to effect and without delay and that if defendant recovers
> judgment against him in the action, he will return the property, if return thereof is
> adjudged, and will pay defendant all sums of money recovered against plaintiff by
> defendant in the action. Fla. Stat. Ann. §78.07 (Supp. 1972-1973).

On the sole basis of the complaint and bond, a writ is issued "command[ing]
the officer to whom it may be directed to replevy the goods and chattels in possession of defendant . . . and to summon the defendant to answer the complaint." If
the goods are "in any dwelling house or other building or enclosure," the officer
is required to demand their delivery; but if they are not delivered, "he shall cause
such house, building or enclosure to be broken open and shall make replevin
according to the writ. . . ."

Thus, at the same moment that the defendant receives the complaint seeking
repossession of property through court action, the property is seized from him.
He is provided no prior notice and allowed no opportunity whatever to challenge
the issuance of the writ. *After* the property has been seized, he will eventually
have an opportunity for a hearing, as the defendant in the trial of the court action
for repossession, which the plaintiff is required to pursue. And he is also not
wholly without recourse in the meantime. For under the Florida statute, the
officer who seizes the property must keep it for three days, and during that period
the defendant may reclaim possession of the property by posting his own security
bond in double its value. But if he does not post such a bond, the property is transferred to the party who sought the writ, pending a final judgment in the underlying action for repossession. . . .

IV

For more than a century the central meaning of procedural due process has been
clear: "Parties whose rights are to be affected are entitled to be heard; and in order
that they may enjoy that right they must first be notified." It is equally fundamental that the right to notice and an opportunity to be heard "must be granted at a
meaningful time and in a meaningful manner." . . .

If the right to notice and a hearing is to serve its full purpose, . . . it must be
granted at a time when the deprivation can still be prevented. At a later hearing,
an individual's possessions can be returned to him if they were unfairly or mistakenly taken in the first place. Damages may even be awarded to him for the wrongful deprivation. But no later hearing and no damage award can undo the fact that

the arbitrary taking that was subject to the right of procedural due process has already occurred. "This Court has not . . . embraced the general proposition that a wrong may be done if it can be undone."

This is no new principle of constitutional law. . . . Although the Court has held that due process tolerates variances in the *form* of a hearing "appropriate to the nature of the case," Mullane v. Central Hanover Tr. Co., and "depending upon the importance of the interests involved and the nature of the subsequent proceedings [if any]," Boddie v. Connecticut, the Court has traditionally insisted that, whatever its form, opportunity for that hearing must be provided before the deprivation at issue takes effect. "That the hearing required by due process is subject to waiver, and is not fixed in form does not affect its root requirement that an individual be given an opportunity for a hearing *before* he is deprived of any significant property interest, except for extraordinary situations where some valid governmental interest is at stake that justifies postponing the hearing until after the event."

The Florida and Pennsylvania prejudgment replevin statutes fly in the face of this principle. To be sure, the requirements that a party seeking a writ must first post a bond, allege conclusorily that he is entitled to specific goods, and open himself to possible liability in damages if he is wrong, serve to deter wholly unfounded applications for a writ. But those requirements are hardly a substitute for a prior hearing, for they test no more than the strength of the applicant's own belief in his rights.[13] . . .

The minimal deterrent effect of a bond requirement is, in a practical sense, no substitute for an informed evaluation by a neutral official. More specifically, as a matter of constitutional principle, it is no replacement for the right to a prior hearing that is the only truly effective safeguard against arbitrary deprivation of property. While the existence of these other, less effective, safeguards may be among the considerations that affect the form of hearing demanded by due process, they are far from enough by themselves to obviate the right to a prior hearing of some kind.

V

The right to a prior hearing, of course, attaches only to the deprivation of an interest encompassed within the Fourteenth Amendment's protection. In the present cases, the Florida and Pennsylvania statutes were applied to replevy chattels in the appellants' possession. The replevin was not cast as a final judgment; most, if not all, of the appellants lacked full title to the chattels; and their claim even to continued possession was a matter in dispute. Moreover, the chattels at stake were nothing more than an assortment of household goods. Nonetheless, it is clear

---

13. They may not even test that much. For if an applicant for the writ knows that he is dealing with an uneducated, uninformed consumer with little access to legal help and little familiarity with legal procedures, there may be a substantial possibility that a summary seizure of property—however unwarranted—may go unchallenged, and the applicant may feel that he can act with impunity.

that the appellants were deprived of possessory interests in those chattels that were within the protection of the Fourteenth Amendment.

Possesory intersts within protection of (life) honerd

A

[The Court ruled that even temporary deprivation of property, so long as it was significant, was subject to the constraints of due process.] The Fourteenth Amendment draws no bright lines around three-day, 10-day or 50-day deprivations of property. Any significant taking of property by the State is within the purview of the Due Process Clause. While the length and consequent severity of a deprivation may be another factor to weigh in determining the appropriate form of hearing, it is not decisive of the basic right to a prior hearing of some kind.

B

[Nor did the fact that those possessing the goods had not fully paid for them, and that they were being seized by persons (the sellers) claiming that partial ownership justify the seizures.] The Fourteenth Amendment's protection of "property," however, has never been interpreted to safeguard only the rights of undisputed ownership. Rather, it has been read broadly to extend protection to "any significant property interest," including statutory entitlements. . . .

C

[The Court refused to limit the protection to "necessities" (however these might be defined) on the grounds that] "under our free enterprise system, an individual's choices in the market place are respected, however unwise they may seem to someone else. It is not the business of a court adjudicating due process rights to make its own critical evaluation of those choices and protect only the ones that, by its own rights, are 'necessary.'"

VI

There are "extraordinary situations" that justify postponing notice and opportunity for a hearing. These situations, however, must be truly unusual.[22] Only in a

---

22. A prior hearing always imposes some costs in time, effort, and expense, and it is often more efficient to dispense with the opportunity for such a hearing. But these rather ordinary costs cannot outweigh the constitutional right. Procedural due process is not intended to promote efficiency or accommodate all possible interests: it is intended to protect the particular interests of the person whose possessions are about to be taken.

The establishment of prompt efficacious procedures to achieve legitimate state ends is a proper state interest worthy of cognizance in constitutional adjudication. But the Constitution recognizes higher values than speed and efficiency. Indeed, one might fairly say of the Bill of Rights in general, and the Due Process Clause in particular, that they were designed to protect the fragile values of a vulnerable citizenry from the overbearing concern for efficiency and efficacy that may characterize praiseworthy government officials no less, and perhaps more, than mediocre ones.

Stanley v. Illinois, 405 U.S. 645, 656.

few limited situations has this Court allowed outright seizure[23] without opportunity for a prior hearing. First, in each case, the seizure has been directly necessary to secure an important governmental or general public interest. Second, there has been a special need for very prompt action. Third, the State has kept strict control over its monopoly of legitimate force: the person initiating the seizure has been a government official responsible for determining, under the standards of a narrowly drawn statute, that it was necessary and justified in the particular instance. Thus, the Court has allowed summary seizure of property to collect the internal revenue of the United States, to meet the needs of a national war effort, to protect against the economic disaster of a bank failure, and to protect the public from misbranded drugs and contaminated food.

The Florida and Pennsylvania prejudgment replevin statutes serve no such important governmental or general public interest. They allow summary seizure of a person's possessions when no more than private gain is directly at stake. . . .

Nor do the broadly drawn Florida and Pennsylvania statutes limit the summary seizure of goods to special situations demanding prompt action. There may be cases in which a creditor could make a showing of immediate danger that a debtor will destroy or conceal disputed goods. But the statutes before us are not "narrowly drawn to meet any such unusual condition." And no such unusual situation is presented by the facts of these cases.

The statutes, moreover, abdicate effective state control over state power. Private parties, serving their own private advantage, may unilaterally invoke state power to replevy goods from another. No state official participates in the decision to seek a writ; no state official reviews the basis for the claim to repossession; and no state official evaluates the need for immediate seizure. There is not even a requirement that the plaintiff provide any information to the court on these matters. The State acts largely in the dark.[30]

23. Of course, outright seizure of property is not the only kind of deprivation that must be preceded by a prior hearing. In three cases, the Court has allowed the attachment of property without a prior hearing. In one, the attachment was necessary to protect the public against the same sort of immediate harm involved in the seizure cases — a bank failure. Coffin Bros. & Co. v. Bennett, 277 U.S. 29. Another case involved attachment necessary to secure jurisdiction in state court — clearly a most basic and important public interest. Ownbey v. Morgan, 256 U.S. 94. It is much less clear what interests were involved in the third case, decided with an unexplicated per curiam opinion simply citing Coffin Bros. and Ownbey. McKay v. McInnes, 279 U.S. 820. As far as essential procedural due process doctrine goes, McKay cannot stand for any more than was established in the Coffin Bros. and Ownbey cases on which it relied completely.

30. The seizure of possessions under a writ of replevin is entirely different from the seizure of possessions under a search warrant. First, a search warrant is generally issued to serve a highly important governmental need — e.g., the apprehension and conviction of criminals — rather than the mere private advantage of a private party in an economic transaction. Second, a search warrant is generally issued in situations demanding prompt action. The danger is all too obvious that a criminal will destroy or hide evidence or fruits of his crime if given any prior notice. Third, the Fourth Amendment guarantees that the State will not issue search warrants merely upon the conclusory application of a private party. It guarantees that the State will not abdicate control over the issuance of warrants and that no warrant will be issued without a prior showing of probable cause. Thus, our decision today in no way implies that there must be opportunity for an adversary hearing before a search warrant is issued. But cf. Quantity of Books v. Kansas, 378 U.S. 205.

VII

Finally, we must consider the contention that the appellants who signed conditional sales contracts thereby waived their basic procedural due process rights. The contract signed by Mrs. Fuentes provided that "in the event of default of any payment or payments, Seller at its option may take back the merchandise. . . ." The contracts signed by the Pennsylvania appellants similarly provided that the seller "may retake" or "repossess" the merchandise in the event of a "default in any payment." These terms were parts of printed form contracts, appearing in relatively small type and unaccompanied by any explanations clarifying their meaning. . . .

The facts of the present cases are a far cry from those of [cases in which the Court has approved such waivers.] There was no bargaining over contractual terms between the parties who, in any event, were far from equal in bargaining power. The purported waiver provision was a printed part of a form sales contract and a necessary condition of the sale. The appellees made no showing whatever that the appellants were actually aware or made aware of the significance of the fine print now relied upon as a waiver of constitutional rights. . . .

The conditional sales contracts here simply provided that upon a default the seller "may take back," "may retake" or "may repossess" merchandise. The contracts included nothing about the waiver of a prior hearing. They did not indicate how or through what process — a final judgment, self-help, prejudgment replevin with a prior hearing, or prejudgment replevin without a prior hearing — the seller could take back the goods. Rather, the purported waiver provisions here are no more than a statement of the seller's right to repossession upon occurrence of certain events. The appellees do not suggest that these provisions waived the appellants' right to a full post-seizure hearing to determine whether those events had, in fact, occurred and to consider any other available defenses. By the same token, the language of the purported waiver provisions did not waive the appellants' constitutional right to a preseizure hearing of some kind.

VIII

We hold that the Florida and Pennsylvania prejudgment replevin provisions work a deprivation of property without due process of law insofar as they deny the right to a prior opportunity to be heard before chattels are taken from their possessor. Our holding, however, is a narrow one. We do not question the power of a State to seize goods before a final judgment in order to protect the security interests of creditors so long as those creditors have tested their claim to the goods through the process of a fair prior hearing. The nature and form of such prior hearings, moreover, are legitimately open to many potential variations and are a subject, at this point, for legislation — not adjudication.[33] Since the essential reason for the

---

33. Leeway remains to develop a form of hearing that will minimize unnecessary cost and delay while preserving the fairness and effectiveness of the hearing in preventing seizures of goods where the party seeking the writ has little probability of succeeding on the merits of the dispute.

requirement of a prior hearing is to prevent unfair and mistaken deprivations of property, however, it is axiomatic that the hearing must provide a real test. "[D]ue process is afforded only by the kinds of 'notice' and 'hearing' that are aimed at establishing the validity, or at least the probable validity, of the underlying claim against the alleged debtor before he can be deprived of his property. . . ." Sniadach v. Family Finance Corp. (Harlan, J., concurring).

For the foregoing reasons, the judgments of the District Courts are vacated and these cases are remanded for further proceedings consistent with this opinion.

It is so ordered.

Vacated and remanded.

Mr. Justice POWELL and Mr. Justice REHNQUIST did not participate in the consideration or decision of these cases.

[The dissenting opinion of Justice WHITE is omitted.]

NOTES AND PROBLEMS

1. What did the court hold in *Fuentes*? One way of getting at that answer is to imagine yourself on the staff of a Florida legislative committee shortly after the statutes had been held unconstitutional.

a. What changes would render the statutes constitutional?

b. Suppose, realistically, that your legislator-boss tells you that she is under great pressure from finance companies, banks, and large retailers to achieve the necessary changes at minimum cost; what is the *smallest* change in procedures that would render them constitutional?

2. Can the parties negotiate around the requirements of *Fuentes*? The Court discusses the possibility of a waiver of the rights of the defendant.

a. Can you draft a waiver clause that would stand up to the Court's discussion in Fuentes?

b. Would it make a difference if the appliance store offered stoves at two prices — one, the regular "with hearing" price and a second, discounted price available if the customer signed a waiver?

3. *Fuentes* is important in its own right and also as a representative of many circumstances in which due process regulates government actions. In the debtor-creditor context the cases have established the proposition that, except in unusual circumstances, prejudgment seizure of a debtor's property without notice and an opportunity for a hearing is unconstitutional. Mitchell v. W.T. Grant Co., 416 U.S. 600 (1974); North Georgia Finishing Inc. v. Di-Chem, Inc., 419 U.S. 601 (1975). But collection attempts do not begin to exhaust the circumstances in which one must consider the meaning of due process.

a. Connecticut v. Doehr, 501 U.S. 1 (1991), considered a due process challenge to a Connecticut statute permitting the attachment of real estate at the instance of a plaintiff in any civil action. The lawsuit was a battery action unrelated to the real estate. The "attachment" consisted of the filing of a lien against the property rather than physical occupation or deprivation of the land; the defendant continued to live in the house throughout the attachment. The Court nevertheless held that, without either a pre-attachment hearing or a bond, there was too serious a risk of error in depriving defendant of a significant asset. On the basis of *Doehr,* can one say that any seizure without the opportunity for a hearing needs special justification?

b. In United States v. Good, 510 U.S. 43 (1993), the Court held that the exigency of a civil forfeiture action — in which property used for unlawful purposes is seized and forfeited to the government — did not justify the seizure without notice of real property.

4. *Fuentes* says situations in which the state may seize property without prior notice or hearing are "truly unusual." That may overstate the matter; the Court has proved quite flexible about due process, particularly in administrative settings.

a. Since *Fuentes* the Supreme Court has articulated a generalized framework for deciding when and what sort of hearing is required by due process:

> In Mathews v. Eldridge, 424 U.S. 319, 335 (1976), the Court set forth three factors that normally determine whether an individual has received the "process" that the Constitution finds "due":
>
> > "First, the private interest that will be affected by the official action; second, the risk of an erroneous deprivation of such interest through the procedures used, and the probable value, if any, of additional or substitute procedural safeguards; and finally, the Government's interest, including the function involved and the fiscal and administrative burdens that the additional or substitute procedural requirement would entail."
>
> By weighing these concerns, courts can determine whether a State has met the "fundamental requirement of due process" — "the opportunity to be heard 'at a meaningful time and in a meaningful manner.'"

City of Los Angeles v. David, 123 S. Ct. 1895, 1896 (2003).

b. How would you apply the Mathews v. Eldridge test to the facts of City of Los Angeles v. David? David's car was towed from a tow-away zone. Did that towing, which occurred without notice (except insofar as a partially obscured street sign gave general notice), violate due process? Work through the three *Mathews* factors.

c. David then paid $134 to retrieve his car, and asked for a hearing to get his money back, contending that his vehicle had been erroneously towed. That hearing occurred 27 days after the towing. David's suit contended that the length of the delay in a post-seizure hearing violated due process. Who should prevail?

d. Consider another situation in which there is government action but no judicial involvement. The county health department, in the course of a routine restaurant inspection, finds inadequate refrigeration and rampant Salmonella infestation, and orders immediate closure. Is that act unconstitutional because there was no opportunity for a prior hearing? Would the answer be different if the only defect identified by the inspector was a rusty knife blade?

5. The injunctive equivalent of a seizure without a hearing is a temporary restraining order (or TRO). TROs may be issued with even less process than preliminary injunctions. Indeed, under limited circumstances a TRO may be

issued ex parte — that is, without the presence or knowledge of the other party. Situations that might call for such drastic action include those in which there is not time to schedule a hearing (for example, bulldozers are about to excavate an area in which rare and legally protected Native American artifacts have just been discovered) or in which notice itself might trigger the action to be restrained (for example, in the case of a battering spouse).

a. How can such an ex parte TRO be squared with the principles of due process established in cases like *Fuentes*?

b. Read Rule 65(b), which governs the issuance of TROs in the federal courts. Which of its provisions are constitutionally required?

c. Plaintiff chicken farmer appears in court seeking an ex parte TRO to restrain defendant from conducting excavations by dynamite on defendant's adjacent land. The affidavits submitted with the application say that plaintiff's poultry will have their laying cycles seriously disrupted by such activities and that a two-day delay will enable the plaintiff to move them and prevent this harm. With which requirement of Rule 65(b) does plaintiff's affidavit fail to comply?

6. Review footnote 23 of *Fuentes*. Note that attachment for the purpose of obtaining jurisdiction is upheld on the basis of a compelling public interest. If a long-arm statute is available as an alternative means for obtaining jurisdiction, can the need for attachment be said to be compelling? After Shaffer v. Heitner (see Chapter II), does it follow that prejudgment attachment without hearing for the purpose of obtaining jurisdiction should no longer be available in a state whose long-arm statute reaches the limits of due process? Consider: There either are or are not minimum contacts. If there are, the long-arm statute should be available and there exists no compelling need for attachment. *Fuentes* thus forbids the attachment. If there are not, *Shaffer* forbids the use of attachment for obtaining jurisdiction.

Even if a state's statute does not reach the limits of due process, may a state argue that its need for attachment for jurisdictional purposes is therefore compelling when the state has the option of extending its statute?

7. Notice that *Fuentes* is a step in a centuries-long process back-and-forth between private action and judicial process.

a. Replevin arose as a response to creditor's self-help; replevin was a way of getting back goods a creditor had taken to induce payment of a debt.

b. By the time of *Fuentes* replevin is being used instead as a creditor's remedy, and the debtors are challenging its constitutionality.

c. But the *Fuentes* line of cases is based on the Due Process Clause, which forbids only a "state" from denying due process, leaving private action, entirely unsupervised by the judiciary, untouched, so long as the private actors do not violate civil or criminal statutes. Self-help repossession, authorized by UCC §9-503 when it can be accomplished without breach of the peace, does not involve state action.

d. Apply this understanding to the world of repossession. Explain why *Fuentes* will leave those repossessing automobiles largely unaffected but will change practices for those who sell household appliances and furniture.

8. Keep in mind that the issue in *Fuentes* was the constitutionality of prejudgment remedies. Attachment, garnishment, and the like continue to be widely used as means for victorious plaintiffs to collect their judgments.

This chapter has explored the reasons people litigate. That exploration has taken us from the global and statistical to the minutely doctrinal. We have begun to examine the lawyer's role in litigation by considering the fee system and its potential for linking or separating lawyer and client, but we have not yet begun to examine what lawyers actually do in litigation. The next chapter begins that inquiry by looking at the first step in a lawsuit—the ancient and honorable practice of pleading.

PLEADING

VI

To start a lawsuit, one has to know what one can ask for — the topic of the preceding chapter — and how to ask for it — the focus of this one. Not too long ago, the main task of a course in procedure would have been to learn the special formulas necessary to bring thirty or so kinds of claims, each of which had special, formulaic language associated with it. Today that is neither necessary nor possible. The problems of today's pleading are less complex but more subtle. In exploring this topic we shall use "pleading" to refer not only to the complaint but to the exchange of initial papers in a lawsuit. Those initial stages did — and sometimes still do — a good deal of sorting and defining.

A. The Story of Pleading

1. Telling Stories

Pleaders tell stories designed to get a court to give them something they want. Once upon a time, those stories were oral and relatively free-form, with the pleader telling the court what had happened and what he wanted the court to do about it. For many centuries now, pleading has been written, and the stories they tell have become conventions — fixed patterns that require certain plot elements. Some of these conventions are sufficiently important that a pleading will fail if it ignores them.

Consider two complaints, one old and one contemporary: What stories are they telling, and why do they tell them this way?

The King to the Sheriff of Nottinghamshire: greeting. If John Smith shall make you secure to prosecute his claim, then put by gages and safe pledges Richard Jones that he be brought before us on the octave of St. Michael, wheresoever we shall then be in England, to shew wherefore, whereas the same John had delivered a certain horse to the said Richard, at Nottingham, well and sufficiently to

Plaintiff John Smith (hereinafter "Plaintiff") alleges:

1. Plaintiff is a citizen of California and Defendant Barbara Jones is a citizen of New York. The matter in controversy exceeds, exclusive of interest and costs, the amount specified by 28 U.S.C. §1332.

2. On July 1, 2003, in a public highway called Wilshire Boulevard in Los Angeles, California, defendant

shoe, the same Richard fixed a certain nail in the quick of the foot of the aforesaid horse in such a manner that the horse was in many ways made worse, to the damage of him the said John one hundred shillings, as he saith. And have there the names of the pledges and this writ.

negligently drove a motor vehicle against plaintiff who was then crossing the highway.

3. As a result, plaintiff was thrown down, suffered a concussion, a broken leg and arm and severe internal injuries and was otherwise injured, was prevented from transacting his business, suffered great pain of body and mind, and incurred expenses for medical attention and hospitalization in the amount of $85,000.

Wherefore plaintiff demands judgment against defendant in the sum of $125,000.

NOTES AND PROBLEMS

1. The first sample is taken from a listing of all the common law writs — some thirty-odd different kinds of legal "story" — compiled in 1531, in the reign of Henry VIII. The second sample is adapted from the sample forms published 400 years later with the Federal Rules of Civil Procedure.

a. Both tell stories about something that happened (or, more precisely, something that the plaintiff *says* or "alleges" happened) before the lawsuit. Start by describing to yourself, in words you would use in a conversation with a friend, what those two stories were.

b. Both stories also include material you would be unlikely to include if you were describing things to your friend. For example, the first complaint contains a greeting to the sheriff of Nottingham (the villain of the Robin Hood legends, but also an actual royal official) and a reference to "gages and safe pledges." The second complaint tells us about the states of which the two parties are "citizens."

2. In both cases these "extras" reveal much about the legal system and provide clues to some of the procedural matters that may be disputed as the case proceeds.

a. The king's greeting to the sheriff provides one example. In medieval England right after the Norman Conquest (in 1066), royal justice (administered by the king, his sheriffs, and judges) was, in theory, special, something extraordinary. Ordinary cases were, again in theory, to be dealt with in local courts and would not involve royal officials. Plaintiffs who wanted to get royal justice — and many did because it quickly gained a reputation as fairer, faster, and generally more efficacious — had to take two steps. First, they had to convince the royal officials that the case was one that warranted royal justice. In early medieval times, this question was debated. Everyone agreed that the royal courts should attend to allegations of breaches of the peace — what today we might call violent crime. Even as royal justice extended to more "peaceful" forms of unlawfulness — failure to pay debts, breach of contract, and negligent injury — the pleadings retained the flavor of outrage. The defendant has not merely failed to keep his word or pay his debt; he has made things worse. Can you see this in the first pleading?

The second thing the plaintiff seeking royal justice had to do was to pay for it. Administering justice was a source of income to the crown, and a plaintiff wanting access to the royal courts had to pay. The writ issued only when the fee was paid, and the "greeting" to the sheriff was also an implicit assurance that the royal coffers had received the right number of shillings — what we would call today a filing fee — from the plaintiff.

b. Another striking characteristic of medieval royal justice was that — except in cases involving land — there was no such thing as a default judgment: The defendant had to appear for the court to proceed further. Defendants who thought they might lose were understandably reluctant to appear, and so early common law procedure devoted much effort to "encouraging" them to appear. The first stage was, as now, for the sheriff to summon them, and to require that they give him some assurance that they would show up on the date set for trial. The complaint sets the "octave of St. Michael," the week after the feast of St. Michael, on September 29, as the time when the defendant should appear before "us," meaning not the king (though in the middle ages the king himself occasionally heard lawsuits) but the royal justices. Defendants assured their appearance in court by two means — by posting what we would now call a bond, called a "gage" (bail bonds are still common in criminal cases, where they assure that defendant will appear) as well as by supplying persons, known as "pledges," who would personally promise to assure defendant's appearance. The writ above thus refers to "gages and safe pledges."

c. Consider now the modern pleading. It is addressed to the court, not to the sheriff, and, because we now have default judgments, it seems unconcerned with gages, pledges, and the like. On the other hand, it begins with a recitation of the state citizenship of the two parties, something that seems quite peripheral to the question of whether Jones's negligence caused Smith's injuries. In fact, that allegation is analogous to the king's greeting to the sheriff: It establishes the court's jurisdiction. In the twenty-first-century United States, federal courts (like medieval royal courts) have limited jurisdiction. One basis for that jurisdiction is "diversity of citizenship," defined in the Constitution and in 28 U.S.C. §1332, to which the complaint refers.

If the medieval complaint focuses on getting the defendant to appear, the modern one seems more concerned with the other end of the lawsuit — the nature of injuries and amount of damages claimed by the plaintiff. As we'll see, this "factuality" is a hallmark of modern lawsuits.

3. The ingredients of a modern complaint are relatively straightforward. Rule 8(a) contains the recipe — a recitation of the basis for jurisdiction, a "short and plain statement of the claim showing that the pleader is entitled to relief," and "a demand for judgment for the relief the pleader seeks." States adapting the Rules as their procedural guidelines usually omit the need to plead jurisdiction; do you understand why? The sample forms following the Rules give examples of some common complaints. The modern recipe is simple. But just as it is deceptively simple to say that a recipe for a soufflé involves only a sauce and some eggs, drafting a complaint requires a bit of art. Perhaps the best way to get started is by trying your own hand, by turning a story about spring break gone sour into a complaint.

a. Paul Pearson is a college student who resides in New York. He is a sophomore at St. Albans College, also in New York. Paul goes to Ft. Lauderdale,

Florida, on April 5, 2004, for spring break week. He rents a car, a blue Chevrolet. Early on the morning of April 8, 2004, at approximately 1:30 A.M., after waiting for the light to change at the intersection of First Avenue and Main Street in Ft. Lauderdale, Paul proceeds into the intersection after the light turns green, and his car is struck on the driver's side by a 1997 Ford van that ran the red light.

At the scene of the accident, the police interview the two teenage occupants of the Ford van, Diana Drip and Debbie Dolt. Drip states in her interview that the van is owned by an incorporated business, which is owned and operated by her parents, David and Dorothy Drip. The business is Drip Electrical Corp. The Drips and Dolt are all residents of the State of Florida. Drip Electrical Corp. is incorporated under the laws of the State of Florida and has its principal place of business in Ft. Lauderdale, Florida. Under Florida law, the driver of a motor vehicle and the owner of the vehicle are both liable for injuries proximately caused by negligent operation of the vehicle.

According to the police report, there are conflicting statements as to who was driving the van at the time of the accident. (Pearson himself did not have the opportunity to see who was driving). Drip said that she was using the van with her parents' permission the night of April 7, that she picked up her friend Debbie Dolt, the two of them went to some spring break parties, that Drip felt she had too much to drink to drive safely and she asked Dolt to drive them both back to Dolt's house where Drip planned to stay until morning. According to Drip's statement to the police, Dolt ran the red light and struck Pearson's vehicle.

Dolt told the police that Drip picked her up the night of April 7 and the two of them went to some spring break parties, that Dolt felt that Drip had too much to drink to drive safely, that Dolt offered to drive them both back to Dolt's house, but Drip refused to let Dolt drive because Drip's father had told her not to allow friends to drive the company van. According to Dolt's statement to the police, Drip was driving at the time of the accident and ran the red light and struck Pearson's vehicle.

Three insurance policies are potentially implicated. The Ford van owned by Drip Electrical Corp. has liability insurance coverage issued by Acme Insurance with limits of $100,000 per person/$200,000 per accident. Drip's parents also own another vehicle personally, which is insured by Beacon Insurance with liability limits of $30,000 per person/$60,000 per accident. Debbie Drip is an insured driver on the Beacon Insurance policy, and the liability coverage applies if she is driving some other vehicle. Dolt's parents also own a vehicle which is insured by Countrywide Insurance with liability limits of $50,000 per person/$100,000 per accident. Dolt is an insured driver on the Countrywide Insurance policy, and the liability coverage applies if she is driving some other vehicle. All three insurance companies are incorporated in the State of Delaware and have their principal place of business in Omaha, Nebraska.

As a result of the accident, Paul Pearson has several broken bones and lacerations. He is hospitalized for 7 days (the bill is $20,000) and his injuries force him to drop out of college for the rest of the spring semester (without any refund of his tuition of $8000/per semester). His injuries heal, but he is left with some scarring on his left arm and with intermittent pain in his right knee. The prognosis regarding the right knee is uncertain. It is possible that the pain will be permanent, but it might get better over time. Paul plans on going to graduate school after college, but he is uncertain as to his planned field of studies. Because he has lost an undergraduate semester, Paul fears that his post-graduate studies will be delayed for a full year, and that he will lose one year of potential income in whatever career he pursues after college and graduate school.

b. Suppose that Paul consults a lawyer in Florida, who decides that federal court is the right place for the lawsuit (perhaps because the federal docket moves somewhat faster than that of the state courts). You are working as a summer associate for Paul's lawyer, who hears that you've had an excellent civil procedure class and asks you to draft a complaint for his review. Draft it.

4. As you drafted, you doubtless had to decide which of the details in the narrative account to include and which to omit. Too little and it's hard for the recipient or the court to know what the dispute about. Too much and it violates the short, plain statement rule and perhaps commits you to proving things that may be difficult. Thus a complaint that said merely, "Defendant has wronged me" would be insufficient. And a complaint that described every event in all the parties' lives for the preceding year would lose the forest for the trees. So how much detail is enough without being too much? Speaking broadly, this is the central problem with which pleading in the English-speaking world has wrestled over the past several hundred years.

a. The common law writs (like the one from the sixteenth century quoted above) suffered from what might be called hardening of the arteries. The forms had been fixed for so many centuries that pleaders knew exactly what allegations would be held sufficient but were fearful to depart from these well-trodden paths, even if the facts of their case made the stock allegations deceptive. For example, by the eighteenth century a pleader might allege that defendant "with force and arms broke and entered the close [i.e., fenced property], trampled on, consumed, and spoiled the grass and herbage of the property. . . ." Such allegations stated a claim for a form of trespass. In fact, the dispute might be over who really owned the property in question, and the allegations of trampling and the like were just conventions, designed to get a court to decide who owned the property. Under such conditions a pleading revealed almost nothing about the real dispute.

b. One solution, espoused by David Dudley Field, a leading lawyer and law reformer of the mid-nineteenth century, was to require not formulas but facts. The procedural reforms he sponsored, known as the "Field Codes" (codes, because they were statutes rather than common law rules), stressed facts:

California Code of Civil Procedure (West 2003)

§425.10. A complaint or cross-complaint shall contain both of the following:
(a) A statement of the facts constituting the cause of action, in ordinary and concise language.
(b) A demand for judgment for the relief to which the pleader claims he is entitled. . . .

Nebraska Revised Statutes (2003)

§25-802. The rules of pleading formerly existing in civil actions are abolished and hereafter the forms of pleading of civil actions in courts of record, and the rules by which their sufficiency may be determined are those prescribed by this code.

§25-804. The petition must contain . . . a statement of the facts constituting the cause of action, in ordinary and concise language, and without repetition; and . . . a demand for the relief to which the party supposes himself entitled. . . .

The Codes thus replaced the formulas of the writs with "facts" and the forms of actions with the "cause of action." Both changes aimed at correcting what was thought to be a major failing of the common law system, but each created problems of its own. Thus, despite the reforms, pleading litigation did not go away. One source of the litigation was the circumstance that, although technical pleading had been abolished, the substantive law as incorporated into the forms of action had not. Moreover, courts interpreted the phrase "cause of action" to refer to this substantive law and treated each cause of action as mutually exclusive. For example, one finds a court insisting that a complaint setting forth the elements of a fraud claim could be treated only as a fraud claim, even if plaintiff proved breach of contract. Ross v. Mather, 51 N.Y. 108 (1872).

Another source of litigation was the requirement for stating "*facts* constituting the *cause of action*" (emphasis added). Assuming one knew what the cause of action was, when were allegations considered either too specific ("mere evidence," as the cases sometimes called them) or too general ("mere conclusions") to fit the requirement of "facts"? Either failing could lead to the sustaining of a demurrer to the complaint. For example, in Gillispie v. Goodyear Service Stores, 258 N.C. 487, 128 S.E.2d 762 (1963), the court upheld the dismissal of a complaint in trespass, noting that the plaintiff alleged, "in a single sentence, that defendants, 'without cause or just excuse and maliciously,' trespassed upon premises occupied by [plaintiff] as a residence." The court ruled that "[t]he complaint states no facts upon which these legal conclusions may be predicated." 128 S.E.2d at 765-766.

c. The Federal Rules, adopted in 1938, sought a way between the formulas of the writs and the "facts" of the Codes:

Federal Rule of Civil Procedure 8(a)

Claims for Relief. A pleading which sets forth a claim for relief . . . shall contain (1) [an allegation of jurisdiction], (2) a short and plain statement of the claim showing that the pleader is entitled to relief, and (3) a demand for judgment for the relief the pleader seeks. Relief in the alternative or of several different types may be demanded.

5. Rule 8 is in one respect a masterful piece of evasion.

a. First, consider the attempt to evade. Suppose a member of the bar suggests to the Rules Advisory Committee (which considers revisions to the Rules) that Rule 8(a)(2) be revised to refer to "facts" and to "claim constituting a cause of action"? On the basis of experience with the Field Codes, what points of controversy would you expect to arise?

b. How does the existing Rule seek to avoid those problems?

6. But does the effort to evade really work?

a. Suppose a pleading in which the complaint, after the requisite jurisdictional allegations, stated, "Defendant has long persisted in a series of unlawful actions which have cost plaintiff many thousands of dollars" and then asked for damages. Would such a complaint be adequate?

b. Your intuitive answer to the preceding question is likely to be "no." But it's slightly more difficult to ground this (correct) intuition in the language of Rule 8. The imagined complaint is certainly "short," as the Rule requires. And it is "plain," if that word denotes unadorned, everyday language rather than legal jargon.

c. So what's wrong? The answer has to be either that the language in question is not a "claim" or, if it's a claim, it does not "show[] that the pleader is entitled to relief." That's because a complaint, even one without fancy or archaic language, has to do two things:

- invoke, at least by reference, a body of substantive law;
- sketch a factual scenario that, if shown to be true, falls within that body of law.

The problem with the complaint in Note 5a is that it does neither of those things. It does not refer to any identifiable body of law, and it does not sketch any facts that would fall within such a legal framework.

d. If the conclusory allegations in Note 5a are fatally lacking in detail, consider the opposite problem — a complaint that is too detailed. In Gordon v. Green, 602 F.2d 743 (5th Cir. 1979), plaintiff's complaints in five consolidated securities fraud cases totaled 4,000 pages, occupied eighteen volumes, and required a hand truck or cart to move. After finding noncompliance with Rule 8 and noting that such pleadings would "hasten the speed at which our country's trees are being transformed into sheets of legal jargon," the court dismissed the complaint with leave to file an amended complaint. According to the court, counsel were lucky that the discipline was not akin to that meted out by the chancellor in 1596 who "decided to make an example of a particularly prolix document filed in his court. The chancellor first ordered a hole cut through the center of the document, all 120 pages of it. Then he ordered that the person who wrote it should have his head stuffed through the hole, and the unfortunate fellow was led around to be exhibited to all those attending court at Westminster Hall."

7. For a contrast to the excessively cursory and the excessively detailed, look again at the two pleadings at the start of this section.

a. What body of law do they invoke?

b. What factual occurrences do they depend on?

c. As a general proposition, if a complaint doesn't invoke a framework of substantive law or provide facts that fit inside that framework, it's defective. As we'll see, sometimes the defect is a result of lawyer's carelessness and can be fixed by better drafting. Other times the problem is that the substantive law doesn't stretch to cover the facts in question; if that's the problem, even the most artful drafting won't solve the problem: The case simply lacks merit.

8. For the student, probably the most difficult aspect of pleading under the Rules is that complaints need not explicitly invoke a legal framework. A complaint, for example, need not say "Claim for Negligence" (though some lawyers do include such helpful labels). The complaint adequately invokes the law of negligence if it simply, in reciting the facts, states that "defendant negligently operated his vehicle." An experienced lawyer draws from that single adverb a whole framework of the law of negligence; the student often has more trouble.

a. Be patient with yourself; you will soon be able to identify the substantive law behind most complaints.

b. For practice, look again at the complaints at the start of this section. What bodies of substantive law do they invoke? In which of your first-year courses would you expect to learn the requirements of the two bodies of law that lie behind these short accounts?

c. Finally, take comfort from the fact that at least one state has agreed with your frustration, and has established a series of forms that (a) make explicit the body of law being invoked and (b) seek to make the initial pleading as routine as possible. Suppose you sold a used car to a former friend, who hasn't paid you the agreed-on price. Imagine how you would fill out the following form.

SHORT TITLE:		CASE NUMBER:

_____ **CAUSE OF ACTION**—Breach of Contract _____ Page _____
    (number)

ATTACHMENT TO ☐ Complaint ☐ Cross-Complaint

(Use a separate cause of action form for each cause of action.)

BC-1. Plaintiff *(name):*

    alleges that on or about *(date):*
    a ☐ written ☐ oral ☐ other *(specify):*
    agreement was made between *(name parties to agreement):*

    ☐ A copy of the agreement is attached as Exhibit A, or
    ☐ The essential terms of the agreement ☐ are stated in Attachment BC-1 ☐ are as follows *(specify):*

BC-2. On or about *(dates):*
    defendant breached the agreement by ☐ the acts specified in Attachment BC-2 ☐ the following acts
    (specify):

BC-3. Plaintiff has performed all obligations to defendant except those obligations plaintiff was prevented or excused from performing.

BC-4. Plaintiff suffered damages legally (proximately) caused by defendant's breach of the agreement
    ☐ as stated in Attachment BC-4 ☐ as follows *(specify):*

BC-5. ☐ Plaintiff is entitled to attorney fees by an agreement or a statute
    ☐ of $
    ☐ according to proof.

BC-6. ☐ Other:

Form Approved by the
Judicial Council of California
Effective January 1, 1982
Rule 982.1(21)   **CAUSE OF ACTION**—Breach of Contract   WEST GROUP Official Publisher   CCP 425.12

2. The Functions of Pleading

In speaking of the substantive law and of its relation to the facts of a case we have begun to move from the technique of pleading to a theory of its functions.

At common law, the royal courts, once they had concluded that the case belonged to them, faced a second decision: what to do with it. To help with this decision, they put the litigants through an elaborate dance of pleading. It is sometimes said that common law pleading aimed at defining precisely the issue in contention between the parties. That assertion is only partly true. Common law pleading aimed, above all, at separating two different kinds of disputes: those that focused on law and those that focused on fact. Disputes about law were supposed to be settled by judges; those about fact by juries. The pleading system isolated the area of dispute sufficiently so that judges could determine, first, whether there was a factual dispute for the jury to hear, and, second, what that dispute was.

To perform this isolating function, the pleading system put the parties to a series of stark choices. Unlike contemporary pleading, early common law pleading forced parties to stake their whole case on either law or fact, by requiring the parties to trade responses until they had, in effect, agreed on what they were disagreeing about. In principle, common law pleading permitted a limited number of quite simple responses to allegations, many of which survive in our current system, though under different names:

1. Challenges to the *jurisdiction* of the court. Translated into contemporary colloquialism, these pleas said, "Not here."
2. *Pleas in suspension* challenged the plaintiff's right to bring the action until some problem was resolved; suppose, for example, the defendant claimed he was an enemy alien who could not defend himself until hostilities ceased. "Not now," such pleas said.
3. *Pleas in abatement* challenged various other procedural defects in the complaint, ranging from the incorrect spelling of defendant's name to the pendency of another action on the same claim between the same parties. "Not until this defect has been fixed," such a plea responded.

[handwritten margin note: pleas not based on merit — dilatory pleas]

These first three pleas have something in common: None of them approaches the merits of the case. They take no position on either the facts or the law. As a consequence, they were known as *dilatory pleas*, responses that delayed the suit, perhaps permanently, but did not constitute a resolution of its merits. A defendant could make multiple dilatory pleas, but they had to be presented one at a time in a specified order. Dilatory pleas made too late were waived.

If a defendant could not dispose of a pleading through a dilatory plea, he had to make a series of choices. Essentially, these choices forced the pleader to decide between resting on the facts and resting on the law, and, as to the facts, between denying the other side's facts and pleading additional facts of one's own. These responses were called *peremptory* pleas; unlike pleas in abatement they grappled with the merits of the claim:

[handwritten margin note: peremptory pleas — based on merit]

4. A *demurrer*, which conceded the truth of the opponent's factual allegations but challenged their legal sufficiency. "So what?" serves as a rough translation of the demurrer.

5. A *traverse*, the opposite of a demurrer, conceded the legal sufficiency of the plea but denied its factual allegations. "Not true," captures the idea behind a traverse.

6. A plea of *confession and avoidance* conceded the legal sufficiency and the factual truth of the preceding plea, but alleged additional facts that changed their significance. "Yes but," serves as a rough paraphrase of the confession and avoidance. For example, if the plaintiff pleaded trespass to land, the defendant might, by way of confession and avoidance, plead that the plaintiff had granted him an easement on the land. See Layman v. Southwestern Bell, infra page 387. This plea conceded that there was a cause of action for trespass and that the defendant had entered the plaintiff's land but, by alleging the grant of an easement, sought to "avoid" the effect of these concessions.

The system of common law pleading has vanished, but its structure remains. Read Federal Rules of Civil Procedure 8(b), (c), 12(b). Today, pleading gives the plaintiff the first official opportunity to tell his story and gives defendants a chance for quick, inexpensive victory.

NOTES AND PROBLEMS

1. Compare Rule 8 and Rule 12(b).
a. Where are the old "dilatory" pleas?
b. Which of the defenses enumerated in Rule 8 corresponds to the traverse?
c. Which of the defenses in Rule 8 corresponds to the plea in confession and avoidance?
d. Read Federal Rule of Civil Procedure 12(b)(6). What was its common law analogue?
2. Consider which of the common law pleas and which of their Rules analogues the defendant should enter in each of the following circumstances:
a. Plaintiff alleges that defendant insulted him in public; defendant believes that the law does not permit recovery for verbal insults unaccompanied by violence.
b. Plaintiff alleges that defendant struck her; defendant says he was not present at the time and place alleged.
c. Plaintiff alleges that defendant and plaintiff signed a contract, whose terms defendant then violated. Defendant contends that she refused to honor the agreement because the plaintiff forced her to sign at gunpoint.
3. Explain why a defendant at common law, in deciding whether to demur or traverse, was also choosing who would decide the case. Explain why, in filing a Rule 12(b) motion, the defendant is similarly telling the court who should decide the case.

The question in Note 3 points to a continuing strategic significance of the common law structure of pleading. Lawsuits can involve two kinds of disputes:

- those about the content of law: What events have to occur for a contract to be formed? When is a person liable for negligently inflicted emotional distress?
- those about the reconstruction of historical events: Did Dolt run through a red light just before the accident? Were the widgets delivered to buyer defective?

By and large, disputes about the content of law are faster and cheaper to decide. Two lawyers and a judge, aided by a law library, can work out most questions of law faster than it will take to interview witnesses, gather documents and physical evidence to reconstruct facts, and invoke procedures for deciding disputed facts. This discrepancy becomes even larger if the witnesses have to testify in person at a hearing or before a jury (which itself must be assembled).

And here lies the great strategic importance of the Rule 12(b) motions — the old dilatory pleas and one of the three peremptory pleas. All of them, if granted, either delay or end the lawsuit — giving the defendant either a temporary or a permanent victory. Even better, from the defendant's standpoint (and even worse from that of the plaintiff), they do so at an early stage of the proceedings. Even better than that — again from the defendant's point of view — they do so cheaply.

Their cheapness resides in the circumstance that one of these motions, the 12(b)(6) motion to dismiss for failure to state a claim, is entirely a matter of law: No contested historical facts are involved. The complaint either states a claim or it doesn't — a question that can be resolved by a judge and a pile of law books. The other 12(b) motions may require some facts (Did the defendant do enough business in the forum state to satisfy the requirements of personal jurisdiction? Was the defendant served with process?), but these facts will often be easy to present and, even if they are contested, they will be decided by the judge on the basis of files and documents, not witnesses testifying in open court. So all of these motions give the defendant an early and a relatively cheap victory — making them understandably popular with the defendants' bar. Conversely, a case that has survived a Rule 12 motion is likely in for a long haul and therefore has a higher settlement value. It's in the right court, there is no glaring procedural problem, and it is, by definition, a case about disputed facts.

NOTES AND PROBLEMS

1. Paul Pearson, using the complaint you drafted for him in the preceding section of this chapter, files a lawsuit in Federal District Court in the Southern District of Florida.

a. Debbie Dolt, one of the defendants, files a 12(b)(6) motion to dismiss. Explain what will happen if Dolt wins her motion.

b. Explain why her lawyer, probably hired by Dolt's insurance carrier, will be particularly happy if this motion succeeds.

2. Before the Rule 12(b)(6) motion, Dolt's insurance carrier has made an offer to settle for $1,000. Pearson, the plaintiff, has turned down the offer to settle on these terms.

a. If the court denies Dolt's motion to dismiss, would you expect the carrier's next offer to be higher or lower? Why?

b. If the court denies Dolt's motion, how will this change the insurance carrier's litigation budget for this case? Why?

c. If the court denies Dolt's motion, what changes is this likely to make in the plaintiff's lawyer's litigation budget for the case? Why?

Modern pleading and motion practice fulfills three functions. It quickly eliminates cases that suffer from significant procedural defects — those captured in Rule 12(b)(1), (3), (4), (5), and (7). It shapes the discovery process that will be the central feature of many cases. Finally, via Rule 12(b)(6) pleading can occasionally eliminate a claim entirely, saving substantial public and private dollars. But this latter possibility comes with a danger: Because pleading occupies a very early stage of a lawsuit, one risks cutting off claims that, with further development, could prove meritorious. In particular, there is a risk of eliminating claims that, though badly pleaded, could be repaired. Take, again as an example, a hypothetical pleading in the case of Paul Pearson v. Diana Drip. Suppose, in the central paragraph of the complaint, Pearson's lawyer pleads as follows:

¶3. On a public road at the intersection of First Avenue and Main Street in Ft. Lauderdale, Florida, on or about April 8, 2003, defendant Dolt or defendant Drip collided with a vehicle driven by Plaintiff which was then lawfully entering said intersection.

¶4. Plaintiff was severely injured.

Wherefore plaintiff demands judgment against defendant Dolt Electrical, and against either defendant Dolt or defendant Drip, according to proof, in the sum of at least $200,000 and costs of suit and for such other and further relief as the Court may deem just and appropriate.

NOTES AND PROBLEMS

1. What is wrong with these paragraphs? Concretely, why would the claim be dismissed on a demurrer or Rule 12(b)(6) motion?

2. Can the defects in these paragraphs be cured? This is the critical question.

a. Procedurally the answer is yes, but. . . . A court will almost never dismiss a complaint without granting the plaintiff leave to amend. But a court will not grant leave to amend unless the plaintiff's lawyer can, within the constraints of truthfulness and professional ethics, amend the complaint in such a way that it will withstand a second motion to dismiss.

b. If the problem lies solely in the lawyer's incompetence, the necessary additional language can be added to these paragraphs and they will be demurrer-proof.

c. If the problem lies instead in the historical record, then the problem is not one of technical incompetence. To put it concretely, if the reason the complaint is drafted this way is that there is no reason to believe defendant was driving negligently or that her negligence caused the accident, there is no ethical way to amend the complaint in a way that will withstand the demurrer.

d. Many lawyers think that if a defective complaint is a result only of the drafter's technical incompetence, a motion to dismiss is not a worthwhile effort. "There is no sense in using your client's money to educate your adversary's lawyer," the saying goes. What's the idea behind this bit of folklore?

e. Read the following complaint and the litigation it produced, asking yourself what the defendant sought to gain by the motion to dismiss.

In the United States District Court for the Southern District of Georgia

p. 340

MICHAEL A. HADDLE,
    Plaintiff

vs.   Civ. No. 96-00029-CV-1-AAA

JEANETTE G. GARRISON [et al.]
    Defendants.   *federal question*

COMPLAINT FOR DAMAGES PURSUANT TO 42 U.S.C. §1985(2) (THE CIVIL RIGHTS ACT OF 1871), THE GEORGIA RICO STATUTE AND GEORGIA LAW OF TORTIOUS INTERFERENCE AND FRAUDULENT CONVEYANCE

NOW COMES Plaintiff MICHAEL A. HADDLE and for this his complaint against Defendants JEANETTE G. GARRISON ("Garrison"), DENNIS KELLY ("Kelly"), PETER MOLLOY ("Molloy"), HEALTHMASTER, INC. ("Healthmaster"), and shows as follows:

Introductory Statement

1. Plaintiff is a citizen and resident of the State of Georgia.

2. Defendant Garrison is a resident of the State of South Carolina.

3. Defendants Molloy [and] Kelly are residents of the Southern District of Georgia.

4. Defendant Healthmaster is a corporation organized and existing under the laws of the State of Georgia with its principal place of business within the Southern District of Georgia.

5. Jurisdiction is proper in this Court over Count I of this Complaint (the Civil Rights Act of 1871) by virtue of 28 U.S.C. §1331. Jurisdiction over Count II (Georgia RICO), Count III (Tortious Interference) and Count IV

All Counts
relate
back to
Count 1

Federal
Civil
Rights/SEL

(Fraudulent Conveyance) is proper in this Court because these Counts are
pendent to Count I.

6. Venue is proper in this Court in that most Defendants reside within the
Southern District of Georgia and in that the actions of all Defendants as
alleged below occurred within the Southern District of Georgia.

General Factual Allegations

7. From September 22, 1986 until approximately April 13, 1995, Plaintiff
was employed by Defendant Healthmaster.

8. From approximately April 13, 1995, until his discharge as alleged
below, Plaintiff was employed by Healthmaster Home Health Care, Inc., a
Georgia corporation whose stock is owned entirely by Defendant
Healthmaster.

9. Defendant Garrison has at all relevant times owned 50% of the stock of
Healthmaster and controlled Healthmaster until April or May, 1995, when
a trustee was appointed for Healthmaster, then a debtor in possession under
Chapter II of the federal Bankruptcy Code, by the United States Bankruptcy
Court for the Southern District of Georgia.

10. The individual Defendants herein have all served in various capacities as corporate officers and directors of Defendant Healthmaster and of
Healthmaster Home Health Care, Inc.

11. Defendant Molloy has at all relevant times been employed by
Defendant Healthmaster or Healthmaster Home Health Care, Inc.

12. On March 8, 1995, a grand jury convened in the United States
District Court for the Southern District of Georgia, Augusta Division, filed
an indictment against Defendants Garrison, Kelly, Healthmaster, and others
charging a total of 133 counts of fraud against various defendants, which
indictment is enumerated as number CR-195-11 in this Court.

13. Although not indicted, Defendant Molloy was, on information and
belief, a target of the ongoing criminal investigation.

14. Plaintiff cooperated with the investigation by federal agents which
preceded this indictment and testified pursuant to subpoena before said grand
jury and appeared pursuant to subpoena to testify before said grand jury,
although his testimony was not actually taken due to the press of time.[*]

15. As a result of their indictment, Defendants Garrison and Kelly were
banned from any participation in the affairs of Healthmaster Home Health
Care, Inc., by order of said Bankruptcy Court.

16. On June 21, 1995, after Defendants had become aware that Plaintiff
would appear as a witness at the criminal trial of Indictment No. CR 195-11,
Defendant Molloy, who was then President of Defendant Healthmaster,
having been retained in said position by the trustee, but acting at the direction of Defendants Garrison and Kelly and pursuant to a prior understanding

---

* [Sic. A conversation with plaintiff's lawyer suggested this inconsistent language may be the
result of an early, unamended pleading being made part of the record on appeal. — Ed.]

and agreement between these three persons, terminated Plaintiff from his employment at Healthmaster Home Health Care, Inc.

Count I — Conspiracy in Violation of 42 U.S.C. §1985(2)
(The Civil Rights Act of 1871)

17. The allegations contained in paragraphs numbered "1" through "16" are incorporated herein by reference.

18. The decision to terminate Plaintiff was made by Defendants and others not in furtherance of the business interests of Defendant Healthmaster, but instead for the purpose of retaliating against Plaintiff for his cooperation with federal agents and his testimony under subpoena to the federal grand jury, and in order to intimidate Plaintiff and others from cooperating with federal agents or testifying in any criminal matters against them including said indictment.

19. Defendants participated in and carried out the decision to terminate Plaintiff, not in furtherance of the business interests of Defendant Healthmaster, but rather to protect themselves as criminal defendants or potential criminal defendants.

20. By means of the described actions, and their agreement and plan to do the same, Defendants have violated 42 U.S.C. §1985(2), in that they have conspired within the State of Georgia to deter, by force, intimidation or threat, a party or witness in the United States District Court for the Southern District of Georgia, from attending such court, or from testifying in any matter pending therein, freely, fully, and truthfully, or to injure such party or witness in his person or property on account of his having so attended or testified, or to influence the verdict, presentment, or indictment of the grand jurors of such court.

21. Plaintiff has been injured in his person and property by the acts of Defendants in violation of 42 U.S.C. §1985(2), and Plaintiff is entitled to recover his damages occasioned by such injury and deprivation against Defendants jointly and severally.

22. Because said Defendants' acts were willful, intentional and malicious, Plaintiff is entitled to recover punitive damages against Defendants jointly and severally.

23. Pursuant to 42 U.S.C. §1988, Plaintiff is entitled to recover his expenses of litigation including a reasonable attorney's fee from said Defendants jointly and severally.

[The Counts alleging statutory and common law claims under Georgia state law are omitted.]

PRAYER FOR RELIEF

WHEREFORE, Plaintiff demands trial by jury on all counts and judgment as to all Defendants jointly and severally for money damages in such amount for actual damages as the evidence may show and as to all Defendants, jointly and severally, judgment for punitive damages and reasonable attorneys' fees and expenses of litigation, together with all costs of Court and such other and further relief as the Court may deem equitable and just.

NOTES AND PROBLEMS

1. To see the issue raised by this complaint, one must start with the text and history of 42 U.S.C. §1985(2). The statute was enacted in the wake of the Civil War and aimed at those who sought to intimidate newly freed former slaves by preventing them from using courts to enforce newly granted constitutional rights.
a. The statute provides:

> If two or more persons in any State or Territory conspire to deter, by force, intimidation, or threat, any party or witness in any court of the United States from attending such court, or from testifying to any matter pending therein, freely, fully, and truthfully, or to injure such party or witness in his person or property on account of his having so attended or testified . . . the party so injured or deprived may have an action for the recovery of damages, occasioned by such injury or deprivation, against any one or more of the conspirators.

b. As with any statute creating a claim, one has to analyze the terms in which the claim is created, considering which, if any, of them will raise issues on the facts alleged. To use an easy example, on the facts as alleged no problem of pleading arises as to the number of conspirators: If all happened as plaintiffs alleged, "two or more persons" — as required by the statute — conspired to have Michael Haddle fired. Is there a problem with the pleading insofar as it alleges that the firing was retaliation for Haddle's testimony before the grand jury? Does the statutory phrase "attend[] any court . . . [and] testify[] to any matter" cover such a situation?

2. Focus now on the statutory phrase "to injure such party or witness in his person or property on account of his having so attended or testified."
a. Haddle does not allege that anyone threatened him physically, so we can disregard the statutory phrase "in his person." His claim must be that the firing injured him "in his . . . property." What "property"?
b. Now consider Georgia's law of employment. Under the relevant Georgia labor statutes, any employment agreement that is not for a specified term is considered to be at will — that is, terminable by the employer for any reason or for no reason at all.
c. Based on the preceding analysis, construct an argument for the defendants that — however unadmirable their actions may have been — those actions did not violate the federal civil rights statute quoted above.

3. You represent the defendant. Your client denies that she fired Haddle in retaliation for his willingness to testify, and you are prepared to present that defense on the facts. But you also realize that the sequence of events look bad; moreover, your client has since pleaded guilty to federal felony charges and you will therefore be asking the jury to believe the testimony of a criminal, in a case where on cross-examination the plaintiff will be able to introduce the following testimony from Jeanette Garrison before the U.S. Senate Committee on Aging:

> My name is Jeanette Garrison. I am a nurse by training. I am married to Joseph Garrison, a now retired anesthesiologist. . . . I was the Chair of the Board and

President of Healthmaster, Inc., a Medicare paid home health care company. I also am a convicted felon. I pleaded guilty in July 1995 to ten (10) counts of Medicare fraud. My company and I have repaid the federal and state government sixteen million five hundred thousand dollars ($16,500,000.). I currently am serving a thirty-three (33) month sentence in a federal prison.

So, if there is a defense that will not involve a credibility contest between your client and her adversary, you would like to take advantage of it.

a. Is there? What is it?

b. The next case describes what the defendant did and the district court's response.

Haddle v. Garrison (S.D. Ga. 1996)

Rule 8   After motion to dismiss

Unpublished Opinion. Docket No. 96-00029-CV-1 (S.D. Ga. 1996)

ALAIMO, J.

Plaintiff, Michael A. Haddle, has brought the current litigation seeking damages under Section 1985(2) of Title 42 of the United States Code, and state law. Presently before the Court are four [defendants'] motions to dismiss for failure to state a claim upon which relief can be granted under Rule 12(b)(6) of the Federal Rules of Civil Procedure. For the reasons stated below, Defendants' motions will be GRANTED.

Facts

Haddle is a former employee of Healthmaster Home Health Care, Inc. He claims that he was improperly discharged from his employment by Defendants in an attempt to deter his participation as a witness in a Federal criminal trial. At the times relevant to this litigation, Haddle concedes that he was an at-will employee.

Discussion

I.   Rule 12(b)(6)

Rule 12(b)(6) permits a defendant to move to dismiss a complaint on the grounds that the plaintiff has failed to state a claim upon which relief can be granted. A motion under Rule 12(b)(6) attacks the legal sufficiency of the complaint. In essence, the movant says, "Even if everything you allege is true, the law affords you no relief." Consequently, in determining the merits of a 12(b)(6) motion, a court must assume that all of the factual allegations of the complaint are true. A court should not dismiss a complaint for failure to state a claim unless it is clear that the plaintiff can prove "no set of facts in support of his claim which would entitle him to relief." Conley v. Gibson, 355 U.S. 41, 45-46 (1957).

II.   42 U.S.C. §1985(2). . . .

In the case at bar, Haddle asserts that he can maintain an action under Section 1985(2) despite the fact that he was defined as an at-will employee during the term of his employment. This is directly contrary to binding precedent of the Eleventh Circuit. Case law states:

> [T]o make out a cause of action under §1985(2) the plaintiff must have suffered an actual injury. Because [Plaintiff] was an at-will employee . . . he has no constitutionally protected interest in continued employment. Therefore, [Plaintiff's] discharge did not constitute an actual injury under this statute.

Morast v. Lance, 807 F.2d 926, 930 (11th Cir. 1987). Given the clear language of Morast, the Court is required to DISMISS Haddle's claim under Section 1985(2).

[The district court declined to exercise supplemental jurisdiction over the state law claims.]

Conclusion

The Court has determined that, under Rule 12(b)(6) Haddle has failed to state a federal claim upon which relief can be granted. His claim under Section 1985(2) is DISMISSED with respect to the above named Defendants. Additionally, all state law claims are DISMISSED WITHOUT PREJUDICE.

NOTES AND PROBLEMS

1. In what respect did the district court find that Haddle's case was deficient?

a. Did the district court make a factual determination that Haddle had not been fired? That he had not cooperated with the federal investigation? That he had not agreed to testify before the grand jury? That he had not been fired because of his cooperation with the federal investigation and prosecution?

b. If not, why was the complaint dismissed? Which element did the district court find to be missing from the complaint?

2. The district court cites well-settled law that, in deciding a motion under Rule 12(b)(6), the "court must assume that all of the factual allegations of the complaint are true." That phrase is the key to understanding what a 12(b)(6) motion, or its analogue, the demurrer, is about.

a. Is the allegation in Paragraph 21 that Haddle was "injured in his person or property" a factual allegation?

b. If it is a factual allegation, should the district court have dismissed the complaint? If it is not a factual allegation, what is it?

3. The district court's order states that Haddle conceded he was an at-will employee.

a. Does the complaint itself state that Haddle was an at-will employee?

b. Is it reasonable to treat the complaint as conceding that Haddle was an at-will employee because it does not allege that his employment was for a specified

term? Is it possible that the concession the district court refers to was made somewhere other than in the complaint itself? Imagine oral argument on the motion
to dismiss, at which the judge asked Haddle's lawyer if he was contending that his
client had some form of protected employment. The lawyer says no. At that point
the judge could ask that the complaint be amended to make that clear or could
simply treat the concession as part of the pleading as it stood.

4. To distinguish a 12(b)(6) motion from other attacks on plaintiff's claim,
imagine some alternative scenarios. Suppose the defendants had moved to
dismiss on the ground that Haddle had quit his job and had not been fired, and
defendants had submitted in support of the motion a letter signed by Haddle
admitting he had quit. Explain why, in such a scenario, the district court could
not have granted a motion to dismiss under Rule 12(b)(6) on the ground that
Haddle had quit and not been fired. See the second sentence of Rule 12(c).

5. Is there anything Haddle's lawyer could have put into the complaint that
would have cured the problem that led the district court to dismiss?

a. Suppose Haddle's lawyer concluded that the judge was about to dismiss his
complaint because he had not alleged that his client held a job more permanent
than at-will employment — that, for example, he had a contract stating that the
employer could dismiss him only for "good cause."

b. Imagine a conversation between a law student and Haddle's lawyer:

Student: Let me see if I understand what's going on. The case was dismissed
because the complaint failed to allege some things — that Mr. Haddle had a
certain kind of clause in his employment contract or understanding with his
employer that he would be fired only for good cause.
Lawyer: Right.
Student: Do you have to prove things in a complaint?
Lawyer: No; proof comes later — during discovery, summary judgment, and
trial, if things come to that. Complaints are just allegations — things you
write down on paper, not evidence.
Student: So what's the problem? As I understand it, a judge will almost always
allow leave to amend either before or after a 12(b)(6) dismissal. Now that
you know what you should have alleged, all you need to do is to get leave
to amend, and then write down the things — about Haddle's terms of
employment — that will satisfy the judge. Just say that he had a written
contract guaranteeing that he would be fired only for good cause. Why the
fuss?
Lawyer: Hold on. It's not quite that simple. Read Rule 11(b) before you tell me
to do that. Do you see what would happen if I took your advice?
Student: I guess it's not quite as simple as I thought.

6. After the District Court's dismissal, the lawyers in Haddle v. Garrison might
be having quite different reactions to the case.

a. Defendant's lawyers might be breathing a deep sigh of relief and maybe even
congratulating themselves a little. Why? Obviously they won the motion, but why
might they be pleased about the way they themselves won?

b. Plaintiff's lawyer would obviously have a different reaction. How bad a loss is this? For a plaintiff and his lawyer, the worst loss is one that has also been expensive, in the sense that lawyer and client have invested heavily in the case before the loss. Does this loss fall into that category? Why not?

c. What can plaintiff do now? Probably because of the constraints suggested in the preceding note, plaintiff did not seek to amend the complaint, and it was dismissed. Plaintiff appealed.

d. If plaintiff did not seek to amend, why did he appeal? What was he trying to accomplish? On what point of law would the appeal turn?

e. The Court of Appeals gave short shrift to Haddle's appeal. The following is the entire text of its unpublished opinion:

Haddle v. Garrison (11th Cir. 1997)

Unpublished Opinion. Docket No. 96-8856 (11th Cir. 1997)

PER CURIAM:

Michael A. Haddle appeals following the district court's dismissal of his 42 U.S.C. §1985(2) claim for failure to state a claim. We conclude that Haddle's arguments on appeal are foreclosed by this court's decision in Morast v. Lance, 807 F.2d 926 (11th Cir. 1987). The judgment of the district court is therefore affirmed.

NOTES AND PROBLEMS

1. Why might the 11th Circuit have thought this was such an easy case that it could be disposed of in a three-sentence per curiam opinion, one perhaps drafted by a law clerk?

2. At this point plaintiff has lost again, but in a much more final way. In recent years the federal courts have disposed of about 250,000 civil cases annually. The district court dismissal would count as one of those cases. A losing litigant has the right to appeal that loss to a U.S. Court of Appeal. In recent years the courts of appeal have disposed of about 55,000 appeals each year; the per curiam affirmance of Garrison v. Haddle would count as one of those cases. A losing litigant in an ordinary civil case does not have the *right* to have his case heard by the U.S. Supreme Court. He may petition for a writ of certiorari, which the Court may grant if it believes the question presented is important enough. In recent years the U.S. Supreme Court has agreed to review and decide between 90 and 100 cases each year.

a. Explain why at this point the plaintiff's lawyer would be telling his client that they still had a chance, but that it was a long shot.

b. Plaintiff sought a writ of certiorari from the U.S. Supreme Court, which granted certiorari.

c. With the grant of certiorari the relative strategic advantage of the parties shifted dramatically. One cannot be sure that the Supreme Court will reverse, but in recent years it has reversed or vacated the judgment below at least twice as often as it has affirmed.

3. Suppose yourself hired by the defendant in Haddle v. Garrison to argue in the Supreme Court. You conclude that you have a client whose factual circumstances are unattractive: It is hard to be sympathetic to a defendant accused first of engaging in criminal activity and then of firing an employee who cooperated with the prosecution in exposing those activities. (And recall that you cannot at this stage of the proceedings argue that your client didn't do any of the things he was accused of: The case arises on a 12(b)(6) motion — on which, as the opinion below notes, "We must, of course, assume that the facts as alleged in petitioner's complaint are true. . . .). In such circumstances many lawyers would say that the best argument focuses not on this client, but on the bad consequences of a legal principle resulting from a decision against this client.

a. Can you frame an argument focusing on such a rule of law? Suppose that the decision goes against the defendant. Can you predict a series of claims brought by other plaintiffs? How might those plaintiffs be less attractive than Michael Haddle?

b. You are a Supreme Court justice considering how to decide Haddle v. Garrison. The plaintiff stresses the intuitive justice of his client's case: Shouldn't one interpret the statute to provide a remedy for an honest employee fired for cooperating with a criminal investigation of his employer? In briefs and in oral argument defendant's counsel takes a different tack, stressing the flood of trivial or unattractive cases that will result from a decision in plaintiff's favor. How should a judge think about the relation between the specific case before the court and the long-term consequences of a rule of law?

c. The Supreme Court heard oral argument, and issued the following opinion as one of the 88 cases it decided that year.

Haddle v. Garrison (p. 352)

525 U.S. 121 (1998)

Chief Justice REHNQUIST delivered the opinion of the Court.

Petitioner Michael A. Haddle, an at-will employee, alleges that respondents conspired to have him fired from his job in retaliation for obeying a federal grand jury subpoena and to deter him from testifying at a federal criminal trial. We hold that such interference with at-will employment may give rise to a claim for damages under the Civil Rights Act of 1871, Rev. Stat §1980, 42 U.S.C. §1985(2).

According to petitioner's complaint, a federal grand jury indictment in March 1995 charged petitioner's employer, Healthmaster, Inc., and respondents Jeanette Garrison and Dennis Kelly, officers of Healthmaster, with Medicare fraud. Petitioner cooperated with the federal agents in the investigation that preceded the indictment. He also appeared to testify before the grand jury pursuant to a subpoena, but did not testify due to the press of time. Petitioner was also expected to appear as a witness in the criminal trial resulting from the indictment.

Although Garrison and Kelly were barred by the Bankruptcy Court from participating in the affairs of Healthmaster, they conspired with G. Peter Molloy, Jr., one of the remaining officers of Healthmaster, to bring about petitioner's termination. They did this both to intimidate petitioner and to retaliate against him for his attendance at the federal-court proceedings.

Petitioner sued for damages in the United States District Court for the Southern District of Georgia, asserting a federal claim under 42 U.S.C. §1985(2) and various state-law claims. Petitioner stated two grounds for relief under §1985(2): one for conspiracy to deter him from testifying in the upcoming criminal trial and one for conspiracy to retaliate against him for attending the grand jury proceedings. As §1985 demands, he also alleged that he had been "injured in his person or property" by the acts of respondents in violation of §1985(2) and that he was entitled to recover his damages occasioned by such injury against respondents jointly and severally.

Respondents moved to dismiss for failure to state a claim upon which relief can be granted. Because petitioner conceded that he was an at-will employee, the District Court granted the motion on the authority of Morast v. Lance, 807 F.2d 926 (1987). In Morast, the Eleventh Circuit held that an at-will employee who is dismissed pursuant to a conspiracy proscribed by §1985(2) has no cause of action. The Morast court explained that "to make out a cause of action under §1985(2) the plaintiff must have suffered an actual injury. Because Morast was an at-will employee, he had no constitutionally protected interest in continued employment. Therefore, Morast's discharge did not constitute an actual injury under this statute." Relying on its decision in Morast, the Court of Appeals affirmed.

The Eleventh Circuit's rule in Morast conflicts with the holdings of the First and Ninth Circuits. We therefore granted certiorari, to decide whether petitioner was "injured in his property or person" when respondents induced his employer to terminate petitioner's at-will employment as part of a conspiracy prohibited by §1985(2).

The statute provides that if one or more persons engaged in such a conspiracy "do, or cause to be done, any act in furtherance of the object of such conspiracy, whereby another is injured in his person or property, . . . the party so injured . . . may have an action for the recovery of damages occasioned by such injury . . . against any one or more of the conspirators." §1985(3).

Petitioner's action was dismissed pursuant to Federal Rule Civil Procedure 12(b)(6) because, in the Eleventh Circuit's view, he had not suffered an injury that could give rise to a claim for damages under §1985(2). We must, of course, assume that the facts as alleged in petitioner's complaint are true and that respondents engaged in a conspiracy prohibited by §1985(2). Our review in this case is accordingly confined to one question: Can petitioner state a claim for damages *Question* → by alleging that a conspiracy proscribed by §1985(2) induced his employer to terminate his at-will employment.

We disagree with the Eleventh Circuit's conclusion that petitioner must suffer an injury to a "constitutionally protected property interest" to state a claim for damages under §1985(2). Nothing in the language or purpose of the proscriptions in the first clause of §1985(2), nor in its attendant remedial provisions, establishes such a requirement. The gist of the wrong at which §1985(2) is directed is not deprivation of property, but intimidation or retaliation against witnesses in federal-court proceedings. The terms "injured in his person or property" define the harm that the victim may suffer as a result of the conspiracy to intimidate or retaliate. Thus, the fact that employment at will is not "property" for purposes of the Due Process Clause, does not mean that loss of at-will employment may not "injur[e] [petitioner] in his person or property" for purposes of §1985(2).

We hold that the sort of harm alleged by petitioner here — essentially third-party interference with at-will employment relationships — states a claim for relief under §1985(2). Such harm has long been a compensable injury under tort law, and we see no reason to ignore this tradition in this case. As Thomas Cooley recognized:

> One who maliciously and without justifiable cause, induces an employer to discharge an employee, by means of false statements, threats or putting in fear, or perhaps by means of malevolent advice and persuasion, is liable in an action of tort to the employee for the damages thereby sustained. *And it makes no difference whether the employment was for a fixed term not yet expired or is terminable at the will of the employer.*

2. T. Cooley, Law of Torts 589-591 (3d ed. 1906) (emphasis added).
This Court also recognized in Truax v. Raich, 239 U.S. 33 (1915):

> The fact that the employment is at the will of the parties, respectively, does not make it one at the will of others. The employee has manifest interest in the freedom of the employer to exercise his judgment without illegal interference or compulsion and, by the weight of authority, the unjustified interference of third persons is actionable although the employment is at will.

The kind of interference with at-will employment relations alleged here is merely a species of the traditional torts of intentional interference with contractual relations and intentional interference with prospective contractual relations. See Restatement (Second) of Torts s 766, Comment g, pp. 10-11 (1977); see also id., §766B, Comment c, at 22. This protection against third-party interference with at-will employment relations is still afforded by state law today. See W. Keeton, D. Dobbs, R. Keeton, & D. Owen, Prosser and Keaton on Law of Torts §129, pp. 995-996, and n. 83 (5th ed. 1984) (citing cases). For example, the State of Georgia, where the acts underlying the complaint in this case took place, provides a cause of action against third parties for wrongful interference with employment relations.

Thus, to the extent that the terms "injured in his person or property" in §1985 refer to principles of tort law, see 3 W. Blackstone, Commentaries on the Laws of England 118 (1768) (describing the universe of common law torts as "all private wrongs, or civil injuries, which may be offered to the rights of either a man's person or his property"), we find ample support for our holding that the harm occasioned by the conspiracy here may give rise to a claim for damages under §1985(2).

The judgment of the Court of Appeals is reversed, and the case is remanded for further proceedings consistent with this opinion.

NOTES AND PROBLEMS

1. Why did the Supreme Court reverse?

a. Did the Supreme Court take issue with the district court's application of the standard for granting a motion to dismiss under Rule 12(b)(6)? If not, what aspect of the court decisions was the Supreme Court rejecting?

b. The Supreme Court's opinion was unanimous. Does that circumstance suggest that the Eleventh Circuit was too hasty in its per curiam decision of the case without oral argument? Or is the Supreme Court's disagreement with the Circuit about an issue as to which more deliberate consideration would have made no difference?

2. What will happen now?

a. This is obviously a victory for the plaintiff. How big and what kind of victory? Explain why plaintiff's lawyer, after allowing his colleagues to congratulate him, will be lining up financing for the next stage of the case, which will likely be more expensive that the proceedings up to now.

b. You represent the defendant. In spite of your best efforts, you have lost in the U.S. Supreme Court. Explain to your client what that means, what will happen now, and what her possible courses of action are. She asks you for a recommendation; what additional information would you want to know before responding?

3. Haddle v. Garrison went to a jury after a hard-fought pretrial stage.

a. A few days before Christmas, 1999, The Augusta (Georgia) Chronicle carried the following report:

Whistle-Blower Wins Case

Sandy Hodson, Staff Writer

A U.S. District Court jury sided with Michael Haddle on Friday afternoon, finding his former bosses fired him for helping uncover corporate crimes that cost taxpayers more than $ 10 million.

But in the same verdict, the jury awarded Mr. Haddle just $65,000 in compensatory damages against Jeannette Garrison, founder and owner of the now-defunct Healthmaster Inc., the company, and her corporate legal counsel and top executive, G. Peter Molloy.

"You won again," defense attorney David Hudson told Mrs. Garrison after the jury verdict was announced at the conclusion of a five-day federal court trial. The low amount of damages left the defense team in smiles, extremely pleased with the jury's decision about damages. But they still intend to challenge the verdict, Mr. Hudson said.

Afterward, Mr. Haddle smiled, too. "I'm pleased with the verdict. It vindicated me.

"Sometimes those things are more important than money."

The article went on to report that the verdict was several hundred thousand dollars less than plaintiff had sought. Observers speculated that the verdict may have resulted from the jury's conclusion that, even without the retaliatory firing, Mr. Haddle would have lost his job a few months later when the corporation went bankrupt in the wake of the federal investigation and conviction of its president.

b. The defendants may, however, have been a bit premature in their self-congratulation. The statute that provided a basis for the suit carries with it a fee-shifting statute (see pages 299-308 supra). Having prevailed in the judgment, the plaintiff's lawyer asked for fees, with the result appearing in *The Augusta Chronicle* on March 30, 2000:

> A federal magistrate judge has recommended that the attorneys who successfully represented Healthmaster whistle-blower Michael Haddle receive $258,113 in legal fees [to be paid by the defendants]. . . .
>
> In a report issued Monday, U.S. Magistrate Judge W. Leon Barfield wrote Mr. Haddle's legal team has earned more than a quarter-million dollars for their work during the past four years on Mr. Haddle's behalf—a legal battle that included a successful trip to the U.S. Supreme Court. . . .
>
> In addition to the attorneys fees for the work done for Mr. Haddle by Charles C. Stebbins III, C. Thompson Harley and Richard Miley, Judge Barfield recommended that the three receive an additional $15,475 from Atlanta attorneys Phillip A. Bradley and Barry J. Armstrong.
>
> Before the civil trial began in December, Judge Alaimo found that Mr. Bradley and Mr. Armstrong, who represented Mrs. Garrison, had violated a specific court order to turn over evidence to Mr. Haddle's attorneys. The judge sanctioned the pair and ordered them [not their clients, as with the other fees] to pay Mr. Haddle's expenses and attorney fees connected with this issue.

NOTE: CONSISTENCY IN PLEADING (356)

A common law pleader had to worry about the consistency of his complaint. If plaintiff said defendant trespassed on Blackacre, defendant could not simultaneously deny that he had entered the land in question and assert that he had an easement. The attractiveness of this insistence on a single consistent story is obvious: We expect people in ordinary life not to vary their version of the facts from moment to moment. A person may legitimately assert either that she made a promise or she didn't; that she kept her promise or she didn't; but not that she didn't make a promise *and* that she kept it.

Yet modern pleading rules, of which Rule 8(e)(2) is one example, permit just this sort of apparent duplicity: "[a] party may set forth two or more statements of a claim or defense alternately or hypothetically [and a] party may also state as many separate claims or defenses as he has regardless of consistency." As a result, a defendant may deny that she ever entered into a contract with plaintiff and at the same time assert that she kept her side of the bargain; similarly, a plaintiff may seek to recover on the ground that a written contract provides "X" and simultaneously seek to have the court reform the contract so that the crucial clause reads "not X" rather than "X."

Understanding why the Federal Rules condone behavior that one would condemn in everyday life requires the student to recall the role of the pleadings in the lawsuit. First, pleadings come very early in the case, often before the parties know all that they will by the time the case comes to trial or to the point of serious settlement discussions. The lawyer is therefore often setting forth what seem to her to be the possible versions of the law and the facts that appear plausible at the time the pleading is filed. Second, allegations in pleadings are tempered by burdens of proof. Thus a lawyer who entirely believes her client's story that he had, but lost, a signed, written contract may allege that in her pleadings but, as a safety net, may also seek to recover on a quantum meruit count in case she decides she cannot convince a jury that the written contract existed. Finally, one has to remember that however inconsistent and contradictory the pleadings, the lawyer will often have to settle on a single version of the story before the case comes to trial. Both judge and jury are likely to look with disfavor on a case that rests on logically inconsistent versions of the facts. (In a multiparty case the plaintiff might conceivably try different versions of the facts against different defendants, but this tactic has its limits.) Thus inconsistent pleadings reflect not lawyers' propensity to talk out of both sides of their mouths but a pleading system that requires lawyers to make allegations before they are certain of the facts and the law. Inconsistent pleadings represent alternative drafts of a story, one version of which the advocate hopes ultimately will persuade a judge or jury.

A real-life example of alternate pleading appears in ¶14 of the Haddle v. Garrison complaint (supra page 342). It alleges both that Haddle testified before the grand jury and that he did not testify but was prepared to do so. Obviously both of these cannot be true. Presumably Haddle's lawyer drafted the complaint at a stage where he was not entirely clear what happened, so included both versions in his complaint. By the time the case reached trial he would have decided which version to rest on.

The fact that inconsistent pleading does not rise to the level of a moral offense, however, does not give the lawyer complete license in the matter. Consider, for example, the lawyer retained by the family of an injured, unconscious person. Knowing only that his client was hurt in an automobile accident and the name of the other driver, could the lawyer file a complaint alleging, alternatively, that the other driver was negligent and that he intentionally ran down the plaintiff? Delay your response until after reading the next section.

3. Ethical Limitations

Given the breadth and apparent ease of notice pleading under the federal regime and the apparent fluidity of theories and stories made possible by Rule 8(e)(2), the student may wonder what the limits are: Short of incoherence or allegations that do not come close to describing a claim, what would constitute a bad pleading? One answer to that question involves an examination both of ethical constraints on lawyers.

As you saw in Bridges v. Diesel Service Inc. in Chapter I, Rule 11 restricts the lawyer's ability to file a pleading when he has no more than a hope that favorable facts or law will emerge as the case progresses. That by itself makes it an unusual Rule of procedure. Most of the Rules tell lawyers how to operate the system: where to file papers, how to join parties, how to plead, what counts as a preanswer defense, how to conduct discovery, and the like.

Rule 11 is different. It regulates the way lawyers and clients conduct themselves, establishing standards for investigation of law and facts. In so doing, it embodies in a procedural rule a standard that might otherwise be found in a standard of professional conduct, or in the tort of malicious prosecution. In fact, the language of Rule 11 echoes language that is found in the professional standards of many bars. One might ask whether such a principle in a Rule violates the Rules Enabling Act, 28 U.S.C. §2072(b), which provides that the Rules shall not "abridge, enlarge, or modify any substantive right." The Supreme Court considered and somewhat curtly dismissed that contention:

> This Court[] . . . in Burlington Northern R. Co. v. Woods, 480 U.S. 1, (1987) . . . held, in a unanimous decision, that "Rules which *incidentally* affect litigants' substantive rights do not violate this provision if reasonably necessary to maintain the integrity of that system of rules." Id., at 5 (emphasis added). There is little doubt that Rule 11 is reasonably necessary to maintain the integrity of the system of federal practice and procedure, and that any effect on substantive rights is incidental. We held as much only last Term in *Cooter & Gell*: "It is now clear that the central purpose of Rule 11 is to deter baseless filings in district court and thus, consistent with the Rule Enabling Act's grant of authority, streamline the administration and procedure of the federal courts."

Business Guides v. Chromatic Communications Enterprises, 498 U.S. 533, 552 (1991).

By bringing such a standard into a procedural rule, Rule 11 makes those standards immediately relevant in the conduct of litigation. That can potentially change the balance of power between the parties.

Rule 11 is distinctive in another respect. It establishes an interlocking set of standards, procedures, and sanctions — a miniature regulatory regime all its own, a regime that affects but does not directly regulate the entire conduct of litigation. Read the Rule and respond to the following questions.

NOTES AND PROBLEMS

1. Start with the question of what conduct is covered by the Rule.

a. Party calls Opponent on the telephone, threatening her with a lawsuit that Party knows to be groundless. May Party be sanctioned under Rule 11? Is there a different result if Lawyer rather than Party makes the telephone call?

b. Party files a groundless interrogatory. May Party be sanctioned under Rule 11? (See Rule 11(d) and 26(g).)

2. Client rushes into lawyer's office, telling him a story of defendant's actions that suggest several forms of liability. Lawyer drafts a complaint embodying the claims described by client. Defendant moves for summary judgment, attaching documents, photographs, and affidavits from disinterested persons indicating that most of Client's story was entirely false.

a. Who has violated Rule 11?

b. If under these conditions Lawyer has violated Rule 11, how will his stance toward future clients change? Does the Rule require that the lawyer be suspicious of clients' stories?

3. Lawyer files an answer alleging the statute of limitations as an affirmative defense. At the time Lawyer filed the answer, she reasonably believed that the facts warranted such a response. Lawyer later learns that a salient event occurred later than she previously thought, and that the statute of limitations therefore has not run. Does Lawyer violate the Rule by failing to file an amended answer? Does Lawyer violate the Rule by orally asserting this defense at a subsequent pretrial conference?

4. Knowing the structure of the Rule is important, but still does not give the student a sense of the kind of conduct for which lawyers and clients find themselves in trouble. Consider some cases that canvass the range of behavior violating the Rule, the procedural issues of enforcing it, and the sanctions available. We start with a case that reminds the student of the risks of not mastering Civil Procedure.

Walker v. Norwest Corp.

108 F.3d 158 (8th Cir. 1996)

JOHN R. GIBSON, Circuit Judge.

Jimmy Lee Walker, III, his guardian, Cynthia Walker, and their attorney, James Harrison Massey, appeal from the district court's award of sanctions against Massey for filing a diversity case in which he failed to plead complete diversity of citizenship, and indeed, pleaded facts which tended to show there was not complete diversity. The Walkers and Massey contend that the district court erred in awarding sanctions at all, in determining the amount of sanctions, and in not allowing the Walkers to amend their complaint. We affirm.

[In a dispute over a minor's trust fund] Massey filed a complaint in the district court for the District of South Dakota on behalf of the Walkers, alleging breach of fiduciary duty and other state law causes of action . . . [against Norwest Corporation and numerous individual officers and employees.] The complaint stated that jurisdiction was based on diversity, since "the Plaintiff and *some of the Defendants* are citizens of different states." (Emphasis added). The Walkers are both South Dakotans. The complaint averred that one of the defendants, Norwest Corporation, was a Minnesota corporation. The complaint did not allege the other defendants'[2] citizenship precisely, but stated that many of them were South Dakota "residents." . . .

Upon receiving the complaint, the attorney for Norwest Corporation and its subsidiaries and officers wrote Mr. Massey informing him that his complaint showed on its face that there was no diversity jurisdiction. The letter asked Massey to dismiss the complaint, and warned that if he did not, Norwest would seek sanctions, including attorneys' fees. Massey's only answer was a letter that acknowledged Norwest's correspondence, but made no substantive response to the deficiency counsel had pointed out.

2. The defendants are: Norwest Corporation, Richard Kovacevich, Norwest Bank South Dakota, N.A., Gary Olson, Kirk Dean, Norwest Investment Management & Trust, Dennis Hoffman, Tom Naasz, Beal Law Offices, and George Beal. The individual defendants were sued individually and as trustees or corporate agents.

After Massey failed to offer any explanation for his defective complaint or to move to amend or dismiss it, Norwest moved to dismiss and for an award of sanctions, as it had promised to do.

The district court granted the Fed. R. Civ. P. 12(b)(1) motion to dismiss for lack of jurisdiction and sanctioned attorney Massey under Fed. R. Civ. P. 11. . . . [awarding $4,800 in fees and expenses.]

The Walkers and Massey appeal.

I

They . . . contend that Rule 11 does not require the kind of "complicated, in-depth, and possibly impossible inquiry" that would have been necessary to determine the defendants' citizenship before filing a complaint based on diversity of citizenship.

We review the district court's decision in a Rule 11 proceeding for abuse of discretion. Cooter & Gell v. Hartmarx Corp., 496 U.S. 384, 399-405 (1990). A district court necessarily abuses its discretion if it bases its ruling on an erroneous view of the law.

It was the Walkers' burden to plead the citizenship of the parties in attempting to invoke diversity jurisdiction. . . .

Furthermore, even though it is the Walkers' burden to plead, and if necessary, prove diversity, they did not allege that all of the defendants are domiciled in a state other than South Dakota. Instead, they argue that finding out the defendants' citizenship would be more trouble than they should be expected to take. This is a burden that plaintiffs desiring to invoke diversity jurisdiction have assumed since the days of Chief Justice Marshall. See Strawbridge v. Curtiss, 7 U.S. at 267. The fact that the Walkers did not allege the citizenship of the defendants convinces us that the district court did not abuse its discretion in determining that Rule 11 sanctions were appropriate.

II

The Walkers and Massey next contend that the district court abused its discretion in awarding monetary sanctions, since dismissal of the complaint would have been adequate. . . . They also argue that the district court should have inquired into Massey's financial circumstances, and that if it had done so, it would have found that he "is presently experiencing financial hardships and is unable to pay this sanction." Not only did Massey fail to argue this point to the district court, but there is no record evidence to support the argument before this court. . . . We see no abuse of discretion in awarding monetary sanctions.

III

The Walkers and Massey contend that the district court abused its discretion in denying their request to amend their complaint. . . . After the dismissal and denial of the motion to reconsider, the district court held a hearing on the amount of attorneys' fees to be awarded. At that hearing, Massey began to reargue the merits of the dismissal. The court stated that some of the individual defendants were South Dakota residents. Mr. Massey replied: "I think an appropriate step for the Court to have taken would have been to dismiss those individuals that the Court considered that it could not bring into the diversity statute through pendent jurisdiction which is within the discretion of the Court." Massey still had not alleged a citizenship for many of the defendants and did not identify which defendants should be dismissed to create diversity jurisdiction. The district court is not obliged to do Massey's research for him, especially at such a late date.[4] There was no abuse of discretion. . . .

We affirm the district court's entry of Rule 11 sanctions in the amounts provided.

NOTES AND PROBLEMS

1. What portion of Rule 11 did the plaintiff violate?

2. Did the defendants comply with the steps set forth in Rule 11(c)(1)(A)?

a. They sent plaintiff's lawyer a letter with notice of the complaint's deficiencies. But the opinion does not say that they gave the plaintiff an actual Rule 11 motion, which they then filed with the court after waiting the requisite 21 days.

b. If the defendants did not comply with this requirement, did the district court err by imposing sanctions? See Rule 11(c)(1)(B).

c. Suppose defendant had not raised the issue in any way but the judge had directed his law clerk to scan all complaints for apparent failure of subject matter jurisdiction (as many federal judges do), so he could dismiss them on his own initiative, as Rule 12(h)(3) directs. Could the judge, having detected the problem of incomplete diversity, have imposed Rule 11 sanctions on his own motion?

d. Who is responsible for paying the fees assessed by the court? The Walkers (Massey's clients)? Or Massey himself? Explain why Rule 11 (c)(2) would not permit an order that the Walkers pay this sanction.

3. Rule 11 explicitly applies to defenses as well as to claims. Consider the fate of a law firm that responded to a complaint of sexual harassment and retaliation claims brought by one of its lawyers:

> Defendants moved to dismiss the retaliation claims for lack of subject matter jurisdiction and the individual defendants moved to dismiss all claims against them for failure to state a claim. In support of the motion to dismiss for lack of jurisdiction, defendants submitted affidavits from the two individual defendants, other Wilson Elser partners, and Wilson Elser's chief executive officer. These affidavits denied the factual allegations in the Amended Complaint and asserted additional facts which, according to defendants, demonstrated that no adverse employment action had been taken against plaintiff. . . . Defendants contended that all of these facts established

---

4. Although it is possible for this court to dismiss nondiverse parties on appeal, see Newman-Green, Inc. v. Alfonzo-Larrain, 490 U.S. 826, 836-37 (1989), the Walkers have not asked us to do so and therefore the issue has not been briefed.

that they did not retaliate against plaintiff, and therefore, plaintiff's allegations of retaliation did not amount to a constitutional case or controversy and the court lacked subject matter jurisdiction over the claims. . . .

To determine whether Rule 11 has been violated, courts apply an objective standard of reasonableness. Sanctions under Rule 11 may be imposed upon lawyers, law firms, and parties who violate the rule or who are responsible for the violation. Fed. R. Civ. P. 11(c). "Absent exceptional circumstances, a law firm shall be held jointly responsible for violations committed by its partners, associates, and employees." Id. 11(c)(1)(A). Monetary sanctions for violation of Rule 11(b)(2) may not be awarded against a represented party. Id. 11(c)(2)(A).

Defendants' argument that the court lacked subject matter jurisdiction over plaintiff's retaliation claims was frivolous under an objective standard of reasonableness. Defendants' argument was not a contention about subject matter jurisdiction. It was simply a contention that plaintiff would be unable to prove her claims on the merits. Arguments about the merits of plaintiff's claims, of course, do not go to the court's power to entertain them, and are not appropriately raised on a motion to dismiss the complaint. No competent lawyer, after reasonable inquiry, would have concluded that this argument was warranted by existing law or by a nonfrivolous argument for the extension, modification, or reversal of existing law or the establishment of new law. . . .

Because defendants presented to the court a written motion asserting frivolous legal contentions, plaintiff's motion for sanctions under Rule 11(b)(2) is granted. Moreover, I am persuaded that defendants' motion and supporting papers were presented for an improper purpose; namely, to harass plaintiff and to increase needlessly the cost of litigating her claims.[1] Accordingly, plaintiff's motion for sanctions under Rule 11(b)(1) is also granted.

Defendants' motion was submitted and signed by James D. Harmon, Jr. of The Harmon Firm. Accordingly, sanctions are imposed against The Harmon Firm and Mr. Harmon under Rule 11(b)(1) and (2).

Sanctions are also imposed against Wilson Elser, Fuerth, and Anesh under Rule 11(b)(1) for presenting papers to the court for an improper purpose. Defendants are experienced lawyers who can fairly be held responsible for papers submitted to the court on their behalf. Moreover, defendants supported their motion with affidavits signed by the individual defendants and other agents of the defendant law firm. . . .

Wright v. Wilson, Elser, Moskowitz, Edelman & Dicker, 71 Fair Empl. Prac. Cas. 902 (S.D.N.Y. 1996)

4. The preceding cases deal primarily with inadequate knowledge concerning well-established law. Probably the most common Rule 11 violation involves the failure to conduct adequate factual investigation. The next case displays that problem. Before reading it, consider the incentives created by the current Rule. Party files a groundless paper. Opponent challenges it, giving Party the required notice and 21-day period before filing the Rule 11 motion; Party perseveres in groundless paper. Opponent makes the necessary substantive motion to defeat the groundless paper (12(b)(1) motion, Rule 56 motion, etc.). Ideally, Party

---

1. At oral argument, I stated that my preliminary view was that I did not believe that the motion to dismiss was made in bad faith. I always prefer to believe that, but on further reflection, I cannot rationally support that tentative wishful opinion.

would like to be able to collect its legal fees for opposing the groundless paper. But the court need not impose any sanction at all; if it does, that sanction may not require any payment to Party. Even if awarded, monetary sanctions are presumptively to be paid to the court—like a criminal fine—rather than to the adversary —like a civil damage award. See Rule 11(c)(2). Moreover, Party cannot combine its Rule 11 motion with the substantive motion because of the separate-motion requirement. Under those circumstances, if Party has already won the underlying lawsuit, when is it worth the effort to bring a separate Rule 11 motion?

Christian v. Mattell, Inc.

286 F.3d 1118 (9th Cir. 2003)

McKEOWN, Circuit Judge.

It is difficult to imagine that the Barbie doll, so perfect in her sculpture and presentation, and so comfortable in every setting, from "California girl" to "Chief Executive Officer Barbie," could spawn such acrimonious litigation and such egregious conduct on the part of her challenger. In her wildest dreams, Barbie could not have imagined herself in the middle of Rule 11 proceedings. But the intersection of copyrights on Barbie sculptures and the scope of Rule 11 is precisely what defines this case.

James Hicks appeals from a district court order requiring him, pursuant to Federal Rule of Civil Procedure 11, to pay Mattel, Inc. $501,565 in attorneys' fees that it incurred in defending against what the district court determined to be a frivolous action. . . .

Mattel is a toy company that is perhaps best recognized as the manufacturer of the world-famous Barbie doll. Since Barbie's creation in 1959, Mattel has outfitted her in fashions and accessories that have evolved over time. . . . Mattel has sought to protect its intellectual property by registering various Barbie-related copyrights, including copyrights protecting the doll's head sculpture. Mattel has vigorously litigated against putative infringers.

In 1990, Claudene Christian, then an undergraduate student at the University of Southern California ("USC"), decided to create and market a collegiate cheerleader doll. The doll, which the parties refer to throughout their papers as "Claudene," had blonde hair and blue eyes and was outfitted to resemble a USC cheerleader. . . .

In the complaint, which Hicks signed, Christian alleged that Mattel obtained a copy of the copyrighted Claudene doll in 1996, the year of its creation,[2] and then infringed its overall appearance, including its face paint, by developing a new Barbie line called "Cool Blue" that was substantially similar to Claudene. Christian sought damages in the amount of $2.4 billion and various forms of injunctive relief. . . .

---

2. The United States Copyright Office issued a certificate of registration on November 20, 1997, for "Claudene Doll Face and Head." The certificate specified the work's nature as "sculpture," and the "nature of authorship" as "3-dimensional sculpture."

Two months after the complaint was filed, Mattel moved for summary judgment. In support of its motion, Mattel proffered evidence that the Cool Blue Barbie doll contained a 1991 copyright notice on the back of its head, indicating that it predated Claudene's head sculpture copyright by approximately six years. Mattel therefore argued that Cool Blue Barbie could not as a matter of law infringe Claudene's head sculpture copyright. . . .

At a follow-up counsel meeting required by a local rule, Mattel's counsel attempted to convince Hicks that his complaint was frivolous. During the videotaped meeting. . . . Hicks declined Mattel's invitation to inspect the dolls and, later during the meeting, hurled them in disgust from a conference table.

Having been unsuccessful in convincing Hicks to dismiss Christian's action voluntarily, Mattel served Hicks with a motion for Rule 11 sanctions. . . . Hicks declined to withdraw the complaint during the 21-day safe harbor period provided by Rule 11, and Mattel filed its motion. . . .

The district court granted Mattel's motions for summary judgment and Rule 11 sanctions. The court ruled that Mattel did not infringe the 1997 Claudene copyright because it could not possibly have accessed the Claudene doll at the time it created the head sculptures of the Cool Blue (copyrighted in 1991) and Virginia Tech (copyrighted in 1976) Barbies. . . .

As for Mattel's Rule 11 motion, the district court found that Hicks had "filed a meritless claim against defendant Mattel. A reasonable investigation by Mr. Hicks would have revealed that there was no factual foundation for [Christian's] copyright claim." Indeed, the district court noted that Hicks needed to do little more than examine "the back of the heads of the Barbie dolls he claims were infringing," because such a perfunctory inquiry would have revealed "the pre-1996 copyright notices on the Cool Blue and [Virginia Tech] Barbie doll heads."

Additionally, the district court made other findings regarding Hicks' misconduct in litigating against Mattel, all of which demonstrated that his conduct fell "below the standards of attorneys practicing in the Central District of California." The district court singled out the following conduct:

- Sanctions imposed by the district court against Hicks in a related action against Mattel for failing, among other things, to file a memorandum of law in support of papers styled as a motion to dismiss and failing to appear at oral argument;
- Hicks' behavior during the Early Meeting of Counsel, in which he "toss[ed] Barbie dolls off a table";
- Hicks' interruption of Christian's deposition after Christian made a "damaging admission . . . that a pre-1996 Barbie doll allegedly infringed the later created Claudene doll head. . . ." When asked whether the prior-created Pioneer Barbie doll infringed Claudene, Christian stated, "I think so . . . [b]ecause it's got the look. . . ." At that juncture, Hicks requested an immediate recess, during which he lambasted his client in plain view of Mattel's attorneys and the video camera.
- Hicks' misrepresentations during oral argument on Mattel's summary judgment motion about the number of dolls alleged in the complaint to be

infringing and whether he had ever reviewed a particular Barbie catalogue (when a videotape presented to the district court by Mattel demonstrated that Hicks had reviewed it during a deposition);

- Hicks' misstatement of law in a summary judgment opposition brief about the circuit's holdings regarding joint authorship of copyrightable works.

After Mattel submitted a general description of the fees that it incurred in defending against Christian's action, the court requested Mattel to submit a more specific itemization and description of work performed by its attorneys. Mattel complied.

The district court awarded Mattel $501,565 in attorneys' fees. . . .

The district court did not abuse its discretion in concluding that Hicks' failure to investigate fell below the requisite standard established by Rule 11. . . .

Hicks argues that even if the district court were justified in sanctioning him under Rule 11 based on Christian's complaint and the follow-on motions, its conclusion was tainted because it impermissibly considered other misconduct that cannot be sanctioned under Rule 11, such as discovery abuses, misstatements made during oral argument, and conduct in other litigation.

Hicks' argument has merit. While Rule 11 permits the district court to sanction an attorney for conduct regarding "pleading[s], written motion[s], and other paper[s]" that have been signed and filed in a given case, Fed. R. Civ. P. 11(a), it does not authorize sanctions for, among other things, discovery abuses or misstatements made to the court during an oral presentation. . . .

The orders clearly demonstrate that the district court decided, at least in part, to sanction Hicks because he signed and filed a factually and legally meritless complaint and for misrepresentations in subsequent briefing. But the orders, coupled with the supporting examples, also strongly suggest that the court considered extra-pleadings conduct as a basis for Rule 11 sanctions. . . .

The laundry list of Hicks' outlandish conduct is a long one and raises serious questions as to his respect for the judicial process. Nonetheless, Rule 11 sanctions are limited to "paper[s]" signed in violation of the rule. Conduct in depositions, discovery meetings of counsel, oral representations at hearings, and behavior in prior proceedings do not fall within the ambit of Rule 11. Because we do not know for certain whether the district court granted Mattel's Rule 11 motion as a result of an impermissible intertwining of its conclusion about the complaint's frivolity and Hicks' extrinsic misconduct, we must vacate the district court's Rule 11 orders.[10]

We decline Mattel's suggestion that the district court's sanctions orders could be supported in their entirety under the court's inherent authority. To impose sanctions under its inherent authority, the district court must "make an explicit finding [which it did not do here] that counsel's conduct constituted or was tantamount to bad faith." Primus Auto. Fin. Serv., Inc. v. Batarse, 115 F.3d 644, 648

---

10. We emphasize that the district court's underlying order regarding summary judgment is not affected by this opinion. Nor do we disturb the district court's finding that Hicks filed "a case without factual foundation" or its other findings as to Hicks' misconduct.

(9th Cir.1997) (internal quotation marks omitted). We acknowledge that the district court has a broad array of sanctions options at its disposal: Rule 11, 28 U.S.C. § 1927,[11] and the court's inherent authority. Each of these sanctions alternatives has its own particular requirements, and it is important that the grounds be separately articulated to assure that the conduct at issue falls within the scope of the sanctions remedy. See, e.g., B.K.B. v. Maui Police Dep't., 276 F.3d 1091, 1107 (9th Cir. 2002) (holding that misconduct committed "in an unreasonable and vexatious manner" that "multiplies the proceedings" violates §1927); Fink v. Gomez, 239 F.3d 989, 991-992 (9th Cir. 2001) (holding that sanctions may be imposed under the court's inherent authority for "bad faith" actions by counsel, "which includes a broad range of willful improper conduct"). On remand, the district court will have an opportunity to delineate the factual and legal basis for its sanctions orders. . . .

NOTES AND PROBLEMS

1. Notice how defendant deployed Rule 11.

a. Mattel served plaintiff with its motion for summary judgment and followed that with a Rule 11 motion, served first on the plaintiff, and then after a lapse of 21 days, filed it with the court. After granting Mattel's summary judgment motion, the court considered and acted on its Rule 11 motions. That order of events caused Mattel to have its lawyers incur about half a million dollars in legal fees, the fees they are now seeking to recover from Christian and his lawyer.

b. Suppose Mattel had, as soon as it read the complaint, prepared and served (but not filed) the Rule 11 motion, sending it to plaintiff and his lawyer together with affidavits and the evidence concerning the date of the two Barbie copyrights in question. If plaintiff withdrew the complaint, Mattel would have saved itself (and the court) a great deal of trouble. If plaintiff refused to withdraw its complaint, Mattel could then prepare the summary judgment motion. Is there any strategic reason not to do this?

c. Why did Mattel bother to file the Rule 11 motion? One answer might be that Mattel wanted its attorney's fees and that investing a bit more lawyers' time in a motion for such fees would be worthwhile. But even if sanctions took the form of a fine, it might go the court rather than the defendant. And even if the court awarded fees to the defendant, Hicks might well be judgment proof. Why was Mattel willing to run the risk of throwing good money (in the form of lawyers' time) after bad? Reread the third paragraph of the opinion; does it suggest that the Rule 11 motion was itself part of a long-range litigation strategy? What message does this motion send to other would-be litigants? Should the court have taken that strategy into account in ruling on the motion?

2. *Christian* reveals a court deploying the full power of Rule 11 economic sanctions. Assume that either the judge or the opposition believes a lawyer has violated

---

11. Section 1927 provides for imposition of "excess costs, expenses, and attorneys' fees" on counsel who "multiplies the proceedings in any case unreasonably and vexatiously."

one of the provisions of Rule 11(b). After the appropriate procedural opportunities (notice and a chance to withdraw, opportunity to respond to charges), the judge finds that the lawyer has violated the rule. What follows from that finding? See Rule 11(c)(2).

a. Need the court impose any sanction at all? Rule 11(c) provides that "the court may . . . impose an appropriate sanction. . . ."

b. The current version of the Rule requires that sanctions be "limited to what is sufficient to deter repetition" of the offending conduct and mentions nonmonetary sanctions (presumably such as requiring the lawyers to take additional training). Some appellate courts have urged trial courts to consider "which sanction 'constitutes the least severe sanction that will adequately deter the undesirable conduct.'" Kirk Capital Corp. v. Bailey, 16 F.3d 1485, 1490 (8th Cir. 1994) (quoting Pope v. Federal Express, 974 F.2d 982, 984 (8th Cir. 1992)).

c. One district court, faced with the prospect of invoking Rule 11 under these circumstances, remarked, "This court is disinclined to bring Rule 11's mechanisms into play to consider the imposition of nonmonetary sanctions on [Name of Party] or her lawyer (an action that would most likely compel [Name of Party] to send good money after bad by having to become involved in such proceedings) — it is enough that the publication of this opinion names [Name of Party's] counsel for what it is." Pierre v. Inroads, Inc., 858 F. Supp. 769,775)(N.D. Ill. 1994). Such a statement may not be toothless if the lawyer in question practices in one of the states that requires lawyers to notify the state bar if they have been sanctioned by any court, with that information becoming part of their file.

d. Another court, in a child custody case in which one branch of the family sought to challenge a child custody order by filing a federal civil rights suit, dismissed the complaint, then ordered a lawyer to apologize:

> The court finds that the minimum sanction necessary to deter repetition by Fichtner and others similarly situated is completion of continuing legal education in federal civil rights law and Texas tort law, and submission of letters of apology to Katherine, the Armstrongs, and their counsel for asserting the claims that the court has held above are sanctionable. . . . As the court stated in *Holmes*:
>
>> This court has recognized that requiring counsel to apologize for errant conduct can have an exquisite impact and, in turn, a strong deterrent effect. A learned professional who is required by a tribunal to apologize for his conduct will not soon forget either the requirement that he apologize or the conduct that prompted the sanction. And the obligation that [counsel] fulfill a continuing legal education requirement should serve the salutary purpose of educating him concerning [the applicable] law.
>
> Accordingly, within 30 days of the date this memorandum opinion and order is filed, Fichtner shall submit to defendants, through their counsel of record, and to their counsel of record, letters of apology for asserting the claims that the court has held above are sanctionable. The letters shall not contain qualifying or conditional language. [A footnote gave examples of inadequate apologies: "Because the court has required that I do so, I am apologizing . . ." or "Although I disagree with the court's decision, I am apologizing. . . ."] Within one year of the date of this opinion, Fichtner shall complete 30 hours of continuing legal education in federal civil rights law (at least 15 of the required hours) and Texas tort law. These hours shall be in addition to any other continuing legal education required of him by any state or

other licensing authority to which he is subject. None of the hours required by this order may be satisfied by self-study or in-office seminars. Fichtner shall advise the court by letter of the title, date, and sponsoring body of each program attended, and of the number of hours attended at each such program.

Crank v. Crank, 1998 WL 713273 (N.D. Tx 1998).

Even if a lawyer has carefully adhered to the requirements of Rule 11, complaints in some categories get closer scrutiny. The question in such cases is whether that heightened scrutiny violates either the letter or the spirit of Rule 8.

4.   Special Claims: Requiring and Forbidding Specificity in Pleading

Stradford v. Zurich Insurance Co.

2002 WL 31027517 (S.D. N.Y. 2002).

BUCHWALD, J.

. . . Dr. Stradford[, the plantiff] is a dentist who maintains an office in Staten Island, New York. . . . Defendants are affiliated corporate insurers. Northern issued a policy of insurance . . . on Dr. Stradford's office effective August 18, 1999, thereby insuring the premises until August 19, 2000. During this term, Dr. Stradford apparently failed to pay the required insurance premiums, and Northern cancelled the Policy from October 10, 1999 to December 13, 1999. On or about December 6, 1999, however, Dr. Stradford submitted a "no claims" letter certifying that he had no losses from October 19, 1999, to that date. He also apparently resumed paying the premiums, and National reinstated the Policy on or about December 14, 1999. Dr. Stradford was notified of the reinstatement on or about January 9, 2000.

Less than ten days later, Dr. Stradford filed a claim on the Policy. Dr. Stradford notified Northern that, "[o]n January 17, 2000, [he] returned to his office from his vacation and found water dripping from frozen pipes and extensive water damage to his personal property and the interior of his office." He further notified Northern that certain dental implants, worth more than $100,000, which had apparently been stored in his office, "had become wet and [therefore] ruined." Dr. Stradford submitted a claim under the Policy for $151,154.74, and Northern made payments to Dr. Stradford in this amount. After receiving these payments, Dr. Stradford "submitted a revised claim under the Policy totaling $1,385,456.70, consisting of $168,000.00 for property damage, and a business interruption claim of $1,209,456.70."

Northern continued to investigate Dr. Stradford's claimed loss. [The insurer concluded that the damage had occurred during the period when the insurance had lapsed because Dr. Stratford had not paid the premium and disclaimed coverage.]

Slightly less than one year later, plaintiffs commenced this suit seeking $1,385,456.70 on the Policy, less the $151,154.74 already paid, or $1,234,301.96. Defendants counterclaimed, asserting, inter alia, that Dr. Stradford "knowingly and willfully devised a scheme and artifice . . . to defraud defendants and obtain money by false pretenses and representations," and seeking the return of the $151,154.74, punitive damages, and investigation expenses. Dr. Stradford now moves, inter alia, to dismiss those counterclaims that are based in fraud for failure to state their claims with sufficient "particularity" under Rule 9(b), and to dismiss certain other counterclaims for failure to state a claim.

Rule 9(b) provides, "In all averments of fraud or mistake, the circumstances constituting fraud or mistake shall be stated with particularity. Malice, intent, knowledge, and other condition of mind of a person may be averred generally." Here, defendants' counterclaims succeed in alleging facts that "give rise to a strong inference of fraudulent intent" as required by the second sentence of Rule 9(b). The timing of Dr. Stradford's claim, just ten days after the policy was reinstated, his alleged refusal to cooperate with National's investigation . . . and the size of his claim can fairly be said to satisfy this requirement.

We find, however, that the counterclaims do not satisfy the first sentence of Rule 9(b), which requires that the "time, place, and nature of the [alleged] misrepresentations" be disclosed to the party accused of fraud. Ross v. Bolton, 904 F.2d 819, 823 (2d Cir. 1990). Here, defendants' counterclaims simply fail to identify the statement made by Dr. Stradford that they claim to be false. Thus, it is unclear from the face of the counterclaims whether defendants assert that Dr. Stradford's claimed losses are improperly inflated, that Dr. Stradford's office never even flooded, or that the offices flooded, but not during the term of the Policy. In essence, defendants claim that Dr. Stradford lied, but fail to identify the lie.

The "primary purpose" of Rule 9(b) is to afford a litigant accused of fraud "fair notice of the [ ] claim and the factual ground upon which it is based." Here, defendants' counterclaims fail to provide Dr. Stradford with fair notice of precisely which statement, or which aspect of his claim on the Policy, they allege to be false. The counterclaims are therefore insufficient under Rule 9(b), and must be dismissed.

Nevertheless, it is the usual practice in this Circuit, when there was no prior opportunity to replead,[3] to grant a litigant who has suffered a dismissal under Rule 9(b) leave to amend so that he may conform his pleadings to the Rule. Fed. R. Civ. P. 15(a) ("leave [to amend] shall be freely given when justice so requires"). Indeed, defendants have already moved for leave to amend and submitted a proposed amended pleading. This pleading cures the defects we found in the counterclaims dismissed above because it makes clear that defendants allege that

3. While defendants have already amended their counterclaims once, they did so before receiving notice that Dr. Stradford intended to challenge their claims on Rule 9(b) grounds. In such a circumstance, we see no reason to dismiss defendants' counterclaims with prejudice. The better course, we believe, is to give defendants a chance to properly conform their counterclaims to the requirements of Rule 9(b).

Dr. Stradford's office was flooded at a time when he permitted the Policy to lapse, and that Dr. Stradford "misrepresented the date of the loss in an effort to bring the date of loss within the coverage period." Accordingly, we hereby grant defendants leave to amend their counterclaims. . . .

Conclusion

For the reasons stated above . . . [d]efendants are granted leave to serve their proposed Second Amended Answer and Counterclaims, in substantially the same form as presented to the Court. . . .

Furthermore, defendants have requested permission to move for summary judgment pursuant to Fed. R. Civ. P. 56(b). Defendants assert that plaintiffs breached their contractual obligations under the Policy by failing to cooperate in the investigation of the claim, and that this breach precludes plaintiffs from recovering on the Policy. Defendants' request is hereby granted. . . .

IT IS SO ORDERED.

NOTES AND PROBLEMS

1. This case did not start as a fraud claim. How did fraud come into the picture?

a. The policy and the claims forms undoubtedly contained clauses requiring Dr. Stradford to be truthful in his dealings with the insurer. If he had been untruthful, the insurer would have a defense to the plaintiff's breach of contract claims and could recapture any money already paid out. So why did the insurer allege fraud? Start with remedies. What would be the insurer's remedy for breach of contract? For fraud?

b. Now think about strategy. Disputes like this one will be presented at least to a judge, and perhaps to a jury as well. No one likes an insurance company that collects premiums but then is reluctant to pay claims. How might the fraud claim help the insurer here?

2. Consider this bit of pretrial maneuvering as a struggle for advantage, and consider who won.

a. Who started this fight over pleading?

b. Who won this round? Are there any signs in the opinion that the defendant insurer has won not just this pleading skirmish but a larger victory for the judge's good opinion?

c. What will happen now?

3. *Stradford* turns on a special pleading rule for fraud cases. The effect of that rule emerges most clearly if one imagines that Dr. Stradford had simply tried to have the insurer's fraud claims dismissed under Rule 12(b)(6).

a. Recall the language of the counterclaim, quoted in the opinion above, that Dr. Stradford "knowingly and willfully devised a scheme and artifice . . . to defraud defendants and obtain money by false pretenses and representations." As a quick review of the principles of "ordinary pleading," explain why the court would have found such a general allegation adequate under Rule 8.

b. How did the insurer need to amend its pleadings as a result of Rule 9(b)?

c. Another case summarizes the kind of specificity typically required in Rule 9(b) cases:

> Taking into consideration all of the allegations in Lanco's answer, defendant nonetheless failed to plead specific facts regarding the fraud such as the identity of Sheraton's agents or employees making the fraudulent representations, the identity of Lanco agents to whom the statements were made, the dates or locations of meetings between the parties, or the exchange of any documents during negotiations. The alleged misrepresentations themselves also are vague and fail to specify the obligations that Sheraton agreed to undertake. Courts have dismissed fraud claims pursuant to Rule 9(b) even where the pleader alleged specific communications because the claims lacked "particularized facts to support the inference that [a party] acted . . . with fraudulent intent." *Shields*, 25 F.3d at 1128-29 (party cited press releases and publicly filed corporate documents to establish fraudulent statements or nondisclosures). See also M. H. Segan Ltd. Partnership v. Hasbro, Inc., 924 F. Supp. 512, 526-27 n. 20 (S.D.N.Y. 1996) (holding that plaintiff satisfied Rule 9(b) because party deposition supplemented pleadings to establish time and place of meeting and people who were present). The affidavit that Lanco submitted in connection with this motion provides no additional information regarding the alleged fraud. Moreover, Lanco's general allegation that Sheraton "knew the representations made were false, fraudulent and made with the intent to defraud" is insufficient pleading of scienter. See *Shields*, 25 F.3d at 1129 (holding that Rule 9(b) was not satisfied where plaintiff alleged that defendants "knew but concealed" some things and "knew or were reckless in not knowing" other things).

ITT Sheraton Corp. v. Lanco Inns, Inc., 1998 WestLaw 187430 (N.D.N.Y. 1998).

4. Why does Rule 9(b) require more specificity in pleading?

a. For the fraud plaintiff the problem is that, if fraud occurred, plaintiff is likely still to be in the dark about some of the salient facts. In the actual case, Northern was able to get some prefiling "discovery" from Dr. Stradford under the terms of the insurance policy. In most fraud causes that won't be true. In those "average" cases the fraud plaintiff's lawyer wants to get to discovery to uncover information proving that defendant was misrepresenting the facts. But discovery will be unavailable if the complaint is dismissed for failure to plead with sufficient specificity to comply with Rule 9(b).

b. For the defendant the problem is that fraud cases threaten to turn contract claims into punitive damage actions. Like contract, fraud grows from some dealing between the parties but has consequences quite different from contract. The point emerges perhaps most clearly in cases in which a "contract" plaintiff alleges that the defendant committed fraud because, even "during the negotiation and formation of the contract . . . defendants materially misrepresented facts so as to induce plaintiff . . . to pay for said goods when defendants had no intention of delivering the goods as promised." Event Marketing Concepts, Inc. v. East Coast Logo, Inc., 1998 WestLaw 414657, *2 (E.D. Pa. 1998). If such a pleading states a fraud claim, what happens to the law of expectation damages in contract cases?

5. Although Rule 9(b) is the only federal Rule requiring such specificity, there are other state and federal laws that have adopted special pleading requirements for certain claims.

a. For example, California Code of Civil Procedure §§425.13(a) (Deering 2003) provides that no complaint may state a claim for punitive damages against a health care provider "unless the court enters an order allowing an amended pleading," and that the court may enter such an order only after "supporting and opposing affidavits [show] that the plaintiff has established that there is a substantial probability that the plaintiff will prevail. . . ." Like Rule 9(b), such procedures seek to prevent insubstantial claims from advancing to discovery. Are such provisions desirable? Would the California approach (amend after presenting evidence) be preferable to the federal approach (plead specifically)?

b. In one specialized area involving fraud — securities — Congress has gone well beyond the Requirements of Rule 9(b). The Private Securities Litigation Reform Act of 1995 sets forth elaborate pleading requirements that apply to claims alleging fraud under federal securities statutes. Among those requirements is that the complaint "shall specify each statement alleged to have been misleading, the reason or reasons why the statement is misleading, and, if an allegation regarding the statement or omission is made on information and belief, the complaint shall state with particularity all facts on which that belief is formed." 15 U.S.C. §§78u-4(b)(1)(B). The same statute replaces the requirements of Rule 9(b) as to states of mind, requiring that a plaintiff "state with particularity facts giving rise to a strong inference that the defendant acted with the required state of mind." Id. at (b)(2). According to one comment, "The interpretation of this 'strong inference' pleading requirement has become one of the most contested issues in federal securities law." Grundfest & Pritchard, Statutes with Multiple Personality Disorders: The Value of Ambiguity in Statutory Design and Interpretation, 54 Stanf. L. Rev. 627, 633 (2002). Like the California medical malpractice statute noted above, the Act also requires the district court to stay any discovery until any challenge to the pleadings has been decided.

c. Specificity can also be a trap for the pleader. Suppose a civil rights organization brings suit against a hospital under federal antidiscrimination legislation. The plaintiffs believe that the hospital pervasively discriminates against patients with HIV and AIDS. The complaint lists four specific types of allegedly discriminatory behavior by defendant, but contains no generalized allegation of discrimination. The defendant, wishing to get rid of the suit with a minimum of expense and bad publicity, announces a immediate change of policy with respect to the four allegations, then moves to dismiss the suit as moot. What can plaintiff do?

d. Finally, remember that "specific" does not mean "long." As one court noted, after dismissing a long complaint that appended 62 newspaper articles, "A complaint can be long-winded, even prolix, without pleading with particularity. Indeed, such a garrulous style is not an uncommon mask for an absence of detail. The amended complaint here, although long, states little with particularity." Williams v. WMX Technologies Inc., 112 F.3d 175 (5th Cir. 1997).

6. In some areas, courts, legislatures and drafters of Rules have gone in the other direction, either forbidding specificity or making clear that it was not required.

a. Occasionally one finds a statute *forbidding* certain kinds of specificity in pleading. Responding to reports in which defendants fainted or had cardiac episodes after reading the amount of damages demanded in personal injury and wrongful death complaints, the California legislature has forbidden a plaintiff seeking damages in such cases from stating any specific amount in the initial complaint, instead allowing the defendant, after receiving the complaint, to demand a statement of damages. CA C. Civ. Proc. §§425.10; 425.11 (West 2002).

b. Civil rights complaints were for several decades at the end of the twentieth century an arena for struggle over the amount of detail required in a complaint. The contest occurred both because some courts were initially hostile to this relatively new claim and because in one area of civil rights the substantive law seems to require specificity of a sort at odds with Rule 8.

Various government officials can be liable for violations of citizen's civil rights. In a complex series of cases, the Supreme Court has said: (a) that such officials are liable if their actions or orders violate constitutional rights but (b) that they enjoy a "qualified immunity" if those actions took place under a reasonable misapprehension of the law. To use an example, a school principal who unlawfully ordered the search of student lockers would be able to avoid liability if, when she gave the order to search, she reasonably believed that the order was constitutional, even if it was not. This "immunity," the Supreme Court has said, is more than an ordinary defense; it is "the right not to stand trial," and, in particular, the right not to be subjected to discovery proceedings. Mitchell v. Forsyth, 472 U.S. 511, 526 (1985).

Reasoning that such an immunity against the post-pleading stage of litigation could be enforced only by requiring specific pleadings, some courts sought to enforce such immunities by requiring more specific pleading, so that plaintiff can show that the official could not reasonably have believed his acts to be constitutional. In several cases the U.S. Supreme Court has rejected such heightened pleading standards for civil rights claims:

> We think that it is impossible to square the "heightened pleading standard" applied by the Fifth Circuit in this case with the liberal system of "notice pleading" set up by the Federal Rules. Rule 8(a)(2) requires that a complaint include only "a short and plain statement of the claim showing that the pleader is entitled to relief." In Conley v. Gibson, 355 U.S. 41, 47 (1957), we said in effect that the Rule meant what it said: The Federal Rules of Civil Procedure do not require a claimant to set out in detail the facts upon which he bases his claim. To the contrary, all the Rules require is "a short and plain statement of the claim" that will give the defendant fair notice of what the plaintiff's claim is and the grounds upon which it rests.
>
> Rule 9(b) does impose a particularity requirement in two specific instances. It provides that "in all averments of fraud or mistake, the circumstances constituting fraud or mistake shall be stated with particularity." Thus, the Federal Rules do address in Rule 9(b) the question of the need for greater particularity in pleading certain actions, but do not include among the enumerated actions any reference to complaints alleging municipal liability under §1983. Expressio unius est exclusio alterius.[*]

[* A canon of statutory construction: Expressing only one of two related ideas implies the exclusion of the other. — Ed.]

. . . Perhaps if Rules 8 and 9 were rewritten today, claims against municipalities under §1983 might be subjected to the added specificity requirement of Rule 9(b). But that is a result which must be obtained by the process of amending the Federal Rules, and not by judicial interpretation. In the absence of such an amendment, federal courts and litigants must rely on summary judgment and control of discovery to weed out unmeritorious claims sooner rather than later.

Leatherman v. Tarrant County Narcotics Intelligence & Coordination Unit, 507 U.S. 163 (1993)

Lest anyone miss the point the Court reiterated it a few years later in an employment discrimination case. In Swierkiewicz v. Sorema, N. A., 534 U.S. 506 (2002), the Court held that Rule 8(a) also governed in employment discrimination cases, where case law had established that to prevail on such a claim, a plaintiff lacking proof of intentional discrimination had to prove a "prima facie" case by showing (1) membership in a protected group; (2) qualification for the job in question; (3) an adverse employment action; and (4) circumstances that support an inference of discrimination. The Court distinguished between proof and pleading; though the plaintiff might have to produce evidence of each of these elements to survive summary judgment, he need not include them in the complaint:

> Other provisions of the Federal Rules of Civil Procedure are inextricably linked to Rule 8(a)'s simplified notice pleading standard. Rule 8(e)(1) states that "no technical forms of pleading or motions are required," and Rule 8(f) provides that "all pleadings shall be so construed as to do substantial justice." Given the Federal Rules' simplified standard for pleading, "[a] court may dismiss a complaint only if it is clear that no relief could be granted under any set of facts that could be proved consistent with the allegations." Hishon v. King & Spalding, 467 U.S. 69, 73 (1984). If a pleading fails to specify the allegations in a manner that provides sufficient notice, a defendant can move for a more definite statement under Rule 12(e) before responding. Moreover, claims lacking merit may be dealt with through summary judgment under Rule 56. The liberal notice pleading of Rule 8(a) is the starting point of a simplified pleading system, which was adopted to focus litigation on the merits of a claim. ("The Federal Rules reject the approach that pleading is a game of skill in which one misstep by counsel may be decisive to the outcome and accept the principle that the purpose of pleading is to facilitate a proper decision on the merits".)

Id. at 513-14.

5.   Allocating the Elements

Thus far we have considered the regime of notice pleading and its requirements and the added considerations introduced by Rule 11. An important piece of the picture is still missing. The substantive law tells the parties in general what issues matter in the lawsuit: In a contract claim, whether the parties agreed, whether the agreement reflected a bargain, and so on; in a negligence claim, whether the defendant fell below ordinary standards of care, whether that carelessness caused harm to the plaintiff, and so on. But knowing what issues will matter in the suit does not answer all the questions in a system driven by party initiative, for one must also ask which party has the responsibility for which of those issues. To put that question into technical procedural terms, which party has the burden of pleading, producing evidence, or proving a particular element of a claim?

The U.S. legal system assigns these tasks to the parties and penalizes them for their failure to fulfill their assignments. As the next case demonstrates, logic does not entirely explain the system of assigning burdens to parties. One could imagine a system in which the plaintiff identified the general contours of the claim and then left it to the judge to direct whatever investigations were necessary. Many civil law countries operate under such a system, and at early common law the jury was told to decide the claims based on its own knowledge of events or to conduct whatever inquiries seemed likely to uncover the truth. Those two systems do not need to allocate burdens between the parties. Only when trials become a structured contest between two adversaries, each of whom tries to demonstrate the truth or falsity of various propositions, does a second-order question emerge: Which party bears initial responsibility for which element of a given claim? That question arises at several points in litigation and first surfaces at the pleading stage. Where the burden of pleading and proving particular elements of a claim rests may be important, both as a procedural and a substantive matter.

One final note is in order. Lawyers usually distinguish among three burdens: the burden of pleading, the burden of production, and the burden of persuasion. To have the burden of pleading means that one must allege that element of the claim or defense; one cannot expect the other party to do so. To have the burden of production means that at trial one must produce evidence — witnesses, documents, and the like — that tend to demonstrate the proposition at stake. To have the burden of persuasion in a civil case means, generally, that one must persuade the trier of fact that one's version of the facts is more likely than not to be true. Usually, though not invariably, the three burdens go together: The party with the burden of pleading an element will also have the burden of producing evidence to prove that element, and, assuming the facts are disputed, of persuading the trier that its version of the facts is more likely than not to be true. Gomez v. Toledo purports to be only about the first of these burdens, that of pleading. For the reader of this text, *Gomez* has another feature: It is an early case in the battle over procedural aspects of civil rights claims, struggles that have reflected themselves in many stages of litigation.

Gomez v. Toledo

446 U.S. 635 (1980)

Mr. Justice MARSHALL delivered the opinion of the Court.

The question presented is whether, in an action brought under 42 U.S.C. §1983 against a public official whose position might entitle him to qualified immunity, a plaintiff must allege that the official has acted in bad faith in order to state a claim for relief or, alternatively, whether the defendant must plead good faith as an affirmative defense.

I

Petitioner Carlos Rivera Gomez brought this action against respondent, the Superintendent of the Police of the Commonwealth of Puerto Rico, contending that respondent had violated his right to procedural due process by discharging him from employment with the Police Department's Bureau of Criminal Investigation. Basing jurisdiction on 28 U.S.C. §1343(3),[2] petitioner alleged the following facts in his complaint.[3] Petitioner had been employed as an agent with the Puerto Rican police since 1968. In April 1975, he submitted a sworn statement to his supervisor in which he asserted that two other agents had offered false evidence for use in a criminal case under their investigation. As a result of this statement, petitioner was immediately transferred from the Criminal Investigation Corps for the Southern Area to Police Headquarters in San Juan, and a few weeks later to the Police Academy in Gurabo, where he was given no investigative authority. In the meantime respondent ordered an investigation of petitioner's claims, and the Legal Division of the Police Department concluded that all of petitioner's factual allegations were true.

In April 1976, while still stationed at the Police Academy, petitioner was subpoenaed to give testimony in a criminal case arising out of the evidence that petitioner had alleged to be false. At the trial petitioner, appearing as a defense witness, testified that the evidence was in fact false. As a result of this testimony, criminal charges, filed on the basis of information furnished by respondent, were brought against petitioner for the allegedly unlawful wiretapping of the agents' telephones. Respondent suspended petitioner in May 1976 and discharged him without a hearing in July. In October, the District Court of Puerto Rico found no probable cause to believe that petitioner was guilty of the allegedly unlawful wiretapping and, upon appeal by the prosecution, the Superior Court affirmed. Petitioner in turn sought review of his discharge before the Investigation, Prosecution, and Appeals Commission of Puerto Rico, which, after a hearing, revoked the discharge order rendered by respondent and ordered that petitioner be reinstated with back pay.

Based on the foregoing factual allegations, petitioner brought this suit for damages, contending that his discharge violated his right to procedural due process, and that it had caused him anxiety, embarrassment, and injury to his reputation in the community. In his answer, respondent denied a number of petitioner's allegations of fact and asserted several affirmative defenses. Respondent then moved to dismiss the complaint for failure to state a cause of action, see Fed. Rule Civ. Proc. 12(b)(6), and the District Court granted the motion. Observing that respondent was entitled to qualified immunity for acts done in good faith within the scope of his official duties, it concluded that petitioner was required to

---

2. That section grants the federal district courts jurisdiction "[t]o redress the deprivation, under color of any State law, statute, ordinance, regulation, custom or usage, of any right, privilege or immunity secured by the Constitution of the United States or by any Act of Congress providing for equal rights of citizens or of all persons within the jurisdiction of the United States."

3. At this stage of the proceedings, of course, all allegations of the complaint must be accepted as true.

plead as part of his claim for relief that, in committing the actions alleged, respondent was motivated by bad faith. The absence of any such allegation, it held, required dismissal of the complaint. The United States Court of Appeals for the First Circuit affirmed.

We granted certiorari to resolve a conflict among the courts of appeals.

II

Section 1983 provides a cause of action for "the deprivation of any rights, privileges, or immunities secured by the Constitution and laws" by any person acting "under color of any statute, ordinance, regulation, custom, or usage, of any State or Territory."[6] This statute, enacted to aid in "'the preservation of human liberty and human rights,'" Owen v. City of Independence, 445 U.S. 622, 636 (1980), reflects a congressional judgment that a "damages remedy against the offending party is a vital component of any scheme for vindicating cherished constitutional guarantees." As remedial legislation, §1983 is to be construed generously to further its primary purpose.

In certain limited circumstances, we have held that public officers are entitled to a qualified immunity from damages liability under §1983. This conclusion has been based on an unwillingness to infer from legislative silence a congressional intention to abrogate immunities that were both "well-established at common law" and "compatible with the purposes of the Civil Rights Act." Finding of immunity have thus been "predicated upon a considered inquiry into the immunity historically accorded the relevant official at common law and the intentions behind it." Imbler v. Pachtman, 424 U.S. 409, 421 (1976). In Pierson v. Ray, 386 U.S. 547, 555 (1967), for example, we concluded that a police officer would be "excus[ed] from liability for acting under a statute that he reasonably believed to be valid but that was later held unconstitutional, on its face or as applied." And in other contexts we have held, on the basis of "[c]ommon-law tradition . . . and strong public-policy reasons," Wood v. Strickland, 420 U.S. 308, 318 (1975), that certain categories of executive officers should be allowed qualified immunity from liability for acts done on the basis of an objectively reasonable belief that those acts were lawful. See Procunier v. Navarette, 434 U.S. 555 (1978) (prison officials); O'Connor v. Donaldson, 422 U.S. 563 (1975) (superintendent of state hospital); Wood v. Strickland, 420 U.S. 308 (1975) (local school board members); Scheuer v. Rhodes, 416 U.S. 232 (1974) (state Governor and other executive officers). Cf. Owen v. City of Independence, supra (no qualified immunity for municipalities).

Nothing in the language or legislative history of §1983, however, suggests that in an action brought against a public official whose position might entitle him to

---

6. Section 1983 provides in full: "Every person who, under color of any statute, ordinance, regulation, custom, or usage, of any State or Territory, subjects, or causes to be subjected, any citizen of the United States or other person within the jurisdiction thereof to the deprivation of any rights, privileges, or immunities secured by the Constitution and laws, shall be liable to the person injured in an action at law, suit in equity, or other proper proceeding for redress."

immunity if he acted in good faith, a plaintiff must allege bad faith in order to state a claim for relief. By the plain terms of §1983, two — and only two — allegations are required in order to state a cause of action under that statute. First, the plaintiff must allege that some person has deprived him of a federal right. Second, he must allege that the person who has deprived him of that right acted under color of state or territorial law. Petitioner has made both of the required allegations. He alleged that his discharge by respondent violated his right to procedural due process, and that respondent acted under color of Puerto Rican law.

Moreover, this Court has never indicated that qualified immunity is relevant to the existence of the plaintiff's cause of action; instead we have described it as a defense available to the official in question. Since qualified immunity is a defense, the burden of pleading it rests with the defendant. See Fed. Rule Civ. Proc. 8(c) (defendant must plead any "matter constituting an avoidance or affirmative defense"); 5 C. Wright & A. Miller, Federal Practice and Procedure §1271 (1969). It is for the official to claim that his conduct was justified by an objectively reasonable belief that it was lawful. We see no basis for imposing on the plaintiff an obligation to anticipate such a defense by stating in his complaint that the defendant acted in bad faith.

Our conclusion as to the allocation of the burden of pleading is supported by the nature of the qualified immunity defense. As our decisions make clear, whether such immunity has been established depends on facts peculiarly within the knowledge and control of the defendant. Thus we have stated that "[i]t is the existence of reasonable grounds for the belief formed at the time and in light of all the circumstances, coupled with good-faith belief, that affords a basis for qualified immunity of executive officers for acts performed in the course of official conduct." Scheuer v. Rhodes. The applicable test focuses not only on whether the official has an objectively reasonable basis for that belief, but also on whether "[t]he official himself [is] acting sincerely and with a belief that he is doing right." Wood v. Strickland. There may be no way for a plaintiff to know in advance whether the official has such a belief or, indeed, whether he will even claim that he does. The existence of a subjective belief will frequently turn on factors which a plaintiff cannot reasonably be expected to know. For example, the official's belief may be based on state or local law, advice of counsel, administrative practice, or some other factor of which the official alone is aware. To impose the pleading burden on the plaintiff would ignore this elementary fact and be contrary to the established practice in analogous areas of the law.[8] The decision of the Court of Appeals is reversed, and the case is remanded to that court for further proceedings consistent with this opinion.

It is so ordered.

---

8. As then-Dean Charles Clark stated over forty years ago, "It seems to be considered only fair that certain types of things which in common law pleading were matters in confession and avoidance — i.e., matters which seemed more or less to admit the general complaint and yet to suggest some other reason why there was no right — must be specifically pleaded in the answer, and that has been a general rule."

Mr. Justice REHNQUIST joins the opinion of the Court, reading it as he does to leave open the issue of the burden of persuasion, as opposed to the burden of pleading, with respect to a defense of qualified immunity.

NOTES AND PROBLEMS

1. As a point of departure for analyzing the case, test your understanding of demurrers and Rule 12(b)(6) motions by briefly explaining why the assertion in footnote 3 is true.

2. With the fundamentals in mind, the first difficulty in understanding this case is seeing what the fight was about. The difference between a complaint that Toledo would have found sufficient and the one actually filed might have been a matter of a single sentence. Consider the following: "In taking the actions alleged in paragraphs 1-6, Defendant Toledo acted in bad faith."

a. If that was the only problem with the complaint, and recalling the adage that demurrers about matters of form are usually not worth the expense, why did defendant think it worthwhile to make the Rule 12(b)(6) motion?

b. Once the court granted Toledo's motion, plaintiff could have added such a sentence when he was given leave to amend by the district court. Instead he incurred many thousands of dollars in costs and fees by taking the case to the Supreme Court. Why? Recalling that pleadings generally serve as a blueprint for discovery and trial, consider what plaintiff might have thought was at stake.

c. What will happen now?

3. Once one understands why the parties thought this issue was worth disputing, one then has to confront the Court's resolution of it.

a. What does the Court mean when it calls good faith an affirmative defense? What consequences does that have for the parties and for future parties bringing or defending such a claim?

b. Why should "qualified immunity for actions in good faith" be an affirmative defense rather than a part of plaintiff's claim?

c. Much scholarly and some judicial analysis of burdens suggests that courts resolve most disputes about burdens of pleading and proof by using value-free analyses. While courts sometimes write in value-free terms (there are hints of such language in *Gomez*), such discourse is deceptive. At root, decisions about burdens of pleading and proof are decisions about which party, in a close case, should win. The answer to that question is anything but value-free. Yet courts frequently express only the value-neutral features of their decisions, and the student accordingly needs to master that discourse.

4. At the time of *Gomez* the good faith defense consisted of two elements: (1) that the defendant subjectively believed in the propriety of his actions; and (2) that such a belief was objectively reasonable. In *Gomez*, defendant Toledo could have maintained such a defense only if he showed that: (1) he believed that he did not need to give Gomez a hearing; and (2) this belief was reasonable. Since *Gomez*, the Court has redefined the good faith defense. It now consists only of the objective reasonableness of the defendant's actions. Harlow v. Fitzgerald, 457

U.S. 800 (1982). If one believed that the Court's primary reason for assigning the burden of pleading good faith to the defendant was that he had easier access to his own mental processes, the changed definition of "good faith" might lead one to expect that the plaintiff would now have the burden of showing bad faith. That has not occurred so far. Does that tell us something about the real reasons for assigning burdens?

5. Try your hand at a couple of run-of-the-mill problems in assigning burdens. Where should the burden of pleading lie in these cases? On what theory?

a. Adams, a lawyer, sues his cousin, Davis, for professional services. Who, if anyone, must allege that the services were (or were not) intended as a gift?

b. Bellows, a disc jockey, sues his employer, WFCP, for failure to pay the amount of overtime compensation required by the Fair Labor Standards Act. Who must allege that Bellows is (or is not) a professional employee and therefore is not (or is) subject to the act?

6. A typical construction contract contains a number of promises by the contractor. If a contractor sues a homeowner for failure to make the payments under the contract, must the contractor allege specific performance of those conditions that are the subject of the homeowner's complaints or must he allege something else? See Rule 9(c).

7. Assume E sues R for breach of an oral employment contract, but the statute of frauds requires all employment contracts to be in writing. Or assume P sues D for damages suffered in an accident that occurred in 1992, and the statute of limitations for negligence actions is two years. Although both the statute of frauds and statute of limitations are listed as affirmative defenses in Rule 8(c), the complaints may be said to include "built-in" affirmative defenses — that is, the basis for the affirmative defense is clear from the complaint. In such a case, plaintiff may be required to negate the built-in defense by an additional allegation, such as fraud, estoppel, or waiver.

B.   Responding to the Complaint

We already have observed that no a priori reason compels the defendant to respond to the plaintiff's complaint. We might simply assume that defendant denied the significant allegations, and no further response would be required. In such a system, any objections to the bringing of the lawsuit or further clarification of issues would arise at a later pretrial stage (for example, by requiring defendant to file a piece of paper at a later date), the pretrial hearing, or the trial itself. In fact, this is precisely the procedure that is followed by small claims courts as well as by some informal dispute settlement mechanisms (for example, arbitration).

Instead, we take the opposite course, using the threat of a default judgment to force defendant to reply; as you will see in Chapter VIII, a defendant who fails to respond to the complaint can have judgment entered against her. Rule 55. For defendants who do want to respond, we grant two opportunities. The *pre-answer motion* permits defendant to raise certain types of objections to the action at a very early stage of the litigation. If the defendant makes no such motion or if it is denied, the defendant must file an additional pleading, usually called an answer. The answer responds to the allegations of the complaint and asserts any additional information or affirmative claims that the defendant may have against the plaintiff. Both the pre-answer motion and the answer serve as key strategic early moments of the lawsuit, as the parties define the contours of their disagreement and maneuver for early advantage.

NOTES AND PROBLEMS

1. Defendant receives the complaint, either by mail (see Rule 4(d)) or in person (see Rule 4(c)).

a. The complaint will arrive with a summons (see Form 1), which tells the defendant to respond or face a default judgment.

b. For a defendant who is a repeat litigant (virtually all large organizations, whether public or private, profit or non-profit), receiving a complaint, though never welcome, is a routine experience. For individuals, it can be an unexpected and unsettling experience. Suppose a friend came to you carrying a complaint and summons she had just received, and asked you what she should do; advise her (remembering that you are not yet licensed to practice law).

2. Who draws up the answer?

3. How long does he have to do it? See Rule 12(a)(1).

4. What does he do with the answer once it is drawn up? See Rules 12(a)(1) and 5(a).

1.   Pre-Answer Motion

We already have had a chance to consider defendant's possible responses to plaintiff's complaint. Briefly, these responses include: (a) reasons why the court should not proceed with the action; (b) assertions that the complaint, even if true, provides no basis for legal relief; (c) denials; (d) affirmative defenses; and (e) requests for clarification and more information. How and in what order can defendant make these responses? What opportunities do they hold for defendants, and what dangers for plaintiffs?

A defendant can simply proceed to answer the complaint. All the responses listed above except (e) — a request for clarification or more information — may be included in the defendant's answer. In addition, Rule 12(b) permits certain defenses to be raised by a pre-answer motion. Read Rule 12(b).

NOTES AND PROBLEMS

1. Why would a defendant want to bother with a pre-answer motion instead of just bundling all his defenses, objections, and the like into the answer?

a. Plaintiff's lawyer, unless the statute of limitations is about to run when his client appears, has a fair amount of time to investigate the facts and the law surrounding the claim.

b. By contrast, defendant's lawyer will have less than three weeks, unless the defendant waives service of process pursuant to Rule 4(d) (which extends the time to answer the complaint to 60 days) or the plaintiff stipulates to an extension of time, or the court orders such an extension. Recall that in some cases defendant may take some time just to locate and speak with a lawyer. Within that period, defendant's lawyer has to investigate the claim, decide which defenses are available, decide whether defendant has any claims against the plaintiff, and answer.

c. What happens to the defendant's obligation to answer the complaint if he makes a pre-answer motion? Read Rule 12(a)(4).

2. Besides time, money makes the pre-answer motion attractive to defendants. Factual investigation and gathering evidence usually takes more time, and thus costs more in fees, than does preparation based solely on law. Some of the grounds for a pre-answer motion, like the demurrer or 12(b)(6) motion, require no factual investigation at all. Others, such as challenges to jurisdiction will require very limited factual groundwork — where did defendant conduct its business? Is this the judicial district where the claim arose? If a defendant can produce a victory with an inexpensive preanswer motion, she has served her client in two ways, not just prevailing, but prevailing inexpensively.

The previous section presented examples of how pre-answer motions can be used to object to plaintiff's failure to state a claim upon which relief can be granted, Rule 12(b)(6). Chapters II and III showed pre-answer motions being used to raise objections to jurisdiction, venue, and service of process. Chapter XIII contains examples of pre-answer motions used to raise questions relating to the failure to join parties. Each of these instances concerns questions such as whether the complaint stated a claim, whether jurisdiction was proper, whether other parties may or must be joined and so on, rather than with the actual mechanics of making the motion. Let us now focus on this latter point.

What is a "motion"? Rule 7 states that a motion is a request to the court for an order. Rule 7 does not specify what kinds of documents constitute the motion. Ordinarily a motion consists of several different documents, although in many districts several may be combined in one document. First is the motion itself or, in other words, a request for the specific relief sought. (Form 19 is an example of a motion. Second is the notice of the motion.) This document tells the opposing party when the motion will be heard. In some districts, by local rule, the motion and the notice are combined in a single document. Third, if the motion in question requires or permits affidavits setting forth any factual information necessary for granting the motion, they will be included. An *affidavit* is a sworn statement by someone competent to testify, that she has observed certain facts. (As a test of your understanding, explain why one would not expect a 12(b)(6) motion to have any affidavits.) The affidavit ordinarily will be made by one of the parties or by an attorney for the moving party. Fourth is a memorandum explaining, with reference to the facts of the case and to supporting authorities, the basis for the motion. Finally, many lawyers say it's good practice to prepare a "Proposed Order," a document the judge can sign on the spot if she grants the motion.

NOTES AND PROBLEMS

1. A motion — any motion — is a request for a court to make an order of some kind.

a. What kind of order does a defendant seek in a pre-answer motion?

b. How long does defendant have to make a pre-answer motion?

2. What happens if the 12(b) motion is denied?

3. What happens if the 12(b) motion is granted?

4. Rule 12(e), the motion for a more definite statement, is best understood in historical terms. Under early common law and Code pleading systems, the complaint bore much of the weight of narrowing the parties' contentions and exposing the issues in dispute. Under such circumstances it was frequently a fair request, as well as a good tactic, to ask the pleader to "make more definite and certain" his contentions. Such motions served as a form of discovery not otherwise permitted. Though it seems inconsistent with the idea of notice pleading, an analogous motion was carried over into the original Federal Rules; there it proved to be the subject of more judicial rulings than any other part of the Federal Rules, often at the hands of judges unfamiliar with the philosophy underlying the Rules. At present, Rule 12(e) is rarely, and almost never successfully, invoked. If the claim is truly so vague as to make a response impossible, it will be subject to a 12(b)(6) motion. In the far more frequent circumstance, in which the pleader has a good idea what the claim is about but wants to know more about the precise nature of the pleader's case, discovery beckons.

5. Another pre-answer motion, Rule 12(f)'s "motion to strike" has two quite different uses.

a. Suppose A's wife is killed in an accident with B, and A sues for wrongful death and seeks punitive damages. If, under the applicable tort law, punitive damages are not recoverable, defendant may move to strike, not the whole claim, but the allegations relating to punitive damages. See Mills v. Fox, 421 F. Supp. 519 (E.D.N.Y. 1976). In this sense, Rule 12(f) acts like a Rule 12(b)(6) motion directed to a single allegation. See Fry v. Lamb Rental Tools, 275 F. Supp. 283 (W.D. La. 1967) (claimed damages for sorrow, grief, loss of love, affection, and companionship not recoverable under state law).

b. A less common use of Rule 12(f) occurs when it is used to strike any "redundant, immaterial, impertinent, or scandalous matter." Courts will grant such a motion if allegations in the complaint have no relation to the case or are unnecessarily confusing: if the complaint is overly long and detailed (especially if it contains excessive evidentiary information) or if allegations are unnecessarily derogatory. See, e.g., Hughes v. Kaiser Jeep Corp., 40 F.R.D. 89, 93 (D.S.C. 1966) (reference to car as "death trap"); Budget Dress Corp. v. ILGWU, 25 F.R.D. 506 (S.D.N.Y. 1959) (defenses based on alleged conspiracy between plaintiff and underworld elements described as "strong arm men" and "racketeers"). It is frequently pointed out that such motions are not favored, waste time, should not be granted as to background information, and should not be granted if the court is at all in doubt. See, e.g., Fuchs Sugars & Syrups, Inc. v. Amstar Corp., 402 F. Supp. 636 (S.D.N.Y. 1975). Accordingly, the decision to strike may depend on whether the allegations are likely to prejudice the moving party, which might occur if the pleadings will be read or given to the jury, and, if so, whether limiting instructions will be given.

6. We have focused most of our attention thus far on the tactical advantages Rule 12 offers to defendants — early, cheap termination of the case. Recall, however, that many of the Rule 12 defenses are the old "dilatory pleas," which lawyers with good reason viewed as ways of dragging a case out without approaching its merits. The Rule drafters, while allowing defendants to use these motions, tried to prevent their abuse by defendants. These regulations, which constitute a trap for the unwary defendant, appear in Rule 12(g) and (h), which set out a fairly elaborate set of "consequences" of making and not making a Rule 12 motion. Read these sections carefully and avoid malpractice by answering the following questions.

a. Arthur sues Betty. Before answering, Betty moves to dismiss for failure to state a claim upon which relief can be granted. The motion is denied.

(1) Can Betty now move to dismiss for improper venue? *No — 12(g) and 12(h)(1)*

(2) Can Betty now move to dismiss for failure to join an indispensable party? *Yes — 12(h)(2)*

(3) Can Betty now move, under Rule 12(e), for a more definite statement?

(4) Can Betty include the defense of insufficiency of service of process in her answer? *No 12(h)(1)*

(5) Can Betty include the defense of failure to join an indispensable party in her answer? *Yes 12(h)(2)*

(6) Can Betty now move to dismiss for lack of subject matter jurisdiction? *Yes 12(h)(3)*

b. Charles sues Dan. Without making a pre-answer motion, Dan answers. The answer consists solely of denials of the material elements of the complaint.

(1) Can Dan move to dismiss for improper venue? *No — must include in original answer*

(2) Dan wants to have the complaint dismissed for failure to state a claim upon which relief can be granted. Rule 12(h)(2) preserves this defense, but it is too late for a pre-answer motion. How does Dan achieve the desired result? See Rule 12(h)(2) and 12(c). *Motion for judgement on pleadings*

(3) Can Dan move three months later to amend her answer to include the defense of improper service of process? See Rule 15(a). *Yes - if court says Ok*

c. Earl sues Frances, and, within the proper time, Frances answers, denying the material elements of the complaint and including the defense of improper venue. What happens to that defense from here on? See Rule 12(d).

Court has hearing of reserves right to decide until later or

2. Answer

If the defendant cannot demur to the complaint (or make an equivalent 12(b)(6) motion) or dispose of it on any of the grounds listed in 12(b), she must respond to its factual allegations. At common law the most common responses were the traverse and the plea in confession and avoidance; they live on, though under their less colorful modern names of denial and affirmative defense. The ensuing sections explore the contours of each.

a.   Denials

In most cases, the defendant denies many of the allegations of the complaint. Rule 8(b) and (d). In essence, Rule 8(b) requires the defendant to deny only those allegations that he actually disputes, and Rule 8(d) provides that any allegation that is not denied is deemed admitted.

These principles, however, conflict with defendants' understandable tendency to "deny everything." At common law, the form of plea called the general issue was permitted for many forms of action; this plea placed all allegations of the declaration at issue. The modern analogue is the general denial, an allegation that denies each and every allegation of the complaint. A more limited form of general denial denies each and every allegation of a specific paragraph or group of paragraphs.

There is nothing bad in theory about the general denial. The problem is that extremely few cases arise in which the defendant can plausibly deny each and every allegation or, as is more common, each and every allegation not relating to the names and citizenship of the parties. Nevertheless, it is still not uncommon for parties to interpose a general denial when they deny the major operative allegations of the complaint. Courts condemn casual, blanket denials because they require parties to spend needless time ferreting out the real items in dispute. A defendant who enters such a general denial may well find himself on the wrong end of a Rule 11 inquiry.

The next case deals with the converse problem — the inclusion of an absolutely accurate denial that proves, however, to be remarkably deceptive. The case asks you to consider the purpose of denials in litigation.

Zielinski v. Philadelphia Piers, Inc.

139 F. Supp. 408 (E.D. Pa. 1956)

VAN DUSEN, J.

Plaintiff requests a ruling that, for the purposes of this case, the motor-driven fork lift operated by Sandy Johnson on February 9, 1953, was owned by defendant and that Sandy Johnson was its agent acting in the course of his employment on that date. The following facts are established by the pleadings, interrogatories, depositions and uncontradicted portions of affidavits:

1. Plaintiff filed his complaint on April 28, 1953, for personal injuries received on February 9, 1953, while working on Pier 96, Philadelphia, for J.A. McCarthy, as a result of a collision of two motor-driven fork lifts.

2. Paragraph 5 of this complaint stated that "a motor-driven vehicle known as a fork lift or chisel, owned, operated and controlled by the defendant, its agents, servants and employees, was so negligently and carelessly managed . . . that the

same . . . did come into contact with the plaintiff causing him to sustain the injuries more fully hereinafter set forth."

3. The "First Defense" of the Answer stated "Defendant . . . (c) denies the averments of paragraph 5. . . ."

4. The motor-driven vehicle known as a fork lift or chisel, which collided with the McCarthy fork lift on which plaintiff was riding, had on it the initials "P.P.I."

5. On February 10, 1953, Carload Contractors, Inc. made a report of this accident to its insurance company, whose policy No. CL 3964 insured Carload Contractors, Inc. against potential liability for the negligence of its employees contributing to a collision of the type described in paragraph 2 above.

6. By letter of April 29, 1953, the complaint served on defendant was forwarded to the above-mentioned insurance company. This letter read as follows:

Gentlemen:

As per telephone conversation today with your office, we attach hereto "Complaint in Trespass" as brought against Philadelphia Piers, Inc. by one Frank Zielinski for supposed injuries sustained by him on February 9, 1953.

We find that a fork lift truck operated by an employee of Carload Contractors, Inc. also insured by yourselves was involved in an accident with another chisel truck, which, was alleged [sic], did cause injury to Frank Zielinski, and same was reported to you by Carload Contractors, Inc. at the time, and you assigned Claim Number OL 0153-94 to this claim.

Should not this Complaint in Trespass be issued against Carload Contractors, Inc. and not Philadelphia Piers, Inc.?

We forward for your handling.

7. Interrogatories 1 to 5 and the answers thereto, which were sworn to by defendant's General Manager on June 12, 1953, and filed on June 22, 1953, read as follows:

1. State whether you have received any information of an injury sustained by the plaintiff on February 9, 1953, South Wharves. If so, state when and from whom you first received notice of such injury. A. We were first notified of this accident on or about February 9, 1953 by Thomas Wilson.

2. State whether you caused an investigation to be made of the circumstances of said injury and if so, state who made such investigation and when it was made. A. We made a very brief investigation on February 9, 1953 and turned the matter over to (our insurance company) for further investigation. . . .

8. At a deposition taken August 18, 1953, Sandy Johnson testified that he was the employee of defendant on February 9, 1953, and had been their employee for approximately fifteen years.

9. At a pre-trial conference held on September 27, 1955, plaintiff first learned that over a year before February 9, 1953, the business of moving freight on piers in Philadelphia, formerly conducted by defendant, had been sold by it to Carload Contractors, Inc. and Sandy Johnson had been transferred to the payroll of this corporation without apparently realizing it, since the nature or location of his work had not changed. . . .

11. Defendant now admits that on February 9, 1953, it owned the fork lift in the custody of Sandy Johnson and that this fork lift was leased to Carload

Contractors, Inc. It is also admitted that the pier on which the accident occurred was leased by defendant.

12. There is no indication of action by either party in bad faith and there is no proof of inaccurate statements being made with intent to deceive. Because defendant made a prompt investigation of the accident . . . its insurance company has been representing the defendant since suit was brought, and this company insures Carload Contractors, Inc. also, requiring defendant to defend this suit, will not prejudice it. Under these circumstances, and for the purposes of this action, it is ordered that the following shall be stated to the jury at the trial:

> It is admitted that, on February 9, 1953, the towmotor or fork lift bearing the initials "P.P.I." was owned by defendant and that Sandy Johnson was a servant in the employ of defendant and doing its work on that date.

This ruling is based on the following principles:

1. Under the circumstances of this case, the answer contains an ineffective denial of that part of paragraph 5 of the complaint which alleges that "a motor driven vehicle known as a fork lift or chisel (was) owned, operated and controlled by the defendant, its agents, servants and employees."

F. R. Civ. P. 8(b), 28 U.S.C. provides:

> A party shall state in short and plain terms his defenses to each claim asserted and shall admit or deny the averments upon which the adverse party relies. . . . Denials shall fairly meet the substance of the averments denied. When a pleader intends in good faith to deny only a part or a qualification of an averment, he shall specify so much of it as is true and material and shall deny only the remainder.

For example, it is quite clear that defendant does not deny the averment in paragraph 5 that the fork lift came into contact with plaintiff, since it admits, in the answers to interrogatories, that an investigation of an occurrence of the accident had been made and that a report dated February 10, 1953, was sent to its insurance company stating "While Frank Zielinski was riding on bumper of chisel and holding rope to secure cargo, the chisel truck collided with another chisel truck operated by Sandy Johnson causing injuries to Frank Zielinski's legs and hurt head of Sandy Johnson." Compliance with the above-mentioned rule required that defendant file a more specific answer than a general denial. A specific denial of parts of this paragraph and specific admission of other parts would have warned plaintiff that he had sued the wrong defendant.

Paragraph 8.23 of Moore's Federal Practice (2nd Edition) Vol. II, p. 1680, says: "In such a case, the defendant should make clear just what he is denying and what he is admitting." This answer to paragraph 5 does not make clear to plaintiff the defenses he must be prepared to meet.

Under circumstances where an improper and ineffective answer has been filed, the Pennsylvania courts have consistently held that an allegation of agency in the complaint requires a statement to the jury that agency is admitted where an attempt to amend the answer is made after the expiration of the period of limitation. Although the undersigned has been able to find no federal court decisions on this point, he believes the principle of these Pennsylvania appellate court decisions may be considered in view of all the facts of this case, where jurisdiction is based on diversity of citizenship, the accident occurred in Pennsylvania, and the federal district court is sitting in Pennsylvania. . . .

2. Under the circumstances of this case, principles of equity require that defendant be estopped from denying agency because, otherwise, its inaccurate statements and statements in the record, which it knew (or had the means of knowing within its control) were inaccurate, will have deprived plaintiff of his right of action.

If Interrogatory 2 had been answered accurately[10] by saying that employees of Carload Contractors, Inc. had turned the matter over to the insurance company,[11] it seems clear that plaintiff would have realized his mistake. The fact that if Sandy Johnson had testified accurately, the plaintiff could have brought its action against the proper party defendant within the statutory period of limitations is also a factor to be considered, since defendant was represented at the deposition and received knowledge of the inaccurate testimony.

At least one appellate court has stated that the doctrine of equitable estoppel will be applied to prevent a party from taking advantage of the statute of limitations where the plaintiff has been misled by conduct of such party. See, Peters v. Public Service Corporation. In that case, the court said, "Of course, defendants were under no duty to advise complainants' attorney of his error, other than by appropriate pleadings, but neither did defendants have a right, knowing of the mistake, to foster it by its acts of omission."

This doctrine has been held to estop a party from taking advantage of a document of record where the misleading conduct occurred after the recording, so that application of this doctrine would not necessarily be precluded in a case such as this where the misleading answers to interrogatories and depositions were subsequent to the filing of the answer, even if the denial in the answer had been sufficient.

Since this is a pre-trial order, it may be modified at the trial if the trial judge determines from the facts which then appear that justice so requires.

NOTES AND PROBLEMS

1. Start by getting clear about the real problem in this case and how it arose.

a. For purposes of tort law, an employer is responsible for the negligent torts of an employee while at work. Whoever ran the business — "operated and controlled" the forklift, in the language of the complaint — was therefore responsible if Sandy Johnson had been negligent.

---

10. At least one federal district court case has suggested that a contempt proceeding under 18 U.S.C. §401 is the proper procedure to compensate the attorneys for one party who had been misled to their pecuniary damage by inaccurate answers to interrogatories. It suggested the imposition of a fine to be paid as civil liability to the attorneys for the complaining party. . . .

11. Pages 73 and 85 of the depositions of October 14, 1955, indicate that the answer to Interrogatory 2 was also inaccurate in saying that defendant made the investigation of the accident; but actually the employees of Carload Contractors, Inc. made the investigation.

b. When plaintiff read the answer, what do you suppose he thought defendant meant by denying the allegations of ¶5 of the complaint (quoted in ¶2 of the opinion)?

c. At some point before trial, the confusion about who was responsible for the forklift became obvious to both parties. Why didn't plaintiff at that point simply voluntarily dismiss the suit against Philadelphia Piers (Rule 41(a) permits such dismissals) and file a new complaint naming the correct defendant, Carload Contractors? What prevented this course of action?

2. Now focus on the court's dilemma.

a. Wasn't the denial by Philadelphia Piers that it operated and controlled the forklift "true"? If so, the judge's order is forcing the defendant at trial to admit something that is false: Why?

b. The court's action would be easy to understand if the court had found that the defendant purposely misled the plaintiff, but that explanation fails on two accounts. First, the opinion specifically rejects that possibility: "There is no indication of action by either party in bad faith and there is no proof of inaccurate statements being made with intent to deceive." Second, as between the parties, what argument can one make that it was *plaintiff's* fault that the denial was deceptive? Redraft the complaint in a way that would make it much less likely that a hastily drafted answer would unintentionally deceive.

3. In spite of the court's order that Philadelphia Piers admit a fact that wasn't true, the result of the case is probably just.

a. Why? Why does the court's order not harm an innocent party?

b. What change in facts would have led the court to permit Philadelphia Piers to stand by its deceptive but truthful denial?

4. *Zielinski* is a case in which defendant with complete certainty could have denied the allegation of operation and control, had it focused on that allegation. What happens if defendant is not sure, or if she believes that plaintiff's allegations may be true? Some defendants seek to evade the requirements of Rule 8 by "putting plaintiff to his proof." That practice, at odds with the spirit of Rule 8(b), drew a spirited rebuke from one federal judge who had seen it tried in one case too many:

> This is it. For too many years and in too many hundreds of cases this Court has been reading, and has been compelled to order the correction of, allegedly responsive pleadings that are written by lawyers who are either unaware of or who choose to depart from Rule 8(b)'s plain roadmap. It identifies only three alternatives as available for use in an answer to the allegations of a complaint: to admit those allegations, to deny them or to state a disclaimer (if it can be made in the objective and subjective good faith demanded by Rule 11) in the express terms of the second sentence of Rule 8(b), which then entitles the pleader to the benefit of a deemed denial.
>
> Here [defendants'] counsel has engaged in a particularly vexatious violation of that most fundamental aspect of federal pleading. It is hard to imagine, but fully 30 of the Response's 35 paragraphs . . . contain this nonresponse, in direct violation of Rule 8(b)'s express teaching:
>
>> Neither admit nor deny the allegations of said Paragraph — but demand strict proof thereof.

It is time for this Court to follow the Rules itself, in this instance Rule 8(d):

> Averments in a pleading to which a responsive pleading is required, other than those
> as to the amount of damage, are admitted when not denied in the responsive pleading.

> . . . Accordingly all of the allegations of Complaint ¶¶6-12, 17, 25-26 and 33-34
> are held to have been admitted by [defendants], and this action will proceed on that
> basis.

King Vision Pay Per View, Ltd. v. J.C. Dimitri's Restaurant, Inc., 180 F.R.D. 332
(N.D. Ill. 1998)

5. In light of the excerpt above, consider how a defendant should respond in
the following situation. Suppose A, a jogger, is injured when B's car swerves off
the road and hits A. A sues B. After reviewing the text of Rule 11(b), decide how B
should respond to the following allegations:

a. The complaint alleges that B has not had his car serviced for the past two
years. Although this allegation is true, B knows that it will be impossible for A to
prove it.

b. The complaint alleges that A was running north (the same direction B was
driving). B does not doubt that this is true but did not actually see A running.

c. Same as in (b), except that X, a friend of A, has told B that he was standing
20 feet away and saw A running north.

b.   *Affirmative Defenses*

Zielinski demonstrates that the traverse lives on in the form of the general or
specific denial. The following case asks where the borderline lies between a
denial and an affirmative defense — the old plea in confession and avoidance. As
a way of understanding it, suppose that in Gomez v. Toledo, the defendant superintendent, instead of demurring to the complaint, had simply denied its central
allegations. When the case came to trial, Toledo's lawyer had then sought to introduce evidence that the superintendent had acted in good faith, even though erroneously. Could Gomez have objected to the introduction of this evidence?

Layman v. Southwestern Bell Telephone Co.

554 S.W.2d 477 (Mo. Ct. App. 1977)

WEIER, J.

This court-tried case comes to us on appeal from a judgment in favor of
defendants Southwestern Bell Telephone Company and Wright Tree Service of
Iowa, Inc., and against the plaintiff Eileen Layman. Plaintiff's petition
contained two counts. In Count I she alleged that she was the owner of real
estate in Jefferson County, Missouri, and that the defendants had trespassed
upon this land and had installed underground telephone wires and cables
without her consent. She further alleged that the defendants continued to enter
upon this land and maintained the wires and cables. As to damages she stated

that by reason of the trespass the property had depreciated in value in the amount of $7,500. She prayed judgment for this sum together with $2,000 for punitive damages because of the willful and forceful nature of the acts of defendants. . . . After hearing the evidence, there being no request for findings of fact and conclusions of law, the court rendered judgment in favor of defendants stating that there was "insufficient evidence to establish the trespass pleaded and sought to be proved."[1] . . .

The evidence indicated that plaintiff had received a title to the 10.3 acres of land by deed on March 8, 1956. Although unsupported by record evidence, in cross-examination, she admitted conveying a remainder interest in the land in 1967 without consideration to her son and daughter retaining a life estate. On July 11, 1973, she saw some men and equipment digging across the south boundary of her land and destroying trees. They dug a trench about a foot wide and some three feet deep and anywhere from eight to twelve feet from the south boundary line. Mrs. Layman testified that prior to July 11, 1973, the fair market value of her property was $35,000 and that thereafter, after telephone wires had been laid in the ditch and covered up, the market value was $20,000 or a difference of $15,000. By answers to interrogatories directed to Southwestern Bell Telephone Company, this defendant admitted that it had employed Wright Tree Service to perform the work of installing the telephone wires on the property of the plaintiff. Defendant Wright Tree Service also admitted installing the wires under contract with Southwestern Bell Telephone Company.

The theory of the defendants in defense of their action in going upon plaintiff's property and installing a telephone cable beneath the surface of the ground was that defendant Southwestern Bell Telephone Company had received an assignment of an easement originally executed by owners of the land prior to the conveyance to plaintiff Layman and further that Mrs. Layman had given her permission for the installation of the cable across her land. In support of their easement defense, a recorded instrument entitled "Easement" executed by Ferdinand Kramme and his wife to Union Electric Company of Missouri dated March 1, 1946, was introduced in the evidence. Defendants claimed assignment of this easement by a document entitled "Joint Use Agreement" between Southwestern Bell Telephone Company and Union Electric Company. It is in the introduction of these documents, the easement to Union Electric and the alleged assignment of the easement rights of Union Electric to Southwestern Bell by the Joint Use Agreement, that plaintiff's contentions on appeal are grounded. . . .

Plaintiff's first point relied on to reverse the trial court contends that the court erred when it permitted the defendant Southwestern Bell to introduce evidence of an easement when it had pleaded only a general denial and not an affirmative defense of easement to plaintiff's claim of trespass. It was the theory of Southwestern Bell that it had a right of easement across plaintiff's land and that

---

1. Although this case has been considered as a trespass case by both parties and the court, because permanent damages were sought and proven under the value formula, it would actually seem to be a suit in the nature of inverse condemnation.

this right of easement was supported by two documents. As previously described, one was an easement which had been granted to Union Electric Company and the other was an assignment of this easement right by a joint use agreement. When defendant Southwestern Bell attempted to introduce the easement as its first exhibit, plaintiff objected on the grounds that an easement is an affirmative defense and that the answers of both Southwestern Bell and Wright Tree Service failed to set this defense out affirmatively. The court overruled the objection and allowed the introduction of the easement. The question now posed is whether right of entry by easement is an affirmative defense in an action for trespass.

Rule 55.08 [similar to Rule 8(c)] specifies that certain named affirmative defenses shall be pleaded to a preceding pleading. In addition to those named, which does not include "easement," the rule specifies "and any other matter constituting an avoidance or affirmative defense." In applying Rule 55.08 and in determining what defenses must be affirmatively pleaded as a condition to the admissibility of such evidence at the trial, the test applied is whether the defendant intends to rest his defense upon some fact not included in the allegations necessary to support the plaintiff's case. A general denial places in issue all of the material allegations contained in plaintiff's petition necessary to support his claim and the defendant is entitled to prove any fact which tends to show plaintiff's cause of action never had any legal existence. On the other hand, if the defendant has a defense in the nature of a confession of the facts of the plaintiff's petition but avers that the plaintiff's theory of liability even though sustained by the evidence does not apply to it because of additional facts which place defendant in a position to avoid any legal responsibility for its action, then such defense must be set forth in his answer. It seems clear that the right of defendant to enter upon the land to which plaintiff has indisputable possessory right would have to be proven by some competent evidence which would give that right to defendant. This would not be in derogation of plaintiff's claim by way of showing that her claim was nonexistent but rather that despite her claim, the defendant had a positive right to enter and disturb the possessory rights of the plaintiff. Thus it is the obligation of a defendant in an action for trespass to affirmatively plead and prove matters in justification. It should also be noted that another form of authority, to go upon land, that is a license, is specifically mentioned in Rule 55.08 as an affirmative defense. The conclusion is therefore inescapable that plaintiff's objection to the introduction of the easement evidence when it was not pleaded in justification of the trespass should have been sustained. . . .

The judgment is reversed and the cause remanded for new trial.

NOTES AND PROBLEMS

1. Start by seeing the role that pleading plays in this case.
a. At what stage of the litigation did the plaintiff object?
b. Why, at this stage, did the court refer all the way back to the pleadings to decide the issue raised by plaintiff's objection?
2. What did defendant do wrong?

a. Would the court have reached the same result if the defendant had simply denied trespass, but, in response to an interrogatory about the basis for its denial, had produced a copy of the purported easement?

b. Learn to be a little suspicious when courts or lawyers pronounce, as in *Layman*, that a "conclusion is therefore inescapable." In fact, one can find numerous cases that, if not directly contradicting *Layman*, at least appear inconsistent with it. For example, Denham v. Cuddeback, 210 Or. 485, 311 P.2d 1014 (1957), held that defendants who had denied the allegations in a trespass action would be permitted to prove title by adverse possession.

c. Does that make *Layman* wrongly decided? Or does that depend on whether the plaintiff was unfairly surprised by the introduction of the easement?

3. In ruling on cases like *Layman* and *Denham*, courts tend to make broad pronouncements about how one aspect of proof or another is inherently part (or not part) of the elements of the claim — and therefore (or therefore not) put at issue by a general denial. It may prove more helpful to think about the role that pleading plays in modern litigation.

a. For an example of a case taking such an approach, consider Harris v. Secretary, U.S. Dept. of Veterans' Affairs, 126 F.3d 339 (D.C. Cir. 1997). Plaintiff, suing the Department alleging racial discrimination in employment, filed her complaint after the statute of limitations had run. Defendant failed to assert the statute of limitations as an affirmative defense, as required in Rule 8(c), but after discovery did so in a motion for summary judgment. Like *Layman*, the *Harris* court insisted that defendant had erred by not pleading the statute; unlike *Layman*, the *Harris* court gave a reason for this rule and suggested that some flexibility might be in order on remand:

> Rule 8(c) means what it says: affirmative defenses must be raised in a responsive pleading, not a dispositive motion. This requirement permits the parties to chart the course of litigation in advance of discovery and motions thereon. Because the Department did not raise the defense in a responsive pleading and did not apply to the District Court for leave to amend its answer under Rule 15(a), the Court should not, without more, have considered the defense of untimeliness. However, this procedural error need not necessarily cause loss of the defense. On remand, the government may seek leave to amend its answers.

Is this solution close to what will happen in *Layman* on remand?

b. To the extent that discovery and pretrial conferences expose the areas of controversy, it shouldn't matter a great deal whether something is pleaded as a denial or an affirmative defense. It does matter in a case in which little discovery or other pretrial process has occurred; there the pleadings will bear the entire burden of exposing the issues in dispute, as they did at common law. *Layman* may be such a case: The small amount at stake makes it likely that neither party did much discovery or conferring, in which case the plaintiff may have been genuinely surprised by the evidence produced at trial.

Is it possible to frame any general principle to cover such situations? Consider the ordinary contract case in which defendant pleads a general denial. The plaintiff will expect defendant to try to show that the negotiations did not amount to an agreement or that the agreement was performed. Much less expected would be an assertion by defendant that the parties had already entered into a binding settlement of the dispute. Look at the list of affirmative defenses in Rule 8(c): Is the list really one of "unexpected" defenses? Section 3018(b) of N.Y. Civ. Prac. L. & R. (McKinney 1974 & Supp. 1987), which requires pleading of "all matters which if not pleaded would be likely to take the adverse party by surprise or would raise issues of fact not appearing on the face of a prior pleading," makes such a principle explicit.

4. If the "surprise" principle were in effect, which of the following would have to be pleaded as an affirmative defense?

a. Plaintiff sues for damages caused by water that overflowed from a dam on defendant's land. Defendant claims that the overflow was caused by an "act of God" and that an even higher dam would have been inadequate.

b. Plaintiff sues for damages caused when defendant's car suddenly swerved into plaintiff's lane. Defendant claims he swerved to avoid hitting a child.

c. Plaintiff sues for medical malpractice resulting from an operation. Defendant claims that plaintiff planned the lawsuit before the surgery and that she faked the injury.

d. Plaintiff sues for damages caused in an automobile accident. Defendant claims that the negligence of X, rather than his own, was the proximate cause of the accident.

e. Plaintiff sues defendant for repayment of a loan. Defendant claims that she and plaintiff formed a joint venture to purchase property and that the funds were plaintiff's contribution to the capital of the venture.

f. Plaintiff sues for breach of contract and seeks recovery of certain expenses incurred in performing the contract. Defendant claims that such expenses are not mentioned in the contract and that recovery is barred by the parol evidence rule.

5. The defendant faces a dilemma in each of the preceding cases. What happens if the defendant decides to take the "safe" course and plead the particular issue as an affirmative defense but later learns that a denial would have been adequate? Has the defendant lost anything by pleading it as an affirmative defense? At common law the answer was clear: A plea of confession and avoidance (see supra page 338) expressly admitted the facts constituting the "confession." That is no longer true, but some courts take the view that by pleading the matter as an affirmative defense, the defendant has assumed the burden of proof on the issue, even though defendant would not have had such a burden had he pleaded a denial. In fact, modern writers urge that defendants plead any doubtful matters as affirmative defenses in order to avoid the possibility of a waiver. See 5 Wright and Miller §1278, at 344.

6. There are a few special situations in which the plaintiff must allege a certain matter, and the defendant must allege the opposite in the form of an affirmative defense, rather than simply denying plaintiff's allegation. For example, the plaintiff in a defamation suit must allege the falsity of the statement, but the truth of the statement is an affirmative defense that must be pleaded. Similarly, although a plaintiff suing on a debt must allege nonpayment, the defendant must assert payment as an affirmative defense. The rationale for these quirks seems to be that the facts in question are such an integral part of the claim that the plaintiff must

make the initial allegation, but courts have applied the allocation rules discussed earlier in such a way as to place responsibility for pleading and proving such matters upon the defendant.

7. Assume *P* sues *D* for breach of an oral contract, and *D* interposes the affirmative defense of statute of frauds. What happens if *P* claims that *D*'s affirmative defense does not state a valid defense to *P*'s claim because the statute of frauds does not apply to the contract alleged by *P*? A procedural device is available to *P* that is analogous to the defense of failure to state a claim: *P* may make a motion to strike the affirmative defense. See Rule 12(f). This device allows *P* to attack the legal sufficiency of *D*'s affirmative defense.

3. Reply

In most cases, the pleadings stop with the answer. This is true whether the answer simply denies certain allegations of the complaint or contains new matter in the form of various affirmative defenses. We have already noted that allegations relating to such new matter are considered as "denied or avoided."

Suppose however, the answer contains a counterclaim. Rule 7(a) requires a reply if the answer contains "a counterclaim denominated as such." In other words, a reply is required only if the answer contains a counterclaim that is labeled as a counterclaim. If the answer contains an ostensible counterclaim that is not a counterclaim but an affirmative defense, then a reply technically is not required, although a cautious lawyer may well decide to reply. Similarly, if the answer contains allegations that are labeled as affirmative defenses, then no reply is required even though such matters should have been labeled as counterclaims. Professor Wright has suggested that when a reply to a counterclaim is required, such reply should be only to the counterclaim. Wright, Federal Courts 456-457. Frequently, however, lawyers will reply to all new matter to avoid a possible inadvertent admission.

In addition to mandatory replies, Rule 7(a) permits the court to order a reply on its own motion or on the motion of a party. In practice, replies rarely are ordered, and the mere fact that the answer raises affirmative defenses ordinarily is an insufficient basis on which to order a reply. One court has suggested the reply as a solution to the tension between substantive law and pleading rules in the civil rights/official immunity cases. In Schultea v. Wood, 47 F.3d 1427 (5th Cir. 1995) (en banc), the court suggested that it was possible to reconcile the "plain, short statement" requirements of Rule 8 with the substantive law of civil rights cases by permitting the plaintiff initially to plead generally, but if the defendant then raised an official immunity defense, to require that the plaintiff reply to the answer and in the reply to supply the specificity not required by Rule 8. Is this a fair solution?

NOTES AND PROBLEMS

As a test of your comfort with the materials on pleading examined thus far, try your hand with some problems.

1. Plaintiff files a complaint against an automobile Dealer and automobile Manufacturer. The complaint, which is properly before the court under diversity jurisdiction, alleges that Plaintiff was injured in an accident caused by a defect in the vehicle's steering mechanism. Manufacturer wants to assert that the vehicle was not defective when delivered to Dealer and that any defect must have been introduced by Dealer when the vehicle was being prepared for delivery to customer. What pleading, if any, should Manufacturer file?

2. Plaintiff files a complaint against Landlord alleging that Plaintiff was injured when a water heater on Landlord's premises exploded and injured Plaintiff. The complaint invokes diversity jurisdiction, alleging that the water heater was defective and asserts that Landlord is liable for having a defective water heater. Landlord files an answer asserting that the complaint fails to state a claim upon which relief can be granted because the doctrine of strict liability for defective products only applies to manufacturers and sellers of products, not to a landlord. At trial, Plaintiff proves that the heater was defective but Landlord continues to assert that it is not liable because strict liability does not apply to landlords. Plaintiff moves the court to strike this defense on the ground that it should have been made in a Rule 12(b)(6) motion, prior to answering, and was therefore waived. What result?

3. Same as preceding question, except that Landlord's answer denies liability but fails to assert that the complaint fails to state a claim upon which relief can be granted. Is the defense waived?

4. Plaintiff files a complaint for breach of contract. Defendant files an answer asserting, as an affirmative defense, that the complaint is barred by a one-year statute of limitations. Upon receiving the answer, Plaintiff's attorney concludes that the affirmative defense is totally without merit. The statute of limitations applicable to a breach of contract claim is four years; the one-year statute cited in the answer's affirmative defense applies only to negligence claims. Should Plaintiff file a Rule 12(b) motion to dismiss the affirmative defense? If not, what pleading should Plaintiff file to assert that the affirmative defense is without merit? *Rule 12(f)*

4.   Amendments

Pleadings provide at least a preliminary definition of what a lawsuit is about. Because that definition may change as the suit develops, particularly as discovery reveals facts unknown at the time of the original pleadings, parties may seek to change their stories. Rule 15 governs such amendments. A reading of the Rule suggests a tension between two goals: easy amendment, which allows the pleadings to reflect the parties' changed view of the case as it develops; and the notion of "prejudice," which reflects the idea that at some point the other side has to make decisions about how to present its case, decisions that become difficult if the story it has to meet continually shifts. Before dealing with the difficult issues, read the Rule and use the following problems to orient you to its structure.

NOTES AND PROBLEMS

1. Plaintiff files a complaint against First Defendant for breach of contract. Before Defendant's time to answer, Plaintiff's attorney realizes that, in addition to being able to claim breach of contract, plaintiff also has a claim for negligence against both First Defendant and Second Defendant.

a. What should plaintiff do?

b. Alternatively, suppose First Defendant answers before Plaintiff's lawyer realizes he has a claim for negligence against the two defendants. How does this affect plaintiff's course of action and the arguments he will use to support them?

2. Plaintiff files a complaint. Defendant answers denying liability. Ten days after filing the answer, Defendant's lawyer realizes that she negligently failed to include the affirmative defense of statute of limitations in the answer. What should Defendant's lawyer do?

3. The next case arises from a collision between Rule 15 and the statute of limitations. Recall Zielinski v. Philadelphia Piers (supra page 382). Suppose that defendant, making the same mistake plaintiff did, admitted that it operated and controlled the forklift, but denied negligence. Then a year later, after the statute of limitations had run, defendant discovered its mistake and sought permission to amend its answer to deny operation and control of the forklift. What should the court have done? The next case wrestles with that problem.

a.   The Basic Problem: Prejudice

Beeck v. Aquaslide 'N' Dive Corp.

562 F.2d 537 (8th Cir. 1977)

BENSON, J.

This case is an appeal from the trial court's exercise of discretion on procedural matters in a diversity personal injury action.

Jerry A. Beeck was severely injured on July 15, 1972, while using a water slide. He and his wife, Judy A. Beeck, sued Aquaslide 'N' Dive Corporation (Aquaslide), a Texas corporation, alleging it manufactured the slide involved in the accident, and sought to recover substantial damages on theories of negligence, strict liability and breach of implied warranty.

Aquaslide initially admitted manufacture of the slide, but later moved to amend its answer to deny manufacture; the motion was resisted. The district court granted leave to amend. On motion of the defendant, a separate trial was held on the issue of "whether the defendant designed, manufactured or sold the slide in question." This motion was also resisted by the plaintiffs. The issue was tried to a jury, which returned a verdict for the defendant, after which the trial court entered summary judgment of dismissal of the case. Plaintiffs took this appeal, and stated the issues presented for review to be:

> Where the manufacturer of the product, a water slide, admitted in its answer and later its answer to interrogatories both filed prior to the running of the statute of

limitations that it designed, manufactured and sold the water slide in question, was it an abuse of the trial court's discretion to grant leave to amend to the manufacturer in order to deny these admissions after the running of the statute of limitations?

After granting the manufacturer's motion for leave to amend in order to deny the prior admissions of design, manufacture and sale of the water slide in question, was it an abuse of the trial court's discretion to further grant the manufacturer's motion for a separate trial on the issue of manufacture?

I. Facts

A brief review of the facts found by the trial court in its order granting leave to amend, and which do not appear to have been in dispute, is essential to a full understanding of appellants' claims.

In 1971 Kimberly Village Home Association of Davenport, Iowa, ordered an Aquaslide product from one George Boldt, who was a local distributor handling defendant's products. The order was forwarded by Boldt to Sentry Pool and Chemical Supply Co. in Rock Island, Illinois, and Sentry forwarded the order to Purity Swimming Pool Supply in Hammond, Indiana. A slide was delivered from a Purity warehouse to Kimberly Village, and was installed by Kimberly employees. On July 15, 1972, Jerry A. Beeck was injured while using the slide at a social gathering sponsored at Kimberly Village by his employer, Harker Wholesale Meats, Inc. Soon after the accident investigations were undertaken by representatives of the separate insurers of Harker and Kimberly Village. On October 31, 1972, Aquaslide first learned of the accident through a letter sent by a representative of Kimberly's insurer to Aquaslide, advising that "one of your Queen Model #Q-3D slides" was involved in the accident. Aquaslide forwarded this notification to its insurer. Aquaslide's insurance adjuster made an on-site investigation of the slide in May 1973, and also interviewed persons connected with the ordering and assembly of the slide. An inter-office letter dated September 23, 1973, indicates that Aquaslide's insurer was of the opinion the "Aquaslide in question was definitely manufactured by our insured." The complaint was filed October 15, 1973.[3] Investigators for three different insurance companies, representing Harker, Kimberly and the defendant, had concluded that the slide had been manufactured by Aquaslide, and the defendant, with no information to the contrary, answered the complaint on December 12, 1973, and admitted that it "designed, manufactured, assembled and sold" the slide in question.[4]

The statute of limitations on plaintiff's personal injury claim expired on July 15, 1974. About six and one-half months later Carl Meyer, president and owner of Aquaslide, visited the site of the accident prior to the taking of his deposition by the plaintiff.[5] From his on-site inspection of the slide, he determined it was

[handwritten margin note: Admits designing + manufactur?]

3. Aquaslide 'N' Dive Corporation was the sole defendant named in the complaint.
4. In answers to interrogatories filed on June 3, 1974, Aquaslide again admitted manufacture of the slide in question.
5. Plaintiffs apparently requested Meyer to inspect the slide prior to the taking of his deposition to determine whether it was defectively installed or assembled.

not a product of the defendant. Thereafter, Aquaslide moved the court for leave to amend its answer to deny manufacture of the slide.

II.   Leave to Amend

Amendment of pleadings in civil actions is governed by Rule 15(a), F. R. Civ. P., which provides in part that once issue is joined in a lawsuit, a party may amend his pleading "only by leave of court or by written consent of the adverse party; and leave shall be freely given when justice so requires."

In Foman v. Davis, 371 U.S. 178(1962), the Supreme Court had occasion to construe that portion of Rule 15(a) set out above:

> Rule 15(a) declares that leave to amend "shall be freely given when justice so requires"; this mandate is to be heeded. . . . If the underlying facts or circumstances relied upon by a plaintiff may be a proper subject of relief, he ought to be afforded an opportunity to test his claim on the merits. In the absence of any apparent or declared reason — such as undue delay, bad faith or dilatory motive on the part of the movant, repeated failure to cure deficiencies by amendments previously allowed, undue prejudice to the opposing party by virtue of allowance of the amendment, futility of amendment, etc. — the leave sought should, as the rules require, be "freely given." Of course, the grant or denial of an opportunity to amend is within the discretion of the district court. . . .

This court in Hanson v. Hunt Oil Co. held that "[p]rejudice *must be shown.*" (Emphasis added). The burden is on the party opposing the amendment to show such prejudice. In ruling on a motion for leave to amend, the trial court must inquire into the issue of prejudice to the opposing party, in light of the particular facts of the case.

Certain principles apply to appellate review of a trial court's grant or denial of a motion to amend pleadings. First, as noted in Foman v. Davis, allowance or denial of leave to amend lies within the sound discretion of the trial court and is reviewable only for an abuse of discretion. The appellate court must view the case in the posture in which the trial court acted in ruling on the motion to amend.

It is evident from the order of the district court that in the exercise of its discretion in ruling on defendant's motion for leave to amend, it searched the record for evidence of bad faith, prejudice and undue delay which might be sufficient to overbalance the mandate of Rule 15(a), F.R. Civ. P., and Foman v. Davis, that leave to amend should be "freely given." Plaintiffs had not at any time conceded that the slide in question had not been manufactured by the defendant, and at the time the motion for leave to amend was at issue, the court had to decide whether the defendant should be permitted to litigate a material factual issue on its merits.

In inquiring into the issue of bad faith, the court noted the fact that the defendant, in initially concluding that it had manufactured the slide, relied upon the conclusions of three different insurance companies,[6] each of which had

---

6. The insurer of Beeck's employer, the insurer of Kimberly Village, as well as the defendant's insurer had each concluded the slide in question was an Aquaslide.

conducted an investigation into the circumstances surrounding the accident. This reliance upon investigations of three insurance companies, and the fact that "no contention has been made by anyone that the defendant influenced this possibly erroneous conclusion," persuaded the court that "defendant has not acted in such bad faith as to be precluded from contesting the issue of manufacture at trial." The court further found "[t]o the extent that 'blame' is to be spread regarding the original identification, the record indicates that it should be shared equally."

No bad faith shown

In considering the issue of prejudice that might result to the plaintiffs from the granting of the motion for leaving to amend, the trial court held that the facts presented to it did not support plaintiffs' assertion that, because of the running of the two-year Iowa statute of limitations on personal injury claims, the allowance of the amendment would sound the "death knell" of the litigation. In order to accept plaintiffs' argument, the court would have had to assume that the defendant would prevail at trial on the factual issue of manufacture of the slide, and further that plaintiffs would be foreclosed, should the amendment be allowed, from proceeding against other parties if they were unsuccessful in pressing their claim against Aquaslide. On the state of the record before it, the trial court was unwilling to make such assumptions,[7] and concluded "[u]nder these circumstances, the court deems that the possible prejudice to the plaintiffs is an insufficient basis on which to deny the proposed amendment." The court reasoned that the amendment would merely allow the defendant to contest a disputed factual issue at trial, and further that it would be prejudicial to the defendant to deny the amendment.

To agree to prejudice claim, court would have to make assumptions

The court also held that defendant and its insurance carrier, in investigating the circumstances surrounding the accident, had not been so lacking in diligence as to dictate a denial of the right to litigate the factual issue of manufacture of the slide.

On this record we hold that the trial court did not abuse its discretion in allowing the defendant to amend its answer.

III. Separate Trials

After Aquaslide was granted leave to amend its answer, it moved pursuant to Rule 42(b), F. R. Civ. P. for a separate trial on the issue of manufacture of the slide involved in the accident. The grounds upon which the motion was based were:

> (1) a separate trial solely on the issue of whether the slide was manufactured by Aquaslide would save considerable trial time and unnecessary expense and preparation for all parties and the court, and

7. The district court noted in its order granting leave to amend that plaintiffs may be able to sue other parties as a result of the substituting of a "counterfeit" slide for the Aquaslide, if indeed this occurred. The court added:

> [A]gain, the court is handicapped by an unclear record on this issue. If, in fact, the slide in question is not an Aquaslide, the replacement entered the picture somewhere along the Boldt to Sentry, Sentry to Purity, Purity to Kimberly Village chain of distribution. Depending upon the circumstances of its entry, a cause of action sounding in fraud or contract might lie. If so, the applicable statute of limitations period would not have run. Further, as defendant points out, the doctrine of equitable estoppel might possibly preclude another defendant from asserting the two-year statute as a defense.

(2) a separate trial solely on the issue of manufacture would protect Aquaslide from substantial prejudice.

The court granted the motion for a separate trial on the issue of manufacture, and this grant of a separate trial is challenged by appellants as being an abuse of discretion.

A trial court's severance of trial will not be disturbed on appeal except for an abuse of discretion.

The record indicates that Carl Meyer, president and owner of Aquaslide, designs the slides sold by Aquaslide. The slide which plaintiff Jerry A. Beeck was using at the time of his accident was very similar in appearance to an Aquaslide product, and was without identifying marks. Kimberly Village had in fact ordered an Aquaslide for its swimming pool, and thought it had received one. After Meyer's inspection and Aquaslide's subsequent assertion that it was not an Aquaslide product, plaintiffs elected to stand on their contention that it was in fact an Aquaslide. This raised a substantial issue of material fact which, if resolved in defendant's favor, would exonerate defendant from liability.

Plaintiff Jerry A. Beeck had been severely injured, and he and his wife together were seeking damages arising out of those injuries in the sum of $2,225,000.00. Evidence of plaintiffs' injuries and damages would clearly have taken up several days of trial time, and because of the severity of the injuries, may have been prejudicial to the defendant's claim of non-manufacture. The jury, by special interrogatory, found that the slide had not been manufactured by Aquaslide. That finding has not been questioned on appeal. Judicial economy, beneficial to all the parties, was obviously served by the trial court's grant of a separate trial. We hold the Rule 42(b) separation was not an abuse of discretion.

The judgment of the district court is affirmed.

NOTES AND PROBLEMS

[margin handwritten note: Prejudice = not hurting other side's case too much]

1. Rule 15 says that "leave [to amend] shall be freely given when justice so requires." The courts have read this phrase to mean: (a) that the would-be amender should have a good reason for not getting the pleading right the first time; and (b) that allowing the change now shouldn't hurt the other side too much. That latter requirement is often captured in the not very illuminating word "prejudice."

a. State simply how the court concluded that the first requirement was met.

b. Without deciding whether the prejudice to the plaintiff was too much, explain simply what it was. How was plaintiff hurt by permitting this amendment to the answer?

2. Is it true, as the court suggests, that the parties are equally to blame for the misidentification of the slide?

a. First assume, as the district court found, that Aquaslide and its insurers acted in completely good faith and that it was in fact difficult to tell the real from the counterfeit slide. Surely the defendant was in a better position to find this out than was the plaintiff. Moreover, once Aquaslide had admitted manufacture in its answer, could one expect any rational plaintiff to invest additional effort in making sure that the admission was accurate?

b. Later phases of this lawsuit revealed that Aquaslide and its president were aware that other manufacturers had been copying their slides; there had been several other lawsuits in which it had turned out that the slides were made by competitors. Beeck v. Aquaslide 'N' Dive Corp. 350 N.W.2d 149 (Iowa 1984). Assume that information had been presented to the court in this lawsuit. Under those circumstances would it have been an abuse of discretion had the trial court denied permission to amend?

3. If one accepts the argument implicit in the preceding two notes, the case presents a problem. The defendant has questionable excuse for having mispleaded in the first place, and the plaintiff will suffer crushing prejudice if amendment is allowed. The court nevertheless permitted amendment. Perhaps the court was simply wrong. But before you conclude that, consider whether there is another, deeper justification for the court's decision.

a. One answer appears if one conducts a thought experiment. Assume the amendment had been denied, and the wrong defendant had remained in the case. How would defendant have responded to the claim of negligent manufacture? Would it have shown its own design, testing, manufacturing, and safety procedures or those of the actual manufacturer? Assuming the latter, what would happen if it didn't know who manufactured the slide? How, in other words, could the defendant have conducted itself during litigation if it had been forced to stand by its erroneous admission of manufacture?

b. Compare *Beeck* to Zielinski v. Philadelphia Piers, which appears earlier in this chapter. In that case the court required the defendant to admit an allegation that was demonstrably false. Is *Zielinski* the right analogy? What key fact differed between the circumstances of that case and those of *Beeck*?

4. The *Beeck* opinion reproduced above did not end this litigation. The Beecks filed a second suit in state court, still against Aquaslide. This time, however, they did not claim a defective product but reckless misrepresentation made in the pleadings in the federal litigation. Plaintiffs' theory was that misrepresentations in the answer (inaccurately admitting that the product was made by Aquaslide) had caused the Beecks to lose their chance to sue the real manufacturer within the statute of limitations. The Beecks presented evidence summarized in Note 2b — showing that Aquaslide should have been on notice that there were counterfeit slides on the market. Plaintiffs argued that defendants were reckless in admitting manufacture without a more complete investigation.

The case came before the Iowa Supreme Court twice, once in 1981 and again in 1984. That court upheld a recovery based on a misrepresentation theory. However, analogizing the Beecks' claim to a legal malpractice action, the court also said that, in order to prevail, the plaintiffs would have to show not only that they would have recovered a judgment against the actual manufacturer but also that the judgment would have been collectible. Beeck v. Aquaslide 'N' Dive Corp., 350 N.W.2d 149 (Iowa 1984). Would you expect the Beecks to be able to make this showing?

5. Review your understanding of this chapter so far with a problem. Plaintiff files a complaint. Defendant answers, denying liability, and the case proceeds. After the close of discovery at the time the court has set for such motions, Defendant files a motion for summary judgment arguing that the complaint is barred by the statute of limitations. On the merits, Defendant has a strong case. Plaintiff argues, however, that because the statute of limitations was not specifically stated as an affirmative defense in Defendant's answer, it was waived. What result?

b. Statutes of Limitations and Relation Back

Beeck v. Aquaslide derived its bite from the possibility that the plaintiff, having suffered a dismissal, would be unable to refile its complaint against the right defendant before the statute of limitations had run. Rule 15(c) gives plaintiffs some leeway in this respect, but the flexibility is not limitless, as the next cases demonstrate. Central to the decision is the question of what constitutes a "claim," a question that takes us back to the beginning of this chapter. Compare the approach taken by the next two cases: Are they consistent?

Moore v. Baker

989 F.2d 1129 (11th Cir. 1993)

MORGAN, Senior Circuit Judge.

[Judith Moore consulted Dr. Baker about a blockage of her carotid artery. Baker recommended surgery and warned her about its risks. Moore signed a consent form. The operation went badly and left Moore severely and permanently disabled. Moore sued Dr. Baker. Her initial complaint alleged that he had violated Georgia's informed consent law by failing to advise her of an alternative therapy.]

On August 6, 1991, Dr. Baker filed a motion for summary judgment on the issue of informed consent. On August 26, 1991, Moore moved to amend her complaint to assert allegations of negligence by Dr. Baker in the performance of the surgery and in his post-operative care of Moore. . . .

I

Moore claims that the district court abused its discretion by . . . denying Moore's motion to amend her complaint. . . . on the ground that the newly-asserted claim was barred by the applicable statute of limitations. . . .

Moore filed her original complaint on the last day permitted by Georgia's statute of limitations. Accordingly, the statute of limitations bars the claim asserted in Moore's proposed amended complaint unless the amended complaint relates back to the date of the original complaint. An amendment relates back to the original filing "whenever the claim or defense asserted in the amended pleading arose out of the conduct, transaction, or occurrence set forth or attempted to be set forth in the original pleading." Fed. R. Civ. P. 15(c). The critical issue in Rule 15(c) determinations is whether the original complaint gave notice to the defendant of the claim now being asserted.

Moore relies heavily on Azarbal v. Medical Center of Delaware, Inc., 724 F. Supp. 279 (D. Del. 1989), which addressed the doctrine of relation back in the context of a medical malpractice case. In *Azarbal*, the original complaint alleged negligence in the performance of an amniocentesis on the plaintiff, resulting in injury to the fetus. After the statute of limitations had expired, the plaintiff sought to amend the complaint to add a claim that the doctor failed to obtain her informed consent prior to performing a sterilization procedure on her because the doctor did not tell her that the fetus had probably been injured by the amniocentesis. The district court [in *Azarbal*] found that "the original complaint provided adequate notice of any claims Ms. Azarbal would have arising from the amniocentesis, including a claim that Dr. Palacio should have revealed that the procedure had caused fetal injury."

The instant case is clearly distinguishable from *Azarbal*. Unlike the complaint in *Azarbal*, the allegations asserted in Moore's original complaint contain nothing to put Dr. Baker on notice that the new claims of negligence might be asserted. Even when given a liberal construction, there is nothing in Moore's original complaint which makes reference to any acts of alleged negligence by Dr. Baker either during or after surgery.[1] The original complaint focuses on Baker's actions before Moore decided to undergo surgery, but the amended complaint focuses on Baker's actions during and after the surgery. The alleged acts of negligence occurred at different times and involved separate and distinct conduct. In order to recover on the negligence claim contained in her amended complaint, Moore would have to prove completely different facts than would otherwise have been required to recover on the informed consent claim in the original complaint.

We must conclude that Moore's new claim does not arise out of the same conduct, transaction, or occurrence as the claims in the original complaint. Therefore, the amended complaint does not relate back to the original complaint, and the proposed new claims are barred by the applicable statute of

---

1. Moore's original complaint is very specific and focuses solely on Dr. Baker's failure to inform Moore of EDTA therapy as an alternative to surgery. Although the complaint recounts the details of the operation and subsequent recovery, it does not hint that Dr. Baker's actions were negligent. In fact, the only references in the original complaint relating to the surgery or postoperative care suggest that Dr. Baker acted with reasonable care. The complaint states that "the nurses noticed a sudden onset of right sided weakness of which they immediately informed Defendant Baker." (Complaint, P 18). "Upon being informed of this [right sided weakness], Defendant Baker immediately caused Plaintiff to be returned to the operation suite. . . . Although the clot was promptly removed by Defendant Baker. . . ." (Complaint, P 19).

limitations. Since the amended complaint could not withstand a motion to dismiss, we hold that the district court did not abuse its discretion in denying Moore's motion to amend her complaint. . . .

Bonerb v. Richard J. Caron Foundation

159 F.R.D. 16 (W.D. N.Y. 1994)

CAROL E. HECKMAN, Magistrate Judge. . . .

In this diversity action, plaintiff seeks damages for personal injuries allegedly sustained when he slipped and fell while playing basketball on defendant's recreational basketball court on November 29, 1991. Defendant is a not-for-profit corporation licensed and doing business as a drug and alcohol rehabilitation facility in Westfield, Pennsylvania. Plaintiff is a resident of Western New York.

The original complaint, filed on October 1, 1993, alleges that plaintiff was injured while he was a rehabilitation patient at defendant's Westfield facility, and was participating in a mandatory exercise program. Plaintiff claims that the basketball court was negligently maintained by defendant.

On July 25, 1994, this court granted plaintiff's motion for substitution of new counsel. On September 1, 1994, plaintiff moved to amend his complaint to add a new cause of action for "counseling malpractice." According to plaintiff's counsel, investigation and discussions undertaken after his substitution as counsel indicated to him that a malpractice claim was warranted under the circumstances. Defendant objects to the amendment on the grounds that the counseling malpractice claim does not relate back to the original pleading and is therefore barred by Pennsylvania's two-year statute of limitations.

Discussion

Rule 15 of the Federal Rules of Civil Procedure provides that once time for amending a pleading as of right has expired, a party may request leave of court to amend, which "shall be freely given when justice so requires." Fed. R. Civ. P. 15(a). . . .

The relation back doctrine is based upon the principle that one who has been given notice of litigation concerning a given transaction or occurrence has been provided with all the protection that statutes of limitation are designed to afford. Thus, if the litigant has been advised at the outset of the general facts from which the belatedly asserted claim arises, the amendment will relate back even though the statute of limitations may have run in the interim.

An amendment which changes the legal theory of the case is appropriate if the factual situation upon which the action depends remains the same and has been brought to the defendant's attention by the original pleading. . . .

In this case, the original complaint alleges that plaintiff was injured when he slipped and fell on a wet, muddy basketball court "while participating in a mandatory exercise program . . ." at defendant's rehabilitation facility. Plaintiff alleges several instances of defendant's negligent conduct, such as failure to maintain the premises safely, failure to warn, failure to inspect and failure to "properly supervise and/or instruct plaintiff. . . ." The proposed amendment seeks to allege that plaintiff "was caused to fall while playing in an outdoor basketball court . . . in an exercise program mandated as part of his treatment in the rehabilitation program . . . ," and that "the rehabilitation and counseling care rendered . . . was negligently, carelessly and unskillfully performed".

The allegations in the original and amended complaints derive from the same nucleus of operative facts involving injury suffered by plaintiff on November 29, 1991. It is true that a claim for professional malpractice invokes an entirely different duty and conduct on the part of the defendant than does a claim for negligent maintenance of the premises. However, the original complaint advised defendant of the same transaction or occurrence giving rise to these different theories of negligence. Indeed, the original complaint alleged that participation in the exercise program was mandatory, and that the injury was caused by defendant's failure to "properly supervise and/or instruct plaintiff. . . ." These allegations not only gave defendant sufficient notice of the general facts surrounding the occurrence, but also alerted defendant to the possibility of a claim based on negligent performance of professional duties. This is all that is required for relation back under Rule 15(c).

Defendant contends that it will be unduly prejudiced by the amendment because it will have to return to the drawing board to prepare an entirely new defense. However, as plaintiff points out, the period for discovery has not yet expired, depositions of defendant's personnel have not yet been taken, and expert witness information has not been exchanged. In addition, the parties have consented to trial before the undersigned, thereby simplifying any further supervision of discovery and the conduct and review of pretrial matters and dispositive motions.

Finally, there has been no showing of undue delay or bad faith on the part of plaintiff. . . .

NOTES AND PROBLEMS

1. Relation-back cases test our belief in statutes of limitations and our idea of a claim.

a. What are statutes of limitations for? Why do we have them?

b. How is that justification linked to the relation-back doctrine? One could, theoretically, have a doctrine that permitted relation back of any subsequent amendment, no matter how unrelated to the original claim. What is the argument against such a doctrine?

2. If one has decided that relation back should apply only to "related" claims, the question is how to define "relatedness." One possibility would be on the basis of legal theory: Any tort claim could be joined to an initial claim for a tort, and so on. As a review of this chapter, explain why such a theory is incompatible with the idea of notice pleading.

3. That leaves us with Rule 15(c), which defines the line between permitted and unpermitted amendments in terms of "the conduct, transaction, or occurrence set

forth or attempted to be set forth in the original pleading." That language is purposely general, and courts will inevitably perceive "conduct, transaction, [and] occurrence" in different-sized packages.

4. In Moore v. Baker, the court finds that the allegations of medical malpractice did not relate back to the allegations of failure to get informed consent for the operation. In Bonerb v. Richard J. Caron Foundation, the court finds that the claim of "counseling malpractice" did relate back to the allegations of negligent maintenance of the basketball court.

a. Are the cases distinguishable? If one focuses just on the "conduct, transaction, or occurrence" language, one might think not. In both cases people presented themselves to health care professionals for treatment and are alleging bad outcomes caused by those professionals. But one plaintiff gets to amend and the other does not. That seems unjustified.

b. Nor does it help to point out that in *Moore* the plaintiff is trying to change the legal theory of her case while in *Bonerb* the plaintiff is merely shifting from one set of facts to another to support the claim of negligence. Rule 15(c) specifically rejects the idea that amendments should turn on legal theories.

c. Focus instead on the stage of litigation at which the motions came in the two cases. Articulate an argument that the cases are both correctly decided because of the timing of the motions to amend.

5. Some of the most spectacular relation-back cases occur when the plaintiff wants to change not just a legal theory, but the party sued. One might think that basic ideas of fair notice would prevent such amendments. But even such an amendment can relate back under some conditions. Read carefully Rule 15(c)(3).

a. The ordinary version of such cases involves a corporation sued under the wrong name or an individual whose name is misspelled. In such instances the "right" defendant is served with process, knows of the suit, and knows of plaintiff's mistake; the courts have often allowed such amendments to relate back.

b. Apply Rule 15(c)(3) to the facts of Zielinski v. Philadelphia Piers, supra page 382. The present version of this Rule was not in effect at the time *Zielinski* was decided. Suppose it had been. Could the court have avoided the awkward step of forcing the defendant to admit a false statement by instead permitting an amendment to change the defendant? Do you need any additional facts to decide whether this approach would work?

c. More dramatic are the cases where the real defendant wasn't served with process because the plaintiff served the person named in the complaint rather than the "real" defendant. In those cases courts wrestle with the question of whether the newly named party knew enough about the suit that she wouldn't be prejudiced in her defense and knew that she would have been named but for a mistake of the plaintiff. Among the most difficult of these are suits against institutions where the plaintiff initially names the institution but for various reasons decides later to sue individuals within that institution — for example, specific police officers rather than the police department or city. Consider, for example, Worthington v. Wilson, 790 F. Supp. 829 (C.D. Ill. 1992), in which the court concluded that the defendant officers had known of the suit — and thus had received the requisite notice — but that the failure to name the officers had not been a "mistake" but a conscious strategic decision by plaintiff's counsel and that the amended complaint therefore did not relate back.

———————————

As we have seen, modern pleading has eliminated most of the rigidities and trapdoors that characterized its common law predecessors. Pleading is no longer a technical game. It continues, however, to serve two central functions. First, it can eliminate some legal theories, sharpen the basis of dispute, and thereby enable the parties to reach converging estimates of a case's values. Second, it can define the ground to be covered in the ensuing discovery phase. Equally important is what modern pleading does not do. In "off-the-rack" litigation about, for example, auto accidents, it usually does not define particular facts in dispute. And, by the same token, it does not convey substantial factual information about the case.

This situation requires other procedural devices to convey information about the lawsuit and to end meritless cases short of trial. The following two chapters describe the answers modern procedure has given to the problems posed by contemporary pleading. The next chapter, on discovery, displays the system's response to the scanty information conveyed by pleading. The one after that, on resolution without trial, discusses ways in which contemporary litigators can seek to eliminate meritless claims and defenses. As you consider these topics, bear in mind that they are in substantial part responses to decisions made about the pleading system.

DISCOVERY

VII

A hundred years ago, if a complaint survived demurrer, the case would go to trial if the plaintiff wanted it to. That is no longer true. In contemporary litigation the chief significance of a complaint's surviving dismissal is that it enables the plaintiff to reach the "pretrial" stage — the intermediate stage between pleading and trial. Today, most lawsuits end at this pretrial stage. In part, they end at this stage *because* of the procedural device explored in this chapter — discovery. Discovery ends lawsuits for two reasons; one of them good, the other not. First, discovery produces information about the merits of the lawsuit and permits parties to make informed judgments about the strength of their and their opponent's positions; such information can end either in settlement or in summary judgment, both of which are explored in the next chapter. Second, because discovery costs time and money, it also enables one of the parties simply to wear the other down — or both sides to wear each other down — without regard to the merits of the case. This chapter explains why discovery has both these potentials and explores ways in which the Rules try to maximize the first reason and minimize the second reason that lawsuits can end at this stage.

A. Modern Discovery

Contemporary civil discovery permits parties to compel the disclosure of witnesses, evidence, documents, and other matters before trial. Under previous practice, only a limited range of discovery devices was available and only against some persons, in some kinds of actions. Discovery was not always a matter of right, and was often limited to a scope narrower than the issues relevant at trial. This recipe could produce good courtroom drama, but not, critics argued, truth or justice.

The institution of modern discovery has changed that picture. Both state courts and the federal system have adopted broad civil discovery rules that permit a lawyer to uncover, in advance of trial, enormous amounts of information. The scope and depth of modern U.S. discovery practice make it unique among today's legal systems. This scope permits the bringing and defense of claims where all or much of the relevant information lies in the possession of the other side. Outside the United States, neither common law nor civil law systems permit the searching scrutiny of material in the possession of the opposing party, and American lawyers often encounter strong resistance when they seek to use discovery techniques in multinational litigation.

As an introduction to these changes a short history of the debates surrounding the discovery portion of the Rules is helpful. The desirability of amendments to the discovery rules has been under debate for more than twenty years. Roughly speaking, one could see the two sides as disagreeing about whether it was possible to throw out the bathwater without harming the baby and, if so, how. The "baby" in this debate was the general acknowledgement that the U.S. discovery system (every state has adopted something like the broad discovery regime of the Rules) makes it possible to ferret out much information and thus to allow parties with good counsel and adequate resources to litigate in full possession of the relevant information. The "bathwater" is composed of several elements, depending on who was doing the analysis. One group focused on the extent of expensive "over-discovery," another on "under-discovery" and stonewalling, a third on the asserted decline of professional civility and cooperation, a fourth on the failure of judicial supervision. These different definitions of the problem led to differing remedies. The 2000 amendments, promulgated after an elaborate process of hearings and comment, had four central features: changes in required disclosures by the parties; a narrowing of the definition of material discoverable without judicial order; imposition of national restrictions on the number of interrogatories and depositions and the length of depositions in the absence of judicial order; and a set of changes designed to encourage judicial monitoring and possible cost-sharing of discovery.

B. The Possibilities and Limits of Discovery: Relevance and Privilege

Both the power and the destructive potential of discovery hinge on the principles governing its use. Rule 26(b)(1) allows the parties, without court approval, to seek discovery "regarding any matter, not *privileged*, that is *relevant* to the claim or defense of any party." If a party shows "good cause" the court may grant even broader discovery "of any matter relevant to the *subject matter* involved in the action." (Rule 26(b)(1); emphasis added.) In either formulation the concept of relevance both grants power and limits it; privilege operates solely as a limitation.

1. Relevance

To be discoverable, information must be relevant, either to a "claim or defense," or, if judicial permission is granted, to the "subject matter" of the lawsuit. "Relevance" thus links discovery to the law of pleading, to the law of evidence, and to common sense. Relevance defines a relationship between pieces of information: How I tie my shoelaces is irrelevant to whether it will rain today; how the sky looks is highly relevant to that question. But legal relevance demands more than this. For a piece of information to be relevant to a legal proposition means, according to the governing substantive law — enforced by the rules of evidence — that the information tends to prove or disprove something the law says matters. For example, if in a contract dispute, the defendant contends that he failed to pay for goods because the goods were defective, the condition of the goods will be relevant. If the defendant instead contends that he failed to pay for the goods because he used the money to support a sick relative, the state of the relative's health would be irrelevant. Its irrelevance flows from the law of contract, which says that one's motives for breaching a contract don't matter. Finally, consider the new role of pleading in defining relevance for the purposes of discovery. In the contract case imagined above, suppose the defendant pleaded, as its sole defense, the running of the statute of limitations. On the basis of that pleading, would information about whether the plaintiff had fulfilled his part of the agreement be "relevant to a claim or defense"?

Davis v. Precoat Metals

2002 WL 1759828 (N.D. Ill. 2002)

NOLAN, Magistrate J.

Plaintiffs Nicholas Davis, L.C. Alexander, Deon Page, George Hollins, and Tina Williams sued their employer Precoat Metals, alleging race and national origin discrimination and retaliation in violation of Title VII of the Civil Rights Act of 1964. Before the Court is Plaintiffs' Motion to Compel Discovery.

Background

For purposes of this order, the Court assumes that the following facts taken from the plaintiffs' complaint are true. The plaintiffs — African-American and Latino employees who worked at the defendant's Chicago plant — allege that they have *Facts* been exposed to a hostile working environment, including being subjected to racially insulting and derogatory comments by the defendant's management level employees. The plaintiffs also claim that the defendant discriminated against African American and Latino employees in terms of entry level place-ment, work assignments, promotions, and discipline and that the defendant retaliated against them after they complained about the company's discrimina-tory practices. . . .

Discussion

Federal Rule of Civil Procedure 26(b)(1) permits discovery into "any matter, not privileged, that is relevant to the claim or defense of any party." Discoverable information is not limited to that which would be admissible at trial. Information is relevant for purposes of Rule 26 "if the discovery appears reasonably calculated to lead to the discovery of admissible evidence." Fed. R. Civ. P. 26(b)(1). However, a plaintiff is not necessarily entitled to all discovery that is relevant under Rule 26. A court can limit discovery if it determines, among other things, that the discovery is unreasonably cumulative or duplicative, obtainable from another source that is more convenient, less burdensome, or less expensive, or the burden or expense of the proposed discovery outweighs its likely benefit. Fed. R. Civ. P. 26(b)(2).

The plaintiffs' motion seeks . . . discrimination complaints made against the defendant by non-clerical/non-administrative employees who worked at the same plant as the plaintiffs (i.e., the Chicago plant). . . .

The parties disagree on whether a plaintiff is entitled to discovery regarding other employees' complaints of discrimination against a defendant. In their motion, the plaintiffs have limited their requests to: (i) the 1998-to-February 2002 time period; (ii) complaints by employees who worked at the same Chicago plant where the plaintiffs worked; and (iii) complaints of race and national origin discrimination — the same types of discrimination alleged in the plaintiffs' complaint. The defendant argues that the plaintiffs' requests are overbroad in that they improperly seek information regarding all allegedly discriminatory actions by the defendant. The Court concludes that the plaintiffs' requests seek discoverable information and that those requests (as limited by the plaintiffs in their motion) are narrowly tailored to the specific claims of the case.

The plaintiffs are correct that other employees' complaints of discrimination may be relevant to establish pretext. See McDonnell Douglas Corp. v. Green, 411 U.S. 792, 804-05 (1973) (stating that an employer's general policy and practice with respect to minority employment may be relevant to establish pretext); Phillip v. ANR Freight Sys., Inc., 945 F.2d 1054, 1056 (8th Cir. 1991) (reversing district court's exclusion of other employees' age discrimination complaints filed against defendant).

The two cases cited by the defendant — Chavez v. DaimlerChrysler Corp., 206 F.R.D. 615 (S.D. Ind. 2002), and Sidari v. Orleans County, 180 F.R.D. 226 (W.D.N.Y. 1997) — do not persuade the Court that other employees' complaints of discrimination are not discoverable. . . . The *Chavez* court did not hold that the other employees' complaints are never discoverable; the court held that the plaintiff in that case had not established that he was entitled to company-wide discovery of this information, i.e., the plaintiff failed to establish that he was entitled to discover complaints filed by employees who did not work at the same manufacturing plant as the plaintiff. In this case, the plaintiffs limited their requests to discrimination complaints, charges, and grievances filed by employees who worked at the same plant as the plaintiffs. In *Sidari*, the . . . court rejected the plaintiff's argument, stating that:

> [T]he plaintiff in this case is entitled only to discovery as to whether he has been discriminated against because of his national origin (Italian) or religion (Catholic). Although the plaintiff may be afforded some latitude to determine a pattern or practice by his employer to discriminate against Italians or Catholics, the plaintiff can not [sic] conduct an across-the-board attack on any and all alleged unequal employment practices by his employer.

Id. at 237. In this case, the plaintiffs do not seek discovery related to all alleged unequal employment practices by the defendant, e.g., the plaintiffs do not seek information regarding other employees' age or sex discrimination complaints, nor do they seek complaints by employees who did not work at the Chicago plant. Rather, the plaintiffs have limited their discovery requests to complaints alleging race and national origin discrimination filed by other employees who worked at the same plant as the plaintiffs. Unlike the requests at issue in *Chavez* and *Sidari*, the Court concludes that the requests in this case are narrowly tailored to the specific allegations of the plaintiffs' complaint. Accordingly, the Court grants the plaintiffs' motion to compel to the extent it seeks production of documents responsive to requests 7, 8, 13, and 21 from Plaintiffs' First Request for Production of Documents. . . .

Steffan v. Cheney

920 F.2d 74 (D.C. Cir. 1990)

PER CURIAM.

Joseph C. Steffan resigned from the United States Naval Academy in 1987, after an administrative board recommended that he be discharged. The board's recommendation was based solely upon Steffan's statements proclaiming himself a homosexual; he was not charged with any homosexual conduct. In 1988 he filed this action, claiming that he was constructively discharged and challenging the constitutionality of the regulations that provided for the discharge of admitted homosexuals. The factual and procedural background of the case is set out in the opinion of the district court, and will not be repeated in detail here.

The matter is before this court now because Steffan, claiming his Fifth Amendment privilege against self-incrimination, refused to answer deposition questions directed to whether he had engaged in homosexual conduct during or after his tenure as a midshipman. He also objected that the questions were not relevant to the legality of his separation. The district court, having issued a prior warning, dismissed Steffan's action for failure to comply with its discovery order, see Fed. R. Civ. P. 37(b)(2), and Steffan appeals. Although the district court has broad discretion in choosing a sanction under Rule 37, no sanction may be upheld if its imposition was based upon an error of law. Because this is such a case, we reverse.

The district court acknowledged that "the record is clear that [Steffan] was separated from the Naval Academy based on his admissions that he is a homosexual rather than on any evidence of misconduct." Nevertheless, the court thought that the questions about homosexual conduct were "highly relevant" because, it believed, the Navy could "refuse reinstatement on the grounds that an individual has engaged in homosexual acts." The court held that "in seeking reinstatement and award of his diploma, [Steffan] through his claims has placed in issue whether he is qualified for such relief."

Judicial review of an administrative action is confined to "the grounds . . . upon which the record discloses that [the] action was based." SEC v. Chenery Corp., 318 U.S. 80, 87 (1943). This rule applies with equal force to judicial review of administrative actions by the military.

Here Steffan is challenging the Navy's administrative determination that he is unfit for continued service because he stated that he is a homosexual. That he seeks reinstatement as relief for an allegedly invalid separation does not put into issue the question whether he engaged in potentially disqualifying conduct unless such conduct was a basis for his separation. See White v. Secretary of the Army, 878 F.2d 501, 505 (D.C. Cir. 1989).* If Steffan was discharged wrongfully, he "has never been discharged[;] . . . in the eyes of the law, [he] remains in service." Dilley v. Alexander, 627 F.2d 407, 411 (D.C. Cir. 1980).

The district court therefore erred in finding the inquiry into homosexual conduct vel non to be relevant on the ground asserted in its opinion. Should the district court find that the questions are relevant on any other ground, it must of course balance anew the interests of the parties before deciding upon a sanction. We reverse the judgment of the district court and remand for further proceedings consistent with this opinion.

So ordered.

NOTES AND PROBLEMS

1. Explain the different outcomes.

a. In *Davis* the plaintiff is given access to information about other employees who are not parties to the suit.

b. In *Steffan* the defendant is prohibited from asking plaintiff a question whose answer was, at the time of the lawsuit, a basis for dismissal from the military.

c. Explain why the information sought in *Davis* was relevant and that in *Steffan* not?

2. Since the decision in this phase of *Steffan* the Supreme Court has held that state laws criminalizing private sexual conduct between consenting adults are unconstitutional. Lawrence v. Texas, 123 S. Ct. 2472 (2003). The implications of that decision for the military are still unclear. Suppose that Steffan is reinstated and again discharged, this time for sexual behavior. He sues and the government again deposes him and asks about instances of sexual conduct. Must he answer?

3. Focus on the procedural moves that led these two courts to issue their discovery rulings.

a. Which actions by which parties led the district court to issue its ruling?

b. Suppose the defendant in *Davis* wanted to challenge the district court ruling. Could it have sought review in the court of appeals?

c. How did *Steffan* reach an appellate court? Would you recommend this as a tactic to your clients who wanted to appeal a discovery ruling?

d. What do your answers tell you about the power of district courts in discovery matters?

---

* The Government now argues that Steffan's admission of homosexuality raised a "rebuttable regulatory presumption that he had a predilection [sic] to commit, and had committed, homosexual acts." This argument, not raised in the district court, finds no support in the record. Cf. Ben-Shalom v. Marsh, 881 F.2d 454, 457 (7th Cir. 1989) (soldier given written notice of presumption).

4. Develop your understanding of the concept of relevance by working through the following problems:

a. Albert and Barbara are involved in an automobile collision. Albert sues Barbara, alleging negligence. Barbara denies liability. Albert seeks to discover the size of Barbara's bank account. (He wants to know whether she will be capable of satisfying a damage judgment.) Is this information "relevant to a claim or defense" and thus discoverable?

b. Same facts as in Problem 3a, except that in addition to asserting negligence, Albert alleges that Barbara intentionally collided with him. Intentional torts carry with them punitive damages, and in many jurisdictions a jury asked to award punitive damages may consider the wealth of the defendant, the idea being that the punishment should be tailored to the defendant's circumstances. Albert again seeks to discover the size of Barbara's bank account. Is it now "relevant to a claim or defense" and thus discoverable?

c. Same lawsuit as in Problem 4a — that is, a negligence action, with no allegations of intentional harm. Albert, fearing that Barbara may lack assets to pay damages, seeks to discover whether Barbara has a liability insurance policy that would be available to satisfy a damage judgment if he wins the suit. If one considers only relevance to a claim or defense, is the policy discoverable? Now consider how Rule 26(a)(1)(D) changes this result. What might justify this exception to the ordinary rules of relevance?

5. Now consider a variation on this problem, one in which you begin to confront some of the techniques of discovery. The current version of Rule 26 provides for a two-stage discovery process. In the first, set forth in Rule 26(a), the parties come forward with certain basic information "that the disclosing party may use to *support* its claims or defenses" (emphasis added); in the second stage, they may ask each other for additional information under the guidelines described in Rule 26(b)(1). Read those provisions and answer the following questions:

a. Albert alleges that Barbara "negligently collided" with his car; Barbara's answer has denied negligence. Albert's lawyer has interviewed him, obtained copies of his medical and wage records, and has spoken with various other potential witnesses. Albert's lawyer intends to present a straightforward version of the case: Barbara ran a red light, collided with Albert, who as a result lost wages and incurred medical expenses. A witness at the intersection will testify that Barbara ran the light. There are, however, some soft spots in the case: Albert has a poor driving record and has himself been cited for running red lights; his job situation has been precarious, and Albert thinks that his boss might testify that he was about to be fired (thus reducing potential damages for lost wages). What disclosures must Albert make under 26(a)(1)?

b. Now consider Barbara's disclosures. Her lawyer has interviewed her and knows the name and address of a mechanic who can testify about the maintenance of her car (he will say it was well maintained), her boss (with whom she had a major argument just before the accident), and a bystander who saw the accident. The bystander, let us suppose, is not the same one located by Albert. This witness is not an attractive one — a vagrant with a long history of minor drug arrests — but he says he thinks the light was green for Barbara when she entered the intersection. Explain how each of these witnesses might have information relevant to the lawsuit. Which of their names should Barbara's lawyer supply at the time appropriate for the disclosure required in Rule 26(a)(1)(A)?

6. Notice that the 2000 revisions of the disclosure provisions require parties to disclose information that they "may use" "to support" their claims or defenses. By contrast, the general discovery provisions of 26(b)(1) require discovery of any unprivileged matter "relevant to the claim or defense of any party." Consider how those provisions would bear on the following problems:

a. Barbara has told her lawyer that she had a violent argument with her boss just before the accident and was still fuming as she drove. Her lawyer is also debating whether to use the testimony of the vagrant who will testify that the traffic light was in her favor. Must she disclose her boss as a witness pursuant to 26(a)(1)? The vagrant?

b. Suppose, after the initial disclosures, Barbara is served with an interrogatory asking her to supply the name of any witness with information relevant to plaintiff's claim. Must she now list her boss as such a witness?

2. Privilege

Rule 26(b)(1) contains an explicit exception: It makes discoverable "any matter, *not privileged*, which is relevant. . ." (emphasis added). The law of evidence creates privileges — protections for information *from certain sources*. We have already seen a civil litigant invoking a privilege in discovery: Though the case did not turn on this issue, the plaintiff in *Steffan* invoked a privilege as one ground for refusing to answer. In a criminal case the prosecutor cannot call the defendant to the stand and ask her if she committed the crime; such an action would violate the constitutional privilege against self-incrimination. Notice first that this objection on the grounds of a privilege has nothing to do with relevance: Whether the defendant committed the crime is highly relevant. Second, note that privileges typically block information from a particular source; privileges are not meant to block the underlying facts. Thus the prosecution in a criminal case, though barred by the Fifth Amendment from asking the defendant about her guilt, can introduce evidence from other, unprivileged sources.

Besides the privilege against self-incrimination, some of the more common privileges are attorney-client, doctor-patient, and psychotherapist-patient. Discussing all of the privileges and the conditions for their invocation is far beyond the scope of a course in civil procedure. Our focus instead is on the interaction of privileges and discovery in civil lawsuits.

NOTES AND PROBLEMS

1. Albert and Barbara are involved in an automobile collision. Albert sues Barbara, alleging that Barbara intentionally drove her car into Albert's. Barbara

denies liability. In a deposition Albert's lawyer asks Barbara, "Did you intentionally collide with Albert?"

a. Can Barbara object on the grounds that the question is irrelevant?

b. Barbara objects on grounds of privilege. What privilege?

2. Often the existence of a privilege only begins an inquiry. All privileges can be waived, either explicitly by the party entitled to use it or implicitly by an action inconsistent with the privilege. Moreover, privileges cannot be abused.

a. For example, a party invoking a privilege against self-incrimination may waive that privilege by taking the stand and denying the crime. Having started to testify about the crime, he cannot then invoke the privilege when the other side seeks to cross-examine. Or a client can waive the attorney-client privilege by disclosing to some third party the contents of his statements to his lawyer — statements that would otherwise be privileged.

b. Same lawsuit as in Problem 1, except that in addition to negligence and battery, Albert alleges that Barbara intentionally inflicted emotional distress. Barbara's answer denies causation and her lawyer plans to argue at trial that Albert has been emotionally unstable for years. During discovery, Barbara's lawyer learns that Albert has been in psychotherapy for some time. (The state in question recognizes a privilege for patient-psychotherapist communications.) Should Albert be allowed to claim privilege as a basis for refusing to answer questions about his therapy?

3. The discussion above contrasts relevance and privilege. In a few unusual cases a party has plausible objections on both grounds. Recall Steffan v. Cheney, in which the Navy sought to depose Steffan about his sexual behavior. Steffan objected on grounds both of relevance and privilege.

a. As a review, explain why relevance was a plausible objection given the law governing the case.

b. Because the court found the question irrelevant, it did not have to decide on the claim of privilege. Assume that the court reached a different decision on relevance. At the time of the case the Supreme Court had not yet ruled that adult, consensual sexual behavior was constitutionally protected. Under these circumstances, construct Steffan's argument that he had a basis in privilege for refusing to answer the government's question about his sexual conduct.

4. One evidentiary privilege arises frequently in a discovery context and deserves special note. The attorney-client privilege protects communications between lawyers and clients concerning the matters the lawyer is handling for the client. Such a privilege does not, of course, prevent discovery of underlying facts ("How fast were you driving, Ms. Defendant?"), but it does prevent inquiries about communications to one's lawyer ("What did you tell your lawyer about how fast you were driving?"). The scope of the attorney-client privilege in corporate contexts forms the center of a case with significant discovery implications. In Upjohn Co. v. United States, 449 U.S. 383, 391-393 (1981), the Court held that the corporation's attorney-client privilege extended beyond the "control group" (top management):

> Middle-level — and indeed lower-level — employees can, by actions within the scope of their employment, embroil the corporation in serious legal difficulties, and it is only natural that these employees would have the relevant information needed by

corporate counsel if he is adequately to advise the client with respect to such actual or potential difficulties. . . .

The control group test adopted by the court below thus frustrates the very purpose of the privilege by discouraging the communication of relevant information by employees of the client to attorneys seeking to render legal advice to the client corporation. The attorney's advice will also frequently be more significant to noncontrol group members than to those who officially sanction the advice, and the control group test makes it more difficult to convey full and frank legal advice to the employees who will put into effect the client corporation's policy. . . .

a. Notice an implication of the *Upjohn* holding: Suppose an individual and a firm in litigation with each other on a matter in which the proper accounting treatment of a particular transaction is in dispute. The corporation's lawyer interviews the accountant, who is an employee of the firm. The individual's lawyer interviews the individual's accountant, a professional who, like the lawyer, works for many clients. Now suppose that each lawyer seeks to discover the contents of the opposing lawyer's interview with the accountant. Will the corporation's lawyer's conversation be privileged? Will that of the individual's lawyer? (As you will see later in this chapter, there may be other barriers to discovery in the latter situation, but not the attorney-client privilege.)

b. Recognize the limitations of the *Upjohn* holding as well: Suppose that, before any litigation is in sight, both the corporation and the individual consulted their respective accountants about how to treat the transaction. When litigation is underway, both sides are deposed. In the deposition the opposing lawyer states, "Describe your conversation with the accountant concerning this transaction." Explain why neither side can claim a privilege in this situation.

C.   Surveying Discovery: Procedures and Methods

Lawyers need to understand the interplay of relevance, privilege, and judicial discretion in discovery. They also need to understand the more specific workings of the discovery rules. The easiest way to grasp these rules is first to read Federal Rules 26-37; then, refer again to specific rules as this survey touches them. As you read, consider why the discovery rules contain more detail than, say, the pleading rules.

Rule 26 is the master rule: It provides a catalogue of disclosure and discovery methods (in 26(a) and (b)) and defines the ground rules. These ground rules establish three stages: a requirement of mandatory disclosure (in 26(a)), a provision for further discovery without any special showing (but limited by relevance to "claims and defenses"), and a provision for broader discovery (into "the subject matter involved in the action") if a party demonstrates "good cause" to the court.

1.   Required Disclosures

Rule 26(a)(1) describes the first stage, which it calls "required disclosures." For types of cases in which disclosure is required, the parties must meet early in the suit; within 14 days after that meeting, each party must offer the other side the names of witnesses and descriptions of documents "that the disclosing party may use to support its claims or defenses," as well as calculations of damages, and copies of insurance agreements. The parties must exchange such information without its having been requested by their opponent. Once these initial disclosures have occurred, the parties may then request additional information using interrogatories, depositions, requests for inspection of documents and physical objects, requests for physical and mental examinations, and for admissions. All this requires cooperation by the lawyers, a timetable, and mechanisms for enforcing discovery and disclosure obligations.

NOTES AND PROBLEMS

1. Your client, Baker, gives you a state court complaint from a state employing the current version of the discovery rules. The plaintiff, Alice, alleges that Baker agreed to sell her his car, and then refused to go through with the transaction; Alice seeks damages. Baker tells you that he and Alice discussed such a possibility, but that they never agreed. In response to your questions, Baker tells you no one witnessed their discussion. You file an answer denying that there was a contract. You know that Rule 26(a)(1) requires some disclosures.

a. On this state of the pleadings, what information would you have to prepare for disclosure?

b. On this state of the pleadings, what would be the only information you would be confident Alice would have to disclose to you?

c. What does "unless solely for impeachment," a phrase used in Rules 26(a)(1)(A) and (B), mean? Suppose that Baker's lawyer has learned that Alice has a reputation for lying, and that a prior lawsuit of a similar sort was dismissed when the judge found that she was not a credible witness. If we imagine that Baker will use this information solely to attack Alice's credibility if she testifies, then Baker need not disclose it as part of the initial disclosures. What if the central element of Baker's defense is that Alice is lying when she says she and Baker agreed to the sale? Is her credibility now "solely for impeachment"?

2. Assuming a party must make some disclosure, when must that disclosure occur? Answering this question requires a close reading of Rules 4, 16(b), 26(a)(1), and 26(f). Together these provisions establish a time line that starts when the defendant has been served or has "appeared" in the lawsuit. Service occurs when the defendant has been served or when the defendant, pursuant to Rule 4(d), has waived formal service. Appearance refers to the defendant's filing some paper or motion that evinces its participation in the lawsuit; it would include an answer as well as various Rule 12(b) motions.

At this point a series of time sequences that govern pretrial procedure begins to run. One appears in Rule 16(b), which requires that within 90 days after a defendant's appearance or 120 days after service, the judge shall hold a "scheduling conference," to discuss the way discovery and other pretrial matters should proceed. Rule 26(f) requires the parties meet themselves, without the judge, to discuss the case "as soon as practicable and in any event at least 21 days before a scheduling conference is held." Finally, to complete the link to disclosure, Rule 26(a)(1) requires the parties, at this meeting or within 14 days after it, to exchange disclosure lists.

The result of these interlocking provisions is to require the parties to exchange the required disclosures at least seven days before the scheduling conference and, at the latest, four months after the complaint is served on defendant. More commonly, where defendant has appeared, the disclosure will occur no later than 85 days after that appearance.

3. Disclosure will not occur in all cases. The 2000 revisions made disclosure mandatory in all federal court cases but at the same time suggested that very small and very large cases will be exempted from disclosure. Rule 26(b)(1)(E) lists a number of exempt categories — smaller claims and those in which either a well-developed record or the absence of counsel make disclosure unnecessary or potentially unfair. The advisory committee notes suggest that very large cases, in which one imagines that close judicial supervision will displace the Rules, may also be exempted.

4. Rule 26(d) says that the parties may not use other forms of discovery — depositions, interrogatories, etc. — until after the meeting required by Rule 26(f). The exchange of disclosures must closely follow the Rule 26(f) meeting. The other forms of discovery will thus come into play only after the initial disclosures.

5. Suppose a party has fully complied with its disclosure requirements, but then learns of an additional witness or document. Read Rule 26(e) and Rule 37(c)(1).

a. Albert, suing Barbara for negligently inflicted injuries in an auto accident, supplies her with all of his medical bills pursuant to Rule 26(a)(1)(B). Thereafter, he receives a substantial new bill from the treating surgeon. What must Albert do?

b. Albert does not inform Barbara of the new surgeon's bill, but its existence comes to light in a deposition of the surgeon. Thereafter, Barbara seeks to block admission of the bill as part of the evidence on damages. How should the judge rule?

Rule 26 defines the broad guidelines for discovery. Rules 27-36 spell out the ways to obtain information and the protocol for using each of the discovery devices. Finally, Rules 26(g) and 37 provide for enforcement of the discovery rules.

There are generally three ways of obtaining information: by asking questions; by examining documents, physical objects, and persons; and by asking one's opponent to admit contentions. Each method has its advantages and problems.

2. Asking Questions: Interrogatories and Depositions (Rules 28, 30, 31, 32, 33, and 37)

One may send one's opponent a list of questions to answer (interrogatories) or one may take a witness's deposition ("depose" him or her). What is the difference between the two? The answer usually involves balancing utility and cost; in discovery one often gets what one pays for.

Interrogatories (Rule 33) are typically much cheaper for the interrogator (the "propounder" of the interrogatories) because one can inexpensively frame a set of appropriate questions, send it to an adverse party, and sit back and wait for the answers; the recipient (and his lawyer) must either answer the questions or object to them. A drawback to interrogatories is that, because the questioner cannot follow up evasive answers with a question designed to pin things down, interrogatories that go beyond fairly routine specific information — such as the names and addresses of witnesses — may yield little valuable information. And because much routine information will ordinarily emerge as part of the disclosure required by Rule 26(a)(1), there may be only a few situations in which interrogatories serve a useful role. Moreover, parties must seek permission of the court — or a stipulation from their opponents — before propounding more than 25 questions. Note also that interrogatories may be sent only to a party; nonparty witnesses may be deposed but need not answer written interrogatories.

Depositions (Rules 28, 30, 31, 32) present the opposite balance of cost and usefulness. A deposition is like questioning a witness at trial without the judge: Depositions usually occur in lawyers' offices, and the lawyers are present, as are the witness and a court reporter or recording device. The lawyers ask questions that the witness must answer under oath. The advantage is that the lawyer can ask a series of questions that force the witness to take a position as to the matters at issue, and the lawyer can follow up with further questions if the witness is evasive, or if the witness's testimony opens up new avenues of inquiry. The disadvantage is expense to all concerned. In a full-blown deposition both sides have their lawyers there; if the witness is not one of the parties he or she may also be represented by a lawyer. In addition, the deposing party must arrange for some form of recording or transcription of the deposition. In a case with multiple parties, each hour of deposition time may amount to thousands of dollars in legal fees and costs. As with interrogatories, the Rules place limits on depositions. Without seeking permission, the total number of depositions taken by one side (plaintiff(s), defendant(s), third-party defendant(s)) may not exceed 10, no deposition may exceed a day of seven hours, and no person may be deposed a second time without the permission of the court or the other side.

Halfway between interrogatories and a deposition is a deposition on written questions (Rule 31); in this rarely-used procedure the lawyer writes down the questions and sends them to the court reporter presiding at the deposition who asks the questions and records the witness's answers. This is a good deal cheaper than a deposition on oral examination but usually yields less information than a "live" deposition. To understand the reason for this low yield, think how difficult it would be to compose such a set of questions: The first one or two inquiries are straightforward, but how does one frame follow-up questions without knowing what the witness will say to the initial inquiry? A related question is what happens if there is a disagreement about whether a question in a deposition or an interrogatory is justified? The procedure differs according to the device being used.

Read Rules 30(d) and 33(b), together with Rule 37(a)(2) and (4), and apply them to the questions below.

NOTES AND PROBLEMS

1. Having sustained injuries from a household appliance, Cora sues Manufacturer. The required discovery conference and the ensuing disclosures occur. Cora then serves 55 interrogatories on Manufacturer and 20 interrogatories on Department Store, which sold her the product. Both Store and Manufacturer refuse to answer.

a. Explain why Store needn't answer even if the questions are relevant and not privileged. By what step might Cora induce Store to answer?

b. Can Cora get a court to compel Manufacturer's answers?

2. Pursuant to Rule 30(b)(6), Cora serves on Manufacturer a request to depose an employee or officer responsible for the "design and safety engineering" of the appliance in question. Manufacturer designates Geraldine Chen, a vice president for product design. At the deposition, Cora's lawyer asks Chen a series of questions about her qualifications and responsibilities. She then asks Chen a question about the financial structure of the company. Manufacturer's lawyer believes that question is outside the subject matter specified in the Rule 30(b)(6) notice (and Chen is therefore less well prepared to answer).

a. May Manufacturer's lawyer instruct Chen not to answer the line of questions to which he objects? See Rule 30(d)(1).

b. What should Manufacturer's lawyer do? See Rule 30(d)(3).

c. In part because Manufacturer's lawyer has lodged numerous objections to the questions asked by Cora's lawyer, the deposition, which started at 9 A.M., ends at 5 (having been interrupted only for a lunch hour) without Cora's lawyer having reached her most important questions. When Cora's lawyer asks that the deposition be continued, Manufacturer's lawyer refuses, citing Rule 30(d)(2). What can Cora's lawyer do? What is Cora's lawyer's strongest argument for a continuation of the deposition?

3. In the same deposition, Cora's lawyer asks Chen a series of questions that Manufacturer's lawyer believes constitute violations of the attorney-client privilege ("Have you consulted with counsel about potential liability for a product with this design characteristic?"). Many lawyers would respond to such a question by instructing their client not to answer the question, a course of action explicitly permitted by Rule 30(d)(1). Having elicited this response to a series of similar questions, Cora's lawyer moves to another subject and thereafter ends the deposition. If Cora's lawyer believes that some of the unanswered questions were not subject to any privilege, how should she proceed to require answers?

4. One should not overlook the deposition as a source of unintentional humor. Consider the following excerpts, collected by Mary Louise Gilman, the editor of National Shorthand Reporter and published in Richard Lederer, Anguished English (1987):

Q.   Doctor, did you say he was shot in the woods?
A.   No, I said he was shot in the lumbar region.

Q.   What is your name?
A.   Ernestine McDowell.

Q.   And what is your marital status?
A.   Fair.

Q.   Mrs. Smith, do you believe that you are emotionally unstable?
A.   I should be.
Q.   How many times have you committed suicide?
A.   Four times.

Q.   When he went, had you gone and had she, if she wanted to and were able, for the time being excluding all the restraints on her not to go, gone also, would he have brought you, meaning you and she, with him to the station?

Mr. Brooks: Objection. That question should be taken out and shot.

Finally, consider what Professor Richard Friedman reports as "an actual trial transcript," whose accuracy he has confirmed with one of the lawyers:

The Court: Next witness.
Ms. Olschner: Your Honor, at this time I would like to swat Mr. Buck in the head with his client's deposition.
The Court: You mean read it?
Ms. Olschner: No, sir. I mean to swat him [in] the head with it. Pursuant to Rule 32, I may use the deposition "for any purpose" and that is the purpose for which I want to use it.
The Court: Well, it does say that.
(Pause.)
The Court: There being no objection, you may proceed.
Ms. Olschner: Thank you, Judge Hanes.
(Whereupon Ms. Olschner swatted Mr. Buck in the head with a deposition.)
Mr. Buck: But Judge. . . .
The Court: Next witness.
Mr. Buck: We object.
The Court: Sustained. Next witness.

3.   Examining Things and People: Production and Inspection of Documents and Things; Physical and Mental Examinations (Rules 34 and 35)

Sometimes a lawsuit turns on the condition of a physical object (the wrecked automobile, the allegedly defective computer chip); sometimes the condition of land is at issue (How deep is the hole into which plaintiff fell? Is it concealed by grass?). Rule 34 permits inspection of land and objects. In addition, documents often provide important evidence, and discovery in most lawsuits will include requests for documents in the possession of the opposing party, or third parties. It is important to keep in mind that the term "documents" is a bit of a misnomer, as it includes not only what we traditionally think of as documents (sheets of paper such as letters, notes, drafts, and manuals), but any medium for recording data or information. An email message stored on a computer's hard drive, or on a backup tape made for crash-recovery purposes is a "document," as is a photograph or videotape.

Documents frequently relate to issues of damages. Medical records, for example, are typically the backbone of damage discovery in personal injury cases, whereas accounting records would be the core of discovery in a case involving a claim of lost profits. Documents may also be critical to liability issues. In a contract dispute over the interpretation of an ambiguous provision of a contract, for example, each side will want to see any drafts, memos, or notes that might reflect the other side's interpretation of the disputed provision, and will want to use such documents in the depositions it might take of the opposing side's witnesses.

Note the procedure for requesting documents differs slightly according to whether one is requesting them from a party or a nonparty. For a party, one simply sends a Rule 34 request, specifying the documents sought. For a nonparty, one makes a similar request but embodies it in a subpoena issued under Rule 45(a)(1)(C). As with both depositions and interrogatories, requests for documents from parties may not be made before the disclosures required by Rule 26(a). It is also important to bear in mind that, unlike interrogatories and depositions, the number of document requests is not limited by the Rules. Because of the central role that documents play, parties will typically want to make comprehensive document requests and want to review the documents produced in response to the request before proceeding with depositions. For such an instance and one court's response to it, see Poole v. Textron, Inc. at the end of this chapter (infra page 457).

The difficulties surrounding requests for documents can resemble those that might be encountered in a large library staffed by hostile librarians who respond to research queries only if asked precisely the right question. Some document production disputes are akin to those in interrogatory practice: How exactly must the requester identify the record in question? In practice, very broad requests are usually allowed, because the party propounding the request does not know what records the responding party has. A typical request might seek all documents in the custody or control of the responding party that "refer, relate or pertain in any manner" to subject X. Such broad requests might end up calling for hundreds, thousands, or even millions of documents, only a small portion of which bear even the remotest potential relevance to the lawsuit. The responding party might then object to the request on the grounds that it is overbroad, or begin a negotiation process whereby it seeks to have the propounding party redefine or narrow the request. The propounding party, however, is suspicious that the responding party is seeking to have the request redrawn in a manner that will insulate the production of relevant and damaging evidence. To the extent that such documents fall within the disclosures required by Rule 26(a), these problems may subside slightly.

Other difficulties with Rule 34 requests arise from issues of who will bear the cost of production: May the party on whom the discovery request is served simply point to a warehouse full of files (or to a computer data bank)? Note that the last sentence of Rule 34(b) requires that the producing party produce the documents "as they are kept in the usual course of business or shall organize and label them to correspond with the categories in the request."

One of the more delicate Rule provisions concerns the physical and mental examinations of parties. Unlike other discovery provisions, Rule 35 requires a special application to the court and a showing of "good cause." The disputes here focus on what constitutes "good cause."

PROBLEMS

1. Alice brings suit against Centerville Village, claiming that its police officers assaulted her during an afternoon political demonstration. Her complaint alleges that the assault "severely injured her." The city attorney assigned to the case uncovers a photograph of Alice, taken the night after the incident, showing her participating enthusiastically in a local dance contest. At the Rule 26(f) conference with Alice's lawyer, Centerville's lawyer learns that she will contend that the police assault injured her leg.

a. Centerville's lawyer would very much like to hold back the photograph — perhaps until a devastating cross-examination of Alice. Must the defendant produce the photograph as part of the disclosures required within ten days of the lawyers' conference? Read Rule 26(a)(1)(B) and think about what Centerville's possible defense strategies might be and what role the photo would play in each of them.

b. What risk does defendant run if it does not disclose the photograph? Read Rule 37(c)(1).

c. Assume that the defendant does not disclose the existence of the photograph in the initial round of disclosures. Thereafter Alice makes a Rule 34 demand that Centerville produce "all documents, memoranda, and reports relating to the incident." As attorney for Centerville, must you now produce the photograph?

d. Suppose Centerville produces the photograph in response to the Rule 34 demand. Can Alice seek sanctions? Of what sort? Read Rule 37(c)(1). Can Centerville argue that any failure to disclose initially is harmless because the evidence eventually came to light?

2. Randolph files suit for damages after being injured in an accident with a truck owned and operated by Craven. Randolph has reason to think that Craven's truck was serviced at Elaine's Garage and wants to see the service record. Randolph doubts Elaine will produce it voluntarily. What steps can Randolph take to obtain the documents?

3. Pat is injured in an automobile crash with Dunham; Pat sues. Dunham seeks to have Pat examined by a physician.

a. Should the court grant permission?

b. If the examination takes place, is Pat entitled to see a copy of the physician's report to Dunham?

c. Pat requests a copy of the physician's report and receives it. Dunham then requests from Pat copies of *her* physician's reports on her injury. Is Dunham entitled to these?

4. Rather than move for a physical examination, Dunham's lawyer in the Rule 26(f) conference suggests that Pat submit voluntarily to a physical examination. If Pat's attorney agrees, can he obtain a copy of the report? Can he take the examining doctor's deposition?

5. A key witness in Pat's suit against Dunham is Jones, who allegedly saw "everything that happened" from a position more than 100 feet away. Can Dunham require Jones to take an eye examination? What happens if Jones is an employee of Dunham?

4.   Asking Your Opponent to Admit Things: Requests for Admission (Rule 36)

One can consider Rule 36 as much a pleading rule as a discovery device: It does not uncover evidence so much as it makes evidence irrelevant by taking an issue out of controversy. Notice that, because of Rule 37(c), Rule 36 has teeth. Rule 36 has functioned best when used to eliminate essentially undisputed issues—for example, that the defendant is incorporated in Washington or that at the time in question the automobile was registered to Martha. In a regime that required detailed pleading, these issues might be disposed of at the pleading stage. The adoption of notice pleading makes a device like Rule 36 useful.

The disputes over Rule 36 have arisen when, either by design or inadvertence, one party has asked the other to admit a fact that seemed to be at the core of the case. One type of such a question might be normative: "Were you driving negligently?" "Did defendant breach the contract?" Another type might be historical: "Were you driving 50 M.P.H. at the time of the accident?" "Did defendant on February 22 deliver the 500 rolls of paper?" In either case the question may lie at the center of the case. How should a party respond to such a question?

Matters become worse when the party served with such a request has simply let the time for reply elapse without responding. Read literally, the Rule suggests that the requested facts should be deemed admitted, and occasionally courts have so held. For example, see Morast v. Auble, 164 Mont. 100, 519 P.2d 157 (1974). Other courts have ignored the literal language or have glossed it with an interpretation suggesting that admissions were meant to deal with peripheral rather than central issues in the case. See Pickens v. Equitable Life Assurance Society, 413 F.2d 1390 (5th Cir. 1969). The Rule states that such an interpretation is erroneous and that a party who wishes in good faith to contest an issue may, if the facts permit, deny it and thereby put the other side to its proof.

PROBLEMS

1. Could plaintiff ask defendant to admit that there was a contract and defendant had breached it, and then, if defendant refused to admit that and plaintiff won the ensuing trial, ask for attorneys' fees for all the legal work done after the refusal to admit? Cf. Marchand v. Mercy Medical Center, 22 F.3d 933 (9th Cir. 1994) (imposing $205,000 attorneys' fees and costs on physician who failed to admit that he was negligent in treating plaintiff).

2. Greg is injured on a scout outing when he stumbles on a tent wire after returning from a late night raid on the campsite of another troop. He brings suit

against the Boy Scouts of America, Inc. A young boy tells defense counsel he saw four other boys trip over the same wire. Plaintiff serves a notice to admit that, prior to this incident, four boys had stumbled on the same wire. Must defendant admit this "fact"?

3. Assume that defendant makes the admission, and one of the other trippers sues. Is the admission binding on defendant?

4. What is the difference between the effect of an interrogatory asking defendant some question and a request for an admission as to the same thing? The answer will emerge if one remembers that an admission is very much like a pleading, while an interrogatory is merely a bit of evidence. An admission takes a matter entirely out of controversy, while an interrogatory answer is a piece of evidence that may be contradicted by other pieces of evidence.

5.   Ensuring Compliance

All the discovery methods discussed above need enforcement mechanisms. The rules contain two — a general provision in Rule 26(g) and more specific provisions in Rule 37. Parties engaged in discovery often want information, and Rule 37 sets forth a series of devices designed either to elicit the information or to respond to parties' refusal to supply it. Under Rule 37, a court may impose punishments ranging from awards of expenses to dismissals of an entire case or the entry of a default judgment. Under Rule 37(d) and (g), some sanctions are available on the occurrence of misbehavior. Under Rule 37(b), however, other sanctions cannot be sought until after the court orders a party to comply. (Put another way, Rule 37(b) sanctions come into play not when a party initially fails to comply with some discovery rule but when the party refuses to comply with a specific court order.) If this feature is a weakness, it is partially remedied by Rule 26(g), which (like Rule 11) requires parties to sign disclosures, discovery requests, and objections and punishes the parties for unjustified requests and refusals even when the parties' behavior does not violate a court order. Unlike Rule 11, Rule 26(g) suggests that attorneys' fees will be an appropriate sanction for most violations of its obligations. Reread Rules 26(g) and 37 and consider their operation in the following problems.

PROBLEMS

1. Producer Corp. sues Supplier, Inc., alleging failure to fulfill the conditions of a contract; Supplier denies the allegations of the complaint and counterclaims for Producer's alleged failure to pay for goods delivered. As soon as pleadings have closed, and before the disclosures have occurred, Producer *notices* (that is, notifies of the intention to take) the depositions of several of Supplier's officers and employees.

   a. Explain why Supplier can object to this course of action. See Rule 26(g)(3).

   b. After the initial round of disclosures, Producer again seeks to depose the officers and employees. Supplier objects to this course of action, believing that without more groundwork these depositions will prove a waste of time and expense — and will have to be repeated later in the action once Producer has developed more information. Can Supplier refuse to attend the depositions and avoid sanctions on the grounds that Producer should first have built a stronger foundation for an efficient use of deposition time? If not, what can Supplier do? See Rule 26(b)(2) and Rule 26(c).

2. In the lawsuit described in Problem 1, Producer's disclosures fail to list a former officer who was present at the negotiations of the agreement and who could testify as to the parties' intent. At trial Producer seeks to have this person testify. What objection can Supplier make? See Rule 37(c)(1).

3. Suppose the same situation as in the preceding problem. After initial disclosures Supplier sends Producer an interrogatory asking for the name of any witness with information about the contract negotiation. Producer fails to supply witness's name; Supplier nonetheless learns of the witness at a subsequent deposition. What sanction can the court can impose on Producer for its failure to disclose the identity of this witness in the original interrogatory?

4. As the lawsuit described in Problem 1 proceeds, Supplier serves Producer with a request to produce documents relevant to the suit.

a. First suppose that Producer simply fails to respond to the requests for documents. What steps must Supplier follow to force Producer either to comply or suffer sanctions? Read carefully Rule 37 (a)(1)-(2). See Shuffle Master Inc. v. Progressive Games, Inc., 170 F.R.D. 166 (D. Nev. 1996) (refusing to order sanctions in the absence of a certificate demonstrating good faith effort to confer with adversary).

b. Now suppose two of the documents sought are letters from Producer's lawyer to Producer, answering questions about the interpretation of the contract in question; Producer believes that both documents are protected by the attorney-client privilege. How should Producer raise such a contention? See Rules 26(c) and 37(a). What tactical advantages might accrue from using Rule 26(c) rather than 37(a) as the setting in which to raise the privilege?

c. Producer's response to Supplier's request states simply, "The requested documents have not been produced because they are protected by the attorney-client privilege." What should Supplier do? See Rules 26(b)(5), 37(a)(2)(B).

Despite the provision for judicial supervision and sanctions in Rules 26(g) and 37, what is most remarkable about discovery is the extent to which the parties run the system without court supervision. Rule 26(f) requires parties to confer about the case and about discovery plans as a prelude to a subsequent scheduling conference with the judge. Rules 26(a) and 29 give the parties the power to write their own discovery rules.

Finally, it is well worth remembering that the formal devices for discovery do not exhaust the possibilities for factual investigation. Independent factual investigation is entirely possible and in many cases is far more important than formal discovery. Legwork, telephone calls, informal interviews, examination of public records, and the like will often yield enormous amounts of information. It is important for the beginning lawyer not to become so mesmerized by the tool kit of formal discovery as to forget the existence of other means of gathering information.

D.   Discovery and Privacy

Discovery aims at uncovering truth and permitting lawsuits to be decided on their merits. But truth sometimes hurts, and one can ask as to any given disclosure whether the gain in relevant information offsets the embarrassment, pain, and possible consequences of revealing tangentially relevant information.

The system seeks to shield parties from such excessive discovery. The question of what discovery is excessive is of course difficult. The general proposition underlying the discovery rules is that people can be required to reveal relevant information, even when the information is embarrassing or "confidential," in the ordinary sense of that word. But the Rules also recognize that sometimes a zealous or ill-meaning adversary will use discovery not to uncover relevant information but to harass. Beyond the general provisions in Rule 26(g) forbidding abusive discovery, the Rules use two devices to control such behavior. Rule 26(c) permits a party to seek a protective order and gives the judge broad power to prevent abusive discovery. Rule 35 places special limits on the use of discovery to compel physical or mental examinations. This section explores both provisions.

1.   The General Problem of Privacy

Rule 26(c) gives a judge power to enter "any order which justice requires to protect a party or person from annoyance, embarrassment, oppression, or undue burden or expense." Those terms are broad and undefined. The next case wrestles with what they might mean in the context of a specific case raising sensitive personal issues.

Stalnaker v. Kmart Corp.

71 Fair Empl. Prac. Cas. (BNA) 705 (D. Kan. 1996)

RUSHFELT, Magistrate Judge.

Under consideration is Defendant's First Motion For Protective Order. Pursuant to Fed. R. Civ. P. 26(c), defendant thereby seeks an order protecting non-party witnesses Lea Rozenberg, Rhonda Hyde, Gloria Olivares, and Lonny Casaert from discovery concerning voluntary romantic conduct or their sexual-related [sic] activities. Plaintiff has noticed depositions for these witnesses. She opposes the motion.

Plaintiff claims sexual harassment. She alleges that Donald Graves, an employee in the Receiving Department of defendant, created a hostile working environment and sexually harassed her by inappropriate touching. She has made no allegations against any of the proposed deponents.

Defendant asserts that plaintiff has not alleged that any of the witnesses had romantic or sexual involvement with her, created or contributed to the alleged hostile work environment, or otherwise wronged her. It further states that none of them have complained to it of sexual harassment. It contends that any voluntary romantic or sexual activities of the witnesses are irrelevant. It suggests, furthermore, that inquiry into such activities will invade their privacy rights. It argues that the embarrassment, humiliation, and invasion of privacy which would result from such inquiry substantially outweighs the probative value, if any, of such activities. . . .

Plaintiff asserts that investigation has revealed potential harassment by Mr. Graves towards Ms. Rozenberg. Plaintiff suggests that the other witnesses may possess relevant information about sexual harassment at Kmart. She would agree to a protective order preventing dissemination of discovery to third parties. She suggests that such an order would alleviate the concern for privacy. . . .

Fed. R. Civ. P. 26(b) permits a broad scope of discovery. The information sought need not be admissible at trial if it appears reasonably calculated to lead to the discovery of admissible evidence. Despite the broad scope of permissible discovery, the court may enter protective orders totally prohibiting certain discovery or limiting the scope of discovery to certain matters. Fed. R. Civ. P. 26(c)(1) and (4).

Whether to enter a protective order is within the sound discretion of the court. Fed. R. Civ. P. 26(c) provides that the court, upon a showing of good cause, "may make any order which justice requires to protect a party or person from annoyance, embarrassment, oppression, or undue burden or expense." "[A] party is entitled to request a protective order to preclude any inquiry into areas that are clearly outside the scope of appropriate discovery." Caldwell v. Life Ins. Co. of N. Am., 165 F.R.D. 633, 637 (D. Kan. 1996). The party seeking a protective order, however, has the burden to show good cause for it. To establish good cause, that party must submit "a particular and specific demonstration of fact, as distinguished from stereotyped and conclusory statements." Gulf Oil Co. v. Bernard, 452 U.S. 89, 102 n.16 (1981).

Even when a motion arises in the context of discovery under Rule 26 of the Federal Rules of Civil Procedure, the Court must remain mindful of Rule 412 and its implications. Fed. R. Evid. 412(a) provides that "[e]vidence offered to prove that any alleged victim engaged in other sexual behavior" or "to prove any alleged victim's sexual predisposition" is not admissible in any civil or criminal proceeding involving alleged sexual misconduct except as provided in subdivisions (b) and (c). . . .

. . . [R]ule [412] aims to safeguard the alleged victim against the invasion of privacy, potential embarrassment and sexual stereotyping that is associated with public disclosure of intimate sexual details and the infusion of sexual innuendo into the factfinding process. By affording victims protection in most instances, the rule also encourages victims of sexual misconduct to institute and to participate in legal proceedings against alleged offenders. . . .

Although Fed. R. Evid. 412 applies generally to sexual harassment cases, the court does not find it controlling the present motion for protective order. The rule does not apply . . . "unless the person against whom the evidence is offered can reasonably be characterized as a 'victim of alleged sexual misconduct.'"

Fed. R. Evid. 412 aside, defendant has demonstrated good cause to bar discovery of voluntary romantic and sexual activities of the four non-party witnesses to the extent they have no relationship to the allegations against Kmart. Those activities appear generally irrelevant to any issue in this action. Any sexual harassment by Graves is relevant, however, whether of plaintiff or of others. Consequently, the court will not preclude inquiry about any voluntary romantic or sexual activities with Mr. Graves to the extent they show any conduct on his part to encourage, solicit, or influence any employee of defendant to engage or continue in such activities. Such discovery is potentially embarrassing and annoying, both to the deponents and to defendant. The parties shall use such discovery, therefore, only for purposes of this litigation and shall not disclose it to anyone outside this litigation.

For the foregoing reasons the court sustains in part and overrules in part Defendant's First Motion For Protective Order. Plaintiff may not pursue discovery from Lea Rozenberg, Rhonda Hyde, Gloria Olivares, or Lonny Casaert about any voluntary romantic or sexual activities, except to the limited extent indicated in this order. The parties, furthermore, shall use discovery from such witnesses only for purposes of this litigation and shall not otherwise disclose it.

IT IS SO ORDERED.

NOTES AND PROBLEMS

1. Be clear about the procedural setting and the nature of the argument.

a. What information was the plaintiff seeking?

b. Why did plaintiff think that information was relevant?

c. Was the defendant claiming that the information was privileged?

2. What did the protective order forbid?

a. Imagine that you are at the deposition of Ms. Rozenberg. What type of questions about her relationship, if any, with Mr. Graves would be allowed under the order? What type of questions would not be allowed?

b. Would it be proper for plaintiff's counsel to begin the deposition by asking "Did you ever have a romantic or sexual relationship with Mr. Graves?"

c. What about asking "Did you ever have a romantic or sexual relationship with Mr. Graves that he in any way encouraged or solicited?" Is there any difference between these two questions?

3. The court took note that the proposed deponents had not themselves sought a protective order. Is it fair to infer that they didn't care about providing the type of information the plaintiff was seeking?

4. Consider the tactics of discovery employed in *Stalnaker*.

a. Plaintiff had a plausible argument for the relevance of the information sought. But think about what other purposes, beyond that of winning on the merits, plaintiff might have hoped to gain from seeking this information.

b. Suppose Rozenberg, the proposed deponent, after being informed of the court's order, retains you as her attorney, telling you she doesn't want to answer questions about her romantic or sexual activities with Mr. Graves. What would you advise her to do? See Rule 26(c).

c. What would happen if she refused to show up for her deposition, or refused to answer questions about her relationship with Mr. Graves? See Rules 37(a), (d).

5. Suppose the plaintiff's or defendant's lawyer disagrees with the magistrate judge's ruling in *Stalnaker*. Can he appeal? The answer to that question requires one to understand the judicial office of the person who makes discovery rulings.

a. If the ruling were made by a district judge, the answer to the question would be easy: No. A nonfinal order cannot be appealed. 28 U.S.C. §1291.

b. The *Stalnaker* ruling, however, was made by a magistrate judge, whose jurisdiction is defined by 28 U.S.C. §§636 et seq. One of the provisions of that jurisdiction is that a magistrate judge may hear nondispositive motions. 28 U.S.C. §636(b)(1)(A). (A dispositive motion is a motion that has the potential to end the case. Discovery orders serve as a prime example of nondispositive motions. Consequently many magistrates hear most or all discovery matters in many cases.)

c. The section defining the magistrate's jurisdiction also provides for limited review of the magistrate's orders by *the district court judge*: "A judge of the [district] court may reconsider any pretrial matter under this subparagraph [providing for magistrate judges' jurisdiction over nondispositive motions] where it has been shown that the magistrate's order is clearly erroneous or contrary to law."

6. Because Rule 26(c) and similar provisions in state procedural rules are cast in terms of the courts' discretion, one cannot set forth clear rules for the granting or denying of protective orders. Consider how you, as the district court or magistrate judge, would respond to a request for a protective order in the following hypothetical case:

Nancy Clark has an abortion at Thomas Jefferson Hospital (TJH) and afterward suffers various complications that lead to a hysterectomy. Clark brings suit against TJH and the operating doctor, claiming that the hysterectomy was made necessary by the negligent treatment that she received after the abortion. The complaint seeks damages for being rendered sterile and for severe mental depression. Defendant seeks information on the name of the putative father, Clark's social relationships, and other facts relating to her emotional state. Does she have to answer the questions? If the doctor and hospital are asked to identify prior patients who have undergone abortions, must they do so? What if such information is revealed and either Clark or the hospital wants to depose one of the former patients to learn of any side effects?

7. The preceding problem illustrates an easily misunderstood point: how the discovery system treats information that is relevant and unprivileged (and not covered by a protective order) but which is confidential. Does Rule 26 exclude confidential information from discovery? Consider some situations in which such an issue might arise.

a. Plaintiffs sue Blood Bank, alleging negligent testing resulted in the transfusion of HIV-contaminated blood. Plaintiff seeks disclosure of the identity of the donor so that plaintiffs can discover from him facts bearing on their contention that Blood Bank failed to screen donors properly. Blood Bank argues that donors will not give blood if they believe their personal lives will thereby become the subject of lawsuits. How should the court rule? See Long v. American Red Cross, 145 F.R.D. 658 (S.D. Ohio 1993) (ruling that discovery — with unspecified protective order — permissible in part because deceased donor had diminished privacy interest).

b. A dismissed professor sues University alleging wrongful refusal to grant tenure. The plaintiff professor seeks to discover confidential tenure review files of others granted tenure at the same time, alleging that comparison will show that he was better qualified than they. The other professors intervene to seek a protective order. See Blum v. Schlegel, 150 F.R.D. 38 (W.D.N.Y.) (granting protective order to prevent discovery of embarrassing "sensitive, scholarly critiques . . . [and] personal observations" of reviewers).

c. At State University, Abrams and Braun have an altercation that results in serious injuries to Abrams. The dean recommends that Braun be suspended for one semester; pursuant to the student code, a hearing is to be held before the student court. The dean tells all parties to testify freely and calls attention to a provision in the student code that all testimony given at the hearing will be "privileged and confidential." As attorney for Braun, should you permit him to testify?

8. Protective orders will not solve all clashes between the broad scope of discovery and clients' interests in keeping certain matters confidential. An example arose in connection with Coca-Cola Bottling Co. v. Coca-Cola Co., 107 F.R.D. 288 (D. Del. 1985), in which Coca-Cola bottlers sued the manufacturer over the division of profits from Diet Coke. The primary issue in contention was "whether the contractual term 'Coca-Cola Bottler's Syrup' includes the syrup used to make Diet Coke." Id. at 289. The bottlers contended that the question could be resolved by discovering the ingredients used in both drinks. The defendant manufacturer strongly resisted the effort, for reasons the opinion explains:

> The complete formula for Coca-Cola is one of the best kept trade secrets in the world. . . . The ingredient that gives Coca-Cola its distinctive taste is a secret combination of flavoring oils and ingredients known as "Merchandise 7X." The formula for Merchandise 7X has been tightly guarded since Coca-Cola was first invented and is known by only two persons within The Coca-Cola Company. . . . The only written record of the secret formula is kept in a security vault . . . which can only be opened upon a resolution from the Company's Board of Directors.

The court, ruling that the formula was relevant and unprotected by any privilege, ordered disclosure but also scheduled hearings on ways in which to protect the trade secret from disclosure to third parties. Defendant still refused to comply:

> By letter . . . counsel for the Company informed the Court that the Company would not disclose its formulae, "[i]n light of the overriding commercial importance of the secrecy of the formulae to the entire Coca-Cola system . . . even under the terms of a stringent protective order. . . ."

Coca-Cola Bottling Co. v. Coca-Cola Co., 110 F.R.D. 363, 366 (D. Del. 1986). The court held a hearing on sanctions and concluded that it would not impose a default judgment but would order that plaintiffs were entitled to any favorable inference from the assumption that the formulas were identical. It also ordered the defendant to pay attorneys' fees and costs on the motion to compel, though not the costs related to its original resistance to discovery.

9. A frequent reason for requesting protective orders is to prevent discovery in one case from being available in another, similar case. Suppose attorney represents plaintiff in a suit alleging a defect in a widely sold automobile. In discovery defendant produces much information about the design and testing of the vehicle.

a. Attorney A wants to use the discovery in other cases he is handling. As a practical matter, it scarcely matters what rule one frames about this situation. Even if one formally prohibits the lawyer from using the information directly, she knows exactly which questions to ask in other cases.

b. Can Attorney A disseminate the information to other lawyers? Lawyers with expertise in particular areas of litigation often give seminars for other lawyers, charging sometimes-hefty fees for their knowledge. Can Attorney A "sell" the discovery information in this way?

c. One answer to the last question is that attempts to sell information will fail if it is available free in court records where other lawyers can review it if they know of its existence. In some jurisdictions, discovery material must be filed with the court and be available for inspection unless the court issues a protective order. Rule 5(d) forbids filling discovery material unless used in a motion or at trial.

10. Finally, consider a common effort to achieve a privately negotiated protective order. Suppose the parties settle the case. One of the terms of the settlement agreement calls for the plaintiff's lawyers to return all originals and copies of discovery documents and not to disclose their contents to any other person. The agreement provides that breach of this term gives rise to liquidated damages of $25,000. Such an agreement is a contract between the parties and is enforceable like any other contract unless one of its terms violates public policy. Alternatively, the parties may seek to have such an agreement made part of a consent judgment and thus enforceable by contempt power. Should the court enter such a judgment?

a. Should the Rules or legislation prohibit such agreements?

b. Such questions have two sides. On the one hand, any term that protects defendants against future liability will encourage them to settle and will result in a higher settlement payment to plaintiffs. (Think how reluctant defendants would be to settle if the terms of each settlement and the underlying information were automatically available to the public.) On the other hand, some discovery will apply to many similar lawsuits, and it is inefficient to require each set of new parties to go through the same discovery routine. How should courts weigh such matters of public concern against the desires of the plaintiff and defendant before the court — both of whom are, for different reasons, seeking to prevent disclosure of the discovery information?

2.   A Special Instance: Physical and Mental Examinations

All uses of discovery conflict with the values of privacy, if one uses that term in a broad sense. The previous section explores how judges must balance this broad interest in privacy against the goals of discovery. Our culture places the highest value on privacy, however, when the question involves individual bodily or psychic integrity, and here the tension between the goals of disclosure and those of privacy seems greatest. Read Rule 35, which attempts to balance those interests, and consider this clash in the next case.

Schlagenhauf v. Holder

379 U.S. 104 (1964)

Mr. Justice GOLDBERG delivered the opinion of the Court. . . .

I

An action based on diversity of citizenship was brought in the District Court seeking damages arising from personal injuries suffered by passengers of a bus which collided with the rear of a tractor-trailer. The named defendants were The Greyhound Corporation, owner of the bus; petitioner, Robert L. Schlagenhauf, the bus driver; Contract Carriers, Inc., owner of the tractor; Joseph L. McCorkhill, driver of the tractor; and National Lead Company, owner of the trailer. Answers were filed by each of the defendants denying negligence. . . .

[Parties] petitioned the District Court for an order directing petitioner Schlagenhauf to submit to both mental and physical examinations by one specialist in each of the following fields:

(1)   Internal medicine;
(2)   Ophthalmology;
(3)   Neurology; and
(4)   Psychiatry. . . .

The petition alleged that the mental and physical condition of Schlagenhauf was "in controversy" as it had been raised by Contract Carriers' answer to Greyhound's cross-claim. This was supported by a brief of legal authorities and an affidavit of Contract Carriers' attorney stating that Schlagenhauf had seen red lights 10 to 15 seconds before the accident, that another witness had seen the rear lights of the trailer from a distance of three-quarters to one-half mile, and that Schlagenhauf had been involved in a prior accident. . . .

The District Court, on the basis of the petition filed by Contract Carriers, and without any hearing, ordered Schlagenhauf to submit to nine examinations—one by each of the recommended specialists — despite the fact that the petition clearly requested a total of only four examinations.[3]

Petitioner applied for a writ of mandamus [which] [t]he Court of Appeals denied. . . .

We granted certiorari to review undecided questions concerning the validity and construction of Rule 35. . . .

III

Defendant Claim — applying Rule 35 to defendant is unconst.

Rule 35 on its face applies to all "parties," which under any normal reading would include a defendant. Petitioner contends, however, that the application of the Rule to a defendant would be an unconstitutional invasion of his privacy, or, at the least, be a modification of substantive rights existing prior to the adoption of the Federal Rules of Civil Procedure and thus beyond the congressional mandate of the Rules Enabling Act. . . .

These same contentions were raised in Sibbach v. Wilson & Co., 312 U.S. 1 (1941) by a plaintiff. . . .

Denies defendant driver claim

Petitioner does not challenge the holding in *Sibbach* as applied to plaintiffs. He contends, however, that it should not be extended to defendants. We can see no basis under the *Sibbach* holding for such a distinction. Discovery "is not a one-way proposition." Hickman v. Taylor. Issues cannot be resolved by a doctrine of favoring one class of litigants over another. . . .

These statements demonstrate the invalidity of any waiver theory. The chain of events leading to an ultimate determination on the merits begins with the injury of the plaintiff, an involuntary act on his part. Seeking court redress is just one step in this chain. If the plaintiff is prevented or deterred from this redress, the loss is thereby forced on him to the same extent as if the defendant were prevented or deterred from defending against the action. . . .

Holding! Petitioner Claim I

We hold that Rule 35, as applied to either plaintiffs or defendants to an action, is free of constitutional difficulty and is within the scope of the Enabling Act. . . .

Petitioner next contends that his mental or physical condition was not "in controversy" and "good cause" was not shown for the examinations, both as required by the express terms of Rule 35. . . .

[T]he "in controversy" and "good cause" requirements of Rule 35 . . . are not met by mere conclusory allegations of the pleadings — nor by mere relevance to the case — but require an affirmative showing by the movant that each condition as to which the examination is sought is really and genuinely in controversy and that good cause exists for ordering each particular examination. Obviously what may be good cause for one type of examination may not be so for another. The ability of the movant to obtain the desired information by other means is also relevant.

Rule 35, therefore, requires discriminating application by the trial judge, who must decide, as an initial matter in every case, whether the party requesting a

---

3. After the Court of Appeals denied mandamus, the order was corrected by the District Court to reduce the number of examinations to the four requested.

mental or physical examination or examinations has adequately demonstrated the existence of the Rule's requirements of "in controversy" and "good cause." . . .

Of course, there are situations where the pleadings alone are sufficient to meet these requirements. A plaintiff in a negligence action who asserts mental or physical injury, places that mental or physical injury clearly in controversy and provides the defendant with good cause for an examination to determine the existence and extent of such asserted injury. This is not only true as to a plaintiff, but applies equally to a defendant who asserts his mental or physical condition as a defense to a claim. . . . Here, however, Schlagenhauf did not assert his mental or physical condition either in support of or in defense of a claim. His condition was sought to be placed in issue by other parties. Thus, under the principles discussed above, Rule 35 required that these parties make an affirmative showing that petitioner's mental or physical condition was in controversy and that there was good cause for the examinations requested. This, the record plainly shows, they failed to do.

The only allegations in the pleadings relating to this subject were the general conclusory statement in Contract Carriers' answer to the cross-claim that "Schlagenhauf was not mentally or physically capable of operating" the bus at the time of the accident and the limited allegation in National Lead's cross-claim that, at the time of the accident, "the eyes and vision of . . . Schlagenhauf were impaired and deficient."

The attorney's affidavit attached to the petition for the examinations provided:

> [T]hat . . . Schlagenhauf, in his deposition . . . admitted that he saw red lights for 10 to 15 seconds prior to a collision with a semi-tractor trailer unit and yet drove his vehicle on without reducing speed and without altering the course thereof.
>
> The only eye-witness to this accident known to this affiant . . . testified that immediately prior to the impact between the bus and truck that he had also been approaching the truck from the rear and that he had clearly seen the lights of the truck for a distance of three-quarters to one-half mile to the rear thereof.
>
> . . . Schlagenhauf has admitted in his deposition . . . that he was involved in a [prior] similar type rear end collision. . . .

This record cannot support even the corrected order which required one examination in each of the four specialties of internal medicine, ophthalmology, neurology, and psychiatry. Nothing in the pleadings or affidavit would afford a basis for a belief that Schlagenhauf was suffering from a mental or neurological illness warranting wide-ranging psychiatric or neurological examinations. Nor is there anything stated justifying the broad internal medicine examination.

The only specific allegation made in support of the four examinations ordered was that the "eyes and vision" of Schlagenhauf were impaired. Considering this in conjunction with the affidavit, we would be hesitant to set aside a visual examination if it had been the only one ordered. However, as the case must be remanded to the District Court because of the other examinations ordered, it would be appropriate for the District Judge to reconsider also this order in light of the guidelines set forth in this opinion. . . .

Vacated and remanded.

Justice BLACK, with whom Justice CLARK joins, concurring in part and dissenting in part.

. . . Unlike the Court . . . I think this record plainly shows that there was a controversy as to Schlagenhauf's mental and physical health and that "good cause" was shown for a physical and mental examination of him, unless failure to deny the allegations amounted to an admission that they were true. While the papers filed in connection with this motion were informal, there can be no doubt that other parties in the lawsuit specifically and unequivocally charged that Schlagenhauf was not mentally or physically capable of operating a motor bus at the time of the collision, and that his negligent operation of the bus caused the resulting injuries and damage. The other parties filed an affidavit based on depositions of Schlagenhauf and a witness stating that Schlagenhauf, driving the bus along a four-lane highway in what apparently was good weather, had come upon a tractor-trailer down the road in front of him. The tractor-trailer was displaying red lights visible for at least half a mile, and Schlagenhauf admitted seeing them. Yet after coming in sight of the vehicle Schlagenhauf continued driving the bus in a straight line, without slowing down, for a full 10 or 15 seconds until the bus struck the tractor-trailer. Schlagenhauf admitted also that he had been involved in the very same kind of accident once before. Schlagenhauf has never at any time in the proceedings denied and he does not even now deny the charges that his mental and physical health and his eyes and vision were impaired and deficient.

In a collision case like this one, evidence concerning very bad eyesight or impaired mental or physical health which may affect the ability to drive is obviously of the highest relevance. It is equally obvious, I think, that when a vehicle continues down an open road and smashes into a truck in front of it although the truck is in plain sight and there is ample time and room to avoid collision, the chances are good that the driver has some physical, mental or moral defect. When such a thing happens twice, one is even more likely to ask, "What is the matter with that driver? Is he blind or crazy?" Plainly the allegations of the other parties were relevant and put the question of Schlagenhauf's health and vision "in controversy." The Court nevertheless holds that these charges were not a sufficient basis on which to rest a court-ordered examination of Schlagenhauf. It says with reference to the charges of impaired physical or mental health that the charges are "conclusory." I had not thought there was anything strange about pleadings being "conclusory" — that is their function, at least since modern rules of procedure have attempted to substitute simple pleadings for the complicated and redundant ones which long kept the common-law courts in disrepute. . . .

Justice DOUGLAS, dissenting in part.

While I join the Court in reversing this judgment, I would, on the remand, deny all relief asked under Rule 35.

I do not suppose there is any licensed driver of a car or a truck who does not suffer from some ailment, whether it be ulcers, bad eyesight, abnormal blood pressure, deafness, liver malfunction, bursitis, rheumatism, or what not. If he or she is turned over to the plaintiff's doctors and psychoanalysts to discover the cause of the mishap, the door will be opened for grave miscarriages of justice.

When the defendant's doctors examine plaintiff, they are normally interested only in answering a single question: Did plaintiff in fact sustain the specific injuries claimed? But plaintiff's doctors will naturally be inclined to go on a fishing expedition in search of *anything* which will tend to prove that the defendant was unfit to perform the acts which resulted in the plaintiff's injury. . . . The doctor or the psychiatrist has a holiday in the privacy of his office. The defendant is at the doctor's (or psychiatrist's) mercy; and his report may either overawe or confuse the jury and prevent a fair trial. . . .

[handwritten: Will go fishing for something so defendents shouldn't undergo examinations]

NOTES AND PROBLEMS

1. Rule 35 contains two requirements in addition to those in the general provisions of Rule 26. The first is that the mental or physical condition be "in controversy"; the second is that the party seeking such discovery show "good cause."

a. How does *Schlagenhauf* deal with each of these requirements?

b. What does it mean for a physical or mental condition to be in controversy?

c. If such condition is in controversy, what *additional* showing does a party have to make to demonstrate good cause?

2. *Schlagenhauf* is unusual in an important respect: It reached an appellate court while discovery was still going on.

a. Why won't that happen in the great majority of cases?

b. In *Schlagenhauf* the appellant used an extraordinary writ, mandamus. Mandamus is, technically, not an appeal but an independent action against the court or judge, alleging that the order is unlawful. The granting of such writs is in the discretion of the appellate courts, and they are rarely granted. Why do you suppose it was granted in this case?

3. Pat is injured in a collision with a truck owned by Dunham and sues for personal injuries. Dunham moves to take Pat's physical examination.

a. Can Pat's lawyer or doctor attend the physical examination? Justice Douglas, in his dissent, assumes not. Compare Langefeldt-Haaland v. Saupe Enterprises, 768 P.2d 1144 (Alaska 1989) (presence of attorney during physical exam ordered), with Wheat v. Biesecker, 125 F.R.D. 479 (N.D. Ind. 1989) (attorney had no right to be present during exam), and Di Bari v. Incaica Cia Armadora, S. A., 126 F.R.D. 12 (E.D.N.Y. 1989) (magistrate denied request for attorney's presence but allowed stenographer).

b. What happens if Pat claims that it violates her religious principles to be examined by a doctor not of her sect, and she attaches appropriate supporting documents attesting to this religious belief?

c. What happens if Pat agrees that there is good cause for a physical examination but contends that the form of examination proposed will place dangerous stress on her weak heart?

4. Assume the Pat-Dunham litigation is settled. Pat's husband, Mike, brings an action against Dunham for loss of consortium (affection and sexual relations between spouses). Can Dunham obtain a physical or mental examination of Pat?

E.   Discovery in an Adversary System

The preceding section examined two situations in which discovery rules balance the privacy of witnesses and parties against the other goals of discovery. Another problem arises because discovery lies within a system in which the opposing parties must represent their own interests while conducting the case in conformity with the Rules. Discovery thus poses a question about what it means to be an "adversary" in litigation. Some lawyers have difficulty reconciling the required disclosure of potentially harmful information to one's adversary with the competitive stance that adversarial litigation otherwise fosters. Moreover, the present scheme of discovery often requires opposing counsel to cooperate with each other. This section will examine several contexts in which discovery clashes with adversarial impulses and with other social goals.

1.   Privilege and Trial Preparation Material

Hickman v. Taylor is the leading discovery case; as you read it consider why that might be. It may be helpful to note that the original Rules had no provision covering trial preparation materials. (Rule 26(b)(3) did not become effective until 1970.)

Hickman v. Taylor

329 U.S. 495 (1947)

Mr. Justice MURPHY delivered the opinion of the Court.

This case presents an important problem under the Federal Rules of Civil Procedure, as to the extent to which a party may inquire into oral and written statements of witnesses, or other information, secured by an adverse party's counsel in the course of preparation for possible litigation after a claim has arisen. . . .

On February 7, 1943, the tug "J.M. Taylor" sank while engaged in helping to tow a car float of the Baltimore & Ohio Railroad across the Delaware River at Philadelphia. The accident was apparently unusual in nature, the cause of it still being unknown. Five of the nine crew members were drowned. Three days later the tug owners and the underwriters employed a law firm, of which respondent Fortenbaugh is a member, to defend them against potential suits by representatives of the deceased crew members and to sue the railroad for damages to the tug.

A public hearing was held on March 4, 1943, before the United States Steamboat Inspectors, at which the four survivors were examined. This testimony was recorded and made available to all interested parties. Shortly thereafter, Fortenbaugh privately interviewed the survivors and took statements from them with an eye toward the anticipated litigation; the survivors signed these statements on March 29. Fortenbaugh also interviewed other persons believed to have some information relating to the accident and in some cases he made memoranda of what they told him. At the time when Fortenbaugh secured the statements of the survivors, representatives of two of the deceased crew members had been in communication with him. Ultimately claims were presented by representatives of all five of the deceased; four of the claims, however, were settled without litigation. The fifth claimant, petitioner herein, brought suit in a federal court under the Jones Act on November 26, 1943, naming as defendants the two tug owners, individually and as partners, and the railroad.

One year later, petitioner filed 39 interrogatories directed to the tug owners. The 38th interrogatory read: "State whether any statements of the members of the crews of the Tugs 'J.M. Taylor' and 'Philadelphia' or of any other vessel were taken in connection with the towing of the car float and the sinking of the Tug 'John M. Taylor.' [Plaintiff also asked for]" exact copies of all such statements if in writing, and if oral, set forth in detail the exact provisions of any such oral statements or reports." . . .

The tug owners, through Fortenbaugh, . . . while admitting that statements of the survivors had been taken, they declined to summarize or set forth the contents. They did so on the ground that such requests called "for privileged matter obtained in preparation for litigation" and constituted "an attempt to obtain indirectly counsel's private files." It was claimed that answering these requests "would involve practically turning over not only the complete files, but also the telephone records and, almost, the thoughts of counsel." . . .

[When the district court ordered Fortenbaugh to produce the requested statements, he refused, and the court ordered him imprisoned until he complied (but stayed the order pending an appeal).]

The pre-trial deposition-discovery mechanism established by Rules 26 to 37 is one of the most significant innovations of the Federal Rules of Civil Procedure. Under the prior federal practice, the pre-trial functions of notice-giving issue-formulation and fact-revelation were performed primarily and inadequately by the pleadings. Inquiry into the issues and the facts before trial was narrowly confined and was often cumbersome in method. The new rules, however, restrict the pleadings to the task of general notice-giving and invest the deposition-discovery process with a vital role in the preparation for trial. The various instruments of discovery now serve (1) as a device, along with the pre-trial hearing under Rule 16, to narrow and clarify the basic issues between the parties, and (2) as a device for ascertaining the facts, or information as to the existence or whereabouts of facts, relative to those issues. Thus civil trials in the federal courts no longer need be carried on in the dark. The way is now clear, consistent with recognized privileges, for the parties to obtain the fullest possible knowledge of the issues and facts before trial. . . .

In urging that he has a right to inquire into the materials secured and prepared by Fortenbaugh, petitioner emphasizes that the deposition-discovery portions of the Federal Rules of Civil Procedure are designed to enable the parties to discover the true facts and to compel their disclosure wherever they may be found. It is said that inquiry may be made under these rules, epitomized by Rule 26, as to any relevant matter which is not privileged; and since the discovery provisions are to be applied as broadly and liberally as possible, the privilege limitation must be restricted to its narrowest bounds. On the premise that the attorney-client privilege is the one involved in this case, petitioner argues that it must be strictly confined to confidential communications made by a client to his attorney. And since the materials here in issue were secured by Fortenbaugh from third persons rather than from his clients, the tug owners, the conclusion is reached that these materials are proper subjects for discovery under Rule 26.

As additional support for this result, petitioner claims that to prohibit discovery under these circumstances would give a corporate defendant a tremendous advantage in a suit by an individual plaintiff. Thus in a suit by an injured employee against a railroad or in a suit by an insured person against an insurance company the corporate defendant could pull a dark veil of secrecy over all the pertinent facts it can collect after the claim arises merely on the assertion that such facts were gathered by its large staff of attorneys and claim agents. At the same time, the individual plaintiff, who often has direct knowledge of the matter in issue and has no counsel until some time after his claim arises, could be compelled to disclose all the intimate details of his case. By endowing with immunity from disclosure all that a lawyer discovers in the course of his duties, it is said, the rights of individual litigants in such cases are drained of vitality and the lawsuit becomes more of a battle of deception than a search for truth.

But framing the problem in terms of assisting individual plaintiffs in their suits against corporate defendants is unsatisfactory. Discovery concededly may work to the disadvantage as well as to the advantage of individual plaintiffs. Discovery, in other words, is not a one-way proposition. It is available in all types of cases at the behest of any party, individual or corporate, plaintiff or defendant. The problem thus far transcends the situation confronting this petitioner. And we must view that problem in light of the limitless situations where the particular kind of discovery sought by petitioner might be used.

We agree, of course, that the deposition-discovery rules are to be accorded a broad and liberal treatment. No longer can the time-honored cry of "fishing expedition" serve to preclude a party from inquiring into the facts underlying his opponent's case. Mutual knowledge of all the relevant facts gathered by both parties is essential to proper litigation. To that end, either party may compel the other to disgorge whatever facts he has in his possession. The deposition-discovery procedure simply advances the stage at which the disclosure can be compelled from the time of trial to the period preceding it, thus reducing the possibility of surprise. But discovery, like all matters of procedure, has ultimate and necessary boundaries. As indicated by Rules 30(b) and (d) and 31(d) [now Rules 26(c) and 30(d)], limitations inevitably arise when it can be shown that the examination is being conducted in bad faith or in such a manner as to annoy, embarrass or oppress the person subject to the inquiry. And as Rule 26(b) provides, further limitations come into existence when the inquiry touches upon the irrelevant or encroaches upon the recognized domains of privilege.

We also agree that the memoranda, statements and mental impressions in issue in this case fall outside the scope of the attorney-client privilege and hence are not protected from discovery on that basis. It is unnecessary here to delineate the content and scope of that privilege as recognized in the federal courts. For present purposes, it suffices to note that the protective cloak of this privilege does not *Hold?* extend to information which an attorney secures from a witness while acting for his client in anticipation of litigation. Nor does this privilege concern the memoranda, briefs, communications and other writings prepared by counsel for his own use in prosecuting his client's case; and it is equally unrelated to writings which reflect an attorney's mental impressions, conclusions, opinions or legal theories.

But the impropriety of invoking that privilege does not provide an answer to the problem before us. Petitioner has made more than an ordinary request for relevant, non-privileged facts in the possession of his adversaries or their counsel. He has sought discovery as of right of oral and written statements of witnesses whose identity is well known and whose availability to petitioner appears unimpaired. He has sought production of these matters after making the most searching inquiries of his opponents as to the circumstances surrounding the fatal accident, which inquiries were sworn to have been answered to the best of their information and belief. Interrogatories were directed toward all the events prior to, during and subsequent to the sinking of the tug. Full and honest answers to such broad inquiries would necessarily have included all pertinent information gleaned by Fortenbaugh through his interviews with the witnesses. Petitioner makes no suggestion, and we cannot assume, that the tug owners or Fortenbaugh were incomplete or dishonest in the framing of their answers. In addition, petitioner was free to examine the public testimony of the witnesses taken before the United States Steamboat Inspectors. We are thus dealing with an attempt to secure the production of written statements and mental impressions contained in the files and the mind of the attorney Fortenbaugh without any showing of necessity or any indication or claim that denial of such production would unduly prejudice the preparation of petitioner's case or cause him any hardship or injustice. For aught that appears, the essence of what petitioner seeks either has been revealed to him already through the interrogatories or is readily available to him direct from the witnesses for the asking. . . .

In our opinion, neither Rule 26 nor any other rule dealing with discovery *Hold?* contemplates production under such circumstances. That is not because the subject matter is privileged or irrelevant, as those concepts are used in these rules. Here is simply an attempt, without purported necessity or justification, to secure written statements, private memoranda and personal recollections prepared or formed by an adverse party's counsel in the course of his legal duties. As such, it falls outside the arena of discovery and contravenes the public policy underlying the orderly prosecution and defense of legal claims. Not even the most liberal of discovery theories can justify unwarranted inquiries into the files and the mental impressions of an attorney.

Historically, a lawyer is an officer of the court and is bound to work for the advancement of justice while faithfully protecting the rightful interests of his clients. In performing his various duties, however, it is essential that a lawyer work with a certain degree of privacy, free from unnecessary intrusion by opposing parties and their counsel. Proper preparation of a client's case demands that he assemble information, sift what he considers to be the relevant from the irrelevant facts, prepare his legal theories and plan his strategy without undue and needless interference. That is the historical and the necessary way in which lawyers act within the framework of our system of jurisprudence to promote justice and to protect their clients' interests. This work is reflected, of course, in interviews, statements, memoranda, correspondence, briefs, mental impressions, personal beliefs, and countless other tangible and intangible ways — aptly though roughly termed by the Circuit Court of Appeals in this case as the "work product of the lawyer." Were such materials open to opposing counsel on mere demand, much of what is now put down in writing would remain unwritten. An attorney's thoughts, heretofore inviolate, would not be his own. Inefficiency, unfairness and sharp practices would inevitably develop in the giving of legal advice and in the preparation of cases for trial. The effect on the legal profession would be demoralizing. And the interests of the clients and the cause of justice would be poorly served.

We do not mean to say that all written materials obtained or prepared by an adversary's counsel with an eye toward litigation are necessarily free from discovery in all cases. Where relevant and non-privileged facts remain hidden in an attorney's file and where production of those facts is essential to the preparation of one's case, discovery may properly be had. Such written statements and documents might, under certain circumstances, be admissible in evidence or give clues as to the existence or location of relevant facts. Or they might be useful for purposes of impeachment or corroboration. And production might be justified where the witnesses are no longer available or can be reached only with difficulty. Were production of written statements and documents to be precluded under such circumstances, the liberal ideals of the deposition-discovery portions of the Federal Rules of Civil Procedure would be stripped of much of their meaning. But the general policy against invading the privacy of an attorney's course of preparation is so well recognized and so essential to an orderly working of our system of legal procedure that a burden rests on the one who would invade that privacy to establish adequate reasons to justify production through a subpoena or court order. . . .

But as to oral statements made by witnesses to Fortenbaugh, whether presently in the form of his mental impressions or memoranda, we do not believe that any showing of necessity can be made under the circumstances of this case so as to justify production. . . .

Denial of production of this nature does not mean that any material, non-privileged facts can be hidden from the petitioner in this case. He need not be unduly hindered in the preparation of his case, in the discovery of facts or in his anticipation of his opponents' position. Searching interrogatories directed to Fortenbaugh and the tug owners, production of written documents and statements upon a proper showing and direct interviews with the witnesses themselves all serve to reveal the facts in Fortenbaugh's possession to the fullest possible extent consistent with public policy. Petitioner's counsel frankly admits that he wants the oral statements only to help prepare himself to examine witnesses and to make sure that he has overlooked nothing. That is insufficient under the circumstances to

[handwritten marginal note:] Exceptions to rule

permit him an exception to the policy underlying the privacy of Fortenbaugh's professional activities. If there should be a rare situation justifying production of these matters, petitioner's case is not of that type. . . .

Mr. Justice JACKSON, concurring. . . .

"Discovery" is one of the working tools of the legal profession. It traces back to the equity bill of discovery in English Chancery practice and seems to have had a forerunner in Continental practice. See Ragland, Discovery Before Trial (1932) 13-16. Since 1848 when the draftsmen of New York's Code of Procedure recognized the importance of a better system of discovery, the impetus to extend and expand discovery, as well as the opposition to it, has come from within the Bar itself. It happens in this case that it is the plaintiff's attorney who demands such unprecedented latitude of discovery and, strangely enough, amicus briefs in his support have been filed by several labor unions representing plaintiffs as a class. It is the history of the movement for broader discovery, however, that in actual experience the chief opposition to its extension has come from lawyers who specialize in representing plaintiffs because defendants have made liberal use of it to force plaintiffs to disclose their cases in advance. Discovery is a two-edged sword and we cannot decide this problem on any doctrine of extending help to one class of litigants. . . .

Counsel for the petitioner candidly said on argument that he wanted this information to help prepare himself to examine witnesses, to make sure he overlooked nothing. He bases his claim to it in his brief on the view that the Rules were to do away with the old situation where a law suit developed into "a battle of wits between counsel." But a common law trial is and always should be an adversary proceeding. Discovery was hardly intended to enable a learned profession to perform its functions either without wits or on wits borrowed from the adversary.

The real purpose and the probable effect of the practice ordered by the district court would be to put trials on a level even lower than a "battle of wits." I can conceive of no practice more demoralizing to the Bar than to require a lawyer to write out and deliver to his adversary an account of what witnesses have told him. . . .

Mr. Justice FRANKFURTER joins in this opinion.

To require disclosure would be demoralizing to bar

NOTES AND PROBLEMS

1. It is easy to miss the point of *Hickman* unless one focuses on the precise question decided.

   a. What information was sought?

   b. Was it relevant?

   c. Was it privileged?

   d. Why wasn't it discoverable?

2. At the time of *Hickman*, Rule 26 did not deal specifically with the topic of trial preparation materials. It now does. Read Rule 26(b)(3) and answer the following questions:

   a. Does the doctrine apply to nonlawyers, such as insurance adjusters and investigators?

b. What if a party or witness makes a written statement to the lawyer? Is that discoverable?

c. What about factual information, as opposed to mental impressions — is that undiscoverable if the facts were uncovered by a lawyer?

d. Unlike privileges, which are absolute unless waived, trial preparation material is sometimes discoverable: When?

3. Most of the following problems deal with the variations on these themes. Work through the problems to see how Rule 26 applies in litigation settings. Start with a routine setting. *P* was injured when struck by a bus owned by *B* Bus Co.; *P* then sued *B*. The litigation raises the following discovery issues:

a. Immediately after the accident, a vice president of *B* went to the scene and made a full investigation, including interviews with witnesses and measurements of the accident location. He then made a written report to the directors of *B*. Can *P* obtain the report? Would it make any difference if *B* has a claims department and the vice president is "attached" to that department? See Rakus v. Erie-Lackawanna Railroad, 76 F.R.D. 145 (W.D.N.Y. 1977) (employees' accident reports to claims department are discoverable); Spaulding v. Denton, 68 F.R.D. 342 (D. Del. 1975) (marine surveyors' report, made in regular course of business without attorney's legal expertise when insurers were trying to find out about unusual accident, is discoverable).

b. Through the expenditure of more than $10,000, *B*'s attorney has uncovered another eyewitness to the accident. *P* serves an interrogatory asking for the names of all eyewitnesses, and *B* objects on the ground of "trial preparation materials." Must *B* disclose the witness's name?

4. In *Hickman*, Fortenbaugh interviewed the witnesses and took notes but apparently did not ask the witnesses to write out statements or tape-record the witnesses' statements. Many lawyers will do so in order to have a basis for subsequent examination or impeachment of the witness. Are such statements discoverable? See Rule 26(b)(3).

a. Boris is seriously injured in an automobile accident with Charles. In the hospital Boris is visited by an investigator for State Farm Insurance Co., which had insured Charles's car. Boris thinks he gave a videotaped statement to the investigator and knows that he talked to the investigator about the accident. As attorney for Boris, (a) can you find out whether Boris gave a statement?; (b) if so, can you obtain a copy of the statement before Boris's scheduled deposition next month?; and (c) if Boris did not give a statement, can you find out what he told the investigator?

b. In Boris's suit against Charles, Frank, a friend of Boris, will testify on his behalf. Frank gave a written, signed statement to Charles's attorney but does not remember what he said. As attorney for Boris, can you obtain the statement? How?

5. What does it take to overcome a claim of work product? How special must the circumstances be?

a. Try first two variations on the facts of *Hickman*. What if Fortenbaugh had interviewed the crew members in the hospital, and they had died before giving their testimony?

b. What if the crew members were still alive but there had been no public hearing on the accident, and the witnesses claimed not to be able to remember events clearly?

c. Plaintiff claims personal injuries in a bus crash. Defendant assigns an investigator to film plaintiff scuba diving while on vacation. Plaintiff seeks both the film and the investigator's report. Substantial need and undue hardship? Freiman v. USAIR Group, Inc., 1994 U.S. Dist. LEXIS 16994 (1994) (work product protection overcome for videotape but not for investigator's report, since he could be deposed). Gibson v. National Rail Pass. Corp., 170 F.R.D. 408 (E.D. Pa. 1997) (surveillance reports discoverable only if defendant plans to offer in evidence, but defendant must disclose a reasonable time before trial whether it plans to offer surveillance in evidence).

6. A common work product problem is the so-called contention interrogatory, in which one party seeks to discover the facts that underlie broad allegations. Thus, for example, in an auto negligence case like Bell v. Novick Transfer (see Chapter I), the defendant might ask plaintiff whether he contended that defendant had driven too fast, failed to maintain his brakes, or failed to heed a traffic signal. The purpose of such interrogatories is to expand on the generalities of the pleading and to prepare for the lines of proof one will need to meet at trial. But do such questions delve impermissibly into the opposing lawyer's mental impressions and legal theories? Sometimes the recipients of such interrogatories refuse to answer on the grounds that such questions reveal their theory of the case and therefore constitute protected work product. Is such an objection justified? Consider how Rule 33(c) bears on your answer:

> An interrogatory otherwise proper is not necessarily objectionable merely because an answer to the interrogatory involves an opinion or contention that relates to fact or the application of law to fact, but the court may order that such an interrogatory need not be answered until after designated discovery has been completed or until a pre-trial conference or other later time.

Does this modify what might otherwise be the effect of Rule 26(b)(3) on such an interrogatory? See Rifkind v. Good, 27 Cal. Rptr. 2d 822 (CA 2d Dist. 1994) (in action between attorneys on fee dispute, proper to seek by interrogatory list of documents supporting affirmative defenses; not proper to ask same question in deposition).

7. This chapter does not seek to explore the doctrines of evidentiary privilege, but you should know that one U.S. Supreme Court opinion on privilege significantly affects discovery. In Upjohn Co. v. United States, 449 U.S. 393 (1981), noted supra on page 415, the Court held that the attorney-client privilege extended to communications between counsel and all corporate employees, not just managers.

a. Recall that *Hickman* rejected the claim that the crew's conversations with Fortenbaugh came under the attorney-client privilege. Explain why, under *Upjohn*, the tugboat company in *Hickman* might have had a stronger argument for privilege. And recall that privilege, unlike trial preparation protection, cannot be pierced by a showing of need. Privilege, unless waived, is absolute.

b. If corporate employees are "clients," another rule, this one concerning lawyers' ethical responsibilities, comes into play. To prevent overreaching and back-door negotiations, professional rules prohibit lawyers from communicating directly with a party represented by another lawyer, unless that lawyer consents. See, e.g., Model Rule of Professional Conduct 4.2.

c. As a review of this section, consider the facts of *Hickman* after *Upjohn*. What new argument against disclosure of the interview notes does Fortenbaugh now have? At one point in *Hickman*, in explaining why plaintiff's lawyer cannot have Fortenbaugh's notes, the Court points out that the plaintiff's lawyer can simply interview the surviving crew members himself. How is this argument complicated after *Upjohn*? Finally, does anything in *Hickman* or *Upjohn* prevent plaintiff's lawyer from deposing the crew members? Why not?

2. Expert Information

In many cases the parties hire experts to analyze the case and, perhaps, to testify. Such experts range from the standard professionals — physicians, accountants, engineers — to exotics who claim expertise in "accident reconstruction" and "brand name identification." Experts typically testify to the inferences one can draw about causes of an event by applying their special knowledge to the evidence available. Before a court will let an expert testify, the party presenting such testimony must establish that he or she is an expert and that the expertise is relevant to contested issues.

The problems posed by expert testimony resemble those of the work product doctrine. Both involve relevant, unprivileged information "produced" by the efforts of one of the adversaries. The clash is between two assumptions of the system. We hope that each side will do its own preparation and neither will "freeload" on the efforts of the other. On the other hand, we want parties to have access before trial to information on which the trial outcome may turn. Issues posed by expert testimony have become especially heated as more experts testify at trials.

Two portions of Rule 26 speak to the problems of expert testimony. Rule 26(a)(2) requires, as part of the initial disclosures, information about experts who may testify and about the basis for their testimony, including a requirement that the adversary receive "a written report prepared and signed by the witness . . . contain[ing] a complete statement of all opinions to be expressed and reasons therefor. . . . Rule 26(b)(4) provides for additional discovery from experts: The Rule requires that testifying experts submit to pretrial deposition but erects special barriers around the opinions of nontestifying experts.

NOTES AND PROBLEMS

1. Before dealing with borderline cases, consider some straightforward applications of the discovery provisions on experts. Perhaps the most significant but

nonobvious point is that the Rule grants its protections not to experts per se but to experts who have developed their information in preparation for litigation. The rule is in that respect like the trial preparation doctrine, which shields not the underlying facts but only the mental processes of those who are using those facts to prepare for litigation.

2. John is seriously injured in an automobile accident and is taken to Coral Hospital for emergency care. In the emergency room, he is examined by Dr. Kildare, who subsequently operates on John's back. Three months later, John's back is examined by Dr. Welby, an orthopedic specialist. John brings suit against Mary, the driver of the other car. Dr. Welby has been hired by John's lawyer and has prepared a report on John's condition.

a. Suppose John's lawyer expects to call both physicians to testify at trial.

(1) What information about which physician must John's lawyer give to Mary's as part of the initial disclosure required by Rule 26(a)(1)?

(2) What information about which physician must John's lawyer supply as part of the disclosure required by Rule 26(a)(2)?

(3) Can Dr. Kildare be required to prepare a written report on his findings?

(4) May Mary's lawyer depose Dr. Welby?

b. Suppose now that John's lawyer does not plan to call Dr. Welby at trial. Need John's lawyer supply any information about him as part of the disclosures required by Rule 26(a)?

c. Same assumptions as in Note 2b, but Mary's lawyer, in deposing John, learns that he has been examined by Dr. Welby, and seeks to depose Welby on his medical opinion of John's injuries. (Mary's lawyer is eager to do this because she infers from the fact that John does not plan to present Welby's testimony that it will not be favorable to John.) Can Mary depose Welby? See Rule 26(b)(4)(B).

3. The most difficult questions arise in connection with Rule 26(b)(4)(B), which tries to balance the adversaries' abilities to prepare their cases against the possibility that a nontestifying expert may have the only access to facts. The next two cases deal with such situations.

Thompson v. The Haskell Co.

65 F. Empl. Prac. Cas. (BNA) 1088 (M.D. Fla. 1994)

SNYDER, Magistrate Judge.

This cause is before the Court on Plaintiff's Motion for Protective Order filed on May 13, 1994 (hereinafter Motion). Plaintiff seeks to shield from discovery documents related to her in the possession of Lauren Lucas, Ph.D., a psychologist. She contends that Rule 26(b)(4) of the Federal Rules of Civil Procedure (FRCP) protects the psychological records in Dr. Lucas' possession. In particular, Plaintiff represents Dr. Lucas was retained by her prior counsel to perform a diagnostic review and personality profile, and that, after seeing Plaintiff on one occasion on June 15, 1992, Dr. Lucas prepared a report for her prior counsel.

Facts

Rule 26(b)(4)[(B)] of the FRCP provides:

> A party may, through interrogatories or by deposition, discover facts known or opinions held by an expert who has been retained or specially employed by another party in anticipation of litigation or preparation for trial and who is not expected to be called as a witness at trial only as provided in Rule 35(b) or upon a showing of exceptional circumstances under which it is impracticable for the party seeking discovery to obtain facts or opinions on the same subject by other means.

Assuming arguendo that Dr. Lucas' report is covered by Rule 26(b)(4), it would nevertheless be discoverable under the circumstances presented in this case. In the instant lawsuit, Plaintiff alleges that, as a result of sexual harassment by co-defendant Zona, a supervisor in the employ of the Defendant, she was "reduced to a severely depressed emotional state and her employment was terminated when she did not acquiesce to the advances of [Zona]." Complaint, filed on September 23, 1993, at 6. According to a complaint filed with the Jacksonville Equal Opportunity Commission, Plaintiff apparently was terminated from her position with Defendant Haskell Company on June 5, 1992. Thus, her mental and emotional state ten days later on June 15, 1992, the date on which she was examined by Dr. Lucas, is highly probative with regard to the above-quoted allegation, which is essential to her case.

This highly probative information is discoverable notwithstanding Rule 26(b)(4), moreover, given the nature of the report at issue. Apparently, no other comparable report was prepared during the weeks immediately following Plaintiff's discharge. Thus, the Defendant could not obtain the information contained in Dr. Lucas' report by other means. In a case almost on all fours with the instant one, the Court recognized that even "independent examinations . . . pursuant to Rule 35 would not contain equivalent information." Dixon v. Cappellini, 88 F.R.D. 1, 3 (M.D. Pa. 1980). Under these facts, it appears there are exceptional circumstances favoring disclosure of Dr. Lucas' report, and that the Defendant could not obtain comparable information by other means. Accordingly, the Motion is DENIED. . . .

Chiquita International Ltd. v. M/V Bolero Reefer

1994 U.S. Dist. LEXIS 5820 (S.D. N.Y. 1994)

FRANCIS, Magistrate Judge.

This is a maritime action in which the shipper, Chiquita International Ltd. ("Chiquita"), sues the carrier, International Reefer Services, S.A. ("International Reefer"), for cargo loss and damage. Chiquita alleges that International Reefer was engaged to transport 154,660 boxes of bananas from Puerto Bolivar, Ecuador to Bremerhaven, Germany aboard the M/V Bolero Reefer. However, because of alleged malfunctions of the vessel's loading cranes and side-ports, only 111,660 boxes were loaded. Thus, 43,000 boxes of bananas were left on the wharf and were later disposed of. The cargo that did arrive in Germany was allegedly in poor condition.

International Reefer has submitted a letter in support of an application to compel discovery of Joseph Winer. Mr. Winer is a marine surveyor who examined the vessel and loading gear at Chiquita's request shortly after the vessel arrived in Bremerhaven. International Reefer seeks Mr. Winer's deposition and production of the file he assembled in connection with his inspection. Chiquita has objected to these demands on the ground that Mr. Winer is a non-testifying expert as to whom discovery is closely circumscribed by Rule 26(b)(4)(B) of the Federal Rules of Civil Procedure. International Reefer replies that Mr. Winer is a fact witness rather than an expert. Moreover, even if he is an expert, International Reefer argues that the fact that he is the only surveyor who observed the vessel shortly after it docked is an exceptional circumstance warranting discovery. . . .

[The opinion quoted Rule 26(b)(4)(B).]

Thus, a non-testifying expert is generally immune from discovery.

Mr. Winer qualifies as such an expert. He is a marine engineer who was specifically engaged by Chiquita to examine the vessel in connection with the cargo loss claim. He is clearly an "expert" in that he brought his technical background to bear in observing the condition of the gear and offering his opinion to Chiquita. He does not forfeit this status merely because he made a personal examination of the vessel and therefore learned "facts," rather than simply offering an opinion based on the observations of others. Rule 26(b)(4)(B) generally precludes discovery of "facts known or opinions held" by a non-testifying expert, and so it anticipates that such an expert may make his or her own investigation. Thus, the relevant distinction is not between fact and opinion testimony but between those witnesses whose information was obtained in the normal course of business and those who were hired to make an evaluation in connection with expected litigation. See Harasimowicz v. McAllister, 78 F.R.D. 319, 320 (E.D. Pa. 1978) (medical examiner subject to ordinary discovery on routine autopsy); Congrove v. St. Louis-San Francisco Railway, 77 F.R.D. 503, 504-05 (W.D. Mo. 1978) (treating physician subject to ordinary discovery). Here, Mr. Winer falls into the latter category and Rule 26(b)(4)(B) therefore applies.

International Reefer nevertheless contends that discovery should be permitted under the "exceptional circumstances" clause of the rule, since no other marine surveyor viewed the vessel shortly after docking. This argument would have merit if International Reefer had been precluded from sending its own expert to the scene by forces beyond its control. Thus, for example, in Sanford Construction Co. v. Kaiser Aluminum & Chemical Sales, Inc., 45 F.R.D. 465, 466 (E.D. Ky. 1968), the court found there to be exceptional circumstances where the plaintiff allowed its own expert to examine the item at issue while barring the defendant's experts until the item was no longer accessible.

However, that is not the case here. The vessel and equipment were at least as available to International Reefer as to Chiquita from the time of loading. Indeed, during the three-week voyage to Bremerhaven, International Reefer's employees had the exclusive opportunity to examine the loading cranes. Under these circumstances, the failure of International Reefer to engage its own marine surveyor in a timely manner should not be rewarded by permitting discovery of

Chiquita's expert. To do so would permit the exceptional circumstances exception to swallow Rule 26(b)(4)(B).

Finally, International Reefer maintains that even if it is foreclosed from deposing Mr. Winer, it should be given access to his file. However, Rule 26(b)(4)(B) applies to document discovery as well as to depositions. Nevertheless, International Reefer is correct that information does not become exempt from discovery merely because it is conveyed to a non-testifying expert. Thus, while the file may contain Mr. Winer's recorded observations and opinions which need not be disclosed, it may also include discoverable information provided to Mr. Winer by others. Such documents shall be produced.

Conclusion

For the reasons set forth above, International Reefer's application to take the deposition of Joseph Winer is denied. By May 13, 1994, Chiquita shall produce from Mr. Winer's file those documents that do not reflect his observations and opinions or are otherwise privileged. Chiquita shall prepare a log of any documents withheld, identifying them with the specificity required by Local Rule 46(e).

SO ORDERED.

NOTES AND PROBLEMS

1. Focus first on what was being sought in each case:

a. What was the defendant seeking in *Thompson*?

b. What was the plaintiff's argument in *Thompson* that the report was undiscoverable?

c. What was the defendant seeking in *Chiquita*?

d. What did the court order discovered in *Chiquita*? Why?

2. *Thompson* and *Chiquita* deal with similar information, which the respective courts concede is relevant and unprivileged. But the *Thompson* court orders disclosure, while the *Chiquita* court denies disclosure.

a. Why?

b. What facts would one change about each case to reach a different result?

c. In *Chiquita* the views of someone familiar with crucial facts are suppressed. How does one justify that result, given the general thrust toward disclosure of the discovery rules?

3. In *Chiquita* the court suggests there is no question that Mr. Winer is a Rule 26(b)(4) expert. In *Thompson* the court suggests in passing that Dr. Lucas might not be: "Assuming arguendo that Dr. Lucas' report is covered by Rule 26(b)(4), it would nevertheless be discoverable under the circumstances presented in this case." If Dr. Lucas's report weren't covered by 26(b)(4), under what discovery provision would it fall? See Problem 2, page 447.

4. *Thompson* and *Chiquita* deal with attempts to discover the reports of nontestifying experts. What if the parties try to go one step further and, with or without

the reports, actually try to compel the opposition's experts to testify at trial? The argument for doing so looks straightforward: These people have unprivileged information relevant to the case. The law is anything but straightforward, as it jumbles together considerations of litigative fairness with a sense that the expert "owns" the subject of her expertise:

> As at least one commentator has noted, the case law dealing with the question whether a party to a lawsuit may obtain discovery of or testimony from an expert consulted by the other, but not to be called at trial by the consulting party, is confused at best. Note, Must the Show Go On? Defining When One Party May Call or Compel An Opposing Party's Consultative Expert to Testify, 78 Minn. L. Rev. 1191, 1199-1203 (1994).
>
> Experts enjoy no constitutional or statutory immunity from compulsory process. Moreover, the desire for all probative information in service of the overall search for truth weighs in favor of compelled testimony and, indeed, discovery even from consultative experts. On the other hand, several considerations may cut the other way, depending upon the particular circumstances.
>
> First, there is an important interest in allowing counsel to obtain the expert advice they need in order properly to evaluate and present their clients' positions without fear that every consultation with an expert may yield grist for the adversary's mill. This policy underlies Fed. R. Civ. P. 26(b)(4)(B)'s severe limitation on the discovery of consultative, as opposed to testifying, experts. . . .
>
> Second, the Federal Rules of Civil Procedure reflect a view that it would be unfair to allow a party to benefit from the effort and expense incurred by the other in preparing its case. In other words, the general policy, which is not without exceptions, is that each side should prepare its own case at its own expense.
>
> Third, there are concerns peculiar to the issue of compelled testimony from nontestifying experts. Some have suggested that allowing the use of compulsion might diminish the willingness of experts to serve as consultants and, in any case, that it is unfair to the experts. . . .
>
> Fourth, and perhaps most pertinent, permitting one party to call an expert previously retained or consulted by the other side entails a risk of very substantial prejudice stemming from the fact of the prior retention, quite apart from the substance of the testimony. One leading commentator aptly has characterized the fact of the prior retention by the adversary as "explosive." 8 C. Wright et al., Federal Practice and Procedure: Civil §2032, at 447 (1994).

Rubel v. Eli Lilly & Co., 1995 U.S. Dist. LEXIS 3456 (S.D. N.Y. 1995).

F. Ensuring Compliance and Controlling Abuse of Discovery

Even with the preceding doctrinal framework in mind, one of the hardest concepts for the student to grasp is the "culture" of discovery. *Hickman*'s fears that the advent of discovery would mean the demise of the adversary system appear to have been greatly exaggerated. Instead, discovery has become the field on which some of unrestrained advocacy's least attractive features have displayed themselves. Delay, evasiveness, abusive use of various discovery devices, use of discovery to buy time or to force a hard-pressed opponent to settle for less, and the like appear on lawyers' lists of such tactics. Such depressing behavior has several sources, some of which lie in the design of the discovery system itself. The Federal Rules envisioned discovery's operating largely without judicial supervision, and the Rules therefore speak of lawyers exchanging various discovery requests without intervention by the court. Judges become involved only when the system breaks down — for example, in the event of a motion for a protective order, a request to compel discovery, or a motion for sanctions. But when such judicial intervention comes, the judge must step into a dispute about which she may know little, and may therefore be inclined to tread rather warily. Moreover, many judges routinely assign discovery matters to federal magistrate judges and hear only appeals from their orders. Thus judges faced with discovery battles often have very little feel for the dispute before them.

1. An Anatomy of Discovery Abuses

Before assessing the effectiveness of these efforts, it may help to construct an anatomy of discovery abuses. There are three basic patterns: too little discovery, too much discovery, and mismatched discovery. The first, sometimes called "stonewalling," occurs when one party refuses or resists appropriate requests for discovery. The second occurs when one party seeks more discovery than the case justifies so as to discourage or hamper the opponent. The last pattern, "mismatched" discovery, occurs when the two parties have significantly unequal wealth; the richer party, even if it does not abuse discovery, may seem to have an unfair advantage. The Rules offer partial solutions to the first two problems but deal less well with the third. The Rules employ three tools: limits on discovery, sanctions for bad behavior, and judicial supervision.

Start with stonewalling. Refusal to cooperate with justifiable discovery requests can subject a party to sanctions. Read Rules 26(g) and 37, noting the range of propositions to which the signature of the lawyer certifies under 26(g). Some report that early judicial supervision is effective in reducing stonewalling; if so, the mandatory scheduling conference required by the 2000 revisions, combined with the mandatory disclosures, may have the desired effect.

Over-discovery has a similar set of control mechanisms. If the information requested is irrelevant or privileged, one may simply decline to answer; the 2000 revisions further limited the scope of material discoverable without a judicial order to "matter relevant to [a] claim or defense," requiring a judicial order to broaden the scope. Discovery can also be excessive because cumulative or burdensome; note the provision in Rule 26(g) in which the signing lawyer certifies that discovery is not "unreasonable or unduly burdensome or expensive, given the needs of the case." The Rules also impose some mechanical limits — 25 interrogatories and a single seven-hour deposition of each witness.

For cases in which these provisions fail to solve the problem, Rule 26(c) permits any party to seek a protective order. That Rule permits a court to limit discovery, even though the information sought might otherwise be discoverable, if it would produce "annoyance, embarrassment, oppression, or undue burden or expense." For problems that do not fit neatly into any of these categories, one might consider a discovery conference (under Rule 16), which involves the judge in the framing of a discovery plan. Such a conference may be convened by the court on its own motion; judges who wish to manage discovery may use such conferences as a tool. Indeed, the 2000 revisions, without explicitly saying so, have divided discovery into two sorts — that which can occur without judicial supervision or permission, and a second phase in which judicial permission and, probably, supervision will be required.

PROBLEMS

1. Having filed a complaint against Baxter Corp. for breach of contract and received the required disclosures, Arthur Corp. sends Baxter a set of additional interrogatories seeking some routine information about the details of company organization, such as which officers and employees are responsible for which aspects of the company's affairs. Baxter refuses to answer any of the questions, noting in its response that these matters are not relevant to the claims and defenses of the action. Arthur's lawyer believes that such questions are entirely proper because they enable her to decide which officers to depose — and that they are thus included within Rule 26(b)(1) as "reasonably calculated to lead to the discovery of admissible evidence."

   a. How should Arthur's lawyer proceed to get answers to his interrogatories?

   b. Can Arthur seek sanctions? Under what Rule(s)?

2. Baxter serves a notice to take the deposition of Alice Arthur, the President of Arthur Corp. On the appointed day, Arthur doesn't show up. As attorney for Baxter, what remedies would you seek? See Rule 37(d).

3. When Baxter seeks sanctions, Arthur claims that Baxter purposefully scheduled the deposition at an extremely inconvenient place and requests that the location be changed. Should that argument, if true, block or mitigate sanctions?

4. When Baxter deposes Alice Arthur, her lawyer interposes numerous objections, with the result that at the end of seven hours, the deposition is just getting into the core inquiries Baxter has planned. Alice and her lawyer stand, call for the end of the deposition, and draw Baxter's attention to the seven-hour provision of Rule 30(d)(2). What should Baxter do?

5. Arthur and Baxter serve a series of requests for discovery on each other, including interrogatories, notices of depositions, and various requests for the production of documents. Arthur believes that it has responded in good faith to Baxter's requests but that Baxter has been systematically uncooperative, raising many barely tenable objections, declining to produce documents until threatened with a court order, producing incomplete sets of documents, then producing overwhelming quantities of documents in which the relevant material is buried, and similar tactics. What should Arthur do?

6. The amount at stake in Arthur v. Baxter is $80,000 — all but $5,000 of that amount representing Arthur's claim against Baxter. In connection with its counterclaim, Baxter serves on Arthur notices for a series of depositions of

Arthur's officers. When Arthur's lawyer calls Baxter's lawyer to discuss the scheduling of these depositions, she learns that the series of depositions will take 30 hours to complete. Given the billing rates of the two attorneys and the cost of a stenographer, the cost of such a series of depositions could exceed $10,000. Is that troubling? Is there anything Arthur's lawyer can do about it?

We have not yet addressed one of the more difficult discovery problems — how the legal system should cope with substantial imbalance in the parties' wealth. Because discovery is conducted by the parties' lawyers, the litigants must bear the costs. Some of the more elaborate forms, particularly depositions, can cost a lot. Can the wealthier party prevail simply by dint of greater resources? The problem has two versions. First, what happens if one party lacks resources to do adequate discovery? The most troubling case would arise if most of the likely evidence was in defendant's hands, and the case suggested that assembly of evidence would be complex — perhaps in a product liability or environmental hazard claim. Without access to discovery, such a claim has no chance of succeeding. Although the Rules nowhere address this problem specifically, several possibilities present themselves. The party with fewer resources may be able to conduct "discovery" from various public sources — government or public documents, press sources, and the like. Digital media and the Internet have made such searches much faster and cheaper than they were fifty years ago. Moreover, a disciplined discovery scheme making maximum use of "cheap" discovery (such as document requests and interrogatories) may yield a good deal. With large public and private institutions, well-planned document requests can produce rich veins of information. Finally, it may be possible to ride free on the discovery efforts of other parties if they are involved: A deposition conducted by one party will likely yield useful information. One change in the 2000 amendments to the Rules made this avenue more difficult to pursue. Rule 5(d) now forbids parties from filing any discovery materials with the court until they are used in a "proceeding" (including a pretrial motion). The motivation behind this amendment was simple: Courts were running out of space to store such documents. But the consequences may be to curtail the availability of discovery materials in separate but factually related cases, making it harder for an ill-funded party to "piggy-back" on another's previous efforts.

2. Remedies: Management and Sanctions

The ultimate incentive to comply with discovery obligations is the court's power to punish violations of the discovery rules. Even though the rules give district courts a broad range of options — from dismissal or a default judgment to requiring a litigant to pay an opponent's costs and expenses incurred as a result of a failure to make discovery — there remains a widespread sense that much discovery abuse goes unchecked. Some observers suggest that judges tend to accept delay and lame excuses on the part of litigants and their attorneys until the court is provoked beyond endurance, at which point the court punishes one side or the other with a termination of the lawsuit by default or dismissal. Judges may be reluctant to mete out less draconian orders for "routine" discovery abuse for fear that such would only compound the burden of discovery disputes by adding a contest over cost-shifting to every underlying discovery problem. Finally, discovery disputes tend to be very fact-intensive and time-consuming for judges. It is often difficult for a judge to figure out which side is being unfair or unreasonable in any particular dispute. The next two cases, both decided in the same district within a year of each other, display two Magistrate Judges dealing with discovery disputes in quite different ways.

Thompson v. Department of Housing & Urban Development

199 F.R.D. 168 (D. Md. 2001)

GRIMM, United States Magistrate Judge.

Plaintiffs are class representatives of African American residents of Baltimore's public housing developments. They filed suit in January, 1995 against the U.S. Department of Housing and Urban Development and its secretary (the "federal defendants") and the Housing Authority of Baltimore City ("HABC"), its executive director and the Mayor and City Council of Baltimore (the "local defendants"). The class action lawsuit alleged that the defendants and their predecessors, from 1933 through the present, established and perpetuated *de jure* racial segregation in Baltimore's public housing. . . .

Pending is the motion by plaintiffs to compel the local defendants to provide responsive answers to Rule 33 and Rule 34 discovery requests. . . . The dispute presents issues of first impression regarding the December 1, 2000 changes to the Federal Rules of Civil Procedure governing the scope of discovery. . . .

. . . The most recent revisions to the discovery rules imposed changes intended to reach lingering concerns about the overbreadth and expense of discovery, and remind the courts and litigants of the fact that in determining what discovery should take place in a particular case, Rule 26(b)(1) is but the first step, necessarily followed by balancing the Rule 26(b)(2) factors. Accordingly, the December 1, 2000 changes to Rule 26(b)(1) restricted the scope of discovery to unprivileged facts relevant to "the claim or defense of any party," unless the court determines that there is "good cause" to permit broader discovery relevant to the subject matter of the action, but not more directly connected to the particular claims and defenses. . . .

[C]ounsel should be forewarned against taking an overly rigid view of the narrowed scope of discovery. While the pleadings will be important, it would be a mistake to argue that no fact may be discovered unless it directly correlates with a factual allegation in the complaint or answer. Such a restrictive approach would run counter to the underlying purpose of the rule changes, as explained by the commentary, run afoul of Fed. R. Civ. P. 1, and undoubtedly do disservice to the requirement of notice pleading in Rule 8, as parties would be encouraged to plead evidentiary facts, unnecessary to a "short and plain statement of the claim showing that the pleader is entitled to relief," Rule 8(a)(2), simply to increase the likelihood of getting broader discovery. It equally is clear, however, that the new rule represents a change from the old version, and that, unless expanded by the court for good cause shown, it is intended that the scope of discovery be narrower than it was, in some meaningful way.

Lest litigants and the court become consumed with the philosophical exercise of debating the difference between discovery relevant to the "claims and defenses" as opposed to the "subject matter" of the pending action — the juridical equivalent to debating the number of angels that can dance on the head of a pin — the practical solution to implementing the new rule changes may be to focus more on whether the requested discovery makes sense in light of the Rule 26(b)(2) factors, than to attempt to divine some bright line difference between the old and new rule. Under this approach, when confronted with a difficult scope of discovery dispute, the parties themselves should confer, and discuss the Rule 26(b)(2) factors, in an effort to reach an acceptable compromise, or narrow the scope of their disagreement.

For example, if the plaintiff seeks discovery of information going back 20 years, and the defendant objects on the grounds of burden, a possible solution may be to agree first to produce information going back 5 years. Then, depending on the results of a review of the more recent information, if more extensive disclosure can be justified, based on the results of the initial, more limited, less burdensome, examination, it should be produced. . . .

The pending discovery dispute illustrates the points raised above. The plaintiffs have filed a sweeping lawsuit alleging discriminatory action by the defendants covering three quarters of a century, and involving all aspects of the public housing programs in Baltimore. . . . Plaintiffs, justifying their discovery requests, argue their broad entitlement to discovery relating to the whole of the dispute that is the basis for the litigation, without once attempting to identify which claims that survived the partial consent decree will be furthered by the requested information, or addressing the burden to the local defendants to produce it. Both parties seem content to leave it to the court to sift through the 56 page complaint and the 74 page partial consent decree to determine what discovery should be allowed. Moreover, although counsel for the parties undoubtedly have conferred in an effort to resolve or narrow the dispute, they have provided the court with nothing to show whether they have attempted to apply the Rule 26(b)(2) balancing factors to try to reach common ground, at least as to some of the areas of dispute. This will not do.

I am returning this dispute to the parties with guidance as to how they should meet and confer to attempt to resolve or narrow their differences. . . . [T]he parties are expected to focus their discussions not on their scope differences under Rule 26(b)(1), but instead on a particularized analysis of the burden/benefit factors of Rule 26(b)(2). In this regard, it seems clear that the challenged requests are too broad as stated, and need to be narrowed by a good faith analysis of which claims that survived the partial consent decree will be furthered by the discovery sought. Additionally, the local defendants are cautioned that, provided the plaintiffs

[handwritten marginal note: Plaintiff argument]

accommodate legitimate concerns of the local defendants regarding burden and expense, it is likely that for each of the discovery requests challenged on the basis of scope or burden, some discovery will be appropriate. However, unparticular-ized claims of burden or expense, as the court stated in *Marens*, will not suffice. If the local defendants claim that they cannot produce requested information because of burden, they must justify this claim with specific details that can be evaluated by the plaintiffs, and, if necessary, the court.

This means that the parties must set aside their differences as adversaries and make a good faith effort to reach common ground on the disputes. It strikes me that this case is a perfect example of how creative counsel can employ the phasing methods used by the Court in *Marens* to permit the plaintiffs to have access to some, but less than all, of the information they seek, with the understanding that if, following the initial, limited review, additional discovery would make sense under the Rule 26(b)(2) factors, it will be provided. Cost shifting or sharing also should be considered.

If, following their consultations, counsel find that there still are differences that cannot be overcome by negotiation, as likely will be the case, they will contact me, and a discovery conference will be set promptly. While I am mindful of the fact that the commentary to the recent rule changes emphasizes the need for the court actively to be involved in applying the Rule 26(b)(2) factors, this involve-ment necessarily must follow, not precede, the parties' own good faith efforts to do so. Therefore, if there is to be a discovery conference, the court will expect counsel to demonstrate that they have fully considered the cost/benefit factors, and made reasonable modifications of their positions to accommodate them. . . .

Poole v. Textron, Inc.

192 F.R.D. 494 (D. Md. 2000)

GAUVEY, United States Magistrate Judge.

This is a product liability case in which the plaintiff, Ryan W. Poole ("Poole"), has sued Textron, Inc. ("Textron") for alleged defects in a golf car, which resulted in serious injuries to him. . . .

Before the Court is plaintiff's request for attorneys' fees and other expenses related to the three substantive discovery motions and other sanctions: the motion for sanctions raising six instances of discovery abuse,[1] the motion to compel production of documents and the motion to determine sufficiency of answers and objections to requests for admissions. . . .

---

1. These instances of discovery abuse are incomplete document production, failure to provide accurate interrogatory answers, lack of diligent search for documents and failure to provide a corpo-rate designee able to address all specified areas of inquiry, defendants' refusal to answer questions at the deposition, defendants' lack of candor with the Court and counsel and Textron's attempt to conceal the existence of the 1998 GX-440 golf car in its possession.

For the reasons stated below, the Court awards $37,258.39 in expenses, including attorneys' fees, but declines to award any other sanction under the rules or its inherent power.

II.   *Governing Law* . . .

As Textron acknowledged, this Court has authority to redress discovery misconduct under the Federal Rules as well as under its inherent powers, and can impose a range of sanctions from award of expenses against both a party and its counsel to an entry of a default judgment. The sanction, of course, depends on the nature of the discovery abuse. . . .

As to plaintiff's motions to compel and to test the sufficiency of the answers and objections to the request for admission, Fed. R. Civ. P. 37 governs both the entitlement to expenses and the amount of such expenses. If such a motion is granted, the Rule provides, in pertinent part:

> [T]he Court *shall* . . . require the party or deponent whose conduct necessitated the motion or the party or attorney advising such conduct or both of them to pay to the moving party the *reasonable expenses* incurred in making the motion, *including attorneys' fees, unless* the Court finds that the motion was filed without the movant's first making a good faith effort to obtain the disclosure or discovery without court action, or that the opposing party's non disclosure, response or objection was substantially justified, or that other circumstances make an award of expenses unjust.

Fed. R. Civ. P. 37(a)(4)(A) (emphasis added). Where, as here, the motion is granted in part and denied in part, the court shall "apportion the reasonable expenses incurred in relation to the motion among the parties and persons in a just manner." Fed. R. Civ. P. 37(a)(4). The Court has determined that there was no substantial justification for Textron's nondisclosure, responses and objections and that there were no circumstances that made an award of expenses unjust.

Similarly, Rule 26(g)(3) provides, in pertinent part, that "if without substantial justification a certification is made in violation of the rule, the Court, upon motion or upon its own initiative *shall* impose upon the person who made the certification, the party on whose behalf the disclosure request, response, or objection is made, or both, an *appropriate sanction* which *may* include an order to pay the amount of *reasonable expenses* incurred because of the violation, *including a reasonable attorney's fee*." (emphasis added). By its language, Rule 26(g)(3) does not limit a court to the award of expenses only, but gives the Court latitude to fashion an "appropriate sanction," in addition to an award of expenses. Nevertheless, an award of attorneys' fees appears to be the sanction most commonly imposed in reported decisions. See Gregory P. Joseph, Sanctions: The Federal Law of Litigation Abuse §44(B) (3d ed. 2000). The Court has determined that while counsel for Textron signed the various discovery responses, counsel had not conducted the requisite "reasonable inquiry" and that the quality of the responses suggested an improper purpose, specifically "to cause unnecessary delay or needless cost of litigation." Fed. R. Civ. P. 26(g). Accordingly, there was no substantial justification for the certifications in violation of the rule. Thus, in the absence of certain findings (which the court does not make here), the rules direct the imposition of a sanction. . . .

III.   Plaintiff's Motion for Determination of Sufficiency of Answers and Objections to Plaintiff's Request for Admissions

Regarding plaintiff's motion for determination of the sufficiency of Textron's answers and objections to plaintiff's request for admissions, the Court finds under Rule 37, in conjunction with Rule 36, that Textron's responses or objections were not substantially justified. To the contrary, with one exception, the responses and objections appeared crafted to sabotage the legitimate use of request for admissions. Under the plain language of the rule, a party must *either* lodge an objection *or* an answer to a request, but cannot do both.

Pursuant to the requirements of Rule 36(a), the answering party that objects to a request for admissions does so at its own peril. That is, Rule 36(a) mandates that a *"matter is admitted unless . . . a written answer or objection"* is served on the requesting party. (Emphasis added). Rule 36 also states, in detail, the requirements for denials, objections, partial admissions, and qualified answers. Failure to adhere to the plain language of this statute requires that the fact in question be admitted.

Rule 36 expressly permits a party to qualify an answer, but only "when good faith requires." . . .

In almost every response, Textron impermissibly lodged both an objection and an answer. Moreover, when Textron filed an answer, its complexity "undermine[d] the efficacy of the rule by crediting disingenuous, hairsplitting distinctions whose unarticulated goal is unfairly to burden an opposing party." *Thalheim*, 124 F.R.D. at 35 (citations omitted).

Accordingly, this Court believes the defendant's responses and objections lacked substantial justification. As the Court granted relief as to 12 out of the 13 contested requests (or 92% of the requests), the Court grants that percentage of the attorney time and expenses reasonably related to this motion. See Fed. R. Civ. P. 37(a)(4).

IV.   Plaintiff's Motion for Sanctions

In his motion for sanctions filed pursuant to Rule 37 and the inherent powers of the Court, plaintiff charged that defendant Textron engaged in "improper discovery tactics [which] were willful, inexcusable and not in good faith" and asked for a finding of liability, or alternatively certain relief tailored to each of the alleged instances of discovery abuse. The Court found that many of plaintiff's complaints of discovery abuse were meritorious, and ordered considerable relief in terms of further investigation and production of discovery responses.

A.   Textron's Lack of Diligence in Providing Key, Requested Information

The conduct this Court has found sanctionable violates Fed. R. Civ. P. 37, and, in some instances, Fed. R. Civ. P. 26(g) as well. Particularly egregious was

Textron's lack of diligence in providing key, requested information, such as prior litigation involving the golf car model or testing whether in its response to requests for production of documents or its identification of designees for the corporation's deposition on these same subjects.

1. Textron's Responses to Plaintiff's Requests for Production

This Court has concluded, as plaintiff states, that "Textron did not perform an even minimally-adequate search for documents prior to Plaintiff's Motion for Sanctions." At the Court's request, Textron described its efforts to locate documents and information requested by plaintiff. Review of Textron's seven page single space letter showed half-hearted, scatter-shot inquiries prior to the court-ordered investigation and inquiry efforts — oftentimes only reacting to leads that plaintiff's counsel provided about Textron's prior litigation involving the same or similar golf cars or testing of the golf car type at issue. That letter did not dispel the Court's previously held impression that Textron's initial inquiry in response to written discovery requests (as well as Rule 30(b)(6) corporate designation) started and largely, if not entirely, stopped with an inquiry to Mr. Gerald W. Powell, a Textron reliability engineer and EZGo's designee in golf car litigation since 1981 and with a review of the official corporate records of Textron. It appears that Textron did not even contact its own employees in other corporate departments, such as the manager of Textron's Commercial and Media Relations, to respond to the document requests or requests attached to the corporate designee notice. While Textron did contact some prior counsel to locate documents in prior lawsuits (but not to prepare Mr. Powell to testify more knowledgeably on prior lawsuits), it appears that those contacts were in response to information that plaintiff's counsel provided, not the result of any systematic inquiry to fully answer the discovery.

[The opinion detailed the voluminous documents produced after a court order and plaintiff's suggestions about various sources of information within the defendant corporation.]

Rule 26(g) of the Federal Rules of Procedure defines the duty of counsel in responding to discovery requests. That is, counsel must make "a reasonable effort to assure that the client has provided all the information and documents responsive to the discovery demand." Advisory Committee Notes to 1983 Amendments to Rule 26(g). "What is reasonable is a matter for the Court to decide on the totality of the circumstances." Id.[11] "[U]nder Rule 26(g)(2) . . . [the subject of the

---

11. The objective standard requires that the attorney signing the discovery documents under Rule 26(g)(2) make only a reasonable inquiry into the facts of the case. Counsel need not conduct an exhaustive investigation, but only one that is reasonable under the circumstances. Relevant circumstances may include: (1) the number and complexity of the issues; (2) the location, nature, number and availability of potentially relevant witnesses or documents; (3) the extent of past working relationships between the attorney and the client, particularly in related or similar litigation; and (4) the time available to conduct an investigation. Dixon v. Certainteed Corp., 164 F.R.D. 685, 691 (D. Kan. 1996); see also 6 Moore's Federal Practice, §26.154 [a]. Here, the Court ordered the detailed, documented search it did in part due to its loss of confidence in the good faith efforts of defendant to that date.

inquiry] is the thoroughness, accuracy and honesty (as far as counsel can reasonably tell) of the responses and the process through which they have been assembled." (G. Joseph §42(c), p. 541). In this case, it is clear that defendant's counsel did not make a reasonable effort under the Rule to assure that its client had complied fully with plaintiff's discovery requests and obtained all documents within its possession, custody and control. . . .

[The opinion went on to identify several other substantial and unjustified failures as described in footnote 1 to comply with plaintiff's discovery requests.]

VI. *An Award of Reasonable Attorneys' Fees and Costs Is the Appropriate Sanction*

In an attempt to ward off any sanction, Textron represents to this Court that its counsel spent at least 154.6 hours on document collection and investigation efforts to comply with the Court's May 22, 1999 Order, at a cost to Textron of $23,260, and argues that "it has now cured (at considerable expense) all deficiencies found by the Court and that an award of sanctions could, under the circumstances, be unjust." Such an interpretation of the rules would encourage sharp practices and dilatory responses to legitimate discovery demands. If the only sanction for failing to comply with the discovery rules is having to comply with the discovery rules if you are caught, the diligent are punished and the less than diligent, rewarded. Indeed, Rule 37 itself defeats such an interpretation, as it provides, *inter alia*, that the Court shall award the moving party fees if the discovery is provided by ruling or simply after the motion is filed. Fed. R. Civ. P. 37(a)(4)(A). *[handwritten in margin: Defense arguments]*

This is clearly not a situation where justice should be tempered by mercy, given the comparative resources of the plaintiff and defendant, and the inescapable conclusion that Textron's stonewalling on discovery played on that disparity. . . .

However, the Court declines to award sanctions beyond those provided in Rules 37(a) and 26(g) because this Court has stopped short of finding that Textron or its counsel acted with bad faith, and because Textron has not directly violated a court order, as it had in the case of Winters v. Textron, Inc., 187 F.R.D. 518 (M.D. Pa. 1999). In cases of bad faith, courts have ordinarily found direct (and often repeated) violation of court orders. . . .

However, the fact that the Court did not find bad faith does not minimize the wrongheadedness of the conduct of Textron and its counsel or suggest lenience in the imposition of the Rule delineated sanctions. The Court recognizes there is an unquantifiable but real prejudice to plaintiff in the motions practice that Textron's conduct necessitated and the litigation disadvantages of the delayed and staged receipt of discovery that was its consequence. For example, depositions are taken without the benefit of later received discovery. That later received discovery might have eliminated whole areas of inquiry or suggested entirely different questioning at deposition. In that situation, a lawyer is faced with the dilemma of whether to spend the time and expense to seek another deposition session or "to make do." Or, belatedly received information may impact an expert's opinion, requiring additional analysis and a further report and even a further deposition. . . .

A significant sanction award is crucial to vindicate the important principles of fair play in the largely private world of civil discovery. In complex litigation such as this, cases are shaped, if not won or lost, in the discovery phase. The rules of discovery must necessarily be largely self enforcing. The integrity of the discovery process rests on the faithfulness of parties and counsel to the rules — both the spirit and the letter. . . . The rules of procedure (and attorneys' duty to adhere to them) apply with equal force to decisions made in private discussions behind closed doors in a client's office on how much effort to expend to answer the opposing party's discovery, as to attorney conduct in the bright light of open court. . . .

Based on its independent analysis [which included affidavits from lawyers in the Baltimore area about the hourly fees customary for lawyers with the experience of plaintiff's and a consequent reduction of some of the fees sought by plaintiff], this Court has concluded that the attorneys' fees and other expenses requested are, in the main, justifiable. . . .

For all these reasons, the Court imposes a monetary sanction of $37,258.39 jointly and severally against Andrew Gendron of Goodell, DeVries, Leech and Gray and Textron, Inc.[24] Mr. Thomas M. Goss is jointly and severally liable with Mr. Gendron and Textron for $4,206.24 of that $37,258.39, which are the fees and costs associated with the motion to determine the sufficiency of answers and objections to requests for admission. . . .

NOTES AND PROBLEMS

1. Two judges in the same judicial district face similar discovery disputes: Defendants have failed to produce documents sought by plaintiffs. One judge declines to rule on the motion and sends the case back with a lecture on cooperation and creativity; the other imposes substantial monetary sanctions. Why the difference in treatment?

a. Both judges are applying the same Rules, which give the court broad discretion over discovery. In part, the difference may be a matter of judicial "style." If so, do you think one is preferable to the other?

b. Or, the difference may have to do with the stage at which the dispute comes to the court. At what stage of litigation did the *Thompson* plaintiff seek judicial intervention? The *Poole* plaintiff?

2. Both rulings are interlocutory, a circumstance that has at least two implications.

a. Neither ruling will be immediately appealable to a court of appeals. Because these cases were decided by federal magistrate judges, the losing parties may seek relief from the federal district judge who assigned these matters to the magistrate, but

---

24. While the Court would have preferred to award the expenses against the firm and its client, the language of Rules 37 and 26 does not permit that. Unlike Fed. R. Civ. P. 11 which specifically authorizes the imposition of the sanction on the law firm, in addition to or in lieu of the individual lawyer, neither Rule 37 nor Rule 26 contains such a specific authorization. In light of that fact and the precedent of Pavelic & LeFlore v. Marvel Entertainment Group, 493 U.S. 120, 110 S. Ct. 456, 107 L. Ed. 2d 438 (1989), this Court is constrained to award the expenses against the specific lawyers representing Textron and/or Textron itself.

that judge may overturn the magistrate only if it is shown that "the magistrate's order is clearly erroneous or contrary to law." 28 U.S.C. §636(b)(1)(A).

b. Neither ruling ends the case on the merits. Both cases will continue, perhaps requiring further hearings before the magistrate judge or federal district judge. Because the cases will continue, it is easy to overlook the effect of these rulings. Suppose you represent either of the parties in *Thompson*, and have another discovery dispute: How comfortable will you be seeking relief from Magistrate Judge Grimm? Or suppose you are Textron's lawyers in *Poole* and have a situation like that in Beeck v. Aquaslide, in Chapter VI, in which you seek to amend your answer to deny manufacture of the golf cart that allegedly cause the injuries. Rule 15 says that amendments should be granted "freely when justice so requires." How might this discovery ruling affect the court's view of what "justice . . . requires"?

3. Both cases also exemplify a problem facing any lawyer representing a large institution — public or private. Institutions run on documents and records, both paper and digital.

a. The institution's lawyer will at an early stage of the case identify and disclose those documents that support her client's claim or defense, as required by Rule 26(a)(1).

b. But the other side will of course be much more interested in documents that harm your client. A natural tendency, though one to be avoided if you want to stay out of the kind of trouble in which Textron's lawyers found themselves, is to respond to requests for documents by contacting only the most obvious persons and to produce only what they deliver.

c. The *Poole* court implies that course of action was part of a conscious pattern of nonresponsiveness, and perhaps it was. But it can also result from the failure to confront one's own client, to push past the obvious and to identify all possible sources of information. That can involve some uncomfortable conversations with the client, but it has two virtues to recommend it.

d. First, it can avoid the kind of sanctions imposed in *Poole*. There's much to be said for that as a matter of professional standing: The bars of many states require lawyers to report to the state bar all instances of sanctions imposed.

e. Second, knowing the worst early can avoid nasty surprises further down the line. We can assume that Textron's lawyers had decided, on the basis of then-available documents, on a defense strategy. Suppose that strategy was that there were no engineering studies identifying the hazard that allegedly injured Poole, and that, in the absence of any such studies, the product was not unreasonably dangerous under the prevailing standards of product liability. If Textron's lawyers plan their strategy in this way and then, in addition to having to pay $35,000 in sanctions, learn that there were engineering studies suggesting the defect, they have even bigger problems.

f. Does this scenario suggest what the lawyers for the defendants in *Thompson* should do, well before they meet with the other side to explore creative and cooperative resolutions to their discovery problems?

4. *Thompson* also suggests a potential problem in lawyer interaction. The judge has ordered the parties to cooperate in resolving their discovery issues. But

suppose they meet and one side behaves as if it has seen too many *Rambo* movies: demanding information that is clearly undiscoverable, refusing to supply information that is clearly discoverable, missing deadlines, making oral agreements that it then "forgets" if they are not put in writing, and so on.

a. How does the other side respond? One possibility is to play tit for tat, behaving as unreasonably and outrageously as one's adversary. That's tempting, but probably a mistake. The difficulty is that, when one of you finally drags the other into court, the judge may reasonably conclude that both sides are behaving like infants and refuse to help either one. That won't advance your cause much.

b. The much more difficult but ultimately effective approach is to behave reasonably and cooperatively yourself, carefully documenting both your own reasonableness and your adversary's unlawful pattern of behavior. You want, if the case finally comes before the judge, for it to be equally clear that you have behaved cooperatively and that your adversary has not. That course of action will require great self-restraint, but is likely to be more effective than hurling yourself into the mud with your adversary.

Having looked at some of the obstacles to the smooth functioning of discovery, step back and consider its place in the larger scheme. If pleading and discovery do their job, the lawsuit will be in a paradoxical state: It will be ready for trial, but trial will probably not occur. The next three chapters focus on those outcomes and explain the paradox. Chapter VIII looks at formal and informal ways in which the parties may avoid trial. Chapters IX and X look at trial itself.

The paradoxical consequences of discovery come from its dual role. It aims to prevent surprise at trial and to assure that cases will be resolved justly on their merits. Surprise witnesses make good courtroom drama but do not reassure us that justice has been done. In this trial-oriented role, discovery aims at laying bare both the parties' positions and the facts of the case.

In its other guise, discovery aims to put the parties in a position from which they can realistically assess the merits. In an ideal world such assessments would match (that is, the parties would both accurately predict the results of a trial). When that happens, the parties will often settle. The next chapter explores the dynamics of settlement. When the parties' assessments of the merits are inaccurate or mismatched, settlement is unlikely, but other mechanisms, like summary judgment, may use the products of discovery to end the case.

Still other parties may be so averse to the litigation process — including abuses of discovery — that they seek to take themselves outside the adjudicatory system. United States law gives them amazing freedom to do so in recognizing a number of contractual alternatives to litigation.

The next chapter explores both the voluntary and involuntary ways in which litigation may be avoided altogether or in which it can end without a trial.

RESOLUTION WITHOUT TRIAL

VIII

"A trial is a failure,"* write two lawyers. What they might mean and whether they are right will provide the focus of this chapter. Applied to contemporary U.S. litigation, the quoted statement looks in two directions. It can refer, as the authors of the statement intended, to the parties' inability to settle or, failing that, their inability to agree on a method of resolving their dispute outside the formal litigation processes. Alternatively, it can refer to the procedures that the formal litigation process itself uses to end lawsuits without a trial.

The last few decades have seen new interest in unofficial ways of resolving disputes. Such systems have grown in number and interest in them has intensified. This world, which some say is replacing ordinary litigation, presents both the best and worst of potential human creativity. On the one hand, it suggests that people can resolve disputes economically and creatively. Imaginative arbitration and mediation systems and creative settlements exemplify this side of the coin. On the other hand, it can demonstrate one-sidedness, greed, and disregard for basic human fairness, samples of which we shall also see in this chapter.

In other cases, however, parties cannot agree either on a system of dispute resolution or a settlement, creative or otherwise. What then? A hundred and fifty years ago, the answer was clear: trial. But trials are expensive; even a short trial will cost thousands of dollars in lawyers', witnesses' and jurors' fees, and judicial time. So in the last half-century procedural systems have consequently sought to avoid unnecessary trials. In this aim they largely succeed, some say too well; in the last fifty years the civil trial rate in the federal courts has fallen from about 20 percent — one in five filed suits — to just under 2 percent — one in fifty filed suits. Figures for the state courts, which handle about 98 percent of civil litigation, are comparable.

What happens to the rest of the lawsuits — those that don't settle? Many filed cases end with adjudicated dispositions other than trial. Although trial rates have dropped, the rate of adjudicated cases in federal courts has remained constant for about fifty years, at about 30 percent of filed cases. Some of these adjudications will result from applications of principles you have already explored — Rule 12(b)(6) motions or dismissals for failure to comply with discovery orders, for example. Another possibility is the motion for summary judgment, a device invented in the nineteenth century and given new life (and teeth) in the last two decades.

---

* Samuel Gross & Kent Syverud, Getting to No: A Study of Settlement Negotiations and the Selection of Cases for Trial, 90 Mich. L. Rev. 319 (1991).

We start and end with the official litigation system, venturing outside it after we have established some baselines and some points of connection between the official and the alternative systems.

A.   The Pressure to Choose Adjudication or an Alternative

Why do lawsuits ever proceed beyond the complaint? Defendants accused of wrongdoing might just ignore the allegations, if there were no way of forcing a response. Conversely, plaintiffs might file meritless suits that they would leave hanging over defendants' heads were there not some way of forcing them to proceed to a conclusion. The procedural devices that force the parties to engage and respond to each other are the bookends of an adversarial system in which the parties rather than the court have primary responsibility for the progress of litigation. There are two such devices: the default judgment, designed to goad the defendant into action; and the involuntary dismissal, intended to keep the plaintiff from going to sleep at the litigative switch. Versions of such principles are found in Rule 55 (for default judgments) and Rule 41(b) (involuntary dismissal).

1.   Default and Default Judgments

Read Rule 55 and consider the following problems.

NOTES AND PROBLEMS

1. Your client, Paula Houston, is involved in an automobile accident with Darlene Magnus. Darlene's insurance carrier, Ace Insurance Company, contacts your client after the accident. You discuss the case with Ace and exchange some letters and medical reports. About six months after the accident, you conclude that the case can't be settled without litigation, and you bring a claim in the appropriate federal district court.

a. You serve Magnus with process. Read Rule 12(a)(1)(A). Twenty days pass, and you have not heard from defendant. What, if anything, should you do? See *First Interstate Bank v. Service Stores of America*, 128 F.R.D. 679 (W.D. Okla. 1989) (unprofessional conduct to take default on first possible day).

b. You request a waiver of service (see Rule 4(d) and Form 1A), and the defendant signs and returns the waiver form (see Form 1B) but files no answer. How long must you wait before being justified in seeking a default judgment?

2. It is now three months after filing the complaint and serving Magnus, and you still have heard nothing. You decide to take a default judgment.

a. State precisely the steps you must take to obtain it.

b. Rule 55(a) provides that the clerk may "enter [a] . . . default" against a party who has failed "to plead or otherwise defend." Rule 55(b)(1) provides that a "default judgment" for a sum certain may be entered against a defendant who "has been defaulted for failure to appear." Rule 55(b)(2) has a similar reference to "appearance." What does it mean to "appear" in an action where one has failed to plead or defend?

3. Defendants often ask plaintiffs for more time to answer than is provided for in Rule 12(a). Plaintiffs are often ready to grant such extensions, particularly if they think that defendant will use that time to decide whether to make a settlement offer. Suppose you represent a defendant who comes to you with a complaint.

a. Time is running: In the absence of an extension, how long do you have to file an answer?

b. After discussing the case with your client, you call the plaintiff's attorney, with whom you've not previously dealt, and have a relatively cordial conversation, in which she agrees to extend the time to answer for a month. Relieved, you hang up and turn to some other pressing work on your desk. What risk are you running, and what should you have done to avoid it?

4. Assume plaintiff obtains a default judgment. What does it actually accomplish? See Rules 55(c) and 60(b).

a. In some civil law systems, default operates as a general denial — that is, the plaintiff must still satisfy the court that the facts justify granting relief. By contrast, in the United States a default operates as an admission of liability. See Hughes Tool Co. v. Trans World Airlines, 409 U.S. 363 (1973). What does this contrast say about party responsibility, the role of the court, and the concept of a lawsuit?

b. Even though a default judgment resolves the question of liability, questions can arise when the court is asked to grant relief. See Rule 55(b)(2). In an action to recover a debt, for example, the judgment will be for the amount owed plus statutory or contractual interest. The situation becomes more complicated when the amount of damages is uncertain, as in a typical accident case. Under these circumstances, the plaintiff must then "prove up" damages. See Rule 55(b)(2). In *Hughes Tool*, supra, a special master heard extensive testimony before awarding $145 million in antitrust damages after the defendant defaulted by refusing to cooperate with discovery. What are the limits on defendants' ability to use this "prove-up" stage to avoid the default judgment? For example, in a libel case, could a defendant try to minimize damages by showing that there was no libel?

5. Despite the system's reliance on default to force the defendant to get on with the job, the courts display real discomfort at entering judgment for reasons that fall so far short of the merits. The next case explores limits on the courts' power to force the parties toward adjudication on the merits.

Peralta v. Heights Medical Center

485 U.S. 80 (1988)

Justice WHITE delivered the opinion of the Court.

Heights Medical Center, Inc. (hereafter appellee) sued appellant Peralta in February 1982, to recover some $5600 allegedly due under appellant's guarantee of a hospital debt incurred by one of his employees. Citation issued, the return showing personal, but untimely, service. Appellant did not appear or answer, and on July 20, 1982, default judgment was entered for the amount claimed, plus attorney's fees and costs.

In June 1984, appellant began a bill of review proceeding in the Texas courts to set aside the default judgment and obtain the relief. In the second amended petition, it was alleged that the return of service itself showed a defective service[2] and that appellant in fact had not been personally served at all. The judgment was therefore void under Texas law. It was also alleged that the judgment was abstracted and recorded in the county real property records, thereby creating a cloud on appellant's title, that a writ of attachment was issued, and that, unbeknownst to him, his real property was sold to satisfy the judgment and for much less than its true value. Appellant prayed that the default judgment be vacated, the abstract of judgment be expunged from the county real property records, the constable's sale be voided, and that judgment for damages be entered against the Medical Center and Mr. and Mrs. Paul Seng-Ngan Chen, the purchasers at the constable's sale and appellees here.

Appellee filed a motion for summary judgment asserting that in a bill of review proceeding such as appellant filed, it must be shown that the petitioner had a meritorious defense to the action in which judgment had been entered, that petitioner was prevented from proving his defense by the fraud, accident, or wrongful act of the opposing party, and that there had been no fault or negligence on petitioner's part. Although it was assumed for the purposes of summary judgment that there had been defective service and that this lapse excused proof of the second and third requirement for obtaining a bill of review, it was assertedly necessary, nevertheless, to show a meritorious defense, which appellant had conceded he did not have.

. . . . "An elementary and fundamental requirement of due process in any proceeding which is to be accorded finality is notice reasonably calculated, under the circumstances, to apprise interested parties of the pendency of the action and afford them the opportunity to present their objections." Mullane v. Central Hanover Bank & Trust Co. [supra page 146]. Failure to give notice violates "the most rudimentary demands of due process of law."Armstrong v. Manzo, 380 U.S. 545, 550 (1965). See also . . . Pennoyer v. Neff.

The Texas courts nevertheless held, as appellee urged them to do, that to have the judgment set aside, appellant was required to show that he had a meritorious defense, apparently on the ground that without a defense, the same judgment would again be entered on retrial and hence appellant had suffered no harm from the judgment entered without notice. But this reasoning is untenable. As appellant asserts, had he had notice of the suit, he might have impleaded the employee whose debt had been guaranteed, worked out a settlement, or paid the debt. He

---

2. The petition alleged that the record contained a return of service of process, showing that service was effected more than 90 days after its issuance, contrary to Texas Rule of Civil Procedure 101. . . . Texas courts have held that service after the 90th day is a nullity, depriving the court of personal jurisdiction over the defendant.

would also have preferred to sell his property himself in order to raise funds rather than to suffer it sold at a constable's auction.

Nor is there any doubt that the entry of the judgment itself had serious consequences. It is not denied that the judgment was entered on the county records, became a lien on appellant's property, and was the basis for issuance of a writ of execution under which appellant's property was promptly sold, without notice. Even if no execution sale had yet occurred, the lien encumbered the property and impaired appellant's ability to mortgage or alienate it; and state procedures for creating and enforcing such liens are subject to the strictures of due process. Here, we assume that the judgment against him and the ensuing consequences occurred without notice to appellant, notice at a meaningful time and in a meaningful manner that would have given him an opportunity to be heard. . . .

. . . The Texas court held that the default judgment must stand absent a showing of a meritorious defense to the action in which judgment was entered without proper notice to appellant, a judgment that had substantial adverse consequences to appellant. By reason of the Due Process Clause of the Fourteenth Amendment, that holding is plainly infirm. Where a person has been deprived of property in a manner contrary to the most basic tenets of due process, "it is no answer to say that in his particular case due process of law would have led to the same result because he had no adequate defense upon the merits." Coe v. Armour Fertilizer Works, 237 U.S. 413, 424 (1915). As we observed in Armstrong v. Manzo, supra, at 552, only "wip[ing] the slate clean . . . would have restored the petitioner to the position he would have occupied had due process of law been accorded to him in the first place." The Due Process Clause demands no less in this case.

The judgment below is reversed.

NOTES AND PROBLEMS

1.   *Peralta* has several layers.

a. As the Court frames the case, Mr. Peralta received no notice of the pending action. Thus framed, the argument for setting aside any resulting judgment seems easy. Recall the facts of Pennoyer v. Neff, which is cited in the opinion: So far as the record showed, Neff had never received notice of Mitchell's lawsuit. Could *Pennoyer* have been dealt with in the same way as *Peralta*, without the need to invent the law of personal jurisdiction?

b. The *Peralta* Court has to work hard to frame the issue that way, since, as the case's first paragraph and footnote 2 suggest, Mr. Peralta apparently did receive actual notice of the suit. Because the service took place beyond the 90-day period in which Texas deems the service to be effective it was, however, under Texas law "a nullity." If one views the case as one in which actual notice — though not valid service — was received, the case becomes harder. If one assumes that Mr. Peralta did receive such notice but took no steps to answer or otherwise defend the suit, does it really deny him due process to require that he show a meritorious defense as a prerequisite to setting aside the default judgment?

c. The Court's answer to that question is phrased in terms of "might haves": Mr. Peralta might have impleaded the employee; he might have worked out a settlement; he might have paid the debt; he might have sold the property himself. Would it be unconstitutional to ask Mr. Peralta to show that any of these events were likely? Would it be fair to ask him why he had ignored the summons?

2. *Peralta* demonstrates that courts, while prepared to enter default judgments, greatly prefer to see the parties engage on the merits of the dispute.

a. This preference means that parties seeking relief from defaults get them set aside if they can show some plausible reason (such as illness or family emergency) for failing to respond to the summons. See Rule 55(c).

b. Rule 55(c) also points to Rule 60(b), which permits the reopening of the case even after judgment is entered on a default. The easy Rule 60(b) cases are situations in which the defendant can show that she did not receive notice. Almost all courts hold the defendant's neglect in such circumstances to be "excusable" under Rule 60(b)(1).

c. Much harder are the cases in which the defendant is served and retains a lawyer — who then fails to respond to the complaint or to judicial orders. Some state statutes extend lenient treatment to some such instances; see, for example, California Code of Civil Procedure §473(b), which directs a court to set aside a default if defendant moves within six months and pays the other side's legal fees, unless it finds that the failure to answer was not the result of an attorney's mistake.

d. A harder-nosed approach is to leave the default in place and tell the client to sue his lawyer for malpractice. In theory damages in a successful malpractice action would cover any damages suffered as a result of the improperly entered default. And blown deadlines are a common staple of malpractice suits. But lawyers who habitually fail clients in such elementary ways are disproportionately likely to be uninsured or otherwise judgment-proof. Should the court then relieve the defendant of the default, thus burdening the plaintiff, who may have changed his position in reliance on the default judgment?

e. Consider the contortions of the Ninth Circuit in Community Dental Services, Inc. v. Tani, 282 F.3d 1164 (9th Cir. 2002). One dentist sued another for allegedly infringing his trademark, "SmileCare." The defendant's lawyer made some early appearances but repeatedly failed to file and serve an answer or otherwise comply with court orders; eventually the court entered a $2 million default judgment against Dr. Tani, who had been assured by his lawyers that the case was proceeding smoothly. With a new lawyer, Tani invoked Rule 60(b)(6) to have the judgment reopened. Tani conceded that his lawyers' actions were beyond the range of "excusable neglect" that would warrant reopening under Rule 60(b)(1). Instead, he argued that they constituted gross neglect, thus falling within the "other reason(s)" language of Rule 60(b)(6). A divided panel of the Ninth Circuit agreed, parting company with other circuits that take a harder line. The dissent protested that the *Tani* result made oatmeal out of the law, classifying lawyers' negligence as "excusable" (and thus within (b)(1)), inexcusable but not "gross" (and thus not warranting relief because not yet "extraordinary"), "gross" and therefore extraordinary and entitled to relief, or willful (which under existing case law would not warrant relief). A footnote in the case tells us that Tani's original lawyer — the one who failed to answer the complaint — resigned from the state bar with charges pending against him; it's a fair guess that he carried no malpractice insurance. Suppose Tani's lawyer had been a member of a prosperous and well-insured firm; would the court have come to the same result?

3. One circumstance distinguishes Mr. Peralta from that of other defendants who suffer default judgments: He challenged it. The vast number of such judgments are entered and not challenged; frequently these defendants do not consult lawyers. The most common default case involves a creditor's suit over an unpaid consumer debt. The debate is over the number of these defendants who have plausible defenses or counterclaims. If the number of such defenses is very low (if, that is, most defendants would inevitably suffer an adverse judgment), then the default judgment represents merely a shorter, cheaper route to that result. If, however, substantial numbers of these defendants have viable defenses, the entry of a default judgment represents a reproach to the legal system. The empirical data are scanty.

2.   Failure to Prosecute: Involuntary Dismissal

Involuntary dismissal does to plaintiffs what default does to defendants: It forces them to pursue the lawsuit to some resolution. In our largest state court system such dismissals occurred in almost 8 percent of all civil filings.* They sometimes result from plaintiffs' discovery that their cases are weaker than previously thought, sometimes from realization that litigation will be more expensive than thought.

In an ordinary lawsuit, defendant has something that plaintiff wants and can get only if the lawsuit proceeds. One might therefore think that a defendant would be quite happy to have a plaintiff who, after filing and serving the complaint, did nothing. Why might a defendant nevertheless feel aggrieved if a plaintiff commenced but then, perhaps distracted by other business, did nothing to prosecute the suit for several years? Imagine a variation on the facts in *Peralta*: The plaintiff files the suit, serves the defendant and puts a lien on his property, but instead of proceeding to a judgment, the plaintiff simply sits and waits. Mr. Peralta can't get the suit dismissed on the merits (recall he has no meritorious defense), but meanwhile he can't sell the property or borrow money on it because of the lien.

What can a defendant in such a situation do about it? Rule 41(b) provides for involuntary dismissal "for failure of the plaintiff to prosecute" (as well as on other grounds). Such a dismissal takes the lawsuit off the books. The question is, how lax must a plaintiff be before a judge should enter such a dismissal? In other words, when does "standard" foot-dragging become abandonment?

NOTES AND PROBLEMS

1. Consider some possible scenarios: In which ones would involuntary dismissal for failure to prosecute be justified?

* Judicial Council of California, Court Statistics Report (2002), Table 5a, 47-1.

a. *K* files suit against *F* in March 2004 (just as the statute of limitations is about to run), claiming fraud in a corporate transaction. Not all the named defendants are served, and at the end of June plaintiff seeks additional time for service because he needs to use discovery to find the present locations of some defendants. The extension is granted; in December 2004 plaintiff sends a defendant an interrogatory seeking the other defendants' addresses. It's returned in mid-January 2005. The remaining defendants are served in March and April 2005. In November 2005 the defendants move to dismiss the action for failure to prosecute, alleging that they have been prejudiced by the delay in service of process. Dismissal; long-footdragging showed bad faith.

b. Three years after a copyright infringement suit is filed, little action has taken place, in part because the parties assure the judge that they are close to settling. The judge orders plaintiff's counsel to report within thirty days about the progress toward settlement. He doesn't, and the judge dismisses the case for failure to prosecute and to obey court orders. Plaintiff appears pro se, alleging that his lawyer deceived him as to his diligence in prosecuting the case, and seeks relief under Rule 60(b)(6). Should the motion be granted?

2. As the preceding examples suggest, the cases involve widely differing factual situations, making it hard to pin down differences in legal standards for granting or denying involuntary dismissal. Moreover, trial courts frequently do not explain why they have dismissed a case, and appellate courts often state that they simply are deciding whether the trial court properly exercised its discretion.* In addition to relying on judicial discretion, some states attempt to deal with less than diligent plaintiffs by setting absolute deadlines. The California Code of Civil Procedure (West 2002) contains two examples:

> §583.210(a). The summons and complaint shall be served upon the defendant within three years after the action is commenced against the defendant.
> §583.310. An action shall be brought to trial within five years after the action is commenced against the defendant.

Even in the face of such absolute statements, however, much litigation has occurred over whether the opposing party has explicitly or impliedly waived such a deadline.

3. Default judgments and involuntary dismissals may present both claim preclusion and issue preclusion issues if plaintiff starts over or if there is litigation on a closely related matter. If, for example, plaintiff's action is dismissed for one of the reasons already discussed, should she be free to start over? If so, what issues, if any, have been determined in the prior "litigation"? See Chapter XII.

---

* Note that a trial court decision denying dismissal is not immediately appealable because, under 28 U.S.C. §1291, appeals lie only from "final decisions." This means that, in practice, a denial of dismissal will be reviewed only if the victorious party on the motion also wins the case on the merits. In such a case, the appellate court is most unlikely to find an abuse of discretion.

3.   Voluntary Dismissal

On the basis of the exposition so far, one might assume that both plaintiff and defendant were locked in adversarial combat until a conclusion of the suit. Not quite. Rule 41(a)(1)(i) allows a plaintiff to dismiss any time before the defendant answers, and Rule 41(a)(1)(ii) permits the plaintiff to dismiss a suit at any time if all the parties agree. Why would they agree? Suppose, as in Note 1(b) in the previous section, the parties are close to settling and want more time without distractions like discovery in which to negotiate. Such stipulated dismissals do not bar a later refiling of the suit unless there has been a previous dismissal or the dismissal itself contains a provision that bars refiling. Provisions barring refiling frequently result from successful settlement negotiations: In return for satisfaction, the plaintiff gives up her chance to pursue the suit or to refile it later.

What about the plaintiff who files suit, then realizes she needs to gather more evidence? The defendant is unlikely to agree to a dismissal for such purposes. Rule 41(a)(2) authorizes a voluntary dismissal after defendant answers only by permission of the court.

NOTES AND PROBLEMS

1. Two kinds of questions present themselves about such cost-free voluntary dismissals. First, one can ask why they are ever permitted. At common law, such dismissals made sense because they enabled a plaintiff who had a good claim but had brought the wrong writ to replead (e.g., to replead trespass instead of trespass on the case, assumpsit instead of debt). The justification for such false starts is much less clear in a system that permits easy joinder of claims and easy amendment. In such a system, one could easily justify a door that locked behind the plaintiff once she had begun a lawsuit: "Either pursue it to a judgment or settlement, or, if you abandon the suit, do so irrevocably." Why permit even one costless voluntary dismissal?

a. One possible reason is to give plaintiff a little breathing room to consider changed circumstances. Suppose software Inventor, having sued SoftWare Co. for infringement, learns that Inventor Two is about to sue *him* for infringement. Inventor may need some time to decide whether his suit should be dropped entirely, or, by contrast, whether he should now add Inventor Two as another defendant, perhaps bringing a more complex suit in a different jurisdiction.

b. Rule 41(a)(1)(i) allows the plaintiff voluntarily to dismiss at any time before the defendant has answered; after that point the court's permission or agreement of the other side is necessary. In one notorious case the availability of voluntary dismissal proved catastrophic for the defendant. In corporate control litigation between Texaco and Pennzoil — Texaco Inc. v. Pennzoil, 481 U.S. 1 (1987) — the plaintiff filed originally in a Delaware state court seeking a preliminary injunction. Defendant opposed the injunction but did not answer the complaint. When the court denied the injunction, using language suggesting the plaintiff would lose on the merits, the plaintiff quickly took a voluntary dismissal and refiled in Texas. A Texas jury eventually awarded the plaintiff $10 billion. This maneuver by the plaintiff would have been unavailable had Texaco answered the Delaware complaint. One account described the defendant's failure to answer as "one of the most expensive tactical errors ever committed in a lawsuit." * The moral, apparently, is that if a voluntary dismissal will harm your case, answer the complaint promptly and lock plaintiff into the forum.

2. Suppose defendant has answered and won't stipulate to a dismissal, thus making a Rule 41(a)(1) dismissal unavailable. Can the plaintiff still dismiss and then restart the litigation? Rule 41(a)(2) gives the judge broad discretion in deciding when to grant a voluntary dismissal after the defendant has answered. The case law surrounding this discretion does not produce clear rules but suggests that plaintiffs should not be permitted to bail out simply to avoid a loss on the merits. To use an extreme example, it would be an abuse of discretion for a trial court to permit a plaintiff to dismiss the suit voluntarily after the jury has returned a verdict for the defendant but before judgment has been entered. The hard questions arise not when there have been such determinations on the merits but when significant procedural issues have been decided. Consider two cases, in both of which the plaintiff sought to dismiss voluntarily after a procedural ruling that made plaintiff's case more difficult.

a. Maurice Manshack, the employee of an electrical contractor, was severely burned while working on Utility Co.'s high-voltage electrical pole and line in Louisiana. The Manshacks filed a lawsuit in the U.S. District Court for the Eastern District of Texas. Shortly after suit was filed, Mrs. Manshack was fired from her job with Utility Co. In the pretrial stage a critical issue was whether Texas or Louisiana law would apply. Louisiana law would handle Manshack's injury under workers' compensation, barring a tort suit; Texas would permit a tort suit. After the district court ruled that Louisiana law applied, the Manshacks sought voluntarily to dismiss the suit, refiling it in Texas state courts. The Fifth Circuit affirmed a district court order permitting the voluntary dismissal. Manshack v. Southwestern Electric Power Co., 915 F.2d 172 (5th Cir. 1990).

b. A child and his parents sued a pharmaceutical company, alleging injuries as a result of the child's grandmother's ingesting a drug given while she was pregnant with the child's mother. Ohio law applied to the case, and a diversity action was brought in federal court. Uncertain what Ohio law was on liability for preconception conduct, the district court certified the question to the Ohio Supreme Court. (For a description of certification of state law questions, see page 253). The Ohio Supreme Court held that the state recognized no such cause of action. The plaintiff thereupon sought permission to dismiss voluntarily, to allow him to file again in an Ohio state court in case the legislature changed Ohio law before the statute of limitations expired. The Sixth Circuit held that permitting a voluntary dismissal under those circumstances was an abuse of discretion. Grover v. Eli Lilly & Co., 33 F. 3d 716 (6th Cir. 1994).

c. Can *Grover* and *Manshack* be reconciled? Both deal with plaintiffs who sought to dismiss after adverse rulings on choice of law questions that looked bad

* Timothy Feltham, Tortious Interference with Contractual Relations: The Texaco Inc. v. Pennzoil Litigation, 33 N.Y.L. Sch. L. Rev. 111, 117, Note 65 (1988).

for the plaintiff. Was the Ohio Supreme Court decision more dispositive than the *Manshack* decision that Louisiana law applied? Or is it bad form to fire the wife of a badly injured plaintiff and then expect the court to be generous in rulings about whether one's litigative position has been "prejudiced"?

3. Many courts routinely require plaintiffs seeking a voluntary dismissal to pay the defendant's attorney's fees as a condition of granting the motion. The logic is fairly clear: Plaintiff initially chose the time and place of suit and has caused defendant at least the expense of retaining a lawyer and answering the complaint (recall that voluntary dismissals before an answer do not require leave of court). Now plaintiff has changed his mind, but remains free to sue again. Shouldn't plaintiff have to pay the cost of this vacillation? Should the Rule make this explicit? If the Rule did make it explicit, would it violate the Rules Enabling Act, 28 U.S.C. §2072(b) (prohibiting any Rule from modifying a "substantive" right)?

B. Avoiding Adjudication

Faced with the products of discovery and kept in engagement by procedural rules, parties may decide that they want to avoid adjudication. Indeed, given foreknowledge about procedural rules, they may decide well before any dispute arises that they wish to avoid litigation. The contemporary U.S. legal regime offers parties a broad set of ways to avoid litigation altogether or to escape from it once involved. Some would add that these alternatives have prevailed and that for most disputes adjudication occurs only under unusual conditions.

These escapes from adjudication, sometimes known as alternative dispute resolution (ADR), take us into a realm that lies beyond the boundaries of formal procedure. But even these alternatives depend on law for their effectiveness. They rely principally on contract: Because the courts will enforce contracts not to litigate or to litigate using special procedures, parties can choose some other mechanism to resolve their disputes. By refusing to hear a lawsuit filed in breach of such an agreement, courts force parties to use the agreed-on procedure or to abandon their dispute.

As a consequence, parties have enormous freedom to write their own procedural rules. To put the matter starkly, one can think of existing procedural rules as principles that come into play only if the parties have not otherwise agreed. The remaining parts of this section explore some of the paths opened by judicial enforcement of such alternative processes.

1. Negotiation and Settlement: Why Settle? And How?

Since the beginning of recorded legal systems, parties have regularly settled most of their disputes informally, without adjudication. Behind this fact lies a normative question. Settlements are cheaper and faster than trials. Are they also better — or are they merely a capitulation to expediency? Some argue that settlements are not just faster and cheaper but also qualitatively better, because consent is a basic principle of justice, and because settlements can take account of nuances and subtleties in the facts and in the parties' interests that would be lost at trial. On the other side are those who argue that settlement leaves the parties less satisfied than if a trier heard their stories, permits might to triumph over right, and deprives the public of definitive adjudication of issues that may reach beyond the individual case.

Whether because settlements are good or merely because they are cheap, lawyers frequently use them. They use them for at least two reasons. One reason for settlement is unattractive: What if a party simply runs out of funds to pursue the litigation? A settlement, getting something, may be better than getting nothing, which is what will happen if the case is dismissed, or being stuck with a default judgment, if the defendant is the side unable to pursue the case. How often does this happen? Reliable estimates are hard to come by, but there's evidence that cases collapsing without regard to the merits is a much rarer event than it used to be. As the materials in Chapter IV, suggest, modern litigation finance is relatively creative, the plaintiffs' bar better capitalized, and therefore the stock story of the meritorious plaintiff crushed by defendant's vastly superior resources is less true today than it once was.* It happens — particularly in bet-the-company cases, in which a defendant with ample resources thinks its continued existence is threatened by a lawsuit — but it's unlikely to occur in most litigation.

That leaves a second, more common and thus more important, reason for settling. Settlements control risk. Trial outcomes have two characteristics that make them risky: (a) they are significantly unpredictable and (b) they tend to be all-or-nothing. Even experienced lawyers have a hard time predicting how juries will decide a given case — keep in mind that summary judgment (infra page 513) will eliminate the clear cases, so the only cases that make it to trial should be those where the evidence doesn't point clearly in one direction. And the nature of substantive law tells judge and jury not to split the difference, but either to hold the defendant liable for all proximately caused damages or to find for the defense. That means that trial can result in either a catastrophe or a windfall for both parties, and no one knows which one. Exacerbating these two risks is the fact that trial is expensive. Not only is lawyers' time in trial expensive, but expert witnesses have to be paid, exhibits prepared, and witnesses' memories refreshed (in most jurisdictions a trial will come at least a year after suit is filed, which may be several years after the events in question). Moreover, in spite of judicial efforts to get parties to get discovery done well before trial, in many cases the approach will set off a flurry of additional discovery as lawyers scurry to shore up weak points in their cases, thus running expenses higher. So for many parties settlement is appealing because it provides a way of avoiding an expensive and risky ordeal — trial.

If they are to achieve their goals, whether of risk avoidance or of consensual justice, settlements have to be technically competent. Settlement agreements require both negotiating skill and knowledge of how parties can achieve their

---

* See Stephen Yeazell, Refinancing Civil Litigation, 51 DePaul L. Rev. 183 (2001).

goal once they come to agreement in principle. Unlike parties who are negotiating the sale of a building or the terms of an employment agreement, parties who are negotiating when a lawsuit is imminent or actually has been filed are likely to be somewhat annoyed with each other. Lawyers can contribute to negotiations by interposing a professional role that keeps the disputants from each others' throats long enough to work out an agreement. Or they can make things worse by becoming so personally embroiled with their counterparts that they prevent two clients, who might otherwise have agreed, from doing so! Whether they help or hinder agreement, however, lawyers can contribute expertise to the terms and the form of settlement, anticipating problems and preventing the settlement of one dispute from becoming the start of another.

Consider the problems in the context of an example that will provide a framework for the next several sections.

JANE SMART v. GROWCO, INC.

Jane Smart is a plant botanist. Until recently she worked at GrowCo, a relatively new, profitable, and expanding firm specializing in genetically modified crops. GrowCo has been much in the news recently, with favorable press reports and significant investor interest. Smart has been deeply involved in developing some of GrowCo's most successful crops. A dispute with the scientific director leads to her dismissal. Dr. Smart consults a lawyer and threatens to bring an action for unlawful discharge and employment discrimination, invoking Title VII of the federal Civil Rights Act. As the lawyers for both sides speak with their clients, the facts aren't one-sided. Plaintiff's story suggests that the senior vice-president and chief scientist at GrowCo has behaved in a way that's at least obnoxious (and will sound terrible to a jury) and is perhaps unlawful. But plaintiff's story also has some problems. It's not clear that she was an excellent employee before her dismissal, and her past involves some breaches of scientific ethics in testing genetically modified crops on humans that will make it easy for defendant to challenge her testimony and portray her as an untrustworthy person.

a. Contracting to Dismiss

The simplest form of settlement is a contract (sometimes called a release) in which the plaintiff (or prospective plaintiff) agrees not to bring a lawsuit or to drop one already filed. Most plaintiffs want something, typically money, in return for such agreements.

NOTES AND PROBLEMS

1. What does a settlement do for the parties?

a. For GrowCo? Besides the possibility of losing, what risks does a trial hold for this defendant?

b. For Smart? Does she have anything to lose besides a lawsuit?

c. For the parties' lawyers? Clients, not lawyers, are empowered to make settlement decisions, but clients often ask lawyers for advice. In the example above, it's likely that Smart's lawyer is working on a combination of fee arrangements — part retainer (many plaintiff's lawyers in such cases require some plaintiff contribution to these fairly risky cases), part contingent fee, both modified by the possibility that a prevailing plaintiff in a Title VII suit can collect reasonable attorney's fees from the losing defendant. (See Chapter IV, supra.) GrowCo's lawyer is probably being paid by the hour, perhaps by GrowCo directly, perhaps by its liability insurer, if it has coverage that includes such claims. If an insurer is involved, its lawyer may be operating with a fairly tight litigation budget, requiring the insurer's permission to take depositions, hire experts, or make certain kinds of motions.

2. Suppose, as often happens, the parties reach a settlement before suit is filed.

a. The parties might do so in a number of ways: a meeting of the lawyers, a series of telephone calls, an exchange of documents. One firm has opened an Internet site dedicated to settling lawsuits. Lawyers log on to the Web site and get a password. The defendant must list three possible settlement figures, in an ascending dollar order for which she will settle. Without knowing the defendant's figures, the plaintiff must list three figures in descending order for which he will settle. The program then matches each of the rounds of offers and "settles" the case if any set of figures falls within 20 percent or $5,000 of each other. The Web site claims to "eliminat[e] egos and posturing" (*http://www.cybersettle.com/about/about.asp*, site visited May 30, 2003).

b. Whether they reach agreement through an old-fashioned handshake or through cyberspace, do the parties need approval of their deal? No: In an ordinary case, the judge need not examine or approve the settlement, though they must grant — usually routinely — plaintiff's request to dismiss the case if that is part of the deal. Plaintiffs needing immediate funds may settle meritorious claims for trivial sums; defendants eager to get on with other matters may offer meritless or fraudulent plaintiffs substantial sums to end litigation. The exceptions to this "freedom to settle" arise in class actions (where Rule 23(e) requires judicial approval of settlements), in cases involving minors, where the court is required to approve settlements (see, e.g., Cal. Prob. Code §3500(b) (West 1999)), and in some multidefendant cases (see, e.g., Cal. Code Civ. Proc. §887.6 (West 1999)). What theory underlies these exceptions to the general rule of judicial indifference to the fairness of settlements?

c. Is the usual practice of judicial indifference defensible? Should judges be required to scrutinize all settlements for fairness? Before answering, imagine yourself as judge. Suppose a very common case — a rear-end vehicle collision in which plaintiff alleges soft-tissue injuries. Such injuries are common, but also commonly feigned. Defendant, represented by an insurer, has answered denying liability but has offered a small settlement. You, the judge, are asked to approve or disapprove the settlement. How would you reach a decision? What information would you want to have? Would your concern be substantive (is the settlement fair?) or procedural (did both parties know the material facts?)? Would the cost of gathering and presenting this information eliminate two of the chief advantage of settlement, speed and cheapness?

d. As a half-way step between trying to police all settlements and leaving matters entirely to the law of contract, legislators can build procedural protections into settlements of certain kinds of claims. For example, federal legislation regulates settlements releasing Age Discrimination in Employment Act (ADEA) claims: Offers must be clearly written; they must remain in effect for stated periods of time; they must advise employees to consult a lawyer; and they must give settling employees at least a week in which to revoke a signed settlement agreement. 29 U.S.C. §626(f). In Oubre v. Entergy Operations, Inc., 522 U.S. 422 (1998), the Court held that an employee who had released ADEA claims without these procedures could, without tendering back the money paid for a settlement, bring suit under the act.

e. Although there is no general doctrine requiring judicial approval of settlements, settlements are contracts and can be attacked on any of the grounds on which one can attack any contract: fraud, duress, mistake, incapacity, unconscionability, and the like.

3. Suppose you represent GrowCo in the hypothetical case of Smart v. GrowCo. You think the plaintiff's case is weak, but your client understands that litigating it will require hours of lost time consumed in depositions and may undermine the morale of other employees. She asks you to see if you can settle the case, inquiring what you think it will cost her.

a. How do you answer her question about cost? A good deal of it will depend on the merits of the case: How "good" or "bad" are the facts? How sympathetic and credible will the plaintiff and her supervisor be as witnesses? But some part of the response will depend on other factors. With all but the most sophisticated clients, one will need to persuade the plaintiff's lawyer as well as the plaintiff that the offer is good, if for no other reason than that the client is likely to ask the lawyer whether to accept the offer. The lawyer in turn may be influenced by such factors as how much effort he has already expended on the case. All other things being equal, the same settlement offer coming in before dollars and hours are invested in discovery or pretrial motions will look more attractive than it does on the eve of trial. For the same reason most defendants will offer somewhat less at the very early stages of a case.

b. After discussion, your client gives you a dollar figure she is willing to offer the Plaintiff to settle. You contact Smart's lawyer (ethical rules prohibit a lawyer's directly contacting a represented client), discuss a series of depositions you want to take, and, at the end of the conversation, ask whether there's any point in discussing settlement. (Some negotiation literature, and much lawyer's lore, says that one should never be the first to utter the dreaded "s" word, but you are unpersuaded by this.) The plaintiff says it might be possible, and after some haggling you reach a figure that the plaintiff's counsel is willing to recommend to his client. Assuming the plaintiff accepts, how will you actually effect the settlement?

c. The simplest way would be an oral agreement that plaintiff will drop the suit when she receives your client's check. This route is also an excellent way to assure that your former client sues you for malpractice. Why?

4. Assume now that you think you should draft a written settlement agreement. What should it say?

a. That the plaintiff should agree not to file a threatened lawsuit?

b. That, having filed suit, the plaintiff should seek a voluntary dismissal and agree not to refile the suit?

c. That, having filed suit, the plaintiff should consent to a dismissal with prejudice and, as added assurance, also agree not to refile the suit?

d. That, having filed suit, the plaintiff should stipulate to a judgment against her and also agree not to refile the suit?

5. All of these techniques are used to create settlements. Consider some of their advantages and disadvantages and the problems entailed by each.

a. Take first the prefiling agreement not to sue. In some respects this is the simplest and best form of settlement: By definition it eliminates all litigation costs. But this form of agreement also requires the lawyer carefully to define the scope of the threatened lawsuit. Consider the language of a stock auto accident release:

KNOW ALL MEN BY THESE PRESENTS: That the Undersigned, being of lawful age, for sole consideration of $ 2,431.18 TWO THOUSAND FOUR HUNDRED THIRTY ONE AND 18/100 DOLLARS to be paid to [Plaintiff] do/does hereby and for my/our/its heirs, executors, administrators, successors and assigns release, acquit and forever discharge [Defendant] his, her, their, or its agents, principals, servants, successors, [and a bunch more boilerplate variations] from any and all claims, actions, causes of action, demands, rights, damages, [and more boilerplate variations] whatsoever, which the undersigned now has/have or which may hereafter accrue on account of or in any way growing out of any and all known and unknown, foreseen and unforeseen bodily and personal injuries and property damage and the consequences thereof resulting or to result from the accident, casualty or event or the handling of any insurance claim or the defense of any legal proceeding arising out of said accident, which occurred on or about the 8th day of June 2004, at or near 1ST AT LARCHMONT, LOS ANGELES CA.

It is understood and agreed that this settlement is the compromise of a doubtful and disputed claim, and that the payment made is not to be construed as an admission of liability on the part of the party or parties hereby released, and that said releasers deny liability therefore and intend merely to avoid litigation and buy their peace.

b. First, suppose an unlikely occurrence: Having signed this release, plaintiff nevertheless files a lawsuit arising out of the same fender-bender. How does defendant get the court to give effect to the release? Read Rule 8(c) to see what allegations defendant would put in her answer. Then read Rule 56(b) and think about what documents would be attached to defendant's motion for summary judgment.

c. A more difficult problem arises if the parties have several claims, only some of which they want to settle. Suppose that Jane Smart has claims to a pension and that neither side wants now to calculate the value of that entitlement, which may involve complex contingencies. In such a situation, the lawyers will have to carve those other claims out of the agreement unless they can reach a global settlement. How would you redraft the release quoted in Note 5a so that it released the discrimination claims but left the pension issues unresolved?

6. Once suit has been filed, a settlement will call for an end to the lawsuit. A settlement achieved at this point saves less in the way of litigation costs, but it also has some advantages: It may save the defendant the cost and publicity of filing an answer — only the plaintiff's complaint will be on file with the court. Voluntary dismissal will end the lawsuit. But recall that Rule 41(a) permits a plaintiff taking a voluntary dismissal to refile the suit — just the result that a settlement seeks to avoid. To avoid this result, a settlement agreement at this stage will require the plaintiff to refrain from refiling this or any related lawsuit.

a. Suppose the defendant wants the lawsuit not only to go away but for the court to enter a judgment on the merits. A voluntary dismissal does not achieve that; involuntary dismissal, with prejudice, under Rule 41(b) does. An involuntary dismissal solves another problem as well: It acts as a judgment on the merits and allows the scope of the claim to be defined by the doctrines of former adjudication rather than by the contract of settlement. As you will see in Chapter XII, under modern doctrines of former adjudication, a claim adjudicated on the merits bars all related claims, whether or not they were stated in the complaint. Such a mode of dismissal also means that if the plaintiff files a second lawsuit, the defendant can invoke not just the contract of settlement but the doctrines of former adjudication to have the suit dismissed. Courts are often quite protective of suits that seem to be flouting their former judgments — an advantage to the defendant.

b. Consider one possible disadvantage of the simple dismissal with prejudice: Imagine that the settlement agreement calls for the parties to take some future action, perhaps to assist the employee to gain other employment, or perhaps to continue medical benefits for some period of time. The employer breaches that duty and the former employee wants to enforce it. How does he do so?

c. The usual answer is that the party seeking to enforce the settlement must sue for breach of contract, the contract in question being the settlement agreement. That suit must take its place at the back of the line of pending litigation: It gets no special attention by virtue of being a suit to enforce a settlement. Indeed, in federal court it may suffer a disadvantage. Jane Smart's original suit, for employment discrimination, could invoke federal question jurisdiction. But the suit to enforce the settlement contract does not arise under federal law, so Employee can invoke federal jurisdiction only if there is diversity between her and her employer and the amount in controversy is satisfied — probably not the case if only a continuation of medical benefits are at stake. See Langley v. Jackson State University, 14 F. 3d 1070 (5th Cir. 1994) (no federal jurisdiction to enforce settlement of federal civil rights claims).

d. If one anticipates such a problem, there is a solution. Suppose the obligation to pay medical benefits had been embodied in a judgment; in those circumstances either party can invoke the court's jurisdiction to enforce its own judgments. One can achieve the same effect through what is called a stipulated judgment or consent decree, a judgment that embodies the parties' agreement:

> The situation [of no jurisdiction to enforce the settlement] would be quite different if the parties' obligation to comply with the terms of the settlement agreement had been made part of the order of dismissal — either by separate provision (such as

a provision "retaining jurisdiction" over the settlement agreement) or by incorporating the terms of the settlement agreement in the order. In that event a breach of the agreement would be a violation of the order, and ancillary jurisdiction to enforce the agreement would therefore exist.

Kokkonen v. Guardian Life Insurance Co., 511 U.S. 375 (1994).

7. We have thus far assumed that settlement will end a lawsuit. That's not always so. Several forms of partial settlement have the effect not of avoiding but of guaranteeing trial.

a. The parties can agree — stipulate — to liability, but contest damages, leaving them to be tried. Why would a defendant do that? Consider the facts surrounding the wreck of the Exxon Valdez, an oil supertanker that ran aground in Alaskan water, polluting miles of shoreline and ocean. The captain of the vessel was shown to be drunk in his cabin during the critical time when course should have been changed through the tricky channel; worse, there was evidence suggesting that the defendant knew of the captain's alcoholism but continued to employ him. Why might Exxon decide to try only the question of damages?

b. Alternatively, the parties can do the opposite, stipulate to one of two damage figures, trying only the question of liability to the jury. Suppose plaintiff is severely injured in an auto accident, but liability is hotly contested. The parties might enter into a "high-low" agreement, in which defendant promises to pay a minimum amount (say $250,000) to plaintiff even if the jury returns a defense verdict. In return, plaintiff agrees that he will accept, say $750,000 (substantially less than the full cost of lifetime care) if the jury returns a plaintiff's verdict. Explain what each party is gaining from such a settlement.

8. Return to the facts of Jane Smart v. GrowCo. GrowCo wants the terms of the settlement — and even the fact of the suit — to remain confidential if possible. Smart wants compensation and continuing health coverage until she finds new employment, and for the employer not to give her a bad reference with other prospective employers.

a. Which form of settlement would best suit GrowCo's interests?

b. Which form would best suit Smart's interests?

b.   *Third-Party Participation in Settlement: Facilitation, Encouragement, and Coercion*

Settlement negotiations sometimes fail. Generally one can trace the failure of negotiations to two causes: divergent estimates of the outcome and bad communication. The parties may have different estimates of the result of litigation. For example, in Smart v. GrowCo either Smart or her lawyer may misjudge the likely reaction of a jury to her story. Or GrowCo's general counsel, perhaps because she is determined to show the board of directors that she is a strong executive, or to accede to the demands of the scientific director who threatens otherwise to quit, may be unwilling to settle. Alternatively, the parties may have similar guesses about the outcome of litigation but may not be communicating clearly, perhaps because their lawyers have taken a dislike to one another. Any of these circumstances can lead to the collapse of negotiations.

Sometimes, however, negotiations that would otherwise fail can succeed if the parties have help. Help comes in several forms, depending on the nature of the problem and the source of help. If the problem is communication, someone who can facilitate those communications may be able to help. Generically, such facilitators are called mediators. What does a mediator do? The narrowest definition of "mediation" sees it as assisted negotiation, aid in overcoming barriers to agreement.

One way to describe a mediator's role is to frame it entirely in terms of process: The mediator seeks to engage the parties in a structured set of discussions leading to agreement. Because the goal is an agreement of the parties, the mediator does not rule on the rights and wrongs of the dispute or tell the parties what to do. But the mediator's limited role is also a function of the fact that she has no coercive power: The mediator succeeds only if the parties agree. The mediator typically talks with the parties (sometimes together, sometimes individually, sometimes both), to ferret out areas of agreement and possible starting points for negotiations, to discover the respective parties' goals, and to suggest ways to accommodate these goals. The success of mediation depends partly on the level of trust the mediator is able to establish and partly on the distance separating the parties' goals.

In recent decades a cadre of professional mediators — many with legal training — has emerged, who offer their services to parties for a fee. Courts and legislatures have shown significant interest in the power of mediation to achieve settlements, and in some cases have established what sounds like a contradiction: mandatory mediation. For example, California statutes require all cases with less than $50,000 in controversy be sent to early mediation; only if the mediator reports that the parties have been unable to reach agreement will the case be calendared for trial. Cal. Code Civ. Proc. §§1730, 1775 et seq. (West 2002). In federal law the Alternative Dispute Resolution Act of 1998, 28 U.S.C. §§651 et seq. goes further by requiring each federal district court to "authorize[], . . . devise, and implement its own alternative dispute resolution program." 28 U.S.C. §651(b). The legislative intent becomes clear from a section instructing district courts to adopt a local rule that "require[s] litigants in all civil cases to consider the use of an alternative dispute resolution process at an appropriate state in the litigation" and to "provide litigants in all civil cases with at least one alternative dispute resolution process. . . ." The act goes on to require training of "neutrals," to help the parties come to agreement.

Family law — divorce, support, and custody disputes — has been a frequent target for such efforts. In one view, the popularity of mediation in this context reflects the fact that family conflicts by their nature are ideal for mediation; in another view, it is said to reflect the low importance attached to such cases by some judges and lawyers. Bear in mind, too, that some efforts described as mediation would be more accurately described as settlements arrived at under heavy pressure, in which the mediator threatens to report to the judge that one or another party is behaving unreasonably (sometimes called "muscle mediation").

NOTES AND PROBLEMS

1. Imagine that in Smart v. GrowCo the two parties, unsure whether to settle, have chosen a mediator, or that a court under one of the statutes described above has assigned one.

a. To begin work, what would Mediator want to know from the parties?

b. Some mediators might proceed by asking the parties how much (or how little) they would accept to settle the claim. Such mediation is sometimes called "positional" and treats settlement as a pie to be divided, in which anything gained by one party is lost by the other. Such mediators can be useful if the parties have engaged in significant bluffing, failing to disclose their true settlement positions.

c. Other mediators will proceed by trying to discover the parties' goals, defining these less in monetary than in other terms. This approach is sometimes called "interest" mediation. Suppose, for example, mediator learns from Jane Smart, the plaintiff, that she is primarily interested in coming away from this dispute with a clean reference that will enable her to find another job and the dignity of not having been fired for cause. GrowCo, on the other hand, wants to be able to recruit future plant botanists. Can you think of settlements that would achieve both goals?

2. After gathering and digesting information from Smart and GrowCo, Mediator works out a solution that maximizes each side's interest and announces the solution to the parties. Why might they be justifiably upset with Mediator's behavior?

3. As mediation proceeds, the parties come close to an agreement. Mediator believes, however, that GrowCo is taking unfair advantage of Smart's momentary financial weakness to drive a hard bargain.

a. Should that be a concern to Mediator if the two parties are satisfied with the agreement?

b. If so, on what theory?

4. How should a lawyer conduct herself in mediation? Some approach it like a case — presenting facts and arguments. Many mediators, particularly those employing interest mediation (see note 1c above) resist this, asking lawyers and parties to talk entirely of goals and desired outcomes, not facts and rights.

5. What if a party or lawyer in the course of mediation makes a statement of fact. If the mediation fails, can the other side later introduce the statement in evidence? Mediation agreements and statutes typically create evidentiary privileges for such statements.

6. How and when should judges act as mediators?

a. One might take the view that they never should — that judges should be adjudicators, pure and simple, and should leave any settlement to the parties or to figures like court-appointed mediators.

b. Whatever the merits of such a view, current procedural law does not support it. Two bodies of law allow a judge actively to manage litigation, personally and through delegates. Rule 16 (Pretrial Conferences; Scheduling; Management) establishes as one of its objectives "establishing early and continuing control so that the case will not be protracted because of lack of management" (Rule 16(a)(2)). Rule 16(c) contains a shopping list of management techniques ranging from establishing time limits to encouraging settlement. The Alternative Dispute

Resolution Act of 1998, 28 U.S.C. §§651 et seq., requires federal judicial districts to offer the parties, even after they have filed a suit, alternatives to litigation, such as mediation or non-binding arbitration (described below).

c. The Act's reference to "early neutral evaluation," §651(a), embodies a simple idea: Parties tend to have excessively optimistic evaluations of their cases; presenting one's case briefly to a neutral party who assesses its strengths and weaknesses will lead to a more realistic negotiating position. Such evaluators are typically volunteer lawyers or magistrate judges not otherwise involved in the case. By listening to the parties' cases, they offer the parties a reality check, enabling them to see their own cases' weaknesses and their adversaries strengths. Notice that with neutral evaluation we are moving away from the world of mediation, in which the effort is to help the parties find a mutually satisfactory solution, and toward a sneak preview of litigation.

d. A variation on early neutral evaluation is nonbinding arbitration, in which, as a condition of going to trial, the parties are required to present their cases to an arbitrator, who issues a decision. This decision, however, does not bind the parties unless they accept it. Federal law permits either party to insist on trial without any penalty. 28 U.S.C. §657(c). Some states using the nonbinding arbitration device provide that a party who insists on trial but does not do better at trial than he did in arbitration — even if he wins — will be liable for costs. Cal. Code Civ. Proc. §1141.21 (West 2003) (costs to include fees of expert witnesses as well as arbitrator's fee).

e. A third variation is the summary jury trial as a settlement device. In summary jury trials a small jury (usually of eight or fewer members) is chosen, and the parties present their cases to the jury in very abbreviated form (usually with the lawyers narrating what the evidence will show rather than calling actual witnesses). The "jury" is charged, deliberates, and returns its verdict, which, however, is not binding. Instead the verdict serves as a basis for further negotiation: The plaintiff who thought his case was worth $250,000 discovers the jury was willing to award only $50,000; the defendant who thought she would win a defense verdict finds herself stung for significant damages. Both return to the negotiating table sadder but better informed. The hope underlying all these processes is that actually "losing" a case (or winning less than was hoped for) may cause the parties to settle.

7. So far we have considered devices that, even if they are administered by a judge, do not directly involve that judge. Should they? Should a judge, in a settlement conference, tell the parties how much she thinks the case is "worth"? Should she go further, telling the parties that they are behaving unreasonably if they do not settle? Consider one judge managing a medical malpractice case. He held settlement conferences, a summary jury trial, and finally,

> directed the defense attorney to attend a settlement conference on November 3 . . . and to bring with him the representative of the insurance company from the home office who had issued these instructions, or one with equal authority. The court specifically and formally admonished defense counsel: "Tell them no[t] to send some flunky who has no authority to negotiate. I want someone who can enter into a settlement in this range [between $125,000 and $175,000] without having to call anyone else."

November 3 arrived, and so did the defense attorney. But the representative from St. Paul's home office did not. Instead, an adjuster from the local office appeared. She advised the court that her instructions from the officials at the home office were to reiterate the offer previously made and not to call them back if it were not accepted.

When asked by the court whether there was some misunderstanding that it had stated a representative from the home office was required to attend, the adjuster replied, "I doubt if anyone from the home office would have come down even if in fact this is what you said." . . .

Accordingly, the court forthwith struck the pleadings of the defendant and declared him in default. The court further ordered that the trial set for the next day would be limited to damages only and that a hearing to show cause why St. Paul should not be punished for criminal contempt be held on December 12, 1986. Later that day, St. Paul settled with the plaintiff for $175,000.

Lockhart v. Patel, 115 F.R.D. 44 (E.D. Ky. 1987)

a. In collective bargaining under the National Labor Relations Act, the parties have a legal obligation to engage in "good faith bargaining." Neither employer nor union is obliged to accept any particular offer, but they must remain open to considering offers. Was the *Lockhart* judge seeking to impose a similar obligation on parties to litigation?

b. Supposing the insurer did not want to settle for more than $125,000, what should it have instructed its adjuster to say?

8. Suppose in the GrowCo v. Smart dispute Jane Smart's lawyer files her lawsuit in Texas state court, dropping the federal sex discrimination claims and alleging only wrongful discharge. As the case develops, it emerges that in the background of the dispute is disagreement about the scope of a plant patent. GrowCo believes that Jane did the work leading to the patent on their time and that it therefore belongs to them; Jane believes she had done the critical work before arriving at GrowCo. Federal courts have exclusive jurisdiction over patent litigation. GrowCo files a federal patent action. Meanwhile, the state action develops and, with the assistance of a court-appointed mediator, the parties make a final effort to settle it.

a. Smart wants easy enforcement of GrowCo's continuation of her medical benefits (a term the employer agrees to), and GrowCo wants an injunction against Smart's disclosure of its trade secrets (a term she is willing to agree to). What form of settlement will satisfy their goals?

b. As they arrive on the brink of agreement, GrowCo insists that the federal patent claims be included in a global settlement. Smart is willing to drop her patent claim. Can the parties settle the patent claim as part of the state court suit?

Matsushita Elec. Industrial Co. v. Epstein

516 U.S. 367 (1996)

Justice THOMAS delivered the opinion of the Court.

This case presents the question whether a federal court may withhold full faith and credit from a state-court judgment approving a class-action settlement simply because the settlement releases claims within the exclusive jurisdiction of the federal courts. The answer is no. Absent a partial repeal of the Full Faith and Credit Act, 28 U.S.C. §1738, by another federal statute, a federal court must give the judgment the same effect that it would have in the courts of the State in which it was rendered.

[The dispute arose from Matsushita's acquisition of MCA, an entertainment company. Two sets of lawsuits were filed on behalf of MCA shareholders — both consisting of class actions. One such group of federal actions alleged breach of federal securities laws. A second group of class actions, filed in Delaware state court, alleged breaches of various state-law fiduciary responsibilities of directors. The claims in the federal actions all fell within the federal courts' exclusive jurisdiction. After the federal district court granted summary judgment to the defendants in the federal cases, but while those cases were on appeal to the Ninth Circuit, the parties to the Delaware action negotiated "a global release of all claims arising out of the Matsushita-MCA acquisition." After notifying the class members of the pending settlement, and holding the required fairness hearing, the Delaware court approved the settlement as fair. In reaching the conclusion of fairness, the Delaware chancellor engaged in a process required by state law in which he assessed the fair value of the claims — including the federal claims — that were being settled.]

The order and final judgment of the Chancery Court incorporated the terms of the settlement agreement, providing:

> All claims, rights and causes of action (state or federal, including but not limited to claims arising under the federal securities law, any rules or regulations promulgated thereunder, or otherwise), whether known or unknown that are, could have been or might in the future be asserted by any of the plaintiffs or any member of the Settlement Class . . . in connection with or that arise now or hereafter out of the Merger Agreement, the Tender Offer, the Distribution Agreement, the Capital Contribution Agreement, the employee compensation arrangements, the Tender Agreements, the Initial Proposed Settlement, this Settlement . . . including without limitation the claims asserted in the California Federal Actions . . . are hereby compromised, settled, released and discharged with prejudice by virtue of the proceedings herein and this Order and Final Judgment.

The Ninth Circuit [before which the federal securities claims were pending, ruled that] the preclusive force of a state-court settlement judgment is limited to those claims that "could . . . have been extinguished by the issue preclusive effect of an adjudication of the state claims." [Determining that the issues in the state and federal cases were distinct, the Ninth Circuit held that adjudication of the state claims could have had no preclusive effect on issues in the federal case. Nor, because of exclusive federal jurisdiction, could Delaware courts have adjudicated the federal securities claims. Accordingly, reasoned the Ninth Circuit, Delaware's approval of the settlement could not bar litigation of the federal claims in federal court. The Supreme Court reversed.]

II

The Full Faith and Credit Act mandates that the "judicial proceedings" of any State "shall have the same full faith and credit in every court within the United States . . .

as they have by law or usage in the courts of such State . . . from which they are taken." 28 U.S.C. §1738. The Act thus directs all [federal] courts to treat a state-court judgment with the same respect that it would receive in the courts of the rendering state. Federal courts may not "employ their own rules . . . in determining the effect of state judgments," but must "accept the rules chosen by the State from which the judgment is taken." Kremer v. Chemical Constr. Corp., 456 U.S. 461(1982). Because the Court of Appeals failed to follow the dictates of the Act, we reverse. . . .

[The opinion examined the somewhat ambiguous Delaware precedents.] Given these statements of Delaware law, we think that a Delaware court would afford preclusive effect to the settlement judgment in this case, notwithstanding the fact that respondents could not have pressed their [federal] claims in the [state] Court of Chancery. [The Supreme Court opinion then looked to the text and statutory history of the federal securities law to determine whether, in providing for exclusive federal jurisdiction over such claims, Congress impliedly repealed 28 U.S.C. §1738 insofar as it would defeat the statutory scheme of exclusive federal jurisdiction. Noting that it had previously held that such claims could be arbitrated or waived, the Court concluded:] Taken together, these cases stand for the general proposition that even when exclusively federal claims are at stake, there is no "universal right to litigate a federal claim in a federal district court." Allen v. McCurry, 449 U.S., at 105, [1980.]

The judgment of the Court of Appeals is reversed, and the case is remanded for proceedings consistent with this opinion.

It is so ordered.

[Justices GINSBURG, STEVENS, and SOUTER wrote separately, disagreeing with the Supreme Court's reading of Delaware law and emphasizing that a judgment is entitled to full faith and credit only if it was rendered in accord with due process (and doubting that the Delaware court had assured that the plaintiff class was adequately represented).]

NOTES AND PROBLEMS

1. What does Matsushita hold?

2. Apply Matsushita's principle to Smart v. GrowCo. How would the parties, assuming they wanted a global settlement, pull it off? What questions would you want to answer about Texas law?

3. Notice several points of apparent agreement in Matsushita:

a. The opinion did not question the parties' ability to settle any pending litigation of any sort by contract. Ordinary settlement agreements every day end cases of all sorts. If the litigation in question had not been a class action (which requires judicial approval of settlements), the parties could have reached an out-of-court settlement of their state claims that included the federal claims as well.

b. The opinion did not question the exclusivity of federal jurisdiction for the adjudication of the federal securities claims at issue. No one said that Delaware could *adjudicate* these claims. See Gargallo v. Merrill, Lynch, et al., infra page 683 for an analogous situation.

c. The opinion suggested that Congress could, by appropriate legislation, have prevented state court decrees from settling federal securities claims.

d. Majority and dissents seemed to agree that a state court judgment (embodying a settlement agreement) could settle claims that the state court had no jurisdiction to adjudicate and that §1738 says that the effect of such a settlement depends on the respect it would be given by Delaware law. The Delaware judgment would not have settled the federal claims unless Delaware preclusion principles had purported to do so.

4. That left two areas of disagreement:

a. Did Delaware preclusion law bar actions that the Delaware courts could not have tried? Notice that to answer this question, the Supreme Court had to guess what Delaware courts would do; this task, like that facing federal courts in diversity cases where they must apply state law, has sometimes been called "metaphysical." The majority said Delaware would bar the federal claims; the dissenters thought that question had received inadequate attention and would have remanded on that question.

b. Had the members of the Delaware class in fact received adequate representation? The majority's only discussion of this question came in footnote 5:

> Apart from any discussion of Delaware law, respondents contend that the settlement proceedings did not satisfy due process because the class was inadequately represented. Respondents make this claim in spite of the Chancery Court's express ruling, following argument on the issue, that the class representatives fairly and adequately protected the interests of the class. We need not address the due process claim, however, because it is outside the scope of the question presented in this Court. While it is true that a respondent may defend a judgment on alternative grounds, we generally do not address arguments that were not the basis for the decision below. See Peralta v. Heights Medical Center, Inc., [supra page 467].

516 U.S. at 379. On remand, the plaintiffs asked the Ninth Circuit to declare that they had been inadequately represented in the Delaware case and were thus not bound by the settlement-judgment. In a split decision, the Circuit said that the Supreme Court had decided that the Delaware court had decided that there was adequate representation — and that the matter was therefore closed. Epstein v. MCA, Inc., 179 F. 3d 641 (9th Cir. 1999). Is that a good reading of the footnote above?

5. So what was all the fuss about in *Matsushita*? Consider two possibilities.

a. Was the Delaware court doing something that looked very much like trying the federal claims? To decide the fair value of the federal claims, as the Delaware judge is required to do in approving a class action settlement, the Delaware court had to "value" them. To value them, it had to decide whether they were based on a viable interpretation of federal law and whether the facts available suggested defendant's liability. Is that getting too close for comfort to trespassing on exclusive federal jurisdiction over securities claims?

b. The state and federal lawsuits, both class actions, were being handled by different sets of lawyers who represented overlapping groups of clients. Suppose the Delaware lawyers thought that their state law claims hadn't much settlement value (the state judge had previously said as much), and that by adding in the federal claims were hoping to raise the amount of settlement. Was that a nice bit of lawyering, getting something extra for their clients while eliminating duplicate litigation? Or was it a bit of professional piracy, "stealing" the federal claims out from under other lawyers who were actually litigating them in federal court?

c.   Contracting for Confidentiality

One settlement goal shared by many defendants, and some plaintiffs, is that the settlement be confidential. What they mean by confidentiality differs from case to case. At its maximum, such a desire means that the parties want not even the fact of a dispute to become public, much less the terms of its compromise. More commonly, confidentiality agreements seek to prevent information or documents from public exposure. Consider again our hypothetical case, Smart v. GrowCo. Suppose that Smart files her unlawful discharge action, and GrowCo counterclaims for an injunction forbidding Smart from disclosing any trade secrets. As in many such cases, discovery yields information that makes both sides unhappy (see Stalnaker v. Kmart Corp., supra page 827). Depositions suggest that the head of GrowCo's research & development group (where Jane Smart was employed), though brilliant, exhibits behavior toward women that may look quite bad to a jury and which might make it hard to recruit future plant geneticists. Depositions and documents also suggest that Smart, in addition to great talent and skill in plant genetics, has unorthodox work habits and a very free hand with expense accounts that may not endear her to future employers. In addition, there is the matter of the disputed patents and trade secrets.

NOTES AND PROBLEMS

1. First, as review, explain why settlement might look like a good resolution to both sides, even though they strongly believe in the merits of their respective claims. How would settlement eliminate some of the risks they are facing?

2. Now consider whether a confidentiality agreement would add value to the settlement.

a. Which of Jane Smart's possible concerns would be solved by a confidentiality agreement?

b. Which of GrowCo's would be solved by a confidentiality agreement?

c. Would anyone lose anything by a confidentiality agreement?

3. How might a settlement agreement be drafted to assure that the parties maintain confidentiality? Suppose that one of the parties' lawyers, rummaging in his files, finds the following example and fills in the names of the present

parties. He gives it you for review, asking whether it will fulfill the clients' expectations:

7. *Return of Documents.* Both parties agree to return all originals and copies of all documents and data, obtained from Jane Smart or GrowCo, directly or indirectly, at any time, by either party, or any agent, attorney, representative, or anyone else acting or purporting to act on his or her behalf. Insofar as they apply to Jane Smart, the obligations of this Paragraph 7 are cumulative to other existing obligations that Smart has as a result of her employment with GrowCo.

8. *Confidentiality.*

8.1 Parties and their attorneys, and each of them, expressly agree that this Agreement and the terms and conditions of this Settlement are confidential, and agree not to disclose, publicize, or cause to be disclosed or publicized the fact of settlement or any of the terms or conditions of this Agreement, including but not limited to the amounts received pursuant to Paragraph 1 of this Agreement or the amounts paid in connection with the Workers' Compensation Claims, except as required by judicial process, or as otherwise required by law. Notwithstanding the foregoing, it is hereby expressly understood and agreed that the parties and their attorneys may need to disseminate certain information concerning the settlement to their accountants, auditors, attorneys, and/or other entities as necessary in the regular course of business. While such disclosures are expressly permitted under the terms of this Agreement, parties and their attorneys shall insure that information deemed confidential under this Agreement is treated as confidential by the recipients thereof. Except as required by judicial process, or as otherwise required by law, if any of the parties or their attorneys or any recipient of information from parties or their attorneys concerning the Settlement is asked about the disposition of the action, such Party, attorney, or recipient shall state the following in substance: "I am not at liberty to discuss it."

8.2 Each disclosure by Parties or their attorneys or by any recipient of information from Plaintiff or their attorneys concerning this Settlement other than a disclosure expressly permitted by subparagraph 8.1 shall be considered a material breach of this Agreement. For each such breach of the confidentiality provision set forth in subparagraph 8.1, the Party who breaches such confidentiality provision shall be solely liable to the other Party for Twenty-Five Thousand Dollars ($25,000.00) in liquidated damages. Parties, and each of them, agree that said sum represents a reasonable estimate of the actual damages which would be suffered by as a result of a violation of subparagraph 8.1 and that this sum is not punitive in any way. In the event a Party is required to file suit or otherwise seek judicial enforcement of its rights under this paragraph 8, the Party who breaches such confidentiality provision shall be solely liable for attorneys' fees and costs incurred as a result thereof.

NOTES AND PROBLEMS

1. Consider several features of this agreement:

a. Why did the agreement call for the return of documents? What might the parties be worried about?

b. Why the liquidated damages provision? How would one enforce such an agreement were there not a liquidated damages clause? Consider the different kinds of disclosures that GrowCo and Smart might make; will this clause deal well with all of them? Notice that the answer matters, because under contract law an unreasonable estimate of liquidated damages may void the whole clause.

2. As matters now stand, such contractual confidentiality agreements are generally enforceable, but what exactly do they protect against? At a minimum, they would prohibit the plaintiff from holding a news conference to announce the terms of the settlement. What could defendant do if, after entering into such a settlement, plaintiff took such an action?

3. Why did the lawyer who drafted this agreement create an exception for disclosures "as required by judicial process, or as otherwise required by law"? Suppose that one of GrowCo's competitors sues it for abusive deployment of one of its patents — behavior thought by some to violate the antitrust laws. In the course of that lawsuit, the competitor seeks to depose Jane Smart about her lawsuit and the patent dispute she had with GrowCo. Assume that a court rules that GrowCo's treatment of Smart's patent claims is relevant to show a pattern of abusive use of patents. Can Smart refuse to answer on grounds of her confidentiality agreement? Can GrowCo get a court to prevent Competitor from taking Jane's deposition? Respond after reading the next case.

Kalinauskas v. Wong

151 F.R.D. 363 (D. Nev. 1993)

JOHNSTON, Magistrate Judge.

This matter was submitted to the undersigned Magistrate Judge on a Motion for a Protective Order filed by defendant Desert Palace, Inc., doing business as Caesars Palace Hotel & Casino (Caesars). . . .

The plaintiff, Ms. Lin T. Kalinauskas (Kalinauskas), a former employee of Caesars, has sued Caesars for sexual discrimination in the instant case. As part of discovery Kalinauskas seeks to depose Donna R. Thomas, a former Caesars employee who filed a sexual harassment suit against Caesars last year. Ms. Thomas's suit settled without trial pursuant to a confidential settlement agreement[,] which the court sealed upon the stipulated agreement of the parties.

This court has examined, in camera, sealed materials relating to Ms. Thomas's case and settlement. The in camera submission included: Stipulation for & Order for Dismissal, Protective Order and Confidentiality Order, Stipulation for Protective Order and Confidentiality Order, and Settlement Agreement. [The Stipulation for a Protective Order provided] that the plaintiff "shall not discuss any aspect of plaintiff's employment at Caesars other than to state the dates of her employment and her job title." Identical language appears in the Protective Order and Confidentiality Order. . . .

Discussion

In general, the scope of discovery is very broad. "Parties may obtain discovery regarding *any matter, not privileged, which is relevant to the* [claim or defense of any party]. . . ." Fed. R. Civ. P. 26(b)(1) (emphasis added). The primary goal of the court and discovery is "to secure the just, speedy, and inexpensive determination of every action." Fed. R. Civ. P.1.

The public interest favors judicial policies which promote the completion of litigation. Public interest also seeks to protect the finality of prior suits and the secrecy of settlements when desired by the settling parties. However, the courts also serve society by providing a public forum for issues of general concern. The case at bar presents a direct conflict between these crucial public and private interests.

To allow full discovery into all aspects of Ms. Thomas's case could discourage similar settlements. Confidential settlements benefit society and the parties involved by resolving disputes relatively quickly, with slight judicial intervention, and presumably result in greater satisfaction to the parties. Sound judicial policy fosters and protects this form of alternative dispute resolution. See, e.g., Fed. R. Evid. 408 which protects compromises and offers to compromise by rendering them inadmissible to prove liability. The secrecy of a settlement agreement and the contractual rights of the parties thereunder deserve court protection.

On the other hand, to prevent any discovery into Ms. Thomas's case based upon the settlement agreement results in disturbing consequences. First, as pointed out by Kalinauskas, preventing the deposition of Ms. Thomas would condone the practice of "buy[ing] the silence of a witness with a settlement agreement." This court harbors little doubt that preventing the dissemination of the underlying facts which prompted Ms. Thomas to file suit is in Caesars's interest, and formed an important part of the agreement to Caesars. Caesars avers that without the confidentiality order the *Thomas* case would not have settled. Yet despite this freedom to contract, the courts must carefully police the circumstances under which litigants seek to protect their interests while concealing legitimate areas of public concern. This concern grows more pressing as additional individuals are harmed by identical or similar action.

Second, the deposition of Ms. Thomas is likely to lead to relevant evidence. Preventing the deposition of Ms. Thomas or the discovery of documents created in her case, could lead to wasteful efforts to generate discovery already in existence. . . .

Caesars argues that Kalinauskas must intervene in the Thomas case and seek a modification of the confidentiality order to depose Thomas. . . .

This court rejects Caesars's first argument regarding intervention. Intervention was appropriate in [a cited case] because that case was ongoing at the time the New York plaintiffs sought discovery. Contrastingly, in this situation the Thomas action had concluded before Kalinauskas filed her discovery motion. Hence, requiring intervention under these circumstances would be wasteful and cause needless delay, especially in light of the fact that no live controversy exists in which Kalinauskas can properly intervene. . . .

Next, [Caesar's] argument that Kalinauskas must show a compelling need to obtain discovery applies to discovery of the specific terms of the settlement agreement (i.e., the amount and conditions of the agreement), not [to] factual information surrounding Thomas's case. Caesars should not be able to conceal basic facts of concern to Kalinauskas in her case, and of legitimate public concern, regarding employment at its place of business.

Accordingly, keeping in mind the liberal nature of discovery, this court will allow the deposition of Ms. Thomas. Kalinauskas has already acquired information about Ms. Thomas's case gleaned through publicly available documents, including Ms. Thomas's original complaint filed in state court. Moreover, Kalinauskas' case even involves at least one Caesars supervisory employee in common with Ms. Thomas's.

The deposition of Ms. Thomas and any further discovery into the Thomas case must not, however, disclose any substantive terms of the Caesars-Thomas settlement agreement. Naturally, Ms. Thomas may answer questions regarding her employment at Caesars and any knowledge of sexual harassment. . . .

While settlement is an important objective, an overzealous quest for alternative dispute resolution can distort the proper role of the court. Furthermore, settlement agreements which suppress evidence violate the greater public policy. . . .

Based on the foregoing . . . IT IS HEREBY ORDERED . . . that the Defendant's Motion for Protective Order is granted to the extent that during the deposition of Ms. Donna R. Thomas, no information regarding the settlement agreement itself shall come forth [and] that the Defendant's Motion for Protective Order is denied as to all other requests. . . .

NOTES AND PROBLEMS

1. See the case as a strategic dance.

a. What did Kalinauskas's lawyer want to do? What were the arguments in plaintiff's favor?

b. How did defendant's lawyer try to stop her? What were defendant's arguments?

2. How did the confidentiality-enforcing mechanism in the Thomas v. Caesars litigation (the case whose confidential settlement is discussed in *Kalinauskas*) differ from those in the sample confidentiality agreement quoted in the preceding section?

a. What did the parties do that went beyond a contract to maintain confidentiality? What did they want the *Thomas* court to do when they submitted a "Stipulation for Protective Order and Confidentiality Order, and Settlement Agreement"?

b. Why did the parties in the *Thomas* litigation seek a protective order? What were they trying to protect from disclosure? Consider the discovery taken in the case: interrogatories, perhaps document discovery, maybe depositions. A contractual confidentiality provision would prohibit the parties from telling others about the contents of such discovery, but it would not prevent other parties from looking over these documents, if they were on file with the court. Do you see now why the parties wanted a court order as well an agreement?

c. "If the documents were on file with the court. . . ." Would they be? Read Rule 5(d). Suppose that in the *Thomas* case there had been a deposition of the supervisor allegedly responsible for the harassment. Could Kalinauskas's lawyer find that deposition in the courthouse files? What if, after that deposition, Caesars had moved for summary judgment, using portions of the supervisor's deposition to support their motion; would that change your answer to the preceding question? Now, suppose that these documents were on file, but covered by a protective order. What will happen when Kalinauskas's lawyer asks to see them?

d. Consider a case in which a party went well beyond a protective order to assure confidentiality. General Motors and Elwell, one of its engineers, had a falling out. Elwell sued GM in a Michigan court. The parties settled that case, and as part of the settlement the Michigan court entered an injunction prohibiting Elwell from "testifying, without the prior written consent of [GM], . . . as . . . a witness of any kind . . . in any litigation . . . involving [GM] as an owner, seller, manufacturer, and/or designer. . . ." As in *Kalinauskas*, a second suit occurred, when the Bakers brought a diversity action in federal court alleging deaths from a defectively designed GM vehicle. They sought to depose Elwell as a fact witness concerning the design of the vehicle. GM contended that his testimony would violate the Michigan injunction — and that the federal court was bound by the Full Faith and Credit Clause and 28 U.S.C. §1738 to enforce the ban on Elwell's testimony. No, said the U.S. Supreme Court, in a somewhat opaque opinion: Although there is no "public policy exception" to the Full Faith and Credit Clause (as the plaintiffs had argued), "Michigan's judgment cannot reach beyond [that] controversy to control proceedings against GM brought in other states. . . ." Baker v. General Motors, 522 U.S. 222 (1998). Suppose that, as part of the settlement in Smart v. GrowCo, our hypothetical case, a Texas court enters an injunction forbidding Smart from disclosing any of GrowCo's trade secrets (see Sigma Chemical v. Harris, supra page 282 for a similar injunction). Does *Baker* mean that injunction is unenforceable?

e. Finally, explain how the outcomes in *Kalinauskas* and *Baker* compare with the results under the work product doctrine. Under that doctrine, announced in Hickman v. Taylor (supra pages 438) and codified in Rule 26(b)(3), a lawyer is protected against disclosure in discovery of information generated by the litigation process itself but not against disclosure of underlying historical facts. Don't the rulings in *Kalinauskas* and *Baker* achieve the same result?

3. What's behind the fight over protective orders?

a. Defendants say that plaintiffs want access to prior discovery merely to give them a "road map" for their own cases — to be able to use the discovery in the preceding case to sort out the most effective strategy and to lower the cost of discovery. By allowing the parties protective orders, the argument continues, we encourage faster settlements: Defendants who cannot get confidentiality may well decide to go to trial, or, at least, engage in protracted wrangling over whether to produce the information in the first place. Finally, privacy is a core value of our society, and courts should be willing to protect it.

b. Plaintiffs stress that sealed discovery may delay public knowledge of dangerous or unlawful situations. Suppose, they say, a defendant makes a widely defective product or engages in a pattern of unlawful employment practices that affect many employees. Even if some plaintiffs come forward and are successful, sealed discovery prevents the knowledge from spreading quickly and delays the time when defendant must change its practices. Courts should not be in the business of abetting such concealment. Moreover, if discovery in prior cases is available, it will reduce the expense of subsequent, similar lawsuits — a desirable outcome.

c. As things now stand Rule 26(c), the provision governing *Kalinauskas*, allows a court to enter a protective order "which justice requires to protect a party or person from annoyance, embarrassment, oppression, or undue burden or expense. . . ." Some states have gone further, most notably Washington, where a statute declares that the public has a right to information "necessary for a lay member of the public to understand the nature, source, and extent of the risk from alleged hazards" and requires a court considering a protective order to weigh that public interest. Wash. Rev. Code Ann. §4.24.611(1)(b) (West 2003). The federal courts in the District of South Carolina have adopted a local rule that providing that an order to seal documents can be entered only after a motion by the parties, who as part of that motion must: "(1) identify, with specificity, the documents or portions thereof for which sealing is requested; (2) state the reasons why sealing is necessary; (3) explain (for each document or group of documents) why less drastic alternatives to sealing will not afford adequate protection; and (4) address the factors governing sealing of documents reflected in controlling case law," attaching to the motion a nonconfidential description of the documents in question. The clerk must post public notice of the motion to seal. D.S.C. Local Civil R. 5.03 (A).

2.   Contracting for Private Adjudication: Arbitration and Its Variants

Parties can enter contracts to settle lawsuits, and they can employ mediators to help them reach such settlements. But what if the parties cannot agree, even with the help of a mediator, or can agree only that they want to have their disputes decided by a third party. Must they then resort to the courts? No; one of the oldest and best-established alternatives to litigation is arbitration. Unlike a mediator, an arbitrator decides a dispute and issues an oral or a written decision after having heard from both sides. Arbitration, in other words, closely resembles adjudication — private, nonjudicial adjudication, but still adjudication.

Why, if it is so much like adjudication, do the parties not simply use the ordinary court system? First, unlike court-controlled adjudication, arbitration permits the parties to design their own procedure. Sometimes that results in processes that are scarcely distinguishable from judicial adjudication, including the rules of evidence and various formal stages of procedure. In other cases arbitration may depart dramatically from legal process. The parties may agree that the arbitrator will be bound by precedent or that he can ignore it — with a number of intermediate variations. Second, the parties may, to an even greater extent than in courts, control the applicable substantive law — they can insist, for example, that the arbitrator will not refer to the ordinary rules of contract but instead will adhere to the traditions that have developed around this particular relationship. Third, arbitration may be faster, cheaper, and more private than ordinary adjudication. The parties may be able to dispense with the rules of discovery or with other procedural stages and insist on a quick decision of their dispute. They may also be able to insist that the arbitrator disclose neither the existence of a dispute nor his decision. Fourth, because the parties may arrange to have only experienced and known arbitrators decide their disputes, they can both ensure a decision maker who is experienced in the field (be it medical malpractice, engineering, or securities) and eliminate the vagaries in outcome that a jury may introduce. In the process, however, they may also deprive one side of the larger damages a jury might award. Finally — and this may be either an advantage or a disadvantage — the arbitrator, though deciding the dispute, may decide it more "softly" than a court:

> It is said of the American commercial arbitrator that he may "do justice as he sees it, applying his own sense of the law and equity to the facts as he finds them to be and making an award reflecting the spirit rather than the letter of the agreement." Many awards resulting from such proceedings might also be described as Solomonic, halving the objects in dispute.

Paul Carrington & Paul Haagen, Contract and Jurisdiction, 1996 Sup. Ct. Rev. 331, 345, quoting Silverman v. Benmor Coats, 61 N.Y.2d 299 (1984).

These features of arbitration will emerge only if the courts are willing to require parties who have agreed to arbitrate to submit their disputes to arbitration when a question arises. Judicial attitudes toward arbitration have undergone a great swing from which the pendulum may now be returning. In the nineteenth and early twentieth centuries many courts widely refused to enforce pre-dispute arbitration agreements; they would enforce arbitration only if the parties chose the method after the dispute had arisen. By case law and statute, however, the rule has generally been changed in favor of arbitration even if agreed to by the parties before any dispute has arisen. For example, the U.S. Supreme Court, which once viewed with suspicion the arbitration of claims arising under federal statutes, has enforced agreements to arbitrate many kinds of claims. And in recent years an increasing number of employers and medical service providers — particularly health maintenance organizations — have included arbitration provisions in their employment manuals and policies.

As a consequence of such cases, parties who have entered a predispute arbitration agreement may be required to use arbitration as their exclusive forum, and a party bound by the agreement may be enjoined from litigating instead of arbitrating. The Federal Arbitration Act, 9 U.S.C. §§2 et seq., allows for enforcement of arbitration agreements in the federal courts. The Act's structure is designed to force the parties to honor their agreement to arbitrate, relying on three basic sections:

- §2 consists of substantive law, broadly declaring agreements to arbitrate valid as a matter of federal law: "A written provision in any . . . contract evidencing a transaction involving commerce to settle by arbitration a controversy thereafter arising out of such contract or transaction . . . shall be valid, irrevocable, and enforceable, save upon such grounds as exist at law or in equity for the revocation of any contract."

- §3 tells the federal courts what to do if a party, in spite of an arbitration agreement, instead files a lawsuit: "If any suit or proceeding be brought in any of the courts of the United States upon any issue referable to arbitration . . . , the court in which such suit is pending . . . shall on application of one of the parties stay the trial of the action until such arbitration [occurs], providing the applicant for the stay is not in default in proceeding with such arbitration."
- §4 tells the courts what to do if a party neither invokes arbitration nor files suit: "A party aggrieved by the alleged failure, neglect, or refusal of another to arbitrate under a written agreement for arbitration may petition any United States district court which, save for such agreement, would have jurisdiction under Title 28 . . . , for an order directing that such arbitration proceed in the manner provided for in such agreement."

That structure provides a roadmap for a party seeking to enforce an arbitration agreement, but it leaves out one ingredient that will doubtless have occurred to the eager civil procedure student — jurisdiction:

> The Arbitration Act is something of an anomaly in the field of federal-court jurisdiction. It creates a body of federal substantive law establishing and regulating the duty to honor an agreement to arbitrate, yet it does not create any independent federal-question jurisdiction under 28 U.S.C. §1331 or otherwise. Section 4 provides for an order compelling arbitration only when the federal district court would have jurisdiction over a suit on the underlying dispute; hence, there must be diversity of citizenship or some other independent basis for federal jurisdiction before the order can issue. Section 3 likewise limits the federal courts to the extent that a federal court cannot stay a suit pending before it unless there is such a suit in existence. Nevertheless, although enforcement of the Act is left in large part to the state courts, it nevertheless represents federal policy to be vindicated by the federal courts where otherwise appropriate.

Moses H. Cone Memorial Hosp. v. Mercury Constr. Corp., 460 U.S. 1, 24 (1983); the Court has suggested that state courts are also bound to enforce this national policy. Id. at 26. In several cases the Supreme Court has required state courts to enforce arbitration agreements even when they contravene state law if the underlying transaction involves interstate commerce. The result is that in any contract involving such commerce (which, given other decisions, covers most commercial transactions), arbitration clauses will be enforceable.

NOTES AND PROBLEMS

1. Consider this framework in relation to some elementary problems of arbitration enforcement. Suppose that Jane Smart, the botanical geneticist, and GrowCo, the biotechnology firm, have entered into an employment contract, which contains a provision that "all disputes arising out of this agreement shall be referred to arbitration conducted under the rules of the American Arbitration Association."

a. When the dispute arises, Smart files a state court lawsuit alleging unlawful discharge. If GrowCo wants to arbitrate rather than litigate the suit, what should it do?

b. If Smart has moved away from GrowCo's home state, can it ask a federal court to enforce the arbitration clause? If Smart is still in GrowCo's state, can it do so? If GrowCo cannot invoke federal jurisdiction, can it still enforce the FAA? How?

c. Suppose in its action to enforce the arbitration clause GrowCo invokes §2 of the Federal Arbitration Act; does the language of that Act give Smart any grounds to argue that it does not apply to her? Does the courts' history of interpreting the act give GrowCo any response to Smart's argument?

2. Suppose that while the dispute is in arbitration GrowCo files suit in federal court against Smart, alleging that, having left the company, she is now engaged in violation of its patents and theft of trade secrets by communicating GrowCo's growing techniques to her new employer. How can Smart make this suit go away, at least temporarily?

3. As the material in this section suggests, courts over recent decades have been broadly ready to enforce arbitration clauses. But that readiness is not absolute. Two kinds of limitations have arisen — those on the nature of claims that can be arbitrated and those on the nature of the arbitration process.

4. What sorts of claims are not arbitrable? It is hard to imagine an arbitration agreement between the president of the United States and the Congress, providing that impeachment proceedings should be submitted to arbitration.

a. In more private matters, the history is more complex. A case refusing to enforce arbitration on other grounds described the history of this limitation:

> Mandatory arbitration of federal statutory claims continues to generate considerable debate among courts and commentators. At bottom, this debate centers on the efficacy of resolving *"public disputes in private fora."* Harry Edwards, *Where Are We Heading With Mandatory Arbitration of Statutory Claims in Employment?*, 16 Ga. St. U.L. Rev. (2000) (emphasis in original).
>
> With its informal nature, arbitration is widely-accepted as a sound method for resolving essentially private disputes, such as those arising from collective bargaining agreements and other contracts. Yet, for some, this informality renders arbitration suspect as a forum for resolving statutory claims, which typically implicate important public interests. As one jurist and commentator has explained:
>
>> When public laws are enforced in private fora, however, we have no assurance that the underlying *public interests* are fully satisfied. This is not to say that private fora are incapable of resolving disputes in a manner protective of the public interest. However, conflicts that are resolved through mediation and arbitration usually are not subject to public scrutiny, so we do not know whether such resolutions are consistent with prevailing interpretations of public law or whether the procedures followed were inequitable.
>
> *Id.* (emphasis in original) (footnote omitted).

For a time, skepticism regarding the role of arbitration in resolving statutory claims held sway. This skepticism is perhaps best reflected in the Supreme Court's approach to the mandatory arbitration of statutory claims. The Court rejected arbitration as the lone forum for vindicating claims under Title VII of the 1964 Civil Rights Act and the Securities Act of 1933. In so holding, the Court explained that arbitrators' inexperience with legal concepts coupled with the lack of stringent procedural safeguards rendered an arbitral forum, in the context of the statutory claims at issue, an unsuitable replacement for a court of law.

However, the tide soon turned. In a trio of cases decided in the 1980s, the Supreme Court enforced arbitration agreements covering claims under the Sherman Act, the Securities Act of 1933, the Securities Exchange Act of 1934, and the civil provisions of the Racketeering Influenced Corrupt Organizations Act ("RICO"). These holdings led the Court to declare in 1991 that "[i]t is now well settled that statutory claims may be the subject of an arbitration agreement, enforceable by the FAA." Gilmer v. Interstate/Johnson Lane Corp., 500 U.S. 20, 26 (1991).

The Court addressed its growing acceptance of mandatory arbitration for statutory claims in *Gilmer v. Interstate/Johnson Lane Corp.*, in which the Court upheld the mandatory arbitration of claims under the Age Discrimination in Employment Act. In permitting the compulsory arbitration of statutory claims, the Court recognized that by "'agreeing to arbitrate a statutory claim, a party does not forgo the substantive rights afforded by the statute; it only submits to their resolution in an arbitral, rather than a judicial, forum.'" And the Court dismissed generalized attacks on the suitability of arbitral fora as arising from a "'suspicion of arbitration as a method of weakening the protections afforded in the substantive law to would-be complainants.'" Such a suspicion, the Court observed, was "far out of step" with the "current strong endorsement" of arbitration.

Yet not all statutory claims are amenable to mandatory arbitration. In creating a statutory cause of action, Congress may choose to mandate a judicial forum for its resolution. Such an intent is typically evidenced in the statutory text, legislative history, or by an "inherent conflict" between arbitration and the underlying purposes of the statute. . . .

Floss v. Ryan's Family Steakhouses, Inc., 211 F.3d 306, — (6th Cir. 2000).

b. Suppose you represent Jane Smart, in her continuing dispute with GrowCo. She wants to submit both her unlawful discharge and her patent dispute with GrowCo to arbitration, but to take her federal gender discrimination claim to federal court. GrowCo, by contrast, wants to deal with the unlawful discharge claim and gender discrimination claim in arbitration but to take the patent claim to federal court. If both parties argue the non-arbitrability of some claims to a federal court, what is the likely outcome?

5. The second category of claims where courts have denied arbitration involves procedural unfairness in the arbitration process. What if, instead of the standard arbitration clause cited in Note 1 above, Jane's employment contract required her (but not GrowCo) to submit all disputes to DecideAll, a private arbitration services. After Jane agreed to this arrangement DecideAll sent her its brochure, which provided:

> 1. Any employment-related dispute between GrowCo, Me, and/or other signatories which would otherwise be brought in State or Federal court will be brought ONLY in the DecideAll arbitration forum and under DecideAll Rules and Procedures, as modified or amended from time to time. . . .
>   2. . . .
> A. Except as to claims or charges actually handled within a State or Federal agency, any and all disputes I may have with GrowCo, or in that company, its supervisors,

managers or other agents may have with Me which would otherwise be decided in court, shall be resolved only through arbitration in the DecideAll forum and NOT THROUGH LITIGATION IN STATE OR FEDERAL COURT. . . .

 E. I absolutely *must* use the DecideAll forum for any and all employment-related disputes and/or claims and/or related tort claims I may have against GrowCo and all other signatories to this Agreement which would otherwise be brought in court, even if the Agreement has been terminated since the date of the claim.

If Jane files suit in federal court and GrowCo seeks to enforce the arbitration agreement, who will prevail? Consider the following two cases.

Floss v. Ryan's Family Steak Houses, Inc.

211 F.3d 306 (6th Cir. 2000)

GWIN, District Judge.

 With these appeals . . . the Court reviews whether employees effectively waived their rights to bring actions in federal court under the Americans with Disabilities Act and the Fair Labor Standards Act, 29 U.S.C. §201, *et seq.* ("FLSA"). At the district court, the plaintiffs attempted to sue their former employer, Ryan's Family Steak Houses, Inc. ("Ryan's"). However, when applying for employment at Ryan's, both plaintiffs had signed a form indicating they would arbitrate all employment-related disputes. In both cases, Ryan's filed a motion to compel arbitration.

 Finding no valid arbitration agreement, the United States District Court for the Eastern District of Tennessee refused to require Plaintiff-Appellee Kyle Daniels to arbitrate his claim under the ADA. In contrast, the United States District Court for the Eastern District of Kentucky found that Plaintiff-Appellant Sharon Floss was required to arbitrate her dispute and could thus not pursue her claim under the FLSA in federal court.

 Ryan's now appeals the district court's refusal to require Daniels to arbitrate his ADA claim. Similarly, Floss appeals the district court's order requiring her to submit her FLSA claim to arbitration. Because we find neither Daniels nor Floss validly waived their right to bring an action in federal court, we REVERSE the district court's order requiring Floss to arbitrate her claim, and AFFIRM the district court's order refusing to require Daniels to submit his claim to arbitration.

I.

In support of its argument that the plaintiffs agreed to waive their right to bring an action in federal court and instead agreed to arbitrate all employment disputes, Ryan's relies upon a document identified as the "Job Applicant Agreement to Arbitration of Employment-Related Disputes." Ryan's includes this purported agreement in its employment application packet. Only those applicants who sign the agreement are considered for employment at Ryan's.[1] Both Daniels and Floss acknowledge signing the agreement.

The employee's agreement to arbitrate is not with Ryan's. Instead, the agreement runs between the employee and a third-party arbitration services provider, Employment Dispute Services, Inc. ("EDSI"). In the agreement, EDSI agrees to provide an arbitration forum in exchange for the employee's agreement to submit any dispute with his potential employer to arbitration with EDSI. Although Ryan's is not explicitly identified as a party to the agreement, the agreement says the employee's potential employer is a third-party beneficiary of the employee's agreement to waive a judicial forum and arbitrate all employment-related disputes.

The agreement gives EDSI complete discretion over arbitration rules and procedures. The agreement says that all arbitration proceedings will be conducted under "EDSI Rules and Procedures." The agreement then gives EDSI the unlimited right to modify the rules without the employee's consent. . . .

[Both employees signed the agreement, left Ryan's, and then sought to file a federal lawsuit, which Ryan's sought to have arbitrated with EDSI.]

IV.

A.

In deciding whether to compel arbitration of a federal statutory claim, we initially consider whether the statutory claim is generally subject to compulsory arbitration. . . . [After reciting the history contained in Note 4a above, the opinion found both claims potentially subject to arbitration.]

However, even if arbitration is generally a suitable forum for resolving a particular statutory claim, the specific arbitral forum provided under an arbitration agreement must nevertheless allow for the effective vindication of that claim. . . .

Both Floss and Daniels argue that the specific arbitration forum provided by the current version of the EDSI Rules and Procedures does not allow them to effectively vindicate their claims under the FLSA and the ADA. They say the procedures allow for the appointment of a biased and incompetent panel of arbitrators,[7] as well as unduly limit the participants' discovery opportunities.

The selection process begins with EDSI furnishing both parties a list of potential adjudicators organized according to each selection pool. Information regarding each adjudicator's recent employment history and related biographical information is provided to the parties along with this list. The parties may then move to strike

---

1. A notice on the inside cover of the packet informs applicants that they must agree to the terms and conditions outlined in the agreement in order to be considered for employment with Ryan's.

7. Under EDSI's current procedures, a panel of three "adjudicators" presides over every arbitration proceeding. Each adjudicator is selected from one of three "selection pools." One pool consists of supervisors or managers of an employer who has entered into an arbitration agreement with EDSI. A second pool consists of nonsupervisory employees of an employer who is a signatory to an EDSI arbitration agreement. A third pool consists of attorneys, retired judges, and "other competent professional persons" not associated with either party. If the dispute involves more than $20,000, only licensed attorneys are included in this third pool.

any adjudicator for cause. Following the removal of any adjudicators for cause, the parties each strike a name from the list until only one name remains from each selection pool.

We have serious reservations as to whether the arbitral forum provided under the current version of the EDSI Rules and Procedures is suitable for the resolution of statutory claims. Specifically, the neutrality of the forum is far from clear in light of the uncertain relationship between Ryan's and EDSI. Floss and Daniels suggest that EDSI is biased in favor of Ryan's and other employers because it has a financial interest in maintaining its arbitration service contracts with employers. Though the record does not clearly reflect whether EDSI, in contrast to the American Arbitration Association, operates on a for-profit basis, the potential for bias exists. In light of EDSI's role in determining the pool of potential arbitrators, any such bias would render the arbitral forum fundamentally unfair.

Moreover, EDSI's current rules require an employee to generally pay one-half of the arbitrators' fees as a condition of pursuing a dispute. Such a fee structure could potentially prevent an employee from prosecuting a federal statutory claim against an employer. Recognizing as much, the District of Columbia Circuit has refused to countenance an employer's requirement that employees submit their disputes to arbitration as a condition of employment absent that employer's agreement to bear the full costs of the arbitrators' fees.

Though we have concerns with both the fee structure and potential bias of EDSI's arbitral forum, we need not decide whether these deficits prevent the arbitration of Floss and Daniels's statutory claims. As explained below, Floss and Daniels are not contractually obligated to submit their federal statutory claims to arbitration in EDSI's arbitral forum. Thus, Floss and Daniels need not establish the unsuitability of EDSI's arbitral forum in order to litigate their statutory claims in federal court.

B.

The Federal Arbitration Act declares that arbitration agreements "shall be valid, irrevocable, and enforceable, save upon grounds that exist at law or in equity for the revocation of any contract." 9 U.S.C. §2. However, "the FAA was not enacted to force parties to arbitrate in the absence of an agreement." . . .

Consideration is an essential element of every contract. . . .

A promise constitutes consideration for another promise only when it creates a binding obligation. Thus, absent a mutuality of obligation, a contract based on reciprocal promises lacks consideration. . . .

Promises may fail to create legally binding obligations for a variety of reasons. Most notably, a promise may in effect promise nothing at all. . . .

In the purported agreement at issue in this case, EDSI offered its promise to provide an arbitral forum as consideration for Floss and Daniels's promise to submit any dispute they may have with their employer to arbitration with EDSI. In ruling in favor of Daniels, the district court found that EDSI's promise did not create a binding obligation. We agree.

EDSI's promise to provide an arbitral forum is fatally indefinite. Though obligated to provide some type of arbitral forum, EDSI has unfettered discretion in choosing the nature of that forum. Specifically, EDSI has reserved the right to alter the applicable rules and procedures without any obligation to notify, much less receive consent from, Floss and Daniels. EDSI's right to choose the nature of its performance renders its promise illusory. . . .[8]

V.

Ryan's has pursued an acceptable objective in an unacceptable manner. An employer may enter an agreement with employees requiring the arbitration of all employment disputes, including those involving federal statutory claims. Yet an employer cannot seek to do so in such a way that leaves employees with no consideration for their promise to submit their disputes to arbitration. Here, we find that Floss and Daniels did not receive any consideration for their promise to arbitrate their disputes. We thus refuse to enforce their promise in favor of Ryan's.

Lyster v. Ryan's Family Steak Houses, Inc.

239 F.3d 943 (8th Cir. 2001)

JOHN B. JONES, District Judge.

Kathy Lyster filed this action alleging unlawful sexual harassment against her former employer, Ryan's Family Steak Houses, Inc. [Lyster's agreement and its circumstances were identical to those in Floss. After her termination she submitted a claim of sexual harassment to the federal Equal Opportunity Employment Commission and received a "right to sue" letter, a routine communication telling the recipient that the Commission will not pursue her claim but that she may do so on her own.]

The district court concluded under the Agreement Lyster was required to arbitrate her claim only if she filed her claim with the EEOC and the MCHR before she was terminated . . . [and therefore denied] Steak House's petition to compel arbitration and motion to dismiss, or alternatively, to stay the proceedings.

Steak House appeals. . . . Lyster argues the Agreement is an unconscionable adhesion contract. . . .

[The court determined that the claim was arbitrable.]

State contract law governs whether an arbitration agreement is valid. . . .

[After quoting the portions of the agreement cited above in Note 5 (with EDSI as the arbitrator) the court considered Lyster's claim of unconscionability.]

Lyster's final argument, that the Agreement is an unconscionable adhesion contract, lacks merit. Pursuant to Missouri law, "[a] contract is substantively unconscionable if there is undue harshness in the terms of the contract. Or, as

8. Floss insists that the district court erred in determining as a matter of law that she was not fraudulently induced to sign the agreement. Because the agreement is unenforceable on other grounds, we do not address this argument.

more colorfully stated, an unconscionable contract is one, such as no man in his senses and not under delusion would make, on the one hand, and as no honest and fair man would accept on the other, . . ." We recognized the potential that substantial arbitration fees may make an arbitration agreement unconscionable in Dobbins v. Hawk's Enterprises, 198 F.3d 715, 717 (8th Cir.1999). However, Lyster has not established on the record before us that undue harshness exists in the terms of the Agreement in light of Missouri law governing unconscionability.

Based upon the above discussion it is clear that Lyster executed a valid arbitration agreement and her claim of unlawful sexual harassment against Steak House falls within the scope of the Agreement. Therefore, Steak House is entitled to an order, pursuant to Section 4 of the FAA, 9 U.S.C. §4, compelling Lyster to pursue her sexual harassment claim in an arbitral, rather than a judicial, forum. Lyster requests if we find the FAA applicable to this case we enter an order requiring the arbitration be conducted in Joplin, Missouri, the city in which Lyster was employed by Steak House. During oral argument, counsel for Steak House stated the arbitration proceedings would be conducted in Missouri, in the city where Lyster was employed. We reverse the district court's denial of Steak House's petition to compel arbitration and stay proceedings. . . .

NOTES AND PROBLEMS

1. Same agreement, similar claims, different outcomes. Why?

a. Technically, these two cases are not in conflict. It is possible for a contract to be enforceable under the laws of one state but not of another, and the laws of different states governed in these two cases.

b. The plaintiff's lawyers in the two cases made slightly different arguments, one stressing the failure of consideration, the other the unconscionability of the agreement. Is it easier for a court to accept one of these arguments? Note too that Lyster's lawyer apparently did not cite *Floss*, which was decided the year before; precedent from a sister circuit isn't binding, but it's often influential.

c. Do you suppose the *Floss* court would have come to the same result if the agreement had contained a statement that EDSI, the arbitrator, promised "promptly and fairly to decide the dispute"? Or was there something else about the agreement that made the court ready to look for reasons not to enforce?

d. Suppose you were advising Ryan's or EDSI; are there changes you would recommend?

2. *Floss, Lyster*, and similar cases represent what might be called a third wave in arbitration. In the early part of the twentieth century courts enforced arbitration agreements only reluctantly. In the middle part of the century they began to embrace such agreements. That readiness to enforce arbitration agreement still holds true in the vast majority of cases. But in the past few years a note of wariness has emerged; courts have begun to discriminate among arbitration agreements on the basis of the fairness of the procedures they employ, and to refuse to enforce agreements they find fundamentally unfair. For example:

a. One court found an arbitration agreement unenforceable because blatantly one-sided:

> The [Employer's] rules when taken as a whole, however, are so one-sided that their only possible purpose is to undermine the neutrality of the proceeding. The rules require the employee to provide the company notice of her claim at the outset, including "the nature of the Claim" and "the specific act(s) or omissions(s) which are the basis of the Claim." [Employer] on the other hand, is not required to file any responsive pleadings or to notice its defenses. Additionally, at the time of filing this notice, the employee must provide the company with a list of all fact witnesses with a brief summary of the facts known to each. The company, however, is not required to reciprocate.
>
> The [Employer's] rules also provide a mechanism for selecting a panel of three arbitrators that is crafted to ensure a biased decisionmaker. . . . Under the rules, [Employer] is free to devise lists of partial arbitrators who have existing relationships, financial or familial, with [Employer] and its management. In fact, the rules do not even prohibit [Employer] from placing its managers themselves on the list. . . .
>
> Nor is fairness to be found once the proceedings are begun. Although [Employer] may expand the scope of arbitration to any matter, "whether related or not to the Employee's Claim," the employee cannot raise "any matter not included in the Notice of Claim." Similarly, [Employer is:] permitted to move for summary dismissal of employee claims before a hearing is held whereas the employee is not permitted to seek summary judgment. . . . The rules also grant Hooters the right to bring suit in court to vacate or modify an arbitral award when it can show, by a preponderance of the evidence, that the panel exceeded its authority. No such right is granted to the employee.
>
> In addition, the rules provide that upon 30 days notice [Employer], but not the employee, may cancel the agreement to arbitrate. . . .

Hooters of America, Inc. v. Phillips, 173 F. 3d 933 (4th Cir. 1999).

b. Reasoning similar to that in *Floss* and *Hooters* appears in Showmethemoney Check Cashers, Inc. v. Williams, 342 Ark. 112, 27 S.W.3d 361 (2000). A check cashing/lending service asked its customers to sign a document in which they agreed to submit any claim they had against the firm to arbitration. But the firm reserved the right to use the courts to collect any debts owed it. The Arkansas court held that in the absence of mutual obligations, there was no contract to enforce.

c. Other courts have refused to enforce arbitration agreements that set forth arbitration procedures less hospitable to the claims than a court would have been. In one case the "inhospitability" consisted of a clause requiring that the claimant pay half of the arbitrator's fees up front, where the cost of adjudication would have been borne by the government. Cole v. Burns Int'l Security Services, 105 F.3d 1465, 1482 (D.C. Cir. 1997).

d. Another form of inhospitality consists of limitations on remedies. In Armendariz v. Foundation Health Psychcare Services, 24 Cal. 4th 83, 6 P.3d 669 (2000), the court held invalid an employment arbitration agreement that limited damages to back pay (thus barring punitive damages), forbade any order of reinstatement (which would have been available in a judicial proceeding), and did not provide for the award of attorney's fees to a prevailing plaintiff (as the statute in question did for adjudicated cases).

3. Suppose you are advising a group of employers in an industry concerning arbitration agreements for their employees. Not surprisingly, they want the process to be as inexpensive (for them) as possible. They also desire confidentiality, as much restriction of discovery as possible, and speed. What can you tell them?

4. In the preceding cases the arbitration processes, whether enforced or not, were relatively traditional: One or more arbitrators, often chosen by the parties, would hear witnesses and receive evidence followed by argument by parties, usually represented by lawyers, and would then render a decision. On the basis of what you have read so far, how would you expect a court to react to a system of arbitration in which the parties were forbidden to present witnesses' live testimony, were never told the identity of the arbitrators, who never met to discuss the case (and were not even told of each other's identities) but were required to tell a third party of their decision without supplying any support or reasons and which could not be appealed? Is it an unenforceable nightmare? Or a monument of dispute-resolving creativity? Read the next case.

Ferguson v. Writers Guild of America, West

226 Cal. App. 3d 1382, 277 Cal. Rptr. 450 (1991)

KLEIN (B.), J. A.*

I

Larry Ferguson appeals from a judgment of the superior court denying his petition for a writ of mandate directed to respondent Writers Guild of America, West, Inc.

Ferguson, a screenwriter, was engaged by Paramount Pictures Corporation to write a screenplay for a feature-length theatrical motion picture entitled "Beverly Hills Cop II." When the picture was completed, the Writers Guild, on April 27, 1987, determined the writing credits for the picture as follows: Screenplay by Larry Ferguson and Warren Skaaren; Story by Eddie Murphy & Robert D. Wachs.

Ferguson then commenced this proceeding by filing a petition for writ of mandate in the superior court on May 15, 1987. In his petition he asked the court to issue a peremptory writ of mandate requiring the Writers Guild to set aside its credit determination and make a new determination giving Ferguson sole screenplay credit and sole story credit. . . .

II

The process for determining writing credits for theatrical motion picture scripts is governed in this case by two documents. The first is the 369-page theatrical and

* Assigned by the Chairperson of the Judicial Council.

television basic agreement, reached in 1985 by 241 producing companies, represented by the Alliance of Motion Picture and Television Producers, Inc.; 3 television networks; Writers Guild of America, West, Inc.; and Writers Guild of America, East, Inc. The second document is the Writers Guild West's 11-page credits manual, dated December 31, 1980.

The basic agreement contains, in a section entitled theatrical schedule A, detailed provisions concerning writing credits for feature-length theatrical photoplays. Under schedule A, the production company must notify all participating writers of its tentative credits determination. Any of the writers may then file with the production company and the Writers Guild a written request for arbitration of credits. . . .

The credits manual, discussed below, sets forth the procedures the Writers Guild has adopted. . . . The credit arbitration is administered by the Writers Guild's credit arbitration secretary. When a credit arbitration is requested, this officer sends the parties to the arbitration a screen arbiter's list, containing the names of all potential arbitrators. These are Writers Guild members with credit arbitration experience or with at least three screenplay credits of their own. This list comprised at least 400 names in 1987. Each party can peremptorily disqualify a reasonable number of persons from the list. From the remaining potential arbitrators, the secretary selects three, endeavoring to select individuals experienced in the type of writing involved in the particular case.

The secretary delivers to the three arbitrators all script, outline, and story material prepared or used in the creation of the screenplay, together with source material (writings upon which the screenplay or story is based). These documents are supplied to the Writers Guild by the production company, and each participant in the credit arbitration may examine them to assure the inclusion of everything he or she has written. Any dispute over the "authenticity, identification, sequence, authorship or completeness" of literary material to be included is resolved by a special three-member committee, which conducts for that purpose a prearbitration hearing, at which all affected writers may present testimony and other evidence.

The arbitrators also receive the production company's statement of tentative credits; a copy of the credits manual; and the statements of the parties, which are confidential. The secretary designates a member of the Writers Guild's Screen Writers' credits committee to act as consultant to the arbitrators on procedure, precedent, policies, and rules, and to aid the arbitrators toward a majority decision.

The three arbitrators hold no hearing, and they deliberate independently of each other. Indeed, each remains unaware of the identity of the other two (unless, after they reach their decisions, the consultant convenes a meeting with the three). Each arbitrator notifies the secretary of his or her determination. The secretary then informs the parties of the decision of the majority of the arbitrators.

Within 24 hours thereafter, any party may request the convening of a policy review board, consisting of three members of the Writers Guild's credits committee including that committee's chairman or vice-chairman. The policy review board does not examine the script, story, or source material; indeed, its members are forbidden to read these. Its function is solely to detect any substantial deviation from the policy of the Writers Guild or from the procedure set forth in the credits manual. The policy review board has authority to direct the arbitration committee to reconsider the case or to order a fresh arbitration by a new triumvirate. The policy review board is not empowered to reverse the decision of an arbitration committee in matters of judgment. A decision of the policy review board approving a credit determination is final.

III

With his petition, Ferguson furnished the . . . court with all screenplay and story materials, so the court could make the proper credit decisions under Writers Guild standards. Thus, to determine the correct story credit, the court was invited to ascertain which writings represented "a contribution distinct from screenplay and consisting of basic narrative, idea, theme or outline indicating character development and action." . . .

Ferguson contends, in the alternative, that the Writers Guild's credit determination process was infected by procedural improprieties and irregularities, and asks us to order the Writers Guild to conduct the credit arbitration anew. The asserted procedural defects are these: (1) the credit arbitration secretary improperly cast herself in the role of consultant to the arbitration committee and had improper substantive communications with the three arbitrators; (2) Ferguson was unfairly denied a postponement of the arbitration to assemble additional story materials and prepare his confidential statement for the arbitrators; (3) the arbitrators were given insufficient time to review the materials Ferguson submitted; (4) the Writers Guild took no steps to ensure the three arbitrators were disinterested and unbiased; (5) the arbitrators were not provided with copies of schedule A or the credits Manual; (6) the Writers Guild incorrectly treated as story material a memorandum in which Paramount executive David Kirkpatrick recounted a story idea told him orally by Murphy and Wachs; and (7) the Writers Guild improperly denied Ferguson's request that the arbitrators be given a second memorandum in which Paramount executive Michael Roberts remarked that Paramount "threw out" the screenplay drafted by the writers it had previously engaged and hired Ferguson "to write an entirely new draft."

Ferguson presents a final contention, challenging as error the rulings of the superior court denying his requests (a) to take the deposition of Warren Skaaren, the writer awarded shared screenplay credit, and (b) to compel the Writers Guild to reveal the identity of the three arbitrators, presumably so Ferguson could take their depositions.

IV

Before ruling on these contentions, we must consider the proper scope of judicial review of the Writers Guild's credit determination in this case. We agree with the Writers Guild's position that under schedule A and the credits manual, disputes over writing credits for feature-length photoplays are nonjusticiable. As judges we are no doubt as capable as any lay person of studying screenplays, outlines, and other literary material to assess the relative contributions of the participating writers. The membership of the Writers Guild, however, have agreed among themselves (by approving the credits manual) and with the producers' association (by entering into schedule A of the basic agreement) that this delicate task is to be performed by arbitration committees composed of experienced Writers Guild members. The professional writers who constitute the Writers Guild have thus decided[,] quite appropriately we think[,] that the credit-determination process can be handled both more skillfully, more expeditiously, and more economically by Writers Guild arbitration committees than by courts. The finality provisions of schedule A and the credits manual, quoted earlier, demonstrate the Writers Guild membership's intention that credit disputes be resolved without resort to ruinously expensive litigation. (See Code Civ. Proc., §§1286-1286.8; Morris v. Zuckerman, 69 Cal. 2d 686, 691 (1968).)

V

In examining Ferguson's claims of procedural irregularities, we bear in mind that the procedures employed in the present arbitration have already been reviewed for correctness by the Writers Guild's own policy review board. The court accords considerable deference to the decision of the policy review board, because of its members' expertise in the interpretation and application of schedule A and the credits manual. . . .

Even were we to reach the merits of Ferguson's seven claims, we would find them devoid of merit. Judicial review of the Writers Guild's credits determination is restricted to considering whether the party challenging the determination has demonstrated a material and prejudicial departure from the procedures specified in the credits manual. Applying this standard, we have determined that the record sustains none of Ferguson's seven procedural contentions.

Ferguson's remaining grievance is that he should have been told the names of the arbitrators. . . . We reject this position. . . .

With respect to the identity of the arbitrators, the credits manual unequivocally specifies that the three arbitrators are not to be informed of each other's identities, and the Writers Guild has sufficiently established that, though not also stated in the credits manual, its unvarying and well-known rule has long been that the identities of the arbitrators are also not disclosed to the parties to the arbitration nor to anyone else inside or outside the Writers Guild. The Writers Guild's insistence on this practice is supported by important and legitimate considerations, including the necessity that arbitrators be entirely freed from both real and perceived dangers of pressure, retaliation, and litigation. While it is unusual to have an arbitration procedure in which the parties cannot appear in person before the arbitrators and cannot learn the arbitrators' identities, discovery of the names of the arbitrators in a Writers Guild credit arbitration could serve no legitimate function. Ferguson apparently wishes to ask the arbitrators, inter alia, to explain and justify their conclusions regarding the various writers' contributions to the final screenplay. Even when an arbitration is conducted under more familiar rules, though, such as the commercial arbitration rules of the American

Arbitration Association, the losing party is not permitted to conduct an inquisition into the arbitrators' thought processes in reaching their award.

Appellant's request to dismiss the appeal is denied, and the judgment is affirmed. . . .

NOTES AND PROBLEMS

1. Imagine that a state legislature adopted the Writers Guild procedure for its court system: litigants limited to written submission to an anonymous panel of judges; no opportunity to appear, summon witnesses, or present testimony; and the court's judgment rendered without explanation.

a. Would such a procedure be held to violate due process?

b. If so, why is such a process permissible here?

2. Closer to our specific topic, compare the Writers' Guild process with far less dramatic or unusual features of "standard" arbitration agreements described in the cases and Notes preceding, a number of which were held unenforceable for procedural unfairness.

a. Should the Writers' Guild system have been enforced? Why?

b. If so, what is it that makes the Guild arbitration system, which has been in effect for several decades, fair while the others are not?

3. Could the Guild have adopted even more streamlined procedures — eliminating, for example, the right to exercise peremptory challenges to names on the panel and the right of appeal to the policy review board?

4. If one believed the answer to the preceding question is no, how would one challenge such a process? In a judicial system the Due Process Clause lies at hand, but in private arbitration the clause does not apply because the requisite state action is absent. Because most arbitration agreements result from such contractual provisions, they are subject to attack on the same fronts as are other contractual clauses. As we have already seen, one can attack an arbitration clause on grounds of contractual doctrines like the failure of consideration, unconscionability, and the like in the same way one might attack consent to jurisdiction. See Carnival Cruise Lines v. Shute, Chapter II, supra page 141. Ferguson did not mount such an attack. Why do you suppose his lawyer decided against this? Would it matter whether he could demonstrate that membership in the Guild, which includes agreeing to consent to its credit arbitration procedures, was required by the studios who buy scripts? Should it matter that the Writers Guild's members have in repeated elections endorsed the arbitration system by large majorities?

5. The preceding discussion of arbitration assumes agreement (or purported agreement) to arbitrate entered into before the dispute arises. Other scenarios are possible.

a. Suppose the parties have no prior agreement to arbitrate, but, after the dispute arises, agree to mediate. The mediation is unsuccessful — the parties cannot agree — but both parties develop trust in the mediator. They decide, therefore, to ask the mediator to switch hats, and to arbitrate the dispute, perhaps with the stipulation that she will limit her decision to the range between the parties' lowest demand and highest offer.

b. Suppose the parties have no prior agreement, a claim arises out of a traffic accident, and a lawsuit is filed. After pleadings close and some discovery has occurred, there are settlement discussions. The parties make some progress, having agreed on a range of settlement, but they are still too far apart to reach a deal. They do agree, however, that the judge assigned to the case is bad news — arbitrary, not very bright, and entirely unpredictable. They might agree to halt the lawsuit and instead arbitrate. That would, among other things, give them a way of selecting another person to decide the case.

c. Alternatively, in the same setting, suppose the parties agree that defendant is liable, but remain far apart on damages: That can happen when there are contested future medical or other expenses. Under these circumstances they might agree to a special form of arbitration, in which both parties present evidence and submit a damage proposal to the arbitrator, who must then choose either the plaintiff's or defendant's figure — nothing in between. (This variation is sometimes called high-low or "baseball" arbitration because the major league owners and the player's union have agreed on it to settle salary disputes.) The advantage of this feature is that, first, it gives the parties incentive to submit a reasonable figure (lest the arbitrator reject it out of hand) and second, it guards against what some believe to be a temptation of arbitrators, to split the difference.

6. If a judge renders a decision, in most U.S. jurisdictions the decision can be appealed. What about arbitrators' awards? The general proposition, illustrated by *Ferguson*, is that appeal to a court is possible but not generally useful because the court will narrowly restrict the scope of its review.

a. *Ferguson* actually offers three different descriptions of judicial review of arbitration awards. At one point it says, "Disputes over writing credits for feature-length photoplays are nonjusticiable." At another it describes its review as "limited to a determination whether there has been a material breach of the terms of the credits manual, which binds the Writers Guild as well as its members." Finally, it compares this review to that employed in "more traditional arbitrations": "The court does not review the merits of the arbitrators' award; it examines only whether the parties in fact agreed to submit their controversy to arbitration, whether the procedures employed deprived the objecting party of a fair opportunity to be heard, and whether the arbitrators exceeded their powers."

b. These three formulations have a similar core idea: The court's reviewing powers are limited to whether the parties actually agreed to submit this particular dispute to arbitration and to whether the arbitrator exceeded the power granted by the agreement.

c. Two cases give a sense of how hesitant courts are to review the substance of arbitration awards and of how expansively they interpret arbitrators' powers. In Advanced Micro Devices, Inc. v. Intel Corp., 36 Cal. Rptr. 2d 581 (Cal. 1994), the California Supreme Court upheld an arbitrator's award that gave not damages but a royalty-free license to the intellectual property of a competitor. Such an award would, the dissent pointed out, be beyond the powers of a court and was not specifically conferred by the contract to arbitrate. In Mastrobuono v. Shearson Lehman

Hutton, 115 S. Ct. 1212 (1995), the U.S. Supreme Court upheld an arbitrator's award that gave a brokerage house customer punitive damages, despite a clause in the arbitration agreement specifying application of New York law, which does not permit arbitrators to award punitive damages. The *Mastrobuono* Court ruled that the choice of law clause clearly governed the substantive law to be applied by the arbitrator but did not clearly specify that it should govern remedial choices as well; the arbitrator's award was therefore not clearly beyond the scope of his jurisdiction. Suppose the brokerage houses now insert a clause clearly saying that punitive damages are unavailable in such arbitrations; do plaintiffs now have an argument that the arbitration agreement should be unenforceable? See Note 2 following Lyster v. Ryan's Family Steak House, supra pages 505-506.

C.   Curtailed Adjudication: Summary Judgment

Suppose there is no arbitration agreement, or that it has features that lead to a court's refusal to enforce it. Litigation ensues. Your client is open to settlement, but negotiations prove fruitless. Or your client wants something that only adjudication can deliver — for example, a binding public declaration of rights. Is trial inevitable? No. Curtailed adjudication — typically known as summary judgment — is an adjudicative alternative to trial for cases so one-sided that trial would be pointless. This section explores the possibilities and limits of summary adjudication.

Rule 56 governs the making and granting of motions for summary judgment. The key provision, in Rule 56(c), provides that such motions are to be granted when the record "show[s] that there is no genuine issue as to any material fact and that the moving party is entitled to judgment as a matter of law." That terse language means that summary judgment reaches both the legal and factual merits of the case. Consider how it does so.

NOTES AND PROBLEMS

1. Start with a simple case that reflects the historical origins of summary judgment. A plaintiff sues the defendant, alleging that the defendant executed a promissory note that is now due and unpaid.

a. The defendant files a Rule 12(b)(6) motion. That motion will be denied. Why?

b. Now explain why the denial of the Rule 12(b)(6) motion does not mean that the plaintiff will prevail at trial. What does a trial test that a 12(b)(6) motion does not?

2. Assume that in this case the defendant answers the complaint by denying liability.

a. Unlike a 12(b)(6) motion, a denial puts the facts of the case at issue.

b. Under the governing substantive law, only a few factual issues are relevant on this state of the pleadings: Was the note actually signed by the defendant? Has the defendant repaid the money owed under the note? (Note that other issues that might arise — the defendant's contention that the plaintiff had previously sued on this same note; his allegation that the parties had agreed to arbitrate their dispute or that the plaintiff had forged defendant's signature — are specified as affirmative defenses under Rule 8(c) and therefore are not raised by an answer that simply denies liability.)

c. If you were a plaintiff faced with a denial in such a case, what information would you want to find out during discovery?

3. Assume that disclosure and discovery yield the note itself, whose validity the defendant does not contest, and the defendant's answer to an interrogatory in which he does not claim to have repaid the note.

a. If the parties go to trial, the plaintiff will presumably introduce the note, defendant's interrogatory answer admitting that he signed it, and testify that the defendant has not paid the money owed under the note. At that point the plaintiff will rest his case. Unless the defendant changes his story from that revealed in the interrogatory answers, he has no defense, because he acknowledges having signed the note and does not claim to have repaid it. Accordingly, the plaintiff will prevail at trial, either because the trier of fact (judge or jury) returns a verdict or judgment in his favor, or, more likely, because the judge uses Rule 50 to order "judgment as a matter of law" — the equivalent of saying that the defendant has not presented a case that would permit a jury to decide in his favor.

b. Under these circumstances summary judgment prevents a futile trial. If the plaintiff properly moved for summary judgment on these facts, the court would grant it, entering judgment in the plaintiff's favor and obviating the necessity of a trial. The court would take this action because, in the hypothetical case, the plaintiff established all the elements of the claim beyond genuine dispute, or, in the language of Rule 56(c), "there is no genuine issue of material fact."

4. How would a plaintiff make such a motion? What would he have to present to the court?

a. Courts decide summary judgment motions on the basis of various documents (affidavits, deposition transcripts, copies of relevant documents). No witnesses testify in court, and no jury is present. Because we bar judges from making assesments of credibility in cases to be tried by juries, the law responds by allowing summary judgment only in cases where we need no such assessments.

b. One of the most common documents in summary judgment motions is an affidavit. An affidavit is a written document in which the affiant swears under penalty of perjury that the statements made are true. Typically, affidavits are drafted by lawyers who review them with the affiants, who then sign them, attesting that they are true.

5. Read Rule 56(e) and answer the following questions.

a. In the hypothetical case described above, recall that one of the issues was whether the defendant had signed the promissory note. Suppose the plaintiff's lawyer presented to the court an affidavit in which the lawyer swore, "Plaintiff told me he watched the defendant personally sign the promissory note." What's the problem?

b. Suppose the plaintiff signs an affidavit whose core statement is, "I know that defendant signed the promissory note." What's the problem?

c. Suppose the plaintiff's lawyer has learned from interviewing his client that the plaintiff watched the defendant sign the note. To support the contention that the defendant signed the note, what statements should plaintiff's affidavit contain?

d. Suppose that in a deposition of the defendant, he said, "I signed the note." Could the transcript (or audio- or videotape) of that deposition be presented instead of the plaintiff's affidavit? In addition to it?

6. Finally, consider what a defendant must present to avoid summary judgment. In our hypothetical case, assume that plaintiff has presented evidence sufficient to warrant a grant of summary judgment. That evidence includes an affidavit from the plaintiff stating that he watched the defendant sign the promissory note. The defendant tells his lawyer that he did not sign the note.

a. To defeat the motion for summary judgment, can he submit an affidavit saying, "I can prove I didn't sign the note"? Why not?

b. What should the affidavit say?

c. Notice a crucial point: If in opposition to a plaintiff's motion for summary judgment, the defendant submits an affidavit denying that he signed the note, the judge will deny the plaintiff's motion. That is true even if the plaintiff bolsters his own affidavit with affidavits of twenty-six disinterested witnesses, each of whom swears to having watched the defendant sign the note. For the defendant to prevail in opposing the plaintiff's motion for summary judgment does not mean that defendant will prevail at trial. It simply means that there is something to have a trial about — here, about the defendant's credibility in denying that he signed the note and about the accuracy of perception and credibility of the witnesses contradicting the defendant.

7. Having cleared this preliminary ground, let us consider summary judgment in action. We do so in two cases. The first, Celotex Corp. v. Catrett, focuses on what the party moving for summary judgment must (in the absence of any opposition) do to justify a court's granting its motion. The second case, Bias v. Advantage International, Inc., focuses on what a party opposing the motion must do to defeat it.

Before *Celotex*, the leading case on federal summary judgment was Adickes v. S. H. Kress & Co., 398 U.S. 144 (1970). *Adickes* grew out of a civil rights demonstration in which plaintiff, refused service at a racially segregated lunch counter, sued the restaurant owner. At the time, the federal public accommodations laws provided no damages remedy for private discrimination, and the liability of the business therefore depended on whether it had acted in concert with the local authorities, thereby fulfilling the state action requirement of 42 U.S.C. §1983. All agreed that there had been a police officer in the store at the time service was refused, but plaintiff produced no evidence showing communication between the officer and any store employee. The defendant submitted affidavits and deposition transcripts from the store manager and the police officer that they had not communicated with each other and that the manager had refused service because he was concerned about "a riot." The Supreme Court held that it was inappropriate to grant summary judgment because defendant "did not carry its burden [on summary judgment] because of its failure to foreclose the possibility that . . . this policeman reached an understanding with some Kress employee that petitioner not be served." 398 U.S. at 157. For *Adickes*, then, the defendant moving for summary judgment had the burden of showing that plaintiff could not prevail at trial. The *Celotex* case asserts that it does not overrule *Adickes*. Is that correct?

Celotex Corp. v. Catrett

477 U.S. 317 (1986)

REHNQUIST, J.

. . . Respondent commenced this lawsuit in September 1980, alleging that the death . . . of her husband . . . resulted from his exposure to products containing asbestos manufactured or distributed by 15 named corporations. . . . Petitioner's motion [for summary judgment] . . . argued that summary judgment was proper because respondent had "failed to produce evidence that any [Celotex] product . . . was the proximate cause of the injuries alleged. . . ." In particular, petitioner noted that respondent had failed to identify, in answering interrogatories specifically requesting such information, any witnesses who could testify about the decedent's exposure to petitioner's asbestos products. In response to petitioner's summary judgment motion, respondent then produced three documents which she claimed "demonstrate that there is a genuine material factual dispute" as to whether the decedent had ever been exposed to petitioner's asbestos products. The three documents included a transcript of a deposition of the decedent, a letter from an official of one of the decedent's former employers whom petitioner planned to call as a trial witness, and a letter from an insurance company to respondent's attorney, all tending to establish that the decedent had been exposed to petitioner's asbestos products in Chicago. . . .

. . . The District Court granted . . . the motion . . . because "there [was] no showing that the plaintiff was exposed to the defendant Celotex's product in the District of Columbia or elsewhere within the statutory period." [The court of appeals reversed.]

. . . In our view, the plain language of Rule 56(c) mandates the entry of summary judgment, after adequate time for discovery . . . against a party who fails to make a showing sufficient to establish the existence of an element essential to that party's case, and on which that party will bear the burden of proof at trial. In such a situation, there can be "no genuine issue as to any material fact," since a complete failure of proof concerning an essential element of the nonmoving party's case necessarily renders all other facts immaterial. The moving party is "entitled to judgment as a matter of law" because the nonmoving party has failed to make a sufficient showing on an essential element of her case with respect to which she has the burden of proof. "[The] standard [for granting summary judgment] mirrors the standard for a directed verdict under Federal Rule of Civil Procedure 50(a). . . ." Anderson v. Liberty Lobby, 477 U.S. 242, 250 (1986).

Of course, a party seeking summary judgment always bears the initial responsibility of informing the district court of the basis for its motion, and identifying those portions of "the pleadings, depositions, answers to interrogatories, and admissions on file, together with the affidavits, if any" which it believes demonstrate the absence of a genuine issue of material fact. But unlike the Court of Appeals, we find no express or implied requirement in Rule 56 that the moving party support its motions with affidavits or other similar materials *negating* the opponent's claim. On the contrary, Rule 56(c), which refers to "the affidavits, *if any*," (emphasis added), suggests the absence of such a requirement. . . . One of the principal purposes of the summary judgment rule is to isolate and dispose of factually unsupported claims or defenses, and we think it should be interpreted in a way that enables it to accomplish this purpose. . . . We do not mean that the nonmoving party must produce evidence in a form that would be admissible at trial in order to avoid summary judgment. Obviously, Rule 56 does not require the nonmoving party to depose her own witness. Rule 56(e) permits a proper summary judgment motion to be opposed by any of the kinds of evidentiary materials listed in Rule 56(c), except the mere pleadings themselves. . . .

The Court of Appeals in this case felt itself constrained, however, by language in Adickes v. S. H. Kress & Co., 398 U.S. 144 (1970). There we held that summary judgment had been improperly entered in favor of the defendant. . . . *Adickes* . . . said . . . "both the commentary on and the background of the 1963 Amendment conclusively show that it was not intended to modify the burden of the moving party . . . to show initially the absence of a genuine issue concerning any material fact." We think that this statement is accurate in a literal sense. . . . But we do not think the *Adickes* language quoted above should be construed to mean that the burden is on the party moving for summary judgment to produce evidence showing the absence of a genuine issue of material fact, even with respect to an issue on which the nonmoving party bears the burden of proof. Instead, as we have explained, the burden on the moving party may be discharged by "showing" — that is, pointing out to the District Court — that there is an absence of evidence to support the nonmoving party's case. . . .

Respondent commenced this action in September 1980, and petitioner's motion was filed in September 1981. The parties had conducted discovery, and no serious claim can be made that the respondent was in any sense "railroaded" by a premature motion for summary judgment. . . .

In this Court, respondent's brief and oral argument have been devoted as much to the proposition that an adequate showing of exposure to petitioner's asbestos products was made as to the proposition that no such showing should have been required. But the Court of Appeals declined to address either. . . . We think the Court of Appeals . . . is better suited than we are to make these determinations in the first instance. . . . Summary judgment procedure is properly regarded not as a disfavored procedural shortcut, but rather as an integral part of the Federal Rules as a whole, which are designed "to secure the just, speedy and inexpensive determination of every action." Fed. Rule Civ. Proc. 1. Before the shift to "notice pleading" accomplished by the Federal Rules, motions to dismiss a complaint or to strike a defense were the principal tools by which factually insufficient claims or defenses could be isolated and prevented from going to trial. . . . But with the advent of "notice pleading," the motion to dismiss seldom fulfills this function any more, and its place has been taken by the motion for summary judgment. . . .

[Reversed and remanded.]

Justice WHITE, concurring.

[I agree with the holding, but] the movant must discharge the burden the rules place upon him: It is not enough to move for summary judgment without supporting the motion in any way or with a conclusory allegation that the plaintiff has no evidence to prove his case. . . .

. . . Celotex does not dispute that if respondent has named a witness to support her claim, summary judgment should not be granted without Celotex['s] somehow showing that the named witness' possible testimony raises no genuine issue of material fact. . . .

Justice BRENNAN, with whom THE CHIEF JUSTICE and Justice BLACKMUN join, dissenting.

. . . I do not disagree with the Court's legal analysis [but believe the majority gives insufficient guidance to district courts. Moreover] I believe that Celotex did not meet its burden of production under Federal Rule of Civil Procedure 56. . . .

. . . If the burden of persuasion at trial would be on the *nonmoving* party, [the *moving*] party . . . may satisfy Rule 56's burden of production in either of two ways. First, the moving party may submit affirmative evidence that negates an essential element of the nonmoving party's claim. Second, the moving party may demonstrate to the Court that the nonmoving party's evidence is insufficient to establish an essential element of the nonmoving party's claim. . . .

Where the moving party adopts this second option . . . a conclusory assertion that the nonmoving party has no evidence is insufficient. . . . Rather, as the Court confirms, a party who moves for summary judgment on the ground that the nonmoving party has no evidence must affirmatively show the absence of evidence in the record. This may require the moving party to depose the nonmoving party's witnesses or to establish the inadequacy of the documentary evidence. [Or] the moving party may demonstrate this by reviewing for the court the admissions, interrogatories and other exchanges between the parties that are in the record. Either way, however, the moving party must affirmatively demonstrate that there is no evidence in the record to support a judgment for the nonmoving party.

. . . [T]he nonmoving party may defeat a motion for summary judgment that asserts the nonmoving party has no evidence by calling the court's attention to supporting evidence in the record that was overlooked or ignored by the moving party. . . .

[Justice BRENNAN's dissent was based on Celotex's failure to discharge its burden as he understood it; he pointed to the failure to deal with the testimony expected to be given by plaintiff's former supervisor. Justice Brennan stated that the supervisor could "describe asbestos products to which decedent had been exposed." Justice STEVENS's dissent is omitted.]

NOTES AND PROBLEMS

1. What was the fight about in *Celotex*?

a. Everyone agreed that, to recover, Mrs. Catrett had to show that her husband had been exposed to asbestos manufactured by Celotex. (A subsidiary issue concerned the date of that exposure. Had it been within the statue of limitations?)

b. Everyone agreed that Celotex could defeat recovery by showing that Mr. Catrett had not been exposed to asbestos manufactured by it (or one of its predecessors).

c. So what were the parties disagreeing about?

2. *Celotex* becomes easier to understand if one bears in mind that summary judgment operates to eliminate trial. At trial Celotex, the defendant, could prevail in two ways. It could prove that Mr. Catrett was not exposed to its asbestos; for example, it might demonstrate that it neither it nor its predecessor companies had ever manufactured asbestos. Or it could prevail if Mrs. Catrett *failed to show* that Mr. Catrett was exposed to its asbestos; for example, it might convince a jury that the sole testimony linking Mr. Catrett to Celotex asbestos was not credible because the witness had been bribed.

a. Explain why these two routes lead to the same result.

b. As a matter of practice (if we eliminate the dramatic and unlikely examples above and suppose that one of Celotex predecessor firms did distribute asbestos but that the evidence linking Celotex to Mr. Catrett is thin), which of these routes to the same result is likely to be easier for Celotex to demonstrate?

c. According to *Celotex*, the defendant Celotex can certainly win its summary judgment motion by making the first showing — that Mr. Catrett was not exposed to its product. That is no news: *Adickes* had said as much. Can Celotex also win with the second showing — that Mrs. Catrett has failed to show that Mr. Catrett was exposed? Explain how this development — whether or not it overrules *Adickes* — could affect the number of cases in which courts will grant summary judgment.

3. *Adickes* was willing to speculate about what the plaintiff might uncover between summary judgment and trial. *Celotex* looks at the state of the evidence at the time of summary judgment.

a. Notice the implication of *Celotex*'s focus on the state of evidence at summary judgment: It will not suffice for the party resisting summary judgment to say, "I'm planning to look into that before trial." Unless the party can show that it has had insufficient time for discovery, it will lose. How would a party that believed it had had insufficient opportunity for discovery ward off summary judgment? See Rule 56(f).

b. A strong way to state the proposition explored in this note is to say that *Celotex* made effective use of discovery not just an option, but virtually mandatory. See Rule 56(f) and explain.

4. Notice the *Celotex* formulation: The party that will have the burden of proof at trial has the equivalent burden at summary judgment — the burden of "mak[ing] a showing" of evidence sufficient to let a rational trier of fact find in its favor. This alignment of burdens at summary judgment with burdens at trial means that the

standard for summary judgment will apply differently depending on which party is moving for summary judgment. To see this point, suppose that one of the issues in contention is whether asbestosis (as opposed to some other disease process) caused Mr. Catrett's death. Mrs. Catrett's complaint alleges that asbestosis caused her husband's death; Celotex denies that allegation in its answer. Mrs. Catrett as the plaintiff will have the burden of proof at trial on that issue.

a. First suppose that Celotex, the defendant, moves for summary judgment on this issue of causation. In its supporting papers, it reviews all the discovery documents (including experts' reports) and points out that no medically qualified expert has opined that asbestosis caused Mr. Catrett's death. In her response, Mrs. Catrett produces the affidavit of a pathologist who recites his professional qualifications, examination of the relevant tissue samples, and comes to the conclusion that the laboratory findings are "consistent with Mr. Catrett's having died as a result of asbestosis." Explain why the court should deny Celotex's motion for summary judgment.

b. Now suppose that it is Mrs. Catrett, not Celotex, who moves for summary judgment on the issue of causation. In support of this motion she produces the same affidavit. In response, Celotex produces no affidavit or other evidence contradicting plaintiff's expert. Explain why the court should deny Mrs. Catrett's motion for summary judgment.

c. Why does the same affidavit lead to the same result (denial of summary judgment) even though different parties are moving for summary judgment?

5. The Court in *Celotex* did not actually decide who should prevail on the defendant's motion for summary judgment. It contented itself instead with setting out a new standard for summary judgment and remanding for the lower courts to decide the case using that new standard. Suppose that Celotex had made an adequate initial showing under that new standard to justify the grant of summary judgment — unless plaintiff in response produced evidence that would entitle a rational trier of fact to find in its favor. Such a situation would frame a question for the lower court: Did the material presented by Mrs. Catrett in response to the motion for summary judgment suffice? That topic is the focus of the next case.

As a bridge to that case, imagine several possibilities. The key piece of evidence was a letter to which both the dissent and majority refer — a letter written by a Mr. Hoff, an executive for a company that had once employed Mr. Catrett. The issue, you recall, is whether Mr. Catrett was exposed to a Celotex asbestos product.

a. Suppose the letter said, "I bought asbestos from Celotex and gave it to Catrett for use on the job." Sufficient to avoid summary judgment? The underlying factual assertion clearly would be. But recall that the letter is not an affidavit — that is, it is not a sworn statement. Will the sufficiency of the letter turn on whether it would be admissible as evidence, as specified in Rule 56(e)?

b. Suppose the letter said, "I don't know what asbestos products Catrett used while employed here, but I think our records will contain that information." Sufficient to avoid summary judgment?

c. What if the letter said, "I wasn't in direct contact with this part of the operation, but I understand that Catrett used Celotex products." Sufficient to avoid summary judgment?

d. The next case assumes that the defendant's initial showing is sufficient to warrant summary judgment unless the plaintiff rebuts that showing and focuses on the adequacy of the plaintiff's response.

Bias v. Advantage International, Inc.

905 F.2d 1558 (1990)

SENTELLE, Circuit Judge:

This case arises out of the tragic death from cocaine intoxication of University of Maryland basketball star Leonard K. Bias ("Bias"). James Bias, as Personal Representative of the Estate of Leonard K. Bias, deceased ("the Estate"), appeals an order of the District Court for the District of Columbia which granted summary judgment to defendants Advantage International, Inc. ("Advantage") and A. Lee Fentress. . . . For the reasons which follow, we affirm. . . .

I. Background

On April 7, 1986, after the close of his college basketball career, Bias entered into a representation agreement with Advantage whereby Advantage agreed to advise and represent Bias in his affairs. Fentress was the particular Advantage representative servicing the Bias account. On June 17 of that year Bias was picked by the Boston Celtics in the first round of the National Basketball Association draft. On the morning of June 19, 1986, Bias died of cocaine intoxication. The Estate sued Advantage and Fentress for . . . injuries allegedly arising out of the representation arrangement between Bias and the defendants.

[T]he Estate alleges that, prior to Bias's death, Bias and his parents directed Fentress to obtain a one-million dollar life insurance policy on Bias's life, that Fentress represented to Bias and Bias's parents that he had secured such a policy, and that in reliance on Fentress's assurances, Bias's parents did not independently seek to buy an insurance policy on Bias's life. . . . [D]efendants . . . did not secure any life insurance coverage for Bias prior to his death. . . .

The District Court awarded the defendants summary judgment. . . . With respect to the [life insurance] claim, the District Court held, in effect, that the Estate did not suffer any damage from the defendants' alleged failure to obtain life insurance for Bias because, even if the defendants had tried to obtain a one-million dollar policy on Bias's life, they would not have been able to do so. The District Court based this conclusion on the facts, about which it found no genuine issue, that Bias was a cocaine user and that no insurer in 1986 would have issued a one-million dollar life insurance policy, or "jumbo" policy, to a cocaine user unless the applicant made a misrepresentation regarding the applicant's use of drugs, thereby rendering the insurance policy void. . . .

The Estate appeals . . . the District Court's conclusions, arguing that there is a genuine issue as to Bias's insurability. . . .

II.   Summary Judgment Standard . . .

Sum Judg
Stndo'

The Supreme Court has stated that the moving party always bears the initial responsibility of informing the district court of the basis for its motion and identifying those portions of the record which it believes demonstrate the absence of a genuine issue of material fact. Celotex Corp. v. Catrett. The Supreme Court also explained that summary judgment is appropriate, no matter which party is the moving party, where a party fails to make a showing sufficient to establish the existence of an element essential to that party's case, and on which that party will bear the burden of proof at trial. Thus, the moving party must explain its reasons for concluding that the record does not reveal any genuine issues of material fact, and must make a showing supporting its claims insofar as those claims involve issues on which it will bear the burden at trial.

Once the moving party has carried its burden, the responsibility then shifts to the nonmoving party to show that there is, in fact, a genuine issue of material fact. The Supreme Court has directed that the nonmoving party "must do more than simply show that there is some metaphysical doubt as to the material facts." Matsushita Elec. Industrial Co. v. Zenith Radio, 475 U.S. 574, 586 (1986). The nonmoving party "must come forward with 'specific facts showing that there is a *genuine issue for trial.*'"(emphasis in original). In evaluating the nonmovant's proffer, a court must of course draw from the evidence all justifiable inferences in favor of the nonmovant. Anderson v. Liberty Lobby, Inc., 477 U.S. 242, 255 (1986).

III.   The Insurance Issue

The District Court's determination that there was no genuine issue involving Bias's insurability rests on two subsidiary conclusions: First, the District Court concluded that there was no genuine issue as to the fact that Bias was a drug user. Second, the District Court held that there was no dispute about the fact that as a drug user, Bias could not have obtained a jumbo life insurance policy. We can only affirm the District Court's award of summary judgment to the defendants on the insurance issue if both of these conclusions were correct.

A.   Bias's Prior Drug Use

The defendants in this case offered the eyewitness testimony of two former teammates of Bias, Terry Long and David Gregg, in order to show that Bias was a cocaine user during the period prior to his death. Long and Gregg both described numerous occasions when they saw Bias ingest cocaine, and Long testified that he was introduced to cocaine by Bias and that Bias sometimes supplied others with cocaine.

Although on appeal the Estate attempts to discredit the testimony of Long and Gregg, the Estate did not seek to impeach the testimony of these witnesses before the District Court, and the Estate made no effort to depose these witnesses. Instead, the Estate offered affidavits from each of Bias's parents stating that Bias was not a drug user; the deposition testimony of Bias's basketball coach, Charles "Lefty" Driesell, who testified that he knew Bias well for four years and never knew Bias to be a user of drugs at any time prior to his death; and the results of several drug tests administered to Bias during the four years prior to his death which may have shown that, on the occasions when the tests were administered, there were no traces in Bias's system of the drugs for which he was tested.

Because the Estate's generalized evidence that Bias was not a drug user did not contradict the more specific testimony of teammates who knew Bias well and had seen him use cocaine on particular occasions, the District Court determined that there was no genuine issue as to the fact that Bias was a drug user. We agree.

There is no question that the defendants satisfied their initial burden on the issue of Bias's drug use. The testimony of Long and Gregg clearly tends to show that Bias was a cocaine user. We also agree with the District Court that the Estate did not rebut the defendants' showing. The testimony of Bias's parents to the effect that they knew Bias well and did not know him to be a drug user does not rebut the Long and Gregg testimony about Bias's drug use on particular occasions. The District Court properly held that rebuttal testimony either must come from persons familiar with the particular events to which the defendants' witnesses testified or must otherwise cast more than metaphysical doubt on the credibility of that testimony. Bias's parents and coach did not have personal knowledge of Bias's activities at the sorts of parties and gatherings about which Long and Gregg testified. The drug test results offered by the Estate may show that Bias had no cocaine in his system on the dates when the tests were administered, but, as the District Court correctly noted, these tests speak only to Bias's abstention during the periods preceding the tests. The tests do not rebut the Long and Gregg testimony that on a number of occasions Bias ingested cocaine in their presence.

The Estate could have deposed Long and Gregg, or otherwise attempted to impeach their testimony. The Estate also could have offered the testimony of other friends or teammates of Bias who were present at some of the gatherings described by Long and Gregg, who went out with Bias frequently, or who were otherwise familiar with his social habits. The Estate did none of these things. The Estate is not entitled to reach the jury merely on the supposition that the jury might not believe the defendants' witnesses. We thus agree with the District Court that there was no genuine issue of fact concerning Bias's status as a cocaine user.

B.   The Availability of a Jumbo Policy in Light of Bias's Prior Drug Use . . .

The defendants offered evidence that *every* insurance company inquires about the prior drug use of an applicant for a jumbo policy at *some point* in the application process. . . . The Estate's evidence that some insurance companies existed in 1986 which did not inquire about prior drug use at certain particular stages in the application process does not undermine the defendant's claim that at *some point* in the process *every* insurance company did inquire about drug use, particularly where a jumbo policy was involved. The Estate failed to name a single particular company or provide other evidence that a single company existed which would have issued a jumbo policy in 1986 without inquiring about the applicant's drug use. Because the Estate has failed to do more than show that there is "some metaphysical doubt as to the material facts," *Matsushita Elec.*, the District Court properly concluded that there was no genuine issue of material fact as to the insurability of a drug user. . . .

In order to withstand a summary judgment motion once the moving party has made a prima facie showing to support its claims, the nonmoving party must come forward with specific facts showing that there is a genuine issue for trial. Fed. R. Civ. P. 56(e). The Estate has failed to come forward with such facts in this case, relying instead on bare arguments and allegations or on evidence which does not actually create a genuine issue for trial. For this reason, we affirm the District Court's award of summary judgment to the defendants in this case.

NOTES AND PROBLEMS

1. Start by framing the claim and defense, around which the summary judgment revolve.

a. Bias's estate sues for breach of contract. What contract? What are the damages sought?

b. How did defendants respond? What parts of the claim did defendants attack?

c. How did plaintiff seek to avoid defendants' response?

2. *Bias* takes us through the trilogy of summary cases handed down the same year as *Celotex*. Summarized in Part II of the opinion, *Liberty Lobby*, *Matsushita Electric*, and *Celotex* establish the current framework for federal summary judgments (as well as for a number of state courts that have followed the same course).

a. What did the defendants do with the discovery process and the products of discovery that enabled them to move for summary judgment? Explain how they used this evidence to attack plaintiff's claim.

b. Explain how *Celotex* enabled them to make such an attack.

3. Once defendants made this motion for summary judgment, *Celotex* and its companion cases allow the nonmoving party (here the plaintiff) to respond in either of two ways. He can argue that party moving for summary judgment has not adequately demonstrated a deficiency in the evidence available to the party resisting summary judgment. Or, he can present evidence to counter the movant's evidence, in the hope of demonstrating the existence of an issue of fact.

a. The plaintiff in *Bias* obviously took the latter course. Explain why that was almost certainly the right move to make, even though it did not succeed.

b. Why does the plaintiff lose? Is the court correctly interpreting the statute and case law?

c. The opinion recites the black letter law for the proposition that the nonmoving party, once properly challenged, must squarely meet the evidentiary issues raised by the moving parties. The nonmoving party can do so by presenting evidence that creates an issue of fact for trial. In seeking to demonstrate that there is a factual dispute, the nonmoving party gets the advantage that the court must draw all justifiable inferences in its favor (Anderson v. Liberty Lobby), but the nonmoving party has to do more than create "metaphysical doubt" (*Matsushita Electric*). Is the court correctly interpreting these cases?

d. The best demonstration of what these phrases mean, as well as of how close the decision in *Bias* comes to the line, emerges if we think about some variations on the facts of the case. Start by supposing that the sole evidence of drug use presented by the defendants was the testimony of Bias's friends, who said under oath that they had on several specific dates seen Bias use cocaine. Further suppose that plaintiff had presented evidence of other persons, present at the same times, who unequivocally testified that they had been in Bias's company the whole time and that he had not used drugs. Explain why summary judgment would not be appropriate.

e. Now come closer to the actual case, in which there was testimony that Bias had ingested cocaine on specific dates, that he had provided drugs for others; there was also evidence (the negative drug tests) that he had been drug-free on other days, and that close associates and family did not believe him to have used drugs. Why does this state of evidence not create a similar conflict for a trier of fact to resolve?

f. The court's answer to that question is that the evidence of drug use was specific, while the evidence of non-use was general, and that the specific trumps the general — and that there really isn't a conflict for the trier to resolve. Suppose that Bias died when he was struck by a car while crossing the street. Under those circumstances if the defendants had moved for summary judgment by introducing evidence of drug use and arguing that he would not have been able to obtain a life insurance policy, do you suppose the case would have come out the same way? Or would plaintiff have been able to argue, first, that, at worst, defendants' evidence showed occasional exposure to the drug and, second, that the defendants were trying to avoid their own breach of contract by posthumously smearing the name of a great African-American athlete? Moreover, the defendants were doing so with the testimony of persons who, by their own account, were habitual drug users, and perhaps paid by the defendants for their testimony; shouldn't Bias's estate be able to put them on the stand before a jury and probe their veracity?

g. In the real world, we know that Bias did not die in a car accident, but from a drug overdose. Is the court, without explicitly saying so, inferring from the cocaine-related death, that Bias must have been a *habitual* user, that drugs would inevitably have showed up in any insurance physical, and that he was therefore uninsurable? If so, is such an inference permissible?

4. Given the facts of the case, is there any way plaintiff could have avoided summary judgment?

a. We are told that Bias was given "several" drug tests, all of which were negative. The court says that this demonstrates only that Bias had not used drugs recently on the days the tests were given and that is not enough to overcome specific testimony by the associates of drug use. But suppose the tests had been administered randomly, some of them in the same months where the other witnesses testified to drug use. Would that be enough cast doubt on the picture of habitual drug use? Recall that the question on summary judgment is whether there is an issue of fact to try.

b. We are also told that the plaintiff did not depose the two friends who testified as to Bias's drug use or attack their credibility. What sort of deposition questions might have shed enough doubt on their credibility to create a triable issue of fact? What if they admitted that they felt Bias' parents had mistreated and taken advantage of him, and that they didn't like the parents and would be happy if the parents lost the suit? Would that be enough?

D.   Judicial Management of Litigation

Lying in the background of judicial discussions of summary judgment as well as of arbitration is a fact that does not often get articulated in judicial opinions: Courts are very busy. In 2002 the federal courts saw 275,000 civil and 67,000 new criminal cases filed; that gave the average federal district judge a bit over 500 cases for which she was responsible. Judges in state courts, where most litigation occurs, often have larger caseloads; in 2000 judges in courts of general jurisdiction (where felonies and large-stake civil litigation occurs) had caseloads ranging from the mid-400s (Alaska and Idaho) to 3,800 (South Carolina), with most large states in the 1,500-2,000 range.* Such caseloads make for judges who are (a) busy, sometimes to the point of frazzled impatience; and (b) eager to manage their cases in such a way that the backlog does not grow.

Just how bad are the backlogs? Judicial administrators speak of "clearance" rates: If 100,000 cases are filed in a given year and 100,000 disposed of, the clearance rate is 100 percent. (Notice that the cases "cleared" needn't be the same ones filed; a clearance rate measures not speed of disposition but whether the system as a whole is gaining ground or falling behind.) In recent years civil filings have dropped slightly. Perhaps as a consequence, a dozen states reported in 2001 that they were gaining ground or staying even, and all but three reported clearance rates of over 90 percent.

How judges cope with their dockets and the implication of those steps for litigants is the subject of this section. Perhaps the first thing to recognize is that many of these cases will go away by themselves, even if a judge does nothing. Typically that happens because the plaintiff has filed suit to get the defendant's attention, and the ensuing negotiations will yield a quick resolution. In the federal system just under 20 percent of civil cases end this way, in an average of six months. Another very large group — almost 70 percent of dispositions — requires some court action but ends before pretrial; these end in an average time of 7.7 months. Thus almost 90 percent of cases end with modest judicial intervention in less than 8 months. The remainder — just over 10 percent of the federal civil cases — take more time: An average of 13.5 months for those that end during the pretrial stage and almost 21 months for the 2 percent of civil cases that go to trial.

* National Center for State Courts, Examining the Role of State Courts 2001, 12. (2001)

State court processing time reveals a similar picture. According to two studies conducted in the 1990s of the 75 largest counties in the United States, about 45 percent of tort and 65 percent of contract cases terminated in less than a year; 75 percent and 85 percent were the respective figures for terminations within two years. For the small percentage of cases going to trial, the timelines are longer. For these tried cases the median time to final judgment was 22 months for torts and 19 months for contract cases; and about 13 percent of tort trials and 5 percent of contract trials took four years or more to complete.*

NOTES AND PROBLEMS

1. What does this time line mean for a litigator?

a. One of your first clients is a small business person involved in a dispute with one of her suppliers. She asks you how long the case will take; what can you tell her?

b. You represent a person injured in an auto accident. The defendant's insurer has offered a settlement — not ridiculously low but not particularly generous. You believe you can do better at trial, or at least close to trial. Your client asks you how long it will take if he doesn't settle now.

2. What does the time to resolution mean for the judicial system?

a. The largest difference in time to termination is between cases that end with little or no judicial intervention and those that require more judicial time. Depending on the specific system, the "judgeless" proportion ranges between 75 percent and 90 percent. Given the effectiveness of what might be called benign neglect, how should a judge "manage" her docket? An elaborate set of studies commissioned by the Congress has found that early judicial management reduced time to disposition but increased litigation cost: Faster but more expensive litigation resulted from judicial management."** How should a judge behave in the face of such studies?

b. According to the cited studies, the single management technique that consistently speeded litigation (though it increased costs) was setting an early date for trial; other techniques yielded the worst of both worlds, increasing cost without speeding disposition. Many judges wishing to establish such deadlines divide cases into categories: simple cases with an early trial date, cases of "ordinary" complexity with a mid-range trial date, and complex cases with a more distant trial date. Linked to trial dates would be other deadlines: for joinder and dismissal motions, for disclosure and discovery cut-off, for pretrial conferences, accordingly. The underlying assumption is that the setting of firm trial dates will prevent counsel (and judges) from procrastinating; deviations from schedules have to be

---

* U.S. Dept. of Justice Bureau of Justice Statistics, Tort Cases in Large Counties 1992; Contract Cases in Large Counties 1992; Contract Trials & Verdicts in Large Counties 1996; Tort Trials and Verdicts in Large Counties 1996.

** James Kakalik et al., Just, Speedy and Inexpensive? An Evaluation of Judicial Case Management Under the Civil Justice Reform Act (Rand Institute for Civil Justice 1996).

justified. Effective though they may be at speeding disposition, such schedules can yield stark results in the hands of a judge determined to enforce them.

Sanders v. Union Pacific Railroad Co.

154 F.3d 1037 (9th Cir. 1998)

PER CURIAM.

Phillip Sanders appeals the district court's dismissal of his action with prejudice for failure to comply with the court's pretrial preparation order. . . . Finding no abuse of discretion by the district court, we affirm.

Background

In June 1995, Sanders sued his employer, Union Pacific Railroad Co., under the Federal Employer's Liability Act, following a work-related back injury. The district judge set a trial date of November 19, 1996. He also scheduled a pretrial conference for November 8, 1996, and issued a form order concerning preparation for that conference. The order set forth a schedule for the filing of various motions, oppositions, proposed instructions, and other trial-related documents. The order's introduction warned the parties that a failure to comply could result in sanctions. The order repeated this admonition in its final paragraph, which stated in bold letters:

> **SANCTIONS. Counsel are advised that failure to comply with the procedures set forth in this order, including the duty to provide the court with updated documents as necessary, may result in sanctions, including but not limited to monetary sanctions, adverse evidentiary rulings, trial continuance, and dismissal of the action.**

Several of the items required by the order, such as the proposed pretrial order, stipulated instructions, and list of stipulated exhibits, called for joint preparation. . . . Sanders's counsel failed to comply with almost all of the requirements of the pretrial order.

The district court's order required motions in limine to be filed twenty-one days before trial. Union Pacific filed eleven motions in limine on time; Sanders's counsel filed one motion in limine six days late. The order required the parties to meet and confer regarding jury instructions, and to submit joint instructions fourteen days before trial. Sanders's counsel did not meet and confer, and submitted about fifty unilateral jury instructions. He submitted his exhibit, witness and expert witness lists two days late. The order required counsel to submit a trial brief fourteen days before trial; Sanders's counsel never submitted a trial brief. The order required joint preparation of a trial notebook, to be submitted fourteen days prior to trial; Sanders's counsel never conferred on the trial notebook and offered to submit a unilateral one only at the pretrial conference. Sanders's counsel never submitted oppositions to Union Pacific's motions in limine, which were due fourteen days before trial. At no time prior to the pretrial conference did Sanders's counsel request a continuance.

Judge Ideman's law clerk presided over the pretrial conference, without any objection by Sanders. Sanders's counsel explained during the conference that he had been representing plaintiffs in a lawsuit in Nebraska involving a multiple-death train collision. His responsibilities in that other matter had lasted longer than he could have anticipated, and he therefore was unable to meet the pretrial order's deadlines. He further asserted that Union Pacific's attorneys were partially responsible for his failure to comply with the order because they had been uncooperative with him. Sanders's counsel made it clear that he was not ready to go to trial; he had further work to do on the case. He suggested a dismissal without prejudice; Union Pacific declined to agree to one. At the conclusion of the pretrial hearing, the presiding law clerk indicated that the case would be removed from the trial calendar, and that the judge would probably take additional action.

About a week after the pretrial conference, the district court dismissed Sanders's action with prejudice as a sanction for failure to comply with the pretrial order. . . . He levied the sanction . . . because (1) Sanders's counsel had completely failed to comply with the pretrial order, (2) Union Pacific had already incurred "great pain and expense in preparing for trial," (3) other litigants before the district court would be inconvenienced by a delay in the present case, and (4) Sanders's case did not involve important questions of public policy. . . .

Discussion . . .

"[T]he key factors [in deciding to dismiss a case for failure to comply with a court order] are prejudice [to the defendant created by the disobedience] and availability of lesser sanctions."

In the present case, by the time of the pretrial conference, Sanders's . . . multiple failures undoubtedly impaired the defendant's efforts to prepare for trial.

. . . By neglecting to alert the court or opposing counsel to his impending total failure to meet pretrial and trial deadlines, Sanders's counsel deprived the court of its best opportunity to impose lesser sanctions to force the litigation back onto track or to make timely alternative arrangements. Counsel's conduct left the court only with last-minute notice of a total failure of preparation, with a consequent disruption of the trial calendar. In these circumstances, we conclude that the district court did not abuse its discretion in rejecting lesser sanctions than dismissal. Trial judges are constantly struggling to avoid the increasing problems of delay and expense that threaten to overwhelm the courts. In our continuing efforts to achieve justice for individual litigants, we must not allow the flagrant disobedience of judges' orders to bring about further delay and expense. . . .

CANBY, Senior Circuit Judge, dissenting:

The position of the majority is understandable; district courts must be able to manage their dockets, and conduct such as that of Sanders' counsel cannot be tolerated. Dismissal, however, "is so harsh a penalty it should be imposed as a sanction only in extreme circumstances." Thompson v. Housing Authority, 782 F.2d 829, 831 (9th Cir. 1986). Although Sanders's counsel was guilty of multiple failures, they all occurred at once as part of his general failure to be ready for the pretrial conference and trial. This is not a case where the court was met with repeated instances of dilatory behavior over a span of time, nor has the litigation been inordinately delayed. In these circumstances, I believe that dismissal with prejudice was an abuse of discretion.

The dismissal was entered by the court sua sponte, which means that counsel should have been warned that a dismissal was imminent. A boilerplate warning in a preprinted order, distributed before any problem has arisen, does not advise counsel that dismissal is imminent. . . . I would . . . reverse and remand for the imposition of other sanctions.

NOTES AND PROBLEMS

1. What was the district court's authority for the original scheduling order whose violation led to dismissal? See Rule 16(b).

2. Sanders sought an en banc rehearing by the Ninth Circuit. The en banc panel reversed the district court with terse explanation:

> We decline to dissect what happened in this case and to prescribe a recipe for how and when an action may be dismissed, with or without prejudice, for failure to follow the pretrial rules. This is a unique case. Suffice it to say that where, as here, the district judge allows his law clerk to conduct the final pretrial conference, declines to give counsel an opportunity to be heard before the court, and then dismisses the action *sua sponte* with prejudice, we cannot let the dismissal stand.
>
> Counsel was plainly derelict in meeting his Rule 16 obligations, but so was the district judge. In different circumstances, where the district court exercises its own discretion in a deliberate, informed and reasonable way, we would accord it considerable deference. But we cannot see how any deference is warranted in these circumstances.
>
> Accordingly, we vacate all orders entered after the pretrial conference and remand for another district judge to consider afresh how to proceed. In so doing, we express no opinion about how the new judge's discretion should be exercised. Rather, we simply put the parties back to square one.

Sanders v. Union Pacific Railroad Co., 193 F.3d 1080 (9th Cir. 1999) (en banc).

a. You are the district judge to whom the case has been newly assigned. What do you do? Can you dismiss the case, as the first judge did? Can you decide to ignore the behavior of plaintiff's lawyer and set the case for trial?

b. If not, is there a sanction less than dismissal that would be just?

3. To answer the preceding question, take the case and the problem it presents in stages.

a. Begin at the point that plaintiff's lawyer saw that his Nebraska case would take longer than he had anticipated and prevent his meeting the pretrial order deadlines. What should he have done?

b. Suppose that, before any deadlines had passed, plaintiff's lawyer approached the other side and explained his problem. In the ensuing conversation the opposing lawyer tells plaintiff's lawyer that she's been working late into every night and all weekend for several weeks to comply with the deadline, and isn't inclined to stipulate to an extension just because plaintiff's lawyer took on more work than he could handle. What should plaintiff's lawyer do now?

c. Besides irritation at having worked hard to meet a deadline the other side ignored, defendant's lawyer has an argument about unfairness. Most lawyers will tell you that there's an enormous difference between simultaneous exchange of information — briefs, witness and exhibit lists, etc. — and having the luxury of being able to prepare your documents after you have already seen the other side's. Had the trial court not dismissed, plaintiff's lawyer's delay would have enabled him to prepare his trial brief after seeing the defendant's, to choose his witnesses after seeing whom the defendant was planning to introduce, and so on. Had plaintiff's lawyer moved for an extension of time, the defendant's lawyer could have averted this unfairness by withholding her materials until plaintiff had prepared his.

4. Now consider the consequences for plaintiff and his lawyer.

a. Suppose the original opinion — dismissing the case — had stood. Imagine a meeting between the plaintiff, Mr. Sanders, and his lawyer after this case. What should the lawyer tell him?

b. Further suppose that after the dismissal Mr. Sanders consulted another lawyer. What should that lawyer tell him?

5. Many lawyers think that the federal court system operates somewhat more formally, with tighter deadlines, than do state courts, though there are very wide variations among individual judges in both systems.

a. One consequence is that in many state courts it takes longer to bring a case to trial than it does in federal courts. Does that justify the harshness of an occasional case like *Sanders*?

b. Was the real failure of "due process" in *Sanders* the judge's failure to warn Sanders's lawyer (supposing he didn't already know it) that he was entering a different zone of "legal culture" than the one he was used to? Does a judge have an obligation to let lawyers know that he or she really means it when a deadline is imposed?

6. Pretrial orders like those in *Sanders* will end some litigation, but their overt aim is different — to prepare parties for the actual trial by encouraging both a winnowing of legal theories and factual disputes and a precise identification of questions to be contested at trial. Note that practices vary among judges using the pretrial conference in this way. Some courts require parties to submit elaborate pretrial statements defining the issues and proof and specifying the admitted and disputed facts. Others conduct a number of conferences throughout the progress of the case. The hope is that such conferences will both reduce the time required for trial and enhance the eventual quality of the trial. The leading study of pretrial in negligence cases* found that only half of these hopes were realized. It concluded that trial time of pretrial cases was not reduced when the time spent in pretrial was taken into account (and that the chances for settlement were not enhanced) but that the quality of trials was improved in terms of party preparation and effective presentation.

---

* Maurice Rosenberg, The Pretrial Conference and Effective Justice (1964).

When the pretrial conference serves this latter function, one major issue is the precise scope of pretrial and, particularly, of the pretrial order. Appellate courts, on occasion, have cautioned judges both against turning the pretrial order into a common law pleading in disguise and against overzealous attempts to encourage admissions on disputed issues. The most commonly litigated issue involves a situation in which the pretrial order specifies that certain issues will be tried, certain witnesses will testify, or certain evidentiary items will be introduced, and one party then seeks to raise matters or present evidence not within the scope of the order.

McKey v. Fairbairn

345 F. 2d 739 (D.C. Cir. 1965)

MILLER, J.

[Mrs. Littlejohn, a tenant, notified her landlord of a leak in one room of her apartment. Before he fixed it] an all-night rain fell, as a result of which the roof developed a leak and the floor of Mrs. Littlejohn's bedroom became wet. Upon arising the next morning and discovering the floor's condition,[1] Mrs. Littlejohn went over it twice with a mop. Having left the room for a short time, she returned to awaken her grandson, who was sleeping there, and to get her coat. She slipped on the wet floor and fell, sustaining certain injuries.

On April 24, 1959, Mrs. Littlejohn brought this suit to recover damages from the owner of the house and her agent. In her complaint, she alleged that the floor on which she slipped and fell

was wet and dangerous due to a leaking roof which the defendants, or either of them, knew or should have known in time to have repaired said damage; that actually defendants, or either of them, had notice of said defect. . . .

The statement of the pretrial proceedings filed March 12, 1963, contains the following:

Plaintiff asserts that on February 27, 1958, Agnes Littlejohn slipped and fell on the wet floor in her second floor bedroom on premises 814 Constitution Avenue, N. E.; that the wet floor was caused by a leaking roof and wall; that her fall and resulting injuries and damages were caused by the following negligence of D: Failure to repair roof and eliminate dangerous condition of roof and walls allowing entry of water, after notice thereof and promise by the Ds to make such repairs, in breach of duty owed under the lease.

During the progress of the trial, the District Judge asked appellant's [Mrs. Littlejohn's] counsel this question:

Do you agree that the allegation of negligence in this case is as set forth in the pretrial order, which reads as follows: Failure to repair roof and eliminate dangerous condition of roof and walls allowing entry of water, after notice thereof and promise

---

1. It was not a puddle, she said, and was not actually running water. She merely said, "It was wet."

by the defendants to make such repairs, in breach of duty owed under the lease? That is your contention?

To which he replied, "Yes, sir, Your Honor." The judge then asked:

Do you both agree on that, that is the allegation of negligence, that is the issue in the case?

Again appellant's counsel answered, "Yes, sir." Later in the trial, counsel for appellant moved to amend the pretrial order to permit him to introduce certain sections of the District of Columbia Housing Regulations, particularly Section 2507 which requires that roofs shall be leakproof, and that rain water shall be drained so as not to cause wet walls or ceilings. The trial judge denied the motion, and directed a verdict for the defendants.

[On appeal] the questions presented [are]:

1. Did the Court err in directing a verdict for appellees where evidence was presented that said appellees — landlords — had notice of a leakage in the roof, which leakage caused plaintiff to slip and suffer injuries, and where said landlords had promised to repair said condition?

2. Did the Court err in refusing to admit into evidence pertinent housing regulations where counsel for plaintiff first became aware of them during the course of trial and proffered them while still putting on plaintiff's evidence; particularly where counsel for defendants had admittedly been familiar with these regulations?

[The court first held that the landlord had no notice of the problem and therefore no liability under the lease to make repairs.]

The second question presented by the appellant remains to be answered. Appellant refers to the housing regulations which she offered as "pertinent." It is suggested the proffered regulations relate only to multiple-unit dwellings and are not pertinent here. Whether so or not, we need not decide because we hold . . . the trial judge in this case did not abuse his "justifiably large discretion" in refusing to permit appellant to change her theory during the trial.

In addition to the foregoing, there is another reason for upholding the trial court's action in directing a verdict for the defendants. There was no possibility of constructive notice to the landlord about the wetness of the floor of Mrs. Littlejohn's room. But she was well aware of the condition, as shortly before she had mopped the floor twice. . . .

Affirmed.

FAHY, J. (dissenting).

The service performed by pre-trial procedure is of unquestionable value. A case arises occasionally, however, in which the latitude granted to the trial judge by Rule 16, Fed. R. Civ. P., to depart from the pre-trial order should be used. The Rule provides that the order controls the subsequent course of the action "unless modified at the trial to prevent manifest injustice." There is no touchstone by which to determine when "manifest injustice" would be prevented by permitting modification. A case must be judged according to its circumstances. The circumstances which lead me to dissent include the important one that the law in this jurisdiction applicable to the legal obligations of a landlord to a tenant includes our decision in Whetzel v. Jess Fisher Management Co. We there held his obligations embrace those imposed by applicable Housing Regulations. Those urged to apply here were not referred to in the pre-trial order. Nevertheless they are public regulations, and Whetzel v. Fisher is a decision of this court. A question for determination at the trial should have been whether the regulations applied and, if so, whether the injury of the tenant was proximately caused by their violation. In deciding the matter of "manifest injustice," or, otherwise stated, "manifest justice," the failure of counsel specifically to bring forth this theory of liability until during the trial must be weighed against the possible prejudice to defendant in then permitting departure from the pre-trial order. The defendants could have been given opportunity to meet the case sought to be based on the regulations; but unless plaintiff were permitted to seek reliance upon them he was, of course, "out of court" entirely with respect to them.

Failure to include the regulations in the pre-trial order appears not to have been deliberate. Plaintiff is thus made to suffer from an inadvertence counsel sought to have remedied at the trial. Any possible disadvantage to experienced counsel for defendants, by permitting the requested departure from the pre-trial order, could have been obviated by a continuance if counsel so desired. In any event the disadvantage to defendants is more than outweighed, it seems to me, by the disadvantage to plaintiff in unnecessarily limiting consideration of her case to only a part of the law which might be found applicable. Manifest injustice is more likely to occur when the applicable law is precluded from consideration because not referred to in the pre-trial order than when the preclusion is of evidentiary matter which takes the adversary by surprise. . . .[1]

NOTES AND PROBLEMS

1. Be clear about the consequences of the judge's failure to amend the pretrial order. The plaintiff had, potentially, two theories of liability — one relying on the lease and the other on the housing code.

a. The plaintiff started by relying exclusively on the lease.

b. When the plaintiff, during trial, sought to introduce into evidence parts of the housing code, the judge refused to permit it. Why?

2. If plaintiff had sought to amend her pleading to allege violation of the housing code, would her motion have been granted? See Rule 15(a). If so, why could she not amend the pretrial order?

3. The conflict that gave rise to this opinion would have been avoided if, during the pretrial conference, the judge had explicitly drawn plaintiff's attention to the housing statute and pointed out that it obviated the necessity to prove negligence. Most judges will not take such an action, arguing that to do so is tantamount to

---

1. I have not sought to solve the problem on the theory, not urged, that the pre-trial order might be read to allow the inclusion of the Housing Regulations in evidence without necessity for its amendment.

"trying the party's case" for her and that it is inconsistent with the premises of the adversary system. Is there an inconsistency between the relatively active role taken by some judges in the settlement phase of pretrial conferences and the disinclination to guide the parties regarding the merits of their cases?

As you have seen, most lawsuits filed in U.S. courts will end by the time they have reached the stage described in this chapter. But don't stop reading: Those suits will end because the parties know about the processes discussed in the next several chapters. One can, therefore, think about those processes in two ways. From one point of view, they will yield results so predictable that parties can settle without regret. From another point of view, they are so unpredictable and so dangerous that parties will settle even strong cases to avoid them. As you read, consider which point of view seems closest to the truth.

IDENTIFYING THE TRIER

IX

At the end of the pretrial stage and on the brink of trial, we focus on an issue that has lurked in the background throughout our consideration of the litigation process: the identity of the trier of fact. Some lawyers assert that the identity of the trier is the most important single factor in determining the outcome of the case; others go even further, asserting that it is the only thing that matters. Even if this view is exaggerated, in close cases it matters who holds the power of decision; small differences in perspective may determine the outcome of cases involving such questions as whether witnesses are trustworthy or what behavior is "reasonable." Notice that we have already approached this topic in exploring jurisdiction, arbitration, mediation, and settlement. Jurisdictional challenges, if successful, take a case out of one court system—and its trier—and put it in another. In negotiated and arbitrated disputes the parties, by taking their case out of the court system, are also taking it out of a judge's hands. This chapter examines a set of issues that arise when a dispute stays within the court system. Even within that system there can be a choice among judges, a further choice between judge and jury, and still further choices among jurors.

A. Judging Judges: Bias and Recusal

We start with the key figure in any case—the judge. The central importance of the judge derives from two circumstances. First, as we have seen, most contemporary lawsuits do not reach trial. Consequently, the potential counterbalance offered by jury trial, where that is available, will not come into play. In most cases the only decisions made by anyone other than a party will be made by a judge. That includes rulings on almost every topic addressed thus far: jurisdiction and venue, choice of law, the pleadings, discovery motions, and motions for summary judgment. Second, even if there is a jury, the judge not only rules on various challenges to jurors but also has the power of setting aside jury verdicts and ordering new trials. The identity of the judge becomes vital to the litigants, and the possibility of a biased judge can be terrifying. Professional training may help keep judges focused on factors the law defines as permissible, but judges are human, and humans are fallible. How does the system seek to protect litigants against biased judges?

Some states permit peremptory challenges of judges simply by the filing of a timely affidavit alleging in conclusory terms that the judge is prejudiced against the party. Cal. Civ. Proc. Code §170.6 (West 2003) (permitting one such peremptory challenge of a judge per case). Such legislation has been proposed in Congress, but at present the federal system permits challenges only for cause. The procedure and standards are set forth in 28 U.S.C. §§144 and 455. The latter statute establishes two broad categories for disqualifying a judge. One contains specific guidelines barring, for example, a judge's hearing a case "where he has served as lawyer in the matter in controversy" before becoming a judge or "[w]here he has served in governmental employment and . . . expressed an opinion concerning the merits of the particular case or controversy." It also bars decisions in cases in which a judge or her family has a financial interest. 28 U.S.C. §455(b). The other category is much broader: "Any justice, judge, or magistrate of the United States shall disqualify himself in any proceeding in which his impartiality might reasonably be questioned." 28 U.S.C. §455(a). As a build-up to the case law, use the following problems to familiarize yourself with the statute.

NOTES AND PROBLEMS

1. In most federal and state courts, where there is more than one judge, the clerk's office will assign each case to a judge by a system of random assignment (unless the case is connected with a previously filed action, in which case it will go to the judge already dealing with the related matter). Suppose you represent a small business owner—a local franchisee of a national firm—in contract claim where you have drawn one of the two following judges; the question is whether either judge must "recuse" him- or herself from the case.

a. Judge Hott, whose name strikes dread in lawyers' hearts, is intemperate, abusive to lawyers, not given to reading briefs or listening to oral argument, and thought not to have studied law deeply either during or after law school. Lawyers with whom you practice report that Judge Hott appears to issue rulings almost randomly. Can you recuse Judge Hott?

b. Judge Wize is well liked by lawyers, listens carefully even to ill-prepared arguments, rules promptly, and, even the losers concede, usually correctly. As required by Rule 7.1 you have filed a Disclosure Statement indicating that 45 percent of your client is owned by Franchisor Corp. Judge Wize indicates that she owns 10 shares of Franchisor Corp. Both you and your adversary would be delighted to keep Judge Wize on the case; can you?

2. Your analysis of the statutes has likely led you to counterintuitive results.

a. Start with Judge Hott. The recusal statutes do not protect litigants against bad judges—only against biased ones; unfortunately, the hypothetical Judge Hott does not appear to be biased against any particular litigant—just generally unsuited to be a judge. Most states and the federal judiciary have procedures for invoking discipline against judges who, though unbiased, fail to comply with the Judicial Canons of Ethics, one of whose provisions requires judges to be "patient, dignified, and courteous to litigants, jurors, witnesses, lawyers, and others with whom the judge deals in an official capacity." Canon 3B(4).

A violation of any of the canons can provide the basis for a disciplinary complaint and investigation of a judge. States have various mechanisms for receiving, investigating, and acting upon complaints against state judges. In the federal judiciary, 28 U.S.C. §372 sets forth a procedure by which persons can file complaints against judges, and requires the chief judge of each circuit to investigate the charges and to take various actions — ranging from dismissal of the complaint, to a declaration that the judge in question is disabled, to censure or reprimand, to referral of the case to the House of Representatives for impeachment proceedings.

The validity of disciplinary rules and mechanisms in the state courts is relatively clear. In the federal courts §372 was long questioned as in possible conflict with Article III of the Constitution, which gives judges life tenure and provides for removal from office only by impeachment. In one fiercely contested case, the D.C. Circuit upheld the right of the Judicial Conference, acting on the recommendation of the Fifth Circuit, to impose on a judge a public reprimand, a withdrawal of all new cases for a year, and a three-year moratorium on sitting in cases in which any of the twenty-three lawyers who had testified against him were involved. The Hon. John McBryde v. Committee to Review Circuit Council Conduct, 264 F.3d 52 (D.C. Cir. 2001).

But violation of the Canons, while perhaps a basis for complaint and discipline against a judge, does not remove that judge from your particular case. Only recusal does that.

b. Must Judge Wize recuse herself? Analytically, that question has two parts. First, locate the portion of §455 that says she has a problem; which clause applies? Second, read §455(e); does it provide a way for the parties to allow Judge Wize to sit?

3. The most difficult applications of §455 involve situations involving the general standard — "might reasonably be questioned" — of §455(a). In the next case a judge trying to prevent public misunderstanding of a ruling runs afoul of §455(a).

In re Boston's Children First

244 F.3d 164 (1st Cir. 2001)

TORRUELLA, Chief Judge.

This petition involves the difficult question of whether a sitting district court judge should have recused herself after commenting publicly on a pending matter. Because we find that it was, in this case, an abuse of discretion for the judge not to recuse herself based on an appearance of partiality, we grant the writ of mandamus. . . .

Background . . .

Petitioners filed suit challenging Boston's elementary school student assignment process . . . claiming that they had been deprived of preferred school assignments based on their race, in violation of state and federal law. The case was assigned to District Judge Nancy Gertner. . . . [Plaintiffs filed both a motion for a preliminary injunction and for class certification.] The court . . . offered petitioners a choice: it would either rule on their pending motion for a preliminary injunction at that time, despite the "relatively truncated record," or it would defer the motion until further discovery had occurred. Petitioners chose to conduct further discovery . . . [but their counsel nevertheless, in an interview with a newspaper reporter] made the provocative claim[, complaining about the judge's failure to issue a preliminary injunction immediately,] that "[i]f you get strip-searched in jail, you get more rights than a child who is of the wrong color," a reference to the facts of the *Mack* case. Dave Wedge, *Lawyer Fights School Ruling*, Boston Herald, July 26, 2000, at 5. The article said that:

> According to [counsel's] motion, Gertner refused to hear arguments to expand the school suit to a class action because the affected students may no longer have standing in the case. But in the strip-search case [*Mack*], Gertner held just the opposite opinion.

Id. The article then noted that "Gertner could not be reached for comment."

In a July 28, 2000 letter to the Herald (with copies sent to both parties), Judge Gertner responded to what she viewed as inaccuracies in the July 26 article. She noted, correctly, that she had not denied class certification, but had postponed ruling on class certification until further discovery had occurred. She also noted that, as of the date of the reporter's interview with counsel, counsel for petitioners had not yet filed the motion in question. She included with the letter a copy of her procedural order providing for a hearing on class certification after the issue of standing had been resolved.

On August 4, 2000, the Herald published a follow-up article, which, based on a telephone interview with Judge Gertner, quoted her as saying:

> In the [*Mack*] case, there was no issue as to whether [the plaintiffs] were injured. It was absolutely clear every woman had a claim. This is a more complex case.

Dave Wedge, *Race-based Admissions Case To Be Heard*, Boston Herald, August 4, 2000, at 24. It is not entirely clear from the record whether Judge Gertner called the Herald reporter, or merely returned an outstanding phone call[.] [N]either party was made aware of her comments prior to their August 4 publication. . . .

Based on Judge Gertner's comments as reported in the August 4 article, petitioners then moved that the judge recuse herself because her "impartiality might reasonably be questioned." 28 U.S.C. §455(a). Specifically, petitioners claimed that the ex parte conversation between Judge Gertner and the Herald reporter, in which she described the current proceeding as "more complex" than *Mack*, was "specifically proscribed by the Code of Judicial Conduct," constituted a comment on the merits of a pending motion, and meant that the court had "placed itself in the apparent position of advising the defendants."

Judge Gertner denied the motion [to recuse]. She acknowledged that she had made the reported statements, characterizing them as attempts to correct a record suffering from gross misrepresentation by counsel for the petitioners. She noted that "[n]othing in the Code of Judicial Conduct" made such a correction improper; moreover, that it was her "obligation to make certain that people receive accurate information regarding the proceedings over which [she] preside[s]." As to the specific comment about the complexity of the instant case, Judge Gertner admitted that a conversation had taken place, but said:

> My comments in court, in the myriad decisions since the inception of the case, reflected precisely that theme — that the case raised complex questions of standing and liability, and that it deserved careful and thoughtful consideration.

As a result, Judge Gertner concluded that she had simply complied with the judicial canon allowing judges to explain "for public information the procedures of the court."

Discussion

We begin, as we must, with the statute. Section 455(a) requires "[a]ny justice, judge or magistrate of the United States [to] disqualify himself in any proceeding in which his impartiality might reasonably be questioned." This statute seeks to balance two competing policy considerations: first, that "courts must not only be, but seem to be, free of bias or prejudice"; and second, the fear that recusal on demand would provide litigants with a veto against unwanted judges. We have thus considered disqualification appropriate only when the charge is supported by a factual basis, and when the facts asserted "provide what an objective, knowledgeable member of the public would find to be a reasonable basis for doubting the judge's impartiality." . . .

Moreover, a petition for a writ of mandamus raises additional hurdles for the party seeking recusal. . . .

The crux of petitioner's complaint is that Judge Gertner's statement — that the present case is "more complex" than *Mack* because in *Mack* "there was no issue as to whether [the plaintiffs] were injured" — could be construed as a comment on the merits of the pending motions for preliminary injunction and class certification. In other words, by calling this case "more complex," Judge Gertner arguably suggested that the petitioner's claims for certification and temporary injunctive relief were less than meritorious; by comparing the case (less than favorably) to *Mack*, Judge Gertner signaled that relief was unlikely to be forthcoming. . . .

Although Canon 3(A)(6) of the Code of Judicial Conduct instructs that "[a] judge should avoid public comment on the merits of a pending or impending action," it does not extend this proscription to "public statements made in the course of the judge's official duties, to the explanation of court procedures, or to a scholarly presentation made for purposes of legal education." . . .

We have little guidance on when public comments, even those on the merits of a pending action, create an appearance of partiality for which §455(a) recusal is the appropriate remedy. [The court discussed one case in which a judge, having learned of a plan to violate his injunction against abortion protesters, went on national television] where he stated that "these people are breaking the law." [*Cooley*.]

Although the media contact in this case was less inflammatory than that in *Cooley*, we see the same factors at work, albeit on a smaller scale. First, the Boston school assignment program is a matter of significant local concern, generating at least two prominent articles in the Boston Herald. Judge Gertner viewed this prominence as all the more reason to correct misrepresentations by petitioners' counsel. However, *Cooley* counsels that in newsworthy cases where tensions may be high, judges should be particularly cautious about commenting on pending litigation. Interested members of the public might well consider Judge Gertner's actions as expressing an undue degree of interest in the case, and thus pay special attention to the language of her comments. With such public attention to a matter, even ambiguous comments may create the appearance of impropriety that §455(a) is designed to address. In fact, the very rarity of such public statements, and the ease with which they may be avoided, make it more likely that a reasonable person will interpret such statements as evidence of bias. . . .

Second, the "appearance of partiality" at issue here, as in *Cooley*, stems from the real possibility that a judge's statements may be misinterpreted because of the ambiguity of those statements. In both cases, the judge's public comments could easily be characterized as legitimate efforts to explain operative law. . . . Still, in both cases the comments were sufficiently open to misinterpretation so as to create the appearance of partiality, even when no actual prejudice or bias existed. In *Cooley*, a reasonable person might interpret the comments as an affirmative effort to enforce the law, and an indication that a guilty verdict would be forthcoming. Here, a reasonable person might interpret Judge Gertner's comments as a preview of a ruling on the merits of petitioner's motion for class certification, despite the fact that defendants had not yet filed a response to that motion. . . .

The fact that Judge Gertner's comments were made in response to what could be characterized as an attack by counsel on the procedures of her court did not justify any comment by Judge Gertner beyond an explanation of those procedures. Whether counsel for petitioners misrepresented the facts or not is irrelevant: the issue here is whether a reasonable person could have interpreted Judge Gertner's comments as doing more than correcting those misrepresentations and creating an appearance of partiality. We feel that, on these facts, a reasonable person could do so.

Again, we underscore that this ruling in no way intimates any actual bias or prejudice on the part of Judge Gertner. . . . "Such a stringent rule may sometimes bar trial by judges who have no actual bias and who would do their best to weigh the scales of justice equally between contending parties." *In re Murchison*. We have every confidence that Judge Gertner is one such judge. "But to perform its high function in the best way, 'justice must satisfy the appearance of justice,'" id., and thus we must grant the writ. . . .

NOTES AND PROBLEMS

1. What did Judge Gertner do wrong?

a. Suppose the plaintiff's lawyer had made his statements in the courtroom, and that Judge Gertner had made the same comments explaining and correcting him. Such judicial statements in court would certainly not provide the basis for recusal. How did the actual case differ?

b. Suppose that Judge Gertner was understandably upset at the potential for public misunderstanding of her rulings in a case that may inflame public passions. With the hindsight of this opinion, she knows that any comment to the press is likely to result in her recusal; is there anything she can do? Can she call the plaintiff's lawyers in and ask that they correct their misstatements? Or will this give them even stronger grounds for recusal? Can she cite these comments as reasons for imposing a "gag order," forbidding both sides from any public comment?

c. Does the opinion suggest a strategy for litigants unhappy with the judge they have drawn: make intentionally false statements about pending proceedings, bait the judge into a public correction, and then move for recusal? How would you counsel a litigant who drew that lesson from the case?

2. The First Circuit went to great lengths to say, repeatedly, that it does not believe that Judge Gertner was in any way biased in fact.

a. Suppose that the appellate judges are absolutely sincere in this belief. They are, then, requiring the recusal of a judge whom they believe is entirely unbiased. What theory underlies recusal for the appearance of bias, when it does not actually exist?

b. In an appendix attached to the opinion after denial of rehearing, the court said:

> After this opinion was prepared and initially released, the court received a petition for rehearing en banc from the district judge. Although the basis for filing such a petition may be open to dispute, cf., Fed. R. App. P. 21(b)(4), the panel sua sponte has consulted informally with the three non-panelist active judges, a practice that this court has followed in other cases.
>
> Those active judges who are not members of the panel are currently of the view that, even if the district court's statement to the reporter comprised a comment on the merits, it does not create an appearance of partiality such as to require mandatory recusal under 28 U.S.C. §455(a). They are particularly concerned that section 455(a) not be read to create a threshold for recusal so low as to make any out-of-court response to a reporter's question the basis for a motion to recuse. However, they share fully the panel's view that when a judge makes public comments to the press regarding a pending case, he or she invites trouble, and that this comment was at the very least particularly unwise.
>
> For the reasons stated, the panel reads section 455(a) as requiring recusal based on the particular events in, and character of, a highly idiosyncratic case. In the circumstances, however, it seemed to the panel fair to acknowledge a difference of view among the active judges, and the continuing need for a case-by-case determination of such issues.

3. *In re Boston's Children First* was a mandamus action, in which the plaintiff sought and the appellate court granted, an extraordinary writ. One result of this procedure is that the appellate court was hearing the case before significant rulings had occurred. In many recusal cases reviewing courts won't have this luxury. In such after-the-fact cases appeals will often involve two questions: (1) should the judge have recused himself? (2) if so, did the failure to recuse

involve a sufficiently serious likelihood of injustice as to overturn or reopen the case? Courts sometimes answer the first question positively but the second negatively.

a. In In re Chevron U.S.A., 121 F.3d 163 (5th Cir. 1997), the court of appeals granted mandamus in mid-trial to consider defendant's claims that, in a racially charged case, the judge had made a number of statements suggesting racial bias in favor of the African-American plaintiffs. After condemning the statements by the judge and saying that they would cause an objective observer to suspect partiality, the court of appeals nevertheless refused to order the judge's recusal. The opinion noted that a jury had been picked and that recusal would require repeating thirty-one days of trial and the testimony of fifty-eight witnesses. The court contented itself with warning the judge to control himself and noting that it was reserving the right to reverse on appeal after final judgment.

b. By contrast, the leading Supreme Court case interpreting §455, Liljeberg v. Health Services Acquisition Corp., 486 U.S. 847 (1988), reopened a judgment under unusual circumstances. Judge Collins sat on the board of directors of a university that stood to profit or lose depending on the decision of the case — clear grounds for recusal under §455(b)(4). But §455(b)(4) requires that the judge know of the interest in the case, and Judge Collins claimed that he had neither attended the board meetings nor read the mail that would have revealed the university's interest — and consequently lacked the requisite knowledge. Some time after Judge Collins had entered a judgment that would benefit the university, the losing party learned of the link and moved to reopen the judgment. A second district judge, after hearings, made factual findings in accord with Judge Collins's assertions that he lacked the actual knowledge required by §455(b)(4). The Supreme Court accepted those findings but nevertheless required reopening of the judgment, not under §455(b) but under §455(a). Essentially the Court held that, while it accepted Judge Collins's protestations of ignorance, "an objective observer would have questioned Judge Collins's impartiality," and that the judgment must therefore be set aside.

4. Notice that an unarticulated assumption stands behind every recusal motion against a federal trial or appellate court judge: that there is another judge without the asserted bias who is available to replace him or her. Consider two situations where that assumption does not hold:

a. What if a challenged judge cannot be replaced? District court and court of appeals judges can fill in for each other, even when a judge has to be brought from another district or circuit to do so. But there are only nine Supreme Court justices: Unlike some state systems, the Constitution does not provide for temporary appointment from a lower court. If a justice is unavailable, by reason of disability or recusal, the Court simply operates with a smaller number of justices. (In such a circumstance a tie vote affirms the result in the lower court.) Does that mean that it should be more difficult to recuse a Supreme Court justice? The justices regularly recuse themselves from cases in circumstances in which §455(b) might apply, generally without announcing publicly their reasons for doing so. Suppose, however, a situation in which only §455(a) applies. In 1993 the Court promulgated an unusual document, a Statement of Recusal Policy, 114 S. Ct. (No. 3) cix (1993). In the statement the justices announced a policy that would govern their recusal when a relative is a lawyer at a firm involved in litigation before the Supreme Court, but where the relative is not working directly on the case involved:

> We do not think it would serve the public interest to go beyond the requirements of the statute, and to recuse ourselves, out of an excess of caution, whenever a relative is a partner in the firm before us. . . . In this court, where the absence of one justice cannot be made up by another, needless recusal deprives the litigants of the nine Justices to which they are entitled. . . .

Id. at cx. Is this the right result?

b. What if a judge can be replaced, but only with a substitute who will have either the same challenged characteristic or its mirror image? A version of such a situation occurred in Blank v. Sullivan & Cromwell, 418 F. Supp. 1 (S.D.N.Y. 1975). In employment discrimination litigation, the defendant law firm moved to disqualify Judge Motley because, as a black woman, she "strongly identified with those who suffered discrimination in employment because of sex or race." Judge Motley denied the motion:

> It is beyond dispute that for much of my legal career I worked on behalf of blacks who suffered race discrimination. I am a woman, and before being elevated to the bench, was a woman lawyer. These obvious facts, however, clearly do not, ipso facto, indicate or even suggest the personal bias or prejudice required [for disqualification]. The assertion, without more, that a judge who engaged in civil rights litigation and who happens to be of the same sex as a plaintiff in a suit alleging sex discrimination on the part of a law firm, is, therefore, so biased that he or she should not hear the case, comes nowhere near the standards required for recusal. Indeed, if background or sex or race of each judge were, by definition, sufficient grounds for removal, no judge on this court could hear this case, or many others, by virtue of the fact that all of them were attorneys, of a sex, often with distinguished law firm or public service background.

Id. at 4. Right result?

5. *In re Boston's Children First* tiptoes around a very difficult problem. Most disqualification cases concern knowledge and attitudes gained by the judge before the litigation started. What about an attitude gained in the course of litigation itself? Can that ever be a basis for disqualification? Suppose Judge Gertner, ordinarily a model judge, becomes truly irritated at plaintiff's counsel for what she believes to be willful misrepresentations of her rulings.

a. Theoretically, one might not call this attitude "bias" at all:

> . . . Not all unfavorable disposition towards an individual (or his case) is properly described by those terms. One would not say, for example, that world opinion is biased or prejudiced against Adolf Hitler. The words connote a favorable or unfavorable disposition or opinion that is somehow wrongful or inappropriate, either because it is undeserved, or because it rests upon knowledge that the subject ought not to possess (for example, a criminal juror who has been biased or prejudiced by receipt of inadmissible evidence concerning the defendant's prior criminal activities), or because it is excessive in degree (for example, a criminal juror who is so

inflamed by properly admitted evidence of a defendant's prior criminal activities that he will vote guilty regardless of the facts).

Liteky v. United States, 510 U.S. 540, 550 (1994).

b. The U.S. Supreme Court has rejected this proposition and is prepared to hold that at least some judicial attitudes acquired during litigation itself ("intrajudicial" bias) can be so disproportionate as to be grounds for recusal. But it has narrowly circumscribed such cases, probably out of fear that every adverse ruling would otherwise lead to a disqualification motion. To require recusal as a result of information gained during trial, "judicial remarks" must "reveal such a high degree of favoritism or antagonism as to make fair judgment impossible." Liteky v. United States, 510 U.S. 540, 555 (1994). One would not expect to find many such cases.

6. Both §144 and §455 of 28 U.S.C. provide for the disqualification of judges. Section 144 is short and is cast in broad language; §455, as you have already seen, is considerably more detailed. Despite this difference in specificity, the courts have held that §144 incorporates the detailed substantive provisions of §455 such that the substantive standards for disqualification are the same under both sections. Section 144, however, permits a party to seek recusal by bringing specific issues to the court's attention. Section 144 also contains a provision not found in §455: When a judge is challenged under that section, "such judge shall proceed no further therein, but another judge shall be assigned to hear such proceeding." On its face, such language might suggest that the question of recusal itself must be decided by another judge. The statute has not been so interpreted. The leading case, Berger v. United States, 255 U.S. 22 (1921), held that the challenged judge rules on the challenge to impartiality. In many districts judges always ask colleagues to rule on recusal motions, but that practice varies. Should Congress amend the statute to require that another judge hear the challenge?

7. Finally, as a transition to the next section, consider whether it should make a difference in §455(a) cases that in some of them — but not all — there will be another decision maker: the jury. Does this cancel out some kinds of judicial bias?

B.   Judge or Jury: The Right to a Civil Jury Trial

In the United States the jury — an ancient, almost unique, and contested institution — counterbalances the judge's power in some cases. The material that follows explores the law governing the choice and the qualifications of the jury, but at the outset you should bear in mind some demographic and structural differences between these two types of decision makers. In this country judges are still predominantly male, white, and at least middle-aged. Equally important, they are all likely to have specialized education and half a lifetime of professional experience in law — with all the habits of mind that implies — behind them. Juries, because they are drawn from the community at large and serve only for a short time, may vary widely from this profile. Juries deliberate in secret and generally announce their verdicts only in general terms. They also are unburdened by the requirement that they describe each link in the chain of fact and law that leads them to their conclusions. Both trial and appellate courts are bound to give jury verdicts wide deference. It therefore makes a difference — sometimes a great difference — whether a litigant can have a jury decide her case.

1.   Historical Reconstruction and the Seventh Amendment

The civil trial jury flourishes only in the United States. Although we inherited the institution from English law, it is available there only in a few specialized cases (for example, in libel actions). But in the United States jury trials are widely available in both state and federal courts. This availability results from provisions in a state and the federal Constitution granting the right to jury trial in certain cases. In the debates attending the adoption of the federal Constitution in 1789 and the Bill of Rights in 1791, much attention was paid to the jury trial. Some opponents of the Constitution cited the omission of a jury trial provision as an argument for not ratifying the document:

> [T]he crux of the objection lay in the political significance of the jury trial. While an adequate representation in at least one branch of the legislature was indispensable at the top, law-making level, the jury trial provided the people's safeguard at the bottom, administrative, level. A [Maryland] Farmer argued, indeed, that the jury trial is more important than representation in the legislature, because "those usurpations, which silently undermine the spirit of liberty, under the sanctions of law, are more danger-ous than direct and open legislative attacks. . . ."*

Beyond its place in the structure of government, those seeking to include the right to jury trial in the Constitution believed that it would affect the outcome of certain cases. In particular, many of the jury's champions believed that juries would be sympathetic to the claims of rural debtors when sued by big-city or foreign creditors. As one authority points out:

> [I]nconveniences [of jury trial were] accepted precisely because, in important instances, through its ability to disregard substantive rules of law, the jury would reach a result that the judge either could not or would not reach. Those who favored the civil jury were not misguided tinkerers. [T]hey were, for their day, libertarians who avowed that important areas of protection for litigants . . . would be placed in grave danger unless it were required that juries sit in civil cases.**

The proponents of jury trial won an important battle: The Seventh Amendment became part of the Bill of Rights. They did not win the war, however, because the amendment did not make all cases triable to a jury. The

---

* H. J. Storing, What the Anti-Federalists Were For: The Political Thought of the Opponents of the Constitution 18-19 (1981).
** Wolfram, The Constitutional History of the Seventh Amendment, 57 Minn. L. Rev. 639, 668-705 (1973).

amendment was a compromise between those who thought jury trial at best a nuisance, at worst an invitation to lawlessness, and those who thought it a vital structural and substantive principle of government. The compromise is embedded in a deceptively short text of the Seventh Amendment:

> In suits at common law, where the value in controversy shall exceed twenty dollars, the right of trial by jury shall be preserved. . . .

The language of the Seventh Amendment reflects this compromise in two phrases: "suits at common law" and "shall be preserved." Unlike other provisions of the Bill of Rights that guarantee various rights, the Seventh Amendment purports to preserve a right but does not indicate the scope of the right being preserved. The English judicial system, whose organization was echoed by colonial courts in the period immediately before the Revolution, was divided into several jurisdictions. In courts of law, jury trial was widely available on most of the writs commonly in use by the eighteenth century. A full list is not possible here, but some of the more common writs will give the student a flavor: trespass (with several subcategories); debt (to recover sums owed); covenant (to remedy breaches of written, sealed contracts); ejectment (to recover land unlawfully occupied); trover and replevin (to recover for unlawful takings of personal property); and assumpsit (meaning "he (or she) promised," used to recover for breaches of informal, usually oral, contracts).

In chancery (which administered various equitable remedies), however, the judge (the chancellor) sat without a jury. The constitutional compromise, then, "preserved" as triable to a jury those cases that could have been brought in a court of common law. If, however, the claim would have fallen into the jurisdiction of the court of chancery, the Seventh Amendment did not extend the right to jury trial. As you will see, courts dealing with this issue distinguish between legal and equitable claims and remedies. By so doing they are simply using a shorthand form of reference: "Legal" in this context means a claim recognized by a court of law (where juries sat), and "equitable" means that the claim or remedy would have been in chancery (where no juries sat).

In Chapter V we noted the development of elaborate doctrine concerning what cases could be brought in equity. The result was that remedies such as injunctions, specific performance, rescission, and accountings and procedural devices such as derivative suits, class actions, bills of peace, and bills of interpleader were within equity jurisdiction. A given plaintiff had to show that the traditional legal remedy of money damages was inadequate and that he otherwise qualified for equitable relief.

It is important to emphasize that most cases within equity jurisdiction did not wind up there because of anyone's conviction that the judge was better suited than a jury to decide a particular type of claim. Although the judge may have been more qualified to sort out fiduciary relationships, probate matters, or multiparty actions, many other branches of equity jurisdiction involved the same questions of fact—what happened, how it happened, and who was telling the truth—as legal actions. For example, injunctive actions frequently involved questions of land ownership or commission of a tort, and specific performance claims usually involved the construction and meaning of contracts. As time went on, distinctions between the two jurisdictions blurred even further: Legal claims in general assumpsit (money had and received) tended to parallel equitable remedies for restitution, and traditionally equitable defenses such as fraud, duress, and illegality came to be recognized at law. In sum, the law-equity jurisdictional distinction was far from hard and fast, and whatever distinction existed was more a result of history than of logic or function.

Given the constitutional language "preserving" rights at "common law," it is not surprising that the courts adopted a historical test for deciding the right to jury trial under the Seventh Amendment. Under the historical test, courts seek to give parties the same right of jury trial as they had in 1791. Presumably, the drafters of the Seventh Amendment were thinking of a world in which there were separate courts of law and equity, a world in which one could only "preserve" a right to jury trial in suits at common law. Because there had never been a right to jury trial in equity, there was nothing to preserve and no right to jury trial.

Consequently, courts applying the historical test do not directly inquire about jury trial. Instead, they ask a related question: whether a given claim lay within the jurisdiction of the common law courts in 1791. If so, the parties have the right to a jury; if not — if only a court of equity would have heard the claim — there is no right to a jury. Equitable jurisdiction generally turned on whether the plaintiff wanted injunctive or other relief available only in equity, wanted to use a procedural device that was available only in equity, or had a claim that could be brought only in equity. Before you despair of sorting all this out, be comforted by the thought that a very large portion of claims fit neatly into well-established historical patterns. Having mastered that pattern, you will have answers for most jury trial questions you will ever encounter. The problems that follow cover this ground.

NOTES AND PROBLEMS

In each of the following problems, the question is whether the parties are entitled to a jury trial under the Seventh Amendment. In answering the questions, assume that if the action could have been brought in a court of common law in 1791, the parties are entitled to a jury; otherwise they are not so entitled. Before answering, you may wish to review the material on equitable remedies, supra pages 279-280.

1. Plaintiff and defendant sign a contract.

a. Plaintiff, alleging breach of contract, seeks money damages.

b. Plaintiff, alleging breach of contract, seeks a decree of specific performance.

c. Plaintiff contends that the agreed price of the goods in question was $200,000 but that through a typing error the contract read "$100,000." Plaintiff seeks to have the contract reformed.

d. Plaintiff, alleging that defendant tricked her into signing the contract by fraud, seeks to have the purported agreement rescinded.

2. Plaintiff and defendant own adjoining real property. Plaintiff alleges that defendant is committing a nuisance on real estate adjoining plaintiff's land.

   a. Plaintiff seeks damages for harm caused by the nuisance.
   b. Plaintiff seeks an injunction against the continuation of the nuisance.
  3. Plaintiff alleges that defendant has taken his diamond ring.
   a. Plaintiff seeks to recover its value.
   b. Plaintiff seeks an order restoring the ring to his possession.
  4. Plaintiff alleges that defendant wrongfully occupies Blackacre.
   a. Plaintiff seeks damages resulting from defendant's wrongful possession.
   b. Plaintiff seeks to eject defendant from the property.

2. Applying the Historical Test to New Claims

Each of the claims in the preceding set of problems could have arisen in 1791. Determining the availability of jury trial for such claims is therefore a matter of recognizing the type of claim involved and knowing whether it would have been brought in a court of law or in a court of equity. That may require refreshing one's historical memory, but it presents no conceptual difficulties.

Knottier problems emerge when one considers claims that did not exist at the time the Bill of Rights was adopted, particularly those created by statute. The next case faces that difficulty, illustrating both the prevailing historical approach to such new claims and an alternative to that approach.

Chauffeurs, Teamsters & Helpers, Local No. 391 v. Terry

494 U.S. 558 (1990)

Justice MARSHALL delivered the opinion of the Court except as to Part III-A.

This case presents the question whether an employee who seeks relief in the form of back pay for a union's alleged breach of its duty of fair representation has a right to trial by jury. We hold that the Seventh Amendment entitles such a plaintiff to a jury trial.

I

McLean Trucking Company and the Chauffeurs, Teamsters, and Helpers Local Union No. 391 were parties to a collective-bargaining agreement that governed the terms and conditions of employment at McLean's terminals. The 27 respondents were employed by McLean as truck drivers in bargaining units covered by the agreement, and all were members of the Union. In 1982 McLean implemented a change in operations that resulted in the elimination of some of its terminals and the reorganization of others. As part of that change, McLean transferred respondents to the terminal located in Winston-Salem and agreed to give them special seniority rights in relation to "inactive" employees in Winston-Salem who had been laid off temporarily.

After working in Winston-Salem for approximately six weeks, respondents were alternately laid off and recalled several times. [As a result of these layoffs and the

ensuing loss of seniority, workers filed grievances with the union. The union prosecuted two of these grievances. When the workers filed a third grievance, the
union refused to prosecute it, arguing that the previous grievance decisions had
settled the issue. At that point the workers sued both the trucking company and
the union. They alleged that the company had violated the collective bargaining
agreement and that the union had violated the duty of fair representation. Before
the case came to trial, the trucking company filed for bankruptcy, and plaintiffs
voluntarily dismissed the case against the company.]

III

We turn now to the constitutional issue presented in this case — whether respondents are entitled to a jury trial.[3]

To determine whether a particular action will resolve legal rights, we examine
both the nature of the issues involved and the remedy sought. "First, we compare
the statutory action to 18th-century actions brought in the courts of England prior
to the merger of the courts of law and equity. Second, we examine the remedy
sought and determine whether it is legal or equitable in nature." Tull [v. United
States, 481 U.S. 412 (1987)]. The second inquiry is the more important in our
analysis. Granfinanciera, S. A. v. Nordberg, 492 U.S. 33, 47-48 (1989).[4]

A

An action for breach of a union's duty of fair representation was unknown in
18th-century England; in fact, collective bargaining was unlawful. See N.
Citrine, Trade Union Law 4-7 (2d ed. 1960). We must therefore look for an analogous cause of action that existed in the 18th century to determine whether the
nature of this duty of fair representation suit is legal or equitable.

The Union contends that this duty of fair representation action resembles a
suit brought to vacate an arbitration award[, which would have been brought in
equity in the eighteenth century].

The arbitration analogy is inapposite, however, to the Seventh Amendment
question posed in this case. No grievance committee has considered respondents'
claim that the Union violated its duty of fair representation; the grievance process
was concerned only with the employer's alleged breach of the collective-bargaining agreement. . . .

---

3. Because the National Labor Relations Act, 49 Stat. 449, 29 U.S.C. §159(a) (1982 ed.), does
not expressly create the duty of fair representation, resort to the statute to determine whether
Congress provided for a jury trial in an action for breach of that duty is unavailing. Cf. Curtis v.
Loether, 415 U.S. 189, 192, n. 6 (1974) (recognizing the "'cardinal principle that this Court will
first ascertain whether a construction of the statute is fairly possible by which the [constitutional]
question may be avoided'" (quoting United States v. Thirty-Seven Photographs, 402 U.S. 363, 369
(1971)).

4. Justice Stevens's analysis emphasizes a third consideration, namely whether "the issues
[presented by the claim] are typical grist for the jury's judgment." This Court, however, has never
relied on this consideration "as an independent basis for extending the right to a jury trial under the
Seventh Amendment." Tull v. United States, 481 U.S. 412, 418, n. 4 (1987). . . .

. . . The Union next argues that respondents' duty of fair representation action is comparable to an action by a trust beneficiary against a trustee for breach of fiduciary duty. Such actions were within the exclusive jurisdiction of courts of equity. 2 Story, [Commentaries on Equity Jurisprudence], §960, p. 266 [(13th ed. 1886)]; Restatement (Second) of Trusts §199(c) (1959). This analogy is far more persuasive than the arbitration analogy. Just as a trustee must act in the best interests of the beneficiaries, a union, as the exclusive representative of the workers, must exercise its power to act on behalf of the employees in good faith. Moreover, just as a beneficiary does not directly control the actions of a trustee, an individual employee lacks direct control over a union's actions taken on his behalf.

The trust analogy extends to a union's handling of grievances. In most cases, a trustee has the exclusive authority to sue third parties who injure the beneficiaries' interest in the trust, including any legal claim the trustee holds in trust for the beneficiaries. The trustee then has the sole responsibility for determining whether to settle, arbitrate, or otherwise dispose of the claim. Similarly, the union typically has broad discretion in its decision whether and how to pursue an employee's grievance against an employer. . . .

Respondents contend that their duty of fair representation suit is less like a trust action than an attorney malpractice action, which was historically an action at law. [The Court had suggested this analogy in an earlier case.] Presented with a more complete range of alternatives, we find that. . . .[t]he attorney malpractice analogy is inadequate in several respects. Although an attorney malpractice suit is in some ways similar to a suit alleging a union's breach of its fiduciary duty, the two actions are fundamentally different. The nature of an action is in large part controlled by the nature of the underlying relationship between the parties. Unlike employees represented by a union, a client controls the significant decisions concerning his representation. Moreover, a client can fire his attorney if he is dissatisfied with his attorney's performance. This option is not available to an individual employee who is unhappy with a union's representation, unless a majority of the members of the bargaining unit share his dissatisfaction. Thus, we find the malpractice analogy less convincing than the trust analogy.

Nevertheless, the trust analogy does not persuade us to characterize respondents' claim as wholly equitable. The Union's argument mischaracterizes the nature of our comparison of the action before us to 18th-century forms of action. As we observed in Ross v. Bernhard, 396 U.S. 531 (1970), "The Seventh Amendment question depends on the nature of the issue to be tried rather than the character of the overall action." Id., at 538 (emphasis added) (finding a right to jury trial in a shareholder's derivative suit, a type of suit traditionally brought in courts of equity, because plaintiffs' case presented legal issues of breach of contract and negligence). As discussed above . . . , to recover from the Union here, respondents must prove both that McLean violated §301 by breaching the collective-bargaining agreement and that the Union breached its duty of fair representation. When viewed in isolation, the duty of fair representation issue is analogous to a claim against a trustee for breach of fiduciary duty. The §301 issue, however, is comparable to a breach of contract claim — a legal issue.

Respondents' action against the Union thus encompasses both equitable and legal issues. The first part of our Seventh Amendment inquiry, then, leaves us in equipoise as to whether the respondents are entitled to a jury trial.

B

Our determination under the first part of the Seventh Amendment analysis is only preliminary. In this case, the only remedy sought is a request for compensatory damages representing back pay and benefits. Generally, an action for money damages was "the traditional form of relief offered in the courts of law." Curtis v. Loether, 415 U.S. 189, 196 (1974). This Court has not, however, held that "any award of monetary relief must *necessarily* be 'legal' relief." Ibid. (emphasis added). Nonetheless, because we conclude that the remedy respondents seek has none of the attributes that must be present before we will find an exception to the general rule and characterize damages as equitable, we find that the remedy sought by respondents is legal.

First, we have characterized damages as equitable where they are restitutionary, such as in "action[s] for disgorgement of improper profits," *Tull*, 481 U.S., at 424. The back pay sought by respondents is not money wrongfully held by the Union, but wages and benefits they would have received from McLean had the Union processed the employees' grievances properly. Such relief is not restitutionary.

Second, a monetary award "incidental to or intertwined with injunctive relief" may be equitable. Because respondents seek only money damages, this characteristic is clearly absent from the case. . . .[8]

We hold, then, that the remedy of back pay sought in this duty of fair representation action is legal in nature. Considering both parts of the Seventh Amendment inquiry, we find that respondents are entitled to a jury trial on all issues presented in their suit.

IV

On balance, our analysis of the nature of respondents' duty of fair representation action and the remedy they seek convinces us that this action is a legal one. Although the search for an adequate 18th-century analog revealed that the claim

---

8. Both the Union and the dissent argue that the backpay award sought here is equitable because it is closely analogous to damages awarded to beneficiaries for a trustee's breach of trust. Such damages were available only in courts of equity because those courts had exclusive jurisdiction over actions involving a trustee's breach of his fiduciary duties.

The Union's argument, however, conflates the two parts of our Seventh Amendment inquiry. Under the dissent's approach, if the action at issue were analogous to an 18th-century action within the exclusive jurisdiction of the courts of equity, we would necessarily conclude that the remedy sought was also equitable because it would have been unavailable in a court of law. This view would, in effect, make the first part of our inquiry dispositive. We have clearly held, however, that the second part of the inquiry — the nature of the relief — is more important to the Seventh Amendment determination. The second part of the analysis, therefore, should not replicate the "abstruse historical" inquiry of the first part, *Ross*, 396 U.S., at 538, n. 10, but requires consideration of the general types of relief provided by courts of law and equity.

includes both legal and equitable issues, the money damages respondents seek are the type of relief traditionally awarded by courts of law. Thus, the Seventh Amendment entitles respondents to a jury trial, and we therefore affirm the judgment of the Court of Appeals.

It is so ordered.

Justice BRENNAN, concurring in part and concurring in the judgment.

I agree with the Court that respondents seek a remedy that is legal in nature and that the Seventh Amendment entitles respondents to a jury trial on their duty of fair representation claims. I therefore join Parts I, II, III-B, and IV of the Court's opinion. I do not join that part of the opinion which reprises the particular historical analysis this Court has employed to determine whether a claim is a "Suit at common law" under the Seventh Amendment, because I believe the historical test can and should be simplified. . . .

I believe that our insistence that the jury trial right hinges in part on a comparison of the substantive right at issue to forms of action used in English courts 200 years ago needlessly convolutes our Seventh Amendment jurisprudence. For the past decade and a half, this Court has explained that the two parts of the historical test are not equal in weight, that the nature of the remedy is more important than the nature of the right. Since the existence of a right to jury trial therefore turns on the nature of the remedy, absent congressional delegation to a specialized decisionmaker, there remains little purpose to our rattling through dusty attics of ancient writs. The time has come to borrow William of Occam's razor and sever this portion of our analysis. . . .

To rest the historical test required by the Seventh Amendment solely on the nature of the relief sought would not, of course, offer the federal courts a rule that is in all cases self-executing. Courts will still be required to ask which remedies were traditionally available at law and which only in equity. . . .[7]

7. There are, to be sure, some who advocate abolishing the historical test altogether. See, e.g., Wolfram, The Constitutional History of the Seventh Amendment, 57 Minn. L. Rev. 639, 742-747 (1973). Contrary to the intimations in Justice Kennedy's dissent, I am not among them. I believe that it is imperative to retain a historical test, for determining when parties have a right to jury trial, for precisely the same reasons Justice Kennedy does. It is mandated by the language of the Seventh Amendment and it is a bulwark against those who would restrict a right our forefathers held indispensable. Like Justice Kennedy, I have no doubt that courts can and do look to legal history for the answers to constitutional questions, and therefore the Seventh Amendment test I propose today obliges courts to do exactly that.

Where Justice Kennedy and I differ is in our evaluations of which historical test provides the more reliable results. That three learned Justices of the Supreme Court cannot arrive at the same conclusion in this very case, on what is essentially a question of fact, does not speak well for the judicial solvency of the current test. My concern is not merely the competence of courts to delve into this peculiarly recalcitrant aspect of legal history and certainly not, as Justice Kennedy summarizes it, the "competence of the Court to understand legal history" in general. My concern is that all too often the first prong of the current test requires courts to measure modern statutory actions against 18th-century English actions so remote in form and concept that there is no firm basis for comparison. In such cases, the result is less the discovery of a historical analog than the manufacture of a historical fiction. By contrast, the nature of relief available today corresponds more directly to the nature of relief available in Georgian England. Thus the historical test I propose, focusing on the nature of the relief sought, is not only more manageable than the current test, it is more reliably grounded in history.

If we are not prepared to accord the nature of the historical analog sufficient weight for this factor to affect the outcome of our inquiry, except in the rarest of hypothetical cases, what reason do we have for insisting that federal judges proceed with this arduous inquiry? It is time we read the writing on the wall, especially as we ourselves put it there.

Justice STEVENS, concurring in part and concurring in the judgment.

Because I believe the Court has made this case unnecessarily difficult by exaggerating the importance of finding a precise common-law analogue to the duty of fair representation, I do not join Part III-A of its opinion. Ironically, by stressing the importance of identifying an exact analogue the Court has diminished the utility of looking for any analogue.

As I have suggested in the past, I believe the duty of fair representation action resembles a common law action against an attorney for malpractice more closely than it does any other form of action. Of course, this action is not an exact counterpart to a malpractice suit. Indeed, by definition, no recently recognized form of action — whether the product of express congressional enactment or of judicial interpretation — can have a precise analogue in 17th- or 18th-century English law. Were it otherwise the form of action would not in fact be "recently recognized."

But the Court surely overstates this action's similarity to an action against a trustee. Collective bargaining involves no settlor, no trust corpus, and no trust instrument executed to convey property to beneficiaries chosen at the settlor's pleasure. Nor are these distinctions reified matters of pure form. The law of trusts originated to expand the varieties of land ownership in feudal England, and evolved to protect the paternalistic beneficence of the wealthy, often between generations and always over time. Beneficiaries are protected from their own judgment. The attorney-client relationship, by contrast, advances the client's interests in dealings with adverse parties. Clients are saved from their lack of skill, but their judgment is honored. Union members, as a group, accordingly have the power to hire, fire, and direct the actions of their representatives — prerogatives anathema to the paternalistic forms of the equitable trust. . . .

Justice KENNEDY, with whom Justice[s] O'CONNOR and SCALIA join, dissenting.

This case asks whether the Seventh Amendment guarantees the respondent union members a jury trial in a duty of fair representation action against their labor union. The Court is quite correct, in my view, in its formulation of the initial premises that must govern the case. Under Curtis v. Loether, 415 U.S. 189, 193 (1974), the right to a jury trial in a statutory action depends on the presence of "legal rights and remedies." To determine whether rights and remedies in a duty of fair representation action are legal in character, we must compare the action to the 18th-century cases permitted in the law courts of England, and we must examine the nature of the relief sought. I agree also with those Members of the Court who find that the duty of fair representation action resembles an equitable trust action more than a suit for malpractice.

I disagree with the analytic innovation of the Court that identification of the trust action as a model for modern duty of fair representation actions is insufficient to decide the case. . . . Having made this decision in favor of an equitable action, our inquiry should end. Because the Court disagrees with this proposition, I dissent. . . .

NOTES AND PROBLEMS

1. The parties fought this case to the Supreme Court over an issue that seems rather far from the merits. Why did the plaintiffs want a jury so badly? Why did the union think it worthwhile to spend many thousands of dollars resisting one? What assumptions are the parties making about the likely sympathies of a jury?

2. To understand how *Terry* illustrates the application of the historical test, follow its analytic steps:

a. The union, resisting the jury demand, first contended that the action resembled a suit brought to vacate an arbitration award. If this contention had been accepted, why would it have defeated plaintiff's demand for a jury?

b. The union's second analogy was to an action brought against a trustee. If this contention had been accepted, why would it have defeated plaintiff's demand for a jury?

c. Terry and his coplaintiffs countered with still another analogy: to a malpractice action brought against a lawyer by his clients. If this contention had been accepted (as Justice Stevens argues it should have been), why would it have assured the plaintiffs a jury?

d. Offered these three analogies, the majority finds that of the trust most apt. Why?

3. Having accepted the trust analogy, the Court might have stopped there — as Justice Kennedy thinks it should have.

a. Instead, the Court found that the trust analogy was imperfect because the facts of the case involved two claims — one against the employer for breach of contract (the collective bargaining agreement) and another against the union for breach of the duty of fair representation. To recover from the union the plaintiffs had to show, first, that they had a good contract claim against the employer and, second, that the union breached its fiduciary duty in failing to press that claim.

b. The majority fails to ask a question about this analysis: Suppose one could demonstrate that such a claim — breach of fiduciary duty by failing to pursue a contract claim held by the beneficiary — would have been handled as a single equitable action. Would that argue in favor of a no-jury result?

4. The majority doesn't take that step. Instead, it moves from a consideration of analogues to the entire action to a consideration of remedy alone. Why? Why does the Court find that the remedy sought in this case was "legal," thus entitling the plaintiffs to a jury?

5. Finally, what is Justice Brennan's position — to which only he subscribes?

6. The Supreme Court has fiercely protected the right to a jury trial, but, like other constitutional rights, the parties can waive it by failing to raise the issue. In the case of the right to trial by jury, Rule 38 reaffirms the constitutional status of

jury trial while insisting on a timely demand and establishing waiver as the penalty for failing to do so. See how the Rule works in two cases:

a. Plaintiff sues, seeking damages for breach of contract. Within the twenty-day limit set forth in Rule 12(a), defendant answers, denying various allegations. Assuming no amendments to the pleadings, how long do the parties have in which to demand a jury trial?

b. Plaintiff sues, alleging breach of contract and seeking specific performance; defendant answers, denying breach and alternatively contending that specific performance is not an available remedy. Plaintiff receives leave to amend and adds a claim for damages. May defendant now demand a jury trial?

c. A party can insert a demand for a jury directly into its pleading. In Note 6a, for example, the plaintiff who sought damages for breach could have in his complaint demanded a jury trial, and the defendant could equally have done so in her answer.

7. *Terry* fits a pattern: For most newly created claims that seek money damages as a remedy, the Court has found a right to jury trial under the Seventh Amendment.

a. For example, in Curtis v. Loether, 415 U.S. 189 (1974) (cited in *Terry*), the Court found that in civil actions brought under Title VIII of the Civil Rights Act of 1968, the parties had a right to jury trial. The Court reached a similar result under the Age Discrimination in Employment Act (ADEA) in Lorillard v. Pons, 434 U.S. 575 (1978). *Lorillard* relied heavily on the fact that Congress borrowed the remedy provisions of ADEA from the Fair Labor Standards Act, which carried a right to jury trial. The Court concluded:

> This inference [that jury trial would be available] is buttressed by an examination of the language Congress chose to describe the available remedies under the [Act]. Section 7(b) empowers a court to grant "legal or equitable relief" and §7(c) authorizes individuals to bring actions for "legal or equitable relief" (emphasis added). The word "legal" is a term of art: In cases in which legal relief is available and legal rights are determined, the Seventh Amendment provides a right to jury trial. . . . We can infer, therefore, that by providing specifically for "legal" relief, Congress knew the significance of the term "legal," and intended that there would be jury trial on demand to "enforc[e] . . . liability for amounts deemed to be unpaid minimum wages or unpaid overtime compensation."

Id. at 583.

b. By contrast, Title VII, which prohibits discrimination in employment, has led a far more tortured existence. Title VII provides that:

> [T]he court may enjoin the respondent from engaging in such unlawful employment practice, and order such affirmative action as may be appropriate, which may include, but is not limited to, reinstatement or hiring of employees, with or without back pay . . . , or any other equitable relief as the court deems appropriate.

If the relief sought is limited to reinstatement or promotion, courts have been uniform in concluding that the relief is equitable and thus not triable to a jury. But what about claims for back pay? The Supreme Court has thus far been silent, leaving lower courts to struggle. Congress has also gotten into the act without bringing much more clarity to the issue. A 1991 amendment to Title VII, 42 U.S.C. §1981a, allowing a plaintiff to seek "compensatory and punitive damages" for intentional discrimination in employment, explicitly provides that such claims for compensatory and punitive damages are to be tried to a jury. 42 U.S.C. §1981a(c).

c. So far, one might assume that Congress had brought Title VII into conformity with the rest of the Civil Rights Act—that all claims of employment discrimination, like suits seeking damages for discrimination in housing, accommodations, education, and the like, were all now triable to a jury. But things are not that simple, for in defining "compensatory damages" in §1981a(b)(2), the statute provides that "[c]ompensatory damages shall not include back pay. . . ." How, then, should one treat a case in which a plaintiff sought reinstatement, back pay, and damages for intentional discrimination?

8. In one notable area, the Supreme Court has appeared to cut back on the extent of jury trial. Patents existed at the time of the ratification of the Seventh Amendment and claims of patent infringement were regularly tried to juries for almost two centuries. But in Markman v. Westview Instruments, 517 U.S. 370 (1996), the Court reanalyzed patent cases in a way that dramatically reduced the jury's scope. By way of background, note that a patent applicant files with the Patent Office a "claim," in which the inventor defines the scope of his invention —what it does and what its advantages are. Markman revolved around whether the jury would construe the meaning of such "claims." The Court held that it would not. The opinion had four steps.

a. In the first, after conceding that patent infringement cases had long been tried to juries, the Court distinguished between the case as a whole and a particular part of the case:

> This conclusion raises the second question, whether a particular issue occurring within a jury trial (here the construction of a patent claim) is itself necessarily a jury issue, the guarantee being essential to preserve the right to a jury's resolution of the ultimate dispute. In some instances the answer to this second question may be easy because of clear historical evidence that the very subsidiary question was so regarded under the English practice of leaving the issue for a jury.

Id. at 377.

b. The second step involved finding that because these "claims" had over the years become much more technical than they were in 1791, there was in fact no clear historical answer to the Seventh Amendment inquiry:

> But when, as here, the old practice provides no clear answer, we are forced to make a judgment about the scope of the Seventh Amendment guarantee without the benefit of any foolproof test.

Id.

c. Having found that they were writing on a clean slate, the justices engaged in an unusual form of analysis:

> We accordingly consult existing precedent and consider both the relative interpretive skills of judges and juries and the statutory policies that ought to be furthered by the allocation. . . .

Where history and precedent provide no clear answers, functional considerations also play their part in the choice between judge and jury to define terms of art. We said in Miller v. Fenton, 474 U.S. 104 (1985), that when an issue "falls somewhere between a pristine legal standard and a simple historical fact, the fact/law distinction at times has turned on a determination that, as a matter of the sound administration of justice, one judicial actor is better positioned than another to decide the issue in question." So it turns out here, for judges, not juries, are the better suited to find the acquired meaning of patent terms.

The construction of written instruments is one of those things that judges often do and are likely to do better than jurors unburdened by training in exegesis. . . .

Finally, we see the importance of uniformity in the treatment of a given patent as an independent reason to allocate all issues of construction to the court. . . . It was just for the sake of such desirable uniformity that Congress created the Court of Appeals for the Federal Circuit as an exclusive appellate court for patent cases, [29 U.S.C. §1295 (1981)], observing that increased uniformity would "strengthen the United States patent system in such a way as to foster technological growth and industrial innovation."

Uniformity would, however, be ill served by submitting issues of document construction to juries.

Id. at 381-384.

d. In most infringement cases the only significant question is whether Device A falls within the scope — the "claim" — of Device B and therefore infringes. Only rarely will there be a dispute about whether Device A was actually manufactured. As a result, judges, not juries, will decide most significant patent issues — a clear change from the situation in 1791.

e. Note that the functional reasoning — that judges are better than juries at construing written documents — would apply as well to many situations in which juries regularly operate when they construe deeds, contracts, and the like. The *Markman* opinion is careful to limit its holding to the patent area, but its reasoning, if extended, could swallow up a lot of the Seventh Amendment.

9. Though they differ in outcome, *Markman* and *Terry* have an important similarity: Both explore the right to jury trial in the face of statutory silence. The 1991 amendment to the Civil Rights Act, discussed in Note 7(b), contains an explicit statutory provision of jury trial. What if the statute had instead forbidden jury trial? What if it had required jury trial of a clearly equitable claim? For example, could Congress order juries in Title VII cases where the only remedy sought is reinstatement? Is there, in other words, a constitutional right to a nonjury trial? The holdings on this question are sparse, but dicta suggest there is no constitutional right to trial by a judge, even in cases traditionally equitable. See, e.g., Beacon Theatres v. Westover, 359 U.S 500, 510 (1959) ("the right to jury trial is a constitutional one . . . while no similar requirement protects trials by the court"). Assuming that this sentence reflects the law, which of the following situations presents a Seventh Amendment issue?

a. Congress passes a statute creating a new private right of action for sexual harassment and authorizing both injunctive relief and damages. The statute provides that all questions of fact shall be tried by a jury, no matter what remedies are sought.

b. Congress passes the same statute, but it provides that all questions of fact shall be tried by a judge, regardless of the remedies sought.

10. Noticeably absent from the Court's Seventh Amendment opinions has been any discussion of the strengths and weaknesses of the jury as a factfinding body: *Markman* is a rare exception. Such discussions occasionally do, however, creep into opinions.

a. One district court, in a Title VII case, noted that fear of racial prejudice by the jurors, particularly in the South, had led earlier courts to shy away from juries and to construe the Seventh Amendment narrowly in light of those fears. The judge noted that today many plaintiffs are seeking jury trials and that the jury question accordingly ought to be reconsidered. Beesley v. Hartford Fire Insurance Co., 717 F. Supp. 781, on reconsideration, 723 F. Supp. 635 (N.D. Ala. 1989).

b. Contrast the preceding view with United States v. Schay, 746 F. Supp. 877 (E.D. Ark. 1990), which suggests that some judges think jury prejudice is a continuing problem in discrimination cases. The plaintiffs in *Schay* sued for housing discrimination under Title VIII. The principal plaintiff, a law clerk to a federal judge, wished to rent a house in a predominantly white section of Little Rock, Arkansas. He telephoned and was told the house was available, but when he arrived and the broker saw his skin color, the house was declared to be already rented. Returning to the office, the plaintiff asked colleagues to make the same inquiry. They were told the house was still available. At trial, the explanation for these discrepancies was that one Frank Daley had rented it before the plaintiff met the broker but had afterward changed his mind, thus accounting for its subsequent availability. After very brief deliberation, a jury found for the white defendant. The district judge, ruling on motions for judgment notwithstanding the verdict and new trial, found the defendant's witnesses barely credible. He remarked of Mr. Daley, "In respect to the testimony and actions of Frank Daley, it might be an exaggeration to say that he was the least credible witness appearing in this court during the last nine years that the writer of this opinion has held this office, but he would certainly be within the top five." Id. at 884. Because of the factfinding power vested in the jury, however, the judge found himself constrained to let the verdict stand.

11. The law-equity jury trial issue also arises in state courts. Unlike the Sixth Amendment (dealing with criminal juries), the Seventh Amendment does not apply to the states. As a consequence, there is no federal constitutional requirement that states accord the right of jury trial in any civil case. State courts may thus reach conclusions under their own laws that differ from those reached by the federal courts under the Seventh Amendment.

a. In many instances state courts have proved substantially less enthusiastic about jury trials in civil cases than have the federal courts. As examples of cases in which state courts rejected claims of entitlement to a jury, consider: C & K Engineering Contractors v. Amber Steel Co., 23 Cal. 3d 1 (1978) (contract actions based on promissory estoppel); Strauss v. Summerhays, 157 Cal. App. 3d 806 (1984) (quiet-title actions); Robair v. Dahl, 80 Mich. App. 458 (1978) (constructive trusts); State ex rel. Willman v. Sloan, 574 S.W.2d 421 (Mo. 1978) (calculation of damages after breach of a contractual covenant not to compete);

Pelfrey v. Bank of Greer, 270 S.C. 691 (1978) (explicitly rejecting, as a matter of state law, Ross v. Bernhard, 396 U.S. 531 (1970), which held that shareholders' derivative actions were triable to a jury); State Bank of Lehi v. Woolsey, 565 P.2d 413 (Utah 1977) (mortgage foreclosure).

b. Why have state courts embraced the civil jury less warmly than the federal courts have? Two possibilities — one political, one practical — come to mind. First, the special history of the Seventh Amendment, whose absence was thought by some to be so important as nearly to scuttle the ratification of the federal Constitution, might cause the federal courts to err on the side of the jury when in doubt. There was no equivalent controversy in most state constitutional debates: Civil juries were taken to be a matter of course. Second, federal courts can more easily absorb the costs of additional jury trials; federal courts are generally better financed than their state counterparts. Every time a state court creates a new right to civil jury trial, it is adding a strain on court budgets.

c. State independence works both ways, sometimes yielding a jury where federal courts would deny one. In Hodgdon v. Mt. Mansfield Co., 624 A.2d 1122 (Vt. 1992) the Vermont Supreme Court held that under its state constitution claims brought under a state statute closely modeled on federal Title VII were triable to a jury, although the equivalent claim brought in a federal court would not have been (see Note 7b above).

3. Applying the Historical Test to New Procedures

The preceding section illustrates the difficulty posed by changes in substantive law that have forced the courts to grasp at sometimes slippery analogies to causes of action that existed in 1791. Procedural changes have occurred as well, and they create equally challenging problems in applying the Seventh Amendment. Some changes have occurred outside the judicial system, as Congress has created administrative agencies to do things that once were, or could have been, done by courts. Other changes have occurred within the judicial system itself, with the merger of law and equity and the abolition of the writ system. Both kinds of procedural change have created tensions in the doctrine surrounding jury trial.

a. The Seventh Amendment and Changes in Judicial Procedure

At the time of the Seventh Amendment there were, of course, separate courts of law and equity. If a litigant needed relief from both (for example, first the reformation of a contract, then suit for damages on the reformed agreement), he would have to file two suits. Moreover, a good deal of adversarial jockeying could arise, with one party seeking remedies at law while the other sought equitable relief. In such cases, which court took precedence? In American Life Insurance Co. v. Stewart, 300 U.S. 203 (1937), the Court ruled that the way to settle such questions was to grant considerable discretion to the trial court, guided by an appeal to historical practice. The judge sitting in equity might decide to restrain the legal action; alternatively, he might decide to let the jury trial proceed while holding the equitable relief in abeyance. Either decision, *Stewart* suggested, would be consistent with the Seventh Amendment.

The Federal Rules of Civil Procedure, which resulted in the merger of law and equity, became effective one year after *Stewart*. Cases that were formerly legal or equitable could now arise in one suit, and the courts were given little guidance as to when a jury trial was required in a merged procedure. The constitutional right to jury trial still applied. The trouble was that the right that was "preserved" came from a system that no longer existed — that is, the right was preserved but the underlying procedural system was not. There was no particular difficulty in applying the historical approach to actions that could be denominated as clearly legal or equitable. For example, the typical personal injury suit was cognizable at law, and a suit seeking only injunctive relief was cognizable in equity. In such cases, a jury trial was granted or denied in accordance with the premerger practice.

But what happened when legal and equitable claims and defenses found their way into the same case? Some examples might be helpful:

(1) Plaintiff joins legal and equitable claims. For example, plaintiff might sue to enjoin a nuisance and simultaneously seek damages for past harm.

(2) Plaintiff brings legal claim; defendant has equitable defense. For example, plaintiff might sue for breach of contract, and defendant might claim mistake and seek reformation of the instrument.

(3) Plaintiff brings a legal (or equitable) claim; defendant brings equitable (or legal) counterclaim. For example, plaintiff might sue for damages while defendant seeks specific performance of the agreement.

In each of these situations the legal and equitable phases of the case had common issues: For example, did the defendant's behavior constitute a nuisance? The merger of law and equity forced courts to think about jury trial in situations such as these with little guidance either from the rule makers who had preserved the right but destroyed the system or from the Supreme Court's opinion in *Stewart*. The next case exemplifies the approach finally adopted.

Amoco Oil Co. v. Torcomian

722 F.2d 1099 (3d Cir. 1983)

BECKER, Circuit Judge.

The question presented by this appeal is whether the district court erred in refusing to afford defendants John Torcomian and Albert Torcomian a jury trial with respect to both the complaint of plaintiff Amoco and the Torcomians' compulsory counterclaim. The basis of the denial was that the claims, which arose out of the parties' dealings concerning an Amoco service station, were equitable in nature. The district court, following a bench trial, found for Amoco on all issues, and the Torcomians appeal. . . . [T]he district court erred in refusing to grant the defendants a jury trial. And because the district court could not properly have granted Amoco a directed verdict on either its claim or the Torcomians' counterclaim, the denial of a jury trial was not harmless error. The defendants' seventh amendment rights were therefore violated. Accordingly, the district court's judgment must be vacated and the entire case remanded for further proceedings.

I. The Record Relevant To The Jury Trial Issue

[The underlying dispute was between Amoco, which owned the service station, and the Torcomians, father and son, who wanted to take the station over from its previous operators and become Amoco's franchised dealers. The Torcomians actually operated the station for some months while negotiations were going on, but they never executed the franchise agreement. The parties disagreed about whether an Amoco representative had ever promised the plaintiffs would be accepted as franchisees and whether they met the stated qualifications for franchisees.]

Amoco originally sought extensive relief including: (1) ejectment of the defendants from the service station; (2) a permanent injunction restraining defendants from continued use, enjoyment and possession of Parkside Amoco; (3) a permanent injunction restraining defendants from use of the Amoco logo, trade name, service mark or trademark; (4) judgment in the amount of $46,675 for profits lost as a result of defendants' wrongful possession and fraudulent misrepresentations; (5) judgment for $12,000 for defendants' mesne profits and wrongful use of the Amoco logo, trade name, service mark or trademark; and (6) attorneys' fees. At the beginning of trial, however, Amoco attempted to orally amend its complaint to delete . . . portions of its complaint that sought money damages other than for mesne profits so as to eliminate any claims that might be construed as legal and to thereby foreclose the defendants' right to a jury trial.

Defendants' pleadings and their submissions in the pre-trial order state a claim that the defendants had a franchise relationship with Amoco at least until July 1984. These claims are based upon negotiations with and representations allegedly made by two Amoco agents. . . . Based on these allegations, the defendants sought "(1) [an] injunction enjoining plaintiff to comply with its franchise agreement with John Torcomian; (2) [a] judgment against plaintiff in an amount in excess of $100,000.00 for profits lost by John Torcomian as a result of plaintiff's failure to comply with its franchise agreement and for plaintiff's fraudulent misrepresentations; [and] (3) [a] judgment against plaintiff in the amount of defendants' reasonable attorneys' fee[s] and other costs involved in defending this action." . . .

II. Were The Components Of Amoco's Claim Legal Or Equitable?

It has long been settled law that neither joinder of an equitable claim with a legal claim nor joinder of a prayer for equitable relief with a claim for legal relief as to a legal claim can defeat an otherwise valid seventh amendment right to a jury trial. See Beacon Theatres, Inc. v. Westover, 359 U.S. 500 (1959); Dairy Queen,

Inc. v. Wood, 369 U.S. 469 (1962). Thus, in order to assess the district court's denial of the defendants' demand for a jury trial as to the main claim, we must consider whether it comprised any legal claims seeking legal relief. If we find such claims, we must vacate the judgment, at least as to those claims, unless we are persuaded that Amoco was entitled to a directed verdict on those claims.

At the outset, we note that on its surface Amoco's complaint appears to present a number of essentially legal claims.[6] The complaint sought ejectment, a form of action long regarded as legal. It also sought damages, a form of relief usually treated as legal. Plaintiff offers several theories, however, to counter this surface interpretation.

To rebut the normal rule that ejectment is an action at law, plaintiff cites two Pennsylvania cases. These cases purportedly hold that, where actual title to property is not in doubt, an action for injunction against defendant's continued possession of property leased to plaintiff is equitable. While our preliminary reading of the cited cases suggests that Amoco's interpretation and conclusions are dubious, there is a more telling problem with its argument: Pennsylvania's characterization of ejectment is irrelevant. As the Supreme Court [has] held, "in diversity cases, of course, the substantive dimension of the claim asserted finds its source in state law . . . but the characterization of that state-created claim as legal or equitable for purposes of whether a right to jury trial is indicated must be made by recourse to federal law." And federal law, as we have indicated, unequivocally holds actions seeking ejectment to be legal, not equitable. . . .

III.   Were The Components Of The Defendants' Counterclaim Equitable Or Legal?

It is settled law in this Circuit and elsewhere that even an equitable main claim cannot preclude a jury trial on a legal counterclaim, at least when the counterclaim is compulsory.[10] A rule to the contrary would enable the preemptive filing of a complaint by the holder of an equitable claim, coupled with the doctrine of res judicata, to deprive the holder of a legal claim of his seventh amendment right to a jury trial. Accordingly, we must consider whether there was an element present in the counterclaim which would have given rise to a right to jury trial.

Although the defendants did ask for equitable relief in their counterclaim (i.e., fulfillment of Amoco's obligation under the alleged franchise agreement), defendants also sought damages for the past breach of that agreement. A routine claim such as that presented here for damages stemming from breach of contract is

---

6. Defendants apparently admit that at least some of the plaintiff's claims (such as equitable relief for trademark infringement and restitution of mesne profits) would not require a jury trial if they stood alone. Nothing we say here is intended to prevent the district court from resolving these components of the complaint without a jury. . . .

10. The counterclaim is clearly compulsory here because it arose out of the same transactions and occurrences that were the subject matter of Amoco's claim. See Fed. R. Civ. P. 13(a). The whole case revolves around the parties' dealings with each other in 1981 with respect to Parkside Amoco.

legal. As we have noted in Part II of this opinion, the fact that equitable relief is sought in addition to substantial legal relief does not eliminate a right to a jury trial. . . .

IV. *Was a Directed Verdict Appropriate?*

We have now certainly found a sufficient admixture of law in Amoco's main claim and the defendants' counterclaim to render erroneous the district court's denial of a jury trial over at least those elements of the two claims. The error is harmless, however, if we are convinced that the evidence was such that Amoco would have been entitled to a directed verdict anyway.

Unfortunately for Amoco, disposition of both its claim and the counterclaim — which, as Amoco confesses, was in many ways the "mirror image" of the main claim — rested largely on issues of credibility. . . .

Viewing the evidence most favorably to the defendants . . . as a trial judge would be obliged to do in considering a motion for a directed verdict, the district court would have had to conclude that a jury could have found a lease or dealership agreement to have existed between Amoco and the defendants. . . . Consequently, we do not believe that a directed verdict could properly have been granted by the district court in this case on either the claim or counterclaim. . . . Nor can we say that a directed verdict was warranted for Amoco on grounds that Arata and Plocki[, Amoco's agents,] had no authority to bind it. For, according to the testimony of John Torcomian, Arata had said that he (Arata) had "the authority to approve me or anybody else as a dealer," and we cannot say, on the basis of the evidence of the course of dealings between the parties, that a jury could not reasonably have believed that Arata had apparent authority to bind Amoco or that the defendants reasonably relied upon his representations. . . .

V. *Conclusion*

We have concluded that both Amoco's main claim and the defendants' counterclaim contained a number of legal components to which the defendants were entitled to a jury trial under the seventh amendment. Accordingly, the judgment of the district court will be vacated and the case remanded for a new trial.

NOTES AND PROBLEMS

1. *Torcomian* involves a review of principles already discussed, a basic holding about a new situation, and some complications.

a. As a quick review of the materials in the preceding section, explain why Amoco thought it might be able to avoid a jury trial by amending its complaint.

b. Now focus on the new aspect of the case. Begin by charting each of plaintiff's claims and each of defendant's counterclaims. Identify each of them as either legal or equitable.

c. Suppose the only claim in the lawsuit was plaintiff's prayer for an injunction preventing defendants from using the Amoco brand on the grounds that they were not official franchisees. Explain why there would have been no right to trial by jury.

d. Now suppose defendants had then filed a single counterclaim, seeking solely an order of specific performance requiring Amoco to honor its alleged agreement with them. Explain why there would have been no right to trial by jury.

e. Finally, suppose that plaintiff amended its complaint to add the claim for ejectment. Explain how this changes the entire complexion of the lawsuit and creates a Seventh Amendment issue.

2. The *Torcomian* opinion makes two statements, both entirely standard, that need to be reconciled.

a. It holds that the district court erred by denying a jury trial.

b. It also says, in footnote 6, "that at least some of the plaintiff's claims (such as equitable relief for trademark infringement and restitution of mesne profits) would not require a jury trial if they stood alone. Nothing we say here is intended to prevent the district court from resolving these components of the complaint without a jury."

c. How could both propositions be true? The resolution lies in understanding an aspect of *Beacon Theatres*, cited in the opinion as the leading case on this aspect of jury trials. *Beacon* laid no new ground in holding that in a case with overlapping equitable and legal claims and counterclaims, a party could get a jury trial on any legal claims. *Beacon*'s importance comes from its second holding: that the jury trial should precede any hearing on the equitable claim and that the jury's findings would control as to any "common" factual issues — disputed issues that might arise both in the legal and in the equitable claims.

d. The negative corollary of *Beacon* is that equitable claims in which there are no such common issues are not subject to jury trial; they will still be decided by the judge alone.

3. To see what these principles mean, apply them to the facts of *Torcomian*. Plaintiff sought ejectment of defendants from the service station premises. Ejectment, held the court, is a legal claim triable to a jury. One of defendants' counterclaims sought a decree of specific performance, requiring Amoco to comply with its purported franchise agreement. Standing alone, such a claim would not be triable to a jury. Under *Beacon* the jury decides any contested issues of fact in the ejectment action, and the jury's determination of *those issues* will control in the equitable claim.

a. Suppose a jury determined that Amoco's apparently authorized representative did agree that the Torcomians could be its franchisee. That would resolve the claim for ejectment: Amoco could hardly eject a lawful franchisee from its premises. What about defendants' counterclaim for specific performance? The judge, in ruling on that claim, could not retry the facts and find that Amoco did not enter into a franchise agreement. He would, however, still have to weigh the equitable considerations required for specific performance. In doing so he *might* reach the conclusion that even though Amoco had agreed to allow the Torcomians to be its franchisee, specific performance was not called for because a legal remedy of damages was adequate or that the difficulties of supervising a franchise between parties already at each other's throats would be too formidable. Such a ruling would respect the jury's finding of an agreement even though it did not grant specific performance.

b. Now consider an alternative scenario. Suppose a jury determined that Amoco's representative had never made such an agreement and that the Torcomians were wrongfully occupying the premises. That would again resolve the ejectment action (this time in plaintiff's favor). But what about plaintiff's claim for $12,000 in mesne profits and wrongful use of the Amoco trademark? The judge would again be bound by the jury's findings that there was no franchise agreement. Footnote 6 suggests that Amoco's claim for restitution remains equitable and could be tried by the judge alone once the jury had resolved the legal claims and made findings on any issues common to the equitable claims.

4. The premise of *Torcomian*, which follows *Beacon* in this respect, is that whichever trier of fact goes first will bind the subsequent trier. Where there are overlapping legal and equitable claims, respect for the jury requires that the jury try *its* claims first. In the preceding example, the ejectment claim was legal. Suppose issues in that claim overlapped with the defendants' claim for specific performance of the alleged franchise agreement. In those circumstances the judge would let the jury try the ejectment claim first and would then be bound by the jury's findings on any issues that overlapped with the claim for specific performance. Sometimes the equitable claim involving the same issue occurs in a completely separate lawsuit. Does it violate the Seventh Amendment to assign preclusive effect to the equitable claim if the same issue arises in a second suit? No, held Parklane Hosiery v. Shore, 439 U.S. 322 (1979), which appears in Chapter XII. The Securities and Exchange Commission (SEC) filed suit for injunctive relief, alleging that a company's proxy solicitation was misleading; the judge ruled for the SEC, finding the proxy misleading. A second suit, brought by a shareholder, sought damages flowing from the same proxy solicitation. In this second suit the defendant would be entitled to a jury trial on whatever issues remained unresolved. The defendant maintained that all issues were unresolved because it would violate the Seventh Amendment to give preclusive effect to the judge's finding that the proxy was misleading. The Supreme Court rejected that contention, holding that the judge's finding in the previous equitable suit controlled in the second action. Parklane was entitled to a jury on the issue of damages but could not relitigate the issues decided by the judge in the equitable claim.

5. After holding that the parties' claims and counterclaims contained a mixture of legal and equitable claims, *Torcomian* goes on to ask whether the court could rightly have disposed of the legal claims on a motion for a directed verdict.

a. Why does the court do that? Suppose that it would have been appropriate to grant a directed verdict — to one party or the other — on each of the legal claims. How and why would that have changed the court's holding?

b. Why on these facts was it inappropriate to grant a directed verdict?

6. According to *Beacon* and *Torcomian*, under which of the following circumstances should a timely demand for jury trial be honored?

a. Plaintiff seeks an injunction; defendant denies allegations of the complaint.

b. Plaintiff seeks an injunction; defendant counterclaims for the imposition of a constructive trust.

c. Plaintiff seeks an injunction; defendant counterclaims for damages.

7. Suppose that, after the dispute arose, one of the parties had brought a single claim, seeking declaratory relief, that Amoco had (or had not) entered into an enforceable franchise agreement. The federal Declaratory Judgment Act, 28 U.S.C. §2201, makes it possible to bring a claim even though one is seeking no coercive relief (damages, an injunction). Declaratory relief, like a counterclaim, is a twentieth-century procedural reform; it was not available in 1791. The legislative history of the act suggests that it was not meant to alter the right to trial by jury. How do the courts think about jury trials in such situations?

a. *Beacon* contained language suggesting that a declaratory judgment action was itself a legal remedy. That statement is inconsistent with the act and has not been widely followed, though it has never been expressly disclaimed by the Court.

b. Most federal courts have asked whether a legal claim would have been possible at the time of the suit. "Thus, in a school desegregation case [seeking injunctive relief], the inclusion of a request for a declaratory judgment does not authorize a jury trial." Richard Bourne & John Lynch, Merger of Law and Equity under the Revised Maryland Rules: Does It Threaten Trial By Jury?, 14 U. Balt. L. Rev. 1, 48 (1984). By contrast, if Amoco had brought an action for declaratory judgment on the facts of *Torcomian*, defendants could have argued that any of several imaginable claims for coercive relief — ejectment, fraud — would have been available, thus entitling either party to a jury trial.

8. All the preceding discussion, in this and the previous section, has assumed that one ought to judge the jury triability of a claim on the basis of the pleader's allegations — accepting at face value the parties' statement of their claims. Courts generally do just that, but a word of caution about one wild-card case is in order:

a. Dairy Queen, Inc. v. Wood, 369 U.S. 469 (1962), suggested that the Court might probe beneath the pleadings, recharacterizing the allegations of the pleadings. Plaintiff, owner of the Dairy Queen trademark, licensed defendant to use the trademark and to franchise others to use it in a specified territory in exchange for certain cash payments. After defendant defaulted, plaintiff terminated the contract and canceled the right to use the trademark; defendant apparently continued, however, to operate under the Dairy Queen name. Dairy Queen thereupon brought suit and sought the following: (a) temporary and permanent injunctions to restrain defendant from using the trademark, (b) an accounting to determine how much defendant owed Dairy Queen and a judgment for that amount, and (c) an injunction pending the accounting to prevent defendant from collecting money from Dairy Queen stores in the territory. All of these claims are generally thought to be equitable, and the district court struck defendant's demand for a jury trial. The Supreme Court reversed:

> The most natural construction of the respondents' claim for a money judgment would seem to be that it is a claim that they are entitled to recover whatever was owed them under the contract as of the date of its purported termination plus damages for infringement of their trademark since that date. . . .

The respondents' contention that this money claim is "purely equitable" is based primarily upon the fact that their complaint is cast in terms of an "accounting" rather than in terms of an action for "debt" or "damages." But the constitutional right to trial by jury cannot be made to depend upon the choice of words used in the pleadings. The necessary prerequisite to the right to maintain a suit for an equitable accounting, like all other equitable remedies, is, as we pointed out in Beacon Theatres, the absence of an adequate remedy at law. . . . The legal remedy cannot be characterized as inadequate merely because the measure of damages may necessitate a look into petitioner's business records.

Id. at 476-479.

b. Notice the potential sweep of *Dairy Queen*. First, aren't all claims and remedies always a function of the way the "complaint is cast"? If courts freely recharacterize complaints to discover their "real" nature, it will become quite difficult to predict jury entitlements. Second, because equitable remedies are available only if legal remedies are inadequate, could a party seeking a jury trial always argue that there was a possibility that the court would award damages and that she was therefore entitled to a jury? Consider, for example, the following hypothetical case: S agrees to sell Blackacre to B for $100,000, but on the appointed day, S refuses to perform the contract. B brings an action against S and alleges in Count I his right to specific performance; in Count II, he seeks monetary damages as an alternative remedy only in the event specific performance is denied. Cf. Rule 8(e)(2). Does B have a right to jury trial? Does S?

c. There is good news for those whose minds threaten to explode at this point: Matters have not gone this far. One does not see many cases in which courts recharacterize pleadings to decide on the basis of what parties are "really" seeking. Combined with *Beacon*, *Dairy Queen* does give lower courts some latitude and creates some potential confusion, but chaos has not resulted.

b. The Seventh Amendment and the Structure of Government

Everyone understands and expects that an amendment about jury trial would have some effect on litigation. The Seventh Amendment also poses a broader, structural challenge that emerges if one thinks of the jury not only as a factfinder but also as an institution of government. Just as the Constitution would forbid combining the Senate and House of Representatives into a single legislative chamber, so some have thought the Seventh Amendment to bar certain changes in the distribution of government powers. Real exploration of this topic would take us far from the boundaries of civil procedure, but the student needs a very brief sketch to understand the importance of the Amendment. One can briefly capture the debate by asking whether the Amendment stands as a barrier to what is sometimes called the administrative state — a system that delegates tasks that look like adjudication to agencies other than courts.

In 1791 government was considerably smaller and less specialized than it is today. By the end of the nineteenth century, however, state and federal governments began to create administrative agencies to regulate and administer large areas of public concern. Congress, in particular, created a number of such agencies dealing with areas ranging from transportation (Interstate Commerce Commission, Federal Aviation Administration) to food (Food and Drug Administration) to public welfare (Social Security Administration) to labor relations (National Labor Relations Board). As these bodies began to appear on the national scene, they raised a number of constitutional questions: How would a Constitution that seemed to establish three branches of government deal with what some have called the fourth branch? Most of these challenges focused on broad issues about the structure of government and lie beyond the province of our discussion. Two, however, bear mention.

You will not be surprised to learn that the Seventh Amendment has not prevented the establishment of administrative agencies, even when those agencies perform adjudication of issues that might, were they in a court setting, trigger jury trial. The issue arises when Congress gives an agency power to resolve the type of question usually decided by a court. For example, was a worker injured in the scope of his employment and thus eligible for federal workers' compensation? Did an employer's actions violate the National Labor Relations Act? Was a workplace unsafe as defined by the Occupational Safety and Health Act? Each of these questions required an agency, usually acting through a hearing officer or administrative law judge, to determine various factual issues and to apply the law to those questions — just the sort of work that a jury might have done had the issue been entrusted to a court. Moreover, such adjudications sometimes resulted in individual liability for money, making the circumstances look even more like traditional adjudication in which juries might be involved.

The Court has spoken with less than complete clarity about this issue. In general, it has upheld the notion of administrative adjudication so long as Congress entirely removes the claim from the court system. To that extent, the Court has endorsed the constitutionality of administrative adjudication (without juries). See, for example, Atlas Roofing v. Occupational Safety & Health Review Commission, 430 U.S. 442 (1977) (holding that the administrative imposition of penalties for violating federal health and safety regulations did not violate the Seventh Amendment):

> At least in cases in which "public rights" are being litigated — e.g., cases in which the government sues in its sovereign capacity to enforce public rights created by statutes within the power of Congress to enact — the Seventh Amendment does not prohibit Congress from assigning the factfinding function and initial adjudication to an administrative forum with which the jury would be incompatible. . . .
>
> [But the appellant employer contends that under this reasoning] Congress could utterly destroy the right to a jury trial by always providing for administrative rather than judicial resolution of the vast range of cases that now arise in the courts. The argument is well put, but it overstates the holdings of our prior cases. . . . Our prior cases support administrative factfinding only in those situations involving "public rights," e.g., where the Government is involved in its sovereign capacity. . . . Wholly private tort, contract, and property cases, as well as a vast range of other cases . . . are not at all implicated. . . .

Id. at 450. Although reality is not as neat as this snippet implies, it is clear that administrative adjudication is constitutional under the Seventh Amendment.

The picture begins to cloud when one moves the site of adjudication from something called an agency into something called a court. The most fertile source of conflicts has been bankruptcy. The Constitution allows Congress to establish a bankruptcy regime; it has done so both by passing legislation regulating the distribution of insolvents' assets and by establishing federal bankruptcy courts. Although bankruptcy tribunals are called "courts," they stand in the constitutional scheme halfway between the Article III federal courts and administrative agencies; more germane to our topic, bankruptcy courts operate without juries. A series of Supreme Court cases have sought to sort out the tangle presented by this situation; two of those cases involved the Seventh Amendment. In Katchen v. Landy, 382 U.S. 323 (1966), a creditor presented his claim to the bankruptcy court seeking to have the claim satisfied out of the assets of the bankrupt's estate. But for the bankruptcy, the claim would have been a legal action for breach of contract, a claim triable to a jury. In bankruptcy, the trustee disallowed the claim in a summary proceeding without a jury. The Supreme Court held this did not violate the Seventh Amendment.

With *Katchen* contrast Granfinanciera, S.A. v. Nordberg, 492 U.S. 33 (1989), which presented facts the converse of *Katchen*. The bankruptcy trustee sued Granfinanciera, alleging that the bankrupt, just before bankruptcy, fraudulently transferred to Granfinanciera assets belonging to the bankruptcy estate, thus depriving other creditors of their fair shares. Granfinanciera denied this fraudulent transfer and demanded a jury trial. The Court held that a jury was required:

> It may be that providing jury trials in some fraudulent conveyance actions . . . would impede swift resolution of bankruptcy proceedings and increase the expense of Chapter 11 reorganizations. But "these considerations are insufficient to overcome the clear command of the Seventh Amendment." . . .

Id. at 63. At one level it is easy to reconcile *Katchen* and *Granfinanciera*: A creditor presenting a claim to the bankruptcy trustee doesn't get a jury trial, while a person against whom the trustee asserts a claim does. At another level the cases are in conflict and stand for a larger tension between the institutional aspects of the Seventh Amendment and contemporary administrative practice.

4. The Jury's Integrity: Size, Rules of Decision, and the Reexamination Clause

Preceding sections have suggested how difficult it is to "preserve" an institution as context changes. That point has double force if the characteristics of the institution also change — as the jury's have. The key elements of this change have been jury size, jury "rule of decision" (unanimity or super-majority?) and the courts' ability to overturn jury verdicts.

At early common law a jury consisted of twelve persons; the verdict was required to be unanimous; and the verdict could be attacked only by "attaint," a process in which a second jury, twice as large, considered charges that the first jury had been deliberately untruthful in its verdict. All these characteristics have undergone significant change since the thirteenth century.

In Colgrove v. Battin, 413 U.S. 149 (1973), a widely criticized decision, the Supreme Court constitutionalized six-person civil juries, and such juries are now in widespread use in federal courts and in some states. What difference does it make? Fundamentally, a smaller jury is less "average," less representative. Smaller juries are less likely to include any given point of view or social charac-teristic—race, political views, and so on. Just as a single individual is more likely to be eccentric than a large group is, so smaller juries are more likely to render aberrant verdicts than larger juries are.

In the federal system, unanimous verdicts are still required unless the parties agree to accept a nonunanimous verdict. See Rule 48. (Some states permit nonunanimous verdicts, usually allowing two or three opposing votes on a twelve-person jury.) Again one can ask what difference it makes. Rules of unanimity will result in more hung juries (a single holdout can block a verdict). Some studies suggest that groups where unanimity is required discuss the evidence with more intensity and in more detail than do groups where a super-majority will suffice.

Notice that, combined, these changes in size and decision rules can magnify each other. Decreasing the size of the jury reduces the likelihood that any given social characteristic will be reflected in the jury's membership. Moreover, abol-ishing the unanimity requirement lessens the effect that social diversity will have on the jury's verdict: If jurors do not have to render a unanimous verdict, the majority can simply ignore the point of view of one or two individuals.

Finally, there have been substantial changes in the assailability of the jury's verdict. By the time of the federal Constitution, courts had some limited power to overturn jury verdicts. Most observers would agree, however, that verdicts have become more vulnerable to attack in the two centuries since the ratification of the Seventh Amendment. That vulnerability has constitutional implications because the Seventh Amendment has two clauses. After granting the right to a jury trial "in suits at common law," the Amendment provides that "no fact tried by a jury, shall be otherwise reexamined in any Court of the United States, than according to the rules of the common law." This language, referred to as the "reexamination clause," serves to bolster jury power by preventing trial and appel-late courts from overturning jury verdicts, except insofar as they traditionally had the power to do so. We shall look at the extent of the courts' power to disturb civil jury verdicts in the next chapter. As you will see, in spite of the language of the reexamination clause, trial and appellate courts today have substantial power to overturn jury verdicts that are found to be without evidentiary support.

5.   Choosing Juries

As jury size and decision rules have changed, so have the rules about its compo-sition. At common law, the sheriff was given very wide discretion in summoning jurors, and it was understood that he would summon people with both feet firmly planted in the established order: A medieval sheriff would have greeted the idea of a demographic cross section first with incomprehension, then with horror. That outlook long prevailed. Not long ago, racial minorities, women, and members of the working class were often omitted from juries, sometimes intentionally. The past forty years have seen vast changes in such practices, both in the states and in the federal system. It is unconstitutional to discriminate on the basis of race or gender in compiling the list from which jurors are summoned. Most jurisdictions go further by statutorily requiring jury selection pools that represent broad cross sections of the community. See 28 U.S.C. §§1861 et seq. Along with these changes in the idea of the ideal jury have come changes in how much freedom parties have in challenging jurors. Fifty years ago a party could challenge jurors without restraint; today that freedom is more limited — at least in theory.

a.   Assembling and Challenging a Jury Pool

Choosing a jury involves two phases: First, a pool of prospective jurors is summoned; second, the members of the trial jury are selected from the pool. Law regulates each phase, but the bodies of law regulating the two phases reflect conflicting pictures of the ideal jury — one striving for inclusiveness, the other allowing the parties to eliminate jurors.

To assemble a pool of prospective jurors, a decision must be made about whom to call to the courthouse. While it is clear that no group of mentally competent adult citizens can be systematically excluded from selection,[*] the general composition of the jury can differ substantially, depending on the type of list used and the method of choosing whom to summon. For example, summoning jurors exclusively from voters' rolls, lists of Social Security recipients, telephone books, driver's license lists, welfare lists, or college registration rolls would yield juries with substantially different characteristics. The federal courts' policy about jury pools appears at 28 U.S.C. §1861: "[L]itigants . . . entitled to trial by jury shall have the right to . . . juries selected at random from a fair cross section of the community. . . ." What is the theory behind applying such a requirement to civil cases? Why is it not adequate that jurors merely be unbiased? The manner in which such cross-sectional summonses are derived is set forth at 28 U.S.C. §§1863-1864 and §1866. The method for challenging a jury pool appears at 28 U.S.C. §1867(c). Examine these statutes and apply them to the following problems.

NOTES AND PROBLEMS

1. Alberta Student leads a campus demonstration protesting University's failure to discipline fellow students allegedly guilty of acts of sexual harassment.

---

[*] In Thiel v. Southern Pacific Co., 328 U.S. 217 (1946), the Supreme Court held that the practice of excluding all persons who worked for a daily wage from the jury list was improper. As a consequence, the Court exercised its supervisory power to reverse a judgment for defendant railroad; the fact that the actual jury contained five persons who would identify with workers was irrelevant.

University sues Student in federal court, invoking diversity jurisdiction and seeking damages for University property Student allegedly destroyed while leading the protest.

a. Student's lawyer believes that the facts are very closely balanced and that the composition of the jury may make a significant difference in the outcome. When must Student's lawyer raise her challenge to the composition of the pool?

b. Pursuant to 28 U.S.C. §1867(d), Student's lawyer presents the affidavit of a demographer stating that college students constitute 5 percent of the population of the district but that a sampling of the list used by the jury commissioner indicates that fewer than 1 percent of those summoned for service are college students. The court must now decide whether "if true, [these allegations] would constitute a substantial failure to comply with the provisions" of §§1861 et seq. Assume that the judge finds Student's statistics trustworthy; the only question to be decided is whether the district's selection processes violate the requirement that juries be "selected at random from a fair cross section of the community." What is the issue? How should the judge rule?

c. Would your answer be different if Student's lawyer had instead shown that women constituted 52 percent of the community but that only 40 percent of those summoned as jurors were women?

2. The judge in University v. Student rules that Student has made a prima facie case under 28 U.S.C. §1867(d), with the consequence that Student may depose the jury commissioner and have access to documentary records. Commissioner testifies that he works from voter registration lists and that many students either do not register to vote or maintain their registration in their hometowns.

a. Should the judge accept this as an adequate response to Student's challenge?

b. If the judge does not accept this response, how should he order the list to be revised or supplemented? See 28 U.S.C. §1863(b)(2).

c. What would happen if the commissioner testified that he sent jury questionnaires (the first step to summoning jurors) to proportional numbers of students, but, having been advised that failure to return the questionnaire usually meant that they would not be called for jury service, the students threw the questionnaires away?

3. At one time many jury service statutes categorically exempted large groups of people, ranging from police officers to mothers to physicians. In recent decades state and federal statutes have dramatically reduced these occupational exemptions. The current federal list exempts only active members of the armed services, police and fire officers, and public officials. The result is jury pools that reflect a broader array of occupations, education, and wealth. What, if any, effect on verdicts would you expect such changes to have?

b.   Challenging Individual Jurors

Even if the jury pool is impeccably cross-sectional, not all of its members can try every case. Just as judges can be recused, so jurors can be challenged for cause. As an obvious example of this principle, a juror cannot decide a case in which he or she is a party. But how much further does this "principle of the unbiased trier" extend? Is the ideal trier neutral as between the parties but acquainted with the law and with the life situation from which the dispute arises? Or is the ideal trier one who requires education in both the facts and the law? The issue is important both to individual litigants — it is terrifying to have one's case depend on a trier one believes to be biased — and to the system of justice. This section explores the question of the "unbiased trier," and in the process extends the understanding of neutrality we began to explore in somewhat different expectations we have of judges and jurors. Once the pool is chosen, jurors must be selected to sit in a particular case. This selection occurs in a process called *voir dire*.[*] Generally, a certain number of those in the pool are called into a particular courtroom, and twelve are selected to sit in the jury box for initial questioning. After general statements about the parties and issues are given, some jurors may be disqualified from service. Parties are not required to accept all jurors. They may challenge an unlimited number of jurors "for cause," that is for an articulated reason involving the prospective juror's bias. In addition, the parties have limited numbers of "peremptory challenges," for which they need give no reason. The next case reveals these two conceptions of jury challenges in interplay.

Thompson v. Altheimer & Gray

248 F.3d 621 (7th Cir. 2003)

POSNER, Circuit Judge.

The plaintiff brought suit against her employer under Title VII of the Civil Rights Act of 1964, charging racial discrimination. The case was tried, the jury returned a verdict for the defendant, and the plaintiff appeals, arguing that a juror named Leiter should have been struck for cause. If the plaintiff is right, she is entitled to a new trial without having to show that Leiter's presence on the jury caused the jury to side with the defendant. Denial of the right to an unbiased tribunal is one of those trial errors that is not excused by being shown to have been harmless. . . .

During the voir dire of the jury, the judge asked the members of the venire whether "there is something about this kind of lawsuit for money damages that would start any of you leaning for or against a particular party?" Leiter raised her hand and explained that she has "been an owner of a couple of businesses and am currently an owner of a business, and I feel that as an employer and owner of a business that will definitely sway my judgment in this case." The judge asked her whether "if I instructed you as to what the law is that you would be able to apply the law recognizing that you are a business owner?" To which she replied, "I think my experience will cloud my judgment, but I can do my best." The judge

---

[*] The term comes from law French, an artificial blend of English and French terms used in medieval English courts; it means "to speak the truth" and dates to an age when jurors were as much witnesses as they were deciders of fact.

permitted the lawyers also to ask questions of the prospective jurors and Thompson's lawyer asked Leiter, "And you said earlier that you were concerned that your position as a business owner may cloud your judgment. Can you tell me how?" And she replied, "I am constantly faced with people that want various benefits or different positions in the company [which is what Thompson was seeking from her employer, the defendant, Altheimer & Gray] or better contacts or, you know, a myriad of issues that employers face on a regular basis, and I have to decide whether or not that person should get them." The lawyer then asked Leiter whether she was concerned "that if somebody doesn't get them [benefits sought from their employer] they're going to sue you," and she answered, "Of course." Asked then whether "you believe that people file lawsuits just because they don't get something they want?", she answered, "I believe there are some people that do." In answer to the next and last question, "Are you concerned that that might cloud your judgment in this case?" she said, "I think I bring a lot of background to this case, and I can't say that it's not going to cloud my judgment. I can try to be as fair as I can, as I do every day."

That was the end of the voir dire of Leiter. After refusing to strike her for cause (though urged to do so by the plaintiff's lawyer), and releasing the jurors who had not been selected for the jury (the defendant had also exercised its three peremptory challenges, none overlapping with the plaintiff's), the judge asked the eight remaining jurors, that is, the jurors selected to hear the case, whether they would follow his instructions on the law even if they didn't agree with them and whether they would be able to suspend judgment until they had heard all the evidence. The question was asked to the jurors at large and all either nodded their heads or said yes. The defendant, again perhaps dropping the ball, makes nothing of Leiter's failure at this stage to reiterate her doubts about her ability to exercise an unclouded judgment. The defendant is content to argue that the answers that Leiter gave to the earlier questions by the judge, and the questions by Thompson's lawyer, did not require that Leiter be struck for cause.

Our review of the trial judge's ruling with respect to a challenge for cause is deferential, but not completely supine, and it is pertinent to note that no issue of credibility is presented. There is no argument that Leiter was not telling the truth. The issue is interpretive: did what she say manifest a degree of bias such that the judge abused his discretion in failing to strike her for cause? . . .

When Leiter said that she believed that some people sue their employer just because they haven't gotten a promotion or a raise or some other benefit, she was not manifesting bias. She was expressing a prior belief (prior, that is, to hearing any evidence in this case) that was not only not irrational, but was undoubtedly true — there are indeed some people who will sue their employer just because of disappointment over the failure of the employer to give them something they want. In other words, there are spurious suits, in the employment domain as elsewhere. Leiter could not be thought biased for holding a true belief, or even for holding it unshakably if it is indubitably true. The belief that some employees make bogus claims against employers is so obviously true that it could not be shaken; but inability to set aside a clearly sound belief does not make for a biased juror. It makes for a realistic one.

Suppose a member of the venire in a case involving alleged sex discrimination by a fire department stated his belief that men on average have greater upper-body strength than women. Suppose he added that this belief was unshakable in the sense that if some social scientist testified otherwise, he would conclude that he was being fed junk science. Should this juror be disqualified? Not automatically, surely. The relevant questions would be whether he could distinguish averages from individuals, and thus recognize the possibility that a given woman might have greater upper-body strength than a given man, and whether he was so fixated on the average sex difference in upper-body strength that he was not open to the possibility that a woman whose upper-body strength was indeed less than that of the least strong firefighter in the fire department could nevertheless be as good a firefighter, or even a better one.

The question in this case was not whether Leiter's belief that some claims against employers are spurious was true or false (it was, as we have noted, true), but whether this belief would somehow impede her in giving due weight to the evidence and following the judge's instructions. That question was not adequately explored. . . .

Had she said she could *not* be fair, the judge would of course have had to strike her for cause. She did not say that, and so the judge (the defendant, though citing *Ricketts*, does not argue that the plaintiff's lawyer was at fault in failing to follow up his question whether Leiter's background would cloud her judgment) should have followed up by asking her, as he later asked the jury *en masse*, whether she would follow his instructions on the law and suspend judgment until she had heard all the evidence. . . .

Had the judge pushed Leiter and had she finally given unequivocal assurances that he deemed credible, his ruling could not be disturbed. But he failed to do that. The venire contained 20 prospective jurors, and more than enough were left to make up a full jury of 8 when he refused to excuse her. A candid and thoughtful person, if one may judge from the transcript, Leiter would probably have made an excellent juror — in another case. . . .

REVERSED AND REMANDED.

DIANE P. WOOD, Circuit Judge, concurring. . . .

I agree wholeheartedly with the majority's conclusion that the plaintiff, Rhodda Thompson, is entitled to a new trial on her Title VII claims because the district court permitted Juror Leiter to sit without obtaining the kind of unequivocal assurances of impartiality that are required to assure an unbiased trier of fact. . . .

The one issue that I regard as more complex concerns a plaintiff who does not exhaust her peremptory challenges. That is not Thompson's situation, but it occasionally happens that not all peremptories are used. If there are left-over peremptories and the plaintiff has failed to convince the court to strike a certain juror for cause, it is at least imaginable that a decision not to use an available peremptory challenge on that juror might amount to a waiver of the right to assert that the juror should not have sat. As I said, that is not this case. It is possible that there might be further complications in an actual case that I cannot envision at this time that would justify even this kind of strategic decision. . . .

NOTES AND PROBLEMS

1. Clear away the easy cases first, so as to concentrate on the contested terrain.

a. Suppose in response to voir dire, Leiter had revealed that she was the defendant's sister. Plaintiff would challenge for cause and the judge would unquestionably grant that challenge. Why?

b. The same result would probably occur if Leiter said that she was at the very moment involved in a similar suit brought by one of her employees.

2. Notice that in both of these clear cases, it would not matter whether Leiter said that in spite of these circumstances she could be fair and open-minded. What's the assumption about human psychology underlying this rule?

3. Come now to the facts of the case.

a. Consider first what Leiter said: She owns a small business and "that will definitely sway my judgment in this case," a statement that she then qualified by saying that it might "cloud" her judgment.

b. Why did she say this? First, it may well be true, and she simply may be acting as a conscientious juror. If that is true, we may face a paradox: The most fair-minded among us may be most likely to articulate doubts about our own fair-mindedness. If that is the case, we may spend way too much time examining the scruples of essentially fair people such as Ms. Leiter.

c. A second possibility: Most small business owners (and many other persons) view jury duty as an unpleasant way to spend their time, and will often dredge their minds for any possible circumstance that might result in being excused. If so, Leiter isn't really "biased," except against jury service. One can imagine a busy trial judge, concerned mostly to seat a jury that isn't obviously biased, might take this view and accordingly fail to follow up as the Seventh Circuit directs. If this is an accurate view, does the case reach the wrong result?

4. The Seventh Circuit holds that the judge's failure to elicit from Leiter a statement that she could be open-minded was reversible error. What assumptions about human psychology underlie such a ruling?

a. The most cynical view is that people are incapable of overcoming biases but that it is for public relations purposes important to have them pledge allegiance to fairness. In such a view, the "error" would be one only of appearance, since the juror would behave the same regardless of what she said.

b. A different view is that people, when their possible biases are brought to their attention, can to some extent overcome them, and that the public commitment to open-mindedness itself will reinforce this commitment. On this view, it is important that the judge elicit the public commitment, and the failure is significant.

c. What if Leiter had instead responded by saying, "I recognize that I may have some unconscious identification with the defendant, but I will do everything in my power not to let it influence my judgment." Should the judge excuse that juror? Or has the judge just found the ideal juror? Is this pretty close to what Leiter really said?

5. What if jurors conceal or lie on voir dire?

a. The first question is how a lawyer would find out. Jurors answer the voir dire questions under oath, but there is no official investigation of their accuracy. Consequently, lawyers find out about anomalies mostly by chance.

b. Once a lawyer determines that a juror was not candid during voir dire, what recourse does she have? The leading case on that question, McDonough Power Equipment v. Greenwood, 464 U.S. 548 (1984), established the standard for challenging a verdict on the basis of inaccurate answers on voir dire:

> We hold that to obtain a new trial in such a situation, a party must first demonstrate that a juror *failed to answer honestly a material question* on voir dire, and then further show that *a correct response would have provided a valid basis for a challenge for cause.*

Id. at 555 (emphasis added).

c. Would you expect many verdicts to be upset under this standard?

6. Do not be deceived by *Thompson*. If the trial judge does her job, challenges for cause are difficult to win. That does not make lawyers less interested in voir dire, which, in practice, has two purposes other than developing challenges for cause.

a. Lawyers use voir dire to begin presenting their cases. They cannot be too overt about this; a question such as "You would be sympathetic to my client, wouldn't you?" would be improper. Nor can lawyers make statements about the facts: "Do you understand that defendant was blind drunk at the time of the accident?" But questions designed to frame the client's story, to get the jurors thinking, for example, about the ways in which injuries had shaped the lives of their families, will generally slide by.

b. The second function of voir dire is to let the parties develop a list of jurors whom they would like to strike as one of the peremptory challenges. Unlike a challenge for cause, a peremptory challenge allows lawyers to strike a juror for any reason or for no reason at all. In the federal courts, 28 U.S.C. §1870 gives each side three peremptory challenges and additional challenges if alternate jurors are selected; in a federal six-person jury, all of the initial jury selections can be replaced via peremptory challenges. The court usually has broad discretion to allocate peremptory challenges or to permit additional challenges in multiparty actions.

What is the justification for peremptory challenges? One view is that peremptories in effect allow the parties to choose their juries, thus giving any ensuing verdict legitimacy in their eyes. A softer justification is that peremptories allow parties to excuse a juror about whom they have a hunch that does not rise to the level of a challenge for cause, or whom they may have offended through vigorous (but unsuccessful) voir dire questioning. Taken to the extreme, however, peremptories may conflict with the ideas of the cross-sectional jury embodied in statutes like 28 U.S.C. §1861. If society believes that juries composed of many different viewpoints are desirable, does it make sense to allow parties to negate that goal through the use of peremptories?

In the last few decades the Supreme Court (as well as statutes or common law decisions in many states have changed the law and the landscape regarding peremptory challenges. Not long ago the lawyers had unfettered freedom in exercising their peremptory challenges. That is still largely true, but a body of law has begun to impose some restrictions.

It is well established that court officials may not intentionally exclude any group from a jury panel. But can the parties accomplish the same result by the use of peremptory challenges? A party ordinarily need not explain or justify the use of such challenges; a party could, for example, strike all blue-eyed panelists from the jury on the basis of whimsy. War stories among trial lawyers suggest the frequent use of peremptories based on hunches about the predilections of various social groups: Are blue-collar, rural whites of Northern European extraction likely to be more defense-oriented than African-American Catholics? Elderly accountants less generous than young race car drivers? And so on. How far does this unaccountability extend?

One answer is that unaccountability stops when race enters the picture. In *Batson v. Kentucky*, 476 U.S. 79 (1986), the Court in a criminal case held that the prosecution's systematic striking of black jurors without a justification based on nonracial factors violated the defendant's right to equal protection. *Edmonson v. Leesville Concrete Co.*, 500 U.S. 614 (1991), extended *Batson* to civil cases, and subsequent cases have expanded the impermissible categories to include gender. *J.E.B. v. Alabama*, 511 U.S. 127 (1994).

7. *Batson*, *Edmonson*, and *J.E.B.* open the door for one party to object to the other's use of peremptory challenges. How do such objections to challenges work? According to *Batson*, a party must first make an initial showing (a "prima facie case") that allows a court to infer a pattern based on race or gender. Suppose that Bertha, a dismissed employee of a state university, sues, alleging wrongful discharge. After voir dire comes the time for the parties to exercise their peremptory challenges.

a. Defendant (the state university) exercises its first peremptory challenge against a male African-American juror. Bertha objects, citing *Edmonson*. Explain why her objection will be overruled.

b. Defendant then challenges a second African-American juror. Bertha renews her objection, now citing the pattern of peremptory challenges. Should defendant now be required to justify the challenges in nonracial terms?

8. *Batson*, *Edmonson*, and *J.E.B.* open a previously closed procedural door, permitting opponents to question the exercise of peremptories and forcing the parties to give nondiscriminatory justifications. But none of these cases devotes much consideration to what ought to count as a good excuse, an acceptable alternative reason for an apparently unacceptable use of a peremptory challenge. What will count as an acceptable justification of an apparently racial or gender-based challenge?

a. Imagine a challenged peremptory. Asked to justify what is an apparently race- or gender-based pattern, lawyer responds, "I didn't like the way she looked at me during voir dire." If the court accepts that justification, what becomes of the principles enunciated in *Edmonson* and *J.E.B.*?

b. Alternatively, suppose that counsel replies, "Yes, it's true that both challenged jurors were men [or African-Americans], but my real reason was that they occupied managerial positions, and I am therefore concerned that they will not be sympathetic to my client's claim of wrongful discharge from her job." If courts refuse to accept such justification, they will effectively eliminate peremptory challenges. When voir dire is brief, counsel will rarely have any but stereotypical information on which to base their challenges.

c. In Purkett v. Elem, 514 U.S. 765 (1995), the Supreme Court suggested how relaxed a standard it was prepared to apply to a "race-neutral explanation." In *Purkett* the convicted defendant complained that the prosecutor had offered inadequate explanations for peremptory strikes of black jurors. When asked to explain the peremptories, the prosecutor replied:

> I struck [juror] number twenty-two because of his long hair. He had long curly hair. He had the longest hair of anybody on the panel by far. He appeared not to be a good juror for that fact, the fact that he had long hair hanging down shoulder length, curly, unkempt hair. Also he had a mustache and goatee type beard. Those are the only two people on the jury . . . with facial hair. . . . And I don't like the way they looked, with the way the hair is cut, both of them. And the mustaches and the beards look suspicious to me.

Id. at 766. The Supreme Court summarily affirmed the conviction, reversing the Eighth Circuit, which had found such an explanation insufficient. Justices Breyer and Stevens dissented on the grounds that the Court's summary action had effectively overruled part of *Batson*. Does *Purkett* suggest that the Court is having second thoughts about the difficulty of the inquiry required by *Batson* and *Edmonson*?

d. Requiring any explanation for the exercise of peremptories poses a challenge of courtroom etiquette. Suppose that a lawyer, asked in the jury's presence to justify a proposed peremptory challenge, says, "Frankly, Your Honor, Juror #3 didn't seem very intelligent, and I think I need smart jurors on this case." Having heard this explanation, Juror #3 might well form a substantially negative view of counsel — perhaps so negative that it would be difficult for her to keep an open mind about the case. At that point, the lawyer would have a valid basis for challenging the juror for cause. In order to prevent such sequences, many judges insist that all discussions of peremptory challenges occur at sidebar (out of the jury's hearing) or in chambers.

9. One explanation for *Purkett* in Note 8c is that the Court worked itself into a corner with this series of cases by purporting to preserve the peremptory challenge but hedging its exercise sufficiently to make it difficult to use. One can imagine a range of solutions:

a. Reverse or curtail *Batson*. The *Purkett* dissenters thought that was happening in that case.

b. Expand voir dire. *J.E.B.* hinted at such a development:

> If conducted properly, voir dire can inform litigants about potential jurors, making reliance upon stereotypical and pejorative notions about a particular gender or race both unnecessary and unwise. Voir dire provides a means of discovering actual or implied bias and a firmer basis upon which the parties may exercise their peremptory challenges intelligently.

517 U.S. at 143-144. Behind such a suggestion is the idea that a lawyer, asked to justify a peremptory challenge, could reply, "It's not her race, Your Honor; it's her attitude toward punitive damages." Many courts in busy metropolitan areas do not conduct extensive voir dire. Must they now change this practice?

c. Abolish the peremptory challenge. The reasoning would be that peremptories are necessarily exercised on scant evidence (given the usually cursory nature of voir dire) and therefore reflect no more than the lawyer's stereotypes. Moreover, if it is important to have widely representative juries, the peremptory works at cross purposes with such a goal by encouraging lawyers to exercise group-based stereotypes. Under such a proposal, Congress (or a state legislature) would simply abolish peremptories, thus obviating the inquiry into motive and speeding jury selection.

d. Combine the two previous suggestions — to eliminate peremptories but compensate by expanding the basis for challenges for cause. The argument in favor of this course is that it would eliminate the impermissible bases for voir dire while preserving the legitimate ones. Nancy Marder, Beyond Gender: Peremptory Challenges and the Role of the Jury, 73 Tex. L. Rev. 1041 (1995).

This chapter began and ended with cases examining the idea of objectivity in the trier: what does it mean for a judge or a juror to be unbiased? That question is important because the entire procedural system works to prevent one-sided cases from reaching trial. As a result, only those cases where there is something to be said on both sides will reach the final — but increasingly rare — stage of litigation, to which we now turn.

TRIAL

X

Trials occupy a paradoxical status in American law. They occur infrequently in relation to lawsuits filed, but they shape almost every aspect of procedure. It is common to point out that only about 3 percent of claims filed in the United States end in trials.* Yet the elaborate provisions for discovery have as one of their primary goals the uncovering of information to be presented at trial, and much of the law of evidence is aimed at controlling the flow of information during a trial. Likewise, the emphasis on the presentation of live witnesses (rather than depositions or other documentary evidence) — which brings with it the opportunity for theatrical displays by lawyers — stems from a conception of the trial as the culmination of litigation. Even the adversarial stance of the lawyers — perhaps more marked in Anglo-American law than in other systems — may flow in part from the realization that the whole case rides on a single presentation in a comparatively short time span before a trier of fact. In this chapter we focus on an especially procedural aspect of trial: the extent of the controls placed on the finder of fact, with a focus on the jury a distinctive feature of U.S. civil practice. We shall examine the procedural mechanisms that empower and control the jury. In doing so, however, we must not lose sight of a larger question: What conceptions of truth, of justice, of democratic decision making underlie jury power and control?

A. The Limits of Rational Inference

Contemporary U.S. procedure aims at assuring that judgments will be based only on inferences that a reasonable person could rationally draw from the evidence presented at trial. Excluded by this formulation are judgments that could only have come from hunch, partiality, whim, and disregard of the law, even when that disregard flows from a sense of higher justice. Substantive law provides the framework for this inferential process, and the law of evidence screens out information that might tempt the trier to decide on criteria forbidden by the substantive law.

---

* Be careful not to equate trials with adjudication. As you have already learned, it's possible for a court to pass on the merits of a case without having held a trial: 12(b)(6) dismissals and motions for summary judgment are two of the more common means by which a court may adjudicate a dispute without its having gone to trial. If one adds such adjudicated dispositions to the figure for trials, data for the federal courts suggest that approximately 30 percent of filed cases end with an adjudicated disposition — of which only 10 percent are trials.

For example, if the law of contract states that good intentions do not excuse a breach, the law of evidence will prevent the defendant from explaining that her failure to make a required payment occurred because she had donated the money to charity.

Guarding the boundaries of rationality is often not so easy as in the preceding example. Tort law says that a defendant shall not be liable for harm unless the plaintiff proves that negligence caused the harm for which he is suing. Suppose that the facts are essentially undisputed; the question then becomes what inferences one can draw from those facts and, more particularly, whether one can infer causation from those facts.

Reid v. San Pedro, Los Angeles & Salt Lake Railroad

39 Utah 617, 118 P. 1009 (1911)

This action was brought by respondent to recover damages for the killing of certain cattle by the trains of appellant. . . .

It is alleged in the first cause of action that appellant's railroad passes through certain lands in Salt Lake County, Utah, owned and improved by private owners; that appellant carelessly and negligently permitted the fence along its line of railroad where the same passes through the lands mentioned to be broken and in poor repair and become down so that cattle had an easy passage through the same; that appellant "carelessly and negligently left and permitted to remain open a gate along the line of said railway at said point and plaintiff (respondent) does not know, and therefore is unable to state, whether the fence was down or the gate left open, and because thereof a three year old heifer of the plaintiff strayed on the right of way of said defendant company, and defendant so carelessly and negligently operated its train that it ran on and over said heifer". . . .

[There was a verdict for plaintiff, and defendant appealed from the judgment entered on the verdict.]

McCARTY, J. (after stating the facts as above).

It is contended on behalf of appellant that the evidence is insufficient to support the verdict because it fails to show where and under what circumstances the cattle sued for got upon the right of way.

The evidence shows that the cow mentioned in the first cause of action was being pastured on land that was fenced, improved, and owned by a private party, and through which appellant's railroad was constructed and maintained; that respondent did not own the land, but was pasturing her stock thereon by permission of the owner at the time the cow was killed; that the fence inclosing appellant's right of way was down and out of repair about one mile west of the point where the cow was killed; that two gates opening into the right of way in the immediate vicinity of the place where the accident occurred, which were installed and maintained by appellant for the benefit and convenience of the owner of the land through which the railroad passes and upon which the cow was being pastured, had been left open almost continuously prior to the accident.

It is not contended, nor even suggested, that these gates, which were in good condition, were used or left open by appellant. In fact, the evidence, what there is on this point, tends to show that the appellant was in no wise responsible for the gates being left open. Respondent contends that the judgment, in so far as it is based on the first cause of action, should be affirmed regardless of whether the cow got on the right of way through the broken fence or the open gate. In his brief counsel for respondent says: "In the first cause of action the evidence showed the fence down and gate open. . . . It is immaterial whether the heifer strayed on through an inviting open gate or an enticing open fence; . . . either gives the verdict to the plaintiff."

Comp. Laws 1907, §456xl, provides:

> Whenever such railroad company shall provide gates for private crossings for the convenience of the owner of the lands through which such railroad passes, such owner shall keep such gates closed at all times when not in actual use, and if such owner fail to keep such gates closed, and in consequence thereof his animal strays upon such railroad, and is killed or injured, such owner shall not be entitled to recover damages therefor.

Under this statute, if the cow entered upon the right of way through the open gate, appellant cannot be held liable for her loss; there being no evidence of negligence on the part of trainmen at the time she was killed.

There is no direct evidence as to where the cow got on to the right of way. It is conceded, however, that she was killed in the immediate vicinity of the gate mentioned, and, as shown by the evidence, about one mile from the point where the fence inclosing the right of way was down and out of repair. The inference, therefore, is just as strong, if not stronger, that she entered upon the right of way through the open gate as it is that she entered through the fence at the point where it was out of repair. The plaintiff held the affirmative and the burden was on her to establish the liability of the defendant by a preponderance of the evidence. It is a familiar rule that where the undisputed evidence of the plaintiff, from which the existence of an essential fact is sought to be inferred, points with equal force to two things, one of which renders the defendant liable and the other not, the plaintiff must fail. So in this case, in order to entitle respondent to recover, it was essential for her to show by a preponderance of the evidence that the cow entered upon the right of way through the broken down fence. This the respondent failed to do.

We are of the opinion that the verdict rendered on the first cause of action is not supported by the evidence, and that the trial court should have directed a verdict for appellant on that cause of action in accordance with appellant's request. . . .

NOTES AND PROBLEMS

1. Start with the substantive law of railroads and livestock in Utah at the turn of the 20th century.

a. If the animal reaches the tracks by coming through an open gate, who bears the loss?

b. If the animal reaches the tracks by coming through a hole in the fence, who bears the loss?

2. The appellate court held that the trial court should have "directed a verdict" for the defendant. As we shall see, that statement is tantamount to saying that a rational trier of fact could not have reached a verdict for the plaintiff, and the judge should therefore have taken the case away from the jury.

a. Why not?

b. The animal *could* have been killed in a way that made the railroad liable. Why not let a jury conclude that it was?

3. Notice that all the discussion (that of the court and in the preceding notes) is necessarily hypothetical. We don't know how the jury reached its decision.

a. The jurors might have concluded that railroads as a group were richer than ranchers' widows.

b. They might have decided on the basis of information provided by a rancher-juror, that the cows never went through gates if fences were available.

c. They might have decided, on the basis of information provided by another juror, that the cow was more likely to have come through the fence than the gate because the gap in the fence was near a salt lick (which cows like).

d. They might have misunderstood the judge's instructions.

e. They might have remembered the testimony differently from the judge.

f. The appellate court has no idea what the jurors thought. As you will later see, even if it is available, evidence of juror deliberations is typically unavailable to impeach a verdict. See infra pages 611-617. As a consequence, in considering a directed verdict, a trial or appellate court knows what went into the black box — evidence, instruction, and argument — and what came out — the verdict. In deciding whether a verdict may stand the court must engage in hypothetical reconstruction: Could a rational factfinder have concluded X, given evidence of A, B, and C and law consisting of G and F? If so, the verdict stands. If not, either a directed verdict or a new trial is in order.

4. In *Reid*, what additional evidence should be present before the court can enter judgment on the verdict for the plaintiff?

a. What if the animal were found twenty-five feet from the broken fence and half a mile from the open gate?

b. What if the animal were equidistant between the fence and the gate, but a veterinarian testified that cattle are unlikely to go over a broken fence if there is a nearby open gate?

5. Two taxicab companies, White Cab Co. and Yellow Cab Co., operate in Provo, Utah. White Cab Co. owns approximately 75 percent of the cabs. The physical appearance of the cabs is identical except that the White cabs have a white "in service" light, and the Yellow cabs have a yellow "in service" light. P is seriously injured in a hit-and-run accident. W, a witness, is sure that P was hit by a taxicab.

a. If P sues White Cab Co. and there is no other evidence, must a judge enter judgment for White?

b. If you say yes to the hypothetical in a., would your answer be different if White owned 95 percent of the cabs?

c. If you would still enter judgment for White in b., would you change your mind if White owned all cabs in Provo — allowing for the possibility that the cab was from another nearby community or Salt Lake City?

d. Same facts as in a., except W says that he got a quick glimpse of the "in service" light and thinks it was white. On cross-examination, W says he isn't sure.

e. In the preceding versions of this problem, does your answer change if the plaintiff can also show that he diligently sought, through discovery and investigation, other evidence, such as examining the taxis for dents and marks, seeking witnesses, looking at the accident site for paint chips and the like? Most courts would not permit a plaintiff to offer evidence of his attempts to locate such information, on the ground that it was irrelevant.

6. Although *Reid*'s facts sound quaint, they present a problem with modern implications. Suppose a person dies from a rare form of cancer. The deceased lived in a small town where the only major change in the past decade was the construction of a uranium milling plant. Decedent's family sues the plant for wrongful death. Plaintiff's evidence of liability consists of medical testimony establishing the decedent's death from the rare cancer in question and that nothing in the health history or habits suggested any special risk. Plaintiff follows this evidence with public health and demographic experts, who establish that the background rate for this form of cancer in the town was three deaths annually per 10,000 persons before defendant's plant was built, and that it is now seven deaths per 10,000, and that some public health and medical studies have linked increases in this form of cancer to inevitable atmospheric discharges of the uranium milling process. Plaintiff rests; defendant moves for a directed verdict. What decision?

7. The initial decision in *Reid* was made by a jury. Suppose neither party had requested a jury and the case had been tried by a judge (called a "bench" trial); would that have affected the outcome?

a. Probably not — at least if one understands the *Reid* court as saying that there simply was no evidence from which a rational trier of fact could have inferred railroad negligence. The appellate court would, however, have had a different problem to deal with. When a case is tried by a judge, Rule 52(a) requires that "the court shall find the facts specially and state separately its conclusions of law thereon. . . ." So the court would have had, perhaps with some assistance from the plaintiff, to spell out the steps of inference by which it concluded that the railroad was negligent. Perhaps this exercise would have convinced the judge that one simply couldn't reach such a conclusion. Alternatively, it would have exposed the judge's reasoning — flaws and all — to the appellate court. We do not impose such a requirement of "showing your work" on juries, and to that extent we give them more slack than judges. If a jury reaches a defensible conclusion, appellate courts affirm without requiring that the jury have reached its outcome by a defensible route: It is enough that it could reasonably have reached that conclusion.

b. Rule 52(a) further provides that a finding of fact made by a trial judge can be set aside on appeal if it is "clearly erroneous," giving the judge's factual conclusions the same insulation from review as a jury's. If it would be irrational speculation for a jury to find that the cow got on the track in a particular way, it would be "clearly erroneous" for a judge to make the same finding.

c. Judges, like juries, must not only decide disputed facts; they must apply the law to those facts. In a jury case, the trial judge instructs the jury on the law it should apply. If the trial judge's instructions do not correctly state the law and the appellate court concludes that there is a likelihood that the error affected the jury's verdict, the judgment will be set aside and a new trial will be ordered. In a bench trial, the judge's "conclusions of law" provide an analogous road map; if the judge gets the law wrong, he or she will be similarly subject to reversal.

B.   Procedural Control of Rational Proof

Reid asks when a chain of inferences drawn by the factfinder strays beyond the bounds of rationality. In the U.S. legal system courts regularly face that question, but it comes to them embedded in a set of procedural institutions. The most important of these are the tradition of adversarial responsibility for proof and the system of jury trial. Both of these dictate the particular forms by which the system tries to assure rationality — and the limits of those efforts.

1.   Juries, Democracy, and Rationality

The contemporary jury embodies several contradictory goals. At one level we speak of it simply as a factfinding body, although finding facts in the midst of conflict and perjury is hardly simple. But we also have other aspirations for it: The jury is the voice of the community, tempering and making acceptable applications of law that might otherwise be resented or resisted. Finally, it is a temporary, lay, and democratic institution that stands at the core of a permanent, professional, and elite institution — the judiciary. The two latter roles conflict at times with factfinding, at least if that task is understood in a limited way. To ask juries to decide cases, then, is to permit them — or perhaps to require them — to do something more than find facts.

If one accepts this proposition, the task of procedure becomes more difficult. The litigation system is dedicated to rationality. It is also, however, committed to a model of factfinding that blends rationality with other goals. How does one frame procedural rules that give juries sufficient leeway to perform the political tasks we have set for them without irreparably compromising the rationality of verdicts?

2.   Adversarial Responsibility for Proof

Part of the answer to the question just posed lies in shifting responsibility from the court to the parties. One hopes that trials frequently arrive at something like truth. But procedures like summary judgment will weed out the easy, clear cases: Procedural principles dictate that the only cases reaching trial will be those in which a rational trier of fact could decide for *either* party. Under these circumstances, litigation becomes "a system for managing doubt," [*] and trial procedure aims at fairness as much as at truth. Trials in the United States are framed not as inquiries but as contests. The adversaries have the opportunity to present competing versions of their stories within the limits permitted by the rules of evidence and other procedural constraints that seek to assure the parties an equal and fair opportunity. Experienced observers of trials can easily recall cases in which an unbiased and credible witness was not called because neither side wanted the whole truth to come out. As a result, a verdict may not be an announcement about truth, but a judgment about who presented the more credible version of the case.

One need not be cynical about this approach; experienced observers often report that they think that the result of trial is usually a judgment that comes as close as humanly possible to the truth. The point is rather that any system seeking to bring rationality to this contest has to take into account the adversarial mode by which proof is presented. Throughout the trial the parties take turns: They take turns in conducting voir dire (if the court permits lawyers to ask questions directly of jurors), in exercising peremptory strikes of jurors, and in presenting what they think will be the most convincing evidence from among what is available to them. They take turns in presenting their cases and, within their respective turns, take further turns in examining and cross-examining witnesses. The system seeks to take account of this symmetrical, game-like quality of trial by devising procedures that fit the adversarial presentation of proof. Assigning to the parties tasks of presenting evidence and argument makes sense in a system that requires the parties to gather information and to plan litigation strategy. In this respect, burdens of proof follow from the design of entire procedural system.

3. Burdens

. The most important of these procedures goes under the term "burden of proof." We assign to one of the parties the burden of proving some aspect of the case. If the trier of fact finds that the party has not offered the required proof, that party loses. We are all familiar with one such burden, the burden on the prosecution in a criminal case to prove the guilt of the defendant beyond a reasonable doubt. According to the doctrine, if a trier of fact thinks it is probable but not certain that the defendant is guilty, the defendant should be acquitted. Burdens in civil cases play a different though no less important role. Lawyers typically distinguish between the two forms that the burden of proof can take, the burden of persuasion and the burden of production.

[*] Geoffrey C. Hazard, Jr., Res Nova in Res Judicata, 44 S. Cal. L. Rev. 1036, 1042 (1971).

a. Burden of Persuasion

We start with the burden of persuasion because it is more familiar from the criminal context (a familiarity that can make it harder to understand civil litigation). The burden of persuasion defines the extent to which a trier of fact must be convinced of some proposition in order to render a verdict for the party who bears it. In civil cases the burden of persuasion is lower than "beyond a reasonable doubt." It is variously defined as "the preponderance of evidence," "more probable than not," or "more likely than not." (In a few specialized circumstances — will contests, fraud — courts or legislation sometimes require "clear and convincing evidence," a standard thought to lie somewhere between preponderance and beyond a reasonable doubt.) As interpreted by the courts, the preponderance standard means that a trier of fact can find for the party with the burden of persuasion if the trier finds the material fact merely "probable." Consider what that means.

NOTES AND PROBLEMS

1. In a negligence case the plaintiff bears the burden of persuading the trier that the defendant was negligent. Such a finding would in turn rest on at least two subsidiary findings: (a) that the defendant committed some act (or failed to take some precaution) and (b) that the act (or omission) created an unreasonable danger. The strictly factual part of that finding concerns the defendant's act or omission. Imagine a simple case in which the plaintiff claims that the defendant ran a red light and collided with the plaintiff's car. Suppose the trier was prepared to find that if the defendant ran the red light, she was negligent. The issue then turns on whether she did. Further suppose conflicting evidence: The plaintiff testifies that the defendant did run the light; defendant testifies that she didn't; and other witnesses give stories that partially corroborate both parties' stories — in short, a very typical case. The judge instructs the jury on the burden of persuasion in a civil case. An example of such an instruction is:

> When I tell you that a party must prove something, I mean that the party must persuade you, by the evidence presented in court, that what he or she is trying to prove is more likely to be true than not true. This is sometimes referred to as "the burden of proof."
>
> After weighing all of the evidence, if you cannot decide whether a party has satisfied the burden of proof, you must conclude that the party did not prove that fact. You should consider all the evidence that applies to that fact, no matter which party produced the evidence.

Judicial Council of California Civil Jury Instructions (2003-2004) CACI No. 200.

a. The jury sifts the evidence and concludes that it thinks the defendant probably did run the light. The jurors aren't sure, but they think it likely. Explain why the outcome will not depend on which party bears the burden of persuasion.

b. The jury sifts the evidence and concludes that it thinks the defendant probably did *not* run the light. The jurors aren't sure but they think it likely.

Explain why the outcome will not depend on which party bears the burden of persuasion.

c. The jury sifts the evidence and concludes that it simply can't decide whether the defendant ran the light. It finds the evidence absolutely evenly balanced. Explain why in this situation — and only in this situation — will the outcome depend on which party bears the burden of persuasion.

d. Now suppose that the defendant were being prosecuted criminally for negligent operation of a motor vehicle. In which of the scenarios would the burden of persuasion determine the outcome of the case? Why?

2. In light of the preceding problem, be prepared to explain why lawyers will tell you that the burden of persuasion in a civil case almost never matters.

b. Burden of Production

By contrast, the burden of production in a civil case often matters a great deal. Unlike the burden of persuasion, which comes into play only when all the evidence is in and the trier of fact has to decide what it all means, the burden of production requires a party to "produce," to find and present evidence in the first place.

Because you have examined the pretrial process, you can now understand what this means. Summary judgment relies on this idea. At the heart of Celotex Corp. v. Catrett, supra page 516, lies the proposition that a party with the burden of production can lose even before trial if she fails to demonstrate, among the facts uncovered by investigation and discovery, sufficient evidence to allow a rational trier of fact to find in her favor. For example, if the plaintiff has the burden of production on the question of whether the defendant ran the red light, it is up to him to find the witness, to interview or depose her, to make sure that she comes to court on the day of trial, to conduct the direct examination in a way that makes her statement admissible. If the plaintiff fails in any of these steps, he loses — even though, as a matter of historical fact, the defendant did run the red light. The plaintiff loses because he has failed to satisfy the burden of production — of coming forward with evidence from which a rational trier of fact could conclude some proposition of material fact.

NOTES AND PROBLEMS

1. You have already encountered a case about the burden of production — Reid v. San Pedro, Los Angeles & Salt Lake Railroad (supra page 584).

a. In *Reid* the plaintiff lost because she did not produce — come forward with — evidence that permitted one rationally to conclude that more probably than not the railroad's negligence had caused the death of the animal.

b. By contrast, the plaintiff *had* met her burden of production on the question of whether the railroad was negligent. Explain what evidence satisfied the burden of production on that issue.

2. Different parties may have the burden of production on different issues. For example, in a negligence case, the plaintiff will have the burden of production on the defendant's negligence. By contrast, if the defendant pleads the statute of limitations as a defense, she will have the burden of production as to the facts material to that defense. Suppose that the plaintiff was exposed to some allegedly toxic chemicals, perhaps as a result of the defendant's negligence. More than a year after that exposure, the plaintiff manifested some physical symptoms that she is now alleging resulted from the exposure. The statute of limitations is one year, and the state in question says that the statute runs from the time the plaintiff should reasonably have realized that she was injured.

a. The plaintiff has the burden of producing evidence that the defendant negligently handled or used the chemicals in question and that the exposure caused the symptoms complained of.

b. The defendant has the burden of producing evidence that the plaintiff should reasonably have realized that she was injured more than a year before the case was filed.

c. Under those circumstances both parties have the burden of producing evidence — and therefore the risk of losing if they fail to do so — about material facts best known to the adversary. Whether they can bear their burdens may depend on how well they can use discovery.

d. Finally, integrate your understanding of the burdens of production and persuasion by considering what would happen if *both* parties met their burdens of production in the hypothetical toxic chemical case. Both parties have presented evidence sufficient to allow a rational trier of fact to conclude (a) that the defendant had negligently handled the chemical (which had caused the plaintiff harm) and (b) that more than a year had elapsed between the time the plaintiff should reasonably have realized that she had been harmed and the filing of the case. Given this information, can one determine who wins the case?

e. The answer is that one cannot: To say that a trier of fact might rationally conclude X is not to say that it must conclude X. Satisfying a burden of production means only that a trier might rationally decide the case in one's favor, not that it must. In any given case, it is entirely possible for both parties to have satisfied their burdens of production — to have produced enough evidence that a rational jury could find for either party. To understand that one cannot, you have to take a final step, as described in the next section.

4.   Controlling Juries Before the Verdict

To define the boundaries of jury rationality, courts employ five procedural devices. Two of these, the law of evidence and the power of instructing the jury on the law and of commenting on the evidence, are designed to control the flow of information that reaches the jury. Three other devices — the directed verdict, the judgment notwithstanding the verdict, and the grant of new trials — are designed to control what the jury does with that information, and, specifically, to prevent it from drawing the "wrong" conclusions. Each of these latter three devices is triggered by a party's argument that the jury should not be permitted to decide in favor of the other side given the evidence it has heard, or that the jury was subject to improper influences. All three devices thus rest on the idea that under some circumstances a jury could not rationally decide in a particular way.

In reading the materials in this section, you should keep two issues separate: First, consider whether the court is limiting what the jury is to consider or whether it is trying to regulate the jury's process of decision making; second, note which procedural device the court is using.

a.   Judgment as a Matter of Law (Directed Verdict)

In the hypothetical case of the negligently handled chemical, suppose the plaintiff has presented all her evidence: that the defendant manufactured toxic chemicals, that the plaintiff has experienced physical symptoms or respiratory distress, and that the symptoms are of a sort that can be caused by the chemical. The defendant believes that the plaintiff has failed to meet her burden of production on the issue of negligence. In so asserting, the defendant is saying that a rational jury could not, from the evidence presented, conclude that the defendant had been negligent either in the manufacture of the chemical or in warning users about precautions.

Procedurally, the defendant makes that assertion by moving for what is commonly known as a directed verdict. Rule 50 permits a party at the close of the other party's case to move for "judgment as a matter of law," sometimes abbreviated as "j.m.l." In so moving, the defendant would be asking the judge to take the case away from the jury to prevent it from considering the evidence and reaching a verdict. The ground for the motion would be that the evidence presented would support only one result: In the words of Rule 50(a), "there is no legally sufficient evidentiary basis for a reasonable jury to find for that party on that issue." That being the case, the judge should save everyone's time by announcing the result that a properly functioning jury would inevitably reach.* To grant such a motion results in final judgment being entered against the party with the burden that she has failed to carry.

The question, of course, is when should the judge do so? The black-letter law is easy to state but quite unhelpful: A judge should direct a verdict only if there is no rational basis for a jury to find in favor of the party against whom the verdict is directed. Applying that standard requires courts to define its meaning in widely varying factual situations. Tens of thousands of reported cases have passed on the

---

* Historically, judges accomplished this result by "directing" the jury to bring in a verdict for one party or the other. Most juries were delighted to be spared the trouble of deliberating, but occasional juries have refused. The judge was then faced with various uncomfortable alternatives — hectoring the jurors, threatening them with contempt, and the like. Accordingly, the current version of Rule 50 substitutes the term "judgment as matter of law" for the more traditional "directed verdict." Many states — and most lawyers — still use the older term, whose meaning and significance is identical.

question whether to grant judgment as a matter of law. One can, at best, acquire a rough sense of the problems, bearing in mind Wigmore's dictum that each case will "depend entirely on the nature of the evidence offered in the case in hand; and it is seldom possible that a ruling can serve as a precedent." 9 J. Wigmore, Evidence §2492, at 296 (3d ed. 1940). Part of the problem comes from the circumstance that a motion for judgment as a matter of law can raise several different issues: credibility (which witness is telling the most convincing story?); inference (what conclusions can one rationally draw from undisputed facts?); evaluation (do the physical facts constitute, for example, negligent behavior?); and substance (for example, is knowledge by the defendant an element of the claim?). Which of these issues does the next case raise?

Pennsylvania Railroad v. Chamberlain

288 U.S. 333 (1933)

Mr. Justice SUTHERLAND delivered the opinion of the Court.

This is an action brought by respondent against petitioner to recover for the death of a brakeman, alleged to have been caused by petitioner's negligence. The complaint alleges that the deceased, at the time of the accident resulting in his death, was assisting in the yard work of breaking up and making up trains and in the classifying and assorting of cars operating in interstate commerce; that in pursuance of such work, while riding a cut of cars, other cars ridden by fellow employees were negligently caused to be brought into violent contact with those upon which deceased was riding, with the result that he was thrown therefrom to the railroad track and run over by a car or cars, inflicting injuries from which he died.

At the conclusion of the evidence, the trial court directed the jury to find a verdict in favor of petitioner. Judgment upon a verdict so found was reversed by the court of appeals, Judge Swan dissenting.

That part of the yard in which the accident occurred contained a lead track and a large number of switching tracks branching therefrom. The lead track crossed a "hump," and the work of car distribution consisted of pushing a train of cars by means of a locomotive to the top of the "hump," and then allowing the cars, in separate strings, to descend by gravity, under the control of hand brakes, to their respective destinations in the various branch tracks. Deceased had charge of a string of two gondola cars, which he was piloting to track 14. Immediately ahead of him was a string of seven cars, and behind him a string of nine cars, both also destined for track 14. Soon after the cars ridden by deceased had passed to track 14, his body was found on that track some distance beyond the switch. He had evidently fallen onto the track and been run over by a car or cars.

The case for respondent rests wholly upon the claim that the fall of deceased was caused by a violent collision of the string of nine cars with the string ridden by deceased. Three employees, riding the nine-car string, testified positively that no such collision occurred. They were corroborated by every other employee in a position to see, all testifying that there was no contact between the nine-car string and that of the deceased. The testimony of these witnesses, if believed, establishes beyond doubt that there was no collision between these two strings of cars, and that the nine-car string contributed in no way to the accident. The only witness who testified for the respondent was one Bainbridge; and it is upon his testimony alone that respondent's right to recover is sought to be upheld. His testimony is concisely stated, in its most favorable light for respondent, in the prevailing opinion below by Judge Learned Hand, as follows:

> The plaintiff's only witness to the event, one Bainbridge, then employed by the road, stood close to the yardmaster's office, near the "hump." He professed to have paid little attention to what went on, but he did see the deceased riding at the rear of his cars, whose speed when they passed him he took to be about eight or ten miles. Shortly thereafter a second string passed which was shunted into another track and this was followed by the nine, which, according to the plaintiff's theory, collided with the deceased's. After the nine cars had passed at a somewhat greater speed than the deceased's, Bainbridge paid no more attention to either string for a while, but looked again when the deceased, who was still standing in his place, had passed the switch and onto the assorting track where he was bound. At that time his speed had been checked to about three miles, but the speed of the following nine cars had increased. They were just passing the switch, about four or five cars behind the deceased. Bainbridge looked away again and soon heard what he described as a "loud crash," not however an unusual event in a switching yard. Apparently this did not cause him at once to turn, but he did so shortly thereafter, and saw the two strings together still moving, and the deceased no longer in sight. Later still his attention was attracted by shouts and he went to the spot and saw the deceased between the rails. Until he left to go to the accident, he had stood fifty feet to the north of the track where the accident happened, and about nine hundred feet from where the body was found.

The court, although regarding Bainbridge's testimony as not only "somewhat suspicious in itself, but its contradiction . . . so manifold as to leave little doubt," held, nevertheless, that the question was one of fact depending upon the credibility of the witnesses, and that it was for the jury to determine, as between the one witness and the many, where the truth lay. The dissenting opinion of Judge Swan proceeds upon the theory that Bainbridge did not testify that in fact a collision had taken place, but inferred it because he heard a crash, and because thereafter the two strings of cars appeared to him to be moving together. It is correctly pointed out in that opinion, however, that the crash might have come from elsewhere in the busy yard and that Bainbridge was in no position to see whether the two strings of cars were actually together; that Bainbridge repeatedly said he was paying no particular attention; and that his position was such, being 900 feet from the place where the body was found and less than 50 feet from the side of the track in question, that he necessarily saw the strings of cars at such an acute angle that it would be physically impossible even for an attentive observer to tell whether the forward end of the nine-car cut was actually in contact with the rear end of the two-car cut. The dissenting opinion further points out that all the witnesses who were in a position to see testified that there was no collision; that respondent's evidence was wholly circumstantial, and the inferences which might otherwise be drawn from it were shown to be utterly erroneous unless all of petitioner's witnesses were willful perjurers. "This is not a case," the opinion proceeds, "where direct testimony to an essential fact is contradicted by direct testimony of other witnesses, though even there it is conceded a directed verdict might be proper in some circumstances. Here, when all the testimony was in, the circumstantial evidence in support of negligence was thought by the trial judge to be so insubstantial and insufficient that it did not justify submission to the jury."

We thus summarize and quote from the prevailing and dissenting opinions, because they present the divergent views to be considered in reaching a correct determination of the question involved. It, of course, is true, generally, that where there is a direct conflict of testimony upon a matter of fact, the question must be left to the jury to determine, without regard to the number of witnesses upon either side. But here there really is no conflict in the testimony as to the *facts*. The witnesses for petitioner flatly testified that there was no collision between the nine-car and the two-car strings. Bainbridge did not say there was such a collision. What he said was that he heard a "loud crash," which did not cause him at once to turn, but that shortly thereafter he did turn and saw the two strings of cars moving together with the deceased no longer in sight; that there was nothing unusual about the crash of cars — it happened every day; that there was nothing about this crash to attract his attention except that it was extra loud; that he paid no attention to it; that it was not sufficient to attract his attention. The record shows that there was a continuous movement of cars over and down the "hump," which were distributed among a large number of branch tracks within the yard, and that any two strings of these cars moving upon the same track might have come together and caused the crash which Bainbridge heard. There is no direct evidence that *in fact* the crash was occasioned by a collision of the two strings in question; and it is perfectly clear that no such fact was brought to Bainbridge's attention as a perception of the physical sense of sight or of hearing. At most there was an inference to that effect drawn from observed facts which gave equal support to the opposite inference that the crash was occasioned by the coming together of other strings of cars entirely away from the scene of the accident, or of the two-car string ridden by deceased and the seven-car string immediately ahead of it.

We, therefore, have a case belonging to that class of cases where proven facts give equal support to each of two inconsistent inferences; in which event, neither of them being established, judgment, as a matter of law, must go against the party upon whom rests the necessity of sustaining one of these inferences as against the other, before he is entitled to recover.

The rule is succinctly stated in Smith v. First National Bank in Westfield, 99 Mass. 605, 611-612, quoted in the *Des Moines National Bank* case [United States F. & G. Co. v. Des Moines National Bank, 145 F. 273, 280 (8th Cir. 1906)]:

> There being several inferences deducible from the facts which appear, and equally consistent with all those facts, the plaintiff has not maintained the proposition upon which alone he would be entitled to recover. There is strictly no evidence to warrant a jury in finding that the loss was occasioned by negligence and not by theft. When the evidence tends equally to sustain either of two inconsistent propositions, neither of them can be said to have been established by legitimate proof. A verdict in favor of the party bound to maintain one of those propositions against the other is necessarily wrong.

[Margin handwritten notes: "General rule for conflict of testimony"; "Reasoning"; "Rule when plaintiff doesn't meet BoP"]

That Bainbridge concluded from what he himself observed that the crash was due to a collision between the two strings of cars in question is sufficiently indicated by his statements. But this, of course, proves nothing, since it is not allowable for a witness to resolve the doubt as to which of two equally justifiable inferences shall be adopted by drawing a conclusion, which, if accepted, will result in a purely gratuitous award in favor of the party who has failed to sustain the burden of proof cast upon him by the law.

And the desired inference is precluded for the further reason that respondent's right of recovery depends upon the existence of a particular fact which must be inferred from proven facts, and this is not permissible in the face of the positive and otherwise uncontradicted testimony of unimpeached witnesses consistent with the facts actually proved, from which testimony it affirmatively appears that the fact sought to be inferred did not exist. . . .

Not only is Bainbridge's testimony considered as a whole suspicious, insubstantial and insufficient, but his statement that when he turned shortly after hearing the crash the two strings were moving together is simply incredible, if he meant thereby to be understood as saying that he saw the two in contact; and if he meant by the words "moving together" simply that they were moving at the same time in the same direction but not in contact, the statement becomes immaterial. As we have already seen he was paying slight and only occasional attention to what was going on. The cars were 800 or 900 feet from where he stood and moving almost directly away from him, his angle of vision being only 3°03′ from a straight line. At that sharp angle and from that distance, near dusk of a misty evening (as the proof shows), the practical impossibility of the witness being able to see whether the front of the nine-car string was in contact with the back of the two-car string is apparent. And, certainly, in the light of these conditions, no verdict based upon a statement so unbelievable reasonably could be sustained as against the positive testimony to the contrary of unimpeached witnesses, all in a position to see, as this witness was not, the precise relation of the cars to one another. The fact that these witnesses were employees of the petitioner, under the circumstances here disclosed, does not impair this conclusion. Chesapeake & Ohio Ry. v. Martin, 283 U.S. 209, 216-220. . . .

Leaving out of consideration, then, the inference relied upon, the case for respondent is left without any substantial support in the evidence, and a verdict in her favor would have rested upon mere speculation and conjecture. This, of course, is inadmissible.

The judgment of the Circuit Court of Appeals is reversed and that of the District Court is affirmed.

Mr. Justice STONE and Mr. Justice CARDOZO concur in the result.

NOTES AND PROBLEMS

1. Focus first on the procedural steps that frame the issue.

a. A trial typically consists of the plaintiff's presentation of his case, the defendant's of its case, closing argument, and jury instructions. When in the course of this sequence did the defendant move for a directed verdict? Locate the portion of Rule 50 that permits a party to make a motion at this point.

b. Could the defendant have moved for a directed verdict earlier? When?

2. To understand the force of *Chamberlain*, consider a variation on the facts.

a. Suppose at the time of the accident Bainbridge had not been standing several hundred feet away from the scene on a misty evening but instead had been standing ten feet away. He testifies that he clearly saw the collision and that Chamberlain's death had been caused by the following car string's overtaking his string and crushing him between the cars. But suppose further that at the time of the accident a group of clergy had been taking a tour of the rail yards. These clergy also saw the accident clearly, and all testify under oath that the following string did not come near Chamberlain's and that the deceased fell onto the tracks when he waved to a friend. Would this testimony warrant granting a judgment for defendant?

b. The commonly accepted answer to this question is no. This answer is a result of the courts' insistence that in directing verdicts they not make judgments about the credibility of witnesses, even when the case seems strongly one-sided.

c. Is that black-letter statement consistent with *Chamberlain*?

3. Cases such as *Chamberlain* have been thought to raise two related issues. The first is the precise standard for taking the case from the jury — more particularly, which evidence should be considered. There is general agreement that the court should consider all evidence favorable to the plaintiff, all inferences from that evidence, and all undisputed evidence. But should the court also consider testimonial and disputed evidence in favor of the defendant? Closely related is the matter of evaluating the evidence. Many courts have stated that the basic test is whether reasonable persons could differ; if they could, the court should defer to the jury on the ground that its members are reasonable persons whose verdict represents one of several reasonable views. The leading case articulating the prevailing view is Boeing Co. v. Shipman, 411 F.2d 365, 374-375 (5th Cir. 1969):

> On motions for directed verdict and for judgment notwithstanding the verdict the Court should consider all of the evidence — not just that evidence which supports the non-mover's case — but in the light and with all reasonable inferences most favorable to the party opposed to the motion. If the facts and inferences point so strongly and overwhelmingly in favor of one party that the Court believes that reasonable men could not arrive at a contrary verdict, granting of the motions is proper. On the other hand, if there is substantial evidence opposed to the motions, that is, evidence of such quality and weight that reasonable and fair-minded men in the exercise of impartial judgment might reach different conclusions, the motions should be denied, and the case submitted to the jury. A mere scintilla of evidence is insufficient to present a question for the jury. The motions for directed verdict and judgment n. o. v. should not be decided by which side has the better of the case, nor should they be granted only when there is a complete absence of probative facts to support a jury verdict. There must be a conflict in substantial evidence to create a jury question. However, it is the function of the jury as the traditional finder of the facts, and not the Court, to weigh conflicting evidence and inferences, and determine the credibility of witnesses.

4. The question in *Chamberlain*, then, is whether, using the standard articulated above, one can construct the evidence presented into a story that makes it reasonable to infer that the fellow workers' negligence caused Chamberlain's death.

a. In constructing such a story, consider a snippet from the opinion below, by Judge Learned Hand:

> It does not appear to us impossible, or indeed improbable, that one in [Bainbridge's] position could tell whether the two strings were together. The intervals between cars in a train are uniform; they may be detected by the straight sides. Certainly a gap of four or five car lengths, when the nine cars came to rest, would have been easily observable; and this was the story of the defendant. What Bainbridge saw, coupled with what he had heard, if uncontradicted, would be enough to support a finding that the nine cars had collided with the deceased's and thrown him off. There is no inherent impossibility in the story.

Chamberlain v. Pennsylvania R.R., 59 F.2d 986, 987 (2d Cir. 1932).

b. Is the Supreme Court in fact making a comparative assessment of witness credibility? N̄ɔ

c. As the Supreme Court describes the case, Bainbridge's testimony is suspicious because of his inadequate opportunity to observe, while the fellow workers' contrary testimony is taken at face value. Is there reason to suspect the other workers' testimony? Is there reason to credit Bainbridge's inference that the two strings collided?

5. *Chamberlain* has to avoid questions of credibility because the jury is the undoubted arbiter of credibility. But we ask jurors to do much more than to decide who is telling the truth. We also give to the jury many questions that require them to apply general, open-ended standards to the facts of the case. Was it negligent under these circumstances to be driving five miles faster than the speed limit? Was the behavior of one of the contracting parties unreasonable? To arrive at answers to such questions, juries may have to decide questions of fact. But even after doing so they must then apply the open texture of law to those facts.

a. Because of this role, courts often give to juries cases where the facts are undisputed. A classic example is Railroad Co. v. Stout, 84 U.S. (17 Wall) 657 (1873). A child was injured while playing on a railroad turntable located at the edge of a sparsely populated rural settlement. The turntable was not locked or fenced. No one contested any of these facts; the case went to the jury, which found negligence. Rejecting the railroad's contentions that the judge should have taken the case from the jury, the Supreme Court wrote:

> Upon the facts proven in such cases, it is a matter of judgment and discretion, of sound inference, what is the deduction to be drawn from the undisputed facts. Certain facts we may suppose to be clearly established from which one sensible, impartial man would infer that proper care had not been used, and that negligence existed; another man equally sensible and equally impartial would infer that proper care had been used, and that there was no negligence. It is this class of cases and those akin to it that the law commits to the decision of a jury. Twelve men of the average of the community, comprising men of education and men of little education, men of learning and men whose learning consists only in what they have

themselves seen and heard, the merchant, the mechanic, the farmer, the laborer; these sit together, consult, apply their separate experience of the affairs of life to the facts proven, and draw a unanimous conclusion. This average judgment thus given it is the great effort of the law to obtain. It is assumed that twelve men know more of the common affairs of life than does one man, that they can draw wiser and safer conclusions from admitted facts thus occurring than can a single judge.

Railroad Co. v. Stout, 84 U.S. at 663. Note that the assumption about the gender of jurors rests on premises since held to be unconstitutional. See supra page 573.

b. Given this practice, note that to describe the jury as merely a factfinding body is deceptive. Isn't the jury's role in such cases very close to making "law"?

b.   Excluding Improper Influences

Judges prefer not to enter judgments as a matter of law. It goes against the grain to require citizens to take time from family and work to decide a case only to yank it out from under them. Moreover, someone is going to get bad news at the end of the case, and most judges would rather have the jury deliver it to them. Judges therefore do everything they can to assure that jurors won't reach verdicts that can't be sustained by the evidence. Besides entering a judgment as a matter of law, a judge has some less drastic procedural tools to use.

The process starts before trial gets under way. Screening the jury through voir dire (see pages 575 supra) seeks to eliminate jurors whose sympathies or inability to understand the evidence might cause them to reach irrational verdicts. During the trial judges try to assure that jurors will consider only information screened through the law of evidence (many of whose parts can be explained as efforts to insulate jurors from information that might be misleading). Even good faith efforts by jurors that bring to their fellow jurors information not filtered through the evidentiary and adversarial screens may result in new trials. For example, in a case that turned on whether aluminum electrical wiring was dangerous, one juror, after hearing testimony to that effect, went home, examined the wiring in his own home, and reported his findings to his fellow jurors the next day. The appellate court ordered a new trial. In re Beverly Hills Fire Litigation, 695 F.2d 207 (6th Cir. 1982). Judges try to avoid such outcomes by instructing the jurors not to discuss the case with others and to decide only on the basis of evidence presented in the courtroom. In extreme instances, where the case is the subject of much public discussion, the judge can sequester the jury.

c.   Instructions and Comment

The judge also teaches the jury by framing the questions for decision and, perhaps, commenting on the evidence. The judge frames the question by instructing the jury on the law. Rule 51. Notice that even this part of the process depends on the parties, who must request instructions, and, in the absence of an objection, may not complain that the judge has wrongly instructed the jury.

Instructions explain the substantive law that applies to the case, and the judge explains in a sequential way the decisions the jury must reach in a given case. For example, if the jury determines that the defendant was negligent, it must then decide whether the defendant's negligence caused the injury of which the plaintiff is complaining.

Jury instructions have two audiences. Their first audience is the jury itself, who may have an intuitive understanding of the law (quite likely in a negligence case) or none at all (as, for example, in antitrust). The second audience for jury instructions is the appellate court, which will reverse a case if an instruction misstates the law in a material way. These audiences have essentially incompatible requirements. The jury wants a simplified, easy-to-follow path through the wilderness of evidence to help it distinguish the central from the peripheral and to explain what factors should go into its decision on each question. The appellate court wants a nuanced, perfectly balanced, all-inclusive statement of the law. The clash between these contradictory requirements means that most instructions are compromises.

Besides telling the jury what the law is, the judge can, if she is very careful, tell the jury what she thinks of the evidence. Here the law speaks to the judge with a mixed voice. In federal courts at least, the judge has the theoretical power to comment on the evidence. That power is hedged, however, with many qualifications and with exhortations that the judge not trespass into the jury's autonomous decision-making space. Judges who do so egregiously — like the judge who solemnly informed a jury that in his experience witnesses who wiped their hands while testifying were liars, Quercia v. United States, 289 U.S. 466, 468 (1933) — are reversed.

5.   Controlling Juries After the Verdict

What does a judge do if, after carefully screening the jury, watching the evidence like a hawk, refraining from impermissible comment, and giving a legally impeccable but easily understood set of instructions, gets an absolutely insupportable verdict from the jury? What can a party on the losing end of such a verdict do about it? If the trial judge committed error at trial, an appeal is a possibility. But suppose there is no such error. In that situation, there are two procedural devices for rectifying the problem: the motion for a judgment notwithstanding the verdict and the motion for a new trial. We consider them in turn.

a.   Judgment as a Matter of Law (Judgment Notwithstanding the Verdict)

Suppose a verdict is insupportable because there was simply no evidence from which a rational person could have found for the party who won the verdict. The plaintiff put on evidence of an auto accident and her injuries, but nothing from which one could infer that the defendant had been negligent — yet the jury returned a plaintiff's verdict. How could that happen? An attentive reader of this and the preceding chapters will realize that, in theory, such a case would never reach the jury. If the defendant made a motion for summary judgment, the case would not reach trial. If it did reach trial (perhaps because defendant failed to move for summary judgment), at trial the defendant would move for judgment as a matter of law before the case went to the jury, and the court would grant it, thus ending the case.

As often, practice is messier than theory. Judges faced with a pretrial summary judgment motion or a preverdict Rule 50 motion, believing that the party with the burden of production has failed to meet it, will sometimes nevertheless deny the motion. Why? If the judge grants the motion and an appellate court reverses, a whole new trial will be necessary—a big waste of time. If the judge denies the motion, one of two things can happen. If the evidence is as one-sided as the judge believes, the jury will likely return a verdict for the "proper" party without any judicial intervention. If something goes wrong, however, the judge can always rescue the case by granting a judgment notwithstanding the verdict (j.n.o.v.)*— essentially a late ruling on the earlier motion for judgment as a matter of law. The grounds for a j.n.o.v. are identical to those for a preverdict judgment as a matter of law: "that there is 'no legally sufficient evidentiary basis for a reasonable jury to find for th[e] party'" against whom the motion is made. Rule 50(a). Only the timing of the two motions differs—one coming before the verdict, the other after.

NOTES AND PROBLEMS

1. In an automobile negligence case, the plaintiff presents evidence of an accident and of her injuries, and then rests her case. The defendant presents his case, which tends to show that the plaintiff, not the defendant, was negligent. The case goes to a jury, which returns a verdict for the plaintiff. The defendant then moves for judgment notwithstanding the verdict. Why must the judge deny this motion, even though the plaintiff has presented no evidence of the defendant's negligence? Rule 50(b).

2. The requirement of a Rule 50(a) motion (for a directed verdict) before the verdict as a prerequisite for granting a Rule 50(b) motion (for judgment notwithstanding the verdict) after trial has constitutional foundations. The Seventh Amendment provides that "no fact tried by a jury, shall be otherwise reexamined in any court of the United States, than according to the rules of common law."

a. The U.S. Supreme Court has held that common law had an analogue to the directed verdict, but none to the judgment notwithstanding the verdict. Does that make the j.n.o.v. unconstitutional? No, said the Supreme Court, if the j.n.o.v. is merely a delayed ruling on the motion for a directed verdict. Baltimore & Carolina Line v. Redman, 295 U.S. 654 (1935). For it to be a delayed ruling, however, there must have been a motion preceding the submission of the case to the jury. Explaining the reasons for this requirement—in a case in which a defendant

---

* So-called from its Latin initials: judgment *non obstante veredicto*.

had failed to make a preverdict Rule 50 motion and thereby missed the chance to challenge a million-dollar punitive damage verdict—a court explained:

> The purpose of this rule is twofold. First it preserves the sufficiency of the evidence as a question of law, allowing the district court to review its initial denial of judgment as a matter of law instead of forcing it to "engage in an impermissible reexamination of facts by the jury." Second, it calls to the court's and the parties' attention any alleged deficiencies in the evidence at a time when the opposing party still has an opportunity to correct them.

Freund v. Nycomed Amersham, 2003 U.S. App. LEXIS 21233.*16-*17 (9th Cir. 2003).

b. This rule is enshrined in Rule 50(b). Do not, therefore, in the heat of your first federal trial, forget to make a Rule 50(a) motion before the case is submitted to the jury, or you will have waived the right to make a Rule 50(b) motion and may find yourself having to answer some very unpleasant questions from your client, your malpractice insurer, and perhaps the state bar.

b.   New Trial

Suppose that the trial judge cannot conscientiously say that there is no evidence to support the jury verdict. She thinks, however, that the case was very strong on one side and very weak on the other, but the wrong side won. Must the verdict stand because the judge could not properly grant a j.n.o.v.? Not necessarily: The judge has another weapon in her arsenal of post-trial motions — the new trial.

Rule 59 governs the granting of new trials, which the judge may order on her own initiative (Rule 59(d)) or on a party's motion. Rule 59 does not specify the grounds for which a new trial may be ordered, but there is a well-developed body of common law on the issue. That law indicates two reasons for granting new trials, one focusing on the procedure leading up to the verdict, the other on the correctness of the verdict itself.

(1)   Flawed procedures

New trials may be granted when the judge concludes that the process leading up to the verdict has been flawed. For example, the judge may conclude that a lawyer has made an impermissible argument to the jury. Or, on reflection after the trial is over, the judge may conclude that she erred in admitting a piece of evidence or that she gave the jury erroneous instructions. Or a judge may discover that a juror, although he was properly selected, misbehaved during the trial, perhaps by visiting the accident scene himself. Ordering a new trial gives the judge a chance to correct herself. Thus a judge who admitted evidence or gave an instruction over an objection may, after the verdict, conclude that the ruling was wrong and grant a new trial to cure the error. Rule 59 explicitly gives the judge power to order a new trial even if neither party so moves.

(2)   Flawed verdicts

Even if the trial was perfect, however, the judge may conclude that the result of that trial — the verdict — is unjustifiable. One example is the verdict that splits the difference between two parties when the law says one or the other must take all — the $500 verdict on the $1,000 bad check. Such a verdict tells the judge that the jury either misunderstood or ignored the instructions. But less blatant errors also will provoke the grant of a new trial.

Probably the most common ground for granting a new trial is that the verdict is against the weight of the evidence. Understanding this idea requires a glance back at the directed verdict and j.n.o.v. Although both result from verdicts lacking evidentiary support, it is important to understand the difference between them and the grant of a new trial. In granting a j.n.o.v., a court is saying that the winner of the verdict had no evidentiary support for at least one essential element of the claim or defense. The consequences of each reflect this difference. A j.n.o.v. results not in a new trial but in an immediate entry of judgment for the loser of the verdict. By contrast, the grant of a new trial does not make a winner out of a loser; it merely begins the contest again. The standard is accordingly lower: As most courts would put it, a judge may grant a new trial when the verdict is "against the great weight of the evidence." Those same courts would agree, however, that the trial judge may not simply decide how she would have voted as a juror and order a new trial if the jury disagrees. Where the standard lies between these two poles is harder to say.

Lind v. Schenley Industries

278 F.2d 79 (3d Cir. 1960)

[Lind, a sales manager for the defendant liquor company, alleged that it had promised him an increase in pay and a share of commissions but had then breached that promise. The alleged promises were oral. Lind and his then-secretary, Mrs. Kennan, testified to such promises. Schenley's agents denied making them. The jury found a contract; a damage award followed. Schenley moved both for judgment notwithstanding the verdict and, alternatively, for a new trial. The trial judge granted the j.n.o.v., and, in the alternative, a new trial. The plaintiff appealed.]

BIGGS, C.J. . . .

The district court granted the alternative motion for a new trial because it found the jury's verdict (1) contrary to the weight of the evidence, (2) contrary to law and (3) a result of error in the admission of evidence. Our conclusion that the verdict was not contrary to law automatically eliminates ground (2).

It is convenient to consider the evidentiary issue relating to point (3) first. [The court held that a tabulated summary of liquor sales had been properly admitted into evidence as a business record.]

The remaining basis for ordering a new trial is that the verdict was against the weight of the evidence. It is frequently stated that a motion for a new trial on this ground ordinarily is nonreviewable because within the discretion of the trial court. But this discretion must still be exercised in accordance with ascertainable legal standards and if an appellate court is shown special or unusual circumstances which clearly indicate an abuse of discretion in that the trial court failed to apply correctly the proper standards, reversal is possible. Concededly appellate courts rarely find that the trial court abused its discretion.

In Commercial Credit Corp. v. Pepper, Judge Borah stated:

> It is a principle well recognized in the federal courts that the granting or refusing of a new trial is a matter resting within the discretion of the trial court. The term "discretion," however, when invoked as a guide to judicial action, means a sound discretion, exercised with regard to what is right and in the interests of justice. And an appellate court is not bound to stay its hand and place its stamp of approval on a case when it feels that injustice may result. Quite to the contrary, it is definitely recognized in numerous decisions that an abuse of discretion is an exception to the rule that the granting or refusing of a new trial is not assignable as error.

Thus an appellate court must still rule upon the propriety of an order for a new trial, even though the grounds for reversal are exceedingly narrow. But before any rational decision can be made, the reviewing court must know what standards the trial judge is bound to apply when ruling upon a motion for a new trial. These standards necessarily vary according to the grounds urged in support of the new trial. There is, however, little authority on what standards are to be applied in ruling on a motion for new trial on the grounds that the verdict is against the weight of the evidence beyond the simple maxim that the trial judge has wide discretion. The few available authorities are conflicting. Professor Moore concludes that while the trial judge has a responsibility for the result at least equal to that of the jury he should not set the verdict aside as contrary to the weight of the evidence and order a new trial simply because he would have come to a different conclusion if he were the trier of the facts. Professor Moore states in this connection:

> [S]ince the credibility of witnesses is peculiarly for the jury it is an invasion of the jury's province to grant a new trial merely because the evidence was sharply in conflict. The trial judge, exercising a mature judicial discretion, should view the verdict in the overall setting of the trial; consider the character of the evidence and the complexity or simplicity of the legal principles which the jury was bound to apply to the facts; and abstain from interfering with the verdict unless it is quite clear that the jury has reached a seriously erroneous result. The judge's duty is essentially to see that there is no miscarriage of justice. If convinced that there has been then it is his duty to set the verdict aside; otherwise not.

Professor Moore's views are logical and persuasive and buttressed by some decisional authority. . . .

What we have stated demonstrates that there is no consensus of opinion as to the exact standards to be used by a trial court in granting a new trial and that the criteria to be employed by an appellate tribunal charged with reviewing the trial judge's decision in this respect are equally indefinite. New trials granted because (1) a jury verdict is against the weight of the evidence may be sharply distinguished from (2) new trials ordered for other reasons: for example, evidence improperly admitted, prejudicial statements by counsel, an improper charge to the jury or newly discovered evidence. In the first instance given it is the jury itself which fails properly to perform the functions confided to it by law. In the latter instances something occurred in the course of the trial which resulted or which may have resulted in the jury receiving a distorted, incorrect, or an incomplete view of the operative facts, or some undesirable element obtruded itself into the proceedings creating a condition whereby the giving of a just verdict was rendered difficult or impossible. In the latter instances, (2), supra, the trial court delivered the jury from a possibly erroneous verdict arising from circumstances over which the jury had no control. Under these conditions there is no usurpation by the court of the prime function of the jury as the trier of the facts and the trial judge necessarily must be allowed wide discretion in granting or refusing a new trial.

But where no undesirable or pernicious element has occurred or been introduced into the trial and the trial judge nonetheless grants a new trial on the ground that the verdict was against the weight of the evidence, the trial judge in negating the jury's verdict has, to some extent at least, substituted his judgment of the facts and the credibility of the witnesses for that of the jury. Such an action effects a denigration of the jury system and to the extent that new trials are granted the judge takes over, if he does not usurp, the prime function of the jury as the trier of the facts. It then becomes the duty of the appellate tribunal to exercise a closer degree of scrutiny and supervision than is the case where a new trial is granted because of some undesirable or pernicious influence obtruding into the trial. Such a close scrutiny is required in order to protect the litigants' right to jury trial.

Where a trial is long and complicated and deals with a subject matter not lying within the ordinary knowledge of jurors a verdict should be scrutinized more closely by the trial judge than is necessary where the litigation deals with material which is familiar and simple, the evidence relating to ordinary commercial practices. An example of subject matter unfamiliar to a layman would be a case requiring a jury to pass upon the nature of an alleged newly discovered organic compound in an infringement action. A prime example of subject matter lying well within the comprehension of jurors is presented by the circumstances at bar.

The subject matter of the litigation before us is simple and easily comprehended by any intelligent layman. The jury's main function was to determine the veracity of the witnesses: i.e., what testimony should be believed. If Lind's testimony and that of Mrs. Kennan, Kaufman's secretary, was deemed credible, Lind presented a convincing, indeed an overwhelming case. We must conclude that the jury did believe this testimony and that the court below substituted its judgment for that of the jury on this issue and thereby abused its legal discretion.

The judgment of the court below will be reversed and the case will be remanded with the direction to the court below to reinstate the verdict and judgment in favor of Lind.

HASTIE, J., with whom KALODNER, J., joins (dissenting).

. . . I think the majority make a serious mistake when they take the extraordinary additional step of reversing the alternative order of the trial judge, granting a new trial because he considered the verdict against the weight of the evidence.

This court has never before reversed an order of a trial judge granting a new trial because of his conclusion on all of the evidence that the jury had reached an unjust result. At least, neither I nor any of my colleagues can find a precedent in our court for such action. Rather, we have recognized that the function in question is broadly discretionary, "requir[ing] that the trial judge evaluate all significant evidence, deciding in the exercise of his own best judgment whether the jury has so disregarded the clear weight of credible evidence that a new trial is necessary to prevent injustice." The opinions of other courts cited by the majority not only recognize that discretion but also emphasize its extreme breadth.

This traditional conception of the role of the trial judge has provided the one important limitation on the power of the jury to make an unimpeachable decision on the facts, even where the evidence is conflicting. The judge may not substitute the verdict he would have rendered on the evidence for that actually rendered by the jury. But he may avoid what in his professionally trained and experienced judgment is an unjust verdict by vacating it and causing the matter to be tried again by a second jury. Thus, the essential institution of jury trial is respected and an expedient middle ground is maintained between the absence of any control over a jury's verdict on conflicting evidence, on the one hand, and judicial usurpation of the fact finding function, on the other.

Under this scheme the only function of a reviewing court, once the trial court has ordered a new trial, is to see whether there can have been any basis in reason for the trial judge's conclusion as to the weight of the evidence and the injustice of the verdict. The majority do not challenge this view, though they do not state explicitly what their understanding of our role is.

The present record discloses a sharp conflict of testimony whether Kaufman, the metropolitan sales manager, ever promised plaintiff, his subordinate district manager, a 1% commission on all gross sales of agents working under plaintiff. There are several remarkable aspects of this alleged promise which could reasonably have influenced the trial judge on this decisive issue. This commission would have more than quadrupled plaintiff's salary of $150 per week, making him much higher paid than his immediate superior, Kaufman, or any other company executive, except the president. No other sales manager or supervisor received any such commission at all. Moreover, after the alleged promise was made, month after month elapsed with no payment of the 1% commission or indication of any step to fulfill such an obligation. Yet plaintiff himself admits that he made no formal demand for or inquiry about the large obligation for several years, and said nothing even informally about it to anyone for many months save for an occasional passing verbal inquiry said to have been addressed to Kaufman. The trial court may have reasoned that the amount said to have been promised was so abnormally large and plaintiff's concern about nonpayment so unnaturally small as to make it incredible that the promise ever was made. In addition, the very vagueness of the alleged promise and the absence of any mention of time in it may have increased the incredulity of the judge who heard the evidence.

In such circumstances it was neither arbitrary nor an abuse of discretion for the trial judge to grant a new trial. Whether in the same circumstances some other trial judge or any member of this court would have let the verdict stand is beside the point.

The majority think the trial judge usurped the function of the jury. I think it is we who are impinging upon the function and discretion of the trial judge in a way that is serious, regrettable and without precedent in this court.

NOTES AND PROBLEMS

1. Why did the trial court grant a new trial?

2. Why did the appellate court reverse the grant of a new trial?

3. The *Lind* opinion merges three separate issues: (1) what standard the trial court should apply in setting aside verdicts as being against the weight of the evidence, (2) how the trial court should apply that standard to the case at hand, and (3) what standard the appellate court should apply in reviewing new trial rulings. How does the *Lind* court resolve each of these issues?

4. The *Lind* opinion also illustrates another part of the relation between directed verdicts and orders for new trials. Notice that defendant, having lost the verdict, made both motions, and the trial court granted both.

a. Why? If the trial judge granted defendant a j.n.o.v., that would end the case. Why bother also ruling on a motion for a new trial? Rule 50(c) contains the answer, permitting a party moving for a j.n.o.v. to make (and the court to rule on) a *conditional* motion for a new trial. This alternative comes into play only if "the judgment [notwithstanding the verdict] is thereafter vacated or reversed." *Lind* illustrates the point of such a conditional ruling because the j.n.o.v. was in fact reversed. Without Rule 50(c), the defendant would have had to return to the trial court and, perhaps some years after the trial, make its motion for a new trial. Rule 50(c), permitting a losing party to make all its post-trial motions at once, allows the trial judge to rule on them with the case still fresh in mind and allows the appellate court to consider all of them at once — as it did in *Lind*.

b. Notice that while the grant of a judgment as a matter of law constitutes a final judgment from which an appeal may be taken, the grant of a new trial, standing alone, does not create a final judgment — this will not happen until the new trial has occurred.

c. The interaction of the final judgment rule and Rule 50(c) creates four possible combinations of grants and denials of judgment as a matter of law and new trial: denial of both motions (probably the most common result); denial of judgment as a matter of law and grant of a new trial; grant of judgment as a matter of law with conditional denial of a new trial; and grant of judgment as a matter of law with conditional grant of a new trial. Which of these are immediately appealable?

5. Suppose a jury returns a defense verdict. The judge, believing that the evidence strongly favored the plaintiff, orders a new trial. The second jury agrees with the first. Should the judge order still a third trial or simply conclude that he was wrong about the weight of the evidence? Because the new trial order is not appealable, the length of such a sequence is theoretically indefinite. In practice, one of three things is likely to happen: the judge may finally get a jury that agrees with him, or the judge may decide that the juries were right and he was wrong. If neither of these occurs, the defendant might eventually get an appellate court to grant a writ of mandamus (see page 644 infra) to put him out of his misery.

6. Consider the procedural dilemmas of a plaintiff, who, having won a trial court verdict, finds it attacked on appeal. Chad Weisgram's mother died in an apartment fire; he sued the manufacturer of an allegedly defective electric baseboard heater. To prove the defect in the heater, Weisgram offered at trial three expert witnesses, whose testimony the defendant challenged. The jury returned a verdict for plaintiff and defendant moved for new trial and for judgment as a matter of law (renewing a similar preverdict motion), which the trial court denied, instead entering judgment on the verdict for the plaintiff. Defendant appealed, contending that the experts' testimony should not have been admitted.

a. Consider the strategic choice confronting Weisgram. He has the right to cross-appeal, arguing that *if* the trial court ruling is reversed, there were other errors that entitled him to a new trial. But as a matter of strategy it is awkward to argue that the trial court judgment was correct and at the same time to contend that there were sufficient errors in various rulings to entitle him to a new trial if the judgment is reversed. Weisgram chose not to make such an argument.

b. That may have been a bad choice, because the appellate court reversed on the ground that the experts' testimony should not have been admitted (because their testimony was scientifically unsound and speculative) and that without that testimony there was no evidence that defendant was responsible for the death. The appellate court then faced the question of whether it should simply grant judgment for the defendant or remand for the trial court to allow Weisgram to move for a new trial; circuits had split on the issue. Resolving a split in the circuits, the Supreme Court unanimously affirmed the appellate court's power to enter judgment for defendant without remanding. Weisgram v. Marley Company, 528 U.S. 440 (2000).

c. Conditional New Trials

Up to now we have dealt with cases in which grants of new trials involved retrying the entire case. Consider a judge who concludes that the jury reasonably could have reached a verdict for the plaintiff but that its damage calculations are unreasonably low or high. May the judge grant a new trial limited to the issue of damages? The answer is yes, though the problems involved in reaching that answer are considerable.

(1)   New trial limited to damages

Consider the logical underpinnings of such a ruling. To be prepared to order a new trial limited to the issue of damages, the judge must be convinced that whatever influences led the jury astray on damages did not infect the judgment on liability as well. Take, for example, a verdict for the plaintiff combined with clearly insufficient damages. Can the judge be certain that the low award did not reflect considerable jury uncertainty that the plaintiff should recover at all—uncertainty that should have been reflected in a judgment for the defendant? The same doubt can exist in the case of clearly excessive damages; a jury so passionately disposed toward the plaintiff may have been so influenced on the issue of liability as well.

Yet courts do order such partial new trials. Pingatore v. Montgomery Ward & Co., 419 F.2d 1138 (6th Cir. 1969), cert denied, 398 U.S. 928 (1970), serves as an example. A rat leapt on and bit plaintiff's knee while she was leaving the department store premises. She developed complications leading to partial paralysis in an arm and leg. Testimony divided over whether the damage was attributable to the treatment for the bite (a series of rabies inoculations), to "conversion hysteria" or "psychosis," or to "malingering." After a trial in which the plaintiff's attorney ranted and swore at the defendant corporation, the jury awarded plaintiff $126,000 in damages and $25,000 to her husband. The court of appeals reversed the judgment on account of the plaintiff's attorney's misbehavior. But, without explaining more than that "there is substantial evidence to support the verdict of the jury on the question of liability," the court limited the new trial to damages. Why was liability so clear? Because it was obvious that the plaintiff should get *something* for being bitten by a rat?

(2)   Remittitur and additur

Instead of ordering a new trial on damages, could the Pingatore court simply have reduced the amount of the damage award to one it thought reasonable? The answer is yes—under some circumstances. In such an action, known as *remittitur*, the judge orders a new trial unless the plaintiff agrees to accept reduced damages. Its damage-increasing analogue is *additur*. Both involve many of the problems inherent in the partial new trial as well as some special difficulties.

If the jury renders a verdict that is arguably excessive, the trial judge faces several questions. These questions apply, in reverse, to additur, the less common of the two devices. Essentially the questions are: first, when should one grant such a reduction (or addition) in damages?; and, second, how does one calculate the amount?

Consider the choice to which the grant of remittitur puts a plaintiff. Assume a verdict of $150,000 for the plaintiff that the court orders remitted to $75,000. If the plaintiff refuses the remittitur, the consequence is, of course, that the court will grant a new trial. The Supreme Court has held that a plaintiff must get a choice between a new trial and accepting reduced compensatory damages. Hetzel v. Prince William County, 523 U.S. 208 (1998). What about punitive damages? In several cases (see Chapter V) the Supreme Court has held that due process requires judicial scrutiny of punitive damage awards. One court has found that this line of cases overcomes what would otherwise be a Seventh Amendment requirement that the court give plaintiff a choice between reduced punitive damages and a new trial. Johansen v. Combustion Engineering, Inc., 170 F.3d 1320 (11th Cir. 1999).

Suppose the plaintiff accepts the remittitur. May she condition her acceptance on a right to appeal? If not, may the plaintiff at least raise the matter if the defendant appeals the remitted verdict? The Supreme Court has checked the attempt of a number of lower courts to permit appeals from conditionally accepted verdicts; according to the Court, the plaintiff had a choice: Accept the remittitur or prepare for a new trial. Donovan v. Penn Shipping Co., 429 U.S. 648, 649 (1977).

Are remittitur and additur constitutional? Some years ago, the Supreme Court held that additur violates the Seventh Amendment but that remittitur does not. The theory was that remittitur simply involves modifying a decision actually made by a jury, while additur involves making an award that no jury has ever made. See Dimick v. Schiedt, 293 U.S. 474, 483 (1935). Critics have suggested that this is a distinction without a meaning, but it is still the law in federal courts. Many states permit additur as well as remittitur. See, e.g., Jehl v. Southern Pacific Co., 66 Cal. 2d 821, 427 P.2d 988, 59 Cal. Rptr. 276 (1967).

C.   The Limits of the Law's Control: The Jury as a Black Box

What happens if the evidence admitted at trial provides some basis for finding for either side? Suppose the jury is properly instructed in the law, proceeds to deliberate, and then returns a verdict. Suppose the losing party's attorney interviews all the jurors after the verdict, and all the jurors admit that they misunderstood or disregarded one or more of the jury instructions. Suppose the jurors further say that they would have decided the case for the losing party if they had properly understood or followed the instructions. Suppose the jurors go one step further and each executes a sworn affidavit to that effect. Should the court grant judgment notwithstanding the verdict or grant a new trial to ensure a rational result under the applicable law?

Peterson v. Wilson

141 F.3d 573 (5th Cir. 1998)

WIENER, J. . . .

I.   Facts and Proceedings

Peterson filed this suit in district court under 42 U.S.C. §§1983 and 1988, as well as the First, Fifth, and Fourteenth Amendments of the United States Constitution after he was fired as grant director at Texas Southern University (TSU). He claims that his property interest in his employment at TSU was damaged or destroyed when it was arbitrarily and capriciously terminated. . . . After five days of trial, conducted by the magistrate judge with the consent of the parties, the jury found for Peterson and awarded him $152,235 for lost pay and benefits and $35,000 for past and future mental anguish. Following the verdict, Wilson renewed his motion for j.m.l. and supplemented it with his bare-bones alternative motion for a new trial.

Some four months later, in January 1996, the district court granted the new trial, ostensibly in response to Wilson's motion, but in actuality on its own motion: The substantive language of the district court's order granting a new trial eschews any conclusion other than that the ruling was granted sua sponte, and that it was not granted for insufficiency of the evidence or because the jury verdict was against the great weight of the evidence, but rather for the following reason:

> The court concludes, based on the jury's verdict and *comments the jurors made to the court after returning the verdict* [and outside the presence of the parties and their respective counsel], that the jury completely disregarded the Court's instructions. Instead, it appears that the jury considered improper factors in reaching its verdict. Accordingly, the Court deems it in the interest of justice to grant a new trial (emphasis added).

. . . The inference is inescapable that, to impeach the jury's verdict, the district court relied on information gleaned from the jurors themselves during the court's post-verdict, ex parte meeting with the jury. The court voided the verdict because, in the court's own words, the jury "completely disregarded the Court's instructions."

Peterson timely filed a motion for reconsideration, which the district court did not grant. The case was re-tried in June 1996, and ended in a jury verdict in favor of Wilson, rejecting Peterson's claims. . . .

The jury, as the finder of facts and the maker of all credibility calls, reached its verdict in the first trial on the basis of the following record facts and inferences.

Peterson is well educated, well trained, and widely experienced in his field of concentration, which is grant administration for institutions of higher education. When Peterson joined TSU in 1983 he assumed responsibility for administering grants, principally Title III grants. In addition, he was in charge of student affairs and was responsible for determining the residency status of foreign students. Peterson also supervised finances of the university and was in charge of Institutional Research. As Title III Director, Peterson generally reported directly to the Vice President for Academic Affairs: first Clarkson, then Moore, and eventually, Wilson. The programs supported by Title III grants included faculty development, equipment purchases, and institutional research, providing millions of dollars annually for expenditures at TSU. . . .

Without reiterating every detail of the relevant testimony and documents, it suffices that the evidence heard and obviously credited by the jury painted a picture of Peterson as a highly principled, apolitical, objective grant administrator who repeatedly refused to "play ball" with high ranking TSU administrators when they attempted to obtain expensive equipment for unauthorized personal use or sought to have unauthorized job positions created and funded with grant money for their special "friends."

The jury also heard and obviously credited testimony of both direct and implied threats by Wilson of adverse job actions, including firing, that Peterson was in jeopardy of incurring if, on reflection, he should fail or refuse to accede to requests that would require the unauthorized expenditure of grant funds.

The termination letter of January 3, 1991, from Wilson to Peterson purported to outline nine items constituting "cause" for the firing, each of which was set forth in a report prepared and submitted on request by one Joyce Deyon with whom, it turned out, Wilson never conferred after receiving the report. Wilson testified that he accepted the report and made his judgment based on it.

The jury heard testimony and saw documents which, if believed — as the jury apparently did — methodically refuted or explained away each of the nine purported causes for termination and revealed that Wilson did not even understand some of the items. The jury also heard evidence which, if credited, was sufficient to support a conclusion that the termination and its purported causes were pretext intended to cover Wilson's retaliation and desire to accomplish his actual or implied threats of getting rid of Peterson and replacing him with a grant director who would be more of a team player, i.e., would be more amenable to funding equipment purchases and job creations for "friends" of the higher-ups in the TSU administration with grant money.

That the jury unquestionably credited the testimony and documentation supporting Peterson's version of the facts and rejected Wilson's is confirmed by the "Yes" answer to Interrogatory No. I-A, "Do you find from a preponderance of the evidence that Dr. Bobby Wilson acted arbitrarily and capriciously in terminating Dr. Peterson?" In the interrogatory that followed, the jury awarded Peterson $152,235 in lost pay and benefits, and $35,000 for past and future mental anguish.

II. Analysis

. . . . We review the district court's grant of a new trial for abuse of discretion. "It is a well-settled rule in this circuit that 'a verdict can be against the "great weight of the evidence," and thus justify a new trial, even if there is substantial evidence to support it.'" What courts cannot do — and what the district court here never purported to do — is to grant a new trial "simply because [the court] would have come to a different conclusion than the jury did." . . .

The district court's succinct but cryptic, three-sentence explanation for granting a new trial demonstrates beyond question that, following the verdict, the court impermissibly met with and interrogated the jurors outside the presence of the parties and their respective counsel, and then proceeded to act in direct reliance on the jurors' comments as though they constituted newly discovered evidence of a kind that the court could properly consider. It was not. The conclusion is inescapable that, in impeaching the jury's verdict in this case, the district court relied on information obtained from the jurors in the court's post-verdict, ex parte meeting with them and that, by definition, any information thus obtained had to come directly from their internal deliberations qua jurors.

1.   Jury Impeachment

Rule 606(b) of the Federal Rules of Evidence (F.R.E.) tightly controls impeachment of jury verdicts. This rule states, in pertinent part:

> Upon an inquiry into the validity of a verdict . . . , a juror may not testify as to any matter or statement occurring during the course of the jury's deliberations or to the effect of anything upon that or any other juror's mind or emotions as influencing the juror to assent to or dissent from the verdict . . . or concerning the juror's mental processes in connection therewith, except that a juror may testify on the question whether extraneous prejudicial information was improperly brought to the jury's attention or whether any outside influence was improperly brought to the jury's attention or whether any outside influence was improperly brought to bear upon any juror. Nor may a juror's affidavit or evidence of any statement by the juror concerning a matter about which the juror would be precluded from testifying be received for these purposes. . . .

The landmark Supreme Court case on this issue is Tanner v. United States. After acknowledging that "[b]y the beginning of this century, if not earlier, the near-universal and firmly established common-law rule in the United States flatly prohibited the admission of juror testimony to impeach a jury verdict," the Court observed that "Federal Rule of Evidence 606(b) is grounded in the common-law rule against admission of jury testimony to impeach a verdict and the exception for juror testimony relating to extraneous influences." Following *Tanner*, and more closely on point, we held in Robles v. Exxon Corp. that receiving testimony from the jurors after they have returned their verdict, for the purpose of ascertaining that the jury misunderstood its instructions, is absolutely prohibited by F.R.E. 606(b). We underscored that holding by noting that "the legislative history of the rule unmistakably points to the conclusion that Congress made a conscious decision to disallow juror testimony as to the jurors' mental processes or fidelity to the court's instructions." What is pellucid here, from the court's own unequivocal and unambiguous words, is that the jurors' statements to the court related directly to matters that transpired in the jury room, that these matters comprehended the mental processes of the jurors in their deliberations on the case, and that the jurors' statements formed the foundation of the court's impeachment of the verdict grounded in the jury's lack of "fidelity to the court's instructions." We cannot conceive of an example more explicitly violative of *Robles*. . . .

[The Court of Appeals concluded that the district court did not find that the verdict was against the great weight of the evidence and that, even if it had, such a decision was contrary to the record.]

We are thus left with no choice but to reverse the district court's grant of a new trial, vacate the court's judgment rendered on the basis of the jury verdict in the second trial, and reinstate the results of the first trial. We therefore remand this case to the district court for entry of judgment in favor of Peterson and against Wilson in the principal sum of $187,235 ($152,235 for lost pay and benefits and $35,000 for past and future mental anguish), and for the assessment of appropriate interest and costs, including reasonable attorneys' fees incurred by Peterson in both trials and on appeal.

NOTES AND PROBLEMS

1. *Peterson* serves both as a review of the preceding chapter and as an embodiment of an important principle about jury integrity. Begin with reviewing some fundamental propositions:

a. Explain why plaintiff could not appeal after the first trial.

b. Explain why the result would have been different had the appellate court found — as defendant urged it to — that the trial court had granted a new trial because the first verdict was "against the great weight of the evidence."

c. Explain why the trial judge, after interviewing the jurors in the first trial and ascertaining that they had misunderstood the instructions, could not simply grant judgment as a matter of law (j.n.o.v.) for defendant.

2. The principle elaborated in *Peterson* has to do with the inviolability of jury deliberations, but also with the limits on the law's insistence on rationality.

a. It was not unlawful, though it was unusual, for the trial judge to interview the jurors to ascertain whether they understood the instructions. In the more usual situation the lawyers rather than the judge interview the jurors. Most lawyers are interested in how their case looked through jurors' eyes. Win or lose, they are usually interested in finding out what persuaded the jury. Jurors have no obligation to speak to the lawyers after the trial, but they are often willing to do so, as they did here to the judge.

b. Why, having learned through these interviews that the jury misunderstood instructions, could the trial court not grant a new trial on that basis?

c. Distinguish *Peterson* from *In re Beverly Hills Fire Litigation*, supra page 600. In the latter case a juror performed home experiments on aluminum electrical wiring (the dangerousness of which was a contested issue at trial) and reported his findings to the other jurors. The appellate court held it an abuse of discretion not to grant a new trial. Why is it erroneous to grant a new trial when a juror misunderstands instructions and erroneous not to grant a new trial when a juror performs such experiments? Explain the distinction.

3. What interests are served by prohibiting impeachment of a jury's verdict through postverdict statements by the jurors regarding their deliberations?

a. One can explain F.R. Evid. 606 cynically: Too many jury verdicts would fall if we delved into jury deliberations deeply.

b. A different explanation is also possible. As you have already seen, if summary judgment and judgment as a matter of law are operating properly, only close cases — cases that could rationally be decided either way — will go to the jury. In such cases, any verdict should be sustainable. And, some would add, in such cases the soft variables that constitute the jury's sense of justice should come into play, even when those variables are hard to justify from the lofty plane of rationalism. By preventing too close an inquiry into jury's decision processes, one allows these variables some free play.

c. Finally, one can justify the rule as a matter of court administration. Many people are reluctant to serve on juries: it disrupts lives and schedules and involves them in making difficult decisions. If one added to these inconveniences the possibility that one could be questioned by a disappointed loser about jury deliberations, it might become very difficult to fill jury boxes.

4. Distinguish two issues that courts sometimes conflate: what constitutes jury conduct sufficiently improper to require a new trial; and when the court will hear evidence about jury conduct from a *juror*. F.R. Evid. 606 governs the latter but has nothing to say about the former.

a. To sharpen the distinction, imagine a case in which evidence of jury conduct came from two sources — a bailiff who overheard deliberations while stationed outside the room and a juror herself. Rule 606 bars testimony from the latter but not from the former.

b. In fact, because juries deliberate in private, only in the very rare case will anyone other than a juror know what happened in the jury room.

5. In contrast to information about jury deliberations, Rule 606 does allow a verdict to be impeached by evidence that there was some improper "outside influence" on the jury.

a. Bribery obviously meets that criterion. So do threats to jurors by outsiders.

b. What about evidence that a majority of jurors badgered a holdout juror until the holdout caved in and went along with the majority? Is there any basis for treating an outside threat to a juror differently from a threat by a fellow juror? A survey found the courts divided and could offer only the not very helpful observation that the cases seemed fact-specific. Impeachment of Verdict by Juror's Evidence That He Was Coerced or Intimidated by Fellow Juror, 39 A.L.R. 4th 800 (1996).

6. It may already have occurred to you that one might make jury verdicts less opaque by asking the jury to explain how it reached its verdict. There are in fact two ways to do just that — the special verdict and the general verdict with special interrogatories. See Rule 49.

a. Which of these procedures was used in *Peterson*?

b. In a special verdict the jury does not render a general verdict at all. Instead it answers a series of questions about the evidence: "Was the defendant negligent? If so, did the defendant's negligence cause the plaintiff's injuries? If so, was the plaintiff also negligent? If so, did the plaintiff's negligence in some part contribute to his injuries?" When the jury has answered all the questions — or all those that are necessary — it delivers them as the verdict. In a general verdict with interrogatories, the jury renders a general verdict but also answers particular questions.

c. The concept of the special verdict and general verdict with interrogatories is simple: One gives the jurors a road map of the relevant legal issues, helping them to focus on each question as (and if) it becomes relevant.

d. The practice surrounding these procedures has been much less happy. Jurors regularly become confused by the questions. The nightmare outcome — one too often realized in the cases — is that juries give inconsistent answers. In one notorious case the jury said (a) that the defendant was negligent but (b) that it was impossible for the defendant to have foreseen any danger from a particular condition on its property — that condition being the only way in which the jury could have found the defendant negligent! Gallick v. B&O Railroad, 372 U.S. 108 (1963). As a consequence of these problems, judges, in whose discretion the decision to allow a special verdict lies, often avoid them.

Though trial by ordeal — drowning, burning, and the like — was abolished by the Lateran Council of 1215, lawyers tell us that even ordinary trials are ordeals of anxiety, weariness, and, for one side, disappointment. The one thing most civil trials are not is dramatic. Witnesses can change their stories and an occasional surprise will appear, but a well prepared civil trial where both sides have made effective use of discovery will not look like a *Perry Mason* episode.

Real trials differ from those in drama in another respect. In drama, the trial is the end of the road: The winners rejoice; the losers slink away in shame or defiance. In litigation the trial is a rare event, but even when it occurs, it is often not the end. In part because trials are so rare, parties who have been unable to settle their differences beforehand are unlikely to do so just because a judge or jury has announced a winner. For many, an appeal lies ahead.

APPEAL

XI

Appeals in U.S. litigation are a booming business. Over the past fifty years federal civil appeals have increased at a rate one and one-half times faster than the increase in lawsuits filed. This increase has come even though one may appeal only from a judgment and, as we have seen, only about a third of federal civil cases end in a judgment. Moreover, this increase has come even though most cases are affirmed on appeal — between 80 and 90 percent in the federal system.

Appeals are the setting for particularly fierce battles between two salient goals of civil procedure: fairness and justice. Fairness dictates that parties should win or lose depending on their compliance with procedural rules and the quality of their argument. Justice dictates that the "right" party should prevail, regardless of such technicalities. Because the system embraces both goals, one must frequently yield to the other, and the conflict appears starkly in appellate litigation.

In many respects appealing a U.S. civil judgment is more like starting a new lawsuit than like continuing the same one. Moreover, that "new suit" (the appeal) is brought in a system that often applies procedural rules in a more technical fashion than do the trial courts. Unlike some other legal systems, the U.S. litigation system operates with a heavy presumption that the trial court decision is correct. U.S. appellate courts do not supervise trial courts. They have jurisdiction only to review specific trial court decisions claimed to be in error. And when they do so, they may reverse only if the error in question was harmful.

This chapter focuses on the doctrinal walls that shield U.S. trial court decisions. These walls restrict the availability of review in three ways: *Who* — which persons who can seek review of a trial court decision? *When* may one appeal a trial court decision? And, *How* — with what depth will an appellate court scrutinize an appealable decision?

Understanding these doctrines has two virtues. It is obviously essential for any lawyer who wants to appeal a trial court decision. It is equally important for another reason: Understanding the barriers to appellate review helps one to comprehend that, as a practical matter, the trial court's decision on most procedural and substantive matters will likely be the only decision. This practical autonomy of the trial court puts enormous weight on the trial judge — to make the right decision — and on the lawyers — to give the judge all the information needed to make the right decision.

A. Who Can Appeal?

In theory, one could imagine appellate courts functioning as the supervisors of trial courts, automatically reviewing cases to assure both that the result is correct and that the trial judge is following appropriate procedure. Or one might imagine a judicial inspector general who would have the power and duty to bring to the attention of appellate courts instances of where either the process or the result of a trial court decision seem questionable. Administrative systems follow such models, and some civil law systems approximate them.

The U.S. courts do not. Even a blatantly erroneous decision may be appealed only by a party to the lawsuit, a party, that is, who has not settled. Even more striking, a losing party who has not settled may nevertheless be unable to gain appellate reversal of a clearly erroneous trial court decision. Two doctrines create this result: those that allow appeals only by parties who have suffered an adverse decision, and those that deter appeals with various penalties.

1. A Losing Party: Adversity

A hallmark of modern procedure is the ease with which parties can join multiple claims and theories of recovery in a single lawsuit. This poses a problem for appellate review: If one wins on one theory but loses on others, may the party in such a situation appeal the unsuccessful claims and contentions? Contemporary appellate review is result-oriented, so the answer to this question requires one to look at the relief sought by the party prevailing on one but not all theories. If the relief sought under the other, losing theories was identical to that awarded, no appeal will lie, even if the appellate court thinks the trial court erred. If, on the other hand, the rejected theory would have entitled the appealing party to more or different relief — to a different judgment — then appeal lies. One can describe the principle as the requirement of an "adverse" judgment, a judgment granting relief different from what one requested.

NOTES AND PROBLEMS

1. Apply this principle to the cases below:

a. Tenant is injured when she slips on a pool of water formed as a result of a leaky apartment roof. She sues landlord for personal injuries, invoking two theories under which the landlord had a duty to repair the roof — a duty arising under the lease, and a duty arising under the municipal housing code. (See McKey v. Fairbairn, supra page 532.) Suppose the trial court rules that a duty is owed under the lease but that there is no duty under the municipal housing code. The court awards damages for personal injury. May plaintiff appeal, contending that a duty arose under the housing code as well? Plaintiff's lawyers, representing other tenants without leases, will wish to establish a precedent under the housing code. Can they appeal?

b. Plaintiff, alleging that automobile dealer sold her a used car when she paid for a new one, sues. She alleges two theories: that the dealer (1) breached a contract; (2) committed fraud. Contract damages call for the plaintiff to recover the difference between the value of the car she received and a new one — $3,000 in this instance. Punitive damages lie for fraud, and are measured not by plaintiff's loss but by magnitude of the wrong committed by defendant. The court finds that punitive damages are inappropriate, but awards plaintiff damages for breach of contract. May plaintiff appeal?

c. Consider the defendants in the two preceding problems. They have "won" parts of both cases, avoiding liability under the housing code in one case and avoiding punitive damages in the other. May they appeal?

2. The "losing party" principle described above comes under tension when a party has won the judgment but where a theory rejected by the trial court will have collateral consequences. In Aetna Casualty & Surety Co. v. Cunningham, 224 F.2d 478 (5th Cir. 1955), an insurance company sued one of its insureds, a building contractor. The contractor had failed to complete a building project, as a result of which the insurer had to pay for its completion. The insurer sought to recover its loss from the contractor, using two theories: (1) that the contractor was required to repay the insurer under the terms of the policy; and (2) that the insured contractor had committed fraud in applying for the policy. The insurer won on the contract theory but lost on the fraud theory. May the insurer appeal?

a. Applying the principle of the adverse judgment, the answer would be no. Since the insurer was seeking only compensatory damages, the amount of recovery on the contract claim was identical to that under the fraud claim. Winning on the fraud count would therefore not have increased the judgment.

b. Insurer argued, however, that the builder was about to file for bankruptcy. In bankruptcy a fraud claim receives more generous treatment than does a contract claim. Consequently the effect of the judgment would be different if the insurer prevailed on the fraud claim. In Cunningham the Fifth Circuit accepted the insurer's argument and permitted an appeal as to the fraud theory.

c. Suppose the insurer's lawyer had foreseen the probability of bankruptcy and the difficulty of appealing on an alternative ground. How could the plaintiff have framed the prayer for damages so as to assure appealability if the plaintiff lost on the fraud count? (See Note 1b above.)

d. Consider whether Forney v. Apfel, 524 U.S. 266 (1998), changes your response to the preceding questions. Sandra Forney applied for Social Security disability benefits. The Social Security Administration denied her claim, and she sued in federal district court, seeking either an order compelling payment of benefits or, in the alternative, a new administrative hearing. The district court ruled that the evidence of alternative employment for Ms. Forney was inadequate and remanded for a new administrative hearing. She appealed. The Ninth Circuit held the case unappealable on the grounds that, having won on at least part of her claim, she was a prevailing party. The Supreme Court unanimously reversed:

> [F]rom Forney's perspective, the second "alternative," [remand rather than an order compelling benefits], which means further delay and risk, is only half a loaf. Thus,

the District Court's order gives petitioner some, but not all, of the relief she requested; and she consequently can appeal the District Court's order insofar as it denies her the relief she has sought.

Id. at 271.

3. Retailer sues Buyer for nonpayment of a bill. Buyer counterclaims for breach of warranty. The trial court enters judgment for Retailer on its claim but also awards damages to Buyer on its warranty claim. Buyer appeals. On appeal, Retailer will argue the correctness of the trial court's rulings on the claim of nonpayment. Retailer may also *cross-appeal*, arguing that the court erred in upholding the breach of warranty claim against it. As to that part of the case Retailer has suffered an adverse judgment.

4. Another aspect of the requirement that the judgment be adverse is the doctrine of mootness, which holds that one may not appeal from a judgment when circumstances have changed in such a way that relief is no longer possible. The doctrine affects not only appeals but also the justiciability of the suit because mootness undercuts the existence of an actual case or controversy required by Article III of the Constitution. There are, however, numerous exceptions to the doctrine.

a. One of the most important exceptions is the case in which the plaintiff's claim has been satisfied despite an adverse ruling by the lower court, but the question raised by the claim is likely to recur, and application of the mootness doctrine would effectively prevent the question from receiving appellate review. In Sosna v. Iowa, 419 U.S. 393 (1975), for example, the plaintiff challenged Iowa's one-year residency requirements for obtaining a divorce. The lower court upheld the requirement, but during the litigation the year passed and the plaintiff became able to obtain her divorce. The Supreme Court nevertheless refused to dismiss the case as moot, reasoning that other plaintiffs would find themselves in the same situation.

b. Mootness can also result from settlement. Parties who settle cannot continue to appeal. Can they, as part of their settlement, ask an appellate court to set aside a lower court's action? The U.S. Supreme Court has said no. In U.S. Bancorp Mortgage Co. v. Bonner Mall, 513 U.S. 18 (1994), a unanimous Court refused the request of a settling party to vacate an appellate decision below. In a slightly different setting the California Supreme Court set aside a trial court judgment when asked by both of the settling parties to do so. Neary v. University of California, 3 Cal. 4th 273, 834 P.2d 119, 10 Cal. Rptr. 2d 859 (1992).

5. Class actions present special problems of appealability. Formally, only the named class representatives are parties. Does that mean that only they can appeal? Does a represented absentee class member have to intervene, thus becoming a formal party, before he can appeal? Suppose a class action comes to a proposed settlement, of which the class members receive notice. One such member objects to the settlement but does not intervene. Can he nevertheless appeal? Yes; in Devlin v. Scardelletti, 536 U.S. 1 (2002), over a dissent arguing that the ruling upset long-standing rules of appealability, the Court held that such a class member could bring an appeal:

> What is most important to this case is that unnamed class members are parties to the proceedings in the sense of being bound by the settlement. It is this feature of class

action litigation that requires that class members be allowed to appeal the approval of a settlement when they have objected at the fairness hearing. To hold otherwise would deprive unnamed class members of the power to preserve their own interests in a settlement that will ultimately bind them, despite their expressed objections before the trial court.

Id. at 17.

2. Who Raised the Issue Below: Waiver

In *Cunningham* (the case of the insurer alleging fraud, described in Problem 2 in the preceding section), suppose that at trial the insurer's evidence of fraud consisted not of misstatements by the contractor but of his failure to disclose the extent of his debts. Some jurisdictions accept such nondisclosure as evidence of fraud. Suppose the contractor's lawyer does not object to the evidence, though he strenuously argues that the undisclosed information was not material. If the trial court finds against the defendant on the fraud count, may the contractor challenge the judgment on the basis that nondisclosure was not sufficient to show fraud in that jurisdiction?

Generally not: a party must present to the trial court the contentions on which it wants rulings. Failure to do so results in waiver of the contention. A century ago the party had not only to raise the contention below but then to make a formal "exception" to the trial court ruling in order to preserve the issue for appeal. Rule 46 did away with the need for exceptions; the party need only "make known to the court the action which the party desires the court to take. . . ." The abolition of the formal requirement did not, however, abolish the doctrine of waiver.

NOTES AND PROBLEMS

1. How persistently must one party object? Suppose that in *Cunningham* (the insurance fraud case) the defendant filed a 12(b)(6) motion challenging the complaint on the grounds that it alleged only failure to disclose, not affirmative misrepresentation. Having lost the 12(b)(6) motion, would the defendant thereafter have to object to the plaintiff's evidence in order to preserve the issue for appeal? Yes, at least to be on the safe side:

To preserve the point the moving party can, and in general is required, upon the trial to renew and support his pleaded objections by objections to evidence, and by requesting rulings and instructions from the Court to the jury which he deems necessary to protect and preserve the point asserted by his motion to dismiss or to strike. In the present case the points asserted by motion were not again presented by any request for instructions, or by any effort to have the Court direct the jury to pass separately upon the question of whether the actions should be merely abated or determined upon its merits. Therefore, since the point was not properly urged and presented, there is no occasion to determine the validity of the fifth defense. Likewise, as to the objections now urged to the charge (which in some portions apparently gave effect to this defense) since no objection was presented to the trial

Court, the appellant can not here properly complain of the alleged erroneous instruction. We cannot accept the contention that the assertion of the objection by motion to strik[e] properly presented and preserved the point throughout the proceedings of the subsequent trial.

Mims v. Central Mfrs. Mut. Ins. Co., 178 F.2d 56, 59 (5th Cir. 1949).

2. An appellant cannot on appeal use an argument not made below. How about an appellee, the party seeking to support the judgment? If appellee lost on a defense or claim below and wants to preserve the objection in case the case is reversed, he must cross-appeal. But suppose appellee wants to use a new argument in *support* of the judgment? For an example, recall again the facts of *Cunningham*. Suppose that the insurer contended that the insured's fraud had consisted of failure to disclose certain information. Further suppose there was a question of whether the law of Connecticut (the insurer's base) or Texas (the insured's) applied. At trial insurer argued that Connecticut law applied and that it recognized nondisclosure as fraud. Insurer wins a judgment on the fraud claim and the defendant appeals.

a. On appeal, appellee insurer wants to argue in support of the judgment that Texas also recognizes nondisclosure as fraud so that an appellate ruling that Texas law applies would not require reversal of the judgment. Can it do so? Yes:

> It is true that a party who does not appeal from a final decree of the trial court cannot be heard in opposition thereto when the case is brought here by appeal of the adverse party. In other words, the appellee may not attack the decree with a view either to enlarging his own rights thereunder or of lessening the rights of his adversary, whether what he seeks is to correct an error to supplement the decree with respect to a matter dealt with below. But it is likewise settled that the appellee may, without taking a cross-appeal, urge in support of a decree any matter appearing in the record, although his argument may involve an attack upon the reasoning of the lower court or an insistence upon a matter overlooked or ignored by it.

United States v. American Ry. Exp. Co., 265 U.S. 425, 435 (1923).

b. The same principle requiring an issue be raised below applies to cross-appeals. If a party who prevails at trial cross-appeals, it can on its cross-appeal raise only those arguments made at trial. Again using *Cunningham* as an example, suppose that the insurer prevailed at trial on the contract but not on the fraud count, and the contractor-defendant appealed. Insurer could cross-appeal, contending that the trial court was correct in awarding judgment on the contract count but that the insurer should also have won on the fraud claim. On this cross-appeal the insurer could make only those contentions made below.

3. Another test of the courts' adherence to the requirement that an appellate issue be raised below comes when there has been a change in the law between the time of trial and the appeal.

a. Arthur applies for Social Security disability benefits, and his claim is denied. He sues, challenging the determination that he is not disabled. He loses in trial court and appeals. While his appeal is pending, a case comes down holding that the administrative procedure by which such claims are determined is unconstitutional. May Arthur on appeal raise this constitutional issue, which he did not raise below?

b. A hard-nosed advocate of the adversary system would say no — that Arthur could have raised such a claim below and cannot now seek to ride on the coat-tails of a more enterprising or imaginative litigant.

c. Courts waver in their willingness to entertain such late-maturing grounds for appeal. If the change in law is sufficiently fundamental, they may hear an argument on appeal that was not raised below. See Carson Products Co. v. Califano, 594 F.2d 453 (5th Cir. 1979) (drug company challenges FDA determination that product ingredient is not a trade secret; on appeal permitted to raise contention that FDA procedures denied due process). But no litigant should count on this grace.

4. The "plain error" rule is another exception to the general requirement that an issue must be raised in the trial court as a predicate to appeal.

a. The doctrine is most commonly applied to criminal cases, where the courts are thought to have a special duty to assure that defendants are not convicted unfairly. Its basis was nicely stated by Judge Frank in Troupe v. Chicago, Duluth & Georgian Bay Transit Co., 234 F.2d 253, 261 (2d Cir. 1956): "[A] litigant surely has the right to assume that a federal trial judge knows the elementary substantive legal rules, long established by the precedents, and . . . will act accordingly, without prompting by the litigant's lawyer." Before you conclude that such a doctrine will save you from failure to object, note that this ringing endorsement of the principle came in a concurring opinion — in a case where the majority held that the doctrine did not apply to a clearly erroneous jury instruction. The rule is typically invoked "where the error has seriously affected the fairness, integrity, or public reputation of judicial proceedings." 9 Wright and Miller §2558, at 675. For a statement of the rule in a civil context, see the following opinion:

> We hold that failure to object timely to a magistrate judge's report and recommendation bars a party, except upon grounds of plain error . . . from attacking on appeal not only the proposed factual findings . . . but also the proposed legal conclusions, accepted . . . by the district court, provided that the party has been served with notice that such consequences will result from a failure to object. . . .

Douglas v. U.S.A.A., 79 F.3d 1415 (5th Cir. 1996).

b. The plain-error doctrine tests how U.S. appellate courts balance the principle of fairness to the parties against the correctness of the result. To say that the failure to object is excused (because an error is "plain") is to say that the appellate courts assume some degree of responsibility for assuring the correctness of the outcome, not just fairness to the parties.

c. In addition to raising the matter in the trial court, counsel usually must also raise an issue in the appellate court before the appellate court will consider it. There are exceptions, however. The matter is discussed in Vestal, Sua Sponte Consideration in Appellate Review, 27 Fordham L. Rev. 477 (1959).

d. Having virtually assaulted the student with the proposition that appellate courts will not consider arguments not made at trial, we should note a glaring exception: Erie Railroad v. Tompkins, supra page 224. In that landmark decision neither party had raised the choice of law question, nor had the Supreme Court granted certiorari to consider it. The Court thus made its landmark decision on a basis not argued or briefed by either party. One can reconcile *Erie* with the preceding discussion: A court may decide on a basis not raised by the parties, but a party must consistently raise an issue he wants to argue. Nevertheless, one might think that the concept of fair notice that applies to the parties might also apply to the court.

5. Recall from Chapter III that there is one issue — the court's subject matter jurisdiction — that the federal courts are required to raise on their own and that may be raised for the first time on appeal by either the parties or the appellate court.

3. Who Was Not Deterred

The increasing rate of appeals has caused many jurisdictions to discourage them. The Supreme Court has never held that there is a constitutional right to appeal a civil case, so a jurisdiction could in theory either forbid civil appeals absolutely or, less dramatically, make all civil appeals a matter of discretion rather than of right. No jurisdiction has to date taken either step. Every jurisdiction in the United States grants the right of at least one appeal in civil cases; further appeal is often discretionary.

Even though they permit appeals, however, judicial systems can discourage them. Are there limits on these burdens? The U.S. Supreme Court has faced that issue in several cases. In Lindsey v. Normet, 405 U.S. 56 (1972), the Court invalidated a state statute that required tenants appealing an eviction judgment to post a bond twice as great as the rent expected to accrue during the appeal. By contrast, in Bankers Life & Casualty Co. v. Crenshaw, 486 U.S. 71 (1988), the Court rejected a similar challenge to a Mississippi statute that imposed a 15 percent penalty on an unsuccessful appeal of a judgment for money damages. The penalty was imposed regardless of the merits of the appeal so long as the appellate court affirmed the damages award without alteration. Bankers Life suffered a $1.6 million punitive damage judgment, which it unsuccessfully appealed, with the appellate court adding a $243,000 penalty to the judgment because the original award was affirmed. Bankers Life argued that the statute had denied it equal protection of the law "because it singles out appellants from money judgments, and because it penalizes all such appellants who are unsuccessful, regardless of the merits of their appeal." 486 U.S. at 81. The Supreme Court rejected this contention in language that revealed its general stance toward appeals:

> Under this Court's equal protection jurisprudence, Mississippi's statute is "presumed to be valid and will be sustained if the classification . . . is rationally related to a legitimate state interest." The state interests assertedly served by the Mississippi statute were detailed by the Mississippi Supreme Court in Walters v. Inexco Oil Co., 440 So. 2d 268 (1983). The penalty statute . . . "expresses the state's interest in discouraging frivolous appeals. It likewise expresses a bona fide interest in providing a measure of compensation for the successful appellee, compensation for his having endured the slings and arrows of successful appellate litigation." In a similar vein the statute

protects the integrity of judgments by discouraging appellant-defendants from prolonging the litigation merely to "squeeze a favorable settlement out of an impecunious" appellee. Also, the penalty statute "tells the litigants that the trial itself is a momentous event, the centerpiece of litigation, not just a first step weighing station en route to endless rehearings and reconsiderations." Finally, in part because it serves these other goals, the penalty statute furthers the State's interest in conserving judicial resources.

Id. at 81-82. The *Bankers Life* Court distinguished *Lindsey* on the grounds that the Oregon statute in *Lindsey* arbitrarily discriminated against tenants (because it applied only to them among all appellants) and was not needed to effectuate the state's purpose of preserving the property at issue.

Lindsey and *Banker's Life* involved "extra" appellate costs. What about ordinary costs that rest on all litigants? Can they ever be unconstitutional? In M.L.B. v. S.L.J., 519 U.S. 102 (1996), the indigent petitioner sought to appeal from a trial court order terminating her parental rights on the grounds she was unfit as a mother. To appeal the state court decision, M.L.B. would have had to pay filing and transcript fees of about $2,300. The state supreme court refused to waive the fees. The U.S. Supreme Court reversed, basing its decision on a combination of due process ("a family association so undeniably important is at stake") and equal protection, the six-to-three majority held "that Mississippi may not withhold from M.L.B. a record of sufficient completeness to permit proper consideration of her claims."

Read together, *Lindsey*, *Bankers Life*, and M.L.B. suggest that some burden on appeals is constitutional. Should legal systems seek generally to discourage appeals by requiring, for example, that the loser pay the winner's attorneys' fees? Federal Rule of Appellate Procedure (Fed. R. App. P.) 38 permits a court of appeals to award "just damages and single or double costs to the appellee" if the appellate courts "determine[s] that an appeal is frivolous." One finds occasional invocation of this rule, but it is used far less frequently than is Rule 11, its analogue at the district court level.

A quite different sort of sanction for meritless appeals that is increasingly used by state and federal appellate courts is the summary affirmance or unpublished decision. Such orders, which go under different names in different systems, often involve denial of the right to oral argument, a decision on the briefs and record alone, and either a one-word order ("affirmed") or a short unpublished opinion. For an example, see Haddle v. Garrison, supra page 348. Some would argue that such "appeals" exist in name only. Would it be preferable for courts to impose sanctions?

B. When a Decision May Be Reviewed: "Finality"

The single most significant rule of appellate procedure in the United States is one that purports to be only about the timing of appeal. Under 28 U.S.C. §1291, appeals lie only from final decisions of the district courts (with some significant exceptions). Most, but not all, states follow a similar pattern.

The final judgment rule affects not just the technique of appeal but its availability. What purport to be timing rules are in fact rules that effectively bar appellate review of most trial court decisions. That may be a good thing: Appeals take time, and most are unsuccessful. So the unavailability of appeal may merely make justice faster and cheaper. Alternatively, one can see it as empowering trial judges to be petty dictators who can be secure in the knowledge that most of their rulings will never reach appellate scrutiny.

The final judgment rule had its origins in a procedural system in which most trial court decisions were made at trial. In such a system, decisions were promptly reviewable because the trial resulted in a judgment from which an appeal would lie. Modern procedure changes that pattern: Discovery and the pretrial process now dominate the procedural landscape. Most rulings entered at this stage do not immediately produce final judgments, and many will never produce final judgments because the case settles. Under such circumstances the final judgment rule does not just defer but eliminates appellate review.

Any rule that has such effects will generate tensions and exceptions. This section explores the contours of the basic rule and some exceptions generated by the pressure to escape it.

1. The Final Judgment Rule

A final decision "is one which ends the litigation on the merits and leaves nothing for the court to do but execute the judgment." Catlin v. United States, 324 U.S. 229, 233 (1945). That's the easy part; the hard part is determining which decisions are "final." Although at first glance the problem may seem to center on premature attempts at appeal, which entail unnecessary cost and delay, the more serious problem is late appeals: There are cases in which litigants waited for a document labeled as a "final decree" only to learn that earlier orders disposing of their claims were deemed to be a final judgment and that the time for appeal had run in the meantime.

a. Appellate Jurisdiction and the Final Judgment Rule

Section 1291, which contains the final judgment rule, has two functions: It defines the moment at which an appeal is proper; and it grants jurisdiction for the appellate courts to hear that appeal. The next case demonstrates the consequences that a wrong guess about the first function can have on the second.

Liberty Mutual Insurance Co. v. Wetzel

424 U.S. 737 (1976)

Mr. Justice REHNQUIST delivered the opinion of the Court.

Respondents filed a complaint in the United States District Court for the Western District of Pennsylvania in which they asserted that petitioner's employee insurance benefits and maternity leave regulations discriminated against women in violation of Title VII of the Civil Rights Act of 1964, as amended by the Equal Employment Opportunity Act of 1972. The District Court ruled in favor of respondents on the issue of petitioner's liability under that Act, and petitioner appealed to the Court of Appeals for the Third Circuit. That court held that it had jurisdiction of petitioner's appeal under 28 U.S.C. §1291, and proceeded to affirm on the merits the judgment of the District Court. We granted certiorari and heard argument on the merits. Though neither party has questioned the jurisdiction of the Court of Appeals to entertain the appeal, we are obligated to do so on our own motion if a question thereto exists. Because we conclude that the District Court's order was not appealable to the Court of Appeals, we vacate the judgment of the Court of Appeals with instructions to dismiss petitioner's appeal from the order of the District Court.

Respondents' complaint, after alleging jurisdiction and facts deemed pertinent to their claim, prayed for a judgment against petitioner embodying the following relief:

> (a) requiring that defendant establish non-discriminatory hiring, payment, opportunity, and promotional plans and programs;
> (b) enjoining the continuance by defendant of the illegal acts and practices alleged herein;
> (c) requiring that defendant pay over to plaintiffs and to the members of the class the damages sustained by plaintiffs and the members of the class by reason of defendant's illegal acts and practices, including adjusted back pay, with interest, and an additional equal amount as liquidated damages, and exemplary damages;
> (d) requiring that defendant pay to plaintiffs and to the members of the class the costs of this suit and a reasonable attorney's fee, with interest; and
> (e) such other and further relief as the Court deems appropriate.

After extensive discovery, respondents moved for partial summary judgment only as to the issue of liability. Fed. Rule Civ. Proc. 56(c). The District Court on January 9, 1974, finding no issues of material fact in dispute, entered an order to the effect that petitioner's pregnancy-related policies violated Title VII of the Civil Rights Act of 1964. It also ruled that Liberty Mutual's hiring and promotion policies violated Title VII. Petitioner thereafter filed a motion for reconsideration which was denied by the District Court. Its order of February 20, 1974, denying the motion for reconsideration, contains the following concluding language:

> In its Order the court stated it would enjoin the continuance of practices which the court found to be in violation of Title VII. The Plaintiffs were invited to submit the form of the injunction order and the Defendant has filed Notice of Appeal and asked for stay of any injunctive order. Under these circumstances the court will withhold the issuance of the injunctive order and amend the Order previously issued under the provisions of Fed. R. Civ. P. 54(b), as follows:
>
>> And now this 20th day of February, 1974, it is directed that final judgment be entered in favor of Plaintiffs that Defendant's policy of requiring female employees to return to work within three months of delivery of a child or be terminated is in violation of the provisions of Title VII of the Civil Rights Act of 1964; that Defendant's policy of denying disability income protection plan benefits to female employees for disabilities related to pregnancies or childbirth is in violation of Title VII of the Civil Rights Act

of 1964 and that it is expressly directed that Judgment be entered for the Plaintiffs upon these claims of Plaintiffs' Complaint; there being no just reason for delay.

It is obvious from the District Court's order that respondents, although having received a favorable ruling on the issue of petitioner's liability to them, received none of the relief which they expressly prayed for in the portion of their complaint set forth above. They requested an injunction, but did not get one; they requested damages, but were not awarded any; they requested attorneys' fees, but received none.

Counsel for respondents when questioned during oral argument in this Court suggested that at least the District Court's order of February 20 amounted to a declaratory judgment on the issue of liability pursuant to the provisions of 28 U.S.C. §2201. Had respondents sought only a declaratory judgment, and no other form of relief, we would of course have a different case. But even if we accept respondents' contention that the District Court's order was a declaratory judgment on the issue of liability, it nonetheless left unresolved respondents' requests for an injunction, for compensatory and exemplary damages, and for attorneys' fees. It finally disposed of none of respondents' prayers for relief.

The District Court and the Court of Appeals apparently took the view that because the District Court made the recital required by Fed. Rule Civ. Proc. 54(b) that final judgment be entered on the issue of liability, and that there was no just reason for delay, the orders thereby became appealable as a final decision pursuant to 28 U.S.C. §1291. We cannot agree with this application of the Rule and statute in question.

Rule 54(b)[2] "does not apply to a single claim action. . . . It is limited expressly to multiple claims actions in which 'one or more but less than all' of the multiple claims have been finally decided and are found otherwise to be ready for appeal." Sears, Roebuck & Co. v. Mackey.[3]

Here, however, respondents set forth but a single claim: that petitioner's employee insurance benefits and maternity leave regulations discriminated against its women employees in violation of Title VII of the Civil Rights Act of 1964. They prayed for several different types of relief in the event that they sustained the allegations of their complaint, see Fed. Rule Civ. Proc. 8(a)(3), but their complaint advanced a single legal theory which was applied to only one set

---

2. "Judgment upon multiple claims or involving multiple parties."

"When more than one claim is presented for relief in an action, whether as a claim, counter-claim, cross-claim, or third-party claim, or when multiple parties are involved, the court may direct the entry of a final judgment as to one or more but fewer than all of the claims or parties only upon the express determination that there is no just reason for delay and upon an express direction for the entry of judgment. In the absence of such determination and judgment, any order or other form of decision, however designated, which adjudicates fewer than all the claims or the rights and liabilities of fewer than all the parties shall not terminate the action as to any of the claims or parties, and the order or other form of decision is subject to revision at any time before the entry of judgment adjudicating all the claims and the rights and liabilities of all the parties."

3. Following *Mackey*, the Rule was amended to insure that orders finally disposing of some but not all of the parties could be appealed pursuant to its provisions. That provision is not implicated in this case, however, to which Mackey's exposition of the Rule remains fully accurate.

of facts.[4] Thus, despite the fact that the District Court undoubtedly made the findings required under the Rule had it been applicable, those findings do not in a case such as this make the order appealable pursuant to 28 U.S.C. §1291.

We turn to consider whether the District Court's order might have been appealed by petitioner to the Court of Appeals under any other theory. The order, viewed apart from its discussion of Rule 54(b), constitutes a grant of partial summary judgment limited to the issue of petitioner's liability. Such judgments are by their term interlocutory, see Fed. Rule Civ. Proc. 56(c), and where assessment of damages or awarding of other relief remains to be resolved have never been considered to be "final" within the meaning of 28 U.S.C. §1292. Thus the only possible authorization for an appeal from the District Court's order would be pursuant to the provisions of 28 U.S.C. §1292.

If the District Court had granted injunctive relief but had not ruled on respondents' other requests for relief, this interlocutory order would have been appealable under §1292(a)(1).[5] As noted above, the court did not issue an injunction. It might be argued that the order of the District Court, insofar as it failed to include the injunctive relief requested by respondents, is an interlocutory order refusing an injunction within the meaning of §1292(a)(1). But even if this would have allowed respondents to then obtain review in the Court of Appeals, there was no denial of any injunction sought by Petitioner and it could not avail itself of that grant of jurisdiction.

Nor was this order appealable pursuant to 28 U.S.C. §1292(b).[6] Although the District Court's findings made with a view to satisfying Rule 54(b) might be viewed as substantial compliance with the certification requirement of that section, there is no showing in this record that petitioner made application to the Court of Appeals within the 10 days therein specified. And that court's holding that its jurisdiction was pursuant to §1291 makes it clear that it thought itself obliged to consider on the merits petitioner's appeal. There can be no

4. We need not here attempt any definitive resolution of the meaning of what constitutes a claim for relief within the meaning of the Rules. It is sufficient to recognize that a complaint asserting only one legal right, even if seeking multiple remedies for the alleged violation of that right, states a single claim for relief.

5. The courts of appeals shall have jurisdiction of appeals from:

(1) Interlocutory orders of the district courts of the United States, the United States District Court for the District of the Canal Zone, the District Court of Guam, and the District Court of the Virgin Islands, or of the judges thereof, granting, continuing, modifying, refusing or dissolving injunctions, or refusing to dissolve or modify injunctions, except where a direct review may be had in the Supreme Court.

6. When a district judge, in making in a civil action an order not otherwise appealable under this section, shall be of the opinion that such order involves a controlling question of law as to which there is substantial ground for difference of opinion and that an immediate appeal from the order may materially advance the ultimate termination of the litigation, he shall so state in writing in such order. The Court of Appeals may thereupon, in its discretion, permit an appeal to be taken from such order, if application is made to it within ten days after the entry of the order Provided, however, That application for an appeal hereunder shall not stay proceedings in the district court unless the district judge or the Court of Appeals or a judge thereof shall so order.

assurance that had the other requirements of §1292(b) been complied with, the Court of Appeals would have exercised its discretion to entertain the interlocutory appeal.

Were we to sustain the procedure followed here, we would condone a practice whereby a district court in virtually any case before it might render an interlocutory decision on the question of liability of the defendant, and the defendant would thereupon be permitted to appeal to the court of appeals without satisfying any of the requirements that Congress carefully set forth. We believe that Congress, in enacting present §§1291 and 1292 of Title 28, has been well aware of the dangers of an overly rigid insistence upon a "final decision" for appeal in every case, and has in those sections made ample provision for appeal of orders which are not "final" so as to alleviate any possible hardship. We would twist the fabric of the statute more than it will bear if we were to agree that the District Court's order of February 20, 1974, was appealable to the Court of Appeals.

The judgment of the Court of Appeals is therefore vacated, and the case is remanded with instructions to dismiss the petitioner's appeal. It is so ordered.

Mr. Justice BLACKMUN took no part in the consideration or decision of this case.

NOTES AND PROBLEMS

1. The *Wetzel* Court was unanimous. What is so important about the finality principle that it elicits such unanimity? Some states, most notably New York, allow interlocutory appeals in a wide range of situations. Since the Judiciary Act of 1789, the policy in the federal courts has been to wait until a final judgment.

a. The basic argument for the final judgment rule can be explained on a cost-benefit basis. The costs of allowing interlocutory appeals are the costs of an unnecessary extra appeal if the trial judge turns out to have been correct. The costs of not allowing interlocutory appeals are those of an unnecessary or an unnecessarily long trial if the trial judge turns out to have been wrong. Is it possible, before deciding the particular appeal, to determine which of these costs is greater? If we assume that the costs of an unnecessary extra appeal are approximately the same as the costs of the unnecessary or unnecessarily long trial, the overall costs are proportional to the number of times the trial judge is right versus the number of times he is wrong. If trial judges are right more often than they are wrong (measured by eventual reversal when appeal finally occurs), then the general policy should disfavor interlocutory appeals. In fact, trial judges are reversed far less often than they are affirmed (the federal courts report a reversal rate of only 10 percent), and many decisions are not even appealed. Thus the general policy seems to be a wise one.

b. Against this argument one can suggest, first, that some of its premises are wrong: Trials, which require elaborate pretrial preparation, witnesses and sometimes juries, will generally be much more expensive than appeals. Second, in some undetermined number of cases, parties will abandon meritorious positions (that is, settle the case) because they cannot afford to wait for vindication on appeal. To point to the absence of appeal in such cases as evidence of a satisfactory trial is to ignore reality.

c. Beyond that, one can make a historical argument. Whatever one thinks of the original merits of the final judgment rule, its effect has changed dramatically with the advent of modern procedure. Before the Federal Rules (and equivalent state systems' rules of procedure) came into effect, there were essentially two stages in litigation, pleading and trial. If a case ended at the pleading stage, appeal was immediately available. If it didn't, trial would follow shortly, after which appeal was again available to the loser. Modern procedure, with its emphasis on discovery and a multistage pretrial process, adopts many of the main features of equity practice. Unlike the common law, equity permitted appeal from all interlocutory rulings. By adopting equity procedure but retaining the common law rule for appealability, modern process has delegated substantial amounts of unreviewable power to the trial court.

d. As noted, New York has formally rejected the final judgment rule. Its procedural code lists a series of pretrial orders from which a losing party may take immediate appeal, including such broad categories as any order that "involves some part of the merits or . . . affects a substantial right." N.Y. Civ. Prac. L.&R. 5701 (Mathew Bender 2003). Other states may, less formally, have created substantial loopholes by manipulating the availability of the extraordinary writs of mandamus and prohibition (see infra page 644).

2. In *Wetzel*, who raised the question of appealability in the Supreme Court?

a. Because the governing statute, §1291, frames appealability in jurisdictional terms, appellate courts have the power and duty to consider appealability even if neither party raises the issue.

b. Compare Rule 12(h)(3), which provides that the district court may raise questions of subject matter jurisdiction sua sponte.

3. A salient characteristic of modern procedure is its allowance of multiple claims and parties. How should we adapt the final judgment rule to such a situation?

a. One extreme would be to allow no one to appeal until after all claims of all parties had been resolved. Rule 54(b) rejects this solution, allowing the court to enter a final judgment as to "one or more but fewer than all of the claims or parties." If such a judgment is entered, it becomes appealable.

b. Rule 54(b) fits into the analysis in Note 1(a), supra, because it covers situations in which matters that could have been raised separately have been joined in one case under liberal joinder rules.

c. But the Rule requires the judge entering such partial final judgment to exercise discretion and to make "an express determination that there is no just reason for delay" in making the decision appealable.

d. Suppose a case involving several plaintiffs against a single defendant. The court grants summary judgment against one of the plaintiffs. Or imagine a case involving one plaintiff against several defendants in which the court grants summary judgment in favor of one defendant. If the court so certifies under Rule 54(b), the loser can immediately appeal. What should guide the judge's discretion in deciding whether to issue a Rule 54(b) certification in such a case? There are efficiency considerations: If the potential appeal contains an issue that persists in the remaining claims, an appellate decision may clarify them before trial. Or a judge might decide on precisely the opposite grounds — that the issues involved as to the loser are entirely different from those for the remaining case — and a decision won't complicate the case for the remaining parties.

e. Finally, suppose a more ordinary case, in which a plaintiff has several claims against a defendant — perhaps a claim of copyright infringement and several state law contract claims. The defendant wins partial summary judgment on the copyright claim, which the plaintiff would like to appeal. But the judge does not certify that claim under Rule 54(b). Can the plaintiff voluntarily dismiss the remaining claims (thus enabling him to refile them if the statute of limitations has not run) and thus create an appealable final judgment? Held, yes, absent evidence of intent to manipulate appellate jurisdiction. James v. Price Stern Sloan, Inc., 283 F.3d 1064 (9th Cir. 2002). How would the court decide whether there was an intent to manipulate appellate jurisdiction?

4. If some means existed for identifying cases in which the trial judge is particularly likely to be wrong, such cases might pose exceptions to the final judgment rule. Under 28 U.S.C. §1292(b), discussed in the *Wetzel* Court's opinion and at further length later in this section, the trial judge may certify (among other things) that her order involves "a controlling question of law as to which there is substantial ground for difference of opinion" and "that an immediate appeal from the order may materially advance the ultimate termination of the litigation." Under such circumstances, the assumptions stated in Note 1(a) no longer apply, and an interlocutory appeal is allowed.

b.   Defining the Moment of Judgment

Even when one is alert to the dire jurisdictional consequences of failure to heed the final judgment rule, it is not always easy to locate the precise point at which a judgment becomes final — or even, for that matter, to identify the judicial act that constitutes a judgment. One difficulty is that the judge's belief that she is entering a judgment can be second-guessed by the appellate court. Recall that in *Wetzel*, both parties understandably thought that the judge's announcement that "final judgment be entered" meant what it said, but the Supreme Court ruled otherwise.

Consider the matter from the perspective of a party wishing to appeal. The only step required to bring an appeal from a ruling of the district court is the timely filing of a notice of appeal with the clerk of the district court. Fed. R. App. P. 3(a). That notice must be filed within the time allowed by Fed. R. App. P. 4(a)(1) — 30 days for the typical appeal; 60 days for an appeal involving the United States. The issue of timing is critical, because, as you have seen, the courts of appeals have repeatedly held that the time limits are "jurisdictional" — that is, that the court of appeals has no jurisdiction to hear the appeal if the notice of appeal is filed too late. Two provisions of 28 U.S.C. §2107 and the appellate rules slightly alleviate the problem of late filings. The cited statute and Fed. R. App.

P. 4(a)(6) empower the district court to let a trial judge extend this time for a party who did not receive notice of the entry of the judgment in question if no prejudice to other parties results. The cited statute and Fed. R. App. P. 4(a)(5) also allow the district court to extend the time for filing the notice of appeal up to 30 days on a showing of "excusable neglect or good cause."

An equally serious problem confronts litigants who file their appeals *too early*. As we have seen, under 28 U.S.C. §1291, appeals lie "from all final decisions of the district courts." By negative implication appeals do not lie from decisions of the district courts that are not final. In the distinction lies what the comments to Fed. R. App. P. 4 term "a trap for an unsuspecting litigant." Before the 1993 amendments, the trap was sprung if the appellant filed a notice of appeal after the judgment but while a post-trial motion for j.n.o.v. or new trial was pending. Until these motions are decided, the final outcome — and judgment — in the case has not occurred. A number of unfortunate would-be appellants discovered this point in sorrow-producing ways. Fed. R. App. P. 4(a)(4) alleviates the difficulty by providing that when a party seeks to appeal from an order that would be final but for the interposition of one of these common post-trial motions, the appeal is held in abeyance until the disposition of these motions, at which point it becomes effective, thus preserving the jurisdiction of the court of appeals.

Even with these provisions, timing remains critical, and rulemakers have therefore tried to make the moment of judgment extremely clear. Rule 58 requires that "every judgment and amended judgment must be set forth on a separate document. . . ." In United States v. Indrelunas, 411 U.S. 216 (1973), the Court said that the separate-document requirement must be "mechanically applied." The problem is that the separate document rule applies not to litigants but to court clerks and judges. Unfortunately, these officials don't always do what the rules require. As the Rules Advisory Committee noted in 2002, "This simple separate document requirement has been ignored in many cases. . . . [with the result that] there have been many and horridly confused problems under Appellate Rule 4(a)." Advisory Committee Notes to 2002 Amendments to Rule 58. The 2002 amendments to Rule 58 tried to set guidelines for some of the worst problems.

NOTES AND PROBLEMS

1. Suppose the judge announces what she and the parties intend as a final judgment; the clerk duly enters that judgment on the docket (as required by Rule 79(a)); but the "separate document" required by Rule 58 never appears. The parties appeal.

a. What result?

b. Read Rule 58(b)(2); does this solve the appellant's problem at least as to timing?

2. FirsTier Mortgage Co. v. Investors Mortgage Insurance Co., 498 U.S. 269, 272 (1991), deals with the opposite problem — the premature appeal. In *FirsTier* the trial judge announced that he would grant summary judgment on all counts for the defendant and asked the parties to submit proposed findings of fact. Before

the trial judge had issued his findings, the plaintiff appealed—"close to a month before the entry of judgment."

a. The Court held that Fed. R. App. P. 4(a)(2) ("A notice of appeal filed after the court announces a decision or order but before the entry of the judgment or order is treated as filed on the date of and after the entry") applied, even though the judge had announced only his intent to enter summary judgment, not the summary judgment itself, much less the separate document embodying the judgment.

b. The *FirsTier* opinion evinces a certain amount of nervousness about the implications of its holding:

> This is not to say that [Fed.] Rule [App. P.] 4(a)(2) permits a notice of appeal from a clearly interlocutory decision—such as a discovery ruling or a sanction order under Rule 11 of the Federal Rules of Civil Procedure—to serve as a notice of appeal from the final judgment. A belief that such a decision is a final judgment would *not* be reasonable.

(Emphasis added.)

c. Is the rule now that a premature notice of appeal is saved by Fed. R. App. P. 4(a)(2) if the appellant reasonably believed that what the judge had issued was a final order? Is that a workable standard?

2.   Exceptions to the Final Judgment Rule

The adoption of the Federal Rules in 1938 greatly increased the importance of the stage between pleading and trial, in which substantial numbers of important but nonfinal rulings would occur. That circumstance placed substantial pressure on legislatures and courts to find exceptions to the rule. The efforts to define exceptions without abandoning the rule has not been easy. We survey the major exceptions below, starting with the one that has caused the greatest difficulty.

a.   Practical Finality

Lauro Lines s.r.l. v. Chasser

490 U.S. 495 (1989)

Justice BRENNAN delivered the opinion of the Court.

We granted certiorari to consider whether an interlocutory order of a United States District Court denying a defendant's motion to dismiss a damages action on the basis of a contractual forum-selection clause is immediately appealable under 28 U.S.C. §1291 as a collateral final order. We hold that it is not.

I

The individual respondents were, or represent the estates of persons who were, passengers aboard the cruise ship Achille Lauro when it was hijacked by terrorists in the Mediterranean in October 1985. Petitioner Lauro Lines s.r.l., an Italian company, owns the Achille Lauro. Respondents filed suits against Lauro Lines in the District Court for the Southern District of New York to recover damages for injuries sustained as a result of the hijacking, and for the wrongful death of passenger Leon Klinghoffer. Lauro Lines moved before trial to dismiss the actions, citing the forum-selection clause printed on each passenger ticket. This clause purported to obligate the passenger to institute any suit arising in connection with the contract in Naples, Italy, and to renounce the right to sue elsewhere.

The District Court denied petitioner's motions to dismiss, holding that the ticket as a whole did not give reasonable notice to passengers that they were waiving the opportunity to sue in a domestic forum. Without moving for certification for immediate appeal pursuant to 28 U.S.C. §1292(b), Lauro Lines sought to appeal the District Court's orders. The Court of Appeals for the Second Circuit dismissed petitioner's appeal on the ground that the District Court's orders denying petitioner's motions to dismiss were interlocutory and not appealable under §1291. The court held that the orders did not fall within the exception to the rule of nonappealability carved out for collateral final orders in Cohen v. Beneficial Industrial Loan Corp., 337 U.S. 541 (1949). We granted certiorari to resolve a disagreement among the Courts of Appeals. We now affirm.

II

Title 28 U.S.C. §1291 provides for appeal to the courts of appeals only from "final decisions of the district courts of the United States." For purposes of §1291, a final judgment is generally regarded as "a decision by the District Court that 'ends the litigation on the merits and leaves nothing for the court to do but execute the judgment.'" Van Cauwenberghe v. Biard, 486 U.S. 517, 521 (1988), quoting Catlin v. United States, 324 U.S. 229, 233 (1945). An order denying a motion to dismiss a civil action on the ground that a contractual forum-selection clause requires that such suit be brought in another jurisdiction is not a decision on the merits that ends the litigation. On the contrary, such an order "ensures that litigation will continue in the District Court." Gulfstream Aerospace Corp. v. Mayacamas Corp., 485 U.S. 271, 275 (1988). Section 1291 thus permits an appeal only if an order denying a motion to dismiss based upon a forum-selection clause falls within the "narrow exception to the normal application of the final judgment rule [that] has come to be known as the collateral order doctrine." Midland Asphalt Corp. v. United States, 489 U.S. 794, 798 (1989). That exception is for a "small class" of prejudgment orders that "finally determine claims of right separable from, and collateral to, rights asserted in the action, [and that are] too important to be denied review and too independent of the cause itself to require that appellate consideration be deferred until the whole case is adjudicated." Cohen, supra, at 546. We have held that to fall within the Cohen exception, an order must satisfy at least three conditions: "It must 'conclusively determine the disputed question,' 'resolve an important issue completely separate from the merits of the action,' and 'be effectively unreviewable on appeal from a final judgment.'" Richardson-Merrell Inc. v. Koller, 472 U.S. 424, 431 (1985), quoting

Coopers & Lybrand v. Livesay, 437 U.S. 463, 468 (1978). For present purposes, we need not decide whether an order denying a dismissal motion based upon a contractual forum-selection clause conclusively determines a disputed issue, or whether it resolves an important issue that is independent of the merits of the action, for the District Court's orders fail to satisfy the third requirement of the collateral order test.

We recently reiterated the "general rule" that an order is "effectively unreviewable" only "where the order at issue involves 'an asserted right the legal and practical value of which would be destroyed if it were not vindicated before trial.'" Midland Asphalt Corp., supra, at 798, quoting United States v. MacDonald, 435 U.S. 850, 860 (1978). If it is eventually decided that the District Court erred in allowing trial in this case to take place in New York, petitioner will have been put to unnecessary trouble and expense, and the value of its contractual right to an Italian forum will have been diminished. It is always true, however, that "there is value . . . in triumphing before trial, rather than after it," MacDonald, supra, at 860, n.7, and this Court has declined to find the costs associated with unnecessary litigation to be enough to warrant allowing the immediate appeal of a pretrial order. See Richardson-Merrell Inc., supra, at 436 ("the possibility that a ruling may be erroneous and may impose additional litigation expense is not sufficient to set aside the finality requirement imposed by Congress" in §1291). Instead, we have insisted that the right asserted be one that is essentially destroyed if its vindication must be postponed until trial is completed.

We have thus held in cases involving criminal prosecutions that the deprivation of a right not to be tried is effectively unreviewable after final judgment and is immediately appealable. Similarly, in civil cases, we have held that the denial of a motion to dismiss based upon a claim of absolute immunity from suit is immediately appealable prior to final judgment, "for the essence of absolute immunity is its possessor's entitlement not to have to answer for his conduct in a civil damages action." Mitchell v. Forsyth, 472 U.S. 511, 525 (1985). And claims of qualified immunity may be pursued by immediate appeal, because qualified immunity too "is an immunity from suit."

On the other hand, we have declined to hold the collateral order doctrine applicable where a district court has denied a claim, not that the defendant has a right not to be sued at all, but that the suit against the defendant is not properly before the particular court because it lacks jurisdiction. In Van Cauwenberghe v. Biard, 486 U.S. 517 (1988), a civil defendant moved for dismissal on the ground that he had been immune from service of process because his presence in the United States had been compelled by extradition to face criminal charges. We noted that, after Mitchell, "[t]he critical question . . . is whether 'the essence' of the claimed right is a right not to stand trial," 486 U.S., at 524, and held that the immunity from service of process defendant asserted did not amount to an immunity from suit—even though service was essential to the trial court's jurisdiction over the defendant.

Lauro Lines argues here that its contractual forum-selection clause provided it with a right to trial before a tribunal in Italy, and with a concomitant right not to be sued anywhere else. This "right not to be haled for trial before tribunals outside the agreed forum," petitioner claims, cannot effectively be vindicated by appeal after trial in an improper forum. There is no obviously correct way to characterize the right embodied in petitioner's forum-selection provision: "all litigants who have a meritorious pretrial claim for dismissal can reasonably claim a right not to stand trial." *Van Cauwenberghe*. The right appears most like that to be free from trial if it is characterized—as by petitioner—as a right not to be sued at all except in a Neapolitan forum. It appears less like a right not to be subjected to suit if characterized—as by the Court of Appeals—as "a right to have the binding adjudication of claims occur in a certain forum." Even assuming that the former characterization is proper, however, petitioner is obviously not entitled under the forum-selection clause of its contract to avoid suit altogether, and an entitlement to avoid suit is different in kind from an entitlement to be sued only in a particular forum. Petitioner's claim that it may be sued only in Naples, while not perfectly secured by appeal after final judgment, is adequately vindicable at that stage—surely as effectively vindicable as a claim that the trial court lacked personal jurisdiction over the defendant—and hence does not fall within the third prong of the collateral order doctrine.

Petitioner argues that there is a strong federal policy favoring the enforcement of foreign forum-selection clauses, citing The Bremen v. Zapata Off-Shore Co., 407 U.S. 1 (1972), and that "the essential concomitant of this strong federal policy . . . is the right of immediate appellate review of district court orders denying their enforcement." A policy favoring enforcement of forum-selection clauses, however, would go to the merits of petitioner's claim that its ticket-agreement requires that any suit be filed in Italy and that the agreement should be enforced by the federal courts. Immediate appealability of a prejudgment order denying enforcement, insofar as it depends upon satisfaction of the third prong of the collateral order test, turns on the precise contours of the right asserted, and not upon the likelihood of eventual success on the merits. The Court of Appeals properly dismissed petitioner's appeal, and its judgment is affirmed.

Justice SCALIA, concurring.

I join the opinion of the Court, and write separately only to make express what seems to me implicit in its analysis.

The reason we say that the right not to be sued elsewhere than in Naples is "adequately vindicable," by merely reversing any judgment obtained in violation of it is, quite simply, that the law does not deem the right important enough to be vindicated by, as it were, an injunction against its violation obtained through interlocutory appeal. The importance of the right asserted has always been a significant part of our collateral order doctrine. When first formulating that doctrine in Cohen v. Beneficial Industrial Loan Corp. we said that it permits interlocutory appeal of final determinations of claims that are not only "separable from, and collateral to, rights asserted in the action," but also, we immediately added, "*too important* to be denied review" (emphasis added). Our later cases have retained that significant requirement. . . .

While it is true, therefore, that the "right not to be sued elsewhere than in Naples" is not fully vindicated—indeed, to be utterly frank, is positively destroyed—by permitting the trial to occur and reversing its outcome, that is vindication enough because the right is not sufficiently important to overcome the policies militating against interlocutory appeals. We have made that judgment when the right not to be tried in a particular court has been created through jurisdictional limitations established by Congress or by international treaty. The same judgment applies — if anything, a fortiori — when the right has been created by private agreement.

NOTES AND PROBLEMS

1. One should begin by noting that the events leading to this case also inspired an opera: *The Death of Klinghoffer*, composed by John Adams, libretto by Alice Goodman. Synopses of this tragedy do not indicate that the question of appealability figures in the plot.

2. *Lauro Lines* tells us that it is one of a series of cases delineating judicially created exceptions to the final judgment rule.

a. The attraction of such an exception is easy to understand: Some district court decisions seem to cry out for reversal before trial is over.

b. The difficulties of creating exceptions are equally obvious: Can one define a coherent set of cases that will be entitled to review before the final judgment?

c. If not, one has neither the draconian simplicity of a final judgment rule nor the "accuracy" of immediate review; rather, one has constant bickering that comes from the necessity of deciding which cases fall on which side of an indistinct line.

3. The Court in *Lauro Lines* held that the order was not appealable and therefore did not decide whether the forum selection clause was valid. That ruling has the same practical effect as holding the order appealable but affirming the trial court decision on the merits. In some cases it is difficult to overcome the sense that denials of review are made with at least an over-the-shoulder glance at the merits. Such a glance may be particularly important in a case like *Lauro Lines*. Such cases are very unlikely to go to trial, and a settlement will not be appealable. Thus the interlocutory review of the court order is likely to be the only review. Is this the point of Justice Scalia's concurrence?

4. The cases that have posed the most severe problems in defining "practical finality" have been those concerning the official immunity defense for government officials. Government officials sued for violating the constitutional rights of citizens have a powerful defense: "official immunity." That doctrine not only them from liability if they reasonably believed they were acting constitutionally. It also, the courts have said, frees them from liability but also from the obligation to stand trial — including the necessity to endure discovery.

But, as *Lauro Lines* recognizes, the "right not to stand trial," can only be vindicated if immediate appeal lies from a trial court order that — erroneously — holds that official immunity does not apply. Two cases have so held. Nixon v. Fitzgerald, 457 U.S. 731 (1982) (immediate appeal of trial court refusal to dismiss, on grounds of absolute official immunity in a suit brought against the president of the United States); Mitchell v. Forsyth, 472 U.S. 511 (1985) (immediate appeal of trial court refusal to dismiss, on the ground of qualified official immunity in a suit brought against a former attorney general of the United States).

a. *Nixon* and *Mitchell* opened Pandora's box. Like *Lauro Lines*, they deal with defendants who argue that they have the "right not to stand trial." If one conceives of such a right, then its vindication *after* trial and final judgment seems futile and self-defeating. But one could describe many defendants in such terms. For example, any defendant who moves to dismiss on any of the grounds listed in Rule 12 (and loses the motion), could argue that her "right not to stand trial" has been violated. Likewise, so could a defendant who made an unsuccessful motion for summary judgment. The defendant in *Lauro Lines* unsuccessfully made such an argument, to the effect that it had, at least, the right not to stand trial anywhere but in Naples.

b. In applying *Mitchell*, the Supreme Court has sought to draw a line between two kinds of cases in which immunity might be asserted. In Johnson v. Jones, 515 U.S. 304 (1995), the court held *not* immediately appealable a rejection of the official immunity defense that turned on facts rather than on the law — what the court called a "we didn't do it" case. In holding that no appeal lay from a denial of defendants' motion for summary judgment, the Court recognized that it might prove difficult to separate immediately reviewable "law" cases from the "fact" cases that would be reviewable only on final judgment. Almost immediately, the Court had to make such a distinction. In Behrens v. Pelletier, 516 U.S. 299 (1996), another qualified immunity case, the Court held that the official asserting immunity was entitled to not one but two interlocutory appeals. The defendant had first asserted his immunity at the pleading stage and had appealed the trial court's rejection of this contention. The appellate court affirmed, and the case proceeded to discovery and a summary judgment motion. When defendant lost that motion, he again sought a *Cohen* appeal. The Ninth Circuit ruled that one interlocutory appeal was enough, but the Supreme Court disagreed. It distinguished *Johnson* on the grounds that the case at hand involved a determination by the district court that, as a matter of law, the official's conduct "constituted a violation of clearly established law." Will this distinction — which, you'll recall, is jurisdictional — prove sustainable?

5. An incomplete list of other orders that have been held to be practically final under the *Cohen* doctrine includes:

a. *Cohen* itself: A trial court decision declining to apply in federal court a state statute requiring the posting of a bond in shareholder derivative actions brought by plaintiffs owning small amounts of stock. Cohen v. Beneficial Industrial Corp., 337 U.S. 541 (1949).

b. Orders vacating the attachment of a vessel. Swift & Co. v. Compania Columbiana de Caribe, 339 U.S. 684 (1950).

c. Orders denying a party leave to proceed in forma pauperis. Roberts v. United States District Court, 339 U.S. 844 (1950).

d. An order remanding a diversity action on grounds of abstention. Quackenbush v. Allstate Insurance Co., 517 U.S. 706 (1996).

6. Contrast with the cases listed in Note 5 a series of examples in which the Court, as in *Lauro Lines*, has held the order in question not to be practically final:

a. Orders refusing to certify class actions. Coopers & Lybrand v. Livesay, 437 U.S. 463 (1978). As the next section explains, this ruling has partly been reversed by an amendment to Rule 23.

b. Orders disqualifying or refusing to disqualify trial counsel for alleged conflicts of interest. Richardson-Merrell v. Koller, 472 U.S. 424 (1985); Flanagan v. United States, 465 U.S. 259 (1984); Firestone v. Risjord, 449 U.S. 368 (1981).

c. Orders denying permission to intervene as of right under Rule 24(a) while granting permissive intervention under Rule 24(b). Stringfellow v. Concerned Neighbors in Action, 480 U.S. 370 (1987).

d. Orders denying a motion to dismiss on grounds of immunity from service of process and forum non conveniens. Van Cauwenberghe v. Biard, 486 U.S. 517 (1988).

e. Orders requiring class action defendants to bear the cost of notifying members of the class. Eisen v. Carlisle & Jacquelin, 417 U.S. 156 (1974). (See Chapter XIII.)

f. Judicial rescission of a dismissal pursuant to settlement. Digital Equipment Corp. v. Desktop Direct, Inc., 511 U.S. 863 (1994).

7. And there is, predictably, a list of topics on which the circuits have split on the question of appealability. One example: the appealability of an order requiring the discovery of material claimed to be protected by attorney-client privilege. See United States v. Phillip Morris, Inc., 314 F.3d 612 (D.C. Cir. 2003) (appealable; acknowledging that six other circuits had reached opposite conclusion).

8. The difficulty of satisfactorily distinguishing between the cases in the two preceding notes may have led to a 1990 amendment to 28 U.S.C. §2072. Congress extended the Supreme Court's rulemaking power under the Rules Enabling Act to include rules "defin[ing] when a ruling of a district court is final for the purposes of appeal under section 1291 of this title." Is the invitation to engage in rulemaking perhaps a subtle suggestion that, in writing the rules, the Court eliminate some of the twists and turns in the *Cohen* doctrine by overruling some decisions in this line? No Rule has to date taken up Congress's challenge. One Rule, 23(f), discussed below, takes a half-step in this direction by creating a new category of interlocutory appeals for class action certification decisions.

b. Injunctions

An important exception to the final judgment rule appears in 28 U.S.C. §1292(a), which allows appeals from interlocutory orders of the district courts "granting, continuing, modifying, refusing or dissolving injunctions, or refusing to dissolve or modify injunctions." Recall that this was one of the argued grounds for appealability in *Wetzel*, supra page 628. Such review is thought to be appropriate because of the special nature of injunctions and their potential for harm.

NOTES AND PROBLEMS

1. Section 1292(b) does not apply to a temporary restraining order, though it does to a preliminary injunction. Presumably the basis for this distinction is the short duration of a TRO — 10 days under Rule 65.

2. The Supreme Court has held that denial of summary judgment in favor of one seeking a permanent injunction does not give rise to the right to immediate appeal under this section because the ruling is simply a step on the way to trial rather than a rejection of the claim on the merits. Switzerland Cheese Association v. E. Horne's Market, Inc., 385 U.S. 23 (1966).

3. Suppose a district court, acting pursuant to Rule 16, orders the parties to refrain from any discovery while they discuss settlement or submit to court-ordered mediation. Is that an injunction? Or just an unappealable pretrial order?

c.   Interlocutory Appeals

Efforts to release some of the tension created by the final judgment rule are found in several statutes. The terms of 28 U.S.C. §1292(b) permit a district court to certify interlocutory appeals from nonfinal judgments. A district court judge wishing to create the possibility for such an interlocutory appeal must certify that the order "involves a controlling question of law as to which there is a substantial ground for difference of opinion" and that "an immediate appeal from the order may materially advance the ultimate termination of the litigation." For the inter-locutory appeal to occur, not only must the district court judge so certify, but the appellate court must agree.

The statute is not heavily used. A study at the close of the 1980s, a period when overall appeals increased dramatically, revealed that out of the 40,000+ federal appeals in an average year only about 300 §1292(b) were certified by district courts, and of those only about a third, 100 cases, were accepted by the courts of appeals. Michael Solomine, Revitalizing Interlocutory Appeals in the Federal Courts, 58 Geo. Wash. L. Rev. 1165 (1990).

Given parties' (and sometimes judges') almost feverish efforts to escape the rigidities of the final judgment rule, why are there not more interlocutory appeals? One possibility is that the same period in which interlocutory appeals were available coincides with exploding appellate caseloads and increased inter-est in trial judge management. The latter development may make appellate courts reluctant to add to their docket; the former may make trial courts more reluctant to release cases to the interference of appellate courts. Professor Solomine's study found that appellate courts were restricting interlocutory appeals to "big, exceptional" cases — mass torts, class actions, and the like — where proceedings are likely to be protracted.

Another possibility for the "failure" of §1292(b) is its requirement that both trial and appellate courts agree that the question is worth certification. A headstrong or defiant judge will not seek appellate review, and an indecisive or timorous one will be seen by appellate judges as a nuisance. If this hypothesis is correct, amended

Rule of Civil Procedure 23(f) may yield better — or at least different — results. As noted in Note 8, page 642 supra, 28 U.S.C. §2072(c) permits Rules to define "when a ruling of a district court is final for purposes of appeal." Acting pursuant to that authority, Rule 23(f) in 1998 was amended to give a court of appeals "discretion to permit an appeal from an order of a district court granting or denying class certification. . . ." The district court need not agree. Should §1292(b) be amended in a similar fashion? Or should Congress await the experience under Rule 23(f)?

NOTES AND PROBLEMS

1. Probably the most common ground for rejecting certification under §1292(b) is that resolution of the issue in question will not in fact "materially advance the ultimate termination of the litigation." For example, in Atlantic City Electric Co. v. General Elec. Co., 337 F.2d 844 (2d Cir. 1964), the court refused to hear an appeal after certification by the trial judge of an issue concerning discovery in antitrust litigation. The judge had refused discovery relating to the defense of "passing on" (the defense, now generally not available, that the plaintiff was not injured by the defendant's price fixing because the plaintiff passed the price increases on to its customers). The availability of the defense had not been settled at that time. The court of appeals emphasized that the case would be a simple one if discovery did not take place and that the error, if any, could be cured quickly on final review. If the trial court had granted discovery, would appeal have been appropriate?

2. In which of the cases considering finality — Liberty Mutual Insurance Co. v. Wetzel and Lauro Lines s.r.l. v. Chasser — would §1292(b) review have been appropriate if the trial judge had certified the issue under the statutory procedure?

3. In addition to 28 U.S.C. §1292(b), other statutes regulating particular areas make certain trial court orders immediately appealable. For example, 9 U.S.C. §15(a) makes a trial judge's refusal of an order to arbitrate immediately appealable. Section (b) of the same statute makes unappealable an order directing arbitration unless it is certified under §1292(b).

4. Suppose the parties agree that a trial court ruling cries out for interlocutory review, but the trial court refuses to certify it, perhaps in the belief that a difficult case will settle if the judge holds the parties' feet to the fire. Is there any way in which the parties can force the trial judge to certify an interlocutory appeal? Consider whether the next section casts light on that question.

d. Mandamus

A *writ of mandamus*, obtained in an original proceeding in the court that issues the writ, orders a public official to perform an act required by law. The public official may be a judge of a lower court. For example, in LaBuy v. Howes Leather, 352 U.S. 249 (1957), where the district court had declined to try an antitrust case, instead referring it to a special master, the court of appeals issued the writ, and it was upheld by the Supreme Court. The Seventh Circuit had previously expressed its displeasure with referral of such cases to masters, and the Supreme Court was even more emphatic in describing the district court's action as an "abdication of the judicial function."

The difficulty with mandamus arises because it can become a tempting route for the avoidance of the rules against interlocutory appeals explored in the preceding material. To prevent this evasion of the final judgment rule, the availability of the writ must be limited:

> The remedy of mandamus is a drastic one, to be invoked only in extraordinary situations. As we have observed, the writ "has traditionally been used in the federal courts only 'to confine an inferior court to a lawful exercise of its prescribed jurisdiction or to compel it to exercise its authority when it is its duty to do so.'" And, while we have not limited the use of mandamus by an unduly narrow and technical understanding of what constitutes a matter of "jurisdiction," the fact still remains that "only exceptional circumstances amounting to a judicial 'usurpation of power' will justify the invocation of this extraordinary remedy."

Kerr v. United States District Court, 426 U.S. 394, 402 (1976).

In spite of such limitations, one does find cases where appellate courts are prepared to issue writs of mandate. One area in which mandamus seems freely available, with little discussion of the usual stated limitations, is that in which the trial judge has denied a jury trial. Thus in Beacon Theatres v. Westover, 359 U.S. 500 (1959) (granting a jury trial in a case combining legal and equitable claims; see Chapter IX), the propriety of interlocutory appellate intervention was largely assumed. Another exception to the general stinginess of the courts in issuing the writ is to prevent the transfer of a case, under 28 U.S.C. §1404(a), out of the circuit. The rationale is that the statutory basis for the writ, 28 U.S.C. §1651, authorizes writs to be issued by courts "in aid of their respective jurisdictions." Because a transfer out of the circuit would deprive the court of appeals of its eventual jurisdiction on appeal, the appellate court has jurisdiction to consider the propriety of such a transfer order. The Seventh Circuit has adopted an apparently unique use of mandamus. In seeking the recusal of judges under 28 U.S.C. §455(a) (on the broad ground that "impartiality might reasonably be questioned"), that Circuit requires parties to use mandamus rather than appeal. The Circuit's theory is that in such broadly based recusal motions, an aggrieved party will never be able to demonstrate an effect on his "substantial rights." As you will see in the next section, only such an effect will constitute reversible error; therefore, in order to create some avenue by which §455(a) can be vindicated, mandamus is available. However tortured the Seventh Circuit's reasoning, the result makes sense: In most cases mandamus will be sought early in the case, before time has been wasted on proceedings that must be set aside.

NOTES AND PROBLEMS

1. Reconsider the problem posed at the end of the preceding section: should an appellate court issue mandamus to force a district court to certify an inter-

locutory appeal under §1292(b)? Can one frame that refusal in such terms as to invoke mandamus?

2. One way in which an appellate court might have its cake and eat it too — refuse to issue mandamus but achieve the same practical effect — is to write an opinion refusing the writ and in the process discussing the course it "hopes" the district court will take. One can find several Supreme Court opinions taking such a tack.

a. In Kerr v. United States District Court, supra, the Supreme Court upheld the Ninth Circuit's refusal to issue mandamus requiring the district court to vacate a discovery order that would have required the California prison system to turn over all of its personnel files. The defendant prison system resisted on grounds that the files were covered by various privileges. The Supreme Court "upheld" the refusal of the writ in terms that came close to granting it:

> Petitioners ask in essence only that the District Court review the challenged documents in camera before passing on whether each one individually should or should not be disclosed. But the Court of Appeals' opinion dealing with the Adult Authority files did not foreclose the possible necessity of such in camera review. . . . The court apparently left open the opportunity for petitioners to return to the District Court, assert the privilege more specifically . . . and then have their request for an in camera review . . . reconsidered in a different light. . . .

Theoretically, the district court remains free after this opinion to refuse in-camera review of the files. Do you suppose it would so refuse after reading this opinion?

b. A similar approach was used in Schlagenhauf v. Holder, appearing in Chapter VII (supra page 433). The principal issue in *Schlagenhauf* was whether the district court could order a series of mental and physical examinations of a defendant bus driver whose bus had collided with another vehicle that he later claimed he did not see. The Supreme Court ruled that, of the numerous examinations ordered by the district court, only the eye examination was justified. The court of appeals had refused to issue a writ of mandamus ordering the district court to rescind its order for the additional examinations. One would therefore expect the Supreme Court to remand to the court of appeals for it to issue the writ of mandamus. Instead the Court remanded the case to the district court for proceedings consistent with its opinion. The Court did not note that the mandamus action before it, being an original action in the court of appeals, could not be remanded to the district court and that the original action was still in the district court.

c. Why are procedural rules bent in order to avoid issuance of the writ of mandamus, at least at the Supreme Court level? Two factors stand out. First, if extraordinary circumstances must be shown in order for the court of appeals to issue the writ, its issuance can be read as a censure of the district judge. Second, the appellate standard of review — that is, the standard that the Supreme Court applies in reviewing the action of the court of appeals — is abuse of discretion, because issuance of the writ is said to be discretionary. Under appropriate circumstances, finding an abuse of discretion may not be too difficult when the court of appeals rules that there are extraordinary circumstances and the Supreme Court thinks that there are not. Ordering the court of appeals to issue the writ requires a finding that there were extraordinary circumstances in the district court and, further, that, given those circumstances, the court of appeals abused its discretion in failing to use the writ of mandamus in response. How much easier it is to affirm denial of the writ but hint broadly at the proper outcome of the dispute in the district court.

C. Scope of Review

Even if a decision is final or otherwise reviewable, and even if the lower court decision is flawed, it does not follow that an appellate court will reverse the judgment. For that to happen, the error must fall into a sometimes elusive category.

1. Law and Fact

Anderson v. Bessemer City

470 U.S. 564 (1985)

Justice WHITE delivered the opinion of the Court.

[A] District Court's finding of discriminatory intent in an action brought under Title VII of the Civil Rights Act of 1964 . . . is a factual finding that may be overturned on appeal only if it is clearly erroneous. In this case, the Court of Appeals for the Fourth Circuit concluded that there was clear error in a District Court's finding of discrimination and reversed. Because our reading of the record convinces us that the Court of Appeals misapprehended and misapplied the clearly-erroneous standard, we reverse.

I

[Bessemer City sought a new Recreation Director. Ms. Anderson was the only woman to apply for the job. A five-member committee (chaired by its only female member) interviewed the eight applicants and chose a male, and Ms. Anderson sued, alleging discrimination.]

. . . After a 2-day trial, during which the court heard testimony from petitioner, Mr. Kincaid [the successful applicant], and the five members of the selection committee, the court issued a brief memorandum of decision setting forth its finding that petitioner . . . had been denied the position . . . on account of her sex. . . . [The judge also requested] that petitioner's counsel submit proposed findings of fact and conclusions of law expanding upon those set forth in the memorandum. . . . [This procedure led to several rounds of proposed findings by plaintiff and objections by defendant. Finally] the court issued its own findings of fact and conclusions of law.

. . . [T]he court's finding that petitioner had been denied employment . . . because of her sex rested on a number of subsidiary findings[: (1) that Ms. Anderson "had been better qualified than Mr. Kincaid" (the court detailed the careers of each); (2) that "male committee members had in fact been biased against" Ms. Anderson because she was a woman, a finding based "in part on the testimony of one of the committee members that he believed it would have been 'real hard' for a woman to handle the job and that he would not want his wife to have to perform" its duties; (3) that Ms. Anderson "alone among the applicants . . . had been asked whether she realized the job would involve night work and travel and whether her husband approved of her applying for the job" (there was some dispute about whether Mr. Kincaid was asked an analogous question but the trial court concluded that it was "not a serious inquiry"); and (4)] that the reasons offered by the male committee members for their choice of Mr. Kincaid were pretextual. The court rejected the proposition that Mr. Kincaid's degree in physical education justified his choice, as the evidence suggested that where male candidates were concerned, the committee valued experience more highly than formal education. . . .

The Fourth Circuit reversed . . . [holding that three of] the District Court's crucial findings were clearly erroneous: the finding that petitioner was the most qualified candidate, the finding that petitioner had been asked questions that other applicants were spared, and the finding that the male committee members were biased against hiring a woman. . . .

II

We must deal at the outset with the Fourth Circuit's suggestion that "close scrutiny of the record in this case [was] justified by the manner in which the opinion was prepared" — that is, by the District Court's adoption of petitioner's proposed findings of fact and conclusions of law.

We too, have criticized courts for their verbatim adoption of findings of fact prepared by prevailing parties. . . . Nonetheless, our previous discussions of the subject suggest that even when the trial judge adopts the proposed findings verbatim, the findings are those of the court and may be reversed only if clearly erroneous. . . .

In any event, the District Court in this case does not appear to have uncritically accepted findings prepared without judicial guidance. . . .

III

Because a finding of intentional discrimination is a finding of fact, the standard governing appellate review . . . is that set forth in Federal Rule of Civil Procedure 52(a): "Findings of fact shall not be set aside unless clearly erroneous, and due regard shall be given to the opportunity of the trial court to judge the credibility of the witnesses." . . .

Although the meaning of the phrase "clearly erroneous" is not immediately apparent, certain general principles . . . may be derived from our cases. The foremost of these principles, as the Fourth Circuit itself recognized, is that a "finding is 'clearly erroneous' when although there is evidence to support it, the reviewing court on the entire evidence is left with the definite and firm conviction that a mistake has been committed." United States v. United States Gypsum Co., 333 U.S. 364, 395 (1948). . . . Where there are two permissible views of the evidence, the factfinder's choice between them cannot be clearly erroneous.

This is so even when the district court's findings do not rest on credibility determinations, but are based instead on physical or documentary evidence or inferences from other facts. To be sure, various Courts of Appeals have on occasion asserted the theory that an appellate court may exercise de novo review over findings not based on credibility determinations. . . .

The rationale for deference to the original finder of fact is not limited to the superiority of the trial judge's position to make determinations of credibility. The trial judge's major role is the determination of fact, and with experience in fulfilling that role comes expertise. Duplication of the trial judge's efforts in the court of appeals would very likely contribute only negligibly to the accuracy of fact determination at a huge cost in diversion of judicial resources. . . . As the Court has stated in a different context, the trial on the merits should be "the 'main event' . . . rather than a 'tryout on the road.'" Wainwright v. Sykes, 433 U.S. 72, 90 (1977). . . .

IV

Application of the foregoing principles to the facts of the case lays bare the errors committed. . . . [T]he Fourth Circuit improperly conducted what amounted to a de novo weighing of the evidence in the record. The District Court's finding was based on essentially undisputed evidence regarding the respective backgrounds of petitioner and Mr. Kincaid and the duties . . . of Recreation Director. The District Court, after considering the evidence, concluded that the position . . . carried with it broad responsibilities for creating and managing a recreation program involving not only athletics, but also other activities for citizens of all ages and interests. The court determined that petitioner's more varied educational and employment background and her extensive involvement in a variety of civic activities left her better qualified to implement such a rounded program. . . .

The Fourth Circuit, reading the same record, concluded that the basic duty of Recreation Director was to implement an athletic program. . . . Accordingly, it seemed evident to the Court of Appeals that Mr. Kincaid was in fact better qualified than [Ms. Anderson].

Based on our reading of the record, we cannot say that either interpretation of the facts is illogical or implausible. Each has support in inferences that may be drawn from the facts in the record. . . . The question we must answer, however, is not whether the Fourth Circuit's interpretation of the facts was clearly erroneous, but whether the District Court's finding was clearly erroneous. . . .

Somewhat different concerns are raised by the Fourth Circuit's treatment of the District Court's finding that petitioner, alone among the applicants . . . , was asked questions regarding her spouse's feelings. . . . Here the error of the Court of Appeals was its failure to give due regard to the ability of the District Court to interpret and discern the credibility of oral testimony. . . . The Court of Appeals rested its rejection of the District Court's finding . . . on its own interpretation of testimony by Mrs. Boone. . . .

Mrs. Boone's testimony on this point, which is set forth in the margin,[3] is certainly not free from ambiguity. But Mrs. Boone several times stated that other candidates had not been questioned about the reaction of their wives — at least "not in the same context." . . . Whether the judge's interpretation is actually correct is impossible to tell from the paper record, but it is easy to imagine that the tone of voice in which the witness related her comment, coupled with her immediate denial that she had questioned Mr. Kincaid on the subject, might have conclusively established that the remark was a facetious one. We therefore cannot agree that the judge's conclusion that the remark was facetious was clearly erroneous. . . .

The Fourth Circuit's refusal to accept the District Court's finding that the committee members were biased against hiring a woman was based to a large extent on its rejection of the finding that petitioner had been subjected to questioning that the other applicants were spared. Given that that finding was not clearly erroneous, the finding of bias cannot be termed erroneous. . . .

Our determination that the findings of the District Court regarding petitioner's qualifications, the conduct of her interview, and the bias of the male committee members were not clearly erroneous leads us to conclude that the court's finding that petitioner was discriminated against on account of her sex was also not clearly erroneous. . . .

---

3. Q.   Did the committee members ask that same kind of question of the other applicants?
   A.   Not that I recall. . . .
   Q.   Do you deny that the other applicants, aside from the plaintiff, were asked about the prospect of working at night in that position?
   A.   Not to my knowledge.
   Q.   Are you saying they were not asked that?
   A.   They were not asked, not in the context that they were asked of Phyllis. I don't know whether they were worried because Jim wasn't going to get his supper or what. You know that goes both ways.
   Q.   Did you tell Phyllis Anderson that Donnie Kincaid was not asked about night work?
   A.   He wasn't asked about night work.
   Q.   That answers one question. Now, let's answer the other one. Did you tell Phyllis Anderson that, that Donnie Kincaid was not asked about night work?
   A.   Yes, after the interviews — I think the next day or sometime, and I know — may I answer something?
   Q.   If it's a question that has been asked; otherwise no. It's up to the Judge to say.
   A.   You asked if there was any question asked about — I think Donnie was just married, and I think I made the comment to him personally — and your new bride won't mind.
   Q.   So you asked him yourself about his wife's reaction?
   A.   No, no.
   Q.   That is what you just said.
   Mr. *Gibson*: Objection, Your Honor.
   [The] Court: Sustained. You don't have to rephrase the answer.

App. 108a, 120a-121a.

In so holding, we do not assert that our knowledge of what happened 10 years ago in Bessemer City is superior to that of the Court of Appeals; nor do we claim to have greater insight than the Court of Appeals into the state of mind of the men on the selection committee. . . . Even the trial judge, who has heard the witnesses directly . . . cannot always be confident that he "knows" what happened. Often, he can only determine whether the plaintiff has succeeded in presenting an account of the facts that is more likely to be true than not. Our task — and the task of appellate tribunals generally — is more limited still: we must determine whether the trial judge's conclusions are clearly erroneous. On the record before us, we cannot say that they are. Accordingly, the judgment of the Court of Appeals is reversed.

[The concurring opinion of Justice POWELL and the dissent of Justice BLACKMUN are omitted.]

NOTES AND PROBLEMS

1. Consider two readings of *Anderson*:

a. The Court's holding might rest on the empirical belief that the trial judge is more likely than an appellate court to be correct in his judgments about which witnesses are telling the truth. If so, then the holding could be challenged by a showing that people in general, even judges, are in fact rather bad at detecting lies, even when they see the witness face to face. There is some empirical evidence that most people lack the capacity to detect untruth. Indeed, that same evidence suggests that people are *better* at detecting lies when they read a transcript than when they hear and see the witnesses. Guy Wellborn, Demeanor, 76 Cornell L. Rev. 1075 (1991) (reviewing a substantial body of essentially unanimous social science literature). If the clearly erroneous rule rests on such an empirical belief, it is itself clearly erroneous.

b. Alternatively, the holding may have a different justification. Under Rule-driven procedure, cases that get to trial will have evidence supporting both sides, or else summary judgment would have occurred. So in such cases a rational trier of fact could come down on either side. Notwithstanding this uncertainty, a judgment has to be rendered. Precisely because of this uncertainty, it makes sense to adopt the view of the first hearer of the case unless there is powerful reason for thinking him wrong. Is that what the "clearly erroneous" rule is about?

2. *Anderson* grows out of a practice that has its roots in the distinction between law and equity. Because cases in equity were originally considered only on a written record and the appellate court was as able to read the record as the trial court, the rule evolved in equity that the appellate court reviewed equity decisions de novo. That standard came to dominate appellate review not just of decisions in equity but of all decisions by a judge sitting without a jury. An example of the stance is Orvis v. Higgins, 180 F.2d 537, 539-540 (2d Cir.), cert. denied, 340 U.S. 810 (1950):

> We must sustain a general or a special jury verdict when there is some evidence which the jury might have believed, and when a reasonable inference from that

evidence will support the verdict, regardless of whether that evidence is oral or by deposition. In the case of findings by an administrative agency, the usual rule is substantially the same as that in the case of a jury, the findings being treated like a special verdict. Where a trial judge sits without a jury, the rule varies with the character of the evidence: (a) If he decides a fact issue on written evidence alone, we are as able as he to determine credibility, and so we may disregard his finding. (b) Where the evidence is partly oral and the balance is written or deals with undisputed facts, then we may ignore the trial judge's finding and substitute our own, (1) if the written evidence or some undisputed fact renders the credibility of the oral testimony extremely doubtful, or (2) if the trial judge's finding must rest exclusively on the written evidence or the undisputed facts, so that his evaluation of credibility has no significance. (c) But where the evidence supporting his finding as to any fact issue is entirely oral testimony, we may disturb that finding only in the most unusual circumstances.

Which of these assertions does *Anderson* overrule?

3. Rule 52(a) now codifies one of *Anderson*'s points: "Findings of fact, *whether based on oral or documentary evidence*, shall not be set aside unless clearly erroneous." (Emphasis added.)

4. Cooter & Gell v. Hartmarx Corp., 469 U.S. 384 (1990), divided into three layers the appellate scrutiny of a trial court's decision to apply Rule 11 sanctions: (a) determinations of historical fact (what investigation did the lawyer do before filing the complaint?); (b) determinations of legal sufficiency (was the complaint warranted by existing law or a good faith extension thereof?); and (c) the fashioning of the sanction. The Court held that the first determination (correctness of factual findings) was reviewable under the clearly erroneous standard (citing *Anderson*). The second and third were reviewable under an abuse-of-discretion standard. The Court also held that in this context all three standards were essentially identical. Justifying the application of the abuse-of-discretion standard to the second question, the Court ruefully noted the difficulty of determining between legal and factual questions.

5. As in *Cooter & Gell*, many decisions are up to the sound discretion of the trial judge. Appellate courts can review such decisions for abuse of discretion. As in *Anderson*'s insistence that factual findings be reversed only if clearly erroneous, the Supreme Court has expressed its impatience with appellate courts that "cheat" on the abuse-of-discretion standard by applying it too stringently. In General Electric v. Joiner, 522 U.S. 136 (1997), a trial court had refused to allow some expert witnesses to testify. Such decisions are within the court's discretion. The Eleventh Circuit reversed, citing a generalized preference for admissibility, and conceding that it was applying a particularly stringent standard of review. The Supreme Court reversed, ordering that the usual abuse-of-discretion standard be applied.

6. When a jury rather than a judge has found the fact in question, the principle of *Anderson* may be constitutionally required. The "reexamination clause" of the Seventh Amendment provides that "no fact, tried by a jury, shall be otherwise reexamined in any Court of the United States, than according to the rules of common law." The Supreme Court has said that this clause permits trial

court scrutiny of jury verdicts via Rules 50 and 59 motions. The Court has also suggested, however, that the same reexamination by an appellate court, because it has not been historically sanctioned, is at least doubtful. Gasperini v. Center for the Humanities, Inc., supra page 245. Does this come close to saying that the clearly erroneous rule is required by the Seventh Amendment in a jury case?

7. *Anderson* deals with one side of the law-fact distinction, holding that findings of fact are entitled to a deferential standard of review. The other side of that distinction is equally important: the proposition that trial court conclusions of law are not entitled to any deference. That statement may seem to be obvious, but in at least one application it has not been clear to many courts of appeals. Diversity actions often involve interpretations of state law. In such cases *Erie* puts the federal appellate court in the same position as the district court — seeking to predict how the state courts would decide the question. In such circumstances some courts of appeals have sometimes deferred to the district courts, whose judges usually come from the state in question, on the ground that they are in a better position to predict state law rulings. These courts are in effect treating questions of state law as factual for purposes of appellate review. In Salve Regina College v. Russell, 499 U.S. 225 (1991), the Supreme Court held that such deference was inappropriate: "We conclude that a court of appeals should review de novo a district court's determination of state law."

a. Isn't *Salve Regina* the mirror image of *Anderson*? One requires that appellate courts defer to district courts on questions of fact, even when the appellate court thinks it could do a better job; the other requires appellate courts not to defer to district courts, even when the appellate court does not think it can do a better job.

b. Is either rule sensible?

2. Harmless Error

Even if an appellate court applying the appropriate standard of review determines that the trial court committed error, it will not necessarily reverse. Federal courts are forbidden to reverse for "errors or defects that do not affect the substantial rights of the parties." 28 U.S.C. §2111. This statute was enacted to reverse the so-called Exchequer Rule,[*] which had presumed that any error was harmful and required reversal. As a consequence of §2111, a court must, after concluding there was error, also decide whether that error was harmful.

Courts typically do so by speculating about the likely outcome of the case in the absence of the error. One can see the difficulty inherent in such speculation in Mehojah v. Drummond, 56 F.3d 1213 (10th Cir. 1995). Plaintiffs had been injured when their car struck cattle that had wandered onto the road. The case turned on whether the fencing was unreasonably inadequate. Plaintiffs sought to introduce into evidence testimony showing that, the day after the accident, the

---

[*] So-called from the name of the English court that had originated the practice.

fencing had been improved. The trial judge excluded this testimony; the majority regretted this exclusion but thought it harmless:

> While we conclude that the court should not have excluded the evidence, we do not believe that the exclusion constituted reversible error. . . .
>
> Having reviewed the entire record including the pleadings, we are of the view that the dispositive fact question in this trial was whether the [defendant] was negligent in placing cattle in a pasture where one end was secured only by a water gap fence. Indeed, at trial, [plaintiff's] counsel stated that the "negligence . . . is not so much the lack of Drummond building the fence, the negligence is placing the cattle on property which was improperly maintained. . . ." Given the material issue at trial, the evidence about construction of the wing fence by Mr. Fairweather (the non-party property owner) the following day would not have helped the [plaintiff's] case. . . .
>
> 28 U.S.C. §2111 requires us to "give judgment after an examination of the record without regard to errors or defects which do not affect the substantial rights of the parties." See also Fed. R. Civ. P. 61. The statute applies to both criminal and civil cases. Applying the nonconstitutional standard for harmless error, we are satisfied that the erroneous exclusion of the evidence did not have a substantial influence on the verdict, nor do we have grave doubt as to whether it had such an effect.

The dissent agreed that the evidentiary ruling was error but thought it harmful:

> Incredibly, the majority holds that the evidence should have been admitted for all purposes, including proof of negligence, but then finds that the error was harmless. How the majority can conclude that the plaintiffs were deprived of their legal right to show graphically both negligence and control by the act of Mr. Fairweather and then conclude that both of these deprivations singly and cumulatively are harmless is beyond me. . . . Since the [defendant] had a non-delegable duty to take reasonable care, it was essential for the jury to know if it would have been feasible for the [defendant] to do more than it did (i.e., inspect the fence) (and, under the majority view, for the jury to be told that they could consider the subsequent actions in determining negligence). . . .
>
> Since the exclusion of the evidence and the resulting impression essentially removed the question of negligence from the jury, the error affected a substantial right of the plaintiffs, and thus, was far from harmless. In fact, since the judge properly instructed the jury that, under Oklahoma law, the defendants had a non-delegable duty to keep the cattle from escaping, I am unable to discern any other basis for the jury to have found for the defendants. I would therefore vacate the judgment and remand for a new trial.

NOTES AND PROBLEMS

1. How should an appellate court decide such questions?

a. A statute, 28 U.S.C. §2111, tells appellate courts not to be trigger-happy in reversing.

b. In the absence of evidence about how the jury actually reached its decision, how does a court responsibly speculate about "what would have happened if . . . ?" An appellate judge with extensive trial court experience might have some basis for a guess; a judge without such experience is likely to be clueless.

2. Should certain kinds of errors, such as errors affecting jury deliberations, be considered intrinsically more serious than others, such as confusing jury instructions? Not all errors affecting jury deliberation are found to constitute prejudicial error.

a. In Gertz v. Bass, 59 Ill. App. 180, 208 N.E.2d 113 (1965), the appellate court reversed because a jury asked to decide whether defendant's behavior was "willful" or "wanton," had obtained from a bailiff a dictionary containing definitions of those terms that differed from the definitions in the jury instructions.

b. In Aetna Casualty & Surety Co. v. Perez, 360 S.W.2d 157 (Tex. Civ. App. 1962), the decision of the lower court was affirmed even though the bailiff had said to some of the jurors, "If you guys are just a couple of thousand dollars apart why don't you settle it?" and "What in the world is the matter with you in there; are you fighting over two or three thousand dollars?" None of the jurors discussed the comments with each other or the other jurors. It should be noted that Texas allows examination of the jurors after the trial for evidence of impropriety and that such an investigation was undertaken in *Perez*. Should that matter?

c. Extrinsic policies occasionally dictate that an error be considered reversible even though no prejudice is demonstrated. In Javis v. Board of Education, 393 Mich. 689, 227 N.W.2d 543 (1975), for example, the Michigan Supreme Court ruled that failure to give any of the Michigan Standard Jury Instructions that are (1) requested by a party, (2) relevant to the case, and (3) a correct statement of the law is presumed to be prejudicial (and therefore reversible error) even if another instruction, otherwise correct and adequate, is given.

RESPECT FOR JUDGMENTS

XII

Procedural rules serve two masters. They aim to air disputes completely and to reach an accurate and just outcome. They also seek to end disputes even if the resting condition is less than optimal. Writers sometimes loftily describe this latter goal as "finality" or "repose." Several branches of law serve the goal of finality. Statutes of limitations forbid litigation entirely if it begins too late. And, as we saw in the preceding chapter, appellate courts have only limited power to overturn trial court findings. This chapter focuses on two other doctrines that serve to bring lawsuits to an end: *claim preclusion* and *issue preclusion*.

Both doctrines are part of the broader topic of *former adjudication*—the effect of judgments on subsequent litigation. These doctrines answer a pair of related questions: What does it mean for a lawsuit to be over? What does a concluded lawsuit decide? Suppose, for instance, that Pamela sues Donald for injuries sustained in an auto accident, and the case goes to a final judgment. The loser can, of course, appeal. But can there be a second lawsuit? For example, may Pamela bring a second suit concerning the same accident, this time seeking recovery for damage to her automobile? Today, most states would say no, citing the principles of claim preclusion. Claim preclusion forbids a party from relitigating a claim that should have been raised in former litigation.

Issue preclusion comes into play when a claim is not barred but when some issue involved in that claim has been previously litigated. If Pamela and Donald had the misfortune to become involved in a second collision the week after the first, Pamela's suit against Donald for injuries sustained in the first accident would not prevent her from bringing suit concerning the second one. But she and Donald might find themselves prevented from relitigating issues decided in that first suit that are relevant to the second, such as whether at the time of the accidents either was required to wear corrective lenses while driving.

Much of this chapter will be devoted to exploring the conditions that enable a party to invoke issue or claim preclusion. You will find that in examining these questions courts sometimes use an older set of terminology to refer to these concepts. They refer to claim preclusion as res judicata and to issue preclusion as *collateral estoppel.* They also occasionally use "res judicata" to refer to the entire topic of former adjudication. The underlying ideas are identical; only the terminology varies.

Handwritten margin notes: Can't relitigate Claim that should have been raised in former lawsuit · Can't relitigate issue that has been litigated in prior suit · claim preclusion = res judicata · issue preclusion = collateral estoppel

657

A.   Claim Preclusion

Claim preclusion has several goals: efficiency, finality, and the avoidance of inconsistency. Efficiency comes most strongly into play when a party that should have raised a claim in previous litigation failed to do so. The exact point at which one claim stops and another begins is not always clear; thus this section pays close attention to the scope of a cause of action.

1.   Precluding the "Same" Claim

The standard doctrinal formulation says that claim preclusion bars the same claim from relitigation. Thus stated, the principle sounds both uncontroversial and obvious. In practice, matters become much more interesting because claim preclusion has two goals — the fostering of efficiency and the prevention of inconsistency. In pursuit of these goals doctrines of claim preclusion go a good deal further than a simple statement of the doctrine might suggest.

a.   Efficiency

Claim preclusion grows from pleading. A common law pleader could not combine different writs in a single suit. Because it seemed unfair to block a second suit if the pleader's only mistake lay in selecting the wrong writ, common law courts precluded a plaintiff only from bringing a second claim on the same writ; the plaintiff remained free to try a different writ on the same facts. This narrow scope of preclusion thus flowed from narrow joinder of claims rules at common law.

The two great pleading reforms of the past 150 years, the Field Codes in the nineteenth century and the Federal Rules in the twentieth, freed pleaders from the confines of the writs. But to the extent they thereby made pleading easier, they made claim preclusion more difficult. A pleader under the Codes or the Rules was free to combine different claims. Did she therefore *have* to do so at the risk of finding them precluded? To put the problem at its most extreme, under Rules 8 and 18, a pleader may state as many claims as she has against the opposing party: If she brings only one such claim, are all others forever precluded? No court has ever gone this far, but, short of this extreme, how broadly should preclusion sweep? In the next case the court contrasts two answers to that question.

Frier v. City of Vandalia

770 F.2d 699 (7th Cir. 1985)

EASTERBROOK, Circuit Judge.

The City of Vandalia is fairly small (the population is less than 2,500), and apparently its police have maintained informal ways. When Charles Frier parked one of his cars in a narrow street, which forced others to drive on someone else's lawn to get around Frier's car, the police left two notes at Frier's house asking him to move the car. That did not work, so an officer called a local garage, which towed the car back to the garage. The officer left a note, addressed to "Charlie," telling him where he could find the car. The officer did not issue a citation for illegal parking, however; he later testified that he wanted to make it easier for Frier to retrieve the car.

Frier balked at paying the $10 fee the garage wanted. He also balked at keeping his cars out of the street. The police had garages tow four of them in 1983 — a 1963 Ford Falcon, a 1970 Plymouth Duster, a 1971 Opal GT, and a 1971 Dodge van. Instead of paying the garages, Frier filed suits in the courts of Illinois seeking replevin. Each suit named as defendants the City of Vandalia and the garage that had towed the car.

One of the suits (which sought to replevy two cars) was dismissed voluntarily when Frier got his cars back. We do not know whether he paid for the tows and the subsequent daily storage fees or whether the garage thought it cheaper to surrender the cars than to defend the suit. The other two cases were consolidated and litigated. The police testified to the circumstances under which they had called for the tows. The court concluded that the police properly took the cars into the City's possession to remove obstructions to the alley, and it declined to issue the writ of replevin because the City had the right to remove the cars from the street. Frier then retrieved another car;[1] so far as we can tell, a garage still has the 1970 Plymouth Duster.

After losing in state court, Frier turned to federal court. His [federal] complaint maintained that the City had not offered him a hearing either before or after it took the cars and that it is the "official policy" of the City not to do so. The complaint invoked the Due Process Clause of the Fourteenth Amendment and 42 U.S.C. §1983, and it sought equitable relief in addition to $100,000 in compensatory and $100,000 in punitive damages. The district court, after reviewing the transcript of the replevin action, dismissed the complaint for failure to state a claim on which relief may be granted. (Because the judge considered the transcript he should have treated the motion to dismiss as one for summary judgment. We analyze the decision as if he had done so.) The court found that Frier had notice of each tow and knew how to get his cars back. Frier also had a full hearing in the replevin action on the propriety of the tows. Although the judicial hearing came approximately one month after the tows, the court thought the delay permissible.

A month is a long wait for a hearing when the subject is an automobile. The automobile is "property" within the meaning of the Due Process Clause, and the City therefore must furnish appropriate process. Sutton v. City of Milwaukee, 672 F.2d 644 (7th Cir. 1982), holds that a hearing is not necessary before the police tow a car but suggests that one must be furnished promptly after the tow. Sutton also suggests, in line with many other cases, that the City must establish the process and tender an opportunity for a hearing; it may not sit back and wait for the aggrieved person to file a suit.

---

1. One garage told Frier he could come and get his car anytime he wanted, without paying a fee.

The City, for its part, maintains that a few isolated tows without hearings are not the "policy" of the City and may not be imputed to it, and that anyway a month's delay in holding a hearing about seized property is permissible. . . .

A court ought not resolve a constitution[al] dispute unless that is absolutely necessary. Here it is not. Frier had his day in court in the replevin action. The City has argued that this precludes further suits. (The City raised this argument in the motion to dismiss, which is irregular but not fatally so. See Fed. R. Civ. P. 8(c).) The district court bypassed this argument because, it believed, Frier could not have asserted his constitutional arguments in a replevin action. This is only partially correct.

Frier could not have obtained punitive damages or declaratory relief in a suit limited to replevin. But he was free to join one count seeking such relief with another seeking replevin. See Welch v. Brunswick Corp., 10 Ill. App. 3d 693 (1st Dist. 1973), revd. in part on other grounds, 57 Ill. 2d 461 (1974); Hanaman v. Davis, 20 Ill. App. 2d 111 (2d Dist. 1959), both of which allow one count seeking replevin to be joined with another count seeking different relief. As we show below, the law of Illinois, which under 28 U.S.C. §1738 governs the preclusive effect to be given to the judgment in the replevin actions, see Marrese v. American Academy of Orthopaedic Surgeons, 470 U.S. 373 (1985), would bar this suit. The City therefore is entitled to prevail on the ground of claim preclusion, although the district court did not decide the case on that ground. See Massachusetts Mutual Life Insurance Co. v. Ludwig, 426 U.S. 479 (1976).

Illinois recognizes the principles of claim preclusion (also called res judicata or estoppel by judgment). Jones v. City of Alton, 757 F.2d 878, 884-85 (7th Cir. 1985) (summarizing the law of preclusion in Illinois). One suit precludes a second "where the parties and the cause of action are identical." "Causes of action are identical where the evidence necessary to sustain a second verdict would sustain the first, i.e., where the causes of action are based upon a common core of operative facts." Two suits may entail the same "cause of action" even though they present different legal theories, and the first suit "operates as an absolute bar to a subsequent action . . . 'not only as to every matter which was offered and received to sustain or defeat the claim or demand, but as to any other admissible matter which might have been offered for that purpose.'" More[over], as we pointed out in Hagee [v. City of Evanston], 729 F.2d 510, 513 [(7th Cir. 1984)], some cases in Illinois recognize preclusion when both suits arise out of the same transaction. This ground of preclusion is potentially broader than the "same evidence" ground.

The City was a defendant in each replevin action. Frier could have urged constitutional grounds as reasons for replevin.[2] He also could have joined a

---

2. At one point in the argument before the state court, Frier's lawyer invoked the constitution, saying that the towing was "the taking of a man's property without due process of law and . . . they have taken [the cars] illegally and are holding [them] illegally" (Tr. 48). This is too fleeting to amount to a formal request for a constitutional ruling, but it does show the pertinence of the constitution to the replevin action.

constitutional claim seeking punitive damages and declaratory relief to his demand for replevin, and therefore he had a full and fair opportunity to litigate (unlike Jones v. City of Alton, where procedural obstacles impeded litigation of the federal claim). The actions also involve both the same "common core of operative facts" and the same transactions. Frier argues that the City towed his cars wrongfully. Each complaint seeking replevin asserted [that] Frier owned each car and that it had not been "seized under lawful process" — in other words, that there had been no citation and no hearing at which anyone had found that the cars were illegally parked. The replevin statute requires a plaintiff to show that the property was taken without "lawful process." Ill. Rev. Stat., ch. 110, §19-104. "Process," even in its technical sense, initiates or follows a hearing. Had there been process and a hearing at which a magistrate found the cars to have been illegally parked, Frier would have had no claim for replevin no matter how strongly he contested the substantive issue. The "operative facts" in the replevin and §1983 actions therefore are the same. Frier urges that he owned the car (the property interest) and that the City did not offer him a hearing to adjudicate the legality of his parking (the absence of due process).

The replevin actions diverged from the path of this §1983 suit only because the state judge adjudicated on the merits the propriety of the seizures. Having found the seizures proper, the judge had no occasion to determine whether the City should have offered Frier an earlier hearing. But this divergence does not mean that the two legal theories require a different "core of operative facts." The courts of Illinois sometimes put the inquiry as whether the two theories of relief "allege the same conduct" by the defendant. Frier has attacked the "same conduct" — towing and detaining the cars without a determination of a parking violation — in all of his suits.

To an extent there is any doubt about this, we look (as we did in Hagee) to the purpose of doctrines of preclusion. Claim preclusion is designed to impel "parties to consolidate all closely related matters into one suit" (Hagee, 729 F.2d at 514; note omitted). This prevents the oppression of defendants by multiple cases, which may be easy to file and costly to defend. There is no assurance that a second or third case will be decided more accurately than the first and so there is no good reason to incur the costs of litigation more than once. When the facts and issues of all theories of liability are closely related, one case is enough. Here the replevin theory contained the elements that make up a due process theory, and we are therefore confident that the courts of Illinois would treat both theories as one "cause of action."

The final question is whether it makes a difference that only two of the replevin actions went to judgment, while here Frier challenges the towing of four cars. Under Illinois law the answer is no. The defendant may invoke claim preclusion when the plaintiff litigated in the first suit a subset of all available disputes between the parties. See Baird & Warner, Inc. v. Addison Industrial Park, Inc., 70 Ill. App. 3d 59 (1st Dist. 1979), which holds that a suit on three of six disputed parcels of land precludes a subsequent suit on all six. We doubt that Illinois would see difference between three lots out of six and two cars out of four.

If Frier had filed the current suit in state court, he would have lost under the doctrine of claim preclusion. Under 28 U.S.C. §1738 he therefore loses in federal court as well.

Affirmed.

SWYGERT, Senior Circuit Judge, concurring in the result.

In my view, the majority has simply applied the wrong analysis to the problem at hand. Rather than trying to squeeze a res judicata solution into a mold that does not fit, I would review the facts to determine whether Frier's procedural due process claims could withstand a summary judgment motion. Because I believe the City was entitled to summary judgment, I concur in the result.

I

In determining whether the disposition of a claim in State court precludes a subsequent suit on the same claim in federal court, the federal court must apply the State's law of res judicata. Because Illinois continues to adhere to the narrow, traditional view of claim preclusion, as opposed to the broader approach codified in the Restatement (Second) of Judgments §§24, 25 (1982), I would hold that Frier's substantive traffic law claim does not preclude this subsequent procedural due process claim. Under the more modern view of the new Restatement, all claims arising from a single "transaction" — broadly defined to include matters related in time, space, origin, and motivation — must be litigated in a single, initial lawsuit, or be barred from being raised in subsequent litigation. There was only one transaction in the case at bar: the seizure of Frier's cars. Accordingly, Frier should have raised both his substantive and procedural objections to the seizure in one initial lawsuit.

Illinois, however, has not adopted the view of the new Restatement.[1] Rather, as the majority recognizes, the Illinois courts focus on the similarities between the causes of action alleged in both suits, not on whether there is a common factual transaction. One suit precludes a second "where the parties and the cause of action are identical." Redfern v. Sullivan, 111 Ill. App. 3d 372, 444 N.E.2d 205, 208 (1983). "Causes of action are identical where the evidence necessary to sustain a second verdict would sustain the first, i.e., where the causes of action are based upon a common core of operative facts." Id. . . .

In sum, the common set of facts that must be shown to invoke Illinois' doctrine of claim preclusion is defined as those facts necessary to sustain the cause of action, not as those facts that could be conveniently litigated in one lawsuit. This focus on the elements of the causes of action and the proofs at trial — rather than on the policy advantages of trying both actions in one suit — dooms any attempt to invoke claim preclusion in the case at bar. To be sure, both actions arise from the same seizure of the same cars. Yet, both the theory of

---

1. No Illinois court has ever cited the new Restatement. The first Restatement, which follows the traditional "cause of action" approach, see Restatement of Judgments §61 (1942), has been cited several times.

recovery and focus of factual inquiry are dramatically different in each case. Frier's replevin claim was substantive in nature; to replevy property, the claimant must show his superior possessory rights. Frier's possessory rights turned on the legality of his parking. Because the trial court found that "the officer reasonably believed and had a right to believe that . . . [Frier's] vehicle obstructed the free use and passage way of that street at that time," it concluded that, therefore, Frier did not enjoy the "superior right to possession of the property" necessary to sustain a replevin action.

Frier's procedural due process claim requires an entirely different factual showing. The legality or reasonableness of the seizure is irrelevant. Because of the "risk of error inherent in the truth-finding process," an individual is entitled to certain procedural safeguards regardless of whether the deprivation of property was substantively justified. The focus of the inquiry, then, is the adequacy of procedures attending the seizure, not the seizure itself.

Due process Claim requires different factual Showing

The majority urges that Frier could have joined a separate constitutional claim to his replevin action. This precise argument was rejected in *Fountas*, 455 N.E.2d at 204. . . .

[Nor does *Hagee*, discussed by the majority, help.] *Hagee* . . . merely repudiated those appellate court cases that relied on technical differences between theories of relief or remedies to avoid invoking claim preclusion despite a substantial overlap in the operative facts necessary to sustain both actions. This court did not, and could not, repudiate Illinois' consistent emphasis on the underlying cause of action, as opposed to the underlying transaction. . . .

II

It was established at Frier's replevin trial that the City police caused various service station owners to tow four of Frier's cars and, in lieu of a traffic citation, left written notice of the reason for the towing and the whereabouts of the cars. Frier eventually recovered two of his cars. Thus, the replevin action, and this action, concern only two of the cars. Frier could have recovered one of those cars immediately by paying a $10.00 towing fee to the owner of the service station that towed the car. However, Frier was informed that any further delay in reclaiming the car would result in a $2.50 per day storage charge. Frier was free to reclaim the other car without paying any fee. I would hold that, on the basis of these uncontested facts, the City was entitled to summary judgment against Frier's procedural due process claim. . . .

[Judge Swygert analyzed the line of cases interpreting the Due Process Clause as they related to plaintiff's claim.]

I would hold, then, that notice of towing, the availability of an expedited State tort suit that can make the petitioner whole, and the ability to reclaim the towed cars immediately at a cost of $10.00 together constitute adequate postdeprivation process as long as the $10.00 fee does not present a financial hardship. This holding would not necessarily conflict with recent decisions of other courts requiring more immediate and elaborate postdeprivation process. More elaborate process may well be required in those cases because the towing practices of the various municipalities were more burdensome on the respective petitioners: Immediate reclamation required significantly more than $10.00 and the litigants had standing to represent indigents who could afford no fee. We need not reach such troublesome issues in the case at bar.

I would find, as a matter of law, no procedural due process violation under these facts. Accordingly, I concur with the majority's decision to affirm the judgment below.

NOTES AND PROBLEMS

1. Why does Frier lose?

a. Does the majority reject his constitutional claim? No – doesn't answer it

b. Does anyone assert that he actually litigated his constitutional claim in the first lawsuit?

c. If not, is it fair now to prevent him from doing so in a second action?

2. The majority and concurrence debate the difference (if any) between the Illinois definition of "claims" for purposes of preclusion and that of the Restatement (Second) of Judgments §24.

a. What is the point of that debate?

b. Notice that the doctrines of claim preclusion discussed in *Frier* do not flow from the Rules or from statute but from common law. One could imagine an amendment to Rule 8 stating that a final judgment on a claim barred the refiling of that claim or any other arising from the same transaction or occurrence. Should the Rules explicitly so state? Would such an amendment violate the Rules Enabling Act, 28 U.S.C. §2072(b), which specifies that the Rules may not "abridge, enlarge, or modify any substantive right"?

c. The Restatement (Second), which seeks to summarize the common law of claim and issue preclusion, sets forth a broad definition of "claims":

> (1) When a valid and final judgment rendered in an action extinguishes a plaintiff's claim . . . , the claim extinguished includes all rights of the plaintiff to remedies against the defendant with respect to all or any part of the transaction, or series of connected transactions, out of which the claim arose.
>
> (2) What factual grouping constitutes a "transaction," and what groupings constitute a "series," are to be determined pragmatically, giving weight to such considerations as whether the facts are related in time, space, origin, or motivation, whether they form a convenient trial unit, and whether their treatment as a unit conforms to the parties' expectations or business understanding or usage.

d. What considerations ought to determine whether a given jurisdiction adopts a transactional test or a narrower one?

e. Should it matter whether the jurisdiction uses a broad, general definition of "claim" for pleading purposes (like that set forth in Rule 8) or a narrower, more focused one? Illinois employs a variation on Code pleading:

> (a) All pleadings shall contain a plain and concise statement of the pleader's *cause of action*, counterclaim, defense or reply.

735 Ill. Con. Stat. 5/3-603 (West 2003) (emphasis supplied). Does the reference to "cause of action" focus more on the legal theory than on the underlying transaction and thus justify a narrow doctrine of preclusion?

3. The opinion identifies some of the bases of claim preclusion:

> Claim preclusion is designed to impel "parties to consolidate all closely related matters into one suit[.]" This prevents the oppression of defendants by multiple cases, which may be easy to file and costly to defend. There is no assurance that a second or third case will be decided more accurately than the first and so there is no good reason to incur the costs of litigation more than once.

Would any of these principles be violated by permitting Frier to raise his constitutional challenge to Vandalia's towing practices?

4. If the purpose of claim preclusion is to prevent inefficiency by forcing a party to bring all its closely related claims together, who is the intended beneficiary of this efficiency — the courts, the opposing party, or both?

a. If the doctrine of claim preclusion is intended to protect the courts, why can it be waived by the opposing side? See Rule 8(c).

b. If it's the other side, would most of the concerns be met by requiring the party seeking to avoid preclusion to pay all the expenses of the first lawsuit?

5. Many states and the federal court system use the transactional definition of "claim" for preclusion purposes. Both *Frier* opinions agree that, under the transactional test, Frier's second claim would have been precluded. Is this a sensible result? Assuming that plaintiff wants to challenge the city's entire procedure for towing cars, should he have to do so when he tried to retrieve his car from the garage? Would it make as much sense to permit him to get his car back and then bring a second, broad-based constitutional challenge to the underlying process?

6. The standard answer to the questions posed in the preceding Note is that forcing a plaintiff to combine all the claims arising out of a transaction does not force the court to try all those claims in a single suit. Rule 42(b) (or an equivalent state rule) gives the trial court authority to sever parts of a complaint for trial. One can imagine a court's wishing to separate the question whether Frier could have his car back from the question whether the city's towing process was unconstitutional. If that is so, however, it casts some doubt on whether the two claims should be treated as one for preclusion purposes. Notice that Restatement (Second) of Judgments §24(b) specifies that "whether [the claims] form a convenient trial unit" is one of the factors to be considered in deciding whether they ought to be precluded.

7. When courts conclude that a second claim ought to be precluded under the applicable test for preclusion, they often describe the precluded plaintiff as trying to split her claim between two lawsuits. Most "splitting" cases are analyzed as involving (a) different theories of recovery, (b) arithmetical splitting, or (c) splitting of relief.

a. Common examples of separate theories are attempts to recover in contract in one action and in quasi-contract in a second, or in conversion in the first action and restitution in the second. For example, see Ley v. Boron Oil Co., 454 F. Supp. 448 (W.D. Pa. 1978) (first action determined that defendant's inquiries about plaintiff did not violate the Fair Credit Reporting Act; second action based on invasion of privacy barred by claim preclusion). Is *Frier* an example of a split theory? Most would answer no because, unlike the standard instances of split theories, Frier sought different remedies in his two claims: replevin to get the cars back, then §1983 for damages.

b. Arithmetical splitting occurs when a plaintiff tries to recover for separate damages from the same incident in separate actions. Clearly, if a plaintiff is injured in an accident, he cannot seek damages for a broken hand in one action and a broken foot in another. Similarly, most courts would not permit a plaintiff to sue for personal injuries and property damage in separate actions. See Rush v. City of Maple Heights in Chapter I. In the case of a series of obligations, such as installment payments on a debt or rent, a plaintiff is required to sue for all installments already due at the time of bringing the action. If the contract has a so-called acceleration clause that makes all installments due if one or two are missed, plaintiff must sue for all installments. This rule does not apply if the acceleration is optional and the option has not been exercised; nor does it apply if the installment obligations are represented by separate notes. Why are separate notes given this treatment?

c. Splitting of relief occurs when a plaintiff asserts one remedy in one action and seeks an alternative or supplemental remedy in a second action. *Frier* has elements of such splitting: There the plaintiff sought one remedy (replevy of his cars) in the first suit and then, deploying constitutional theories in a second suit, sought damages for the same acts of allegedly unlawful towing. For example, a plaintiff who lost a contract action could not later bring an action to reform the same contract. Gatzemeyer v. Vogel, 589 F.2d 360 (8th Cir. 1978). Similarly, a plaintiff who sues to enjoin State University from charging him out-of-state tuition would not be allowed to sue again to recover past overcharges.

8. Having grasped the counterintuitive idea that unlitigated claims can be precluded, do not overstate the principle. Before a claim can be precluded by a lawsuit, it must *be* a claim at the time of that suit. The rule that installments not yet due need not be joined (see Note 7(b)) thus illustrates the broader principle that any claims that could not be brought in an action will not be deemed to be merged into it. The principle in question is not limited to issues of a claim's ripeness; they may also involve the first tribunal's competency. For example, claims for equitable relief would not be precluded as a result of a suit in a court that had no power to grant equitable relief.

9. The transactional definition of claims does not extend to claims by different parties but arising from the same episode. For example, if *H* and *W* were injured when a car they were riding in was hit by *T*'s truck, each can sue *T* separately. The Supreme Court of New Hampshire has suggested that a compulsory joinder of parties rule might be desirable in certain cases. But in Reid v. Spadone Machine Co., 119 N.H. 198, 400 A.2d 54 (1979), the court, noting that no such compulsory joinder rule exists, allowed a wife to sue for loss of consortium after her husband had won a claim for an employment-related injury. For another example, see Illinois Central Gulf R. v. Parks, infra, page 688. Would such a rule create problems that do not exist for compulsory joinder of claims?

10. *Frier* silently assumes that in trying to decide the preclusive effect of a judgment one should look to the court rendering that judgment.

a. For the *Frier* court the question is thus whether the courts of Illinois, which rendered the first judgment in the preclusion action, would bar the civil rights claim. That is almost always the right analysis. So if Frier had first brought his civil rights claim in federal court, then brought a state law replevin action, the Illinois state court would have faced the question of what preclusive effect a federal court would assign to its judgment in the first case. (As a quick review, explain what the answer to that question is.)

b. The United States Supreme Court has said the matter is more complicated than that in federal diversity cases.

c. In Semtek Intl. Inc. v. Lockheed Martin Corp., 531 U.S. 497 (2001), supra 245, the Court held that the preclusive effect of a federal judgment rendered in a diversity action should be the same that would be attached to that judgment if a *state* court in the forum state had rendered it. Thus a Maryland court should give to a federal court judgment rendered in California (in a diversity action), the same effect as would be accorded to a California state court rendering the same judgment. According to the unanimous opinion of the Court, that result flows neither from statute nor the Constitution but from the federal common law of former adjudication.

d. That common law, however, said *Semtek*, has some flexibility: "This federal reference to state law will not obtain, of course, in situations in which the state law is incompatible with federal interests. If, for example, state law did not accord preclusive effect to dismissals for willful violations of discover orders, federal courts' interest in the integrity of their own processes might justify a contrary federal rule."

e. As you will see when we consider the meaning of "on the merits," infra page 680, *Semtek* introduces some wrinkles when state and federal preclusion law differ in a diversity case. For now, it is enough to note the general rule — the preclusion law of court rendering the judgment applies — and the exception — in a diversity action the scope of the judgment, whether rendered by a state or a federal court, should be measured as if the state court had rendered it.

b. Consistency — The Logical Implications of the Former Judgment

Claim preclusion encourages parties to bring claims in efficiently large packages — by threatening them with preclusion if they do not. The same doctrine also aspires to prevent at least the most egregious forms of inconsistency in successive judgments.

Martino v. McDonald's System, Inc.

598 F.2d 1079 (7th Cir.), cert. denied, 444 U.S. 966 (1979)

PELL, J.

The plaintiffs, Louis J. Martino and McDonald's Drive-In of Ottumwa, Iowa, Inc. (McDonald's Ottumwa) appeal from the district court's entry of summary judgment against them on one count of their two count antitrust complaint against the defendants, McDonald's System, Inc. (McDonald's System) and Franchise Realty Interstate Corporation (FRIC). The only issue before this court is whether a 1973 consent judgment against Martino precludes the cause of action set forth in Count I of the present complaint. The district court held that both res judicata and the compulsory counterclaim rule of Fed. R. Civ. P. 13(a) barred the plaintiffs from suing on their first cause of action.

In 1962 the plaintiff Louis Martino and three brothers not involved in this action entered into a franchise and lease agreement with the defendants.[1] Martino and his brothers then organized McDonald's Ottumwa, the corporate plaintiff here, to operate the business. The contract to which Martino and the defendants were parties provided that neither Martino nor a member of his immediate family would acquire a financial interest in a competing self-service food business without the written consent of McDonald's System and FRIC. In 1968 Martino's son purchased a Burger Chef franchise in Pittsburg, Kansas. Martino financed this transaction.

On the basis of this transaction FRIC and McDonald's System brought a federal diversity action in Iowa against Martino and his three brothers, charging that Martino had violated the contract provision restricting acquisitions described above. This lawsuit, commenced in 1972, ended in 1973 with a consent judgment to which the district court appended findings of fact and conclusions of law. The court order also provided that the parties had entered an agreement for the sale of McDonald's. . . .

Martino and McDonald's Ottumwa brought this action in 1975. Count I of their complaint alleges that the enforcement of the restriction on acquisition in the franchise and lease agreements violated Section 1 of the Sherman Act, 15 U.S.C. §1. As a basis for damages, Martino claims profits he would have earned as owner of the McDonald's franchise. Both plaintiffs claim damages for having had to sell the franchise, allegedly below its market value.

The defendants have presented two theories for barring Count I of the plaintiffs' antitrust complaint. The first theory is based on the preclusive effect of Fed. R. Civ. P. 13(a), applying to compulsory counterclaims. The second theory is based on the principle of res judicata. We shall now consider the merits of each theory.

The defendants argue that the district court correctly held that Count I is precluded by Fed. R. Civ. P. 13(a).[2] Claims coming within the definition of "compulsory counterclaim" are lost if not raised at the proper time. According to the defendants, Rule 13(a) required Martino to raise this antitrust challenge to

---

1. The defendant McDonald's System, Inc. licensed the McDonald's franchise, and the defendant FRIC leased the property for the franchise.

2. Rule 13(a) provides in pertinent part:

> A pleading shall state as a counterclaim any claim which at the time of serving the pleading the pleader has against any opposing party, if it arises out of the transaction or occurrence that is the subject matter of the opposing party's claim and does not require for its adjudication the presence of third parties of whom the court cannot acquire jurisdiction.

the contract provision in the earlier suit based on the same provision. If Rule 13(a) were applicable to these facts, the defendants' argument might have merit. Rule 13(a), however, by its own terms does not apply unless there has been some form of pleading.

The rule expressly says that "a *pleading* shall state as a counterclaim any claim which at the time of serving the *pleading* the *pleader* has against any opposing party. . . ." (Emphasis added.) In the prior Iowa action at issue here, Martino filed no pleading as the word is defined in Fed. R. Civ. P. 7(a).[4] For this reason, Martino argues that we must not apply Rule 13(a) to the claim stated in Count I of his complaint. We agree.

Rule 13(a) is in some ways a harsh rule. It forces parties to raise certain claims at the time and place chosen by their opponents, or to lose them. The rule, however, is the result of a balancing between competing interests. The convenience of the party with a compulsory counterclaim is sacrificed in the interest of judicial economy. We do not believe that the drafters of Rule 13 chose the term "pleading" unadvisedly. It no doubt marks, although somewhat arbitrarily, a point at which the judicial burden of the earlier lawsuit outweighs the opposing party's interest in bringing an action when and where it is most convenient. The earlier action between these parties was terminated by a consent judgment before the answer was filed. . . .

Although Rule 13(a) does not dispose of Martino's antitrust claim, longstanding principles of res judicata establish a narrowly defined class of "common law compulsory counterclaims." See Restatement (Second) of Judgments §56.1(2)(b), Reporter's Note on Comment f (Tent. Draft No. 1, 1973). We hold that the antitrust claim set forth in Count I of Martino's complaint falls within this narrow class of claims and that the res judicata effect of the earlier consent judgment is a bar to raising it now.

The principle of res judicata at issue here treats a judgment on the merits as an absolute bar to relitigation between the parties and those in privity with them of every matter offered and received to sustain or defeat the claim or demand and to every matter which might have been received for that purpose.

The conclusion of the earlier contract lawsuit with a consent judgment does not prevent the earlier judgment from having a res judicata effect. . . . Although the earlier judgment at issue here was entered pursuant to the agreement of the parties, it was accompanied by judicial findings of fact and conclusions of law that go to the merits of the controversy. The court described Martino's actions as "a material breach of the agreements sufficient to justify termination." The trial "court is not properly a recorder of contracts, but is an organ of government constituted to make judicial decisions and when it has rendered a consent judgment it has made an adjudication." 1B Moore's Federal Practice ¶0.409[5] at 1030 (2d ed. 1974).

Having determined that the prior consent judgment is an adjudication on the merits, we conclude that this judgment precludes Count I of the antitrust action.

4. Rule 7(a) defines the following as pleadings: an answer, a reply to a counterclaim, an answer to a cross-claim, a third party complaint, and a third party answer.

As a predicate for our discussion of the res judicata effect of the prior judgment we turn to the basis of Martino's present antitrust claim.

The gravamen of Count I of Martino's antitrust complaint is the 1973 lawsuit. In paragraph 12 of Count I, the complaint describes the 1973 lawsuit seeking termination of the franchise. Paragraph 15 alleges that

> By enforcing the provisions of the franchise agreement and the sub-lease that prohibited the acquisition of any financial interest in a non-McDonald's self service food and beverage establishment against plaintiffs, defendants discouraged competition and unreasonably restrained trade and commerce in violation of Section 1 of the Sherman Act (15 U.S.C. §1).

Paragraph 16 concludes Count I, alleging that Martino lost profits he would have earned as owner of the McDonald's franchise and that Martino was forced to sell the franchise at below its market value.

It is impossible to interpret this count as anything but a direct challenge to the outcome of the 1973 lawsuit. The 1973 lawsuit concluded that termination was justified. The plaintiff now contends that termination was not justified, because the federal antitrust laws forbade it. If Martino's antitrust theory had merit, it would have been a defense in 1973, changing the outcome of the litigation.

The well-settled rule for the purpose of determining the res judicata effect of a judgment is that a "cause of action" comprises defenses, such as the alleged antitrust violation here, that were or might have been raised. As the Supreme Court said long ago:

> [A judgment on the merits] is a finality as to the claim or demand in controversy, concluding parties, and those in privity with them, not only as to every matter which was offered and received to sustain or defeat the claim or demand, but as to any other admissible matter which might have been offered for that purpose. Thus, for example, a judgment rendered on a promissory note is conclusive as to the validity of the instrument and the amount due upon it, although it be subsequently alleged that perfect defenses actually existed, of which no proof was offered, such as forgery, want of consideration, or payment. If such defenses were not presented in the action, and established by competent evidence, *the subsequent allegation of their existence is of no consequence*

Cromwell v. County of Sac, 94 U.S. 351, 352 (1876) (emphasis added).

Because the alleged antitrust violation constitutes a separate ground for recovery as well as a defense to the suit to terminate the franchise, however, Martino argues that Count I of this action constitutes a different "cause of action" for the purpose of res judicata and that the prior judgment does not preclude relitigation of the defendants' termination rights under the antitrust laws. For cases like this one, to which Rule 13(a) is inapplicable, Martino's argument correctly states the general rule. When facts form the basis of both a defense and a counterclaim, the defendant's failure to allege these facts as a defense or a counterclaim "does not preclude him from relying on those facts in an action subsequently brought by him against the plaintiff." Restatement (Second) of Judgments §56.1(1), Comment b (Tent. Draft No. 1, 1973). The logic of this rule in circumstances not subject to Rule 13(a) is manifest. Should the earlier litigation end in its very first stage, no great burden on the courts results from permitting a counterclaim to be raised at a more convenient time and place. Notions of judicial economy give way to fairness. The defendant in the earlier action has his day in court when and where he sees fit.

The rule is not absolute, however. Both precedent and policy require that res judicata bar a counterclaim when its prosecution would nullify rights established by the prior action. Judicial economy is not the only basis for the doctrine of res judicata. Res judicata also preserves the integrity of judgments and protects those who rely on them. McDonald's System and FRIC have terminated and repurchased Martino's franchise in reliance on the trial court's 1973 judgment telling them they were justified in doing so. Now Martino seeks to impose significant financial liability on the defendants for these actions. We cannot hold that the counterclaim exception to the res judicata rule, based merely on notions of convenience, permits the plaintiff here to wage this direct attack on the rights established by the prior judgment. . . .

. . . Concluding that Martino's claim set forth in Count I of his complaint is a direct attack on the termination rights established in the earlier judgment, we hold that Martino is barred from raising that claim. . . .

Accordingly, the judgment of the district court is affirmed.

NOTES AND PROBLEMS

1. Martino asserted that the contractual provision barring his relatives from owning competing franchises violated the U.S. antitrust laws.

a. Did any court ever rule on the merits of that contention?

b. If not, why was the claim barred?

2. *Martino* analyzes two problems: the operation of Rule 13(a) and the operation of what the opinion calls the "common law compulsory counterclaim."

a. First work through the analysis of Rule 13(a). If Rule 13(a) applied to this case, why would it have barred the second claim?

b. Why didn't Rule 13(a) apply?

3. If Rule 13(a) does not apply, why is the second claim barred?

a. The *Martino* opinion refers to "a narrowly defined class of common law 'compulsory counterclaims.'" It may be helpful to ignore this awkward phrase and focus instead on the broader question: Why does the court think that the integrity of the judicial system requires it to bar Martino's second action?

b. Martino in the second lawsuit contended that the "one-franchise" clause in the McDonald's contract violated the federal antitrust laws. That argument could have been used a defense to McDonald's original action, and as a counterclaim: If the clause was unlawful, McDonald's could not force Martino to sell the second franchise. Martino didn't assert that defense, perhaps because his lawyer at the time didn't think of it. Now he wants to use the antitrust argument, not as a defense to the first action, but as the basis of an independent claim. Why does the court forbid him from doing so?

4. As explored in Chapter VIII, consent judgments are a common way of implementing settlement agreements when the terms of settlement require parties to do or refrain from doing something in the future.

a. Embodying the agreement in a consent judgment enables the parties to get quick enforcement of their agreement.

b. Such consent judgments sometimes recite that the agreement is without prejudice to the parties' other legal rights, but one must choose language with care. In Coker v. Jay Hambridge Art Foundation, 144 Ga. App. 660, 242 S.E.2d 323 (1978), the defendant foundation had sought in a previous action to enjoin the present plaintiffs from occupying a cottage on the defendant's property. The previous case was settled with an agreement that an injunction would issue after one month. The agreement further recited that "nothing herein contained shall preclude either party from pursuing against the other any legal remedy the respective parties hereto may have, if any." In the cited action plaintiffs sued the defendant foundation on their employment contract. It was admitted that the claim would have been compulsory but for the language just quoted. The Georgia Court of Appeals held the second action was barred and upheld the trial court's interpretation of the language as allowing the present plaintiffs to have asserted their contract claim as a counterclaim in the original suit but not as a claim in a separate action. Should the intent of the parties control? If so, is it likely that the parties would actually intend, without saying, that the employment issue be raised in the first action but not in a second?

2.   Between the "Same" Parties

Most commonly, claim preclusion will operate only between those who were the parties to both the first and second lawsuits; by contrast, different parties possess different claims for preclusion purposes, even when those claims arise out of the same transaction. Thus in Rush v. City of Maple Heights, supra page 46, if Mr. and Mrs. Rush are both injured in a motorcycle accident caused by the City's negligence, Mr. Rush not barred from bringing a suit even though Mrs. Rush has previously sued the City for her injuries. The proposition that claim preclusion operates only between the same parties has, however, several exceptions. Imagine, for example, that the owner of Suburbanacre sues Neighbor for trespass, and the court rules that Neighbor enjoys a permanent easement over Owner's land. If Owner sells Suburbanacre to Buyer, Buyer will be bound by the judgment, even though he was not a party to the action. In buying the land, he "buys" the result of litigation defining the nature of Owner's rights. Courts describe Buyer has being bound because he is "in privity" with Owner, a phrase that makes sense given the transaction between Owner and Buyer. Courts sometimes go even further than this: They sometimes note that it is possible for someone not formally named as a party to be so closely connected to a suit that it is appropriate to treat her as if she were named. When they do so, they use the same phrase, "in privity," to describe the party bound by the first suit. That term is harmless as long as one understands that it merely expresses the conclusion that the person whose name was not on the caption of the first case should nevertheless be bound. When that should happen is the issue in the next case.

Searle Brothers v. Searle

588 P.2d 689 (Utah 1978)

[Edlean Searle sued Woodey Searle for a divorce. In that case, the court determined that a piece of property known as the Slaugh House, which was recorded in Woodey's name, was part of the marital property; Woodey argued that he had a one-half interest in the property and that the other half was owned by a partnership with his sons as partners. The court awarded the entire property to Edlean to "even out" the distribution of marital property.

This action was brought against Edlean by the partnership (Searle Bros.), which claimed an undivided one-half interest in Slaugh House. It was alleged that Slaugh House had been paid for with partnership funds. The trial court held that claim and issue preclusion barred this action.]

ELLETT, C.J.:

Appellants [the partnership] have appealed this judgment, claiming that the trial court erred in that the appellants were not parties to the divorce action and could not be bound by the decree entered therein.

In general, a divorce decree, like other final judgments, is conclusive as to parties and their privies and operates as a bar to any subsequent action. In order for res judicata to apply, both suits must involve the same parties or their privies and also the same cause of action; and this precludes the relitigation of all issues that could have been litigated as well as those that were, in fact, litigated in the prior action. If the subsequent suit involves different parties, those parties cannot be bound by the prior judgment.

Collateral estoppel, on the other hand, arises from a different cause of action and prevents parties or their privies from relitigating facts and issues in the second suit that were fully litigated in the first suit. This means that the plea of collateral estoppel can be asserted only against a party in the subsequent suit who was also a party or in privity with a party in the prior suit.

In Bernhard v. Bank of America Natl. Trust & Savings Assoc. the California Supreme Court considered the question of the applicability of res judicata as a basis for applying the collateral estoppel doctrine and identified the following three tests as being determinative:

1. Was the issue decided in the prior adjudication identical with the one presented in the action in question?
2. Was there a final judgment on the merits?
3. Was the party against whom the plea is asserted a party or in privity with a party to the prior adjudication?

In a subsequent opinion, the California Supreme Court recognized the necessity for a fourth test: "Was the issue in the first case competently, fully, and fairly litigated?" These four tests have been adopted by the majority of jurisdictions as the correct standard to apply. As to the second test above, there is no dispute that the divorce decree rendered in the former suit was a final judgment on the merits. Points One and Four will be discussed infra. Under the third test, it is clear that the appellants in this action were not parties to the first action; hence, the only way they can be barred or estopped from pursuing the second suit is if they were "in privity" with the parties to the divorce action.

The legal definition of a person in privity with another, is a person so identified in interest with another that he represents the same legal right. This includes a mutual or successive relationship to rights in property. Our Court has said that as applied to judgments or decrees of court, privity means "one whose interest has been legally represented at the time."

In the case before us, appellants' interest was neither mutual nor successive. They claim no part of the interest owned by Woodey B. Searle, but assert their own, independent and separate partnership interest in 50 percent of the property involved. The rights are similar but not identical. The property interest arose before the commencement of the first action, not subsequent thereto, so that appellants cannot be regarded as in privity and subject to the judgment rendered therein. Furthermore, under U.C.A. [Utah Code Ann.], 1953, as amended, 48-1-22(1), partners are co-owners of specific partnership property which is directly opposite to successive interests.

The first and fourth tests previously outlined also do not permit the application of collateral estoppel in this case. The partnership interest was not legally represented in the prior divorce suit. Woodey B. Searle, the defendant in the prior action, was acting in his individual capacity as the husband of the plaintiff and was not acting in a representative capacity for the partnership. Respondent urges that Woodey B. Searle was acting as *agent* for the partnership; hence, the partnership is bound by his action or inaction in the prior litigation. However, the general rule is that agents and principals do not have any mutual or successive relationship to rights of property and are not, as a consequence thereof, in privity with each other. Therefore, the principal is not bound by any judgment obtained against an agent, unless the principal became a party or privy thereto by actually and openly defending the action.

The right to intervene as a party in the prior suit does not bind the party in the subsequent suit where he failed to so intervene. . . .

The foregoing rule has been adopted by this Court.[13]

Collateral estoppel is not available to defeat appellants' claim since the partners were not made parties to the first suit and there is not sufficient evidence in the record to show that the interest of the partnership in the "Slaugh House" was ever litigated. The standard rule was reiterated by this Court earlier this year in

13. [C]f. also Rule 19(b), Utah Rules of Civil Procedure which provides that persons who ought to be made parties but who are nonetheless outside the jurisdiction of the court, are not affected by any judgment rendered therein.

Ruffinengo v. Miller when we said: "Collateral estoppel is not a defense against a litigant who was not a party to the action and judgment claimed to have created an estoppel." . . .

Appellants cannot be bound by the decree entered in the previous suit nor are they estopped from litigating their own claim against the property in a subsequent suit since they were not parties or privies in the first action, and the issue raised in the second action was never litigated in the prior proceeding. The trial court erred in holding that the doctrines of res judicata and collateral estoppel barred the appellants from pursuing their suit. In making this ruling, we do not express an opinion as to whether or not the property in question was an asset of the partnership.

The judgment is reversed and remanded for trial. Costs are awarded to appellants. WILKINS and HALL, JJ., concur.

CROCKETT, J. (dissenting):

I am unable to agree with the main opinion that the trial court erred when it held that the doctrine of collateral estoppel barred the plaintiffs. It is my judgment that the ruling was in conformity with principles of equity and justice.

It is to be conceded that the judgment in the divorce action would not normally bar the plaintiffs' action here because they were not parties thereto. However, upon a survey of the total circumstances I think the trial court was justified in its ruling. The main opinion correctly indicates that the doctrine of collateral estoppel is applicable when it is shown that: (1) the prior judgment is on the same issue and the same facts; (2) the issue thus litigated was essential to support the prior judgment; and (3) that it was between parties who were the same, or in privity with them. . . .

The more critical question is to whether these plaintiffs, the sons of the parties to the divorce action, were sufficiently involved and interested therein that they should properly be regarded as parties in privity thereto.

It appears that this matter was submitted to the trial court on the basis of the testimony given in the divorce action. The court's order recited that "The transcript of testimony of the previous divorce action between the plaintiff's parents was referred to" and that "after full consideration . . . the court further finds that the doctrine of collateral estoppel . . . is a bar to plaintiff's claim." It is incontestably plain that the members of the family, including the plaintiffs herein, were actively involved in that suit, which in turn involved whatever interest any of them had in the family assets. Further, they were fully aware of the adverse claims being asserted to the Slaugh House which is the subject of this suit. Two of the sons, Randy and Rhett, were called to testify on behalf of their father in that trial. . . .

This is a situation where the plaintiffs are seeking the aid of equity to assert ownership in property which stood of record only in their father's name. Even under the facts as contended by them, he was the managing partner of the claimed partnership, who had control of the property in dispute and the income therefrom; and he thus should be regarded as representing and protecting whatever interests they and the claimed partnership had therein. Further, plaintiffs themselves were fully aware of the disputation concerning the ownership of this property. They actively participated in that lawsuit, but asserted no claim for themselves. Instead of doing so, they stood by until the determination was made adverse to their father's (and their own) interests. Such claim as they have in contesting the record title to the property is based solely upon supposed oral declarations made within the family, and self-serving declarations at that.

The purpose of the doctrine of collateral estoppel is to protect a party from being subjected to harassment by being compelled to litigate the same controversy more than once. This case impresses me as being a very good example of a situation where the trial court was justified in applying that doctrine and, consistent therewith, concluding that in equity and good conscience the plaintiffs should now be estopped from seeking the relief they asked against their mother.

For the reasons stated above I would affirm the dismissal of the case.

MUGHAN, J., concurs in the views expressed in the dissenting opinion of CROCKETT, J.

NOTES AND PROBLEMS

1. The majority opinion speaks both in terms of res judicata (claim preclusion) and collateral estoppel (issue preclusion). One can make an argument for both labels. On the one hand, claim preclusion requires an identity of causes of action, and different parties are generally thought to have different causes of action. Thus one might conclude that claim preclusion is not the question and that issue preclusion must be. On the other hand, if the parties to the present litigation were in fact in privity with those to the former litigation, one can think of them as legally identical, eliminating the objection to the claim preclusion label.

As far as privity is concerned, the label doesn't matter. Thus the following Notes freely mix cases referring to claim preclusion and issue preclusion. A detailed consideration of issue preclusion, which comes later in the chapter, should not be necessary to understand the cases.

2. We do not ordinarily preclude witnesses from bringing claims similar to those in the case in which they testified. For example, if two cars collide and Passenger testifies when Driver One sues Driver Two, Passenger remains free to bring her own lawsuit.

a. The Searle brothers were asserting that they were, in effect, just like Passenger—mere witnesses in the first lawsuit who should not be barred from bringing a suit on their own behalf. What does that characterization leave out?

b. Can the brothers make convincing arguments that they did not have an opportunity to litigate fully the question of ownership in the first action? As nonparties, could they have appealed the first judgment?

3. The case holds that Randy and Rhett can sue their mother. If the outcome of that suit matches the prior one—ruling that Slaugh House was Woodey's sole property—there is no problem except the added expense to Edlean from having to litigate twice.

a. Suppose, however, that the second court sides with the sons. Edlean, who now has less property than the first court awarded her, seeks to reopen the marital property decree to have Woodey turn over assets matching the half interest in Slaugh House of which she has now been deprived. In this action Woodey can successfully argue that he is not bound by the judgment in the litigation between Edlean and the two sons. Explain why.

b. Now suppose that Edlean's lawyer had seen this train wreck of litigation approaching and realized that what was needed was a proceeding in which all four family members were parties. That can't be done in a divorce action; however interested children may be in such litigation, they are not parties. Can you construct a lawsuit to which all four would be parties — a suit settling the ownership of the property — whose results could then be used in the marital property litigation?

4. *Searle* stands for the proposition that a strong legal relationship is required to bind someone to a judgment in a case to which he was not a party. The Supreme Court has reminded us that this proposition has a constitutional dimension. Richards v. Jefferson County, 517 U.S. 793 (1996), arose from an Alabama county's imposition of an "occupation tax" to finance construction of a new civic center. Several lawsuits challenging the legality of the tax were filed. The first of these, Bedingfield v. Jefferson County, 520 So. 2d 1270 (Ala. 1988), went to the Alabama Supreme Court, which upheld the tax. When Richards filed a second action, raising federal law challenges to the tax, the Alabama Supreme Court held "that the federal claims as well as the state claims were barred by the adjudication in *Bedingfield* . . . [because a] judgment is generally 'res judicata not only as to all matters litigated and decided by it, but as to all relevant issues which could have been but were not raised and litigated in the suit,'" quoting Jefferson County v. Richards, 662 So. 2d 1127 (Ala. 1995).

a. As a quick review, explain why the Alabama Supreme Court was on solid ground in this part of its ruling. Which case in this chapter is most squarely on point?

b. Even though the Alabama Court was entirely conventional in its statement of claim preclusion doctrine, the U.S. Supreme Court reversed. It did so because Alabama had applied claim preclusion not to the original parties in the suit but to new parties. The Alabama Supreme Court had applied claim preclusion to new plaintiffs on the grounds that there was "substantial identity of the parties" to the first and second lawsuits — *Bedingfield* and *Richards*.

> State courts are generally free to develop their own rules for protecting against the relitigation of common issues or the piecemeal resolution of disputes. We have long held, however, that extreme applications of the doctrine of res judicata may be inconsistent with a federal right that is "fundamental in character." . . .
>
> The limits on a state court's power to develop estoppel rules reflect the general consensus "'in Anglo-American jurisprudence that one is not bound by a judgment in personam in a litigation in which he is not designated as a party or to which he has not been made a party by service of process.' Hansberry v. Lee, [infra page 807]. . . . This rule is part of our 'deep-rooted historic tradition that everyone should have his own day in court.'" Martin v. Wilks, [infra page 779]. . . .
>
> Of course, these principles do not always require one to have been a party to a judgment in order to be bound by it. Most notably, there is an exception when it

can be said that there is "privity" between a party to the second case and a party who is bound by an earlier judgment. For example, a judgment that is binding on a guardian or trustee may also bind the ward or the beneficiaries of a trust. Moreover . . . the term "privity" is now used to describe various relationships between litigants that would not have come within the traditional definition of that term. See generally Restatement (Second) of Judgments, ch. 4 (1980). . . .

We begin by noting that the parties to the *Bedingfield* case failed to provide petitioners with any notice that a suit was pending which would conclusively resolve their legal rights. That failure is troubling because, as we explained in Mullane v. Central Hanover Bank & Trust Co. [supra page 146], the right to be heard ensured by the guarantee of due process "has little reality or worth unless one is informed that the matter is pending and can choose for himself whether to appear or default, acquiesce or contest." . . .

Nevertheless, respondents ask us to excuse the lack of notice on the ground that petitioners, as the Alabama Supreme Court concluded, were adequately represented in *Bedingfield*. . . .

. . . [O]ur opinion in *Hansberry* . . . explained that a prior proceeding, to have binding effect on absent parties, would at least have to be "so devised and applied as to insure that those present are of the same class as those absent and that the litigation is so conducted as to insure the full and fair consideration of the common issue." It is plain that the *Bedingfield* action . . . does not fit such a description. . . .

. . . [T]here is no reason to suppose that the *Bedingfield* court took care to protect the interests of petitioners in the manner suggested in *Hansberry*. Nor is there any reason to suppose that the individual taxpayers in *Bedingfield* understood their suit to be on behalf of absent county taxpayers. Thus, to contend that the plaintiffs in *Bedingfield* somehow represented petitioners, let alone represented them in a constitutionally adequate manner, would be "to attribute to them a power that it cannot be said that they had assumed to exercise." *Hansberry* . . . .

Of course, we are aware that governmental and private entities have substantial interests in the prompt and determinative resolution of challenges to important legislation. We do not agree with the Alabama Supreme Court, however, that, given the amount of money at stake, respondents were entitled to rely on the assumption that the *Bedingfield* action "authoritatively established" the constitutionality of the tax. A state court's freedom to rely on prior precedent in rejecting a litigant's claims does not afford it similar freedom to bind a litigant to a prior judgment to which he was not a party. That general rule clearly applies when a taxpayer seeks a hearing to prevent the State from subjecting him to a levy in violation of the Federal Constitution.

Id. at 797-805.

c. First focus on the implication of the holding in *Richards*. At a minimum it means that Randy and Rhett Searle, had the Utah Supreme Court not decided in their favor, could have appealed to the U.S. Supreme Court on due process grounds (assuming, of course, they had not waived that contention by failing to raise it below). *Richards* does not, of course, hold that the Searle brothers would have prevailed on such an appeal. They had notice of the prior suit, and the argument that their father had represented them was much stronger than for the litigants in *Richards*. The difficult question is where the line between constitutional and unconstitutional representation lies.

5. As *Richards* notes, courts regularly bind nonparties to judgments in a number of circumstances. Three broadly defined situations result in binding a nonparty to the results of a lawsuit. Explain whether and why each of these passes the test of due process.

a. *Substantive legal relationships.* Successive owners of property supply a common example. Alice owns Blackacre. During her ownership a lawsuit between her and Ben establishes that Ben has a prescriptive easement in Blackacre. Ben records that judgment on the title of Blackacre. When Caroline buys Blackacre, she takes subject to the easement. Restatement (Second) of Judgments §44.

Other such substantive relationships can lead to similar results. In Albright v. R.J. Reynolds Tobacco Co., 463 F. Supp. 1220 (W.D. Pa. 1979), the court held that an action for injuries (brought by a person who later died) was the same claim as a wrongful death action brought by the person's survivors. The court further decided that the administrator of the decedent's estate was in privity with the decedent, so that the administrator's wrongful death action was barred by the decedent's previous loss of an action against the same defendant for the same acts causing injury. Other such substantive relationships include beneficiary and trustee and heirs and executors of estates. By contrast, in Arsenault v. Carrier, 390 A.2d 1048 (Me. 1978), a child was allowed to sue his father for support through his mother as "next friend" even though the mother had previously settled an action against the father. The rights of the mother and child for support were held to be distinct.

Co-ownership, joint obligation, vicarious liability (like that of an employer for the acts of an employee), and indemnification present some special problems. But the principles are the same as with successive owners of property: *If the substantive law of the relationship treats A as a substitute for B, B will be bound by the results of a lawsuit in which A participated.* Thus, in Jones v. Bradley, 366 So. 2d 1266 (Fla. Dist. Ct. App. 1979), an insurance company was barred from suing an alleged tortfeasor on a subrogation theory after the insured, to whom the company was subrogated, had previously lost an action against the tortfeasor.

b. *Express agreement to be bound by a decision to which one is not a party.* Ann and Ben, both passengers in a car, are injured in a collision with a vehicle driven by Charles, against whom they bring separate lawsuits. In return for Charles's agreement not to contest the extent of her injuries, Ann agrees to be bound by the court's determination of Charles's liability in the suit brought by Ben. Restatement (Second) of Judgments §40.

c. *Instances of "procedural representation."* In contrast to the previous categories, here the binding effect is the result not of the substantive law or agreement, but of something that happens in the lawsuit itself. Examples include guardians ad litem appointed by the court to represent an incompetent or minor, class actions (considered at length in the next chapter), and an ephemeral category sometimes called "virtual representation." Classically, courts of equity used virtual representation to determine future or contingent interests in property. Suppose many contingent beneficiaries of a trust, all with identical interests. It may be impossible to locate or identify all of them. If a sufficient number can be identified and appear in the suit to determine their interests, the others will be bound because they are "virtually represented." In re Estate of Lange, 75 N.J. 464, 383 A.2d 1130 (1978) (potential takers from an estate who could not be identified and who might not even have been born at the time of litigation were represented by other members of the same class of takers who could be identified at the time of litigation). See Mullane v. Central Hanover Bank & Trust, supra page 146.

Courts have occasionally used the term "virtual representation" to describe another situation, in which someone, though not a party to a lawsuit, so guides and controls it that a court treats him as if he were a party. For example, in Rynsburger v. Dairymen's Fertilizer Cooperative, 266 Cal. App. 2d 269, 72 Cal. Rptr. 102 (1968), the court barred a homeowners' group from bringing an action to enjoin an alleged nuisance when the group had earlier gathered evidence and requested that the city bring a similar action and where some of the group's members had testified in the city's action. In Montana v. United States, 440 U.S. 147 (1979), the United States was held to be bound by a previous judgment upholding the constitutionality of a state tax imposed on contractors for public but not private construction projects. The United States was bound, the Court ruled, because the issues were the same and the previous litigation (brought by a contractor) had been financed and controlled by the United States. Is *Searle* distinguishable?

3.   After a Final Judgment

It is sometimes said that the doctrine of claim preclusion requires a prior final judgment. Like the proposition that claim preclusion applies only between the same parties, the final judgment requirement does not receive a completely literal interpretation. Thus, certain kinds of administrative determinations may be entitled to claim-preclusion effect. For example, see South Bend Federation of Teachers v. National Education Association, 180 Ind. App. 299, 389 N.E.2d 23 (1979).

A more important question involving finality is the effect of an appeal on a judgment's status. The usual rule is that a judgment is final even though an appeal is pending; in a few states, however, the mere pendency of an appeal voids a judgment. What should be done if a judgment is given claim-preclusion effect and then reversed on appeal? Some courts solve the problem by postponing the decision on claim preclusion until the appeal is resolved. For another approach see Rule 60(b)(5). Should the trial in the second action go forward although the issue of claim preclusion is being held in abeyance?

4.   After a Judgment "on the Merits"

Not all final judgments, even though they involve the same claim and the same parties, receive preclusive effect. All agree that a judgment after a full trial is undoubtedly entitled to preclusive effect. Short of that, however, when ought preclusive effect to attach? The problem is difficult because courts might want to assign preclusive effect to a judgment for at least two quite different reasons. One reason, of course, is that the court considered and decided the merits of the lawsuit. A different reason would be that the party had misbehaved (for example, refused to obey court orders) and the court dismissed the suit as a sanction; such a dismissal would have nothing to do with the merits of the complaint, but the sanction would be futile unless it barred the refiling of the suit. Unfortunately, courts sometimes discuss this problem by stating that preclusive effect ought to attach only to judgments "on the merits." Like "in privity," this phrase conceals more than it explains, because it begs the real question: For what reasons should we attach preclusive effect to a judgment?

NOTES AND PROBLEMS

1. As a matter of principle, which of the following stages of litigation ought to preclude filing of a second suit by the same party on the same claim?
    a. Full jury trial.
    b. Directed verdict.
    c. Summary judgment.
    d. Dismissal after a Rule 12(b)(6) motion for failure to state a claim.
    e. Dismissal after a Rule 12(b)(2) motion for want of personal jurisdiction.
    f. Dismissal for failure to prosecute.
2. Consider whether Rule 41 changes your answers to the previous Note. Rule 41(b) provides:

> Unless the court in its order for dismissal otherwise specifies, a dismissal under this subdivision and any dismissal not provided for in this rule, other than a dismissal for lack of jurisdiction, for improper venue, or for failure to join a party under Rule 19, operates as an adjudication on the merits.

3. How did you answer problem 1(d)? Its problem — how to treat a judgment following a dismissal for failure to state a claim upon which relief can be granted under Rule 12(b)(6) — creates difficulties, which arise because one can see such a dismissal in two ways.
    a. On the one hand, such a dismissal can be for essentially formal reasons: The plaintiff's lawyer forgot that one must allege an agreement as part of a breach of contract suit. If the underlying facts suggest an agreement, it seems unjust to preclude when a sentence added to the pleading would cure the problem. On the other hand, if the plaintiff's lawyer has alleged all that can truthfully be alleged and the complaint is still dismissed, isn't that a statement about the merits of a claim?
    b. Is the question answered for the federal courts by Rule 41(b)? Does the argument that a complaint should not be dismissed for failure to state a claim unless there is no possible basis for relief have anything to do with the issue? A further justification for treating Rule 12(b)(6) dismissals as claim-preclusive is the ease of

amendment. It is axiomatic that a trial court should not dismiss a pleading for failure to state a claim without granting plaintiff at least one leave to amend. Suppose plaintiff does amend, and the trial court nevertheless dismisses the amended complaint. Is the opportunity to amend — after being instructed by the trial court what was wrong with the original complaint — a sufficient assurance that plaintiff has stated any possible claim, and therefore justification for assigning preclusive effect? In Federated Department Stores v. Moitie, 452 U.S. 394 (1981), the Supreme Court apparently accepted such reasoning, in a footnote that, in its entirety, reads: "The dismissal for failure to state a claim under Fed. Rule Civ. Proc. 12(b)(6) is a 'judgment on the merits.'" Id. at 399 n.3. The statement was necessary to the decision of the case and is thus a holding, but it was unexplained and unelaborated.

c. Not all states adhere to the same rule. For example, see In re Estate of Cochrane, 72 Ill. App. 3d 812, 391 N.E.2d 35 (1979) (under Illinois procedural law, which differs somewhat from the Federal Rules, dismissal for failure to plead enough facts to state a claim does not bar a second suit with the necessary facts added; presumably it would bar bringing a suit based on an identical complaint); Keidatz v. Albany, 39 Cal. 2d 826, 249 P.2d 264 (1952) (dismissal on demurrer bars subsequent action on complaint alleging same facts but does not bar claim raising new issues or new facts in support of same claim). Is it possible to decide which rule is preferable without taking into account the pleading regime of the jurisdiction in question?

4. To this mix now add the principle of Semtek Intl. Inc. v. Lockheed Martin Corp., 531 U.S. 497 (2001), supra 245. As noted in connection with Frier v. City of Vandalia, supra page 658, Semtek establishes a departure from the usual choice of law rules in diversity cases: It held that the scope of a federal court judgment in a diversity case should be the same as it would have been had the case been adjudicated in state court. Notice the result of Semtek, as applied to some of the hypothetical cases above. For federal claims the preclusive effect of a Rule 12(b)(6) dismissal bars not only the claim pleaded but all claims arising from the same transaction or occurrence. But some states have different rules (see Note 3c).

a. In a federal court lawsuit based on federal claims, a 12(b)(6) dismissal will bar a new complaint based on the same occurrence.

b. Suppose a diversity action is brought in federal district court in California (whose state courts apparently would not bar a repleaded complaint in such circumstances). Would a 12(b)(6) dismissal bar a new claim, based on the same transaction, but now properly pleaded?

c. The answer may not be clear. On one hand, if California would permit such a repleading of the case, Semtek says that the federal court should do likewise in a diversity action. What, though, should we make of Semtek's caution that state preclusion law should not apply if it is "incompatible with federal interests"? It gives as an example of such incompatibility a situation in which the federal court dismissed the case for plaintiff's failure to comply with discovery orders. The federal courts almost invariably allow plaintiffs an opportunity to amend their complaints, and they have less technical pleading requirements than some states. Is the federal "interest" in getting all the pleading out of the way in a single suit enough of a federal interest to justify disregarding state law? Or would such an approach be insufficiently deferential to state law?

d. *Semtek* raises still another set of questions when a federal judgment is entered in a case in which the court's jurisdiction rests both on federal questions and diversity. Does the preclusive effect of the judgment differ by claim? Or is less deference to state preclusion law required when the federal courts' jurisdiction rests on a basis other than diversity?

e. The next case tries to extract itself from the quicksand of the opposite situation: a *state court* dismissal of a claim for noncompliance with discovery, with the added attraction that the claim dismissed ought not to have been in state court in the first place.

Gargallo v. Merrill Lynch, Pierce, Fenner & Smith

918 F.2d 658 (6th Cir. 1990)

RYAN, J.

This case presents the interesting dual questions 1) whether a federal court must apply federal or state claim preclusion law in deciding 2) whether a prior state court judgment upon subject matter over which only a federal court has jurisdiction is a bar to a subsequent federal court claim upon the identical cause of action. . . . The district court dismissed the suit below on grounds of res judicata as to Merrill Lynch. . . .

I

Miguel Gargallo opened a "margin brokerage account" with Merrill Lynch in 1976. He maintained the account until 1980, when his investments apparently went awry and losses occurred, resulting in a debt of some $17,000 owed to Merrill Lynch. . . . When the obligation was not paid, the brokerage firm filed suit for collection in the Court of Common Pleas, Franklin County, Ohio. In response, Mr. Gargallo filed an answer and counterclaim against Merrill Lynch, alleging that Merrill Lynch caused his losses through "negligence, misrepresentations, and churning," and that the firm had violated . . . federal securities laws. After a considerable history of discovery difficulties, the state court dismissed Mr. Gargallo's counterclaim "with prejudice," citing Ohio Civil Rule 37 [substantially identical to Federal Rule 37], for refusal to comply with Merrill Lynch's discovery requests and the court's discovery orders. . . .

Mr. Gargallo . . . then filed a complaint in the United States District Court, Southern District of Ohio, charging Merrill Lynch and its account executive, Larry Tyree, with violating [federal securities laws] . . . based on the same transactions at issue in the state litigation. After preparing a thoughtful written opinion, the district court dismissed the suit against Merrill Lynch on res judicata grounds, finding that the "issues, facts and evidence to sustain this action are identical to the claims asserted [against the brokerage firm] in [Mr. Gargallo's] counterclaim that was dismissed with prejudice by the state court." This appeal followed.

II

There is no dispute in this case about the essential facts relating to the summary judgment, and the ultimate issue is: whether the district court correctly dismissed the plaintiff's claims on res judicata . . . grounds. . . .

A.   Claim Preclusion

The federal securities law violations asserted against Merrill Lynch . . . in this litigation are the same, for all practical purposes, as those Mr. Gargallo previously asserted in the counterclaim he filed in the Franklin County court. For reasons we shall discuss shortly, Ohio claim preclusion law ultimately determines the outcome of this case. Consequently, we must decide whether the Franklin County court judgment dismissing Mr. Gargallo's first lawsuit would operate as a bar, under Ohio claim preclusion rules, to the action brought in the district court, now under review, had it been brought in an Ohio court. . . .

In Ohio, the requirements for application of the doctrine of claim preclusion, or res judicata as the earlier Ohio court termed it, are the same as those applicable in a federal court:

> The doctrine of res judicata is that an existing final judgment rendered upon the merits, without fraud or collusion, by a court of competent jurisdiction, is conclusive of rights, questions and facts in issue, as to the parties and their privies, in all other actions in the same or any other judicial tribunal of concurrent jurisdiction.

Norwood v. McDonald, 142 Ohio St. 299, 305, 52 N.E.2d 67, 71 (1943).

Under Ohio law, the dismissal with prejudice of Mr. Gargallo's Common Pleas Court counterclaim for noncompliance with Ohio's Civil Rule 37 was a "final judgment rendered upon the merits."

. . . We agree with the district court that the "issues, facts, and evidence to sustain this action are identical to the claims asserted . . . in [plaintiff's state] counterclaim," and we are satisfied that the federal claim or cause of action giving rise to this appeal is the same claim or cause of action that was asserted in the counterclaim dismissed in the state court litigation.

Thus, we have no question that, absent any regard for subject matter jurisdiction, Ohio claim preclusion law would bar the claim asserted in Mr. Gargallo's district court complaint had it been filed in an Ohio court.

B.   Federal Exclusivity

However, the district court in which plaintiff brought his claim is not an Ohio court but a federal tribunal. Consequently, we are faced with the more difficult issue of whether a federal district court may give claim preclusive effect to an Ohio judgment regarding federal securities laws that are within the exclusive jurisdiction of the federal courts. The first rule in determining whether a prior state court judgment has preclusive effect in a federal court is that the full faith and credit statute, 28 U.S.C. §1738,[3] requires a federal court to give a state court judgment the same preclusive effect such judgment would have in a state court. . . .

In Marrese v. [American] Academy of Orthopaedic Surgeons, 470 U.S. 373 (1985), the Court [held] . . . that federal courts are required under 28 U.S.C. §1738 to determine the preclusive effect of prior state court judgments, pursuant to the law of the state in which the judgment was entered, even as to claims within the exclusive jurisdiction of the federal courts. Marrese requires, therefore, that a federal court must determine whether to give claim preclusive effect to a state court judgment upon a cause of action over which the state court had no subject matter jurisdiction by determining whether the state court would give preclusive effect to such a judgment. . . .

Ohio appears to subscribe to the Restatement (Second) of Judgments position that a judgment rendered by a court lacking subject matter jurisdiction ought not be given preclusive effect. . . . It seems clear, therefore, that in Ohio a final judgment by a court of that state, upon a cause of action over which the adjudicating court had no subject matter jurisdiction, does not have claim preclusive effect in any subsequent proceedings. . . .

In summary, we hold that the Ohio court judgment, dismissing, with prejudice, Mr. Gargallo's federal securities law claims against Merrill Lynch . . . may not be given claim preclusive effect in a subsequent federal court action asserting those same claims because Ohio courts would not give claim preclusive effect to a prior final judgment upon a cause of action over which the Ohio court had no subject matter jurisdiction. . . .

[Reversed and remanded.]

NOTES AND PROBLEMS

1. *Gargallo* has two aspects: (1) whether the original dismissal was "on the merits" for purposes of claim preclusion; and (2) how the jurisdictional defect in the first proceeding ought to affect claim preclusion.

2. Start with the first aspect. Cases like *Gargallo* are easier to understand if one does not become distracted by the misleading phrase "on the merits."

a. Explain why it is fair — and probably necessary — to assign preclusive effect to the dismissal for failure to comply with discovery orders.

b. Explain why it is fair to do so although no one in his right mind would say that the prior suit determined the merits of Gargallo's claim in the ordinary sense of that phrase.

---

3. In pertinent part, 28 U.S.C. §1738 provides that "the Acts of the legislature of any State, Territory, or Possession of the United States" and "the records and judicial proceedings of any court of any such State, Territory or Possession . . . shall have the same full faith and credit in every court within the United States and its Territories and Possessions as they have by law or usage in the courts of such State, Territory or Possession from which they are taken."

3. To understand the force of the principle illustrated in *Gargallo*, suppose that Mr. Gargallo had not waited to be sued by his brokerage and had instead brought his federal securities claims against Merrill, Lynch in a federal court. Further imagine that Mr. Gargallo had been as uncooperative in discovery in federal court as he was in the Ohio courts and suffered a dismissal under Rules 37 and 41 for failure to comply with discovery orders. Now suppose he refiled that suit in federal court — what result?

4. Turn now to the jurisdictional defect in Gargallo's state court counterclaim. Did Mr. Gargallo's mistake ignorance (filing his federal securities claim in the wrong court) save him from the consequences of his behavior (failure to comply with discovery)? The underlying principle may be just — is the result?

5. What procedures did defendant use to raise its argument of claim preclusion?

a. Former adjudication is an affirmative defense. See Rule 8(c).

b. Having raised this defense, how did defendant get a judicial ruling on the question of whether the first suit precluded the second? *Sum Judge*

c. Why is such a case decided on a motion for summary judgment rather than on the pleadings? What "facts" are needed for the court to decide if the claim is precluded?

B.   Issue Preclusion

Issue preclusion has a narrower but deeper bite than claim preclusion. If the conditions for claim preclusion are met, a party will find all her contentions barred from relitigation — those she actually advanced in the first case as well as those that she did not advance. The preclusive effect, however, extends only to the same claim. By contrast, issue preclusion bars from relitigation only those issues actually litigated and determined. But they will be barred from relitigation in all subsequent claims between the parties — and, according to recent doctrine, in some claims that do not involve both parties.

The black letter of issue preclusion is simple:

> When
> [1] an issue of fact or law is
> [2] actually litigated and determined by
> [3] a valid and final judgment, and
> [4] the determination is essential to the judgment,
> the determination is conclusive in a subsequent action between the parties, whether on the same or a different claim.[*]

Each of these four conditions, however, involves some difficulties that we shall examine in turn. We shall first look briefly at what it means for an issue to be the same in successive cases. Second comes an exploration of the boundaries between issue and claim preclusion and an effort to define the conditions under

---

[*] Restatement (Second) of Judgments §27.

which one can say that an issue has been "actually litigated and determined." Then we examine the meaning of "essentiality to the judgment." Finally, we turn to a body of doctrine that severely limits the last of the stated conditions — that the subsequent case be "between the parties."

1.   The Same Issue

A threshold question in all issue-preclusion cases will be the identity of the issue to be precluded. Sometimes the analysis of that question will be easy. For example, suppose the United States sues Student civilly, seeking nonpayment of two student loans, both signed on the same day and containing identical and allegedly fraudulent statements. Student defends on the grounds that the statements in the loan documents are true. If Student loses the first lawsuit, the fraudulence of the statements in question will be precluded in the second suit as well.

But matters can be subtler. Suppose that in the student loan lawsuits, the government prevails, establishing fraudulent misstatements. The United States then prosecutes Student criminally, asserting that he obtained the loans fraudulently. Student defends on grounds that the statements are true. Does the government's previous victory in the civil lawsuit preclude Student from his defense? No: Civil and criminal proceedings operate under different burdens of proof. To prevail, as the government did, on a civil burden of preponderance of the evidence does not mean that one can establish the same issue beyond a reasonable doubt. One must, then, build into one's definition of the "issue" not only its substantive contours but the procedural conditions under which it was determined.

NOTES AND PROBLEMS

1. The federal government criminally prosecutes an IRS agent, accusing her of stealing tax revenues. She is acquitted. The government then sues Agent in a civil suit to recover funds allegedly embezzled in the same criminal acts. Agent seeks to invoke preclusion on the grounds that the previous case demonstrates the acts did not occur. Preclusion?

2. Reverse the order of the civil and criminal actions in the preceding example. Suppose the civil action came first, and the government prevailed, winning a judgment against Agent on the ground that she had embezzled funds. The government now prosecutes Agent criminally, charging her with the same acts of embezzlement. Why doesn't the first case preclude Agent from relitigating the question of embezzlement?

3. Suppose in Problem 1 Agent had been convicted in the criminal prosecution. In the subsequent civil case could the government take advantage of preclusion against Agent?

2. An Issue "Actually Litigated and Determined"

Even if one concludes that the issue at stake in the first and second lawsuits is identical, one must ask a further question: Was that issue actually litigated and determined in the first case? In Gargallo v. Merrill, Lynch, supra page 683, Larry Tyree, a Merrill stockbroker sued by Gargallo, sought to use the issues established in the first suit against Gargallo in the second, federal suit. The court's answer was swift and clear:

> With respect to the summary judgment in favor of Larry Tyree, since Mr. Gargallo's counter claim was dismissed in the state court as a sanction for discovery violations, none of the factual or legal issues he raised were actually litigated and decided. Consequently, the doctrine of collateral estoppel, or issue preclusion, is not applicable.

Gargallo v. Merrill, Lynch, 918 F.2d 658, 664 (6th Cir. 1990) The answer is not always so easy.

Illinois Central Gulf Railroad v. Parks

181 Ind. App. 141, 390 N.E.2d 1078 (1979)

LYBROOK, J.

[Jessie and Bertha Parks were injured when a car driven by Jessie in which Bertha was a passenger collided with an Illinois Central train. Bertha and Jessie sued Illinois Central; Bertha sought compensation for her injuries, and Jessie sought damages for loss of Bertha's services and consortium. Bertha recovered a $30,000 judgment on her claim, and judgment was rendered for Illinois Central on Jessie's claim.

Jessie then sued Illinois Central for his own injuries. On Illinois Central's motion for summary judgment, the trial court held that Jessie's claim was not barred by claim preclusion and that the prior action did not preclude Jessie on the issue of contributory negligence. Illinois Central took an interlocutory appeal.]

. . . Illinois Central Gulf's first allegation of error is an attempt to apply estoppel by judgment [the court's term for claim preclusion] in the case at bar, but the railroad concedes its own argument by admitting that Jessie's cause of action for loss of services and consortium as a derivative of Bertha's personal injuries is a distinct cause of action from Jessie's claim for damages for his own personal injuries.

Estoppel by judgment precludes the relitigation of a *cause of action* finally determined between the parties, and decrees that a judgment rendered is a complete bar to any subsequent action on *the same claim or cause of action.* Jessie's cause of action in the case at bar is a different cause of action from the one he litigated in the companion case; therefore, estoppel by judgment does not apply.

Estoppel by verdict [the court's term for issue preclusion], however, does apply. Using Judge Shake's terminology, the causes of action are not the same but, if the case at bar were to go to trial on all the issues raised in the pleadings and answer, some facts or questions determined and adjudicated in the companion case would again be put in issue in this subsequent action between the same parties.

To protect the integrity of the prior judgment by precluding the possibility of opposite results by two different juries on the same set of facts, the doctrine of estoppel by verdict allows the judgment in the prior action to operate as an estoppel as to those facts or questions actually litigated and determined in the prior action. The problem at hand, then, is to determine what facts or questions were actually litigated and determined in the companion case.

We agree with three concessions made by Illinois Central Gulf as to the effect of the verdict in the prior case: (1) that the verdict in favor of Bertha established, among other things, that the railroad was negligent and that its negligence was a proximate cause of the accident and Bertha's injuries; (2) that, inasmuch as Jessie's action for loss of services and consortium was derivative, if Jessie sustained any such loss it was proximately caused by the railroad's negligence; and (3) that, in order for the jury to have returned a verdict against Jessie, it had to have decided that he either sustained no damages or that his own negligence was a proximate cause of his damages.

This third proposition places upon the railroad the heavy burden outlined by Judge Shake in [Flora v. Indiana Service Co., 222 Ind. App. 253, 256-257 (1944)]:

> ... [W]here a judgment may have been based upon either or any of two or more distinct facts, a party desiring to plead the judgment as an estoppel by verdict or finding upon the particular fact involved in a subsequent suit must show that it went upon that fact, or else the question will be open to a new contention. The estoppel of a judgment is only presumptively conclusive, when it appears that the judgment could not have been rendered without deciding the particular matter brought in question. It is necessary to look to the complete record to ascertain what was the question in issue.

The railroad argues that, because Jessie's evidence as to his loss of services and consortium was uncontroverted, the jury's verdict had to be based upon a finding of contributory negligence. Illinois Central Gulf made this same argument in the companion case[*] in relation to a related issue and Jessie countered, as he does here, with his contention that, although the evidence was uncontroverted, it was minimal and, thus, could have caused the jury to find no compensable damages. We reviewed the complete record in the companion case and held that the jury verdict against Jessie in that cause could mean that he had failed his burden of proving compensable damages....

We hold that Illinois Central Gulf has failed its burden of showing that the judgment against Jessie in the prior action could not have been rendered without deciding that Jessie was contributorily negligent in the accident which precipitated the two lawsuits. Consequently, the trial court was correct in granting partial summary judgment estopping the railroad from denying its negligence and in limiting the issues at trial to whether Jessie was contributorily negligent, whether

---

[* The appeal from the first suit, in which Bertha had recovered for her injuries. — Ed.]

any such contributory negligence was a proximate cause of the accident, and whether Jessie sustained personal injuries and compensable damages. . . .

NOTES AND PROBLEMS

1. *Parks* causes potential confusion for the reader who has just completed the preceding section on claim preclusion.

a. If one were told the facts in the first lawsuit (Bertha and Jessie v. Railroad) and were further told that the railroad asserted a defense of former adjudication in the second suit, what would one expect that defense to be?

b. Why wasn't claim preclusion available to the railroad in Indiana? Indiana applies a definition of claim preclusion that is narrower than that set forth in Restatement (Second) of Judgments §24, supra page 664.

2. Now focus on why Jessie was not precluded from relitigating the issue of his contributory negligence in the second lawsuit. Why did the court reject the railroad's contention that the jury's verdict demonstrated that Jesse was contributorily negligent?

a. Isn't it plausible — indeed, likely — that the jury decided that Jessie was contributorily negligent? So why doesn't the court so conclude?

b. What is the other way a jury could have reached its verdict in the first suit? Should the court interview the jury about how it actually reached its decision?

3. What is the purpose of issue preclusion? A typical opinion explains, "[a]pplication of the doctrine of [issue preclusion] represents a decision that the needs of judicial finality and efficiency outweigh the possible gains of fairness or accuracy from continued litigation of an issue that previously has been considered by a competent tribunal." Nasem v. Brown, 595 F.2d 801 (D.C. Cir. 1979).

a. Professor Martin Shapiro has argued that "it must always be remembered that the basic aim of a trial is to resolve a conflict or to impose social controls, not to find the facts. Much of what may appear to be unsatisfactory as pure fact-finding, if we were applying general scientific canons for empirical inquiry, may be quite satisfactory in the specific context of trials." * If Professor Shapiro's analysis is correct, courts are understandably hesitant to transplant the "findings" to a second dispute because it is a different dispute. The requirements that hedge issue preclusion thus grow from courts' understandable reluctance to equate findings with facts.

b. Does this analysis omit something? Do courts have a right to prevent two successive judgments from finding that fact X both did and did not occur? Is more than judicial face-saving at stake?

4. Assume that Illinois Central had not asserted Jessie's contributory negligence in the first action. Would Illinois Central be precluded from asserting it when Jessie sued for his own injuries? Most courts would say no. Unlike claim preclusion, under which theories are barred even if not raised, issue preclusion only

---

* Shapiro, Courts: A Comparative and Political Analysis 44 (1981).

applies to issues actually decided in the prior action. Why? What is it about a new claim that makes it fair to preclude only those issues in the previous claim that were actually litigated?

5. Should a litigant be allowed to use evidence extrinsic to the record to establish what issues were actually determined in the previous litigation? The answer is yes, according to Restatement (Second) of Judgments §27 Comment f. What kind of extrinsic evidence would be useful to show which issues were determined by previous litigation?

6. What happens if the first action involved a default judgment?

a. Note 4 would imply that no issues are collaterally estopped because no issues were actually decided. Some jurisdictions do recognize an exception for facts that it would have been necessary to prove in the defaulted proceedings if they had been contested. For example, see Braxton v. Litchalk, 55 Mich. App. 708, 223 N.W.2d 316 (1974). This rule seems to arise in cases like *Martino*, supra, in which, if an issue is left open for litigation in the second case, it threatens the integrity of the first judgment.

b. Can there ever be reasons for giving preclusive effect to an issue *not* actually litigated and determined in a prior proceeding? Consider the facts of In re Sammy Daily, 47 F.3d 365 (9th Cir. 1995). The Federal Deposit Insurance Corporation, as receiver for bank loans, sued Daily, alleging he had fraudulently obtained the loans. Daily answered the complaint, then engaged in "a deliberate, dilatory course of conduct" constituting "a strategy of delay and evasiveness . . . [that] significantly prejudiced the plaintiffs [and] the judicial process." As a sanction for this behavior, the trial court, invoking Rule 37, "ordered all allegations of the complaint deemed admitted and entered a default judgment in favor of the FDIC." In the meantime, Daily had filed for bankruptcy. Bankruptcy does not discharge debts resulting from fraudulent acts. The FDIC sought to have the bankruptcy court rule that the judgment could not be discharged in bankruptcy on grounds of fraud. Daily argued that the prior judgment did not establish fraud, because those claims had not been "actually litigated." The Ninth Circuit conceded that ordinarily a default judgment could not serve as a basis for issue preclusion, but ruled that this judgment was different:

> The judgment entered in the [prior] action was not an ordinary default judgment. Daily did not simply decide the burden of litigation outweighed the advantages of opposing the FDIC's claim and fail to appear. He actively participated in the litigation, albeit obstructively, for two years before judgment was entered against him. A party who deliberately precludes resolution of factual issues through normal adjudicative procedures may be bound, in subsequent, related proceedings involving the same parties and issues, by a prior judicial determination reached without completion of the usual process of adjudication. In such a case the "actual litigation" requirement may be satisfied by substantial participation in an adversary contest in which the party is afforded a reasonable opportunity to defend himself on the merits but chooses not to do so.

Id. at 368.

The opinion cited no case directly establishing this proposition; *Gargallo*, supra page 683, is to the contrary. Is the result nevertheless reasonable?

3.   An Issue "Essential to the Judgment"

In *Parks* the court declined to apply preclusion because the opacity of the general verdict made it difficult to determine what the first judgment had decided. Sometimes courts face the opposite problem: too many findings in support of a judgment. In a trial to the bench, Rule 52(a) requires the judge to set forth findings of fact and conclusions of law. Imagine that the trial in *Parks* had taken place before a judge, who had determined (1) that Illinois Central had not been negligent and (2) that Jessie Parks had been contributorily negligent. Under these circumstances, should the court in a subsequent claim between the same parties hold Jessie precluded from relitigating both those issues? Or neither one? That question, though it occurs infrequently, uncovers the values underlying the doctrine. The first Restatement of Judgments took the position that when alternative grounds for decision existed, *both* should be precluded in subsequent litigation. The Restatement (Second) of Judgments §27 Comment i opines that *neither* determination should be binding in subsequent litigation:

> It might be argued that the judgment should be conclusive with respect to both issues. The matter has presumably been fully litigated and fairly decided; the determination does support, and is in itself sufficient to support, the judgment for the prevailing party; and the losing party is in a position to seek reversal of the determination from an appellate court. Moreover, a party who would otherwise urge several matters in support of a particular result may be deterred from doing so if a judgment resting on alternative determinations does not effectively preclude relitigation of particular issues.
>
> There are, however, persuasive reasons for analogizing the case to that of the nonessential determination. . . . First, a determination in the alternative may not have been as carefully or rigorously considered as it would have if it had been necessary to the result, and in that sense it has some of the characteristics of dicta. Second, and of critical importance, the losing party, although entitled to appeal from both determinations, might be dissuaded from doing so because of the likelihood that at least one of them would be upheld and the other not even reached. If he were to appeal solely for the purpose of avoiding the application of the rule of issue preclusion, then the rule might be responsible for increasing the burdens of litigation on the parties and the courts rather than lightening those burdens.

As if to show just how close the question is, a later comment to the same section qualifies the suggested rule:

> [Comment] o [to §27]. Effect of an appeal. . . .
>
> If the judgment of the court of first instance was based on a determination of two issues, either of which standing independently would be sufficient to support the result, and the appellate court upholds both of these determinations as sufficient, and accordingly affirms the judgment, the judgment is conclusive as to both determinations. In contrast to the case discussed in Comment i, the losing party has here obtained an appellate decision on the issue, and thus the balance weighs in favor of preclusion.
>
> If the appellate court upholds one of these determinations as sufficient but not the other, and accordingly affirms the judgment, the judgment is conclusive as to the first determination.

If the appellate court upholds one of these determinations as sufficient and refuses to consider whether or not the other is sufficient and accordingly affirms the judgment, the judgment is conclusive as to the first determination.

To get a grasp of the issues at stake, imagine that in federal district court a defendant makes a pretrial motion seeking to dismiss a case, citing alternative grounds for its decision — lack of federal subject matter jurisdiction and lack of personal jurisdiction. See, for example, Ruhrgas AG v. Marathon Oil, 526 U.S. 574 (1999), noted supra page 192. The district court dismisses and the plaintiff refiles the suit in state court. When he does so, the defendant invokes issue preclusion based on the prior decision.

NOTES AND PROBLEMS

1. Consider several variations on *Ruhrgas*, beginning with the simplest. Suppose the district court had dismissed solely on grounds that federal subject matter jurisdiction was lacking. Under those conditions, what effect will the prior decision have on the state court suit?

2. Now suppose that the federal district court had dismissed solely on grounds that personal jurisdiction was lacking. What effect will the prior decision have on the state court suit?

3. Now suppose that the federal district court had dismissed, citing both grounds, ruling in a written opinion that personal and subject matter jurisdiction were both lacking. What effect should that ruling have in the second lawsuit?

4. Finally, suppose that after the federal district court had dismissed, citing both grounds, the plaintiff had appealed. Suppose the court of appeals affirms.

a. If the appellate court affirms the absence of subject matter jurisdiction without reaching the question of personal jurisdiction, what effect in the second lawsuit?

b. If the appellate court affirms both grounds for dismissal, what effect on the second suit?

5. What idea is behind the importance that the Restatement (Second) attaches not just to the opportunity to appeal but to actual appellate litigation of alternative grounds? Does this suggest a lack of confidence in trial court decisions, or is there something else at work? Put yourself in the position of the plaintiff in the hypothetical lawsuit. You have just lost big in federal district court, with the judge throwing your lawsuit out of court on two alternative grounds. One of those grounds was that the defendant had insufficient contacts with the state to permit personal jurisdiction. You are offended by that finding, so you go to your lawyer and say, "We should appeal."

a. Your lawyer will explain why an appeal claiming that the personal jurisdiction ruling was erroneous has little chance of success. Why?

b. Isn't the Restatement (Second) position based on an image of litigation not as a search for truth but as a set of incentives and disincentives? In that world a judge will have less reason to be careful about any particular finding if there are other independent grounds leading to the same result. The losing litigant will have less incentive to appeal any particular finding if it seems likely that the appellate court will affirm on the basis of the other, independent grounds for decision. Under those circumstances, the theory goes, too few people have an incentive to make sure the findings are accurate. That being the case, we should be reluctant to import them into a second lawsuit.

4.   Between Which Parties?

We have thus far dealt with situations in which the former and the present lawsuits involve the same parties. At common law this identity of parties (called "mutuality") was a requirement for both claim preclusion and issue preclusion. It continues to be a requirement for claim preclusion; in recent decades, however, many courts have abandoned this requirement for issue preclusion.

a.   The "Victim" of Preclusion

To see how such a scheme might operate, consider a variation on the facts in Illinois Central Gulf Railroad v. Parks. Wife sues Railroad for injuries suffered in a crossing collision. Wife wins a judgment. Husband now sues for his injuries, sustained in the same accident. Railroad cannot argue that his claim is precluded by the first lawsuit: Biologically separate individuals possess separate claims, and no rule compels such individuals, even when married to each other, to prosecute their claims together. So Husband's suit can go forward.

In Husband v. Railroad, can either party take advantage of issue preclusion? Fifty years ago, the answer was a clear no. Like claim preclusion, issue preclusion applied only if both parties had been in the first suit, and, because Husband was not a party to that first lawsuit, the conditions for issue preclusion were not met: "Mutuality"—conditions under which both parties could benefit from or be burdened with preclusion—did not exist. The last several decades have seen that principle of mutuality erode. Many courts would today permit Husband, even though he had not been a party to the first suit, to take advantage of an issue fully litigated and determined in that suit. In this case Railroad's negligence, causation, and proximate causation would all be candidates for preclusion in the second action. The rationale for that extension of issue preclusion is that the "victim" of issue preclusion (here, the railroad) had a full and fair opportunity to litigate the matter in the first suit.

Now change one factor: What if Railroad had won the first suit, demonstrating to the jury's satisfaction that it was not negligent? Could it take advantage of that determination in a second action brought by Husband? The answer is no. Whether they attribute this result to simple fairness or to due process, all agree that a party who has never had an opportunity to litigate an issue cannot be precluded from doing so. The abandonment of mutuality thus creates a potential asymmetry: If Railroad loses the first case brought by Wife, it will be saddled by that loss in subsequent litigation with Husband. If it wins against Wife, however, it must still defend against Husband. The anomaly has its logic; as one pioneering decision put it:

> The criteria for determining who may assert a plea of [issue preclusion] differ fundamentally from the criteria for determining against whom [such] a plea . . . may be asserted. The requirements of due process of law forbid the assertion of a plea of . . . [issue preclusion] against a party unless he was bound by the earlier litigation in which the matter was decided. He is bound by that litigation only if he has been a party thereto or in privity with a party thereto. There is no compelling reason, however, for requiring that the party asserting the plea . . . must have been a party, or in privity with a party, to the earlier litigation.
>
> No satisfactory rationalization has been advanced for the requirement of mutuality. Just why a party who was not bound by a previous action should be precluded from asserting it as res judicata against a party who was bound by it is difficult to comprehend. (See 7 Bentham's Works, Bowring's Ed., 171.)

Bernhard v. Bank of America, 19 Cal. 2d 807, 811-812, 122 P.2d 892, 894-895 (1942) (Traynor, J.). Despite this reasoning, the asymmetrical availability of nonmutual preclusion has made some courts and commentators uneasy. The next case explores the problem.

b. The Precluder

Parklane Hosiery Co. v. Shore

439 U.S. 322 (1979)

Mr. Justice STEWART delivered the opinion of the Court.

This case presents the question whether a party who has had issues of fact adjudicated adversely to it in an equitable action may be collaterally estopped from relitigating the same issues before a jury in a subsequent legal action brought against it by a new party.

The respondent brought this stockholder's class action against the petitioners in a Federal District Court. The complaint alleged that the petitioners, Parklane Hosiery Co., Inc. (Parklane), and 13 of its officers, directors, and stockholders, had issued a materially false and misleading proxy statement in connection with a merger.[1] The proxy statement, according to the complaint, had violated §§14(a), 10(b), and 20(a) of the Securities Exchange Act of 1934, as well as various rules and regulations promulgated by the Securities and Exchange Commission (SEC). The complaint sought damages, rescission of the merger, and recovery of costs.

Before this action came to trial, the SEC filed suit against the same defendants in the Federal District Court, alleging that the proxy statement that had been issued by Parklane was materially false and misleading in essentially the same

---

1. The amended complaint alleged that the proxy statement that had been issued to the stockholders was false and misleading because it failed to disclose (1) that the president of Parklane would financially benefit as a result of the company's going private; (2) certain ongoing negotiations that could have resulted in financial benefit to Parklane; and (3) that the appraisal of the fair value of Parklane stock was based on insufficient information to be accurate.

respects as those that had been alleged in the respondent's complaint. Injunctive relief was requested. After a four-day trial, the District Court found that the proxy statement was materially false and misleading in the respects alleged, and entered a declaratory judgment to that effect. The Court of Appeals for the Second Circuit affirmed this judgment.

The respondent in the present case then moved for partial summary judgment against the petitioners, asserting that the petitioners were collaterally estopped from litigating the issues that had been resolved against them in the action brought by the SEC.[2] The District Court denied the motion on the ground that such an application of collateral estoppel would deny the petitioners their Seventh Amendment right to a jury trial. The Court of Appeals for the Second Circuit reversed, holding that a party who has had issues of fact determined against him after a full and fair opportunity to litigate in a nonjury trial is collaterally estopped from obtaining a subsequent jury trial of these same issues of fact. The appellate court concluded that "the Seventh Amendment preserves the right to jury trial only with respect to issues of fact, [and] once those issues have been fully and fairly adjudicated in a prior proceeding, nothing remains for trial, either with or without a jury." Because of an inter-Circuit conflict, we granted certiorari.

I

The threshold question to be considered is whether quite apart from the right to a jury trial under the Seventh Amendment, the petitioners can be precluded from litigating facts resolved adversely to them in a prior equitable proceeding with another party under the general law of collateral estoppel. Specifically, we must determine whether a litigant who was not a party to a prior judgment may nevertheless use that judgment "offensively" to prevent a defendant from relitigating issues resolved in the earlier proceeding.[4]

A

Collateral estoppel, like the related doctrine of res judicata,[5] has the dual purpose of protecting litigants from the burden of relitigating an identical issue

2. A private plaintiff in an action under the proxy rules is not entitled to relief simply by demonstrating that the proxy solicitation was materially false and misleading. The plaintiff must also show that he was injured and prove damages. Mills v. Electric Auto-Lite Co., 396 U.S. 375, 386-390. Since the SEC action was limited to a determination of whether the proxy statement contained materially false and misleading information, the respondent conceded that he would still have to prove these other elements of his prima facie case in the private action. The petitioners' right to a jury trial on those remaining issues is not contested.

4. In this context, offensive use of collateral estoppel occurs when the plaintiff seeks to foreclose the defendant from litigating an issue the defendant has previously litigated unsuccessfully in an action with another party. Defensive use occurs when a defendant seeks to prevent a plaintiff from asserting a claim the plaintiff has previously litigated and lost against another defendant.

5. Under the doctrine of res judicata, a judgment on the merits in a prior suit bars a second suit involving the same parties or their privies based on the same cause of action. Under the doctrine of collateral estoppel, on the other hand, the second action is upon a different cause of action and the judgment in the prior suit precludes relitigation of issues actually litigated and necessary to the outcome of the first action.

with the same party or his privy and of promoting judicial economy by preventing needless litigation. Blonder-Tongue Laboratories, Inc. v. University of Illinois Foundation, 402 U.S. 313, 328-329. Until relatively recently, however, the scope of collateral estoppel was limited by the doctrine of mutuality of parties. Under this mutuality doctrine, neither party could use a prior judgment as an estoppel against the other unless both parties were bound by the judgment. Based on the premise that it is somehow unfair to allow a party to use a prior judgment when he himself would not be so bound,[7] the mutuality requirement provided a party who had litigated and lost in a previous action an opportunity to relitigate identical issues with new parties.

By failing to recognize the obvious difference in position between a party who has never litigated an issue and one who has fully litigated and lost, the mutuality requirement was criticized almost from its inception.[8] Recognizing the validity of this criticism, the Court in Blonder-Tongue Laboratories, Inc. v. University of Illinois Foundation, supra, abandoned the mutuality requirement.... The "broader question" before the Court, however, was "whether it is any longer tenable to afford a litigant more than one full and fair opportunity for judicial resolution of the same issue." . . .

B

The *Blonder-Tongue* case involved defensive use of collateral estoppel — a plaintiff was estopped from asserting a claim that the plaintiff had previously litigated and lost against another defendant. The present case, by contrast, involves offensive use of collateral estoppel — a plaintiff is seeking to estop a defendant from relitigating the issues which the defendant previously litigated and lost against another plaintiff. In both the offensive and defensive use situations, the party against whom estoppel is asserted has litigated and lost in an earlier action. Nevertheless, several reasons have been advanced why the two situations should be treated differently.

First, offensive use of collateral estoppel does not promote judicial economy in the same manner as defensive use does. Defensive use of collateral estoppel precludes a plaintiff from relitigating identical issues by merely "switching adversaries." Bernhard v. Bank of America Natl. Trust & Savings Assn.[12] Thus defensive collateral estoppel gives a plaintiff a strong incentive to join all potential defendants in the first action if possible. Offensive use of collateral estoppel, on the other

---

7. It is a violation of due process for a judgment to be binding on a litigant who was not a party or a privy and therefore has never had an opportunity to be heard. Blonder-Tongue Laboratories, Inc. v. University of Illinois Foundation.

8. This criticism was summarized in the Court's opinion in Blonder-Tongue Laboratories, Inc. v. University of Illinois Foundation, supra. The opinion of Justice Traynor for a unanimous California Supreme Court in Bernhard v. Bank of America Natl. Trust & Savings Assn., made the point succinctly: "No satisfactory rationalization has been advanced for the requirement of mutuality. Just why a party who was not bound by a previous action should be precluded from asserting it as res judicata against a party who was bound by it is difficult to comprehend."

12. Under the mutuality requirement, a plaintiff could accomplish this result since he would not have been bound by the judgment had the original defendant won.

Offensive CE
Will increase litigation / decrease judicial economy

hand, creates precisely the opposite incentive. Since a plaintiff will be able to rely on a previous judgment against a defendant but will not be bound by that judgment if the defendant wins, the plaintiff has every incentive to adopt a "wait and see" attitude, in the hope that the first action by another plaintiff will result in a favorable judgment. Thus offensive use of collateral estoppel will likely increase rather than decrease the total amount of litigation, since potential plaintiffs will have everything to gain and nothing to lose by not intervening in the first action.[13]

A second argument against offensive use of collateral estoppel is that it may be unfair to a defendant. If a defendant in the first action is sued for small or nominal damages, he may have little incentive to defend vigorously, particularly if future suits are not foreseeable. The Evergreens v. Nunan; cf. Berner v. British Commonwealth Pac. Airlines (application of offensive collateral estoppel denied where defendant did not appeal an adverse judgment awarding damages of $35,000 and defendant was later sued for over $7 million). Allowing offensive collateral estoppel may also be unfair to a defendant if the judgment relied upon as a basis for the estoppel is itself inconsistent with one or more previous judgments in favor of the defendant.[14] Still another situation where it might be unfair to apply offensive estoppel is where the second action affords the defendant procedural opportunities unavailable in the first action that could readily cause a different result.[15]

Not fair if D wins all suits except one

Reasoning

Trial courts can choose where to apply (based on fuel)

We have concluded that the preferable approach for dealing with these problems in the federal courts is not to preclude the use of offensive collateral estoppel, but to grant trial courts broad discretion to determine when it should be applied.[16] The general rule should be that in cases where a plaintiff could easily have joined in the earlier action or where, either for the reasons discussed above

13. The Restatement (Second) of Judgments §88(3) (Tent. Draft No. 2, Apr. 15, 1975) provides that application of collateral estoppel may be denied if the party asserting it "could have effected joinder in the first action between himself and his present adversary."

14. In Professor Currie's familiar example, a railroad collision injures 50 passengers all of whom bring separate actions against the railroad. After the railroad wins the first 25 suits, a plaintiff wins in suit 26. Professor Currie argues that offensive use of collateral estoppel should not be applied so as to allow plaintiffs 27 through 50 automatically to recover. Currie, [Mutuality of Collateral Estoppel: Limits of the *Bernhard* Doctrine], 9 Stan. L. Rev. [281, 304 (1957)]. See Restatement (Second) of Judgments §88(4).

15. If, for example, the defendant in the first action was forced to defend in an inconvenient forum and therefore was unable to engage in full scale discovery or call witnesses, application of offensive collateral estoppel may be unwarranted. Indeed, differences in available procedures may sometimes justify not allowing a prior judgment to have estoppel effect in a subsequent action even between the same parties, or where defensive estoppel is asserted against a plaintiff who has litigated and lost. The problem of unfairness is particularly acute in cases of offensive estoppel, however, because the defendant against whom estoppel is asserted typically will not have chosen the forum in the first action. See id., at §88(2) and Comment d.

16. This is essentially the approach of [the Restatement (Second) of Judgments] at §88, which recognizes that "the distinct trend if not the clear weight of recent authority is to the effect that there is no intrinsic difference between 'offensive' as distinct from 'defensive' issue preclusion, although a stronger showing that the prior opportunity to litigate was adequate may be required in the former situation than the latter." Id., Reporter's Note, at 99.

*General
Rule*

or for other reasons, the application of offensive estoppel would be unfair to a defendant, a trial judge should not allow the use of offensive collateral estoppel.

In the present case, however, none of the circumstances that might justify reluctance to allow the offensive use of collateral estoppel is present. The application of offensive collateral estoppel will not here reward a private plaintiff who could have joined in the previous action, since the respondent probably could not have joined in the injunctive action brought by the SEC even had he so desired.[17] Similarly, there is no unfairness to the petitioners in applying offensive collateral estoppel in this case. First, in light of the serious allegations made in the SEC's complaint against the petitioners, as well as the foreseeability of subsequent private suits that typically follow a successful Government judgment, the petitioners had every incentive to litigate the SEC lawsuit fully and vigorously.[18] Second, the judgment in the SEC action was not inconsistent with any previous decision. Finally, there will in the respondent's action be no procedural opportunities available to the petitioners that were unavailable in the first action of a kind that might be likely to cause a different result.[19]

Reasoning

We conclude, therefore, that none of the considerations that would justify a refusal to allow the use of offensive collateral estoppel is present in this case. Since the petitioners received a "full and fair" opportunity to litigate their claims in the SEC action, the contemporary law of collateral estoppel leads inescapably to the conclusion that the petitioners are collaterally estopped from relitigating the question of whether the proxy statement was materially false and misleading.

II

The question that remains is whether, notwithstanding the law of collateral estoppel, the use of offensive collateral estoppel in this case would violate the petitioners' Seventh Amendment right to a jury trial. . . . The Seventh Amendment has never been interpreted in the rigid manner advocated by the petitioners. On the contrary, many procedural devices developed since 1791 that have diminished the civil jury's historic domain have been found not to be inconsistent with the Seventh Amendment. . . .

17. SEC v. Everest Management Corp. ("the complicating effect of the additional issues and the additional parties outweighs any advantage of a single disposition of the common issues"). Moreover, consolidation of a private action with one brought by the SEC without its consent is prohibited by statute. 15 U.S.C. §78u(g).

18. After a four-day trial in which the petitioners had every opportunity to present evidence and call witnesses, the District Court held for the SEC. The petitioners then appealed to the Court of Appeals for the Second Circuit, which affirmed the judgment against them. Moreover, the petitioners were already aware of the action brought by the respondent, since it had commenced before the filing of the SEC action.

19. It is true, of course, that the petitioners in the present action would be entitled to a jury trial of the issues bearing on whether the proxy statement was materially false and misleading had the SEC action never been brought—a matter to be discussed in Part II of this opinion. But the presence or absence of a jury as factfinder is basically neutral, quite unlike, for example, the necessity of defending the first lawsuit in an inconvenient forum.

The *Galloway* case [319 U.S. 372 (1943)] is particularly instructive. There the party against whom a directed verdict had been entered argued that the procedure was unconstitutional under the Seventh Amendment. In rejecting this claim, the Court said: "The Amendment did not bind the federal courts to the exact procedural incidents or details of jury trial according to the common law in 1791, any more than it tied them to the common-law system of pleading or the specific rules of evidence then prevailing. Nor were 'the rules of the common law' then prevalent, including those relating to the procedure by which the judge regulated the jury's role on questions of fact, crystallized in a fixed and immutable system." . . .

The law of collateral estoppel, like the law in other procedural areas defining the scope of the jury's function, has evolved since 1791. Under the rationale of the *Galloway* case, these developments are not repugnant to the Seventh Amendment simply for the reason that they did not exist in 1791. Thus if, as we have held, the law of collateral estoppel forecloses the petitioners from relitigating the factual issues determined against them in the SEC action, nothing in the Seventh Amendment dictates a different result, even though because of lack of mutuality there would have been no collateral estoppel in 1791. . . .

[The Court held that the Seventh Amendment was not a bar to successful assertion of issue preclusion.

Justice REHNQUIST dissented on the ground that preclusion under these circumstances violated the Seventh Amendment.]

[handwritten margin note: 7th Amend not a bar to assertion of issue preclusion]

NOTES AND PROBLEMS

1. Think of *Parklane* as a variation on Illinois Central Gulf v. Parks.

a. Without joining her husband Jessie, suppose Bertha Parks sues the railroad, alleging its negligence as a cause of her injuries. Bertha wins. In *Parklane*, which party is Bertha and which is the railroad?

b. Jessie Parks now sues the railroad, alleging its negligence as a cause of his injuries. Jessie wants to treat the determination of the railroad's negligence and causation as precluded from relitigation. That issue is identical, was actually litigated and determined, and was essential to the judgment in the first case. In *Parklane*, which party to the second lawsuit is in the same position as Jessie, and what issue did that party want to preclude from relitigation?

c. In fact, the *Parklane* opinion suggests a reason for thinking that *Parks* is a *weaker* case for preclusion than is *Parklane* itself. What opportunity did Jessie Parks have that Shore (the plaintiff in the second *Parklane* suit) did not have? Under *Parklane*, would that opportunity have been sufficient reason for denying Jessie the use of nonmutual-issue preclusion?

2. Consider the following situations in which parties might wish to take advantage of preclusion. In which should they be able to do so?

a. The Rushes, riding on a motorcycle, are thrown off when the cycle hits a pothole. Mrs. Rush, the owner of the cycle, sues the city for $1,000 in damages to the machine. See Rush v. City of Maple Heights, supra page 46. Mrs. Rush brings the suit in municipal court, which uses an abbreviated system of discovery and has a jurisdictional limit of $5,000. City loses. Mr. Rush sues for disabling *N₂* spinal injuries suffered in the same accident; he seeks damages of $1.5 million. Mr. Rush seeks to invoke preclusion on the issue of City's negligence.

b. An airplane crashes. The National Transportation Safety Board investigates the accident in a proceeding in which it calls various witnesses (but in which *No* Airline does not have the right to cross-examine). The NTSB makes a finding that the crash occurred as a result of Airline's negligent failure to train its pilots for a particular predictable emergency situation. Passenger's executor sues, invoking the finding as conclusive of Airline's negligence.

c. Finally, a nonmutual variation on a hypothetical case considered earlier in this section. The federal government accuses an IRS agent of certain criminal acts. She is acquitted. The government then sues Accomplice to recover funds allegedly embezzled in the same criminal acts. Accomplice seeks to invoke preclusion on the grounds that the previous case demonstrates the acts did not occur. Standefer v. United States, 447 U.S. 10 (1980) (no preclusion).

d. These hypothetical cases emphasize a point that should by now be familiar: Lawsuits do not decide "what happened" in the abstract; instead, they decide who, given the procedural setting of the case, made a better showing. If one keeps this point in mind, it is easier to understand why procedural settings that differ significantly may supply a reason not to apply preclusion.

3. *Parklane* joins a number of state cases in permitting nonmutual preclusion. Like *Parklane*, these cases generally cite both efficiency and fairness as grounds for applying preclusion. To this judicial enthusiasm for issue preclusion there is, however, one glaring exception: the federal government. In United States v. Mendoza, 464 U.S. 154 (1984), the Court held that the United States could not be subjected to nonmutual-issue preclusion. The ordinary rules of issue preclusion apply if Party and the United States are involved in two successive lawsuits, but if A sues the United States and prevails, B may not in a later suit use against the United States those issues determined in A's favor. Otherwise put, the principles of *Parklane* do not apply to the United States. Why not? The *Mendoza* Court did not do a remarkably good job of justifying its result, but one can imagine two reasons.

a. There is a practical problem. At present the United States appeals selectively, choosing only those cases in which some principle of law or fact important to the United States is at stake. (The office of the Solicitor General makes these discretionary judgments.) The *Mendoza* court worried that applying *Parklane* to the United States would force the government to appeal virtually every case it lost, for fear of its effect in subsequent cases. Note, however, that this same problem afflicts other large litigants — state governments, Microsoft, General Motors, large insurers — but no such exception has been carved out for them.

b. The United States faces another problem. Many of the suits to which it is a party involve constitutional questions. As things now stand, an unappealed decision of a district court involving a constitutional question affects only those involved in the case itself. It does not even bind other courts in the same district.

If one applied *Parklane* to the United States, all that would change. A single district court decision against the United States on a constitutional issue would become — by virtue of issue preclusion — a kind of superprecedent that would bind all other courts, including the U.S. Supreme Court. For example, suppose a district court in the course of a criminal trial ruled that all searches of automobiles without a warrant were unconstitutional. If that ruling stood, it could be applied against the United States by all subsequent defendants. Moreover, unlike ordinary precedent, the ruling would not be subject to reconsideration or "overruling" by the U.S. Supreme Court. Is this a good enough reason not to extend *Parklane* to the United States? Or does it suggest a narrower exception involving only questions of constitutional law?

4. The widespread move to various forms of comparative negligence raises several questions of issue preclusion.

a. Consider a fairly simple case. Two cars collide; Passenger is riding in one of them. The two drivers sue each other and the case goes to judgment. The jury finds that both drivers were negligent and apportions fault at 70 percent to Driver A and 30 percent to Driver B. If Passenger now sues (assuming the state permits such claims), the apportionment of fault from the former suit will bind both drivers. The reasoning is that both had a fair opportunity to litigate an issue essential to the judgment.

b. But what happens if Passenger sues only one driver, perhaps because she is uncertain about the other's negligence and wishes not to complicate an otherwise clear case? May Passenger take advantage of the finding of negligence as against Driver A alone? Presumably so. Is she limited to collecting only 70 percent of her damages? That will depend on the state's regime of joint and several liability, but in many states Passenger (assuming no fault on her part) will be able to collect her total damage bill from Driver A, who may have an action for equitable indemnification against Driver B.

c. Suppose Passenger is in a state that has modified the common law rules of joint and several liability so that she may collect from each driver only in proportion to his fault. Must Passenger accept the finding that Driver A was only 70 percent at fault, or is she free to show that his proportion was greater? Can Passenger have the sweet without the bitter — the determination of liability without the limitation as to its amount?

5. For those who argue that mutuality is an unnecessary constraint on preclusion, there is a nightmare case: several plaintiffs with essentially identical claims against the same defendant. The typical example is a bus or train crash, with multiple suits brought by injured passengers. Why is this example a nightmare? — Because it illuminates the extent to which everything turns on the outcome of the first case.

a. If the plaintiff won the first case and the second through fiftieth plaintiffs now seek to invoke preclusion, what result under the doctrine of *Parklane*?

b. If the defendant won the first case and now seeks to invoke preclusion against subsequent plaintiffs, what result?

c. Lest you think such situations are confined to the teeming brains of law teachers, consider the next case.

State Farm Fire & Casualty Co. v. Century Home Components

275 Or. 97, 550 P.2d 1185 (1976)

HOLMAN, J.

   Defendant appeals from judgments entered in 13 actions for damages resulting from a fire. These actions were among 48 cases consolidated for a single hearing in the court below on the issue of collateral estoppel. The ruling of the trial court that defendant was collaterally estopped from contesting liability in each of the 48 actions forms the basis for defendant's appeal.

   The fire giving rise to this litigation started early one Sunday morning in the summer of 1968. Defendant constructed prefabricated housing in a large shed. Plaintiffs' property was stored in a warehouse which was located approximately 60 feet from defendant's shed and which was connected thereto by a wooden loading dock. On the side of defendant's shed was a wooden box, called a skip box, into which sawdust from a neighboring saw was customarily deposited. On the Saturday evening preceding the fire, defendant's janitor had dumped a mix of linseed oil and dry sawdust into the box. No employees were present at the time the fire started. Whatever its cause and point of origin, and these are in dispute, the fire spread via the loading dock and caused substantial damage to defendant's shed, the warehouse and its contents.

   Shortly thereafter various actions, eventually totaling over 50, were filed against defendant to recover for losses from the fire. Three of these actions proceeded separately through trial to final judgment. In each case the plaintiffs alleged essentially that defendant was negligent with respect to both the start and spread of the fire. The first case to come to trial resulted in a jury verdict for defendant. On appeal this court reversed the judgment for error in failing to compel defendant to produce a statement needed by the plaintiff for purposes of impeaching a defense witness, and remanded for a new trial. Pacific N.W. Bell v. Century Home. During the pendency of the foregoing appeal the second case was tried and produced another jury verdict for defendant. Sylwester v. Century Home Components, Inc. No appeal was taken from that judgment and it became final. Shortly thereafter the third case was tried and a jury verdict was returned for the plaintiff. This judgment was affirmed on appeal. Hesse v. Century Home. The Pacific N.W. Bell case was subsequently retried, this time to the court sitting without a jury, and the court found for the plaintiff. We affirmed on appeal.

   Following entry of final judgment in both Hesse and Pacific N.W. Bell, the present plaintiffs filed amended and supplemental complaints, conforming their allegations to those in the foregoing cases, and asserted that the judgments therein should operate to preclude defendant from again litigating the question of liability. Defendant alleged in defense that it would be unfair to bar relitigation in view of the similarity of issues between those cases and Sylwester and of the existence of the jury verdict and judgment in defendant's favor in Sylwester. In the consolidated hearing on the question of collateral estoppel the parties submitted the records and transcripts of all three cases. The trial court rendered its ruling in favor of plaintiffs, finding inter alia: "That the allegations of the second amended and supplemental complaint raising the issue of collateral estoppel have been established by the greater weight of the evidence, and that the affirmative allegations of the answer thereto have not been established by the evidence. . . ."

To summarize the posture of these cases, the question of defendant's negligence has been tried four times and three final judgments have been rendered. Defendant has procured one favorable judgment (and two jury verdicts) and the claimants have received two judgments. The present plaintiffs, who were not parties to any of the previous actions, seek to utilize the prior claimants' judgments to establish conclusively defendant's negligence and its responsibility for any loss caused by the fire. . . .

The "multiple-claimant anomaly" was first hypothesized by Brainerd Currie as one instance where, absent mutuality, the unrestrained application of collateral estoppel might produce unfair results. Currie, Mutuality of Collateral Estoppel: Limits of the Bernhard Doctrine, 9 Stan. L. Rev. 281 (1957). Currie posed the situation of a train wreck resulting in 50 separate claims being filed against the railroad for negligence. If the defendant railroad won the first 25 cases and subsequently lost the 26th, Currie characterized as an "absurdity" the notion that the remaining 24 claimants could ride in on the strength of the 26th plaintiff's judgment and estop the defendant on the issue of negligence. The reason was that the 26th judgment would clearly seem to be an aberration. Currie then reasoned that, if we should be unwilling to give preclusive effect to the 26th judgment, we should not afford such effect to an adverse judgment rendered in the *first* action brought because "we have no warrant for assuming that the aberrational judgment will not come as the first in the series." Currie, supra. Currie thus concluded that, absent mutuality, collateral estoppel should not be applied where a defendant potentially faces more than two successive actions.

Those courts which have discarded the rule of mutuality and permit the offensive assertion of collateral estoppel have generally rejected Currie's solution to the multiple-claimant anomaly in situations where the *first* judgment is adverse to the defendant, and have precluded a defendant from relitigating multiple claims where it has been concluded that the defendant had in actuality the incentive and complete opportunity to contest the issue fully in the first action. Currie's reservations were based on the apprehension that the first judgment might well be an aberration, but this view failed to recognize that the very notion of collateral estoppel demands and assumes a certain confidence in the integrity of the end result of our adjudicative process. . . .

As the foregoing discussion would indicate, however, we are not free to disregard incongruous results when they are looking us in the eye. If the circumstances are such that our confidence in the integrity of the determination is severely undermined, or that the result would likely be different in a second trial, it would work an injustice to deny the litigant another chance. Thus, where it is apparent that the verdict was the result of a jury compromise, the losing party should not be precluded by the judgment. . . . It has also been held that if the prior determination was manifestly erroneous the judgment should not be given preclusive effect. Restatement (Second) of Judgments §88(7) and Comment i. (Tent. Draft No. 2, 1975). And the existence of newly discovered or crucial evidence that was not available to the litigant at the first trial would provide a basis for denying preclusion where it appears the evidence would have a significant effect on the outcome.

Those courts and commentators which have considered the question are in virtually unanimous agreement that where outstanding determinations are actually inconsistent on the matter sought to be precluded, it would be patently unfair to estop a party by the judgment it lost. Although Currie's initial perceptions provoked much discussion, the problem has remained largely academic because inconsistent verdicts are rarely encountered. Our research has disclosed only one case where inconsistent determinations by separate trial courts were asserted as a reason for denying collateral estoppel. . . .

We agree with the commentators to the extent at least that, where there are extant determinations that are inconsistent on the matter in issue, it is a strong indication that the application of collateral estoppel would work an injustice. There seems to be something fundamentally offensive about depriving a party of the opportunity to litigate the issue again when he has shown beyond a doubt that on another day he prevailed. . . .

Plaintiffs in the present case contend that the determinations are not "inconsistent" because the issues in *Hesse* and *Pacific N.W. Bell* were not identical with the issues in *Sylwester*. It is true, as plaintiffs point out, that the phrasing of the allegations of negligence differed and that certain specifications of negligence were not submitted to the jury in *Sylwester*. We do not give much weight to variations in the wording of the pleadings, however, where essentially the same acts and omissions are alleged. To concentrate on slight discrepancies in the allegations of negligence would put defendant at a distinct disadvantage, for claimants could modify the wording after each judgment for defendant until one claimant prevailed, after which all remaining claimants could conform their complaints to that of the prevailing claimant and could then successfully claim that the prior judgments for defendant were based upon different issues.

The thrust of plaintiffs' argument must be that the jury in *Hesse* and the court in *Pacific N.W. Bell* adjudicated defendant negligent in respects which were not considered by the jury in *Sylwester*. The records of the cases, however, do not permit such a conclusion. Since the jury in *Hesse* returned a general verdict, we do not know in which respects it found defendant negligent and, given the substantial similarity of some of the allegations and the basic thrust of the negligence alleged, we are unable to conclude that it found defendant negligent on the basis of conduct not submitted to the jury in *Sylwester*. In *Pacific N.W. Bell* the court specifically found that the fire started in defendant's skip box; and that defendant was negligent in failing at the close of the preceding work day to remove combustible materials from its plant, in storing them in a box which was not a suitable receptacle or bin, in placing inflammable wastes in such a manner that defendant knew or should have known that any fire in the skip box was likely to spread to adjacent structures, and in failing to empty the trash box before leaving the premises unattended for the night. Allegations of essentially the same conduct were submitted to the jury in *Sylvester* under proper instructions by the court, and the jury obviously found that defendant was not negligent in the respects specified by the court in *Pacific N.W. Bell*. . . .

We conclude that the prior determinations are basically inconsistent and that the circumstances are such that it would be unfair to preclude defendants from relitigating the issue of liability.

Reversed and remanded.

NOTES AND PROBLEMS

1. The court concludes that because there were several lawsuits with varying verdicts, issue preclusion should not apply.

a. Could one argue that this was a stronger case for issue preclusion than in the ordinary case because here one had several verdicts, most pointing in one direction?

b. Does *Century Home Components* suggest that issue preclusion rests as much on the desire to prevent inconsistency as it does on the goal of efficiency?

2. Suppose Baker sues Welch and invokes prior judgments involving identical issues against Welch and in favor of Slater and Schultz. The trial court denies issue-preclusion effect to the earlier judgments, and the action is tried to the jury. Welch prevails. On appeal, Baker demands that the appellate court set aside the judgment of the trial court and order it to enter judgment in Baker's favor. What result? If the appellate court grants Baker's requests, would it thereby promote efficiency and consistency, the twin goals of issue preclusion?

3. Professor Currie doubtless was correct when he observed a certain inconsistency between disallowing issue preclusion (in favor of the plaintiff) when the defendant wins the first nine cases but loses the tenth and allowing it when the defendant loses the first action. Is such a system unfair to the defendant?: "Heads I win; tails we play over and over until I win." Another way of putting the point is to say that the rules of nonmutual preclusion make it very difficult for the defendant to place a value on litigation while it is in progress: A loss can have devastating consequences, but a victory's value is confined to a single case.

4. One solution to the problem posed by *Century Home Components* lies in judicial control of dockets. In many jurisdictions, claims arising out of the same episode — a large building fire, an airplane crash — will be assigned to the same judge for consolidated proceedings. That judge's management of the case can have substantial implications for the application of preclusion.

a. Suppose such consolidation had occurred in *Century Home Components* and that the second *Pacific N.W. Bell* case (recall that plaintiffs contended this was the best-tried of all the cases) had come first. At that point the judge would have been writing on a clean slate: one case, well-tried, with a plaintiff's verdict resulting. Preclusion might have seemed like an attractive possibility.

b. To avoid the premature use of preclusion, some judges faced with these circumstances will purposely set several cases for trial to see if the results are inconsistent or if a pattern develops. Is this a better approach?

5. *Century Home Components* involved a single occurrence affecting several parties; the analogy to a transportation disaster seems apt. But there are other patterns of mass torts, one of the most common of which is the mass product liability case. One of the major areas of such litigation has been claims of asbestos-related injuries. The general fact patterns are similar: Workers in factories, shipyards, or in mining, years after exposure to various forms of asbestos, develop one of several forms of lung disease.

a. One might imagine that such litigation would present an occasion for applying issue preclusion against defendant producers of asbestos. But the courts have not typically done so. Should they?

b. As the asbestos cases have developed, a variation on preclusion has occurred. As hundreds of cases have been tried over a number of years, the lawyers on both sides have come to recognize patterns of verdicts. These patterns include both determinations of liability (was the plaintiff's death caused by, for example, smoking rather than by asbestos?) and of damages. Using these patterns of verdicts, lawyers and judges have begun to develop bases for settling the cases relatively quickly, sometimes without any formal court proceedings.

c. Is such a development a triumph or a failure of the system? On the one hand, it seems clear that the pattern of verdicts provides a much more reliable basis for assessment than a single case, no matter how well tried. On the other hand, the litigants whose cases have produced that pattern have "paid" for the information, sometimes quite literally with their lives.

6. The position of the Restatement (Second) of Judgments on mutuality is as follows:

§29. Issue Preclusion in Subsequent Litigation with Others

A party precluded from relitigating an issue with an opposing party, in accordance with §§27 and 28,* is also precluded from doing so with another person unless he lacked full and fair opportunity to litigate the issue in the first action or other circumstances justify affording him an opportunity to relitigate the issue. The circumstances to which considerations should be given include those enumerated in §28 and also whether:

(1) Treating the issue as conclusively determined would be incompatible with an applicable scheme of administering the remedies in the actions involved;

(2) The forum in the second action affords the party against whom preclusion is asserted procedural opportunities in the presentation and determination of the issue that were not available in the first action and that could likely result in the issue being differently determined;

(3) The person seeking to invoke favorable preclusion, or to avoid unfavorable preclusion, could have effected joinder in the first action between himself and his present adversary;

(4) The determination relied on as preclusive was itself inconsistent with another determination of the same issue;

* See supra page 686 and infra pages 710-712.

(5) The prior determination may have been affected by relationships among the parties to the first action that are not present in the subsequent action, or apparently was based on a compromise verdict or finding;

(6) Treating the issue as conclusively determined may complicate determination of issues in the subsequent action or prejudice the interests of another party thereto;

(7) The issue is one of law and treating it as conclusively determined would inappropriately foreclose opportunity for obtaining reconsideration of the legal rule upon which it was based;

(8) Other compelling circumstances make it appropriate that the party be permitted to relitigate the issue.

Restatement (Second) of Judgments. Do any of these factors justify the result in *Century Home Components*? Is there a common thread running through these exceptions?

7. Should issue preclusion apply if the first case is a criminal proceeding? In Teitelbaum Furs, Inc. v. Dominion Insurance Co., 58 Cal. 2d 601, 375 P.2d 439, 25 Cal. Rptr. 559 (1962), cert. denied, 372 U.S. 966 (1963), Teitelbaum Furs sued to recover on a theft insurance policy. The insurance company sought to invoke a criminal judgment convicting Teitelbaum, plaintiff's president, of stealing the furs. The court applied issue preclusion, finding that Teitelbaum was the alter ego of the company and had been "afforded a full opportunity to litigate the issue of his guilt with all the safeguards afforded the criminal litigant, and . . . he had every possible motive to make as vigorous a defense as possible." 58 Cal. 2d at 606-607, 375 P.2d at 441, 25 Cal. Rptr. at 661. Teitelbaum's decision not to testify was, according to the court, a matter of trial strategy not affecting issue preclusion. Is this an adequate resolution of the differences between civil and criminal proceedings?

C.   The Boundaries of Preclusion

With *Century Home Components* we have already begun to approach the topic of this section — the point at which preclusion doctrines should yield. Both claim and issue preclusion are judge-made doctrines, and neither is engraved in stone. With the exception of the full faith and credit issues, to be considered in the next section, and the due process restrictions on the excessive use of either doctrine, neither has significant constitutional dimensions. Thus it is not surprising that other policies should occasionally challenge the applications of either doctrine.

1.   Claim Preclusion

Claim preclusion, or res judicata, has more stringent requirements than issue preclusion and therefore presents fewer opportunities for anomalous results. Section 26 of the Restatement (Second) of Judgments lists some straightforward reasons for declining to apply claim preclusion: where the parties have expressly or implicitly agreed to allow claim splitting; where a court has in the first action reserved plaintiff's right to bring the second; or where jurisdictional limitations prevented plaintiff from seeking certain forms of relief now sought. Past that point, the Restatement enters uncertain ground:

§26. Exceptions to the General Rule Concerning Splitting

(1) When any of the following circumstances exists, the general rule of §24 does not apply to extinguish the claim, and part or all of the claim subsists as a possible basis for a second action by the plaintiff against the defendant: . . . .

(d) The judgment in the first action was plainly inconsistent with the fair and equitable implementation of a statutory or constitutional scheme, or it is the sense of the scheme that the plaintiff should be permitted to split his claim; or

(e) For reasons of substantive policy in a case involving a continuing or recurrent wrong, the plaintiff is given an option to sue once for the total harm, both past and prospective, or to sue from time to time for the damages incurred to the date of suit, and chooses the latter course; or

(f) It is clearly and convincingly shown that the policies favoring preclusion of a second action are overcome for an extraordinary reason, such as the apparent invalidity of a continuing restraint or condition having a vital relation to personal liberty or the failure of the prior litigation to yield a coherent disposition of the controversy.

The situation imagined in (d) typically involves a broadly applicable law as to which interpretation has changed. Imagine that in the years before Brown v. Board of Education, 347 U.S. 483 (1954), a school child sues seeking racial integration of her school. She loses. The next year *Brown* is decided. It has to be possible for the plaintiff, otherwise bound by the now rejected interpretation of the Constitution, to take advantage of the changed law. Section 26(e) seeks the same result for situations involving repeated interactions between the same parties.

The final catchall exception is designed to help courts out of messes that inconsistent prior decisions can lead to. One prominent example is Adams v. Pearson, 411 Ill. 431, 104 N.E.2d 267 (1952). Adams sold a farm to Pearson for a down payment of $4,000 and a balance of $14,600, to be paid when Pearson sold a farm in Indiana. The contract required Adams and his wife to sign a warranty deed. When Mrs. Adams refused to sign, Pearson sued for specific performance. Adams counterclaimed, seeking rescission of the contract in a counterclaim to Pearson's suit for specific performance. The court denied specific performance because it was unavailable in Illinois at that time in cases in which the wife had not waived her dower right. The court also denied the counterclaim, however, because there was no showing of fraud on Pearson's part. Pearson had been in possession of the farm since the time of the signing of the contract but had refused to pay the balance of the contract price without the warranty deed. Adams then brought an action in ejectment; Pearson counterclaimed for specific performance in the form of a warranty deed signed by Adams alone. Both parties pleaded claim preclusion as a defense to the claim of the other. As the Illinois Supreme Court noted, application of the doctrine would have been standard under most circumstances but would have left Pearson, after ten years of litigation, with possession but not title, and Adams, after ten years, with title but no money. The court decided that application of claim preclusion was inappropriate and that the equities of the case lay with Pearson, who was allowed to prevail in his counterclaim for a warranty deed signed by Adams but not his wife.

Apart from these rather unusual circumstances, courts take claim preclusion very seriously, even when the prior decision has obviously been erroneous. Recall Gargallo v. Merrill, Lynch, Pierce, Fenner & Smith, supra page 683, in which the Sixth Circuit was prepared to give preclusive effect to a state court judgment on a claim over which federal courts have exclusive jurisdiction. Matsushita Elec. Industrial Co. v. Epstein, supra page 486, provides another example. Again, there was a state court judgment embodying a settlement of a securities claim over which the federal courts have exclusive jurisdiction. For the majority in *Matsushita*, the only question to be discussed was whether the state courts would assign preclusive effects to such a judgment.

2.   Issue Preclusion

Exceptions to the application of issue preclusion, or collateral estoppel, are more numerous than exceptions to claim preclusion. The Restatement (Second) of Judgments §28, excerpts of which are reprinted below, provides a guide to the terrain:

§28. Exceptions to the General Rule of Issue Preclusion

Although an issue is actually litigated and determined by a valid and final judgment, and the determination is essential to the judgment, relitigation of the issue in a subsequent action between the parties is not precluded in the following circumstances:

   (1) The party against whom preclusion is sought could not, as a matter of law, have obtained review of the judgment in the initial action. . . .

An example of this principle may be found in Murphy v. Andrews, 465 F. Supp. 511 (E.D. Pa. 1979), in which the plaintiff charged various police officials with violation of his civil rights by beating him in an attempt to obtain a confession from him. In the criminal proceedings against him, plaintiff sought to suppress his confession on those grounds but lost the motion on a finding that illegal duress had not taken place. Subsequently, another party confessed to the murder, and plaintiff was acquitted. Plaintiff then brought the civil action in question, and defendants argued that the ruling in the criminal case settled the question of the legality of the interrogation. The court ruled otherwise, suggesting that even if plaintiff had appealed the denial of the suppression order, the appeal would have been useless because of the acquittal. Note that this latter rationale suggests a principle somewhat broader than that set out in §28 of the Restatement. The original draft of this section specified that the review of the judgment should be "by an appellate court"; the deletion presumably indicates that the drafters may have had in mind proceedings in which a federal district court reviews a magistrate judge's findings or in which a trial court reviews an administrative agency's findings.

(2) The issue is one of law and (a) the two actions involve claims that are substantially unrelated, or (b) a new determination is warranted in order to take account of an intervening change in the applicable legal context or otherwise to avoid inequitable administration of the laws. . . .

In Commissioner v. Sunnen, 333 U.S. 591 (1948), a device for attributing certain income to a wife instead of her husband (in order to pay a lower rate on it) had been upheld by a decision of the Board of Tax Appeals. The device was used for many years, and the IRS challenged it again after a series of decisions had undercut the reasoning of the original decision. The Supreme Court denied application of issue preclusion against the IRS on several grounds, including the change in the applicable law. Why is *Sunnen* an issue-preclusion rather than a claim-preclusion case?

(3) A new determination of the issue is warranted by differences in the quality or extensiveness of the procedures followed in the two courts or by factors relating to the allocation of jurisdiction between them. . . .

Newport News Shipbuilding and Drydock Co. v. Director, 583 F.2d 1273 (4th Cir. 1978), illustrates the point relating to jurisdiction of the two courts. Plaintiff had sought damages for a work-related lung disease from the Virginia Industrial Commission, a tribunal with jurisdiction only over workers' injuries and with limited appellate review. He lost on a finding that the injury did not arise in the course of employment. The plaintiff subsequently sought compensation in federal court under the federal Longshoremen's and Harbor Workers' Compensation Act. The finding of the state industrial commission that the injury did not arise out of the plaintiff's employment was not given issue-preclusion effect because of the commission's limited jurisdiction.

In another common application of this principle, actions in small claims or traffic courts do not have issue-preclusion effect. Thus the defendant's conviction in traffic court for speeding will not give rise to issue preclusion in a subsequent negligence action. This result is a practical recognition of the informal procedures and lack of adequate opportunity for discovery that often prevail in such courts.

(4) The party against whom preclusion is sought had a significantly heavier burden of persuasion with respect to the issue in the initial action than in the subsequent action; the burden has shifted to his adversary; or the adversary has a significantly heavier burden than he had in the first action. . . .

Newport News Shipbuilding also illustrates this principle, because the worker had the burden of showing by a preponderance of the evidence before the state industrial board that his injury arose out of his employment, while his burden in the federal action was much weaker.

(5) There is a clear and convincing need for a new determination of the issue (a) because of the potential adverse impact of the determination on the public interest

or the interests of persons not themselves parties in the initial action, (b) because it was not sufficiently foreseeable at the time of the initial action that the issue would arise in the context of a subsequent action, or (c) because the party sought to be precluded, as a result of the conduct of his adversary or other special circumstances, did not have an adequate opportunity or incentive to obtain a full and fair adjudication in the initial action.

Points (b) and (c) are discussed in both *Parklane Hosiery* and *Century Home Components*. Point (a) was an alternative basis for the holding for the *Sunnen* tax case: The public interest in the evenhanded application of the tax laws suggested that a taxpayer should not be able to take perpetual advantage of an earlier superseded decision. A similar rationale has been applied to decisions categorizing goods for import duty purposes. Assume *A* and *B* import the same products. *A* engages in litigation with the government and obtains a favorable ruling concerning import duties, and *B* litigates with the government and receives an unfavorable decision. Giving permanent issue-preclusion effect to *A*'s judgment will give *A* a permanent competitive advantage over *B*. United States v. Stone & Downer Co., 274 U.S. 225 (1927). Note also that the public interest may also call for application of issue preclusion and even the abandonment of mutuality. The decision in Blonder-Tongue, discussed extensively in Parklane Hosiery, was based partially on the public interest in consistent adjudications with respect to the same patent: If some manufacturers are bound by a patent while others have won adjudications of its invalidity, the market will be distorted by the unequal costs of the suppliers, some of whom have to pay royalties while others do not.

3. The Law of the Case and "Judicial Estoppel"

Two doctrines logically and technically distinct from claim and issue preclusion sometimes play roles resembling them: the law of the case and "judicial estoppel" (also sometimes known as preclusion of inconsistent positions). A brief survey may help to clarify their rather narrow roles and to distinguish them from claim and issue preclusion.

The law of the case functions within a single case to prevent relitigation of decided points of law. Suppose that plaintiff seeks injunctive relief concerning an allegedly unconstitutional municipal hiring practice — perhaps a requirement that city police officers be residents of the city. The district court grants a preliminary injunction, and, pursuant to 28 U.S.C. §1292(a)(1), the loser appeals. The appellate court affirms the district court's interpretation of the law and remands for a trial on final injunctive relief. Neither the doctrine of precedent nor the doctrine of issue preclusion would prevent the loser from seeking to re-argue his position on remand to the district court nor on a subsequent appeal of the final judgment. Precedent would not apply because it is the same case, and issue preclusion would not apply because there would as yet be no final judgment. Enter the law of the case, which serves to stabilize such a legal ruling once it has been made. That doctrine essentially says that the parties get a single appellate shot at their legal contentions and that, once they have achieved such an appellate ruling, it continues to govern in subsequent trial and appellate proceedings. If the loser does not like the initial appellate ruling, his remedy lies in a petition for certiorari to the U.S. Supreme Court. What he may not do is to continue to argue the question in the lower courts.

The doctrine of judicial estoppel (or preclusion of inconsistent positions) lacks the sharp definition of the law of the case. Not all courts apply it, and those that do cannot entirely agree on its definition. Courts typically invoke judicial estoppel when a party has taken a sworn position in a prior proceeding, benefited from that position by receiving a judgment or other official award, and now seeks to take a differing position in the present proceeding in order to win a judgment that would rest on a basis inconsistent with his prior position. One court has sought to describe judicial estoppel by contrasting it with issue preclusion:

> Collateral estoppel forecloses "the relitigation of issues of fact or law that are identical to issues which have been actually determined and necessarily decided in prior litigation in which the party against whom [issue preclusion] is asserted had a full and fair opportunity to litigate." . . .
>
> . . . [By contrast, "j]udicial estoppel precludes a party from adopting a position that is inconsistent with a stance taken in prior litigation," John S. Clark Co. v. Faggert & Frieden P.C., 65 F.3d 26, 28 (4th Cir. 1995), and is designed to prevent a party from "playing fast and loose" with the courts and "protect the essential integrity of the judicial process." Allen v. Zurich Ins. Co., 667 F.2d 1162, 1166 (4th Cir. 1982). Although "courts have had difficulty in formulating a specific test for determining when judicial estoppel should be applied," at least three elements must always be satisfied. First, the party sought to be estopped must assert a position inconsistent with that taken in prior litigation and the position must be one of fact rather than law or legal theory. Second, the prior inconsistent position must have been accepted by the court. And third, the party sought to be estopped must intentionally have misled the court to gain unfair advantage.

Sedlack v. Braswell Services Group Inc., 134 F.3d 219 (4th Cir. 1998). To this definition one should add that the party has benefited from the court's adopting its factual contention.

Some cases have invoked judicial estoppel in the context of successive actions by former employees who have obtained Social Security benefits (SSDI) — on grounds of total disability — and then have sued their employers under the Americans with Disabilities Act (ADA) or the Age Discrimination in Employment Act, alleging fitness for employment. The Supreme Court has tried to sort out circumstances in which judicial estoppel is appropriate:

> We believe that, in context, these two seemingly divergent statutory contentions are often consistent, each with the other. Thus pursuit, and receipt, of SSDI benefits does not automatically estop the recipient from pursuing an ADA claim. Nor does the law erect a strong presumption against the recipient's success under the ADA. Nonetheless, an ADA plaintiff cannot simply ignore her SSDI contention that she was too disabled to work. To survive a defendant's motion for summary judgment, she must explain why that SSDI contention is consistent with her ADA claim that

714 XII. Respect for Judgments

she could "perform the essential functions" of her previous job, at least with "reasonable accommodation."...

This case does not involve ... directly conflicting statements about purely factual matters, such as "The light was red/green," or "I can/cannot raise my arm above my head." An SSA representation of total disability differs from a purely factual statement in that it often implies a context-related legal conclusion, namely "I am disabled for purposes of the Social Security Act." And our consideration of this latter kind of statement consequently leaves the law related to the former, purely factual, kind of conflict where we found it....

Nonetheless, in some cases an earlier SSDI claim may turn out genuinely to conflict with an ADA claim. Summary judgment for a defendant is appropriate when the plaintiff "fails to make a showing sufficient to establish the existence of an element essential to [her] case, and on which [she] will bear the burden of proof at trial." Celotex Corp. v. Catrett, [supra page 516]. An ADA plaintiff bears the burden of proving that she is a "qualified individual with a disability"—that is, a person "who, with or without reasonable accommodation, can perform the essential functions" of her job. And a plaintiff's sworn assertion in an application for disability benefits that she is, for example, "unable to work" will appear to negate an essential element of her ADA case—at least if she does not offer a sufficient explanation. For that reason, we hold that an ADA plaintiff cannot simply ignore the apparent contradiction that arises out of the earlier SSDI total disability claim. Rather, she must proffer a sufficient explanation....

When faced with a plaintiff's previous sworn statement asserting "total disability" or the like, the court should require an explanation of any apparent inconsistency with the necessary elements of an ADA claim. To defeat summary judgment, that explanation must be sufficient to warrant a reasonable juror's concluding that, assuming the truth of, or the plaintiff's good faith belief in, the earlier statement, the plaintiff could nonetheless "perform the essential functions" of her job, with or without "reasonable accommodation."

Cleveland v. Policy Management Systems, 119 S. Ct. 1597 (1999).

Note that with issue preclusion an issue must have been contested and decided *against* the party burdened with preclusion; with judicial estoppel the party burdened has typically *prevailed* in the prior litigation, with a court adopting its position. Thus, for example, two successive cases involved a the question of whether a pension plan was subject to ERISA, a federal statute regulation retirement and health benefits. In the first suit the employer denied that ERISA applied, but settled the suit. In the second, the employer, now a plaintiff, sued an insurer, this time arguing that the plan was subject to ERISA. No judicial estoppel, said the Third Circuit. The two positions were entirely inconsistent, but no court had ever adopted the employer's position in the first suit, and the settlement left it free to pursue a different argument in the second case. Montrose Medical Group v. Bulger, — F.3rd — (3d Cir. 2001).

Judicial estoppel, whatever its exact contours, is in some tension with Rule 8(e)(2), which permits a party to state as many claims as it has, "regardless of consistency." As you have seen, the explanation of this rule lies in the parties' uncertainty about which set of facts they will be able to persuasively present. Can one reconcile the apparent conflict between Rule 8(e)(2) and the doctrine of judicial estoppel? Judicial estoppel applies not to pleadings but to sworn positions taken in actual proceedings. Many courts further limit it to situations in which those sworn statements have resulted in a judgment or award to the party now taking the inconsistent position. Are the values protected by judicial estoppel sufficiently important to warrant its elaboration? Or can we rely on the opposing party and factfinder's good sense to discredit parties who talk — under oath — out of both sides of their mouths?

D. Repose: Collateral Attack and Reopened Judgments

This chapter has focused on a pair of common law doctrines that prevent subsequent lawsuits from undermining judgments. Claim preclusion, by preventing subsequent litigation on the same claim, requires the parties to include related grievances in the same suit. Issue preclusion prevents inconsistent findings when subsequent litigation is permitted. We turn now to two principles that ensure that courts heed the doctrines of former adjudication without producing unfair hardship.

To see their relationship, consider a hypothetical case. Motorists from New York and New Jersey collide with each other. New Jersey plaintiff sues New York defendant in New Jersey state court and loses. Could plaintiff try again by going to New York and suing there in either state or federal court? Or suppose that after the original case has gone to judgment, plaintiff discovers a witness who supplies the crucial missing evidence of defendant's negligence; moreover, plaintiff discovers that defendant knew of the witness but failed to reveal his existence in response to interrogatories. Can plaintiff somehow bring this evidence before the court? The doctrines of claim preclusion do not answer the first question because, as common law doctrines, they speak only to the courts of a given jurisdiction. As the next section shows, principles of full faith and credit back up the common law by insisting that courts of one jurisdiction heed the judgments of another. But the doctrines of former adjudication, reinforced by full faith and credit, have the potential to work injustice if they perpetuate defendant's fraudulent concealment of evidence in the second case. To prevent that, legislatures have created the opportunity, in limited circumstances, to reopen a judgment.

1. Full Faith and Credit as a Bar to Collateral Attack

The common law doctrines of claim and issue preclusion require courts of any given political unit to heed the judgments of courts of that unit. However, they give no guidance respecting the judgments of sister jurisdictions — other states or the federal government. Two provisions of law fill that silence. Section 1738 of 28 U.S.C. demands that federal courts give the same full faith and credit to state court judgments as those states would give. Though the statute does not mention full faith and credit to federal court judgments, that requirement has always been assumed and is not questioned. The Constitution itself, in Article IV, places the same obligation on state courts to recognize sister-state judgments.

If one puts these provisions together with the common law of preclusion, they create an apparently seamless web. Within any given political unit, the law of preclusion prevents attacks on the judgment: Anything that was or could have been litigated in the previous case may not be relitigated. Across the boundaries of political units, the principles of full faith and credit require that the courts of one unit give to sister courts' judgments the same credence they would have in the unit that rendered them. We have already seen these principles in operation in Gargallo v. Merrill, Lynch, Pierce, Fenner & Smith and Matsushita Elec. Industrial Co. v. Epstein, supra pages 683 and 486.

There is, however, a hole — of indeterminate size — in this doctrinal tapestry. That hole is created by a nineteenth century doctrine that has been eroded but not entirely eliminated. As you will recall from the study of jurisdiction, under some circumstances one may collaterally attack a judgment on the grounds that the court rendering it lacked jurisdiction. (That is one of the holdings of Pennoyer v. Neff, supra page 61.) Nineteenth century courts often asserted this proposition in sweeping terms, saying that a judgment entered without jurisdiction was "void." One implication of that proposition was that such a judgment was not entitled to full faith and credit.

Put in the most general terms, the objection that a judgment was invalid for want of jurisdiction created a sizable hole in the doctrines of finality. Twentieth century courts have begun, cautiously, to patch some of the hole. The next case describes the extent of this patching.

Durfee v. Duke

375 U.S. 106 (1963)

Mr. Justice STEWART delivered the opinion of the Court.

The United States Constitution requires that "Full Faith and Credit shall be given in each State to the . . . judicial Proceedings of every other State." The case before us presents questions arising under this constitutional provision and under the federal statute enacted to implement it.

In 1956 the petitioners brought an action against the respondent in a Nebraska court to quiet title to certain bottom land situated on the Missouri River. The main channel of that river forms the boundary between the States of Nebraska and Missouri. The Nebraska court had jurisdiction over the subject matter of the controversy only if the land in question was in Nebraska. Whether the land was Nebraska land depended entirely upon a factual question — whether a shift in the river's course had been caused by avulsion or accretion.[3] The respondent appeared in the Nebraska court and through counsel fully litigated the issues, explicitly contesting the court's jurisdiction over the subject

---

3. Throughout this litigation there has been no dispute as to the controlling effect of this factual issue.

matter of the controversy.[4] After a hearing the court found the issues in favor of the petitioners and ordered that title to the land be quieted in them. The respondent appealed, and the Supreme Court of Nebraska affirmed the judgment after a trial de novo on the record made in the lower court. The State Supreme Court specifically found that the rule of avulsion was applicable, that the land in question was in Nebraska, that the Nebraska courts therefore had jurisdiction of the subject matter of the litigation, and that title to the land was in the petitioners. The respondent did not petition this Court for a writ of certiorari to review that judgment.

Two months later the respondent filed a suit against the petitioners in a Missouri court to quiet title to the same land. Her complaint alleged that the land was in Missouri. The suit was removed to a Federal District Court by reason of diversity of citizenship. The District Court after hearing evidence expressed the view that the land was in Missouri but held that all the issues had been adjudicated and determined in the Nebraska litigation, and that the judgment of the Nebraska Supreme Court was res judicata and "is now binding upon this court." The Court of Appeals reversed, holding that the District Court was not required to give full faith and credit to the Nebraska judgment, and that normal res judicata principles were not applicable because the controversy involved land and a court in Missouri was therefore free to retry the question of the Nebraska court's jurisdiction over the subject matter. We granted certiorari to consider a question important to the administration of justice in our federal system. For the reasons that follow, we reverse the judgment before us.

The constitutional command of full faith and credit, as implemented by Congress, requires that "judicial proceedings . . . shall have the same full faith and credit in every court within the United States . . . as they have by law or usage in the courts of such State . . . from which they are taken." Full faith and credit thus generally requires every State to give to a judgment at least the res judicata effect which the judgment would be accorded in the State which rendered it. "By the Constitutional provision for full faith and credit, the local doctrines of res judicata, speaking generally, become part of national jurisprudence, and therefore federal questions cognizable here."

It is not questioned that the Nebraska courts would give full res judicata effect to the Nebraska judgment quieting title in the petitioners. It is the respondent's position, however, that whatever effect the Nebraska courts might give to the Nebraska judgment, the federal court in Missouri was free independently to determine whether the Nebraska court in fact had jurisdiction over the subject matter, i.e., whether the land in question was actually in Nebraska.

In support of this position the respondent relies upon the many decisions of this Court which have held that a judgment of a court in one State is conclusive upon the merits in a court in another State only if the court in the first State had power to pass on the merits — had jurisdiction, that is, to render the judgment.

4. This is, therefore, not a case in which a party, although afforded an opportunity to contest subject-matter jurisdiction, did not litigate the issue. Cf. Chicot County Drainage Dist. v. Baxter State Bank, 308 U.S. 371.

As Mr. Justice Bradley stated the doctrine in the leading case of Thompson v. Whitman, 18 Wall. 457 [(1873)], "we think it clear that the jurisdiction of the court by which a judgment is rendered in any State may be questioned in a collateral proceeding in another State, notwithstanding the provision of the fourth article of the Constitution and the law of 1790, and notwithstanding the averments contained in the record of the judgment itself." The principle has been restated and applied in a variety of contexts.

However, while it is established that a court in one State, when asked to give effect to the judgment of a court in another State, may constitutionally inquire into the foreign court's jurisdiction to render that judgment, the modern decisions of this Court have carefully delineated the permissible scope of such an inquiry. From these decisions there emerges the general rule that a judgment is entitled to full faith and credit — even as to questions of jurisdiction — when the second court's inquiry disclosed that those questions have been fully and fairly litigated and finally decided in the court which rendered the original judgment.

With respect to questions of jurisdiction over the person,[8] this principle was unambiguously established in Baldwin v. Iowa State Traveling Men's Assn., 283 U.S. 522 [(1931)]. There it was held that a federal court in Iowa must give binding effect to the judgment of a federal court in Missouri despite the claim that the original court did not have jurisdiction over the defendant's person, once it was shown to the court in Iowa that that question had been fully litigated in the Missouri forum. "Public policy," said the Court, "dictates that there be an end of litigation; that those who have contested an issue shall be bound by the result of the contest, and that matters once tried shall be considered forever settled as between the parties. We see no reason why this doctrine should not apply in every case where one voluntarily appears, presents his case and is fully heard, and why he should not, in the absence of fraud, be thereafter concluded by the judgment of the tribunal to which he has submitted his cause."

Following the Baldwin case, this Court soon made clear in a series of decisions that the general rule is no different when the claim is made that the original forum did not have jurisdiction over the subject matter. In each of these cases the claim was made that a court, when asked to enforce the judgment of another forum, was free to retry the question of that forum's jurisdiction over the subject matter. In each case this Court held that since the question of subject-matter jurisdiction had been fully litigated in the original forum, the issue could not be retried in a subsequent action between the parties. . . .

In Treinies [v. Sunshine Mining Co., 308 U.S. 66 (1939)], the rule was succinctly stated: "One trial of an issue is enough. 'The principles of res judicata apply to questions of jurisdiction as well as to other issues,' as well to jurisdiction of the subject matter as of the parties." . . .

To be sure, the general rule of finality or jurisdictional determinations is not without exceptions. Doctrines of federal pre-emption or sovereign immunity may

---

8. It is not disputed in the present case that the Nebraska courts had jurisdiction over the respondent's person. She entered a general appearance in the trial court, and initiated the appeal to the Nebraska Supreme Court.

in some contexts be controlling. Kalb v. Feuerstein, 308 U.S. 433 [(1940)]; United States v. United States Fidelity Co., 309 U.S. 506 [(1940)].[12] But no such overriding considerations are present here. . . .

It is to be emphasized that all that was ultimately determined in the Nebraska litigation was title to the land in question as between the parties to the litigation there. Nothing there decided, and nothing that could be decided in litigation between the same parties or their privies in Missouri, could bind either Missouri or Nebraska with respect to any controversy they might have, now or in the future, as to the location of the boundary between them, or as to their respective sovereignty over the land in question. Either State may at any time protect its interest by initiating independent judicial proceedings here.

For the reasons stated, we hold in this case that the federal court in Missouri had the power and, upon proper averments, the duty to inquire into the jurisdiction of the Nebraska courts to render the decree quieting title to the land in the petitioners. We further hold that when that inquiry disclosed, as it did, that the jurisdictional issues had been fully and fairly litigated by the parties and finally determined in the Nebraska courts, the federal court in Missouri was correct in ruling that further inquiry was precluded. Accordingly the judgment of the Court of Appeals is reversed, and that of the District Court is affirmed.

It is so ordered.

Mr. Justice BLACK, concurring.

Petitioners and respondent dispute the ownership of a tract of land adjacent to the Missouri River, which is the boundary between Nebraska and Missouri. Resolution of this question turns on whether the land is in Nebraska or Missouri. Neither State, of course, has power to make a determination binding on the other as to which State the land is in. U.S. Const., Art. III, §2; 28 U.S.C. §1251(a). However, in a private action brought by these Nebraska petitioners, the Nebraska Supreme Court has held that the disputed tract is in Nebraska. In the present suit, brought by this Missouri respondent in Missouri, the United States Court of Appeals has refused to be bound by the Nebraska court's judgment. I concur in today's reversal of the Court of Appeal's judgment, but with the understanding that we are not deciding the question whether the respondent would continue to be bound by the Nebraska judgment should it later be authoritatively decided, either in an original proceeding between the States in this Court or by a compact between the two States under Art. I, §10, that the disputed tract is in Missouri.

NOTES AND PROBLEMS

1. Begin by framing the issue clearly.

a. *Durfee* seems to be a simple case: The contesting party appeared, specifically litigated the issue of jurisdiction (both at trial and on appeal), and lost. There had been a full judicial airing of the contested matter.

12. It is to be noted, however, that in neither of these cases had the jurisdictional issues actually been litigated in the first forum. . . .

b. Suppose that the question a party sought to relitigate was an ordinary factual one: the date of a purported deed conveying the land. If a Nebraska court had decided that question, ordinary preclusion doctrine would bar its relitigation in any subsequent action between the same parties. The Full Faith and Credit clauses would require that a Missouri court (or a federal court) give the same effect to that decided issue as a Nebraska court.

c. In fact the Nebraska court had decided an issue — whether it had jurisdiction over the subject matter of the case.

d. So why did Duke think he could relitigate the question in another court?

2. Suppose the Missouri parties had not appeared in the Nebraska action (believing that the Nebraska court had no jurisdiction over them or their property), and the Nebraska parties did not appear in the Missouri federal court proceedings on a similar ground. Each court, believing the land to be located within its jurisdiction, could claim jurisdiction based on the fact that ownership of the land was directly in dispute (citing Shaffer v. Heitner. See Chapter II). But neither side could invoke the principle of *Durfee*, could it? What would be the result if the Nebraska court ordered its sheriff to protect the possession of the Nebraska parties and the federal court ordered the federal marshal to evict the Nebraska parties?

3. Suppose the Missouri parties had appeared in the Nebraska proceedings but failed to raise the jurisdictional issue. There would be no issue preclusion because the issue was not actually litigated and determined. Is there nevertheless waiver of the jurisdictional defense?

The answer to that question is cloudy because of the maneuvering room created by nineteenth century courts that had declared that judgments entered without jurisdiction were "void," with the corollary that they could be attacked (or ignored) in subsequent litigation. Because the issue decided in the Missouri proceeding could be described as jurisdiction, Duke could argue that he was free to challenge it collaterally.

4. Understanding this maneuvering room requires a review of the half-steps by which the Court has almost — but not quite — assimilated jurisdictional challenges to other preclusion doctrine.

a. The starting point is Pennoyer v. Neff, which states that an unnotified party over whom the court lacks personal jurisdiction may collaterally challenge the resulting judgment.

b. The opposite proposition — that a party who appears and contests personal jurisdiction is bound by the court's decision on the jurisdictional question — was decided in Baldwin v. Iowa State Traveling Men's Assn., described in the *Durfee* opinion.

c. *Durfee* itself extends the *Baldwin* holding to subject matter jurisdiction: A party who appears and litigates a challenge to subject matter jurisdiction is bound by the resulting decision.

d. Defendants who appear but fail to raise a challenge to personal jurisdiction are universally treated as having waived their objections. Rule 12(h).

5. The principles thus far described leave gaps: How does one treat a defendant who was properly notified but failed to raise an objection to subject matter

jurisdiction? (One might further subdivide matters by distinguishing between defendants who defaulted and those who appeared but defended on other, nonjurisdictional grounds.) It is here that the Supreme Court has wavered — almost but not quite endorsing the ordinary rules of preclusion — that would preclude relitigation of jurisdictional issues under these circumstances.

a. The Court's nearest approach to this "ordinary principles of preclusion" position came in Chicot County Drainage District v. Baxter State Bank, 308 U.S. 371 (1940). In that case two defendants were notified of the action but did not appear. The Court held that they were bound by the resulting decree even though the statute under which that decree was rendered was declared to be unconstitutional.

b. Had matters remained there, *Durfee* might have been a brief per curiam opinion. But in the same term as *Chicot County* the Court decided Kalb v. Feuerstein, 308 U.S. 433 (1940). In *Kalb* the Court held that a properly notified defendant who had not appeared could nevertheless challenge the decree collaterally, because the statute specifically created an exception to the principles forbidding collateral attack. Thus stated, *Kalb* sounds easy to reconcile with *Chicot County*. The difficulty is that the statute did not state in unequivocal — or even in equivocal — terms that it overcame preclusion; instead the Court implied the exception to preclusion from the statute's purposes.

c. There matters stand. One can say that a litigant who litigates jurisdiction, whether subject matter or personal, is bound by the decision. One can say that a defendant who does not appear can raise a collateral challenge to personal jurisdiction and that a defendant who appears but does not challenge personal jurisdiction thereby waives her objection. One cannot, however, be certain about collateral challenges to subject matter jurisdiction. *Chicot County* suggests that ordinary preclusion rules will apply to bar afterthought challenges. *Kalb* stands as a reminder that there will be exceptions, either by virtue of specific statutory exemptions or those implied by the importance of the jurisdictional challenge.

d. One may not collaterally attack subject matter jurisdiction for failure of diversity, Des Moines Navigation & Railroad v. Iowa Homestead Co., 123 U.S. 552 (1887), even though a court may dismiss sua sponte for lack of diversity on appeal in the original case, Capron v. Van Noorden, 6 U.S. 126 (1804).

e. Conversely, states may choose to declare judgments of their own courts void when they lack subject matter jurisdiction; such judgments are subject to attack at any time. See the discussions in Gargallo v. Merrill, Lynch, Pierce, Fenner & Smith, supra page 683. Under the full faith and credit statute, 28 U.S.C. §1738, and its requirement to give the "same" full faith and credit as the rendering state, the second state must look to the effect that the first state gives its own judgments from courts lacking subject matter jurisdiction.

f. Even if a court has jurisdiction over the defendant and the subject matter, the defendant may collaterally attack the judgment in another state by showing that it was procured fraudulently, Bondeson v. Pepsico, Inc., 573 S.W.2d 842 (Tex. Civ. App. 1978) (summary judgment in favor of plaintiff on Florida judgment denied where defendant alleged that plaintiff had promised to dismiss the Florida action and not prosecute it further).

6. Fraud aside, the requirement of full faith and credit to judgments is a strict one, as illustrated by Fauntleroy v. Lum, 210 U.S. 230 (1908). The parties had made a contract in Mississippi that was illegal (in fact, criminal) under Mississippi law. Plaintiff sued defendant in Mississippi but voluntarily dismissed the case before judgment on the merits. Then plaintiff sued in Missouri, apparently on the basis of transient jurisdiction, and the Missouri courts enforced the contract. It is likely that if the illegality of the contract had been raised in the Missouri proceedings, the principle requiring full faith and credit to the laws (as opposed to the judgments) of another state would have required Missouri to apply Mississippi law and to refuse enforcement of the contract. Nonetheless, plaintiff took his Missouri judgment to Mississippi for enforcement. The Mississippi courts balked, but the Supreme Court ruled that they were required to enforce the Missouri judgment because the Missouri court had jurisdiction. In effect, the Court said that all but the jurisdictional questions had to be raised and appealed in the first action.

7. Although by ignoring several bases for refusing enforcement of the Missouri judgment, *Fauntleroy* establishes a strict principle for judgments, the law of recognition of equitable decrees is not nearly so severe. The majority of American courts hold that a decree is entitled to full faith and credit with respect to the circumstances and issues as of the time of the decree. But since decrees are generally modifiable because of changed circumstances in the courts that rendered them, changed circumstances subsequent to the rendition of the decree allow its modification in another state. See, for example, Ashwood v. Ashwood, 371 So. 2d 924 (Ala. Civ. App. 1979) ("best interests" of a child in a custody determination can never be finally determined).

The changed-circumstance rule plays a large role in one of the most frequent and bitter disputes over interstate enforcement of equitable decrees — battles over child custody and support decrees. The intensity of the parties' feelings and the frequency of changed residence of at least one party combine to create opportunity for contest and bitterness. Several legislative efforts have sought to alleviate at least the jurisdictional battles arising from these unhappy circumstances. The adoption of the Uniform Reciprocal Enforcement of Support Act and the Uniform Child Custody Jurisdiction Act by some states has had a limited effect in solving problems of interstate jurisdiction and relitigation of facts in cases involving children. Federal legislation — 28 U.S.C. §§1738A and 1738B — requires state courts to enforce without modification a decree entered by another court if that court has met certain prerequisites. Those prerequisites include not only the obvious — jurisdiction — but also that the decree have been entered in the child's home state (except under unusual circumstances).

8. Foreign country judgments present special problems. If the United States and the foreign nation have entered into a treaty requiring reciprocal enforcement of each other's judgments, that treaty binds state and federal courts. In the absence of such a treaty, neither state nor federal courts are required to give full faith and credit under the terms of 28 U.S.C. §1738 or Article IV of the Constitution. In Hilton v. Guyot, 159 U.S. 113 (1895), however, the Supreme Court applied notions of comity and reciprocity to give some effect to foreign

country judgments. Specifically it held that if a foreign country judgment resulted from proceedings that comported with broad notions of due process, the judgment would be enforced if the foreign country recognized American judgments. As noted above, comity describes the voluntary recognition of judgments. The limitation to judgments of countries that recognize American judgments is called *reciprocity*. State courts are usually held not to be bound by Hilton v. Guyot — for example, Nicol v. Tanner, 310 Minn. 68, 256 N.W.2d 796 (1976). Should the federal courts be bound by the state rule in a diversity case? Note that *Hilton* was decided before *Erie*.

2.   The Reopened Judgment as an Alternative to Collateral Attack

Claim and issue preclusion combine with requirements of full faith and credit to force litigants and courts to honor judgments. In the great majority of cases, litigants wishing to challenge the correctness of a judgment must appeal the decision to a higher court rather than file a second lawsuit. This principle, intended to force challenges into regular channels, can itself work injustice. Consider the case of a litigant who discovers that her opponent has won a victory by unlawful means: Perhaps he failed to serve her with process and thus obtained a default judgment; perhaps he concealed a crucial piece of evidence by failing to produce it in response to an appropriate discovery request. In such a case appeal will not work because the original court committed no error; the complaint is instead about evidence that never reached the court's attention. But if the plaintiff simply begins a second lawsuit, she will face the defense of claim preclusion.

The escape from this dilemma lies in the opportunity to reopen a judgment. See Rule 60(b). We approach this subject gingerly because any discussion of it tends to overstate its practical availability. The basic mechanisms for correcting errors are post-trial motions in the trial court and appeals. To the extent that another postjudgment remedy is available, it necessarily undercuts the appellate system. For this reason, courts insist repeatedly that relief under Rule 60(b) is not a substitute for appeal.

Scan Rule 60(b) and note the different grounds for which relief may be granted. Consider its effort to define the line between finality of adjudication and the sense that an injustice has occurred. Now consider what should happen, under Rule 60, if, after a final judgment, the losing litigant discovers that the opposition has failed during discovery to produce highly relevant, perhaps dispositive, materials in its possession. Compare your intuition to the results of the next case.

United States v. Beggerly

524 U.S. 38 (1998)

Chief Justice REHNQUIST delivered the opinion of the Court.

[In assembling the lands for a National Seashore, the federal government in 1979 brought a quiet title action (the *Adams* litigation) in the Southern District of

Mississippi against respondents. The case turned on whether, before the date of the Louisiana Purchase in 1803, the land had been deeded to a private individual. If so, it would belong to Beggerly, and the United States would have to purchase it; if not, the U.S. government would already own it. That case settled on the eve of trial for a relatively modest sum, reflecting the uncertainty of Beggerly's title.] Judgment was entered based on this settlement agreement. In 1994, some 12 years after that judgment, respondents sued in the District Court to set aside the settlement agreement and obtain a damage award for the disputed land. . . .

During discovery in the *Adams* litigation, respondents sought proof of their title to the land. Government officials searched public land records and told respondents that they had found nothing proving that any part of Horn Island had ever been granted to a private landowner. Even after the settlement in the *Adams* litigation, however, respondents continued to search for evidence of a land patent that supported their claim of title. In 1991 they hired a genealogical record specialist to conduct research in the National Archives in Washington. The specialist found materials that, according to her, showed that on August 1, 1781, Bernardo de Galvez, then the Governor General of Spanish Louisiana, granted Horn Island to [a private party].

Armed with this new information, respondents filed a complaint in the District Court on June 1, 1994. They asked the court to set aside the 1982 settlement agreement and award them damages. . . . The District Court concluded that it was without jurisdiction to hear respondents' suit and dismissed the complaint.

The Court of Appeals reversed. It concluded that there were two jurisdictional bases for the suit. First, the suit satisfied the elements of an "independent action," as the term is used in Federal Rule of Civil Procedure 60(b). . . .

The Government's primary contention is that the Court of Appeals erred in concluding that it had jurisdiction over respondents' 1994 suit. It first attacks the lower court's conclusion that jurisdiction was established because the suit was an "independent action" within the meaning of Rule 60(b). . . . [The Government argued that although] the District Court had jurisdiction over the original Adams litigation because the United States was the plaintiff, 28 U.S.C. §1345, there was no statutory basis for the Beggerlys' 1994 action, and the District Court was therefore correct to have dismissed it.

We think the Government's position is inconsistent with the history and language of Rule 60(b). Prior to the 1937 adoption of the Federal Rules of Civil Procedure, the availability of relief from a judgment or order turned on whether the court was still in the same "term" in which the challenged judgment was entered. . . . If the term had expired, resort had to be made to a handful of writs, the precise contours of which were "shrouded in ancient lore and mystery." . . .

The 1946 Amendment [to Rule 60] . . . made clear that nearly all of the old forms of obtaining relief from a judgment, i.e., coram nobis, coram vobis, audita querela, bills of review, and bills in the nature of review, had been abolished. The revision made equally clear, however, that one of the old forms, i.e., the "independent action,"[2] still survived. The Advisory Committee notes confirmed this,

---

2. This form of action was also referred to as an "original action."

indicating that "if the right to make a motion is lost by the expiration of the time limits fixed in these rules, the only other procedural remedy is by a new or independent action to set aside a judgment upon those principles which have heretofore been applied in such an action.". . .

The Government is therefore wrong to suggest that an independent action brought in the same court as the original lawsuit requires an independent basis for jurisdiction. This is not to say, however, that the requirements for a meritorious independent action have been met here. If relief may be obtained through an independent action in a case such as this, where the most that may be charged against the Government is a failure to furnish relevant information that would at best form the basis for a Rule 60(b)(3) motion, the strict 1-year time limit on such motions would be set at naught. Independent actions must, if Rule 60(b) is to be interpreted as a coherent whole, be reserved for those cases of "injustices which, in certain instances, are deemed sufficiently gross to demand a departure" from rigid adherence to the doctrine of res judicata. Hazel-Atlas Glass Co. v. Hartford-Empire Co., 322 U.S. 238 (1944).

Such a case was Marshall v. Holmes, 141 U.S. 589 (1891), in which the plaintiff alleged that judgment had been taken against her in the underlying action as a result of a forged document. The Court said:

> According to the averments of the original petition for injunction . . . the judgments in question would not have been rendered against Mrs. Marshall but for the use in evidence of the letter alleged to be forged. The case evidently intended to be presented by the petition is one where, without negligence, laches or other fault upon the part of petitioner, [respondent] has fraudulently obtained judgments which he seeks, against conscience, to enforce by execution.

Id., at 596.

The sense of these expressions is that, under the Rule, an independent action should be available only to prevent a grave miscarriage of justice. In this case, it should be obvious that respondents' allegations do not nearly approach this demanding standard. Respondents allege only that the United States failed to "thoroughly search its records and make full disclosure to the Court" regarding the Boudreau grant. Whether such a claim might succeed under Rule 60(b)(3) we need not now decide; it surely would work no "grave miscarriage of justice," and perhaps no miscarriage of justice at all, to allow the judgment to stand. We therefore hold that the Court of Appeals erred in concluding that this was a sufficient basis to justify the reopening of the judgment in the *Adams* litigation.

The judgment of the Court of Appeals is therefore reversed, and the case is remanded for further proceedings consistent with this opinion.

[Justice STEVENS'S concurring opinion is omitted.]

NOTES AND PROBLEMS

1. *Beggerly* deals with several distinct problems in reopening judgments. Start with the issue that faced the plaintiff and the Supreme Court. The plaintiffs had found significant evidence not disclosed by their adversary in the prior litigation

that might well have led to the award of damages many times the amount for which they had settled twelve years previously.

a. Examine Rule 60(b) carefully and explain why "an independent action," described in the Court's opinion, was the only avenue of relief open to them under the Rule.

b. Now explain the basis for the federal district court's jurisdiction to hear this "independent action."

c. Finally, approach the merits. Why does the Court conclude that these facts do not satisfy the criteria for reopening the judgment under the murky criteria for an independent action? Why does it not work a "grave miscarriage of justice" for the federal government to have taken the plaintiffs' land for an alleged fraction of its value?

d. The materials bearing on the case were apparently in the National Archives, which are open to anyone armed with the determination, bibliographic, and linguistic skills to make use of them. Should the case have come out differently if the same information had existed solely in confidential or secret files, such as those of the Federal Bureau of Investigation or Central Intelligence Agency?

2. Return now to the text of Rule 60(b) and consider how it might have applied had the Beggerlys uncovered the archival evidence within months after the first judgment.

a. Which sections of the Rule might apply?

b. The opinion mentions Rule 60(b)(3). Is that the most obvious one?

3. As implied in *Beggerly*, courts treat the one-year statute of limitations applying to sections (1)-(3) as meaning what it says.

a. Consider the case of the unfortunate Lorenzo Brandon:

> Lorenzo Brandon sought Rule 60 relief from a judgment entered against him for failure to prosecute his case. The district court denied relief and Brandon now appeals. The facts are unusual. Indeed, Brandon claims they are unique. Brandon filed his Americans with Disabilities action against the Chicago Board of Education on August 2, 1995. His attorneys, Paul F. Peters and James C. Reho, entered appearances in the case, listing as their address the Law Offices of Paul F. Peters, One North LaSalle Street, Chicago. It is undisputed that in docketing the case, the Clerk of the United States District Court erroneously entered Paul A. Peters, another Chicago attorney, who is located at 10 South LaSalle Street, Chicago, as attorney for the plaintiff. As a result of this error, subsequent mailings from the court were directed to the wrong attorney at the wrong address. . . .
>
> A little more than a year passed before plaintiff's counsel began to wonder what happened to the case. Upon visiting the Clerk's office in late 1996, he discovered his case had been quite active without him. Included in the court's file was . . . the order dismissing the case for want of prosecution.

Brandon v. Chicago Board of Education, 143 F.3d 293 (7th Cir. 1998). The Court of Appeals affirmed the dismissal. It held that a case can fall into only a single category of Rule 60(b) and that this one fell into 60(b)(1). Because it fell into (b)(1), it could not also fall into (b)(6). The one-year limit applicable to (b)(1) but not (b)(6) was therefore in effect, and because Brandon's lawyer had filed the Rule 60 motion three days after the one-year period had run, the motion was barred.

b. Can Brandon recover against his lawyer for malpractice? Would a reasonably competent lawyer have realized that he hadn't heard from the court and inquired early enough to prevent dismissal?

4. What principles or values justify holdings like those in *Beggerly* and *Brandon*? It is easy to pillory the courts for adhering to mindless technicality in upholding unjust judgments.

a. Consider the consequences of an opposite rule: that a judgment could be reopened at any time a party had additional relevant information to present.

b. Once one rejects such a rule, there is going to be a difficult line-drawing problem. Does Rule 60 put the lines in the right places?

5. Underlying some decisions in the Rule 60 area is realism (or cynicism) about the limits of adversarial factfinding and advocacy — a line between, if you will, litigation and science. In scientific inquiry, no evidence ever comes in too late, and no conclusion is barred from reexamination.

a. Litigation is different. We bring some disputes to an end not because we're sure we're right, but because we're sure there has to be an end to the dispute so people can move on with their lives. In such a view only a genuinely egregious mistake (and perhaps one that the other side caused) is enough to upset the judgment.

b. Moreover, the passage of time itself confers legitimacy: Old law is good law in part because we develop reliance on it.

6. Such responses seem most convincing, however, only if the litigant seeking relief has had at least one fair shot at the adversarial system. Perhaps as a consequence, although the Rule itself does not make any distinction between judgments entered at different stages of the litigative process, the courts have made a very sharp distinction between default judgments and others. The effect has been to make it comparatively easy to open a default judgment on the showing of some negligence and meritorious defense. Numerous decisions state, in one way or another, a very strong policy against judgments without consideration of the merits. Indeed, this policy is so strong that some practitioners advise against taking a default judgment unless there is absolutely no alternative. These lawyers have seen too many default judgments taken and defended in clear and justifiable circumstances, only to be set aside in the trial court or on appeal. The net result is considerable expense and a multi-year delay in the litigation.

7. As a review, imagine that *P* and *D* are involved in an automobile accident. *P* sues *D*, claiming that *D* was intoxicated at the time and that the accident resulted from *D*'s failure to keep a proper lookout and his inability to keep the car in his lane. At the trial, *P* and *D* testify, and the jury renders a verdict for *D*. Within one year, *P* moves to set aside the judgment. Under which of the following circumstances should it be vacated?

a. *D* bribed the judge.

b. *D* lied when he said he had been at home prior to the accident; in fact, *D* had just left his girlfriend's apartment.

c. *W* witnessed the event and observed *D*'s negligent driving and intoxicated state. *P* had taken the deposition of *X*, who was at the scene of the accident, but *X* said he did not see anything and no other person was there. It now turns out that X lied because W told X he didn't want to get involved.

d. Same facts except W actually testified at the trial that he didn't see anything.

e. In any of the preceding cases, would the answer differ if the motion had been made more than one year after judgment?

PART C

TESTING THE BOUNDARIES: ADDITIONAL CLAIMS AND PARTIES

This section combines the approaches taken in the two sections that precede it. Part A took a top-down view in looking at the ways in which the U.S. Constitution establishes constraints for civil litigation. Part B started at the bottom, taking the individual lawsuit as its unit of examination.

We turn now to opportunities and problems that arise when procedural rules open the confines of a lawsuit. Our forum for that examination is the rules of joinder, the principles that allow parties to modern civil litigation to combine claims and add additional parties. Those principles constitute one of the respects in which contemporary civil litigation differs sharply from its predecessors: A modern lawsuit can, to a large extent, aim at resolving an entire dispute by encompassing all the claims and all the parties involved.

Those same principles, however, challenge both the jurisdictional scheme elaborated in Part A and the litigation process explored in Part B. In many cases jurisdictional problems will either limit or defeat joinder that would otherwise be available. From one standpoint, these limitations are undesirable restrictions on a lawsuit that would otherwise provide a comprehensive resolution to a dispute. From another standpoint, jurisdictional limits prevent what might otherwise become a monster from devouring both the court system and the litigants swept into it. Joinder poses a similar issue for the design of the procedural system. Flexible joinder rules permit parties to frame issues broadly and to include everyone who has a stake in the resolution of those issues. Carried to its logical conclusion, however, this principle of inclusion can create a lawsuit that cannot resolve anything — because it is unmanageable. The Rules consequently establish a fine line by seeking broad inclusion but trying to keep inclusiveness from preventing resolution of the dispute.

The issues thus raised require the student to review much of the course. At the threshold of many cases will be both a pleading problem and a jurisdictional problem. The pleading problem will require the student to consider whether the party or claim fits within the joinder rule's definition. If it does, there will sometimes be a second level of inquiry: Assuming that the party or claim can be joined as a matter of pleading, does the court's jurisdictional reach extend sufficiently far to encompass this joinder? Just beyond the pleading and jurisdictional inquiries may lie a question about preclusion: Joinder is often sought in order to achieve claim or issue preclusion, and the preclusive effects of the case may supply an additional reason for joining (or not joining) a claim or party. This interplay among principles already explored makes joinder challenging — and useful as a test of one's grasp of the preceding material.

JOINDER

XIII

Modern civil procedure in the United States has two distinguishing features. One, discovery, increases the depth of any given lawsuit. The other, broad joinder of claims and parties, increases the breadth of a suit. To achieve this breadth, modern process turned from the single-mindedness of common law procedure and focused on the transaction rather than on the writ or legal theory. This focus permits parties to combine various claims and to add additional parties. A larger litigative "package" confers advantages: It allows a single suit to adjudicate multiple claims against multiple parties and permits litigation to reflect some of life's complexity. Disadvantages can also flow from this freedom: Litigation can become intricate, and considerable procedural skirmishing can occur long before the merits come into view, as parties dispute whether a given effort at joinder is permitted.

A. Joinder of Claims

In our exploration of procedure up to this point, we have for the most part assumed a simple case in which one plaintiff had a single claim against one defendant, and the defendant did not have a claim against the plaintiff. But, as the reader will already have seen, many lawsuits are not that simple: A plaintiff may have more than one claim against a defendant, and a defendant may have claims against the plaintiff. We first consider joinder issues in the context of a lawsuit between a single plaintiff and a single defendant. The ensuing sections will examine the questions that arise when additional parties are joined.

1. Joinder of Claims by Plaintiff

a. Historical Background

At common law the rules governing joinder of claims were simple: Plaintiff could join only claims using the same writ but could do so regardless of whether the claims were factually related. For example, plaintiff could join claims for assaults on two separate occasions or a slander on one day and an act of negligence months later (both actions brought under the *in consimile casu* writ), but could not join a claim for assault with a claim for slander, even if both were part of the same incident, because the writ for assault was trespass and the writ for slander was case. Plaintiff also could join alternative versions of the same grievance by alleging each in a separate count, as if each count referred to a separate occurrence. But, again, each version had to be within the same form of action; plaintiff could not set forth one count in assumpsit and another in trover. This principle becomes more understandable if one remembers that different writs used different forms of pretrial and trial process and that the goal of much common law procedure was to frame a single, straightforward question for the jury. Also bear in mind that the scope of former adjudication was correspondingly narrow (see supra page 658).

At common law a mistake in joinder had severe consequences. Misjoinder could lead to a successful demurrer or even the upsetting of a verdict; the defect was not waived by failure to make an early objection. One can find cases in the early twentieth century throwing out verdicts for plaintiff because of misjoinder.

Equity was more relaxed than common law in this respect; indeed, its broader scope was one reason for parties' resort to equity. Although standards for joinder in equity were never made completely clear, joinder was generally permitted when claims shared a transactional relationship and raised common issues. There were limits, however, and a bill in equity could be found objectionable for *multifariousness*, meaning that it combined too many claims.

b.   The Federal Rules

The Rules changed all this: They eliminated all barriers to joinder of claims by a plaintiff. Read Rule 18. A single plaintiff can join any and all claims he has against a single defendant. This freedom can create trial management problems. If one imagines a case between Microsoft and one of its major business partners, the possibilities are mind-boggling. The Rules solve this problem by permitting the judge, under Rule 42(b), to sever claims for trial convenience. Such severed claims may, of course, be as distinct for pretrial and trial purposes as if the plaintiff had brought entirely separate suits.

Although Rule 18 permits joinder, it does not compel it. So far as the *Rules* are concerned there is no compulsory joinder of claims. The Rules do not, however, tell the whole story. The principles of former adjudication, explored in Chapter XII, often require a plaintiff to join related claims, especially when they arise out of the same incident. Moreover, a plaintiff's own interest is often served by joinder of all claims, or at least all related claims, he has against a defendant. The combination of these two factors creates a powerful incentive for plaintiffs to join claims, even in the absence of a Rule requiring that they do so. If preclusion and litigative strategy encourage broad joinder, jurisdiction often supplies an obstacle.

c.   Joinder and Jurisdiction

The most difficult joinder issues often involve jurisdictional considerations. Review of a few fundamental propositions may be helpful in setting the stage.

Assume A, a citizen of Illinois, sues B, also a citizen of Illinois, on a federal claim. Can A join a state claim against B? That question poses two subquestions: (1) Do the principles of joinder, governed by the Rules, permit combining these claims; and (2) Assuming that joinder is allowed by the rules, does the federal court have jurisdiction over the state claim thus joined?

Rule 18 creates no joinder problem in this situation. Recall that the Rule permits a plaintiff to join as many claims as she wishes, whether related or unrelated. The problem is jurisdictional: The court may lack subject matter jurisdiction over A's state law claim.

Such problems often prove important in federal litigation. The basic proposition to bear in mind is that federal courts are tribunals of limited jurisdiction: They do not have jurisdiction unless a provision of the Constitution and a statute grant it to them. In the example above, the basis for jurisdiction over the plaintiff's original claim is straightforward: It arises under federal law, over which Article III and 28 U.S.C. §1331 confer jurisdiction.

Jurisdiction over the state law claim is more difficult. There is no diversity of citizenship between plaintiff and defendant. The claim arises under state rather than federal law, so there is no original federal question jurisdiction. If there is jurisdiction, it exists, therefore, only by virtue of the supplemental jurisdiction conferred by 28 U.S.C. §1367. Read that statute and consider what question would have to be answered to resolve the jurisdictional issue here.

Rule 15
= Joinder

Section 1367 has a particularly important feature for our exploration of joinder. Its grant of supplemental jurisdiction depends on three variables: (1) the basis of the original jurisdiction over the case; (2) the identity of the party — plaintiff or defendant — seeking to invoke supplemental jurisdiction; and (3) the Rule authorizing the joinder of the party or claim over whom supplemental jurisdiction is sought. In the sections below we shall have repeated occasion to explore these variables; in order to gain a basic orientation, consider some elementary problems. In answering each, be prepared to explain which provision of §1367 governs and how you believe that section resolves the question.

NOTES AND PROBLEMS

1. In this and the next four problems, assume the litigation occurs in federal district court. Ann, a citizen of Illinois, sues Barbara, also a citizen of Illinois, alleging that Barbara violated federal civil rights statutes in firing her. Ann seeks to add a state law claim alleging that her firing also violated a state wrongful discharge law. Is there supplemental jurisdiction?

2. Ann, a citizen of Illinois, sues Barbara, also a citizen of Illinois, alleging that Barbara violated federal civil rights statutes in firing her. Ann seeks to add a state law claim alleging that Barbara caused her injuries when her car backed into Ann's in the company parking lot. Is there supplemental jurisdiction?

3. Ann, a citizen of Illinois, sues Barbara, also a citizen of Illinois, alleging that Barbara violated federal civil rights statutes by permitting co-workers to engage in sexual harassment. Ann seeks to join Charles, a co-worker, who actually engaged

in the harassment. State tort law is the basis of Ann's claim against Charles. Because Charles is not Ann's employer, the claim against him does not arise under federal law. Assume that the claim against Charles presents sufficiently common issues to qualify for joinder under Rule 20. Is there supplemental jurisdiction over the claim against Charles?

4. Ann, a citizen of Illinois, sues Barbara, a citizen of Wisconsin, alleging breach of an employment contract and seeking a recovery in excess of $75,000. Ann seeks to join Charles, a citizen of Illinois; Ann alleges that Charles conspired with Barbara to breach the employment contract. Assume that the claim against Charles presents sufficiently common issues to qualify for joinder under Rule 20. Is there supplemental jurisdiction over the claim against Charles?

5. We have focused on the interplay between joinder rules and federal subject matter jurisdiction. As you will see, joinder can also raise issues of personal jurisdiction. In the hypothetical case explored above, suppose that Ann, a citizen of Illinois, wants to sue Barbara, a citizen of Wisconsin, and Charles, a citizen of Illinois, on a federal civil rights claim.

a. Joinder will present no problem if the claims against the two defendants arise from the same transaction and share common questions of law and fact. On these facts subject matter jurisdiction will present no obstacle because the claim arises under federal law.

b. But if the suit is brought in Illinois, there may be a question of whether the court has personal jurisdiction over Barbara, the citizen of Wisconsin. Such problems of personal jurisdiction will affect both state and federal courts. As a quick review of jurisdictional concepts, explain why 1367 will not help with such problems of personal jurisdiction.

6. In addition to issues of personal jurisdiction, state courts will occasionally need to consider issues of subject matter jurisdiction in connection with joinder. Suppose in a state court operating under the Federal Rules plaintiff sues a publisher for breach of contract, alleging defendant failed to publish her book as promised.

a. Now suppose that plaintiff proposes in an amended complaint to add a copyright infringement claim. Does Rule 18 pose any problem?

b. What is the objection to this claim? See 28 U.S.C. §1338(a); cf. Gargallo v. Merrill Lynch, supra page 683.

2. Claims by the Defendant: Counterclaims

In examining pleading we considered the responses that defendant might make to plaintiff's complaint, but we did not explore the possibility that defendant might have claims against plaintiff. At common law the rules governing such claims were simple: They did not exist. The defendant who had such a claim could bring a separate suit or, in a limited number of cases, "set off" her claim against the plaintiffs (that is, reduce the plaintiff's recovery) but could not herself recover in the original action. Today Rule 13 permits defendants to assert such claims.

Rule 13 divides counterclaims into two categories, *compulsory* and *permissive*. As you read the next case, consider what it means for a counterclaim to be compulsory and why it matters.

Plant v. Blazer Financial Services

598 F.2d 1357 (5th Cir. 1979)

RONEY, J.

In this truth-in-lending case, we resolve . . . important issues to this field of the law. First, we decide that an action on the underlying debt in default is a compulsory counterclaim that must be asserted in a suit by the debtor on a truth-in-lending cause of action. . . .

On July 17, 1975 plaintiff Theresa Plant executed a note in favor of defendant Blazer Financial Services, Inc. for $2,520.00 to be paid in monthly installments of $105.00. No payments were made on the note. In March 1976 plaintiff commenced a civil action under §1640 of the Truth-in-Lending Act, 15 U.S.C.A. §1601 et seq., for failure to make disclosures required by the Act and by Regulation Z, 12 C.F.R. §226.1 et seq. (1978) promulgated thereunder. Defendant counterclaimed on the note for the unpaid balance. Based on defendant's failure to disclose a limitation on an after-acquired security interest, the trial court held the disclosure inadequate and awarded plaintiff the statutory penalty of $944.76 and $700.00 in attorney's fees. . . . [Defendant appealed this ruling.]

The trial court, however, offset the plaintiff's award and the attorney's fee award against the judgment for defendant on the counterclaim. From this judgment and setoff, plaintiff appeals on three issues: (1) the jurisdiction of the court to entertain the counterclaim, (2) defenses to the counterclaim under Georgia law, and (3) the offset of attorney's fees.

I. Counterclaim

Plaintiff challenges the trial court's ruling that defendant's counterclaim on the underlying debt was compulsory. The issue is jurisdictional. A permissive counterclaim must have an independent jurisdictional basis, while it is generally accepted that a compulsory counterclaim falls within the ancillary jurisdiction of the federal courts even if it would ordinarily be a matter for state court consideration. In the instant case there is no independent basis since neither federal question nor diversity jurisdiction is available for the counterclaim. Consequently, if the counterclaim were to be treated as permissive, defendant's action on the underlying debt would have to be pursued in the state court.

The issue of whether a state debt counterclaim in a truth-in-lending action is compulsory or permissive is one of first impression in this Circuit, has never, to our knowledge, been decided by a court of appeals, and has received diverse treatment from a great number of district courts. . . .

Rule 13(a), Fed. R. Civ. P., provides that a counterclaim is compulsory if it "arises out of the transaction or occurrence" that is the subject matter of plaintiff's claim. Four tests have been suggested to further define when a claim and counterclaim arise from the same transaction:

1) Are the issues of fact and law raised by the claim and counterclaim largely the same?

2) Would res judicata bar a subsequent suit on defendant's claim absent the compulsory counterclaim rule?

3) Will substantially the same evidence support or refute plaintiff's claim as well as defendant's counterclaim?

4) Is there any logical relation between the claim and the counterclaim?

6 Wright & Miller, Federal Practice and Procedure §1410 at 42 (1971). An affirmative answer to any of the four questions indicates the counterclaim is compulsory.

The test which has commended itself to most courts, including our own, is the logical relation test. Revere Copper & Brass, Inc. v. Aetna Casualty & Surety Co., 426 F.2d at 714; 6 Wright & Miller at 48. The logical relation test is a loose standard which permits "a broad realistic interpretation in the interest of avoiding a multiplicity of suits." "The hallmark of this approach is its flexibility."

In *Revere Copper & Brass* this Court added a third tier to the counterclaim analysis by further defining "logical relationship" to exist when the counterclaim arises from the same "aggregate of operative facts" in that the same operative facts serve as the basis of both claims or the aggregate core of facts upon which the claim rests activates additional legal rights, otherwise dormant, in the defendant.

Applying the logical relationship test literally to the counterclaim in this case clearly suggests its compulsory character because a single aggregate of operative facts, the loan transaction, gave rise to both plaintiff's and defendant's claims. Because a tallying of the results from the district courts which have decided this question, however, shows that a greater number have found such a counterclaim merely permissive, we subject the relationship between the claims to further analysis.

The split of opinion on the nature of debt counterclaims in truth-in-lending actions appears to be, in large part, the product of competing policy considerations between the objectives of Rule 13(a) and the policies of the Truth-in-Lending Act, and disagreement over the extent to which federal courts should be involved in state causes of action for debt. While Rule 13(a) is intended to avoid multiple litigation by consolidating all controversies between the parties, several courts and commentators have observed that accepting creditors' debt counterclaims may obstruct achievement of the goals of the Truth-in-Lending Act.

Various arguments are made compositely as follows: The purpose of the Act is

to assure a meaningful disclosure of credit terms so that the consumer will be able to compare more readily the various credit terms available to him and avoid the uninformed use of credit.

15 U.S.C.A. §1601. This purpose is effectuated by debtors' standing in the role of private attorneys general not merely to redress individual injuries but to enforce

federal policy. The success of this private enforcement scheme would be undermined if debtors were faced with counterclaims on debts often exceeding the limits of their potential recovery under the Act. The purpose of the Act would suffer further frustration if federal courts were entangled in the myriad factual and legal questions essential to a decision on the debt claims but unrelated to the truth-in-lending violation. In Roberts v. National School of Radio & Television Broadcasting, the court also noted the incongruity of enlisting the federal court's resources to assist in debt collection by the very target of the legislation which gives the plaintiff its cause of action.

Several other factors have been cited to offset the attractiveness of treating all related disputes in a single action under Rule 13. For example, courts have predicted a flood of debt counterclaims, greatly increasing the federal court workload. Furthermore, permitting debt counterclaims might destroy truth-in-lending class actions by interjecting vast numbers of individual questions. The judicial economy of consolidated litigation might be countered by the delay of having to provide a jury trial for the debt claim though none is available to the truth-in-lending plaintiff. Other courts have suggested that regarding such debt counterclaims as compulsory would infringe on the power of states to adjudicate disputes grounded in state law.

Courts which have concluded debt counterclaims to be permissive have found the nexus between the truth-in-lending violation and debt obligation too abstract or tenuous to regard the claims as logically related. One claim, they reason, involves the violation of federal law designed to deter lender nondisclosure and facilitate credit shopping and the other concerns merely a default on a private duty.

After careful consideration of the factors relied upon in these cases to find counterclaims permissive, we opt for the analysis applied by district courts in Louisiana, Alabama, Texas and Georgia in determining debt counterclaims to be compulsory. . . .

The results reached in *Carter* [v. Public Finance Corp.] were found "inescapable" in George v. Beneficial Finance Co. of Dallas. Emphasizing the goal of judicial economy furthered by a single presentation of facts, the court observed that "suits on notes will inevitably deal with the circumstance of the execution of the notes and any representation made to 'induce' the borrowing.". . .

We add to these arguments the observation that one of the purposes of the compulsory counterclaim rule is to provide complete relief to the defendant who has been brought involuntarily into the federal court. Absent the opportunity to bring a counterclaim, this party could be forced to satisfy the debtor's truth-in-lending claim without any assurance that his claims against the defaulting debtor arising from the same transaction will be taken into account or even that the funds he has been required to pay will still be available should he obtain a state court judgment in excess of the judgment on the truth-in-lending claim. In addition, a determination that the underlying debt was invalid may have a material effect on the amount of damages a debtor could recover on a truth-in-lending claim.

To permit the debtor to recover from the creditor without taking the original loan into account would be a serious departure from the evenhanded treatment afforded both parties under the Act. Truth-in-lending claims can be brought in either state or federal court. To the extent this dual jurisdiction was intended to permit litigation of truth-in-lending claims in actions on the debt, it reflects a purpose that the debt claim and the truth-in-lending claims be handled together. To the extent it was intended to relieve federal courts of any of this litigation, the purpose would be frustrated by providing a sanctuary from the creditor's claims in one jurisdiction but not in the other. State courts would always have jurisdiction of a creditor's counterclaim. Had Congress intended to insulate recovery in truth-in-lending actions in federal court from the counterclaims of creditors, of which it surely was aware, it could have easily done so.

We conclude that the obvious interrelationship of the claims and rights of the parties, coupled with the common factual basis of the claims, demonstrates a logical relationship between the claim and counterclaim under the test of *Revere Copper & Brass*.[13] We affirm the trial court's determination that the debt counterclaim is compulsory. . . .

NOTES AND PROBLEMS

1. What is the practical significance of this decision?

a. If Plant had not paid the loan, why had Blazer not already brought suit?

b. Suppose the court had decided that the counterclaim was not compulsory. So what? Rule 13(b) permits a defendant to bring as a permissive counterclaim any claim, related or unrelated, against a plaintiff. What difference would it have made to Blazer if the court had called the debt a permissive rather than a compulsory counterclaim?

c. What difference would it have made to permit Plant to maintain her action without Blazer's counterclaim rather than require her to defend against the counterclaim?

2. The opinion refers to "competing policy considerations between the objectives of Rule 13(a) and the Truth-in-Lending Act." What does this mean?

a. The Seventh Circuit addressed a similar question in the context of another statute regulating credit, the Consumer Leasing Act, 15 U.S.C. §1667-1667e. Discussing whether a counterclaim for an unpaid lease should be compulsory to a claim for violating the Act's disclosure regulations (and therefore within the grant of supplemental jurisdiction), the court said:

> Plaintiffs contend—presumably invoking [28 U.S.C.] §1367(c)(4), though they do not discuss it—that a court should not entertain a counterclaim on the lease

---

13. State courts, which share jurisdiction over truth-in-lending actions, have considered the nexus between such claims in the opposite procedural posture. Where creditors bring actions on the debt, state courts have split on the question of whether the debtor may assert a truth-in-lending counterclaim otherwise barred by the Act's one-year statute of limitations. 15 U.S.C.A. §1640(e). Where the counterclaim can be regarded as arising from the same transaction as the claim, courts have permitted the counterclaim as a "recoupment" or "setoff" without regard to the statute of limitations. The similarity between the requirements for recoupment and those for Rule 13(a) compulsory counterclaims has been noted. . . .

because the threat of an adverse judgment [on the counterclaim] would unduly discourage enforcement of the Consumer Leasing Act.

Channell v. Citicorp Natl. Services, Inc. 89 F.3d 379, 386 (7th Cir. 1996)

b. As a sample of the reasoning that led one court to reach a conclusion opposite that of Plant, consider Whigham v. Beneficial Finance Co. of Fayetteville, 599 F.2d 1322, 1323-1324 (4th Cir. 1979):

> We conclude that a lender's claim for debt against a borrower who sues for violation of the Truth-in-Lending Act has none of the characteristics associated with a compulsory counterclaim. First, the lender's counterclaim raises issues of fact and law significantly different from those presented by the borrower's claim. The only question in the borrower's suit is whether the lender made disclosures required by the federal statute and its implementing regulations. The lender's counterclaim, on the other hand, requires the court to determine the contractual rights of the parties in accordance with state law.
>
> Second, the evidence needed to support each claim differs. The borrower need produce only the loan documents for consideration in light of the federal requirements. The lender, however, must verify the obligation and prove a default on loan payments.
>
> Third, the claim and the counterclaim are not logically related. The lender's counterclaim alleges simply that the borrower has defaulted on a private loan contract governed by state law. The borrower's federal claim involves the same loan, but it does not arise from the obligations created by the contractual transaction. Instead, the claim invokes a statutory penalty designed to enforce federal policy against inadequate disclosure by lenders. To let the lender use the federal proceedings as an opportunity to pursue private claims against the borrower would impede expeditious enforcement of the federal penalty and involve the district courts in debt collection matters having no federal significance.

3. Notice that *Whigham* and *Plant* reach opposite conclusions while quoting the same "test" — whether a counterclaim arises out of the same transaction or occurrence and is therefore compulsory. *Plant* sets forth four such tests. How helpful are these formulations?

a. Aren't the first and the third tests mirror images of each other? That is, if there is significant overlap of law and fact (test 1), doesn't it follow that the same evidence would be relevant (test 3)?

b. Isn't the second test just a restatement of the question? That is, *if* both claims arise out of the same transaction or occurrence, they *will* involve the same claim and *therefore* will be subsequently barred.

c. Isn't the fourth test essentially meaningless as interpreted by the court? There is no logical relationship between a Truth-in-Lending claim and one for an unpaid debt, if "logical" refers to an analytically strict set of relationships like those of formal logic. If "logical" instead means "sensibly related," then this test, like the second, becomes a restatement of the question: Just what claims are "sensibly related" to each other?

4. *Plant* posits that two consequences flow from deciding a counterclaim is compulsory.

a. First, it must be brought at the risk of losing it.

b. Second, if it is brought, supplemental jurisdiction extends to cover it.

c. Under those circumstances, there is a penalty for omitting a counterclaim that is later held to be compulsory, but no penalty for including a counterclaim that is found not to be compulsory. Do you see why?

d. As a result of this asymmetrical penalty, most cases presenting the issue whether a counterclaim is compulsory or permissive do not arise in situations in which defendant has omitted the counterclaim in one action and attempted to assert it in a later action. Martino v. McDonald's System, Inc., Chapter XII, is a rare exception. Instead, most cases are similar to *Plant*, in which plaintiff asserts a federal claim; defendant interposes a counterclaim under state law for which there is no independent federal jurisdiction; plaintiff moves to dismiss the counterclaim for lack of subject matter jurisdiction; and defendant argues that the counterclaim is a compulsory one within the supplemental jurisdiction of the federal court. Such an attack is, of course, based on the premise that there is no supplemental jurisdiction over permissive counterclaims.

5. Supplemental jurisdiction today is codified in 28 U.S.C. §1367. That statute speaks of supplemental jurisdiction's extending to any claims that "form part of the same case or controversy under Article III." Consult the statute, and consider two issues it raises with respect to counterclaims.

a. Is "case or controversy," a reference to Article III of the federal Constitution, meant to be broader than "same transaction or occurrence" or "common nucleus of operative facts"? If so, then it will change some results in cases presenting issues analogous to those in *Plant*. It will do so wherever joinder rules are more liberal than the existing jurisdictional rules. In the case of counterclaims, Rule 13(b) permits joinder of any counterclaim, regardless whether related to plaintiff's claim. Does §1367 extend supplemental jurisdiction to all such counterclaims? To some of them?

b. Section 1367(b) proposes a narrower role for supplemental jurisdiction in cases based solely on diversity jurisdiction. But this narrowing does not apply to counterclaims by defendants. Why?

6. *Plant* represents a straightforward, if subtle, counterclaim problem. To test your understanding of the doctrine, consider a complex manifestation of the doctrine found in Great Lakes Rubber Corp. v. Herbert Cooper Co., 286 F.2d 631 (3d Cir. 1961). This case arose after two key employees of Great Lakes left to form Herbert Cooper. An active competition for contracts relating to the manufacture of flexible rubber tubing followed. Initially, Great Lakes sued Herbert Cooper for (1) unfair competition in stealing trade secrets and customers, (2) unfair competition in bidding for contracts on the basis of prices that would involve infringing patents, and (3) disparagement of Great Lakes's product. Cooper then interposed an antitrust counterclaim alleging that Great Lakes was trying to monopolize the relevant market by (1) making false statements to Cooper's suppliers that the suppliers were contributory infringers and (2) bringing a series of unjustified lawsuits to harass Cooper. Great Lakes's claim was dismissed for lack of jurisdiction, but the antitrust counterclaim, with an independent basis for federal jurisdiction, remained. Great Lakes then interposed essentially the same allegations in the form of a

counterclaim to the antitrust claim, and the court found the counterclaim compulsory:

> We have indicated that a counterclaim is compulsory if it bears a "logical relationship" to an opposing party's claim. . . . The phrase "logical relationship" is given meaning by the purpose of the rule which it was designed to implement. Thus, a counterclaim is logically related to the opposing party's claim where separate trials on each of their respective claims would involve a substantial duplication of effort and time by the parties and the courts. Where multiple claims involve many of the same factual issues, or the same factual and legal issues, or where they are offshoots of the same basic controversy between the parties, fairness and considerations of convenience and of economy require that the counterclaimant be permitted to maintain his cause of action. Indeed the doctrine of res judicata compels the counterclaimant to assert his claim in the same suit for it would be barred if asserted separately, subsequently.
>
> Cooper alleges that the claims originally asserted in Great Lakes' amended complaint, reiterated in substance in its counterclaim, are "unjustified" and were brought in "bad faith and without color of right with the sole object of harassing and preventing defendant [Cooper] from competing in the manufacture and sale of flexible hose." These are the only allegations set out by Cooper's counterclaim which demonstrate a relationship within the purview of Rule 13(a) to Great Lakes' amended complaint or counterclaim. But that they do demonstrate a relationship is unquestionable. It is clear that a determination that Cooper's claims that the claims asserted in Great Lakes' amended complaint and reiterated in substance in its counterclaim are harassing will entail an extensive airing of the facts and the law relating to Great Lakes' counterclaim. It follows that the court below was in error in dismissing Great Lakes' counterclaim on the ground that it was permissive. We hold that Great Lakes' counterclaim was a compulsory one within the meaning of Rule 13(a).

Id. at 634. Would the result have been different if Cooper's complaint had not alleged the unjustified lawsuits?

7. The material so far has suggested great breadth for compulsory counterclaims. Some limitations on the doctrine are illustrated in the following questions:

a. In 2003, B purchased a house from S and gave a promissory note for $50,000, payable on January 2, 2004, for the unpaid balance of the purchase price. In 2003, alleging numerous defects in the house, B sued S for breach of contract and breach of warranty. Is S's claim on the unpaid promissory note a compulsory counterclaim?

b. Same facts as in (a), except that the suit was brought in February 2004 after S had commenced an action on the note in another court.

8. Assume Passenger is injured in a collision between Driver 1 and Driver 2 and brings suit against both. Driver 1 may have no counterclaim against Passenger but may have her own claim against Driver 2.

a. The Rules refer to Driver 1's claim against Driver 2 as a *cross-claim*. See Rule 13(g).

b. Some states do not make such fine distinctions in their joinder terminology. California, for example, uses "cross-claim" to refer both to what a federal court would call a "counterclaim" and to what a federal court would call a "cross-claim."

9. As a review both of the joinder material thus far examined and their interplay with pleading, consider the following problems. Plaintiff files a complaint against an automobile Dealer and automobile Manufacturer. The complaint, which is properly before the court under diversity jurisdiction, alleges that Plaintiff was injured in an accident caused by a defect in the vehicle's steering mechanism.

a. Manufacturer wants to assert that the vehicle was not defective when delivered to Dealer and that any defect must have been introduced by Dealer when the vehicle was being prepared for delivery to customer. What pleading, if any, should Manufacturer file?

b. Manufacturer wants to assert that Dealer has failed to pay for several vehicles that Manufacturer delivered to Dealer (not including the vehicle at issue in the action). Can it do so? What pleading, if any, should Manufacturer file?

c. Dealer wants to assert that Plaintiff owes Dealer money for a breach of contract that has no relationship whatsoever to the vehicle or accident at issue in Plaintiff's complaint. Can Dealer do so? What pleading, if any, should it use?

d. Dealer and Manufacturer both want to assert that there was no defect in the vehicle and that the accident was solely the result of Plaintiff's negligence. What pleading, if any, should Dealer and Manufacturer use?

B.   Joinder of Parties

1.   By Plaintiffs

Mosley v. General Motors Corp.

497 F.2d 1330 (8th Cir. 1974)

Ross, J.

Nathaniel Mosley and nine other persons joined in bringing this action individually and as class representatives alleging that their rights guaranteed under 42 U.S.C. §2000e et seq. and 42 U.S.C. §1981 were denied by General Motors and Local 25, United Automobile, Aerospace and Agriculture Implement Workers of America [Union] by reason of their color and race. Each of the ten named plaintiffs had, prior to the filing of the complaint, filed a charge with the Equal Employment Opportunity Commission [EEOC] asserting the facts underlying these claims. Pursuant thereto, the EEOC made a reasonable cause finding that General Motors, Fisher Body Division and Chevrolet Division, and the Union had engaged in unlawful employment practices in violation of Title VII of the Civil Rights Act of 1964. Accordingly, the charging parties were notified by EEOC of their right to institute a civil action in the appropriate federal district court. . . .

In each of the first eight counts of the twelve-count complaint, eight of the ten plaintiffs alleged that General Motors, Chevrolet Division, had engaged in unlawful employment practices by: "discriminating against Negroes as regards promotions, terms and conditions of employment"; "retaliating against Negro employees who protested actions made unlawful by Title VII of the Act and by discharging some because they protested said unlawful acts"; "failing to hire Negro employees as a class on the basis of race"; "failing to hire females as a class on the basis of sex"; "discharging Negro employees on the basis of race"; and "discriminating against Negroes and females in the granting of relief time." Each additionally charged that the defendant Union had engaged in unlawful employment practices "with respect to the granting of relief time to Negro and female employees" and "by failing to pursue 6a grievances." The remaining two plaintiffs made similar allegations against General Motors, Fisher Body Division. All of the individual plaintiffs requested injunctive relief, back pay, attorneys' fees and costs. Counts XI and XII of the complaint were class action counts against the two individual divisions of General Motors. They also sought declaratory and injunctive relief, back pay, attorneys' fees and costs. . . .

The district court ordered that "insofar as the first ten counts are concerned, those ten counts shall be severed into ten separate causes of action," and each plaintiff was directed to bring a separate action based upon his complaint, duly and separately filed. . . .

In reaching this conclusion on joinder, the district court followed the reasoning of Smith v. North American Rockwell Corp. which, in a somewhat analogous situation, found there was no right to relief arising out of the same transaction, occurrence or series of transactions or occurrences, and that there was no question of law or fact common to all plaintiffs sufficient to sustain joinder under Federal Rule of Civil Procedure 20(a). Similarly, the district court here felt that the plaintiffs' joint actions against General Motors and the Union presented a variety of issues having little relationship to one another; that they had only one common problem, i.e., the defendant; and that as pleaded the joint actions were completely unmanageable. Upon entering the order, and upon application of the plaintiffs, the district court found that its decision involved a controlling question of law as to which there is a substantial ground for difference of opinion and that any of the parties might make application for appeal under 28 U.S.C. §1292(b). We granted the application to permit this interlocutory appeal and for the following reasons we affirm in part and reverse in part.

Rule 20(a) of the Federal Rules of Civil Procedure provides:

> All persons may join in one action as plaintiffs if they assert any right to relief jointly, severally, or in the alternative in respect of or arising out of the same transaction, occurrence, or series of transactions or occurrences and if any question of law or fact common to all these persons will arise in the action. . . .

Additionally, Rule 20(b) and Rule 42(b) vest in the district court the discretion to order separate trials or make such other orders as will prevent delay or prejudice. In this manner, the scope of the civil action is made a matter for the discretion of the district court, and a determination on the question of joinder of parties will be reversed on appeal only upon a showing of abuse of that discretion. To determine whether the district court's order was proper herein, we must look to the policy and law that have developed around the operation of Rule 20.

The purpose of the rule is to promote trial convenience and expedite the final determination of disputes, thereby preventing multiple lawsuits. 7 C. Wright, Federal Practice and Procedure §1652 at 265 (1972). Single trials generally tend to lessen the delay, expense and inconvenience to all concerned. Reflecting this policy, the Supreme Court has said: "Under the Rules, the impulse is toward entertaining the broadest possible scope of action consistent with fairness to the parties; joinder of claims, parties and remedies is strongly encouraged." United Mine Workers of America v. Gibbs, 383 U.S. 715 (1966).

Permissive joinder is not, however, applicable in all cases. The rule imposes two specific requisites to the joinder of parties: (1) a right to relief must be asserted by, or against, each plaintiff or defendant relating to or arising out of the *same transaction or occurrence, or series of transactions or occurrences*; and (2) *some question of law or fact common* to all the parties must arise in the action.

In ascertaining whether a particular factual situation constitutes a single transaction or occurrence for purposes of Rule 20, a case by case approach is generally pursued. 7 C. Wright, Federal Practice and Procedure §1653 at 270 (1972). No hard and fast rules have been established under the rule. However, construction of the terms "transaction or occurrence" as used in the context of Rule 13(a) counterclaims offers some guide to the application of this test. For the purposes of the latter rule, "'Transaction' is a word of flexible meaning. It may comprehend a series of many occurrences, depending not so much upon the immediateness of their connection as upon their logical relationship." Moore v. New York Cotton Exchange, 270 U.S. 593 (1926). Accordingly, all "logically related" events entitling a person to institute a legal action against another generally are regarded as comprising a transaction or occurrence. 7 C. Wright, Federal Practice and Procedure §1653 at 270 (1972). The analogous interpretation of the terms as used in Rule 20 would permit all reasonably related claims for relief by or against different parties to be tried in a single proceeding. Absolute identity of all events is unnecessary.

This construction accords with the result reached in United States v. Mississippi, 380 U.S. 128 (1965), a suit brought by the United States against the State of Mississippi, the election commissioners, and six voting registrars of the State, charging them with engaging in acts and practices hampering and destroying the right of black citizens of Mississippi to vote. The district court concluded that the complaint improperly attempted to hold the six county registrars jointly liable for what amounted to nothing more than individual torts committed by them separately against separate applicants. In reversing, the Supreme Court said:

> But the complaint charged that the registrars had acted and were continuing to act as part of a state-wide system designed to enforce the registration laws in a way that would inevitably deprive colored people of the right to vote solely because of their color. On such an allegation the joinder of all the registrars as defendants in a single suit is authorized by Rule 20(a) of the Federal Rules of Civil Procedure. . . . These registrars were alleged to be carrying on activities which were part of a series of transactions or occurrences the validity of which depended to a large extent upon "question[s] of law or fact common to all of them."

Here too, then, the plaintiffs have asserted a right to relief arising out of the same transactions or occurrences. Each of the ten plaintiffs alleged that he had been injured by the same general policy of discrimination on the part of General Motors and the Union. Since a "state-wide system designed to enforce the registration laws in a way that would inevitably deprive colored people of the right to vote" was determined to arise out of the same series of transactions or occurrences, we conclude that a company-wide policy purportedly designed to discriminate against blacks in employment similarly arises out of the same series of transactions or occurrences. Thus the plaintiffs meet the first requisite for joinder under Rule 20(a).

The second requisite necessary to sustain a permissive joinder under the rule is that a question of law or fact common to all the parties will arise in the action. The rule does not require that *all* questions of law and fact raised by the dispute be common. Yet, neither does it establish any qualitative or quantitative test of commonality. For this reason, cases construing the parallel requirement under Federal Rule of Civil Procedure 23(a) provide a helpful framework for construction of the commonality required by Rule 20. In general, those cases that have focused on Rule 23(a)(2) have given it a permissive application so that common questions have been found to exist in a wide range of contexts. 7 C. Wright, Federal Practice and Procedure §1763 at 604 (1972). Specifically, with respect to employment discrimination cases under Title VII, courts have found that the discriminatory character of a defendant's conduct is basic to the class, and the fact that the individual class members may have suffered different effects from the alleged discrimination is immaterial for the purposes of the prerequisite. Hicks v. Crown Zellerbach Corp. In this vein, one court has said:

> [A]lthough the actual effects of a discriminatory policy may thus vary throughout the class, the existence of the discriminatory policy threatens the entire class. And whether the Damoclean threat of a racially discriminatory policy hangs over the racial class is a question of fact common to all the members of the class.

The right to relief here depends on the ability to demonstrate that each of the plaintiffs was wronged by racially discriminatory policies on the part of the defendants General Motors and the Union. The discriminatory character of the defendants' conduct is thus basic to each plaintiff's recovery. The fact that each plaintiff may have suffered different effects from the alleged discrimination is immaterial for the purposes of determining the common question of law or fact. Thus, we conclude that the second requisite for joinder under Rule 20(a) is also met by the complaint.

For the reasons set forth above, we conclude that the district court abused its discretion in severing the joined actions. The difficulties in ultimately adjudicating damages to the various plaintiffs are not so overwhelming as to require such severance. If appropriate, separate trials may be granted as to any particular issue after the determination of common questions.

The judgment of the district court disallowing joinder of the plaintiffs' individual actions is reversed and remanded with directions to permit the plaintiffs to proceed jointly. . . .

NOTES AND PROBLEMS

1. *Mosley* is an unusual case in at least one respect: The district and appellate courts thought the issue of joinder important enough to certify an interlocutory appeal, something that happens only about 300 times each year among the 250,000 civil suits filed annually in the federal system. Why did the litigants think the question important? If you were the plaintiffs' lawyer, would you rather try these cases together or separately? If you were General Motors' lawyer, which would you prefer? If the decision about joinder is going to make it much more likely that plaintiffs will prevail, it becomes important to be sure that the decision is right. Is it?

a. The court says "[e]ach of the ten plaintiffs alleged that he had been injured by the same general policy of discrimination on the part of General Motors and the Union." Consider who the plaintiffs are:

- African-Americans who worked for GM but alleged they had not been promoted;
- African-American workers who alleged they had been punished for protesting unlawful actions by GM;
- African-Americans who had applied for but not been hired by GM;
- Women (presumably both African-American and white) who had applied for jobs but not been hired by GM;
- African-American employees who had been fired;
- African-Americans and women employees who alleged they had not been granted "relief time" on the same terms as white males.

What "question of law or fact common to all those persons will arise in the action"? (Rule 20.)

b. The Eighth Circuit reversed the district court, ordering joinder. Suppose the case proceeds, with discovery focusing on the defendant's alleged refusal to hire or promote African-Americans and women. Imagine the suit goes to trial (or, more likely a settlement that is embodied in a consent decree, which has the same preclusive effect as a judgment). Thereafter, one of the female plaintiffs brings a second suit alleging that GM's maternity leave policies during the period at issue in the first lawsuit constituted a violation of Title VII, the same statute invoked in the first suit. Is that claim precluded? Could GM argue that the breadth of joinder in the first suit meant that it precluded relitigation of any claim involving prohibited race- or gender-based discrimination?

c. What would have happened in *Mosley* if the court had found joinder improper? See Rule 21.

d. Courts are not always so flexible as *Mosley* in finding common links among plaintiffs:

> The Plaintiffs in this case, all female, are employed by or were formerly employed by AT&T as sales persons in a small, distinct business organization within AT&T known as the Profile Initiative Program (PIP). The Plaintiffs are residents of five different cities and four different states who worked in four separate AT&T offices

located in three states. While the Plaintiffs were directly supervised by different managers in each office, it appears they were indirectly supervised by the same centralized PIP upper management group. The Plaintiffs contend the PIP management systematically discriminated against them because of their sex and allege discriminatory actions by some of the same individuals in PIP management. However, the Plaintiffs identify no specific discriminatory policy or practice to which they were all subjected. In addition to the claims of sex discrimination, Plaintiff Harryman asserts claims of race, age, and national origin discrimination, while Plaintiff Bryan asserts a claim of age discrimination. All the Plaintiffs also assert various state law claims against the Defendants. Thus, AT&T is faced with five individual Plaintiffs asserting a total of more than twenty claims against it. . . .

AT&T contends the Plaintiffs are misjoined and request that this Court sever the claims of each Plaintiff and proceed with five separate trials. . . . AT&T argues the jury may improperly conclude that it is guilty of wrongdoing simply because so many Plaintiffs will complain of discrimination and so many different witnesses will testify in support of the Plaintiffs' claims. AT&T further contends that in a single trial, the jury will hear evidence that may be relevant to the claims of one Plaintiff, but that is completely irrelevant and prejudicial to the claims of the remaining Plaintiffs. According to AT&T, a single trial will unnecessarily complicate evidentiary rulings and will deprive this Court of its discretion to rule on the admissibility of marginally relevant but highly prejudicial evidence.

Henderson v. AT&T Corp., 918 F. Supp. 1059, 1061 (S.D. Tex. 1996). Recognizing that *Mosley* was the leading case on joinder of plaintiffs in employment discrimination cases, the court allowed the joinder under Rule 20 but went on to sever three of the five cases for pretrial and trial.

2. *Henderson* (supra) reminds us that joinder is a game that three can play.

a. Initially plaintiff has the choice, subject to the constraints of Rule 20.

b. Like in *Mosley* and *Henderson*, defendant can challenge joinder of parties, with the result, under Rule 21, that the parties found to be improperly joined will have their cases severed.

c. The third player is the judge, who rules on any challenges to joinder under Rule 20 but also exercises independent power to consolidate and sever claims under Rule 42. Suppose that the *Mosley* plaintiffs had filed nine separate lawsuits and the trial judge had concluded that they were in fact closely related and should be consolidated. Under Rule 42(a) the judge can order "a joint hearing or trial of any or all matters in issue in the actions."

d. Conversely, even if the parties are content with the party structure as it stands, a court acting under the authority of Rule 42(b) may sever claims.

e. Finally, in many federal districts there are local rules that require parties to identify a case that is factually related to any other case currently pending in the district. The purpose of this identification is to allow consolidation of related claims — and to prevent judge-shopping by filing several similar claims and then dismissing all but the one that draws the friendliest judge.

f. Given this judicial discretion, is Rule 20 necessary? Should there be unlimited joinder of parties — just as there is of claims — with the question of joinder treated as one of trial convenience? Are Rules 20 and 21 consistent with Rule 42? A concrete way of putting this question is to ask whether, after the *Mosley* opinion, the trial court, invoking the authority of Rule 42, could still sever the claims for trial.

3. Assume A has similar claims against B and C. What is the practical difference between one action by A against B and C and consolidation of separate actions by A v. B and A v. C under Rule 42(a)? Some possible differences include requirements of serving papers, Rules 5(a), 30(b)(1); right to cross-examine at depositions, cf. Rule 30(c); and right of discovery by B against C and vice versa, Rules 33, 34, 35. In practice, the court consolidating the two cases may order that B and C be treated as co-parties for such matters, thus minimizing the differences.

2.   By Defendants: Third-Party Claims

Although modern procedure accords plaintiffs great autonomy, it does not give them the last word about parties to the suit. The next case illustrates defendants' ability to join additional parties — and the limits to that ability.

Price v. CTB, Inc.

168 F. Supp. 2d 1299 (M.D. Ala. 2001)

DE MENT, District Judge. . . .

[Price, a chicken farmer, hired Latco to build a new chicken house. Alleging that the structure was defective, Price sued CTB, which equips poultry houses, and] Latco . . . [as the] . . . original defendant in the underlying action concerning the quality of its workmanship when it constructed chicken houses for various Alabama farmers. The causes of action against Latco include breach of the construction contract, fraudulent misrepresentation of the caliber of materials to be used, and negligence and wantonness in the construction. Latco moved to file a Third Party Complaint against, inter alios, ITW on February 21, 2001, approximately six months after the case had been removed to the Middle District of Alabama. . . . In the Third Party Complaint, Latco alleges that ITW, a nail manufacturer, defectively designed the nails used in the construction of the chicken houses. The specific causes of action include breach of warranty, violation of the Alabama Extended Manufacturer's Liability Doctrine, and common law indemnity. ITW argues that it was improperly impleaded under Rule 14 of the Federal Rules of Civil Procedure, or, alternatively, that the Third Party Complaint is barred by the equitable doctrine of laches.

Under Rule 14(a), a defendant may assert a claim against anyone not a party to the original action if that third party's liability is in some way dependent upon the outcome of the original action. There is a limitation on this general statement, however. Even though it may arise out of the same general set of facts as the main claim, a third party claim will not be permitted when it is based upon a separate and independent claim. Rather, the third party liability must in some way be derivative of the original claim; a third party may be impleaded only when the original defendant is trying to pass all or part of the liability onto that third party.

Latco argues that ITW is the prototypical third party defendant under Rule 14. It asserts that ITW can be found liable for the warranty surrounding its products if Latco is first found liable for faulty construction. Furthermore, insists Latco, this derivative liability merely involves a shift in the overall responsibility of the allegedly defective chicken houses. ITW contends, however, that because Rule 14 is merely a procedural rule, the propriety of its application depends upon the existence of a right to indemnity under the substantive law. ITW accurately states the law in this regard, but its conclusion that there is no viable substantive claim under Alabama law is incorrect.

Conceding that Alabama does not recognize a right to contribution among joint tortfeasors, Latco directs the court's attention to the concept of implied contractual indemnity. Under this doctrine, Alabama courts recognize that a manufacturer of a product has impliedly agreed to indemnify the seller when 1) the seller is without fault, 2) the manufacturer is responsible, and 3) the seller has been required to pay a monetary judgment. Under Latco's theory, should it be found liable for its construction of the chicken houses, it can demonstrate that the true fault lies with the nail guns and the nails manufactured by ITW.

Alabama case law, not to mention the parties' briefs, is especially sparse with respect to the contours of the doctrine of implied indemnity. . . . [The opinion went on to find that Alabama's law resembled that of Illinois on the point in question and that Illinois would permit a claim for implied indemnity under the circumstances of the case.] The court finds that Alabama law provides Latco a cause of action under common law indemnity against ITW.

It must be noted, however, that, under Alabama law, the doctrine permits recovery only when the party to be indemnified is "without fault." Whether, in fact, such a factual scenario will be proven at trial is irrelevant for present purposes. The only issue before the court is whether there exists a legal basis to implead ITW, not whether ITW is, in fact, liable to Latco. Since Rule 14 permits Latco to implead any party who "may be liable," Fed. R. Civ. P. 14(a), it follows that the court must permit development of the factual record so the extent of that liability may be determined. . . .

Furthermore, since Latco has established a basis upon which it may properly implead ITW, the court need not address the applicability of Rule 14 to the other claims in Latco's Third Party Complaint. It is well established that a properly impleaded claim may serve as an anchor for separate and independent claims under Rule 18(a).[3] . . . In short, the court finds that Latco has properly impleaded ITW under Rule 14(a).

---

3. The court finds it necessary to dispel any worry that its rule might permit defendants to improperly encumber ongoing lawsuits by simply asserting claims of implied contractual indemnity. Rule 14(a) grants federal courts discretion in determining the propriety of a third party complaint, and in making its determination, a court may consider the burden upon the litigation that might ensue, as well as the merit of the third party complaint. . . . Rules 21 and 42 further provide original plaintiffs protection against vexatious litigation by permitting the court to drop parties or to sever claims.

[The opinion went on to reject ITW's claim of laches, finding there had been no undue delay in filing the claim and no prejudice to ITW.]

Accordingly, it is CONSIDERED and ORDERED that ITW's Motion To Dismiss be and the same is hereby DENIED.

NOTES AND PROBLEMS

1. To understand the possibilities and limits of impleader (exemplified in Rule 14), consider a world in which it did not exist.

a. Mr. Price, a chicken farmer, sues Latco for damages suffered when the structures fell apart and the chickens died or fell ill. If Latco wins, there's no problem — at least no procedural problem (Mr. Price may be unhappy).

b. Suppose, however, Latco loses, on a judgment that finds the houses defective and awards damages. In a world without impleader, Latco could still sue the nail manufacturer. But, because the nail manufacturer wasn't a party to the first suit, it would be able in the second suit to argue, for example, that the chicken houses weren't defective at all, or that it was, for example, Mr. Price's poor maintenance that destroyed them. The two lawsuits could thus result in opposed findings — that the houses were defective and that they weren't — with Latco left holding the bag. Or, the jury in the first case might find that Mr. Price suffered very substantial damages — when all his chickens died — while the jury in the second case might find that damages were limited to the cost of a new structure, because the chickens' death had been due to Mr. Price's failure to mitigate damages.

c. Explain how impleader provisions like those found in Rule 14 solve the problem just described.

2. With this understanding, refocus on what is at stake for ITW, the nail manufacturer, now that impleader has been held to be proper.

a. Obviously, it has to defend this case.

b. What other problem for ITW emerges if one rereads the last sentence of footnote 3? How does ITW's problem present a situation that Mr. Price's lawyer might exploit?

c. With this new problem in mind, suppose that, as litigation proceeds, ITW's lawyer decides that things are not going well. The judge has made a number of interlocutory rulings that ITW thinks will make it hard to mount a really effective defense at trial; moreover, he is concerned about how a local jury might react to an out-of-state defendant (the *I* in ITW stands for Illinois). Can you recommend a course of action that might minimize ITW's litigation exposure?

In the present matter, the court deems it appropriate to allow the factual record to develop so that the role of ITW's products in the allegedly defective chicken houses can be determined. Under the rationale that a stitch in time saves nine, the court considers it more efficient to determine liability presently rather than to risk potential relitigation on all the issues at a later date. This conclusion is underscored given that forty identical suits were filed against Latco.

3. As a quick check on your understanding of the principle represented by impleader, imagine that when Mr. Price sued Latco for the collapsed chicken house, Latco investigated and found evidence that the house was in fact destroyed by Farmer Jones, a rival neighbor chicken raiser who sneaked onto Price's property at night and vandalized the house.

a. Latco could *not* implead Jones. This outcome looks at first surprising, but it is well-established:

> It is no longer possible under Rule 14, as it was prior to the 1948 amendment to the rule, to implead a third party claimed to be solely liable to the plaintiff. . . . A proposed third-party plaintiff must allege facts sufficient to establish the derivative or secondary liability of the proposed third-party defendant. . . . Thus, under Rule 14(a), a third-party complaint is appropriate only in cases where the proposed third-party defendant would be secondarily liable to the original defendant in the event the latter is held to be liable to the plaintiff.

Barab v. Menford, 98 F.R.D. 455, 456 (E.D. Pa. 1983) (citations omitted).

> Numerous courts have echoed this principle. . . . Derivative liability is central to the operation of Rule 14. It cannot be used as a device to bring into a controversy matters which merely happen to have some relationship to the original action. . . . In other words, a third party claim is not appropriate where the defendant and putative third party plaintiff says, in effect, "It was him, not me." Such a claim is viable only where a proposed third party plaintiff says, in effect, "If I am liable to plaintiff, then my liability is only technical or secondary or partial, and the third party defendant is derivatively liable and must reimburse me for all or part (one-half, if a joint tortfeasor) of anything I must pay plaintiff."

Watergate Landmark Condominiums Unit Owners' Assoc. v. Wiss, Janey, Elstner Assoc., 117 F.R.D. 576, 578 (E.D. Va. 1987)

b. How, then, can Latco would raise and litigate the issue of Jones's responsibility for the damage?

4. Impleader typically has two substantive foundations, one in tort and the other in contract, both mentioned in the case.

a. The tort doctrine is that of "contribution," a claim that allows one tortfeasor to demand that another fellow wrongdoer "contribute" to the damages payable to the harmed plaintiff. Nineteenth-century law often limited or forbade entirely such contribution on the grounds that no one should be able to avoid the consequences of his wrongdoing. Legislatures and courts in the twentieth- and twenty-first centuries have often been more forgiving, permitting such actions for contribution among joint tortfeasors. But not always; notice that Alabama at the time of the case did not allow for such an action of contribution.

b. The contract doctrine is of indemnity. Suppose Mr. Price, the farmer who sued Latco, did not own the chicken houses but instead leased them from AgriBiz. The lease contains a provision that Price will indemnify and hold AgriBiz harmless from any claim arising out of Price's use of the premises. Price's employee, who works in the building in question, develops cancer and sues AgriBiz claiming that his injury is caused by asbestos-lined ventilation system in the structures. Employee can't bring that claim against his Price because workers' compensation statutes block suits against the employer. When AgriBiz is sued by

Employee, it can implead Price for contractual indemnity. What potential problem does AbriBiz avoid by doing so?

5. Rule 14 has two attractions for persons sued. First, and obviously, it gives them a way of bringing into the suit anyone else who might help them foot all or part of the damage bill. Less obviously, it gives such parties a way of delaying the case and making it more expensive for the plaintiff by adding another party. Inevitably, a three-party case will take longer than a two-party case: for the added party there will be a flurry of pleading and related motions; there will be discovery to be done; scheduling three sets of lawyers' meetings increases time conflicts exponentially; and so on. Moreover, from the plaintiff's standpoint, this added delay and expense does nothing for her, so long as she has identified a solvent defendant and has a strong claim: It's all for defendant's benefit. Not surprisingly, then, plaintiffs are often unenthusiastic about defendant's impleading additional parties. (Footnote 3 of *Price* exemplifies the concerns that plaintiffs may have.) Are there any grounds on which they can resist? Read Rule 14(a).

a. In the jurisdiction in question, third-party plaintiff (the party impleading) isn't entitled to contribution or indemnity from the third-party defendant; therefore impleader is improper. As a quick comprehension check explain briefly why Price lost that argument.

b. A second objection is suggested by the third sentence of Rule 14(a): [If the impleading complaint is not filed within ten days of the answer] "the third party plaintiff must obtain leave on motion upon notice to all parties to the action." One court explained the kinds of things ordinarily considered in connection with such a motion:

> The district court has considerable discretion in deciding whether to permit a third-party complaint. Upon determination that a third-party complaint would be appropriate and foster the interest of judicial economy, the factors to be considered in determining whether to grant leave to implead a third-party defendant are: (i) whether the movant deliberately delayed or was derelict in filing the motion; (ii) whether impleading would unduly delay or complicate the trial; (iii) whether impleading would prejudice the third-party defendant; and (iv) whether the third-party complaint states a claim upon which relief can be granted. "The court must balance the benefits derived from impleader — that is, the benefits of settling related matters in one suit — against the potential prejudice to the plaintiff and third-party defendants." Oliner v. McBride's Industries, Inc., 106 F.R.D. 14, 20 (S.D.N.Y. 1985).

Too, Inc. v. Kohl's Dept. Stores, Inc., 213 F. Supp. 2d 138 (S.D.N.Y. 2003). Suppose defendant makes a motion to implead a third-party defendant a year after the answer is served, after discovery is complete, and a trial date has been set. What would plaintiff's objection sound like? Could there be any circumstances in which such a motion would be granted?

6. Test your understanding by applying it to some potential impleader situations:

a. Andrew sues Blair for assault, in a claim arising out of a scuffle while both were waiting in line to enter a nightclub. Blair seeks to implead Blaine, contending that Andrew has mistaken the identity of his assailant, and that Blaine, not Blair, was the person who struck Andrew. Can Andrew object to Blair's impleader of Blaine?

b. Price sues Latco for defectively constructed chicken houses. Latco promptly impleads Nails, the manufacturer of the nails and nail guns used in constructing the houses, contending that Nails' products were defective. The court permits the impleader of Nails. After six month's investigation of the claims, Nails seeks leave to implead SteelCo, the manufacturer who supplied the metal used in making Latco's nails; Nail's third-party complaint alleges that the metal supplied during the time in question had impurities that caused the nails to corrode when exposed to the weather. Do any of the present parties have grounds to object to Nails's motion to implead SteelCo?

c. In the case described in b., when Price sues Latco, Latco counterclaims against Price for unpaid construction bills, alleging that Price failed to pay the agreed-upon contract price for the construction. In response to Latco's counterclaim, Price seeks to implead Bank, which, Price alleges, failed to fund the line of credit it as it had agreed. Does Rule 14 permit a *plaintiff* to use impleader in this fashion?

7. As we have just seen, parties already in the case may be able to object to a motion to implead either on the grounds that impleader doesn't lie (because the substantive law doesn't allow an action for indemnity or contribution under the circumstances) or because allowing impleader will unjustifiably increase delay or expense. It's less likely that there will be an objection to jurisdiction — either personal or federal subject matter — because statute and Rule grant impleader some special advantages in this respect.

a. Personal jurisdiction over an impleaded third-party defendant (like the nail manufacturer) will usually lie because in many circumstances the third-party defendant will have been involved in the occurrence or transaction that led to the original claim and thus subject to personal jurisdiction under the *International Shoe* line of cases. If that isn't enough, Rule 4(k)(1)(B) gives an extra 100-mile boost to the court's jurisdiction. Read that provision and apply it to the following situation. Plaintiff sues Defendant, a Pennsylvania corporation, in federal court in Philadelphia, alleging a breach of contract, arising out of some work Defendant performed in Wilmington, Delaware, about 35 miles south of Philadelphia. Defendant wants to implead Employee, who lives and works in Wilmington, and has insufficient contacts with Pennsylvania to subject him to personal jurisdiction there. Does Employee have a jurisdictional objection to his joinder? Why?

b. Federal subject matter jurisdiction gets a similar boost from 28 U.S.C. §1367. Reread that provision and explain why a federal district court will always have subject matter jurisdiction over a properly impleaded third-party defendant.

3. More Complex Litigation

Thus far, we have considered what may be called single-issue joinder problems involving a single rule. Many cases, however, involve combinations of the joinder provisions already discussed. As a review of the joinder material so far, respond to the problems below.

NOTES AND PROBLEMS

1. Plaintiff files a complaint against an automobile Dealer and automobile Manufacturer. The complaint, which is properly before the court under diversity jurisdiction, alleges that Plaintiff was injured in an accident caused by a defect in the vehicle's steering mechanism.

a. Dealer wants to assert that Manufacturer is contractually obligated to indemnify Dealer for any liability that Dealer may have to Plaintiff in the action. What pleading, if any, should Dealer file?

b. Manufacturer wants to assert that the vehicle was not defective when delivered to Dealer and that any defect must have been introduced by Dealer when the vehicle was being prepared for delivery to customer. What pleading, if any, should Manufacturer file?

c. Manufacturer wants to assert that Dealer has failed to pay for several vehicles that Manufacturer delivered to Dealer (not including the vehicle at issue in the action). Can it do so? What pleading, if any, should Manufacturer file?

d. Dealer wants to assert that Plaintiff owes Dealer money for a breach of contract that has no relationship whatsoever to the vehicle or accident at issue in Plaintiff's complaint. Can Dealer do so? What pleading, if any, should it use?

e. Dealer and Manufacturer both want to assert that there was no defect in the vehicle and that the accident was solely the result of Plaintiff's negligence. What pleading, if any, should Dealer and Manufacturer use?

2. Plaintiff sues Defendant alleging that Defendant infringed Plaintiff's patent. Defendant wants to assert that Plaintiff and a Competitor of Defendant are liable to Defendant for compensatory and punitive damages for conspiring to use frivolous patent claims to create a monopoly in violation of the antitrust laws. Assume that the court would have personal jurisdiction over Competitor, and that Competitor's addition as a party would not defeat subject matter jurisdiction. What pleading, if any, would Defendant file?

3. Why doesn't Rule 18, permitting the joinder of all claims, counterclaims, and cross-claims, whether or not related, take care of many of these problems? Harmonizing Rules 13, 14, and 18 requires careful analysis.

a. Rule 18 provides that a "party asserting a claim . . . as an original claim, counterclaim, cross-claim, or third-party claim, may join, either as independent or as alternate claims, as many claims, legal, equitable, or maritime as he has against an opposing party."

b. But Rule 13(g) contains a more restrictive provision, limiting cross-claims to those "arising out of the transaction or occurrence that is the subject matter either of the original action or of a counterclaim therein. . . ." Rule 14(a) similarly restricts claims by third-party defendants.

c. Does Rule 18 eliminate the restrictions created by Rules 13 and 14? No; the key to reconciliation lies in the difference between the requirements for the first cross-claim or third-party-defendant claim and any subsequent ones. Thus, in Note 1c above, Manufacturer cannot file a cross-claim against dealer because there is no transactional relationship between Dealer's claim against Manufacturer and the unpaid-for vehicles. But if he had one transactionally related cross-claim, he could join with it another that lacked such a connection.

4. The problems in this Note have thus far focused on the propriety of joinder under the Rules. As we have already seen, federal courts facing joinder questions must often confront a second problem beyond the issue of the propriety of joinder — jurisdiction.

a. If a claim carries with it an independent jurisdictional basis, that question is quickly resolved. For example, if a cross-claim arises under federal law, there will be no problem. Similarly, if a defendant/third-party plaintiff and a third-party defendant meet the requirements of diversity of citizenship, there will be no difficult jurisdictional issue.

b. But what happens if the federal court would not otherwise have jurisdiction over a compulsory counterclaim, third-party claim, or cross-claim? Does supplemental jurisdiction extend to cover these essentially defensive claims? In many circumstances, the answer is yes. Section §1367 of the Judiciary Code (28 U.S.C.) permits many, but not all, such claims to come in under the umbrella of supplemental jurisdiction.

c. Locating the line between permissible and impermissible extensions of supplemental jurisdiction requires (1) a close reading of the statute and (2) a consideration of the concept underlying the statute. It also involves thinking strategically along with the parties as they invoke the Rules and the principles of jurisdiction. The next case, which we examine in several separate phases, explores both the possibilities of impleader and a jurisdictional barrier to its deployment.

Kroger v. Omaha Public Power District

523 F.2d 161 (8th Cir. 1975)

NANGLE, J. . . .

Plaintiff-Appellant, Geraldine Kroger . . . as administratrix of the estate of James Kroger, brought suit based on diversity jurisdiction for damages resulting from decedent's wrongful death by electrocution.

Appellant's decedent was employed by Paxton & Vierling Steel Company at its factory in Carter Lake, Iowa. On January 18, 1972, decedent was involved in the movement of a large steel tank by means of a crane with a 60-foot boom. While one man drove the crane and another operated the boom, decedent walked alongside the tank to steady it. During this maneuver, the boom came close enough to high-tension lines that electricity from those lines arced over to the boom. Another arc of electricity arced from the tank over to decedent and killed him. . . .

NOTES AND PROBLEMS

1. Put yourself in the position of plaintiff's lawyer. Your client has suffered a terrible loss and any success in a lawsuit will be of great help to a young family. You survey potential defendants and learn the following:

The crane involved was owned by the Owen Equipment and Erection Company, and leased by Paxton & Vierling Steel Company (hereafter "Paxton") for heavy lifting.

Kroger v. Owen Equipment & Erection Co., 558 F.2d 417, 418 (8th Cir. 1977).

> Omaha Public Power District [OPPD], a public corporation of the state of Nebraska, had at one time owned the transmission lines involved. On November 14, 1966, however, OPPD sold the lines and equipment to Paxton & Vierling, OPPD thereafter sold electricity to Paxton & Vierling and when so requested made repairs upon the lines and equipment.

Kroger v. Omaha Public Power District, 523 F.2d 161, 162 (8th Cir. 1975). You have, then, three possible defendants: Omaha Public Power, Paxton & Vierling Steel, and Owen Equipment & Erection.

a. If one assumes that each of these entities has assets sufficient to satisfy a judgment, which seems intuitively to be liable for Mr. Kroger's death — if anyone is?

b. Paxton might seem a promising defendant. But in most states, workers' compensation laws give employees the right to receive compensation for on-the-job injuries and death without the necessity of proving fault. In return for this right, workers' compensation laws bar tort suits against employers.

c. Can you identify any reason for not suing Owen Equipment?

d. Mrs. Kroger's lawyer in fact sued only Omaha Public Power District.

2. Now imagine yourself as the lawyer for Omaha Power. Look back at the facts above. Your client has been sued on a claim for which you believe it has no liability.

a. What is your basic strategy for a defense?

b. Explain why, on these facts, it would be plausible to implead Owen Equipment. Why would such a use of impleader not violate the "It was him, not me" stance described in Note 3 following Price v. CTB, supra page 748?

c. Having used impleader as a form of "litigation insurance," Omaha Power returned to its central defense — denial of liability — and successfully sought summary judgment:

> The District Court based its order of summary judgment on the fact that ownership of the transmission lines lay indisputably with Paxton & Vierling, that OPPD had no duty to maintain the lines, that OPPD had not been requested to discontinue the flow of electricity on the date of the accident and that OPPD had not been put on notice that a crane was being operated in the vicinity of the lines. As a result, there was no duty owed by OPPD to decedent, the breach of which would give rise to liability.

Kroger v. Omaha Public Power District, 523 F.2d 161 at 162. The Eighth Circuit affirmed.

3. Switch sides again and return to your original representation of Mrs. Kroger. Omaha Power has impleaded Owen Equipment. Although you did not sue this defendant originally, it is now in the case and you decide to take advantage of the opportunity.

a. Read Rule 14(a) with care and identify the sentence that makes it possible for you to assert a claim against Owen Equipment.

b. Mrs. Kroger's complaint, let us assume, complied with Rule 8(a)(1) by asserting that plaintiff was a citizen of Iowa and that Owen Equipment was a Nebraska corporation with its principal place of business in that state and otherwise satisfied the requirements of 28 U.S.C. §1332. Owen answered Kroger's complaint as follows:

> 1. Admits that Owen Equipment and Erection Company is a corporation organized and existing under the Laws of the State of Nebraska.
> 2. Denies each and every other allegation contained in said Amended Complaint, except those allegations which would be in the nature of admissions against the interest of the plaintiff.

Kroger v. Owen Equipment & Erection Co., 558 F.2d 417, 429 (8th Cir. 1977).

c. Read Rule 8(b), which governs answers, and recall Zielinski v. Philadelphia Piers, Inc., supra page 382. Does this answer — quoted in its entirety — comply with the Rule? Has defendant conceded jurisdiction?

4. Two years after these pleadings — and after Omaha Power had won its summary judgment motion — trial began, with Owen Equipment as the sole defendant. That trial saw a dramatic development:

> So stood the description of the parties [i.e., as of diverse citizenship,] until noon on the third day of the trial. At this juncture, defendant Owen elicited from witness Petersen, Secretary of Owen, that Owen's principal place of business was in Carter Lake, Iowa. Having done so, defendant the same afternoon challenged the jurisdiction of the court on the ground of lack of diversity.

Kroger v. Owen Equipment & Erection Co., 558 F.2d 417 at 419.

a. Note that this evidence does not squarely contradict the answer, which admitted that defendant was a Nebraska corporation and generally — but vaguely — denied everything else, including, by inference, that defendant's principal place of business was in Nebraska.

b. Before asking whether the court should grant Owen's motion, consider why that motion came only at trial. Rule 12(h)(3) specifies that jurisdictional challenges are not waived and can be raised at any time. But why wait? What advantages might accrue to Owen by waiting two years to make this motion?

5. The district court refused to grant Owen's motion to dismiss.

a. The Court of Appeals affirmed. The opinion discussed but did not expressly rely on reasoning like that used in Zielinski to the effect that defendant was estopped from relying on an ambiguous and deceptive pleading. The court said, "The doctrine of the perpetual availability of jurisdictional challenge furnishes no sanctuary to appellant in the light of such conduct." Kroger v. Owen Equipment & Erection Co., 558 F.2d 417 at 427.

b. But the Court of Appeals devoted most of its opinion to another ground. The case, which preceded the enactment of 28 U.S.C. §1367, raises one of the problems the statute now addresses — extending supplemental jurisdiction to a claim asserted by a plaintiff against a nondiverse third-party defendant. The Court of Appeals held that supplemental jurisdiction did extend to Mrs. Kroger's claim against Owen Equipment; the U.S. Supreme Court disagreed.

Owen Equipment & Erection Co. v. Kroger

437 U.S. 365 (1978)

Mr. Justice STEWART delivered the opinion of the Court. . . .

The relevant statute in this case, 28 U.S.C. §1332(a)(1), confers upon federal courts jurisdiction over "civil actions where the matter in controversy exceeds the [requisite amount in controversy] . . . and is between . . . citizens of different States." This statute and its predecessors have consistently been held to require complete diversity of citizenship. That is, diversity jurisdiction does not exist unless *each* defendant is a citizen of a different State from *each* plaintiff. Over the years Congress has repeatedly reenacted or amended the statute conferring diversity jurisdiction, leaving intact this rule of complete diversity. Whatever may have been the original purposes of diversity of citizenship jurisdiction, this subsequent history clearly demonstrates a congressional mandate that diversity jurisdiction is not to be available when any plaintiff is a citizen of the same State as any defendant.

Thus it is clear that the respondent could not originally have brought suit in federal court naming Owen and OPPD as codefendants, since citizens of Iowa would have been on both sides of the litigation. Yet the identical lawsuit resulted when she amended her complaint [to assert a claim against Owen]. Complete diversity was destroyed just as surely as if she had sued Owen initially. In either situation, in the plain language of the statute, the "matter in controversy" could not be "between . . . citizens of different States."

It is a fundamental precept that federal courts are courts of limited jurisdiction. The limits upon federal jurisdiction, whether imposed by the Constitution or by Congress, must be neither disregarded nor evaded. Yet under the reasoning of the Court of Appeals in this case, a plaintiff could defeat the statutory requirement of complete diversity by the simple expedient of suing only those defendants who were of diverse citizenship and waiting for them to implead nondiverse defendants.[17] If, as the Court of Appeals thought, a "common nucleus of operative fact" were the only requirement for ancillary jurisdiction in a diversity case, there would be no principled reason why the respondent in this case could not have joined her cause of action against Owen in her original complaint as ancillary to her claim against OPPD. Congress' requirement of complete diversity would thus have been evaded completely.

---

17. This is not an unlikely hypothesis, since a defendant in a tort suit such as this one would surely try to limit his liability by impleading any joint tortfeasors for indemnity or contribution. Some commentators have suggested that the possible abuse of third-party practice could be dealt with under 28 U.S.C. §1359, which forbids collusive attempts to create federal jurisdiction. See, e.g., 3 J. Moore, Federal Practice para. 14.27[1], p. 14-571 (2d ed. 1974); 6 C. Wright & A. Miller, Federal Practice and Procedure §1444, pp. 231-232 (1971); Note, Rule 14 Claims and Ancillary Jurisdiction, 57 Va. L. Rev. 265, 274-275 (1971). The dissenting opinion today also expresses this view. Post, at 383. But there is nothing necessarily collusive about a plaintiff's selectively suing only those tortfeasors of diverse citizenship, or about the named defendants' desire to implead joint tortfeasors. Nonetheless, the requirement of complete diversity would be eviscerated by such a course of events.

It is true, as the Court of Appeals noted, that the exercise of ancillary jurisdiction over nonfederal claims has often been upheld in situations involving impleader, cross-claims or counterclaims. But in determining whether jurisdiction over a nonfederal claim exists, the context in which the nonfederal claim is asserted is crucial. And the claim here arises in a setting quite different from the kinds of nonfederal claims that have been viewed in other cases as falling within the ancillary jurisdiction of the federal courts.

First, the nonfederal claim in this case was simply not ancillary to the federal one in the same sense that, for example, the impleader by a defendant of a third-party defendant always is. A third-party complaint depends at least in part upon the resolution of the primary lawsuit. Its relation to the original complaint is thus not mere factual similarity but logical dependence. The respondent's claim against the petitioner, however, was entirely separate from her original claim against OPPD, since the petitioner's liability to her depended not at all upon whether or not OPPD was also liable. Far from being an ancillary and dependent claim, it was a new and independent one.

Second, the nonfederal claim here was asserted by the plaintiff, who voluntarily chose to bring suit upon a state-law claim in a federal court. By contrast, ancillary jurisdiction typically involves claims by a defending party haled into court against his will, or by another person whose rights might be irretrievably lost unless he could assert them in an ongoing action in a federal court. A plaintiff cannot complain if ancillary jurisdiction does not encompass all of his possible claims in a case such as this one, since it is he who has chosen the federal rather than the state forum and must thus accept its limitations. "[T]he efficiency plaintiff seeks so avidly is available without question in the state courts."[20]

It is not unreasonable to assume that, in generally requiring complete diversity, Congress did not intend to confine the jurisdiction of federal courts so inflexibly that they are unable to protect legal rights or effectively to resolve an entire, logically entwined lawsuit. Those practical needs are the basis of the doctrine of ancillary jurisdiction. But neither the convenience of litigants nor considerations of judicial economy can suffice to justify extension of the doctrine of ancillary jurisdiction to a plaintiff's cause of action against a citizen of the same State in a diversity case. Congress has established the basic rule that diversity jurisdiction exists under 28 U.S.C. §1332 only when there is complete diversity of citizenship. "The policy of the statute calls for its strict construction." To allow the requirement of complete diversity to be circumvented as it was in this case would simply flout the congressional command.[21]

Accordingly, the judgment of the Court of Appeals is reversed.

It is so ordered.

---

20. Whether Iowa's statute of limitations would now bar an action by the respondent in an Iowa court is, of course, entirely a matter of state law.

21. Our holding is that the District Court lacked power to entertain the respondent's lawsuit against the petitioner. Thus, the asserted inequity in the petitioner's alleged concealment of its citizenship is irrelevant. Federal judicial power does not depend upon "prior action or consent of the parties." American Fire & Cas. Co. v. Finn.

Mr. Justice WHITE, with whom Mr. Justice BRENNAN joins, dissenting.

The Court today states that "[i]t is not unreasonable to assume that, in generally requiring complete diversity, Congress did not intend to confine the jurisdiction of federal courts so inflexibly that they are unable . . . effectively to resolve an entire, logically entwined lawsuit." In spite of this recognition, the majority goes on to hold that in diversity suits federal courts do not have the jurisdictional power to entertain a claim asserted by a plaintiff against a third-party defendant, no matter how entwined it is with the matter already before the court, unless there is an independent basis for jurisdiction over that claim. Because I find no support for such a requirement in either Art. III of the Constitution or in any statutory law, I dissent from the Court's "unnecessarily grudging" approach. . . .

We have previously noted that "[s]ubsequent decisions of this Court indicate that Strawbridge is not to be given an expansive reading." State Farm Fire & Cas. Co. v. Tashire. In light of this teaching, it seems to me appropriate to view §1332 as requiring complete diversity only between the plaintiff and those parties he actually brings into the suit. Beyond that, I would hold that in a diversity case the District Court has power, both constitutional and statutory, to entertain all claims among the parties arising from the same nucleus of operative fact as the plaintiff's original, jurisdiction-conferring claim against the defendant. Accordingly, I dissent from the Court's disposition of the present case.

NOTES AND PROBLEMS

1. Recall that *Kroger* preceded the enactment of 28 U.S.C. §1367. Consider the statute's effect on the factual situation.

a. First confirm the proposition that 28 U.S.C. §1367 codifies *Kroger*. What phrase in what section of the statute codifies the Supreme Court's views in *Kroger*?

b. Contrast the statute's handling of federal question claims. Suppose that Mrs. Kroger's claim had been based on federal rather than state law, in which she alleged that OPPD had violated federal job-site safety regulations and that the violation caused decedent's death. OPPD then impleaded Owen Equipment, alleging that it was directly responsible for the violations, and, once Owen Equipment was in the suit, Mrs. Kroger asserted a claim directly against Owen Equipment. Explain why on those facts there *would be* supplemental jurisdiction over Mrs. Kroger's claim against Owen.

2. The Supreme Court almost entirely ignored the question that had so exercised the district and circuit courts, Owen's misleading answer to the jurisdictional allegations and its late raising of the jurisdictional defense.

a. Footnote 21 suggests, though it does not quite hold, that there could be no such "jurisdictional estoppel." Is that a sound ruling?

b. Could one distinguish between cases in which a party simply failed to raise a jurisdictional defense and those like *Kroger*, in which a party misled the court and other parties? If federal question jurisdiction is a fundamental political boundary line, party behavior should make no difference, should it?

3. Congress, in enacting §1367, could have reversed the result in *Kroger*.

a. As a quick review, explain why Congress had that power.

b. Why do you suppose Congress did not do so? One possibility is the concern about collusive suits, in which A wishing to sue C but lacking jurisdiction to do so, instead sues B, who A knows will implead C, against whom A can then assert a claim under Rule 14(a). Is this a big concern?

4. Test your analysis on a variation on the facts of *Kroger*. Suppose that the third-party defendant had first made a claim against the plaintiff—perhaps an allegation that Mr. Kroger had been vandalizing the crane at the time of the accident.

a. As a matter of pleading, that claim is allowable. Rule 14(a) provides that a third-party defendant "may assert any claim against the plaintiff arising out of the transaction or occurrence that is the subject matter of the plaintiff's claim" against the original defendant. Would supplemental jurisdiction also attach to such a claim? See §1367(b).

b. Now suppose that *after* Owen Equipment asserted such a claim, Mrs. Kroger filed her claim for wrongful death. As a matter of pleading such a claim is again allowable, whether analyzed under 14(a) or under 13(a). (Do you see why both of these sections might plausibly apply?) Would supplemental jurisdiction attach to Mrs. Kroger's claim in these circumstances?

In answering that question, consider the relevance of a passage from *Kroger*:

> [I]n determining whether jurisdiction over a nonfederal claim exists, the context in which the nonfederal claim is asserted is crucial. . . .
>
>   [T]he nonfederal claim here was asserted by the plaintiff, who voluntarily chose to bring suit upon a state-law claim in a federal court. By contrast [supplemental] jurisdiction typically involves claims by *a defending party haled into court against his will*. . . . (Emphasis added.)

When Owen Equipment asserts a claim against Mrs. Kroger, does she then become "a defending party" entitled to invoke supplemental jurisdiction? The straightforward language of the statute suggests not: This is a claim by a plaintiff against a third-party defendant. The rationale of *Kroger* might lead one to a different decision. The statute is more recent than *Kroger*, and Congress has the power to supersede the case law on a matter not governed by the Constitution. But the statutory history of §1367 suggests it intended to codify *Kroger*, not to supersede it. So does one read into the statute *Kroger*'s gloss on the statute? Or follow the text alone?

5. Finally, let us return to the travails of Mrs. Kroger. Having lost on the merits against Omaha Power and against Owen Equipment on a belatedly raised jurisdictional defense, what remedies did she have?

a. The Supreme Court suggested a state court lawsuit. There would be no jurisdictional barrier to such a suit, but what defense could her lawyer anticipate?

b. Iowa, like some but not all states, has "savings statutes" that grant relief from the statute of limitations under some conditions. Such statutes are aimed, among other things, at jurisdictional dismissals. Iowa's statute provides:

> If, after the commencement of an action, the plaintiff, for any cause except negligence in its prosecution, fails therein, and a new one is brought within six months

thereafter, the second shall, for the purposes herein contemplated, be held a continuation of the first.

Iowa Code Ann. §614.10 (2003). Would Mrs. Kroger's claim be saved by this statute? About what clauses might her lawyer be worried?

c. As it happens, Mrs. Kroger's legal travails came to an end that was, if not happy, at least less disastrous than their beginning. Rumor has it that during the pendency of the several phases of the suit, she remarried and moved to Texas. She filed suit again, in state court, successfully invoking the Iowa savings statute as an answer to the statute of limitations defense, and settled the case for what is reported to be somewhat more than the original jury had awarded.

4. Compulsory Joinder

This chapter has thus far concentrated on who can be joined in a suit if someone already a party seeks joinder. We now consider whether there are those who must be joined — even if neither they nor those already in the suit desire to see them there. The topic, sometimes rather confusingly described in terms of "necessary and indispensable parties," has its roots in eighteenth century equity practice. Chancery developed the perfectly sensible notions that: (1) litigation often affected people who weren't formal parties; and (2) if the effects were serious enough and the affected persons could be joined, they should be. Rule 19 now embodies these propositions. Reading the Rule might leave one with the impression that it required courts in every case to consider the most efficient and effective party structure for a lawsuit. That is now how courts have interpreted it.

Temple v. Synthes Corp.

498 U.S. 5, rehg. denied, 498 U.S. 1092 (1990)

PER CURIAM.

Petitioner Temple, a Mississippi resident, underwent surgery in October 1986 in which a "plate and screw device" was implanted in his lower spine. The device was manufactured by respondent Synthes, Ltd. (U.S.A.) (Synthes), a Pennsylvania corporation. Dr. S. Henry LaRocca performed the surgery at St. Charles General Hospital in New Orleans, Louisiana. Following surgery, the device's screws broke off inside Temple's back.

Temple filed suit against Synthes in the United States District Court for the Eastern District of Louisiana. The suit, which rested on diversity jurisdiction, alleged defective design and manufacture of the device. At the same time, Temple filed a state administrative proceeding against Dr. LaRocca and the hospital for malpractice and negligence. At the conclusion of the administrative proceeding, Temple filed suit against the doctor and the hospital in Louisiana state court.

Synthes did not attempt to bring the doctor and the hospital into the federal action by means of a third-part complaint, as provided in Federal Rule of Civil Procedure 14(a). Instead, Synthes filed a motion to dismiss Temple's federal suit for failure to join necessary parties pursuant to Federal Rule of Civil Procedure 19. Following a hearing, the District Court ordered Temple to join the doctor and the hospital as defendants within twenty days or risk dismissal of the lawsuit. According to the court, the most significant reason for requiring joinder was the interest of judicial economy. The court relied on this Court's decision in Provident Tradesmens Bank & Trust Co. v. Patterson, 390 U.S. 102 (1968), wherein we recognized that one focus of Rule 19 is "the interest of the courts and the public in complete, consistent, and efficient settlement of controversies." When Temple failed to join the doctor and the hospital, the court dismissed the suit with prejudice.

Temple appealed, and the United States Court of Appeals for the Fifth Circuit affirmed. The court deemed it "obviously prejudicial to the defendants to have the separate litigations being carried on," because Synthes' defense might be that the plate was not defective but that the doctor and the hospital were negligent, while the doctor and hospital, on the other hand, might claim that they were not negligent but that the plate was defective. The Court of Appeals found that claims overlapped and that the District Court therefore had not abused its discretion in ordering joinder under Rule 19. A petition for rehearing was denied.

In his petition for certiorari to this Court, Temple contends that it was error to label joint tortfeasors as indispensable parties under Rule 19(b) and to dismiss the lawsuit with prejudice for failure to join those parties. We agree. Synthes does not deny that it, the doctor, and the hospital are potential joint tortfeasors. It has long been the rule that it is not necessary for all joint tortfeasors to be named as defendants in a single lawsuit. Nothing in the 1966 revision of Rule 19 changed that principle. The Advisory Committee Notes to Rule 19(a) explicitly state that "a tortfeasor with the usual 'joint-and-several' liability is merely a permissive party to an action against another with like liability." Advisory Committee's Notes on Fed. Rule Civ. Proc. 19, 28 U.S.C. App., p. 594, at 595. There is nothing in Louisiana tort law to the contrary. See Mullins v. Skains, 252 La. 1009, 1014, 215 So. 2d 643, 645 (1968); La. Civ. Code Ann., Arts. 1794, 1975 (West 1987).

The opinion in *Provident Bank*, supra, does speak of the public interest in limiting multiple litigation, but that case is not controlling here. There, the estate of a tort victim brought a declaratory judgment action against an insurance company. We assumed that the policyholder was a person "who, under . . . [Rule 19](a), should be joined if 'feasible.'" and went on to discuss the appropriate analysis under Rule 19(b), because the policyholder could not be joined without destroying diversity. After examining the factors set forth in Rule 19(b), we determined that the action could proceed without the policyholder; he therefore was not an indispensable party whose absence required dismissal of the suit.

Here, no inquiry under Rule 19(b) is necessary, because the threshold requirements of Rule 19(a) have not been satisfied. As potential joint tortfeasors with Synthes, Dr. LaRocca and the hospital were merely permissive parties. The Court of Appeals erred by failing to hold that the District Court abused its discretion in ordering them joined as defendants and in dismissing the action when Temple failed to comply with the court's order. For these reasons, we grant the petition for certiorari, reverse the judgment of the Court of Appeals for the Fifth Circuit, and remand for further proceedings consistent with this opinion.

It is so ordered.

NOTES AND PROBLEMS

1. The opinion does not dispute the lower courts' conclusion that it would be more efficient to have all the litigation in a single forum. It nevertheless holds that it was reversible error to dismiss the case. Moreover, the opinion was *per curiam* (by the court as a whole, rather than signed by an individual justice). Such brief, anonymous opinions are often used in cases for which the court believes the principles are clear beyond doubt and require no extended discussion. What principle is the court valuing more highly than the obvious efficiency of consolidating the cases?

2. What does the court mean when it notes that "Synthes did not attempt to bring the doctor and the hospital into the federal action by means of a third-party complaint, as provided in Federal Rule of Civil Procedure 14(a)."

a. As a review of impleader, recall that Synthes could *not* implead the doctor on the basis that his negligence rather than a defective product caused Billy Temple's injury. (Such a clam would constitute a forbidden "It's him, not me" use of impleader.)

b. So what factual or legal relations would have had to exist for Synthes to be able to implead the doctor or hospital?

3. As further review, consider whether, if the plaintiff had wanted to sue both defendants in the same action, he could have done so.

a. As a matter of pleading?

b. As a matter of jurisdiction?

4. Ordinarily one expects that plaintiffs will be eager to sue as many plausible defendants as possible. The strategy in such a case is to have one defendant — perhaps the surgeon — argue that he was not negligent, but the product was defective, while Synthes contends that its product was fine but that the medical defendants were negligent. In such circumstances the defendants, pointing fingers at each other, do part of plaintiff's work. What risks was Temple's lawyer running by filing separate lawsuits against the two defendant groups?

5. *Temple* stands at least for the proposition that Rule 19 does not require the most efficient possible packaging of lawsuits. Nor does it require the joinder of anyone who might be affected by precedent:

> We are not sure what the district court means by the phrase "persuasive precedent." To the extent it involves the doctrine of stare decisis, we are not inclined to hold that any potential effect the doctrine may have on an absent party's rights makes the absent party's joinder compulsory under Rule 19(a) whenever "feasible." Such a holding would greatly expand the class of "necessary" or compulsory parties Rule 19(a) creates. Moreover, to whatever extent the rule's phrase "as a practical

matter impair or impede" has broader meaning than that given by principles of issue preclusion, we think the effect of the federal decision must be more direct and immediate than the effect a judgment in Shepard Niles' favor would have on Underwood here. They are, after all, separate corporate entities. In any event, we do not believe any possibility of a "persuasive precedent" requires joinder under subsection 19(a)(2)(i).

Janney Montgomery Scott, Inc. v. Shepard Niles, Inc., 11 F.3d 399, 407 (3d Cir. 1993).

6. Given these background understandings, the necessary parties rules therefore typically operate only when "there is some connection of property ownership, contract rights, or obligations between those who are initially made parties and those who have not been joined." James, Hazard & Leubsdorf at 526. Rule 19 seeks to describe the circumstances under which courts should overcome the ordinary presumptions of party autonomy. Read it and apply it to an elementary problem. Buyer enters into a contract with Husband and Wife to purchase Blackacre. The sellers fail to convey the land at the appointed time, and Buyer sues Husband, seeking a decree of specific performance. Assume that the jurisdiction in question requires the signatures of both Husband and Wife to convey ordinary, clean title.

a. According to Rule 19(a), should Wife be joined if that is feasible?

b. Be prepared to explain, using the categories of the Rule, why Wife's joinder is desirable (or not desirable).

7. Notice that Rule 19 is somewhat coy about who is to raise the question of joining additional parties. Unlike rules that empower one of the parties to make a motion, this one says, "a person . . . shall be joined as a party," suggesting the court has independent power (and perhaps a duty) to make inquiry. In practice, courts will do so only in a few quite well-defined circumstances. More frequently, one of the parties, typically the defendant, will raise the objection. The defendant's motive for doing so is frequently less than altruistic, as you will see if you study Rule 19(b).

a. What do you suppose the typical defendant is hoping will happen as a result of a Rule 19 motion?

b. Consider again the case of Buyer's suit for specific performance against Husband. Suppose that the court concludes that (1) Wife should be joined; but (2) the court lacks jurisdiction over her. What should the court do? Dismiss Buyer's suit? Something else?

c. In analyzing the preceding question, consider especially the language in Rule 19(b) requiring the court to think about "the extent to which, by protective provisions in the judgment, by the shaping of relief, or other measures, the prejudice can be lessened or avoided. . . ." Buyer wants Blackacre as contracted for, with a clean title. Husband and Wife are entitled to the purchase price, but Wife is not a party to the suit. About whom should the court be concerned, and what can it do to alleviate these concerns if it goes forward with the suit?

8. In the typical Rule 19 case, the indispensable party issue is raised in the trial court, and it is a given that the assertedly desirable party is not subject to jurisdiction.

The question is then whether it is possible and fair to proceed in his absence. *Helzberg*'s is an example of such a case.

Helzberg's Diamond Shops v. Valley West Des Moines Shopping Center

564 F.2d 816 (8th Cir. 1977)

ALSOP, J.

On February 3, 1975, Helzberg's Diamond Shops, Inc. (Helzberg), a Missouri corporation, and Valley West Des Moines Shopping Center, Inc. (Valley West), an Iowa corporation, executed a written Lease Agreement. The Lease Agreement granted Helzberg the right to operate a full line jewelry store at space 254 in the Valley West Mall in West Des Moines, Iowa. Section 6 of Article V of the Lease Agreement provides:

> [Valley West] agrees it will not lease premises in the shopping center for use as a catalog jewelry store nor lease premises for more than two full line jewelry stores in the shopping center in addition to the leased premises. This clause shall not prohibit other stores such as department stores from selling jewelry from catalogs or in any way restrict the shopping center department stores.

Subsequently, Helzberg commenced operation of a full line jewelry store in the Valley West Mall.

Between February 3, 1975 and November 2, 1976 Valley West and two other corporations entered into leases for spaces in the Valley West Mall for use as full line jewelry stores. Pursuant to those leases the two corporations also initiated actual operation of full line jewelry stores. On November 2, 1976, Valley West and Kirk's Incorporated, Jewelers, an Iowa corporation, doing business as Lord's Jewelers (Lord's), entered into a written Lease Agreement. The Lease Agreement granted Lord's the right to occupy space 261 in the Valley West Mall. Section I of Article V of the Lease Agreement provides that Lord's will use space 261

> . . . only as a retail specialty jewelry store (and not as a catalogue or full line jewelry store) featuring watches, jewelry (and the repair of same) and incidental better gift items.

However, Lord's intended to open and operate what constituted a full line jewelry store at space 261.

In an attempt to avoid the opening of a fourth full line jewelry store in the Valley West Mall and the resulting breach of the Helzberg-Valley West Lease Agreement, Helzberg instituted suit seeking preliminary and permanent injunctive relief restraining Valley West's breach of the Lease Agreement. The suit was filed in the United States District Court for the Western District of Missouri. Subject matter jurisdiction was invoked pursuant to 28 U.S.C. §1332 based upon diversity of citizenship between the parties and an amount in controversy which exceeded [the statutory amount]. Personal jurisdiction was established by service of process on

Valley West pursuant to the Missouri "long arm" statute, Rev. Stat. Mo. §506,500 et seq. (1977). Rule 4(e), Fed. R. Civ. P.

Valley West moved to dismiss pursuant to Rule 19 because Helzberg had failed to join Lord's as a party defendant. That motion was denied. The district court went on to order that

> pending the determination of [the] action on the merits, that [Valley West] be, and it is hereby, enjoined and restrained from allowing, and shall take all necessary steps to prevent, any other tenant in its Valley West Mall (including but not limited to, Kirk's Incorporated, Jewelers, d/b/a Lord's Jewelers) to open and operate on March 30, 1977, or at any other time, or to be operated during the term of [Helzberg's] present leasehold, a fourth full line jewelry store meaning a jewelry store offering for sale at retail a broad range of jewelry items at various prices such as diamonds and diamond jewelry, precious and semi-precious stones, watches, rings, gold jewelry, costume jewelry, gold chains, pendants, bracelets, belt buckles, tie tacs, tie slides and earrings, provided, however, nothing contained herein shall be construed to enjoin [Valley West] from allowing the opening in said Valley West Mall of a small store, known by [Valley West] as a boutique, which sells limited items such as only Indian jewelry, only watches, only earrings, or only pearls.

From this order Valley West appeals.

It is clear that Valley West is entitled to appeal from the order granting preliminary injunctive relief. 28 U.S.C. §1292(a)(1). However, Valley West does not attack the propriety of the issuance of a preliminary injunction directly; instead, it challenges the District Court's denial of its motion to dismiss for failure to join an indispensable party and argues that the District Court's order fails for lack of specificity in describing the acts of Valley West to be restrained. . . .

[The opinion quotes Rule 19.]

Because Helzberg was seeking and the District Court ordered injunctive relief which may prevent Lord's from operating its jewelry store in the Valley West Mall in the manner in which Lord's originally intended, the District Court correctly concluded that Lord's was a party to be joined if feasible. See Rule 19(a)(2)(i), Fed. R. Civ. P. Therefore, because Lord's was not and is not subject to personal jurisdiction in the Western District of Missouri, the District Court was required to determine whether or not Lord's should be regarded as indispensable. After considering the factors which Rule 19(b) mandates be considered, the District Court concluded that Lord's was not to be regarded as indispensable. We agree. . . .

Rule 19(b) requires the court to look first to the extent to which a judgment rendered in Lord's absence might be prejudicial to Lord's or to Valley West. Valley West argues that the District Court's order granting preliminary injunctive relief does prejudice Lord's and may prejudice Valley West. We do not agree.

It seems axiomatic that none of Lord's rights or obligations will be ultimately determined in a suit to which it is not a party. Even if, as a result of the District Court's granting of the preliminary injunction, Valley West should attempt to terminate Lord's leasehold interest in space 261 in the Valley West Mall, Lord's will retain all of its rights under its Lease Agreement with Valley West. None of its rights or obligations will have been adjudicated as a result of the present proceedings, proceedings to which it is not a party. Therefore, we conclude that Lord's will not be prejudiced in a way contemplated by Rule 19(b) as a result of this action.

Likewise, we think that Lord's absence will not prejudice Valley West in a way contemplated by Rule 19(b). Valley West contends that it may be subjected to inconsistent obligations as a result of a determination in this action and a determination in another forum that Valley West should proceed in a fashion contrary to what has been ordered in these proceedings.

It is true that the obligations of Valley West to Helzberg, as determined in these proceedings, may be inconsistent with Valley West's obligations to Lord's. However, we are of the opinion that any inconsistency in those obligations will result from Valley West's voluntary execution of two Lease Agreements which impose inconsistent obligations rather than from Lord's absence from the present proceedings.

Helzberg seeks only to restrain Valley West's breach of the Lease Agreement to which Helzberg and Valley West were the sole parties. Certainly, all of the rights and obligations arising under a lease can be adjudicated where all of the parties to the lease are before the court. Thus, in the context of these proceedings the District Court can determine all of the rights and obligations of both Helzberg and Valley West based upon the Lease Agreement between them, even though Lord's is not a party to the proceedings.

Valley West's contention that it may be subjected to inconsistent judgments if Lord's should choose to file suit elsewhere and be awarded judgment is speculative at best. In the first place, Lord's has not filed such a suit. Secondly, there is no showing that another court is likely to interpret the language of the two Lease Agreements differently from the way in which the District Court would. Therefore, we also conclude that Valley West will suffer no prejudice as a result of the District Court's proceeding in Lord's absence. Any prejudice which Valley West may suffer by way of inconsistent judgments would be the result of Valley West's execution of Lease Agreements which impose inconsistent obligations and not the result of the proceedings in the District Court.

Rule 19(b) also requires the court to consider ways in which prejudice to the absent party can be lessened or avoided. The District Court afforded Lord's an opportunity to intervene in order to protect any interest it might have in the outcome of this litigation. Lord's chose not to do so. In light of Lord's decision not to intervene we conclude that the District Court acted in such a way as to sufficiently protect Lord's interests.

Similarly, we also conclude that the District Court's determinations that a judgment rendered in Lord's absence would be adequate and that there is no controlling significance to the fact that Helzberg would have an adequate remedy in the Iowa courts were not erroneous. It follows that the District Court's conclusion that in equity and good conscience the action should be allowed to proceed was a correct one.

In sum, it is generally recognized that a person does not become indispensable to an action to determine rights under a contract simply because that person's rights or obligations under an entirely separate contract will be affected by the result of the action. This principle applies to an action against a lessor who has entered into other leases which also may be affected by the result in the action in which the other lessees are argued to be indispensable parties. We conclude that the District Court properly denied the motion to dismiss for failure to join an indispensable party. . . .

In view of the foregoing, it follows that the judgment of the District Court is affirmed.

NOTES AND PROBLEMS

1. What is the fight about in *Helzberg's*?

a. Assume the suit proceeds without Lord's, and the court enters a permanent injunction forbidding Valley West to rent to Lord's. When Valley West proceeds to evict Lord's, Lord's sues, alleging that the eviction will be a breach of its lease with Valley West. Valley West points to the injunction, arguing that the court's construction of the lease is binding. What is Lord's response to that contention?

b. Suppose that in Lord's suit against Valley West the court construes the lease differently from the first court and holds that Lord's is entitled to conduct its business in the mall. At this point Valley West is under two conflicting court orders: one requiring that it evict Lord's, the other that it honor its lease with Lord's. Both decrees are valid; what should Valley West do?

c. The opinion in *Helzberg's* seems to concede implicitly that the scenario just sketched is possible. What is its response to the dilemma in which Valley West may find itself?

d. What would have been the alternative to proceeding with the suit in federal district court in Missouri?

e. In light of this alternative, articulate an argument that the court improperly applied Rule 19 and therefore came to the wrong result.

2. With *Helzberg's* contrast Clinton v. Babbitt, 180 F.3d 1081 (9th Cir., 1999), involving what the court described "as claims to exclusive use [of land] . . . between the Hopi Tribe and the Navajo Nation, producing what became known as 'the greatest title problem in the West.'"

a. Members of the Navajo Tribe living on lands that a settlement had awarded to the Hopi Nation sued the Secretary of the Interior, alleging unconstitutional discrimination in the terms of the leases given them as part of the settlement. The Secretary argued that the Hopi Nation, which stood to lose large sums of money if the settlement fell apart, was a necessary party. But, the argument continued, the Hopi Nation could not be joined because of sovereign immunity — and the suit must therefore be dismissed. The Ninth Circuit agreed:

> The plaintiffs seek, at a minimum, a declaration that Secretary Babbitt cannot constitutionally approve any individual leases between HPL Navajos and the Hopi Tribe that use the standard terms of the [settlement]. Such a declaration would prohibit the Tribe from fulfilling its obligations under the Settlement Agreement to enter into such leases and would deprive the Tribe of substantial compensation from the United States (over $25 million and the creation of additional trust lands),

which is conditioned on Secretary Babbitt's approval of certain numbers of such
leases. The Hopi Tribe, therefore, has a legally protected interest relating to the
subject of the action as defined by Rule 19(a)(2). . . .

. . . Although no alternative forum exists for the plaintiffs to seek relief, we
conclude that the Hopi Tribe's interest in maintaining its sovereign immunity
outweighs the interest of the plaintiffs in litigating their claim. See *Quileute*, 18
F.3d at 1460-61 ("'[A p]laintiff's interest in litigating a claim may be outweighed by
a tribe's interest in maintaining its sovereign immunity [because] society has
consciously opted to shield Indian tribes from suit without congressional or tribal
consent.'" (citations omitted)). . . .

Clinton at 1089-1090.

b. *Helzberg's* differs from *Clinton* in an important way: The former case
rejected arguments that an outside party should be joined, while the latter held
that it should be joined. A further contrast is that in *Helzberg's* the court, having
rejected arguments for compulsory joinder, proceeded to judgment with the existing parties; in *Clinton* the court, having held that the outsider should be joined
but could not be, dismissed the entire case, leaving the plaintiff with no forum for
his claim. Notice the striking result of the necessary-parties doctrine in such
conditions: Because the court cannot do perfect justice, it decides it will do
nothing at all. Before it takes such an action, should a court be sure that it is not
doing a worse injustice to the existing parties by dismissing than it would do to
the unjoined party by proceeding in its absence? Consider a footnote in *Clinton*:

Whether the allegations of the plaintiffs' equal protection claim are sufficient to
state a claim upon which relief may be granted is a question we need not reach in
this appeal. We note, however, the apparent lack of substance to the claim. First,
the plaintiffs admit they are in the unique position of being offered free leases to
remain on land to which they have no right, and fail to allege that they are being
treated less favorably than any similarly situated individuals. Second, even if the
plaintiffs make the threshold showing of disparate treatment they fail to show that
this treatment is not rationally related to legitimate legislative goals, such as the
peaceful settlement of the Navajo-Hopi land dispute:

> [The 1996 Settlement Act] will implement a settlement [which is] a consensual reso-
> lution of an age old problem. It creates a way for Navajo families now residing on Hopi
> land to lawfully remain at the home sites where their families have lived for many
> generations. At the same time, it preserves the Hopi Tribe's right to exercise jurisdic-
> tion over its land. It is based on principles of self-determination for the Tribes and
> human dignity for all tribal members. With this settlement, both tribes now will be
> able to devote their efforts and resources to important educational, health, and
> economic developments for the Navajo and Hopi people.

Navajo-Hopi Land Dispute Settlement Act of 1996: Signing Statement of President
William J. Clinton.

Clinton at 1087, n.4. Does this footnote constitute an effort to assure readers that
the court has not lost sight of what Rule 19(b) calls "equity and good conscience"?

3. In *Helzberg's* the asserted jurisdictional obstacle to joinder was personal
jurisdiction. In *Clinton* the obstacle was the sovereign immunity of an Indian
tribe. Because claims of sovereign immunity will be rare, and the reach of

modern long-arm jurisdiction is long, the more common objection is want of subject matter jurisdiction.

a. Take, for example, a variation on the facts of *Helzberg*'s. Suppose that Helzberg's and Lords were both Missouri corporations. Under those circumstances Helzberg's could invoke diversity jurisdiction in its suit against Valley West (an Iowa corporation); joining Lord's as a defendant would, however, destroy diversity.

b. Should the federal courts extend supplemental jurisdiction to cover this situation?

c. In cases relying entirely on diversity jurisdiction, 28 U.S.C. §1367(b) explicitly excludes from supplemental jurisdiction "claims by plaintiff against persons made parties under Rule 14, 19, 20, or 24 . . . or over claims by persons proposed to be joined as plaintiffs under Rule 19 . . . or seeking to intervene as plaintiffs under Rule 24." What is the theory underlying denial of supplemental jurisdiction where there is no independent basis for diversity jurisdiction? Sometimes it is said that if the courts permitted ancillary jurisdiction in this situation, it would open the door to collusive manipulation of jurisdiction: *A*, wishing to sue *B* and *C* but lacking complete diversity, would sue just *B*, hoping that she would plead *C*'s absence and insist on joinder under Rule 19; if ancillary jurisdiction extended to cover this situation, *A* could achieve an otherwise impermissible lawsuit.

d. Another section of the same statute (28 U.S.C. §1367(a)), however, suggests that supplemental jurisdiction will extend to such parties if the plaintiff is not asserting claims against them or if there is a ground for federal jurisdiction other than diversity. Is there a theory underlying such a discrepancy between the treatment of plaintiffs invoking diversity jurisdiction and others?

4. Should federal courts be more willing under Rule 19(b) to dismiss cases in which the reason for nonjoinder is a problem with subject matter jurisdiction than when the difficulty is personal jurisdiction? The argument for such a result would be that there will always be a state court where subject matter jurisdiction is not a problem, but (because the state and federal courts have substantially identical reaches under personal jurisdiction) there may not be a state court that can resolve the lawsuit.

5. Arguments for compulsory joinder are most common in the following situations:

a. Cases involving an obligation on which two or more persons are, originally or by assignment, either joint obligees or joint obligors, but not all joint obligees or joint obligors are joined as parties.

b. Cases involving ownership of, or interests in, real or personal property in which some persons claiming an interest (for example, joint owners, lessees, mortgagees, mortgagors, lienors, and holders of equity of redemption) are not included as parties.

c. Cases involving representative parties in which either the representative or some of the parties being represented are not included.

d. Cases involving claims to a limited fund or pool of assets, such that potential claimants who are not parties will find the funds depleted when their cases are heard.

6. Practice your analysis of compulsory joinder with the following problems.

a. Wyoming Rancher sells interests in her herd to several parties. She also borrows from a bank, using the herd as collateral. When she can't pay the loan, the bank seeks to replevy the cattle. Rancher argues that the joinder of all those claiming an interest in the herd is required, and that, because the presence of some of them would defeat diversity, the lawsuit must be dismissed. Analyze the strength of defendant's argument, bearing in mind that a replevin action determines who has the right to possession of a chattel (the word is derived from the same root as cattle), but does not settle the question of title.

b. Larry is the income beneficiary of a spendthrift trust, and his children have the remainder interest. The trustee has a power to appoint the trust to Larry at any time. Larry, a California resident, sues the trustee, an Illinois resident, seeking a declaration that the trustee abused his power by not appointing the trust to him. Any problems?

c. Prior to 2000, Husband was married to W1 and procured insurance from Insco payable to "my wife." In 2000, Husband procures a Mexican divorce and marries W2. After Husband's death in 2004, W1 brings an action against Insco claiming: a) Husband and she were never properly divorced; and b) even if she and Husband were divorced, his intention was to have the policy payable to her. Insco moves to dismiss for failure to join W2. What result?

C.   Intervention

The joinder devices thus far explored have a common characteristic: They serve to bring into a lawsuit a party who does not want to be there. We turn now to a doctrine with the opposite function: to permit an unjoined party to elbow her way into a suit where no one wants her. Like the doctrines of compulsory joinder, the principles of intervention flow from a recognition that lawsuits may have effects on persons not joined. The effects will not be those of formal preclusion — due process forbids binding one who was not a party — but judgments have broader ripple effects than the formal binding effect of the decree.

To take a common example, suppose that Developer and Zoning Board are engaged in litigation over whether Developer can build an office building on a plot of land bordering a residential area. If Developer wins the suit, Homeowner, whose property lies next to the plot in question, will be affected. If Developer loses the suit, Landowner, who owns another adjacent plot of land that would be more valuable if it can be commercially developed, will be adversely affected. The resulting judgment will not formally bind either Homeowner or Landowner, but it will affect them. Both might wish to influence the outcome of the suit. If they were entitled to intervene, they would thereby become parties to the suit, with the right to present evidence and arguments in the same way as Developer and Zoning Board.

Notice that Developer and Zoning Board (and perhaps the judge as well) may be notably unenthusiastic about intervention. From the standpoint of the existing parties, it complicates and perhaps weakens their litigating strategy. Even an intervenor who seeks the same outcome as one of the parties will have a different perspective and perhaps a different strategy. Moreover, additional parties may make settlement more difficult. Conceptually, intervention means further erosion of the principle of party autonomy, and, carried to a logical extreme, turns every lawsuit into a town meeting at which anyone even distantly "interested" in the topic of litigation becomes a party. The principles of intervention seek to allow some — but not all — who might wish to be involved in a lawsuit to join it. Read Rule 24.

Note the structure of the Rule. It is subdivided into two major categories: intervention of right (Rule 24(a)) and permissive intervention (Rule 24(b)). Intervention of right is designed to give to those with strong interests in the litigation the power to insist on joinder. The terms of Rule 24(a)(2) echo those of Rule 19(a)(2) — "an interest relating to" the pending litigation and a situation in which "disposition of the action may as a practical matter" harm the would-be intervenor. Permissive intervention is the weaker counterpart, as it is designed to capture those with weaker bases for insisting on joinder. As the terms imply, an applicant who meets the criteria of Rule 24(a) must be allowed to join the lawsuit. An applicant who meets only the criteria of Rule 24(b) may be allowed to join, with the judge's decision reviewed only for abuse of discretion.

Most of the reported cases focus on Rule 24(a), the general criteria for intervention as of right. That section contains four requirements. The intervention must be timely — the intervenor may not lie in wait until the litigation is on the brink of resolution. The intervenor must have an "interest" in the property or transaction that is the subject of the suit, and that interest must be in some strong way at risk. Finally, even an applicant meeting all these criteria will be denied intervention if those already in the lawsuit are adequately representing the interest. The next case assumes that intervention is timely and analyzes the other three criteria.

Natural Resources Defense Council v. United States Nuclear Regulatory Commission

578 F.2d 1341 (10th Cir. 1978)

DOYLE, J.

The American Mining Congress and Kerr-McGee Nuclear Corporation seek review of the order of the United States District Court for the District of New Mexico denying their motions to intervene [as] a matter of right or on a permissive basis, pursuant to Rule 24(a)(2) and (b), Fed. R. Civil Proc.

The underlying action in which the movants requested intervention was instituted by the Natural Resources Defense Council, Inc., and others. In the action, declaratory and injunctive relief is directed to the United States Nuclear Regulatory Commission (NRC) and the New Mexico Environmental Improvement Agency (NMEIA), prohibiting those agencies from issuing licenses for the operation of uranium mills in New Mexico without first preparing environmental impact statements. Kerr-McGee and United Nuclear are potential recipients of the licenses.

Congress, in the Atomic Energy Act of 1954, has authorized the NRC to issue such licenses. NMEIA is involved because under §274(b) of the Act, the NRC is authorized to enter into agreements with the states allowing the states to issue licenses. Such agreements have been made with about 25 states including New Mexico. Thus, the action below in effect seeks to prevent the use of §274(b) of the Act so as to avoid the requirement of an impact statement for which provision is made in the National Environmental Policy Act. . . .

The relief sought by the plaintiffs' complaint is, first, that NRC's involvement in the licensing procedure in New Mexico is, notwithstanding the delegation to the state, sufficient to constitute major federal action, whereby the impact statement requirement is not eliminated. Second, that if an impact statement is not required in connection with the granting of licenses, the New Mexico program is in conflict with §274(d)(2) of the Atomic Energy Act of 1954.

The motion of United Nuclear Corporation to intervene is not opposed by the parties and was granted. On May 3, 1977, the date that the complaint herein was filed, NMEIA granted a license to United Nuclear to operate a uranium mill at Church Rock, New Mexico. The complaint seeks to enjoin the issuance of the license thus granted.

It was after that that Kerr-McGee Nuclear Corporation, Anaconda Company, Gulf Oil Corporation, Phillips Petroleum Company, and the American Mining Congress filed motions to intervene. These motions, insofar as they sought intervention as of right, were denied on the ground that the interests of the parties or movants would be adequately represented by United Nuclear. Permissive intervention was also denied. Kerr-McGee and the American Mining Congress both appeal denial of both intervention as of right and permissive intervention.

Our issue is a limited one. We merely construe and weigh Rule 24(a) of the Fed. R. Civ. P. (intervention as of right) and decide in light of the facts and considerations presented whether the denial of intervention was correct. [The court quoted Rule 24(a).]

We do not have a subsection (1) situation involving a statutory conferring of right to intervene. Accordingly, we must consider the standards set forth in subsection (2), which are:

1. Whether the applicant claims an interest relating to the property or transaction which is the subject of the action.

2. Whether the claimants are so situated that the disposition of the action may as a practical matter impair or impede their ability to protect that interest.

3. Whether their interest is not adequately represented by existing parties.

[The district court decided that, even if the first two tests were satisfied,] the interests of the movants were adequately protected by United Nuclear [and therefore denied the motion to intervene.] Our conclusion is that the interests of movants in the subject matter is sufficient to satisfy the requirements of Rule 24 and that the threat of loss of their interest and inability to participate is of such magnitude as to impair their ability to advance their interest.

I

. . . Strictly to require that the movant in intervention have a direct interest in the outcome of the lawsuit strikes us as being too narrow a construction of Rule 24(a)(2). . . .

In our case the matter of immediate interest is, of course, the issuance and delivery of the license sought by United Nuclear. However, the consequence of the litigation could well be the imposition of the requirement that an environmental impact statement be prepared before granting any uranium mill license in New Mexico, or, secondly, it could result in an injunction terminating or suspending the agreement between NRC and NMEIA. Either consequence would be felt by United Nuclear and to some degree, of course, by Kerr-McGee, which is said to be one of the largest holders of uranium properties in New Mexico. It operates a uranium mill in Grants, New Mexico, pursuant to an NMEIA license, which application for renewal is pending. A decision in favor of the plaintiffs, which is not unlikely, could have a profound effect upon Kerr-McGee. Hence, it does have an interest within the meaning of Rule 24(a)(2). This interest of Kerr-McGee is in sharp contrast to the minimal interest which was present in *Allard*, wherein it was an interest of environmental groups in the protection of living birds. This was considered insufficient to justify intervention in a case involving feathers which are part of Indian artifacts. Their interest was said to be limited to a general interest in the public. The interest asserted on behalf of Kerr-McGee and the American Mining Congress is one which is a genuine threat to Kerr-McGee and the members of the American Mining Congress to a substantial degree.

We do not suggest that Kerr-McGee could expect better treatment from state authorities than federal. We do recognize that a change in procedure would produce impairing complications.

II

The next question is whether, assuming the existence of an interest, the chance of impairment is sufficient to fulfill the requirement of Rule 24(a)(2).

. . . If the relief sought by the plaintiffs is granted, there can be little question but that the interests of the American Mining Congress and of Kerr-McGee would be affected. Plaintiffs contend, however, that appellants would not be bound by such a result if they are not participants. Kerr-McGee points out that even though it may not be res judicata, still it would have a stare decisis effect. Moreover, with NRC and NMEIA as parties, the result might be more profound than stare decisis.

It should be pointed out that the Rule refers to impairment "as a practical matter." Thus, the court is not limited to consequences of a strictly legal nature. The court may consider any significant legal effect in the applicant's interest and it is not restricted to a rigid res judicata test. Hence, the stare decisis effect might be sufficient to satisfy the requirement. It is said that where, as here, the case is of first impression, the stare decisis effect would be important.

Finally, the considerations for requiring an environmental impact statement will be relatively the same in respect to the issuance of a uranium mining license in every instance. Hence, to say that it can be repeatedly litigated is not an answer, for the chance of getting a contrary result in a case which is substantially similar on its facts to one previously adjudicated seems remote.

We are of the opinion, therefore, that appellants have satisfied the impairment criterion.

III

The final question is whether the trial court was correct in its conclusion that United Nuclear would adequately represent Kerr-McGee and the American Mining Congress.

The finding and conclusion was that the representation would be adequate because United Nuclear, a fellow member of the industry, has interests which were the same as those of the appellants and possessed the same level of knowledge and experience with the ability and willingness to pursue the matter and could adequately represent Kerr-McGee and the members of the American Mining Congress. . . .

United Nuclear is situated somewhat differently in this case than are the other members of the industry since it has been granted its license. From this it is urged by Kerr-McGee that United Nuclear may be ready to compromise the case by obtaining a mere declaration that while environmental impact statements should be issued, this requirement need be prospective only, whereby it would not affect them. While we see this as a remote possibility, we gravely doubt that United Nuclear would opt for such a result. It is true, however, that United Nuclear has a defense of laches that is not available to Kerr-McGee or the others.

7A C. Wright & A. Miller, Federal Practice & Procedure, §1909, at 524 (1972), says:

> [I]f [an applicant's] interest is similar to, but not identical with, that of one of the parties, a discriminating judgment is required on the circumstances of the particular case, but he ordinarily should be allowed to intervene unless it is clear that the party will provide adequate representation for the absentee.

While the interest of the two applicants may appear similar, there is no way to say that there is no possibility that they will not be different and the possibility of divergence of interest need not be great in order to satisfy the burden of the applicants under *National Farm Lines*.

There are other reasons for allowing intervention. There is some value in having the parties before the court so that they will be bound by the result. American Mining Congress represents a number of companies having a wide variety of interests. This can, therefore, provide a useful supplement to the defense of the case. The same can be said of Kerr-McGee.

The trial court was concerned that the addition of these movants would make the litigation unwieldy. If the intervenors are limited to this group, unwieldiness does not become a problem which the trial court cannot control. It does not appear that there would be a need for additional parties in view of the presence of the American Mining Congress. While we do not express an opinion on the possibilities of further additions, we wish to make clear that the present holdings that the two applicants should be allowed to intervene does not say that others should be added . . .

The order of the district court is reversed and the cause is remanded with instructions to the trial court to grant the appellants, Kerr-McGee's and American Mining Congress', motions to intervene.

NOTES AND PROBLEMS

1. Focus on each of the intervenors separately.

a. United Nuclear's motion to intervene was granted without objection. Why? Analyze United Nuclear's position and explain why it met the categories of Rule 24.

b. Kerr-McGee sought to intervene as of right; the trial court denied the motion. Why? How does the court of appeals deal with the trial court's reason for denying Kerr-McGee's motion?

c. How was the position of the American Mining Congress different from that of any of the other intervenors? Was its case for intervention stronger or weaker than that of Kerr-McGee?

d. Construct an argument that the correct result on these facts was to grant intervention to United Nuclear and the American Mining Congress, but to deny Kerr-McGee's motion.

e. The court holds that all of the would-be intervenors met the criteria of Rule 24(a). Suppose it had come to a different decision. It would then have had to review the decision of the trial court to deny the intervenors permissive intervention under Rule 24(b). Explain why it is likely that the appellate court would have affirmed the trial court's denial of permissive intervention.

2. In Trbovich v. United Mine Workers, 404 U.S. 528 (1972), a union member sought to intervene in an action by the Secretary of Labor to set aside a union election. The Court held that the union member could not intervene to allege additional grounds to set aside the election or to propose safeguards for a future election but could intervene "to present evidence and argument in support of the Secretary's [challenge to the election.]" Id. at 537. In answer to the contention that the Secretary's representation was adequate, the Court stated that "[t]he requirement of the Rule [relating to adequacy of representation] is satisfied if the applicant shows that representation of his interest" may be "inadequate; and the burden of making that showing should be treated as minimal." Id. at 538 n.10. The Court then found this "minimal" burden was satisfied, as the Secretary represented the interests of both the union members and the public; thus, the union member might intervene to assure protection of the union member's interest alone. Does this approach present a difficulty? Is it consistent with *Natural Resources Defense Council*?

3. Rule 24 applies not only to competing claimants to property but, as *Natural Resources Defense Council* indicates, goes far beyond such a situation. How far?

a. Assume *A* and *B* were both injured in a fireworks display held at Memorial Stadium. *A* sues Memorial Stadium and alleges that the stadium was negligent in handling the fireworks, and, in the alternative, that the fireworks display was an extrahazardous activity for which the stadium has absolute liability. *B* seeks to intervene, claiming liability on similar grounds.

b. Plaintiff sues Auto Manufacturer claiming that a defective design led to her injury. Substantial discovery occurs, followed by a settlement agreement that includes a provision requiring that the materials uncovered by plaintiff in discovery remain confidential. Sixteen persons, each claiming injuries in unrelated accidents involving the same design feature, seek to intervene to challenge the protective order that is part of the settlement. See Jochims v. Isuzu Motors, Ltd., 148 F.R.D. 624 (S.D. Iowa 1993) (permissive intervention granted for purpose of challenging motion for protective order).

4. As already noted, intervention under Rule 24 and the compulsory joinder of parties under Rule 19 deal with related problems.

a. The texts of the two Rules closely resemble each other; more fundamentally, the two rules address similar issues, Rule 19 from the viewpoint of those already in the lawsuit, Rule 24 from that of those outside it. How should a court address the problem that arises when someone who might have been joined — but was not — and might have intervened — but did not — now complains of harm suffered from the judgment entered without her participation?

b. Occasionally courts have hinted that knowledge of a pending action in which one could intervene would suffice to make the judgment binding on such a person, even though she had not in fact intervened. Helzberg's Diamond Shops, supra page 766, has language so suggesting. In Provident Tradesmens Bank & Trust, 390 U.S. 101, 114 (1968), the court remarked:

> [I]t might be argued that [a certain nonparty] should be bound by the previous decision because, although technically a nonparty, he had purposely bypassed an adequate opportunity to intervene. We do not now decide whether such an argument would be correct. . . .

Parklane Hosiery v. Shore, supra page 695, contained a similar hint, involving not intervention but the failure to join a prior action. Explaining why it was prepared to allow nonmutual issue preclusion, the *Parklane* Court noted:

> The application of offensive collateral estoppel will not here reward a private plaintiff who could have joined in the previous action, since the respondent probably could not have joined in the injunctive action brought by the SEC even had he so desired.

439 U.S. at 331.

In spite of these hints, neither *Provident Tradesmens* nor *Parklane* decided squarely whether one could bind parties who had knowledge of a suit in which their interests were at stake in a lawsuit but who failed to intervene. When the Supreme Court faced that question squarely, it did not go in the direction suggested by its previous hints. The dispute involved a challenge by racial minorities to the hiring practices of Birmingham, Alabama, a city that had in the preceding generation been at the center of a struggle against racial segregation, a struggle in which the fire and police departments had been deployed on the side of segregation.

Martin v. Wilks

490 U.S. 755 (1989)

Chief Justice REHNQUIST delivered the opinion of the court. . . .

The litigation [that gave rise to the present lawsuit] began in 1974, when the Ensley Branch of the NAACP and seven black individuals filed separate class-action complaints against the City [of Birmingham] and the Board [that made hiring decisions for public employees]. They alleged that both had engaged in racially discriminatory hiring and promotion practices in various public service jobs in violation of Title VII of the Civil Rights Act of 1964, 42 U.S.C. §2000e et seq., and other federal law. After a bench trial on some issues, but before judgment, the parties entered into two consent decrees, one between the black individuals and the City and the other between them and the Board. These proposed decrees set forth an extensive remedial scheme, including long-term and interim annual goals for the hiring of blacks as firefighters. The decrees also provided for goals for promotion of blacks within the department. The District Court entered an order provisionally approving the decrees and directing publication of notice of the upcoming fairness hearings. Notice of the hearings, with a reference to the general nature of the decrees, was published in two local newspapers. At that hearing, the Birmingham Firefighters Association (BFA) appeared and filed objections as amicus curiae. After the hearing, but before final approval of the decrees, the BFA and two of its members also moved to intervene on the ground that the decrees would adversely affect their rights. The District Court denied the motions as untimely and approved the decrees. Seven white firefighters, all members of the BFA, then filed a complaint against the City and the Board seeking injunctive relief against enforcement of the decrees. The seven argued that the decrees would operate to illegally discriminate against them; the District Court denied relief. . . .

A new group of white firefighters, the *Wilks* respondents, then brought suit against the City and the Board in District Court. They too alleged that, because of their race, they were being denied promotions in favor of less qualified blacks in violation of federal law. The Board and the City admitted to making race conscious employment decisions, but argued the decisions were unassailable because they were made pursuant to the consent decrees. A group of black individuals, the *Martin* petitioners, were allowed to intervene in their individual capacities to defend the decrees.

The defendants moved to dismiss the reverse discrimination cases as impermissible collateral attacks on the consent decrees. . . . After trial the District Court granted the motion to dismiss. . . .

On appeal, the Eleventh Circuit reversed. It held that "[b]ecause . . . [the *Wilks* respondents] were neither parties nor privies to the consent decrees, . . . their independent claims of unlawful discrimination are not precluded." . . .

Can't be bound when not a party

We granted certiorari and now affirm the Eleventh Circuit's judgment. All agree that "[i]t is a principle of general application in Anglo-American jurisprudence that one is not bound by a judgment in personam in a litigation in which he is not designated as a party or to which he has not been made a party by service of process." Hansberry v. Lee, 311 U.S. 32, 40 (1940) [see infra page 807]. This rule is part of our "deep-rooted historic tradition that everyone should have his own day in court." 18 C. Wright, A. Miller, & E. Cooper, Federal Practice and Procedure §4449, p. 417 (1981) (18 Wright). A judgment or decree among parties to a lawsuit resolves issues as among them, but it does not conclude the rights of strangers to those proceedings.[2]

Petitioners argue that, because respondents failed to timely intervene in the initial proceedings, their current challenge to actions taken under the consent decree constitutes an impermissible "collateral attack." They argue that respondents were aware that the underlying suit might affect them and if they chose to pass up an opportunity to intervene, they should not be permitted to later litigate the issues in a new action. The position has sufficient appeal to have commanded the approval of the great majority of the Federal Courts of Appeals, but we agree with the contrary view expressed by the Court of Appeals for the Eleventh Circuit in this case.

We begin with the words of Justice Brandeis in Chase National Bank v. Norwalk, 291 U.S. 431 (1934):

> The law does not impose upon any person absolutely entitled to a hearing the burden of voluntary intervention in a suit to which he is a stranger. . . . Unless duly summoned to appear in a legal proceeding, a person not a privy may rest assured that a judgment recovered therein will not affect his legal rights.

Id. at 441.

While these words were written before the adoption of the Federal Rules of Civil Procedure, we think the Rules incorporate the same principle; a party seeking a judgment binding on another cannot obligate that person to intervene; he must be joined. . . . Against the background of permissive intervention set forth in *Chase National Bank*, the drafters cast Rule 24, governing intervention, in permissive terms. See Fed. Rule Civ. Proc. 24(a) (intervention as of right) ("[u]pon timely application anyone shall be permitted to intervene"); Fed. Rule Civ. Proc. 24(b) (permissive intervention) ("[u]pon timely application anyone may be permitted to intervene"). They determined that the concern for finality

Rule 24 drafted in permissive terms

---

2. We have recognized an exception to the general rule when, in certain limited circumstances, a person, although not a party, has his interests adequately represented by someone with the same interests who is a party. See Hansberry v. Lee, 311 U.S. 32, 41-42 (1940) ("class" or "representative" suits); Fed. Rule Civ. Proc. 23 (same); Montana v. United States, 440 U.S. 147, 154-155 (1979) (control of litigation on behalf of one of the parties in the litigation). Additionally, where a special remedial scheme exists expressly foreclosing successive litigation by nonlitigants, as for example in bankruptcy or probate, legal proceedings may terminate pre-existing rights if the scheme is otherwise consistent with due process. See NLRB v. Bildisco & Bildisco, 465 U.S. 513, 529-530, n. 10 (1984) ("proof of claim must be presented to the Bankruptcy Court . . . or be lost"); Tulsa Professional Collection Services, Inc. v. Pope, 485 U.S. 478 (1988) (nonclaim statute terminating unsubmitted claims against the estate). Neither of these exceptions, however, applies in this case.

and completeness of judgments would be "better [served] by mandatory joinder procedures." 18 Wright §4452, p. 453. Accordingly, Rule 19(a) provides for mandatory joinder in circumstances where a judgment rendered in the absence of a person may "leave . . . persons already parties subject to a substantial risk of incurring . . . inconsistent obligations. . . ." Rule 19(b) sets forth the factors to be considered by a court in deciding whether to allow an action to proceed in the absence of an interested party.

[handwritten margin note: Must be joined to have suit enforc]

Joinder as a party, rather than knowledge of a lawsuit and an opportunity to intervene, is the method by which potential parties are subjected to the jurisdiction of the court and bound by a judgment or decree.[6] The parties to a lawsuit presumably know better than anyone else the nature and scope of relief sought in the action, and at whose expense such relief might be granted. It makes sense, therefore, to place on them a burden of bringing in additional parties where such a step is indicated, rather than placing on potential additional parties a duty to intervene when they acquire knowledge of the lawsuit. The linchpin of the "impermissible collateral attack" doctrine — the attribution of preclusive effect to a failure to intervene — is therefore quite inconsistent with Rule 19 and Rule 24. . . .

[handwritten margin note: Burden should be on those in suit to bring in any necessary party]

Petitioners . . . rely on our decision in *Provident Tradesmans Bank*, supra, as authority for the view which they espouse. In that case we discussed Rule 19 shortly after parts of it had been substantially revised, but we expressly left open the question of whether preclusive effect might be attributed to a failure to intervene.

Petitioners contend that a different result should be reached because the need to join affected parties will be burdensome and ultimately discouraging to civil rights litigation. Potential adverse claimants may be numerous and difficult to identify; if they are not joined, the possibility for inconsistent judgments exists. Judicial resources will be needlessly consumed in relitigation of the same question.

[handwritten margin note: π arg]

Even if we were wholly persuaded by these arguments as a matter of policy, acceptance of them would require a rewriting rather than an interpretation of the relevant Rules. But we are not persuaded that their acceptance would lead to a more satisfactory method of handling cases like this one. It must be remembered that the alternatives are a duty to intervene based on knowledge, on the one hand, and some form of joinder, as the Rules presently provide, on the other. No one can seriously contend that an employer might successfully defend against a Title VII claim by one group of employees on the ground that its actions were required by an earlier decree entered in a suit brought against it by another, if the later group did not have adequate notice or knowledge of the earlier suit.

[handwritten margin note: Good arg but not in compliance w/ rules]

The difficulties petitioners foresee in identifying those who could be adversely affected by a decree granting broad remedial relief are undoubtedly present, but

---

6. The dissent argues on the one hand that respondents have not been "bound" by the decree but rather, that they are only suffering practical adverse affects from the consent decree. On the other hand, the dissent characterizes respondents' suit not as an assertion of their own independent rights, but as a collateral attack on the consent decree which, it is said, can only proceed on very limited grounds. Respondents in their suit have alleged that they are being racially discriminated against by their employer in violation of Title VII: either the fact that the disputed employment decisions are being made pursuant to a consent decree is a defense to respondents' Title VII claims or it is not. If it is a defense to challenges to employment practices which would otherwise violate Title VII, it is very difficult to see why respondents are not being "bound" by the decree.

they arise from the nature of the relief sought and not because of any choice between mandatory intervention and joinder. Rule 19's provisions for joining interested parties are designed to accommodate the sort of complexities that may arise from a decree affecting numerous people in various ways. We doubt that a mandatory intervention rule would be any less awkward. As mentioned, plaintiffs who seek the aid of the courts to alter existing employment policies, or the employer who might be subject to conflicting decrees, are best able to bear the burden of designating those who would be adversely affected if plaintiffs prevail; these parties will generally have a better understanding of the scope of likely relief than employees who are not named but might be affected. Petitioners' alternative does not eliminate the need for, or difficulty of, identifying persons who, because of their interests, should be included in a lawsuit. It merely shifts that responsibility to less able shoulders.

Nor do we think that the system of joinder called for by the Rules is likely to produce more relitigation of issues than the converse rule. The breadth of a lawsuit and concomitant relief may be at least partially shaped in advance through Rule 19 to avoid needless clashes with future litigation. And even under a regime of mandatory intervention, parties who did have adequate knowledge of the suit would relitigate issues. Additional questions about the adequacy and timeliness of knowledge would inevitably crop up. We think that the system of joinder presently contemplated by the Rules best serves the many interests involved in the run of litigated cases, including cases like the present one. . . .

Justice STEVENS, with whom Justice BRENNAN, Justice MARSHALL, and Justice BLACKMUN join, dissenting.

As a matter of a law there is a vast difference between persons who are actual parties to litigation and persons who merely have the kind of interest that may as a practical matter be impaired by the outcome of a case. Persons in the first category have a right to participate in a trial and to appeal from an adverse judgment; depending on whether they win or lose, their legal rights may be enhanced or impaired. Persons in the latter category have a right to intervene in the action in a timely fashion, or they may be joined as parties against their will. But if they remain on the sidelines, they may be harmed as a practical matter even though their legal rights are unaffected. One of the disadvantages of sideline-sitting is that the bystander has no right to appeal from a judgment no matter how harmful it may be.

In this case the Court quite rightly concludes that the white firefighters who brought the second series of Title VII cases could not be deprived of their legal rights in the first series of cases because they had neither intervened nor been joined as parties. . . . There is no reason, however, why the consent decrees might not produce changes in conditions at the white firefighters' place of employment that, as a practical matter, may have a serious effect on their opportunities for employment or promotion even though they are not bound by the decrees in any legal sense. The fact that one of the effects of a decree is to curtail the job opportunities of nonparties does not mean that the nonparties have been deprived of legal rights or that they have standing to appeal from that decree without becoming parties. . . .

Regardless of whether the white firefighters were parties to the decrees granting relief to their black co-workers, it would be quite wrong to assume that they could never collaterally attack such a decree. If a litigant has standing, he or she can always collaterally attack a judgment for certain narrowly defined defects. See, e.g., Klapprott v. United States, 335 U.S. 601 (1949). See also Korematsu v. United States, 584 F. Supp. 1406 (N.D. Cal. 1984) (granting writ of coram nobis vacating conviction based on Government concealment of critical contradictory evidence in Korematsu v. United States, 323 U.S. 214 (1944)). On the other hand, a district court is not required to retry a case — or to sit in review of another courts' judgment — every time an interested nonparty asserts that *some* error that might have been raised on direct appeal was committed. Such a broad allowance of collateral review would destroy the integrity of litigated judgments, would lead to an abundance of vexatious litigation, and would subvert the interest in comity between courts. . . .

NOTES AND PROBLEMS

1. Consider both the sequence of litigative events and the identity of the parties involved. The basic lawsuit involved one "entity plaintiff" (the NAACP) and seven individual plaintiffs suing a pair of entity defendants (the City and the County Personnel Board, which was apparently responsible for staffing firehouse positions).

a. The plaintiffs and defendants engaged in considerable litigation — including a trial of some issues — before arriving at a settlement.

b. There were then three separate efforts to challenge the settlement, each by a slightly different set of individual and entity parties. What actions did these groups take, at what stages of the lawsuit, and by what procedural means?

2. Now put yourself in the position of the original parties. They have fought each other to exhaustion and have arrived at a settlement that they are prepared to live with. Now comes a group not previously involved in the litigation, who contend that the terms of the settlement disadvantage them in an unlawful way.

a. Explain why both original parties to the suit would be unhappy about this development.

b. Describe the argument — ultimately rejected by the Court — that the original parties used to explain why the white firefighters should be bound by the settlement agreement, even though they had not participated in the lawsuit or in the settlement negotiations. Though it was rejected by the majority, this argument got four votes. Why?

3. *Wilks* can be understood as a question of who has the responsibility to ensure that the requisite interests are represented in the lawsuit. One view, rejected by the majority, is that the absentees have the burden of invoking Rule 24 to intervene. On this view the penalty for failing to intervene is that one must subsequently suffer under any unfavorable result. The other view, adopted in *Wilks*, is that those in the suit share with the court the responsibility for joining the absentees. On this view the penalty for failing to locate and join all absentee interests is that one must face the prospect of subsequent litigation when the absentees do assert their interests. As a matter of either good judicial administration or due process, is the choice between the two paths clear?

4. The problem in *Wilks* can also be seen as one of respect for judgments as well as of joinder of parties. How one reacts to the first will affect one's response to the second. If one believes that parties should be encouraged or required to intervene in a pending action in which their interests may be affected, one will be tempted to enforce that belief by refusing to hear a later action. If, on the other hand, one believes strongly in party autonomy, one may be reluctant to require intervention in the original suit and accordingly to permit the later action.

5. *Wilks* shifts the "burden of joinder" to the parties in the original action. Consider a similar case arising after the decision in *Wilks*. A group of Hispanic employees sues its employer, alleging discrimination in employment. Both sides agree only that the claims will be difficult to prove. After some discovery, the parties begin to talk about settling. The terms of the tentative settlement may work some practical disadvantage on non-Hispanic employees.

a. Should the parties move to join the non-Hispanic employees on the ground that failure to do so will render any settlement open to challenge?

b. If one or both parties move to join another group, how should that be done? By moving to join them under Rule 19? What happens if the potential opposition is not organized? Can the court simply name one or several non-Hispanic employees and treat them as representing the rest?

c. If the non-Hispanic employees join the lawsuit, either voluntarily or as compulsorily joined parties, how much control do they have over the settlement? May they block the settlement simply by stating that it is disadvantageous to them and that they will not agree to it? Or, in order to prevent the settlement, must they demonstrate that, if adopted, it would result in unlawful discrimination against them?

d. Arriving at a settlement under these conditions will probably be more difficult than it would be with only the original parties. On the other hand, a settlement satisfactory to all the interests will probably be more durable. Do you suppose the Court considered such matters? Should it?

6. In the wake of *Wilks*, Congress enacted and the president signed legislation aimed at, among other things, reversing the holding of the case. 42 U.S.C. §2000e — 2(n). The statute prohibits a collateral challenge to a consent decree in a civil rights case complaining of employment discrimination if the challenger is "a person who, prior to the entry of [the consent decree] had — (i) actual notice . . . of the proposed judgment. . . ; and (ii) a reasonable opportunity to present objections to such judgment or order; or (iii) . . . a person whose interests were adequately represented" in the first action.

a. Explain why, on the facts of *Wilks*, this statute would lead to a result different from that decision.

b. The legislation applies only to employment discrimination consent decrees. It would not apply, for example, to an antitrust consent decree. Should Congress seek to dictate different procedural rules for particular substantive areas?

c. What is the source of law for the decision in *Wilks*? Is it an interpretation of Rule 19 or is it based on the Due Process Clause? If *Wilks* is based on the Due Process Clause, a statute purporting to overrule *Wilks* would be unconstitutional.

D.   Interpleader

In discussing necessary parties, we looked briefly at a case in which a husband made a life insurance policy payable to "my wife." The couple subsequently divorced. Husband remarried and later died. Suppose both wives claim the proceeds of the policy. If they bring separate suits on the policy, it is possible that, to the consternation of the insurance company, both will win. In the past, any possible resolution of the insurance company's dilemma had to overcome two difficulties: (a) the unavailability of an effective procedural device to join both claimants, and (b) jurisdictional and venue limitations in using available procedural devices. Interpleader provides a procedure by which a "stakeholder" — often a bank or insurer — can require the competing claimants to litigate their rights to the fund or property in question. Typically the stakeholder invokes interpleader, joining the claimants as parties. Such a proceeding will, however, fail to yield a stable resolution of the dispute if the forum lacks jurisdiction over the claimants.

As an illustration of the difficulties such limitations could pose, consider New York Life Insurance Co. v. Dunlevy, 241 U.S. 518 (1916). Father, in Pennsylvania, bought an insurance policy that paid a lump sum amount after a set number of years. The sum came due, but Father and Daughter disagreed about whether he or she was entitled to the sum. One of Daughter's creditors brought suit in Pennsylvania. The insurer, knowing of the dispute between Father and Daughter, interpleaded Father, Daughter, and Creditor. The Pennsylvania court ruled that Father was entitled to the proceeds. Daughter, dissatisfied by this result, sued the insurer in California. Insurer contended that the Pennsylvania suit precluded Daughter's claim. Wrong, held the U.S. Supreme Court — because Pennsylvania had not acquired personal jurisdiction over Daughter, who lived in California. The insurer was thus liable — a second time — for the policy proceeds.

Congress responded to the procedural uncertainties and the jurisdictional issues presented in cases like *Dunlevy* by enacting the Federal Interpleader Act, codified at 28 U.S.C. §§1335, 1397, and 2361. This legislation accomplishes several tasks:

a. The Interpleader Act broadens the circumstances in which interpleader is available, eliminating some restrictions that older equity doctrines had imposed. See §1335.

b. The Act removes limitations on federal subject matter jurisdiction. How does it do this? See §1335(a).

c. The Act permits nationwide service of process. See §2361. Thus, in *Dunlevy*, Daughter would be subject to the jurisdiction of the federal courts in Pennsylvania, which could thus resolve all the parties' conflicting claims.

d. The Act expands venue provisions to permit venue where any claimant resides. See §1397. The provisions of Rule 22 closely resemble those of the Interpleader Act. But it is subject to the normal rules for subject matter jurisdiction (diversity between all plaintiffs and all defendants); personal jurisdiction (jurisdiction within the state); and venue (all defendants, or where the claim arises). In practice, Rule 22 interpleader is used when the stakeholder is a citizen of one state and all claimants are citizens of a second state. In such a case, there is no jurisdiction under the Interpleader Act because no two claimants are of diverse citizenship. In such cases, however, the normal rules for jurisdiction and venue can be satisfied by an action in the state of all claimants.

The table below illlustrates some differences between statutory interpleader and Rule 22 interpleader.

Issue	Statutory	Rule 22
Subject Matter Jurisdiction		
— Diversity	Minimal diversity; determined as between claimants	Complete diversity; stakeholder on one side and claimants on the other
— Amount	$500 in controversy	$75,000+
Personal Jurisdiction; service of process	Nationwide service of process	Need personal jurisdiction; service under Rule 4
Venue	Residence of one or more claimants	Residence of any claimants (if all from one state); district where dispute arose; district where property is; district where any claimant found if no other basis for venue
Injunctions	Statutory authority for injunctions (28 U.S.C. §2361)	Only basis is provision in 28 U.S.C. §2283 for stay "where necessary in aid of . . . jurisdiction."

Would statutory or Rule interpleader best have suited the situation described in the next case? The setting of the case involved international politics as well as personal greed. Ferdinand Marcos was the president (and some claimed the corrupt dictator) of the Republic of the Philippines between 1972 and 1986. After Marcos's overthrow, allegations surfaced that he and his wife Imelda had converted government funds to their personal use and had used those funds to acquire everything from 3,000 pairs of shoes for Imelda to real estate and art objects in several nations. Some of those objects are the subject of the next case.

Cohen v. The Republic of the Philippines

146 F.R.D. 90 (S.D.N.Y. 1993)

CONNER, J.

This is an interpleader action initiated by Marc Cohen and Marc Cohen & Co. (collectively "Cohen") against Klaus Braemer (Braemer) and The Republic of the Philippines (the Philippines). The action is presently before the Court on the motion of Imelda R. Marcos (Marcos) for leave to intervene. The motion is granted subject to the conditions outlined below.

Background

At issue in this action is the ownership of four paintings whose total value is nearly $5,000,000.[1] In late 1991 or early 1992, Cohen received the paintings on consignment from Braemer, who was Marcos's agent entrusted to run her New York home in which the paintings had previously hung. Braemer demanded return of the paintings in March of 1992, but Cohen refused because he was uncertain who actually owned the paintings. Consequently, Cohen brought this interpleader action against Braemer and the Philippines.

Braemer claims that Marcos authorized him to sell the paintings, and he asserts a direct interest in the paintings originating from a $300,000 loan made to Marcos and a $500,000 loan which Braemer guaranteed for Marcos, both of which were collateralized by the paintings. The Philippines claims that the paintings were acquired with Philippine Government funds for the benefit of the Philippines, or that the paintings were acquired with funds which Marcos or her husband illegally obtained during Ferdinand Marcos's tenure as President of the Philippines. In either case, the Philippines claims to be the rightful owner of the paintings. Marcos now seeks to intervene in this action, claiming that the paintings were acquired with her personal funds and remain her property. She denies that a lien or security interest in the paintings was given to Braemer and, in the alternative, claims a right to the paintings after payment of the amount due Braemer. . . .

Discussion

Marcos's motion for leave to intervene in this action is granted with conditions because she has complied with the requirements of Rule 24(a), Fed. R. Civ. P. Rule 24(a)(2) allows anyone, upon timely application, to intervene in an action if [t]he applicant claims an interest relating to the property or transaction which is the subject of the action and the applicant is so situated that the disposition of the action may as a practical matter impair or impede the applicant's ability to protect that interest, unless the applicant's interest is adequately represented by existing parties.

Marcos's intervention motion is timely; Marcos has an interest in the paintings that are the subject of this interpleader action; Marcos's interest is likely to be prejudiced by the action; and the existing parties are unlikely to adequately protect Marcos's interest.

Timeliness

Timeliness is a flexible determination made in the discretion of the Court. Among the factors to be considered in determining whether a motion to intervene is timely are (1) how long the applicant knew of his interest before making the motion;

1. The paintings at issue are Georges Braque's "Guitar Valse," Henri Matisse's "Head of a Woman," Pierre Auguste Renoir's "Jeune Fille au Chien," and Pierre Auguste Renoir's "Jeunes Filles au bord de l'eau" (collectively "the paintings").

(2) prejudice to the existing parties from any such delay; (3) prejudice to applicant if the motion is denied; (4) other unusual circumstances. Marcos's decision to apply for intervention was made approximately five months after the initial complaint was filed. However, all parties knew of Marcos's potential intervention from the inception of the action, and the delay was caused by settlement discussions between Marcos and the Philippines in a California action which may have disposed of this matter as well. We believe Marcos's delay was not unreasonable given the complex and politically sensitive international implications of this action. The existing parties have not been unduly prejudiced by the delay because the addition of Marcos does not require altering a scheduled trial date on which they may have relied. However, as stated below, Marcos's interest is very likely to be prejudiced if her intervention is denied.

Interest

Marcos has an interest in the paintings in question. She has filed an affidavit with her motion which claims that the paintings were acquired with her personal funds and hung in her Olympic Tower residence in New York City. In addition, Marcos disputes Braemer's alleged lien on the paintings. The Philippines has submitted a default judgment of July 1987 which indicates that Marcos's Olympic Tower residence was held in a constructive trust for the Philippines. However, this judgment does not make any reference to the contents of the premises, nor do we wish to try the merits of Marcos's interest in determining this motion. Marcos has alleged and affirmed an interest in the paintings sufficient to support her motion to intervene.

Possible Prejudice and Lack of Adequate Representation

Marcos's interest may be impaired by the action and is not adequately protected by the existing parties. Marcos's alleged interest is contrary to the interest of both existing parties. Marcos claims an interest in the paintings superior to that of the Philippines, and she disputes Braemer's alleged security interest in the paintings. Thus, Braemer can not adequately protect Marcos's interest. Furthermore, the Philippines asserts that a joint tentative settlement of this action and the Sotheby's action has been reached and that Marcos's intervention will destroy this agreement. If Braemer were adequately protecting Marcos's interests in these negotiations, the addition of Marcos as a party would not disrupt the agreement. However, since the loan at issue in the Sotheby's action is under-collateralized while the loan at issue here is over-collateralized, we believe that this over-collateralization will be somehow divided among the existing parties to both actions pursuant to the joint settlement agreement. If Marcos has an interest in either the paintings or the over-collateralized portion thereof, this settlement will defeat that interest. We will not deprive Marcos of her day in court simply to allow the speedy but possibly unjust disposition of the two actions before us.[3]

---

3. The Philippines claims that Marcos's interest will not be adversely affected by this action because she is free to pursue her interests in other actions in the Philippines or elsewhere. However, a requirement that Marcos institute a separate action is too great a burden on her interest.

Conclusion

Marcos fulfills all the requirements of Rule 24(a)(2), and her motion to intervene is, therefore, granted subject to the following conditions:

(1) Marcos must make all necessary applications to the Philippine Government to allow her to travel to New York for a deposition in this matter at least 7 days before trial.

(2) If the Government of the Philippines grants her the right to travel, Marcos must appear for a deposition in New York at least 7 days before trial.

(3) If the Government of the Philippines denies Marcos the right to travel to New York for this deposition, Marcos must make herself available for a deposition in the Philippines at least 30 days before trial.

SO ORDERED.

NOTES AND PROBLEMS

1. Consider first the case as things stood before Marcos's intervention.

a. Cohen, the art dealer, had the paintings.

b. He also had two parties, Braemer and the Republic of the Philippines, asserting ownership to them.

c. Suppose Cohen sought your counsel at this stage. What risk would you point out to him?

d. How did Cohen's next procedural move seek to avoid that risk?

e. What is the obstacle — surmounted by the time we read the case — to the use of that procedure?

2. As things turned out, still another party — Marcos — also asserted that she owned the paintings and intervened to protect that interest. The court permitted her to do so. For our purposes the case becomes even more interesting had she not intervened.

a. Suppose the case went to judgment, awarding the paintings to Braemer. Marcos now sues Braemer, alleging that he stole them from her. Can he point to the judgment as proof that they belong to him? Why not?

b. What if Cohen sought to interplead Mrs. Marcos as well as Braemer and the Philippines? As a matter of pleading, she easily satisfies the criteria for a "claimant." But she is located in the Philippines. Nationwide service of process does not reach her. Is there jurisdiction based on her previous residence in New York City, where the paintings were hung?

c. If Cohen knew that the Philippines and Marcos, as well as Braemer, claimed the paintings as theirs, why didn't he try to interplead Marcos as well as the other two claimants?

d. Note that the Philippines objected to Marcos's intervention. From a purely analytic standpoint, it might have wished her presence in the suit, if only to establish ownership firmly. In real life, the Philippines might not have been too worried about a suit by Marcos. Where would such a suit have taken place?

3. Arthur had an insurance policy with Prudential Life Insurance Co. payable to Barbara. The policy terms did not permit him to change beneficiaries.

Sometime before his death, Arthur changed the beneficiary to Grace; and, because of a clerical error, the company did not realize that no changes were permitted. Arthur died, and both Barbara and Grace claimed the proceeds of the policy. In Trowbridge v. Prudential Insurance Co., 322 F. Supp. 190 (S.D.N.Y. 1971), the court held interpleader improper on the ground that Prudential's liability to Barbara was not inconsistent with its also being liable to Grace. This was because liability to Barbara was for failure to follow instructions, and liability to Grace was on the policy. Since both claimants were not claiming the same thing, and Prudential's liability to each was independent, the requirements for interpleader were not met.

4. Imagine that Chicago National Bank holds funds claimed by both Fred, a Kansas resident, and Greta, a Nebraska resident. In which federal courts can the bank file an interpleader action under the Interpleader Act? Under Rule 22? What is the outcome if Fred first sued Chicago National Bank in the U.S. District Court for the District of Kansas?

5. What is the relationship between Rule 19 and interpleader? For example, assume Haas (an Ohio citizen) claimed certain shares of common stock of Jefferson National Bank (for diversity purposes a Florida citizen), pursuant to an agreement with Glueck (an Ohio citizen) for joint purchase of the shares. Assume the shares were held by the bank at the time. Haas maintains that he performed his part of the bargain, the bank had knowledge of his interest, and Glueck requested transfer of the shares to Haas but the bank refused. Jefferson claims it refused because Glueck had owed the bank a debt for which the stock was collateral and that Glueck then withdrew the transfer request and pledged the stock to the bank. On closely related facts, the court in Haas v. Jefferson National Bank, 442 F.2d 394 (5th Cir. 1971), held Glueck an indispensable party based on the possibility that "Glueck, not being bound by res judicata, could theoretically succeed in later litigation against the Bank in asserting ownership of the whole." 442 F.2d at 398. If you had represented Haas, what argument might you have made in response to the court's belief that it had to dismiss the case because the bank risked double liability?

6. Finally, consider a situation that stretches the concept of interpleader to the breaking point. A bus collides with a pickup truck, injuring numerous passengers. The driver of the truck has a liability policy with a maximum of $20,000 in coverage, an amount that will be exhausted many times over if driver is found to be negligent.

a. Can the insurance company interplead all the actual and potential plaintiffs (the bus passengers)? Unlike the usual interpleader situation, there is here no danger that the insurer will be subject to multiple liability: It may have a duty to defend its insured in multiple suits and to minimize his liability, but the insurer's duty to indemnify is limited to the face value of the policy. The virtue of interpleader in this situation is that it assures that the plaintiffs will share proportionately in the policy proceeds rather than have the total amount go to the first plaintiff whose case comes to judgment.

b. Under these circumstances the U.S. Supreme Court said that interpleader would lie. The plaintiffs could not be required to litigate the question of liability in the interpleader action, but interpleader could be used to distribute the policy proceeds equitably. State Farm Fire & Casualty Co. v. Tashire, 386 U.S. 523 (1967).

c. *Tashire* is also notable for an entirely different reason: It held, squarely and definitively, that the requirement of complete diversity was statutory rather than constitutional. The necessary implication is that Congress can amend §1332 to permit federal jurisdiction when some but not all parties are of diverse citizenship.

E.   Class Actions

1.   Introduction

A class action permits, in the words of Rule 23, one or more parties to "sue or be sued as representative parties on behalf" of all those similarly situated. The underlying concept is simple: If many persons find themselves in the same situation, advantages may flow from aggregating many lawsuits into one. In practice, the class action has stimulated comments as favorable as "one of the most socially useful remedies in history" and as negative as "legalized blackmail."[*] Technically a joinder device, the class action has a potential effect on the judicial system and the substantive law unmatched by other joinder devices discussed in this chapter. The class action repays study: It raises some of the most challenging procedural issues on the current legal scene, and it raises questions that lie close to the heart of civil litigation — the nature of representation and the purpose of a lawsuit.

Although one can trace collective litigation into the mists of the common law, the modern class action traces its immediate pedigree only to 1966.[**] The revision of Rule 23 in that year sparked a new interest in and widespread use of class actions, prompting reaction of the type quoted earlier. Class actions clearly differ from the normal litigation model in which an individual plaintiff seeks redress from an individual defendant. The difference is not merely quantitative. For reasons that will become clear in the following materials, the ability to aggregate large numbers of litigants tends to shift the focus from the client to the lawyer, from damages to attorneys' fees, and from litigation to settlement.

The effect of class actions on the substantive law is subtler. It is not that the availability of class actions literally changes the statutes or the content of the case law, but, rather, that rules devised for one-on-one litigation have different effects in the context of mass litigation. For example, in Katz v. Carte-Blanche Corp.,

---

[*] The former comment comes from Pomerantz, New Developments in Class Actions — Has Their Death Knell Been Sounded?, 25 Bus. Law. 1259 (1970); the latter characterization appears in Handler, The Shift from Substantive to Procedural Innovations in Anti-Trust Suits, 71 Colum. L. Rev. 1, 9 (1971).

[**] See generally Stephen C. Yeazell, From Medieval Group Litigation to the Modern Class Action (1987).

496 F.2d 747 (3d Cir.), cert. denied, 419 U.S. 885 (1974), a background issue was whether minimum statutory damages of $100 should be available to each person in a class containing hundreds of thousands of members. More generally, when the availability of class actions increases the number of claims that are brought rather than simply facilitating the bringing of large numbers of claims that would have been brought separately, the impact of the underlying substantive law may be greatly heightened. Some have argued that this effect is a regrettable aspect of the rule. Others have argued that the increased potential for deterring wrongdoers and forcing wider compliance with the law is a powerful argument in favor of the device.

2. Statutory Requirements

To understand the furor, one has first to see how the contemporary class action operates. The starting point is, as always, the text of the Rule. That text establishes a series of hurdles for class actions to surmount, on their way to "certification," a process described in Rule 23(d). To become certified, a class action must meet both the requirements of Rule 23(a) and also fit into one of the three categories of Rule 23(b).

Practitioners refer to the four requirements of Rule 23(a) as numerosity, commonality, typicality, and adequacy of representation. To establish a case as a class action, the person seeking to represent the class must show that each of these requirements is satisfied.

Numerosity (Rule 23(a)(1)) is established if the class representative can show that enough persons are in the class to make joining them as individuals impractical. Courts occasionally certify classes as small as a few score, but typically classes consist of at least hundreds of persons. Commonality is jargon for the idea that the class should be a class — that it should consist of persons who share characteristics that matter in terms of the substantive law involved. This chapter has already encountered this idea in Mosley v. General Motors, supra page 742. Mosley discussed commonality as a requirement for joining individual plaintiffs under Rule 20. The requirement of cohesiveness recurs in class actions. For example, a "class" consisting of all persons who have claims against the United States would not have much in common: One person would be seeking an income tax refund, another compensation for an accident involving a postal truck, and a third might be seeking Social Security benefits. A much-litigated question is whether the members of the class have enough in common to justify class certification. Since virtually all classes proposed will have some characteristics in common and some unshared characteristics, there is much room for argument. Typicality is the requirement that class representatives stand, in significant respects, in the same shoes as the average class member. For example, in a case alleging mismanagement of a pension plan, if most members of the class have lost a few hundred dollars, it would raise a typicality problem if the class representative alleged losses of tens of thousands. The premise underlying the typicality requirement is that the class representative will be controlling the litigation, making the decisions that a client would be making in a one-client suit. In order to protect the interests of the absent class members, one would want the representative client to have the same incentives and motivations as the average class member. In practice, the class representatives have proved far less significant than the lawyers, and judges have consequently been willing to bend the requirements of typicality if they are assured that the last requirement — adequacy of representation — is fulfilled.

Courts have measured adequacy in several ways. The class representative herself must have some stake in the litigation. The representative's relation to the lawyer should be straightforward. For example, the class representative should not be an employee or a relative of the lawyer — relationships that would conflict with the representative's decisions about the litigation. The lawyer should have no conflicts that would cloud the representation. For example, some class representatives have been found inadequate because their real reason for pursuing the class action was to gain additional leverage for an individual client's case. Finally, the lawyer has to be sufficiently skillful and equipped with sufficient support and resources to handle the case. To use an extreme example, it is unlikely that a young lawyer with the ink still drying on her bar certificate would be found to be an adequate representative in a complex class action. Conversely, decisions certifying adequacy typically recite the lawyer's experience with previous similar cases. Decisions also note the lawyer's and firm's financial ability to finance protracted litigation. Added as part of the 2003 revisions, Rule 23(g) establishes both guidelines and a procedure for appointing class counsel. It places substantial weight on the entrepreneurial activity of counsel in unearthing and investigating the claim, on experience in handling class actions, on knowledge of the applicable law, and, in a bow to the expense of class suits, on the resources the lawyer can bring to bear on the case.

Having surmounted the hurdles of Rule 23(a), the lawyer seeking class certification still has to show that the litigation fits within one of the three categories of Rule 23(b). One might ask why: If the case fits the requirements of Rule 23(a), should it not be a class action? The drafters of the Rule were understandably unsure about the potential of the class action — for good or for harm. They had two fairly clear cases in mind that they thought should usually be treated as class actions — the situations described in Rule 23(b)(1) and 23(b)(2) — and a residual category — the (b)(3) cases — where they wanted courts to proceed cautiously.

The first situation — the 23(b)(1) class — is essentially a mass-production version of Rule 19. For example, suppose a city proposes to issue bonds to build a new civic auditorium. One group of citizens sues to block the issuance of the bonds; another group sues the city to insist that it go forward with the bonds and the project. If those suits proceed separately, the city might find itself the subject of incompatible judicial rulings: Issue the bonds; do not issue the bonds. By grouping the challengers and the supporters into classes, the court prevents a situation in which "varying adjudications with respect to individual members of the class" (the taxpayers) "would establish incompatible standards of conduct for the party opposing the class" (the city). Or, to take another example, suppose that a number of claimants all seek to collect on claims that exceed insurance coverage.

Under such circumstances Rule 23(b)(1) provides a way to assure that similarly situated parties are treated alike.

Rule 23(b)(2) provides for class actions where the party opposing the class has acted or refused to act "on grounds generally applicable to the class." The advisory committee notes to the Rule make clear that the drafters had in mind civil rights claims, where the plaintiff class would be alleging that defendants were acting on a racially motivated basis. Note that the availability of Rule 23(b)(2) is limited to cases in which the plaintiffs are seeking injunctive or declaratory relief. Again, such a description fits the standard civil rights case, where the typical relief sought is an injunction requiring some action — voter registration, school integration, changes in employment practices — by a defendant. An often litigated question is how much monetary relief a 23(b)(2) class can seek before the action ceases to be primarily injunctive and therefore ineligible for 23(b)(2) treatment.

The final category of class actions — those brought under Rule 23(b)(3) — has proved the most controversial. It comprises all class actions not captured in 23(b)(1) and 23(b)(2). In particular it includes all claims in which the plaintiffs are seeking primarily money damages. In practice, those actions can be subdivided into two groups. One group consists of what one might call "small claims" lawsuits: actions in which many persons allege small amounts of damage. Examples include such diverse lawsuits as one in which all purchasers of blue jeans in California were alleged to have been overcharged by a dollar or two and a claim in which 5 million purchasers and sellers of small lots of stock were alleged to have been overcharged by an average of $70. Notice that such claims are probably not worth any individual plaintiff's time or money to bring and that only the class action device makes them viable. Notice too that in such actions, the defendant is, as a practical matter, immune from liability unless a class is certified.

At the other end of the scale of Rule 23(b)(3) actions lies what is often called the "mass tort" — an airplane crash, a hotel fire, the exposure of hundreds of thousands of workers to asbestos fibers. The drafters of Rule 23 suggested in the Advisory Committee notes that such cases would not usually be appropriate for class treatment, but in the recent decades courts have increasingly — and controversially — certified class actions in mass torts. Because of the amount of potential damages, each of the individual plaintiffs will have a viable lawsuit. Such lawsuits in the aggregate may, however, drag on for many years and, in extreme cases, threaten to bankrupt the defendants and overwhelm the courts. In these suits the incentives for a class action change. To plaintiffs they continue to offer the increased bargaining power that comes from aggregation and the prospect of a single overwhelming damage judgment. In contrast to the small claims cases, they also offer some advantages to defendants — consolidation (of suits that would have been brought even without the class action), efficiency, and the possibility of a global settlement.

Placing a class action in one of the Rule 23 categories is more than a matter of analytical neatness. Whole cases may stand or fall as a result of the classification. This unexpected consequence flows from two sources. First, Rule 23(b)(3) requires the certifying judge to engage in a complicated weighing of advantages and disadvantages — as a result of which he may rule against certification. Second, Rule 23(c)(2)(B) requires individual notice to class members in all 23(b)(3) cases but not in the other two categories. (Rule 23(c)(2)(A) allows, but does not require, "appropriate notice" to the class in 23(b)(1) and (b)(2) cases.) Because the Supreme Court has held that the representative plaintiff must initially pay for such notice, inability to bear these costs may end the suit. Eisen v. Carlisle & Jacquelin, 417 U.S. 156 (1974).

The notes that follow ask you to consolidate this elementary discussion of Rule 23.

NOTES AND PROBLEMS

1. The regents of State University announce a tuition increase that applies only to out-of-state students. Two thousand such students stand to have their tuition increased. The president of the Student Association, an in-state student, announces that she is filing suit, on behalf of the affected students, to enjoin the regents from implementing the increase.

a. With which of the requirements of Rule 23(a) will the prospective class action have most difficulty?

b. What additional information will the court likely require in order to decide whether the suit meets the criteria of 23(a)?

c. Suppose that after some rearrangement, the court rules that the class meets the requirements of Rule 23(a); into what category of Rule 23(b) would it fall?

2. Assume that the tuition increase described in the preceding note has gone into effect and has been paid by the out-of-state students. One enterprising such student discovers that the regents adopted the increase at a closed meeting — in violation of state law — and that it is therefore unlawful. He proposes to file suit as representative of a class of all out-of-state students.

a. Student (as class representative) proposes to seek refunds in the form of reduced tuition in the following school year. Do you see why such a plan for relief may cause the court to find Student an inadequate representative (and perhaps an atypical one) for at least some members of the class?

b. Suppose Student proposes to remedy the adequacy of representation problems exposed in 2a by seeking cash refunds to all students, present and former, who paid the allegedly unlawful higher fees. What will this change in remedy do to the classification of the lawsuit under Rule 23(b)? What consequences will that change in classification have? (See Rule 23(c)(2)(B).)

c. Suppose Student finally decides to seek certification of a Rule 23(b)(3) class seeking cash refunds to all students who paid the higher fees. The costs of notifying the class are estimated to be in the neighborhood of $10,000. How might this fact cause a court that was otherwise satisfied that Student met the criteria of Rule 23(a)(4) to reconsider its decision and to decertify the class?

3. With these relatively elementary issues under your belt, consider courts struggling with certification in more complex situations.

Communities for Equity v. Michigan High School Athletic Assn.

1999 U.S. Dist. LEXIS 5780 (W.D. Mich. 1999)

ENSLEN, C.J.

This matter is before the Court on the Plaintiffs' Motion for Class Certification. For the reasons which follow, the motion will be granted.

Plaintiffs bring this suit against the Michigan High School Athletic Association and its Representative Council, alleging that they have been excluded from opportunities to participate in interscholastic athletic programs and have received unequal treatment and benefits in these programs. They contend that this putative exclusion and unequal treatment constitute gender discrimination, in violation of (1) Title IX of the Education Amendments of 1972; (2) the Equal Protection Clause of the Fourteenth Amendment; and (3) Mich. Comp. Laws §§37.2302 and 37.2402. The alleged discrimination is made manifest, according to Plaintiffs, in MHSAA's: (1) refusing to sanction girls' ice hockey and water polo; (2) requiring that the Plaintiff Class play its sports in non-traditional seasons; (3) operating shorter athletic seasons for some girls' sports than for boys' sports; (4) scheduling the competitions of the Plaintiff Class on inferior dates; (5) providing, assigning, and operating inferior athletic facilities to the Plaintiff Class in which to play MHSAA-sanctioned games; (6) requiring that the Plaintiff Class play some sports under rules and/or conditions different from those in the NCAA or other governing organizations, unlike boys; and (7) allocating more resources for the support and promotion of male interscholastic athletic programs than for female programs.

Plaintiffs' Motion for Class Certification asks the Court to define the proposed class as follows: all present and future female students enrolled in MHSAA member schools who participate in interscholastic athletics or who are deterred from participating in interscholastic athletics because of Defendants' discriminatory conduct and who are adversely affected by that conduct.

Standard for Class Certification

According to the United States Supreme Court, this Court must conduct a "rigorous analysis" into whether the prerequisites of Federal Rule of Civil Procedure 23 are met before certifying a class action. General Tel. Co. v. Falcon, 457 U.S. 147, 161 (1982). . . . The "rigorous analysis requirement" means that a class is not maintainable merely because the complaint parrots the legal requirements of Rule 23. Although a hearing prior to the class determination is not always required, "it may be necessary for the court to probe behind the pleadings before coming to rest on the certification question." *Falcon* [at 160.] In this case, the extensive briefing filed by the parties, the Court's past review of motions, and the documentary evidence and affidavits filed make the hearing of evidence unnecessary because the Court is able to probe behind the pleadings without additional evidence or argument.[1] . . .

1. Defendants raise a number of liability arguments in their briefing. While these may carry the day ultimately, that day has not yet arrived. The certification determination is not concerned with a plaintiff's success on the merits. See Eisen v. Carlisle & Jacquelin, 417 U.S. 156 (1974) (stating that certification question concerns Rule 23 factors and not an assessment of the merits).

Class Certification

Rule 23(a)(1) — Numerosity/Impracticability of Joinder. . . .

In this case, the numbers themselves justify a conclusion of numerosity and impracticability of joinder. Under Plaintiffs' theory of liability, thousands of female high school athletes and would-be athletes are subjected to Defendants' alleged discriminatory practices. . . . The Court concludes that the numerosity requirement is satisfied by the proposed class. . . .

Rule 23(a)(2) — Commonality

Next, the Rule requires commonality — that there are questions of law and fact common to class members. Not every common question suffices. What is necessary for certification are common issues the resolution of which will advance the litigation. In cases involving the question of whether a defendant has acted through an illegal policy or procedure, commonality is readily shown because the common question becomes whether the defendant in fact acted through the illegal policy or procedure. Where the nature of the legal claims are such that individuals would have to submit separate proofs to establish liability, class actions are disapproved due to lack of commonality. See, e.g., *Sprague* [v. General Motors Corp.], 133 F.3d at 398 (class action disapproved as to estoppel which would require individual proof of reliance). However, the presence of individual questions need not defeat certification. This should be obvious, since Rule 23 requires common questions, not the absence of individual ones. Once it is determined that there are common questions of law and fact as to a legal claim, differences in damages sustained by class members will usually not defeat certification.

Here, the common questions of fact and law are obvious enough. The overarching question is, did MHSAA and its Representative Council act in a manner inconsistent with Title IX, the Equal Protection Clause of the Fourteenth Amendment; and/or Mich. Comp. Laws §§37.2302 and 37.2402? The answer turns on the resolution of factual questions regarding Defendants' decision-making process and outcomes, and determination of the legal consequences of those facts.

Rule 23(a)(3) — Typicality. . . .

The typicality requirement is the one demanding the closest attention in this matter. The Court must determine whether, on the facts of this case, the Supreme Court's *Falcon* decision precludes a finding of typicality, given the breadth of Plaintiffs' claims. In *Falcon*, a Mexican-American employee who alleged that he had been denied a promotion because of race discrimination brought a class action against his employer. The class included all Mexican-American employees and Mexican-American applicants for employment who had not been hired. The class was certified pursuant to a Fifth Circuit rule which permitted "across-the-board" attacks on all racially discriminatory employment practices. The Fifth Circuit had held that it was permissible for " 'an employee complaining of one employment practice to represent another complaining of another practice, if the plaintiff and the members of the class suffer from essentially the same injury. In this case, all of the claims are based on discrimination because of national origin.'" The Supreme Court reversed, holding that:

> Respondent's complaint provided an insufficient basis for concluding that the adjudication of his claim of discrimination in promotion would require the decision of any common question concerning the failure of petitioner to hire more Mexican-Americans. Without any specific presentation identifying the questions of law or fact that were common to the claims of respondent and of the members of the class he sought to represent, it was error for the District Court to presume that respondent's claim was typical of other claims against petitioner by Mexican-American employees and applicants. If one allegation of specific discriminatory treatment were sufficient to support an across-the-board attack, every Title VII case would be a potential company wide class action.

At first blush, the Supreme Court's criticism of the class certification challenged in *Falcon* appears applicable in a case such as this. After all, a number of different harms are alleged here, which have not been suffered uniformly among the proposed class representatives. There are two reasons, however, that *Falcon* does not bar the certification of this class.

First, the various discrete harms alleged by Plaintiffs are all allegedly suffered by members of Communities for Equity, a proposed class representative. "Numerous decisions have recognized the ability of associations, both incorporated and unincorporated, to act as class representatives under Rule 23. . . ." Upper Valley Assoc. For Handicapped Citizens v. Mills, 168 F.R.D. 167, 171 (D. Vt. 1996). . . .

More importantly, however, the mere fact of some distinction between the particular claims of named Plaintiffs and the diverse manifestations of discrimination alleged here is insufficient to extinguish typicality. The *Falcon* Court provided for the possibility of broad-based attacks on discrimination if there were proof of an underlying policy of discrimination. Here, the variety of alleged manifestations of discrimination, such as inequitable facilities, scheduling, sanctioning, and rules, present a sufficient case of an underlying policy or practice of discrimination.[2] The Court determines that differences between sanctioning water polo and scheduling basketball are less significant in this matter than the typicality of claims that female high school athletes are discriminated against in violation of the various laws invoked by Plaintiffs. . . .

Rule 23(a)(4) — Adequacy of Representation

Rule 23(a) requires that the class members and their counsel be prepared to provide fair and adequate representation to the class. In Senter v. General Motors Corp., 532 F.2d 511, 525 (6th Cir. 1976), the Sixth Circuit Court of Appeals articulated two criteria for determining adequacy of representation: "1) the representative must have common interests with unnamed members of the class, and 2) it must appear that the representatives will vigorously prosecute the interests of the class through qualified counsel." . . . Two issues in this matter raise the potentiality for conflict.

---

2. If it should be shown by the conclusion of the litigation that such a policy were absent, there might be cause to remove the individual Plaintiffs as representatives for lack of typicality. CFE, however, might remain a viable representative.

First, it is quite possible that members of the class have no desire to pursue this action, and are not unhappy with the status quo. However, the proposed class purports to include only those who are "adversely affected." . . . As well, even without the limiting language, this sort of putative conflict generally fails to bar class certification. See Newberg at §3.30 ("the class member who wishes to remain a victim of unlawful conduct does not have a legally cognizable conflict with the class representative"). . . .

Moreover, as suggested by Plaintiffs, the interests of those class members who do not consider themselves adversely affected will be adequately represented by Defendants. "As long as both those seeking to uphold and those desiring to strike the particular regulations are adequately represented, the suit may proceed as a class action." 7A Charles Alan Wright, Arthur R. Miller, & Mary Kay Kane, Federal Practice and Procedure §1768 (2nd ed. 1986).

A second type of potential conflict may be that achieving certain types of relief in this case could come at the expense of other types. For instance, MHSAA may experience legally justifiable financial constraints which make it impossible for it to sanction tournaments in both ice hockey and water polo. Should a conflict arise from the limited availability of resources, however, it may be resolved by the creation of subclasses. In this case, the Court believes that the appropriate course is to defer consideration of any subclasses until the relief stage, if any, of this litigation. . . . To the extent that the underlying issue in this case is one of unequal treatment and discrimination, the matter of whether to sanction a particular sport appears to be one relating to relief, rather than liability.

Adequacy of representation is also measured by the quality of class counsel. There is no argument here that counsel for Plaintiffs are unqualified. They are experienced in both Title IX litigation, and litigation generally. The Court determines that the requirements of Rule 23(a)(4) are satisfied.

Rule 23(b)(2) — Injunctive or Declaratory Relief. . . .

Defendants argue that a class is unnecessary, because relief granted to named Plaintiffs would inure to the benefit of the class. The Sixth Circuit has disclaimed any necessity requirement for Rule 23(b)(2) certification. Even if such a requirement existed, mootness concerns would suggest the necessity of certification.

To the extent that Defendants discriminate against female high school athletes through unequal treatment, Defendants act or refuse to act on grounds generally applicable to the class. Injunctive relief is, of course, an appropriate remedy for discriminatory treatment. Rule 23(b)(2) certification is therefore appropriate. . . .

Therefore, it is the conclusion of this Court that the Motion for Class Certification shall be granted. An order shall issue consistent with this Opinion.

Order

In accordance with the Court's Opinion of this date;

IT IS HEREBY ORDERED that the Plaintiffs' Motion for Class Certification is GRANTED and that the Court certifies this matter as a class action pursuant to

Federal Rule of Civil Procedure 23(b)(2). The class action is certified as to the following class: all present and future female students enrolled in MHSAA member schools who participate in interscholastic athletics or who are deterred from participating in interscholastic athletics because of Defendants' discriminatory conduct and who are adversely affected by that conduct.

NOTES AND PROBLEMS

1. Why a class action? Consider the situation before the lawsuit started. The athletes and parents disadvantaged by the association's decisions want to challenge their legality; the association, imagining turmoil if existing arrangements have to be altered, wants to maintain them.

a. A single student or a small group could sue, seeking an injunction. If the court agreed with their claims, the injunction would, as a practical matter, forbid the association and its member schools from conducting women's athletics in the manner the plaintiffs had successfully challenged. If that is so, why should the plaintiffs bother jumping through the class action hoops? Why not just plunge into the merits?

b. Consider the same problem from the defendants' standpoint. It is obvious that there is a group of very unhappy students and parents who will mount a legal challenge to existing arrangements. If that's a given, why not welcome the class action as a way of getting the dispute over with, once and for all, in a way that will bind all concerned?

c. Part of the answer on the plaintiffs' side has to do with mootness. Litigation can drag on, and students graduate or leave sports programs. The plaintiffs don't want to be on the verge of a decision only to find that a student's departure for college moots the whole issue. In many similar circumstances plaintiff classes find themselves involved with institutional defendants on a temporary basis; a class action, by defining the group as those currently involved, prevents mootness.

d. But another part of the answer probably lies outside the courtroom. If you were the defendant, would you rather be dealing with an adversary who, with judicial approval, could describe herself as representing all the women high school athletes in Michigan? Or would you rather be dealing with a dozen plaintiffs whom you could, perhaps with some accuracy, describe as malcontents?

2. The opinion described the question of typicality as the most difficult on these facts.

a. Another district court came to a different certification decision on similar facts, citing concerns about adequacy of representation:

In this case, there is unrebutted evidence of a conflict of interests between the named plaintiffs and other members of the class which precludes certification under Rule 23. The results of the survey related to the court by defendant's expert indicate that plaintiffs do not adequately represent the interests of all the members of their class and that plaintiffs' claims are not typical of their class. A majority of the female public school athletes surveyed expressed a desire to preserve the status quo, meaning that most would not favor the injunctive relief sought by plaintiffs. There is a clear division in the class between those girls whose schools have already been subject to reclassification and those girls whose schools could, potentially, at some future time, be subject to reclassification. Those who have never experienced reclassification prefer not to have the entire system changed to suit the student athletes who have had to stop playing one or more of their preferred sports due to reclassification. Logically, if statewide realignment occurred, many more girls would be faced with the necessity of changing which sports they play. . . .

This conflict prevents plaintiffs from satisfying the typicality requirement as well as the adequacy of representation requirement. Plaintiffs have presented nothing to dispel the defendant's suggestion that there is a schism between girls who may benefit from reclassification and those who are injured by reclassification. A girl who could not previously play two sports because they occurred in the same season may be able to play those two sports when a school is reclassified and the seasons for some sports change. Such girls would not bring claims like the ones brought here by plaintiffs. Thus it cannot be said that as goes the claim of these plaintiffs, so go the claims of all others in the class.

Alston v. Virginia High School League, Inc., 184 F.R.D. 574, 579 (W.D. Va. 1999). Is this point well taken? Suppose that the Virginia arrangements for women high school athletes violate federal law: Does it matter that a number of athletes are satisfied with those arrangements?

b. What factual difference arguably makes *Alston* distinguishable from *Communities for Equity*?

c. The *Communities for Equity* court had three different solutions to the possibility that some women athletes might not share the goals of the class representatives. Explain what they were.

d. Notice that such intraclass conflicts will be particularly severe in 23(b)(1) and (b)(2) cases because those classes lack the possibility of opting out, which is offered by Rule 23(c)(2) for (b)(3) classes. They are necessarily "trapped" in the class.

3. Some conflicts are like those asserted in the *Alston* opinion: Do all the class members want to challenge the legality of the practice in question?

a. Other class conflicts have a more objective quality. In Kohl v. Association of Trial Lawyers, 183 F.R.D. 475 (D. Md. 1998), a former employee challenged the way in which a pension plan made certain distributions; she argued they should include a cost-of-living increase. Her original complaint sought to represent "all . . . who received or who will be eligible to receive in the future" such distributions. That definition thus included present as well as former employees. Defendant objected on grounds of inadequate representation:

> Defendants argue that to the extent that Plaintiff is successful in her suit and obtains some monetary relief, she would be depriving the Plan of a portion of its "finite pool of resources." According to Defendants, if Plaintiff is successful in this lawsuit, and damages are granted, "she will take money [from ATLA employees] that could be used for pay raises and enhanced benefits away from current employees." Thus, Defendants argue that a conflict of interest would exist between Plaintiff and those members of the class that are still employed. . . .
>
> This Court . . . has no real evidence before it that Plaintiff's interests may be antagonistic to the interests of current ATLA employees/future retirees. However, the Court finds no problem with Plaintiff representing the interests of current retirees, like herself.

Id. at 485.

b. The *Kohl* decision just quoted dealt with a potential conflict by narrowing the class. Another technique is to create subclasses, a technique that can be used to deal both with conflicts and with commonality and typicality problems. Of course, if the subclasses become numerous, the whole action threatens to become unmanageable.

c. Notice an odd feature of all such cases. It is the defendant who raises arguments that ostensibly seek to insure that plaintiffs have the best possible representation. In fact, defendants are seeking to avoid class certification and thus to eliminate the lawsuit entirely. In that respect class action certifications resemble Rule 19 cases in which a defendant is typically arguing that because perfect justice cannot be done, the case should be dismissed.

4. The *Communities for Equity* opinion is a typical class action certification decision. The requirement for "rigorous analysis" means that each class certification will travel over the categories of Rule 23(a) and then locate the case in one of the three 23(b) categories. As with this case, sometimes the category requires only cursory discussion, sometimes more.

a. A frequently litigated question is whether the existence of a damage claim alongside a prayer for injunctive relief moves the case from the (b)(2) to the (b)(3) category:

> An action seeking monetary damages cannot fall under (b)(2) unless the final injunctive relief or corresponding declaratory relief is the primary relief sought. . . . The plaintiffs are seeking all the remedies provided by the statute. Consequently, the difficult issue in this case is whether the monetary relief is incidental to the plaintiffs' request for final injunctive or declaratory relief.

Israel v. Avis Rent-A-Car Systems, Inc., 185 F.R.D. 372, 382 (S.D. Fla. 1999). Why do the litigants care?

> An action for money damages and injunctive relief can be certified under Rule(b)(3). To be certified under Rule 23(b)(3), however, the class must meet two prerequisites, neither of which is applicable under (b)(2): (1) the questions of law or fact common to the members of the class must predominate over any questions affecting only individual members; and (2) the class action must be superior to other available methods for the fair and efficient adjudication of the controversy. Actions brought under (b)(3) are also subject to the provisions in Rule 23(c)(2) requiring that notice be given to all members who can be identified through reasonable effort and each member has the option to be excluded from the class.

Id. at 384.

The ferocity of such classificatory fights may subside if a significant number of courts accept the invitation offered in the 2003 revisions; Rule 23(c)(2)(A) now provides that courts "may direct appropriate notice" to (b)(1) and (b)(2) classes. To the extent that courts require individual notice in such cases, they will increase the expense of such cases, and make the distinction between (b)(3) claims and other types less critical.

b. Another recurrent question in class actions is a choice of law problem that some practitioners refer to as the "fifty states" issue. In a nationwide class there can be persons who stand in similar factual circumstances but to whom different state laws apply. For example, suppose a proposed class consisting of cigarette smokers who claim that tobacco is a "defective" or unreasonably dangerous product. In considering whether the claims of such persons have sufficient commonality, a court might conclude that the product liability regimes of the states are sufficiently diverse as to deprive the proposed class of cohesiveness. Costano v. American Tobacco Co., 84 F.3d 734 (5th Cir. 1996) (class certification reversed for failure to consider how variations in state law affect predominance and superiority). A frequent counter to such arguments is the assertion either that state laws are converging or that a class action can resolve a number of common issues before the divergences are encountered.

5. As you will have gathered, the decision to certify (or to refuse to certify) a proposed class action is often critical for the outcome of the litigation. Certification gives the class representative immense bargaining power, refusal to certify means that the defendant is facing only a single plaintiff or a handful of plaintiffs, with much less at stake.

a. Until 1998 a district court's decision on certification was not appealable. If it certified the class, there was no final judgment. If it refused to certify the class, the action, though practically dead, still continued, in theory, as the claim of the representative plaintiff. As a consequence, there is less appellate law than one might think on the question of appropriately certifiable classes.

b. Rule 23(f) changes that situation. Read the Rule to see how. But the amendment also poses an interesting question: When should an appellate court take such appeals?

6. As you can see, even an "ordinary" class action certification has some knotty issues. Consider one made more complicated by procedural maneuvering.

Heaven v. Trust Company Bank

118 F.3d 735 (11th Cir. 1997)

BURNS, J.:

Background

Plaintiff . . . Ranae Heaven . . . leased a Ford Taurus from Sun Trust, signing a preprinted lease form provided by Sun Trust. . . . Later, she brought this action alleging that Sun Trust failed to comply with the strict disclosure requirements of the C[Consumer] L[easing] A[ct, 15 U.S.C. §§1667-67e] and Regulation M [implementing the Act]. Heaven sued for the statutory penalty and attorney fees but alleged no actual damages. She sought to certify a class pursuant to Fed. R. Civ. P. 23(a) and (b)(3).[3]

---

3. Heaven defined the class she sought to represent as:

all persons who satisfy the following criteria: (a) They signed a lease [with Sun Trust] prepared using the same printed form [that Heaven used]; (b) The total payments on the lease were less than $25,000; (c) The lease was for more than four months; (d) The lease is marked as a consumer purpose lease; and (e) The leases were outstanding within one year prior to the filing of this action.

Sun Trust counterclaimed on the alternative grounds that individual class members had (a) defaulted on the terms of their lease agreements, and/or (b) made false statements in their lease applications. The district court denied certification of the class. . . .

Standard of Review

The district court's decision whether to certify a class may only be overturned if it constitutes an abuse of discretion. . . .

Discussion . . .

The district court ruled that Heaven had established the four prerequisites of Rule 23(a). We see no need to revisit that aspect of the court's ruling. The district court concluded Heaven had not established that her action met the requirements of subdivision (b)(3). . . .

The district court recognized that the question of appropriateness of class certification in this case was very close. We agree with that assessment. The court engaged in a lengthy and thoughtful analysis and determined that several factors taken together tipped the balance against certification.

First, the court determined that Sun Trust's counterclaims were compulsory under Fed. R. Civ. P. 13(a). We agree that this conclusion is compelled by the case law of this circuit. See Plant v. Blazer Financial Services, Inc., [supra page 735] (Holding that debt counterclaims are compulsory in Truth In Lending Act (TILA) cases).

Heaven does not dispute that debt counterclaims are compulsory in TILA and CLA cases as a general matter. However, she contends that the presence of counterclaims cannot be a basis for denying class certification. Heaven apparently asserts that Roper v. Consurve, Inc., 578 F.2d 1106 (5th Cir. 1978), aff'd, 445 U.S. 326, (1980) stands for the proposition that Fed. R. Civ. P. 13(a) has no application at all in class certification analysis. We do not believe that Roper states such a universal rule. . . .

The court below considered the nature of Sun Trust's counterclaims and determined that individual lessee counterclaim defendants would be compelled to come forward with individual defenses. This would require the court to engage in multiple separate factual determinations, a proper factor for consideration under Rule 23(b)(3)(D). The court also determined that the interests of some individual class members in controlling their own case would be compromised. Their exposure as counterclaim defendants could well exceed the amount they might recover for statutory penalties as class members. The statutory claims asserted by the class would be against the interests of these individual class members. This is a proper factor for consideration under Rule 23(b)(3)(A). . . .

If this panel had faced the class certification issue in the first instance, we may well have found it appropriate to certify the class or to establish subclasses. However, where the district court has given due consideration to all the

No abuse of discretion

relevant factors within the context of a rigorous analysis and has not relied on impermissible factors, we are unable to find an abuse of discretion. If, after such an evaluation, the district court is convinced that a class action is not superior to other available methods for the fair and efficient adjudication of the controversy, we cannot second guess that conclusion under the applicable standard of review.[7] . . .

Affirmed.

NOTES AND PROBLEMS

1. Explain why the district court declined to certify the class. On what part of Rule 23 did the proposed action founder? Why?

2. There were presumably hundreds of leases in question here, and evidently some substantial number of consumers had not paid in accordance with their lease terms. As to these, Sun Trust counterclaimed.

a. If the leases were unpaid, why had Sun Trust not already brought suit?

b. Was it improper to do so after the class action was filed?

3. Citing Plant v. Blazer Financial Services, supra page 805, *Heaven* takes it as established that the district court has jurisdiction over the compulsory counterclaim, thus making class certification questionable because of the manageability problems. In a case presenting very similar issues, a court declined to exercise supplemental jurisdiction precisely because its exercise would make the class unmanageable:

> The parties did not raise and the court did not address, however, whether the court should decline to exercise jurisdiction pursuant to 28 U.S.C. §1367(c). This court raises the issue sua sponte, and for the reasons set forth below, declines to exercise supplemental jurisdiction over ECS's counterclaims. See 28 U.S.C. §1367(c)(4). Pursuant to section 1367(c)(4): "The district courts may decline to exercise supplemental jurisdiction over a claim under subsection (a) if . . . (4) in exceptional circumstances, there are other compelling reasons for declining jurisdiction."
>
> The court finds that there are compelling reasons for public policy embodied in the [federal disclosure legislation] for declining jurisdiction in this case.
>
> To allow a debt collector defendant to seek to collect the debt in the federal action to enforce the [disclosure statute] might well have a chilling effect on persons who otherwise might and should bring suits such as this. . . . Given the remedial nature of the [statute] and the broad public policy it serves, federal courts should be loath to become immersed in the debt collection suits [brought by] the target of the very legislation under which the . . . plaintiff states a cause of action.

7. We do not intend to suggest that compulsory counterclaims should preclude the maintenance of class actions in cases under the CLA as a general rule. We rule only that it is a proper exercise of discretion for the district court to evaluate the nature of the counterclaims and the difficulties they present and to consider the usefulness of breaking the proposed class into subclasses to avoid those difficulties.

Ballard v. Equifax Check Servs., 1999 U.S. Dist. LEXIS 4071 (E.D. Cal. 1999).

4. The decision to certify or not to certify a proposed class action can have dramatic consequences for both parties.

a. In one category of case — the "small claims" class — that decision is usually dispositive. In such cases, typically (b)(3) actions, a large number of persons seek damages for claims that are individually small. If the individual claims carry no attorneys' fee provision, the plaintiffs will rarely find it economically worthwhile to pursue their claims individually. In such cases a refusal to certify will end not just the class but any individual actions. Conversely, the decision to certify may face the defendant with a potentially huge liability claim, one it feels compelled to settle almost without regard to the merits.

b. Certifying a class has another important consequence. As you will see in the next section, an adequately represented class is bound by a judgment or settlement. Use the facts of *Communities for Equity*, supra page 795, to see this proposition at work. The trial judge certified the case over defendants' objections. The defendants' unhappiness would change, however, if the trial court proceeded, as footnote 1 hinted it might, to find that the defendants' actions were entirely lawful. At that point — if we assume the plaintiffs were adequately represented — no present or future woman high school athlete could challenge Michigan's arrangements on grounds of gender inequity. Do you see why this is so?

c. Because of the important consequences of class certification, Rule 23(c)(1) requires that the court shall determine whether to certify case as a class action "at an early practicable date." Because the certification is difficult, however, and because it so sharply changes the dynamics of the litigation, sometimes parties and judges drag their feet.

d. Such delay can have substantial consequences if the court, with class status still undecided, makes dispositive rulings on the merits. In such circumstances the plaintiff, up until now urging class status, is suddenly happy to have only a decision involving an individual. By contrast, defendant, who has until now been fighting class certification, would now welcome it.

e. What's the difference between being bound by precedent and being bound by claim preclusion? As a formal matter, the distinction is that one can at least try to convince the court that there are arguments it overlooked in its former decision or that the precedent itself is wrong and should be overruled. In claim preclusion the only question that matters is whether this is the same claim between the same parties.

3.   The Class Action and the Constitution

Above the controversy surrounding the class action stand a pair of constitutional arguments that both enable and limit the procedure. Both flow from the Due Process Clause. One argument entails whether a party can be bound by litigation to which he is not a party. The other asks whether due process requires certain procedures within the class action in order for it to be a valid adjudication of the absentees' rights.

a.   Representative Adequacy

Fundamental to the class action is the idea that a suit, conducted by a representative on behalf of a number of persons who are not formal parties, may nevertheless bind the entire represented class. In that respect it represents a departure from the ordinary proposition that one may be bound only by litigation to which one is a party. One might cite any number of cases for this proposition, including Martin v. Wilks, supra page 779. The next case works out the conditions under which such a representative may bind those who are not parties. It limits the class action, but at the same time it gives the class action, thus limited, great potential power.

Hansberry v. Lee

11 U.S. 32 (1940)

Mr. Justice STONE delivered the opinion of the Court.

The question is whether the Supreme Court of Illinois, by its adjudication that petitioners in this case are bound to a judgment rendered in an earlier litigation to which they were not parties, has deprived them of the due process of law guaranteed by the Fourteenth Amendment. . . .

[The case was decided before Shelley v. Kraemer, 334 U.S. 1 (1948), holding racially restrictive covenants unenforceable. The Hansberrys, a black family, bought a house in an area of Chicago allegedly covered by a racially restrictive covenant. The covenant said it did not take effect unless signed by owners of 95 percent of the frontage. In fact, the signers represented only 54 percent. Lee brought an action to enjoin breach of the covenant, naming as defendants both the Hansberrys, who had purchased a home allegedly in violation of the covenant, and the people from whom the Hansberrys had bought the property. One of the Hansberrys' defenses was that the covenant was unenforceable because not enough owners had signed it. Plaintiff countered by referring to Burke v. Kleiman, an earlier suit to enforce the same covenant. In *Burke* a property owner "in behalf of herself and other property owners in like situation" sued four named individuals allegedly in violation of the covenant. Burke was litigated in the Illinois courts, where the parties had *stipulated* (falsely) that the requisite 95 percent had signed, and the earlier court had adopted that stipulation in its findings. Burke upheld the covenant. The Supreme Court of Illinois in the present case determined that Burke had been a class action, that the Hansberrys and their vendors were members of the class of *plaintiffs* in *Burke,* and that they were therefore bound by the findings in the previous action even though those findings were factually erroneous.]

To the defense that the agreement had never become effective because owners of 95 percent of the frontage had not signed it, respondents pleaded that that issue was res judicata by the decree in an earlier suit. To this petitioners pleaded, by way of rejoinder, that they were not parties to that suit or bound by its decree, and that denial of their right to litigate, in the present suit, the issue of performance of the condition precedent to the validity of the agreement would be a denial of due process of law guaranteed by the Fourteenth Amendment. It does not appear, nor is it contended that any of petitioners is the successor in interest to or in privity with any of the parties in the earlier suit.

The [state] . . . court, after a trial on the merits, found that owners of only about 54 per cent of the frontage had signed the agreement, and that the only support of the judgment in the *Burke* case was a false and fraudulent stipulation of the parties that owners of 95 per cent had signed. But it ruled that the issue of performance of the condition precedent to the validity of the agreement was res judicata as alleged and entered a decree for respondents. . . .

From this the Supreme Court of Illinois concluded in the present case that *Burke v. Kleiman* was a "class" or "representative" suit, and that in such a suit, "where the remedy is pursued by a plaintiff who has the right to represent the class to which he belongs, other members of the class are bound by the results in the case unless it is reversed or set aside on direct proceedings"; that petitioners in the present suit were members of the class represented by the plaintiffs in the earlier suit and consequently were bound by its decree. . . .

State courts are free to attach such descriptive labels to litigations before them as they may choose and to attribute to them such consequences as they think appropriate under state constitutions and laws, subject only to the requirements of the Constitution of the United States. But when the judgment of a state court, ascribing to the judgment of another court the binding force and effect of res judicata, is challenged for want of due process it becomes the duty of this Court to examine the course of procedure in both litigations to ascertain whether the litigant whose rights have thus been adjudicated has been afforded such notice and opportunity to be heard as are requisite to the due process which the Constitution prescribes.

It is a principle of general application in Anglo-American jurisprudence that one is not bound by a judgment in personam in a litigation in which he is not designated as a party or to which he has not been made a party by service of process. Pennoyer v. Neff. A judgment rendered in such circumstances is not entitled to the full faith and credit which the Constitution and statutes of the United States prescribe, Pennoyer v. Neff; and judicial action enforcing it against the person or property of the absent party is not that due process which the Fifth and Fourteenth Amendments require.

To these general rules there is a recognized exception that, to an extent not precisely defined by judicial opinion, the judgment in a "class" or "representative" suit, to which some members of the class are parties, may bind members of the class or those represented who were not made parties to it.

The class suit was an invention of equity to enable it to proceed to a decree in suits where the number of those interested in the subject of the litigation is so great that their joinder as parties in conformity to the usual rules of procedure is impracticable. Courts are not infrequently called upon to proceed with causes in which the number of those interested in the litigation is so great as to make difficult or impossible the joinder of all because some are not within the jurisdiction or because their whereabouts is unknown or where if all were made parties to the suit its continued abatement by the death of some would prevent or unduly delay a decree. In such cases where the interests of those not joined are of the same class as the interests of those who are, and where it is considered that the latter fairly represent the former in the prosecution of the litigation of the issues in which all have a common interest, the court will proceed to a decree. . . .

[T]here is scope within the framework of the Constitution for holding in appropriate cases that a judgment rendered in a class suit is res judicata as to members of the class who are not formal parties to the suit. Here, as elsewhere, the Fourteenth Amendment does not compel state courts or legislatures to adopt any particular rule for establishing the conclusiveness of judgments in class suits, nor does it compel the adoption of the particular rules thought by this Court to be appropriate for the federal courts. With a proper regard for divergent local institutions and interests, this Court is justified in saying that there has been a failure of due process only in those cases where it cannot be said that the procedure adopted, fairly insures the protection of the interests of absent parties who are to be bound by it.

It is familiar doctrine of the federal courts that members of a class not present as parties to the litigation may be bound by the judgment where they are in fact adequately represented by parties who are present, or where they actually participate in the conduct of the litigation in which members of the class are present as parties, or where the interest of the members of the class, some of whom are present as parties, is joint, or where for any other reason the relationship between the parties present and those who are absent is such as legally to entitle the former to stand in judgment for the latter.

In all such cases, so far as it can be said that the members of the class who are present are, by generally recognized rules of law, entitled to stand in judgment for those who are not, we may assume for present purposes that such procedure affords a protection to the parties who are represented, though absent, which would satisfy the requirements of due process and full faith and credit. Nor do we find it necessary for the decision of this case to say that, when the only circumstance defining the class is that the determination of the rights of its members turns upon a single issue of fact or law, a state could not constitutionally adopt a procedure whereby some of the members of the class could stand in judgment for all, provided that the procedure were so devised and applied as to insure that those present are of the same class as those absent and that the litigation is so conducted as to insure the full and fair consideration of the common issue. We decide only that the procedure and the course of litigation sustained here by the plea of res judicata do not satisfy these requirements.

The restrictive agreement did not purport to create a joint obligation or liability. If valid and effective its promises were the several obligations of the signers and those claiming under them. The promises ran severally to every other signer. It is plain that in such circumstances all those alleged to be bound by the agreement would not constitute a single class in any litigation brought to enforce it. Those who sought to secure its benefits by enforcing it could not be said to be in the same class with or represent those whose interest was in resisting performance, for the agreement by its terms imposes obligations and confers rights on the owner of each plot of land who signs it. If those who thus seek to secure the benefits of the agreement were rightly regarded by the state Supreme Court as constituting a class, it is evident that those signers or their successors who are interested in challenging the validity of the agreement and resisting its performance are not of the same class in the sense that their interests are identical so that any group who had elected to enforce rights conferred by the agreement could be said to be acting in the interest of any others who were free to deny its obligation.

Because of the dual and potentially conflicting interests of those who are putative parties to the agreement in compelling or resisting its performance, it is impossible to say, solely because they are parties to it, that any two of them are of the same class. Nor without more, and with the due regard for the protection of the rights of absent parties which due process exacts, can some be permitted to stand in judgment for all.

It is one thing to say that some members of a class may represent other members in a litigation where the sole and common interest of the class in the litigation, is either to assert a common right or to challenge an asserted obligation. It is quite another to hold that all those who are free alternatively either to assert rights or to challenge them are of a single class, so that any group, merely because it is of the class so constituted, may be deemed adequately to represent any others of the class in litigating their interests in either alternative. Such a selection of representatives for purposes of litigation, whose substantial interests are not necessarily or even probably the same as those whom they are deemed to represent, does not afford that protection to absent parties which due process requires. The doctrine of representation of absent parties in a class suit has not hitherto been thought to go so far. Apart from the opportunities it would afford for the fraudulent and collusive sacrifice of the rights of absent parties, we think that the representation in this case no more satisfies the requirements of due process than a trial by a judicial officer who is in such situation that he may have an interest in the outcome of the litigation in conflict with that of the litigants.

The plaintiffs in the *Burke* case sought to compel performance of the agreement in behalf of themselves and all others similarly situated. They did not designate the defendants in the suit as a class or seek any injunction or other relief against others than the named defendants, and the decree which was entered did not purport to bind others. In seeking to enforce the agreement the plaintiffs in that suit were not representing the petitioners here whose substantial interest is in resisting performance. The defendants in the first suit were not treated by the pleadings or decree as representing others or as foreclosing by their defense the rights of others; and, even though nominal defendants, it does not appear that their interest in defeating the contract outweighed their interest in establishing its validity. For a court in this situation to ascribe to either the plaintiffs or defendants the performance of such functions on behalf of petitioners here, is to attribute to them a power that it cannot be said that they had assumed to exercise, and a responsibility which, in view of their dual interests it does not appear that they could rightly discharge.

Reversed.

Mr. Justice MCREYNOLDS, Mr. Justice ROBERTS and Mr. Justice REED concur in the result.

NOTES AND PROBLEMS

1. In *The History Behind Hansberry v. Lee*, 20 U.C. Davis L. Rev. 481 (1987), Allen Kamp reveals that the case was one step in a long struggle over the desegregation of Chicago neighborhoods. The Hansberry family itself gave the nation considerably more than a leading case: Lorraine Hansberry, the daughter of the named party, was a leading playwright whose best-known work is *Raisin in the Sun*. In reminiscences about her father she recalled the terrible toll that this fight had on her and her family:

> [T]wenty-five years ago, [my father] spent a small personal fortune, his considerable talents, and many years of his life fighting, in association with NAACP attorneys, Chicago's "restrictive covenants" in one of this nation's ugliest ghettos.
>
> That fight also required that our family occupy with disputed property in a hellishly hostile "white neighborhood" in which literally howling mobs surrounded our house. . . . One of these missiles almost took the life of the then eight-year-old signer of this letter. My memories of this "correct" way of fighting white supremacy in America include being spat at, cursed and pummeled in the daily trek to and from school. And I also remember my desperate and courageous mother, patrolling our household all night with a loaded German [L]uger [pistol], doggedly guarding her four children, while my father fought the respectable part of the battle in the Washington court.

Id. at 488, quoting L. Hansberry, To Be Young, Gifted and Black 20-21 (adapted by R. Nemiroff, 1969).

2. *Hansberry*'s doctrinal equation is simple to state: A judgment in a class action binds absentee members of a class only if they have been adequately represented. For example, imagine that the homeowners in the area had brought a class suit against the property tax assessor, alleging that improper assessment principles had been used in figuring taxes on the tract. Assume the class lost on the merits. If the class of plaintiffs had been adequately represented, a single member of the class would be barred from bringing a second suit challenging the same assessment.

3. Much harder to work out is the application of that principle to the facts of *Hansberry*.

a. Were the Hansberrys and their vendors "represented" in the earlier class action, according to the Illinois courts?

b. On which side? The only plausible class was a group of persons seeking to enforce the covenant against those who wished to buy or sell property free of racial restrictions. Surely the Hansberrys weren't represented by this class.

c. If there had been a defendant class in Burke v. Kleiman as well — a class consisting of all those who challenged the validity of the covenant — one could at least begin to discuss whether the Hansberrys were members of that class. But the defendants in *Burke* were four named individuals who purported to represent only themselves. So on its face it represents massive confusion to describe Burke v. Kleiman as a class suit that bound the Hansberrys.

4. At this point the U.S. Supreme Court had a problem. The Court doesn't have jurisdiction to correct confusion within state courts unless that confusion falls within its jurisdiction. The only way the Court could reach the Illinois judgment was to find a constitutional error.

a. What was the constitutional error?

b. The *Hansberry* opinion tells us that the Illinois Supreme Court deemed the earlier action to have been a class action even though it was not conducted with any real attention to the interests of the "class" members. Couldn't the result in *Hansberry* have rested on the much narrower ground that due process is denied when binding effect is given to a judgment in an action in which no attempt was made to consider the problems of representing a group of absentees? Isn't the real problem that no one tried to represent the Hansberrys' interests in the earlier suit?

5. In explaining why the prior litigation did not bind the Hansberrys, the Court contrasted appropriate class actions with inappropriate ones:

> It is one thing to say that some members of a class may represent other members in a litigation where the sole and common interest of the class in the litigation is either to assert a common right or to challenge an asserted obligation. It is quite another to hold that all those who are free alternatively either to assert rights or to challenge them are of a single class, so that any group, merely because it is of the class so constituted, may be deemed adequately to represent any others of the class in litigating their interests in either alternative.

311 U.S. at 44-45.

a. In the context of the *Hansberry* case itself, the statement has special force. Professor Kamp's research revealed that the Burke family, who sold to the Hansberrys, had been the leaders of the plaintiff class in the first lawsuit and then later changed their minds about the covenant:

> The Court's words, "free to assert or deny" [rights] did not refer to an abstract possibility — that is exactly what had happened. The party enforcing the covenant in Burke was the wife of the person who had sold his house to Carl Hansberry. . . . Although the language is so sweeping it could apply to and invalidate every class action, what actually happened in *Burke* and *Hansberry* was unique — that husband of the class representative in the first action had become a defendant and sought to subvert the goals of the plaintiff class.

20 U.C. Davis L. Rev. 481, 497 (1987).

b. Assume that Rule 23 had been in effect in the Illinois courts that heard Burke v. Kleiman. What portion of that Rule would have been most relevant to the conduct of the case?

6. The problem of the binding power of a class action usually boils down to a question of fairness to parties who may not have been adequately represented. Although the court in the first action can help to ensure adequate representation of such parties, no ruling to that effect in the first action should bind them if in fact they were not adequately represented. (An analogy can be made to attacks on the personal jurisdiction of a court. Recall from pages 716-723 that if the defendant appears in the first action and either raises or has an opportunity to raise the jurisdictional issue, he is bound by the court's determination that it has jurisdiction. But if the defendant does not appear in the first action, no jurisdictional ruling of the first court can bind him.) Thus, *Hansberry* can also be cited for the proposition that a person asserted to be bound by former class litigation has the right collaterally to challenge the adequacy of the representation in the class suit.

A good illustration of this point is Gonzales v. Cassidy, 474 F.2d 67 (5th Cir. 1973), in which an unnamed member of a class was not precluded from bringing a later action even though an earlier class action had failed. The named plaintiff in the earlier action had succeeded in securing relief for himself; at that point, the second court ruled, he had become an inadequate representative of the class by failing to appeal. Failure of the plaintiff in the second action to intervene in the first action for the purpose of appealing was held not to be fatal to his argument that the first decision should not bind him.

b.   Jurisdiction

Hansberry tells us that for a class action to bind absentees the representation of the class must be adequate. Does due process place further constraints on the operation of the class action?

Phillips Petroleum v. Shutts

472 U.S. 797 (1985)

REHNQUIST, J.

[Phillips produces and sells natural gas. During the 1970s it acquired some of this gas by leasing gas-producing lands from others, paying royalties on the gas it extracted from each parcel of leased land. The royalty was based on the price for which the gas was finally sold, and increases in the selling price required approval by a federal agency. While regulatory approval was pending, however, Phillips sold the gas at higher prices but paid royalties only on the lower, already approved prices, paying the incremental royalties only when and if the increase met with regulatory approval. Phillips's defense of this practice rested on the difficulty of obtaining rebates from the royalty owners if the price increases were not approved.

Plaintiff Irl Shutts filed a suit on behalf of himself and 33,000 small royalty owners, claiming that they were entitled to interest on the money during the period when Phillips was awaiting approval of its price increases. The average claim of the class members was $100. Suit was filed in Kansas state court, which certified the action under a state provision substantially resembling Federal Rule of Civil Procedure 23.]

After the class was certified respondents provided each class member with notice through first-class mail. The notice described the action and informed each class member that he could appear in person or by counsel; otherwise each member would be represented by Shutts and the Andersons, the named plaintiffs. The notices also stated that class members would be included in the class and bound by the judgment unless they "opted out" of the lawsuit by executing and returning a "request for exclusion" that was included with the notice. The final class as certified contained 28,100 members; 3,400 had "opted out" of the class by returning the request for exclusion, and notice could not be delivered to another 1,500 members, who were also excluded. Less than 1,000 of the class members resided in Kansas. Only a minuscule amount, approximately one quarter of one percent, of the gas leases involved in the lawsuit were on Kansas land. [After some procedural skirmishing over the class action issue, the case went to trial. On the merits the Kansas court held "as a matter of Kansas equity law" that Phillips owed the royalty owners interest and entered judgment for the plaintiff class.]

Petitioner raised two principal claims in its appeal to the Supreme Court of Kansas. It first asserted that the Kansas trial court did not possess personal jurisdiction over absent plaintiff class members as required by International Shoe Co. v. Washington and similar cases. Related to this first claim was petitioner's contention that the "opt-out" notice to absent class members, which forced them to return the request for exclusion in order to avoid the suit, was insufficient to bind class members who were not residents of Kansas or who did not possess "minimum contacts" with Kansas. Second, petitioner claimed that Kansas courts could not apply Kansas law to every claim in the dispute. The trial court should have looked to the laws of each State where the leases were located to determine, on the basis of conflict of laws principles, whether interest on the suspended royalties was recoverable, and at what rate. . . .

Reduced to its essentials, petitioner's argument is that unless out-of-state plaintiffs affirmatively consent, the Kansas courts may not exert jurisdiction over their claims. Petitioner claims that failure to execute and return the "request for exclusion" provided with the class notice cannot constitute consent of the out-of-state plaintiffs; thus Kansas courts may exercise jurisdiction over these plaintiffs only if the plaintiffs possess the sufficient "minimum contacts" with Kansas as that term is used in cases involving personal jurisdiction over out-of-state defendants. E.g., International Shoe Co. v. Washington, Shaffer v. Heitner, World-Wide Volkswagen Corp. v. Woodson. Since Kansas had no prelitigation contact with many of the plaintiffs and leases involved, petitioner claims that Kansas has exceeded its jurisdictional reach and thereby violated the due process rights of the absent plaintiffs. . . .

Although the cases like *Shaffer* and *Woodson* which petitioner relies on for a minimum contacts requirement all dealt with out-of-state defendants or parties in the procedural posture of a defendant, petitioner claims that the same analysis must apply to absent class-action plaintiffs. In this regard petitioner correctly points out that a chose in action is a constitutionally recognized property interest possessed by each of the plaintiffs. Mullane v. Central Hanover Bank & Trust Co. An adverse judgment by Kansas courts in this case may extinguish the chose in action forever through res judicata. Such an adverse judgment, petitioner claims, would be every bit as onerous to an absent plaintiff as an adverse judgment on the merits would be to a defendant. Thus, the same due process protections should apply to absent plaintiffs: Kansas should not be able to exert jurisdiction over the plaintiffs' claims unless the plaintiffs have sufficient minimum contacts with Kansas.

We think petitioner's premise is in error. The burdens placed by a State upon an absent class-action plaintiff are not of the same order or magnitude as those it places upon an absent defendant. An out-of-state defendant summoned by a plaintiff is faced with the full powers of the forum State to render judgment *against* it. The defendant must generally hire counsel and travel to the forum to defend itself from the plaintiff's claim, or suffer a default judgment. The defendant may be forced to participate in extended and often costly discovery, and will be forced to respond in damages or to comply with some other form of remedy imposed by the court should it lose the suit. The defendant may also face liability for court costs and attorney's fees. . . .

A class-action plaintiff, however, is in quite a different posture. . . .

In sharp contrast to the predicament of a defendant haled into an out-of-state forum, the plaintiffs in this suit were not haled anywhere to defend themselves upon pain of a default judgment. As commentators have noted, from the plaintiffs' point of view a class action resembles a "quasi-administrative proceeding, conducted by the judge."

A plaintiff class in Kansas and numerous other jurisdictions cannot first be certified unless the judge, with the aid of the named plaintiffs and defendant, conducts an inquiry into the common nature of the named plaintiffs and the absent plaintiffs' claims, the adequacy of representation, the jurisdiction possessed over the class, and any other matters that will bear upon proper representation of the absent plaintiffs' interest. See, e.g., Kan. Stat. Ann. §60-223 (1983), Fed. Rule Civ. Proc. 23. Unlike a defendant in a civil suit, a class-action plaintiff is not required to fend for himself. See Kan. Stat. Ann. §60-223(d) (1983). The court and named plaintiffs protect his interest. Indeed, the class-action defendant itself has a great interest in ensuring that the absent plaintiffs' claims are properly before the forum. . . .

The concern of the typical class-action rules for the absent plaintiffs is manifested in other ways. Most jurisdictions, including Kansas, require that a class action, once certified, may not be dismissed or compromised without the approval of the court. In many jurisdictions such as Kansas the court may amend the pleadings to ensure that all sections of the class are represented adequately. Kan. Stat. Ann. §60-223(d) (1983); see also e.g., Fed. Rule Civ. Proc. 23(d).

Besides this continuing solicitude for their rights, absent plaintiff class members are not subject to other burdens imposed upon defendants. They need not hire counsel or appear. They are almost never subject to counterclaims or cross-claims, or liability for fees or costs.[2] Absent plaintiff class members are not subject to coercive or punitive remedies. Nor will an adverse judgment typically bind an absent plaintiff for any damages, although a valid adverse judgment may extinguish any of the plaintiff's claim which was litigated. . . .

In most class actions an absent plaintiff is provided at least with an opportunity to "opt out" of the class, and if he takes advantage of that opportunity he is removed from the litigation entirely. This was true of the Kansas proceedings in this case. . . .

---

2. Petitioner places emphasis on the fact that absent class members might be subject to discovery, counterclaims, cross-claims or court costs. Petitioner cites no cases involving any such imposition upon plaintiffs, however. We are convinced that such burdens are rarely imposed upon plaintiff class members, and that the disposition of these issues is best left to a case which presents them in a more concrete way.

Because States place fewer burdens upon absent class plaintiffs than they do upon absent defendants in nonclass suits, the Due Process Clause need not and does not afford the former as much protection from state-court jurisdiction as it does the latter. The Fourteenth Amendment does protect "persons," not "defendants," however, so absent plaintiffs as well as absent defendants are entitled to some protection from the jurisdiction of a forum State which seeks to adjudicate their claims. In this case we hold that a forum State may exercise jurisdiction over the claim of an absent class-action plaintiff, even though that plaintiff may not possess the minimum contacts with the forum which would support personal jurisdiction over a defendant. If the forum State wishes to bind an absent plaintiff concerning a claim for money damages or similar relief at law,[3] it must provide minimal procedural due process protection. The plaintiff must receive notice plus an opportunity, to be heard and participate in the litigation, whether in person or through counsel. The notice must be the best practicable, "reasonably calculated, under all the circumstances, to apprise interested parties of the pendency of the action and afford them an opportunity, to present their objections." *Mullane*. The notice should describe the action and the plaintiffs' rights in it. Additionally, we hold that due process requires at a minimum that an absent plaintiff be provided with an opportunity to remove himself from the class by executing and returning an "opt out" or "request for exclusion" form to the court. Finally, the Due Process Clause of course requires that the named plaintiff at all times adequately represent the interests of the absent class members. . . .

We think that the procedure followed by Kansas, where a fully descriptive notice is sent first-class mail to each class member, with an explanation of the right to "opt out," satisfies due process. . . .

The Kansas courts applied Kansas contract and Kansas equity law to every claim in this case, notwithstanding that over 97 percent of the gas leases and some 97 percent of the plaintiffs in the case had no apparent connection to the State of Kansas except for this lawsuit. Petitioner protested that the Kansas courts should apply the laws of the States where the leases were located, or at least apply Texas and Oklahoma law because so many of the leases came from those States. The Kansas courts disregarded this contention and found petitioner liable for interest on the suspended royalties as a matter of Kansas law, and set the interest rates under Kansas equity principles. . . .

. . . We make no effort to determine for ourselves which law must apply to the various transactions involved in this lawsuit, and we reaffirm our observation in *Allstate* that in many situations a state court may be free to apply one of several choices of law. But the constitutional limitations laid down in cases such as Allstate and Home Insurance Co. v. Dick must be respected even in a nationwide class action.

---

3. Our holding today is limited to those class actions which seek to bind known plaintiffs concerning claims wholly or predominantly for money judgments. We intimate no view concerning other types of class-action lawsuits, such as those seeking equitable relief. Nor, of course, does our discussion of personal jurisdiction address class actions where the jurisdiction is asserted against a defendant class.

We therefore affirm the judgment of the Supreme Court of Kansas insofar as it upheld the jurisdiction of the Kansas courts over the plaintiff class members in this case, and reverse its judgment insofar as it held that Kansas law was applicable to all of the transactions which it sought to adjudicate. We remand the case to that Court for further proceedings not inconsistent with this opinion.

Justice POWELL took no part in the decision of this case.

Justice STEVENS [concurred with the majority opinion on the class action issue and dissented only on the choice of law question.]

NOTES AND PROBLEMS

1. Start by admiring the defendant's fiendishly clever argument.

a. According to the defendant, how did the plaintiff class members in this case resemble defendants in ordinary cases?

b. According to the defendant, what implication did that resemblance have for the conduct of the class action?

c. How did the Supreme Court disagree with defendant?

2. Now turn to *Shutts*'s implications for our understanding of due process and the class action. What does *Shutts* hold?

a. Does its ruling apply only to class actions in which the members are scattered about the nation? That will include many, but by no means all, class actions.

b. Or does the *Shutts* ruling apply to all class actions, even where the class members are not distant from the forum site? If the latter, *Shutts* has broad implications.

c. The question matters because Rule 23(c)(2)(B) requires individual notice to all members of 23(b)(3) classes but does not apply to (b)(1) and (b)(2) classes. In Eisen v. Carlisle & Jacquelin, 417 U.S. 156 (1974) the U.S. Supreme Court read Rule 23(c)(2) as an inflexible requirement: In all (b)(3) classes, all members of the class must receive individual notice and a chance to opt out of the class. The Kansas courts, operating under an analogous state rule, apparently interpreted the notice requirements for (b)(3) actions in the same way as the *Eisen* court had.

d. *Shutts* might mean that the holding in *Eisen* was constitutionally required — that anything less than individualized notice in (b)(3) classes denies due process. Or it might mean that individual notice satisfies the Constitution but is not required by it. To illustrate, imagine that Kansas had mailed notice to a random sample of the 33,000 class members and taken out ads on radio and television stations where large numbers of them lived. Would that have satisfied the requirements of due process?

3. Another version of the same question would have arisen if Kansas, instead of excluding the 1,500 royalty owners who could not be located, had included them in the class. Would these unnotified absentees have been bound by the resulting judgment? *Shutts* suggests not, but recall the facts of Mullane v. Central Hanover Bank & Trust (Chapter II). In that case the Court held that a number of unnotified trust beneficiaries would be bound by a judgment because they had been adequately represented by those who were notified. If *Mullane* is good law, then

notice to those who can't easily be located is not required. But is that part of *Mullane* still good law after *Shutts*?

4. *Shutts* contains a curious footnote indicating that its decision reaches only class actions involving money damages primarily or exclusively — that is, Rule 23(b)(3) actions. Why this limitation? There seem to be at least two possibilities:

a. The Court may merely be exercising traditional common law restraint in not deciding cases not before it.

b. Or there may be something special about the nature of injunctive relief that makes the requirement of notice and an opportunity to opt out less important or significant than in other cases. If the latter, did that impulse lead the Rules' drafters to treat 23(b)(3) cases differently from the other two sorts?

c. The question of which reading of *Shutts* is correct has substantial implications. If one thinks that *Shutts*'s concerns apply to Rule 23(b)(1) and (b)(2) actions as well as to (b)(3) cases, then Rule 23 provides insufficient constitutional protections to the members of (b)(1) and (b)(2) classes. The 2003 revisions to Rule 23 raise this issue, by providing that in (b)(1) and (b)(2) cases "the court may direct appropriate notice to the class." What notice is appropriate? And when is it appropriate?

NOTE: CLASS ACTIONS IN FEDERAL COURTS

As *Hansberry* and *Shutts* indicate, the federal courts have no monopoly on class actions, but the federal courts have played a particularly important role in the development of the modern class action.

The original Federal Rules of Civil Procedure provided for class actions but did so in a Rule so opaque and confusing that the device was little used before the 1966 revision to Rule 23, in which that Rule took essentially the shape it now has. That revision brought the class action into modern prominence, and since that time the courts and Congress have debated whether the class action is an entirely good thing.

The federal courts have seemed uncertain about how to think about jurisdiction over the class action. Well before the Federal Rules, Supreme Tribe of Ben-Hur[*] v. Cauble, 255 U.S. 356 (1921), held that for purposes of complete diversity, courts should look to the citizenship only of the class representatives and ignore the class members. *Supreme Tribe* thus lowers jurisdictional barriers to the class action. By contrast, on the issue of the amount in controversy, the Court has proved much less accommodating. Snyder v. Harris, 394 U.S. 332 (1969), held that one could not aggregate the claims of all class members for purposes of satisfying the amount in controversy. Zahn v. International Paper Co., 414 U.S. 291 (1973), went further by requiring that not just named plaintiffs but each member of the class satisfy the amount in controversy. Several appellate courts have held that 28 U.S.C. §1367 reverses the result in *Zahn*, though not in *Snyder*. Their reasoning is that §1367(a) extends supplemental

---

[*] The Supreme Tribe was a fraternal organization whose life insurance program was the subject of the lawsuit.

jurisdiction to all but the cases designated in §1367(b), whose exceptions do not cover the class action situation. Compare Free v. Abbott Laboratories, 51 F.3d 524 (5th Cir. 1995) (supplemental jurisdiction over plaintiff class members) with Leonhardt v. Western Sugar Co., 160 F.3d 631 (10th Cir. 1998) (1367 does not overrule *Zahn*).

None of these rulings affect class actions based on federal law. Congress, however, has spoken sharply in one such area. For several years class actions based on alleged violations of federal securities laws have proved controversial. In 1995 Congress, believing that some of these suits lacked merit, acted to tighten pleading requirements for claims alleging violations of federal securities laws. 15 U.S.C. §78u4(b)(1)(B).

Three years later, citing evidence that plaintiffs had reacted to this change by moving their lawsuits to state courts, Congress enacted the Uniform Securities Litigation Standards Act of 1998, 15 U.S.C. §77p(c). That Act uses an interesting repertory of procedural devices to restrict state law securities class actions. First, it states that federal law preempts state securities laws, but only in class actions alleging fraud in the purchase and sale of securities. Second, it provides that all class actions filed in state courts and alleging securities fraud shall be removable to federal district courts without regard to diversity or amount in controversy. Once removed, they should be dismissed unless they fall into a narrow range of permitted claims. The result of this two-step procedure — removal followed by dismissal — essentially eliminates all class actions based on violations of state securities laws.

The student of procedure will find several features of the statute remarkable. Congress has undoubted power to preempt state securities laws. Here, however, Congress has achieved both more and less than preemption. The Act achieves less than preemption because it applies only to class actions rather than to all state law securities claims. It achieves more than ordinary preemption because it assures that all "preempted" claims will be dismissed. With ordinary substantive preemption, Congress relies on state courts to recognize and enforce the preemptive effect of federal law. The Supreme Court acts as the only federal enforcer of preemptive federal law by granting certiorari if state courts fail to recognize federal preemption. But the Supreme Court can hear only about 100 cases a year and thus allows for considerable slippage in the enforcement of preemptive federal laws. In the Act's scheme, removal solves this slippage problem. The federal district courts, not the Supreme Court, enforce federal preemption. Every class action involving state securities laws is removable, thus assuring a federal forum for this federal "defense." The Act demonstrates both the significance of the class action and the use of federal jurisdiction to control it.

4.   Settlement of Class Actions and the "Settlement Class"

The student will already have understood that the effect of the class action is more than the simple gathering together of similar cases. That proposition is particularly true at the settlement stage — the way in which most class actions end. Settlement presents several difficult problems unique to the class action. Most of those problems flow from the circumstance that, in many class actions (especially those created by Rule 23(b)(1) and (b)(3)), the litigative group is organized only for purposes of the lawsuit. In the most extreme cases the "group" may exist only in the abstract — as, for example, the sharers of some hypothesized interest. Yet many of the ordinary rules of litigation assume a client who hires a lawyer, guides the case, authorizes settlement, and benefits directly from the relief, if any.

a.   Fees

In most litigation the client pays the lawyer's fee because she has agreed to do so. While the named representative party in a class action may have such an agreement, that contract does not bind absentees. Yet it may seem that the lawyer whose work has benefited the class should be paid for that work. In class actions that recover money damages, courts apply the "common fund" doctrine, described supra pages 299-300. According to this doctrine, a plaintiff whose efforts create a fund is entitled to have those who benefit contribute to his lawyer's fee. In class actions that create funds for distribution to class members, the doctrine is applied more directly: Courts regularly award the class lawyer a fee taken directly from the fund created by the litigation.

How should the court calculate such a fee? One school holds that a simple percentage is appropriate, using the analogy of contingent fee arrangements. Others point out that the key ingredient in a contingent fee calculation — the agreement between lawyer and client — is missing in the class action context. They argue instead that the proper way to calculate fees is to start with the appropriate hourly rate of the lawyer and then adjust that according to various factors — such as special risks, novelty of the issues, and the like. In practice, the two methods may often arrive at similar results.

Setting these fees presents problems, because most class actions settle, and the fee award is made in the context of a separate hearing specifically focussed on fees as described in Rule 23(h). At that hearing the representatives of the plaintiff and defendant, who will have agreed on an appropriate amount of fees, are unlikely to raise questions casting doubt on the agreed amount. The Rule addresses this problem by requiring notice to the absent class members and permitting them to come forward to object to the settlement terms. The idea is that they will have an incentive to do so because the lawyer's fee is coming out of a fund, the remainder of which will be distributed to the class. In a number of cases objectors have come forward. Consider how some representative problems should be solved.

NOTES AND PROBLEMS

1. Solo Practitioner brings a class action on behalf of a group of plaintiffs, alleging they were overcharged for their automobiles. The case is settled after three years,

during which time Solo has devoted a third of her professional hours to it. The suit grants injunctive relief and $100,000 in compensatory damages. The two hundred members of the class will share in whatever remains of the proceeds after Solo's fee is paid. The judge finds that Solo spent more than 1,500 hours on the case. The court also finds that in her other legal work Solo billed clients at $75 an hour. Finally, the court finds that similarly skilled lawyers working in larger firms typically bill for such work at not less than $150 per hour.

a. Should the court use Solo's actual hourly rate or the higher rate for comparable big-firm lawyers?

b. This was Solo's first piece of comparably complex litigation. The judge finds that a more experienced practitioner would have devoted 200 fewer hours to the case. Should the judge subtract this amount from the hours Solo actually expended?

c. Even using the lower billing rate and a lower number of hours, multiplying the hours times the rate will yield a sum nearly as great as the $100,000 recovery. What should the court do?

2. In a class action seeking several millions of dollars in damages, the defendant offers to settle for a total sum of $100,000, with $95,000 allocated to lawyers' fees and $5,000 to the 500 plaintiffs.

a. Should such separately negotiated attorneys' fees be ethical?

b. If they are, how should the judge decide whether to approve such an offer?

3. Reread Rule 23(g) and 23(h), prescribing standards and procedures for appointing class counsel and fee awards.

a. Suppose that the judge, following the procedures for appointing class counsel, gets a bid and a maximum fee from the lawyer appointed. Thereafter, that lawyer achieves a settlement of the suit, a settlement the judge deems excellent both as a result for the class members and as an example of diligent, creative lawyering. May the judge award more than the amount (or the formula) approved in appointing class counsel?

b. Suppose the court, following the procedures for appointing class counsel, gets a bid and a fee formula from the lawyer appointed. Thereafter the lawyer does what the judge believes is a substandard job of representation. Must the judge award a fee according to the formula approved in the 23(g) hearing?

b.   Damages and Injunctive Relief

In class actions, damages pose an issue that rarely arises in ordinary cases: making sure that the class recovery finds its way into the hands of the class members. Class members often are unaware of the class action and subsequent recovery and consequently don't claim damages. The nature of some types of class actions makes notice difficult. One proposed solution to the problem is the *fluid class recovery*, under which, in the case of a class consisting of past consumers that dealt with a company, damages would be distributed to future consumers through rate reductions lasting long enough to exhaust the recovery. That was the approach taken in Daar v. Yellow Cab Co., 433 P.2d 732 (Cal. 1967), in which the class consisted of overcharged taxicab customers in Los Angeles. The court said it would be appropriate to require the defendant to lower its rates to all customers until the damages had been "paid." At least one district court suggested this approach, which was firmly rejected by the Second Circuit. Eisen v. Carlisle & Jacquelin, 479 F.2d 1003 (1973). Note that the ordinary purpose of litigation — compensation of the plaintiff for a wrong suffered — is not served by the fluid class recovery because some of the beneficiaries are not the people who have suffered the harm but merely people similar to them. Fluid class recovery thus serves to deter the defendants but not to compensate the plaintiffs. Is that a problem? Or is it a virtue?

Rule 23 is silent on the cost of efforts to contact class members after a judgment against a defendant. Should the defendant be required to bear the cost? If so, can such a requirement be squared with the fact that defendants in ordinary litigation bear no analogous cost? Should the cost be deducted from the damages claimed by those who are contacted? Should it come from the entire recovery — even the portion that will not be claimed?

If the relief sought is declaratory or injunctive rather than damages, the problems just discussed do not arise. Instead, problems for class members arise if the judge making a Rule 23(c) (2)(A) ruling, does not notify them. For example, what should be the binding effect of a school busing order on parent members of the plaintiff class who do not wish their children to be bused?

c. Settlement and Dismissal

Class actions are supposed to bind members of the class, so it is particularly important that class members be informed, if possible, of settlement proposals. Rule 23(e) requires court approval for dismissal or compromise, and "notice in a reasonable manner to all class members who would be bound." What happens when someone objects? Rule 23(e) requires the court to approve any settlement or dismissal "only after a hearing and on finding that the settlement . . . is fair" Rule 23(e)(i)(c). Deciding if a settlement is fair is not aided by the circumstance that the previously adverse parties are now both urging approval of the settlement. At fairness hearings a court will typically consider testimony from the plaintiff about how weak her case was — and thus why the settlement is favorable from her standpoint — and from the defendant about how diligent and creative plaintiff was — showing why one could not expect more. If there has been substantial discovery in the case, the judge may be able to make some independent judgment about such matters. What, however, if the parties have conducted little or no discovery? In such a case the judge will have little more than each party's word that the settlement is fair. The most dramatic such problems are presented in the so-called settlement class, in which the motion for class certification is presented simultaneously with a proposed settlement. A celebrated and controversial example follows.

Amchem Products, Inc. v. Windsor

521 U.S. 591 (1997)

Justice GINSBURG delivered the opinion of the Court.

This case concerns the legitimacy under Rule 23 of the Federal Rules of Civil Procedure of a class-action certification sought to achieve global settlement of current and future asbestos-related claims. The class proposed for certification potentially encompasses hundreds of thousands, perhaps millions, of individuals tied together by this commonality: each was, or some day may be, adversely affected by past exposure to asbestos products manufactured by one or more of 20 companies. Those companies, defendants in the lower courts, are petitioners here. . . .

I

A

The settlement-class certification we confront evolved in response to an asbestos-litigation crisis. A United States Judicial Conference Ad Hoc Committee on Asbestos Litigation, appointed by The Chief Justice in September 1990, described facets of the problem in a 1991 report:

> [This] is a tale of danger known in the 1930s, exposure inflicted upon millions of Americans in the 1940s and 1950s, injuries that began to take their toll in the 1960s, and a flood of lawsuits beginning in the 1970s. On the basis of past and current filing data, and because of a latency period that may last as long as 40 years for some asbestos related diseases, a continuing stream of claims can be expected. The final toll of asbestos related injuries is unknown. Predictions have been made of 200,000 asbestos disease deaths before the year 2000 and as many as 265,000 by the year 2015.
>
>   The most objectionable aspects of asbestos litigation can be briefly summarized: dockets in both federal and state courts continue to grow; long delays are routine; trials are too long; the same issues are litigated over and over; transaction costs exceed the victims' recovery by nearly two to one; exhaustion of assets threatens and distorts the process; and future claimants may lose altogether.

Report of The Judicial Conference Ad Hoc Committee on Asbestos Litigation 2-3 (Mar. 1991).

Real reform, the report concluded, required federal legislation creating a national asbestos dispute-resolution scheme. . . . To this date, no congressional response has emerged.

In the face of legislative inaction, the federal courts — lacking authority to replace state tort systems with a national toxic tort compensation regime — endeavored to work with the procedural tools available to improve management of federal asbestos litigation. Eight federal judges, experienced in the superintendence of asbestos cases, urged the Judicial Panel on Multidistrict Litigation (MDL Panel), to consolidate in a single district all asbestos complaints then pending in federal courts. Accepting the recommendation, the MDL Panel transferred all asbestos cases then filed, but not yet on trial in federal courts to a single district, the United States District Court for the Eastern District of Pennsylvania; pursuant to the transfer order, the collected cases were consolidated for pretrial proceedings before Judge Weiner. The order aggregated pending cases only; no authority resides in the MDL Panel to license for consolidated proceedings claims not yet filed.

B

After the consolidation, attorneys for plaintiffs and defendants formed separate steering committees and began settlement negotiations. . . . Settlement talks . . . concentrated on devising an administrative scheme for disposition of asbestos claims not yet in litigation. In these negotiations, counsel for masses of inventory plaintiffs[*] endeavored to represent the interests of the anticipated future claimants, although those lawyers then had no attorney-client relationship with such claimants.

Once negotiations seemed likely to produce an agreement purporting to bind potential plaintiffs, CCR[, a consortium of defendants,] agreed to settle, through separate agreements, the claims of plaintiffs who had already filed asbestos-related lawsuits. . . . After settling the inventory claims, CCR, together with the plaintiffs' lawyers CCR had approached, launched this case, exclusively involving persons outside the MDL Panel's province — plaintiffs without already pending lawsuits.[3]

C

The class action thus instituted was not intended to be litigated. Rather, within the space of a single day, January 15, 1993, the settling parties — CCR defendants and the representatives of the plaintiff class described below — presented to the District Court a complaint, an answer, a proposed settlement agreement, and a joint motion for conditional class certification.

The complaint identified nine lead plaintiffs, designating them and members of their families as representatives of a class comprising all persons who had not filed an asbestos-related lawsuit against a CCR defendant as of the date the class action commenced, but who (1) had been exposed — occupationally or through the occupational exposure of a spouse or household member — to asbestos or products containing asbestos attributable to a CCR defendant, or (2) whose spouse or family member had been so exposed. Untold numbers of individuals may fall within this description. All named plaintiffs alleged that they or a member of their family had been exposed to asbestos-containing products of CCR defendants. More than half of the named plaintiffs alleged that they or their family members had already suffered various physical injuries as a result of the exposure. The others alleged that they had not yet manifested any asbestos-related condition. The complaint delineated no subclasses; all named plaintiffs were designated as representatives of the class as a whole.

[* As the opinion elsewhere explained, the steering committees referred to persons who had already filed claims as "inventory plaintiffs," distinguishing them from those who had not yet experienced illness, to whom they referred as "exposure-only" cases. — Ed.]

3. It is basic to comprehension of this proceeding to notice that no transferred case is included in the settlement at issue, and no case covered by the settlement existed as a civil action at the time of the MDL transfer.

The complaint invoked the District Court's diversity jurisdiction. . . .

A stipulation of settlement accompanied the pleadings; it proposed to settle, and to preclude nearly all class members from litigating against CCR companies, all claims not filed before January 15, 1993, involving compensation for present and future asbestos-related personal injury or death. An exhaustive document exceeding 100 pages, the stipulation presents in detail an administrative mechanism and a schedule of payments to compensate class members who meet defined asbestos-exposure and medical requirements. The stipulation describes four categories of compensable disease: mesothelioma; lung cancer; certain "other cancers" (colon-rectal, laryngeal, esophageal, and stomach cancer); and "non-malignant conditions" (asbestosis and bilateral pleural thickening). Persons with "exceptional" medical claims — claims that do not fall within the four described diagnostic categories — may in some instances qualify for compensation, but the settlement caps the number of "exceptional" claims CCR must cover. . . .

For each qualifying disease category, the stipulation specifies the range of damages CCR will pay to qualifying claimants. Payments under the settlement are not adjustable for inflation. Mesothelioma claimants — the most highly compensated category — are scheduled to receive between $20,000 and $200,000. The stipulation provides that CCR is to propose the level of compensation within the prescribed ranges; it also establishes procedures to resolve disputes over medical diagnoses and levels of compensation.

Class members are to receive no compensation for certain kinds of claims, even if otherwise applicable state law recognizes such claims. . . . Although not entitled to present compensation, exposure-only claimants and pleural claimants may qualify for benefits when and if they develop a compensable disease and meet the relevant exposure and medical criteria. Defendants forgo defenses to liability, including statute of limitations pleas.

Class members, in the main, are bound by the settlement in perpetuity, while CCR defendants may choose to withdraw from the settlement after ten years. A small number of class members — only a few per year — may reject the settlement and pursue their claims in court. Those permitted to exercise this option, however, may not assert any punitive damages claim or any claim for increased risk of cancer. Aspects of the administration of the settlement are to be monitored by the AFL-CIO and class counsel. Class counsel are to receive attorneys' fees in an amount to be approved by the District Court.

D

On January 29, 1993, as requested by the settling parties, the District Court conditionally certified, under Federal Rule of Civil Procedure 23(b)(3), an encompassing opt-out class. . . . Judge Weiner assigned to Judge Reed, also of the Eastern District of Pennsylvania, "the task of conducting fairness proceedings and of determining whether the proposed settlement is fair to the class." [The district court approved the settlement.]

E

The Court of Appeals [reversing] . . . found that "serious intra-class conflicts precluded the class from meeting the adequacy of representation requirement" of Rule 23(a)(4). . . .

III

To place this controversy in context, we briefly describe the characteristics of class actions for which the Federal Rules provide. Rule 23, governing federal-court class actions, stems from equity practice and gained its current shape in an innovative 1966 revision. . . .

In the decades since the 1966 revision of Rule 23, class action practice has become ever more "adventuresome" as a means of coping with claims too numerous to secure their "just, speedy, and inexpensive determination" one by one. See Fed. Rule Civ. Proc. 1. The development reflects concerns about the efficient use of court resources and the conservation of funds to compensate claimants who do not line up early in a litigation queue. . . .

Among current applications of Rule 23(b)(3), the "settlement only" class has become a stock device. Although all Federal Circuits recognize the utility of Rule 23(b)(3) settlement classes, courts have divided on the extent to which a proffered settlement affects court surveillance under Rule 23's certification criteria. . . .

IV

We granted review to decide the role settlement may play, under existing Rule 23, in determining the propriety of class certification. . . .

Confronted with a request for settlement-only class certification, a district court need not inquire whether the case, if tried, would present intractable management problems, see Fed. Rule Civ. Proc. 23(b)(3)(D), for the proposal is that there be no trial. But other specifications of the rule — those designed to protect absentees by blocking unwarranted or overbroad class definitions — demand undiluted, even heightened, attention in the settlement context. Such attention is of vital importance, for a court asked to certify a settlement class will lack the opportunity, present when a case is litigated, to adjust the class, informed by the proceedings as they unfold. See Fed. Rule Civ. Proc. 23(c),(d).[16]

And, of overriding importance, courts must be mindful that the rule as now composed sets the requirements they are bound to enforce. Federal Rules take effect after an extensive deliberative process involving many reviewers: a Rules Advisory Committee, public commenters, the Judicial Conference, this

---

16. Portions of the opinion dissenting in part appear to assume that settlement counts only one way — in favor of certification. To the extent that is the dissent's meaning, we disagree. Settlement, though a relevant factor, does not inevitably signal that class action certification should be granted more readily than it would be were the case to be litigated. For reasons the Third Circuit aired, proposed settlement classes sometimes warrant more, not less caution on the question of certification.

Court, the Congress. The text of a rule thus proposed and reviewed limits judicial inventiveness. Courts are not free to amend a rule outside the process Congress ordered, a process properly tuned to the instruction that rules of procedure "shall not abridge . . . any substantive right." 28 U.S.C. §2072(b).

Rule 23(e) [at the time of the decision,] on settlement of class actions, read[] in its entirety: "A class action shall not be dismissed or compromised without the approval of the court, and notice of the proposed dismissal or compromise shall be given to all members of the class in such manner as the court directs." This prescription was designed to function as an additional requirement, not a superseding direction, for the "class action" to which Rule 23(e) refers is one qualified for certification under Rule 23(a) and (b). . . . The safeguards provided by the Rule 23(a) and (b) class-qualifying criteria, we emphasize, are not impractical impediments — checks shorn of utility — in the settlement class context. . . .

Federal courts, in any case, lack authority to substitute for Rule 23's certification criteria a standard never adopted — that if a settlement is "fair," then certification is proper. Applying to this case criteria the rulemakers set, we conclude that the Third Circuit's appraisal is essentially correct. Although that court should have acknowledged that settlement is a factor in the calculus, a remand is not warranted on that account. The Court of Appeals' opinion amply demonstrates why — with or without a settlement on the table — the sprawling class the District Court certified does not satisfy Rule 23's requirements. . . .

A

We address first the requirement of Rule 23(b)(3) that "[common] questions of law or fact . . . predominate over any questions affecting only individual members." The District Court concluded that predominance was satisfied based on two factors: class members' shared experience of asbestos exposure and their common "interest in receiving prompt and fair compensation for their claims, while minimizing the risks and transaction costs inherent in the asbestos litigation process as it occurs presently in the tort system." . . .

The predominance requirement stated in Rule 23(b)(3), we hold, is not met by the factors on which the District Court relied. The benefits asbestos-exposed persons might gain from the establishment of a grand-scale compensation scheme is a matter fit for legislative consideration, but it is not pertinent to the predominance inquiry. That inquiry trains on the legal or factual questions that qualify each class member's case as a genuine controversy, questions that preexist any settlement. . . .

B

Nor can the class approved by the District Court satisfy Rule 23(a)(4)'s requirement that the named parties "will fairly and adequately protect the interests of the class." The adequacy inquiry under Rule 23(a)(4) serves to uncover conflicts of interest between named parties and the class they seek to represent. . . .

As the Third Circuit pointed out, named parties with diverse medical conditions sought to act on behalf of a single giant class rather than on behalf of discrete subclasses. In significant respects, the interests of those within the single class are not aligned. Most saliently, for the currently injured, the critical goal is generous immediate payments. That goal tugs against the interest of exposure-only plaintiffs in ensuring an ample, inflation-protected fund for the future. . . .

The settling parties, in sum, achieved a global compromise with no structural assurance of fair and adequate representation for the diverse groups and individuals affected. Although the named parties alleged a range of complaints, each served generally as representative for the whole, not for a separate constituency. . . .

The Third Circuit found no assurance here — either in the terms of the settlement or in the structure of the negotiations — that the named plaintiffs operated under a proper understanding of their representational responsibilities. That assessment, we conclude, is on the mark.

C . . .

Because we have concluded that the class in this case cannot satisfy the requirements of common issue predominance and adequacy of representation, we need not rule, definitively, on the notice given here. In accord with the Third Circuit, however, we recognize the gravity of the question whether class action notice sufficient under the Constitution and Rule 23 could ever be given to legions so unselfconscious and amorphous.

V

The argument is sensibly made that a nationwide administrative claims processing regime would provide the most secure, fair, and efficient means of compensating victims of asbestos exposure. Congress, however, has not adopted such a solution. And Rule 23, which must be interpreted with fidelity to the Rules Enabling Act and applied with the interests of absent class members in close view, cannot carry the large load CCR, class counsel, and the District Court heaped upon it. As this case exemplifies, the rulemakers' prescriptions for class actions may be endangered by "those who embrace [Rule 23] too enthusiastically just as [they are by] those who approach [the rule] with distaste." C. Wright, Law of Federal Courts 508 (5th ed. 1994). . . .

Justice O'CONNOR took no part in the consideration or decision of this case.

Justice BREYER, with whom Justice STEVENS joins, concurring in part and dissenting in part.

Although I agree with the Court's basic holding that "settlement is relevant to a class certification," I find several problems in its approach that lead me to a different conclusion. First, I believe that the need for settlement in this mass tort case, with hundreds of thousands of lawsuits, is greater than the Court's opinion suggests. Second, I would give more weight than would the majority to settlement-related issues for purposes of determining whether common issues predominate. Third, I am uncertain about the Court's determination of adequacy of representation, and do not believe it appropriate for this Court to second-guess the District Court on the matter without first having the Court of Appeals consider it. Fourth, I am uncertain about the tenor of an opinion that seems to suggest the settlement is unfair. And fifth, in the absence of further review by the Court of Appeals, I cannot accept the majority's suggestions that "notice" is inadequate. . . .

NOTES AND PROBLEMS

1. *Amchem* exposes numerous issues, some of which challenge the most basic assumptions about the nature of civil litigation. In that respect it is a fitting close both to this chapter on joinder and to the student's exploration of civil procedure.

2. Start by defining the respects in which *Amchem* is an unusual case, even within the category of class actions, which are themselves unusual if measured by ordinary litigation standards.

a. In a typical class action the plaintiff files a complaint; there is a battle over class certification, followed (if the class is certified) by discovery, perhaps a summary judgment motion, and settlement discussions. What happened in *Amchem*?

b. In many ordinary, single-plaintiff-single-defendant cases, the parties settle before any suit is filed. To use the asbestos context, a lawyer for a former shipyard worker alleging injuries from inhalation of asbestos dust could approach an asbestos manufacturer and settle the case without ever filing so much as a complaint. Why didn't the parties do so in *Amchem*? Why *couldn't* they do so if they wanted the settlement to have the intended effect?

c. What did the parties — in particular the defendants — want to get from class certification that they could not have gotten in any other way?

3. To answer Problem 2c, one must be clear about the definition of the class. The persons involved in the *Amchem* litigation comprised two groups.

a. There were individual claimants who had filed complaints against various asbestos manufacturers (the so-called inventory claimants). These cases had been consolidated (under the provision for Multidistrict Litigation, 28 U.S.C. §1407). These claims could have been settled without regard to class certification; indeed, it was the discussion of their settlement that led to the proposed class action.

b. Who, then, were the other members of the class?

c. Put yourself in the position of a defendant. Why would you have wanted the class certification and settlement before being willing to settle the "inventory" of individual cases?

4. You are now in a position to understand the ethical dimension of *Amchem*.

a. The same group of lawyers represented both the individual, already-filed, "inventory" cases and the class of unfiled, often unidentified "exposure-only" cases.

b. What's the problem (which lawyers would refer to as "a conflict")?

c. Why is this problem discussed at length in an opinion on whether a class action should be certified (as opposed, for example, to a state bar disciplinary proceeding against one of the lawyers)? What, in other words, makes this problem part of the law of class actions as well as of professional ethics?

d. The Supreme Court has emphasized that it meant what it said in *Amchem* about the avoidance of conflicts of interest by lawyers representing classes. Striking down another asbestos settlement class in Ortiz v. Fibreboard Corp., 527 U.S. 815 (1999), the Court said:

> One may take a settlement amount as good evidence of the maximum available if one can assume that parties of equal knowledge and negotiating skill agreed upon the figure through arms-length bargaining, unhindered by any considerations tugging against the interests of the parties ostensibly represented in the negotiation. But no such assumption may be indulged in this case, or probably in any class action settlement with the potential for gigantic fees. In this case, certainly, any assumption that plaintiffs' counsel could be of a mind to do their simple best in bargaining for the benefit of the settlement class is patently at odds with the fact that at least some of the same lawyers representing plaintiffs and the class had also negotiated the separate settlement of 45,000 pending claims, the full payment of which was contingent on a successful global settlement agreement or the successful resolution of the insurance coverage dispute. . . . Class counsel thus had great incentive to reach any agreement in the global settlement negotiations that they thought might survive a Rule 23(e) fairness hearing, rather than the best possible arrangement for the substantially unidentified global settlement class. Cf. Cramton, Individualized Justice, Mass Torts, and "Settlement Class Actions": An Introduction, 80 Cornell L. Rev. 811, 832 (1995) ("Side settlements suggest that class counsel has been laboring under an impermissible conflict of interest and that it may have preferred the interests of current clients to those of the future claimants in the settlement class"). The resulting incentive to favor the known plaintiffs in the earlier settlement was, indeed, an egregious example of the conflict noted in *Amchem* resulting from divergent interests of the presently injured and future claimants.

Id. at 852-853.

5. In *Amchem* the district court's response to the adequacy-of-representation problem took two forms. It examined the length and serious quality of the negotiations among counsel, the "maturity" of asbestos litigation (a term used to describe the many litigated cases, whose outcome made it easier to value individual claims), and the relationship of the amounts that had previously been awarded in asbestos verdicts to the amounts proposed to be paid to future claimants. Looking at all these factors, the district judge concluded that the negotiations had led to a fundamentally fair result — and that counsel had therefore been adequate.

a. What part of that reasoning did the Supreme Court attack?

b. Does the majority opinion rest on a conviction that the procedure was fundamentally unfair?

6. A few years after *Amchem*, Rule 23(e), governing the judicial approval of settlements, was amended (after much controversy in the class action bar). Read the current version of the Rule. Does it suggest any change in the outcomes of *Amchem* or *Ortiz*?

7. In the background of *Amchem* is the question of whether any settlement class can ever be approved under Rule 23.

a. Like *Amchem*, Ortiz v. Fibreboard Corp., supra Note 4d, rejected a global settlement class but, also like *Amchem*, did so in terms that stressed the deficiencies of the particular procedure rather than any inherent unlawfulness of the idea:

> This case turns on the conditions for certifying a mandatory settlement class on a limited fund theory under Federal Rule of Civil Procedure 23(b)(1)(B). We hold that applicants for contested certification on this rationale must show that the fund is limited by more than the agreement of the parties, and has been allocated to claimants belonging within the class by a process addressing any conflicting interests of class members.

Fibreboard at 821.

Besides the problem of conflicts of interest among the lawyers representing classes with divergent interests, *Fibreboard* emphasizes the problem of certifying for settlement a 23(b)(1) class. As you will recall, the rationale for (b)(1) classes is that an inherently limited fund must be distributed; the function of the class action is to assure the parties share equitably in the fund. In *Fibreboard* the "limitedness" of the fund resulted from an agreement among two insurance companies and the defendant that they would contribute only a certain amount to settle these claims. For the Supreme Court, this wasn't enough to create a limited fund.

b. Have there been approved settlement classes? Yes. For an example, see Hanlon v. Chrysler Corp., 150 F.3d 1011, 1020-1021 (9th Cir. 1997), in which plaintiffs sued an auto manufacturer alleging a defective latch in a van's door. Affirming the district court's approval of a settlement class, the Ninth Circuit carefully distinguished *Amchem*:

> At the heart of *Amchem* was concern over settlement allocation decisions; asbestos manufacturers had a designated amount of money that was not fairly distributed between present and future claimants. The *Amchem* settlement eliminated all present and future claims against asbestos manufacturers, with class counsel attempting to represent both groups of plaintiffs. The Supreme Court found this dual representation to be particularly troubling, given that present plaintiffs had a clear interest in a settlement that maximized current funds, while future plaintiffs had a strong interest in preserving funds for their future needs and protecting the total fund against inflation.
>
>   Unlike the class in *Amchem*, this class of minivan owners does not present an allocation dilemma. Potential plaintiffs are not divided into conflicting discrete categories, such as those with present health problems and those who may develop symptoms in the future. Rather, each potential plaintiff has the same problem: an allegedly defective rear latchgate which requires repair or commensurate compensation. The differences in severity of personal injury present in *Amchem* are avoided here by excluding personal injury and wrongful death claims. Similarly, there is no structural conflict of interest based on variations in state law, for the named representatives include individuals from each state, and the differences in state remedies are not sufficiently substantial so as to warrant the creation of subclasses. Representatives of other potential subclasses are included among the named representatives, including owners of every minivan model. However, even if the named representatives did not include a broad cross-section of claimants, the prospects for irreparable conflict of interest are minimal in this case because of the relatively small differences in damages and potential remedies.

Is this an adequate response?

8. As one can gather from the disagreement between majority and dissent, the judiciary, academia, and the bar are divided on the desirability of settlements like *Amchem* and *Fibreboard*.

a. One experienced observer of the legal scene described such cases as violations of due process and "the sale of res judicata at a bargain basement price."

b. Others have praised them as embodying the highest traditions of judicial creativity and lawyers' cooperation.

c. In part, one's assessment may depend on one's assumptions about the alternatives. If one thinks that the alternative is an expeditiously conducted civil trial, much of the straining to find that the settlement did not breach either the principles of due process or of professional ethics will seem unnecessary and undesirable. One can find some evidence to support the thesis that the "ordinary" litigation system was developing methods of coping with the asbestos cases.

d. If one thinks that the alternative is the death or financial destitution of those waiting in line for such a civil trial, then the district courts' action in *Amchem* and *Fibreboard* will seem both humane and sensible. One can find some evidence that the litigation system was drowning in asbestos litigation and that litigation expenses, including lawyers' fees, were consuming two-thirds of the amounts recovered.

9. Beyond this level of debate is a subsidiary one about legal institutions. Some who would accept the argument that courts were doing badly with asbestos litigation would nevertheless say that there were other institutions that could and should have responded.

a. One candidate was Congress, which could have created an administrative system (like that for workers' compensation) for dealing with the asbestos claims. The Black Lung Benefits Act, 30 U.S.C. §§901 et seq. might have provided a model. Under the Act, funded by a tax on coal, miners who show disability produced by exposure to coal dust collect benefits from a federal agency. As the opinion in *Amchem* noted, Congress has not acted in a similar way in the case of asbestos. Does that mean that the courts should act on their own? Or has the courts' search for solutions taken the political heat off Congress and thereby thwarted a legislative solution?

b. Another candidate was the bankruptcy courts. John Coffee (who testified — without fee — as an expert in *Amchem*) argues that bankruptcy courts are in the business of collective litigation: They regularly resolve cases in which large numbers of creditors have claims against an entity. Moreover, they are expressly vested with the power to do the sort of quasi-administrative tasks achieved by the proposed settlement. Finally, Coffee argues, the history of a large asbestos bankruptcy suggests that the claimants would get more (and the lawyers less) than under the settlement. One theoretical objection to the settlement class in *Fibreboard* was that by using Rule 23(b)(1) and a limited fund rationale, the defendants were seeking the sort of protection they might have achieved in bankruptcy without subjecting themselves to the powers of a bankruptcy proceeding that might have dug much more deeply into their pockets.

10. As a nice summation of your grasp of civil procedure, be prepared either to defend or to attack the *Amchem* settlement — and explain your grounds for doing so — both as a matter of procedural law and of political theory.

TABLE OF CASES

Principal cases are italicized.

TABLE OF CITATIONS TO THE JUDICIAL CODE (28 U.S.C.)

§133(a)	164	§1397	785
§144	538, 546	§1404	75, 169, 170, 177,
§372	539		178, 244, 245, 645
§455	538, 539, 544, 546, 645	§1406	177, 178
§636	430, 463	§1407	177, 178, 829
§651	483, 485	§1441	212, 213, 217, 218
§657	485	§1442	218
§1253	55	§1445	218
§1254	55	§1446	213, 216
§1255	55	§1447	213
§1256	55	§1631	177
§1257	55	§1651	645
§1258	55	§1652	222
§1291	52, 53, 316, 430, 627,	§1738	489, 495, 685, 715,
	628, 633, 635, 642		721, 722
§1292(a)	316, 642, 712	§1738A	197, 722
§1292(b)	634, 643, 644, 646	§1738B	722
§1331	5, 180, 181, 185, 733	§1861	573, 574, 579
§1332	5, 180, 194-198, 201,	§1863	573, 574
	202, 331, 757, 791	§1864	573
§1332(c)	196	§1866	573
§1332(d)	198	§1867	573, 574
§1333	180	§1870	579
§1334	180	§1920	290
§1335	157, 196, 785	§1961	268
§1337	180	§2072	242, 355, 475, 642,
§1338	180, 734		644, 664
§1341	180	§2107	634
§1359	198	§2111	653, 654
§1367	204-207, 211, 212, 217,	§2201	187, 285, 568
	218, 733, 734, 740, 753,	§2202	187, 285
	755, 757, 760, 761, 771, 819	§2361	120, 153, 163, 785
§1391	11, 164, 165, 168	§2412	307
§1392	165		

TABLE OF CITATIONS TO THE FEDERAL RULES OF CIVIL PROCEDURE

1	280	15	393, 394, 398, 463
3	12, 155, 234, 250, 251	15(a)	23, 381, 534
4	10, 12, 119, 154-159, 163,	15(b)	23
	168, 250, 378, 379, 417, 466, 753	15(c)	23, 400, 403, 404
4.1	157	16	453, 484, 643
5(a)	23, 378, 748	16(b)	417, 530
5(d)	23, 454, 494	16(c)	484
7	379	18	658, 732-734, 754
7(a)	19, 392	18(a)	207
8	334, 335, 338, 365, 367,	19	23, 26, 156, 196, 762,
	370, 386, 392, 658, 664		764, 765, 769, 771, 778, 784,
8(a)	180, 331, 334, 371, 756		790, 793, 802
8(b)	18, 22, 23, 75, 338, 382, 386, 757	19(a)	765, 773
8(c)	16, 18, 338, 377, 390,	19(b)	765, 770, 771
	391, 480, 514, 665, 686	20	23, 24, 28, 206, 734,
8(d)	22, 382		746, 747, 771, 792
8(e)	353, 354, 569, 714	21	746, 747
9(b)	368, 369	22	785, 786, 790
9(c)	377	23	23, 28, 234, 642, 791,
11	13, 14, 16, 75, 347, 354,		794, 795, 805, 812, 818,
	355, 358-360, 363-365, 371,		821, 822, 830
	382, 387, 425, 627, 652	23(a)	792, 793, 795, 802
12	339, 381, 641	23(b)	792-795, 801, 802,
12(a)	19, 75, 155, 378, 379,		806, 817, 818, 820, 831, 832
	466, 467, 557	23(c)	794, 795, 801, 806, 817
12(b)	18, 53, 55, 74, 75, 154,	23(d)	792
	189, 190, 192, 211, 338-340,	23(e)	478, 820, 822
	346, 347, 349, 352, 359, 367,	23(f)	642, 644, 803
	376, 378-381, 393, 417, 465,	23.1	234
	513, 623, 681, 682	24	23, 27, 316, 771, 773,
12(c)	347, 381		777, 778, 783
12(d)	381	24(a)	642, 773, 777
12(e)	18, 380, 381	24(b)	642, 773, 777
12(f)	75, 380, 392	26	31, 413, 416, 418, 430,
12(g)	74, 381		437, 443, 444, 446
12(h)	74, 184, 358, 381, 633, 720, 757	26(a)	29, 413, 414, 416-419,
13	20, 75, 204, 734, 735, 754		422, 423, 426, 446, 447, 463
13(a)	18, 286, 671, 738, 761	26(b)	31, 408, 413, 414, 416,
13(b)	18, 738, 740		418, 426, 438, 443-447,
13(g)	18, 20, 741, 754		450, 453, 495
14	18, 21, 156, 750, 752-754, 771	26(c)	31, 426, 427, 430, 452, 496
14(a)	26, 752, 754, 756, 761, 764	26(d)	418

TABLE OF AUTHORITIES

INDEX